WORLD
THE GLOBAL EXPERIENCE
CIVILIZATIONS

Volume II 1450 to Present

PETER N. STEARNS
CARNEGIE MELLON UNIVERSITY

MICHAEL ADAS
RUTGERS UNIVERSITY

STUART B. SCHWARTZ
UNIVERSITY OF MINNESOTA

HarperCollins*Publishers*

Executive Editor: Bruce Borland
Development Editor: Rebecca Strehlow
Project Coordination, Text and Cover Design:
Proof Positive/Farrowlyne Associates, Inc.
Cover Photo: Jack Demuth
Photo Researcher: Roberta Knauf
Production Manager: Michael Weinstein
Compositor: The Clarinda Company
Printer and Binder: Courier Corporation
Cover Printer: The Lehigh Press, Inc.

World Civilizations: The Global Experience, Volume II
1450 to Present

Library of Congress Cataloging-in-Publication Data

Stearns, Peter N.
World civilizations:the global experience/Peter N. Stearns, Michael Adas, Stuart B. Schwartz.—1st ed.
p. cm.
Also published as a single volume ed.
Includes bibliographical references and index.
Contents: v. 1. Beginnings to 1750—v. 2. 1450 to present.
ISBN 0-06-500260-1 (vol. 1)—ISBN 0-06-500261-x (vol. 2)
1. Civilization—History. 2. Civilization—History—Sources.
I. Adas, Michael. II. Schwartz, Stuart B. III. Title.
CB69.S84 1992
909—dc20 91-33476
CIP

93 94 9 8 7 6 5 4 3

Brief Contents

Detailed Contents

24

25

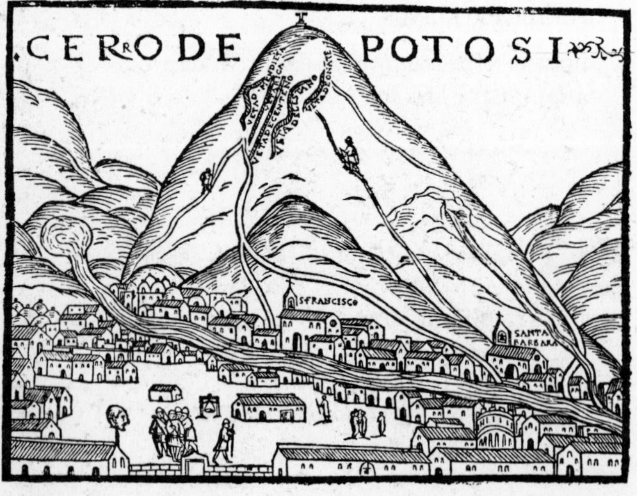
CERRO DE POTOSI
S. FRANCISCO

26

27

28

PART 5

29

Depart des Heroines de Paris pour Versailles le 5 Octobre 1789.

30

31

32

33

PART 6

34

35

36

37

38

39

40

41

42

Maps

PAGE

Preface

World history provides an exciting introduction both to the world and to the historian's craft, and this text builds on these two themes. The survey course in world history has been gaining ground steadily as a staple of the history and social science curriculum. The reasons are immediately evident. First, the composition of the American population perpetually changes, adding to our need for international understanding. The European heritage, though still vital, now logically shares attention with our sources in Africa, various parts of Asia, and Latin America.

Second, American involvement in world affairs continues to grow. Long a Pacific, Caribbean, and Atlantic power, the United States nevertheless has tended to define its primary interests in terms of Europe. In the second half of the 20th century, after participation in three wars in Asia, plus massive economic and cultural interaction around the globe, the United States and its citizens have embraced a global perspective. This perspective involves emphasis on international currents and on a full range of civilizations.

GOALS

To meet the needs of a global perspective—to explain the emergence of the present world and its major civilizations—teachers of world history have created an increasingly sophisticated and comprehensive structure. Several decades of scholarship in world history and in area studies by historians and other social scientists and humanists have yielded a wealth of information and interpretive generalizations. This text reflects a synthesis of teaching and historical scholarship, a synthesis that grasps world history not as a list of facts recorded for routine memorization but as a set of processes open to analysis that builds an understanding of how world study has been shaped.

We have taught and written widely on topics central to world history. This text reflects our experience and our conviction of the role of world history in improving students' ability to handle issues of interpretation. By showing students how to assess change and continuity, the text helps them learn how to relate past to present.

As in many world history texts, we include excerpts from original documents in order to enhance student contact with diverse voices of the past. As with several other writers, we also share a firm commitment to include social history that involves women, the nonelite, and experiences and events outside the spheres of politics and high culture.

This text is no clone, however. It offers a number of distinctive qualities that pioneer in the presentation of world history.

APPROACH

The two most important and distinguishing features of this text involve its genuine global orientation and its analytical style. This is a real *world* history text. It deals seriously with the Western tradition, but does not allocate extra space to it that might blur the distinction between a Western civilization text and a world history text. Correspondingly, civilizations or societies sometimes slighted in world texts—such as the nomadic societies of Asia, Latin American societies, and nations and states of the Pacific Rim—receive additional attention here. This global orientation makes *World Civilizations: The Global Experience* the first of a logical new generation, one that will decide coverage in terms of international criteria, giving the West its respectful due but not pride of place.

This text also seeks to upgrade the analytical level of the presentation of world history. Many world history texts function as factual compendia, leaving analytical challenge to the classroom. Our goal throughout has been to relate fact to interpretation while still allowing ample room for classroom exploration. Analytical emphasis is evident in the attention to periodization, which presents strands of interpretation amid the parade of facts. Comparative issues are strongly emphasized, as a means both of raising the level of reading above that of memorization and of bridging the gap between discrete civilization segments.

By happy accident, this text was written during one of those moments in world history (1989–1991) when all sorts of established patterns seem to change. Thus, the text incorporates the recent upheavals in Russia, Eastern Europe, and the Middle East, not as completed events, to be sure, but in integral relationship with other coverage. The text is thus up-to-date not only in its presentation of facts but also in relating recent events to larger analytical patterns.

THEMES AND STRUCTURE

This text pays a great deal of attention to periodization. Some texts range through one civilization and then the next without much attention to coherent time periods. This book, in contrast, identifies themes for each major period of world history that help locate some common experiences or at least common forces in individual societies. Part introductions set clear definitions for each period, identifying new kinds of global contacts and parallel developments. Basic characteristics of each period are referred to in chapters dealing with specific civilizations and also in a number of crosscutting chapters that return to larger world trends.

The book is divided into six major parts, each defined by fundamental new characteristics in world history. After sketching the hunting-and-gathering phase of the human experience, Part 1 focuses on several major developmental stages. The rise of agriculture and then the development of civilization—with initial examples in different parts of Asia, Africa, Central America, and southeastern Europe—constitute the sequence that set world history in motion, from the origin of the human species until about 3000 years ago.

Part 2 deals with the elaboration of major civilizations in several parts of the world. Civilizations in this classical phase developed a new capacity to integrate large regions and diverse groups of people through overarching cultural and political systems. They also established many durable values that continue to mark the character of major societies to the present day. Part 3 of the book, covering the period from A.D. 500 to A.D. 1400, gains coherence through the spread of major religions to many different societies, by further expansion of the civilization form, and above all by the establishment of new commercial and cultural linkages that brought most civilizations into great contact with each other.

The final three parts of the book deal with world history in the past 550 years. During these years, previous international systems were fundamentally redefined, and well-established traditional civilizations encountered new forces of change. Part 4 of the book deals with the three centuries after 1450, when new technology and modes of military and political organization allowed the establishment of a variety of important empires and when western Europe gained primary control of international trade, redefining its own society in the process. Western global power increased in the 170 years after 1750 (Part 5), mainly through the ramifications of the Industrial Revolution. Other civilizations had to take a position toward Western power and toward industrialization—a common set of pressures that evoked diverse responses.

A new period of world history opened up in the middle decades of the 20th century with the retreat of Western imperialism, the rise of new political systems such as communism, the surge of the United States and the Soviet Union, and a variety of economic innovations including the achievements of Japan and the Pacific Rim. Part 6 deals with this most recent period of world history and some of its portents for the future.

PEDAGOGICAL AIDS

Teachers (and students) of world history come from a wide range of backgrounds, personal and academic. To support the thematic and analytical features of the text and to make all facets of world history as accessible as possible, the authors have integrated a number of pedagogical features into the book.

In addition to narrative part openers that set forth key themes in each unit, parts begin with an extensive but manageable timeline that establishes the period under consideration. The timeline includes events in all the societies involved.

Chapters open with an outline for a quick overview of major topics and with a detailed timeline specific to the groups to be discussed. Chapter introductions highlight key themes and analytical issues to consider in reading.

Within each chapter, one or more documents appear in a discrete section. The documents are preceded by a brief, scene-setting narration and followed by probing questions. Each chapter also contains an analytical essay on a topic of broad application; the essay is followed by questions intended both to probe student appreciation of the topic and to suggest questions or interpretive issues for further thought.

The text is accompanied by photographs, line drawings, and a series of maps specially developed to enhance the global orientation. Maps in the part introductions and in the chapters highlight major developments during each period and familiarize students with many non-Western arenas.

Each chapter ends with a conclusion that goes beyond a mere summary of events. Conclusions reiterate the key themes and issues raised in the chapter and again suggest areas for reflection and anticipation. Obvious examples can be found in the unit on the 20th century, in which conclusions highlight developments leading to events of which students have had first-hand experience. Each chapter also includes several paragraphs of annotated suggested readings, so that readers can pursue additional topics on their own.

At the back of the book (in addition to the index) is a comprehensive glossary, another feature that sets this book apart. It includes conceptual terms, frequently used foreign terms, and names of important geographical regions and key characters on the world stage. Much of world history will be new to most students, and this glossary will greatly assist them in developing a global vocabulary.

ACKNOWLEDGMENTS

Grateful acknowledgment is made to the following colleagues and reviewers, who made many useful suggestions during the development of this book:

Claire Adas
Rutgers University

Jay Pascal Anglin
The University of Southern Mississippi

Norman R. Bennett
Boston University

Deborah D. Buffton
University of Wisconsin—LaCrosse

Victoria Chandler
Georgia College

Allen Cronenberg
Auburn University

Kevin Deuschle
Rutgers University

William T. Eagan
University of Southern Colorado

James Forse
Bowling Green State University

Peter Golden
Rutgers University

Dana Greene
Saint Mary's College—Maryland

William Kent Hackmann
University of Idaho

Eric G. Haines
Bellevue Community College

Howard R. Holter
California State University—Dominquez Hills

Jon E. Mandaville
Portland State University

Robert M. Maxon
West Virginia University

John A. Mears
Southern Methodist University

Vera Blinn Reber
Shippensburg University

Timothy A. Ross
Arkansas State University

John P. Ryan
Kansas City, Kansas Community College

Martin F. Seedorf
Eastern Washington University

S. Henry Tsai
University of Arkansas

Ralph V. Turner
Florida State University

Richard S. Williams
Washington State University

Donald R. Wright
SUNY College—Cortland

Herbert F. Zeigler
University of Hawaii—Manoa

PETER N. STEARNS
MICHAEL ADAS
STUART B. SCHWARTZ

Supplements

The following supplements are available for use in conjunction with this book:

FOR THE STUDENT

Student Study Guide and Practice Quizzes, in two volumes. Volume I (Chapters 1 through 23) and Volume II (Chapters 22 through 42), prepared by John Paul Bischoff, Oklahoma State University. Includes chapter outlines, timeline and map exercises, two multiple-choice practice tests, and sample essay questions.

Mapping World Civilizations: Student Activities. A free student map workbook by Gerald Danzer, University of Illinois, Chicago. Features numerous map skill exercises written to enhance students' basic geographical literacy. The exercises provide ample opportunities for interpreting maps and analyzing cartographic materials as historical documents. The instructor is entitled to one free copy of *Mapping World Civilizations: Student Activities* for each copy of the text purchased from HarperCollins.

SuperShell II Computerized Tutorial. An interactive program for computer-assisted learning, prepared by John Paul Bischoff, Oklahoma State University. Features multiple-choice, true-false, and completion quizzes; comprehensive chapter outlines; "flash cards" for key terms and concepts; and diagnostic feedback capabilities. Available for IBM computers.

Timelink: World History Computerized Atlas, by William Hamblin, Brigham Young University. A highly graphic, Hypercard-based computerized atlas and historical geography tutorial for the Macintosh.

Documents in World History, in two volumes. Volume I, *The Great Traditions—From Ancient Times to 1500*; Volume II, *The Modern Centuries—From 1500 to the Present,* edited by Peter N. Stearns, Carnegie Mellon University. A collection of primary source documents that illustrates the human characteristics of key civilizations during major stages of world history.

FOR THE INSTRUCTOR

Instructor's Resource Manual, by John Paul Bischoff, Oklahoma State University. Includes chapter outlines, discussion, term paper and essay topics. Also bound in the *Instructor's Resource Manual* is the *Experiencing World Music* audio cassette (see below). The *Instructor's Resource Manual* includes a commentary on each piece in the audiocassette.

Experiencing World Music. A 60-minute audiocassette. Contains over 20 selections of important music from a wide range of times and cultures. Selections range between one and four minutes in length. Commentaries about the pieces and suggestions for using them in lectures, prepared by Evan Tonsing, Oklahoma State University, and Jane Adas, Rutgers University, are included in the *Instructor's Resource Manual.* Western pieces include short selections from the medieval period to the present. Non-Western pieces include short selections from China, India, Japan, Iran, Africa, Turkey, and others.

Test Bank, by John Paul Bischoff, Oklahoma State University. A total of 2300 questions, including 50 multiple-choice questions and five essay questions per text chapter. Each test item is referenced by topic, type, and text page number. Available in print and computerized format.

TestMaster Computerized Testing System. A test-generation software package available for IBM and Macintosh computers. Allows users to add, delete, edit, and print test items. Available free to adopters.

World History Through Maps and Views, by Gerald Danzer, University of Illinois, Chicago, winner of the AHA's James Harvey Robinson Award for his work in the development of map transparencies. This set of 100 four-color transparencies from selected sources is bound in a three-ring binder and available free to adopters. Also contains an introduction on teaching history with maps and detailed commentary on each transparency. The collection includes cartographic and pictorial maps, views and photos, urban plans, building diagrams, classic maps, and works of art.

Map Transparencies. A set of 48 two- and four-color transparencies of basic maps designed to be used in teaching world civilization courses.

The HarperCollins World Civilization Media Program. A wide variety of media enhancements for use in teaching world civilization courses. Offered to qualified adopters of HarperCollins's western civilization texts.

Grades. A grade-keeping and classroom management software program that maintains data for up to 200 students.

Prologue

The study of history is the study of the past. Knowledge of the past gives us perspective on our societies today. It shows different ways people have identified problems and tried to resolve them, as well as important common impulses in the human experience. History can inform through its variety, remind us of some human constants, and provide a common vocabulary and examples that aid in mutual communication. One of the ways in which peoples from different cultures understand one another is through shared historical information.

The study of history is also the study of change. Historians seek to describe major changes in the human experience over time and to examine the ways in which those changes connect the past to the present. They try to distinguish between superficial and fundamental change, as well as between sudden and gradual change, and to explain why change occurs and what impact it has. Finally, they are attentive to the ongoing nature of change, pinpointing continuities from the past along with innovations. History, in other words, is a study of human society in motion.

World history is not simply a collection of the histories of various societies, but a subject in its own right. World history is the study of historical events in a global context. It does not attempt to sum up everything that has happened in the past. It focuses on two principal subjects: the evolution of leading civilizations and the framework for international contacts among different societies. In the first category, world history identifies major stages in the development of important societies. In the second category, world history emphasizes major stages in the interaction between different peoples and societies around the globe.

THE EMERGENCE OF WORLD HISTORY

Serious attempts to deal with world history are relatively recent. Many historians have attempted to locate the evolution of their own societies in the context of developments in a larger "known world": Herodotus, though particularly interested in the origins of Greek culture, wrote also of developments around the Mediterranean; Ibn-Khaldūn wrote of what he knew about developments in Africa and Europe as well as in the Muslim world; and unsystematically, European historians in the 18th-century Enlightenment liked to compare the evolution of various societies along with their own. But it was not until the 20th century, with an increase in international contacts and a vastly expanded knowledge of the historical patterns of major societies, that a complete world history became possible. In the West, world history depended on a growing realization that the world could not be understood simply as a mirror reflecting the West's greater glory or as a stage for Western-dominated power politics. This hard-won realization continues to meet some resistance. Nevertheless, at various points since 1900, historians in several societies have attempted to develop an international approach to the subject that includes but goes beyond merely establishing a context for the study of the emergence of their own civilization.

There are many other approaches to the study of history. The most familiar uses a purely national framework, such as the study of American history or French history, which at best is enlivened by some awareness of how one national tradition compares with the traditions of other societies. World history does not replace national histories entirely. The history of the United States, France, or China can be enhanced when there is a larger context to fit it in, for this facilitates more precise comparisons and underlines the ways in which national patterns were shaped by more general forces.

The need to study world history, however, goes beyond the provision of a good starting point for examining one's own society. The surge of interest in world history has been fueled by three other, interrelated factors. The first factor has been an explosion of knowledge about the histories of societies outside the Western tradition, in some cases also older than that tradition. The known past is much larger than ever before. The perspectives and the interpretive insights history provides have greatly expanded. Analysis of a host of issues—the effects of a classical tradition on later cultural development, the relationship between religion and commerce, or the impact of the Industrial Revolution on women—simply cannot be confined to Western examples.

The second factor involves the realization of the increasingly international context in which we live. Much of what happens in the United States can still be explained by national or even local contexts, but our economy and culture, as well as our military and diplomatic framework, are vitally shaped by developments around the world. For example, wars and revolutions in the Middle East and economic and population trends in Latin America have direct impact on the way we live. Living in an international context creates the need to understand this context and to apply to it the knowledge and perspectives of history. We need to know how other traditions besides our own have evolved, what beliefs and attitudes they produce, and what kinds of economic and political behaviors they generate.

One world historian has put the case this way: History in the United States first concentrated on the national experience alone, as part of an attempt at self-understanding and as a means of building agreed-upon national values. In the 20th century Americans realized that they were caught up in a network of which Europe was a vital part. One response was the creation of programs in the study of the history of Western civilization that made us better able to deal with European issues in the post–World War II era. Now we need, and are developing, the same types of programs on a wider international level—and world history plays a key role here.

The third factor follows from the growing analytical challenge world history poses. Historians increasingly understand that key aspects of past and present alike have been shaped by global forces—exchanges of technologies, ideas, religions, foods, and diseases. Defining and assessing the emergence of global forces and tracing their interaction with individual societies stand at the forefront of the world history agenda as a research area. Our understanding of these forces, though still incomplete, is steadily improving.

In addition to explaining the need for world history, it is necessary to offer a few words at the outset about its manageability. No world history includes everything, or even most things, about the past. It focuses on the activities of human civilizations, rather than human history as a whole. No world history would be manageable if this distinction were not kept in mind.

WHAT CIVILIZATION MEANS

In dealing with *civilizations*—societies that generate and use an economic surplus beyond basic survival needs—world history focuses on only a tiny portion of the more than 2.5 million years since the genus *Homo* first appeared in the savanna of eastern Africa. The era of civilized life makes up about 9000 of the 40,000 years that our own human species, *Homo sapiens sapiens*, has inhabited the earth. Civilized life has made possible human population densities unimaginable in precivilized time periods; it has given human groups the capacity to reshape their environments in fundamental ways and to dominate most other living creatures. The history of civilizations embraces most of the people who have ever lived; their literature, formal scientific discoveries, art, music, architecture, and inventions; their most sophisticated social, political, and economic systems; their brutality and destruction caused by conflicts; their exploitation of other species; and their degradation of the environment—a result of advances in technology and economic organization.

To be truly global in scope, our inquiry into the history of civilizations must not be constricted by the narrow, Western-centric standards for determining what is civilized. Many peoples have seen themselves as "civilized," regarding outsiders with different physical features and cultures as uncouth "barbarians" or even subhumans. For example, in awarding a society civilized status, most European and American writers have insisted that monumental buildings, cities, writing, and a high level of technology be present. These criteria banished from the realm of the civilized many societies that were highly advanced in other areas but deficient in the ones Western writers deemed critical. Clearly, another approach to the meaning of civilization has to be taken if one is to write a truly global history of the human experience.

Different civilizations have stressed and therefore excelled in different facets of human creativity. The Chinese have consistently demonstrated the capacity to build large and effective political systems. But Chinese thinkers have formulated only one major religion, Daoism, and this has had only a limited appeal both within and beyond East Asia. By contrast, the peoples of India have produced some of humankind's most sophisticated and sublime religions, but they have rarely known periods of political unity and strong government. The civilizations of the Maya made remarkable discoveries in astronomy and mathematics, but their technology remained roughly equivalent to that of stone-age peoples as late as the arrival of the Spaniards in the 16th century. These examples suggest that, rather than stressing particular attainments such as the capacity to build pyramids or wheeled vehicles, a genuinely global definition of what it means to be civilized should focus on underlying patterns of social development that are common to complex societies throughout history. The attributes that determine whether a particular society is civilized or not should be freed from the *ethnocentrism*—or the tendency to judge other peoples' cultural forms solely on the basis of how they compare to one's own—and sense of moral superiority that have dominated definitions of civilization.

For our purposes, civilization is a form of human social organization that arises from the capacity of certain peoples to produce food supplies beyond their basic needs, and to develop a variety of specialized occupations, a heightened social differentiation on a class and gender basis, intensified economic exchanges between social groups, and regional and long-distance trading networks. Surplus agricultural production spurs the growth of large towns and then cities inhabited by merchants, artisans, ritual specialists, and political leaders. Both specialization and town life contribute to an increase in creativity and innovation that have been characteristic of all civilizations.

THE COMPARATIVE APPROACH TO THE HISTORY OF CIVILIZATIONS

In concentrating on civilizations, world history offers an initial focus that greatly reduces the time period world history covers, and also draws attention to civilizations that covered particularly extensive geographical areas. Even in emphasizing major civilizations, however, world history must offer other ways to select and highlight significant developments. One vital step involves a comparative approach to the major societies. Much of world history can be organized through careful comparisons of the leading characteristics of the principal civilizations, such as formal governments, family structures, and art. Remembering what civilizations have in common helps us to manage the complexity of world history and to highlight key distinctions among major societies. Comparison gives us a means of connecting historical developments within different civilizations and allows us to identify key patterns that ought to be remembered and explained.

Comparison can also help capture the process of historical change. A single civilization can be compared across time, before and after change. Furthermore, a situation new to one society can be compared with similar situations that exist elsewhere. Consider the introduction of a new slave system, as happened in the Americas in the 16th and 17th centuries. By comparing the American slave system with slave systems developed elsewhere, one can get a better fix on what American slavery involved and what changes it brought to the emerging society.

INTERNATIONAL CONTACTS AND TIME PERIODS

World history is not, however, simply a progression of separate civilizations that can be compared in various ways. An understanding of the kinds of contacts different civilizations developed—and their responses to the forces that crossed their boundaries—is as important as the story of the great societies themselves. For example, when the rate of international trade picked up, it presented questions for each major society to answer: How would the society participate in the trading system? What domestic impact did international trade have? How did one society's reactions to the new levels of trade compare with those of other major societies?

World history is organized into major time periods primarily on the basis of changes in the nature and level of international exchange. Because of parallel developments, contacts, and crosscutting global forces, many civilizations display some common chronological features that suggest an international framework encompassing the individual societies. Establishing a sense of each time period of world history in terms of the characteristics of international interactions gives coherence to the larger story of world history. Some time periods see a particular trend toward the formation of empires; others involve the spread of major religions; others stress the impact of new technologies or production systems. Not all societies, in a given time period, neatly responded to the larger world forces—isolation from the wider world remained possible until just a few centuries ago—but enough did to enable us to define the basic chronology of world history.

This book emphasizes six major time periods in world history. The first, covered in Part 1, involved the emergence of civilization. Early civilizations arose after people had formed a wide variety of local societies over most of the inhabitable globe. The early civilizations were regional, but they pulled more localized groups together into some shared institutions and beliefs; some of them developed limited contacts with other civilizations.

The second period of world history saw the formation of much larger civilization units—the great classical societies of China, India, and the Mediterranean. Emphasis in the classical period rests on the integration of and the level of contact among these larger civilization areas. This was the period when elites in many parts of the world created systems of thought and artistic styles that continue to have force today: Confucian ideas about polite behavior and the social good, Greek ideas about nature, and Buddhist ideas about spirituality.

The third, postclassical period in world history emerged as the classical civilizations underwent new challenge and decline. After about A.D. 500, civilization spread to new areas and new kinds of contact developed, involving the spread of novel religious systems, the increase of commercial exchange, and even the acceleration of international disease transmission.

The fourth period of world history, beginning around A.D. 1450, saw the Americas and other previously isolated areas brought into the international framework as trade and exchange reached yet another level of intensity. Humble American crops such as corn and potatoes encouraged massive population growth in many societies—a trend that continues into our own time.

Between about 1750 and 1920, the fifth period of world history was shaped particularly through the advent of industrial society in western Europe. Industrial technology brought new rates of international interaction and a new, and complex, balance of forces among the major civilization areas. Habits of work changed in response to new ideas of discipline and productivity; leisure changed as well. This was the time when key sports won an international audience.

Finally, world history periodization took a sixth turn during the 20th century, again because of complicated changes in the nature of international contacts and the impact these contacts have on particular societies. The new global patterns of this century gain added meaning against the perspective of previous world trends.

The basic framework for managing and understanding world history resembles a weaving loom, in which two sets of threads interweave. One set consists of the major civilizations, identified through their principal characteristics and traced over time; the second set involves parallel processes and contacts that delineate the principal time periods of world history. The interaction between civilizations and international forces form the warp and weave of world history, from civilization's origin to the present day.

ANALYSIS IN WORLD HISTORY

In addition to comparison and periodization, which link the historical experience of individual civilizations, some world historians have been fascinated by a third, even more sweeping formula: regularities in historical development that can be identified and applied on a global basis. Do all civilizations rise, mature, and then fall in a process like that of human growth? Is there a historical law that proves that societies that begin to neglect the welfare of their lowest classes are doomed to decay? A variety of historical laws have been proposed, and even if some of them prove simplistic, the more insightful ones can raise valid questions about the larger processes of world history.

World history involves comparison, assessment of global interaction, and consideration of more general formulas about how human societies operate. There are facts to be learned, but the greater analytical challenge is to use the facts to compare civilizations, to identify key periods of world history and the patterns of change from one period to the next, and to test general propositions about historical causation and development. Using this approach, world history becomes something to think about, not simply something to regurgitate. With this approach the task of learning world history gains focus and purpose.

WORLD
CIVILIZATIONS

1281 **Founding of Ottoman dynasty**

1350s Ottoman invasion of southeastern Europe

1368 Ming dynasty in China

1390 Ming restrictions on overseas trade

1405–1423 Chinese expedition period

1434–1498 Portuguese expeditions down West African coast

1441 Beginning of European slave trade in Africa

1453 Ottoman conquest of Constantinople

1480 Moscow region free of Mongol control

1492 Columbus expeditions

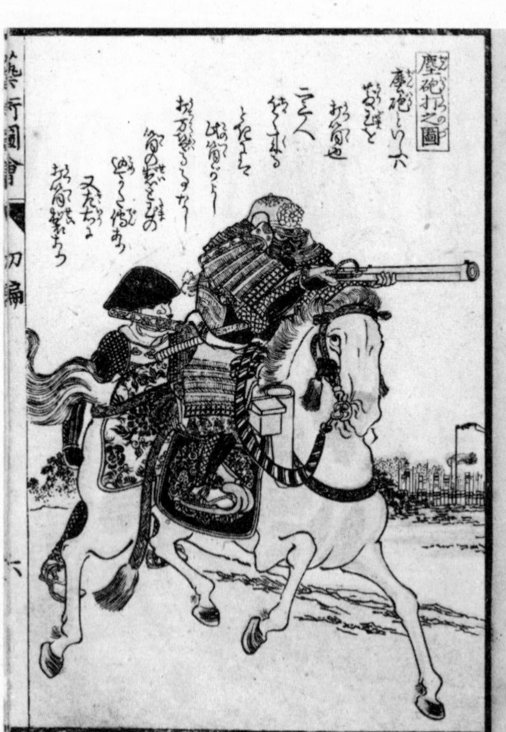

The gun was introduced into Japan in 1542 through the Portuguese. By 1562, 10,000 Japanese soldiers carried muskets. The scenes depicted here are from a military manual written by one of the greatest generals of the period, Nobunaga.

A.D. 1500 A.D. 1550 A.D. 1600 CONTINUED

1500–1600 Europe's commercial revolution
1519–1521 Magellan circumnavigates globe
1552 Russia begins expansion in central Asia and western Siberia
1509 Spanish colonies on American mainland
1498–1499 Vasco da Gama expedition opens seas to Asia
1570 Portuguese colony of Angola (Africa)
1520–1566 Suleiman the Magnificent (Ottoman)
1510–1511 Portugal conquers Goa (India), Malacca (Malaysia)
1526 Babur conquest in northern India (Mughal)
1501–1510 Safavid conquest of Iran
1590 Hideyoshi unifies Japan
1517–1541 Protestant Reformation (Europe)
1548 Portuguese government in Brazil
1533 Pizarro wins Peru
1591 Fall of Songhay (Africa)
1519–1524 Cortes conquers Mexico
1571 Ottoman naval defeat at Lepanto
1600–1690 Scientific revolution (Europe)
1603 Tokugawa shogunate
1608 First French North American colonies
1637 Russian pioneers to Pacific
1600 Dutch and British merchants begin activity in India
1607 First British colonies in North America
1644 Qing dynasty, China
1642–1727 Isaac Newton
1641 Dutch colonies in Indonesia
1640s Japan isolation

PART 4

The World Shrinks, 1450–1750

A number of developments highlighted the three centuries of world history after 1450, marking a major new period—the early modern period—in the global experience. As in most new world history periods, the balance of power among major civilizations shifted; the West became the most dynamic force worldwide. Largely under Western aegis, contacts among many civilizations intensified; the world became smaller, as international trade affected many diverse societies and the speed and range of sailing ships increased. Finally, based mainly on new weaponry, particularly gunpowder, new or revamped empires formed important regional political units in many parts of the world—a set of developments especially significant in Asia. The West built a new colonial empire in various parts of the world, using its new maritime muscle combined with naval gunnery. Land-based empires emerged in Russia—now a rapidly rising power; under the Ottoman Turks, in the Middle East, southwestern Europe, and to an extent North Africa; as well as in India, Persia, and China where this was already a familiar pattern. Gunpowder empires showed new capacities for political integration of substantial territories and cut into traditionally independent areas notably in central Asia.

The rise of the West, the intensification of international contacts on literally a global scale, and the formation of new empires marked off the early modern centuries from the previous postclassical period in world history. The period was launched during the 15th century when Western countries, headed by Portugal and Spain, began new explo-

1652 Dutch colony South Africa

1689–1725 Peter the Great (Russia)

1682–1699 Turks driven from Hungary

1658–1707 Aurangzeb reign, beginning of Mughal decline

1713 New Bourbon dynasty, Spain

1722 Fall of Safavid dynasty (Iran)

1759–1788 Reforms of Latin American colonial administration

1763 Britain acquires"New France"

1764 British East India Company controls Bengal (India)

1756–1763 Seven Years' War

1770s European-Bantu conflicts in southern Africa

1772–1795 Partition of Poland

1775–1783 American Revolution

1781 Indian revolts in New Granada and Peru (Latin America)

1792 Slave uprising in Haiti

rations and soon new colonization efforts around Africa to Asia and to the Americas. It was launched, also, by the formation of the powerful new Ottoman Empire in the Middle East and the emergence of Russia from two centuries of Mongol control.

ON THE EVE OF THE EARLY MODERN PERIOD: THE WORLD AROUND 1450

Important new or expanded civilization areas developed in the postclassical period, in contact with the leading centers. Russia was one such case, as a Russian monarchy formed. Western Europe, slowly recovering from the 5th-century collapse of the Roman Empire, failed to gain political unity. West Europeans built important regional kingdoms, while expanding the role of commerce and city life and establishing an elaborate artistic and philosophical culture around Catholic Christianity. In sub-Saharan Africa, another set of regional kingdoms formed, though there were vital areas organized more loosely; African trade and artistic expression gained ground steadily. Areas in contact with China, finally, built increasingly elaborate societies. Japan, like western Europe, emphasized a rather decentralized, militaristic feudal system in politics, but it copied many aspects of Chinese culture and some social principles, including a more patriarchal approach to the status of women.

A third area of the world featured civilizations or elaborate cultures developing in isolation from any international contacts. This was true of parts of sub-Saharan Africa and of the expanding Polynesian zone in the Pacific Islands. It characterized the brilliant, populous civilizations of the Americas, focused in Central America (under the Aztecs) and in the Andes (by the 15th century under the vast Inca realm).

The structure of the postclassical world began to shift between the 13th and 15th centuries, setting the stage for the new world history period. The isolated civilizations were not affected by these changes, precisely because they were isolated; they continued to follow their own dynamic, which culminated in the great Aztec and Inca empires, both of which were showing signs of strain and overextension by the later 15th century. In Asia, Africa, and Europe, the key development was the decline of Arab political power and cultural dynamism. Islam continued to expand, but its political and commercial units fragmented. At the same time, a new round of invasions from central Asia, under the Mongols, attacked China, the Middle East, and eastern Europe, disrupting established political boundaries and allowing new contacts between Asia and Europe.

By 1400 the Mongol threat was receding, though only slowly in Russia. A new empire emerged in China. The Arab caliphate had perished, but a new Islamic political force, under the Ottoman Turks, was taking shape, unifying much of the Middle East and poised to destroy the venerable Byzantine Empire. Utilizing their growing commercial vigor, but also terrified by the emergence of a new Islamic power, west Europeans cast about for ways to gain greater control over their international trade, while possibly winning new areas for the Christian faith and new territories for the competing regional kingdoms. China briefly experimented with a dominant international role early in the 15th century, sending out a series of mighty trading expeditions across the Indian Ocean, but then it pulled back, deciding to concentrate on its traditions of internal political, cultural, and commercial development. This, as it turned out, left the way open for the west European probes, as Western leaders benefited from a number of technologies newly learned from China and Islam—such as the compass and explosive powder—while adding important innovations such as guns and faster oceangoing ships.

THE RISE OF THE WEST

Between 1450 and 1750 the West, headed initially by Spain and Portugal, then by Britain, France, and Holland, gained control of the key international trade routes. It established colonies in the Americas and, on a much more limited basis, in Africa and parts of Asia.

At the same time, partly because of its new international position and the growing impact of commerce, the West itself changed rapidly, becoming an increasingly unusual kind of agricultural civilization. Commerce began to alter the social structure and also affected basic attitudes toward family life and the natural environment. A host of new ideas, some of them springing from religious reformers, created a novel cultural climate in which scientific principles increasingly held pride of place; the scientific revolution gradually reshaped Western culture as a whole. More effective political structures emerged by the 17th century, as Western monarchs began to introduce bureaucratic principles similar to those pioneered long before in China.

A vital facet of the early modern period, then, consisted of the West's expansion as an international force and its simultaneous internal transformation. Like the previous world-class civilization, Arab Islam, the West developed a diverse and dynamic culture and society, which was both a result and a cause of its ascending international position.

THE WORLD ECONOMY AND GLOBAL CONTACTS

It was as a result of initiatives mainly from the West that the world network set up in the previous period intensified and took on new dimensions. The change involved more than the fact that the Europeans, not the Muslims, dominated international trade. It involved an expansion of the world network to literally global proportions, well beyond the geographical scope of previous linkages. Far more of Africa, and above all the Americas, were brought into contact with other cultures and included in international exchanges for the first time. At the end of the period, in the 18th century, Polynesian and Australian societies began to undergo the same painful integrating experience.

Effectively, by 1750 there were no more fully isolated societies of any great size. The new globalism of human contacts had a host of vital consequences that ran through early modern centuries. The human disease pool became fully international for the first time, and peoples who had previously been isolated from most of the rest of the world suffered immensely from their exposure to diseases for which they had developed no immunities. The global network also permitted a massive exchange of plants and animals. Cows and horses were introduced to the Americas, prompting substantial changes in American Indian habits in economy and warfare alike. American food crops were spread around the world, bringing sweet potatoes, corn, and manioc to China, corn to Africa, potatoes and tobacco to Europe—innovations that in many places prompted great changes in agricultural production. One result through most of the world, beginning in Asia as well as western Europe, was a rapid population expansion that quickly attained unprecedented levels.

Even globalization, though its impact was vast, did not exhaust the changes wrought in the world network during the three centuries after 1450. Far more than in the postclassical era, the period between 1450 and 1750 saw a set of definite and highly unequal relationships established among a number of civilizations. During the postclassical millennium, A.D. 450–1450, a few areas had contributed relatively inexpensive raw materials (including labor power in the form of slaves) to more advanced societies, notably China and the Islamic world; this was true for the West and parts of Africa and Southeast Asia. Though economic relationships in these instances were unequal, they did not constrain the "raw-materials-producing" societies too severely, because international trade was simply not of overriding importance yet. After 1450 or 1500, as Western commerce expanded internationally, the West began to set up relationships with a number of areas that produced pronounced dependence and subordination in the international economy. Areas such as Latin America depended heavily on sales to export merchants, on imports of processed goods, and on Western ships and merchants to handle international trade. Dependence of this sort might have political ramifications in creating weak governments open to foreign intervention; it certainly affected labor relations by encouraging commercial exploitation of slaves and serfs; and it even tied in with cultural impositions from the West on some of the dependent areas. It is vital to stress that much of the world, particularly in the great Asian civilizations, remained outside this set of relationships, but there was a growing tendency to draw closer toward it, as occurred in India and much of Indonesia by the 18th century, as the level of Western overseas expansion increased steadily. The establishment of a new set of international economic relationships, based on Western preeminence, is discussed explicitly in Chapter 23, but it undergirds analysis of many individual civilizations as well.

The linked themes of the rise of the West and the intensification and transformation of the world network accurately convey key international trends during the period

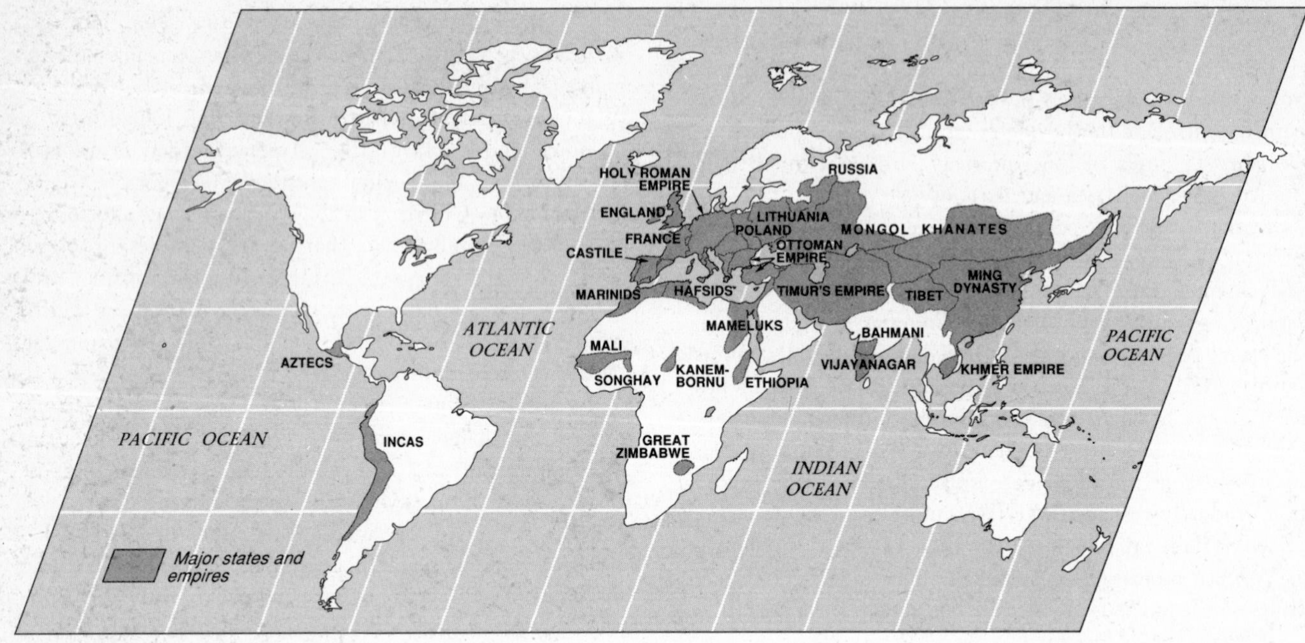

World Boundaries, about 1453

after 1450, supplemented as they were by new food and disease exchanges and resultant population shifts. As before, no simple set of features covers the complexities of developments in the many and diverse areas involved in world history. Particularly because the West's influence varied in different parts of the world, and the relationships between African, Asian, or Amerindian peoples to the Western-dominated international economy varied as well, it is vital to note two other developments that were larger than individual civilizations, but not fully subsumed under the emergence of the Western world system either.

THE GUNPOWDER EMPIRES

The centuries after 1450 could also be designated "the age of the gunpowder empires." The development of cannons and muskets in the 15th and 16th centuries, through the combination of Western technology with previous Chinese invention, obviously spurred the West's expansion. Ship-based artillery was fundamental to the West's mastery of international sea lanes and many ports and islands. But gunnery was picked up by other societies as well. The Ottoman Turks used Hungarian-built cannons to aid their successful siege of Constantinople in 1453. The subsequent Ottoman Empire relied heavily on land-based guns to supplement trained cavalry. The rise of a new Russian Empire after 1480 also built on growing use of guns, and the Russian economy was subsequently reshaped to provide the manufacturing basis for the new military hardware. Three other key empires—the Mughal in India, the Safavid in Persia, and the 17th-century Manchu dynasty in China—relied on the new strength of gun-supported land armies. Guns also played a role in Japanese and African history during the period.

Clearly, guns supported important military changes that in turn supported new political organization—colonial empires in the case of the West, where naval strength played a particularly important role, and new land agglomerations through much of Asia and eastern Europe and, to an extent, in Africa. Here were developments largely independent of Western influence, save for some of the initial technologies, and which in fact counterbalanced the growth of Western power to a considerable degree. The rise of the Russian Empire ran through the whole period, and while not as important as the rise of the West it was certainly a vital theme, involving among other things the progressive elimination of an independent central Asia. The rise of the Ottomans, Safavids, and Mughals was a bit shorter-lived, but echoed through the first two centuries of the period and, in the case of the Ottomans, created one of the most durable empires known in world history.

To the labels "rise of the West" or "new world economy," then, the phrase "age of the gunpowder empires" could quite legitimately be added to describe 1450–1750.

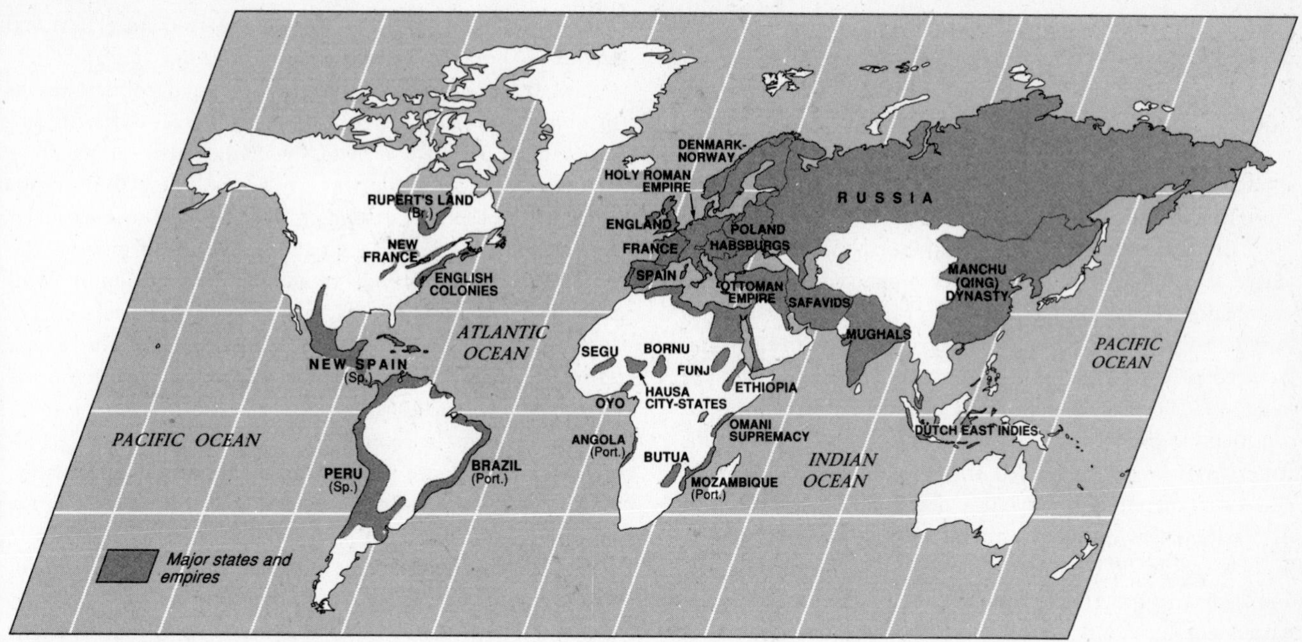

World Boundaries, about 1700

It reflects developments that affected a massive number of people and long overshadowed, at least in the eyes of most Asian leaders, the Western surge.

The period of 1450–1750 saw an unusual number of boundary changes in world history. The spread of Western colonies was the most obvious development, but the establishment or extension of a number of large land-based empires was almost as significant. Compare the two maps by tracing the areas of Western penetration. You will see the different forms this penetration took in different parts of the world. Note also what parts of the world offered particular opportunities for rivalries among the leading Western colonial powers, and what parts were particularly immune to Western expansion of any major sort.

Look also to the land-based empires. What empires were particularly new as they took shape between the 15th and 18th centuries? What parts of the world had the most stable boundaries during these centuries? Why?

Of the boundary changes you can trace during this three-century period, which changes seem particularly important for the world today? What parts of the world look very different today, in terms of the boundaries of major political units, from the form they had achieved by the 18th century?

COMMERCE AND ITS OUTREACH

One other development deserves note: This was also an age of world commercialization. Market exchange played an increasing role in shaping economic activity. The world remained predominantly agricultural, but agriculture was now modified more than ever by specializations that depended on market transactions, as well as by the activities of merchants and the lure of money. Heightened commercial activity was one of the means by which rising populations could be sustained in advance of major technological change in the means of production. Commerce not only spread knowledge of new foodstuffs, but also allowed increased specialization in production that could heighten output, as some regions concentrated on goods they were best suited to grow or manufacture, relying on trade for other materials.

The intensification of international trade, under the sponsorship of Western traders but also involving merchants in other societies, played an important part in the general expansion of commerce. Not only did many Latin Americans produce precious metals and agricultural products for sale to the West; many more Latin Americans produced foods and clothes to sell to workers in the export sectors. Internal trade increased within Latin America, particularly by the 18th century. International trade activities prompted increasing numbers of Westerners, as well, to engage in market activities, at home as well as abroad. Similar patterns emerged in West Africa. Earlier international trade routes, oriented toward North Africa, were diverted to a new Atlantic commerce organized by European merchants. African kings and merchants organized goods to sell in this trade, particularly slaves, and received manufactured products, including guns, in exchange. Again the West was encouraged in its own commercial expansion, as considerable profits could be realized in the slave trade; the Americas were transformed through the introduction of new African populations and a new kind of slavery; and Africa itself was diversely affected by the new exchange.

The spread of commerce went beyond these Western-dominated transactions, however. Both China and Japan witnessed the rapid growth of market exchanges within their own boundaries, as production and sale of foodstuffs, beverages, and the like expanded. A general trend—the Western-dominated international economy and its growth—was thus supplemented by some parallelisms in some other parts of the world, where internal trade far outweighed international exchange. And this meant not only a surprisingly widespread commercial and urban surge, but also some broader effects in terms of culture and society. In most cases without toppling the land-based aristocracy, merchants in a number of societies, not just the West, gained new influence. Growing trade also played a role in some societies (in the West but also, for instance, in Japan) in encouraging some groups to reduce their commitment to religion and other worldly goals in favor of a focus on secular pursuits. The expansion of commerce, in other words, though not producing a uniform new version of an agricultural economy or society, had some wider potential reverberations in many parts of the world.

EVOLUTION OF THE EARLY MODERN PERIOD: CIVILIZATIONS AND LARGER TRENDS

As in earlier world history epochs, many developments during these early modern centuries occurred within individual civilizations, with little or no relationship to more general world trends. Only the Americas came close to being overwhelmed by outside influences. Many of the following chapters, correspondingly, will focus on particular societies.

Nevertheless, the impact of the four international trends—Western expansion, intensification and globalization of the world network, the military and political results of gunpowder, and the spread of commerce—affected patterns in the separate societies in many ways, for the force of international trends was growing. These four trends generate the central questions to be addressed to each major civilization, to see how it fit the larger world picture. Response to the key trends ranged from eager embrace of new international currents, to self-conscious isolation, to forced compliance. A new set of diversities described major societies precisely because of the heightened potency of real or potential international contacts.

The tensions between the West's expansion and its attributes versus more general forces of change—population growth in several societies, commercial expansion, and the power of gunpowder empires—allowed many societies to evolve with scant reference to what the West and its colonies were up to. The period's beginning date—1450—embraces both patterns. It was after 1450 that Western exploration and maritime expansion began to take off with particular rapidity, and it was also then that two of the most important new land-based empires, the Ottoman and the Russian, fully emerged. This already suggests the need to treat these centuries as involving more than the West and world reactions to the West. The balance between Western-sponsored change and more general patterns of development did tend to shift over time, particularly in the final century before 1750.

By 1700 the West's activities were looming larger not just in key areas such as the Americas, the Asian island groups, and the coast of West Africa, but in Asia and eastern Europe as well. A new Russian urge selectively to copy aspects of the West and the establishment of growing British control in parts of India expressed two facets of this shift. Even Japan, which had responded to the new world economy by effective isolation, began to show modest new openness, rescinding a ban on translating Western books.

By 1750 it is fair, with all the advantages historians have of knowing how their stories turn out, to note that civilizations that were not in a position to react effectively to the West's new world role were verging on decline—whereas a mere century before, this would have been a considerable distortion of a more complex international balance. After 1750, in large part because of another major transformation within the West—the emergence of a revolutionary industrial economy—the theme of Western predominance took on new meaning, which is why the periodization of world history breaks at this point once again.

The acceleration of economic change in the West was clearly underway by 1750, but it is important to note that its effects on other societies lagged a bit. In many ways the themes of the early modern period persisted in places, such as Russia and Asia, for a few decades more, which means that chapters covering these societies push beyond 1750 in some respects. Worldwide transition to the effects of pioneering industrialization in western Europe was not an overnight affair, though it was widely underway by 1800.

The chapters in this unit focus first on changes within the West and the emergence of Western colonies and Western-dominated world trade. Then two chapters deal with two societies that had particular links with the West—Russia, whose expansion was such an important theme in its own right, and a new kind of emerging civilization in Latin America. The final group of chapters deals with major societies in Asia and Africa where contacts with the West and the new world economy were significant, particularly as the early modern period wore on, but where separate patterns of activity remained vital.

1300–1450 Italian Renaissance

1450–1600 Northern Renaissance

1452–1519 Leonardo da Vinci

1455 First European printing press in Mainz, Germany

1469–1527 Machiavelli

1475–1514 Michelangelo

1490s France and Spain invade Italian city-states; beginning of Italian decline

1500–1600 "Commercial revolution"

1515–1547 Francis I of France

1517 Luther's 95 theses; beginning of Protestant Reformation

1534 Beginning of Church of England

1541–1564 Calvin in Geneva

1543 "Copernican revolution"; Copernicus' work on astronomy

22 The Transformation of the West, 1450–1750

INTRODUCTION. During the three centuries after 1450, Western civilization—particularly its core areas such as France, Britain, the Low Countries, and much of Germany—changed in dramatic ways. Still a largely agricultural society in 1750, the West had become unusually commercially active and had laid out a growing manufacturing sector. Government powers had expanded, while new political ideas and challenges complicated the picture. Beliefs had altered. Science came to form the centerpiece of Western intellectual life for the first time in the history of any society. The popular outlook, including ideas about personality and family as well as concepts of nature, also had shifted substantially.

In a variety of ways and at various social levels, the West was becoming an unusual kind of agricultural civilization compared to most others in the world at the time. In some areas the West in this period may be seen as incorporating developments, such as increased bureaucratization in the central state, that other more advanced civilizations had already instituted. But in other areas, such as popular belief and family structure, the West was striking out in new directions. Certainly, Western civilization changed more fundamentally in this period than any of the established societies in Asia, and its innovations prepared further changes—notably, the Industrial Revolution—for the future.

Even before 1450 Western culture and the Western economy had been changing. Initially, change focused on Italy and Spain, the former being the leader in cultural innovation, the latter spearheading Europe's overseas expan-

1642–1727 Newton

17th century Scientific revolution

1730–1850 European population boom

1643–1715 Louis XIV in France; absolute monarchy

18th century Enlightenment

1609 Independence of Netherlands

1776 Adam Smith's *Wealth of Nations*

1688–1690 Glorious Revolution in Britain; parliamentary monarchy; some religious toleration; political writing of John Locke

1555–1603 Elizabeth I, England

1588 Defeat of Spanish Armada by English

1780–1790 Joseph II, Austria and Hungary

1733 James Kay invents flying shuttle loom

1550–1649 Religious wars in France, Germany, and Britain

1670–1692 Decline of witchcraft trials

1736 Beginnings of Methodism

1642–1649 English civil wars

1792 Mary Wollstonecraft's *Vindication of the Rights of Women*

1712–1786 Frederick the Great of Prussia; enlightened despotism

1682–1699 Habsburgs drive Turks from Hungary

1564–1642 Galileo

1647–1648 Culmination of popular rebellion

1618–1648 Thirty Years' War

1756–1763 Seven Years' War: France, Britain, Prussia, and Austria

A.D. 1600 A.D. 1750

sion along with Portugal. Increasingly, after 1450, change became more general through Western society, and the center of activity shifted northward to France, Britain, and surrounding areas. Changes within Europe, finally, constantly interacted with overseas expansion and the fruits of European dominance of international trade; Europe's steady evolution resulted from its new world power, and furthered this power in turn.

EPISODES IN THE LARGER PATTERNS OF CHANGE

The new directions taken up in the West were reflected in a host of subperiods, most of which are staples of European history in what is rightly called the West's early modern period. During the 15th century the Renaissance took full shape, spreading to northern Europe from its initial home in Italy. Then came the disruption of religious unity in the West, with the Protestant Reformation and Catholic response. Then came the rise of absolute monarchy in the 17th century and also the scientific revolution. By 1730 this was followed by the Enlightenment and a rather modest, but widely trumpeted, modification of absolute monarchy called *enlightened despotism*.

Key developments occurred at different points; there was no coordinated evolution. The proliferation of subperiods, many with famous labels such as Renaissance or Reformation, suggests that change in the West involved a number of specific stages, each with its own characteristics. Relatedly, change was not uniform or always consistent, nor was it always terribly rapid. The Renaissance, as a cultural movement, suggested more secular art and literature; its writers and artists esteemed human achievements and the human form. The leaders of the Reformation reasserted the primacy of religious values, attacking Renaissance secularism and covering portions of Renaissance paintings that had celebrated the human form too vividly. Changes thus moved unevenly. Overall, Europe's early modern period saw a reduction in the importance of religion, but there were many countercurrents. Amid this complexity, it is important to seize on the four major trends of the period:

- First, the Western economy became steadily more commercial, and this commercialization began to transform the social structure.
- Second, Western culture shifted gears at both the elite and popular levels. This revolution in beliefs had stages and was certainly a gradual process, but its main outlines moved through several of the subperiods of early modern history. People began to look at nature and human society in new ways.
- Third, soon after the economic and cultural changes were launched, the West moved from feudal monarchy as a typical political form to the nation-state unit, with characteristically stronger governments and greater contacts between the state and ordinary people.
- Accompanying these three changes was the major alteration in the West's position in the wider world. From a backwater area, the West became a world trader and colonizer. This role is taken up in Chapter 23, but it must be remembered as, from the West's own standpoint, a fourth major change intertwined with the other three.

FROM RAGS TO RICHES

Western Europe in 1450 was in many ways a poor candidate for great new dynamism. It was politically divided with regional governments rather decentralized through the powers of the Church and feudal aristocracy; feudalism had involved a network of mutual restraints and obligations among landowners, many with their own armies, that seriously constrained even the strongest monarchies. Its economy, though no longer purely agricultural, lagged well behind the major civilizations in technology and commercial experience. Medieval culture had, furthermore, passed its high point. Theology had become less vibrant, more wrapped up in petty debates over trivial definitions. Population and economy had been weakened by major plagues and an inability to produce enough food to sustain previous population growth. Some of these weaknesses, in fact, spurred innovation—including new efforts, through voyages of exploration, to find ways to overcome the West's inferiority in world trade.

The results of change, gradually accumulated, overrode many characteristics of the medieval past. These results explain why the West was able to seize a new world role. They explain also why other societies would seek to copy some of the characteristics the West was now pioneering. Russia launched a selective imitation as early as 1700, and other societies would confront similar agendas after 1800. The transformation of the West, in sum, without defining the whole of subsequent world history, had repercussions well beyond the West.

THE FIRST BIG CHANGES: CULTURE AND COMMERCE

The West's initial moves away from its earlier ideas and institutions as well as the stagnation that had developed in the 14th and early 15th centuries focused on art, religion, popular beliefs, and trade. These changes built on traditional elements, including religious fervor and the important merchant activities that had arisen with the cities of the postclassical period in Europe. The new trends extended from the late 15th century through the subsequent century, embracing thus the Renaissance, Reformation, and Catholic response and what is aptly known as a 16th-century commercial revolution. Some political and technological shifts accompanied the more sweeping developments. By 1600 the West had reluctantly abandoned religious unity, and some people had found religious certainty reduced as well. It had begun to define a new social structure that could accommodate greater commercial activity; new groups of propertyless workers had no choice but to provide labor for profit-seeking merchants. Elements of this social structure continue to describe Western society even today. Its genesis also provoked a massive popular outcry in the name of older values—a sign of the major transformation and disruption involved.

THE RENAISSANCE

The process of moving away from earlier patterns began with the Renaissance, which first developed in Italy during the 14th and 15th centuries. The significance of this "rebirth" should not be exaggerated: more fundamental changes came later and somewhat separately. But the Renaissance did challenge medieval intellectual values and styles. It suggested a certain amount of political innovation and built on a more commercialized economy. The Renaissance also sketched a new, brasher spirit that may have helped create a new Western interest in exploring strange waters or urging that old truths be reexamined.

Italy was already well launched in the development of Renaissance culture by the 15th century, based on its unusually extensive urban, commercial economy and its competitive city-state politics. Writers such as Petrarch and Boccaccio had trumpeted classical literary canons against medieval logic and theology, writing in Italian as well as the traditional Latin and emphasizing secular subjects such as love and pride. Painting turned to new realism and a host of classical and human-centered themes. Religion declined as a central focus.

The Italian Renaissance blossomed further in the 15th century. This was a great age of Western art, as Leonardo da Vinci advanced the realistic portrayal of the human body while Michelangelo applied classical styles in both painting and sculpture. In political theory Niccolo Machiavelli emphasized realistic discussions of how to seize and maintain power; his work *The Prince* resembled earlier Chinese legalism in urging that rulers do what they must do, without scruple, in order to control undisciplined subjects. Like the artists, Machiavelli bolstered his realism with abundant use of Greek and Roman examples. In history, scholars portrayed a past unencumbered by divine intervention and established new critical standards that could be used to disprove traditional Church claims.

Overall, Italian Renaissance culture stressed themes of humanism—a focus on humankind as the center of intellectual and artistic endeavor. Religion was not attacked, but its principles were no longer predominant. Humanists clearly touted the superiority of classical forms over medieval styles. As individuals they could proclaim a pride in their own achievements, which implied an ability of talented people to progress, to advance on the basis of human effort alone.

This religious painting from 15th-century Renaissance Italy depicts the Martyrdom of St. Sebastian. Realism in human figures and careful perspective mark this painting, attributed to Pollaiuolo.

These Renaissance themes had some bearing on politics and commerce. Renaissance merchants improved banking techniques and became more unabashedly capitalist in their profit-seeking than their medieval counterparts had been. City-state leaders experimented with new political forms and functions. They justified their rule not on the basis of heredity or divine guidance, but more on the basis of what they could do to advance general well-being. Thus they sponsored cultural activities and tried to improve the administration of the economy. They also developed more professional armies, for wars among the city-states were common, and gave new attention to military tactics and training. They also rethought the practice of diplomacy, introducing the regular exchange of ambassadors for the first time in the West. Clearly, the Renaissance encouraged innovation, though it could also produce some slavish dependence on classical models.

THE RENAISSANCE MOVES NORTHWARD

Italy began to decline as a Renaissance center by about 1500. French and Spanish monarchs invaded the peninsula, cutting down on political independence. At the same time new Atlantic trade routes reduced the importance of Mediterranean ports, a huge blow to the Italian economy.

As Renaissance creativity faded in its Italian birthplace, it passed northward. The northern Renaissance—focused in France, the Low Countries, Germany, and England—opened up after 1450. Classical styles in art and architecture became the rage. Knowledge of Greek and Latin literature gained ground, though most northern humanists wrote in their vernacular languages. Northern humanists were more religious than their Italian counterparts, trying to blend secular interests with continued Christian devotion. Renaissance writers such as Shakespeare in England, or Rabelais in France, also mixed classical themes with an earthiness, a joy in bodily functions and human passions, that maintained elements of medieval popular culture. Renaissance literature established a new set of classics for literary traditions in the major Western languages: Shakespeare for England, Cervantes for Spain, and so on.

The northern Renaissance produced some political change. Renaissance kings increased their pomp and ceremony. Kings such as Francis I in France became patrons of the arts, even importing Italian sculptors and architects for their classical-style palaces, as these in turn replaced

Western Europe during the Renaissance and Reformation

fortified castles. Many Renaissance monarchs tried to impose new controls over the Catholic church, and they also developed some new functions in the areas of economy and welfare. Many monarchs, by the late 16th century, were sponsoring trading companies and colonial enterprises. Interest in military conquest became more blatant than in the Middle Ages. Francis I was even willing to ally in principle with the Ottoman sultan, the key Muslim leader. His goal was to distract his main enemy, the Habsburg ruler of Austria and Spain. In fact the alliance was in name only, but it illustrated how power politics was beginning to emerge without some of the feudal or religious justifications that had previously clothed it in the West.

Through most of the West, the Renaissance signaled some vital changes in cultural life. The classical styles favored by Renaissance leaders long prevailed over the medieval Gothic. Upper-class education changed, becoming defined in terms of classical precepts—such as Cicero's advice on moderate morals and devotion to the public good—plus literary study as well as an appropriate dose of Christian morality. Elements of this education would continue to describe the experience of upper-class Westerners into the 20th century. A Renaissance spirit of individual excellence and defiance of tradition influenced other facets of life in the West, including new scientific endeavor.

Yet the impact of the Renaissance should not be overdone, particularly outside Italy. Renaissance kings had new ceremonies, but they were still confined by the political powers of feudal landlords—a really new political form had yet to emerge. Ordinary people were little touched by Renaissance values; the life of most peasants and artisans went on much as before. Economic life, too, was little altered, particularly outside the Italian commercial centers. Rural people were sometimes pressed for new taxes to support cities and kings. Women, even in the upper classes, sometimes encountered new limits as Renaissance leaders touted men's public bravado over women's domestic roles.

THE COMMERCIAL ECONOMY

More fundamental changes were brewing in Western society by 1500, beneath the glittering surface of the Renaissance. Spurred by trading contacts with Asia, workers in the West improved the quality of pulleys and pumps in mines and learned how to forge stronger iron products. Printing was introduced in the 15th century, as the German Johannes Gutenberg invented movable type, a much more flexible system than Chinese block printing. Soon books were distributed in new quantities in the West, which helped expand the audience for Renaissance writers but particularly served to disseminate religious ideas. Literacy began to gain ground, a fertile source of new kinds of thinking. Technology clearly began to spur a variety of changes.

Family structure was also changing. A European-style family pattern came into being by the 15th century. It involved, for ordinary people, a relatively late marriage age and a primary emphasis on nuclear families of parents and children, rather than extended families characteristic of most agricultural civilizations. These changes emphasized the importance of husband-wife relations. It also linked the family to individual property holdings with new intensity, for most people could not marry until they had appropriate access to property. Late marriage also provided a certain amount of birth control, which prevented vast overcrowding even as economic activity began to speed up again in the West. By the 16th century most ordinary Europeans did not marry until they were 26 or 27—late by the standards of most societies. Newly formed families were largely independent of older parents, however, which could encourage some sense of division between family and community.

Winds of change were blowing from several directions by the early 16th century. New family habits unseated traditions at one level; new cultural interests challenged them at another. Both elites and ordinary people generated innovation, though in somewhat different manners. It was in the 16th century, however, with religious upheaval and a new commercial surge, that the directions of change began to be more fully defined.

RELIGIOUS AND ECONOMIC LIFE

In 1517 a German monk named Martin Luther nailed a document containing 95 *theses*, or propositions, to the door of the castle church in Wittenberg. He was specifically protesting claims made by a papal representative in selling *indulgences*, or grants of salvation, for money, but in fact his protest went deeper. Luther's reading of the Bible convinced him that only faith could gain salvation. Pious actions or Church sacraments were not the path, for God could not be manipulated. Luther's protest, rebuffed by the papacy, soon led him to challenge many Catholic beliefs, including the authority of the pope himself. Luther would soon argue that monasticism was wrong, that priests should marry (as he did), and that the Bible should be translated from Latin so ordinary people might have direct access to the teachings of the faith. Luther did not want to break Christian unity, but the church he wanted should be on his terms (or, as he would have argued, the terms of the true faith).

THE REFORMATION

Disputes and heresies were not new in Western Christianity, but always before the Catholic church had ultimately managed to contain them. The Renaissance papacy, however, was not interested in compromise as it tried to force Luther to back down. At the same time Luther picked up wide support for his views during the middle decades of the 16th century and beyond. Many Germans resented the authority and taxes of the Roman pope, in something of a nationalist reaction. German princes saw an opportunity to gain more power, for their nominal leader, the holy Roman emperor, remained Catholic. Princes who turned Protestant could increase their independence; they also had an excuse to seize Church lands. The Lutheran version of Protestantism (as the general wave of religious dissent was called) urged state control of the church as an alternative to papal authority, and this had obvious political appeal.

There were reasons for ordinary people to shift as well. Some German peasants saw Luther's attack on authority as a sanction for their own social rebellion against landlords, though Luther specifically renounced this reading. Some townspeople were drawn to Luther's approval of work in the world; since faith gained salvation, Lutheranism could sanction money-making and other earthly pursuits more wholeheartedly than did traditional Catholicism.

Once Christian unity was breached, other Protestant groups sprang forward. In England Henry VIII set up an Anglican church initially to challenge papal attempts to enforce his first marriage, which had failed to produce a male heir. (Henry would ultimately have six wives in sequence, executing two of them.) Henry was also attracted to some of the new doctrines, and his most durable successor, his daughter Elizabeth I, was Protestant outright. The Anglican church became increasingly, though broadly, Protestant in doctrine as well as a separate form of church government. Still more important were the churches inspired by Jean Calvin, a Frenchman who set his base in the Swiss city of Geneva. Calvinism insisted on God's *predestination*, or prior determination, of those who would be saved. Nothing humans could do, and certainly no sacraments, could win God's favor. At the same time those elected to God's grace had the obligation to encourage others to behave morally and to gain knowledge of the Bible. Calvinist ministers became moral guardians and preachers of God's Word. Calvinists sought the participation of all believers in local church administration, which had political implications in encouraging the idea of a wider access to government. They also promoted wider popular education so that more people could read the Bible. Calvinism was accepted not only in part of Switzerland but also in portions of Germany and France (where it produced strong minority groups), in the Netherlands, and in England and Scotland. By the early 17th century it also spread to North America.

The Catholic church did not sit still under Protestant attack. It did not restore religious unity, but it defended southern Europe, Austria, Poland, Hungary, and key parts of Germany for the Catholic faith. Under a Catholic Reformation, Church councils revived Catholic doctrine and refuted key Protestant tenets such as the idea that priests had no special sacramental power and could marry. They also attacked popular superstitions and remnants of animism, which meant that Catholics and Protestants alike were trying to find new ways to shape the outlook of ordinary folk. A new religious order, the Jesuits, became active in politics, education, and missionary work, regaining some parts of Europe for the Church. Jesuit fervor would also sponsor Catholic missionary activity in Asia and the Americas.

THE END OF CHRISTIAN UNITY IN THE WEST

The Protestant and Catholic Reformations had a number of results within Europe during the later 16th and early 17th centuries. Most obvious was an important series of religious wars. France was a scene of bitter battles between Calvinist and Catholic forces, intertwined with new rebellions by landed nobles against royal authority. These disputes ended only with the granting of tolerance to Protestants through the edict of Nantes in 1598—though in the next century French kings progressively cut back on Protestant rights. Wars raged recurrently in Germany, punctuated by efforts to agree on which states could be Protestant, which Catholic. In 1618 the Thirty Years' War broke out, pitting German Protestants and allies such as Lutheran Sweden against the holy Roman emperor, backed by Spain. The war was so devastating that it reduced German power and prosperity for a full century. It was ended only by the 1648 Treaty of Westphalia that agreed to the territorial tolerance concept, with some princely states and cities choosing one religion, some another. The treaty also reduced Spain's power, after decades in which Spanish armies had been the most powerful in Europe, in favor of France, which had backed the Protestant side. This treaty also finally settled a rebellion of the Protestant Netherlands against Spain, giving the former its full independence.

Religious fighting, finally, punctuated British history, first before the reign of Elizabeth in the 16th century, then in a civil war in the 1640s. Here too religious issues conjoined with other problems, particularly in a battle between the claims of parliament to rights of controlling royal actions and some rather tactless assertions of authority by a new line of English kings. The fighting of the civil war ended in 1660 (after one king had been beheaded), but full resolution came only in 1688 to 1689, when limited religious toleration was granted to most Protestant (but not Catholic) faiths.

Religious issues thus dominated European politics for almost a century. The religious wars led generally to a grudging and limited acceptance of the idea of religious pluralism: Christian unity could not be restored, though in most individual countries (the Netherlands came closest to a full exception) any idea of full religious liberty was still in the future. The religious wars persuaded some people that religion itself was suspect; if there was no dominant single truth, why all the cruelty and carnage? The wars, finally, affected the power balance and political structure of Europe. France, after a period of weakness during its internal strife, was on the upswing. The Netherlands and Britain were galvanized toward a growing international role. Spain, briefly ascendant, fell back. Internally some kings and princes benefited from the decline of papal authority by taking a stronger role in religious affairs. This was true in many Catholic as well as Protestant domains. In some cases, however, Protestant dissent and Protestant-derived political theory that challenged the idea of one-man rule encouraged popular political movements and enhanced parliamentary power.

Hans Holbein's "The Dance of Death" was encouraged by the continuing plague as well as religious clash.

The impact of religious change went well beyond politics. The way people thought and acted in daily life began to shift toward new forms. Popular mentalities changed most in Protestant areas, but Catholic reform produced new impulses as well. Several basic shifts were set in motion. Western people gradually became less likely to see an intimate connection between God and nature. Protestants believed fervently in God's power—and in important ways the role of religion in popular belief gained ground for at least a century—but they did not focus on miracles or other disruptive interventions in nature's course. Protestant churches, as physical structures, were more isolated than their Catholic counterparts from market activities in the cities, encouraging an idea that religion and daily life were separate. Many Westerners, in sum, gained a new sense of distinction between religious and other activities and tended to see nature in desacralized terms. This could affect, for example, their approach to health problems, encouraging (very gradually) a greater tendency to turn strictly to secular healers rather than religious or religiouslike practitioners when ill.

Religious change also promoted greater concentration on family life. Protestant and Catholic leaders began to talk of the family in more positive terms, not simply as an institution necessary because of human lust. Love between husband and wife was encouraged. As one English writer put it, "When love is absent between husband and wife, it is like a bone out of joint: there is no ease, no order." This promotion of family had ambiguous implications for women. Protestantism, abolishing religious convents, made marriage more necessary for women than before; there were fewer alternatives for women who could not marry. On the other hand, within the family women's emotional role improved with the new emphasis on affection.

Religious change accompanied and promoted growing literacy along with the spread of the printing press. In the town of Durham, England, around 1570 only 20 percent of all people were literate, but by 1630 the figure had climbed to 47 percent. Growing, though still limited, literacy opened people to additional new ideas and ways of thinking. It may have encouraged a new independence, a new belief in the powers of the individual to seek truth. This in turn promoted the idea of the self as a distinct entity, separate from church or community.

Without producing sudden or complete revolution in outlook, religious change obviously stimulated a considerable reorientation of the mental map of many ordinary people in the West. This reorientation followed from the important divisions that opened up in formal religious affiliations and the reduced political power of the Christian churches.

THE COMMERCIAL REVOLUTION

Concurrent with religious upheaval during the 16th century, the economic structure of the West underwent fundamental redefinition. The level of European trade rose sharply, and many Europeans had new goods available to them. Involvement with markets and merchants increased. At the same time western Europe's growing role in international trade furthered the role of commerce at home.

A basic spur to greater commercialization was a substantial price inflation that occurred throughout western Europe during the 16th century. The massive import of gold and silver from Spain's new colonies in Latin America forced prices up. New wealth heightened demand for products to sell both in the colonies and in Europe, but Western production could not keep pace—hence the price inflation. Inflation, in turn, while it hurt groups such as landlords who faced fixed rents, encouraged merchants to take new risks, for borrowing was cheap when money was losing value.

Inflation and the new colonial opportunities led to the formation of great trading companies, often with government backing in Spain, England, the Netherlands, and France. Governments granted regional monopolies to these giant concerns; thus the Dutch East Indies Company long dominated trade with the islands of Indonesia. European merchants increasingly pushed out Arab and Indian traders in East Asia and the Indian Ocean. They brought new profits back to Europe and developed new managerial skills and banking arrangements.

Colonial markets and generally increasing trade stimulated manufacturing. Most peasants continued to produce mainly for their own needs, but agricultural specialty areas developed in the production of wines, cheeses, wool, and the like. Some of these encouraged commercial farming and the use of paid laborers on the land. Shoemaking, pottery, metalworking, and other manufacturing specializations arose both in rural villages and in the cities. Technical improvements followed in many branches of manufacture, particularly in metals and mining.

The spread of markets and considerable manufacturing had a number of sweeping effects. Population grew by about 20 percent between 1500 and 1650, reversing a long period of decline. Several large urban centers arose. Prosperity increased for ordinary people as well as for the great merchants. English farmers, for example, enjoyed pewter tableware, more feather beds, and other amenities.

One historian has estimated that by around 1600 the average Western peasant or artisan owned five times as many "things" as his or her counterpart in southeastern Europe. Landowning peasants began to commission painters to decorate cabinets and other furnishings, in a popular art style that spread through western and central Europe. People were aware of the change in material standards at the time. A 16th-century Englishman noted that whereas in the past a peasant and his family slept on the floor, having only a pan or two as kitchenware, by the final decades of the century a farmer might have "a fair garnish of pewter in his cupboard, three or four feather beds, so many coverlets and carpets of tapestry, a silver salt, a bowl for wine . . . and a dozen spoons." It was around this time that French peasants began to enjoy wine on a fairly regular basis, rather than simply at special occasions—the result of higher productivity and better trade and transport facilities.

There were victims of change as well, however. Growing commercialization created the beginnings of a new proletariat in the West—people without access to producing property. Population growth and rising food prices hit hard at the poor, and many people had to sell their small plots of land. Some proletarians became manufacturing workers, depending on orders from merchant capitalists to keep their tools busy in their cottages. Others became paid labor on agricultural estates, where landlords were eager for a more manipulable work force to take advantage of sales opportunities in the cities. Others pressed into the cities, and a growing problem of wandering poor and beggars began to affect Western society; a new, tough attitude toward poverty crystallized that has lasted to some extent to the present day. New methods of disciplining elements of the proletariat, including institutional prisons, emerged to counter those features of proletarianization that impacted unfavorably on the rest of society. Government began to organize some aid to the poor, an important new function.

Commercialization, besides moving European society farther away from older traditions of community solidarity, had other results. Growing prosperity for some groups helped support a more elaborate family life. Better furnishings encouraged people to spend more time at home, at family meals for example, and many women were prompted to become regulators of domestic social routine. More market involvement encouraged greater belief in personal achievement and in the demystification of nature. Economic change, in other words, intertwined with some of the alterations in mentalities also wrapped up in the religious upheaval.

Finally, the shifts in popular economic and cultural traditions provoked important outcry, for these were fundamental challenges to sanctioned behaviors and values. A huge wave of popular protest in western Europe developed at the end of the 16th century, extending until about 1650. Peasants and townspeople alike rose in defense of noncommercial economic motives and greater protection from poverty and proletarianization. The risings did not deflect the basic currents of change, but they revealed the massive dislocation involved. Not directed against established governments, the riots showed real hatred of the rich merchant classes as well as a sense of popular democracy that would reemerge in the 18th century.

A huge outburst against suspected witches arose in the same decades in various parts of western Europe and also in New England. More than 100,000 suspected witches were accused and killed. The witchcraft hysteria reflected new resentments against the poor, often accused of witchcraft by communities unwilling to accept responsibility for their poverty. The hysteria also reflected new uncertainties about religious truth, for the trials were particularly common in areas converted to Protestantism. It even showed new tensions about family life and the role of women, who were the most common targets of persecution.

The West, in sum, was moving toward new economic structures and a new belief system, both of which promised further change in the future. Many people greeted the changes with dismay and sought ways of expressing their insecurity and fear, for the changes reached deeply into personal life and intimate beliefs.

This 1514 woodcut portrays the European view of witches, concocting an ointment to be used for flying to the Sabbath.

NEW SOCIAL DIVISIONS

Renaissance, Reformation, and economic change had combined to produce a number of new divisions in western Europe. The Renaissance created some new wedges between the educated elite and the mass of ordinary people. Traditionally, Europe's aristocracy had shared in popular culture, enjoying peasant festivals and an earthiness that embraced ribald jokes and even public urination—as in Wales where a young man might urinate on his betrothed's dress as a sign of possession. By the 16th century many aristocrats and religious leaders began to pull away from popular culture, urging more refined manners and/or a purer religious spirit. Both the Protestant and the Catholic Reformation picked up on this latter tone, attacking popular dancing and other customs that had mixed in with religious ceremonies.

In response to elite disapproval and to the growth of a propertyless proletariat, popular rebellions throughout Europe signaled important social tension. Peasant songs expressed such sentiments as this: "The whole country must be overturned, for we peasants are now to be the lords, it is we who will sit in the shade." Risings in 1648 produced demands for a popular political voice; an English group called the Levelers gained 100,000 signatures on a petition for political rights. Elsewhere common people praised the kings while attacking their "bad advisors" and high taxes. One English agitator said that "we should cut off all the gentlemen's heads . . . we shall have a merrier world shortly." In France Protestant and Catholic peasants rose together against landlords and taxes: "They seek only the ruin of the poor people for our ruin is their wealth."

New social divisions were not, however, completely straightforward, which is one reason the popular risings ultimately failed. Growing wealth spread to property-owning peasants and craftsmen, who also gained increasing literacy. These people might be attracted to some of the new ideas, urged by religious leaders, about tighter family structures. These groups could readily share the suspicions of government leaders about the irresponsibility of the poor. Western social alignments were in flux, which most obviously produced impressive popular protest and new divisions over beliefs, but which also generated audiences for various other new ideas.

DOCUMENT
CONTROVERSIES ABOUT WOMEN

Changes in family structure and some shifts in the economic roles of women, plus ambivalent Protestant promptings about women that emphasized the family context but urged affection and respect between wives and husbands, touched off new gender tensions in Western society by the 17th century. Some of these tensions showed in witchcraft trials, so disproportionately directed against women. Other tensions showed in open debate about women's relationship to men, in which new male hostility toward women not content with a docile wifeliness vied with new claims of virtue and prowess by some women. Though the debate centered in the upper class of Protestant nations such as England, it may have had wider ramifications; some of these ramifications, though quieter during the 18th century, would burst forth again in arguments about inequality and family confinement in the 19th century, when a more durable feminist movement took shape in the West. In the selections below, the antiwoman position is set forth in a 1615 pamphlet by Joseph Swetnam; the favorable view implicitly urging new rights is in a 1640 pamphlet pseudonymously authored by "Mary Tattle-well and Ioane Hit-him-home, spinsters."

SWETNAM'S "ARRAIGNMENT OF WOMEN"

Men, I say, may live without women, but women cannot live without men: for Venus, whose beauty was excellent fair, yet when she needed man's help, she took Vulcan, a clubfooted Smith. . . .
For women have a thousand ways to entice thee and ten thousand ways to deceive thee and all such fools as are suitors unto them: some they keep in hand with promises, and some they feed with flattery, and some they delay with dalliances, and some they please with kisses. They lay out the folds of their hair to entangle men into their love; betwixt their breasts is the vale of destruction; and in their beds there is hell, sorrow, and repentance. Eagles eat not men till they are dead, but women devour them alive. . . .

It is said of men that they have that one fault, but of women it is said that they have two faults: that is to say, they can neither say well nor do well. There is a saying that goeth thus: that things far fetched and dear bought are of us most dearly beloved. The like may be said of women; although many of them are not far fetched, yet they are dear bought, yea and so dear that many a man curseth his hard pennyworths and bans his own heart. For the pleasure of the fairest woman in the world lasteth but a honeymoon; that is, while a man hath glutted his affections and reaped the first fruit, his pleasure being past, sorrow and repentance remaineth still with him.

TATTLE-WELL AND HIT-HIM-HOME'S "WOMEN'S SHARP REVENGE"

But it hath been the policy of all parents, even from the beginning, to curb us of that benefit by striving to keep us under and to make us men's mere Vassals even unto all posterity. How else comes it to pass that when a Father hath a numerous issue of Sons and Daughters, the sons forsooth they must be first put to the Grammar school, and after perchance sent to the University, and trained up in the Liberal Arts and Sciences, and there (if they prove not Blockheads) they may in time be book-learned? . . .

When we, whom they style by the name of weaker Vessels, though of a more delicate, fine, soft, and more pliant flesh therefore of a temper most capable of the best Impression, have not that generous and liberal Education, lest we should be made able to vindicate our own injuries, we are set only to the Needle, to prick our fingers, or else to the Wheel to spin a fair thread for our own undoing, or perchance to some more dirty and debased drudgery. If we be taught to read, they then confine us within the compass of our Mother Tongue, and that limit we are not suffered to pass; or if (which sometimes happeneth) we be brought up to Music, to singing, and to dancing, it is not for any benefit that thereby we can engross unto ourselves, but for their own particular ends, the better to please and content their licentious appetites when we come to our maturity and ripeness. And thus if we be weak by Nature, they strive to make us more weak by our Nurture; and if in degree of place low, they strive by their policy to keep us more under.

Now to show we are no such despised matter as you would seem to make us, come to our first Creation, when man was made of the mere dust of the earth. The woman had her being from the best part of his body, the Rib next to his heart, which difference even in our complexions may be easily decided. Man is of a dull, earthy, and melancholy aspect, having shallows in his face and a very forest upon his Chin, when our soft and smooth Cheeks are a true representation of a delectable garden of intermixed Roses and Lilies. . . .

Man might consider that women were not created to be their slaves or vassals; for as they had not their Original out of his head (thereby to command him), so it was not out of his foot to be trod upon, but in a *medium* out of his side to be his fellow feeler, his equal, and companion. . . .

Thus have I truly and impartially proved that for Chastity, Charity, Constancy, Magnanimity, Valor, Wisdom, Piety, or any Grace or Virtue whatsoever, women have always been more than equal with men, and that for Luxury, Surquidant obscenity, profanity, Ebriety, Impiety, and all that may be called bad we do come far short of them.

Questions: Why did such different views about women develop in the 17th century? Why did some women defy patriarchal culture, and what were their main arguments? Did the new arguments in favor of women suggest that their conditions were improving?

SCIENCE AND POLITICS: THE NEXT PHASE OF CHANGE

Religious disruptions had produced major changes in Western intellectual life, and the related shifts in popular mentality involved even more fundamental new directions. It was the revolution in science, culminating in the 17th century, that set the seal on the cultural reorientation of the West. While the scientific revolution most obviously affected formal intellectual life, it also furthered some of the key changes in wider mentalities.

At the same time, after the political upheavals occasioned by the Reformation, a more decisive set of new government forms arose in the West, centering on the emergence of the nation state. The functions of the state and its contacts with popular loyalties expanded. The Western nation state was not a single form, as key variants emerged such as absolute monarchies and parliamentary regimes, but there were some common patterns beneath the surface. Continued cultural change, then, and new roles for the state defined the second major phase in the transformation of the early modern West during the late 17th and early 18th centuries.

SCIENCE

During the 16th century important scientific research had continued the traditions of the later Middle Ages, although the results were somewhat obscured by the more striking developments in art and religion. A Polish monk, Copernicus, used astronomical observation and mathematical calculation to disprove the Hellenistic belief that the earth was the center of the universe. Rather, the earth moved around the sun. Also in the 16th century, anatomical work by the Belgian Vesalius overturned many medical ideas. These key discoveries not only advanced knowledge; they also implied a new power for scientific research in its ability to test and often overrule accepted ideas.

These implications won full attention in a dizzying series of empirical advances and wider theoretical generalizations from the 1590s onward. New instruments such as the microscope and improved telescopes allowed gains in biology and astronomy. Scientists throughout the Western world participated in a surge of excited discovery. The Italian Galileo publicized Copernicus's discoveries while adding his own basic findings about the laws of gravity and planetary motion. Condemned by the Catholic church for his innovations, Galileo nevertheless definitively proved the inadequacy of traditional ideas about the universe. He also showed the new pride in scientific achievement, writing modestly how he, "by marvelous discoveries and clear demonstrations, had enlarged a thousand times" the knowledge produced by "the wise men of bygone ages." Chemical research advanced understanding of the behavior of gases. The English physician John Harvey demonstrated the circular movement of the blood in animals, with the heart as the "central pumping station."

The advances in knowledge were accompanied by important methodological statements about science and its impact. Francis Bacon urged the value of careful empirical research and predicted that scientific knowledge could steadily advance, producing improvements in technology as well. René Descartes established the importance of a skepti-

This 40-foot reflecting telescope was built in Britain in 1789.

cal review of all received wisdom, arguing that human reason could then develop laws that would explain the fundamental workings of nature. Descartes included a proof of God in his rationalistic generalizations, but this system allowed no real room for divine interventions.

The capstone to the 17th-century scientific revolution came with Isaac Newton's publication of his *Principia* in 1687, for this drew the various astronomical and physical observations and wider theories together in a neat framework of natural laws. Newton set forth the basic, simple principles of all motion: that a body in motion maintains uniform momentum unless affected by outside forces, that changes in rates of motion are proportional to the outside force, and that to every action there is always opposed an equal reaction. Newton defined the forces of gravity in great mathematical detail and showed that the whole universe responded to these forces, which among other things explained the planetary orbits. Finally, Newton stated the basic scientific method in terms of a mixture of rational hypothesis and generalization and careful empirical observation and experiment. Here was a vision of a natural universe that could be captured in relatively simple laws (though increasingly complex mathematics accompanied the findings). Here was a vision of a method of knowing that might do away with blind reliance on tradition or an acceptance of the need for religious faith.

The scientific revolution was quickly popularized among educated Westerners, though not yet the wider populace. New scientific institutes were set up, often with government aid, to advance research and disseminate findings. Lectures and easy-to-read manuals publicized the latest advances and communicated the excitement researchers themselves shared. The results fed into some of the wider shifts in outlook, at least among literate, urban people. Attacks on beliefs in witchcraft became more common, and magistrates grew increasingly reluctant to entertain witchcraft accusations in court; the public hysteria began to die down after about 1670. There were growing signs of a new belief that people could control and calculate their environment. Insurance companies sprang up to help guard against risk. Doctors increased their attacks on popular healers in the name of a more scientific diagnosis of illness. Newsletters, an innovation by the late 17th century, began to advertise lost and found items, for there was no point leaving this kind of problem to blind chance.

The scientific revolution had important implications beyond science in terms of how and what people could know. By the 1680s writers affected by the new science, though not themselves scientists, began to attack traditional religious ideas such as miracles, for in the universe of the scientific revolution there was no room for disruption of nature's laws. Some intellectuals held out a new conception of God, called "Deism," arguing that while there might be a divinity its role was simply to set natural laws in motion, not to regulate them once the process was launched. Faith came under direct scrutiny. John Locke, in England, argued that people, through their senses and reason, could learn everything they needed to know; faith was irrelevant. Christian beliefs in human sinfulness crumbled in the view of the ascendant intellectuals, for human nature was basically good, given the capacity to learn. Finally, scientific advance created wider assumptions about the possibility of human progress. If knowledge could advance through concerted human effort, why not progress in other domains? Even literary authorities joined this parade—the idea that past styles set timeless standards of perfection came under growing criticism.

The scientific revolution by no means monopolized the West's intellectual life around 1700. There were important movements in art with the continued reliance on classical styles. Religious authorities were hardly silent, and many attacked the brashness of the new science. Unquestionably, however, the balance of intellectual interests was shifting, and science, with its presumed implications for other kinds of knowledge, increasingly ruled the roost.

This realignment was a first in human history. Science had never before been central to intellectual life. Science had played important roles in other civilizations, as in China, classical Greece, and Islam. Generally, however, wider religious or philosophical interests predominated. In China most notably, despite some real interest in generalizations about the physical universe derived from Daoism, science continued to be construed mainly in terms of practical, empirical advances. Chinese science piled up concrete information about astronomy or medicinal drugs. The Western passion for combining empiricism with more sweeping rational formulations—the idea of general laws of nature—clearly built on specific traditions that had come from Greek thought as mediated by Christian theology and Islamic philosophy during the postclassical period. The West, in sum, was not alone in developing crucial scientific data, but it had become the most vibrant center for scientific advance and its leading thinkers stood alone, for some time, in seeing science as the key to gaining and defining knowledge.

THE NATION-STATE

The feudal monarchy—that balance between king and nobles—that had defined Western politics since the High Middle Ages finally came undone in the 17th century. In most countries, after the passions of religious wars finally cooled, monarchs gained new powers, curtailing the tradition of noble pressure or revolt. At the same time, more ambitious military organization, in states that defined war as a central purpose, required more careful administration and improved tax collection.

The prototype for this new pattern was France, now the West's most important nation. French kings steadily built up their power in the 17th century. They stopped calling the medieval parliament, passing laws as they saw fit, though some provincial councils remained strong. They blew up the castles of dissident nobles, another sign of how gunpowder undercut the military basis of feudalism. They appointed a growing bureaucracy, drawn from the merchants and lawyers. They sent direct representatives to the outlying provinces. They professionalized the army, giving more formal training to officers, providing uniforms and logistical support, and creating military hospitals and pensions. The French kings had larger and more reliable military forces than ever before in Western history.

So great was the power of the monarch, in fact, that the French system became known as *absolute monarchy*. Its most glorious royal proponent, King Louis XIV, summed up its principles succinctly: "I am the state." Louis became a major patron of the arts, giving government a cultural role beyond any previous levels in the West. His academies not only encouraged science but worked to standardize the French language. A sumptuous palace at Versailles was used to keep nobles busy with social functions, so that they could not interfere with affairs of state.

More substantively, using the new bureaucratic structure, Louis and his ministers developed additional functions for the state. They cut down on internal tariffs barriers to trade and created new, state-run manufacturing. The reigning economic theory, called *mercantilism,* held that governments should promote the internal economy in order to improve tax revenues and to limit imports from other nations, lest money be lost to enemy states. Hence absolute monarchs like Louis XIV set tariffs on imported goods, tried to encourage their merchant fleets, and sought colonies to provide raw materials and a guaranteed market for manufactured goods produced at home.

The basic structure of absolute monarchy developed in other states besides France. Spain, after its 17th century decline, tried to imitate French principles in the 18th century, which resulted among other things in efforts to tighten control over its Latin American colonies. The most important spread of absolute monarchy occurred, however, in the central European states that were gaining in importance. A series of kings in Prussia, in eastern Germany, built a strong army and bureaucracy. They promoted economic activity and also began to develop a state-sponsored school system. Habsburg kings in Austria-Hungary, though still officially rulers of the Holy Roman Empire, in fact concentrated increasingly on developing a stronger monarchy in the lands under their direct control. The power of these Habsburg rulers increased after they pushed back the last Turkish invasion threat late in the 17th century, and then added the kingdom of Hungary to their domains.

Absolute monarchy and the classical style in architecture are symbolized by Louis XIV's great 17th-century palace at Versailles.

Absolute monarchy formed a domestic system of government. Most absolute monarchs saw a strong military as a key political goal, and many hoped for territorial expansion. Louis XIV used his strong state as the basis for a series of wars from the 1680s onward. The wars yielded some new territory for France but finally attracted an opposing alliance system that blocked further advance. Prussian kings, though long cautious in exposing their proud military to the risk of major war, turned in the 18th century to a series of conflicts that won new territory.

Britain and the Netherlands, both growing commercial and colonial powers, stood apart from the trend toward absolute monarchy in the 17th century. They, too, emphasized the role of the central state, but they also firmed up parliamentary regimes in which the kings shared power with representatives selected by the nobility and upper urban classes. The English civil wars produced a final political settlement in 1688 and 1689 (the so-called Glorious Revolution) in which parliament won basic sovereignty over the king. The English parliament no longer depended on the king to convene, for regular sessions were now scheduled, and it held assured rights to approve taxation that allowed it to monitor or initiate most major policies.

Furthermore, a growing body of political theory arose in the 17th century that built on these parliamentary ideas. John Locke and others argued that power came basically from the people, not from a divine right to royal rule. Kings should therefore be restrained by institutions that protected the popular interest, including certain general rights to freedom and property. A right of revolution could legitimately oppose unjust rule.

Overall, while the West developed important diversity in political forms, between absolute monarchy and a new kind of *parliamentary monarchy,* a characteristic tension remained between government growth and the idea that there should be some limits to state authority. This tension was expressed in new forms, but it recalled some principles that had originated in the Middle Ages.

Government growth itself should not be exaggerated. While absolute monarchs had torn down some of the characteristic institutions of feudal days, they lacked the means to gain detailed control over their subjects. Nobles in fact

Europe under Absolute Monarchy, 1715

Civil war resulted in the execution of Charles I in London, England, in 1649.

continued to play a considerable role in affairs of state. Furthermore, many of the innovations that did occur simply brought to the West the kinds of bureaucratic structures that other civilizations, particularly China, had developed long before.

It was significant, nevertheless, that at a time in world history when governments in many civilizations were entering a period of decline, those in the West were on the upswing. It was significant also that Western governments gained new powers to influence wider spheres of activity. They affected economic life and the treatment of the poor. They increasingly defined the way prisoners should be treated. They played some role in cultural trends. They also gave merchants a political role, as bureaucrats or parliamentary representatives, that was unusual in world history to that point.

Furthermore, both the absolute monarchies and the parliamentary monarchies shared important characteristics as nation-states. Unlike the great empires of many other civilizations, they ruled peoples who shared a common culture and language, some important minorities apart. They thus could appeal for a certain loyalty that linked cultural and political bonds. This was as true of England, where the idea of special rights of Englishmen helped feed the parliamentary movement, as of France. Not surprisingly, ordinary people in many nation-states, even though not directly represented in government, showed increasing belief that government should act for their interests. Thus Louis XIV faced recurrent popular riots predicated on the assumption that, when bad harvests drove up food prices, it was the obligation of government to help people out. Thus the English parliamentary system, though monopolized by the upper classes, opened the way to frequent popular petitions about various grievances.

Nation-states, in sum, developed a growing list of functions, particularly under the banner of mercantilism whose principles were shared by monarchists and parliamentary leaders alike. They also promoted new political values and loyalties that were somewhat less common among the political traditions of other civilizations. They certainly kept the West divided politically and frequently at war.

ANALYSIS
ELITES AND MASSES

What caused the end of witchcraft hysteria in the West by the later 17th century? One explanation focuses on new efforts by elites, such as local magistrates, to discipline mass impulses. Authorities stopped believing in demonic disruptions of natural processes, and so forced an end to persecutions. But many ordinary people were also thinking in new ways. Without converting fully to a scientific outlook, they became open to new ideas about how to handle health problems, reducing their belief in magical remedies; they needed witches less. Early attacks on witches may have changed popular habits, contributing to the reduction of hysteria. Older women, for example, threatened by growing community suspicion, learned to maintain a lower profile, emphasizing benign, grandmotherly qualities rather than seeking a more independent role. Some Western people still believed in witches, and a few believed they were witches themselves. (A few still do, in the later 20th century in the West.) But witchcraft beliefs, once a key element in the Western mentality, and the hysteria specifically characteristic of the 16th and 17th centuries, both declined. This decline reflected new ways of thinking about strangeness and disruption. It involved complex interactions among various segments of Western society—magistrates and villagers, scientists and priests, husbands and widows.

The transformation of Western society after 1450 raises fascinating questions about the role of elites—particularly powerful groups and creative individuals—versus the ordinary run of folk in causing change. The growing importance of social history has called attention to ordinary people, as we have seen, but it has not answered all the questions about their actual role. This role varies, of course, by place and time. But some social historians tend generally to see ordinary people as victims of change, bumped and beleaguered by the power groups. Others, in contrast, tend generally to stress the positive historical role of ordinary people in partly shaping the context of their own lives and affecting the larger course of history as well.

Massive religious change, for example, such as the spread of Islam or the Protestant Reformation in Europe, involved the needs and opportunities of ordinary people in contact with extraordinary religious leaders. Such change has always involved conversion of ordinary people—by persuasion or coercion—the activities of rulers, and indeed a combination of popular impulses and traditions with formal religious doctrine.

It is easy to read the early modern transformation of western Europe as an operation shaped by elites, with the masses as passive or futilely protesting clay. Not only the Renaissance and Reformation, but also the commercial revolution, entailed decisive action by key leadership groups. Leading merchants spurred economic change, and they ultimately began to farm out manufacturing jobs. Resultant proletarianization—which tore a growing minority of west Europeans away from property and so from economic control of their lives—graphically illustrated the disparities of power in Western society, as capitalist merchants and landowners gained a more manipulable labor force. Ordinary people knuckled under or protested, but they were reacting, not initiating.

The rise of science rivets attention on the activities of extraordinarily creative individuals, such as Newton, and elite institutions such as the scientific academies. Some historians have suggested that the rise of science forged a new gap between the way educated upper classes and masses thought.

Yet the ordinary people of western Europe were not inert, nor did they simply and abortively protest change in the name of the tried and true. Widespread shifts came from repeated decisions by nameless peasants and artisans, not just from those at the top. The steady technological improvements in manufacturing thus flowed upward from practicing artisans, not downward from formal scientists. The European-style family, an innovation by ordinary people the elite long ignored, encouraged new parent-child relations, new tensions between young adults and the old, that might spur other innovations—including a willingness to settle distant colonies in search of property. The fact that young people often had to wait to marry until their property-owning fathers died could spur many to seek new lands or new economic methods. Ordinary people, in other words, changed their habits too. They created a new climate for generating as well as receiving new ideas about medicine or witchcraft or about how to handle emotions in the family. They created new motives and rhythms for work. In mentalities, changes at the popular level clearly related to elite currents, despite clashes and discontinuities.

Finally, the dichotomy of elites and ordinary people was bridged in important new ways during the early modern centuries, and particularly after about 1650. The spread of literacy facilitated interchange, first in religion and then in science. While the rise of a proletarian minority constituted a new rift, growing prosperity and commercial mindedness among many middle-level property owners complicated any claim to growing economic inequality overall. Gender divisions increased in some respects, as women became more fully associated with domestic functions, but the emphasis on family values encouraged men and women to participate in some shared experiences. Western society was generating some new middle ground in outlook and power. Commercial contacts even eased, without fully eliminating, one of the oldest divisions in agricultural civilization, that between country and town. Rural people gained access to new (sometimes disturbing) urban habits and leisure forms.

The new Western patterns were obviously complex, as any sweeping transformation must be. Changes emanated from various levels, moved in various directions, and created new groupings as well as new disparities. The active involvement of ordinary people warrants comparison with transformations in other key junctures of world history. It also explains why other civilizations, later seeking to imitate certain features of the new Western society, faced important choices about whether and how to involve the masses—choices in which the masses would have their own contributions to make.

Questions: Did elites gain new power over the masses in early modern Western society? Are ordinary people more conservative by nature, more suspicious of change, than groups at the top? Can you describe at least two other historical cases in which it is important whether change was imposed on ordinary people from above, or whether ordinary people themselves produced important innovations?

THE WEST BY 1750

The three great currents of change—commercialization, cultural reorientation, and the rise of the nation-state—continued to operate in the West after 1700, along with the growing international influence of the West. Each strand, in fact, produced new ramifications that furthered the overall transformation of the West.

POLITICAL PATTERNS

On the whole, during the middle decades of the 18th century political changes seemed least significant. During much of the century English politics settled into a rather turgid parliamentary routine, in which key political groups competed for influence without major policy differences. Some popular concern for greater representation surfaced in the 1760s, as a movement for democracy surged briefly, but there was as yet no consistent reform current. Absolute monarchy in France changed little institutionally, but it became progressively less effective. It was unable to force changes in the tax structure that would give it more solid financial footing, because aristocrats refused to surrender their traditional exemptions.

Political developments were far livelier in central Europe. In Prussia Frederick the Great, building on the military and bureaucratic organization of his predecessors, introduced greater freedom of religion while expanding the economic functions of the state. His government actively encouraged better agricultural methods, as in promoting use of the potato as a staple crop. It also codified its laws toward greater commercial coordination and greater equity; harsh traditional punishments were cut back. Later in the 18th century an Austrian emperor, Joseph II, tried a similar program of state-sponsored improvements, including a major effort to roll back the power of the Catholic church. Rulers of this sort claimed to be enlightened despots, wielding great authority but for the good of society at large.

Enlightened or not, the policies of the major Western nation-states produced recurrent warfare. France and Britain squared off in the 1740s and again in the Seven Years' War (1756–1763); their conflicts focused on battles for colonial empire. Austria and Prussia also fought, with Prussia gaining new land. Wars in the 18th century were carefully modulated, without devastating effects, but they demonstrated the continued linkage between statecraft and war characteristic of the West.

ENLIGHTENMENT THOUGHT

In culture, the aftermath of the scientific revolution spilled over into a new movement known as the *Enlightenment,* centered particularly in France but with adherents throughout the Western world. Enlightenment thinkers continued to support scientific advance. While there were no Newton-like breakthroughs, chemists gained new understanding of major elements and biologists developed a vital new classification system for the natural species.

The Enlightenment also pioneered in applying scientific methods to the study of human society, sketching the modern social sciences. The basic idea here was that rational laws could describe social as well as physical behavior, and that knowledge could be used to improve policy. Thus criminologists wrote about how brutal punishments failed

Enlightenment efficiency and old-fashioned public punishment caused the construction of this "mass production" scaffold, which sped up executions at the Old Bailey, London. Other reformers opposed capital punishment, however quick and humane.

to deter crime, whereas a decent society would be able to rehabilitate criminals through education. Political theorists wrote about the importance of carefully planned constitutions and controls over privilege, though they disagreed about what political form was best. A new school of economists developed. The Scottish philosopher Adam Smith set forth a number of invariable principles of economic behavior, based on the belief that people act according to their self-interest but, through competition, work to promote general economic advance. Government should avoid regulation in favor of the operation of individual initiative and market forces. Here was an important specific statement of economic policy and an illustration of the growing belief that general models of human behavior could be derived from rational thought.

More generally still, the Enlightenment produced a set of basic principles about human affairs. Human beings are naturally good and can be educated to be better. Reason was the key to truth, and religions that relied on blind faith or refused to tolerate diversity were wrong. Enlightenment thinkers attacked the Catholic church with particular vigor. Progress was possible, even inevitable, if people could be set free. Society's goals should center on improvements in material and social life.

Enlightenment thinkers showed great interest in technological change, for greater prosperity was a valid and achievable goal. Coercion and cruelty could be corrected, for the Enlightenment encouraged a humanitarian outlook that was applied in condemnations of slavery and war.

Though not typical of the Enlightenment's main thrust, a few thinkers applied the general principles to other areas. A handful of socialists argued that economic equality and the abolition of private property must become important goals. A few feminist thinkers, such as Mary Wollstonecraft in England, argued that new political rights and freedoms should extend to women, against the general male-centered views of most Enlightenment thinkers.

The Enlightenment, summing up and extending earlier intellectual changes, became an important force for political and social reform. It did not rule unchallenged. Important popular religious movements, such as Methodism in England, showed the continued power of spiritual faith. Many writers, particularly those experimenting with the novel as a new literary form in the West, rebelled against Enlightenment rationality to urge the importance of sentimentality and emotion. These approaches, too, encouraged rethinking of traditional styles.

The popularization of new ideas encouraged further changes in the habits and beliefs of many ordinary people. Reading clubs and coffeehouses allowed many urban artisans and businessmen to discuss the latest reform ideas. Leading writers and compilations of scientific and philosophical findings, such as the *Encyclopaedia Britannica*, won a wide audience and, in a few cases, a substantial fortune due to the sale of books. Groups and individuals formed to promote better agricultural or industrial methods, or bent on winning new political rights, referred directly to Enlightenment thinking. Some groups of artisans and peasants also turned against established churches and even withdrew from religious belief, as secular values gained ground.

Other changes in popular outlook paralleled the new intellectual currents, though they had deeper sources than philosophy alone. Attitudes toward children began to shift in many social groups. Older methods of physical discipline were criticized, in favor of more restrained behavior that would respect the goodness and innocence of children. Swaddling began to decline, as parents were interested in freer movement and greater interaction for young children; no longer were infants tightly wrapped during their first months. Among wealthy families, educational toys and books for children reflected the idea that childhood should be a stage for learning and growth. At the most basic level, parents became increasingly likely to give young children names at birth and to select names different from those of older relatives—a sign of a new affection for children and new belief in their individuality. These changes were gradual, and they involved more adult control of children as well as a more humane outlook. The idea of shaping children and instilling guilt-stimulated consciences gained ground. Unquestionably, the net effect was to alter parent-child relations and also to produce novel personality ideals for adults themselves.

Family life generally was altered by a growing sense that old hierarchies needed to be rethought, toward somewhat greater equality in the treatment of women and children within the home. Love among family members gained new respect, and an emotional bond in marriage became more widely sought. Parents, for example, grew more reluctant to force a match on a son or daughter if the emotional vibrations were not right. Here was a link not only with Enlightenment ideas of proper family relations but with the novels that poured out a sentimental view of life.

Ongoing economic change, finally, paralleled the ferment in popular culture and intellectual life. Commerce continued its spread. Ordinary Westerners began to buy processed products, such as refined sugar and coffee or tea obtained from Indonesia and the West Indies, for daily use. Here was a sign of the growing importance of Europe's new colonies for ordinary life and of the beginnings of mass consumerism in Western society. Another sign of change was the growing use of paid, professional entertainment as part of popular leisure even in rural festivals. Not accidentally, circuses, first introduced in France in the 1670s, began to redefine leisure to include spectatorship and a taste for the bizarre.

Agriculture began to change. Until the later 17th century Western Europe had continued to rely largely on the methods and techniques characteristic of the Middle Ages—a severe economic constraint in a still agricultural society. Now, first in the Netherlands and then elsewhere, new procedures for draining swamps added available land. Nitrogen-fixing crops were introduced to reduce the need to leave land fallow. Stockbreeding improved, and new techniques like seed-drills or simply the use of scythes instead of sickles for harvesting heightened productivity. Some changes spread particularly fast on large estates, which was one reason that in England more and more land was enclosed, with ordinary farmers serving as tenants or laborers rather than owners. Other changes affected ordinary peasants as well. Particularly vital in this category was the spread of the potato from the late 17th century onward. A New World crop, the potato had long been shunned because it was not mentioned in the Bible and was held to be the cause of plagues. Enlightened government leaders and peasant desire to win greater economic security and better nutrition led to widespread adoption of this efficient crop. The West, in sum, improved its food supply and also its agricultural efficiency, leaving more labor available for other pursuits.

These changes, along with the steady growth of colonial trade and internal commerce, spurred increased manufacturing. The 18th century witnessed a rapid spread of household production of textiles and metal products, mostly by rural workers who alternated manufacturing with some agriculture. Hundreds of thousands of people were drawn into this domestic system in which capitalist merchants distributed supplies and orders and workers ran the production process for pay. While manufacturing tools were still hand operated, the spread of domestic manufacturing spurred important technical innovations designed to improve efficiency. In 1733 James Kay in England introduced the flying shuttle, which permitted automatic crossing of threads on looms; with this, an individual weaver could do the work of two. Improvements in spinning soon followed, as the Western economy began to escalate toward a full-fledged Industrial Revolution.

Finally, agricultural changes, commercialism, and manufacturing combined, particularly after about 1730, to produce a rapidly growing population in the West. With better food supplies, more people survived—the potato was a crucial ingredient here. More commercial motives helped prompt landlords and some ambitious peasants to acquire more land and to push unneeded labor off, heightening proletarianization but also reducing the restraints some parents could impose over the sexual behavior of their children: In essence, as some groups grew unsure of inheritance, they sought more immediate pleasures and also hoped to use the labor of the resultant children. Finally, new manufacturing jobs helped landless people support themselves, promoting in some cases earlier marriage and sexual liaisons. Growing population, in turn, promoted further economic change, heightening competition and producing a more manipulable labor force. The West's great population revolution, which would continue into the 19th century, both caused and reflected the civilization's dynamism, though it also produced great strain and confusion.

Western society was still essentially agricultural by the mid-18th century. Decisive new political forms had yet to be introduced, and in many ways government policies failed to keep pace with cultural and economic change after 1700. Established churches were forces to be reckoned with still. Even new developments, such as the spread of domestic manufacturing, functioned because they allowed so many traditional habits to persist. Thus while new market relationships described this growing system, the location and many of the methods of work as well as the association of family with production were not altered. Western society hovered between older values and institutions and the full flowering of change. Decades of outright political and economic revolution, which would build on these tensions and cause a fuller transformation, were yet to come.

CONCLUSION

INNOVATION AND INSTABILITY

Nevertheless, despite important continuities from the past, Western society had by the 18th century become increasingly accustomed to change. Population pressure and the force of new ideas generated additional stimuli. All levels of society were involved. The traditional aristocratic upper class had to think about new values and the challenge of commercial habits; it was also faced with population growth in its own ranks, which raised concern about what to do with surviving younger sons and daughters. Proletarians had to adjust to work without property; they also picked up new ideas about sex and children, and possibly new expectations about government responsibilities.

It was also notable that, by the 18th century, the various strands of change began to intertwine in Western civilization. Stronger governments promoted agricultural improvements that helped prod population growth. Changes in mentalities were fed by new economic structures; both encouraged a reevaluation of the family and the roles of children. New beliefs raised new political challenges. Enlightenment ideas about liberty and some fundamental human equality could obviously be directed against existing regimes. New family practices might have political implications as well. Children, raised with less adult restraint or encouraged to value their individual worth through parental love and careful education, might see traditional political limitations in new ways. There was no perfect fit, no inevitable match, in the three strands of change that had been transforming the West for two centuries or more—the commercial, the cultural, and the political. Clearly, however, by 1750, all were in place. The combination had already produced an unusual version of an agricultural civilization, and it promised more upheaval in the future.

The Western package of change had also produced a society unusually dynamic in the world at large. Two cautions here. First, other societies had changed rapidly before, and some displayed great vigor after 1450; the West in no sense invented change. Second, Western change depended heavily on the position it won in the wider world. Commercialization, for example, built on the West's ability to extract wealth from other societies. It remained true that internal shifts helped explain the West's course in the wider world, and here the key connection was the West's instability and tension, not its smooth course. Religious disputes, political rivalries, and economic dislocations all helped explain why Westerners reached out, as individuals and in groups, for new roles in international trade, explorations, or colonies. International activity flowed not from serene strength, but from recurrent disruption, and this activity in turn served the West as a vital outlet. Only in the 20th century have Westerners faced the obvious resultant question: What will happen to the West and its crosscurrents once the civilization's international role meets new challengers?

FURTHER READINGS

For an overview of developments in Western society during this period, with extensive bibliographies, see Sheldon Watts's *A Social History of Western Europe, 1450–1720* (1984) and Peter N. Stearns's *Life and Society in the West: The Modern Centuries* (1988). Charles Tilly's *Big Structures, Large Processes, Huge Comparisons* (1985) offers an analytical framework based on major change; see also Tilly's edited volume, *The Formation of National States in Western Europe* (1975).

On more specific developments and periods, J. H. Plumb's *The Italian Renaissance* (1986), F. H. New's *The Renaissance and Reformation: A Short History* (1977), O. Chadwick's *The Reformation* (1983), and Stephen Ozment's *The Age of Reform, 1520–1550* (1980) are fine introductions to early changes. See also Hubert Jedin and John Dolan, eds., *Reformation and Counter Reformation* (1980). Later political changes are sketched in G. Clark's *Early Modern Europe* (1960), M. Beloff's *The Age of Absolutism* (1967), and R. Hatton's *Europe in the Age of Louis XIV* (1979).

Key aspects of social change in this period can be approached through Peter Burke's *Popular Culture in Early Modern Europe* (1978), Keith Thomas's *Religion and the Decline of Magic* (1971), and Lawrence Stone's *The Family, Sex and Marriage in England 1500–1800* (1977). On popular protest, see Charles Tilly's *The Contentious French* (1986) and H. A. F. Kamen's *The Iron Century: Social Change in Europe 1550–1660* (1971).

On science, A. R. Hall's *From Galileo to Newton, 1630–1720* (1982) is a fine introduction. Relations between science and technology are covered in C. Cipolla's *Before the Industrial Revolution* (1976).

THE WEST'S FIRST OUTREACH

- **DOCUMENT:** Western Conquerors: Tactics and Motives
- **ANALYSIS:** Causation and the West's Expansion

TOWARD A WORLD ECONOMY

COLONIAL EXPANSION

- **CONCLUSION:** The Impact of a New World Order
- **FURTHER READINGS**

1394–1460 Prince Henry the Navigator

1433 China ends great expeditions

1434 Portugal extends expeditions down West African coast

1488 Portuguese round Cape of Good Hope

1492 Columbus's first expedition

1497–1498 Vasco da Gama to India

1509 First Spanish colonies on Latin American mainland

1514 Expedition to Indonesia

1519–1521 Magellan circumnavigates globe

1534 First French explorations in Canada

1542 Portuguese reach Japan

1562 Britain begins its slave trade

1571 Ottoman fleet defeated in Battle of Lepanto

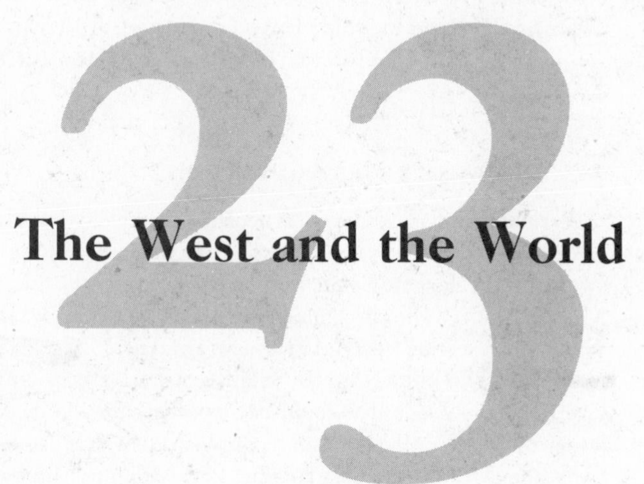

23 The West and the World

INTRODUCTION. One of the ways Westerners long have used history to make themselves feel good involves the recounting of the great explorations and conquests accomplished by Western stalwarts from the late 15th century onward. School children are steeped in the voyages of Columbus, the empires hacked out in Central and South America by Spanish conquerors, and the work of Christian missionaries in Asia and the New World.

The West did become steadily more important in the world in the centuries after 1450. It entered into some contact with every major society, it spurred and largely controlled a growing volume of international trade, and it set up colonies in key areas and outposts in others. The rise of the West between the 15th and the 18th centuries was also wrapped up in other developments of crucial importance in world history: the heightening and redefinition of interchanges among world societies and civilizations.

Previous periods had witnessed important steps toward greater diffusion of goods and ideas. During the classical era, most attention was given to the development of larger regional economies and cultural zones, such as the whole Chinese Middle Kingdom or the Mediterranean basin. Wider international contacts existed, as in the silk trade from China westward or the interaction between India and Hellenistic outposts following the conquests of Alexander the Great; few of these contacts, however, were of fundamental importance to the societies involved.

The level and significance of contacts increased during the postclassical era. Missionary religions spilled across civilizational boundaries, as with Buddhism in eastern and Southeast Asia and above all with Islam. The Indian Ocean became the center for a thriving international trade, which created new feeder regions—notably in East Africa—for

1588 British defeat Spanish Armada

1597 Japan begins isolation policy

1607 First British colony in Virginia

1608 First French colonies in Canada; first trading concession in India to England

1641 Dutch begin conquests on Java, in Indonesia

1652 Dutch launch colony in southern Africa

1744 French-British wars in India

1756 "Black hole" of Calcutta

1756–1763 Seven Years' War, in Europe, India, and North America

1763 British acquire New France

1764 East India Company control of Bengal

1775–1783 American Revolution

A.D. 1600 A.D. 1700

the dominant centers in the Middle East. For the Middle East, parts of Africa, and much of India, international trade became an important feature of the basic economic structure, with some regions garnering particular profits. In other cases wider regional economies developed, notably in trade from the Mediterranean northward in Europe or in the new regional economic zone in eastern Asia. Therefore, these varied economic and cultural exchanges sped up the pace of transfering technology among civilizations—a major boon to Europe in gaining access to earlier Chinese discoveries.

These previous intensifications of world interchange must not be neglected. It remains true, nevertheless, that the kind of world relationships that developed after 1450, mainly though not exclusively sponsored by Western leaders, spelled a new period in world history. Most obviously, new areas of the world were for the first time brought into the international complex, particularly the Americas, but also new parts of Africa and ultimately Polynesia. The rate and impact of international trade also increased in some portions of the Old World, such as the islands of Southeast Asia and India. Further, international trade now became so significant that it forged different relationships among key societies based on the kind of goods and amount of control contributed to the surging world economy. These new economic relationships, in turn, prompted some societies to reconsider older political and cultural traditions in light of patterns—again, particularly those of the West—that seemed compellingly successful. This kind of differential interchange had occurred before in world history—witness the Japanese imitation of China or the impact of Islam in East Africa—but it now spread more widely, more literally internationally.

The rise of the West, important in itself, was thus part of a larger reshuffling of world relationships. The intensification of an international framework became a factor, in some cases a determining factor, in the development of individual societies. Complexity remained. The traditions of individual civilizations, even those most affected by international pressures and Western incursions, were not totally effaced. More important, different civilizations forged different relationships to the international framework, creating various levels of involvement and impact. The story of the rise of the West must be cast in terms of its relationship to new international systems and the distinctions that arose within these systems.

This chapter, accordingly, deals with several interrelated developments during the centuries between about 1450 and 1750—the same centuries when the West was changing rapidly within its own borders. Topic one is simply the West's next explorations and acquisitions as it became the world's leading international trader and colonial power. Topic two involves the larger international economic system the West created, which turned out to have a life of its own. New contacts in terms of exchanges of ideas, foods, and diseases followed from the emergence of this new system. Topic three, finally, involves sorting out the different kinds of responses generated outside the West to the new economic framework and the West's role, ranging from attempts at isolation to outright subjection. The possibilities were considerable, and no society's history was fully described by Western activities or international economics. The new developments did, however, set part of the environment in which individual civilizations continued to evolve.

THE WEST'S FIRST OUTREACH

Various Western leaders, particularly merchants but also some princes and churchmen, had become increasingly aware of the larger world around them since the High Middle Ages. Cultural contacts with Islam and the Byzantine Empire formed part of this new awareness. The Crusades brought knowledge of Islam's superior economic levels and the goods that could be imported, for the delectation of the West's increasingly sophisticated aristocracy, from the Middle East and Asia. The Mongol Empire, which sped up exchanges among the civilizations of Asia, also spurred European interest. The fall of the Khans in China disrupted this interchange, as China became once again a land of mystery as far as Europeans were concerned. Europe's upper classes had by this time become accustomed to imported products from Southeast Asia and India, particularly spices. These goods were transported by sea to the Middle East in Arab ships, then brought overland where they were loaded again onto vessels (mainly from Genoa and Venice, in Italy) for the Mediterranean trade.

Europe entered into this era of growing contacts with the wider world network with a number of disadvantages. Their ignorance of the wider world remained vast. To be sure, Viking adventurers from Scandinavia had crossed the Atlantic in the 10th century, reaching Greenland and then North America, which they named Vinland. They quickly lost interest beyond establishing settlements on Greenland and Iceland, however, in part because they encountered Indian warriors whose weaponry was good enough to cause them serious problems. And many Europeans continued to believe that the earth was flat, though scientists in more advanced civilizations knew otherwise; their beliefs made them fearful of distant voyages, lest they fall off the world's edge.

Europeans did launch a more consistent effort at expansion from 1291 onward, as was discussed in Chapter 21. They were spurred by a new commercial and venturesome spirit, linked to Christian missionary zeal and Renaissance confidence alike. They were also pressed by new problems: fear of the strength of the emerging Ottoman Empire, a major new Muslim power, and the lack of gold to pay for Asian imports. Initial settlements in island groups in the south Atlantic fed hopes for further gains. Though Europeans failed to find the gold explorers kept claiming existed in great abundance somewhere in Africa—playing off the fabled treasures of the kings of Mali and some outright myths—early enterprises did have some concrete economic results. The first expeditions were limited, however, by the small, oar-propelled ships used in the Mediterranean trade, for these could not press far into the oceans.

NEW TECHNOLOGY: A KEY TO POWER

During the 15th century a series of technological improvements began to change the equation. Europeans developed deep-draft, round-hulled sailing ships for the Atlantic, capable of carrying heavier armaments than the ships they or most other societies had previously used. They also began to use a compass for navigation (an instrument they copied from the Arabs, who in turn had gained it from the Chinese). Mapmaking and other navigational devices improved as well. Finally, European knowledge of explosives, another Chinese invention, was adapted into gunnery. European metalwork, steadily advancing in sophistication, allowed Western craftsmen to devise the first guns and cannon. European technology, initially employed to produce bells, had introduced heavier castings than the finer Asian or African metalwork, and those castings were adaptable to gunnery. Though not initially very accurate, this weaponry was awesome by the standards of the time (and more than a bit terrifying to many Europeans, who had reason to fear the new destructive power of their own armies and navies). The West began to forge a weapons advantage over all other civilizations of the world, at first primarily on the seas—an advantage it would retain into the 20th century. With an unprecedented ability to kill and intimidate from a distance, the West was ready for its big push.

PORTUGAL AND SPAIN LEAD THE PACK

The specific initiative came from the small kingdom of Portugal. The rulers of this country had just finished driving out the Muslims, who still threatened from North Africa. This threat, the surge of energy that sometimes accompanies expulsion of an occupation force, and Christian missionary zeal prompted the Portuguese to look for conquests in Africa during the 15th century. Portugal's rulers were drawn by the excitement of discovery, the harm they might cause to the Muslim world, and a thirst for wealth—a potent mix. A Portuguese prince, Henry the Navigator, directed a series of expeditions along the African coast and also outward to islands such as the Azores. Beginning in 1434 the Portuguese began to press down the African coast, each expedition going a little farther than its predecessor. They brought back some slaves, spices such as pepper, and many stories of gold hordes they had not yet been able to find.

Later in the 15th century, Portuguese sailors ventured around the Cape of Good Hope planning to find India, where direct contact would give Europeans easier access to

Prince Henry the Navigator of Portugal sent annual expeditions down the western coast of Africa.

luxury cloths and spices, and also to reach the African east coast, held to be the source of gold. They rounded the Cape in 1488, but weary sailors forced the expedition back before it could see India. Then, after news of Columbus's discovery of America for Spain in 1492, Portugal redoubled its efforts, hoping to stave off the new Spanish competition. Vasco da Gama's fleet of four ships reached India, with the aid of a Hindu pilot picked up in East Africa, in 1497. The Portuguese mistakenly believed that the Indians were Christians, for they were confused by the Hindu temples they saw and thought they were churches. They faced the hostility of Muslim merchants, who had long dominated trade in this part of the world, but they managed to return with a small load of spices.

This success set in motion an annual series of Portuguese voyages to the Indian Ocean. One expedition, blown off course, reached Brazil where it proclaimed Portuguese sovereignty. With growing experience and rapidly improving maps, both Portuguese and Spanish expeditions became increasingly comfortable with voyages in the South Atlantic and the Indian Ocean. Portugal began to set up forts on the African coast and also in India—the forerunners of such Portuguese colonies as Mozambique, in East Africa, and Goa, in India. By 1514 the Portuguese had reached the islands of Indonesia, the center of spice production, and also China. By 1542 one Portuguese expedition arrived in Japan, where a missionary effort was launched that met with some success for several decades. In the space of

This is the earliest European sketch of American Indians at the time of a Portuguese expedition to northern South America about 1500. "The people are thus naked, handsome, brown. . . . They also eat each other, . . . and hang the flesh of them in the smoke. They become a hundred and fifty years of age, and have no government."

roughly a century, Portugal had traveled to almost every part of the world; as a Portuguese poet later said, "And if there had been more world they would have found it."

Meanwhile, only a short time after the Portuguese quest began, the Spanish reached out with even greater force. Here too was a country only recently freed from Muslim rule, full of missionary zeal and a desire for riches. The Spanish had traveled into the Atlantic during the 14th century. Then in 1492—the same year that the final Muslim fortress was captured in Spain—the Italian navigator Christopher Columbus, sailing in the name of the newly united Spanish monarchy and its rulers Ferdinand and Isabella, set sail for a westward route to India, convinced that the round earth would make his quest possible. As is well known, he failed, reaching the Americas instead and mistakenly naming their inhabitants Indians. Although Columbus believed to his death that he had sailed to India, later Spanish expeditions brought a firm realization that they had voyaged to a region in which Europeans and Asians had not traveled previously. One expedition, headed by Amerigo Vespucci, gave the New World its name. Spain, eager to claim this new land, won papal approval for Spanish dominion over most of what is now Latin America, though a later treaty awarded Brazil to Portugal.

Finally, a Spanish expedition under Ferdinand Magellan set sail westward in 1519, passing the southern tip of South America and sailing across the Pacific, reaching the Indonesian islands in 1521 after incredible hardships. It was on the basis of this voyage, ultimately the first trip around the world, that Spain claimed the Philippines, which were to be Spanish territory until 1898.

Portugal emerged from this first round of exploration with coastal holdings in parts of Africa and in the Indian port of Goa, a lease on the Chinese port of Macao, short-lived interests in trade with Japan, and, finally, the claim on Brazil. Spain asserted its hold on the Philippines, various Pacific islands, and the bulk of the Americas. During the 16th century, the Spanish moved to back up these claims by military expeditions to Mexico and South America. The Spanish also held Florida and sent expeditions northward from Mexico into California and other parts of what later became the southwestern United States.

Spain and Portugal: Explorations and Colonies, about 1600

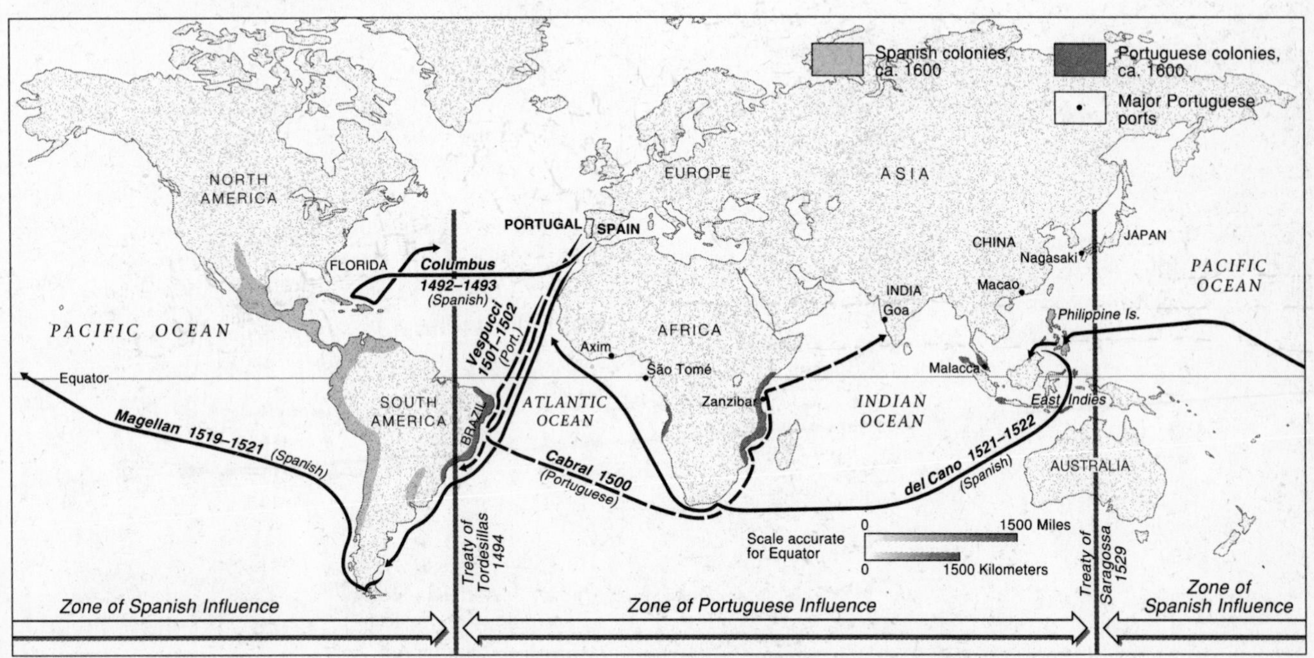

DOCUMENT
WESTERN CONQUERORS: TACTICS AND MOTIVES

In the first passage, Columbus writes to the Spanish monarchy on his way home from his 1492 expedition. In the second passage, the brother of Francisco Pizarro, the Spanish conqueror of Peru, describes in 1533 how the Inca ruler, Atahuallpa, was defeated.

COLUMBUS'S 1492 EXPEDITION

SIR, Believing that you will take pleasure in hearing of the great success which our Lord has granted me in my voyage, I write you this letter, whereby you will learn how in thirty-three days' time I reached the Indies with the fleet which the most illustrious King and Queen, our Sovereigns, gave to me, where I found very many islands thickly peopled, of all which I took possession without resistance for their Highnesses by proclamation made and with the royal standard unfurled. To the first island that I found I gave the name of *San Salvador,* in remembrance of His High Majesty, who hath marvelously brought all these things to pass; the Indians call it *Guanaham*. . . .

Espanola is a wonder. Its mountains and plains, and meadows, and fields, are so beautiful and rich for planting and sowing, and rearing cattle of all kinds, and for building towns and villages. The harbours on the coast, and the number and size and wholesomeness of the rivers, most of them bearing gold, surpass anything that would be believed by one who had not seen them. There is a great difference between the trees, fruits, and plants of this island and those of *Juana*. In this island there are many spices and extensive mines of gold and other metals. The inhabitants of this and of all the other islands I have found or gained intelligence of, both men and women, go as naked as they were born, with the exception that some of the women cover one part only with a single leaf of grass or with a piece of cotton, made for that purpose. They have neither iron, nor steel, nor arms, nor are they competent to use them, not that they are not well-formed and of handsome stature, but because they are timid to a surprising degree. . . .

Although I have taken possession of all these islands in the name of their Highnesses, and they are all more abundant in wealth than I am able to express . . . yet there was one large town in *Espanola* of which especially I took possession, situated in a locality well adapted for the working of the gold mines, and for all kinds of commerce, either with the main land on this side, or with that beyond which is the land of the great Khan, with which there is great profit. . . .

I have also established the greatest friendship with the king of that country, so much so that he took pride in calling me his brother, and treating me as such. Even should these people change their intentions towards us and become hostile, they do not know what arms are, but, as I have said, go naked, and are the most timid people in the world; so that the men I have left could, alone, destroy the whole country, and this island has no danger for them, if they only know how to conduct themselves. . . . Finally, and speaking only of what has taken place in this voyage, which has been so hasty, their Highnesses may see that I shall give them all the gold they require, if they will give me but a very little assistance; spices also, and cotton, as much as their Highnesses shall command to be shipped; and mastic, hitherto found only in Greece . . . slaves, as many of these idolators as their Highnesses shall command to be shipped. . . .

But our Redeemer hath granted this victory our illustrious King and Queen and their kingdoms, which have acquired great fame by an event of such high importance, in which all Christendom ought to rejoice, and which it ought to celebrate with great festivals and the offering of solemn thanks to the Holy Trinity with many solemn prayers, both for the great exaltation which may accrue to them in turning so many nations to our holy faith, and also for the temporal benefits which will bring great refreshment and gain, not only to Spain, but to all Christians.

WHY AND HOW ATAHUALLPA WAS DEFEATED

The messengers came back to ask the Governor to send a Christian to Atahuallpa, that he intended to come at once, and that he would come unarmed. The Governor sent a Christian, and presently

Atahuallpa moved, leaving the armed men behind him. He took with him about five or six thousand Indians without arms, except that, under their shirts, they had small darts and slings with stones.

He came in a litter, and before him went three or four hundred Indians in liveries, cleaning the straws from the road and singing. Then came Atahuallpa in the midst of his chiefs and principal men, the greatest among them being also borne on men's shoulders. . . . A Dominican Friar, who was with the Governor, came forward to tell him, on the part of the Governor, that he waited for him in his lodgings, and that he was sent to speak with him. The Friar then told Atahuallpa that he was a Priest, and that he was sent there to teach the things of the Faith, if they should desire to be Christians. He showed Atahuallpa a book . . . and told him that that book contained the things of God. Atahuallpa asked for the book, and threw it on the ground, saying: "I will not leave this place until you have restored all that you have taken in my land. I know well who you are, and what you have come for. . . ." The Friar went to the Governor and reported what was being done, and that no time was to be lost. The Governor sent to me; and I had arranged with the Captain of the artillery that, when a sign was given, he should discharge his pieces, and that, on hearing the reports, all the troops should come forth at once. This was done, and as the Indians were unarmed, they were defeated without danger to any Christian. Those who carried the litter, and the chiefs who surrounded Atahuallpa, were all killed, falling round him. The Governor came out and seized Atahuallpa, and in protecting him, he received a knife cut from a Christian in the hand. The troops continued the pursuit as far as the place where the armed Indians were stationed, who made no resistance whatever, because it was night. All were brought into town, where the Governor was quartered.

Next morning the Governor ordered us to go to the camp of Atahuallpa, where we found forty thousand pesos worth of gold and two or three pounds of silver. . . . The Governor said that he had not come to make war on the Indians, but that our Lord the Emperor, who was Lord of the whole world, had ordered him to come that he might see the land, and let Atahuallpa know the things of our Faith. . . . The Governor also told him that that land, and all other lands, belonged to the Emperor, and that he must acknowledge him as his Lord. He replied that he was content, and, observing that the Christians had collected some gold, Atahuallpa said to the Governor that they need not take such care of it, as if there was so little; for that he could give them ten thousand plates, and that he could fill the room in which he was up to a white line, which was the height of a man and a half from the floor.

Questions: What were the main bases for initial European judgments about the characteristics of American Indians? How might the Indians have judged the Europeans? What motives does Columbus appeal to in trying to interest Spanish rulers in the new land?

NORTHERN EUROPEAN EXPEDITIONS

Later in the 16th century, the lead in further exploration passed to northern Europe, as newly strong monarchies, such as France and England, got into the act, and zealous Protestants in Britain and Holland strove to rival Catholic gains. In part this shift in dynamism occurred because Spain and Portugal were busy digesting the gains they had already made; in part it was because northern Europeans, particularly the Dutch and the British, improved the design of oceanic vessels, producing lighter, faster ships than those of their Catholic adversaries. Britain won a historic sea battle with Spain in 1588, in which the British navy and adverse weather routed a massive Spanish Armada. From this point onward, the British, the Dutch, and to an extent the French vied for dominance on the seas, though in the Americas they mainly aimed northward because they could not challenge the Spanish and Portuguese colonies. Only in the sugar-rich West Indies did northern Europe seize islands initially claimed by Spain.

French explorers crossed the Atlantic first in 1534, reaching Canada, which was claimed in France's name. French voyages increased in the 17th century, as various expeditions pressed down from Canada into the Great Lakes region and the Mississippi valley.

The British also turned their attention to North America, starting with a brief expedition as early as 1497. The English hoped, in vain, to discover a northwest passage to India, and in fact accomplished little beyond exploration of the Hudson Bay area of Canada during the 16th century. England's serious work began in the 17th century, with the colonization of the east coast of North America. Holland also had holdings in North America and, for a time, in Brazil.

The Dutch entered the picture after winning independence from Spain, and Holland quickly became a major competitor with Portugal in Southeast Asia. The Dutch sent substantial numbers of sailors and ships to the region, ousting the Portuguese from the Indonesian islands by the early 17th century. Voyagers from the Netherlands explored the coast of Australia, though without much immediate result. Finally, toward the middle of the 17th century, Holland established a settlement on the southern tip of Africa, mainly to provide a relay station for its ships bound for the East Indies.

Dutch and British exploration and trade were sponsored by the government, but unlike the Spanish, the Portuguese, and to some extent the French expeditions, they owed much to the private initiative of merchant groups. The Netherlands, Britain, and France all chartered great trading companies such as the Dutch East India Company or the British firm of similar name. These companies were given government monopolies of trade in the regions designated, but they were not rigorously supervised by their own states. Thus semiprivate companies, formed by pooling merchant capital and amassing great fortunes in commerce, long acted almost like independent governments in the regions they claimed. For some time a Dutch trading company virtually ruled the island of Taiwan off the coast of China; the British East India Company played a similar role in parts of India during much of the 18th century. Companies in North America traded actively in furs.

ANALYSIS
CAUSATION AND THE WEST'S EXPANSION

Because of their central interest in social change, historians inevitably deal with causation. What prompted the fall of Rome? Why did Islam spread so widely? What factors explain why most agricultural civilizations developed patriarchal family structures?

Historical causation differs from the kinds of causation many scientists test. When experiments or observations can be repeated, scientists can gain a relatively precise understanding of the factors that produce a phenomenon and their exact priority: Remove an ingredient and the product changes. Historical causation is slippier. Major develop-

French, British, and Dutch Holdings, about 1700

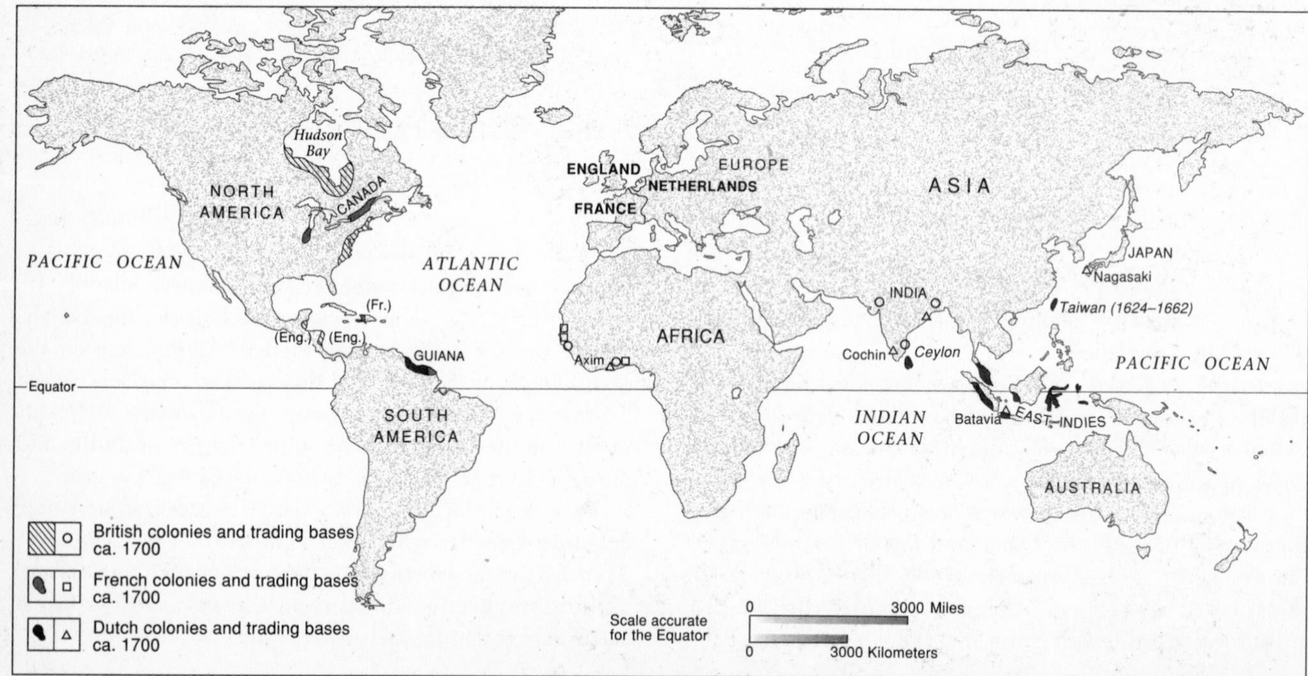

ments may resemble each other but they never happen the same way twice, and so definitive proof that factor *X* explains 40 percent of the spread of Buddhism in East Asia is impossible. Despite the fact that historians cannot prove definitively that they have their causation right—and hence often disagree—the attempt to fathom the process continues, for if precision is impossible, high probability is not. Further, probing causation helps explore the phenomenon itself. We know more about the nature of Western expansion in the 15th and 16th centuries if we discuss what caused it.

Some historians and other social scientists posit a systematic causation. They look to one kind of cause as the key to explanation in a variety of circumstances. Some anthropologists are cultural determinists. They judge that a basic set of cultural factors, usually assumed to be very durable, causes the ongoing differences among societies: Chinese on average respond differently to emotional stimuli from Greeks because of their cultural conditioning. Some historians, in explaining change, also look to the primacy of cultural causation, assuming that a change in ideas or values leads to other developments such as revolutions or inventions. More common is a technological or economic determinism. Some historians regularly look to technological change as setting other changes in motion. Others, including Marxists, argue that economic arrangements, in terms of the way the economy is structured and what groups control it, produce at least the basic framework for innovations in culture, politics, or family life.

At another pole, some historians used to look to "great men" as the prime movers in history. The causes of change thus became Chinggis Khan or Ashoka, with no need to look much farther. While the "great man" approach is less popular today, as most historians prefer more sweeping forces within which individual leaders operate, it has been dressed up by attempts to probe the special psychology of certain movers and shakers such as Martin Luther. One American historian has recently argued that we should pay more attention to great people as causes because we can thus inspire our youth to believe they can shape their destinies and national development through rational planning and ethical behavior.

Various approaches to causation have been applied to the West's explorations and colonial conquests in the early modern period. There is room, certainly, for a great man analysis. Many descriptive accounts that dwell on explorers and conquerors—Vasco da Gama and Cortez, for example—and on leaders who sponsored them—such as Henry the Navigator—implicitly suggest that the key cause of the West's new world role stemmed from the daring and vision of exceptional individuals.

Cultural causation can also be invoked. Somehow Europe's expansion must relate to the wonders of innovation introduced by the Renaissance. A society that spawned humanistic fascination with the power of individuals to achieve and innovate, to challenge past constraints, also yielded efforts to challenge the spatial limits of Western civilization. Not accidentally, key early explorers came from the same kind of Italian city-states as the Renaissance centers. The link with Christian culture is even easier to prove, for a missionary spirit quickly supplemented the efforts of early explorers, leading to more voyages and settlement in Asia and the Americas.

Political causation enters in, if not in causing the initial surge, at least in confirming it. Through the 16th century and beyond, rivalries among the nation-states helped impel a continuing quest for new trade routes and colonies.

There is also room, however, for a simpler, technologically determinist approach. Europe's gains, in this view, came from a handful of new inventions. Benefiting from knowledge of advances in China and the Middle East, Europeans gained improved navigational techniques (the compass). They also adapted explosives by introducing gunnery with special effect in naval cannon. Along with steady improvements in ship design, new techniques explain why Europe gained as it did. Save in the Americas, where they had larger technical and organizational advantages, Europeans advanced in areas they could reach by sea and dominate by ships' cannon—port cities, islands, and trade routes—and not elsewhere. In the simplest rendering of technological determinism, Europe gained simply through these few technical edges.

Like all determinisms, however, this technological approach raises as many questions as it answers. Why were Europeans so ready to adopt new inventions? Why did other societies, such as China, quickly aware of Europe's innovations, show little interest in imitation? Chinese policy successfully aimed at containing Europe's penetration by political arrangements, especially in granting limited access through Macao; it deliberately scorned any adoption of Western naval techniques. Here a different outlook, plus China's past decision not to expand its seaborne trade, determined a reaction different from that of the West. Technology and culture went hand in hand. Clearly, some combined causal framework is required in this case, with room for individual factors such as the special position of Spain and Portugal after the expulsion of the Muslims.

Finally, the world history context requires the addition of causes resulting from the West's ambiguous position in the interchanges among key civilizations by the 15th century. Europe expanded from special weakness as well as some new strengths. Explorations were goaded by a fear of

Muslim superiority, heightened by the impact of the Turkish conquest of Constantinople. Westerners wanted trade routes that would free them from any dependence on the Islamic powerhouse. They also needed new trading strength, for their economic inferiority required them to pay in gold for costly goods such as spices—hence the greed for precious metals that drove so many early expeditions. The results of expansion changed Europe's economic position in the world dramatically, but these should not be confused with initial causation.

All students of history can sort through the factors involved in a development as complex as the West's expansion to refine the list and try to set priorities. Or they can ponder more sweeping theories about what propels a society to new dynamism in world history. We cannot expect uniform agreement on a precise ordering of causation, but we can expect fruitful debate—the kind of debate that already has moved our understanding beyond surface causation, like the powerful personalities of a few people, to a grasp of more underlying context.

Questions: If you had to choose a single determinism (cultural, technological, or economic) as basic to social change, which one would you pick? Why? In what ways might the professed motives of Western explorers and colonists have differed from their real motives? Would they necessarily have been aware of the discrepancy?

TOWARD A WORLD ECONOMY

By the late 16th century, West Europeans had gained control of most of the world's seas. They were moving freely across the Atlantic Ocean and with some regularity across the vast Pacific as well—the first time in world history these oceans had opened to regular human use. Europe's maritime dominance, in turn, had three great effects in world history: It created a new international pool for basic exchanges of foods, diseases, and a few manufactured products. It created a new world economy, involving of course the fuller inclusion of Africa and the first embrace of the Americas in international trade, but setting a different framework even for Europe and Asia. And it created the conditions for direct Western penetration of some parts of the world through the formation of colonies. The consequences of Western colonization, though immense, were largely regional at this point, whereas the first two results more literally recast the framework for much of world history.

THE "COLOMBIAN EXCHANGE" OF DISEASE AND FOOD

The impact of wider exchange became visible quite quickly. Just as earlier European contacts with Asia, a few centuries previously, had helped spread new plagues, so the extension of international interaction facilitated disease. Here the tragic victims were millions of American Indians who had not previously been exposed to diseases such as smallpox and measles and who therefore had no natural immunities. During the 16th and into the 17th centuries, they died in huge numbers. Overall, in North and South America, well over half the native population would perish; some estimates run as high as 80 percent. Whole island populations in the West Indies were wiped out. Here was a major blow to earlier forms of civilization in the Americas, as well as an opportunity for Europeans to forge a partially new population from their own ranks and the ranks of slaves imported from Africa. The devastation occurred over a 150-year period, though some areas were depleted quickly. When Europeans gained contact with north Pacific coast Indians in the 18th century, the same dreadful pattern played out—again cutting back a vibrant culture.

Other exchanges were less dire. New world crops were spread rapidly via Western merchants. American corn was taken up widely in China (where merchants learned of it from Spaniards in the Philippines), the Mediterranean, and parts of Africa. In some cases this productive new crop, along with local agricultural improvements, triggered substantial population increases. China, for example, began to experience long-term population pressure in the 17th century, and new crops played a key role. Europe itself, ironically, was slower to take advantage of new crops. The use of tobacco, sugar, and coffee spread, but corn and particularly the potato began to win adoption only in the late 17th century, at which point they spurred major population upheaval in Europe as well.

Animal husbandry became more similar across the world, as European or Asian animals, such as horses and cattle, were introduced to the New World. Dissemination of basic products and diseases, then, formed an important backdrop to world history from the 16th century on as a phenomenon never before experienced on such a wide scale, and never with such quick and massive results on population structures in various regions.

THE WEST'S COMMERCIAL OUTREACH

The development of a new kind of world economy related more directly to European naval advantages. Here, in turn, the key point was the ability of the Europeans to dominate most international trade while steadily increasing its overall levels. Westerners did not displace all Asian shipping from the coastal waters of China and Japan, nor did they completely monopolize the Indian Ocean (see Chapter 28). Along the East African coast, while a few European bases were established, Muslim traders remained active and the orientation of commerce continued to veer toward the Middle East. Generally, however, the West dominated a great deal of oceanic shipping, even muscling in on trade between other societies (as between India and southeast Asia). This greatly improved Europe's overall profit situation, because even before terms of trade improved in the West's direction with the development of manufacturing exports, profits came back simply for handling commerce. The longer-range result was increased European ability to determine the framework for international trade, based on disproportionate control of the relevant carriers and the companies experienced in the field.

Europe gained its shipping position, of course, through the combination of technology and force that had propelled its initial explorations and conquests. Experienced merchant marines and superior ship design helped undercut competition from other societies. Naval gunnery did the rest. In the Mediterranean, for example, a Spanish-directed fleet inflicted a decisive defeat on the navy of the Ottoman Empire in the battle of Lepanto in 1571. With this setback, any hope of successful Muslim rivalry against European naval power ended. The Turks rebuilt their fleet and continued activity in the eastern Mediterranean just as India and China maintained a stake in Asian shipping, but they could not challenge the Europeans on the larger international routes. Here, competition for international trade continued, but among European powers, not across civilizations. Spaniards vied with English merchant shippers and pirates, and then as Spanish shipping declined, competition among English, Dutch, and French shippers heated up.

Sheer control of the seas and the bulk of international trade involved other incursions of Western power. While the West did not conquer much inland territory in Africa or Asia, it did seek a limited network of secure harbors. Led by Spain and Portugal, then followed by the various northern powers, European ports spread along the west coast of Africa, several parts of the Indian subcontinent, and the islands of Southeast Asia by the 17th century. Even in China, where unusually strong governments limited European ability to seize harbors outright, the Portuguese won effective control over the island port of Macao.

European-controlled ports, in turn, brought some fortifications, plus supplies for the omnipresent shipping. They also served as contact areas with overland traders (usually local merchants) and so brought access to inland goods not directly within the reach of the West.

Where scattered ports were not feasible because of effective governments that did not want this kind of foreign interference, European influence and the lure of the trade involved led to the formation of special Western enclaves in existing cities, where Western traders won special rights including, often, the ability to regulate themselves rather than be subject to local law. This was the pattern in the Ottoman Empire, where Western merchants set up virtual colonies within Constantinople, and also in Russia, where Western factors (shipping agents) set up first in Moscow and then in St. Petersburg. Elements of this system even emerged in Japan after a firm isolationist policy was launched around 1600, as Dutch traders had some special access to the port of Nagasaki. The point was obvious: Virtually worldwide, international trade gained growing importance in supplementing regional economies. Since the West now ran this trade, the West won special rights of access.

IMBALANCES IN WORLD TRADE

What was emerging by the 17th century was a new layering of the world economy, with key Western nations on top, along with the greater extent and volume of world trade. Leading trading states ruled the roost. Spain briefly held this position in the 16th century as it brought in silver from the New World. However, its own economy and banking system could not easily accommodate this new wealth—among other things, there was not enough local manufacturing to meet demand—so Spain, like Portugal, declined in economic vitality even while continuing to administer huge colonial empires. The more durable economically dominant powers emerged with the second round of exploration and commercial expansion led by England, France, and Holland. These nations pulled in the lion's share of profits from world trade. Supremacy as world merchants brought additional earnings through control of international banking and other commercial services. Furthermore, these nations and some other parts of western Europe quickly expanded their manufacturing operations so that they were able to export relatively expensive, processed goods—such as guns or manufactured cloth—as well as some high-fashion artisan products in return for cruder unprocessed goods, such as silver or sugar, traded by many other societies. Here, too, was a tidy profit margin.

These dominant core areas in the new world system supplemented their growing economic prowess by self-serving political policies. The doctrines of *mercantilism,* which urged that a nation-state not import goods from outside its own empire but sell exports as widely as possible in its own ships, both reflected and encouraged the new world system. Tariff policies, designed to discourage manufacturing in colonial areas as well as to compete with other Western nation-states, actively furthered the new layering of the world economy.

Around the core nations of northwestern Europe grew up a hinterland of other European states that did not dominate banking or manufacturing but might still benefit somewhat from the new world system. Spain, even after its post-1600 decline, continued to produce some specialty items, such as high-quality wool, that won it some benefits from the international market. Italy was another area, now lagging somewhat because of political divisions and the decline of the Mediterranean as a commercial focal point, that nevertheless maintained a middle level in world-economic operations.

Beyond this zone, in turn, lay areas that were increasingly enmeshed in the world economy but on a strictly dependent basis. These areas produced low-cost goods in growing quantity—precious metals, cash crops such as sugar and tobacco (and later cotton) from the Americas, or spices and tea from plantations in Southeast Asia and India. These goods were of course carried in European vessels, with shipping arranged by European agents. In a special, though vitally important case, human labor was the item of exchange. Parts of sub-Saharan Africa entered the new world economy mainly on the basis of supplying slaves. In return for relatively unprocessed products—including human beings—Europeans traded their manufactured items while profiting from their control of commercial and shipping services.

The rise of core and dependent economic zones was a vitally important development in world history in the 16th and 17th centuries. It was not absolutely without precedent, though the West had never before been in the economic driver's seat. Greece and Rome had imported cheap foods in return for processed goods in their relationship with colonies elsewhere in the Mediterranean, as in North Africa; in Rome's case this relationship had even encouraged such excessive farming in North Africa that soil quality was permanently damaged. The Muslim Middle East developed a set of dependent areas in Africa that provided slaves or salt or other relatively cheap goods. In this case, Arab "core" traders also organized the ships or caravans in a pattern quite like what the West developed after 1500.

These had been regional relationships, not worldwide, however, and they usually had less impact on the economies involved than the New World economy did. Europe's New World economy uprooted many older trade patterns. In West Africa the earlier orientation toward trading across the Sahara yielded to a dominant focus on the Atlantic, and therefore to activities organized by Western shippers. Some parts of West Africa suffered dearly from the decline of the old routes.

A SYSTEM OF INTERNATIONAL INEQUALITY

Disruptive as they often were at first, the new world economic relationships proved highly durable. Most of the areas established as dependent by the 17th century still, in the late 20th century, suffer some special burdens in world trade. Core and dependent statuses tended to reinforce each other, making it hard to break out of their grasp.

The core-dependent system should not of course be exaggerated, quite apart from the fact that, as we will see, most of the world was not yet fully embraced in it. While the core areas of northwestern Europe drew great profits from international trade and became increasingly commercialized as a result, the benefits were not evenly distributed. Growing interest in commercial production and manufacturing encouraged the growth of a poor, wage-earning proletariat, juxtaposed with the rising standard of living of great merchants and many property owners. Core status was linked to a deterioration of life for some people in the core as well as in the dependent areas.

In dependent areas like Latin America or the slave-supplying parts of Africa, not all people were mired in deepest poverty. African slave traders and princes who taxed the trade might grow rich. In Latin America the silver mines and commercial estates required regional merchants and farmers who supplied food; not all market activity was directly ensnared in Western-dominated world trade, which means that internal social and economic structures could be fairly complex. Further, there were many peasants in Latin America, and even more in Africa, not yet involved in a market economy at all—regional or international—but rather producing for local subsistence with traditional motives and methods. It was true, however, that important minorities were wrapped up in production for the world market. It was also true that most African or Latin American merchants and landlords did not fully control their own terms of trade. They might prosper, but their wealth did not stimulate much local manufacturing or general economic advance. Rather, they tended to import European-made goods, including (in the case of American planters) art objects and luxury items.

Moreover, dependence in the world economy had implications beyond the economy itself. It helped determine a coercive labor system. Because dependent economies relied on cheap production of unprocessed goods, there was an inevitable tendency to build a system of forced labor that would cost relatively little even when the overall labor supply was a bit precarious. In the Americas, given the population loss due to disease, this led to the massive importation of African slaves, which brought Africa as well as the Americas into the dependent economic network. Also in the Americas, for many Indians and *mestizos*, or people of mixed European and Indian blood, systems of estate management developed that exacted large amounts of labor service and high rents (usually through payments in kind). Systems of this sort not only generated marketable foods, such as sugar, but also staffed the great silver mines in the Andes. While outright slavery and coercive estate systems developed most fully in the Americas and West Indies, more limited examples of estate agriculture, with peasants forced into labor without the legal freedom to leave, arose also for the production of spices in the Dutch East Indies and, by the 18th century, in British-dominated agricultural operations in India.

Forced labor plus the high degree of European influence in economic affairs tended to generate or maintain relatively weak government structures in the dependent areas. Weak governments in Latin America, for example, allowed estates a relatively free hand in regulating their labor force, while substantial poverty among the masses limited the tax revenues available to governments—and so limited the effective outreach of governments themselves. In contrast core states, with growing trade revenues, tended to generate increasing government strength, as in France's absolute monarchy or the nation-state operations of Britain or Holland.

Core and dependent areas thus differed in politics, class structure, and labor systems, as well as in their ability to draw profits from the new world trading relationships. The differences resulted from distinctive trading positions, including who actually controlled the shipping and international business operations, but they also reinforced these differences, confirming the framework with each passing decade. During the 16th and 17th centuries, furthermore, the gap between core and dependent areas showed starkly in population trends. In other words, while West Europe's population modestly expanded, the population of Latin America—hit by disease—declined; the population of sub-Saharan Africa, depleted by the huge trade in slaves, at best stagnated.

HOW MUCH WORLD IN THE WORLD ECONOMY?

The idea of a new world economy arising with the West's commercial expansion is not universally accepted by all interested historians. Some historians object that the world-economy notion distracts us from other developments in places like Latin America or (even more) sub-Saharan Africa, as if Western capitalists were calling all the shots. Certainly many people and activities were not directly involved in the world economy. Still more important was the fact that huge areas of the world were not caught up in any intense contact with the world economy. In these areas the new framework did not significantly influence politics or culture, nor did it prevent vigorous regional economic life. The societies that were external to the New World system certainly did not gain ground as rapidly as the core areas of Europe, because they did not have the profit opportunities in international trade. Their commercial operations expanded less rapidly and they did not have the same spurs to additional technological change in transport and manufacturing. Their lag, at least until the 18th century, was relative, not direct; it did not force any particular response, and indeed the societies involved were often blissfully unaware of the gradual shift in relative economic balance.

Dependent economic relationships arose mainly in areas where civilizations had developed late and in some isolation, with resultant technological lags behind the Eurasian world. The leading Asian civilizations, in contrast, had ample political strength and economic sophistication to avoid dependent status. They had little need for goods manufactured in Europe. They might be attracted to some products brought by European shippers, such as a few agricultural items grown in other regions that were not locally available. But the trade that resulted in return for some spices or artistic products, such as Chinese porcelain, even though handled mainly by Western merchants, was not substantial enough to have a major impact on the regional economy. Most trade and production, in other words, was either aimed at local consumption or was destined for regional markets, carried by local shippers overland, by river, or in coastal waters.

East Asia constituted the civilization that remained most fully and consciously external to the burgeoning world economy. The Chinese government, having renounced large-scale international trade of its own early in the 15th century when the great Indian Ocean expeditions were halted just before western Europe began its surge, was resolutely uninterested in elaborate involvement with international trade on someone else's terms. It did copy some firearms manufacturing from the Europeans, though at a fairly low level. Beyond this it depended on extensive government regulation, backed up by a coastal navy, to keep European activities in check. Most of the limited trade that existed was channeled through Macao. European visitors wrote scornfully of China's disdain for military advances—a Jesuit wrote that "The military . . . is considered mean among them"—and for their addiction to tradition. One Western missionary in the 17th century described how, in his opinion, the Chinese could not be persuaded "to make use of new instruments and leave their old ones without an especial order from the Emperor to that effect. They are more fond of the most defective piece of antiquity than of the most perfect of the modern, differing much in that from us who are in love with nothing but what is new."

The German Jesuit missionary Johann Adam Schall became the official astronomer at the Chinese court in the mid-17th century.

So China opted out, not keeping up with European developments but also not subservient to European merchants. The world economy thus had little to do with Chinese history through the 18th century. Indeed at the end of the 18th century a famous British mission, appealing to the government to open the country to greater trade, was treated to a perfectly accurate rebuff, as the imperial court, after insisting on the most abject abasement by the British envoy, haughtily informed him that the Chinese had no need for outside goods. European eagerness for Chinese goods—attested to by the habit adopted in the 17th century of calling fine porcelain "china"—was simply not matched by Chinese enthusiasm, though a trickle of trade continued. Westerners compensated in part by developing their own porcelain industry by the 18th century, which fed into the early Industrial Revolution, particularly in Britain; still there were hopes for commercial entry to China that remained unfulfilled.

Japan, though initially attracted by Western expeditions in the 16th century, also quickly pulled back. The Japanese displayed some openness to Christian missions and they were also fascinated by Western advances in gunnery and shipping. Guns had particular relevance amid Japan's ongoing feudal wars, for there was no disdain here for military life. Yet Japanese leaders soon worried about undue Western influence and the impact this could have on internal divisions among warring lords, as well as the threat guns posed to samurai military dominance. They encouraged a local gun making industry that matched existing European muskets and small cannon fairly readily, but having achieved this they cut off all but the most vestigial contact with any world trade. Japanese were forbidden to travel or trade abroad, the small Christian minority was suppressed and, from the 17th until the 19th centuries, Japan entered a period of almost complete isolation. Important internal changes continued, including expanding national commerce; but only indirectly, by the decision to halt a previous policy of selective imitation and regional trade in East Asia, had the rise of the world economy affected Japan.

Several other societies remained substantially untouched by new world trade, participating if at all at levels too low for significant internal impact. The rulers of India's new Mughal Empire in the 16th century were interested in some contact with Western traders and even encouraged the establishment of small port colonies, but the bulk of their attention was riveted on internal development; world trade was but a sideline. The same held true for the Ottoman and Safavid empires in the Middle East through the 17th

Japanese artists in the 16th century depicted the Europeans and their African slaves as exotic and unfamiliar.

century; the essential dynamics had nothing to do with the West's trading activities, despite the presence of small European enclaves in key cities. Russia also lay outside the world economic orbit. A substantially agricultural society, Russia conducted much of its trade with nomadic peoples in central Asia, which further cushioned it against West European demands. Finally, much of Africa, outside the slave-trading orbit in western regions, was simply untouched by world trade patterns.

Clearly, the salience of the world economic network should not be read as some sudden or complete globalization of the dynamic of history. Societies that remained outside any intense world economic involvement might themselves be expanding as a result of new use of gunpowder for land armies and superior political organization, or they might stagnate or fluctuate, as with the fortunes of several African kingdoms. Whatever their trajectory, they responded primarily to regional changes, not international ones.

THE EXPANSIONIST TREND

Yet the world economy was itself not stationary; it tended to gain ground over time. While South America, the West Indies, a part of North America, and some regions in West Africa were first staked out as dependencies beginning in the 16th century, the list subsequently expanded. Portions of Southeast Asia that produced for world markets, under the dominance of the great Western trading companies, were brought into the orbit by the 17th century.

By the late 17th century Western traders were advancing in India, as the Mughal Empire began falling apart. British and French East India Companies staked out increasing roles in internal trade and administration. Early in the 18th century, Britain began to apply legislation to India clearly designed to fit Britain's holdings into a dependent status in the world economy. Notably, tariffs were passed against the import of cotton cloth manufactured in

India as a means of protecting Britain's own infant cotton textile industry. The intent was to beat down Indian manufacturing that might have export potential in favor of using India as a market for British-processed goods and a source of relatively cheap cash crops such as tea—or as a source of outright payments of gold, which the British were exacting in some quantity by the later 18th century. Indian observers were themselves quite aware of the shifting balance. An 18th century account noted:

> But such is the little regard which they [the British] show to the people of this kingdom, and such their apathy and indifference for their welfare, that the people under their dominion groan everywhere, and are reduced to poverty and distress.

India maintained a complex regional economy still, with much internal manufacturing and trade; it was not forced into such complete dependency as, say, Latin America. Nor did coerced labor become as widespread. Clearly, however, what had initially been a position external to the world economy was being modified, and on the whole to India's disadvantage.

Some similar tendencies emerged in the Ottoman Empire, though they were less marked. Western traders played a growing role by the 18th century, and pressed steadily for further advantages. The stagnation of technology through the Middle East and southeastern Europe contrasted with steady Western gains. The great Ottoman problem, to be sure, was not the world economy but Russia's rising military power, backed as it was by superior artillery. Nevertheless, world economic forces played an increasing role.

Eastern Europe constituted a final area brought into a growing relationship with the world economy and the West European core. The growth of manufacturing in the West, with considerable attendant expansion of cities, created a growing market for imported grains by the 18th century. Much of this market was filled by East European growers, particularly in Prussia and Poland but also to an extent in Russia. Export grains, in turn, were produced mainly on large estates by serfs who were subjected to increasingly coercive controls including prolonged periods of labor service. The exports in turn were handled by Western shippers who also imported Western-made products, including art objects and furnishings for aristocrats. There was no small resemblance between this relationship and that which prevailed in Latin America, with one exception: Outside of Poland, East European governments were considerably stronger than their Latin American counterparts.

The rise and evolution of the world economy thus set a partial, but increasingly important, framework for world history in the centuries after 1500. Along with purely regional developments, as in Japan, it extended the importance of commercial arrangements in many otherwise different societies. It definitely set up a new pecking order among world societies, with the Western core, a number of external societies that lagged compared to the West, and a growing number of societies in considerable economic dependency. Never before had a single economic system exerted so much effect on such a variety of civilizations, while still, admittedly, falling short of fully determining regional patterns.

COLONIAL EXPANSION

Along with the larger world economic system, a new wave of colonialism took shape following the early Spanish and Portuguese explorations. Key Western nations developed direct overseas empires. Their outreach began at the same time as Russian expansion plus the spread of the Ottoman and Mughal empires, which also had vital consequences. But the Western colonial pattern, based as it was on naval supremacy, was unusual in bringing considerable Western dominance over a variety of peoples and cultures. It also reinforced the larger world economy, for most colonial areas were quickly placed in dependent status, with colonial administrations encouraging the production of unprocessed materials and the development of cheap labor systems. The world economic system did not in fact necessitate outright colonies, for certain areas could be brought into partial dependency while retaining their own governments; but colonialism helped, and many Western leaders believed that direct control was the only sure way of guaranteeing markets for European products and assured access to cheap supplies of precious metals, cash crops, timber, and other vital items.

THE AMERICAS

Opportunities for colonies were particularly inviting in the Americas, where European guns, horses, and iron weapons offered special advantages and where in many cases political disarray, soon exacerbated by the population losses caused by new disease, provided openings (see Chapter 25). Spain moved first. The Spanish colonized several West Indian islands soon after Columbus's first voyage, starting with Hispaniola and then extending to Cuba, Jamaica, and Puerto Rico. Only in 1509 did they begin settlement on the mainland, in search of gold; the first colony was established under an able if unscrupulous adventurer, Balboa. Several expeditions fanned out in Central America, and then a separate expedition from Cuba launched the Spanish conquest of the Aztecs in Mexico. Explorations and some settlements in northern Mexico and what is now the American Southwest followed. Another expedition headed toward the Inca realm in the Andes in 1531, where hard fighting was needed before ultimate victory. From this base several colonial expeditions spread to Colombia, other parts of the Andes, and portions of Argentina.

Portugal moved more slowly in Brazil, initially content with a few small coastal settlements. The need to protect their claim against other European powers like the Dutch, plus gradual realization of the wealth that could be found in the interior, caused more substantial settlement and a more formal administration.

Early colonies in the Americas were typically developed by small bands of Europeans, often loosely controlled by colonial administrations in the mainland. Thirst for gold drew many adventurers, whose behavior toward each other, as well as toward American Indians, was frequently violent and duplicitous. Where Indian populations were substantial and not totally decimated by disease, the colonial rulers often established only loose controls at first, content to exact tribute without imposing detailed administration and sometimes leaving existing leaders in place. Gradually somewhat

Europeans in Florida during the 1590s scorned American Indians for worshiping a column set up by an earlier explorer.

more formal administration spread, as agricultural settlements were established and official colonial systems took shape under control of bureaucrats sent from Spain or Portugal. Active missionary endeavor, which formed parish churches and a host of missions designed to Christianize the Indians, added another layer of detailed administration throughout the Spanish holdings in North and South America.

France, Britain, and Holland, though latecomers to the Americas, also staked out colonial settlements. French explorations along the St. Lawrence River in Canada led to small colonies around Quebec, from 1608 onward, plus explorations in the Mississippi River basin. Dutch and English settlers moved into portions of the Atlantic coastal regions early in the 17th century. Also in the 17th century all three countries seized and colonized several West Indian islands, which they soon involved in the growing slave trade.

AFRICA AND ASIA

While Europeans for the most part contented themselves with small coastal fortresses in Africa, negotiating with African kings and merchants but without attempting to claim large territories on their own, there were two important exceptions. From initial coastal settlements, Portugal sent expeditions into Angola in search of slaves. These expeditions had more direct and more disruptive impact in this part of southwestern Africa than was characteristic elsewhere along the Atlantic coast. More important still was a colony planted by the Dutch on the Cape of Good Hope in 1652. The intent was to form another coastal station in order to supply Dutch ships bound for Asia. But some Dutch farmers were sent out, and these Boers (the Dutch word for farmers) began to fan out on large farms in a region still lightly populated by Africans. They clashed with local hunting groups, enslaving some of them. Only after 1770 did the expanding Boer settlements directly conflict with Bantu farmers, opening a long battle for control of southern Africa that still rages today in the nation of South Africa. South Africa was exceptional, however, because of its mild climate and scant population. Generally, Europeans were deterred by climate, disease, and unnavigable rivers from trying to reach into the interior. The real scramble to colonize Africa came later.

European colonies in Asia were also exceptional. Spain set up an administration for the Philippines, while the Dutch East India company, one of the great government-chartered trading units that sprung up all over western Europe, ousted the Portuguese and administered portions of the main islands of present-day Indonesia and also Taiwan, off the China coast. These holdings, while economically important, did not compel extensive government efforts or substantial settlements from Europe, though the Spanish in the Philippines also mounted a substantial and successful missionary effort in the name of the Catholic church.

Colonization in Asia entered a new phase as the British and French began to struggle for control of India, beginning in the late 17th century when the Mughal Empire weakened. Even before the Mughals faltered after their last great emperor Aurangzeb, who died in 1707, French and British forts dotted the east and west coasts, along with Portuguese Goa. (Dutch presence, briefly a factor, had declined given the Netherlands' primary focus in the East Indies.) As Mughal inefficiency increased, with a resultant surge of regional states ruled by Indians, portions of the subcontinent became an arena for the growing international rivalry between Britain and France.

The British East India Company had two advantages in this competition. Through negotiation with local princes it had gained a station at Calcutta, which gave it some access to the great wealth of the Ganges valley. Further, the company had enormous influence over the British government and, through Britain's superior navy, excellent communication on the ocean routes. Its French rivals, in contrast, had less political clout at home, where the government was often distracted by European land wars. The French were also more interested in missionary work than the British, who like most Protestants became deeply committed to efforts at conversion in colonial territories only in the 19th century. Before then, the British were content to leave Hindu customs alone and devote themselves to commercial profits.

French-British rivalry raged bitterly through the middle decades of the 18th century. Each side recruited Indian princes and troops as allies. Outright warfare erupted in 1744 and then again during the Seven Years' War. British officials had become alarmed at growing French influence with local princes and troops. They were also roused by the capture of Calcutta in 1756 by an Indian official, who imprisoned English captives in a "black hole"—an underground chamber originally used as a jail by the English themselves; many English officials suffocated. The East India Company's army recaptured Calcutta and then seized additional French and Indian territory, aided by abundant bribes distributed to many regional princes. French power in India was destroyed, and England was committed—without plan or clear intent as the East India Company dragged the government in its wake—to administration of the region called Bengal, which stretched inland from Calcutta. Soon after this, the British also gained the island of Ceylon from the Dutch. Although the British military force remained small, its superior weaponry, including field artillery, plus tight military organization and alliances with many local leaders had proved decisive in battles with hostile Indian rulers. At the same time, more sophisticated naval power allowed Britain to outdistance its European rivals. Thus, from 1764 onward, a British empire in India was truly launched. Along with Indonesia and the Americas, India became one of the great territorial acquisitions of the West prior to 1800.

This Indian portrait of two ladies in European dress illustrates the English influence in 18th-century India.

The full history of British India did not begin until late in the 18th century when the British government took a more active hand in Indian administration, supplementing the quasi-government of the East India Company. Indeed, British control of the subcontinent was incomplete. The Mughal Empire remained, though it was increasingly hollow and controlled scant territory, as did other regional kingdoms including the Sikh state. Britain gained some new territories by force of arms, but was also content to ally with local princes without disturbing their internal administration.

British, and to an extent French and Dutch, commercial activities in India had an important effect even before the full implications of India's new colonial status were worked out. Throughout the 18th century, much of India was increasingly drawn into the world trading patterns dominated by the West. Like Indonesia, but unlike the Americas, India offered a well-developed manufacturing economy along with a vast population and a solid agricultural base. European merchants were eager to exploit India's wealth, but were concerned lest India compete with their own manufacturing capabilities. This caused the tariff barriers on Indian exports. By limiting Indian access to a British market, London effectively reduced India's opportunities in world trade. British-made goods, including textiles, were widely sold on the subcontinent. In turn, the Indians exported gold and also agricultural products, such as tea, which were grown on commercial estates staffed by low-paid laborers and set up so that Europe might shake off dependence on Chinese-grown tea. British agents also took growing command over Indian textile production, dictating wages and conditions to the workers, while the British East India Company exported Indian gold as a payment for their costs of administration.

By the late 18th century major European colonial holdings had spread through key parts of southern and southeastern Asia as well as the Americas. The Middle East and East Asia were untouched, as was most of Africa. In Africa, however, the expanding Dutch settlement in the south was joined by Portuguese claims in Angola (where effective administration remained confined to coastal regions), and several key ports in West Africa were beginning to develop as urban centers, with some conversions to Christianity and other signs of interest in European culture among a small number of urbanized Africans. French coastal holdings in what is now the nation of Senegal, for example, were beginning to radiate a certain amount of influence.

In most cases European administration of African and Asian colonies remained rather loose. Colonial officials were few in number, backed by small armed forces plus the omnipresent navies that could rush in as enforcers in case of emergency. Most administrations depended heavily on deals with local princes; they did not interfere directly in regional affairs or in most village life. Political and, in many cases, cultural impacts were limited in this situation. In Africa established kingdoms still held sway. In Asia, significant conversions to Christianity occurred only in the Philippines, and they were limited still in Africa. European influence was too small, and attachment to established beliefs too great, to effect extensive change. The chief result of colonial acquisitions for the world at large involved the redirection of economic patterns, as the new colonies were fit into the world economy.

Few colonies received much European settlement. In Asian holdings, a few merchants and planters joined the sketchy governmental staffs and missionary groups. Dutch South Africa was unusual in that an initially small settler group multiplied, joined by some new European immigration (including French Protestants) in the later 17th and 18th centuries. Most West Indian islands drew only small European settlements of plantation owners and the like—though in a few cases, such as Bermuda (previously unpopulated), a larger European percentage lived alongside imported African slaves. Latin America drew somewhat larger groups of Spaniards and Portuguese, and by the 17th century their intermarriage with Indian groups created the largest population segment, the mestizos. People of "pure" European stock continued to hold a special place in Latin American economic and political life, but they were a small minority compared to mestizos, Indians, and (in many areas) imported African slaves. Western impact in terms of sheer numbers of settlers, then, was also limited throughout most of the new colonial holdings.

IMPACT ON WESTERN EUROPE

Western Europe, of course, was affected by its own colonial success not only economically but also diplomatically. Colonial rivalries and wars added to the endemic hostilities among key nation-states. England and Holland early turned against Spanish success, with great effect. The Dutch and the English competed, with many skirmishes in the 17th century. Then attention turned to the growing competition among the British and French. This contest had such extensive geographical ramifications, with the Seven Years' War fought in Europe, India, and North America, that it presaged later world wars precipitated in Europe. Economically, colonies supplemented the effects of the overall world economy by bringing new wealth into Europe, encouraging a merchant class, and promoting domestic manufacturing.

There were humbler effects in European society. For example, from the mid-17th century onward, the use of colonially produced sugar spread widely, particularly in countries like Britain with relatively cold climates. Previously, sugar had been a costly, upper-class item. Now for the first time, except for salt, a basic product available to ordinary people was being traded over long distances. The spread of sugar had cultural as well as social and economic significance in giving ordinary Europeans an ability to obtain pleasurable sensations in relatively quick doses, an interesting foreshadowing of later features of Western consumer behavior.

In the world at large, however, the impact of European expansion must be treated in terms of interaction, not simple Western dominance. European penetrations affected the history of key civilizations, such as India, but they did not bring these civilizations even close to a Western framework. Nor was there any intention of doing so, for the goal was economic differentiation between the West and its colonies, not a merger of equals. Even in Latin America, where the Western impact was far greater than in Africa or Asia, a separate historical record must be written in which the Western share forms only part of a complex story. Western colonialism was an important development in world history by the 18th century, in part because of its role in creating the new world economic system, but it by no means dictated this history even in the regions where it was most pervasive.

BRITISH AND FRENCH NORTH AMERICA

One set of colonies stands out from the general pattern in that a fuller development of Western institutions and values took place as part of the colonial experience. In essence, with important modifications suitable to the new location, Western civilization was extended to the Atlantic coast of North America, in French and particularly British colonies, from the 17th century onward.

Colonial holdings in North America—aside from Spain's crucial Mexican colony with its northerly extensions—were generally of least interest to Western colonial powers in the 17th and even the 18th centuries. The Dutch had settlements in what is now New York and New Jersey, but were more attached to their Asian colonies. British and French leaders valued West Indian holdings well above their North American colonies. North America was judged in terms of mercantilism and the world economy and was regarded as a source of crude goods, such as timber or furs, and as a market for costlier imports. But the fact was that the value of North American products was not nearly as great as those available from the Indies or

Latin America, and so much less attention was given to careful controls—a crucial ingredient in allowing some merchant and manufacturing activities to emerge among new Americans themselves.

North America remained relatively unimportant in world history through the 18th century. The American colonies that would become the United States had a population of a mere three million, far smaller than the powerful colonies in Latin America. The value of imports and exports also remained relatively insignificant. Southern colonies that produced tobacco and sugar, and then cotton, did win importance. Patterns emerged there quite similar to those of Latin America, with large estates based on imported slave labor, a wealthy planter class bent on importing luxury products from western Europe, and relatively weak formal governments. Still, in world historical terms the Atlantic colonies in North America remained something of a backwater amid the larger colonial holdings staked out in the early modern centuries.

Yet, partly because unimportance permitted some freedom of maneuver, the extent to which Western civilization was spread to this new land was important for the future. Driven by religious dissent, ambition, and other motives, a number of Europeans, many from the British Isles, colonized the Atlantic coastal region, where Indian populations were quickly reduced by disease and war. The society that developed in the British colonies was far closer to West European forms than was that of Latin America. The colonies operated their own assemblies, which provided considerable political experience. Local town governments were also active, as in many cases were Calvinist church assemblies that gave governing power to groups of elders or wider congregations. Many colonists thus had reason to share with some West Europeans a sense of the importance of representative institutions and self-government. They were also avid consumers of political theories written in Europe, such as those of John Locke.

Trade and some manufacturing developed widely. While most international trade was carried in British ships, merchants in the mid-Atlantic colonies and New England made forays of their own. By the late 18th century some were even trading with China, their ships picking up medicinal herbs along the Pacific coast and exchanging these for Chinese artifacts and tea. Great Britain attempted to impose firmer limits on this modestly thriving local economy, trying to win greater tax revenues and guarantee markets for British goods and traders, but the effort came too late and helped encourage rebellion in key colonies. Unusually among the West's colonies, North America developed a merchant class and some stake in manufacturing in a pattern similar to that taking shape in western Europe.

North American colonists also retained vigorous cultural ties with western Europe, particularly with Britain and France where so much of the cultural action centered in the 17th and 18th centuries. Thanks to Protestant encouragement, an unusual percentage of the colonists were literate, which promoted this kind of cultural exchange. Most Americans focused primarily on religious writings, but even these gave some link to European religious currents including such later Protestant movements as Methodism. There was also wide reading and discussion of Enlightenment materials, and institutions like the American Philosophical Society formed in the 18th century in deliberate imitation of European scientific institutes. Hundreds of North Americans contributed scientific findings to the British Royal Society. The colonies remained somewhat modest in certain cultural attainments. Art was rather primitive, though stylistic cues came largely from Europe. There was no question that in formal culture North American leaders saw themselves as part of a larger Western world.

The spread of Western values in the Atlantic colonies and in British and French settlements in Canada was also facilitated by the relatively slight ongoing impact of American Indians in these settled areas. The Indian population of this part of North America had always been less dense than in Central America or the Andes region. Because few Indian groups in these regions practiced settled agriculture, instead combining hunting with a slash-and-burn corn-growing complement, European colonists found it relatively easy to displace them from large stretches of territory. The ravages of European-imported disease reduced the Indian population greatly. Further, some Indian groups moved out of the coastal forests spontaneously, from the mid-17th century onward, heading for the plains farther west. Various plains Indians began to adopt the horse after Indians in Mexico first gained its use from the Spanish conquerors. The horse (once known in North America but becoming extinct just as the first Indian settlers arrived from Asia) gave Indian hunters immense advantages in killing bison, and, combined with European pressure on the coasts, this induced many forest people to abandon agriculture. Many territorial wars resulted among North American Indian groups. The net result of all these factors was that, while colonists certainly interacted with Indians, learned from them, and feared and misused them, they did not combine with them to forge a new cultural amalgam as occurred in much of Latin America.

By 1700 the importation of African slaves proved to be a more important modification of Western habits, particularly in the southern colonies. The practice of slave-holding and interactions with African culture would mark off North American life from its European counterpart.

British naval power allowed the light infantry to scale the French Fort from the St. Lawrence River and capture Quebec in 1759.

NORTH AMERICA AND WESTERN CIVILIZATION

On balance, most white settlers intended to transplant key Western habits into their new setting and managed to do so. Family patterns, for example, were similar. American colonists were able to marry slightly earlier than ordinary West Europeans because of greater abundance of land, and they had larger families. Still, they reproduced most features of the European-style family, including primary emphasis on the nuclear unit. The new Americans did display unusual concern for children, if only because they depended so heavily on their work in a labor-scarce environment. European visitors commented on the child-centeredness of American families and the freedom of children to speak up. These variations, while significant, played on trends also becoming visible in Europe, with the new emphasis on family affection. In other respects, as coastal colonies became more crowded in the 18th century, American families reverted more closely to European patterns, as in marrying later in order to limit the pressure of large numbers of children on property. In basic features of life, then, such as family behavior, North American colonists and their European counterparts moved from essentially the same base in very similar directions.

Americans were conscious of some distinctiveness. They lacked Europe's elaborate art and great cities, though they were eager to imitate. They felt somewhat inferior to the more-powerful mother countries, but also took pride in what they claimed was greater freedom (slavery conveniently set apart in a highly racist culture that judged by conditions of whites alone) and a more youthful vigor. The habit of looking to Europe, plus the spontaneous parallels between key European and American developments in economic, social, and intellectual life, modified the claims to a totally new civilization. Even when key colonies rebelled against European control, as they did in 1776, they moved in the name of Western political ideas and economic goals against the dependency the British belatedly tried to impose, and they proceeded to establish a government that, though it pioneered some distinctive features, remained within the range of Western political values.

Crucial diversities arose among the Atlantic colonies. The most important divided the cash-crop, slave-holding colonies, clearly enmeshed as dependents in the European-dominated world economy, and those to the north. There were divisions as well between the colonies that would become the United States and those in Canada.

In Canada, the first substantial European settlements were launched by the French government under Louis XIV. The initial plan involved setting up manorial estates under great lords whose rights were carefully restricted by the state. French peasants were urged to emigrate, though it proved difficult to develop an adequate labor force. However, birth rates were high and by 1755 New France had about 55,000 settlers in a peasant society that proved extremely durable as it fanned out around the fortress of Quebec. Strong organization by the Catholic church completed this partial replica of French provincial society. France lost its colony under the terms of the Treaty of Paris that in 1763 settled the Seven Years' War. France eagerly regained its West Indian sugar islands, along with trading posts in Africa, while Britain took control of Canada and the Mississippi basin. Relations between British officials and the French-Canadian community remained strained as British settlements developed in eastern Canada and in Ontario; the flight of many American loyalists after the 1776 revolution added to the English-speaking contingent in Canada.

Many English colonies along the Atlantic seaboard began much as the French in Canada had begun, with grants of land to major proprietors, such as William Penn, who then set about recruiting settlers. New England was an exception, with its early base in Calvinist refugees from religious tensions in Britain. New York began as a Dutch settlement, but was taken over easily by an English expedition in 1664. Whatever the initial origins, however, the thirteen colonies ultimately set up along the coast all developed local representative assemblies with considerable influence over the governors appointed by the English crown. Economic conditions were considerably more equal than in Europe, and there was no formal aristocracy; only the 23 percent of the population held as slaves stood clearly apart from the mass. This was a new kind of colonial setup, based on significant settlement and displacement, rather than use or conversion, of the original Indian population. This fact, combined with the loose rule of the British crown, assured a trajectory for this part of North America considerably different from that of the other European holdings. One of the first concrete results of this difference came in the rebellious reaction of many colonists when Britain did at last, after its expenses in the Seven Years' War, attempt to treat these colonies more similarly to its other vast holdings in order to win clearer economic advantages and also to recoup administrative costs.

CONCLUSION

THE IMPACT OF A NEW WORLD ORDER

Important as Europe's colonies were in bringing Western influences or a Western outcropping to new areas of the world, the larger development of the world economy stands as the West's most important, and in some ways most durable, incursion onto the world scene during the centuries after 1500. Like all major shifts in human history, the world economy brought both advantages and disadvantages in its wake. Some societies definitely suffered as economic inequalities increased among key regions. Latin America, major parts of Africa, and even the southern colonies of what became the United States were drawn into the world economy as inferiors, with harsh labor systems and political limitations as a result. Many of these economic inferiorities proved to be self-perpetuating, for few of the initially dependent regions have even today fully achieved economic parity with world economic leaders or substantial control over their own economic destinies. Correspondingly the West, ultimately to include much of North America, became a long-term beneficiary in world economic relationships, in a pattern that still substantially prevails today.

The world economy also created new links, mainly through rising commerce, among key societies. Knowledge of new foodstuffs as well as increased trade helped many agricultural societies expand their populations and deal with some problems of scarcity that had previously been irremediable.

Above all, the creation of the world economic framework presented key challenges to virtually every civilization in the world. While not yet a dominant factor in all regions, the world economy, supplemented by the West's military advantages and thirst for colonies, did raise new questions about how to react. Even when the choice involved a new effort at isolation, some innovation was required. The West's new world role, in sum, unleashed an important force for change. Responses varied because of varying conditions and prior traditions, and other changes developed that had little to do with the West one way or the other. Even societies that sought stability above all, however, found their environment shifting, so that some new policies were essential simply to try to stand still.

FURTHER READINGS

Excellent discussions of Western exploration and expansion are Carlo Cipolla's *Guns, Sails and Empires: Technological Innovation and the Early Phases of European Expansion 1400–1700* (1965) and J. H. Parry's *The Age of Reconnaissance* (1982). Somewhat more specific facets are treated in D. K. Fieldhouse's *The Colonial Empires* (1971), J. H. Parry's *The Discovery of South America* (1979), and C. R. Boxer's *Four Centuries of Portuguese Expansion* (1969). A vital treatment of the international results of new trading patterns of foods and disease is Alfred Crosby's *The Columbian Exchange: Biological and Cultural Consequences of 1492* (1972).

On slavery and its trade, see Eric Williams's *Capitalism and Slavery* (1964), Orlando Patterson's *Slavery and Social Death: A Comparative Study* (1982), and D. B. Davis's *Slavery and Human Progress* (1984)—the last two being important comparative and analytical statements in a major field of recent historical study. See also Philip D. Curtin's *Atlantic Slave Trade* (1972) and his edited volume, *Africa Remembered: Narratives by West Africans from the Era of the Slave Trade* (1967). A good recent survey of developments in Africa and in the period is Paul Bohannan and Philip Curtin's *Africa and Africans* (3d ed., 1988).

New world-trading patterns are discussed in K. N. N. Shanduri's *Trade and Civilization in the Indian Ocean* (1985) and Philip Curtin's *Cross-Cultural Trade in World History* (1984). A controversial theoretical statement about new trade relationships and their impact on politics and social structure is Immanuel Wallerstein's *The Modern World System: Capitalist Agriculture and the Origins of the European World Economy in the Sixteenth Century* (1974) and *The Modern World System: Mercantilism and the Consolidation of the European World Economy 1600–1750* (1980); see also his *Politics of the World Economy: The States, the Movements and the Civilizations* (1984).

For discussions on where colonial North America fits in this period of world history, see Jack Greene and J. R. Pole, eds., *Colonial British America: Essays on the New History of the Early Modern Era* (1984).

1462 Much of Russia freed from Tartars by Ivan III (Ivan the Great)

1480 Moscow region free; Russian expansion presses south

1533–1584 Ivan IV (Ivan the Terrible), first to be called tsar; boyar power reduced

1552–1556 Russian expansion in central Asia, western Siberia

1604–1613 Time of Troubles

1613–1917 Romanov dynasty

1637 Russian pioneers to Pacific

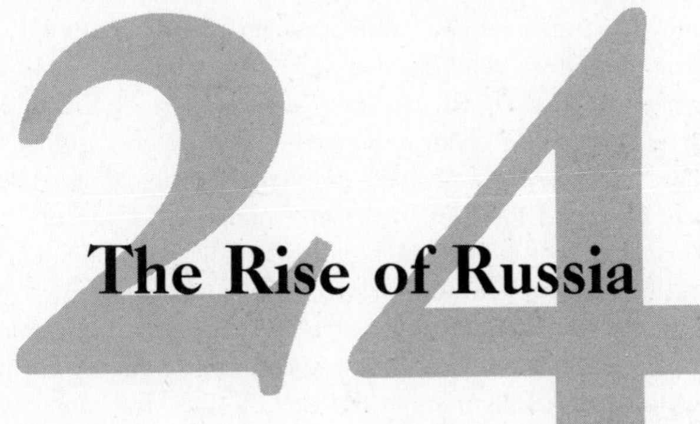

24 The Rise of Russia

INTRODUCTION. World history between 1450 and 1750 was defined by the rise of several empires besides that of the West. New military technologies, particularly the growing use of gunpowder by imperial armies, provided the common means for these expansions. The non-Western empires, however, were largely acquired over land and contiguous, therefore, to their original bases. While they had important economic implications, the commerce of these empires was regional in scope; thus they lacked the worldwide economic influences the Western powerhouses were carving out. Some of the empires, in fact, despite their impressive military and political structures, became enmeshed in the Western-dominated world economy on unfavorable terms.

Of these surging overland empires, the one with the most lasting success and whose achievements changed the map of Europe and Asia most substantially was the new Russian empire. Russian leaders, casting off Tartar domination between 1450 and 1480, proceeded on a fairly steady course of expansion. Much of their new territory was Asian, but their growth soon gave Russia the leading role in eastern Europe as well. Smaller kingdoms remained in eastern Europe, and many of them differed from Russian characteristics in important ways. But Russia was now the focal point, as it became a significant force in world history for the first time.

Russia had been a minor actor on the world stage before the 15th century. Russian culture had developed in close connection with the Byzantine Empire, from roughly the 9th century onward. Russia had also converted to Orthodox Christianity, with its vibrant cultural traditions and rich art (see Chapter 15). Russia's regional kingdom resembled other loose kingdoms in eastern Europe during the postclassical period, such as Lithuania and Hungary. Russia's kingdom weakened, however, as the Byzantine Empire began to collapse, and in the 13th century it was overrun by Mongol invaders. The ensuing two centuries of Mongol,

1649 Law enacted making serfdom hereditary

1689–1725 Peter the Great

1700–1721 Wars with Sweden

1703 Founding of St. Petersburg

1762–1796 Catherine the Great

1773–1775 Pugachev revolt

1772, 1793, 1795 Partition of Poland

1785 Law enacted tightening landlord power over serfs

or Tartar, rule had reduced Russia's cities and trade and lowered its cultural and educational levels. Christianity remained, as did the memory of political independence. However, Tartar rule confirmed Russia's substantial separation from activities in western Europe, and also reduced Russian vitality precisely at a point when Western economic and political institutions were beginning to spring forward.

Russia's evolution after 1450 compels our attention not simply because of territorial expansion and growing importance, but because of the fascinating transformation the nation undertook as part of its surge onto the world scene. Building on older East European traditions, including the glories of the Byzantine Empire, and on a strong sense of separate identity, the Russians also entered into new contacts with Western society. The result established new complexities in the definition of the two European civilizations, for more contacts and more outright imitation developed than had been true prior to 1450. Yet Russia, though the first society consciously and by its own volition to mimic the West, did not become Western. It could not, among other things, gain equality within the world economy, nor did it really strive to do so at this point. In this respect and in the social structure that underlay its economy, Russia and most of eastern Europe drew apart from Western patterns during these centuries. A tension arose concerning Western influence—whether to embrace it, select from it, or shun it—that has continued in Russian culture to this day.

The period from 1450 to 1750, in sum, formed many of the characteristics of East European civilization that have lasted into our own time: the dominance of Russia and the formation of a Eurasian Russian Empire; the capacity for change but a dynamic force rather different from that of the West in the same era; the ambivalence toward the West itself. All of these characteristics became more significant as part of larger world history, as the region moved into greater power and prominence.

This chapter deals with one of the great regional empires formed during the early modern period. Russia's rise was novel, and it involved substantial territorial redefinitions not only in eastern Europe, but also in central and northeastern Asia. Russia's development also brought new contacts with Western civilization and a first case of *Westernization*, as Russia borrowed selectively from Western economic and political techniques and from Western culture, while remaining a distinctive civilization overall. Here was an important forerunner of later developments elsewhere in the world, and also a vital new ingredient in Russian culture that continues to play a role.

RUSSIA'S EXPANSIONIST POLITICS UNDER THE TSARS

Russia's emergence as a new power, first in eastern Europe and central Asia and ultimately on a still-larger scale, initially depended on gaining freedom from Mongol (Tartar) control. The Duchy of Moscow served as the center for the liberation effort beginning in the 14th century. Local princes began to carve out greater autonomy, and the effectiveness of Mongol control began to diminish. Ironically, the Moscow princes initially gained political experience as tax collectors for the Mongols, but gradually they moved toward regional independence. Under Ivan III, or Ivan the Great, who claimed succession from the Rurik dynasty and the old Kievan days, a large part of Russia was freed after 1462. Ivan organized a strong army, giving the new government a military emphasis it would long retain. He also used loyalties to the Orthodox Christian faith and to Russia—that is, to a blend of vague nationalism with religion—to win support for his campaigns. By 1480 Moscow had been freed from any payment to the Mongols and had gained a vast territory running from the borders of the Polish kingdom, in the west, to the Ural mountains.

THE NEED FOR REVIVAL

Mongol control had never reshaped basic Russian values, for the rulers had been interested in tribute, not full government. Many Russian landlords did adopt Mongol styles of dress and social habits. However, most Russians had remained Christians, and many recalled the earlier times in which Russia had ruled itself. Most local administrative issues remained in the hands of regional princes, landlords, or peasant villages. In these senses Russia was set to resume many of its earlier trajectories when full independence was achieved. On the other hand the Mongol period had reduced the vigor of Russian cultural life—worsening, for example, the levels of literacy among the priesthood. An earlier literary and artistic tradition had partially atrophied. Economic life deteriorated as well, with trade down and manufacturing limited; Russia had become a purely agricultural economy, dependent on peasant labor. In these senses independence brought a challenge for revival and reform.

Ivan the Great restored the earlier tradition of centralized rule, which went back to the Rurik dynasty and Byzantine precedents. He added to this a new sense of imperial mission. He married the niece of the last Byzantine emperor, which gave him the chance to claim supervision of all Orthodox churches whether in Russia or not.

Encouraged by his advisors, Ivan also insisted that Russia had succeeded Byzantium as a "third Rome," with all that this implied in terms of grandeur and expansionist potential. Ivan accordingly entitled himself tsar, or Caesar—the "autocrat of all the Russians."

The next important tsar, Ivan IV, justly called Ivan the Terrible, continued the policy of Russian expansion. He also placed still greater emphasis on confirming the power of the tsarist autocracy, earning his nickname by attacking many Russian nobles, or boyars, whom he suspected of conspiracy, and killing a number of them. This obviously reduced potential competition for governing rights. Russian aristocrats lacked the tradition of political assertion of their counterparts in western Europe, and Ivan's policies of terror confirmed this fact.

PATTERNS OF EXPANSION

The territorial expansion policy focused particularly on central Asia. It was motivated by a desire to push the former Mongol overlords farther back as a reaction to previous invasions common in human history, and thus was quite sensible from a strategic point of view. Russia was a country of vast plains, with few natural barriers to invasion. The early tsars turned this drawback to an advantage by pushing southward toward the Caspian Sea; they also moved east, into the Ural mountains and beyond. Both Ivan III and Ivan IV recruited peasants to migrate to the newly seized lands, particularly in the south. These peasant-adventurers, or *cossacks,* were Russian pioneers, combining agriculture with daring military feats on horseback. Expansion territories long had a rough-and-ready frontier quality, only gradually settling down to more regular administration. The cossack spirit provided volunteers to implement further expansion, for many of the pioneers—like their American westward-moving analogies in the 19th century—chafed under detailed tsarist control and were eager to move on to new settlements. During the 16th century the cossacks not only completed the conquest of the Caspian Sea area but also moved into western Siberia, across the Urals, beginning the gradual takeover and settlement of these vast plains, previously sparsely inhabited by nomadic Asian peoples.

Russia's expansionist policy, firmly set by the 16th century, resulted thus from an initial impulse to chase previous overlords farther away, building on the kind of energy that seems often to follow a national liberation (compare, for example, China after periods of foreign control, or Spain and Portugal after the expulsion of the Muslims). The policy was maintained by the development of a powerful military-settler force and spirit. It was also justified by the heady tsarist sense that Russia had succeeded to the mantle of the great Rome. Russia's Christianity and sense of Orthodox mission also provided ideological motivation, although some of the conquered peoples were not brought into a Christian fold; here, nevertheless, was an expansionist element similar to that operating in the West during the same period. Expansion also offered tsars a means of rewarding loyal noblemen and bureaucrats by giving them estates in new territories, and it provided not only new ag-

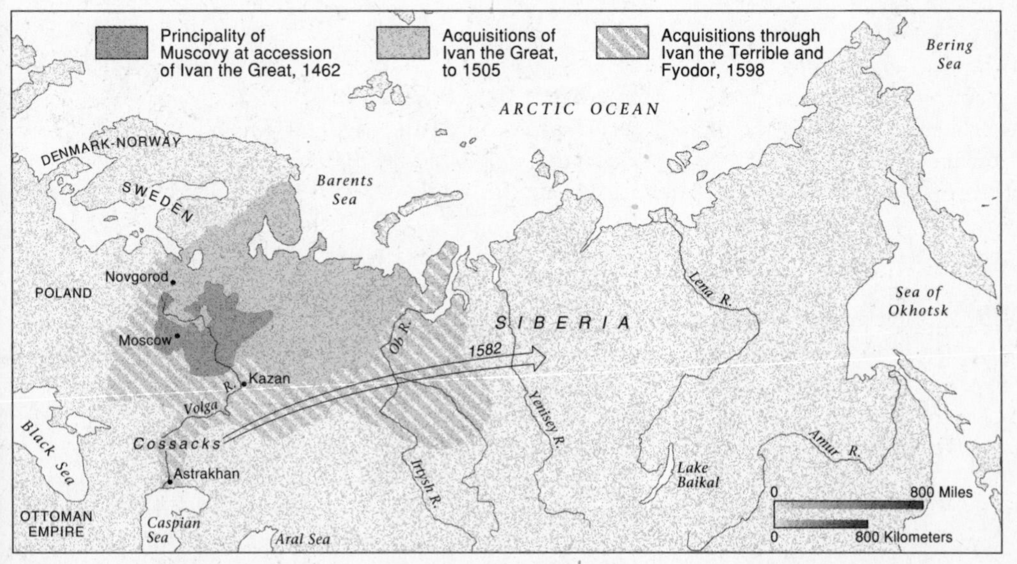

Russian Expansion under the Early Tsars, 1462–1598

ricultural areas but also sources of labor—Russia utilized slaves for certain kinds of production work into the 18th century. While Russia never became as dependent on expansion for social control and economic advance as the later Roman Empire or the Ottoman Empire had, it certainly had abundant reasons to continue the policy. The zeal for conquest, the easy geographic access to surrounding territory, and the economic and technical advantages Russia had over many central and northeast Asian groups facilitated the policy in turn. Russia, though not possessed of advanced manufacturing techniques, did create substantial trading connections with its new Asian territories and their neighbors.

Russia's early expansion, along with that of the Ottoman Empire to the south, eliminated independent central Asia, that age-old source of nomadic cultures and periodic invasions in both the east and the west. The same expansion, while driven by the movement of Russian peasants and landlords to new areas, also added to Russia a diversity of new peoples, making this empire, like that of the Mughals and Ottomans, a real multicultural entity. Particularly important was the addition of a large Muslim minority, overseen by the tsarist government but not pressed to integrate with Russian culture.

RUSSIA AND THE WEST

Along with expansion and enforcement of tsarist primacy, the early tsars added one final policy ingredient to their overall approach: some carefully managed contacts with the West. The tsars realized that Russia's cultural and economic lag under the Mongols had put them at a disadvantage relative to the West, whose commercial expansion and, with the Renaissance, cultural drive could not fail to impress. Ivan III was eager to launch diplomatic missions to the leading Western states, as an emblem of Russia's renewed independence and a sign that it wanted contact with the Western network of international relations. During the

These icons depict Mary and the Christ child, one from the early 15th century, the other from 1655. The Russian icon tradition used styles passed from Byzantine art that under Western influence became more naturalistic by the 17th century.

reign of Ivan IV, British merchants established trading contacts with Russia, selling manufactured products in exchange for furs and other raw materials. Soon, outposts of Western merchants were established in Moscow and other centers. The tsars also imported Italian artists and craftsmen to design church buildings and the magnificent royal palace in the Kremlin in Moscow. The foreign architects modified Renaissance styles to take Russian building traditions into account, producing the ornate, onion-shaped domes that became characteristic of Russian (and other East European) churches and creating a distinctive form of classicism. Nevertheless, the tradition of looking to the West, particularly for emblems of upper-class art and status, was beginning to emerge by the 16th century, along with some reliance on Western commercial initiative.

Ivan IV died, little mourned, without an heir. This set off the Time of Troubles early in the 17th century. The boyars tried to use the vacuum of power to gain governing rights for themselves, in an effort reminiscent of battles between throne and nobility in the West. Several neighboring states, led by Sweden and Poland, also captured Russian territory, for they had worried about the growth of a giant neighbor to their east. In 1613, however, an assembly of boyars chose a member of the Romanov family as tsar. This family was to rule Russia until the great revolution of 1917. While many individual Romanov rulers were weak and tensions with noble claims recurred at various points, the Time of Troubles did not produce any lasting constraints on tsarist power, as did the parliaments that were gaining ground in some Western states at this time.

The first Romanov, Michael, did have to accept a few noble claims, for the autocracy was not fully restored until late in the 17th century, but he established internal order without great difficulty. He also drove out the foreign invaders and resumed the expansionist policy of his predecessors. A successful war against Poland brought Russia part of the Ukraine, including Kiev, and in the south Russia's boundaries were stretched to meet those of the Ottoman Empire. Expansion at this point, obviously, was beginning to suggest new diplomatic implications as Russia encountered other established governments and began to move eastward as well as into parts of Asia.

Alexis Romanov abolished the assemblies of nobles and gained new powers over the Russian church. He was eager to purge the Church of many superstitions and errors that, in his judgment, had crept in during Mongol times. His policies resumed the Orthodox tradition of state control over the Church. It also created new tensions within Russian religion, as hundreds of thousands of Russians, attached to the rituals and beliefs Alexis attacked, tried to resist what they viewed as dangerous innovation. The government, in turn, exiled thousands of these "old believers" to Siberia or to southern Russia, where they maintained their religion but also extended Russia's colonizing activities.

PETER THE GREAT AND WESTERNIZATION

By the end of the 17th century Russia had become, territorially, one of the great land empires, spanning major parts of Europe and Asia. European Russia alone was the largest political unit on this continent. Tsarist autocracy, briefly threatened, had been reasserted. Economically, however, Russia remained unusually agricultural by the standards of the commercializing West and of the great Asian civilizations. A strong Russian cultural voice had yet to redevelop, despite important contacts with the West and a rich popular tradition in music and storytelling.

The reign of Peter I, the son of Alexis and known with some justice as Peter the Great, built a number of new features into this framework between 1689 and 1725. In essence Peter extended his predecessors' policies of building up tsarist control and expanding Russian territory. He added a more definite interest in changing selected aspects of Russian economy and culture through imitation of Western forms.

Peter the Great was an energetic leader of exceptional intelligence and ruthless energy. A giant himself, standing 6 feet 8 inches, he was eager to move his country more fully into the Western diplomatic and cultural orbit, without making it fully Western. He traveled widely in the West, incognito, seeking Western allies for a crusade against Turkish power in Europe—for which he found little enthusiasm. He also visited many Western manufacturing centers, even working as a ship's carpenter in Holland; through these activities he gained an interest in Western science and technology. He brought scores of Western artisans back with him to Russia.

TSARIST AUTOCRACY

In politics Peter was a clear autocrat. He put down revolts against his rule with great cruelty, in one case executing some of the ringleaders personally. He had no interest in the parliamentary features of Western centers such as Holland, seizing instead on the absolutist currents in the West at this time. Peter enhanced the power of the Russian state by using it as a reform force, trying to show that even aristocratic habits could be modified by state decree. Peter also extended an earlier policy of recruiting bureaucrats from outside aristocratic ranks and giving them noble titles to reward bureaucratic service. Here was a key means

This piece of art portrays Peter the Great in heroic pose with his subordinates and his military technology.

of freeing the state from exclusive dependence on aristocratic officials, who might maneuver from their separate power base. Peter imitated Western military organization, creating a specially trained fighting force that put down local militias.

Furthermore, Peter the Great set up a secret police to prevent dissent and to supervise the bureaucracy, here paralleling an earlier Chinese innovation but going well beyond the bureaucratic-control impulses of Western absolutists at this time. Peter's Chancery of Secret Police was to survive, though under different names and with changing functions, to the present day, reinstituted after 1917 by a revolutionary regime that in other respects worked to undo key features of the tsarist regime.

Peter's foreign policy maintained many well-established lines. He attacked the Ottoman Empire (no crusade was involved, but more of a power quest), though he won no great victories. He warred with Sweden, at the time one of the leading northern powers in Europe, and gained territory on the eastern coast of the Baltic Sea, which reduced Sweden to second-rate military status. Russia now had a window on the sea, including an ice-free port, and from this time onward Russia became a major factor in European diplomatic and military alignments. The tsar commemorated both Russia's shift of interests westward and his desire to reform Russia in some Western directions by moving his capital from Moscow to a new Baltic city that he named St. Petersburg.

WHAT WESTERNIZATION MEANT

As a reformist, Peter concentrated on improvements in political organization, on selected economic development, and on cultural change. Peter attempted to streamline Russia's small bureaucracy and alter military structure to take Western organizational principles into account. He created a clearer military hierarchy, while developing separate, functionally specialized bureaucratic departments. He also improved the army's weaponry and, with aid from Western advisors, created the first Russian navy. He completed the elimination of old noble councils, creating a set of advisors under his control. Provincial governors were appointed from St. Petersburg, and while town councils were elected, here too a tsar-appointed magistrate served as final authority. The Russian church was placed still more firmly under state control, with the tsar as head of the church directing a committee of bishops who ran detailed religious affairs. Peter's ministers systematized law codes to extend through the whole empire, and the tax system was revised with taxes on ordinary Russian peasants increasing steadily. New training institutes were established for aspiring bureaucrats and officers, which was one way for more talented nonnobles to be brought into the system.

Peter's economic efforts concentrated on building up metallurgical and mining industries, using Russia's extensive iron holdings that could feed state-run munitions and shipbuilding facilities. Without urbanizing extensively or developing a large commercial class, Peter's reforms did alter the Russian economy. Landlords were rewarded for using serf labor to staff new manufacturing operations. The result gave Russia not a Western-level manufacturing base, but a sufficiently independent operation that avoided the need for imports for military purposes. This was a limited goal, but a very important one in giving Russia the internal economic means of maintaining a substantial military presence for almost two centuries.

Finally, Peter was eager to make Russia culturally respectable in Western eyes. Cultural change would supplement bureaucratic training and provide greater technical expertise—it was not all window dressing. Peter was also eager to cut the Russian elite off from its traditions, to enhance state power, and to commit the elite to new identities. Thus he issued edicts requiring nobles to shave off their beards and wear Western dress; in symbolic ceremonies he cut off the long, Mongol-type sleeves and pigtails that were characteristic of the boyars. Here was the first of many instances in which traditional appearance was forcibly altered as part of Western-oriented change, though in this case only the upper class was involved. Of greater substance were attempts to provide more education in mathematics and other technical subjects for the nobility. Under Peter and his successors scientific institutes and academies were founded along Western lines, and serious discussion of the latest scientific and technical findings became common. At the elite level, indeed, Peter succeeded in building Russia into the Western cultural zone, with fads and fashions extending easily into the glittering new capital city. Ballet, for example, initially encouraged in the French royal court, was imported and made something of a Russian specialty.

This first case of Westernization embodied several features that would be visible in other societies later on. In the first place the changes envisaged were selective. Peter did not try to touch the ordinary people of Russia or to involve them in the kinds of technologies or mentalities becoming current in the West. New manufacturing involved labor that was partially coerced, not the more independent (though not necessarily richly rewarding) system of wage

This contemporary Russian cartoon lampoons Peter the Great's order to his nobility to cut off their beards.

labor spreading in the West. There was no interest in building the kind of worldwide export economy characteristic of the West. Peter wanted economic development to support military strength, rather than for wider commercial goals. Westernization was meant, finally, to encourage the autocratic state, not to challenge it with some of the new political ideas circulating in the West at this time. This was real change, but it did not fold Russia into Western civilization outright; selectivity was crucial, and there was no interest in abandoning particularly Russian goals.

Furthermore, the Westernization that did occur brought hostile response. Many peasants resented the Westernized airs and expenses of their landlords, some of whom no longer even knew Russian but spoke only French. Elements of the elite opposed Peter's thirst for change, arguing that Russian traditions were superior to those of the West and that emphasis should be placed on Russia's distinctive culture, not on its ability to mimic. This tension would continue in Russian history from this point forward, leading to important oscillations between enthusiasm and revulsion where Western values were concerned.

RUSSIA IN THE 18TH CENTURY

The death of Peter the Great in 1724 was followed by several decades of weak rule, dominated in part by power plays among army officers who guided the selection of several ineffective emperors and empresses. The weakness of tsardom in these years encouraged new grumblings about undue Westernization and also some new initiatives by church officials eager to gain more freedom of maneuver, but no major new policy directions were set. Russian territorial expansion continued, with several clashes with the Ottoman Empire and further exploration and settlement in Siberia.

In 1762 Peter III, nephew of Peter the Great's youngest daughter, reached the throne. He was retarded, but his wife, a German-born princess who changed her name to Catherine—later, Catherine the Great—soon took matters in hand and continued to rule as empress after Peter III's death. Catherine resumed Peter the Great's interests in several respects. She defended the powers of the central monarch. She put down a vigorous peasant uprising, led by Emelian Pugachev, butchering Pugachev himself. She used the Pugachev rebellion as an excuse to extend the powers of the central government in regional affairs.

Catherine was also a Westernizer. She flirted vigorously with the ideas of the French Enlightenment, importing several French philosophers for visits and playing the patroness of arts and sciences. She summoned various reform commissions to discuss new law codes and other Western-style measures, including reduction of traditionally severe punishments.

There was more than a bit of facade in Catherine's internal programs, however. A centralizer she was, and certainly an advocate of a strong tsarist hand. But Catherine also gave new powers to the nobility over their serfs, maintaining a kind of trade-off that had been developing over the previous two centuries in Russia. In this trade-off, nobles would acquiesce in strong central government prerogatives and would staff the government as bureaucrats and officers. They were in this sense a service aristocracy, not an independent force. They would also accept into their ranks newly ennobled officials chosen by the tsars. In return, however, most of the actual administration over local peasants, except for those on government-run estates, was wielded by the noble landlords. These landlords could requisition peasant labor, tax in money and in kind, and even exact punishments for crimes since local justice was administered by landlord-dominated courts. Catherine increased the harshness of punishments nobles could decree for their serfs, thus ensuring that, for the majority of the Russian people, government remained effectively decentralized despite the tsarist superstructure.

The central government taxed the peasants and recruited some peasants for military service, but its contacts with many ordinary people were limited. The extensive government tradition of empires, such as China or the more activist governments beginning to develop in the West, were not paralleled in Russia, which combined a real monopoly of formal politics by a central tsarist administration with limited functions and personnel in the outlying provinces. Tsarist administrations controlled some land directly, where labor was performed by state serfs, but its hold over estates owned by nobles was almost nonexistent.

Catherine's Westernization program was extremely shallow, though it did represent a real desire to appear progressive in the eyes of Western intellectuals. The new law codes, when enacted, were not really put into effect. Confirmation of landlord power over serfs moved, in fact, in opposite directions to those preached in Enlightenment theory. Catherine did patronize Western-style art and architecture, continuing to build St. Petersburg in the classical styles popular at the same time in the West and encouraging leading nobles to tour the West or even send children for some Western education. But she also sought to avoid contagion from the West. When political turmoil hit the West in the form of the great French Revolution of 1789, Catherine was quick to close Russia's doors to the "seditious" writings of liberals and democrats. She also censored

The Western fashion and Western painting style that won the Russian elite are shown in this 1762 painting of Catherine the Great.

a small but emerging band of Russian intellectuals who urged reforms along Western lines, prohibiting the publication of critiques of serfdom or the autocratic political system. One of the first Western-inspired radicals, a nobleman named Radishev who sought abolition of serfdom and more liberal political rule, was vigorously harassed by Catherine's police, his writings banned.

Catherine pursued the tradition of Russian expansion with vigor and success. She resumed campaigns against the Ottoman Empire, winning considerable new territories in central Asia including the Crimea, bordering the Black Sea. The Russian-Ottoman contest became a central diplomatic issue for both powers, with Russia increasingly ascendant. She sped the colonization of Russia's holdings in Siberia and encouraged further exploration, claiming the territory of Alaska in Russia's name. Russian explorers also moved down the Pacific coast of North America into what is now northern California, while tens of thousands of pioneers spread over Siberia.

Another sign of Russian expansion was the establishment by a Russian trading company of several forts on the northernmost Hawaiian island around 1800. These forts

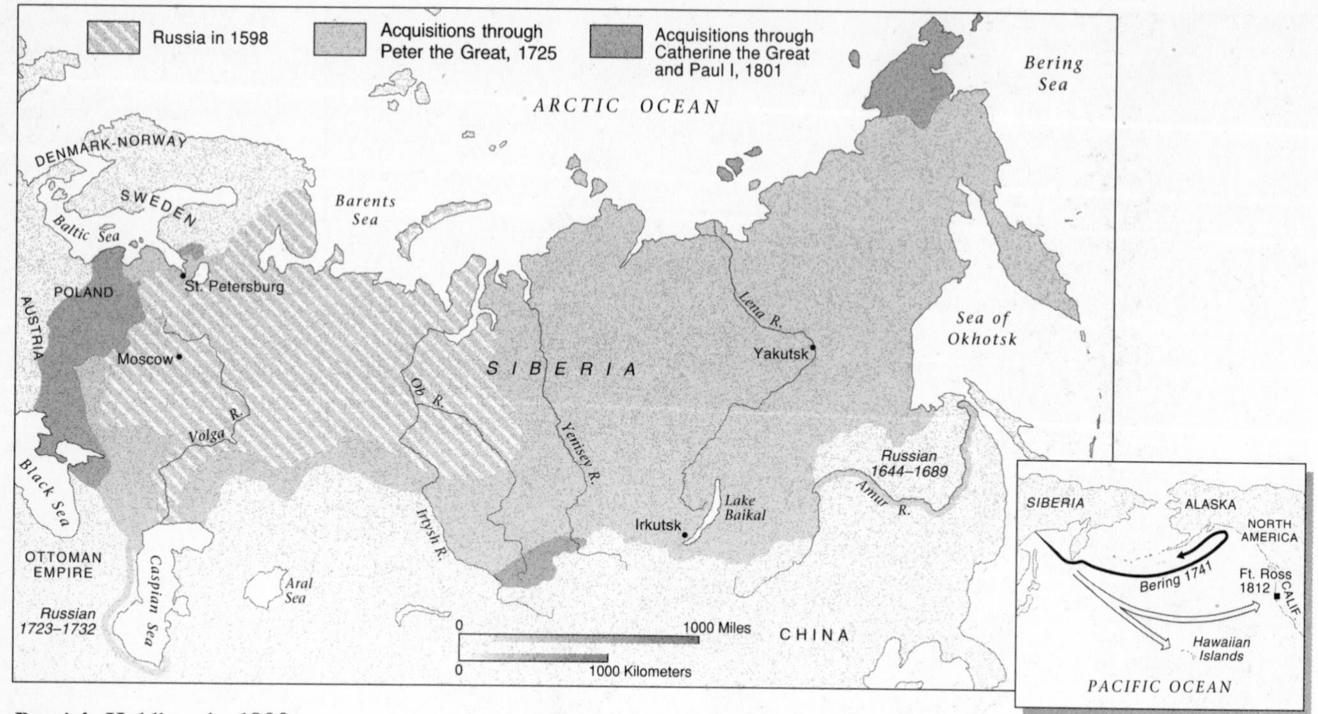

Russia's Holdings by 1800

and trade around them flourished only until 1817 (when a newly unified Hawaiian kingdom under British influence expelled them), but they raised a hope briefly of yet another Russian acquisition. In combination with Russia's push down the North American Pacific coast, these Pacific expeditions showed a dynamism not matched again for one and one-half centuries, as Russia after 1815 would enter a period of growing internal tensions and constraint.

Finally, Catherine pressed Russia's interests in Europe, playing power politics along with Prussia and Austria though without risking major wars. She stepped up Russian interference in Polish affairs. The Polish government was extremely weak, almost paralyzed by a parliamentary system that let noble landowners veto any significant measure, and this invited interest by more powerful neighbors. Russia was able to win agreements with Austria and Prussia to partition Poland. Three partitions, in 1772, 1793, and 1795, eliminated Poland as an independent state, and Russia held the lion's share of the spoils. The basis for further Russian involvement in European affairs had obviously been created, and this would show in Russia's ultimate role in putting down the French armies of Napoleon after 1812, the first time Russian troops moved into the heartland of western Europe.

By the time of Catherine's death in 1796, Russia had passed through three centuries of extraordinary development. It had won independence and constructed a strong central state, though one that had to balance the local political and economic interests of a powerful nobility. It had infused new elements into Russia's culture and economy, in part by borrowing from the West. And it had extended its control over the largest land empire in the world. In the east it now bordered China, where an 18th-century Amur River agreement set new frontiers. It had pressed into central Asia in the south, and was now pushing against the much weaker Ottoman Empire and in fact stimulating its further decline. And of course it had moved west, into the Baltic region and now Poland; by 1796 it was bumping against the borders of Prussia and Habsburg Austria, with most smaller nations of eastern Europe now eliminated. A tradition of careful but successful military aggrandizement had been established, along with a real pioneering spirit of settlement. It is no small wonder that not too long after 1800 a perceptive French observer, Alexis de Tocqueville, would liken the expanded and more important Russia to the new country emerging in the Western hemisphere, the United States of America, as the two new giants of emerging world history.

DOCUMENT
THE NATURE OF WESTERNIZATION

Peter the Great and Catherine the Great were the two chief reformist rulers in Russia before 1800. In the first of the following edicts, Peter focuses on educational change; his approach reflected a real desire for innovation, Russia's autocratic tradition in government, and its hierarchical social structure. Catherine's *Instruction* borrowed heavily from Western philosophers and was hailed by one French intellectual as "the finest monument of the century." This document, too, showed distinctively Russian traditions and problems. Furthermore, the reforms in law and punishment were not put into practice, and indeed the document itself was banned as subversive by Catherine's successor, as Russia's rulers began to fear the subversive qualities of Western influence following the French Revolution.

DECREES ON COMPULSORY EDUCATION OF THE RUSSIAN NOBILITY, JANUARY 12 AND FEBRUARY 28, 1714

Send to every *gubernia* [region] some persons from mathematical schools to teach the children of the nobility—except those of freeholders and government clerks—mathematics and geometry; as a penalty [for evasion] establish a rule that no one will be allowed to marry unless he learns these [subjects]. Inform all prelates to issue no marriage certificates to those who are ordered to go to schools. . . .

The Great Sovereign has decreed: in all *gubernias* children between the ages of ten and fifteen of the nobility, of government clerks, and of lesser officials, except those of freeholders, must be taught mathematics and some geometry. Toward that end, students should be sent from mathematical schools [as teachers], several into each *gubernia*, to prelates and to renowned monasteries to establish schools. During their instruction these teachers should be given food and financial remuneration of three *altyns* and two *dengas* per day from *gubernia* revenues set aside for that purpose by personal orders of His Imperial Majesty. No fees should be collected from students. When they have mastered the material, they should then be given certificates written in their own handwriting. When the students are released they ought to pay one ruble each for their training. Without these certificates they should not be allowed to marry nor receive marriage certificates.

THE "INSTRUCTION" OF 1767

6. Russia is a European State.
7. This is clearly demonstrated by the following Observations: The Alterations which *Peter the Great* undertook in Russia succeeded with the greater Ease, because the Manners, which prevailed at that Time, and had been introduced amongst us by a Mixture of different Nations, and the Conquest of foreign Territories, were quite unsuitable to the Climate. *Peter the First*, by introducing the Manners and Customs of Europe among the European People in his Dominions, found at that Time such Means as even he himself was not sanguine enough to expect.
8. The Possessions of the Russian Empire extend upon the terrestrial Globe to 32 Degrees of Latitude, and to 165 of Longitude.
9. The Sovereign is absolute; for there is no other Authority but that which centers in his single Person, that can act with a Vigour proportionate to the Extent of such a vast Dominion.
10. The Extent of the Dominion requires an absolute Power to be vested in that Person who rules over it. It is expedient so to be, that the quick Dispatch of Affairs, sent from distant Parts, might make ample Amends for the Delay occasioned by the great Distance of the Places.
11. Every other Form of Government whatsoever would not only have been prejudicial to Russia, but would even have proved its entire Ruin.
12. Another Reason is: That it is better to be subject to the Laws under one Master, than to be subservient to many.
13. What is the true End of Monarchy? Not to deprive People of their natural Liberty; but to correct their Actions, in order to attain the *supreme Good*. . . .

272. The more happily a People live under a government, the more easily the Number of the Inhabitants increases. . . .

519. It is certain, that a *high* Opinion of the *Glory* and *Power* of the Sovereign, would *increase* the *Strength* of his Administration; but a *good Opinion of his Love of Justice, will increase it at least as much.*

520. All this will never please those Flatterers, who are daily instilling this pernicious Maxim into all the Sovereigns on Earth, *That their People are created for them only.* But *We* think, and esteem it *Our* Glory to declare, "That *We* are created for *Our* People; and, for this Reason, *We* are obliged to Speak of Things just as they ought to be." For God forbid! That, after this Legislation is finished, any Nation on Earth should be more just; and, consequently, should flourish, more than Russia; otherwise the Intention of *Our* Laws would be totally frustrated; an Unhappiness *which I do not wish to survive.*

Questions: In what sense did reformist measures strengthen Russian autocracy? Why might 18th-century Western thinkers admire reformist tsars? What relationships to the West did the reform measures suggest?

THEMES IN EARLY MODERN RUSSIAN HISTORY

Our attention easily rests on tsarist policies and the series of wars and diplomatic maneuverings that created the great empire. However, the 17th and 18th centuries were also crucial in the development of key features of Russian social and economic life. It was here, more than in the political sphere, that the differences between Russia (plus much of the rest of eastern Europe) and the West were particularly manifest, widening in fact just as political and cultural contacts increased. A key theme running through social and economic relationships and cultural life involved the great gap between Russia's ruling classes and its peasant masses, in a society where only small urban populations existed to provide any intermediary social diversity.

Because of its great estates, its local political power, and its service to the state, the Russian nobility maintained a vital—indeed, unusually important—position in Russian society. In Russia and in eastern Europe generally, landed nobles tended to divide between a minority of great magnates, who lived in major cities and provided key cultural patronage, and smaller landowners whose culture was less Westernized, and whose life-style was considerably less opulent. Despite important periods in which nobles sought an independent political voice, notably during the Time of Troubles early in the 17th century, Russia's nobility did not win a separate institutional role in the central state. Rather, their politics were expressed through service in the tsarist state and the preeminent political power they wielded over the peasant serfs.

SERFDOM: THE LIFE OF EAST EUROPE'S MASSES

This power, furthermore, increased fairly steadily during the 17th and 18th centuries. Again in common with much of eastern Europe, Russia saw a progressive intensification of serfdom during these centuries, precisely as the West was tending toward a relaxation of this institution in favor of different labor systems. Prior to the Mongol conquest Russian peasants had been largely free farmers, their legal position superior to that of their medieval Western counterparts. After the expulsion of the Tartars, however, increasing numbers of Russian peasants fell into debt and had to accept servile status to the noble landowners when they could not repay. They retained access to much of the land, in other words, but not primary ownership. The Russian government actively encouraged this process from the 16th century onward. Serfdom gave the government a means of conciliating the nobility and of regulating peasants when the government itself lacked the means—financial and bureaucratic—to extend controls directly over the common people. As new territories were added to the empire, the system of serfdom was extended accordingly, sometimes after a period of free farming. By 1800 half of Russia's peasantry was enserfed to the landlords, and much of the other half owed comparable obligations to the state. Laws passed during the 17th and 18th centuries tied the serfs to the land and increased the legal rights of the landlords. An act in 1649 fixed the hereditary status of the serfs, so that people born to that station could not legally escape it.

Russia was in the process of setting up a system of serfdom very close to outright slavery in that serfs could be bought and sold, gambled away, as well as punished by their masters. Prompted in part by a labor shortage in the vast, expanding empire, the system constituted a very unusual case in which a people essentially enslaved many of its own number—in contrast to most slave systems, which focused on identifiable "outsiders."

While Russian serfdom was unusually harsh, rural conditions in many other parts of eastern Europe were quite similar. Nobles maintained estate agriculture in Poland, Hungary, and elsewhere. They used the system to support

The tsar's agents collected taxes from the oppressed peasantry in the 17th century.

their political control and distinctive life-style, as in Russia, though the landlord class was divided between sophisticated, Westernized magnates and provincial, cruder gentry types. The intensification of estate agriculture and serf labor also reflected eastern Europe's growing economic subordination to the West. Coerced labor was used to produce grain surpluses sold to Western merchants, to be transported in Western ships to the growing cities of Britain and Holland, as well as other parts of Western Europe. In return, Western merchants brought in manufactured goods, including the luxury furnishings and clothing essential to the aristocratic life-style. This unequal economic relationship, and its dependence on cheap, manipulated serf labor, was more pronounced in Poland and Hungary than in Russia, where economic dependence on the West was less complete, but it increasingly defined aspects of the Russian economy during the 18th century.

Serfs on the estates of eastern Europe were taxed and policed by their landlords and were even bought and sold like ordinary property. In Russia, whole villages were thus sold as manufacturing labor, a process Peter the Great, eager to spur the economy but unable to recruit workers otherwise, actively encouraged. Peasants were not literally slaves. They continued actively to use village governments to regulate many aspects of their lives, relying more heavily on community ties than their analogues in the Western countryside. Yet most peasants were quite poor and illiterate. They paid high taxes or obligations in kind, and they owed extensive labor service to the landlords or the government—a source not only of agricultural production but also of mining and manufacturing. The labor obligation, or *obruk,* could take up to one-tenth of the total work time the serfs had, and it tended to increase. This was the labor that produced grain available for export and that serviced the mines and metallurgical operations. Both the economic and the legal situation of the peasantry continued to deteriorate. While Catherine the Great sponsored a few model villages to display her enlightenment to Western-minded friends, in fact she turned the government of the serfs over to the landlords more completely than ever before. A law of 1785 allowed landlords to punish harshly any serfs convicted of major crimes or rebellion.

Peasant conditions formed both the setting for most peoples' lives and Russia's most pressing social issue by the later 18th century. Peasant rebellions recurred from the 17th century onward, but the Pugachev uprising of the 1770s was unusually menacing. Pugachev, a cossack chieftain who claimed to be the legitimate tsar, promised an end to serfdom, taxation, and military conscription, along with the abolition of the landed aristocracy. His forces roamed over southern Russia until they were finally defeated in pitched battles. Pugachev himself was brought to Moscow in a case and cut into quarters in a public square. The triumph of Catherine and the nobility did not resolve the issue, though it did highlight the mutual dependence of government and upper class. Liberal reformers such as Radishev, though imprisoned for their views, kept the issue alive as they interviewed discontented peasants. Radishev, finding peasants barely able to find enough time to work their own plots of land and sometimes tortured to work harder, thought he saw the handwriting on the wall: "Tremble, cruelhearted landlord! On the brow of each of your peasants I see your condemnation written."

After the great serf revolt, Pugachev was imprisoned and then executed.

TRADE AND ECONOMIC DEPENDENCE

In between serfs and landlords, Russian society offered scant layering. Cities were small, as 95 percent of the population remained rural. (Most manufacturing, obviously, took place in the countryside; hence there was no well-defined artisanal class.) Government growth encouraged some nonnoble bureaucrats and professionals. Small merchant groups existed as well, though most of Russia's European trade was handled by Westerners posted to the main Russian cities and relying on Western shipping. During the 18th century, logically following on Peter the Great's economic development program, an increase of internal trade occurred, which briefly spurred the growth of local merchants, many drawn from peasant origins. But the nobility—concerned about this potential social competition—managed to reduce this group, and a substantial merchant class with any sense of more than local identity simply did not develop.

This meant that much of the task of economic direction outside of agriculture fell either to foreign traders or to the state. The government thus took the leadership in organizing mining, munitions factories, and related iron-processing works, playing a considerably greater relative role in the economy than was common in the more commercially developed West. International trade was organized by Western merchant companies that maintained important privileges in St. Petersburg.

Russia's social and economic system, though distinctive by Western standards, worked well in many respects. It produced enough revenue to support an expanding state and empire. It underwrote the aristocratic magnates and their glittering, Westernized culture. The system, along with Russia's expansion, yielded significant population growth—Russia's inhabitants doubled during the 18th century to 36 million. For an empire burdened by a harsh climate in most regions, this was no small achievement. Periodic famines, as well as epidemics, bedeviled Russia still, but there was no question that the overall economy had advanced.

Yet the system suffered from important limitations. Most agricultural methods were highly traditional, and there was little motivation among the peasantry for improvement—since increased production would likely be taken by state or landlord. Landlords themselves, though like their Western counterparts they debated agricultural improvements in their academies, had little reason to take the trouble of trying to change. For them increased production meant placing greater burdens on the peasantry, not trying to sponsor new methods. Manufacturing, similarly, lagged by Western standards, despite the important extension developed under Peter the Great; again, cheap, unfree labor, not great technical sophistication, served as the key to success.

Russia did have enough economic strength to avoid the elaborate dependence in the world economy characteristic of other world regions, such as Latin America. It did not need massive Western imports; here Peter the Great's promotion of self-sufficiency in metals and weapons was a crucial move. Russia was able to trade in furs and other commodities with areas in central Asia outside its boundaries, which meant that its export economy was not totally oriented toward the more dynamic West. Yet increasing involvement with the Western-dominated world economy, and at an obvious disadvantage, was emerging by the 18th century. Western merchants expanded their operations. Russia did export increasing amounts of raw materials, notably furs, grain, and timber products, to the West, again through Western agents and ships. These exports were crucial to finance the artistic imports cherished by the upper aristocracy, as well as some other manufactured goods. This pattern bore real similarities to the clearly dependent relationships the West had encouraged in other parts of the world. It was marked also by the reliance on cheap, servile labor, with Russian peasants playing a role similar to that of Latin American *hacienda* workers (see Chapter 25).

There is no need to oversimplify. Russia's economy had strength and diversity. Russia's political independence and growing power marked it off from the more fully subordinate areas in the world economy. Other parts of eastern Europe, notably Poland, that converted more fully to grain exports to the West based on serf labor, fell into a dependent role more completely. Still, the trends of the 18th century suggested not only a growing economic weakness, but also a tendency to rigidify internal labor arrangements for world-economic as well as internal political reasons.

SOCIAL UNREST

Russia's economic and social system certainly generated important protest. By the end of the 18th century a small but growing number of Western-oriented aristocrats like Radishev were criticizing the regime's backwardness, urging measures as far-reaching as the abolition of serfdom. Here were the seeds of a radical intelligentsia that, despite government repression, would grow with time.

More significant still were the recurring peasant rebellions. Russian peasants were for the most part politically loyal to the tsar, but they harbored bitter resentments against their landlords, seen as having taken lands that were rightfully theirs. Periodic rebellions, such as those of the mid-17th century or the Pugachev uprising under Catherine, saw peasants destroy manorial records, seize land, and sometimes kill landlords and their officials. Here too was a current of discontent that would grow in the 19th century, again producing important government repression that could prevent peasant gains but could not prevent recurrent outbreaks. Peasants had the sense of grievance and the tight community structure and group traditions ideal for popular rural protest. They maintained strong family ties, extending among collateral relatives, and they preserved active village institutions—both providing a political basis for action.

By the 18th century Russia had developed what would soon be recognized as a "peasant problem" that limited its economic options because of the inflexible labor organization involved. This challenged political and social stability and embarrassed those Russians persuaded by the standards of the Western Enlightenment that a society should work toward greater human freedom and equality. Not surprisingly, it would prove difficult to decide what to do about the peasant issue, even when the issue was recognized.

RUSSIAN CULTURE AND THE TENSIONS OF WESTERNIZATION

Russia's social organization, finally, had important cultural ramifications. Russia's most obvious cultural history, beginning with the Ivans and their contact with Renaissance art and extending through the more pervasive Westernization of taste in the 18th century, involved growing participation in Western cultural forms. By the 18th century increasing numbers of Russians provided an audience for Western literature and philosophy, as well as art, music, and dance. Russia's main contributions to these mainstream Western styles lay in the future; the first great Russian poets and novelists, using Russian themes but largely Western genres, were just emerging in 1800. The same held true in musical composition, where Russia was to win such an important role in the 19th and early 20th centuries. Nor were there, as yet, major scientific contributions, though here too educated Russians attended to the achievements of the Enlightenment.

The movement toward Western cultural forms was not, however, the whole story. In addition, Orthodox priests and some nobles produced objections, fearing outside influence and arguing in the name of special Russian institutions and values. As one priest wrote to tsar Alexis, "You feed the foreigners too well, instead of bidding your folk to cling to the old customs." The attempt to define and preserve a Russian soul would remain a durable part of Russia's cultural development, building on Russia's undeniably distinctive social structure and on the separate Orthodox tradition.

Most ordinary Russians remained far removed from both Westernizing and articulately anti-Western currents. A substantial cultural gap opened between the elite and the masses. Ordinary Russian culture during the early modern centuries meant the Orthodox religion and traditional oral expressions—the heroic epics, rich musical life, and often witty proverbs designed to explain life's vagaries. The carefully structured rituals of the Orthodox church and the worship of saints allowed ordinary Russians to pray for victories or for protection from disease and famine. They represented the focal point of an elaborate system of festivals, more numerous in Russia than in the West, in which feasting and celebration contrasted with the ordinary work routine. Icon painting, resumed as a major art form after the Mongol expulsion and lasting until the later 17th century (at which point Westernizing currents began to capture artistic creativity), linked more formal culture to the popular currents, as did the revival of religious chronicles written by monks.

Religion aside, peasant cultural values also emphasized the importance of community and an earthy appreciation of life's foibles and pleasures. Community harmony was facilitated by informal village government run by peasants themselves. Most villages worked hard to regulate disputes among peasants, often using liberal doses of liquor, consumed before the village court convened, to smooth the process. Strong patriarchal control over the extended family also served as an organizing principle in peasant life. Unlike West European peasants, Russian peasants tended to marry early, through arrangements made by parents; the new household became part of the larger family economy run by the groom's father.

This peasant culture, though linked to the Orthodox church, was largely untouched by the more formal developments sponsored by the tsar. Westernized aristocrats, as a result, might point with horror at the coarseness and superstitiousness of the peasantry, but there were few efforts to bridge the gap by directly challenging traditional popular beliefs. Here too was a significant difference from the admittedly complex elite-popular cultural mixture in the West during the same centuries. Despite Westernization, or almost because of its concentration within the elite, Russia maintained a distinctive, highly traditional peasant culture into the 20th century.

ANALYSIS

RUSSIAN HISTORY AND THE COLD WAR

It is always difficult fully to appreciate traditions other than our own. It is hard to grasp the meanings of ideas and habits that differ from what we're used to, and harder still, in most cases, not to find the differences we do grasp as somehow inferior. Thus China, in not separating state and society as we in the West deem proper, can be criticized for bureaucratic heavy-handedness and lack of innovation—despite the fact that during long historical periods the Chinese record of initiatives and flexibility is considerable.

Consideration of Russian history amplifies the normal problems of interpreting distinctiveness, for Russians can easily be seen not only as different from us in the West, but also as particularly backward and hostile. Since 1947, and to an extent since Russia's communist revolution in 1917, many Westerners have regarded Russia as an overwhelming threat to world peace and independence. In 1947 a "cold war" arose that pitted the Soviet Union and its East European allies in a tense, militarized competition with the West, particularly with the United States. Diplomatic alliances and arms races stood at the core of this competition, but there were also rivalries in economic growth rates, in international sports, and in the arts. While the tensest cold-war mood eased after the 1950s, and lightened still further after the mid-1980s, it continues to affect mutual judgments between Russia and the West.

These judgments can easily spill over into historical interpretation. Recent rivalry between the United States and the Soviet Union might make it comforting to see Russia as traditionally backward, doomed always to lag behind the West. This backwardness judgment picks up earlier Western ideas, dating from before the cold war, that reflected the West's pride in its commercial superiority. Westerners have long seen Russia as underdeveloped, by the West's own standards. Backwardness judgments were also encouraged by a tendency among some Westernized Russians to hold up foreign standards and condemn their own society on this basis.

The cold-war legacy also promotes a more specific tendency toward oversimplification of the Russian past, as if it were locked into institutions and habits different from those in the West and predictive of what many Westerners dislike about what they understand to be Soviet communism. Thus Russians may be dismissed in cold-war commentary as almost inherently docile to authority or suspiciously closed-minded. Important features of Russian history, such as the absence of a Western-style church-state separation, may be magnified into generalizations about the unendingly authoritarian qualities of Russian government.

There are three controls for these kinds of facile generalizations, none of which oversimplifies in the other direction by ignoring the real differences in traditions—the fact that Russia did participate in a civilization distinct from that of the West—that did exist. The first check on simplistic characterizations of the Russian past involves a recognition of diversity and tension. Russia was not a simple society. It was autocratic in government form during the early modern centuries, but it also had a strong popular protest tradition that demonstrated an ability to shake off deference to authority. Russians did manifest some suspicions of foreign influences, but they were also open to selective imitation; again, the cultural qualities were (and remain) complex. Diversity led to many outright disagreements between Westernizers and their opponents, peasants and landlords, conservatives and radicals.

Secondly, Russia could and did change. The powers of tsarist autocrats varied over time. Reformist interests oscillated, rising and falling depending on the personality of the tsar and the larger social context. Russia after Peter the Great was quite different, culturally and economically, from its 17th-century predecessor. The capacity to change would flower again in the 19th century, as part of Russia's successful industrialization, and of course abundantly in the revolutionary era after 1920. Russia's capacity to change blossomed again after 1985. Since the 15th century Russia has probably been one of the more adaptable of the world's societies, without, however, seeking to become thoroughly Western.

Finally, Russia's relationship to the West has not been constant. The movement of Byzantine influence into Russia from the 9th century onward set a base largely separate from the West. But new and abundant contacts opened up from the late 15th century onward. Many Westerners easily accepted Russia as part of a common cultural and political tradition by the 18th century, because of shared Enlightenment beliefs at the elite level and also because of parallel developments in government. Russian absolutists had much in common with counterparts in France and Prussia. Historical patterns in the 19th century tended to reemphasize some distance, despite participation in a common diplomatic framework. Russian politics, like Russian society earlier, did not march to the Western drum at this point. The nature as well as the extent of Russian-Western distinctions were not constant, for the two civilizations had important kinship. Even in the late 20th century some leading West European conservatives, no friends to communism, argued that Russia was more fully a part of a real European tradition than was the brash, consumer-minded United States.

Russian history, in sum, overlaps Western history without merging with it. Its distinctiveness should not be confused with unusual changelessness. Twentieth-century judgments that try to oversimplify Russia's past to argue that a particularly feared regime, such as the Stalinist police state, is an inevitable expression of Russianness risk being as silly as any other culturally determinist approach that fails to allow either for change or for the diversities of the past itself.

Questions: Is there any sense in which Russia and the West were bound to clash as a result of developments visible by the 18th century? What are the best arguments for holding that Russia is a variant of a basic European civilization, not a separate entity?

CONCLUSION

RUSSIA AND EASTERN EUROPE

Russian history did not describe the whole of eastern Europe after the 15th century, though Russia's expansion, particularly its final acquisition of much of Poland, did merge much of the larger region into the Russian embrace. Regions west of Russia continued nevertheless to form something of a fluctuating borderland between West European and East European influences, aside from the Balkan lands that remained part of the Ottoman Empire. Even in this last case, by the 18th century growing trade with the West sparked some new cultural exchange, as Greek merchants, for example, picked up some Enlightenment ideas.

Areas such as present-day Poland or Czechoslovakia were more fully a part of the Western cultural orbit than was Russia, even by the 18th century. Thus a Polish scientist such as Copernicus participated early on in fundamental discoveries in what became the scientific revolution. Western currents such as the Reformation also echoed in parts of east-central Europe such as Hungary.

It was true that the smaller East European nationalities tended to lose political autonomy during the early modern era. Hungary, freed from the Turks, became part of the German-dominated Habsburg Empire. This empire also took over Czechoslovakia (then called Bohemia). Prussian territory pushed eastward into Polish lands. These developments meant also that much of eastern Europe even outside of Russia was described by the trends of absolute monarchy, largely immune to the political diversities and the new political theories current in the West at the same time.

The decline of Poland was particularly striking. In 1500 Poland, formed in 1386 by a union of the regional kingdoms of Poland and Lithuania, was the largest state in eastern Europe aside from Russia. Polish cultural life, linked through shared Roman Catholicism with the West, flourished in the 16th century. By 1600, however, economic and political setbacks mounted. Polish aristocrats, charged with electing the king, began deliberately to choose weak figures. The central government became powerless, while aristocrats ran roughshod over impoverished peasants. As in Russia, urban centers, and thus a merchant class, were lacking. The aristocratic parliament vetoed any reform efforts. As Polish power dwindled, it became ripe for the division by Prussia, the Habsburgs, and particularly Russia, which erased it as an independent country.

Separate cultures survived in the East European borderlands, even if political independence did not. Poles, Czechs, Hungarians, and the southern Slavs under Turkish rule preserved prior religion, language, and folkways, refusing assimilation into the larger empires that had swallowed them up.

At the same time, however, eastern Europe shared with Russia key social and economic patterns that distinguished the region as a whole from western Europe. The landed aristocracy loomed large. Most agriculture was controlled by large estates, with rigid serfdom providing the labor in a pattern pervasive from Prussia eastward through the Russian steppes and southward through Hungary and the Balkans. Western merchants gained increasing roles in eastern Europe because a native commercial class and a significant urban culture were largely absent—stronger in some cases than in Russia but far weaker than in the West.

Despite vital diversities, then, something of an East European economy had emerged by the 18th century that would significantly shape subsequent political and social change, despite internal political and cultural boundaries. For its part, Russia had become more than an East European power. Its achievement of empire was one of the key developments of the centuries after 1500. Here, Russia deserves comparison not so much with the West, whose imperial attainments were rather different, but with the other great landed empires of the period. Like the Mughals or Ottomans, Russia established rule through its armies. Also like these empires, the Russian Empire embraced a number of diverse, indeed potentially conflicting cultures. Expansion into Siberia brought contact with relatively small hunting-and-gathering groups. The movement into southern and central Asia gained Russia its large Muslim minority and a number of distinct racial groups. Fewer Russians moved into central Asia than into Siberia, a fact that sustained great diversity within this multinational empire. Finally, penetration farther into Europe produced control over several different Slavic minorities and some Germans. Many of these minorities were Catholic, not Orthodox Christian.

Russia's push westward also brought it a large Jewish population. Jews, excluded from Russia for religious reasons until the 18th century, were finally admitted as Russia pushed West. Catherine promised some tolerance but, bowing to Christian prejudices, did not allow Jews in key centers such as Moscow. Here, as in other cases, Russia's diversity suggested tensions for the future. Jews did fan out into many other parts of Russia, becoming an important, though often deeply resented, minority element of the multinational empire.

The multicultural character of the new empire proved a lasting feature. Yet Russia's fate obviously differed from that of other such empires in the early modern period, such as the Ottomans or the Mughals. The Russian Empire lasted longer, its vigor lasted longer still. The ethnic Russian presence was larger, for Ottomans and Mughals ruled over a majority of people from other cultures (the Arabs in the Ottoman Empire) or religions (the Hindus in the Mughal realm). Ethnic Russians with their high birthrate formed a larger percentage of the empire's total population. Russia also actively pushed pioneer settlements, which brought Russian presence, and in some cases dominance, in many of the new regions. Economic development, for all its hesitations, was also backed more vigorously, which gave the new empire some coherence and no small energy. Russia, in sum, became not only the new boy on the imperial block during the centuries after 1500, but one of history's unusual imperial success stories—still going strong, though much changed, at least until the end of the 20th century.

The early modern period was obviously a crucial formative era for Russia and for its role in Asia and Europe, despite important traditions from before the Mongol invasions. Tensions and ambiguities in Russia's contacts with the West, created in this period, continue to define Russian society. Questions raised by a multinational empire of the sort Russia so successfully created in this same period rose again to haunt the Russian state at the end of the 20th century. Issues of economic development, and whether or not to define it in strictly Russian terms, were recast in the 20th century, but they retained some of the overtones initially imparted by Peter the Great. Because of the importance Russia also began to acquire in world affairs in the early modern period, Russian questions could easily become issues affecting many other societies around the world.

FURTHER READINGS

For excellent survey coverage on this period, plus additional bibliography, see Nicholas Riasanovsky's *History of Russia* (4th ed., 1984). Two excellent source collections for this vital period of Russian history are T. Riha, ed., *Readings in Russian Civilization*. Vol. II, *Imperial Russia 1700–1917* (1969) and Basil Dmytryshyn's *Imperial Russia: A Sourcebook 1700–1917* (1967).

On important regimes, see J. L. I. Fennell's *Ivan the Great of Moscow* (1961), R. Massie's *Peter the Great* (1981), and N. V. Riasanovsky's *The Image of Peter the Great in Russian History and Thought* (1985). This last book is a very interesting interpretive effort. On Catherine, see I. de Madariaga's *Russia in the Age of Catherine the Great* (1981).

Three good studies deal with cultural history: H. Rogger's *National Consciousness in Eighteenth Century Russia* (1963), Marc Raeff's *Origins of the Russian Intelligentsia: The Eighteenth Century Nobility* (1966), and Marc Raeff, ed., *Russian Intellectual History* (1986).

For economic and social history, A. Kahan's *The Knout and the Plowshare: Economic History of Russia in the 18th Century* (1985) is a major treatment. For the vital peasant question, see Jerome Blum's *Lord and Peasant in Russia from the Ninth to the Nineteenth Century* (1961); see also Richad Hellie's *Slavery in Russia, 1450–1725* (1982). For an analytical overview, see Marc Raeff's *Understanding Imperial Russia; State and Society in the Old Regime* (1984).

1493–1520 Exploration and settlement in the Caribbean

1494 Treaty of Tordesillas

1519–1524 Cortés leads conquest of Mexico

1492 Fall of Granada, last Muslim kingdom in Spain; expulsion of the Jews; Columbus landfall in the Caribbean

1493 Columbus's second expedition; beginnings of settlement in the Indies

1500 Cabral lands in Brazil

1533 Cuzco, Peru falls to Francisco Pizarro

1540–1542 Coronado explores southwestern United States

1549 Royal government established in Brazil

1541 Santiago, Chile founded

1580–1640 Spain and Portugal united under same rulers

1630–1654 Dutch capture northeastern Brazil

Early Latin America

INTRODUCTION. As Russia began to define its new empire in eastern Europe and Asia during the 15th and 16th centuries, other empires took shape in Central and South America—created and controlled by Spain and Portugal. In contrast to Russia, these were dependent empires, and both their economies and their cultural relationships to the West differed accordingly.

The new Latin American empires, like Russia by the 18th century, maintained special contacts with the West—and, as with Russia, this fact has continued to shape key characteristics to the present day. Whereas Russian leaders decided what to borrow, however, Western forms were simply imposed on many Latin American people. The new empires were examples also of the potency of gunpowder, which the conquerors used to establish their sway. Spanish and Portuguese conquerors, however, had advantages besides gunpowder: metal equipment, horses, and the fearsome power of European diseases. This explains why the conquerors were able to force highly unequal relationships on the subject populations.

Latin America was immediately drawn into the New World economy, playing a central role in providing silver, new crops, and other goods. The new hierarchy of world economic relationships, correspondingly, shaped conditions in this new civilization for several centuries.

The societies of Latin America also generated important new political and cultural forms, as conquering Spaniards and Portuguese mixed with Native Americans and their earlier civilization forms, and were influenced by imported African slaves. The formative period for Latin American civilization—the newest on the world's list—extended from initial contacts in the 1490s through the 18th century when colonial structures began to decline. This span ran slightly longer than the early modern period in Europe—

1695 Gold discovered in Brazil

1759–1788 Charles III rules Spain; Bourbon reforms

1763 Brazilian capital moved to Rio de Janeiro

1702–1713 War of the Spanish succession; Bourbon dynasty rules Spain

1767 Jesuits expelled from Spanish America

1756–1763 Seven Years' War

1781 Comunero revolt in New Granada; Tupac Amaru rebellion in Peru

1654 English take Jamaica

1755–1776 Marquis of Pombal, Prime minister of Portugal

1759 Jesuits expelled from Brazil

1788 Conspiracy for independence in Minas Gerais, Brazil the early 1800s, rather than 1750, is the appropriate terminal point. This period also embraced a number of discrete stages, from raw conquest to growing economic and political complexity by the 18th century.

The landfall of Columbus on a Caribbean island in October 1492 began the process of conquest and settlement of what was to become Latin America. New societies, created by the intrusion of Spaniards and Portuguese and by the incorporation or destruction of indigenous Native Americans and their cultures, arose throughout the American continents. Both Europeans and Indians drew heavily on their previous experiences and understandings as they grappled with the problems created by their encounter with each other. Much of what the Iberians (the Spaniards and Portuguese) did in the Americas followed the patterns and examples of their European traditions. The life-styles of Indians who survived, although battered and profoundly transformed, showed a vitality and resiliency that shaped the subsequent societies in many ways. What resulted drew on European and Indian precedents, but was something new—the world's latest addition to the list of distinctive civilizations.

The various European nations essentially sought the same ends in the New World—economic gain and social mobility. The Portuguese, English, Spanish, and French all created large landed estates, or *plantations,* worked by coerced laborers, ultimately African slaves, wherever tropical conditions and European demand combined to make such enterprises feasible. The Europeans exploited precious metals when they were discovered, and those Europeans who did not find the metals followed rumors of gold or emeralds hopefully. The goals and desires formed similar plots, but the stages, settings, and actors differed.

The chronology of events in the areas conquered and colonized by the Spaniards and Portuguese falls roughly into three periods during the early modern centuries. These are: an era of conquest from 1492 to about 1570 during which the main lines of administration and economy were set out; a second phase of consolidation and maturity to about 1700 in which the colonial institutions and societies took their definite form; and finally, during the 18th century, a period of reform and reorganization in both Spanish America and Portuguese Brazil that intensified the colonial relationship and planted the seeds of dissatisfaction and revolt.

SPANIARDS AND PORTUGUESE: BACKGROUND TO CONQUEST

The peoples who inhabited the Iberian peninsula had long lived at the frontier of Mediterranean Europe. The peninsula had known many inhabitants—Phoenicians, Carthaginians, Romans, and Goths—and during the Middle Ages it had become a cultural frontier between Christianity and Islam. Conflict along that frontier created a strong tradition of military conquest and rule over peoples of other beliefs and customs—a tradition that became part of the Iberian experience. A number of Christian kingdoms had emerged. Of these the most important were Portugal on the Atlantic coast, and in the center of the peninsula, Castile, the largest of all. By the mid-15th century, the religious and ethnic diversity in these kingdoms was being submerged by a process of political and religious unification. In 1452, the marriage of Ferdinand—the Prince of Aragon—and Isabella—the Princess of Castile—brought the crowns of Aragon and Castile into close alliance, and in 1492 with the fall Granada, the last Muslim kingdom, the cross had triumphed throughout the peninsula. Political savvy and religious fervor moved Isabella. Immediately upon the fall of Granada, Isabella (now Queen of Castile) ordered the Jews of her realm to convert or leave the country. As many as 200,000 may have left, severely disrupting some aspects of the Castilian economy. It was also in 1492, with the Granada War at an end and religious unification established, that Isabella and Ferdinand were willing to support the project of a Genoese mariner named Christopher Columbus, who hoped to reach the East Indies by sailing westward around the globe.

IBERIAN SOCIETY AND TRADITION

Spanish and Portuguese society had a number of distinctive features that would become part of the American ventures. Like many Mediterranean people they were heavily urban, with many peasants not scattered across the countryside but living in small towns and villages. The desire to live in an urban setting helped set up a pattern of Spanish cities amid a largely Indian countryside in many parts of the Americas.

Emphasis on nobility ran strong in Iberian society, and many Spanish and Portuguese commoners who came to America as conquerors sought to recreate themselves as a new nobility, with Indians as their serfs. Few former Iberian peasants wanted a life of farming in the New World. Patriarchal ideals were also heavily emphasized, though women had an active role in family life. The patriarchal family was readily adapted to Latin America, where large estates and grants of Indian laborers, or *encomiendas,* provided the framework for relations based on economic dominance. The Iberian peninsula maintained a tradition of holding slaves—part of its experience as an ethnic frontier—in contrast to most of medieval Europe, and African slaves had been imported from the trans-Sahara trade. The extension of slavery to America built upon this tradition.

Portugal and Castile were well launched by the 15th century on political centralization and the creation of a professional bureaucracy. Legally trained bureaucrats formed the basis of Iberian rule in Latin America in a process worth comparing with China and other great empires. Religion and the Church served as the other pillar of Iberian politics; close links between Church and state resulted from the reconquest of the peninsula from the Muslims, and these links, including royal nomination of Church officials, were also extended to the New World.

Spanish and particularly Portuguese merchants also shaped traditions that became relevant in the American colonies. Portugal had been pushing down the African coast since 1415, establishing forts for commercial exchange rather than outright colonies. In the Atlantic islands, however, more extensive estates were established, leading to a slave trade with Africa and a highly commercial agricultural system based on sugar. Brazil would extend this pattern, starting out as a trade factory but then shifting, as in the Atlantic islands, to plantation agriculture.

THE CONQUEST OF THE NEW WORLD

The period from 1492 to about 1600 witnessed a remarkable spurt of human energy in destruction and creation. During roughly a century, vast areas of two continents and millions of people were brought under European control. The bases of an economic system that linked these areas to an emerging Atlantic economy were created, and a flow of immigration and commerce was set in motion. These processes were accompanied and made possible by the conquest and destruction of many Indian societies and the transformation of others, as well as by the introduction in some places of forced immigrants, the African slaves. Mexico and Peru, with their large sedentary populations and mineral resources, attracted the Spaniards and became, after the short initial Caribbean stage, the focus of immigration and institution building. Other conquests radiated outward from the Peruvian and Mexican centers.

THE CARIBBEAN CRUCIBLE

The Caribbean experience served Spain as a model for its actions elsewhere in the Americas. From this crucible the foundations of the empire were forged. After Columbus's original voyage in 1492, a return expedition in the next year established a colony on the island of Santo Domingo (Hispaniola). From there and from Spain, expeditions carried out new explorations and conquests. Puerto Rico (1508) and Cuba (1511) fell under Spanish control and by 1513 settlements existed in Panama and on the northern coast of South America.

In the Caribbean, Columbus's attempt to keep the Mediterranean and West African model of trade forts, private investment under royal contract, and a trade in gold and slaves proved unworkable, and a more extensive colonization pattern quickly developed. The agricultural Taino Indians of the islands provided enough surplus labor to make their distribution to individual Spaniards feasible, and thus began what would become the encomienda, or grants of Indians to individual Spaniards in a kind of serfdom. Gold

St. Augustine, Florida, the oldest city in the United States (founded in 1565), reflects its Spanish heritage in the central plaza and the checkerboard layout that can be seen in this 18th-century engraving.

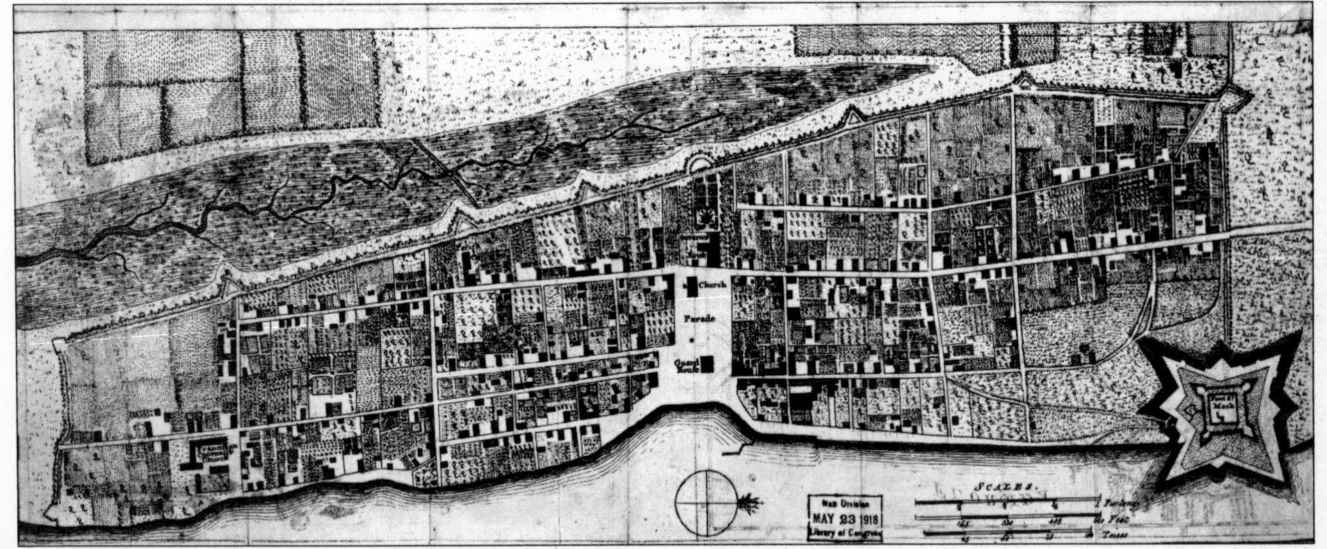

hunting, slaving, and European diseases rapidly depopulated the islands, and there was little left there to hold Spanish attention by the time of Hernán Cortés's conquest of Mexico. A few strongly fortified ports, such as Havana, San Juan, and Santo Domingo, guarded Spain's commercial lifeline, but on the whole the Caribbean became a colonial backwater for the next two centuries until sugar and slaves provided the basis of its resurgence.

In the short period of 40 years between the first voyage of Columbus and the conquest of Mexico by Cortés, the Caribbean served as a testing ground. Iberian-style cities were established. Spaniards had to adapt them to American realities. Hurricanes and Indians caused a number of towns to be moved or abandoned, but the New World also provided opportunities to implant new ideas and forms. Unlike cities in Europe, Spanish American cities were usually laid out according to a grid plan or checkerboard form with the town hall, major church, and governor's palace in the central plaza. Spanish conquerors and administrators applied classical models and rational town planning ideas to the new situation. Using the Caribbean experience, the model of town foundation was carried throughout the Americas, and in 1570 Spain issued a basic set of instructions for setting up towns. Conquest came to imply settlement.

A move from the private control of Columbus and his family to royal administration was marked by the creation of administrative institutions: the governorship, the treasury office, and the royal court of appeals, or *audiencia*, staffed by professional magistrates. Spanish legalism was part of the institutional transfer. Notaries accompanied new expeditions, and a body of laws was developed based on those of Spain and augmented by American experience. The Church, represented at first by individual priests and then by contingents of missionaries such as the Dominicans, participated in the enterprise and by 1530, a cathedral was being built on Hispaniola with a university to follow. The new area had to be provisioned and its commerce regularized. The Genoese participated in this process at first, but by the turn of the century the Board of Trade *(Casa de Contratación)* was operating in Seville and Spanish merchants were fully involved.

Rumors and hopes stimulated immigration from Spain, and by the 1510s this included larger numbers of Spanish women. Also, Spanish and Italian merchants began to import African slaves to work on the few sugar plantations that operated on the islands. The arrival of both Spanish women and African slaves represented a shift from an area of conquest to one of settlement. The same process would be noted elsewhere in the Indies. The gold hunting phase had given out in the islands by the 1520s and was replaced by the establishment of ranches and sugar plantations. The adventurous, the disappointed, and the greedy repeated the pattern. Expeditions spun off in new directions, repeating the processes already set in motion, although in each case drawing on the experience already gained.

Among these experiences was the virtual annihilation of the Indians of the Caribbean. Depopulation of the laboring population led to slaving in other islands, and in a sadly remarkable period of 30 years or so, most of the Indian population had died or been killed. The fewer, less sedentary, and more warlike Caribs of the lesser Antilles (whom the Spanish accused of cannibalism and who were thus always subject to enslavement) held out longer because their islands were less attractive to European settlement. The pattern of European concentration on areas of denser Indian populations was already forming. The destruction of the Indians led to further expeditions toward the mainland; it also caused a transformation of the islands' economies toward activities like sugar production, which called forth the African slave trade.

As early as the 1510s the mistreatment and destruction of the Indians led to attempts by clerics and royal administrators to end the worst abuses. The activities of men such as the Dominican friar Bartolomé de Las Casas (1484–1566), a conquistador turned priest, initiated the struggle for justice that was also to repeat itself elsewhere in the Indies. He became an ardent supporter of conversion through kindness and peaceful means, an opponent of forced labor, and an advocate of Indian rights. His position actually won some support from a Spanish crown interested in limiting the power of the emerging conquistador aristocracy.

Expeditions, formed by a cross section of Spanish society, leapt from island to island. Leadership was personalist, investment was private, and division of spoils was made on a shares basis. An expedition's successful leader quickly sought to ignore the authority of whomever had sent him out and asked for direct power in the king's name. By the time Cortés looked upon the Aztec capital of Tenochtitlan, the techniques of conquest and settlement were already well established. Where the Indian peoples and cultures were more resilient, their impact on the subsequent societies was greater than in the Caribbean, but the process of contact was similar.

By the time of the conquest of Mexico in the 1520s and Peru in the 1530s, all the elements of the colonial system of Latin America were in place. Even in Brazil, which the Portuguese began to exploit after 1500, a period of bartering with the Indians was slowly replaced by increasing royal control and development of a sugar plantation economy. There, as in the Caribbean, Indian resistance and subsequent depopulation led to the importation of African laborers.

CONQUESTS AND CONQUERORS

> No other race can be found that can penetrate through such rugged lands, such dense forests, such great mountains and deserts and cross such broad rivers as the Spaniards have done . . . solely by the valor of their persons and the forcefulness of their breed.

These words, written in the 16th century by Pedro Cieza de Leon, one of the conquistadores of Peru, underlined the pride of the Spaniards in their accomplishments. In less than a century, a large portion of two continents and islands in an inland sea, inhabited by millions of people, was brought under Spanish control. Spanish expeditions, usually from 50 to 500 men, provided the spearhead of conquest, and in their wake followed the women, missionaries, administrators, and artisans who began to form civil society.

The conquest was not a unified movement, but rather a series of individual initiatives that usually operated with government approval. After Columbus's settlement of Santo Domingo, the conquest of the Americas was two-pronged: One prong was directed toward Mexico and the other aimed at South America. From Santo Domingo, expeditions moved to Cuba and then on to Mexico.

We can use the well-documented campaign in Mexico as an example of the conquest. In 1519 Hernán Cortés, a man of some education and considerable ability as a leader, led an expedition of some 600 men to the coast of Mexico. After hearing rumors of a great kingdom in the interior, he destroyed his ships to leave no route of retreat, established a base at Veracruz on the coast, and then began to strike inland. A number of pitched battles were fought with towns subject to the Aztec Empire, but after gaining these victories, Cortés was able to enlist the Indians' support against their overlords. With the help of the Indian allies, Cortes eventually reached the great Aztec island capital of Tenochtitlan. By a combination of deception, boldness, courage, ruthlessness, and luck, the Aztec emperor Moctezuma II was made a captive and then killed. Cortés and his followers were forced to flee the Aztec capital and retreat toward the coast, but with the help of the Aztecs' traditional enemies, Tenochtitlan was cut off and besieged. Although the Aztec confederacy put up a stiff resistance, disease, starvation, and battle brought the city down. The Aztec poets later remembered:

We are crushed to the ground,
we lie in ruins.
There is nothing but grief and suffering
in Mexico and Tlatelolco,
where once we saw beauty and valor.

By 1521, the Spaniards had broken organized Aztec opposition and were beginning to construct their capital, the city of Mexico, on the ruins of Tenochtitlan. By 1535 most of central Mexico with its network of towns and its dense, agricultural populations had been brought under Spanish control as the kingdom of New Spain. From there, the Spanish pushed their conquest southward into Guatemala and Honduras and northward into the area of the nomadic Indians of North-central Mexico.

The second trajectory of conquests led from the Caribbean outposts to the coast of northern South America and Panama. From Panama, the Spaniards followed rumors of a rich kingdom to the south. In 1535, after a false start, Francisco Pizarro led his men to the conquest of the Inca Empire, which was already weakened by a long civil war. Once again, using guile and audacity, fewer than 200 Spaniards and their Indian allies brought a great Indian empire down. The Inca capital of Cuzco, high in the Andes, fell in 1533, but the Spanish decided to build their major city, Lima, closer to the coast. By 1540 most of Peru was under Spanish control, although an active resistance continued in remote areas for another 30 years.

From the conquests of the sedentary Indians' densely populated areas, such as México and Peru, where there were considerable surpluses in food and potential laborers, Spanish expeditions spread out in search of further riches and strange peoples. The conquest of the sedentary Chibcha Indians of New Granada (modern Colombia) in northern South America took place between 1536 and 1538, carried out by expeditions from both the Caribbean and Peru. Spanish expeditions penetrated the zones of semisedentary and nomadic peoples who often offered stiff resistance. Expeditions from Mexico moved into the northern frontiers inhabited by the nomadic Chichimecs. From 1540 to 1542 in one of the most famous expeditions, Francisco Vázquez de Coronado, searching for mythical cities of gold, penetrated what is now southwestern United States as far as Kansas. At the other end of the Americas, Pedro de Valdivia conquered the tenacious Araucanian Indians of central Chile and set up the city of Santiago in 1541, although the Araucanians continued to fight long after. Buenos Aires at the southern end of the continent, founded by an expedition from Spain in 1536, was abandoned because of Indian resistance and only refounded in 1580. Expeditions like that led by Gonzalo Pizarro (1541–1542) penetrated the Amazon basin, and others explored the tropical forests of Central and South America during these years, but there was little there to attract permanent settlement. By the 1550s a string of settlements had been created from Venezuela to Argentina and Chile. By 1570 there were 192 Spanish cities and towns throughout the Americas, one-third of which were in Mexico and Central America.

THE CONQUERORS

We can make some general statements about the conquerors and the organization of conquest. Leadership in the conquests was based on reputation and past achievement. The captains led by force of will and personal power. "God in the sky, the king in Spain, and me here," was the motto of one captain, and sometimes absolute power could lead to tyranny. Usually, an agreement was drawn up between the leader of the conquest and the representatives of the Spanish crown that granted authority for the expedition in return for a promise to pay one-fifth of all treasure or other gains to the crown. Men signed up on a shares basis; those who brought horses or who had special skills might get double shares. Rewards were made according to the contract, with premiums paid for special service and valor. There was a tendency for leaders to reward their friends, relatives, and men from their home province more liberally than others, so that after each conquest there was always a group of unhappy and dissatisfied conquerors ready to organize for a new expedition. As one observer put it, "if each man was given the governorship, it would not be enough."

Few of the conquerors were professional soldiers; they represented all walks of Spanish life, including a scattering of gentlemen. Some of the later expeditions included a few Spanish women such as Ines Suarez, the heroine of the conquest of Chile, but such cases were rare. In general, the conquerors were men on the make, hoping to better themselves and serve God by converting the heathen at the same time. Always on the lookout for treasure, most conquerors were satisfied by grants of Indians who could be taxed or put to work. They took a distinct pride in the fact that they were not paid soldiers, but rather volunteers who risked their lives for king and Church. These adventurous men, many of humble origins, came to see themselves as a new nobility entitled to dominion over a new peasantry—the Indians.

The reasons for Spanish success were varied. Horses, firearms, and more generally steel weapons gave them a great advantage over the stone technology of the Indians. This technological edge, combined with effective and ruthless leadership, produced remarkable results. Europeans were also aided by the silent ally, epidemic disease, which sometimes even preceded a conquest and weakened the In-

Population Decline in New Spain

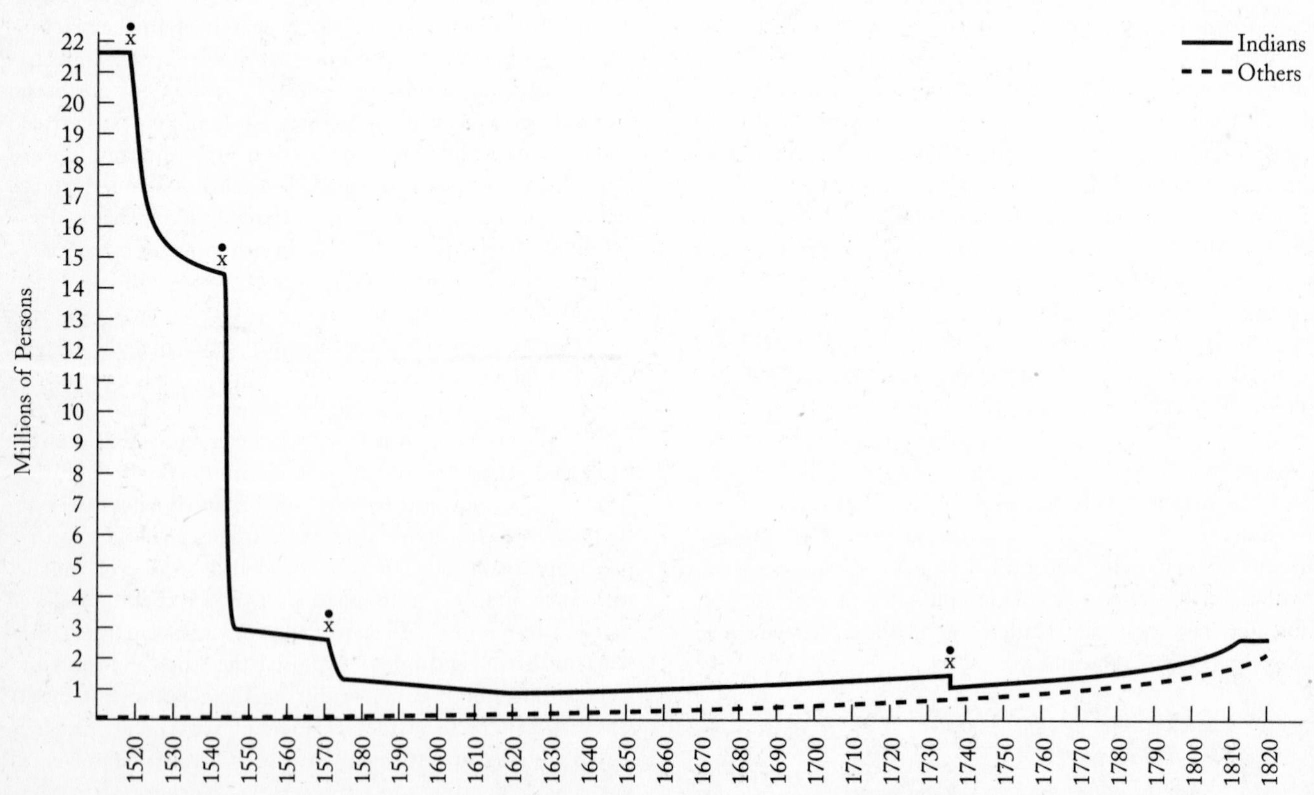

dian resistance. Finally, internal divisions and rivalries within Indian empires and their high levels of centralization made the great civilizations particularly vulnerable. It is not accidental that the Indian peoples who offered the stiffest and most continuous resistance were usually the mobile and tough nomadic tribes rather than the centralized states composed of a sedentary peasantry.

By about 1570, the age of the conquest was coming to a close and the generation of the conquerors was replaced by bureaucrats, merchants, and colonists as the institutions of colonial rule and the basis of the economy were regularized. The transition was not easy. In Peru a civil war erupted in the 1540s, and in Mexico there were grumblings from the old followers of Cortés, but when viceroys were established in the two main colonies and law courts were created in the main centers, the presence and effectiveness of royal government greatly increased. Spanish America became a colony rather than a conquest.

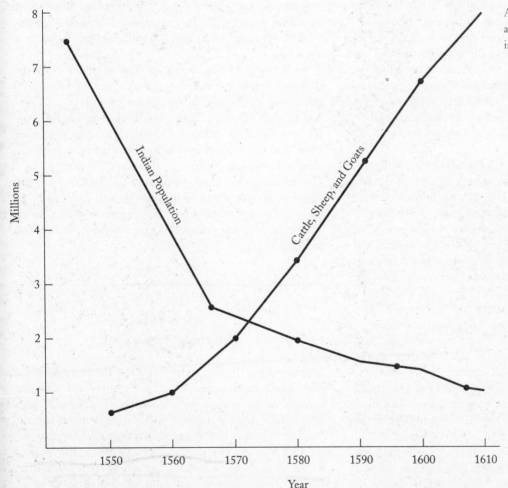

THE DESTRUCTION AND TRANSFORMATION OF INDIAN SOCIETIES

The various Indian peoples responded in many ways to the invasion of America and the transformation of their societies. All of them suffered a severe decline of population. This was a demographic catastrophe of incredible proportions. On the main islands of the Caribbean, the Indian population had virtually disappeared by 1540, a result of slaving, mistreatment, and disease. In central Mexico, war, destruction, and above all disease brought the population from an estimated 25 million in 1519 to less than two million in 1580. In Peru, a similar process brought a loss from 10 million to 1.5 million between 1530 and 1590. Elsewhere in the Americas a similar but less well-documented process took place. Smallpox, influenza, and even measles wreaked havoc on the Indian population, which had developed no immunities against these diseases.

A Comparison of Human and Livestock Populations in Central Mexico

While epidemic disease was the major cause of depopulation, the destruction of the conquest and the weakening of indigenous societies contributed to the mortality and made the Indian populations more susceptible to disease. Population losses of this size disrupted Indian societies in many ways. For example, in central Mexico the contraction of the Indian population led the Spanish to concentrate the remaining population in fewer towns, and this led in turn to the seizure of former communal farming lands by Spanish landowners. Demographic collapse made the maintenance of traditional social and economic structures very difficult.

The case of Mexico is particularly stark. The tremendous decline of the Indian population was matched by the rapid increase in European livestock. Cattle, sheep, and horses flourished on the newly created Spanish farms or on unclaimed lands. In a way, the Indian population of Mexico was replaced by European livestock.

EXPLOITATION OF THE INDIANS

Spanish desires to exploit the Indians as laborers or to extract a tribute from them led to Spanish attempts to maintain those aspects of Indian life that served colonial goals or at least did not openly conflict with Spanish authority or religion. Thus, in Mexico and Peru, while the old Indian religion and its priestly class were eliminated, the traditional Indian nobility remained in place, supported by Spanish authority, as middlemen between the tax and labor demands of the new rulers and the majority of the population.

The enslavement of Indians, except those taken in war, was prohibited by the mid-16th century in most of Spanish America. Instead, different forms of labor or taxation were imposed. At first, encomiendas were given to the individual conquerors of a region. The holders of these grants, or *encomenderos*, were able to use their Indians as workers and servants or to tax them. While in the Inca and Aztec empires commoners had owed tribute or labor to the state, the new demands were arbitrary, often excessive, and usually devoid of the reciprocity of obligation and protection characteristic of the Indian societies. Encomiendas were introduced after the initial conquest of a region from New Mexico in the north to Chile in the south. In general, the encomiendas proved to be destructive to Indian societies, and as depopulation continued, the holders of the grants became dissatisfied. Finally, the Spanish crown, unwilling to see a new nobility arise in the New World among the conquerors with their grants of Indian serfs, moved to end the institution in the 1540s. The crown limited the inheritability of encomiendas and prohibited the right to demand certain kinds of labor from the Indians. While encomiendas continued to exist in marginal regions at the fringes of the empire, in the central areas of Mexico and Peru they were all but gone by the 1620s. With the disappearance of the encomienda, the colonists and descendants of the conquerors increasingly sought grants of land rather than Indians as the basis of wealth.

Meanwhile, the colonial government increasingly extracted Indian labor and tax through local royal officials. In many places, communities were required to send groups of laborers to work on state projects, such as church construction or road building, or in labor gangs for mining or agriculture. This forced labor, called the *mita* in Peru, mobilized thousands of Indians to work in the mines and on other projects. While the Indians were paid a wage for this work, there were many abuses of the system by the local officials, and community labor requirements were often disruptive and destructive to Indian life. By the 17th century, many Indians left their villages to avoid the labor and tax obligations, preferring instead to work for Spanish landowners or to seek employment in the cities. This process eventually led to the growth of a wage labor system in which Indians, no longer resident in their villages, worked for wages on Spanish-owned mines and farms or in the cities.

In the wake of this disruption, Indian culture also demonstrated considerable resiliency in the face of Spanish institutions and forms, adapting and modifying them to Indian ways. In New Spain, the Spanish municipal councils established in Indian towns were staffed by the Indian elite, and their operations reflected preconquest patterns within European forms. In Peru and Mexico, Indians learned to use the legal system and the law courts so that litigation became a way of life. At the local level, many aspects of Indian life remained, and Indians proved to be selective in their adaptation of European foods, technology, and culture.

ANALYSIS
THE GREAT EXCHANGE

The arrival of the Spaniards and the Portuguese in the Americas initiated one of the most extensive and profound changes in the history of humankind. The New World, which had existed in relative isolation since the end of the last Ice Age, was now brought into continual contact with the Old World. The peoples and cultures of Europe and Africa came to the Americas through voluntary or forced immigration. Between 1500 and 1850 perhaps 10 to 15 million Africans and five million Europeans crossed the Atlantic and settled in the Americas as part of the great migratory movement. Contact also initiated a broader biological and ecological exchange that changed the face of both the Old World and the New World—the way people lived, what they ate, and how they died—as the animals, plants, and diseases of the two hemispheres were transferred. Historian Alfred Crosby has called this process the "Columbian exchange," and he has pointed out its profound effects as the first stage of the "ecological imperialism" that accompanied the expansion of the West.

In this chapter we have discussed the devastating impact of Old World disease on Indian peoples. Long separated from the populations of the Old World and lacking immunities to diseases such as measles and smallpox, Indian populations throughout the Americas suffered disastrous losses after initial contact. Not only among the dense populations in Peru and Mexico, but in the forests of Brazil and the woodlands of North America, contact with Europeans and Africans resulted in epidemics that devastated the Indian populations. Only after a number of generations did immunities build up in the remaining population that allowed it to withstand the diseases.

Disease may have also moved in the other direction. Some authorities believe that syphilis had an American origin and was brought to Europe only after 1492. In general, however, forms of life in the Old World—diseases, plants, and animals—were more complex than those that existed in the Americas and thus displaced the New World varieties in open competition. The diseases of Eurasia and Africa had a greater impact on America than vice versa.

With animals also, the major exchange was from the Old World to the New World. From the beginning of contact, Europeans noted with curiosity the strange fauna of America, so different from Europe. The birds were a hit. Parrots were among the first things brought to Europe from America. Many early observers commented on the smaller size of the mammals in the New World and the absence of certain types, not realizing that mastodons, horses, camels, and other animals that had once roamed the Americas had long since disappeared. American Indians had domesticated dogs, guinea pigs, some fowl, and the llama, but in general domesticated animals were far less important in the Americas than in the Old World. Protein resources were thus also more restricted. The absence of cattle and horses had also left the peoples of the Americas without suitable beasts of burden except for the llamas of the Andes.

In the first years of settlement in the Caribbean, the Spanish introduced horses, cattle, sheep, chickens, and domestic goats and pigs, all of which were considered essential for civilized life as the Iberians understood it. Some of these animals thrived in the New World. In the scrub brush and prairies of North America, in the tropical grasslands of Venezuela, and on the South American *pampas* vast herds of cattle began to roam freely. A hundred head of cattle abandoned by the Spanish in the Rio de la Plata area in 1587 had become 100,000 head 20 years later. Both for the consumption of meat, tallow, and hides in the Americas and eventually for the export of hides and meat to Europe and the rest of the world, the arrival of cattle in the Americas was a revolutionary occurence. In Mexico, livestock and Spanish haciendas grew as rapidly as the Indian population declined and Indian communities contracted. The replacement of Indians by cattle became a metaphor of the conquest of Mexico.

The success of other European livestock was no less impressive. In the Andes and in Mexico, sheep thrived and supported an active textile industry which eventually supplied most of the local needs. Horses were quickly adopted by the nomadic peoples of North and South America. This adaptation transformed their societies and gave them added mobility, allowing them to meet the Europeans on an almost equal basis. With horses, the Apaches of Arizona and the Indians of the Argentine pampas were able to hold off the Europeans for 300 years.

European livestock and even animals such as the humble pigs and chickens transformed Indian life in America. Indians acquired some animals, such as oxen, slowly, but other animals, such as horses and sheep, had obvious benefits. The Indian chieftain who answered that the greatest benefit Spain had brought to his people was the chicken egg may have disappointed his questioner, but it reflected a keen appreciation of the importance of the interchange. The newly introduced animals changed the ecological balance in the New World. Not only animals that were purposefully introduced, but species such as the sparrow and the brown rat, whose arrival was unplanned, changed the nature of life in the Americas.

The Europeans also brought their crops. It was hard for Iberians to live without the Mediterranean necessities: wheat bread, olive oil, and wine. Columbus on his second voyage in 1499 had introduced wheat, peas, melons, onions, grapes, and probably olives, as well as sugar cane. Some crops, like sugar cane, thrived and provided the basis for the rise of plantation economies; other crops like wheat, olives, and grapes needed cooler or drier environments and had to wait until the Spanish reached the more temperate zones before they flourished. Subsequently, Europeans introduced all of their own crops and even some crops—bananas, coconut trees, coffee, and breadfruit—that they had encountered in Africa, Asia, and the Pacific.

In the exchange of foods and stimulants, the contribution of America probably outweighed that of Europe, however. It is difficult today to imagine the diet of the Old World prior to the discovery of America. New World plants, such as the tomato, squash, sweet potatoes, types of beans, and peppers, became essential foods in Europe. Tobacco and cacao, or chocolate, both American in origin, became widely distributed throughout the world.

Even more important were basic crops, such as the potato, maize, and manioc, all of which yielded more calories per acre than all the Old World grains except rice. The high yield of calories per acre of maize and potatoes had supported the high population densities of the American civilizations. After the Columbian voyages, these foods began to produce similar effects in the rest of the world. Manioc or casava (we know it as tapioca) was a basic Indian food in the Caribbean and tropical South America. Particularly well-suited to the tropics, manioc was never popular in Europe, but it spread widely in Asia and Africa, where it became a basic food by the 18th century. The potato, a staple of the Andean civilizations, was easy to grow and yielded large numbers of calories. By the 18th century it was well known from Ireland to Russia. Maize was the great success story. It yielded as many calories per acre as rice but it was easier to grow and could flourish in a wide variety of situations. By the 17th century it had spread to Spain and France, and by the 18th century it was found in Italy, Turkey, Greece, and Russia. The Europeans also introduced it to West Africa and China. Maize became a staple across the globe. At present, at least one-third of the crops raised to feed the world's population are of New World origin.

In the period after 1750 the population of the world experienced a dramatic rise. The reasons for this expansion were many, but the contribution of the American foodstuffs with their high yields was a central aspect. Manioc, potatoes, sweet potatoes, and maize—to say nothing of peanuts, beans, and tomatoes—greatly expanded the food resources available to men and women throughout the world and continue to do so today. The balance sheet of the "Columbian exchange" was mixed, but the world was undeniably different after it began.

Questions: Why and in what ways was the "Columbian exchange" a particularly significant case of global contact? Was western Europe the chief beneficiary of the exchange? What balance was there between the economic dependency of the Americas and the ideas, technology, and goods they received from Europe?

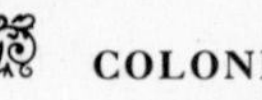

COLONIAL ECONOMIES AND GOVERNMENTS

Spanish America was an agrarian society in which the vast majority of people, perhaps 80 percent of the population, lived and worked on the land. Yet in terms of America's importance to Spain, mining was the essential activity and the basis of Spain's rule in the Indies. Until the 18th century, the whole Spanish maritime commercial system was essentially organized around the mining economy and the exchange of America's precious metals for manufactured goods from Europe. It was this exchange that began to fit Latin America into the New World economy as a somewhat dependent area producing unprocessed exports to trade with western Europe.

While the booty of conquest provided some wealth, most of the precious metal sent across the Atlantic came from the postconquest mining industry. Gold was found in the Caribbean, Colombia, and Chile, but it was silver far more than gold that formed the basis of Spain's wealth in America.

THE SILVER HEART OF EMPIRE

The major silver mining strikes were made in Mexico between 1545 and 1565 and in Peru at roughly the same time. Great silver mining towns developed. Potosí in Upper Peru (in what is now Bolivia) was the largest mine of all, producing about 80 percent of all the Peruvian silver. In the early 17th century over 160,000 people lived and worked in the town and its mine. Peru's Potosí and Mexico's Zacatecas became wealthy mining centers with opulent churches and a luxurious way of life for some, but as one viceroy of Peru commented, it was not silver that was sent to Spain, "but the blood and sweat of Indians."

Mining labor was provided by a variety of workers. The early use of Indian slaves and encomienda workers in the 16th century was gradually replaced by a system of labor drafts. By 1572 the mining mita in Peru was providing about 13,000 workers a year to Potosí alone. Similar labor drafts were also used in Mexico, but by the 17th century the mines in both places also had large numbers of wage workers willing to brave the dangers of mining in return for the relatively good wages.

Although Indian methods were used at first, most mining techniques were European in origin. After 1580, silver mining depended on a process of amalgamation with mercury to extract the silver from the ore-bearing rock. The discovery of a mountain of mercury at Huancavelica in Peru aided American silver production. Potosí and Huancavelica became the "great marriage of Peru" and the basis of silver production in South America.

According to Spanish law, all subsoil rights belonged to the crown, but the mines and the processing plants were owned by private individuals who were permitted to extract the silver in return for paying one-fifth of production to the government, which also profited from its monopoly of the mercury needed to produce the silver.

Although there is considerable debate about Spanish American mining output, some points seem clear. Silver production expanded rapidly after 1580 and crested by 1640. In this period, production from Peru outstripped that in Mexico. Both areas then experienced a steady decline caused by disruption of the mercury supply and mismanagement, although the crisis seems to have been more silver failing to reach Spain rather than difficulties in production. Still, there was decline in silver output until the mid-18th century, when there was a new mining boom. Mexico's mines emerged as the leader of American production.

Mining served as a stimulus to many other aspects of the economy, even in areas far removed from the mines. Workers had to be fed and the mines supplied. In Mexico, where most of the mines were located beyond the area of settled preconquest Indian population, large Spanish-style farms developed to raise cattle, sheep, and wheat. To Peruvian mines high in the Andes from distant regions ran a steady stream of supplies: mercury, mules, food, clothing, and even coca leaves, used to deaden hunger and make the work at high altitudes less painful. From Spain's perspective, mining was the heart of the colonial economy.

HACIENDAS AND VILLAGES

While mining gave America meaning to Spain's colonial enterprise, Spanish America remained predominantly an agrarian economy. In highland Peru, Mexico, Guatemala,

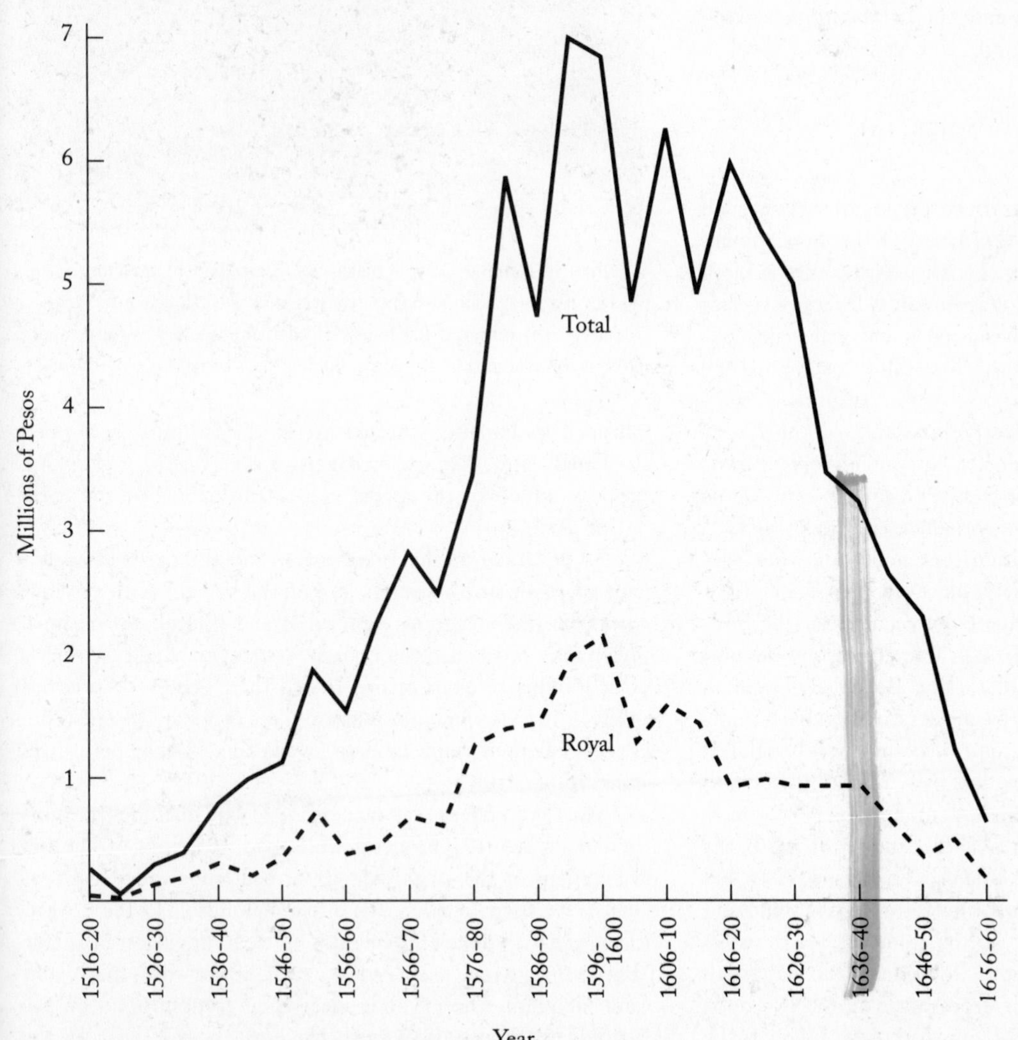

Silver Production in Spanish America, 1516–1660

and New Granada where large sedentary populations existed, Indian communal agriculture of traditional crops continued. As populations dwindled, Spanish ranches and farms began to emerge to feed the populations of the cities. The colonists, faced with declining Indian populations, also found landownership more attractive. Rural estates, based on family ownership and which produced grains, grapes, and livestock, developed throughout the central areas of Spanish America. Most of their labor force came from Indians who had left their communities and from people of mixed Indian and European heritage. These rural estates, or *haciendas,* producing primarily for consumers in America, became the basis of wealth and power for the local aristocracy in many regions. Although some plantation crops, such as sugar and later cacao, were exported to Europe from Spanish America, they made up only a small fraction of the value of the exports in comparison to silver. In some regions where Indian communities continued to hold traditional farming lands, an endemic competition between haciendas and village communities emerged.

Women in colonial Latin America were engaged in agriculture and in manufacturing, especially in textile workshops, but social ideology still reserved the household and the kitchen as the proper sphere for women, as seen in a kitchen of a large Mexican home.

INDUSTRY AND THE COMMERCIAL SYSTEM

Industry was not lacking. Sheep raising in areas, such as Ecuador, New Spain, and Peru, led to the development of small textile sweatshops, or *obrajes,* where common cloth was produced, usually by Indian women workers. America became self-sufficient for its basic foods and material goods and looked to Europe only for fine (and costly) luxury items not locally available.

Still, from Spain's perspective and that of the larger world economy taking shape in the early modern centuries, the American "kingdoms" had a silver heart and the whole Spanish commercial system was organized around that fact. Spain took an exclusivist position, essentially allowing only Spaniards to trade with America and even then under tight restrictions. All American trade from Spain after the mid-16th century was funneled through the city of Seville and, later, the nearby port of Cádiz. The Board of Trade in Seville registered ships and passengers, kept charts, collected duties, and in general controlled the Indies trade. It often worked in conjunction with a merchant guild, or *consulado,* in Seville that had virtual monopoly rights over goods shipped to America and handled much of the silver received in return. Linked to branches in Mexico City and Lima, the consulados kept tight control over the trade and were able to keep prices high in the colonies. For most of the 17th century, for example, the consulado had such power that most goods moving from Spain to the Río de la Plata on the Atlantic coast of South America had to be shipped to Panama, carried across the isthmus, reshipped to Lima, and then carried across the Andes, a trip that greatly added to their cost and to the profits of the merchant guild.

As the trade of the Indies grew and the precious metals flowed to Spain, other Europeans looked on with envious eyes. To discourage foreign rivals and pirates, the Spanish eventually worked out a convoy system in which two fleets sailed annually from Spain, traded their goods for precious metals in Mexico and Panama, as well as silver from Peru, and then rendezvoused at Havana, Cuba, before returning to Spain.

The fleet system was well planned and included a number of elements. The fleets were made possible by the development of the large, heavily armed ships called galleons that were used to carry the silver belonging to the crown. Two great galleons a year also sailed from Manila in the Philippines to Mexico loaded with Chinese silks, porcelain, and lacquer. These goods were then transshipped on the convoy to Spain along with the American silver. In the

Caribbean, heavily fortified ports, such as Havana and Cartegena (Colombia), provided shelter for the treasure ships, while coastguard fleets cleared the waters of potential raiders. Although cumbersome, the convoys (which continued until the 1730s) were relatively successful. While pirates and Spain's European enemies sometimes captured individual ships, and although some ships were lost to storms and other disasters, only one fleet was lost, to the Dutch in 1627.

In general, the supply of American silver to Spain was continuous and made the colonies seem worth the effort, but the reality of American treasure was more complicated. Much of the wealth flowed out of Spain to pay for Spain's European wars, its long-term debts, and the purchase of manufactured goods to be sent back to the Indies. Probably less than half of the silver remained in Spain itself. The arrival of American treasure also contributed to a sharp rise in prices and a general inflation, first in Spain and then throughout western Europe during the 16th century. At no time did the American treasure make up more than one-fourth of Spain's state revenues, which is to say that the wealth of Spain depended more on the taxes levied on its own population than it did on the exploitation of its Indian subjects. The seemingly endless supply of silver did, however, stimulate bankers to continue to loan money to Spain, because the prospect of the great silver fleet was always enough to offset the falling credit of the Spanish rulers and of the sometimes bankrupt government. As early as 1619, Sancho de Moncada wrote that "the poverty of Spain resulted from the discovery of the Indies," but there were few who could see the long-term costs of empire.

DOCUMENT

A VISION FROM THE VANQUISHED

History is usually written by the victors, so it is rare when we have a detailed statement from the vanquished. In the 17th century, Guaman Poma de Ayala, an acculturated Peruvian Indian who claimed to trace his lineage to the provincial nobility of Inca times, composed a memorial outlining the history of Peru under the Incas and reporting on the current conditions under Spanish rule. Guaman Poma was a Christian and a loyal subject. He hoped that his report would reach King Phillip III of Spain who might then order an end to the worst abuses, among which were the Spanish failure to recognize the rank and status of Indian nobles like himself. His book was not published in his lifetime and was only recovered in the 20th century.

In addition to his class pride, Guaman Poma was also an educated, bilingual Indian who spoke Quechua as well as Spanish and who had a profound understanding of Andean culture. His book is remarkable for its revelations of Indian life, for its detailed criticism of the abuses suffered by the Indians, and especially because Guaman Poma illustrated his memorial with a series of drawings that give his words a visual effect. The illustrations also reveal the world view of this interesting character. The drawings and text offer a critical inside view not of the laws, but of the workings of Spain's empire in America from an Indian point of view.

MINERS

At the mercury mines of Huancavelica the Indian workers are punished and ill-treated to such an extent that they die like flies and our whole race is threatened with extermination. Even the chiefs are tortured by being suspended by their feet. Conditions in the silver-mines of Potosí and Chocllococha, or at the gold-mines of Carabaya are little better. The managers and supervisors, who are Spaniards or mestizos have virtually absolute power. There is no reason for them to fear justice, since they are never brought before the courts.

Beatings are incessant. The victims are mounted for this purpose on a llama's back, tied naked to a round pillar or put in stocks. Their hair is cut off and they are deprived of food and water during detention.

Any shortage in the labor gangs is made an excuse for punishing the chiefs as if they were common thieves or traitors instead of the nobility of the country. The work itself is so hard as to cause permanent injury to many of those who survive it. There is no remuneration for the journey to the mines and a day's labor is paid at the rate for half a day.

PROPRIETORS

Your Majesty has granted large estates, including the right to employ Indian labor, to a number of individuals of whom some are good Christians and the remainder are very bad ones. These *encomenderos,* as they are termed, may boast about their high position, but in reality they are harmful both to the labor force and to the surviving Indian nobility. I therefore propose to set down the details of their life and conduct.

They exude an air of success as they go from their card games to their dinners in fine silk clothes. Their money is squandered on these luxuries, as well it may, since it costs them no work or sweat whatever. Although the Indians ultimately pay the bill, no concern is ever felt for them or even for Your Majesty or God himself.

Official posts like those of royal administrator and judge ought not to be given to big employers or mine-owners or to their obnoxious sons, because these peoples have enough to live on already. The appointments ought to go to Christian gentleman of small means, who have rendered some service to the Crown and are educated and humane, not just greedy.

Anybody with rights over Indian labor sees to it that his own household is well supplied with servant girls and indoor and outdoor staff. When collecting dues and taxes, it is usual to impose penalties and detain Indians against their will. There is no redress since, if any complaint is made, the law always favours the employer.

The collection of tribute is delegated to stewards, who make a practice of adding something in for themselves. They too consider themselves entitled to free service and obligatory presents, and they end up as bad as their masters. All of them, and their wives as well, regard themselves as entitled to eat at the Indians' expense.

The Indians are seldom paid the few reales a day which are owed to them, but they are hired out for the porterage of wine and making rope or clothing. Little rest is possible either by day or night and they are usually unable to sleep at home.

It is impossible for servant girls, or even married women, to remain chaste. They are bound to be corrupted and prostituted because employers do not feel any scruple about threatening them with flogging, execution, or burial alive if they refuse to satisfy their master's desires.

The Spanish grandees and their wives have borrowed from the Inca the custom of having themselves conveyed in litters like the images of saints in processions. These Spaniards are absolute lords without fear of either God or retribution. In their own eyes they are judges over our people, whom they can reserve for their personal service or their pleasure, to the detriment of the community.

Great positions are achieved by favour from above, by wealth or by having relations at Court in Castile. With some notable exceptions, the beneficiaries act without consideration for those under their control.

The *encomenderos* call themselves conquerors, but their Conquest was achieved by uttering the words: *Ama mancha noca Inca,* or 'Have no fear. I am the Inca.' This false pretense was the sum total of their performance.

Questions: What are the main abuses Guaman Poma complains about? What remedies does he recommend? What relationship do his views have to traditional Inca values? How might a white landlord or colonial official have answered his attacks?

RULING AN EMPIRE

Spain controlled its American empire through a carefully regulated administrative and bureaucratic system. Sovereignty rested with the crown, based not on the right of conquest, but on a papal grant that awarded the Indies to Castile in return for its services in bringing those lands and peoples into the Christian community. Some Indians found this curious and could not understand how the pope could assign to Castile what was not his in the first place. Some European theologians agreed, but Spain was careful to bolster its rule in other ways. The Treaty of Tordesillas (1494) between Castile and Portugal clarified the spheres of influence and right of possession of the two kingdoms by drawing a hypothetical north-south line around the globe and reserving to Portugal newly discovered lands (and their route to India) to the east of the line and to Castile all lands to the west. Thus, Brazil fell within the Portuguese sphere. France, England, and other European nations would later raise their own objections to the Spanish and Portuguese claims.

The Spanish Empire became a great bureaucratic system built on a juridical core and staffed to a large extent by *letrados*, or university-trained lawyers from Spain. The modern division of powers was not clearly defined in the Spanish system, so that judicial officers also exercised legislative and administrative authority. Spanish society was highly legalistic and the formulation of law was a major attribute of authority. The body of laws for the Indies was so large and varied that it took almost a century to complete a great law code, the *Recopilación* (1681), which despite its defects and inconsistencies became the basis of law in the Indies.

THE STATE AND THE CHURCH

The king ruled through the Council of the Indies in Spain that issued the laws and advised him on all matters dealing with the colonies. Within the Indies, Spain created two viceroyalties in the 16th century, one based on Mexico City and the other on Lima. Viceroys, high-ranking nobles who were direct representatives of the king, wielded broad military, legislative, and, when they had legal training, judicial powers. The viceroyalties of New Spain and Peru were then subdivided into ten judicial divisions controlled by superior courts, or audiencias, staffed by professional royal magistrates who helped to make law as well as apply it. At the local level, royally appointed magistrates in the towns and villages were the direct representatives of the state, applying the laws, collecting taxes, and assigning the work requirements on Indian communities. It is little wonder that they often were highly criticized for bending the law and taking advantage of the Indians under their control. Below them was a myriad of minor officials, customs and tax collectors, municipal officers, and inspectors who made bureaucracy both a living and a way of life.

To some extent the clergy formed another branch of the state apparatus, although, of course, it had other functions and goals as well. The conquest of America had been a remarkable missionary as well as military effort. Catholic religious orders such as the Franciscans, Dominicans, and Jesuits carried out the widespread conversion of the Indians, establishing churches in the towns and villages of sedentary Indians and setting up missions in frontier areas.

Taking seriously the pope's admonition to Christianize the peoples of the new lands as the primary justification for Spain's rule, some of the early missionaries became ardent defenders of Indian rights and even admirers of aspects of Indian culture. For example, the Franciscan priest Fray Bernardino de Sahagún (1499–1590) became an expert in the Nahuatl language and composed a bilingual encyclopedia of Aztec culture, which was based on methods very similar to those used by modern anthropologists. Other clerics wrote histories, grammars, and studies of Indian language and culture. Some were like Diego de Landa, Bishop of Yucatán (1547), who admired much about the culture of the Maya but who so detested their religion and feared its survival that he burned all their ancient books and tortured many Maya suspected of backsliding from Christianity. The recording and analysis of Indian cultures were designed primarily to provide tools for conversion.

In the core areas of Peru and New Spain, the missionary church was eventually replaced by an institutional structure of parishes and bishoprics. Archbishops sat in the major capitals, and a complicated church hierarchy developed, which reflected the demographic and economic realities of each area. Since the holders of all ecclesiastical positions were nominated by the Spanish crown, the clergy tended to be a major support of state policy as well as a primary influence on it. It was no accident that in the *Recopilación*, the great law code of the Indies, the first section dealt with "the Holy Catholic Faith."

The Catholic church profoundly influenced the cultural and intellectual life of the colonies in many ways. The construction of churches, especially the great baroque cathedrals of the capitals, stimulated the work of architects and artists, usually reflective of European models but sometimes taking up local themes and subjects. The printing presses, introduced to America in the early 16th century, always published a high percentage of religious books, as well as works of history, poetry, philosophy, law, and language.

Much intellectual life was organized around religion. Schools—such as those of Mexico City and Lima, founded in the 1550s—were run by the clergy and universities and were created to provide training primarily in law and theology, the foundations of state and society. Eventually, over 70 universities flourished in Spanish America. A stunning example of colonial intellectual life was the nun, Sor Juana Inés de la Cruz (1651–1695), author, poet, musician, and social thinker, who was welcomed at the court of the viceroy in Mexico City where her beauty and intelligence were celebrated. She eventually gave up secular concerns and her library, at the urging of her superiors, to concentrate on purely spiritual matters. Even secular authors were heavily influenced by baroque Catholicism. To control the morality and orthodoxy of the population, the tribunal of the Inquisition set up offices in the major capitals, although Indians were usually exempt from its jurisdiction. Overall, church and state combined to create an ideological and political framework for the society and economy of Spanish America.

Sor Juana Inés de la Cruz was the remarkable Mexican poet and writer whose talents won her recognition rarely given to women for intellectual achievements in colonial Latin America.

BRAZIL: THE FIRST PLANTATION COLONY

The search for gold and silver was a constant theme in overseas expansion, but there were other European demands the New World could also satisfy, which contributed to its growing involvement in the Western-dominated world economy. While Spanish America seemed to fulfill dreams of mineral wealth, Brazil—Portugal's American colony—became the first major plantation zone, organized to produce a tropical crop—sugar—in great demand and short supply in Europe.

Although the Portuguese had already set up small plantation colonies on the little Atlantic islands of Madeira and Sao Tomé, the move toward plantation agriculture in Brazil was gradual. The first official Portuguese landfall on the South American coast took place in 1500 when Pedro Álvares Cabral, leader of an expedition to India, stopped briefly on the tropical Brazilian shore, celebrated a mass, and bartered with the Indians. There was little at first to attract European interest except for the dyewood trees that grew in the forests, and thus for 30 years the Portuguese crown paid little attention to Brazil, preferring instead to grant licenses to merchants who agreed to exploit the dyewood in return for tax benefits and services. Pressure from French merchants also interested in dyewood finally moved the Portuguese crown to military action. The coast was cleared of the French and a new system of settlement was established in 1532. Minor Portuguese nobles were given strips of land along the coast to colonize and develop. The nobles who held these *capitaincies* combined broad, seemingly "feudal" powers with a strong desire for commercial development. Most of them lacked sufficient capital to carry out the colonization and some had continual problems with the local Indian population. In a few places, towns were established, colonists were brought over, relations with the Indians were relatively peaceful, and, most importantly, sugar plantations were established using first Indian, and then imported African, slaves.

The limited success of the captaincies caused the Portuguese crown in 1549 to send a governor general and other royal officials and to create a royal capital at Salvador. The first Jesuit missionaries also arrived. By 1600 Indian resistance had been broken in many places either by military action, missionary activity, or by epidemic disease. A string of settlements extended along the coast, centered on port cities such as Salvador and Rio de Janeiro. These served the roughly 150 sugar plantations, a number which would double by 1630. The plantations were increasingly worked by African slaves. By 1600 the Brazilian colony had about 100,000 inhabitants: 30,000 Europeans, 15,000 black slaves, and the rest Indians and people of mixed origin.

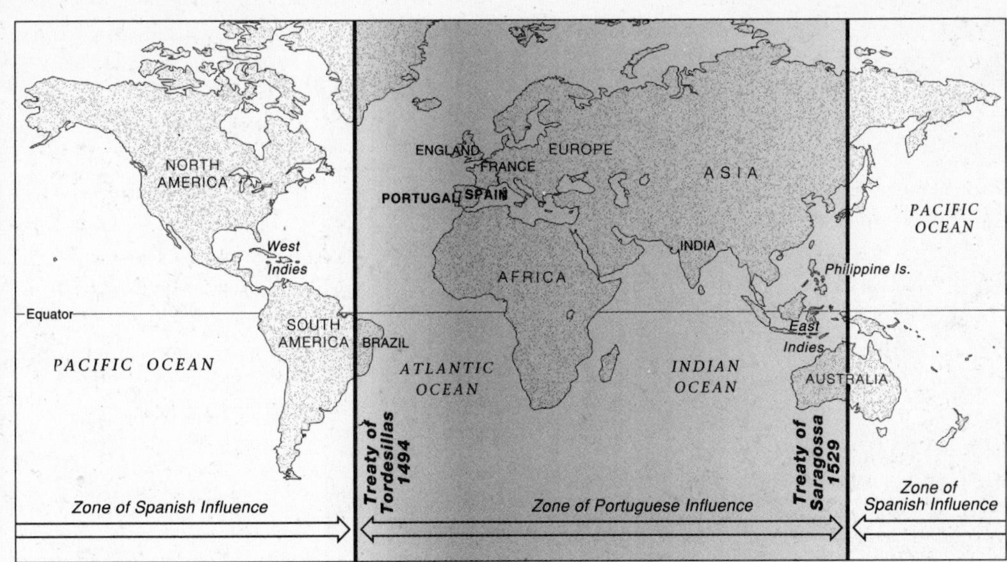

Divisions of the Tordesillas

SUGAR AND SLAVERY

During most of the next century, Brazil held its position as the world's leading sugar producer. Sugar cane had to be processed in the field—cut, pressed in large mills, and the juice then heated before it would crystallize into sugar. This combination of agriculture and industry in the field demanded large amounts of capital for machinery and large quantities of labor for the backbreaking work. While there were always some free workers who had skilled or artisan occupations, slaves did most of the work. During the 17th century, about 7000 slaves a year were imported from Africa. By the end of the century, Brazil had about 150,000 slaves—about half its total population.

Based on a single crop produced by slave labor, Brazil became the first great plantation colony and a model that would later be followed by other European nations in their own Caribbean colonies. Even after the Brazilian economy became more diverse, Brazil's society still reflected its plantation and slave origins. Slavery and the plantation system imposed a strong social hierarchy. The white planter families became an aristocracy that controlled local social and political life. Linked by interest and marriage to resident merchants and to the few Portuguese bureaucrats and officials, this class dominated local institutions. At the bottom of society were the slaves, distinguished by their color and their servile condition as property. There was, however, a growing segment of the population composed of people of mixed origins, the result of miscegenation between whites, Indians, and Africans who—alongside poorer whites, freed blacks, and free Indians—served as artisans, small farmers, herdsmen, and free laborers. In many ways, society as a whole reflected the hierarchy of the plantation.

Like Spain, Portugal created a bureaucratic structure that integrated this colony within an imperial system. A governor general ruled from Salvador, but the governors in each captaincy often acted with independence and reported directly to the overseas council in Lisbon. The missionary orders were particularly important in Brazil, especially the Jesuits. Their extensive cattle ranches and sugar mills supported the construction of churches and schools as well as a network of missions with thousands of Indian residents.

As in Spanish America, royal officials trained in the law formed the core of the bureaucracy. Unlike the Spanish Empire, which was, with the exception of the Phillipines, almost exclusively American, the Portuguese Empire included colonies and outposts in Asia, Africa, and Brazil. Only gradually in the 17th century did Brazil become the predominant Portuguese colony. Even then, Brazil's ties to Portugal were in some ways stronger and more dependent than those between Spanish America and Spain. Unlike Spanish America, neither universities nor printing presses existed in Brazil. Thus intellectual life was always an extension of Portugal, and Brazilians seeking higher education and government offices or hoping to publish always had to turn to the mother country. The general economic dependency of Latin America was matched by an intellectual subordination more intense in Brazil than in Spanish America.

BRAZIL'S AGE OF GOLD

As overseas extensions of Europe, the American colonies were particularly susceptible to changes in European politics. For 60 years (1580–1640), Spain and Portugal were

Sugar was introduced to the Caribbean in 1493, but Brazil became the greatest producer by the next century. Sugar plantations using enslaved workers characterized Brazil and the Caribbean. This early European engraving is wrong in some details, but it does convey an image of the almost factorylike conditions in the sugar mills.

ruled by the same monarchs, a situation that sponsored their cooperation and gave the Habsburg kings of Spain and Portugal a worldwide empire. From 1630 to 1654, as part of a global struggle against Spain, the Dutch seized a portion of northeastern Brazil and controlled its sugar production. Although the Dutch were expelled from Brazil in 1654, by the 1680s the Dutch, English, and French had established their own plantation colonies in the Caribbean and were producing sugar, once again with slave laborers. This competition—which led to a rising price for slaves and a falling world price for sugar—undercut the Brazilian sugar industry, and the colony entered into hard times. Eventually, each European nation tried to establish an integrated set of colonies that included plantations (the Caribbean, Brazil), slaving ports (Africa), and food producing areas (New England, southern Brazil).

Although Brazil's domination of the world sugar market was lost, throughout the 17th century *Paulistas*, hardy backwoodsmen from São Paulo (an area with few sugar plantations), had been exploring the interior, capturing Indians and searching for precious metals. These expeditions not only established Portuguese claims to much of the interior of the continent, but were eventually successful in their quest for wealth. In 1695, gold strikes were made in the mountainous interior in a region that came to be called Minas Gerais (General Mines), and the Brazilian colony experienced a new boom.

A great gold rush began. People deserted coastal towns and plantations to head for the gold washings, and they were soon joined by waves of about 5000 immigrants a year who came directly from Portugal. Labor in the mines, as in the plantations, was provided mostly by slaves. By 1720 there were over 35,000 slaves in Minas Gerais, and by 1775 there were over 150,000 (out of a total population of 300,000 for the region). Wild mining camps and a wide-open society eventually coalesced into a network of towns like the administrative center of Ouro Prêto, and the government, anxious to control the newfound wealth, imposed a heavy hand to collect taxes and reign in the unruly population. Gold production reached its height between 1735 and 1760 and averaged about three tons a year in that period, making Brazil the greatest source of gold in the Western world.

The discovery of gold was a mixed blessing in the long run. Further discovery of gold—and later of diamonds—opened the interior to further settlement, once again with disastrous effects on the Indian population and with the expansion of slavery. The early disruption of coastal agriculture caused by the gold strikes was overcome by government control of the slave trade, and exports of sugar and tobacco continued to be important to the colony. Mining did stimulate the opening of new areas to ranching and farming, to supply the new markets in the mining zone. Cattle ranches appeared in the interior of northeast Brazil, while large herds spread over the grassy plains of the south. Rio de Janeiro, the port closest to the mines, grew in size and importance. It became capital of the colony in 1763. In Minas Gerais a distinctive society developed in the mining towns, where the local wealth was used to sponsor the building of churches, which in turn stimulated many artisan activities and the work of artists, architects, and composers. Like the rest of Brazil, however, the hierarchy of color and the legal distinctions of slavery marked life in the mining zones, which were populated by large numbers of slaves and free persons of color.

Finally, gold allowed Portugal to continue economic policies that were detrimental in the long run. With access to gold, Portugal could purchase the manufactured goods it needed for itself and its colonies. Few industries were developed in the mother country and, with pressures from Portuguese wine producers, a treaty was signed with England in 1703 that guaranteed a trading arrangement with that country. As a result much of the Brazilian gold flowed from Portugal to England to pay for manufactured goods and to compensate for a trade imbalance, since the value of English manufactures was greater than that of Portuguese wine. After 1760 as the supply of gold began to dwindle, Portugal was again in a difficult position, in some ways an economic dependency of England.

MULTIRACIAL SOCIETIES

The conquest and settlement of Latin America created the conditions for the formation of multiethnic societies on a large scale. The three major groups—Indians, Europeans, and Africans—had been brought together under very different conditions: the Europeans as conquerors and voluntary immigrants, the Indians as conquered peoples, and the Africans as slaves. This situation created hierarchies of masters and servants, Christians and pagans that reflected the relationships of power and the colonial condition. In some places like central Mexico, where an Indian nobility had existed, aspects of preconquest social organization were maintained because these served the ends of Spanish government. In theory, there was a separation between the "republic of the Spaniards," which included all non-Indians, and the "republic of the Indians," which was supposed to have its own social rankings and its own rules and laws. This separation was never a reality, however, and the "republic of the Indians" always formed the base on which all society rested. Indians paid tribute, something not required of others in society.

THE SOCIETY OF CASTAS

Spaniards had an idea of society drawn from their own medieval experience, but American realities soon altered that concept. The key was miscegenation. The conquest had involved the sexual exploitation of Indian women as well as occasional alliances formed by the giving of concubines and female servants. Marriages with Indian women, especially with the Indian nobility, were not unknown, and as early as 1516 the Spanish crown tried to sponsor mixed marriages, although later it sought to limit opportunities for mixed offspring. With few European women available, especially in frontier regions, mixed marriages and informal unions were common. The result was the growth of a large population of mixed background, the so-called mestizos. Although always suspected of illegitimacy, their status, especially in the early years, was higher than that of Indians. More acculturated than the Indians, able to operate in two worlds, mestizos became an intermediate category, not fully accepted as equals to Spaniards and yet expected to live according to the standards of Spanish society and often acting as auxiliaries to it. A similar process took place in areas like Brazil and the Caribbean coasts where large numbers of African slaves were imported. Slave owners exploited their female slaves or took slave women as mistresses, and then sometimes freed their mulatto children. The result was the growth of a large population of mixed background, often illegitimate in its origins.

Throughout the Spanish Indies, European categories of noble, priest, and commoner continued, as did hierarchies based on wealth and occupation. But American realities created new distinctions in which race and place of birth played a crucial role. This was the *sociedad de castas,* based on racial origins, in which Europeans or whites were at the top, black slaves or Indians were at the bottom, and the many kinds of mixes filled the intermediate categories. The sexual fusion and mixing accompanied the great cultural fusion in the formation of Latin America.

From the three original ethnic categories, many combinations and crosses were possible: mestizos, mulattoes, zambos (Indian-African parents), castizos (mestizo-Spanish origins), etc. By the 18th century, this segment of the population had grown rapidly and there was much confusion and local variation in terminology. A whole genre of painting developed simply to identify and classify the various

By the 18th century a genre of painting developed to portray the various racial mixtures. In this canvas a *mestizo* father and his Spanish wife are shown with their *castizo* (three-fourths white) daughter. These paintings are also interesting because they show relations between men and women and between adults and children.

combinations. Together, the people of mixed origins were called the *castas*, and they constituted a large and troublesome population; relegated to secondary status, considered dangerous, pushy, and untrustworthy, restricted from certain positions and honors, not fully accepted by Spanish society, and yet needed by it to fill many of the essential positions of artisans, craftsmen, shopkeepers, and small farmers. In 1650 the castas made up perhaps 5 to 10 percent of the population of Spanish America, but by 1750, with considerable regional variation, they constituted 35 to 40 percent. In Brazil, still dominated by slavery, free people of color made up about 28 percent of the population, a proportion equal to that of whites. Together, however, free and slave blacks and mulattoes made up two-thirds of the inhabitants of Brazil in the late 18th century.

As the mixed population grew in Spanish America, increasing restrictions were placed on them, but their social mobility could not be halted. The "racial" labels, in fact, were changed by individuals as their occupations, wealth, or marital status changed. A successful Indian might call himself a mestizo; a mestizo who married a Spanish woman might be called a white. The ranks of the castas were also swelled by former slaves who had been given or had bought their freedom and by Indians who left their communities, spoke Spanish, and lived within the orbit of the Hispanic world. Thus, physical characteristics were only one among many criteria of rank and status, but color and ethnicity mattered and created a pseudoracial hierarchy. European or white status was a great social advantage. Not every person of European background was wealthy, but most of the wealthy merchants, landowners, bureaucrats, and miners were white. As one visitor wrote: "In America, every white is a gentleman."

Originally, all whites had shared the privileged status of Spaniards regardless of the continent of their birth, but over time distinctions developed between *peninsulares*, or those actually born in Spain, and *Creoles*, or those born in the New World. Creoles thought of themselves as loyal American Spaniards, but with so many mestizos around, the shadow of an Indian forbearer and illegitimacy always made their status suspect as far as the Europeans were concerned. Still, creoles dominated the local economies, held sway over large numbers of dependents at their haciendas and mines, and with the exception of the peninsulares, stood at the top of society. Increasingly, they developed a sense of identity and pride in their accomplishments, and

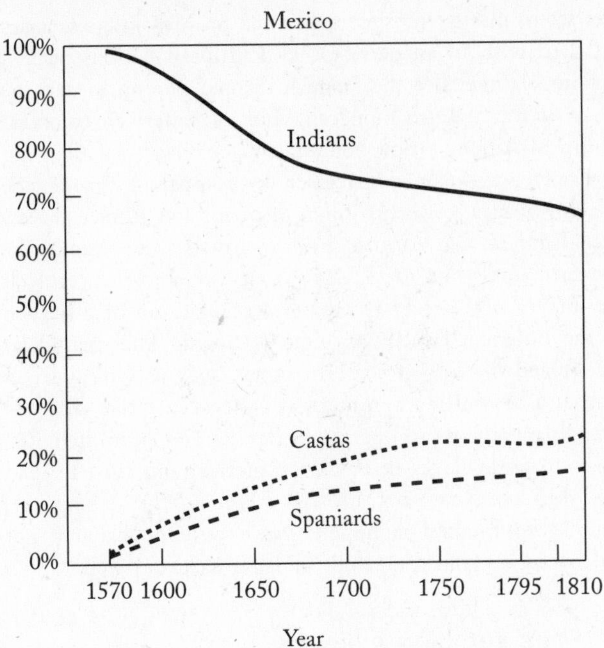

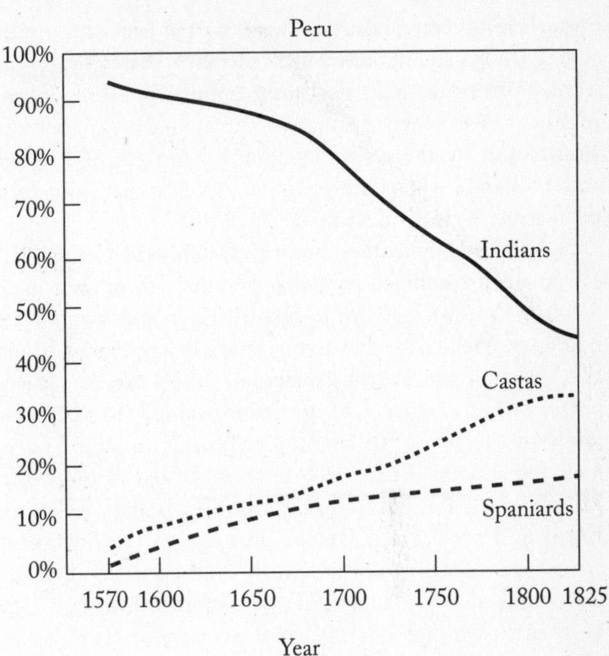

Changing Ratios of Ethnic Categories in Mexico and Peru

they were sensitive to any suggestion of inferiority or to any discrimination because of their American birth. That growing sense of self-identity eventually contributed to the movements for independence in Latin America.

The hierarchy of race intersected with traditional Iberian distinctions based on gender, age, and class. The father of a family had legal authority over his children until age 25. Women were in a subordinate position; they could not serve in government and were expected to assume the duties of motherhood and household. After marriage, women came under the authority of their husbands, but many widows assumed the direction of their family's activities. Lower-class women often controlled small-scale commerce in towns and villages, worked in the fields, or labored at the looms of small factories. Marriages were often arranged and accompanied by the payment of a dowry that remained the property of the women throughout the marriage. Women also had full rights to inheritance. Upper-class women who did not marry at a young age were placed in convents to prevent contacts or marriages with partners of unsuitable backgrounds.

THE 18TH CENTURY REFORMS

No less than in the rest of Europe, the 18th century was a period of considerable intellectual change and ferment in Spain and Portugal as well as in their empires. In Spain and its colonies, small clubs and associations, calling themselves *amigos del país*, or friends of the country, met in many cities to discuss and plan all kinds of improvements and reform. Their programs were for material benefits and improvements, not political changes, and they sometimes had the direct sponsorship of high officials and even the king himself. In Portugal, foreign influences and ideas created a group of progressive thinkers and bureaucrats open to new ideas in economy, education, and philosophy. Much of the change that came in both empires resulted as much from the changing European economic and demographic realities as from new ideas. The expansion of population and economy in Europe and increased demands for American products, along with the long series of wars in the 18th century, gave the American colonies a new importance. The result was a resuscitation of both the Spanish and Portuguese empires, but with some long-term results that eventually led to the disruption and fall of both.

THE SHIFTING BALANCE OF POLITICS AND TRADE

By the 18th century it was clear the colonial system that had linked America to Spain had become outmoded and that Spain's exclusive hold on the Indies was no longer secure. To some extent the problem lay in Spain itself. The

Spanish kings were relatively weak by the late 17th century and did not provide adequate leadership. Beset by foreign wars, increasing debt, declining population, and internal revolts, a weakened Spain was threatened by a powerful France and by the rising mercantile strength of England and Holland, whose intransigent Protestantism also made them natural rivals of Catholic Spain.

Since the 16th century French, Dutch, and English ship captains had combined contraband trade with raiding in the Spanish Empire, and while Spain's European rivals could not seize Mexico or Peru, the sparsely populated islands and coasts of the Caribbean became likely targets. Buccaneers, owing allegiance to no nation, raided the Caribbean ports in the late-17th century. Meanwhile, the English took Jamaica in 1654, the French took control of western Hispaniola (Haiti) by 1697, and other islands fell to the English, French, and Dutch. The age of the buccaneers came to a close in the early 18th century when the other Europeans also had an interest in stopping their raids, but by then Spain and Portugal had permanent rivals in the Americas. Many of the islands turned to sugar production and the creation of slave and plantation colonies much like those in Brazil. These settlements were part of a general process of colonization, in which the English settlement of eastern North America and French occupation of Canada and the Mississippi valley were another part.

Less apparent than the loss of territories, but equally important, was the failure of the Spanish mercantile and political system. Traditional ideas that national wealth consisted primarily of the amount of silver and gold in the royal treasury were no longer adequate, and in England and France they had been replaced by mercantilist concepts in which national wealth was based on the volume of trade. Spain was slow to move toward these new ideas even though the flow of precious metal from the Indies had fallen off. The annual fleets became irregular. Silver remittances from America declined, while most goods shipped to the Indies and even the ships that carried them were non-Spanish in origin. The colonies became increasingly self-sufficient in basic commodities, and as central government became weaker, local aristocrats in the colonies exercised increasing control over the economy and government of their regions, often at the expense of the Indian and the lower-class populations. Graft and corruption were rampant in many branches of government. The empire seemed to be crumbling. What is most impressive is that Spain was able to retain its American possessions for another century.

Even with Spain in decline, the Indies still seemed an attractive prize coveted by other powers, and the opportunity to gain them was not long in coming. A final crisis was set in motion in 1701 when the Spanish king, Charles II, died without an heir. Other European nations backed various claimants to the Spanish throne, hoping to win the prize of the Spanish monarchy and its American colonies. Philip of Anjou, a Bourbon and thus a relative of the king of France, was named successor to the Spanish throne; the possibility of a powerful union of Spain and France threatened England and Austria, France's rivals. The War of the Spanish Succession (1702–1713) ensued, and the result at the Treaty of Utrecht (1713) was recognition of a branch of the Bourbon family as rulers of Spain. The treaty also recognized the loss of some territory, such as Gibraltar, to England as well as commercial concessions that allowed French merchants to operate in Seville and permitted England to trade slaves in Spanish America (and even to send one ship per year to trade for silver in the Americas). Spain's commercial monopoly was now being broken, not just by contraband trade, but by legal means as well.

THE BOURBON REFORMS

In the face of territorial loss and commercial weakness, the new and vigorous Bourbon dynasty in Spain launched a series of reforms aimed at strengthening the state and its economy. In this age of "enlightened despotism" the Spanish Bourbon monarchs, especially Charles III (1759–1788), moved by economic nationalism and a desire for strong centralized government instituted fiscal, administrative, and military reforms in Spain and its empire. The goal of these rulers and their progressive ministers, such as the Count of Floridablanca (1728–1808), was to resuscitate Spain within the framework of its traditional society by applying the principles of rational and planned government. Thus the aim was to make government more effective and more powerful, better able to direct the economy. Certain groups or institutions that opposed these measures or stood in the way might be punished or suppressed. The Jesuit order, for example, with its special allegiance to Rome, its rumored wealth, and its missions in the New World (which controlled almost 100,000 Indians in Paraguay alone) was a prime target. The Jesuits were expelled from Spain and its empire in 1767 as they had been from the Portuguese empire in 1759. In general, however, the entrenched interests of the Church and nobility were not frontally attacked so long as they did not conflict with the authority of the crown. The reforms aimed at material improvements and a more powerful state, not social or political upheaval.

French bureaucratic models were introduced. In Spain, the councils of government were supplanted by ministers who took direct responsibility for policy. The system of

Charles III, King of Spain (1759–1788), ruled Spain and its empire during the most important of the Bourbon reforms.

taxation was tightened. The navy was reformed and new ships built. The convoy fleet system was abandoned and new ports were opened in Spain and America for the Indies trade. In 1778 the policy of *commercio libre* opened trade to many ports in Spain and the Indies, although trade was still restricted to Spaniards or ships sailing under Spanish license. Still, the more open policy undercut the monopoly of the consulados, and by stimulating trade made contraband less attractive.

In the Indies, the Bourbons initiated a broad program of reform. New viceroyalties were created in New Granada (1739) and the Rio de la Plata (1778) to provide better administration and defense to the growing populations of these regions. Royal investigators were sent to the Indies. The most important investigator, José de Gálvez, spent six years in Mexico before returning to Spain to become Minister of the Indies and a chief architect of reform. His investigations as well as reports by others revealed the worst abuses of graft and corruption, which implicated the local magistrates and the Creole American landowners and aristocracy. Gálvez moved to eliminate the Creoles from the upper bureaucracy of the colonies. New offices were created. After 1780 the *corregidores,* or local magistrates, were removed from the Indian villages and that office was replaced by a new system of *intendants,* or provincial governors, based on French models. This intendancy system was introduced throughout the Indies. These well-paid and experienced Spaniards took direct responsibility for tax collection, military matters, and economic development in their regions. Such measures did improve the collection of taxes and made government more effective, but these reforms also disrupted the patterns of influence and power especially among the Creole bureaucrats, miners, and landowners as their political power declined.

Many of the reforms in America were directly linked to defense and military matters. During the century, Spain was often allied with France and the global struggle between England and France for world hegemony made Spain's American possessions a logical target for English attack. During the Seven Years' War (1756–1763) the loss of Florida and the English seizure of Havana shocked Spain into action, particularly because when England held Havana in 1762, Cuban trade boomed. Regular Spanish troops were sent to New Spain, and militia units, led by local Creoles who were given military rank, were created throughout the empire. Frontiers were expanded and previously unoccupied or loosely controlled regions, such as California, were settled by a combination of missions and small frontier outposts. In the case of the Rio de la Plata, foreign competitors were resisted by military means. Spain sought every means to strengthen itself and its colonies.

During the Bourbon reforms the government took an active role in the economy. State monopolies were established on essential items such as tobacco and gunpowder. Whole new areas of Spanish America were opened to development. Monopoly companies were granted exclusive rights to develop certain colonial areas in return for developing the economies of those regions. The Caracas Company, formed in 1728, stimulated the development of cacao production in Venezuela and assured Spain an inexpensive supply of chocolate, but by eliminating contraband and controlling the price of imports it also provoked complaints and even rebellion from the colonists.

The commerce of the Caribbean greatly expanded under the more liberal trading regulations. Cuba now became another full-scale plantation and slave colony, exporting sugar, coffee, and tobacco and importing large numbers of Africans. Buenos Aires on the Río de la Plata proved to be a great success story. Its population had grown rapidly in the 18th century, and by 1790 it had a booming economy based on ranching and on the export of hides and salted beef. The liberalization of commerce meant that Buenos Aires no longer had to depend on the old established trade routes from Peru, and a newly prosperous merchant community in Buenos Aires now dominated the region's trade.

The commercial changes were a double-edged sword. As Spanish and English manufactures became cheaper and more accessible, they undercut locally produced goods so that some regions, such as the interior of the Río de la Plata and Ecuador, that had specialized in producing cloth or other goods now were unable to compete with the European imports. Links to international trade tightened as the diversity of Latin America's economy decreased. Later conflicts between those who favored "free trade" and those who wanted to limit imports and protect local industry were often as much about regional interests as about economic philosophy.

Finally, and most important, the major centers of the Spanish Empire also experienced considerable growth in the second half of the 18th century. As part of the general policy of reform, mining inspectors and experts had been sent to Peru and New Spain to suggest reforms and to introduce new techniques. This plus the discovery of new veins allowed for an expansion of production, especially in New Spain where silver output reached new heights, far outstripping Peru, which itself witnessed increased production.

All in all, the Bourbon reforms must be seen from two vantage points: Spain and America. Undoubtedly, in the short run the restructuring of government and economy resuscitated the Spanish Empire and gave it new life. In the long run, the removal of Creoles from government, the creation of a militia with a Creole officer corps, the opening of commerce, and other such changes contributed to a growing sense of dissatisfaction among the elite, which only their relative well-being and the existing social tensions of the sociedad de castas kept in check.

POMBAL AND BRAZIL

The Bourbon reforms in Spain and Spanish America were paralleled in the Portuguese world during the administration of the Marquis of Pombal (1755–1776), Portugal's authoritarian prime minister. Pombal had lived as ambassador in England and had observed the benefits of mercantilism first hand. He hoped to use these same techniques along with state intervention in the economy to break England's hold on the Portuguese economy, especially on the flow of Brazilian gold from Portugal to England. This became crucial as the production of Brazilian gold began to decline after 1760. In another example of "enlightened despotism," Pombal brutally suppressed any group or institution that stood in the way of royal power and his programs. He developed a particular dislike for the Jesuits because of their allegiance to Rome and their semi-independent control of large areas in Brazil. Pombal expelled the Jesuits from the Portuguese Empire in 1759.

Pombal made Brazil the centerpiece of his reforms. Vigorous administrators were sent to the colony to enforce the changes. Fiscal reforms aimed at eliminating contraband, gold smuggling, and tax evasion. Monopoly companies were formed to stimulate agriculture in older plantation zones and were given the right to import large numbers of slaves. New crops were introduced. Just as in Spanish America, in Brazil new regions began to flourish under the impetus of reform. Rio de Janeiro became the capital and its hinterland was the scene of agricultural growth. The undeveloped Amazonian region, long dominated by Jesuit missionaries, received new attention. A monopoly company was created to develop the region's economy, and it stimulated the development of cotton plantations and the export of wild cacao from the Amazonian forests. These new exports joined the traditional sugar, tobacco, and hides as Brazil's main products.

Pombal was willing to do some social tinkering as part of his project of reform. He abolished slavery in Portugal in order to assure a steady supply of slaves to Brazil, the economic cornerstone of the empire. Because Brazil was vast and needed to be both occupied and defended, he removed Indians from missionary control in the Amazon and encouraged whites to marry them. Immigrant couples from Portugal and the Azores were sent to colonize in the Amazon and the plains of southern Brazil, which now began to produce quantities of wheat and cattle. In 1778 a treaty between Spain and Portugal established the frontier between their American colonies. Like the Bourbons in Spain, Pombal hoped to revitalize the colonies as a way of strengthening the mother country. While new policies were instituted, little changed within society. Brazil was just as profoundly based on slavery in the late 18th century as it had ever been, as levels of slave imports reached 20,000 a year.

Even in the long run Pombal's policies were not fully effective. Although he considerably reduced Portugal's trade imbalance with England in this period, Brazilian trade suffered because demand for its products on the world market remained low. This was a classic problem for the American colonies. Their economies were so tied to the sale of their products on the European market and so controlled by policies in the metropolis that the colonies' range of action was always limited. While for all his efforts Pombal's policies were not immediately successful, they did set the stage and provided the structure for an economic boom in the last 20 years of the 18th century.

REFORMS, REACTIONS, AND REVOLTS

By the middle of the 18th century the American colonies of Spain and Portugal, like the rest of the world, were experiencing considerable growth in population and productive capacity. Scholars disagree on the role of the Bourbon and Pombaline reforms in this process, but the growth was undeniable. By the end of the century, Spanish America had a population of close to 13 million. Between 1740 and 1800 the population of Mexico, the most populous area, increased from 3.5 to almost 6 million, about half of which were Indians. In Brazil, the population reached about 2 million by the end of the century. This overall increase was due to declining mortality rates, increasing fertility levels, increasing immigration from Europe, and the thriving slave trade. The opening of new areas to development and Europe's increasing demand for American products accompanied the growth of population. The American colonies were experiencing a boom in the last years of the 18th century.

Reformist policies, tighter tax collection, and the presence of a more activist government in both Spanish America and Brazil disrupted old patterns of power and influence, raised expectations, and sometimes provoked violent colonial reactions. Urban riots, tax revolts, and Indian uprisings were not unknown before 1700, but after that date serious and more protracted rebellions broke out. In New Granada, popular complaints against the government's control of tobacco and liquor consumption, and rising prices as well as new taxes, led to the widespread Comunero Revolt in 1781. A royal army was defeated, the viceroy fled from Bogotá, and a rebel army almost took the capital. Only tensions among the various racial and social groups and concessions by the government brought an end to the rebellion.

At the same time in Peru, an even more threatening revolt erupted. A great Indian uprising took place under the leadership of Jose Gabriel Condorcanqui, Tupac Amaru. A mestizo with a direct link to the family of the Incas, Tupac Amaru led a rebellion against "bad government." For almost three years the whole viceroyalty was thrown into turmoil as over 70,000 Indians, mestizos, and even a few Creoles joined in rebellion against the worst abuses of the colonial regime. Tupac Amaru was captured and brutally executed, but the rebellion smoldered until 1783. It failed mostly because the Creoles, though they had their own grievances against the government, feared that a real social upheaval might take place.

This kind of social upheaval was not present in Brazil, where a government attempt to collect back taxes in the mining region led in 1788 to a plot against Portuguese control. A few bureaucrats, intellectuals, and miners planned an uprising for independence, but their conspiracy was discovered. The plotters were arrested, and one conspirator, a militia officer nicknamed Tiradentes, was hung.

These movements despite their various social bases, indicated that the activist government increased dissatisfaction in the American colonies. The new prosperity of the late 18th century contributed to a sense of self-confidence and economic interest among certain colonial classes, which made them sensitive to restrictions and control by Spain and Portugal. Different groups had different complaints, but the sharp social and ethnic divisions within the colonies acted as a barrier to common effort and tended to undercut revolutionary movements. Only when the Spanish political system became disrupted by a crisis of legitimacy at the beginning of the 19th century did real separation and independence from the mother countries become a possibility.

CONCLUSION

THE DIVERSE INGREDIENTS OF LATIN AMERICAN CIVILIZATION

During the course of three centuries, Spain and Portugal had created large colonial empires in the Americas. These American colonies had provided a basis of power to their

Iberian mother countries and had taken a vital place in the expanding world economy as suppliers of precious minerals and certain crops to the growing economy of Europe. By the 18th century, the weakened positions of Spain and Portugal within Europe had allowed England and France to benefit directly from the Iberian trade with American colonies.

To their American colonies, the Iberian nations had transferred and imposed their language, laws, forms of government, religion, and institutions. Large numbers of immigrants, first as conquerors and later as settlers, had come to the colonies. Eventually, the whole spectrum of Iberian society was recreated in the New World as men and women came to seek a better life, bringing with them their customs, ideas, religion, laws, and ways of life. By government and individual action, a certain homogeneity was created, both in Spanish America and in Brazil. That seeming unity was most apparent among the Europeanized population.

Underlying the apparent continuity with Spain and Portugal and homogeneity among the various colonies were great variations. Latin America, with its distinct environments, its various economic possibilities, and its diverse Indian peoples imposed new realities. In places like Mexico and Peru, Indian cultures had emerged from the shock of conquest, battered but still vibrant. Indian communities adapted to the new colonial situation. A distinctive multiethnic and multiracial society developed, drawing on Iberian precedents but also dependent on the nature of the Indian population and the proportion of various mixed racial categories. In areas where slavery predominated, African cultures also played a major role. Argentina with few Indians, Cuba with its slaves and plantations, and Mexico with its large rural Indian population all shared the same Hispanic traditions and laws and all had a predominantly white elite, but their social and economic realities made them very different places. Latin America developed as a composite civilization—distinct from the West though related to it—combining in a series of local variations aspects of European and Indian culture and society, or creating the racial hierarchies of slave societies in places like Brazil.

From the perspective of the world economy, despite the decline in production of precious metals, Latin American products remained in great demand in Europe's markets, and as Latin Americans began to seek political independence in the early 19th century, they were confronted by this basic economic fact and by their continued dependence on trade with the developing world economy. Latin America's world economic position, with its labor force organization and outside commercial control, was yet another difference between this new civilization and that of western Europe.

FURTHER READINGS

James Lockhart and Stuart B. Schwartz's *Early Latin America* (1982), provides an interpretation and overview. Lyle N. Macalister's *Spain and Portugal in the New World* (1984) is particularly good on the Iberian background and on the formation of societies in Latin America. John H. Parry's *The Spanish Seabourn Empire* (1966) is well written and particularly good on commerce and government.

On the conquest period there are excellent regional studies. Geographer Carl O. Sauer's *The Early Caribbean* (1966), describes the discovery, settlement, and conquest of that region with much attention to Indian culture. James Lockhart's *Spanish Peru* (1968) is a model reconstruction of conquest society while his *Men of Cajamarca* (1972) is an in-depth look at a group of conquistadores. The conquest of Mexico can be seen from two different angles in Bernal Díaz del Castillo's *The Discovery and Conquest of Mexico*, trans. A. P. Maudsley (1956), and in Miguel López-Portilla's *The Broken Spears. The Aztec Account of the Conquest of Mexico* (1962).

The transformation of Indian societies has been studied in books such as Steve J. Stern's *Peru's Indian Peoples and the Challenge of Spanish Conquest* (1982) on the early colonial era, and William B. Taylor's *Drinking, Homicide, and Rebellion in Colonial Mexican Villages* (1979) on the 18th century. Another approach to the impact of conquest is presented in Noble David Cook's *Demographic Collapse. Indian Peru, 1520–1620* (1981), while Murdo MacLeod's *Spanish Central America* (1973), presents an integrated regional study of society and economy. Particularly sensitive to Indian views is Nancy Farriss's *Maya Society under Colonial Rule* (1984).

Social and economic history have received considerable attention. The establishment of colonial economies has been studied in detail in books such as François Chevalier's *Land and Society in Colonial Mexico* (1963), Stuart Schwartz's *Sugar Plantations and the Formation of Brazilian Society* (1985), and Peter J. Bakewell's *Silver Mining and Society in Colonial Mexico* (1971). Very good social history is now being written. For example, Silvia Arrom's *The Women of Mexico City, 1790–1857* (1985) examines the changing role of women. In Louisa Schell Hoberman and

Susan Migden Socolow, eds., *Cities and Society in Colonial Latin America* (1986), urban social types are examined. A different kind of social history that examines popular thought can be seen in Jacques Lafaye's *Quetzalcóatl and Guadalupe* (1974).

The best starting place on the Bourbon reforms is David Brading's *Miners and Merchants in Bourbon Mexico* (1971), while John L. Phelan's study of the Comunero Revolt, *The People and the King* (1978), examines the Bourbon reforms' unintended effects. Dauril Alden's *Royal Government in Colonial Brazil* (1968) shows Pombal's effects on Brazil.

Ottoman Empire

1243 Mongol invasion of Asia Minor

1281 Founding of the Ottoman dynasty

1350s Ottoman invasion of Europe; conquest of much of the Balkans and Hungary

1402 Timur's invasion; Ottoman setbacks under Bayazid

c. 1450s Beginning of large-scale recruitment of Janissary troops

1453 Ottoman capture of Constantinople

1507 Portuguese victory over Ottoman-Arab fleet at Diu in the Indian Ocean

1514 Ottoman victory over Safavids at Chaldiran

1517 Ottoman capture of Syria and Egypt

1520–1566 Rule of Suleyman the Magnificent; construction of the Suleymaniye mosque in Constantinople

Safavid Dynasty

1334 Death of the first Safavid Sufi master at Ardabil

c. 1450s Shi'ite influences enter Safavid teachings

1501–1510 Safavid conquest of Persia (present-day Iran)

1514 Safavid defeat by Ottomans at Chaldiran

Mughal Dynasty

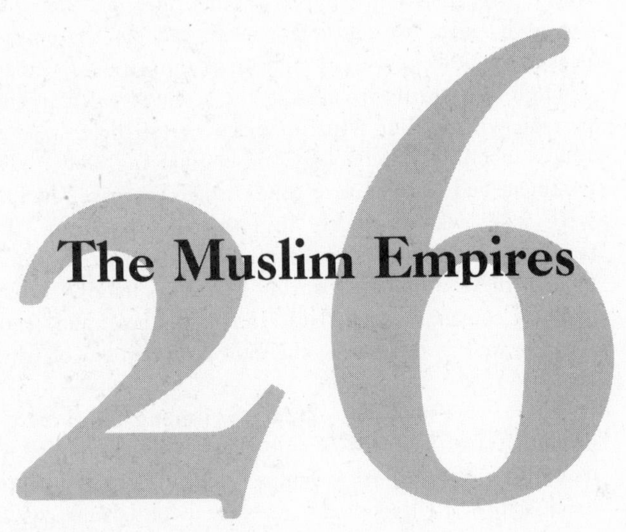

26 The Muslim Empires

INTRODUCTION. Early modern developments in the Islamic world—the Middle East, North Africa, parts of India and island Southeast Asia, and (in terms of political control) southeastern Europe—differed greatly from the dynamics of the new civilization that was developing in Latin America. Muslim civilization encompassed a diverse combination of age-old civilized centers, now reorganized in terms of political boundaries but predominantly Islamic in religion and cultural influences. Intensified trading contacts, the continuing spread of the Islamic faith, and the growth of three great empires dominated the 1450-1750 period in the overall history of the Muslim zone. The rise of the West and the growing world economic links that had been so central to developments in Latin American societies had much less of an impact on Muslim peoples and cultures in this era. But from the eastern Mediterranean to the Java Sea, the expansive Europeans were establishing commercial and military beachheads that would serve as the bases for their growing dominance over some parts of the Islamic world from the early 18th century onward.

The great nomadic invasions by the Mongols in the first half of the 13th century and by the armies of Timur in the last decades of the 14th century had made a shambles of much of the Muslim world. The

1529 First Ottoman siege of Vienna

1571 Battle of Lepanto

1683 Last Ottoman siege of Vienna

1699 Treaty of Carlowitz; Ottomans cede territories in Europe

1727 First Turkish-language printing press founded

1730 Ottoman armies are defeated by Persian forces under Nadir Khan (later Nadir Shah, emperor of Persia)

1730s First Western-modeled military schools established

1540–1545 Mughal ruler Humayan in exile at Safavid court

1588–1629 Reign of Abbas I (the Great)

1722 Fall of the Safavid dynasty

1736–1747 Reign of Nadir Shah

1526 Battle of Panipat; Babur's conquest of India

1540 Babur's successor, Humayan, driven from India

1540–1545 Humayan in exile at the Safavid court

1556 Mughal Empire reestablished in North India

1556–1605 Reign of Akbar

1582 Akbar's proclamation of his new religion

c. 1600s Arrival of Dutch and English merchants in the Mughal Empire

1631–1653 Construction of the Taj Mahal

1640s Rise of Maratta resistance to Mughals in western India

1657–1658 Great war of succession between sons of Shah Jahan

1658–1707 Reign of Aurangzeb

1680s Rajput and peasant revolts in North India

1739 Nadir Shah invades India from Persia, sacks the Mughal capital at Delhi pretence of Muslim unity, which had been preserved by the Seljuk Sultans' retention of the powerless caliphs after 1055, was shattered in 1258 by the conquest and sacking of the Abbasid capital and the extinction of the long-lived caliphate. Regional dynasties in areas as distant as Asia Minor and India were also crushed by nomadic armies, and many splendid Islamic cities were laid to waste. But in the wake of the last and greatest incursions of the nomadic peoples of central Asia into the civilized heartlands of Eurasia, three new Muslim dynasties arose that collectively produced a new flowering of Islamic civilization. Competition between them also led to important political divisions and periodic military clashes, especially between the Ottomans and Safavids, within the Muslim world.

The largest of the three empires, the Ottoman, stretched at its peak in the 17th century from North Africa to southern Russia, and from Hungary to the port of Aden on the southern end of the Red Sea. To the east in what is now Iran and Afghanistan, the Safavid dynasty arose to challenge the Ottomans for leadership of the Islamic world. Finally, in India yet another Muslim empire, centered like most of the earlier ones on the Delhi region of the Gangetic plain, was built under the leadership of a succession of remarkable Mughal rulers.

The combination of these three empires—Ottoman, Safavid, and Mughal—produced the greatest political and military power the Islamic world had yet attained. The Ottomans' armies captured Byzantium in 1453, thus putting an end to the Eastern Roman Empire. They reduced Hungary to vassalage and threatened Austria as late as the end of the 17th century. Farther east, Mughal forces conquered much of the Indian subcontinent, thus building a far larger empire than any previous Muslim or even Hindu dynasty. Muslim naval power was felt in the Mediterranean and the Indian Ocean until late in the 16th century. With those of China, the Ottoman navies were the only ones that stood a chance of blocking European global expansion by sea.

The Ottoman, Safavid, and Mughal Empires

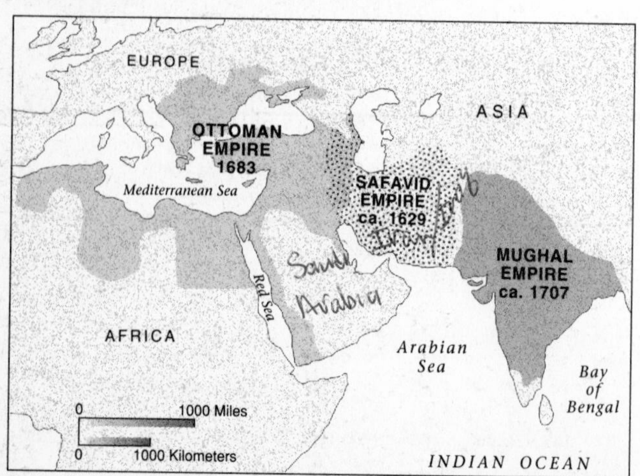

In addition to political and military power, the three empires produced an artistic renaissance in the Islamic world. Particularly in painting, architecture, and literature, the 16th and 17th centuries, when each of the empires peaked in power, were a time of stunning achievement. Though new breakthroughs in the sciences paled in comparison with earlier Muslim discoveries, there were advances in military technology and engineering, and medical treatment and hospital care continued to compare favorably with what was available in Europe and China. The strength and splendor of the three great empires contributed to the continued expansion of Islam, mainly through peaceful conversion in Africa, India, Southeast and central Asia, as well as in some of the European bastions of Christendom.

There were striking similarities among the three empires that are the focus of this chapter. Each empire had its origins in the Turkic nomadic cultures of the central Asian steppe. Religious fervor and zeal for Islamic conversion were central to the rise of both the Ottoman and Safavid dynasties. Though the founders of the Mughal Empire were displaced princes in search of a new kingdom rather than religious zealots, their successors were frequently preoccupied with questions of how far to push conversion efforts aimed at the Hindu majority of the peoples of India. Each empire was based on military conquest, and, at least in its early stages, oriented to the support of its armies and military classes. Both the early conquests and continued strength of each of the dynasties depended on its effective use of firearms on the battlefield and in siege warfare. Each of the Muslim empires was ruled by a succession of absolute monarchs whose imperial pretensions and courtly rituals were patterned in varying degrees after those of earlier Islamic kingdoms. Support of the ever-expanding bureaucracies and military establishments of each empire was drawn primarily from taxes levied on the peoples of the ancient agrarian societies that each empire conquered and ruled. Under each dynasty unique styles of artistic and literary expression developed, which drew both on earlier Islamic expression and on the skills and sensibilities of the conquered peoples, both Muslim and non-Muslim.

These similarities were counterbalanced by significant differences between the rival Muslim empires. Although each dynasty was Muslim, the Mughals, for example, ruled a predominantly non-Muslim population. Thus the political tactics and social policies followed by the Mughal rulers in India differed fundamentally from those pursued by their Safavid rivals in Persia, whose subjects were for the most part followers of Islam. The Ottoman situation in this respect was midway between the Mughals and Safavids. For the first centuries of Ottoman rule, their subjects were largely Christian. Though extensive conversions to Islam from the 15th century onward resulted in a Muslim majority, throughout their reign the Ottoman sultans had to keep the interests and reactions of the empire's large Christian minority in mind. The empires were also divided by the Sunni-Shi'a split that, as we have seen, emerged in the early decades of Islamic history and persisted through the centuries. Enmity was particularly intense between the Ottoman champions of Sunni Islam and the Shi'ite Safavids. These neighboring powers frequently warred over territory and persecuted the adherents of their rivals' brand of Islam. Sunni and Shi'a differences also led to varying religious practices, legal codes, and social organization in each of the Islamic empires.

THE OTTOMANS: FROM FRONTIER WARRIORS TO EMPIRE BUILDERS

For centuries before the rise of the Ottoman dynasty in the 13th and 14th centuries, Turkic-speaking peoples from central Asia had played key roles in Islamic civilization as soldiers and administrators, often in the service of the Abbasid caliphs. In fact, the collapse of the Seljuk Turkic kingdom of Rum in eastern Anatolia in Asia Minor, following the invasion by the Mongols in 1243 described in Chapter 20, opened the way for the Ottomans' rise to power. The Mongols raided but did not directly rule Anatolia, which fell into a chaotic period of warfare between petty, would-be successor states to the Seljuk sultans. Turkic peoples, both those fleeing the Mongols and those in search of easy booty, flooded into the region in the last decades of the 13th century. One of these peoples, called the Ottomans after an early leader named Osman, came to dominate the rest, and within decades they had begun to build a new empire based in Anatolia.

By the 1350s, the Ottomans had advanced from their strongholds in Asia Minor across the Bosporus straits into Europe. Thrace was quickly conquered and by the end of the century large portions of the Balkans had been added to their rapidly expanding territories. The Ottoman rise to power was severely, but only temporarily set back in 1402, when the armies of Timur swept into Anatolia and defeated the Ottoman sultan Bayazid at Angora. For nearly a decade thereafter the region was torn by civil war between Bayazid's sons, each hoping to occupy his father's throne. The victory of Mehmed I led to the reunification of the empire and new conquests in both Europe and Asia Minor.

In moving into Europe in the mid-14th century, the Ottomans had bypassed rather than conquered the great city of Constantinople, long the capital of the once-powerful Byzantine Empire. By the mid-15th century, the Ottomans, who had earlier alternated between alliances and warfare with the Byzantines, were strong enough to undertake the capture of the well-fortified city. For seven weeks in the spring of 1453, the army of Mehmed II, "The Conqueror," which numbered well over 100,000, assaulted the triple ring of land walls that had protected the city for centuries. The undermanned forces of the defenders repulsed attack after attack until the sultan ordered his gunners to batter a portion of the walls with their massive siege cannon. Wave after wave of Ottoman troops struck at

This illuminated French manuscript from the 15th century shows the Ottoman siege of Constantinople in 1453. The Muslim capture of the great eastern bastion of Christian Europe aroused fears throughout the continent, resulting in demands for Crusades to recapture the city.

Jihad: holy war

the gaps in the defenses that had been cut by the guns, overwhelmed the defenders, and raced into the city to loot and pillage for the three days that Mehmed had promised as their reward for victory.

In the two centuries after the conquest of Constantinople, the armies of a succession of able Ottoman rulers extended the empire into Syria and Egypt, across North Africa, thus bringing under their rule the bulk of the Arab world. The empire also spread through the Balkans into Hungary in Europe, and around the Black and Red Seas. The Ottomans also became a formidable naval power in the Mediterranean Sea. Powerful Ottoman galley fleets made it possible to capture major island bases on Rhodes, Crete, and Cyprus; to drive the Venetians and Genoese from much of the eastern Mediterranean; and to threaten southern Italy with invasion on a number of occasions. From their humble origins as frontier vassals, the Ottomans had risen to become the protectors of the Islamic heartlands and the scourge of Christian Europe. As late as 1683, Ottoman armies were able to lay siege to the capital of the Austrian Habsburg dynasty at Vienna. Even though the Ottoman Empire was in decline by this point in time and the threat the assault posed to Vienna was far less serious than a previous attack in the early 16th century, the Ottomans remained a major force in European politics until the late 19th century.

A STATE GEARED TO WARFARE

Befitting an empire that had been founded and extended to spread Islam through the waging of the jihad, or holy war, military leaders played a dominant role in the Ottoman state and the economy of the empire was geared to warfare and expansion. The Turkic cavalrymen, who were chiefly responsible for the Ottomans' early conquests from the 13th to the 16th centuries, gradually developed into a warrior aristocracy. They were granted control over land and peasant producers in annexed areas for the support of their often sizeable households and numerous military retainers. From the 15th century onward, members of the warrior class also vied with religious leaders and administrators drawn from other social groups for control of the ever-expanding Ottoman bureaucracy. As the power of the warrior aristocracy shrank at the center, they sought to build up regional and local bases of support that inevitably competed with the sultans and central bureaucracy for revenue and labor control.

A considerable portion of the economic resources that the Ottoman sultans managed to control themselves was funneled into maintaining the massive armies required both to sustain expansion and protect the territories the Ottomans had won from rivals in all directions. From the mid-15th century, the imperial armies were increasingly

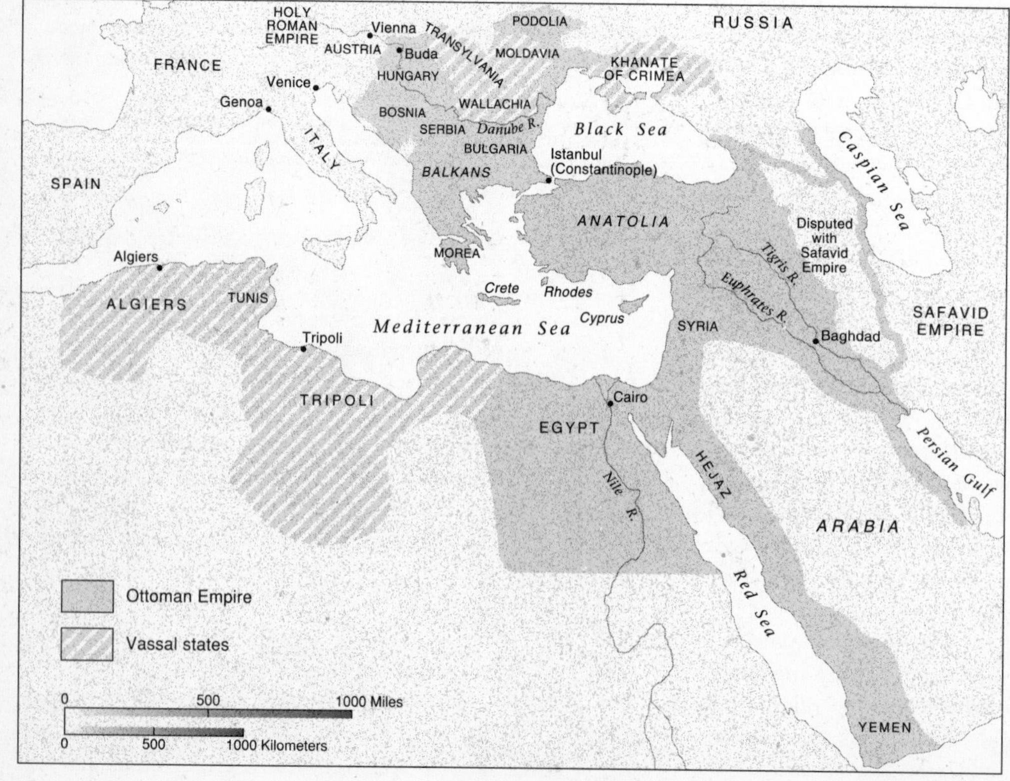

The Ottoman Empire at Its Peak in the 17th Century

dominated by infantry divisions made up of troops called *Janissaries*. Most of the Janissaries had been forcibly conscripted as adolescent boys in conquered areas, such as the Balkans, where the majority of the population retained its Christian faith. Sometimes the boys' parents had willingly turned their sons over to the Ottoman recruiters because of the opportunities for advancement that came with service to the Ottoman sultans. Though legally slaves, the youths were given fairly extensive schooling for the time and converted to Islam. Some of them went on to serve in the palace or bureaucracy, but most became Janissaries.

Because the Janissaries controlled the artillery and firearms that became increasingly vital to Ottoman success in warfare with both Christian and Muslim adversaries, they rapidly became the most powerful component in the Ottoman military machine. Their growing importance was another factor contributing to the steady decline of the role of the aristocratic cavalrymen. Just like the mercenary forces that had earlier served the caliphs of Baghdad, the Janissaries eventually sought to translate military service into political influence. By the late 15th century they were deeply involved in court politics; by the mid-16th century they had the power to depose sultans and decide which one of a dying ruler's sons would mount the throne.

THE SULTANS AND THEIR COURT

The sultans were nominally absolute monarchs, but even the most powerful sultan maintained his position by playing factions in the warrior elite off each other and the warriors as a whole against the Janissaries and other groups. Chief among the latter were the Islamic religious scholars and legal experts, who retained many of the administrative functions they had held under the Arab caliphs of earlier centuries. In addition to Muslim traders, commerce within the empire was in the hands of Christian and Jewish trading groups, who as dhimmis, or "peoples of the Book," were under the protection of the Ottoman rulers. The sultans were also responsible for the prosperity of their subjects and for upholding Islamic law within their domains. Though they have often been depicted as brutal and corrupt despots in Western writings, the Ottoman sultans, especially in the early centuries of their sway, were frequently very capable rulers. Ottoman conquest often meant effective administration and tax relief for the peoples of areas annexed to the empire. This was true for the peasants throughout much of the Balkans, whose Christian overlords had oppressed them with excessive tax and service demands in the decades before the Ottoman takeover.

Like the Abbasid caliphs, the Ottoman sultans grew more and more distant from their subjects as their empire increased in size and wealth. In their splendid marble palaces and pleasure gardens, surrounded by large numbers of slaves and the many wives and concubines of their harems, Ottoman rulers followed elaborate court rituals based on those of earlier Byzantine, Persian, and Arab dynasts. Day-to-day administration was carried out by a large bureaucracy headed by a grand *vizier* (*wazir* in Arabic), the overall head of the imperial administration, who often held more real power than the sultan himself. Early sultans took an active role in political decisions and often personally led their armies into battle. Their sons were usually made provincial administrators or military commanders. This practice gave the potential successors to the ruler vital leadership training, and it does much to explain the high quality of many of the Ottoman monarchs until the late 16th century.

Like earlier Muslim dynasties, however, the Ottomans suffered greatly because they inherited Islamic principles of political succession that remained vague and contested. The existence of many talented and experienced claimants to the throne meant constant danger of civil strife. The death of a sultan could, and increasingly did, lead to protracted warfare among his sons. Defeated claimants sometimes fled to the domains of Christian or Muslim rulers hostile to the Ottomans, thereby becoming rallying points for military campaigns against the son who had managed to gain the throne. The uncertainty of succession and threat of civil strife led some of the early sultans to have all their brothers and other potential family rivals put to death at the time of their accession to the throne. The extent to which fratricide was practiced, however, was greatly exaggerated by the Ottomans' Christian adversaries. From about 1600, rival princes and other possible claimants to the throne were usually confined to the palace and harem, rather than being put to death.

CONSTANTINOPLE RESTORED AND THE FLOWERING OF OTTOMAN CULTURE

An empire that encompassed so many and diverse cultures from Europe, Africa, and Asia naturally varied greatly from one province to the next in its social arrangements, artistic production, and physical appearance. But the Ottomans' ancient and cosmopolitan capital at Constantinople richly combined the disparate elements of their extensive territories. Like the Byzantine Empire as a whole, Constantinople had fallen on hard times in the centuries before the Ottoman conquest in 1453. Soon after Mehmed II's armies had captured and sacked the city, however, the Ottoman ruler set about restoring its ancient glory. He had the cathedral of Saint Sophia converted into one of the grandest mosques in the Islamic world, and new mosques and palaces were built throughout the city, benefiting from architectural advances the Ottomans derived from the Byzantine heritage. Aqueducts were constructed from the surrounding hills to supply the growing population with water, markets were reopened, and the city's defenses were repaired. Each of the sultans who ruled in the centuries after Mehmed strove to be remembered for his efforts to beautify the capital. The most prominent additions were further mosques that represent some of the most sublime contributions of the Ottomans to Islamic and human civilization. The most spectacular of these was the Suleymaniye, built by one of the most successful of the sultans, Suleyman the Magnificent (1520–1566). Though it smacks a good deal of hometown pride, the following description by a 17th-century Ottoman chronicler of the reaction of some Christian visitors to the mosque conveys a sense of the awe that the structure still evokes:

> The humble writer of these lines once himself saw ten Frankish infidels skilful [sic] in geometry and architecture, who, when the door-keeper had changed their shoes for slippers, and had introduced them into the mosque for the purpose of showing it to them, laid their finger on their mouths, and each bit his finger from astonishment when they saw the minarets; but when they beheld the dome they tossed up their hats and cried Maria! Maria! and on observing the four arches which supported the dome . . . they could not find terms to express their admiration, and the ten . . . remained a full hour looking with astonishment on those arches. [One of them said] that nowhere was so much beauty, external and internal, to be found united, and that in the whole of Frangistan [Christian Europe] there was not a single edifice which could be compared to this.

In addition to the mosques, sultans and powerful administrators built mansions, rest houses, religious schools, and hospitals throughout the city. Both public and private gardens further beautified the capital, which Ottoman writers were inclined to compare to paradise itself. The city and its suburbs stretched along both sides of the Bosporus, the narrow strait that separates Europe from Asia. Its harbors and the Golden Horn, a triangular bay that formed the northern boundary of the city, were crowded with merchant ships from ports throughout the Mediterranean and the Black Sea. Constantinople's great bazaars were filled with merchants and travelers from throughout the empire and places as distant as England and Malaya. They offered the seasoned shopper all manner of produce from the spices of the East Indies and the ivory of Africa to slaves and forest products from Russia and fine carpets from Persia. Coffeehouses—places where males gathered to smoke tobacco (introduced from America in the 17th century by English merchants), gossip, do business, and play chess—were found in all sections of the city and were pivotal to the social life of the capital. The coffeehouses also played a major role in the cultural life of Constantinople as centers where poets and scholars could congregate, read their latest works aloud, and debate about politics and the merits of each other's ideas.

Beneath the ruling classes a sizeable portion of the population of Constantinople and other Ottoman cities belonged to the merchant and artisan classes. The Ottoman regime closely regulated both commercial exchanges and handicraft production. Government inspectors were employed to ensure that standard weights and measures were used, to license the opening of new shops and regulate the entry of apprentice artisans into the trades, and to inspect the quality of the goods they produced. Like their counterparts in medieval European towns, the artisans were organized into guilds. Guild officers set craft standards, arbitrated disputes between their members, provided financial assistance for needy members, and even arranged popular entertainments, which were often linked to religious festivals. The guilds of Ottoman towns were much more closely supervised by government officials, and a wider array of occupational groups—including entertainers, prostitutes, and even ordinary laborers—were organized into guilds than was normally the case in Europe.

The early Ottomans had written in Persian, while Arabic remained an important language for works on law and religion throughout the empire's history. But by the 17th century the Turkish language of the Ottoman court had become the preferred mode of expression for poets and historians as well as the language of the Ottoman bureaucracy. In writing, as in the fine arts, the Ottomans' achievements have been somewhat overshadowed by those of their contemporary Persian and Indian rivals. Nonetheless, the authors, artists, and craftsmen of the Ottoman Empire have left a considerable legacy, particularly in poetry, ceramics, carpet manufacturing, and above all in architecture.

THE PROBLEM OF OTTOMAN DECLINE

Much of the literature on the Ottoman Empire concentrates on its slow decline from the champion of the Muslim world and the great adversary of Christendom to the "sick man" of Europe in the 18th and 19th centuries. This approach provides a very skewed view of Ottoman history as a whole. Traced from its origins in the late 13th century, the Ottoman state is one of the great success stories in human political history. Vigorous and expansive until the late 17th century, the Ottomans were able to ward off the powerful enemies that surrounded their domains on all sides for nearly four centuries. The dynasty endured for over 600 years—a feat matched by no other in all human history.

From one perspective the long Ottoman decline, which officials and court historians actively discussed from the mid-17th century onward, reflects the great strength of the institutions on which the empire was built. Despite internal revolts and periodic conflicts with such powerful foreign rivals as the Russian, Austrian, Spanish, and Safavid empires, the Ottomans ruled into the 20th century. Yet centuries earlier the empire had reached the limits of its expansive power, and by the late 17th century the long retreat from Russia, Europe, and the Arab lands had begun. In a sense, some contraction was inevitable. Even when it was at the height of its power, the empire was too large to be maintained given the resource base that the sultans had at their disposal and the primitive state of transport and communications in the preindustrial era.

INTERNAL WEAKNESSES AND IMPERIAL DECLINE

The Ottoman state had been built on war and steady territorial expansion. As possibilities for new conquests ran out and lands began to be lost to the Ottomans' Christian and Muslim enemies, the means of maintaining the oversized bureaucracy and army shrank markedly. The decline in the effectiveness of the administrative system that held the empire together was signaled by the rampant growth of corruption among Ottoman officials. The venality and incompetence of state bureaucrats in turn prompted regional and local officials—in provinces where the population was predominantly European and Arab as well as those with a Turkish majority—to retain increasing amounts of revenue for their own purposes. Revenues that were retained at the local and regional level were, of course, lost to those who sought to run and defend the empire as a whole.

Poorly regulated by the central government, many local officials, who also controlled large landed estates, squeezed the peasants and the laborers who worked their lands for additional taxes and services. At times the oppressive demands of local officials and estate owners sparked rebellions. But more frequently they caused the hard-pressed peasantry to abandon their holdings and flee to those of less rapacious lords or to become vagabonds, bandits, or beggars in the cities. Both responses resulted in the abandonment of cultivated lands and social dislocations that further drained the resources of the empire.

From the 17th century on, the forces that undermined the empire from below were compounded by growing problems at the center of imperial administration. The practice of assigning the royal princes administrative or military positions, in order to prepare them to rule, died out. Instead, possible successors to the throne were kept like hostages in special sections of the palace, where they remained until one of them ascended the throne. The other princes and potential rivals were also, in effect, imprisoned for life in the palace. Though it might have made the reigning sultan more secure, this solution to the problem of contested succession produced monarchs far less prepared to rule than those in the formative centuries of the dynasty. The great warrior-emperors of early Ottoman history gave way, with some important exceptions, to weak and indolent rulers, addicted to drink, drugs, and the pleasures of the harem. In many instances the later sultans were little more than pawns in the power struggles between the viziers and other powerful officials, and the leaders of the increasingly influential Janissary corps. Because the imperial apparatus had been geared to strong and absolute rulers, the decline in the caliber of Ottoman emperors had devastating effects on the strength of the empire as a whole. Civil strife increased and the discipline and leadership of the armies on which the empire depended for survival deteriorated.

MILITARY REVERSES AND THE OTTOMAN RETREAT

Debilitating changes within the empire were occurring at a time when challenges from without were growing rapidly. The Ottomans had made very effective use of artillery and firearms in building their empire. But their addiction to huge siege guns and the Janissaries' determination to block all military changes that might jeopardize the power they had been able to gain within the state caused the Ottomans to fall farther and farther behind their European rivals in the critical art of waging war. With the widespread introduction of light field artillery into the armies of the European powers in the 17th century, Ottoman losses on the battlefield multiplied rapidly and the threat they posed for the West began to recede.

On the sea the Ottomans were eclipsed as early as the 16th century. The end of their dominance was presaged by their defeat by a combined Spanish-Venetian fleet at Lepanto in 1571. Though the Ottomans had completely rebuilt their war fleet within a year after the battle and soon launched an assault on North Africa that preserved that area for Islam, their control of the eastern Mediterranean had been lost. Even more ominously, in the decades before Lepanto, the Ottomans and the Muslim world had been outflanked by the Portuguese seafarers down and then around the coast of Africa. The failure in the early 1500s of the Ottomans and their Muslim allies in the Indian Ocean to drive the Portuguese from Asian waters proved far more disastrous than Ottoman defeats in the Mediterranean.

The clash of the galley fleets at Lepanto was one of the great sea battles in history. But despite devastating losses, the Ottomans managed to replace most of their fleet and go back on the offensive against their Christian adversaries within a year.

Portuguese naval victories in the Indian Ocean revealed the obsolescence of the Ottoman galley fleets and Mediterranean-style warships more generally. The trading goods, particularly spices, that the Portuguese carried back to Europe around Africa enriched the Ottomans' Christian rivals. In addition, the fact that a sizeable portion of the flow of these products was no longer transmitted to European ports through Muslim trading centers in the eastern Mediterranean meant that merchants and tax collectors in the Ottoman Empire lost critical profits and revenues. As if this were not enough, from the late 16th century on, large amounts of silver flowed into the Ottomans' lands from mines worked by Amerindian laborers in the Spanish possessions of the New World. This sudden influx of bullion into the rather rigid and slow growing economy of the Ottoman Empire set off a long-term inflationary trend that further undermined the finances of the empire.

Several able sultans took measures to shore up the crumbling imperial edifice in the 17th century. The collapse of the Safavid dynasty in Persia and conflicts between the European powers at this time also gave the Ottomans hope that their earlier dominance might be restored, but their reprieve proved temporary. With the scientific, technological, and commercial changes occurring in Europe and the overseas expansion that these innovations had made possible, the Ottomans were falling at an accelerating rate behind their Christian rivals in most areas of endeavor, but most critically in trade and making war. The sense the Ottomans inherited from their Arab, Persian, and Turkic predecessors that little of what happened in Europe was important prevented them from taking seriously the revolutionary changes transforming western Europe. The intense conservatism of powerful groups like the Janissaries and, to a lesser extent, the religious scholars reinforced this fatal myopia. Through much of the 17th and 18th centuries, these groups proved able to block most of the Western-inspired innovations that reform-minded sultans or their advisors sought to introduce. As a result of this narrow and potentially dangerous view, the isolated and increasingly fossilized Ottoman imperial system proved incapable of checking the forces that were steadily making for its dismemberment.

DOCUMENT
AN ISLAMIC TRAVELER LAMENTS THE MUSLIMS' INDIFFERENCE TO EUROPE

Though most of the travelers and explorers in this era were Europeans who went out to Africa, Asia, and the Americas, a few individuals from these lands visited Europe. One of these, Abu Taleb, was a scholar of mixed Turkic-Persian descent whose family had settled in India. At the end of the 18th century, Abu Taleb traveled in Europe for three years and later wrote an account in Persian of his experiences there. Though his was one of the few firsthand sources of information about Europe available to Muslim scholars and leaders, Abu Taleb was deeply disturbed by the lack of interest shown by other Muslims in his observations and discoveries.

> . . . when I reflect on the want of energy and the indolent dispositions of my countrymen, and the many erroneous customs which exist in all Mohammedan countries and among all ranks of Mussulmans, I am fearful that my exertions [in writing down his experiences in Europe] will be thrown away. The great and the rich intoxicated with pride and luxury, and puffed up with the vanity of their possessions, consider universal science as comprehended in the circle of their own scanty acquirements and limited knowledge; while the poor and common people, from the want of leisure, and overpowered by the difficulty of procuring a livelihood, have not time to attend to their personal concerns, much less to form desires for the acquirement of information of new discoveries and inventions, although such a passion has been implanted by nature in every human breast, as an honor and an ornament to the species. I therefore despair of their reaping any fruit from my labors, being convinced that they will consider this book of no greater value than the volumes of tales and romances which they peruse merely to pass away their time, or are attracted thereto by the easiness of the style. It may consequently be concluded, that as they will find no pleasure in reading a work which contains a number of foreign names, treats on uncommon subjects, and alludes to other matters which cannot be understood at first glance, but require a little time for consideration, they will, under pretense of zeal for their religion, entirely abstain and refrain from perusing it.

Questions: What reasons does Abu Taleb give for the Muslims' indifference to his account of Europe? What other factors can be added as a result of our study of long-standing Islamic attitudes toward Europe and conditions in the Ottoman Empire in this period? In what ways might the Muslims' neglect of events in Europe hinder their efforts to cope with this expansive civilization in the following centuries?

ABBASID COMPARISONS AND THE OTTOMAN ACHIEVEMENT

We have encountered many of the forces that led to the decline of the Ottoman Empire in earlier Islamic history. In fact, in many ways the Ottoman decline seems to be a replay of the earlier fall of the Abbasid caliphate. At the center of both empires, the forces that sapped their strength included the decreasing ability and reduced powers of the rulers, court intrigues and succession disputes, the growing involvement of mercenary soldiers in politics, and bureaucratic corruption. Away from the capitals at Baghdad and Constantinople, revolts by peasants and townsmen oppressed by the landed classes, the loss of territory to internal rebels, and defeats in wars by foreign powers all contributed to imperial decline.

Though these parallels are striking, they should not blind us to crucial differences between the two cases. These differences arise in part from changes in the international and domestic conditions that each dynasty, which were widely separated in time, had to face. The growing military and economic competition of European rivals, for example, had much more to do with the Ottoman decline than the Abbasid, in which (despite the Crusades) the Europeans did not play a critical role. But they also suggest that the Ottomans had learned a good deal from Abbasid mistakes and improved considerably upon their predecessors' performance.

To begin with, the real power of the Ottoman rulers persisted much longer than that of the Abbasid caliphs—two to three centuries as opposed to three or four generations. In part this was due to the higher caliber of the early Ottoman sultans, which can be traced to the better training that the princes of the royal house were given in the first phase of Ottoman history. In addition, the Ottoman bureaucracy was larger, better organized, and more dedicated than its Abbasid counterpart. It was therefore better able to administer effectively the various parts of the empire and funnel resources to the central government, at least in the early centuries of Ottoman rule. The Ottoman military machine was much better prepared, disciplined, and led than the motley alliance of forces that had brought the Abbasids to power. In the early centuries of Ottoman expansion, a military elite from a single ethnic stock, committed to a common project of religious expansion, directed military operations and discouraged infighting. By contrast, the Abbasid alliance soon broke apart, with Sunni fighting Shi'a and individual commanders seeking to create their own kingdoms. In both cases mercenary forces, which were employed to strengthen the military establishment, became deeply embroiled in politics. But the Janissaries were, initially at least, more effectively controlled by the Ottoman rulers. They also took much longer to become a major political force than the Turkic mercenaries who threatened the Abbassid throne soon after they first entered the service of the caliphate.

Interestingly, the greater political and military success of the Ottomans did not translate into a higher level of intellectual or artistic achievement. Though the Abbasid dynasty was weaker and far less expansive than the Ottoman, its reign witnessed a burst of creativity in the arts, sciences, and philosophy that has seldom been matched by any human society. Though the Ottomans made significant contributions to Islamic architecture, literature, and various crafts, their accomplishments lacked the range, originality, and sheer magnitude of those of the Abbasid age. In the broadest sense, the Ottoman legacy was one in which the restoration and preservation of the Islamic heritage was foremost. For centuries, Ottoman power brought a high level of internal peace and protection from outside invaders to the Islamic heartlands. But the price of security was an inflated bureaucracy and military establishment that proved both an increasing burden for peasants and merchants and a major barrier to creativity and innovation. With the Muslims' old adversaries, the Europeans, forging ahead, the price paid would prove a very high one indeed.

THE SHI'ITE CHALLENGE OF THE SAFAVIDS

Like the Ottomans, the Safavid dynasty arose from the struggles of rival Turkic nomadic groups in the wake of the Mongol and Timurid invasions of the 13th and 14th centuries. Also like the Ottomans, the Safavids rose to prominence as the frontier-warrior champions of a highly militant strain of Islam. But unlike the Ottomans, who became the champions of the Sunni majority of the Muslim faithful, the Safavids espoused the Shi'ite variant of Islam. As we saw in Chapter 12, in the early decades of Muslim expansion a split developed in the community of the faithful between the Sunnis, who recognized the legitimacy of the first three successors to Muhammad (Abu Bakr, Umar, and Uthman) and the Shi'ites, who believed that only the fourth successor (Ali, Muhammad's cousin and son-in-law) had the right to succeed the prophet. Over time, differences in doctrine and ritual were added to the disagreements over succession that had originally divided the Islamic community. Divisions have also arisen within both the Shi'ite and Sunni groupings, but bitter hostility and violent conflict have most often developed along Sunni-Shi'a lines. The long rivalry between the Sunni Ottomans and the Shi'ite Safavids proved to be one of the most pivotal episodes in the long history of these sectarian struggles.

In the first years of the 16th century after decades of warfare against established Muslim states, rival sects, and Christian communities in what is today southern Russia, the Safavids founded a dynasty and conquered the region that comprises the present-day nation of Iran. From that point onward, Iran has been one of the strongest and most enduring centers of Shi'ism within the Islamic world. Under the Safavid dynasty, which lasted until 1722, the Iranian region was also restored as a center of political power and cultural creativity at a level that it had rarely enjoyed since the collapse of the Sassanid Empire in the middle of the 7th century. With the Ottoman and Mughal empires that bordered it on the west and east, Safavid Iran was one of the three core regions of Islamic civilization in the gunpowder age.

SAFAVID BEGINNINGS

The Safavid dynasty had its origins in a family of Sufi mystics and religious preachers, whose shrine-center was at Ardabil near the Caspian Sea. In the early 14th century, one of these Sufis, Safi al-Din, who gave the dynasty its name, began a militant campaign to purify and reform Islam and spread Muslim teachings among the Turkic tribes of the region. In the chaos that followed the collapse of Mongol authority around the mid-14th century, Safi al-Din and other Safavid Sufi leaders gained increasing support. But as the numbers of the "Red Heads" (as the Safavids' followers were called after their distinctive headgear) grew, and as they began in the mid-15th century to preach Shi'ite doctrines, their enemies multiplied. After decades of fierce local struggles in which three successive Safavid leaders perished, a surviving Sufi commander, Ismail, led his Turkic followers to a string of victories on the battlefield. In 1501 Ismail's armies took the city of Tabriz, where he was proclaimed shah, or emperor.

In the next decade, Ismail's followers conquered most of Persia, drove the Safavid's ancient enemies—the Ozbegs, a neighboring nomadic people of Turkic stock—back into the central Asian steppes, and advanced into what is now Iraq. The Safavid successes and the support their followers received in the Ottoman borderlands from Turkic-speaking peoples inevitably brought them into conflict with Ottoman rulers. In August of 1514, at Chaldiran in northwest Persia, the armies of the two empires met in one of the most fateful battles in Islamic history.

Chaldiran was more than a struggle between dynasties: it was a clash between the most powerful adherents of the Shi'a and Sunni variants of Islam. The fervor with which both sides fought the battle was enhanced by the long-standing Safavid persecutions of the Sunnis and the recent slaughter, by the forces of the Ottoman sultan Selim, of the Shi'ias in Anatolia on whom his soldiers could lay their hands. At Chaldiran the Safavid cavalry, which made up the bulk of Ismail's forces, proved no match for the musketeers and cannon of the Ottomans. The Safavids were dealt a devastating defeat that checked the westward advance of Shi'ism and decimated the ranks of the Turkic warriors who had built the Safavid Empire. But the Ottomans were unable to follow up their victory with an occupation that would have put an end to the Safavids. The latter's capital at Tabriz was too far from Ottoman supply areas to be held through the approaching winter. The withdrawal of the Ottoman forces gave the Safavids the breathing space they needed to regroup their forces and reoccupy much of the territory they had originally conquered. Though the two empires would fight wars periodically over the next centuries, Chaldiran had more or less set the limits to which each could expand and extend its variant of the Islamic faith.

POLITICS AND WAR UNDER THE SAFAVID SHAHS

After his defeat at Chaldiran, Ismail, who had once been a courageous warrior and popular leader, retreated to his palace and sought to escape his troubles through drink. His seclusion, and struggles between factions backing each of his sons for the right to succeed him, left openings for subordinate Turkic chiefs to attempt to seize power. After years of turmoil, a new shah, Tahmasp I (1534–1576), won the throne and set about restoring the power of the dynasty. The Turkic chiefs were foiled in their bid for supreme power, and the Ozbegs were again and again driven from the Safavid domains. Under Shah Abbas I (1587–1629) the empire reached the height of its strength and prosperity, though the territories it controlled remained roughly equivalent to those ruled by Ismail and Tahmasp I.

Under Tahmasp I and his successors repeated efforts were made to bring the Turkic chiefs under control. They were gradually transformed into a warrior nobility comparable to that in the Ottoman domains. Like their Ottoman counterparts, the Safavid warrior nobles were assigned vil-

This Persian miniature from 1680 depicts a Safavid notable, probably Shah Suleiman I (1667–1693), with a group of courtiers, which includes (on the right-hand side of the central horseman) a European visitor bearing presents for the Persian leader.

lages, whose peasants were required to supply them and their troops with food and labor. The most powerful of the warrior leaders occupied key posts in the imperial administration, and from the defeat at Chaldiran onward they posed a constant threat to the Safavid monarchs. To counterbalance this threat, Safavid rulers recruited Persians for positions both at the court and in the rapidly expanding imperial bureaucracy. The tug-of-war for power and influence between Turkic and Persian notables was further complicated by the practice, initiated by Ismail's successor Tahmasp I, of recruiting into the bureaucracy and army slave boys, who were captured in campaigns in southern Russia. Like the Janissaries in the Ottoman Empire, many of these slaves rose to positions of considerable power. Also like the Janissaries, the slave regiments soon became a major force in Safavid political struggles.

Of all of the Safavid shahs, Abbas I made the greatest use of the youths captured in Russia, then educated and converted to Islam. They not only came to form the backbone of his military forces, but they were granted provincial governorships and high offices at court. Like the Janissaries, "slave" regiments, which were wholly dependent on Abbas's support, monopolized the firearms that had become increasingly prominent in Safavid armies. The Persians had artillery and handguns long before the arrival of the Portuguese by sea in the first decades of the 16th century. But Abbas and his successors showed little reluctance to call upon the knowledgeable but infidel Europeans for assistance in their wars with the Ottomans. Abbas turned to European advisors, particularly the Sherley brothers from England, for instruction in the casting of cannon and the training of his slave infantrymen and a special regiment of musketeers recruited from the Iranian peasantry. By the end of his reign, Abbas had built up a standing army of nearly 40,000 troops and an elite bodyguard. These measures to strengthen his armies and his victories on the battlefield appeared to promise security for the Safavid domains for decades to come—a promise that was not to be fulfilled.

STATE AND RELIGION

The Safavid family was originally of Turkic stock, and early shahs like Ismail wrote in Turkish, in ironic contrast to their Ottoman rivals who preferred to write in Persian. After Chaldiran, however, Persian gradually supplanted Turkish as the language of the court and bureaucracy. Persian influences were also felt in the organization of court rituals and in the more and more exalted posture of the Safavid shahs. Abandoning all pretense to the egalitarian comradery that had marked their earlier dealings with the warrior chiefs, the Safavids took grand titles, such as *padishah* or king of kings, often derived from those used by the ancient Persian emperors. Like the Ottoman rulers, the Safavids presided from their high thrones over opulent palace complexes, crowded with servants and courtiers. The pattern of palace life was set by elaborate court rituals and social interaction governed by a refined sense of etiquette and decorum. Though the later Safavid shahs played down claims to divinity that had been set forth under Ismail and his predecessors, they continued to claim descent from one of the Shi'ite *imams*, or successors of Ali.

Changes in the status accorded to the Safavid rulers were paralleled by shifts in the religious impulses that had been so critical to their rise to power. The militant, expansive cast of Shi'ite ideology was modified as the faith became a major pillar of dynasty and empire. The early Safavids imported Arabic-speaking religious experts of the Shi'a persuasion, but later shahs came to rely on Persian religious scholars who entered into the service of the state and were paid by the government. *Mullahs*, who were both local mosque officials and prayer leaders, were also supervised by and given some support from the state. All religious leaders were required to curse the first three caliphs and mention the Safavid ruler in the Friday sermon. Teaching in the mosque schools was also planned and directed by state religious officials.

Through these agents the bulk of the Iranian population was gradually converted to Shi'ism during the centuries of Safavid rule. Sunni Muslims, Christians, Jews, Zoroastrians and—ironically, given the Safavids' origins—the followers of Sufi preachers were pressured, and sometimes persecuted, to induce them to convert to Shi'ism. Shi'a religious festivals, such as that commemorating the martyrdom of Husayn that involved public flagellation and passion plays, and pilgrimages to Shi'a shrines, such as that at Karbala in central Iraq, became the focal points of popular religion in Iran. Thus, Shi'ism not only provided ideological and institutional support for the Safavid dynasty, it came to be an integral part of Iranian identity, setting the people of the region off from most of their Arab and Turkic neighbors.

When the dynasty weakened, some of the religious experts and mullahs grew more independent. They found support in their local communities and voiced interpretations of the sacred texts that were based more on their own study than on the dictates of Safavid functionaries. Some religious scholars disputed the legitimacy of the dissolute shahs who occupied the throne in the latter stages of the dynasty. But it would be wrong to equate the power of these religious thinkers with that the *ayatollahs,* or highest religious authorities, have gained in present-day Iran. None tried to seize power in his own right. Most continued to serve the dynasty or the rulers who succeeded the Safavids, or they withdrew from political affairs altogether.

ELITE AFFLUENCE AND ARTISTIC SPLENDOR

Though earlier rulers had erected or restored mosques and religious schools and financed public works projects, Abbas I surpassed them all. After securing his political position with a string of military victories, Abbas I set about the task of establishing his empire as a major center of international trade and Islamic culture. He had a network of roads and rest houses constructed and strove to make merchants and travelers safe within his domains. He set up workshops to manufacture the silk textiles and splendid Persian carpets that then, as now, were in great demand. Abbas I sought to encourage Iranian merchants to trade not only with their Muslim neighbors and India and China to the east, but also with the Portuguese—and later the Dutch and English—whose war and merchant ships were becoming a familiar sight in the Persian Gulf and Arabian Sea.

Though Abbas I undertook building projects throughout his empire, he devoted special attention to his capital at Isfahan. The splendid seat of Safavid power was laid out around a great square, which was lined with two-storied shops interspersed with great mosques, government offices, and soaring arches that opened onto formal gardens. Abbas I oversaw the construction of numerous public baths and rest houses, and founded several colleges. He patronized workshops where intricately detailed and brilliantly colored miniatures were produced by master painters and their apprentices.

It was above all the great mosques Abbas I had built at Isfahan that were the glory of his reign. The vividly colored ceramic tiles, which Iranian builders had begun to use centuries earlier, turned the massive domes and graceful minarets of Safavid mosques and royal tombs into creations of stunning beauty. Geometric designs, floral patterns, and verses from the Quran written in stylized Arabic added movement and texture to the deep blue tiles that distinguished the monumental construction of the Safavid era. Gardens and reflecting pools were built near the mosques and rest houses. By combining graceful arches, greenery, and colorful designs, Persian architects and artisans sought to create lush and cool refuges (perhaps duplicating heaven itself as it is described in the Quran) in a land that is dry, dusty, and predominately gray-brown for much of the year.

SOCIETY AND GENDER ROLES: OTTOMAN AND SAFAVID COMPARISONS

Though the Ottomans and Safavids were bitter political rivals and religious adversaries, the social systems that developed under the two dynasties had much in common. Both were dominated, particularly in their earliest phases, by warrior aristocracies, which shared power with the theoretically absolutist monarchs of each empire and enjoyed the prestige and luxury of elite life in the capital and on rural estates. In both cases the warrior aristocrats gradually retreated to the estates, making life increasingly difficult for the peasants on whom they were dependent for the support of their grand households and many retainers. During the early phases of Safavid and Ottoman rule, the strength of the court and traditional peasant defenses such as the underreporting of crop yields and the threat of flight more or less kept in check the demands of the warrior elite, now predominantly a rural landowning class. But as the real

The great square of the Safavid capital at Isfahan was built by Abbas I to project the splendor and power of his empire. The buildings of the square made up one of the most splendid architectural complexes of the early modern era.

power of the rulers of each empire diminished and population increases reduced the uncultivated lands to which peasants might flee, the exactions of the landlord class grew harsher. Foreign invasions, civil strife, and the breakdown in vital services once provided by the state added to the growing misery of the peasantry. The resulting spread of banditry, peasant uprisings, and flight from the land further drained the resources of each empire and undermined the legitimacy of the rival dynasties.

The early rulers of both the Ottoman and Safavid empires sought to encourage the growth of handicraft production and trade in their realms. Both dynasties established imperial workshops where products ranging from miniature paintings and rugs to weapons and metal utensils were manufactured. The rulers of each empire lavishly patronized public works projects that provided reasonably well-paid work for engineers, stonemasons, carpenters, and other sorts of artisans. Some of the more able emperors of each dynasty also pursued policies that they believed would increase both internal and international trade. In these endeavors, the Ottomans gained in the short run from the fact that large-scale traders in their empire were often from minority groups, such as the Christians and Jews, who had extensive contacts with overseas traders that the bazaar merchants of the Safavid realm normally lacked. Though Safavid cooperation with Portuguese traders remedied this shortcoming to some extent, the Safavid economy remained much more constricted, less market oriented, and more technically backward than that of their Ottoman rivals.

Significantly, the Ottomans' advantages in trade and handicraft production were only relative; they were reversed when comparisons were made with European kingdoms to the west. While European techniques and technology were changing dramatically—even before 1750 and the beginnings of the Industrial Revolution—Ottoman manufacturing stagnated, and its most dynamic trade sectors, still controlled by non-Muslim minorities, developed in increasing isolation from Ottoman society as a whole and often in defiance of imperial restrictions.

Women in Islamic societies under Ottoman or Safavid rule faced legal and social disadvantages that were comparable to those we have encountered in most civilized areas. Within the family women were subordinated to their fathers and husbands; they seldom exercised political or religious power in their own right; and they had surprisingly meager outlets for artistic or scholarly expression. To some extent the great nomadic influx into the Islamic heartlands on the part of both Mongol and Turkic peoples from the 12th to the 15th centuries offset these trends. As we have seen, women generally enjoyed more personal freedom and higher social status in the nomadic societies than in the sedentary societies of the Middle East and central Asia. Much of this was eventually, if not immediately, sacrificed by women of Turkic or Mongol backgrounds when they settled in the towns of conquered areas. There the dictates of increasingly male-centric codes and restrictive practices such as seclusion and veiling were imposed on the women of all classes, but most strictly on those of the elite.

Recent evidence suggests, however, that many women in the Islamic heartlands in this era, perhaps clinging to the memory of the lives their nomadic predecessors had led, struggled against these restrictions. Travelers to Persia in the time of Abbas I remarked on the brightly colored robes worn by women in the capital and elsewhere, and noted that many women made no effort to cover their faces in public. At both the Ottoman and Safavid courts, the wives and concubines of the rulers and royal princes continued to exert considerable influence behind the throne and remained deeply involved in palace conspiracies. More important for ordinary women in each of these societies was the fact that many women were active in trade and some in moneylending. Court records also suggest that women were often able to invoke provisions in Islamic law that protected their rights to inheritance, decent treatment by their spouses, and even divorce in situations that had become intolerable.

How typical these instances of female assertion and fulfillment were is not at all clear. Though some women were a good deal better off than we had once thought and perhaps as well or better off than their counterparts in China and western Europe, most women very likely lived unenviable lives. Limited largely to contacts with their own families and left with little more than household chores and domestic handicrafts like embroidery to occupy their time, the overwhelming majority of women in effect disappeared from the history of two of the great centers of Islamic civilization.

THE RAPID DEMISE OF THE SAFAVID EMPIRE

Given the power and splendor the Safavid Empire had achieved by the end of the reign of Abbas I, its collapse was stunningly rapid. Abbas's fears of usurpation by one of his sons, which were fed by plots on the part of several of his closest advisors, had led during his reign to the death or blinding of all who could legitimately succeed him. A grandson, who was weak and thus thought by high state officials to be easily manipulated, was placed on the throne following Abbas's death. From this point the dynasty's fortunes declined markedly. As was true of the Ottomans, the practice of confining the princes to the atmosphere of luxury and intrigue that permeated the court led to a sharp fall in the quality of Safavid rulers. Able shahs, such as Abbas II (1642–1666), were too few to halt the rot within the imperial administration or to deal effectively with the many foreign threats to the empire. Factional disputes and rebellions shook the empire from within, while nomadic raiders and Ottoman and Mughal armies steadily reduced the territory the Safavids could tap for manpower and revenue.

By March of 1722, Isfahan was besieged by Afghani tribesmen. In October, after over 80,000 of the capital's inhabitants had perished of starvation and disease, the city fell and Safavid power was effectively ended. One of those who fought for the throne in the decade of war and destruction that followed claimed descent from the Safavid line. But a soldier-adventurer named Nadir Khan Afshar eventually emerged victorious from these bloody struggles. Though he began as a champion of Safavid restoration, Nadir Khan proclaimed himself shah in 1736. Despite the title, his dynasty and those that followed were short-lived. The area that had once made up the Safavid Empire was reduced for generations to a battleground for its powerful neighbors and a tempting target for nomadic raiders.

THE MUGHALS AND THE APEX OF MUSLIM CIVILIZATION IN INDIA

Despite the fact that the founder of the Mughal dynasty, Babur, traced his descent on one side from the Mongol khans, the Mughal in the dynasty's name had little to do with the earlier nomadic conquerors. Babur was also descended from Turkic warriors like Timur, and most of his followers were from Turkic or mixed-nomadic origins. Unlike the Ottomans and Safavids, Babur's motives for conquest and empire building had little to do with religious fervor. He led his followers into India in 1526 because he had lost his original kingdom centered on Farghana in central Asia in the preceding decades. On his father's death in 1498, Babur, then only a boy of 16, was thrown into a fierce struggle with the Ozbeg tribesmen for control of his ancestral realm. By 1504 Babur and his supporters had been driven back to Kabul in what is now Afghanistan. Originally, he directed raids into the fertile and heavily populated plains of India only to gain booty to support his campaigns to win back Farghana. Though India had much greater potential as a base on which to build an empire, Babur cared little for the green and well-watered subcontinent. Even after he later conquered India, he continued to long for the arid steppe and blue-domed mosques of his central Asian birthplace. But after decades of wars that repeatedly ended in defeat, he was forced to give up his dream of reclaiming his homeland and to turn his full energies to the conquest of northern India.

In 1526 Babur—by then a seasoned military commander—entered India at the head of a veteran and well-organized army. At Panipat north of Delhi, his army of 12,000 met the huge force of over 100,000 sent to crush it by the last ruler of the Muslim Lodi dynasty, which then ruled much of northern India. Employing gun carts, movable artillery, and cavalry tactics similar to those that had brought the Ottomans victory at Chaldiran, Babur routed the Lodi army. In addition to the superior firepower and mobility of his forces, their victory owed a great deal to the tactic of frightening the hundreds of war elephants that led the Lodi army into battle. The elephants stampeded, trampling thousands of Lodi infantrymen or sending them into flight. A year later, Babur's forces, again vastly outnumbered, decisively defeated a confederation of Hindu warrior-kings at Khanua. Within two years he had conquered large portions of the Indus and Gangetic plains and founded a dynasty that would last over 300 years.

SUCCESSION AND NEAR FATAL IMPERIAL CRISIS

The founder of the Mughal dynasty was a truly remarkable man. A fine military strategist and fierce fighter who went into battle alongside his troops, Babur also managed, in the decades when he was continually fighting for his very life, to cultivate a taste for the arts and music. He wrote one of the great histories of India, was a fine musician, and designed wonderful gardens for his new capital at Delhi. But he proved a better conqueror than administrator. He did little to reform the very ineffective Lodi bureaucracy he had taken over, a project that would have solidified the Mughals' hold on the empire that Babur was soon to pass on to his much-loved son, Humayan. In 1530, at the age of 48, Babur suddenly fell ill and died, leaving Humayan to inherit the newly founded kingdom.

Like his father, Humayan was a good soldier; in fact he had won his first battle at the age of 18. But Babur's death was the signal for his enemies to strike from all sides. One of Humayan's brothers disputed his succession, and armies from Afghanistan and the Rajput states of western India marched on his capital. By 1540, with his armies shattered, Humayan was forced to flee to Persia, where he remained in exile, an embarrassed guest at the Safavid court, for nearly a decade. Having gained a foothold at Kabul in 1545, Humayan launched a series of campaigns into India that restored Mughal rule to the northern plains by 1556. But Humayan did not live to savor his victory. Shortly after entering Delhi in triumph, he was hurrying down his library steps, his arms full of books, to answer the call to prayer. He stumbled and fell, hitting his head. He was dead within days.

AKBAR AND THE BASIS FOR A LASTING EMPIRE

Humayan's sudden death once again imperiled the Mughal dynasty. His son and successor, Akbar, was only 13 years old, and the Mughals' enemies moved quickly to take advantage of what they viewed as a very favorable turn of events. Their expectations were soon dashed because in Akbar, two gifted monarchs were succeeded by one of the great leaders of all history. Interestingly, Akbar's reign was contemporaneous with those of a number of other remarkable monarchs, including Elizabeth I of England, Philip of Spain, and the Muslim rulers, Suleyman the Magnificent and Abbas I. Akbar was a match for any of these very formidable rivals.

Like his father and grandfather, Akbar was a fine military commander who possessed great personal courage. But unlike his predecessors, Akbar also had a vision of empire and sense of mission that hinged on uniting India under his rule. A workaholic who seldom slept more than three hours a night, Akbar personally oversaw the building of the military and administrative systems that would form the backbone of the Mughal Empire for centuries. He also patronized the arts, personally entered into complex religious and philosophical discussions with learned scholars from throughout the Muslim, Christian, and Hindu worlds, and still found time to carry out social reforms and invent his own universalistic religion. Though illiterate—there had been little time for book learning when his father fought for survival in the wilderness—Akbar had an insatiable curiosity and incredible memory. By having others read aloud to him, he became a learned man in a number of fields.

At first with the help of senior advisors but soon on his own, Akbar routed the enemies who had hoped to capitalize on the Mughals' misfortunes. In the decades after 1560, when he took charge of the government, Akbar's armies greatly extended the empire with conquests throughout north and central India. It was Akbar's social policies and administrative genius that made it possible to establish the foundations of a lasting dominion in the subcontinent. He pursued a policy of reconciliation and cooperation with the Hindu princes and the Hindu majority of the population of his realm. He encouraged intermarriage between the Mughal aristocracy and the families of the Hindu Rajput rulers. Akbar also abolished the much-hated head taxes that earlier Muslim rulers had levied on Hindu unbelievers. He promoted Hindus to the highest ranks in the government, ended a long-standing ban on the building of new Hindu temples, and ordered Muslims to respect cows, which the Hindu majority viewed as sacred. Despite all this, Akbar considered his new religion, the Din-i-Ilahi, which blended elements of the many faiths with which he was familiar, as the long-term key to his efforts to reconcile Hindus and Muslims. If he could persuade the adherents of each religion to embrace the common faith he had devised, sectarian quarrels and even violent conflict could be brought to an end.

The Muslim and Hindu warrior aristocracy that formed the core of the supporters of the Mughal dynasty were, like their counterparts in the Ottoman and Safavid empires, granted villages for their support. In turn they were required to maintain a specified number of cavalrymen and

The Growth of the Mughal Empire, from Akbar to Aurangzeb

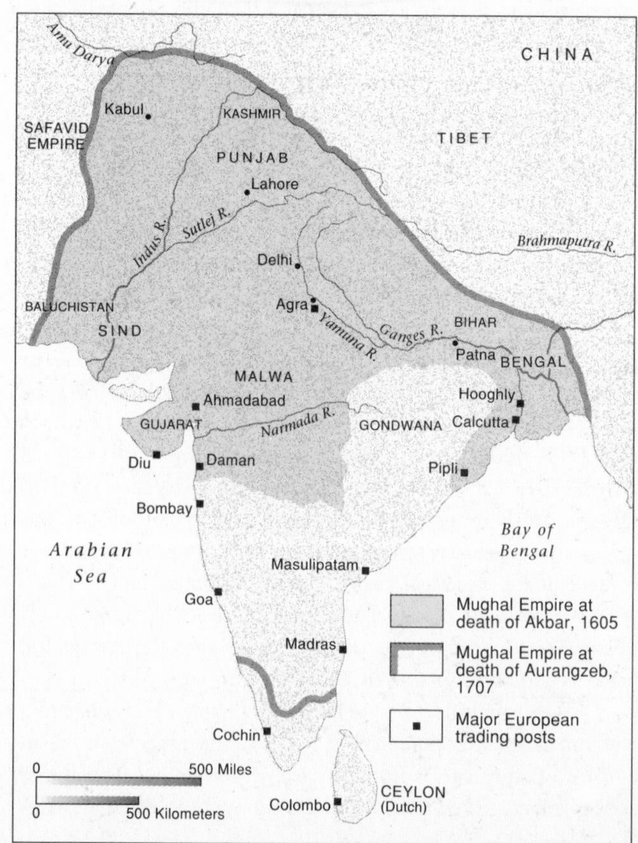

This engraving from a late 16th-century German traveler's account of India shows a European artist's impression of an Indian widow committing *sati*. Not surprisingly, this practice of immolating high-caste widows on their deceased husbands' funeral pyres was frequently described at great length by European visitors in this era.

to be on call should the emperor require their services. The court and central bureaucracy were supported by revenues drawn both from the tribute paid by the military retainers and (especially) from taxes on lands—mostly near the twin capitals at Delhi and Agra—set aside for the support of the imperial household. Due to a shortage of manpower, in most areas local notables, many of whom were Hindu, were left in place as long as they swore allegiance to the Mughal rulers and paid their taxes on time. These arrangements left the control and welfare of the village population largely in the hands of the military retainers of the dynasty and local power brokers. Depending on the leader in a given locality, this could result in strict but paternalistic administration of peasant affairs or blatant corruption and the exploitation of the village population.

SOCIAL REFORM AND SOCIAL CHANGE

In addition to his administrative reforms, Akbar pushed for social changes that he believed would greatly benefit his subjects. Beyond the public works that were typically favored by able Muslim rulers, Akbar sought to improve the calendar, establish living quarters for the rather large population of beggars and vagabonds in the large cities, and regulate the consumption of alcohol. Whatever success the latter campaign may have had in Indian society as a whole, it apparently failed in Akbar's own household for one of his sons was reputed to drink 20 cups of double-distilled wine per day.

More than any of Akbar's many reform efforts, those involving the position of women demonstrated how far the Mughal ruler was in advance of his time. He sought to encourage widow remarriage, at that point taboo for both Hindus and Muslims, and to discourage child marriages. The latter were so widespread among the upper classes that he did not attempt to outlaw them, and it is doubtful that his disapproval did much to curb the practice. Akbar did legally prohibit sati, or the immolation of high-caste Hindu women on their husbands' funeral pyres, even though this custom was deeply entrenched among the Rajput princes and warrior classes that were some of his most faithful allies. Akbar was so determined to eradicate sati, particularly in cases where the widow was pressured to agree to be burned alive, that he once personally rescued a young girl despite the protestations of her angry relatives. He also sought to provide relief for women trapped in *purdah*, or the seclusion from public viewing, by encouraging the merchants of Delhi and other cities to set aside special market days for women only. Even prostitutes were a matter of concern for the emperor. He had special sections in Mughal towns set aside for their brothels; he appointed inspectors to check abuses against both the prostitutes and their clientele; and he even had records kept of those who frequented houses of prostitution, perhaps to discourage the practice.

MUGHAL SPLENDOR AND EARLY EUROPEAN CONTACTS

Despite his many successes and the civil peace and prosperity his reign brought to much of northern India, Akbar died a lonely and discouraged man. By 1605 he had outlived most of his friends and faced revolts by sons eager to claim his throne. Above all, he died knowing that the Din-i-Ilahi, the religion that he had created to reconcile his Hindu and Muslim subjects, had been rejected by both.

Though neither of his successors, Jahangir (1605–1627) or Shah Jahan (1627–1658), added much territory to the empire Akbar had left them, in their reigns Mughal India reached the peak of its splendor. European visitors marveled at the size and opulence of the chief Mughal cities of Delhi, Agra, and Lahore. The huge Mughal armies, replete with elephant and artillery corps, dwarfed those of even the most powerful European rulers at the time. European ambassadors to the great Mughal's court were literally dazzled by the jewel-encrusted palaces of white marble and red sandstone and the large numbers of courtiers who vied for the emperor's favor. Some of the more perceptive of the European observers, such as Francois Bernier, also noted the abject poverty in which the lower classes in both town and countryside lived and the lack of discipline and training of most of the soldiers in the Mughal armies. Perhaps most ominously, Bernier added that in invention and the sciences India had fallen far behind western Europe in most areas. Until the 18th century, however, criticisms by writers like Bernier were drowned out by exclamations of wonder on the part of the merchants, adventurers, and missionaries who visited the empire.

Beyond the (as it turned out false) promise of tens of millions of converts that Mughal India offered to Christian missionaries, it became in the reigns of Akbar's successors one of the major overseas centers for European traders. French, Dutch, and English merchants brought products from throughout Asia, though little from Europe itself, to exchange for a variety of Indian products, particularly the subcontinent's famed cotton textiles. The trade gap that the demand for Indian cotton cloth and clothing had created in the West in Roman times persisted millennia later. The 17th- and 18th-century rage for Indian textile products is reflected in the following ditty from *Prince Butler's Tales*, written in England in 1696:

Our ladyes all were sent a gadding
After these toys they ran a madding
And nothing then would please their fancies
Nor dolls, nor joans [cotton caps]
Nor wanton nancies.
Unless it be of Indian making.

The importance of the Indian textile trade is also indicated by the names we still use for different kinds of cotton cloth, from calico (after the Indian port city of Calicut) to chintz and muslin, as well as by our names for cotton apparel such as pajamas.

Because they were easily washed and relatively inexpensive, Indian textiles first won a large market among the working and middle classes in Britain and elsewhere in Europe. In the reigns of Queen Mary and Queen Anne, fine Indian cloth came into fashion at the court as well. An incident from the reign of the Mughal emperor Aurangzeb, who succeeded Shah Jahan, suggests just how fine the cloth in question was. Aurangzeb, a religious zealot and a bit of a prig, chastised his favorite daughter for appearing in his presence in garments that revealed so much of her body. The daughter protested that she had on three layers of fine cotton clothing. It is thus no wonder that even after industrialization had revolutionized cotton textile manufacture in England, European visitors to India continued to observe and write in great detail about the techniques used by Indian artisans to weave and dye cotton cloth. The popularity of so-called "madras" cloth today demonstrates that this interest has by no means died out.

ARTISTIC ACHIEVEMENT IN THE MUGHAL ERA

Both Jahangir and Shah Jahan continued Akbar's policy of tolerance toward the Hindu majority and retained most of the alliances he had forged with Hindu princes and local leaders. They made little attempt to alter significantly the administrative apparatus they had inherited from Akbar, and fought their wars in much the same way the founders of the dynasty had. Both mounted campaigns to crush potential enemies and in some cases to enlarge the empire, but neither was as interested in conquest and politics as he was in enjoying the good life. Both were fond of drink, dancing girls, and the pleasure gardens they had laid out from Kashmir to Allahabad. Both were delighted

This miniature painting by Bishndas depicts the birth of Prince Jahangir. The mixed reactions of the other members of Akbar's harem, the presence of musicians, and the varied activities of the courtiers in the courtyard below provide wonderful insights into the nature of court life at the height of the Mughal age.

by polo matches (a game invented by the princes of India), ox and tiger or elephant fights, and games of parchesi, which they played on life-sized boards with dancing girls as chips. Both took great pleasure in the elaborate court ceremonies that blended Indian and Persian precedents, in lavish state processions, in their palaces and jewel-studded wardrobes, and in the scented and sweetened ices that were rushed from the cool mountains in the north to their capitals on the sweltering plains.

Jahangir and Shah Jahan are best remembered not for their pleasure-loving ways but as two of the foremost patrons of the fine arts in human history. They expanded the painting workshops that had been started by the early Mughals to the point where thousands of exquisite miniatures could be produced during their reigns. Some of these paintings show the influence of European painting: at times superficial, as in the addition of halos and cherubs to portraits of Jahangir; at times more fundamental, as when Indian artists attempted to introduce true perspective or Christian religious themes into their work. Most of the miniatures, however, are devoted to more traditional Islamic subjects, such as key battles and scenes of life at court or portraits of Mughal noblemen and wonderfully detailed paintings of animals and plants. As these choices of subject matter indicate, Indian artists, such as those in Persia, ignored the prohibition against depicting the human figure that was pushed by some religious authorities from the earliest centuries of Islam. Manuscript illumination was a highly valued art form that was carried to near perfection by the draftsmen and painters at the Mughal court.

Both Jahangir and Shah Jahan also devoted a good deal of personal attention and vast revenues and manpower to building some of the most stunning architectural works of all time. The best known of these is the Taj Mahal, which has come to be a symbol for India itself, as witnessed by Air India advertisements and lists of the wonders of the

Perhaps no single building has come to symbolize Indian civilization more than the Taj Mahal. The grace and elegance of the tomb that Shah Jahan built in his wife's honor provide an enduring source of aesthetic delight.

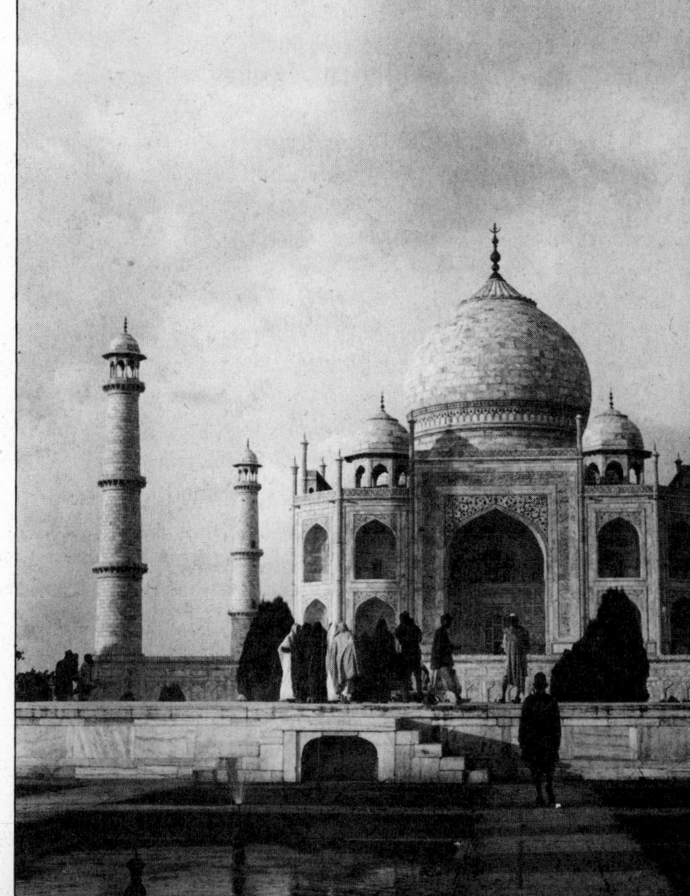

world. But structures, such as the audience hall in the Red Fort at Delhi, Akbar's tomb at Sikandra, and the tomb of Itimad al-Dowleh at Agra, rival the Taj Mahal in design and perhaps surpass it in detail and decoration.

At its best, Mughal architecture blends what is finest in the Persian and Hindu traditions. It fuses the Islamic genius for domes, arches, and minarets and the balance between them with the Hindu love of ornament. In place of the ceramic tiles the Persians used to finish their mosques and tombs, Indian artisans substituted gleaming white marble that was inset with semiprecious stones arranged in floral and geometric patterns. Extensive use was also made of marble reflecting pools, the most famous of which mirrors the beauty of the Taj Mahal. When these pools were inlaid with floral patterns and provided with fountains, the rippling water appeared to give life to the stone plant forms. Like the architects and artisans of the Ottoman Empire and Safavid Persia, those who served the Mughal rulers sought to create paradise on earth—an aspiration that was carved in marble on the audience hall of the Red Fort at Delhi. Around the ceiling of the great hall, it is written "If there is paradise on earth—It is here . . . it is here."

COURT POLITICS AND THE POSITION OF ELITE AND ORDINARY WOMEN

Not surprisingly, two rulers who were so absorbed in the arts and the pursuit of pleasure left most of the mundane tasks of day-to-day administration largely in the hands of subordinates. In both cases strong-willed wives took advantage of their husbands' neglect of politics to win positions of considerable power and influence at the Mughal court. Jahangir's wife, Nur Jahan, continually amassed power as he became more and more addicted to wine and opium. She packed the court with able male relatives, and her faction dominated the empire for much of the later years of Jahangir's reign. Nur Jahan was a big spender, but not only on pomp and luxury. She became a major patron of much-needed charities in the major cities. Despite her considerable success at pursuits that were normally reserved for males, she was defeated in the end by the roles of wife and mother to which many felt she should confine herself. She died giving birth to her 19th child.

Shah Jahan's consort, Mumtaz Mahal, also became actively involved in court politics. But Shah Jahan was a much more engaged and able ruler than Jahangir, and thus her opportunities to amass power behind the throne were more limited. Mumtaz Mahal is remembered not for her political acumen but for the love and devotion that Shah Jahan bestowed upon her—a love literally enshrined in the Taj Mahal, the tomb where she is buried. Shah Jahan's plans to build a companion tomb in black marble across the Jumna River were foiled by the revolt of his sons and his imprisonment. He is buried next to his wife in the Taj Mahal. But her tomb is central and far larger than that of her emperor-husband.

Though the position of women at the Mughal court improved in the middle years of the dynasty's power, that of women in the rest of Indian society declined markedly. Child marriage grew more popular and the age limit was even lowered. It was not unheard of for young girls to be married at the age of nine. Widow remarriage among Hindus virtually died out. Seclusion was more and more strictly enforced for upper-caste women, both Hindu and Muslim. Muslim women rarely ventured forth from their homes unveiled, and those who did risked verbal and even physical abuse. The governor of one of the provinces of the Mughal Empire divorced his wife because she was seen scrambling for her life, but unveiled, from an elephant that had run amuck. Among upper-caste Hindus, the practice of sati spread despite Shah Jahan's renewal of efforts to outlaw it. The dwindling roles left to women and the correspondingly limited productivity permitted them, combined with the burden of the dowry that had to be provided to marry them off, meant that the birth of a girl was increasingly viewed as an inauspicious event. At court or in the homes of ordinary villagers only the birth of a son was greeted with feasting and celebrations.

THE BEGINNINGS OF IMPERIAL DECLINE

Aurangzeb, Shah Jahan's son and successor, seized control of an empire that was threatened by internal decay and growing dangers from external enemies. For decades the need for essential administrative, military, and social reforms had been ignored. The Mughal bureaucracy had grown bloated and excessively corrupt, the army was equally bloated and woefully backward in weaponry and tactics, and the peasants and urban workers had seen their productivity and living standards fall steadily. The Taj Mahal and other wonders of the Mughal artistic imagination had been paid for by the mass of the people at a very high price.

Though far from being the cruel bigot that he is often portrayed as, Aurangzeb was not the man to restore the dynasty's declining fortunes. Courageous, honest, intelligent, and hardworking, he seemed an ideal successor to two rulers who had so badly neglected affairs of state. But Aurangzeb was driven by two ambitions that proved disastrous to his schemes to strengthen the empire. He was determined to extend Mughal control over the whole of the Indian subcontinent, and he believed that it was his duty to purify Indian Islam, to rid it of the Hindu influences he was convinced were steadily corrupting it.

The first ambition increased the number of the empire's adversaries, strained the allegiance of its vassals and allies, and greatly overextended its huge but ponderous and obsolescent military forces. By the time of his death in 1707, after a reign of nearly 50 years, Aurangzeb had conquered most of the subcontinent and extended Mughal control as far north as Kabul in what is now Afghanistan. But the almost incessant warfare of his years in power drained the treasury and further enlarged an already flabby and inefficient bureaucracy and army without generating corresponding increases in revenues to support them.

Equally critical, the long wars occupied much of Aurangzeb's time and energies, diverting him from administrative tasks and reforms essential to the dynasty's continued strength. While he was leading his massive armies in the south, there were peasant uprisings and revolts by Muslim and Hindu princes in the north. Perhaps even more fundamentally harmful to the imperial system was the growing autonomy of local leaders, who were able to divert more and more revenue from the central administration into their own coffers. On the northern borders, incursions by Persian and Afghan warrior bands were on the increase.

While Aurangzeb's military campaigns strained the resources of the empire, his religious policies gravely weakened the internal alliances and disrupted the social peace Akbar had so skillfully established. Aurangzeb continued to employ Hindus in the imperial service—in fact, he did not have the Muslim replacements to do without them. But non-Muslims were given far fewer posts at the upper levels of the bureaucracy and their personal contact with the emperor was severely restricted. Aurangzeb also took measures that he and his religious advisors felt would help rid their Muslim faith and culture of the Hindu influences that had permeated it over the centuries. He forbade the building of new temples and had several demolished. He put an end to Hindu religious festivals at court and strove to reinstate the hated head tax on unbelievers, a measure he hoped might prod them to convert to Islam. The tax fell heavily on the Hindu poor and in some cases drove them to support sectarian movements that rose up to resist Aurangzeb's proselytizing zeal.

By the end of Aurangzeb's reign the Mughal Empire was far larger than it had been under any of the earlier emperors, but it was also a good deal more unstable. Internal rebellions by those such as the Marattas of western India, who claimed to be defending Hinduism against Muslim persecution, put an end to effective Mughal control over large areas. The rise of new sects, such as the Sikhs in the northwest, further strained the declining resources of an imperial system that was clearly overextended. The early leaders of the Sikhs had originally sought to bridge the differences between Hindu and Muslim. But Mughal persecution of the new sect, which was seen as religiously heretical and a political threat to the dynasty, eventually transformed Sikhism into a staunchly anti-Muslim force within the subcontinent. In addition, Muslim kingdoms in the Deccan and Bengal regions continued to resist Mughal hegemony, and Islamic invaders waited at the poorly guarded passes through the Himalayas to strike and plunder once it was clear that the Mughals could no longer effectively fend them off.

From the first decades of the 18th century onward, control and state revenues passed increasingly from the Mughal court and bureaucracy to regional lords, who had once served as Mughal governors but now gave little more than lip service and token tribute payments to the Mughal emperors. As centralized political control broke down and warfare increased markedly throughout much of the subcontinent, these regional lords became the keys to social coherence and cultural creativity. In a sense this shift from fairly centralized to regional political control marked a return to a pattern that had long been predominant in South Asian civilization. However, the fragmentation of political power in the early decades of the 18th century left tempting openings in many parts of India for foreign intervention and the economic exploitation of Indian artisans and peasants by local lords and foreign and local merchants. None would take fuller advantage of these opportunities than the English, who began the century as just one of many Asian and European contenders for the fallen crown of the Mughal emperors. (On England's expansion in India, see Chapters 23 and 30.)

ANALYSIS

THE DECLINE OF EMPIRES—MUSLIM VARIATIONS ON A UNIVERSAL THEME

In their rise and decline, each of the Muslim gunpowder dynasties exhibited common patterns that can tell us a great deal about the dynamics of preindustrial political systems and the difficulties of sustaining empires more generally. Each of the Muslim empires owed its existence to the courage and fighting abilities of frontier warriors, whose nomadic life-style provided extensive training in the arts of war and a high degree of mobility. In each case a succession of strong leaders was able to forge a disciplined and unified military force from disparate bands of fractious herdsmen. The success of these forces in establishing lasting imperial dynasties depended on their combination with regiments equipped with handguns and artillery.

Each of the dynasties was also continuously challenged by the warrior peoples that had been so critical to their rise to power. Measures taken by the rulers of each empire to offset the power of the warrior aristocrats that developed, such as the Safavid and Ottoman recruitment of slave soldiers and Mughal alliances with Hindu princes, eventually contributed to the downfall of their empires. These attempts to develop alternative bases of power weakened the loyalty of the warrior peoples and, by reducing their importance to the state, contributed to a gradual decline in their military preparedness.

Because each of the Muslim empires was built on military conquest and expansion, each was increasingly confronted by a dilemma that none was able to solve. On the one hand, continued wars and annexations were essential to the maintenance of ever larger bureaucracies and military establishments. On the other hand, the preindustrial weaponry and communications technology available made it difficult to control effectively the far-flung territories each claimed. Russia, another gunpowder empire, here gained strengths—by innovations in military technology under rulers like Peter the Great—that the Muslim empires ignored. Efforts to hold the Muslim empires together often used up more resources than new territories generated—again in contrast to the Russian and Western empires in the early modern period. Wars of expansion sustained hostilities with peoples bordering on the empires or created new foes. They also diverted the rulers of each of the empires from much-needed reforms at home and allowed internal competitors to amass strength. When external enemies and logistical limitations blocked its capacity to expand farther, each empire entered into a phase of decline.

Though religious fervor was a key factor in the emergence of only two of the empires, the Ottoman and Safavid, it became an increasingly important factor in the Mughal Empire as well. The frontier-warrior holy war appeals of Osman and the holy men of Ardabil go far to explaining the victories of their followers over often superior armies. Once their successors were established in power, religious justifications for their rule grew hollow as missionary zeal gave way to officially sponsored treatises on Islamic precedents for absolutist rule. The varying strains of Islam the Ottomans and Safavids espoused led to intermittent warfare between the two empires. These clashes further drained their resources and prevented them from paying sufficient attention to other threats, particularly those from an expanding Europe.

The Mughals, who professed the Sunni variant of Islam, clashed on occasion with the Shi'ite Safavids, but their chief religious problems were of a different sort. Despite the heroic efforts of Akbar, no lasting rapprochement could be found with the Hindu majority or minority sects. Thus, key alliances with Hindu princes remained uncertain and religiously inspired rebellions increasingly shook the Mughal imperium. This problem was less serious for the Ottomans and Safavids, but both had to deal with sectarian enemies within their domains and worry about the reliability of support rendered by Christian minorities.

Consistent with the pattern of Islamic political history as a whole, none of the three gunpowder empires solved the critical problem of political succession. Each of the empires was periodically racked by bitter civil wars between the forces backing rival claimants to the throne, who were usually the sons of a recently deceased or gravely ill ruler. Emperors were often forced to kill off or blind (the latter act was sufficient in Muslim law to bar them from succession) their most able sons, who had attempted or were suspected of plotting to attempt to seize their thrones by force. Efforts to establish less violent modes of determining succession, such as the virtual captivity of the Ottoman princes in the palace complex, resulted in other, perhaps more serious problems. The many untested, harem-ridden sultans this seclusion produced from the 17th century onward led to a marked decline in the quality of the sultans—a serious consequence in a system so dependent upon effective autocratic rule.

Questions: To what extent do the forces that led to decline in the Muslim gunpowder empires correspond to those discussed for the civilizations of the classical world? Which of these causes are unique to the Islamic world? Is the larger crisis set in motion by the rising power of the West something new or a phenomenon we have encountered before in global history?

CONCLUSION

THE RISE OF EUROPE AND THE ECLIPSE OF ISLAMIC CIVILIZATION AS THE PIVOT OF THE WORLD ORDER

The causes of decline outlined above were probably in themselves sufficient to destroy each of the great gunpowder empires of Islam. But each was also undermined by further weaknesses that would have profound significance for Islamic civilization as a whole. Captivated by their rivalries with each other and the problems of holding together their empires, none of the dynasties took the rising threat from Europe seriously. Though they called on travelers and missionaries for advice in casting cannon or military tactics, none of the Islamic emperors systematically monitored technological advances in Europe, much less attempted to adopt them on a wide scale. This failure to take strong measures to meet the challenges that European overseas expansion was creating for Islamic civilization as a whole was also responsible for the weakening of the economic basis of each of the empires. Key tax revenues and merchant profits were drained off by the rise of European trading empires in Asia (see Chapter 23). Spiraling inflation and the resulting devaluation of Ottoman currency, brought on by the unchecked importation of precious metals from European colonies in the Americas, priced Ottoman handicraft goods out of the world market and disrupted the agrarian economy throughout their domains. Minority peoples within the Muslim gunpowder empires, from the Christian and Jewish merchants of the Ottoman lands to the Hindu traders of India, increasingly oriented their commercial activities to the more dynamic economies of European nations, overseas colonies, and trading outposts. The Europeans' gains in ways to generate wealth and economic growth meant increasing losses for Muslim societies and political systems, losses that would eventually prove critical to the failure of their efforts to compete successfully with their Christian neighbors and long-standing rivals.

Equally critical, Muslim rulers and scholars continued to take little interest in European learning. Thus, they were largely oblivious to the scientific ideas that were transforming the European world view and steadily enhancing the Westerners' ability to tap new sources of power for production, communications, and war. The Muslims' contempt for the Europeans and their culture was centuries old, but by the 16th century it was also a dangerous anachronism. In the 18th and 19th centuries Muslim peoples and cultures would pay a high price for this arrogance and their leaders' failure to inquire into and match the intellectual and material accomplishments of the West.

FURTHER READINGS

The Lapidus survey suggested in the earlier chapters on Islam provides a fine introduction to the empires that are the focus of this chapter. The best detailed studies of the Ottoman Empire can be found in the works of Halil Inalcik, especially his chapters in *The Cambridge History of Islam*. For a rather different perspective on the Ottomans, see Stanford Shaw's *History of the Ottoman Empire and Modern Turkey*, vol. I (1280–1808) (1976). See Bernard Lewis's *Istanbul and the Civilization of the Ottoman Empire* (1963) for internal views of life at the center of the Ottoman Empire, and Peter F. Sugar's *Southeastern Europe under Ottoman Rule, 1354–1804* (1977) for life in the Christian portions of the Ottoman Empire.

R. M. Savory's writings, including his chapters in *The Cambridge History*, are the most reliable of a very limited literature on the Safavid period. Though quite specialized, Michel Mazzaoui's *The Origins of the Safavids* (1972) provides the fullest account of the origins and rise of the Safavid dynasty. The contributions to the volume that Savory edited on *Islamic Civilization* (1976) include good discussions of the arts and society in the Turkic and Persian sectors of the Islamic heartland. The introductory sections of Nikki Keddi's *Roots of Revolution* (1981) provide a good discussion of the relationship between religion and the state in the Safavid period.

The Ikram and Ahmad books cited in the earlier chapter on Islam in India are also good on the Mughals. Though specialized, the works of Muhammad Habib and Athar Ali on the Mughal Empire are also critical. Of the many works on Mughal art and architecture, the volume by Gavin Hambly on *Mughal Cities* (1968) has some of the better color plates and an intelligent commentary.

Note's

Muslim people's arrogance, led to their own failure, and decline.

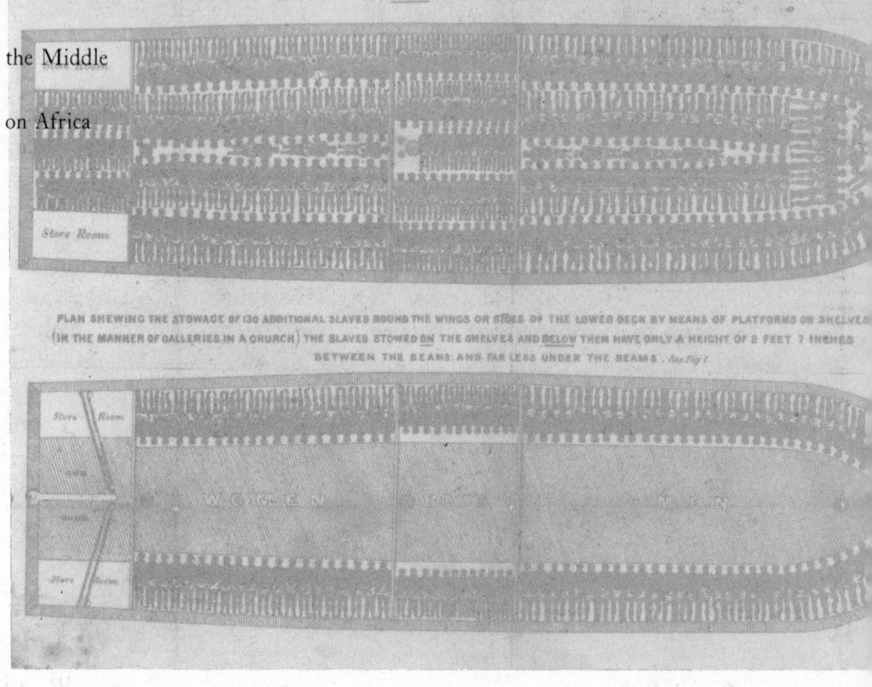

130 OF THESE BEING STOWED UNDER THE SHELVES AS SHEWN IN
Store Room
PLAN SHEWING THE STOWAGE OF 130 ADDITIONAL SLAVES ROUND THE WINGS OR SIDES OF THE LOWER DECK BY MEANS OF PLATFORMS OR SHELVES (IN THE MANNER OF GALLERIES IN A CHURCH) THE SLAVES STOWED ON THE SHELVES AND BELOW THEM HAVE ONLY A HEIGHT OF 2 FEET 7 INCHES BETWEEN THE BEAMS AND FAR LESS UNDER THE BEAMS. See Fig 1.
Store Room
Store Room
WOMEN

1415 Portuguese capture Ceuta (Morocco); beginning of European expansion

1441 First shipment of African slaves brought directly from Africa to Portugal

1481 Portuguese fort established at El Mina

1562 Beginnings of English slave trade

1570 Portuguese establish colony in Angola

1591 Fall of Songhay Empire

27

Africa and the Africans in the Age of the Atlantic Slave Trade

INTRODUCTION. While the new empires dominated the core areas of the Muslim world during the early modern centuries, sub-Saharan Africa, previously linked to the Muslim world in many ways, pulled into a different orbit. Islam remained important, and in eastern Africa so did trade with western Asia, but the rise of the West and of the Western-dominated world economy proved to be a powerful force in recasting the framework of African history. The strength of earlier African cultural and political traditions persisted in many places, but the impact of the West was the newest influence in Africa, and in some respects an immensely powerful one.

African history had its own pace and rhythm and so this chapter will exceed the chronological boundaries of the early modern period. The external influences of Islam and the West initiated or intensified processes of religious conversion, political reorganization, and social transformation that persisted, in some cases, to the 19th century. The distinctive nature and chronology of African history should not blind us, however, to its role in world history.

During the age of European maritime and commercial expansion, large areas of Africa were brought into the orbit of the expanding world economy and were influenced by the transformation taking place. Not all parts of Africa were influenced in the same way nor at the same time. During the period after 1450, the growing and often bitter contacts between Europeans and Africans, primarily through the slave trade, linked the destiny of Africa to broader external trends and resulted in a diaspora of millions of Africans to the Middle East, Europe, and especially the Americas. Not all European contact with Africa was centered on the slave trade, nor was the desire for slaves the only impulse behind European explorations, but the slave trade after 1600 came to predominate other activities until the mid-19th century.

1652 Dutch establish colony at Cape of Good Hope

1700–1717 Osei Tutu unifies the Asante kingdom

1713 English get right to import slaves to Spanish Empire

1720s Rise of the kingdom of Dahomey

1790s Abolitionist movement gains strength in England

1792 Slave uprising in Haiti

1804 Usuman Dan Fodio leads Hausa expansion

1815 Cape colony comes under formal British control

1818–1828 Shaka forges Zulu power and expansion; *Mfecane* under way

1833 Great Britain abolishes slavery in the West Indies

1834 Boers make "great trek" into Natal

This process had a direct impact on certain areas of Africa, and it also made Africans an important element in the changing balance of world civilizations. The forced movement of Africans as captive laborers and the creation of slave-based societies in the Americas were major aspects of the formation of the modern world and the growth of the economies of western Europe. In a way, this forced migration was part of the international exchange of foods, diseases, animals, and ideas that marked the era, and which, as we saw in the case of the Americas, had a profound influence on the indigenous peoples in various regions. Moreover, in large areas of the Americas, colonized by Europeans, where slavery came to be the predominant form of labor, African culture was transferred, contributing to the creation of new cultural forms. In this chapter we will examine, in some detail, the history of parts of Africa in the age of the slave trade and the creation of slave societies in the Atlantic world as part of the general process of European expansion and the creation of a world economy.

While much of the analysis in this chapter emphasizes the increasing linkage between Africa and the wider world, it should be made clear at the outset that many fundamental processes of African development discussed in Chapters 10 and 14 continued throughout this period. It is vital to realize that almost all of Africa remained independent of outside political control and that most cultural development was autonomous as well. Africa differed profoundly from Latin America in these aspects during the early modern centuries.

A variety of trends affected various parts of the sub-Saharan region. Islam consolidated its position in East Africa and the Sudan. In Ethiopia, the Christian kingdom of the highlands continued to hold off its Muslim rivals. In many places in Africa, as in Europe, a tendency for independent states to form and expand in size continued, perhaps as a result of a population expansion that followed the diffusion of iron tools and improved agriculture. Kingdoms spread to new areas. Scholars hold differing opinions on the extent to which these long-term developments were affected by Europeans and the rise of the Atlantic slave trade. Some have argued that the enlarged political scale—the growth of large kingdoms through much of the subcontinent—was the dominant theme of the period, with slavery one of its by-products. Others see European demand as a major impulse in political expansion. In this chapter we emphasize the impact of slavery and the slave trade because our focus is not simply the geographical region of Africa, but the African peoples who were swept into the expanding international economy.

THE PORTUGUESE PENETRATION

As we have seen, the Portuguese were the first Europeans to begin direct contact with black Africa. The Portuguese knew that much of the gold that arrived in North Africa came from beyond the Sahara, and during the difficult years of the 15th century following the Black Death, they were anxious to acquire direct access to this gold. Beginning in 1415, after seizing the Moorish stronghold of Ceuta in Morocco, Portuguese ships began to push down the West African coast in search of gold, ivory, pepper, and other exotic commodities. These voyages were usually private ventures, but were sometimes sponsored and financed by important nobles, such as Prince Henry (called "The Navigator")—a younger son of the Portuguese king—who also seems to have gathered mapmakers, mariners, and scholars together in order to plan and prepare for further voyages. Prince Henry financed about one-third of the voyages personally and granted licenses for most of the others before his death in 1460. Moved also by curiosity and by hopes of finding the fabled Christian kingdom of Prester John, which might eventually have aided in a war against Islam, Portuguese exploration and voyages continued to be primarily commercial in nature.

THE EARLY ATLANTIC SLAVE TRADE

Ships pushed down the West African coast into the region of Senegal and Guinea, and finally reached the Cape of Good Hope in 1487. Along the coast, the Portuguese established trade forts and trading posts with resident merchants. The most important of these was El Mina (1482) in the heart of the gold-producing region of the forest zone. These forts assured arriving ships of a secure landing place where goods could be traded. They also allowed for the exercise of some control or influence with minimum investment of manpower. Although some raiding was carried out by the early voyages, once out of range of their canons, the Portuguese were simply not powerful enough to enforce their will on the larger West African states. Most of the forts, therefore, were established with the agreement or license of local rulers who benefited from the access to European commodities and sometimes from the military support the Portuguese provided in local wars.

Africans acquired cloth, iron, copper, brass, horses, and guns from the Portuguese, who also sometimes provided African rulers with slaves brought from other stretches of the coast. In return the Portuguese received ivory, pepper, animal skins, and gold. From El Mina, Accra, and other trade forts, routes led directly into the gold-producing regions of the interior so that the Portuguese eventually traded with Mande and Soninke merchants from Mali and Songhay. Much of the Portuguese success was due to their ability to penetrate the already existing African trade routes, to which they could also add specialized items. Portuguese and African-Portuguese mulatto traders and middlemen struck out into the interior to establish trade contacts and collection points. These isolated *lançados* provided essential links between the economies of the African interior and the nodules of European mercantilism on the coast.

Trade was the basis of Portuguese relations with Africans but in the wake of commerce came political, religious, and social relations. The small states of the Senegambian coast did not impress the Portuguese, and they were particularly suspicious of Muslims since Iberian Catholics considered Islam a traditional enemy. When they reached the area of the Gold Coast (modern Ghana) and encountered the kingdom of Benin, they were impressed both by the power of the ruler and by the magnificence of his court. Other large African states also provoked similar responses.

Missionary efforts were made to convert the rulers of Benin, Kongo, and other African kingdoms. The Portuguese contacted the Kongo kingdom south of the Zaire River about 1484. The missionaries achieved a major success in Kongo, where members of the royal family were converted and eventually the ruler, Nzinga Mvemba, took the title Afonso I. During his reign (1507–1543) he sought, with the help of Portuguese advisors and missionaries, to convert the whole kingdom to Christianity. Attempts were made to "Europeanize" the kingdom. Portugal and Kongo exchanged ambassadors and dealt with each other with a certain equality in this early period, but eventually enslavement of his subjects led Afonso to attempt to end the slave trade and limit Portuguese activities. In this he was only partially successful because of Portugal's control of Kongo's ability to communicate with the outside world and its dominance over Kongo's trade.

These first contacts were marked by preconceptions as well as an appreciation or curiosity. Africans found the newcomers strange and at first tried to fit them into their existing concepts of the spiritual and natural world. Images of Portuguese soldiers and traders began to appear in the bronzes of Benin and the carved ivory sculptures of other African peoples. The Portuguese looked on Africans as savages and pagans, who were, however, capable of civilized behavior and conversion. African arts were appreciated. Carved elephant tusks, ivory salt cellars, and other items done by African artists in a distinctive Afro-Portuguese style became an item of trade with Europe.

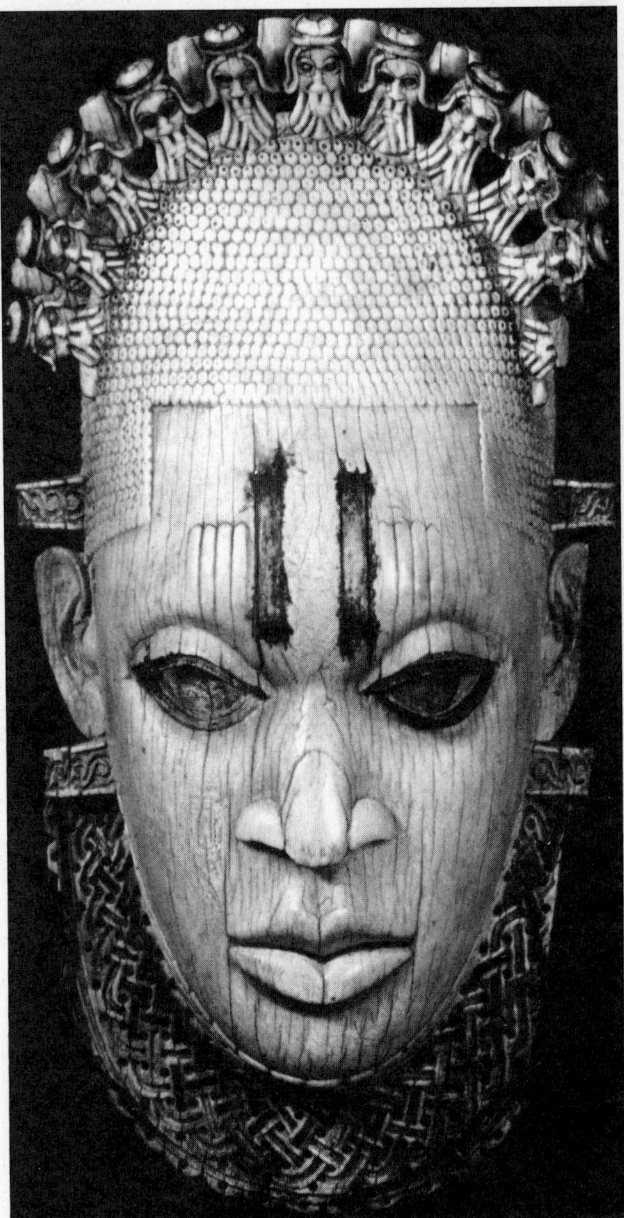

African artists were impressed by the Europeans and sometimes incorporated them in their own work, as can be seen in the headpiece of this beautifully carved ivory head of a Benin monarch. Europeans in turn employed African craftsmen to produce decorative luxury goods.

Portuguese exploration continued southward toward the Cape of Good Hope and beyond in the 16th century. Early contacts were made with the Mbundu peoples south of Kongo in the 1520s, and a more permanent Portuguese presence was established there in the 1570s with the foundation of Luanda on the coast. This became the basis for the Portuguese colony of Angola. We have already seen that, after Vasco da Gama rounded the Cape and reached the trading cities of East Africa on his way to India, the Portuguese sought to impose themselves on the existing trading system of the African ports in the Indian Ocean and Red Sea. They established a base on Mozambique island and then secured bases at Kilwa, Mombasa, Sofala, and other ports that gave them access to the gold trade from Monomotapa (Mwenemutapa) in the interior. In East Africa as on the West African coast, the number of permanent Portuguese settlers was minimal. The Portuguese effort was primarily commercial and military, although it was always accompanied by a strong missionary effort.

The Portuguese were the first Europeans to establish a permanent presence in Africa and as such they established the patterns that were to characterize such contacts for the next 200 years. In the 17th century, other Europeans—the Dutch, English, French, and others—competed with the Portuguese and displaced them to some extent, but the system of fortified trading stations, the combination of force and diplomacy, alliances with local rulers, and the predominance of commercial relations continued as the principal pattern of European contact with Africa.

Portuguese Expansion and Major African Kingdoms

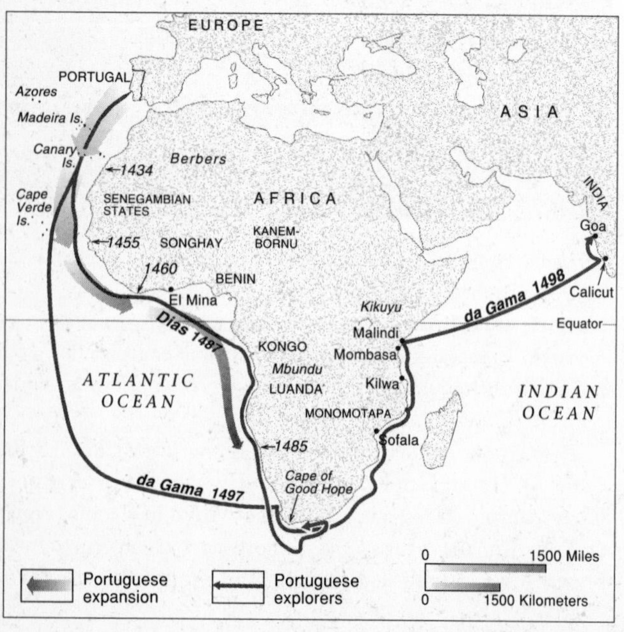

Although for a long time Portugal's major interest was in gold, pepper, and other products, a central element in this pattern was the slave trade. Slavery as an institution had been extensive in the Roman Empire, but had died out in most of Europe during the Middle Ages as it had been replaced by serfdom. In the Mediterranean and in Iberia, however, where there was an active military frontier between Christians and Muslims, it had remained important. Moreover, the trans-Saharan slave trade had brought small numbers of black Africans into the Mediterranean throughout the period. The Portuguese voyages now opened a direct channel to sub-Saharan Africa. The first slaves brought directly to Portugal from Africa arrived in 1441, and after that date slaves became a growing item in trade. The Portuguese and later other Europeans raided for slaves along the coast, but the numbers acquired in this way were comparatively small and after initial raids Europeans found that trade was a much more secure and profitable way to get these human cargoes. The Portuguese, for example, sent about 50 slaves per year to Portugal prior to 1450 when raiding was prevalent, but by 1460 some 500 slaves per year arrived in Portugal as a trade with African rulers developed. Acquired by raiding or trade, the effects on the victims were similar. An eyewitness to the unloading of slaves in Portugal in 1444 wrote:

> But what heart could be so hard as not to be pierced with piteous feelings to see that company? For some kept their heads low and their faces bathed in tears, looking one upon another; others stood groaning very dolorously, looking up to the height of heaven, fixing their eyes upon it, crying out loudly, as if asking help of the Father of Nature.

The trade was given an added impetus when the Portuguese and the Spanish began to develop sugar plantations on the Atlantic islands of Madeira (Portugal), the Canaries (Spain), and off the African coast on Portuguese São Tomé. Sugar production demanded many workers and constant labor under difficult conditions, usually in a tropical or subtropical environment. The plantation system of organization associated with sugar, in which managers were able to control and direct laborers over long periods with little restraint, was later extended to America and then to other crops. While it did not depend only on Africans, they became the primary plantation laborers in the Atlantic world. The slave trade grew significantly in volume and complexity after 1550 as the American plantation colonies, especially Brazil, began to develop. By 1600 the slave trade predominated over all other kinds of commerce on the African coast.

THE STRUCTURE OF THE ATLANTIC SLAVE TRADE

Although considerable debate and controversy surrounds many aspects of the history of slavery, it is perhaps best to start with the numbers. Estimates of the volume of the trade have varied widely and scholars still debate the figures and their implications, but the range of calculations has been narrowed by recent research. Between 1450 and 1850 it is estimated that about 12 million Africans were shipped across the Atlantic, and with a mortality rate of 10 to 20 percent on the ships, about ten or eleven million Africans actually arrived in the Americas. How many people died in Africa as a result of the slaving wars or in the forced marches to the coast is unknown, but estimates have been as high as one-third of the total captured.

TREND TOWARD EXPANSION

The volume changed over time. In the 16th century, numbers were relatively small, but they increased to perhaps 16,000 per year in the 17th century. The 18th century was the great age of the Atlantic slave trade; probably over seven million slaves, or over 80 percent of all those embarked, were exported between 1700 and 1800. By the latter date about three million slaves resided in the Americas. Even in the 19th century, when slavery was under attack, the trade continued in volume to some places. Cuba received some 700,000 slaves and Brazil took over one million in that century alone.

The high volume of the slave trade was a necessity because in most of the slave regimes in the Caribbean and Latin America slave mortality was high and fertility was low (partly because more men than women were imported). Thus, over time there was usually a loss of population. The only way to maintain or expand the number of slaves was by importing more from Africa. The one exception to this pattern was the southern United States, where the slave population had a positive rate of growth due perhaps to the temperate climate and the fact that few worked in dangerous and unhealthy occupations like sugar and mining. By 1860 almost six million slaves worked in the Americas, but about four million of them lived in the southern United States, an area that depended more on natural population growth than on the Atlantic slave trade. In terms of total population, however, slaves in British North America were never more than one-fourth of the whole population, while in the British and French Caribbean they made up between 80 and 90 percent of the population.

The dimensions of the trade varied over time, reflecting the economic and political situation in the Americas. From 1530 to 1650, Spanish America and Brazil received the majority of African slaves, but after the English and French began to cultivate sugar in the Caribbean, the islands of Jamaica, Barbados, and St. Domingue (Haiti) became important terminals for the slavers. By the 18th century, Virginia and the Carolinas in North America had also become major destinations, although they never rivaled the Caribbean or Brazil.

If we view the whole history of the slave trade from about 1550 to 1850, it is possible to see the relative proportions of the trade. Brazil alone received between 3.5 and 5 million Africans, or about 42 percent of all those who reached the New World. The Caribbean islands, dedicated to sugar production, were the other major destination of Africans. The island colonies of St. Domingue and Jamaica each received over one million slaves in the 18th century alone.

It should be emphasized that these figures represent only the volume in the Atlantic slave trade. The older trans-Sahara, Red Sea, and East African slave trades in the hands of Muslim traders continued throughout the period and added another three million people to the total of Africans exported as slaves in this period.

The Atlantic trade drew slaves from across the continent and its concentration shifted over time. In the 16th century, the majority of slaves were exported from the Senegambia region but by the 17th century West-central Africa (modern Zaire and Angola) was the major supplier. It was joined by the areas of the Gold Coast and the Slave Coast—Dahomey and Benin—at the end of the century

TABLE 27.1

Slave Exports from Africa (1500 to the 19th Century)

Region	1500–1600 (1000s)	%	1600–1700 (1000s)	%	1700–1800 (1000s)	%	1800–1900 (1000s)	%	TOTALS (1000s)	%
Red Sea	200	17	200	7	200	3	450	8	1,050	6
Trans-Sahara	550	47	700	24	700	9	1,200	22	3,150	19
East Africa and Indian Ocean	100	9	100	4	400	5	442	8	1,042	6
Trans-Atlantic	325	28	1,868	65	6,133	83	3,330	61	11,656	69
									16,898	

Source: Adapted from Paul Lovejoy, *Transformations in Slavery. A History of Slavery in Africa* (1983).

TABLE 27.2

Destinations of African Slaves in the Atlantic Slave Trade

Region	Number in 1000s	%
British North America	523	5
Spanish America	1,687	15
British Caribbean	2,443	21
French Caribbean	1,655	15
Dutch Caribbean	500	4
Danish Caribbean	50	0.4
Brazil	4,190	37
Old World	297	2.6
	11,345	

Source: James Rawley, *The Transatlantic Slave Trade* (1981), 428.

when Benin alone was exporting over 10,000 slaves per year. In the following century, wars for control of the interior created the large states of Asante among the Akan peoples of the Gold Coast and of Dahomey among the Fon peoples. These wars were both the cause and the result of increasing slave exports from these regions.

DEMOGRAPHIC PATTERNS

The demographic patterns of the Atlantic slave trade also merit discussion. The trans-Saharan slave trade had carried a majority of women to be used as concubines and domestic servants in North Africa and the Middle East, but the Atlantic slave trade concentrated on men. The slave ships carried mostly young men. To some extent this was because planters and mine owners in the Americas were seeking workers for heavy labor and were not anxious to risk the purchase of children due to high levels of mortality. On the other hand, African societies that sold captives into slavery often preferred to sell the men and keep the women and children as domestic slaves or to extend existing kin groups.

The Atlantic trade seems to have had a demographic impact on at least certain parts of West and central Africa. One estimate is that the population of about 25 million in 1850 in those regions was about one-half what it would have been had there been no slave trade. It is true that the trans-Atlantic trade carried more men than women and more women than children, but captive women and children who remained in Africa swelled the numbers of enslaved people and skewed the proportion of women to men in the African enslaving societies. Finally, as the Atlantic trade developed, new crops, such as maize and manioc, were introduced to Africa that provided new food resources for the population and helped it recover from the losses to the slave trade.

ORGANIZATION OF THE TRADE

The patterns of contact and trade established by the Portuguese were at first followed by rival Europeans on the African coast. Control of the slave trade or a portion of it generally reflected the political situation in Europe. For one and one-half centuries until about 1630, the Portuguese controlled most of the coastal trade and were the major suppliers of their own colony of Brazil and the Spanish settlements in America. The growth of slave-based plantation colonies in the Caribbean and elsewhere led other Europeans to compete with the Portuguese. The Dutch became major competitors when they seized El Mina in 1637 and temporarily took Angola (1641–1648) in order to supply their conquests in northeastern Brazil. By the 1660s the English were anxious to have their own source of slaves for their growing colonies in Barbados, Jamaica, and Virginia. The Royal African Company was chartered for that purpose. The French made similar arrangements in the 1660s, but it was not until the 18th century that France became a major carrier. Even smaller European nations like Denmark had its agents and forts on the African coast. Each nation established merchant towns or trade forts at places such as Axim, Nembe, Bonny, Whydah, and Luanda from which a steady source of captives could be obtained.

For the Europeans stationed on the coast, Africa was also a graveyard because of the tropical diseases encountered. Less than ten percent of the employees of the Royal Africa Company who went to Africa ever returned to England, and the majority died in the first year out. European mortality among the crews of slave ships was also very high due to tropical diseases like malaria. The slave trade proved deadly to all involved, but at least for some of the Europeans there was choice, while for the enslaved Africans there was none.

European agents for the companies often had to deal directly with local rulers, paying a tax or offering "gifts." Various forms of currency were used: iron bars, brass rings, cowrie shells. Traders calculated slaves and European goods in units of these currencies. The Spanish developed a complicated system in which a healthy adult male was called an "Indies piece," while children and women were valued at fractions of that value. Slaves were brought to the coast by a variety of means. Sometimes, as in Angola, European military campaigns produced captives for slaves or African and mulatto agents would purchase captives at interior trade centers. In Dahomey, a royal monopoly was established to control the flow of slaves. Some groups used their position to tax or control the movement of slaves from the interior to the coast. Although African and European states sought to establish monopolies over the trade, often private merchants circumvented restrictions.

Clearly, the slave trade was a trade that involved both Europeans and Africans. It was also not always clear which side was in control. One group of English merchants on the Gold Coast complained of African insolence in 1784 because in negotiations the Africans had emphasized that "the country belongs to them." In any case, the result of this collaboration was to send millions of Africans into bondage in foreign lands.

Historians have long debated the profitability of the slave trade. Some have argued that the profits were so great and constant that they constituted a major element in the rise of commercial capitalism and, later, the origins of the Industrial Revolution. Undoubtedly, many people derived a profit from the trade in Africans. An individual slaving voyage might gain a profit of as much as 300 percent and merchants in the ports that specialized in fitting out ships for the slave trade, such as Liverpool, England, or Nantes, France—as well as African suppliers—derived a profit from the slave trade. But the slave trade also involved considerable risks and costs, so that in the long run profitability levels did not maintain such high returns. In the late 18th century, profitability in the English slave trade probably ran between five and ten percent on the average and in the French and Dutch trades it was slightly lower. The slave trade was little more profitable in the long run than most business activities of the age, and as such it alone was not a major source for the capital needed in the Industrial Revolution.

It is more difficult, however, to calculate the full economic importance of slavery to the economies of Europe because it was so directly linked to the plantation and mining economies of the Americas. During some periods a "triangular" trade existed in which slaves were carried to the Americas; sugar, tobacco, and other goods were then carried to Europe; and then European products were sent to the coast of Africa to begin the triangle again. Were profits from the slave trade accumulated in Liverpool invested in the nascent textile industry of England? And if so, how important were these for the growth of that industry? The value of goods produced in Europe for exchange in the slave trade as well as the profits derived from the colonies would need to be calculated in order to adequately measure the importance of slavery to the growth of the European economies. Still, the very persistence of the trade indicates its viability. The slave trade surely contributed to the formation of emerging capitalism in the Atlantic world and made Africa very much a part of the process. In Africa itself, the slave trade often had the effect of deforming economies into dependence on trade with Europeans and suppressing the growth of alternative economic activities.

The debate over the slave trade continues. Whatever its long-range implications, by the late 18th century it is clear that the slave trade and slavery were essential aspects of the economy of the Atlantic basin, and their importance was increasing. Over 40 percent of all the slaves that crossed the Atlantic embarked in the century after 1760, and the plantation economies of Brazil, the Caribbean, and the southern United States were booming in the early 19th century. The slave trade was profitable enough to keep merchants in it, and it contributed in some way to the expanding economy of western Europe. It was also the major way in which Africa was linked to the increasingly integrated economy of the world.

AFRICAN SOCIETIES, SLAVERY, AND THE SLAVE TRADE

Europeans in the age of the slave trade sometimes justified enslavement of Africans by pointing out that slavery already existed on that continent. However, while forms of bondage were ancient in Africa, and the Muslim trans-Saharan and Red Sea trades were long-standing, the Atlantic trade interacted with and transformed these earlier aspects of slavery.

African societies had developed many forms of bondage and servitude that varied from a kind of peasant status to something much more like chattel slavery in which people are considered things—"property with a soul," as Aristotle put it. African states were usually nonegalitarian and since in many African societies all land was owned by the state or the "ruler," the control of slaves was one of the few, if not the only way, in which individuals or lineages could increase their wealth and status. Slaves were employed in many ways as servants, concubines, soldiers, administrators, and field workers. In some cases, as in the ancient empire of Ghana and in Kongo, there were whole villages of enslaved dependents who were required to pay tribute to the ruler. The Muslim traders of West Africa who linked the forest region to the savanna had slave porters as well as villages of slaves to supply their caravans. In a number of situations, these forms of servitude were relatively benign and were an extension of lineage and kinship systems. In others, however, they were exploitative economic and social relations that reinforced the hierarchies of various African

The size of African cities and the power of African rulers often impressed European observers. Here the city of Loango, capital of a kingdom on the Congo coast, is depicted as a bustling urban center. At this time it was a major port in the slave trade.

societies and allowed the nobles, senior lineages, and rulers to exercise their power. Among the forest states of West Africa, such as Benin, and in the Kongo kingdom in central Africa slavery was already an important institution prior to the European arrival, but the Atlantic trade opened up new opportunities for expansion and intensification of slavery in those societies.

Despite considerable variation in African societies and the fact that slaves sometimes attained positions of command and trust, in most cases slaves were denied choice about their lives and actions. They were placed in dependent or inferior positions, and they were often considered aliens. It is important to remember that the enslavement of women was a central feature of African slavery. Although slaves were used in many ways in African societies, domestic slavery and extension of lineages through the addition of female members remained a central feature in many places. Some historians believe that the excess of women led to polygyny and the creation of large harems by rulers and merchants, whose power was increased by this process while the position of women was lowered in some societies.

In the Sudanic states of the savanna, Islamic concepts of slavery had been introduced. Slavery was viewed as a legitimate fate for nonbelievers but an illegal treatment for Muslims. Despite the complaints of legal scholars like the Ahmad Baba of Timbuktu (1556–1627) against the enslavement of Muslims, many of the Sudanic states enslaved their captives both pagan and Muslim. In the Niger Valley many slave communities produced agricultural surpluses for the rulers and nobles of Songhay, Gao, and other states. Slaves were used for gold mining and salt production, and as caravan workers in the Sahara. Slavery was a widely diffused form of labor control and wealth in Africa.

The existence of slavery in Africa and the preexisting trade in people allowed Europeans to mobilize the commerce in slaves relatively quickly by tapping existing routes and supplies. In this venture they were aided by the rulers of certain African states who were anxious to acquire more slaves for themselves and to supply slaves to the Europeans in exchange for aid and commodities. In the 16th century Kongo kingdom, the ruler had an army of 20,000 slaves as part of his household, and this gave him greater power than any Kongo ruler had ever held. In general, African rulers did not enslave their own people, except for crimes or in other unusual circumstances, but rather sought to enslave their neighbors. Thus, expanding, centralizing states were often the major suppliers of slaves to the Europeans as well as to societies in which slavery was an important institution.

SLAVING AND AFRICAN POLITICS

As one French agent put it, "the trade in slaves is the business of kings, rich men, and prime merchants." European merchants and royal officials were able to tap existing routes, markets, and institutions, but the new and constant demand also intensified enslavement in Africa and perhaps changed the nature of slavery itself in some African societies.

In the period between 1500 and 1750 as the gunpowder empires and expanding international commerce of Europe penetrated sub-Saharan Africa, existing states and societies were often transformed. Although, as we saw in Chapter 14, the empire of Songhay controlled a vast region of the western savanna until its defeat by a Moroccan invasion in 1591, for the most part the many states of central and western Africa were relatively small and fragmented. This led to a situation of instability caused by competition and warfare as states sought to expand at the expense of their neighbors or to consolidate power by incorporating subject provinces. The warrior or soldier emerged in this situation as an important social type in states such as the Kongo kingdom and Dahomey, as well as along the Zambezi River. The incessant wars promoted the importance of the military and made the sale of captives into the slave trade an extension of the politics of regions of Africa. Sometimes, as among the Muslim states of the savanna or the Lake Chad region, wars took on a religious overtone of believers against nonbelievers, but in much of West and central Africa that was not the case. Some authors see this situation as an endemic aspect of African politics; others feel it is the result of European demand for new slaves. In either case, the result was the capture and sale of millions of human beings. While increasing centralization and hierarchy could be seen in the enslaving African societies, a contrary trend of self-sufficiency and antiauthoritarian ideas developed among those peoples who bore the brunt of the slaving attacks.

One result of the presence of Europeans on the coast was a shift in the locus of power within Africa. Whereas states like Ghana and Songhay in the savanna had taken advantage of their position as intermediaries between the gold of the West African forests and the trans-Saharan trade routes, now those states closer to the coast or in contact with the Europeans could play a similar role. Those right on the coast tried to monopolize the trade with Europeans, but European meddling in their internal affairs and European fears of any coastal power that became too strong blocked the creation of centralized states under the shadow of European forts. Just beyond the coast it was different. With access to European goods, especially firearms, iron, horses, cloth, tobacco, and other goods, West and central African kingdoms began to redirect trade toward the coast and to expand their influence. Some historians have written of a gun and slave cycle in which increased firepower allowed these states to expand over their neighbors, producing more slaves that then could be exchanged for more guns. The result was unending warfare and the disruption of societies as the search for slaves pushed ever farther into the interior.

ASANTE AND DAHOMEY

Perhaps the effects of the slave trade on African societies are best seen in some specific cases. A number of large states developed in West Africa during the slave trade era. Each, in its own way, represented a response to the realities of the European presence and to the process of state formation long under way in Africa. Rulers in these states grew in power and often surrounded themselves with ritual authority and a luxurious court life as a way of reinforcing the position that their armies had won.

In the area called the Gold Coast by the Europeans, the empire of Asante (Ashanti) rose to prominence in the period of the slave trade. The Asante were members of the Akan people (the major group of modern Ghana) who had settled in and around Kumasi, a region of gold and kola nut production that lay between the coast and the Hausa and Mande trading centers to the north. There were at least 20 small states based on the matrilineal clans that were common to all the Akan peoples, but those of the Oyoko clan predominated. Their cooperation and their access to firearms after 1650 initiated a period of centralization and expansion. Under the vigorous Osei Tutu (d. 1717) the title of *asantehene* was created as supreme civil and religious leader. His golden stool became the symbol of an Asante union that was created by linking the many Akan clans under the authority of the asantehene but recognizing the autonomy of subordinate areas. An all-Asante council advised the ruler, and an ideology of unity was was used to overcome the traditional clan divisions. With this new structure and a series of military reforms, conquest of the area began. By 1700 the Dutch on the coast realized that a new power had emerged, and they began to deal directly with it.

With control of the gold-producing zones and a constant supply of prisoners to be sold as slaves for more firearms, Asante maintained its power until the 1820s as the dominant state of the Gold Coast. Although gold continued to be a major item of export, by the end of the 17th century the value of slaves made up almost two-thirds of Asante's trade.

Farther to the east in the area of the Bight of Benin (between the Volta and Benin rivers on what the Europeans called the Slave Coast), a number of large states developed in the slave trade era. The kingdom of Benin was at the height of its power when the Europeans arrived. It traced its origins to the city of Ife and to the Yoruba peoples that were its neighbors, but it had become a separate and independent kingdom with its own well-developed political and artistic traditions, especially in the casting of bronze. As early as 1516 the ruler, or oba, limited the slave trade from Benin, and for a long time most of the trade with Europeans was controlled directly by the king and was in pepper, textiles, and ivory rather than slaves. Eventually European pressure and the goals of the Benin nobility combined to generate a significant slave trade in the 18th century, but Benin never made the slave trade its primary source of revenue or state policy.

The kingdom of Dahomey, which developed among the Fon (or Aja) peoples, used a different strategy of response to the European presence. It began to emerge as a power in the 17th century from its center at Abomey about 70 miles from the coast. Its kings ruled with the advice of councils that had considerable power, but by the 1720s access to firearms allowed the rulers to create an autocratic and sometimes brutal political regime based on the slave trade. In the 1720s, under king Agaja (1708–1740), the kingdom of Dahomey moved toward the coast, seizing in 1727 the port town of Whydah, which had attracted a large number of European traders. Although Dahomey became to some extent a subject of the powerful neighboring Yoruba state of Oyo, whose cavalry and archers made it strong, Dahomey maintained its autonomy and turned increasingly to the cycle of firearms and slaves. The trade was controlled by the royal court, whose armies (including a regiment of women) were used to raid for more captives. As Dahomey expanded it eliminated the royal families and customs of the areas it conquered and imposed its own traditions. This resulted in the formation of a unified state that proved more lasting than some of its neighbors.

Well into the 19th century, Dahomey was a slaving state. Dependence on the trade in human beings had negative effects on the society as a whole. The large-scale sacrifice of human victims in the annual renewal festival, or Customs, at the royal court was one example of the cheapening of life that the trade produced. Historians argue about whether the expansion of Dahomey was driven by the desire for more slaves or by an attempt to unify all the Aja peoples, but in any case, slavery played a central role in the history of the area. Over 1.8 million slaves were exported from the Bight of Benin between 1640 and 1890.

Emphasis on the slave trade should not obscure the creative process within many of the African states. The growing devine authority of the rulers paralleled in some ways the rise of absolutism in Europe. It led to the development of new political forms, some of which had the power to limit the role of the king. In the Yoruba state of Oyo, for example, a governing council shared power with the ruler. In some states, a balance of offices kept central power in check. In Asante the traditional village chiefs and officials whose authority was based on their lineage were increasingly challenged by new officials appointed by the asantehene, as a state bureaucracy began to form.

The creativity of these societies was also seen in traditional arts. In many places, crafts such as bronze casting, woodcarving, and weaving flourished. Guilds of artisans developed in a number of societies and their specialization produced crafts executed with great skill. In Benin and the Yoruba states, for example, remarkable and lifelike sculptures in wood and ivory continued to be produced. Often, however, the best artisans labored for the royal court, producing objects designed to honor the ruling family and reinforce the civil and religious authority of the king. This was true in architecture, weaving, and the decorative arts as well. Much of this artistic production also had a religious function or contained religious symbolism as African artists made the spiritual world visually apparent.

EAST AFRICA AND THE SUDAN

West Africa was obviously the region most directly influenced by the trans-Atlantic slave trade, but there and elsewhere in Africa, long-term patterns of society and economy continued and intersected with the new external influences.

On the East Coast of Africa, the Swahili trading cities continued their commerce in the Indian Ocean and the Arabian Sea, accommodating to the military presence of the Portuguese and the Ottoman Turks. Trade to the interior continued to bring ivory, gold, and a steady supply of slaves. Many of these slaves were destined for the harems and households of Arabia and the Middle East, but also a small percent were carried away by the Europeans for their plantation colonies. The Portuguese and Indo-Portuguese settlers along the Zambezi River in Mozambique made use of slave soldiers to increase their territories, and certain groups in interior East Africa specialized in supplying ivory and slaves to the East African coast. Europeans did establish some plantation-style colonies on islands like Mauritius in the Indian Ocean, and these depended on the East African slave trade.

On Zanzibar and other offshore islands, and later on the coast itself, Swahili, Indian, and Arabian merchants actually followed the European model and set up plantations producing cloves, using African slave laborers. Some of the plantations were large, and by the 1860s Zanzibar had a slave population of around 100,000. The sultan of Zanzibar alone owned over 4000 slaves in 1870. Slavery became an extensive feature of the East African coast, and the slave trade from the interior to these plantations and to the traditional slave markets of the Red Sea continued until the end of the 19th century.

Much less is known about the interior of eastern Africa. The well-watered and heavily populated region of the great lakes of the interior supported large and small kingdoms. Bantu-speakers predominated but a number of peoples inhabited the region. Linguistic and archeological evidence suggests that pastoralist Nilotic peoples from the Upper Nile Valley with a distinctive late iron age technology had moved southward into what is today western Kenya and Uganda where they came into contact with Bantu-speakers and with the farmers and herdsmen who were speakers of another group of languages called Cushitic. The Bantu states absorbed the immigrants, even when at times the newcomers established ruling dynasties. Later Nilotic migrations, especially of the Luo peoples, resulted in the construction of a number of related dynasties among the states in the area of the large lakes of east-central Africa. At Bunyoro, the Luo eventually established a ruling dynasty among the existing Bantu population. This composite kingdom exercised considerable power in the 16th and 17th centuries. Other related and similar states formed in the region. In Buganda, near Lake Victoria, a strong monarchy ruled a heterogeneous population and dominated the region in the 18th century. These developments in the interior, as important as they were for the history of the region, were less influenced by the growing contact with the outside world than were other regions of Africa.

Across the continent in the northern savanna at the end of the 18th century, the process of Islamization, which had been important in the days of the empires of Mali and Songhay, entered a new and violent stage that not only linked Islamization to both the external slave trades and the growth of slavery in Africa, but also produced other long-term effects in the region. After the break up of Songhay in the 16th century, a number of successor states had developed. Some, such as the Bambara kingdom of Segu, were pagan. Others, such as the Hausa kingdoms in Northern Nigeria, were ruled by Muslim royal families and urban aristocracies but continued to contain large numbers of animist subjects, most of whom were rural peasants. In these states the degree of Islamization was slight, and an accommodation between Muslims and animists was achieved. Beginning in the 1770s Muslim reform movements began to sweep the western Sudan. Religious brotherhoods advocating a purifying Sufi variant of Islam extended their influence throughout the Muslim trade networks in the Senegambia region and the western Sudan. This movement had an intense impact on the Fulani (Fulbe), a pastoral people who were spread across a broad area of the western Sudan.

In 1804 Usuman Dan Fodio, a studious and charismatic Muslim Fulani scholar, began to preach the reformist ideology in the Hausa kingdoms. His movement became a revolution when in 1804, seeing himself as God's instrument, he preached a jihad against the Hausa kings whom he felt were not following the teachings of the Prophet. A great upheaval followed in which the Fulani took control of most of the Hausa states of northern Nigeria in the western Sudan. A new kingdom, based on the city of Sokoto, developed under Dan Fodio's son and brother. The Fulani expansion was driven not only by religious zeal but by political ambitions, as the attack on the well-established Muslim kingdom of Bornu demonstrated. The result of this upheaval was the creation of a powerful Sokoto state under a caliph, whose authority was established over cities such as Kano and Zaria and whose rulers became emirs of provinces within the Sokoto caliphate.

By the 1840s the effects of Islamization and the Fulani expansion were felt across much of the interior of West Africa. New political units were created, a reformist Islam that sought to eliminate pagan practices was spread, and social and cultural changes took place in the wake of these changes. Literacy, for example, became more widely dispersed and new centers of trade, such as Kano, emerged in this period. Later jihads established other new states along similar lines. All of these changes had long-term effects on the region of the western Sudan.

These upheavals—moved by religious, political, and economic motives—were not unaffected by the external pressures on Africa. They fed into the ongoing processes of the external slave trades and the development of slavery within African societies. Large numbers of captives resulting from the wars were exported down to the coast for sale to the Europeans, while another stream of slaves crossed the Sahara to North Africa. In the western and central Sudan the level of slave labor rose, especially in the larger towns and along the trade routes. Slave villages, supplying royal courts and merchant activities as well as a sort of plantation system, developed to produce peanuts and other crops. Slave women spun cotton and wove cloth for sale, slave artisans worked in the towns, and slaves served the caravan traders, but most slaves did agricultural labor. By the late 19th century regions of the savanna contained large slave populations—in some places as much as 30 to 50 percent of the whole population. From the Senegambia region of Futa Jallon, across the Niger and Senegal basins, and to the east of Lake Chad, slavery became a central feature of the Sudanic states and remained so through the 19th century.

WHITE SETTLERS AND AFRICANS IN SOUTHERN AFRICA

One area of Africa little affected by the slave trade in the early modern period was the southern end of the continent. As we saw in Chapter 17 this region was still occupied by non-Bantu hunting peoples, the San (Bushmen), and by the Khoikhoi (Hottentots) who lived by hunting and sheep herding, and, after contact with the Bantu, cattle-herding peoples as well. Peoples practicing farming and using iron tools were living south of the Limpopo River by the 3d century A.D. Probably Bantu-speakers, they spread southward and established their villages and cattle herds in the fertile lands along the eastern coast, where rainfall was favorable to their agricultural and pastoral way of life. The drier western regions toward the Kalahari Desert were left to the Khoikhoi and San. Mixed farming and pastoralism spread throughout the region in a complex process that involved migration, peaceful contacts, and warfare.

By the 16th century, Bantu-speaking peoples occupied much of the eastern regions of southern Africa. They practiced agriculture and herding; worked iron and copper into tools, weapons, and adornments; and traded with their neighbors. They spoke related languages such as Tswana, Sotho, as well as the Nguni languages such as Zulu and Xhosa. Among the Sotho, villages might have contained as many as 200 people, but the Nguni lived in hamlets made up of a few extended families. Men served as artisans and herdsmen; women did the farming and housework, and sometimes organized their labor communally. Politically, chiefdoms of various sizes—many small, but a few with as many as 50,000 inhabitants—characterized the southern Bantu peoples. Chiefs held power with the support of relatives and with the acceptance of the people, but there was considerable variation in chiefly authority. The Bantu-speaking peoples' pattern of political organization and the splitting off of junior lineages to form new villages created a process of expansion that led to competition for land and absorption of newly conquered groups. This situation became intense at the end of the 18th century, either because of the pressures and competition for foreign trade through the Portuguese outposts on the East African coast or because of the growth of population among the southern Bantu. In any case, the result was farther expansion southward into the path of another people who had arrived in southern Africa.

In 1652 the Dutch East India Company established a colony at the Cape of Good Hope to serve as a provisioning ground for ships sailing to Asia. On the fertile lands around this colony relatively large farms developed. The Cape colony depended on slave labor brought from Indonesia and Asia for a while, but it soon enslaved local Africans as well. The expanding colony and its labor needs led to a series of wars with the San and Hottentot populations, who were pushed farther to the north and west. By the 1760s the Dutch, or Boer, farmers had crossed the Orange River in search of new lands. They viewed the fertile plains and hills as theirs, and they saw the Africans only as intruders and as a possible source of labor. Competition and warfare resulted. Around 1800 the Cape colony had about 17,000 settlers (or Afrikaners as they came to be called), 26,000 slaves, and 14,000 Khoikhoi.

At the same time that the Boers were pushing northward, the southern Bantu were extending their movement to the south. Matters were also complicated by European events when Great Britain seized the Cape colony in 1795 and then took it under formal British control in 1815. While the British government helped the settlers to clear out Africans from potential farming lands, government attempts to limit the Boer settlements and their use of African labor were unsuccessful. Meanwhile competition for farming and grazing land led to a series of wars between the settlers and the Bantu during the early 19th century.

Various government measures, the increasing arrival of English-speaking immigrants, and the lure of better lands caused groups of Boers to move to the north. These "voortrekkers" moved into lands occupied by the southern Nguni, eventually creating a number of autonomous Boer states. After 1834, when Britain abolished slavery and imposed restrictions on landholding, groups of Boers staged a "great trek" far to the north to be free of government interference. This movement eventually brought them across the Orange River and into Natal on the more fertile east coast, which the Boers believed to be only sparsely inhabited by Africans. They did not realize at the time that the lack of population was due to a great military upheaval taking place among the Bantu peoples of the region.

THE "MFECANE" AND THE ZULU RISE TO POWER

Among the Nguni peoples, major changes had taken place. A process of unification had begun among some of the northern chiefdoms, and a new military organization had emerged. In 1818 leadership fell to Shaka, a brilliant military tactician who reformed the loose forces into regiments organized by lineage and age. Iron discipline and new tactics were introduced, including the use of a short stabbing-spear to be used at close range. The army was made a permanent institution, and the regiments were housed together in separate villages. The fighting men were only allowed to marry after their service had been completed. Shaka's own Zulu chiefdom became the center of this new military and political organization that began to absorb or destroy its neighbors. Shaka demonstrated considerable talents as a politician, destroying the ruling families of those groups he incorporated into the growing Zulu state. He ruled with an iron hand, destroying his enemies, acquiring their cattle, and crushing any opposition. His policies brought power to the Zulu, but his erratic and cruel behavior also earned him enemies among his own people. Though he was assassinated in 1828, Shaka's reforms remained in place and his successors built on the structure he had created. Zulu power was still growing in the 1840s, and the Zulu remained the most impressive military force in black Africa until the end of the century.

The rise of the Zulu and other Nguni chiefdoms was the beginning of the *mfecane*, or wars of crushing and wandering. As Zulu control expanded, a series of campaigns and forced migrations led to incessant fighting, as other peoples sought to survive by fleeing, emulating, or joining the Zulu. Groups spun off to the north and south, raiding the Portuguese on the coast, clashing with the Europeans to the south, and fighting with neighboring chiefdoms. New African states, such as the Swazi, that adapted aspects of the Zulu model emerged among the survivors. One state, Lesotho, successfully resisted the Zulu example. It combined Sotho and Nguni speakers and defended itself against Nguni armies. It eventually developed as a kingdom far less committed to military organization and one in which the people exercised considerable influence on their leaders.

The whole of the southern continent, from the Cape colony to Lake Malawi, had been thrown into turmoil by raiding parties, remnants, and refugees. Superior firepower allowed the Boers to continue to hold their lands, but it was not until the Zulu Wars of the 1870s that Zulu power was crushed by Great Britain—and even then only at great cost. During the process, the basic patterns of conflict between Africans and Europeans in the largest settler colony on the continent were created. These patterns included a competition between settlers and Africans for

This Zulu royal kraal drawn in the 1830s gives some idea of the power of the Zulu at the time that Shaka was forging Zulu dominance during the *mfecane*.

land, the expanding influence of European governmental control, and the desire of Europeans to make use of Africans as laborers.

ANALYSIS
SLAVERY AND HUMAN SOCIETY

Slavery is a very old and pervasive institution. It has been found at different times all over the globe, among relatively simple societies and in the great centers of civilization. In some of these societies, it has been an essentially marginal or secondary form of labor, while in others it became the predominant labor form or "mode of production" (in the jargon of Marxist analysis). The need for labor beyond the capacity of the individual or the family unit is very old, and as soon as authority, law, or custom could be established to set the conditions for coercion, the tribe, the state, the priests, or some other group or institution extracted labor by force. Coerced labor, of course, could take different forms. There are important distinctions between indentured servants, convict laborers, debt-peons, and chattel slaves.

While most societies placed some limits on the slaveholder's authority or power, the denial of the slave's control over his or her own labor and life choices was characteristic of this form of coercion throughout history. In most societies that had a form of chattel slavery, the slave was denied a sense of belonging in the society, the idea of kinship. The honor associated with family or lineage was the antithesis of slavery. Joseph in Egypt, the viziers of the sultans of Turkey might rise to high positions, but the fact that they were slaves meant that they were essentially instruments of their masters' will. In fact, because they were slaves and thus unconstrained by kinship or other ties and obligations, they could be trusted in positions of command.

Because slaves became nonpersons, or as one modern author has put it, because they suffered a "social death," it was always easier to enslave "others" or "outsiders," those who were different in some way. Hebrews enslaved Canaanites, Greeks enslaved "barbarians," and Muslims made slaves of nonbelievers. If the difference between slave and master was readily seen, it made enforcement of slave status that much easier. Racism as such did not cause modern slavery, but differences in culture, language, color, or other physical characteristics had always facilitated enslavement. The familiarity of Europeans and Muslims with black Africans in an enslaved status contributed to the development of modern racism. To paraphrase the English historian Charles Boxer, no people can enslave another for 400 years without developing an attitude of superiority.

Slavery was not only a general phenomenon that existed in many societies; rarely questioned on any grounds, it was recognized as a necessary and "natural" phenomenon. Slavery appears and is accepted in the texts of ancient India, the Old Testament, and the writings of 5th century Greece. Aristotle specifically argued that some people were born to rule and others to serve. In Christian theology, while all people might be free in spirit in the kingdom of God, in the real world, servitude was a necessary reality. Voices might be raised arguing for fair treatment or against the enslavement of a particular group, but the condition of servitude itself was usually taken as part of the natural order of the world.

In this context, the attack on slavery in Western culture that grew from the Enlightenment and the social and economic changes in western Europe and its Atlantic colonies at the end of the 18th century was really a remarkable turning point in world history. Whether one believes that slavery was an atavistic labor form that was incompatible with industrial capitalism and was, therefore, abolished or that it was destroyed essentially because its immorality became all too obvious, its demise was relatively quick. In about one and one-half centuries, the moral and religious underpining of chattel slavery was cut away and its economic justifications seriously questioned. Although slavery lingered on in at least a few places well into the 20th century, few people were willing to defend the institution publicly.

While slavery historically existed in many places it has become intimately associated with Africa because of the scope of the Atlantic slave trade and the importance of slavery in the formation of the modern world system. There was nothing inevitable about Africa becoming the primary source of laborers in the modern world. Europeans did make use of American Indians and European indentured workers when they could, but historical precedents, maritime technology, and availability all contributed to the process which made Africa the source of labor for the expanding plantation colonies of Europe.

African slavery obviously played an important role in the shaping of the modern world. The African slave trade was one of the first truely international trades, and it created an easy access to labor that enabled Europeans to carry out the exploitation of the Americas. Some have argued that it was an important, even a necessary feature in the rise of capitalism and the international division of labor. Others are less convinced. In this question, as in virtually every other question regarding modern slavery, controversies still abound.

In the context of African history, the interpretation of slavery is still in the process of rapid change. The estimate of the volume involved in the Atlantic trade (10–12 million) has been seriously questioned, especially by African scholars who see these new figures as an attempt to lessen the extent of the exploitation of Africa. Another debate centers on the impact of the trade on the population and societies within Africa. The slave trade was important to the economy of the Atlantic, but how important was this external trade in Africa itself? Early researchers, reacting to the preabolitionist European self-justifications that the slave trade was no great crime because Africans were long familiar with slavery and were selling already enslaved individuals, argued that African "slavery" was often an extension of kinship or other forms of dependency and was quite unlike the chattel slavery of western Europe. But further research has demonstrated that in many African societies, slavery was an integral and essential part of the economy and that while specific conditions might vary considerably from the Americas, the servile condition in Africa had much in common with chattel slavery. The Sokoto caliphate in the 19th century, for example, had a proportion of slaves similar to Brazil or the southern United States. Slave societies did exist in Africa.

Now controversy rages over the extent to which the development of African slavery resulted from the long-term impact of the slave trade and European demand for captive labor. African societies did not live in isolation from the pressures and examples of the wider world economy into which they were drawn. The extent to which that contact transformed slavery in Africa is now in question. These controversies among historians reflect current concerns and a realization that the present social and political situation in Africa and in many places in the Americas continues to bear the burden of a historical past in which slavery played an essential role. In the evaluation of slavery as in all other historical questions, what we think about the present shapes our inquiry and interpretation of the past.

Questions: Why did Africa become the leading source of slaves in the early modern world economy? What are some of the leading issues in the interpretation of African slavery? What were the roles of Africans and Europeans in the early modern slave trade?

THE AFRICAN DIASPORA

The slave trade was the means by which the history of the Americas and Africa became linked and a principal way in which African societies were drawn into the world economy. The import into Africa of European firearms, Indian textiles, Indonesian cowrie shells, and American tobacco in return for African ivory, gold, and especially slaves demonstrated Africa's integration into the mercantile structure of the world. Africans involved in the trade learned to deal effectively with this situation. The price of slaves rose steadily in the 18th century and the terms of trade increasingly favored African dealers. In many African ports, such as Whydah, Porto Novo, and Luanda, an African or Afro-European community developed that specialized in the slave trade and used their position as middlemen to advantage.

SLAVE LIVES

For those carried in the trade, such considerations had little meaning. For them slavery meant destruction of their villages or capture in war, separation from friends and family, and then the forced march to an interior trading town or to the slave pens at the towns or forts of the coast. Conditions during the process were deadly and perhaps as many as one-third of the captives died along the way or in the slave pens. Eventually the slaves were loaded onto the ships. Cargo size varied and could go as high as 700 slaves packed and crowded into the dank, unhealthy conditions of the slave ships, but most cargoes were smaller and overcrowding was less of a factor in mortality than the length of the voyage or the point of origin in Africa—the Bights of Benin and Biafra being particularly unhealthy. The average rate of mortality for slaves varied over time but ran at about 18 to 20 percent until the 18th century when it declined somewhat. Still, on individual ships losses could be catastrophic, as on a Dutch ship of 1737 where 700 of the 716 slaves perished on the voyage.

The so-called Middle Passage, or slave voyage to the Americas, was a traumatic experience for the slaves. Taken from their homes, branded, confined, and shackled, they faced not only the dangers of poor hygiene, dysentery, disease, and bad treatment, but also the fear of being eaten or worse by the Europeans. Their situation led sometimes to suicide or to resistance and mutiny on the ships. However traumatic, the Middle Passage certainly did not strip Africans of their culture, and they arrived in the Americas with their languages, beliefs, artistic traditions, and strong memories of their past.

DOCUMENT
A SLAVE'S DESCRIPTION OF THE MIDDLE PASSAGE

During the era of the slave trade a number of enslaved Africans by one means or another succeeded in telling their stories. These accounts with their specific details of the injustice and inhumanities of slavery became particularly useful in the abolitionist crusade. The biography of Frederick Douglas is perhaps the most famous of these accounts.

The biography of Olaudah Equiano, an Ibo from what is today eastern Nigeria on the Niger River, presents a personal description of the enslavement process in Africa and the terrors of the Middle Passage. Equiano and his sister were kidnapped in 1756 by African slave hunters and sold to British slave traders. Separated from his sister, he was carried to the West Indies and later to Virginia where he became servant to a naval officer. He traveled widely on his master's military campaigns and was later sold to a Philadelphia Quaker merchant who eventually allowed him to buy his freedom. Later in life, he moved to England and became an active member in the movement to end slavery and the slave trade. His biography was published in 1789. The political uses of this kind of biography and Equiano's association with the abolitionists should caution us to take some care in accepting the account at face value, but it does convey the personal shock and anguish of those caught in the slave trade's web.

> The first object which saluted my eyes when I arrived on the coast was the sea, and a slaveship, which was riding at anchor, and waiting for its cargo. These filled me with astonishment, which was soon converted into terror, which I am yet at a loss to describe, nor the then feelings of my mind. When I was carried on board I was immediately handled, and tossed up, to see if I were sound, by some of the crew; and I was now persuaded that I had got into a world of bad spirits, and that they were going to kill me. Their complexions too differing so much from ours, their long hair, and the language they spoke, which was very different from any I had ever heard, united to confirm me in this belief. Indeed, such were the horrors of my views and fears at that moment, that if ten thousand worlds had been my own, I would have freely parted with them all to have exchanged my condition with that of the meanest slave in my own country. When I looked round the ship too, and saw a large furnace or copper boiler, and a multitude of black people of every description chained together, every one of their countenances expressing dejection and sorrow, I no longer doubted my fate; and, quite overpowered with horror and anguish, I fell motionless on the deck and fainted. When I recovered a little, I found some black people about me, who I believed were some of those who brought me on board, and had been receiving their pay; they talked to me in order to cheer me, but all in vain. I asked them if we were not to be eaten by those white men with horrible looks, red faces, and long hair. They told me I was not. . . . I now saw myself deprived of all chance of returning to my native country, or even the least glimpse of hope of gaining the shore, which I now considered as friendly; and I even wished for my former slavery, in preference to my present situation, which was filled with horrors of every kind, still heightened by my ignorance of what I was to undergo. I was not long suffered to indulge my grief; I was soon put down under decks, and there I received such a salutation in my nostrils as I had never experienced in my life; so that with the loathsomeness of the stench, and the crying together, I became so sick and low that I was not able to eat, nor had I the least desire to taste anything. I now wished for the last friend, death, to relieve me; but soon, to my grief two white men offered me eatables; and on my refusing to eat, one of them held me fast by the hands, and laid me across, I think, the windlass, and tied my feet while the other flogged me severely. I had never experienced anything of this kind before; and, although not being used to the water, I naturally feared that element the first time I saw it; yet, nevertheless, could I have got over the nettings, I would have jumped over the side; but I could not; and, besides the crew used to watch us very closely who were not chained down to the decks, lest we should leap into the water; and I have seen some of these poor African prisoners most severely cut for attempting to do so, and hourly whipped for not eating. This, indeed was often the case with myself. In a little time after amongst the poor chained men, I found some of my own nation, which in a small degree gave ease to my mind. I inquired of them what was to be done with us? They gave me to understand we were to be carried to these white people's country to work for them. I then was a little revived, and thought, if it were no worse

than working, my situation was not so desperate: but still I feared I should be put to death, the white people looked and acted, as I thought, in so savage a manner; for I had never seen among any people such instances of brutal cruelty; and this was not only shown to us blacks, but also to some of the whites themselves. . . .

At last when the ship we were in had got in all her cargo, they made ready with many fearful noises, and we were all put under deck, so that we could not see how they managed the vessel. But this disappointment was the least of my sorrow. The stench of the hold while we were on the coast was so intolerably loathsome, that it was dangerous to remain there for any time, and some of us had been permitted to stay on deck for the fresh air; but now the whole ship's cargo was confined together, it became absolutely pestilential. The closeness of the place, and the heat of the climate, added to the number in the ship, which was so crowded that each had scarcely room to turn himself, almost suffocated us. This produced copious perspirations, so that the air soon became unfit for respiration, from a variety of loathsome smells, and brought on a sickness amongst the slaves, of which many died, thus falling victims to the improvident avarice, as I may call it, of their purchasers. This wretched situation was again aggravated by the galling of the chains, now become insupportable; and the filth of the necessary tubs, into which the children fell, and were almost suffocated. The shrieks of the women, and the groans of the dying, rendered the whole a scene of horror almost inconceivable. . . .

Questions: In what ways does Equiano's description alter an understanding of the slave trade? What opportunities existed for the captives to resist? What effect might the experience of Africans on the slave ships have on their perceptions of each other and of the Europeans?

AFRICANS IN AMERICA

The destination of the slaves carried across the Atlantic was principally the plantations and mines of America. Landed estates using large amounts of often coerced labor became characteristic of American agriculture, at first in the production of sugar, and later for rice, cotton, and tobacco. The plantation system already used for producing sugar on the Atlantic islands of Spain and Portugal was transferred to the New World. After attempts to use Indian laborers in places like Brazil and Hispaniola, Africans were brought in. West Africans, in fact, coming from societies in which herding, metallurgy, and intensive agriculture were widely practiced were sought by Europeans for the specialized tasks of making sugar. In the English colonies of Barbados and Virginia, indentured servants from England were eventually replaced by enslaved Africans when either new crops, such as sugar, were introduced or when indentured servants became less available. In any case, the plantation system of farming with a dependent or enslaved work force characterized the production of many tropical and semitropical crops in demand in Europe, and thus the plantation became the locus of African and Afro-American life.

Slaves did many other things as well. As we saw in Chapter 24, gold mining in Brazil made extensive use of black slaves and the Spanish used slaves in the silver mines of Mexico. Urban slavery was characteristic of Latin American cities, where slaves were often artisans, street vendors, and household servants. In early 17th century Lima, Peru, capital of Spain's colony in South America, blacks outnumbered Europeans. Later cities, such as Charleston and New Orleans, would also develop a large slave and free Afro-American population. In short, there was virtually no occupation that slaves did not perform, although the vast majority lived their lives as agricultural laborers.

AMERICAN SLAVE SOCIETIES

Each American slave-based society reflected the variations of its European origin and its component African cultures, but there were certain similarities and common features. Each recognized distinctions between African-born "salt water" slaves who were almost invariably black (by European standards) and their American-born descendants, the Creole slaves, some of whom were mulattoes as a result of sexual exploitation of slave women or the process of miscegenation. In all the American slave societies, a hierarchy of status evolved in which free whites were at the top, slaves were at the bottom, and free people of color had an intermediate position. In this sense color and "race" played a role in American slavery it had not played in Africa. Among the slaves, slaveholders also created a hierarchy based on origin and color. Creole and especially mulatto slaves were given more opportunities to acquire skilled jobs

Africans were set to all kinds of labor in the Americas, from domestic service to mining and shipbuilding, but the vast majority worked on plantations like this sugar mill in the Caribbean.

or to work in the house as servants rather than in the fields or mines. They were also more likely to win their freedom by manumission.

This system of hierarchy was a creation of the slaveholders and did not necessarily reflect perceptions among the slaves. There is evidence that important African nobles or religious leaders, who for one reason or another were sold into slavery, continued to exercise authority within the slave community. Still, the distinctions between Creole and African slaves tended to divide that community, as did the distinctions between different African groups who maintained their ties and affiliations in America. Many of the slave rebellions in the Caribbean and Brazil were organized along African ethnic and political lines. In Jamaica there were a number of Akan-led rebellions in the 18th century and the largest escaped-slave community in 17th century Brazil was apparently organized and led by Angolans.

While economic organization and European concepts of hierarchy imposed a certain similarity in the various colonies in which Africans formed a part, the slave-based societies also varied in their composition. In the 18th century, for example, on the Caribbean islands where the Indian population had died out or had been exterminated and where few Europeans settled, Africans and their descendants formed the vast majority. In Jamaica and St. Domingue, slaves made up over 80 percent of the population, and because mortality levels were so high, a large proportion were African-born. Brazil also had large numbers of imported Africans, but its more diverse population and economy, as well as a tradition of manumitting slaves and high levels of miscegenation, meant that slaves made up only about 35 percent of the population. Free people of color, the descendants of former slaves, however, made up about another one-third, so that together slaves and free colored constituted two-thirds of the total population.

The Caribbean and Brazil differed significantly from the southern colonies of British North America, which depended less on imported Africans because of a positive rate of growth among the slave population. There, Creoles predominated but manumission was less common and free people of color were less than ten percent of the total Afro-American origin. The result was that slavery in North America was less influenced directly by Africa: By the mid-18th century, the slave population in most places in North America was reproducing itself. By 1850 less than one percent of the slaves there were African-born. The combination of natural growth and the relatively small direct trade from Africa reduced the degree of African cultural reinforcement in comparison with Cuba or Brazil.

THE PEOPLE AND GODS IN EXILE

Africans brought as slaves to America faced a peculiar series of problems. Working conditions were exhausting and life for most slaves was often "nasty, brutish, and short." Family formation was made difficult because of the general shortage of women carried in the slave trade, a situation made even worse where the ratio of men to women was sometimes as much as three to one. To this was added the insecurity of slave status in which family members might be separated by sale or by the masters' whim. Still, most slaves lived in family units even if their marriages were not always sanctioned by the religion of their masters.

Throughout the Americas, wherever Africans were brought, aspects of their language, religion, artistic sensibilities, and other elements of culture survived. To some extent the amount of continuity depended on the intensity and volume of the slave trade from a particular area. Yoruba culture, for example, was particularly strong in northeastern Brazil because the trade between it and the Bight of Benin was heavy and continuous in the early 19th century. During certain periods, Akan peoples predominated in Jamaica, while Ewe or Dahomeans predominated in Haiti. Some slaveholders tried to mix up the slaves on their plantations so that strong African identities would be lost, but colonial dependence on slavers who dealt continually with the same region tended to undercut such policies. In the reality of slavery in the Americas, Africans had to adapt and change and to incorporate other African peoples and their ideas and customs. Moreover, there were also the ways and customs of the masters that were both imposed and adopted. Thus, what emerged as Afro-American culture reflected specific African roots adapted to a new reality. Afro-American culture was dynamic and creative in this sense.

Religion was an obvious example of continuity and adaptation. Slaves were converted to Catholicism by Spaniards and Portuguese, and slaves were capable of fervent devotion as members of Black Catholic brotherhoods some of which were organized by African origins. Still, African religious ideas and practices did not die out, and many African slaves were accused of "witchcraft" by the Inquisition in those colonies. In the English islands, *obeah* was the name given to the African religious practices, and the men and women knowledgeable in them were held in high regard within the community. In Brazilian *candomble* (Yoruba) and Haitian *Vodun* (Aja), rather fully developed versions of African religion flourished and continue until the present, despite attempts to suppress them.

The reality of the Middle Passage meant that religious ideas and concepts were easier to transfer than the institutional aspects of religion. Without religious specialists or a priestly class, aspects of African religions were changed or transformed by contact with other African peoples as well as with colonial society. In many cases slaves held their new faith in Christianity and their African beliefs at the same time, and sought to fuse the two. For Muslim Africans this was less possible. In 1835 in Bahia, the largest slave rebellion in Brazil was organized by Muslim Yoruba and Hausa slaves and directed against the whites and against nonbelievers.

Resistance and rebellion were other aspects of African-American history. Recalcitrance, running away, and direct confrontation were present wherever slaves were held. As early as 1508 African runaways disrupted communications on Hispaniola, and in 1527 a plot to rebel was uncovered in Mexico City. Throughout the Americas communities of

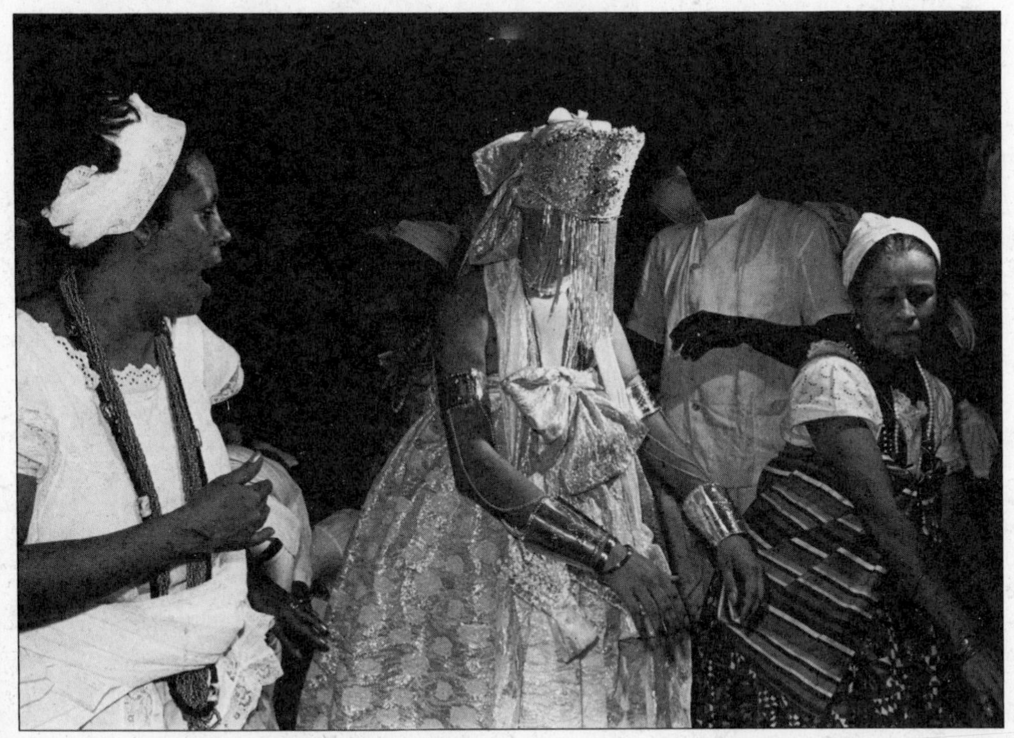

The cultures of Africa brought to the Americas were transformed in the new setting. African religions that were transferred to Brazil, for example, survived and were combined with local elements to form vibrant new faiths. Here a participant who has been "possessed" by one of the goddesses dances in her regalia.

runaway slaves formed. In Jamaica, Colombia, Venezuela, Haiti, and Brazil runaway communities were continuous and persistent. In Brazil, during the 17th century, Palmares, an enormous runaway slave kingdom with numerous villages and a population of perhaps 8,000 to 10,000 people, resisted Portuguese and Dutch attempts to destroy it for a century. Although its inhabitants were both Creoles and Africans of various backgrounds, its origins, organization, and leadership were Angolan. In Jamaica, the runaway "Maroons" were able to gain some independence and a recognition of their freedom. So-called ethnic slave rebellions organized by a particular African group were relatively common in the Caribbean and Brazil in the 18th century. In North America where reinforcement from the slave trade was less important, resistance was also important, but it was based less on African origins or ethnicities.

Perhaps, the most remarkable story of African American resistance is found in the forests of Suriname, a former Dutch plantation colony. There large numbers of slaves ran off in the 18th century and mounted an almost perpetual war in the rain forest against the various expeditions sent to hunt them down. Those captured were brutally executed, but eventually a truce developed. Today about 50,000 Maroon descendants still live in Suriname and French Guiana. The Suriname Maroons maintained many aspects of their West African background in terms of language, kinship relations, and religious beliefs, but these were fused with new forms and ways drawn from European and American Indian contacts resulting from their New World experience. From this fusion based on their own creativity, a truly Afro-American culture was created.

African or American, or both? In Suriname, descendants of escaped slaves maintain many aspects of African culture but have adapted, modified, and transformed them in many ways. This wooden door shows the imaginative skills of African-American carvers.

AFRICA AND THE END OF THE SLAVE TRADE

The end of the Atlantic slave trade and the abolition of slavery in the Atlantic world resulted from economic, political, and religious changes in Europe and in its overseas American colonies and former colonies. These changes, which were manifestations of the Enlightenment, the Age of Revolution, Christian revivalism, and perhaps the Industrial Revolution, were basically external to Africa but once again they determined the pace and nature of transformations within the African continent.

Like much else about the history of slavery, there is considerable disagreement about the end of the slave trade. It is true that some African societies began to export new "legitimate" commodities, such as peanuts, cotton, and palm oil, which made their dependence on the slave trade less important, but the supply of slaves to European merchants was not greatly affected by this development. In general, the British plantation economies were booming in the period from 1790 to 1830, and plantations in Cuba, Brazil, and the South of the United States flourished in the following decades. Thus, it is difficult to find a direct and simple link between economic self-interest and the movement to suppress the slave trade.

Opponents of slavery and the brutality of the trade had appeared in the mid-18th century, in relation to new intellectual movements in the West. The philosopher Jean Jacques Rousseau in France and the political economist Adam Smith in England had both written against it. Whereas in ancient Rome during the spread of Christianity and Islam or in 16th century Europe, enslavement of "barbarians" or nonbelievers was viewed as a positive benefit, a means to civilize others. Slavery during the European Enlightenment and bourgeois revolution came to be viewed as unprogressive, retrograde, and immoral. The slave trade was particularly criticized. It was the symbol of slavery's inhumanity and cruelty.

England, as the major maritime power of the period, was the key to the end of the slave trade. Under the leadership of religious humanitarians, such as John Wesley and William Wilberforce, an abolitionist movement gained strength against its opponents made up of merchants and the "West Indies interests." After considerable parliamentary debate, the British slave trade was abolished in 1807. Having set out on this course, Britain sought to impose abolition of the slave trade on other countries throughout the Atlantic. Spain and Portugal were pressured to gradual suppression, and the British navy was used as a means to enforce these agreements by capturing illegal slave ships, though the full end of slavery in the Americas occurred only in 1888.

CONCLUSION

THE IMPACT OF SLAVERY ON AFRICA

Africa had been drawn into the world economy in the era of the slave trade, at first slowly, but after 1750 with increasing intensity. Its incorporation produced differing effects on African societies, reinforcing authority in some places, creating new states in others, and sometimes provoking social, religious, and political reactions. While many aspects of African life followed traditional patterns, the contact with the world economy forced many African societies to adapt and adjust in ways that often placed them at a later disadvantage and facilitated Europe's eventual colonization of Africa in the 19th century. Well into the 20th century, as forced labor continued in Africa itself under European direction, the legacy of the slave trade era proved slow to die.

FURTHER READINGS

Aside from the general books on Africa already mentioned in the bibliographical suggestions for previous chapters, there are some specific readings that are particularly useful. Martin Hall's *The Changing Past. Farmers, Kings, and Traders in Southern Africa* (1987) discusses the use of archeological evidence in African history. D. Birmingham and Phyllis Martin, eds., *History of Central Africa*, 2 vols. (1983) presents extended essays on a number of regions. On West Africa in the age of the slave trade, a good introduction is J. F. A. Ajayi and Michael Crowder, eds., *History of West Africa*, 2 vols. (1971), especially volume 1. On southern Africa, Leonard Thompson's *A History of South Africa* (1990) presents a broad survey, while J. D. Omer-Cooper's *The Zulu Aftermath* (1969) is a classic account.

There are many histories of the slave trade, but James Rawley's *The Transatlantic Slave Trade* (1981) provides an intelligent overview. On the quantitative aspects of the slave trade, Philip Curtin's *The Atlantic Slave Trade. A Census* (1969) is the proper starting point. Roger Anstey's *The Atlantic Slave Trade and British Abolition* (1975) deals with the economic and religious aspects of the end of the trade.

On Africa, Paul Lovejoy's *Transformations in Slavery. A History of Slavery in Africa* (1983) and Patrick Manning's *Slavery and African Life* (1990) provide comprehensive overviews, while J. E. Inikori's *Forced Migration. The Impact of the Export Slave Trade on African Societies* (1982) brings together essays by leading scholars. Joseph Miller's *Way of Death* (1989) is a detailed study of the effects of the slave trade on Angola and a fine example of an in-depth study of one region.

Walter Rodney's essay, "Africa in Europe and the Americas," *Cambridge History of Africa*, vol. 4, 578–622 is a succinct overview of the African diaspora. Herbert Klein's *African Slavery in Latin America and the Caribbean* (1987) is an up-to-date survey.

On the general theoretical issues of slavery, Orlando Patterson's *Slavery and Social Death* (1982) is a broad comparative sociological study. David B. Davis's *Slavery and Human Progress* (1984) takes a historical approach to many of the same questions and then places the abolitionist movement in context.

 **THE ASIAN TRADING WORLD AND THE COMING OF THE EUROPEANS**

 **MING CHINA: A GLOBAL MISSION REFUSED**

- **DOCUMENT:** Exam Questions as a Mirror of Chinese Values
- **ANALYSIS:** Means and Motives for Overseas Expansion: Europe and China Compared

FENDING OFF THE WEST: JAPAN'S REUNIFICATION AND THE FIRST CHALLENGE

- **CONCLUSION:** Asia and the First Phase of Europe's Global Expansion
- **FURTHER READINGS**

1405–1423 Zhenghe expeditions from China to Southeast Asia, India, and East Africa

1511 Portuguese conquer Malacca on the tip of Malayan peninsula

1573–1620 Reign of the Wanli emperor

1590 Hideyoshi unifies Japan

1510 Portuguese conquest of Goa in western India

1368–1398 Reign of the Hongwu emperor

1592 First Japanese invasion of Korea

1498–1499 Vasco da Gama opens the sea route around Africa to Asia

1403–1424 Reign of the Yunglo emperor in China

1573 End of the Ashikaga Shogunate

1540s Francis Xavier makes mass converts in India

1390 Ming restrictions on overseas commerce

1507 Portuguese defeat a combined Muslim war fleet at Diu off the coast of western India

1368 Ming dynasty comes to power in China

1580s Jesuits arrive in China

28 Asian Transitions in an Age of Global Change

INTRODUCTION. Trends in East and Southeast Asia during the early modern centuries, while highly diverse, compare interestingly with developments in other regions. Island areas, such as Ceylon (or what is today Sri Lanka), Java and the "spice islands" of the Indonesian archipelago, and the Philippines, were quickly involved in the West's overseas expansion and its efforts to redefine the world economy. The results were distinctive, but they can be compared to patterns emerging in parts of Latin America and, by the 18th century, India. China and Japan, however, followed a different path. Like other centers of well-established civilization, such as those in the Middle East, China and Japan were not fundamentally reshaped by the rise of the West in the early modern era. Political consolidation and social and intellectual revival marked most of East Asia during these centuries. In contrast to the Islamic world, however, East Asia not only developed new political and social strengths, but its peoples also pursued a more explicit policy of isolation in response to global trends. This distinctive reaction had great implications for Asian as well as global history in the succeeding centuries.

When Vasco da Gama's ships returned to Lisbon in 1499, it was clear that tiny Portugal rather than mighty Spain had won the race to the fabled Indies. Though Columbus's voyages to the Americas with the support of the Spanish rulers opened up new worlds to the civilizations of Europe, Asia, and Africa, da Gama's voyages accomplished the task that was the ultimate aim of all the explorations launched by the Europeans as early as the 14th century. Da Gama had found a sea link between an expansive and insecure Europe and the Asian sources of power and wealth that the rulers of Christendom hoped to tap to strengthen them in their struggles with the Muslims and their European rivals.

1597 Second Japanese invasion of Korea

c. 1600s Dutch and British assault on Portuguese Empire in Asia; decline of Portuguese power

1603 Tokugawa Shogunate established

1614 Christianity banned in Japan

1619–1620 Dutch East India Company established at Batavia on Java

1640s Japan moves into self-imposed isolation

1641 Dutch capture Malacca from the Portuguese; Dutch confined to Deshima Island off Nagasaki

1644 Nomadic Manchus put an end to the Ming dynasty; Manchu Qing dynasty rules China

1654–1722 Reign of the Kangxi emperor in China

1658 Dutch conquer Portuguese areas on Ceylon

1755–1757 Dutch reign as the paramount power on Java; Qing conquest of Mongolia

Though da Gama's voyage from 1498 to 1499 marked a major turning point for much of western Europe, its impact on most of Asia was a good deal less decisive, at least in the 16th and 17th centuries. The Portuguese and the Dutch, French, and English who followed them into Asia soon found that they had little to offer the Asians in exchange for the silks and spices they risked their lives to carry back to Europe and sell at exorbitant prices. They were disappointed to find that few of the Asian peoples were interested in converting to Christianity, which they deemed the one true religion and sought to spread wherever their ships sailed. They also quickly realized that however feisty and well-armed they might be, they were far too few in numbers to make much headway against even the smaller kingdoms of Asia, such as Siam or Vietnam, much less against mighty empires like those ruled by the Chinese or the Mughals.

The Europeans used their sea power to control the export of specific products like spices and the seaborne commerce found in some sections of the vast Asian trading network that stretched from the ports of the Red Sea to South China. But efforts at trade control proved expensive and were difficult to sustain in the face of widespread Asian resistance. The Portuguese—and after them the Dutch and English—found that it was better to fit themselves into the Asian system rather than to attempt to capture it. They also concluded that they gained a good deal more by doing homage to and serving Asian monarchs than by quarreling with them or becoming involved in madcap schemes to capture their kingdoms or forcibly convert their subjects to Christianity.

For their part, most of the Asian peoples were only marginally, if at all, affected by the coming of the Europeans in the two centuries after da Gama's voyage. The Europeans concentrated their efforts on Ceylon (present-day Sri Lanka) and island Southeast Asia, where the spices were concentrated and where their sea power was the most effective. They also traded in India, mainland Southeast Asia, Persia, and, to a much lesser extent, China and Japan. But they neither controlled the commerce of these areas nor significantly altered the course of their social, economic, or political development. As was the case with the Mughal and Safavid empires (see Chapter 26), the central themes in the history of Asian civilizations in the 16th and 17th centuries often had little or nothing to do with European expansion. They emerged from long-term processes that were rooted in the inner workings of these ancient civilizations and their interaction with neighboring states and nomadic peoples. For example, the Europeans had nothing to do with the impressive expeditions by which the Chinese sought in the first decades of the 14th century, to initiate their own global expansion. A century later, threats from elsewhere in Asia, not Europe, convinced the rulers of China to attempt to shut their kingdom off from the world. Though European missionaries and firearms played important roles in the civil wars that raged in Japan in the 16th century, these struggles were part of a pattern of feudal fragmentation and a quest for political unity that long preceded the coming of the Europeans.

Thus, though the European presence was felt in each of the areas considered in this chapter, the impact of Europe's global expansion remained of secondary importance except in island Southeast Asia, which is the focus of the first section of this chapter. The sections on China and Japan that follow emphasize the longer-term unfolding of the pattern of civilization within each of these areas and the effects of their interaction on each other. The continuing importance of nomadic challenges to Chinese civilization also is stressed. Though fascinating in their own right, European responses to and activities in China and Japan are worked into these larger patterns because this perspective more accurately conveys the actual situation in this era. European seafarers may have sailed out across much of the globe, but European peoples had not yet gained the military strength and economic power to dominate the civilizations of Asia or alter the course of their historical development.

THE ASIAN TRADING WORLD AND THE COMING OF THE EUROPEANS

Vasco da Gama and his Portuguese crew received a rather rude shock soon after arriving in India in 1498. Still congratulating themselves on having found a sea route around Africa, which Portuguese explorers had been seeking for generations, they successfully made their way across the Arabian Sea to India. At Calicut, a prosperous commercial center on the southwest coast, they went ashore to trade for the spices, fine textiles, and other Asian products that were among the main objectives of the voyages of exploration. Reveling in the fine quality and abundance of the products from all over Asia available in the town's great marketplace, the Portuguese were startled to learn that none of the merchants was interested in the products they had brought along to swap for Asian goods. In fact, their cast-iron pots, coarse cloth, and coral beads elicited little more than sneers of contempt from the savvy merchants they approached. Suddenly da Gama and his crews faced the humbling prospect of returning home with little proof that they had actually reached Asia and begun to tap its fabled wealth. Reluctantly, they concluded that they had little choice but to make use of the small supply of silver bullion they had brought along for emergency situations. They found that the Asian merchants were quite willing to take their precious metal, but also that their meager provision did not go very far toward filling the holds of their ships with Asian treasures. Nonetheless, at least there was tangible evidence that they had indeed reached Asia, that Portuguese sailors had succeeded where Columbus and the ships of Spain had failed.

Much of the European enterprise in Asia in the 16th and 17th centuries was devoted to working out the implications of that first encounter in Calicut. The very fact of da Gama's arrival demonstrated both the needs and curiosity that had driven the Europeans halfway around the world as well as the seaworthiness of their ships. The encounter at Calicut introduced the Europeans to the vast and sophisticated trading network that had linked the civilizations of Asia since ancient times. It had made them aware that if they were going to break into that system, they would either have to empty the Portuguese royal treasury of precious metals, an unthinkable alternative at the time, or apply military force to obtain the products they desired. The latter option soon became a major preoccupation of the Portuguese and of the Dutch and English who followed them into Asia in the 17th century.

Their stops at Calicut and other ports on the eastern coast of Africa also made the Portuguese acutely aware of the fact that their old rivals the Muslims had arrived in East Africa and South and Southeast Asia well ahead of them. This unpleasant discovery promised resistance to Portuguese trading and empire building in Asia and major obstacles to their designs for the mass conversion of the peoples of the area to Roman Catholicism. But the Portuguese also observed that the Muslims and the Asian peoples as a whole were deeply divided among themselves, and that they were rarely able to comprehend the potential threat posed by what was after all a handful of strangers from across the world.

BONDS OF COMMERCE: THE ASIAN SEA-TRADING NETWORK, C. 1500

As subsequent voyages by Portuguese fleets quickly revealed, Calicut and the ports of East Africa, which da Gama had encountered on the initial foray into Asia, made up only a small segment of a larger network of commercial exchange and cultural interaction. This trading system stretched thousands of miles from the Middle East and Africa along all the coasts of the giant Asian continent. Both the products exchanged in this network and the main routes followed by those who sailed it had been established for centuries, in many cases millennia.

In general, the trading system can be broken down into three main zones, each of which was focused on major centers of handicraft manufacture. In the west was an Arab zone anchored on the glass, carpet, and tapestry manufacturing Islamic heartlands at the head of the Red Sea and Persian Gulf. India, with its superb cotton textiles, dominated the central portions of the system; and China, which excelled in the production of paper, porcelain, and silk textiles, formed the eastern pole. In between or on the fringes of the three great manufacturing centers were areas such as Japan, the mainland kingdoms and island states of Southeast Asia, and the port cities of East Africa that fed mainly raw materials—precious metals and forest products—into the trading network.

Many products circulated throughout the system. Cotton textiles from India were sold from Egypt (and Europe) to Africa and eastward throughout Southeast Asia. Chinese silks and porcelains were in high demand throughout Asia and on the African coast and found their way, at hugely inflated prices, to the Middle East and Italy. Of the raw materials circulating in the system, the broadest demand and highest prices were paid for spices—such as pepper, cinnamon, nutmeg, and mace—that came mainly from Ceylon and the islands at the eastern end of what is today the Indonesian archipelago. African ivory also found lucrative markets from India to China and Japan. Some products, such as Indian elephants, Arabian horses, European glassware, and African slaves reached only more limited regional markets. Long-distance trade was largely in high-priced commodities such as spices, ivory, and precious stones, but silk and cotton textiles were also traded over long distances. Bulk items, such as rice, livestock, and timber, were normally exchanged between the ports within each of the main trading zones. Though less profitable than luxury commodities, bulk staples made up a substantial portion of the volume of goods traded in some segments of the system.

Since ancient times monsoon winds and the nature of the ships and navigational instruments available to sailors had dictated the main trade routes in the Asian network. Much navigation was of the coasting variety, that is sailing along the shoreline and charting distances and location with reference to towns and natural landmarks. Peoples like the Arabs and Chinese, who possessed compasses and large and well-built ships, could cross large expanses of open water such as the Arabian and South China seas. But even they preferred established coastal routes to navigating in the largely uncharted and less predictable open seas. As the Portuguese quickly discerned, there were a number of crucial points where segments of the trade converged or where geography funneled it into narrow confines. The mouths of

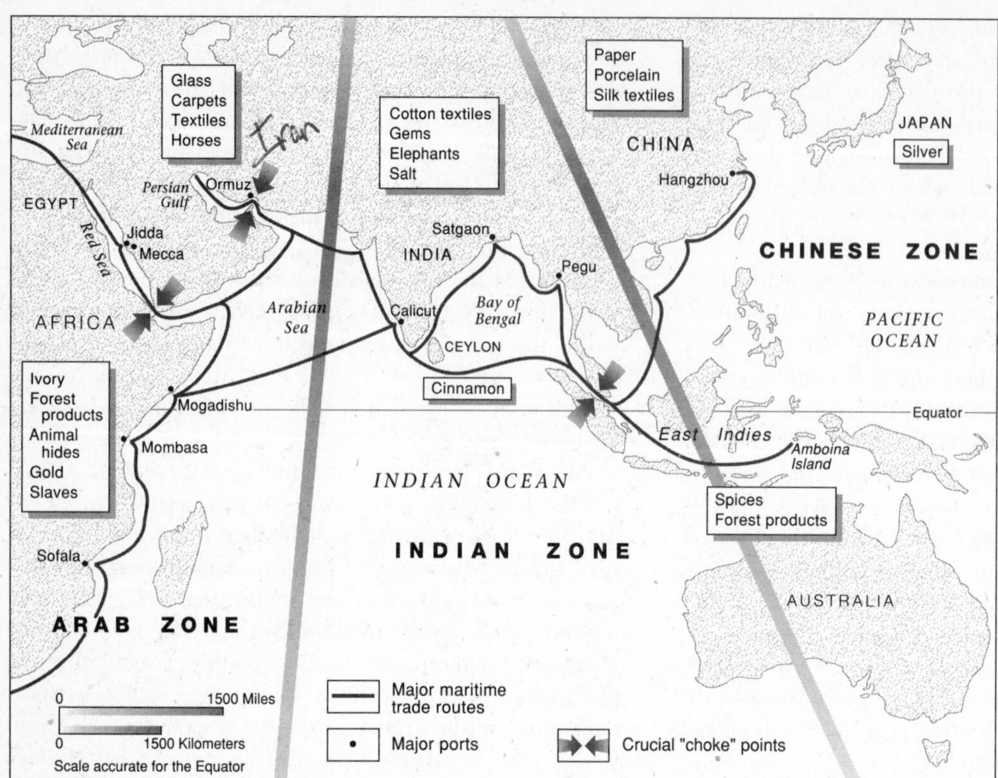

Routes and Major Products Exchanged in the Asian Trading Network, c. 1500

the Red Sea and Persian Gulf were two of these points, as were the straits of Malacca that separated mainland from island Southeast Asia. What had been centers of cross-cultural interaction and exchange in the millennia before da Gama's arrival would become strategic nodes of the sea empires the Europeans sought to build from the 16th to the 18th centuries.

Two general characteristics of the trading system at the time of the Portuguese arrival were critical to subsequent European attempts to regulate and dominate it: There was no central or overall control, and military force was usually absent from commercial exchanges. Though Arab sailors and merchants were found in ports throughout much of the network, they had no sense of common cause. They sailed and traded to provide for their own livelihood and to make profits for individual princes or specific merchants who financed their expeditions. The same was true for the Chinese, Southeast Asian, and Indian merchants and sailors who were concentrated in particular segments of the whole trading complex. Because all the peoples participating in the network had something to exchange for the products they desired from others, exchanges within the system were largely peaceful. Trading vessels were lightly armed, in case they should be attacked by pirates. Though Asian coastal states like Shrivijaya sometimes used war fleets to control trade in limited segments of the network, their efforts were usually short-lived and resented by other participants in the system. The great powers of Asia, such as the Chinese and Safavid empires, were too wealthy and self-sufficient to consider resorting to naval warfare in order to control a trading system in which they already played such prominent roles.

TRADING EMPIRE: THE PORTUGUESE RESPONSE TO THE ENCOUNTER AT CALICUT

The Portuguese were simply not prepared to abide by the informal rules that had evolved over the centuries for commercial and cultural exchanges in the great Asian trading complex. It was apparent after the sobering trip to the market in Calicut that the Portuguese had little, other than gold and silver, to exchange with Asian peoples. In an age where prominent economic theorists, called *mercantilists,* taught that a state's power depended heavily on the amount of precious metals a monarch had in his coffers, a steady flow of bullion to Asia was unthinkable. It was particularly objectionable because it would enrich and thus strengthen merchants and rulers from rival kingdoms and religions, particularly the heretical Muslims, whose position the Portuguese had deliberately set out to undermine through their overseas enterprises. Unwilling to forgo the possibilities for profit that pioneering a sea route to Asia presented, the Portuguese resolved to take by force what they could not get through fair trade.

To a large degree the Portuguese decision to resort to force to extract spices and other market commodities from Asia resulted from their realization that they could offset their lack of numbers and trading goods with their superior ships and weaponry. Though the Chinese had ships that were much larger and in some respects better built, none of the Asian peoples possessed oceangoing vessels that were as swift and maneuverable as the caravels that had carried the Portuguese around Africa. These slender, long-hulled vessels with many triangular, or lateen, sails, which made them highly maneuverable and allowed them to sail against the wind, were a match for any of the vessels they encountered in Asian waters. Navigational advantages combined with the fact that Portuguese ships were increasingly well armed whereas Asian ships were rarely so, made it possible for the Portuguese to build a trading empire in Asia within decades of da Gama's voyage.

Excepting the huge war fleets of Chinese junks, no Asian people could muster fleets able to withstand the firepower and maneuverability of the Portuguese squadrons. Their sudden appearance in Asian waters and their interjection of sea warfare into a trading system that had been overwhelmingly peaceful gained the European intruders an element of surprise that kept their adversaries off balance in the critical early years of empire building. The Portuguese, whose forces were small in numbers but united in their drive for wealth and religious converts, also took advantage of the deep divisions that separated their Asian competitors and their inability to combine their forces effectively in battle. Thus, when da Gama returned on a second expedition to Asian waters in 1502, he was able to force ports on both the African and Indian coasts to submit to a Portuguese tribute regime and to bombard with impunity those towns that refused to cooperate. When a combined Egyptian-Indian fleet was finally sent in reprisal in 1509, it was decisively defeated off Diu on the western Indian coast. The Portuguese would not have to face so formidable an alliance of Asian sea powers again.

The Portuguese soon found that sea patrols and raids on coastal towns were not sufficient to control the trade in the items, especially spices, they desired. Thus, from 1507 onward, the Portuguese strove to capture towns and build fortresses at a number of strategic points on the Asian trading network. In that year they took Ormuz at the southern end of the Persian Gulf; in 1510 they captured Goa on the western Indian coast; and, most critical of all, in the next year they successfully stormed Malacca on the tip of the

In the 15th and 16th centuries, the port of Lisbon in tiny Portugal was one of the great centers of international commerce and European overseas exploration. Though aspects of the early, streamlined caravel design can be detected in the ships pictured here, additional square sails, higher fore and aft castles, and numerous cannons projecting from holes cut in the ships' sides exemplify a later stage of naval development.

Malayan peninsula. These ports served as both naval bases for Portuguese fleets patrolling Asian waters and as "factories" or points where spices and other products could be stored until they were transhipped to Europe to be sold at hefty profits. Ships and naval stations became the key components of a Portuguese trading empire that was financed and directed by the kings of Portugal.

The aim of the empire was to establish Portuguese monopoly control over key Asian products, particularly spices. Ideally, all the spices produced were to be shipped in Portuguese galleons to Asian or European markets. There they would be sold at prices the Portuguese could dictate because they controlled the total supply of these goods. The Portuguese also sought, with little success, to impose a licensing system on all merchant ships that traded in the Indian Ocean from Ormuz to Malacca. The combination of monopoly and the licensing system, backed by force, was intended to give the Portuguese control of a sizeable portion of the Asian trading network.

PORTUGUESE VULNERABILITY AND THE RISE OF THE DUTCH AND ENGLISH TRADING EMPIRES

The plans for empire that the Portuguese drew up on paper were never even close to being translated into reality. Though they managed for some decades to control much of the flow of spices, such as nutmeg and mace that were grown in very limited locales, a corner on the market in key condiments, such as pepper and cinnamon, eluded them. Despite draconian punishments—they were not above cutting off the hands of the rival traders and ships' crews caught transporting spices in defiance of their monopoly—the Portuguese did not have the manpower or the ships to sustain either their monopolies or the even more ambitious licensing system. With just over a million people in all of Portugal and never more than 15,000 Portuguese in Asia at one time, the manpower of the trading empire was stretched thin indeed. Even this relatively small community soon became deeply divided, and many of the Portuguese who went out to serve in the empire became independent traders in defiance of the crown monopoly. The resistance of Asian rivals, military indiscipline, rampant corruption among crown officials, and heavy losses to Portuguese shipping due to overloading and poor design had taken a heavy toll on the empire by the end of the 16th century.

The overextended and declining Portuguese trading empire proved no match for the Dutch and English rivals whose war fleets challenged it in the early decades of the 17th century. The position of the Portuguese had grown so weak that they proved unable to exploit the deep hostility and frequent clashes between their northern European rivals. Of the two, the Dutch emerged, at least in the short term, as the victors. They captured the critical Portuguese port and fortress at Malacca and built a new port of their own in 1620 at Batavia on the island of Java. The latter location, which was much closer to the island sources of key spices, reflected not only the much improved European knowledge of Asian geography but also the Dutch decision to concentrate on the monopoly control of certain spices rather than Asian trade more generally. The English, who fought hard but lost the struggle for control of the spice islands, were forced to fall back on India. At the time this appeared to be a disheartening reversal. In the 18th century, however, when the demand for Indian textiles soared and India emerged as the keystone of Britain's global empire, it came to be seen as an incredible stroke of good fortune.

The Dutch trading empire was made up of the same basic components as those of the Portuguese: fortified towns and factories, warships on patrol, and monopoly control of a very limited number of products. But the Dutch had more numerous and better armed ships and went about the business of monopoly control in a much more systematic fashion. To regulate the supply of cloves, nutmeg, and mace, for example, they uprooted the plants that produced these spices on islands they did not control. They also forcibly removed or wiped out island peoples who cultivated these spices without Dutch supervision and dared to sell them to trading rivals of the Dutch.

Though the very impressive profits from the sale of these spices in Europe in the middle decades of the 17th century helped sustain Holland's golden age, the Dutch found that the greatest profits in the long-run could be gained from peacefully working themselves into the long established Asian trading system. As the demand for spices declined and their futile efforts to gain control over crops, such as pepper, that were grown in many places became more and more expensive, the Dutch came to rely on the fees they charged for transporting products from one area in Asia to another. They also depended on profits gained from buying Asian products, such as cloth, in one area and trading them in other areas for goods that could be sold in Europe at inflated prices. The English also adopted these trading patterns, though their enterprises were concentrated along the coasts of India and on the cloth trade rather than on the spices of Southeast Asia. For both the Dutch and the English peaceful commerce came to be more profitable than forcible control, and monopolistic measures were increasingly aimed at European rather than Asian rivals.

GOING ASHORE: EUROPEAN TRIBUTE SYSTEMS IN ASIA

Although their ships and guns allowed the Europeans to force their way into the Asian trading network in the 16th and 17th centuries, as they moved inland, away from the sea, their military advantages and capacity to dominate Asian peoples rapidly disappeared. Because the vastly superior numbers of Asian armies offset the limited edge the Europeans possessed in weapons and organization for waging war on land, even relatively small kingdoms like those found on Java and throughout mainland Southeast Asia proved able to resist European inroads into their domains. In the larger empires like those in China, India, and Persia—or when confronted by martial cultures like that of Japan—the Europeans quickly learned their place. That they were often reduced to kowtowing or humbling themselves before the thrones of Asian potentates is clearly demonstrated by the following instructions given by a Dutch envoy regarding the proper behavior for a visit to the Japanese court:

> Our ministers have no other instruction to take there except to look to the wishes of that brave, superb, precise nation in order to please it in everything, and by no means to think on anything which might cause greater antipathy to us. . . . That consequently the Company's ministers frequenting the scrupulous state each year must above all go armed in modesty, humility, courtesy, and amity, always being the lesser.

In certain situations, however, the Europeans were drawn inland away from their forts, factories, and war fleets in the early centuries of their expansion into Asia. The Portuguese, and the Dutch after them, felt compelled to conquer the coastal areas of Ceylon in order to control the production and sale of cinnamon, which grew in the forests of the southern portions of that island. The Dutch moved slowly inland from their base at Batavia into the highlands of western Java. They discovered that this area was ideal for the cultivation of coffee, which was in great demand in Europe by the 17th century. By the middle of

This photograph, taken in the era of British colonial rule, shows Sinhalese workers peeling the bark from the branches of cinnamon trees. Much the same techniques were used by cinnamon peelers in the pre-European, the Portuguese, and the Dutch periods to extract the sticks and powder that were in great demand in Europe.

the 18th century, the Dutch not only controlled the coffee-growing areas, but were the paramount power on the island of Java. The Treaty of Gijanti in 1757 reduced the remaining Javanese princes to vassals of the Dutch East Indian Company. The Spanish, taking advantage of the fact that the Philippine islands lay in the half of the world the pope had given them to explore and settle in 1493, invaded the islands in the 1560s. The conquest of Luzon and the northern islands was facilitated by the fact that the animistic peoples inhabiting them lived in small states the Spanish could subjugate one by one. The repeated failure of Spanish expeditions to conquer the southern island of Mindanao, which was ruled by a single kingdom whose Muslim rulers were determined to resist Christian dominance, dramatically underscores the limits of the Europeans' ability to project their power on land in this era.

In each of the areas where the Europeans went ashore in the early centuries of expansion, they set up tribute regimes that closely resembled those the Spanish imposed on the Amerindian peoples of the New World (see Chapter 25). The European overlords were content to let the indigenous peoples live in their traditional settlements, which were controlled largely by hereditary leaders drawn from their own communities. In most areas little attempt was made to interfere in the daily lives of the conquered peoples as long as their leaders met the tribute quotas set by the European conquerors. The tribute was paid in the form of agricultural products that were cultivated by the peasantry under forced labor systems supervised by the peasants' own elites. The Philippines, where a major missionary effort was launched after the conquest, provided an important exception to the pattern of minimal intervention. In some cases the indigenous peoples continued to harvest crops they had produced for centuries, such as the bark of the cinnamon plant demanded of special villages in southwestern Ceylon. In other areas new crops, such as coffee or sugarcane, were introduced. But in all cases, tribute demands took into account the local peasants' need to raise the crops on which they themselves subsisted.

SPREADING THE FAITH: THE MISSIONARY ENTERPRISE IN SOUTH AND SOUTHEAST ASIA

Though the Protestant Dutch and English were little interested in winning converts to Christianity in the early centuries of overseas expansion, the spread of Roman Catholicism was a fundamental part of the global mission of the Portuguese and Spanish. After the widespread conversion of Amerindian peoples, the rather meager returns from the Iberian missionary offensive in Asia were disappointing. The fact that Islam had arrived in much of maritime South and Southeast Asia centuries before da Gama's arrival had much to do with the indifference or open hostility the Portuguese encountered when they attempted to convert the peoples to Christianity. The dream of a Christian Asia joining the Iberian crusade against the Muslims was also dealt a setback by the discovery that the Hindus, whom da Gama and some of his entourage had originally believed to be Christians, possessed a sophisticated and deeply entrenched set of alternative religious ideas and rituals. As a result, widespread conversion in South and Southeast Asia was limited to outcaste groups in Indian coastal areas and peoples, such as the northern Filipinos, who had not previously been exposed to a world religion like Islam or Buddhism and who came under the direct rule of the Europeans.

In India from the 1540s onward, Francis Xavier and his coworkers, who were willing to bring food and care to the poor and low-caste fisherfolk and pariahs along the southwest coast, brought initial conversions in the tens of thousands. But the Franciscans and other missionary orders soon realized that they were making little headway among high-caste groups and, in fact, low-caste conversions made it virtually impossible to even approach upper-caste groups.

In the early 1600s, an Italian Jesuit, Robert di Nobili, attempted a rather different approach. He learned a number of Indian languages, including Sanskrit (which allowed him to read the sacred texts of the Hindus), donned the garments of an Indian brahman, and adopted a vegetarian diet. All of these measures were calculated to win over the upper-caste Hindus in South India where he was based. His strategy to Christianize the Hindus by first converting the elite groups, who, he argued, would then bring the lower Hindu classes into the fold, was to be widely adopted by Jesuits working in various parts of Asia. Despite some early successes, in India di Nobili's strategy was undone by the high-caste Hindus' refusal to worship with low-caste groups and to give up their traditional beliefs and religious rituals. Citing these trends, rival missionaries denounced his approach. Eventually di Nobili was recalled to Rome and his mission collapsed.

Because they had conquered the northern Philippines and then governed them as part of their vast intercontinental empire, the Spanish could take a much more conventional approach to conversion in the islands. Once areas had been "pacified" by Spanish conquistadores, the administration of the Filipinos, or at least of those who lived outside the capital at Manila, was turned over to the missionary orders. The *friars*, as the priests and brothers who went out to convert and govern the rural populace were called, became the main channel for the transmission of European influences. The friars first converted and then administered through local Filipino leaders. These leaders were usually persuaded to order their followers to construct new settlements that were centered, like those in Iberia and the New World, on town squares where the local church, the residences of the missionary fathers, and government offices (if there were any) were located. Beyond tending to the spiritual needs of the villagers in their congregation, the friars in effect served as government officials. They dispensed justice, oversaw the collection of the tribute payments and public works projects, and were responsible for what little education rural Filipinos received. Very often friars were the only Europeans the great majority of the Philippines' population saw for years or even decades.

Like the Amerindian peoples of Spain's New World empire, most of the Filipinos were formally converted to Catholicism. But also like the Amerindians, the Filipinos' brand of Christianity represented a creative blend of their traditional beliefs and customs and the religion preached by the friars. Since key tenets of the Christian faith were taught in Spanish for fear that they would be corrupted if put in the local languages, it is doubtful that most of the converts had a very good grasp of Christian beliefs. Many converted because Spanish dominance and their own leaders' co-optation gave them little choice; others adopted the new faith because they believed that the Christian God could protect them from illness or because they were taken with the notion that they would be equal to their Spanish overlords in heaven.

Almost all Filipinos clung to their traditional ways and in the process seriously compromised Christian beliefs and practices. Most attended confession, for example, at best once a year to be absolved of all the "heathenish" sins the missionaries accused them of committing. Catholic saints easily fused with preconquest idolatry, and Christian miracles were easily assimilated into indigenous magical practices. The Filipinos continued public bathing, which the missionaries condemned as immodest; refused to give up ritual drinking; and continued to commune with deceased members of their families, often in sessions that were disguised as public recitations of the rosary. Thus, even in the Asian area where European control was the strongest and pressures for acculturation to European ways the greatest, much of the preconquest way of life and approach to the world was maintained.

MODEST RETURNS: THE EARLY IMPACT OF EUROPEANS IN MARITIME ASIA

In 1700, after two centuries of European involvement in South and Southeast Asia, most of the peoples of the area had been little affected by efforts to build trading empires and win Christian converts. European sailors had added a number of new routes to the Asian trading network, the most important being the link around the Cape of Good Hope between Europe and the Indian Ocean and the connection between the Philippine islands and Mexico in the New World. The Europeans' need for safe harbors and storage areas had led to the establishment or rapid growth of trading centers, such as Goa, Calcutta, and Batavia, as well as the gradual decline of existing rival centers, such as many of the Gujarati cities in western India, several Muslim centers in East Africa, and, after the arrival of the Dutch, the fortress town of Malacca. Though Europeans reaped most of the profits, they did introduce the principle of sea warfare into what had been a peaceful commercial world. But the Asian trading system as a whole survived the initial shocks, and the Europeans eventually concluded that they were better off accommodating than dismantling the existing commercial arrangements.

Because Europe and Asia had been exchanging plants and diseases for millennia, few new plants and diseases were spread in the era of expansion (except for the New World plants brought to Asia by European merchants), particularly in comparison with the catastrophic exchange between Europe and Africa and the New World. Mostly Europeans died of diseases like new strains of malaria and dysentery that they contracted in Asia. They spread diseases only to the more isolated parts of Asia, such as the Philippines, where the coming of the Spanish was accompanied by a devastating smallpox epidemic. The impact of European ideas, inventions, and modes of social organization was also very limited in the first centuries of expansion. Key European devices, such as clocks, were regarded as toys by Asian rulers to whom they were given as presents. Christianity aroused more hostility than interest from the adherents of the ancient faiths of Asia and the more recent converts to Islam.

MING CHINA: A GLOBAL MISSION REFUSED

With the restoration of ethnic Chinese rule and the reunification of the country under the Ming dynasty in 1368, Chinese civilization seemed ready for a new age of splendor. China's endowment in terms of both human and natural resources was indeed impressive. Its population was the largest of any center of civilization at the time, probably exceeding that of all western Europe combined. Its resources were vast, and it had some of the most advanced technology as well as large numbers of skilled engineers and artisans to put its rich soils and mineral wealth to productive use. China's centralized bureaucracy was the best organized and most efficient in the world. Though the firearms of its armies were somewhat behind those of the West, in numbers, organization, and leadership China possessed a formidable military establishment. A return to the examination system under the Ming rulers ensured that the Chinese elite was one of the largest and best educated of any major civilization. These developments within Chinese civilization will be the focus of the early sections on Ming China.

As China's achievements multiplied and its advantages over neighboring civilizations grew, there was every reason to expect that its internal prosperity and dynamism would be translated into external expansion. In earlier periods, strong dynasties, such as the Han and the Tang, had pursued territorial and commercial expansion overland into central and Southeast Asia and overseas. The century of Mongol rule from 1260 to 1368 reinforced these expansive tendencies by opening China to outside influences from places as distant as the Middle East and Europe and through Mongol military forays in East and Southeast Asia. At the time of the Ming dynasty's assumption of power, however, China had not yet expanded on a global scale. Some of its technology had been widely disseminated, but the spread of the Chinese pattern of civilization had been confined mainly to areas bordering the Middle Kingdom—the nomadic steppe to the north and west, the rice valleys to the east and south, and the Japanese islands off China's northern coast.

In the early Ming era it appeared that China would break out of these regional confines to become one of the great global powers of the coming age. In fact, in the early decades of the 15th century, when the Portuguese had not yet begun to probe the African coastline in search of a route to Asia, a series of major sea expeditions (see Chapter 21) carried the Chinese across the Java Sea and Indian Ocean to the coast of Africa. The hundreds of ships and tens of thousands of officials, sailors, soldiers, and merchants involved in these voyages unquestionably demonstrated China's capacity to expand; to become perhaps the premier global power. These expeditions and China's involvement with the outside world more generally are the focus of the later sections on the Ming period.

If the leaders of China had chosen to follow up on these early initiatives to project the power of their empire and civilization overseas, the subsequent history of the world would have been dramatically altered. At the very least, there would have been, certainly in Asia and perhaps in East Africa, a major countervailing force to check the expansive drive and rise to global dominance of western Europe. Chinese war fleets, for example, which at the time of the Ming were more than a match for those from Europe, might have been able to ward off European attempts to transform key segments of the open, peaceful Asian commercial network into closed trading empires. But the leaders of China did not choose to follow up on these early expeditions. A combination of factors, including old concerns with enemies in the interior of Asia and political rivalries at the Ming court, put an end to Chinese overseas expansion. Significantly, the past successes and the high degree of self-sufficiency of Chinese civilization played vital roles in the decisions to withdraw. In contrast to the Europeans, who had strong motives for their exploration and colonization efforts (see Chapter 23), there seemed to be little China needed from the rest of the world. What little there was, the Chinese could get through peaceful trade with people who were eager to come to China rather than wait for the Chinese to go out to them.

RESTORATION: THE BEGINNINGS OF THE MING ERA

The founding of the Ming dynasty, which would reign for nearly three centuries between 1368 and 1644, meant a good deal more than the restoration of ethnic Chinese rule after yet another period of nomadic dominance. The early Ming emperors sought both to restore key Chinese institutions and practices that had been set aside or neglected by the Mongols and to reform the Chinese polity in major ways. Zhu Yuanzhang, a military commander of peasant origins who was the founder of the Ming dynasty, had suffered a great deal under the Mongol yoke. Both of his parents and two brothers had died in a plague in 1344, and he and a remaining brother were reduced to begging for the land to bury the rest of their family. Threatened with the prospect of starvation in one of the many famines that ravaged the countryside in the later, corruption-riddled reigns of the Mongols, Zhu alternated between begging and living in a Buddhist monastery to survive. When the neighboring countryside rose in rebellion in the late 1340s, Zhu left the monastery to join a rebel band. His courage in combat and natural capacity as a leader had soon made him one of the more prominent of a number of rebel warlords seeking to overthrow the Yuan dynasty. After protracted military struggles against rival rebel claimants to the throne and the Mongol rulers themselves, Zhu's armies conquered most of China, and he declared himself the Hongwu emperor in 1368. He would reign for 30 years.

Immediately following his seizure of the throne, Zhu launched a concerted effort to rid China of all traces of the "barbarian" Mongols. Mongol dress was discarded, Mongol names were both dropped by those who had adopted them and removed from buildings and court records, and Mongol palaces and administrative buildings in some areas were raided and sacked. The nomads themselves fled or were driven beyond the Great Wall, where Ming military expeditions pursued them on a number of occasions in order to raid and intimidate them.

THE SCHOLAR-GENTRY REVIVAL

Because the Hongwu emperor, like the founder of the earlier Han dynasty, was from a peasant family and thus poorly educated, he viewed the scholar-gentry with some suspicion. But he also realized that their cooperation was essential to the full revival of Chinese civilization. Scholars well-versed in the Confucian classics were again appointed to the very highest positions in the imperial government. The generous state subsidies that had provided support for the imperial academies in the capital and the regional colleges were fully restored. Most critically, the civil service examination system, which the Mongols had discontinued, was reinstated and greatly expanded. In the Ming era and the Qing that followed, the examinations played a greater role in determining entry into the Chinese bureaucracy than had been the case under any earlier dynasty. At times, as many as half of all government officials had earned their positions through success in the exam competitions. Though this left many positions to be won by virtue of being born into the right family or of timely "gifts" to high officials, the exams ensured that there was a high level of education and talent for Ming administrators as a whole.

In the Ming era the examination system was routinized and made more complex than before. Prefectural or county exams were held in two of every three years to award the lowest degree, which allowed successful candidates to compete for higher degrees (and positions) and, less commonly, to win appointments to minor offices. Competition was fierce since there could be only 20 to 30 successful candidates. The exams were given in large compounds, surrounded by walls and watch towers from which the examiners could keep an eye on the thousands of candidates. Each candidate was provided with a small cubicle, where he struggled to answer the questions posed, and slept and ate over the several days that it took to complete the exams.

Those who passed and received the lowest degree were eligible to take the next level of exams that were given in the provincial capitals every three years. Only the most gifted and ambitious went on because the odds against success were even higher than at the beginning level. Each province had a quota—in some cases 4000 candidates competed for 150 degrees. Success at the provincial level brought a considerable rise in status and opened the way for appointments to positions in the middle levels of the imperial bureaucracy. It also permitted a particularly talented scholar to take the imperial examinations, which were given in the capital every three years. Those who passed the imperial exams were eligible for the highest posts in the realm and were the most revered of all Chinese, excepting members of the royal family.

This 19th-century engraving shows the cubicles in which Chinese students and bureaucrats took the imperial civil service examinations that were given in the capital at Beijing. Examinees were confined to the cubicles for days and completed their exams under the constant surveillance of official proctors.

DOCUMENT

EXAM QUESTIONS AS A MIRROR OF CHINESE VALUES

The subjects and specific learning tested on the Chinese civil service exams give us great insight into behavior and attitudes expected of the literate, ruling classes of what was perhaps the best educated preindustrial civilization. A reading of sample test questions from these exams can tell us a good deal about what sorts of knowledge were considered important and what kinds of skills were necessary for those who aspired to successful careers in the most prestigious and potentially the most lucrative field open to Chinese youths—administrative service in the imperial bureaucracy. The very fact that such a tiny portion of the Chinese *male* population could take the exams and an even smaller number could successfully pass them says a lot about gender roles and elitism in Chinese society. In addition, the often decisive role of a student's calligraphy, the skill with which he was able to brush the Chinese characters, reflects the emphasis the Chinese elite placed on a refined sense of aesthetics.

Question 1—Provide the missing phrases and elaborate on the meaning of the following:

> The Duke of She observed to Confucius: "Among us there was an upright man called Kung who was so upright that when his father appropriated a sheep, he bore witness against him." Confucius said . . .

(The missing phrases are:

> "The upright men among us are not like that. A father will screen his son and a son his father—yet uprightness is to be found in that.")

Question 2—Write an eight-legged essay [one consisting of eight sections] on the following: Scrupulous in his own conduct and lenient only in his dealings with the people.

Question 3—First unscramble the following characters and then comment on the significance of the quotation from the classics:

> Beginning, good, mutually, nature, basically, practice, far, near, men's

(The correct answer is:

> Men's beginning nature is basically good.
> Nature mutually near.
> Practice mutually far.)

Questions: Looking at the actual content of these questions, what else can we learn about Chinese society and attitudes? Where, for example, do the Chinese look for models to orient their social behavior? What kinds of knowledge are important to the Chinese? Do they stress specialist skills or the sort of learning that we associate with a "broad liberal arts education"? If we take SAT exams as equivalent gauges of our social values, how would you compare Ming China and modern America? What are the advantages and drawbacks of each system?

REFORM: HONGWU'S EFFORTS TO ROOT OUT ABUSES IN COURT POLITICS

Though mindful of his dependence on a well-educated and loyal scholar-gentry for the day-to-day administration of the empire, Hongwu sought to put clear limits on their influence over the emperor and to institute reforms that would check the abuses of other factions at court. Early in his reign he abolished the position of chief minister, which had formerly been the key link between the many ministries of the central government. The very considerable powers that had been amassed by members of the scholar-gentry class who occupied this office were transferred to the emperor himself, who now worked through the Grand Secretary with the heads of each of the secretariats, the six main government departments, and the head of the Censorate. Hongwu also sought to impress all officials with the honesty, loyalty, and discipline he expected from them by introducing the practice of public beatings for bureaucrats found guilty of corruption or incompetence. Officials charged with misdeeds were paraded before the assembled courtiers and beaten a specified number of times on their bare buttocks. Many died of the wounds they received in the ordeal. Those who survived never recovered from the humiliation, which was to a certain extent shared by all the scholar-gentry by virtue of the very fact that such degrading punishments could be meted out to them.

Hongwu also introduced measures to cut down on the court factionalism and never ending conspiracies that had done much to erode the power of earlier dynasties. He decreed that the emperor's wives should come only from humble family origins, in order to put an end to the power plays of the consorts from high-ranking families who built palace cliques that were centered on their influential aristocratic relatives. He warned against allowing eunuchs to occupy positions of independent power and sought to limit their numbers within the Forbidden City. To prevent plots against the ruler and fights over succession, Hongwu established the practice of exiling all the potential rivals to the throne to estates in the provinces, and he forbade them to become involved in political affairs. On the darker side, Hongwu condoned thought control, as when he had some sections from Mencius's writings that displeased him deleted forever from the writings included on the imperial exams. Though many of these measures went far to keep peace at court under Hongwu and his strong successor, the Yunglo emperor (1403–1424), they were allowed to lapse under later, less capable, emperors with devastating consequences for the Ming Empire.

CONTINUITY AND CHANGE: FAMILY, CLASS, AND GENDER UNDER THE MING

Perhaps because his lowly origins and personal suffering made him sensitive to the plight of the peasantry, Hongwu sought to introduce measures that would improve the lot of the common people. Like most strong emperors, he promoted public works projects, including dike building and the extension of irrigation systems aimed at improving the farmers' yields. In order to bring new lands under cultivation and encourage the growth of a peasant class that owned the lands it toiled so hard to bring into production, Hongwu decreed that unoccupied lands would become the tax-exempt property of those who cleared and cultivated them. He also sought to lower forced labor demands on the peasantry by both the government and members of the gentry class, and to promote silk and cotton cloth production and other handicrafts that provided supplemental sources of income for peasant households.

Though these measures led in the short run to some improvement in the peasants' condition, they were all but offset by the growing power of rural landlord families, buttressed by alliances with kinsmen in the imperial bureaucracy. Gentry households with members in government service were exempted from land taxes and enjoyed special privileges, such as permission to be carried about in sedan chairs by their growing retinues of slaves and the right to use fans and umbrellas. Many gentry families engaged in moneylending on the side; some even ran lucrative gambling dens. Almost all sought to add to their estates either by buying up lands held by peasant small landholders or through the foreclosure on loans made to cultivators in times of need in exchange for mortgages on their family plots. Peasants displaced in these ways had little choice but to become tenants of large landowners or landless laborers moving about in search of employment.

More land meant ever larger and more comfortable households for the gentry class, who sought to justify the growing gap between their wealth and the general impoverishment of the peasantry by contrasting their foresight and industry with the lazy and wasteful ways of the ordinary cultivators. The virtues of the gentry class were celebrated in stories and popular illustrations. These show, for example, members of gentry households hard at work weaving and storing grain to see them through the cold weather, while commoners, who neglected these tasks, wandering during the winter months cold and hungry past the walled compounds and closed gates of gentry households.

At most levels of Chinese society, the Ming period saw the continuation of the subordination of youths to elders and women to men that had been steadily intensifying in earlier periods. If anything, neo-Confucian thinking was even more influential than under the late-Song and Yuan dynasties. The remedies of some of its advocates for challenges to the increasingly rigid allocation of social status and roles were truly draconian. Students, for example, were expected to venerate and follow the instructions of their teachers, no matter how muddle-headed or tipsy the latter might be. A terrifying lesson in proper decorum was drawn from an incident in which a student at the imperial academy dared to dispute the findings of one of his instructors. The student was beheaded, and his severed head was hung on a pole at the entrance to the academy. Not surprisingly, this rather unsubtle solution to the problem of keeping order in the classroom merely drove student protest underground. Anonymous letters critical of poorly prepared teachers continued to circulate among the student body.

In a sense women were also driven to underground activities to ameliorate their subordination and, if they dared, expand their career opportunities. At the court, they continued, despite Hongwu's measures, to play strong roles behind the scenes. Even strong rulers like Hongwu were swayed by the advice of favorite wives or dowager mothers and aunts. On one occasion Hongwu chided the empress Ma for daring to inquire into the condition of the common people. She replied that since he was the father of the people, then she was the mother and thus it was quite proper for her to be concerned for the welfare of her children. Weak emperors like Wanli (1573–1620) could become so embroiled in disputes arising from rivalry between their wives and concubines and their allies at court that the rulers' ability to govern was seriously impaired.

Even within the palace, however, the plight of most women was grim. Hundreds, sometimes thousands of comely young women were brought to the court in the hope that they would catch the emperor's fancy and become one of his concubines or perhaps even be elevated to the status of wife. Because few actually succeeded, many spent their lives in loneliness and inactivity, just waiting for the emperor to glance their way.

In society at large, women had to settle for whatever status and respect they could win within the family. As before, their success in this regard hinged largely on being able to bear male children and, when they were married, moving from the status of daughter-in-law to mother-in-law. But the daughters of upper-class families were often taught to read and write by their parents or male siblings, and many composed poetry, painted, or played musical instruments. As in earlier centuries, even well-read women were barred from taking the civil service exams and obtaining positions in the bureaucracy. Though women from the nonelite classes still worked the fields and in some areas sold goods in the local market, the main avenues for some degree of independence and self-expression remained becoming courtesans or entertainers. The former should be clearly distinguished from prostitutes in that they served a very different clientele and were literate and often quite accomplished in painting, music, and poetry writing. Though even the most successful courtesans made their living by gratifying the needs of upper-class males for uninhibited sex and companionship, they often enjoyed lives of considerable luxury and much greater personal freedom than even women from scholar-gentry households.

AN AGE OF GROWTH: AGRICULTURE, POPULATION, COMMERCE, AND THE ARTS

The first decades of the Ming period were an age of buoyant economic growth in China that was both fed by and resulted in unprecedented contacts with other civilizations overseas. The territories controlled by the Ming emperors were never as extensive as those ruled by the Tang emperors. But in the Ming era, the great commercial

The varied diversions of the wives and many concubines of Ming emperors are depicted in this scene of court life. In addition to court intrigues and maneuvers to win the emperor's favor, women of the imperial household occupied themselves with dance, music making, games, and polite conversation.

boom and population increase that had begun in the late-Song was renewed and accelerated. The peopling of the Yangtze region and the areas to the south was given a great boost by the importation, through Spanish and Portuguese merchant intermediaries, of new food crops from the Americas, particularly root crops from the Andes highlands. Three plants—maize (our corn), sweet potatoes, and peanuts—were especially important. Because they could be grown on inferior soils that did not require irrigation, the cultivation of these crops spread quickly through the hilly and marginal areas that bordered on the irrigated rice plots of southern China. They became vital supplements to the staple rice or millet diet of the Chinese people as a whole, but particularly those of the rapidly growing southern regions. Because these plants were less susceptible to drought, they also became an important hedge against famine. The introduction of these new crops was an important factor behind the great surge in population growth that was under way by the end of the Ming era. By 1600 the population of China had risen to about 120 million from 80 to 90 million in the 14th century. Two centuries later in 1800, it had more than doubled and surpassed 300 million.

Agrarian expansion and population increase were paralleled in early Ming times by a renewal of commercial growth. The market sector of the domestic economy became ever more pervasive, and overseas trading links multiplied, particularly to areas in Southeast Asia such as Siam and the Philippines. Because China's advanced handicraft industries produced a wide variety of goods, from silk textiles and tea to fine ceramics and lacquerware that were in high demand throughout Asia and in Europe, the terms of trade ran very much in China's favor. In addition to the Arab and Asian traders, who had long risked arduous and dangerous overland or overseas journeys to trade in China, Europeans arrived in increasing numbers at the only two places—Macao and, somewhat later and more sporadically, Canton—where they were officially allowed to do business in Ming China. From Japan, from the European trading empires in South and Southeast Asia, and especially from Manila in the Spanish-held Philippines, there was a steady flow of precious metals, particularly silver, into China. Though some inflation was inevitable, the vast and sophisticated Chinese economy was much more equipped to handle this influx of new wealth than societies such as Spain and the Ottoman Empire, which had far less-developed market and manufacturing sectors.

Not surprisingly, the merchant classes, particularly those engaged in long-distance trade, reaped the biggest profits from the economic boom. But a good portion of their gains was transferred to the state in the form of taxes and to the scholar-gentry in the form of "gifts" for official favors. Much of the merchant wealth was invested in land, rather than being plowed back into trade or manufacturing, because landowning, not commerce, remained the surest route to social status in China. Though the pattern was not as pronounced as it would become in the Qing era that followed the Ming, the state and scholar-gentry were also enriched by the money paid by prominent merchants to have their sons educated so that they might pass the civil service exams. In some cases, large sums were paid to ensure that merchants' offspring did well; in others, offices were simply bought outright.

Ming prosperity was reflected in the fine arts, which found generous patrons both at court and among the scholar-gentry class more generally. Though the monochro-

Like the Ming courtiers shown here admiring a scroll painting in a carefully arranged garden setting, accomplished members of the scholar-gentry elite cultivated a taste for fine literature and the arts and interacted in accordance with an elaborate code of ritual and etiquette.

matic simplicity of the work of earlier dynasties was sustained by the ink-brush paintings of artists, such as Xuwei, much of the Ming output was busier and more colorful. Portraits and scenes of court, city, or country life were more prominent, though the Chinese delight in depicting individual scholars or travelers—contemplating the beauty of mountains, lakes, and marshes that dwarf the human observers—continued unabated.

While the painters of the Ming era concentrated mainly on developing established techniques and genres, major innovation in the arts came in literature with the full development of the Chinese novel, which had its beginnings in the writings of the Yuan era. The novel was given great impetus by the spread of literacy among the upper classes in the Ming era and by the growing availability of books that had resulted from the spread of woodblock printing from the 10th century onward. Ming novels, such as *The Water Margin*, *Monkey*, and *The Golden Lotus*, were recognized as classics in their own time and continue to set the standard for Chinese prose literature to the present day. Thus, though Chinese inventiveness of a more technical nature seems to have slowed at a critical point in time, given the great advances in science and technology in contemporary Europe, Ming achievements in the fine arts were impressive, even in comparison with those of the glorious Tang and Song eras.

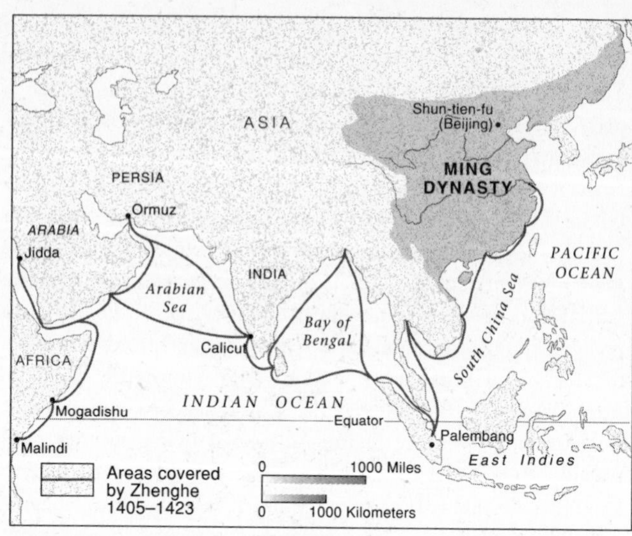

Ming China and the Zhenghe Expeditions, 1405–1423

AN AGE OF EXPANSION: THE ZHENGHE EXPEDITIONS

The seemingly boundless energy of the Chinese in early decades of Ming rule drove them far beyond the traditional areas of expansion in central Asia and the regions south of the Yangtze. In the reign of the third Ming emperor, Yunglo, they launched a series of expeditions that had no precedent in Chinese history. Between 1405 and 1423, a court eunuch named Zhenghe, who was one of Yunglo's most trusted subordinates, led seven major expeditions overseas. A mix of motives, including a desire to explore other lands and proclaim the glory of the Ming Empire to the wider world, prompted the voyages. The early expeditions were confined largely to Southeast Asian seas and kingdoms; the last three expeditions reached as far as Persia, southern Arabia, and the east coast of Africa, distances comparable to those covered by the Portuguese in their early voyages around Africa.

The ships and fleets involved in each of the overseas missions were truly impressive. The initial fleet contained 62 ships—compared to 3 for Columbus in 1492 and 4 for da Gama 6 years later—that accommodated nearly 28,000 sailors, merchants, and soldiers—compared to 150 for da Gama's first voyage around Africa. Some of the larger ships in Zhenghe's fleet were over 400 feet long and displaced up to 1500 tons of water; the largest of da Gama's caravels cannot have been much more than 60 feet in length and displaced around 300 tons of water. Taken together, the expeditions led by Zhenghe leave little doubt that the Chinese had the capacity to expand on a global scale at least a century before the Europeans rounded the Cape of Good Hope and entered Asian waters.

Though they possessed ample means, the Chinese were more than a little ambivalent about the worth of the voyages. It was gratifying to have "barbarian" peoples from the southern seas do homage to the emissaries of the Ming ruler; also, the giraffes and other curious animals that were carried home made interesting additions to the imperial zoo. But there were few tangible returns from what were very expensive undertakings. The scholar-gentry rivals of Zhenghe and other court eunuchs could convincingly argue that the voyages were a luxury that the empire simply could not afford. When they noted that the Mongols were once again restless beyond the defenses of the Great Wall (which was in need of repair and reinforcements), it was hard to refute their insistence that the defense of the empire must come before seemingly frivolous overseas exploration. Though there was one more voyage after the death of Yunglo in 1424, his successors shared little of his enthusiasm for the voyages, and consequently they were abandoned in the early 1430s. China's spectacular entry onto the world stage proved a short run indeed.

ANALYSIS

MEANS AND MOTIVES FOR OVERSEAS EXPANSION: EUROPE AND CHINA COMPARED

Given China's demonstrated capacity for overseas expansion and the fateful consequences for global history that resulted from the fact that Europe, not China, eventually took the lead in this sort of endeavor, the reasons for the Chinese failure to follow up on their early voyages of exploration merit serious examination. The explanations for the Chinese refusal to commit to overseas expansion can be best understood if they are contrasted with the forces that drove the Europeans with increasing determination into the outside world. In broad terms such a comparison underscores the fact that, though both the Europeans and the Chinese had the means to expand on a global scale, only the Europeans had strong motives for doing so.

The social and economic transformations that occurred in European civilization during the late Middle Ages and the early Renaissance had brought it to a level of development that compared favorably with China in many areas (see Chapters 21, 22, and 23). Though the Chinese empire was far vaster and more populous than tiny nation-states, such as Portugal, Spain, and Holland, European kingdoms had grown more efficient at mobilizing their more limited resources. Rivalries between the states of a fragmented Europe had also made for a greater aggressiveness and sense of competition on the part of the Europeans than the rulers of the Chinese monolith could even imagine. China's armies were far larger than those of any of the European kingdoms, but European soldiers were on the whole better led, armed, and disciplined. Chinese wet-rice agriculture was more productive than European dry-land farming, and the Chinese rulers had a far larger population to cultivate their fields, build their dikes and bridges, work their mines, and manufacture tools, clothing, and weapons. But on the whole, the technological innovations of the medieval period had given the Europeans a decided advantage over the Chinese in the animal and machine power they could generate—a capacity that did much to make up for their manpower deficiencies.

Despite differences, both civilizations possessed the means for sustained exploration and expansion overseas, though the Chinese were ready to undertake such enterprises some centuries earlier than the Europeans. As the voyages of da Gama and Columbus on the one side and Zhenghe on the other side demonstrated, both civilizations possessed the shipbuilding and navigational skills and technology to tackle such ambitious undertakings. Why then were the much more impressive Zhenghe expeditions a dead end, while the much more modest probes of Columbus and da Gama were the beginning of a half-millennia of European overseas expansion and global dominance?

The full answer to this question is as complex as the societies it asks us to compare. We can learn a good deal by looking at the groups pushing for expansion within each civilization and the needs that drove them into the outside world. There was widespread support for exploration and overseas expansion in seafaring European nations such as Portugal, Spain, Holland, and England. European rulers financed expeditions they hoped would bring home precious metals and trade goods that could be sold at great profits. Both treasure and profits could be translated into warships and armies that would strengthen these rulers in their incessant wars with both European rivals and, in the case of the Iberian kingdoms, their Muslim adversaries. European traders looked for much the same benefits from overseas expansion. Rulers and merchants also hoped that explorers would find new lands whose climates and soils were suitable for the cultivation of crops, such as sugar, that were in high demand and thus would bring big profits. Leaders of rival branches of the Christian faith believed that overseas expansion would give their missionaries access to unlimited numbers of heathens to be converted, or would put them in touch with the legendary lost king, Prester John, who would ally with them in their struggle with the infidel Muslims.

By contrast, the Chinese Zhenghe expeditions were very much the project of a single emperor and a favored eunuch whose Muslim family origins may go a long way toward accounting for his wanderlust. Yunglo appears to have been driven by little more than curiosity and the vain desire to impress his greatness and that of his empire on peoples whom he considered inferior. Though some Chinese merchants went along for the ride, most felt little need for the voyages. They already traded on favorable terms for all the products that Asia, and in some cases Europe and Africa, could offer. The merchants had the option of waiting for other peoples to come to them, or, if they were a bit more ambitious, of going out in their own ships to maritime Southeast Asia.

The scholar-gentry were actively hostile to the Zhenghe expeditions. The voyages strengthened the position of the much-hated eunuchs who vied with the scholar-gentry for the emperor's favor and the high posts that went with it. In addition, the scholar-gentry saw the voyages as a foolish diversion of resources that the empire could not afford. They believed it would be better to direct the wealth and talents of the empire to building armies and fortifications to keep out the hated Mongols and other nomads. The memory of foreign rule was, after all, quite fresh.

As the foregoing makes clear, the elites of western European nations had very good reasons for pushing voyages of exploration and projects of overseas expansion. The rulers and bureaucrats of China, on the other hand, had no reasons that were very convincing. In fact, there were very persuasive reasons, rooted in centuries of struggle against the nomads, for diverting resources that might have gone into overseas expeditions into projects on the home front. As so often before in their history, the Chinese were drawn inward, fixated on internal struggles and the continuing threat from central Asia. As the Chinese retreated, the Europeans exploded outward. It is difficult to exaggerate the magnitude of the consequences for both civilizations and all humankind.

Questions: How might history have been changed if the Chinese had mounted a serious and sustained effort to project their power overseas in the decades before da Gama rounded the Cape of Good Hope? Why did the Chinese fail to foresee the threat that European expansion would pose for the rest of Asia and finally for China itself? Are there other civilizations that had the capacity for global expansion in this era? What prevented them from launching expeditions similar to those of the Chinese and Europeans? In terms of motivation for overseas expansion, were peoples such as the Muslims, Indians, and Amerindians more like the Europeans or the Chinese?

CHINESE RETREAT AND THE ARRIVAL OF THE EUROPEANS

Just over a half century after the last of the Zhenghe expeditions, China consciously had moved from the position of a great power reaching out overseas to an increasingly isolated empire. In 1390 the first imperial edict aimed at limiting Chinese overseas commerce was issued. In the following centuries, the Ming war fleet declined dramatically in the number and quality of its ships, and strict limits were placed on the size and number of masts with which a seagoing ship might be fitted out. As the Chinese shut themselves in, the Europeans probed ever farther across the globe and were irresistibly drawn to the most legendary of all overseas civilizations, the Middle Kingdom of China. In addition to the trading contacts noted above, Christian missionaries infiltrated Chinese coastal areas and sought to gain access to the court, where they hoped to curry favor with the Ming emperors. While religious orders, such as the Franciscans and Dominicans, toiled to win converts among the common people and made modest progress that could be counted in the tens of thousands, the Jesuits adopted the "top down" strategy that di Nobili had pursued in India. In China, however, a single individual, the Ming emperor, instead of a whole caste, sat at the top of the social hierarchy, and for that reason the rulers and their chief advisors became the prime targets of the Jesuit mission.

Some Chinese scholars showed interest in Christian teachings and Western thinking more generally. But the Jesuit missionaries who managed to make their way to Beijing clearly recognized that their scientific knowledge and technical skills were the keys to maintaining a presence at the Ming court and eventually interesting the Chinese elite in Christianity. Beginning in the 1580s a succession of brilliant Jesuit scholars, such as Matteo Ricci and Adam Schall, spent most of their time in the imperial city correcting faulty calendars, forging cannon, fixing clocks imported from Europe, and astounding the Chinese literati with the accuracy of their instruments and their ability to predict eclipses. They won a few converts among the scholar-gentry, but most of the highest court officials were suspicious of these strange looking "barbarians" with large noses and hairy faces and sought to limit their contacts with the imperial family. Some at the court, especially the scholar-officials, who were humiliated by the foreigners' corrections to their calendars, and many of the eunuchs, were openly hostile to the Jesuits. Despite serious harassment, however, the later Ming emperors remained sufficiently fascinated by these very learned and able visitors that they allowed a handful to remain at court. When the Ming were overthrown by the Manchu nomads from the north, the Jesuits were able to hold and even strengthen their position at court.

MING DECLINE AND THE CHINESE PREDICAMENT

By the late 1500s the Ming retreat from overseas involvement had become just one facet of a familiar pattern of dynastic decline. The highly centralized, absolutist political structure, which had been established by Hongwu and run well by able successors such as Yunglo, became a major liability under the mediocre or incompetent individuals who occupied the throne through much of the last two centuries of Ming rule. Decades of rampant official corruption, exacerbated by the growing isolation of weak rulers by the thousands of eunuchs who gradually came to dominate life within the Forbidden City, eventually eroded the very foundations on which the empire was built.

Public works projects, including the critical dike works on the Yellow River, fell into disrepair, and floods, drought, and famine soon ravaged the land. Peasants in afflicted districts were reduced to eating the bark from trees or the excrement of wild geese. Some peasants sold their children into slavery to keep them from starving, and peasants in some areas resorted to cannibalism. Rapacious local landlords built huge estates by taking advantage of the increasingly desperate peasant population. As in earlier phases of dynastic decline, cultivators who had been turned off their land and tortured for taxes, or had lost most of the crop they had grown, turned to flight, banditry, and finally open rebellion to confiscate food and avenge their exploitation by avaricious landlords and corrupt officials.

True to the pattern of dynastic rise and fall, internal disorder resulted in and was intensified by foreign threats and renewed assaults by nomadic peoples from beyond the Great Wall. One of the early signs of the seriousness of imperial deterioration was the inability of Chinese bureaucrats and military forces to put an end to the epidemic of Japanese (and ethnic Chinese) pirate attacks that ravaged the southern coast in the mid-16th century. Despite an official preoccupation with the Mongols early in the Ming era and with the Jurchens or Manchus to the northeast of the Great Wall in later times, the dynasty was finally toppled in 1644 not by the Mongols in the west but by rebels from within. By that point in time, the administrative apparatus had become so feeble that the last Ming emperor, Chongzhen, did not realize how serious the rebel advance was until enemy soldiers were scaling the walls of the Forbidden City. After watching his wife withdraw to her chambers to commit suicide and bungling an attempt to kill his young daughter, the ill-fated Chongzhen retreated to the imperial gardens and hanged himself rather than face the ignominy of capture.

Though they managed to topple the dynasty, none of the divided rebel forces that challenged the Ming in the 1640s proved a viable replacement. A political vacuum within China once again opened the way for invasions and conquest by a nomadic people from beyond the Great Wall. This time, the Jurchens or Manchus, not the Mongols, seized power following a series of military victories and the capture of the imperial capital. The Manchu leader, Nurhaci, established a new dynasty, the Qing, that would rule China for nearly 3½ centuries and prove to be the last of a succession of imperial houses that extended back more than two millennia. Roughly the first half of the Qing reign, extending to the 1780s, was a time of renewed political strength, economic prosperity, and cultural development for Chinese civilization. Between 1644 and the mid-18th century, China's influence over surrounding areas in East Asia was restored. But by the end of the 18th century, a combination of internal crises and growing external challenges, particularly on the part of the increasingly aggressive European powers, gave rise to fundamental challenges that not only threatened the Qing dynasty but the very foundations of Chinese civilization. In Chapters 32 and 41, we will see how these challenges profoundly shaped the history of Chinese civilization throughout the past two centuries and how they continue to affect it to the present day.

FENDING OFF THE WEST: JAPAN'S REUNIFICATION AND THE FIRST CHALLENGE

Given the deep divisions of the country that resulted from the rise of the warring daimyo households, Japan was fortunate that it appeared to have little to attract the Europeans in the early centuries of their expansion. The islands were off the main trading routes and, compared to their Chinese and Southeast Asian neighbors, had few products to tempt European merchants. In fact, Japan, like Europe, contributed mainly raw materials, especially silver, to the Asian trading system the Europeans were striving to dominate. In comparison with China, the Japanese were few in number. Thus, though Francis Xavier thought them the "best people [the Europeans] had yet discovered," the prospect of their conversion paled in comparison with missionary hopes for Christianizing the multitudes of China or India. In addition, the Europeans soon discovered that the relatively small population of the islands was ruled by one of the most disciplined and fierce military elites that they had encountered anywhere in the world. It is hard to know how the Portuguese or Spanish would have fared if they had attempted to invade the islands as they did the Philippines and coastal Sri Lanka. As European visitors to Japan readily acknowledged, even divided the Japanese would make formidable adversaries.

Fortunately for the Japanese, their ability to defend their island home was not to be tested in the early centuries of expansion. In the decades just after the Europeans began to arrive in the islands in the 1540s, the Japanese found the leaders who had the military and diplomatic skills and ruthlessness needed to restore the shogunate and force the daimyo to acknowledge a supreme commander, if not a true sovereign. By the early 1600s with the potential threat from the Europeans looming ever larger in the Japanese imagination, the new Tokugawa shoguns had gained sufficient control to gradually shut down contacts with outsiders and put into effect a self-imposed isolation of the islands that would last nearly 2½ centuries. One of the main casualties of this move into isolation was the Christian missionary effort, which in the 1580s seemed on the verge of converting the shogun and the majority of his subjects. One of the great advantages of withdrawal from the Japanese point of view was the time it provided for them to recover from the long years of civil war and to build the political and economic infrastructure that was essential for lasting internal peace and the defense of Japan from outside invaders.

THE SHOGUNATE REVIVED: TOWARD THE RETURN OF INTERNAL ORDER

By the 16th century, the daimyo stalemate and the pattern of recurring civil war were so entrenched in Japanese society that it required a succession of three rather remarkable military leaders to restore a semblance of unity and internal peace. Nobunaga, the first of these leaders, was from a minor warrior household, but his skills as a military leader soon vaulted him into prominence in the ongoing struggles for power among the daimyo lords. As a leader Nobunaga combined daringness, a willingness to innovate, and ruthless determination—some would say outright cruelty. He was quite prepared to launch a surprise attack against an enemy that outnumbered him ten to one, and he was one of the first of the daimyos to make extensive use of the firearms that the Japanese had begun to acquire from the Portuguese in the 1540s. The measures Nobunaga took in reprisal against those who resisted him, such as the slaughter of thousands of monks and villagers attached to the Buddhist monastery at Mount Hiei near Kyoto, may well have cowed some of the weaker daimyos into submission. In 1573 Nobunaga deposed the last of the Ashikaga shoguns, who had long ruled in name only, and by 1580 he had unified much of central Honshu under his command. As his armies drove against the powerful western daimyo in 1582, Nobunaga was caught off guard by one of his vassal generals and killed when the Kyoto temple where he had taken refuge was burned to the ground.

At first it appeared that Nobunaga's campaigns to restore central authority to the islands might be undone. But his ablest general, Toyotomi Hideyoshi, moved quickly to punish those who had betrayed Nobunaga and to renew the drive to break the power of the daimyos who had not yet submitted to him. Though the son of a peasant, Hideyoshi matched his master in military prowess and was far more skillful at diplomacy. A system of alliances and a string of victories over the last of the resisting daimyos made Hideyoshi the military master of Japan by 1590.

The ambitious overlord had much more grandiose schemes of conquest in mind. He dreamed of ruling China and even India, though he knew little about either place,

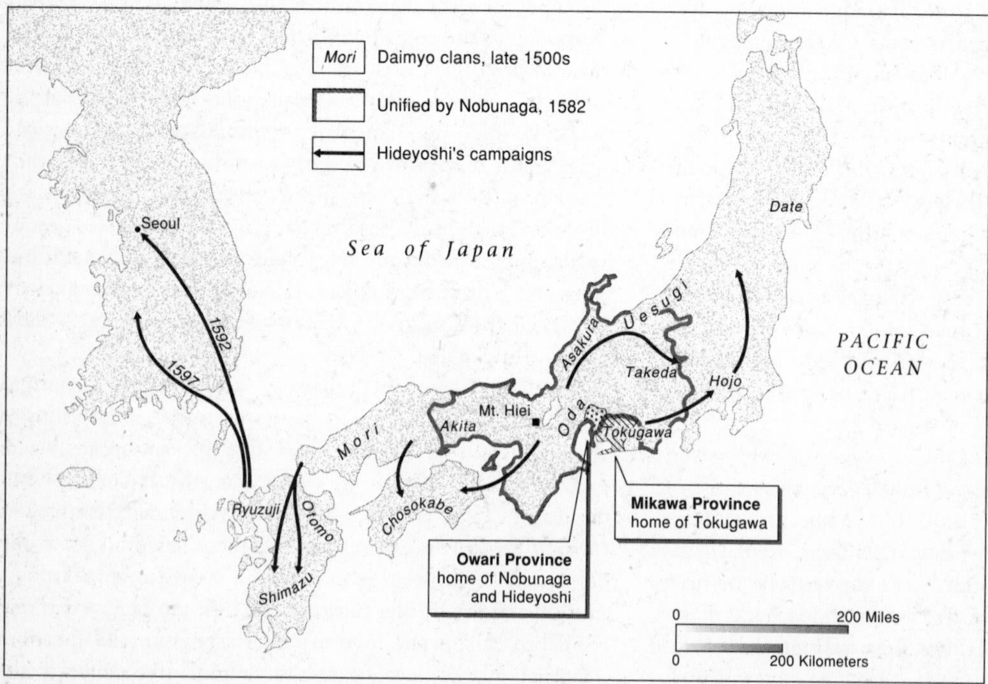

Japan: The Rise of the Tokugawa Shogunate

In this late 16th-century portrait Hideyoshi (1536–1598) grasps the sword that catapulted him to power and exudes the discipline and self-confidence that did much to further his campaigns to unify Japan.

and threatened, among others, the Spanish in the Philippines. Apparently as the first step toward fulfilling this vision of empire-building on a grand scale, Hideyoshi launched two attacks on Korea in 1592 and 1597, each of which involved nearly 150,000 soldiers. After initial successes both campaigns stalled: The first ended in defeat; the second was still in progress when Hideyoshi died in 1598.

Though Hideyoshi had sought to ensure that he would be succeeded by his son, the vassals whom he had appointed to carry out his wishes sought to seize power for themselves after his death. One of these vassals, Tokugawa Ieyasu, who had originally come from a minor daimyo house but as an ally of Hideyoshi, had been able to build up a powerful domain on the heavily populated Kanto plain and emerged triumphant from the renewed warfare that resulted. Rather than continue Hideyoshi's campaigns of overseas expansion, Ieyasu concentrated on consolidating power at home. In 1603 he was granted the title of shogun by the emperor, an act which formally inaugurated 2½ centuries of rule by the Tokugawa family. Under Ieyasu's direction, the remaining daimyos were reorganized. Most of the lands in central Honshu were either controlled directly by the Tokugawa family, who now ruled the land from the city of Edo (later Tokyo), or were held by daimyos who were closely allied with the shoguns. Though many of the outlying or vassal daimyos retained their domains, they were carefully controlled and required to pledge their personal allegiance to the shogun. Over a period of time the estates of numerous vassal daimyos were reduced in size or broken up and absorbed by the Tokugawa family or their close allies. It was soon clear that the Tokugawas' victory had put an end to the civil wars and brought a semblance of political unity to the islands.

DEALING WITH THE EUROPEAN CHALLENGE

All through the decades when the three unifiers were struggling to bring the feisty daimyos under control, they also had to contend with a totally new force in Japanese history, the Europeans. From the time in 1543 when shipwrecked Portuguese sailors were washed up on the shore of Kyushu island, European traders and missionaries visited the islands in increasing numbers. The traders brought the Japanese mainly goods produced in India, China, and Southeast Asia and exchanged them for silver, copper, pottery, and lacquerware. Perhaps more important, the European traders and the missionaries who followed them to the islands brought firearms, printing presses, and other Western devices such as clocks. The firearms, which the Japanese could themselves manufacture within years and were improving in design within a generation, revolutionized Japanese warfare and contributed much to the victories of the unifiers. Commercial contacts with the Europeans also encouraged the Japanese to venture overseas to trade in nearby Formosa and Korea and places as distant as the Philippines and Siam.

Soon after the merchants, Christian missionaries arrived in the islands and set to work converting the Japanese to Roman Catholicism. Beginning in the outlying daimyos' domains, the missionaries worked their way toward the political center that was beginning to coalesce around Nobunaga and his followers by the 1570s. Seeing Christianity as a counterforce to the militant Buddhist orders that were resisting his rise to power, Nobunaga took the missionaries under his protection and encouraged them to preach their faith to his people. The Jesuits, adopting the same "top down" strategy of conversion that they had followed in India and China, converted a number of the daimyos and many of their samurai retainers. Some of the Jesuits were also convinced that they were on the verge of

This 16th-century screen painting shows the arrival of Francis Xavier and his entourage in Japan. The painting conveys a sense of the Japanese perception of these strangers from distant lands as exotic, awkward, and curiously dressed.

winning over Nobunaga, who delighted in wearing Western clothes, encouraged his artists to copy Western paintings of the Virgin Mary and scenes from the life of Christ, and permitted the missionaries to build churches in towns throughout the islands. The missionaries were persuaded that Nobunaga's conversion would bring the whole of the Japanese people into the Christian fold. Even without it, they reported converts in the hundreds of thousands by the early 1580s. After all of the frustrations that the missionaries had experienced as a result of their efforts in India, China, and elsewhere, Japan looked for a time to be the most promising candidate in all of Asia for widespread conversion.

In the late 1580s, quite suddenly, the missionaries saw their carefully mounted conversion campaign collapse. Nobunaga was murdered, and his successor, Hideyoshi, though not yet openly hostile, was lukewarm toward the missionary enterprise. In part the missionaries' fall from favor resulted from the fact that the resistance of the Buddhist sects had been crushed. More critically, Hideyoshi and his followers were alarmed by reports of converts refusing to obey commands, which they believed conflicted with their newly adopted Christian beliefs, from their daimyo overlords or their own parents. Thus, the threat that the new religion posed for the established social order was growing more apparent. That threat was compounded by signs that the Europeans might follow up their commercial and missionary overtures with military expeditions aimed at the conquest of the islands. The Japanese had been strongly impressed with the firearms and pugnacity of the Europeans, and they were therefore not inclined to take threats of invasion lightly.

JAPAN'S SELF-IMPOSED ISOLATION

Growing doubts about European intentions and fears that both merchants and missionaries might subvert the existing social order led, beginning in the late 1580s, to official measures to restrict foreign activities in Japan. First, the Christian missionaries were ordered by Hideyoshi to leave the islands—an order that was not rigorously enforced, at least at the outset. By the mid-1590s, Hideyoshi was actively persecuting both Christian missionaries and converts. His successor Ieyasu continued this persecution and then officially banned the faith in 1614. European missionaries were driven out of the islands; those who remained underground were hunted down and killed or expelled. Japanese converts were compelled to renounce their faith; those who refused, including women and children, were imprisoned, tortured, and executed. By the 1630s the persecutions, even against Christians who attempted to practice their faith in secret, had become so intense that thousands of converts in the western regions joined in hard-fought, but hopeless, rebellions against the local daimyo and the forces of the *shogun*. With the suppression of these uprisings Christianity in Japan was reduced to an underground faith of isolated communities. As in India and China, a promising start toward conversion had come to little.

Under Ieyasu and his successors the persecution of the Christians grew into a broader campaign to utterly isolate Japan from outside influences. In 1616 foreign traders were confined to a handful of cities; in the 1630s all Japanese ships were forbidden to trade or even sail overseas. One after another different European nations were either officially excluded from Japan (the Spanish) or concluded that trading there was no longer worth the considerable risk (the English). By the 1640s only a limited number of Dutch and Chinese ships were allowed to call at and carry on commerce in the small island of Deshima in Nagasaki Bay. The export of silver and copper was greatly restricted, Western books were banned to prevent Christian ideas from reentering the country, and foreigners were permitted to live and travel only in very limited areas.

By the mid-17th century Japan's retreat into almost total isolation was completed. Much of the next century was spent in consolidating the internal control of the Tokugawa Shogunate by extending bureaucratic administration into the vassal daimyo domains throughout the islands. In the 18th century, a revival of neo-Confucian philosophy, which had marked the period of the Tokugawa's rise to power, increasingly gave way to the influence of thinkers who championed the school of "National Learning." As its name implies, the new ideology laid great emphasis on Japan's unique historical experience and the revival of indigenous culture at the expense of Chinese imports such as Confucianism. In the following centuries, through contacts with the small Dutch community at Deshima, members of the Japanese elite also followed developments in the West. Their avid interest in the achievements of the Europeans contrasted sharply with the indifference of the Chinese scholar-gentry in this period to the doings of the "hairy barbarians" from Europe.

The openings the Japanese left to the outside world meant than when the second push by the Western powers for entry into Japan came, beginning in the 1850s, the Japanese knew much more clearly than the Chinese what they were up against. Chinese indifference left them blind to the intentions and power of their European adversaries, and thus unable to deal effectively with European demands and ultimately military incursions in the middle decades of the 19th century. After much debate within the daimyo elite, the Japanese first followed a policy of concession and evasion in the face of the Western challenge, then concentrated on building up their strength by adopting European innovations they had monitored over the centuries through contacts with the Dutch at Deshima.

CONCLUSION

ASIA AND THE FIRST PHASE OF EUROPE'S GLOBAL EXPANSION

During the early modern period in global history, the West's surge in exploration and commercial expansion touched most of Asia only peripherally. This was particularly true of East Asia, where the political cohesion and military strength of the vast Chinese empire and the Japanese warrior-dominated states blocked all hope of European domination. Promising missionary inroads in the 16th century were stifled by hostile Tokugawa shoguns in the early 17th century and carefully contained by the Ming emperors and the nomadic Qing dynasty that succeeded in the mid-1600s. Strong Chinese and Japanese rulers also limited trading contacts with the aggressive Europeans and confined European merchants to one or two ports—Macao and Canton in China, Deshima in Japan—that were remote from their respective capitals. These restrictions and the strength of the regimes and societies able to impose them meant that the European impact on East Asian civilizations was highly selective and limited in the first three centuries of European overseas expansion. Change in China, Japan, Korea, or central Asia was generated mainly by internal factors; continuity was ensured by the persistence of centuries-old cultural and social patterns and techniques of handling alien intruders like the European seafarers.

Even in most of South and Southeast Asia, where the European impact in the early centuries of Western overseas expansion was much more pronounced, Asians retained control over their own destinies and their history was shaped far more by long-standing indigenous patterns of development than by impulses from a vibrant but distant Europe. European control was limited to the island periphery of great empires, such as that built by the Mughals in India, and the kingdoms of mainland and island Southeast Asia. Sea power allowed the Portuguese, and after them the Spanish, Dutch, and English, to control trading outposts in ports such as Goa, Malacca, Batavia, and Bombay, and even to conquer parts of island kingdoms, such as the southwest corner of Ceylon or the northwest end of Java. But little European headway was made until well into the 18th century against even some of the weaker kingdoms of South or Southeast Asia, and Christian missionaries won few converts except in areas, such as the northern Philippines, where one of the major Asian religions had not previously spread. Even in commerce and seafaring, where the influence of the West in Asia was the greatest, the Europeans found that it was better to blend into the existing networks and cooperate with local rulers and merchants than to build expensive and vulnerable trading empires.

Only in the 18th century were first the Dutch and later the English able to begin to dominate some of the core areas of South and Southeast Asian civilization. Even then, as we shall see in Chapter 30, the domination was as much a product of Asian divisions and weaknesses as of decisive European advantages in making war or running bureaucracies.

FURTHER READINGS

C. G. F. Simkins's *The Traditional Trade of Asia* (1968) provides an able overview of the Asian trading network from ancient times until about the 18th century. Much more detailed accounts of specific segments of the system, as well as the impact of the Dutch and Portuguese on it, can be found in the works of J. C. van Leur, M. A. P. Meilink-Roelofsz, K. N. Chaudhuri, Ashin Das Gupta, and Michael Pearson. C. R. Boxer's *The Portuguese Seaborne Empire* (1969) and *The Dutch Seaborne Empire* (1965) are still essential reading, though the latter has little on the Europeans in Asia. Boxer's *Race Relations in the Portuguese Colonial Empire, 1415–1825* (1963) provides a stimulating, if contentious, introduction to the history of European social interaction with overseas peoples in the early centuries of expansion. G. B. Sansom's *The Western World and Japan* (1968) includes a wealth of information on the interaction between Europeans and, despite its title, peoples throughout Asia, and it has good sections on the missionary initiatives in both China and Japan.

The period of the Ming dynasty has been the focus of broad but detailed studies to a greater extent than the dynasties that preceded it. An important early work is Charles O. Hucker's *The Censorial System of Ming China*

(1966). Two essential recent works are Albert Chan's *The Glory and Fall of the Ming Dynasty* (1982) and Edward Dreyer's more traditional political history entitled *Early Ming China, 1355–1435* (1982). There are also wonderful insights into daily life at various levels of Chinese society in Roy Huang's very readable *1587: A Year of No Significance; The Ming Dynasty in Decline* (1981), and into the interaction between the Chinese and the Jesuits in Jonathan Spence's *The Memory Palace of Matteo Ricci* (1984). Frederic Wakeman Jr.'s *The Great Enterprise*, 2 vols. (1985), is essential to an understanding of the transition from Ming to Manchu rule. The early chapters of Jonathan Spence's *The Search for Modern China* (1990) also provides an illuminating overview of that process.

Perhaps the best introductions to the situation in Japan in the early phase of European expansion are provided by G. B. Sansom's survey, *A History of Japan, 1615–1867* (1963), and Conrad Totman's *Politics in the Tokugawa Bakufu, 1600–1843* (1967). Numerous studies on the Europeans in Japan include those by Donald Keene, Grant Goodman, Noel Perrin, and C. R. Boxer. Intellectual trends in Japan in this era are the most fully treated in H. D. Harootunian's *Toward Restoration: The Growth of Political Consciousness in Tokugawa Japan* (1970).

A.D. 1700

A.D. 1800

1770 James Watt's steam engine; beginning of Industrial Revolution

1808–1825 Latin-American wars of independence

1789–1815 French Revolution and Napoleon

1730–1850 Population boom in western Europe

1805–1849 Muhammed Ali rules Egypt

1776–1783 American Revolution

1823 Monroe Doctrine

1812 Napoleon's failed invasion of Russia

1786–1790 First British reforms in India

1822 Brazil declares independence

1815 Vienna settlement

1788 Australian colonization begins

1798 Napoleon's invasion of Egypt

1815 British annexation of Cape Town and region of southern Africa

The Crystal Palace in Hyde Park, London, was constructed for the 1851 World's Fair. The building is almost all glass and was one of the industrial wonders of the time.

1839–1876 Reforms in Ottoman Empire

1848 ff. Beginnings of Marxism

1860–1868 Civil strife in Japan

1840 Semiautonomous government in Canada

1861–1865 American Civil War

1870–1910 Acceleration of "demographic transition" in western Europe and the United States

1853 Perry expedition to Edo Bay in Japan

1863 Emancipation of slaves in U.S.

1839–1841 Opium War with China

1830, 1848 Revolutions in Europe

1854–1856 Crimean War

1835 English education in India

1867 Union of central and eastern Canada

1826 New Zealand colonization begins

1838 Ottoman trade treaty with Britain

1850–1864 Taiping rebellion in China

1868–1912 Meiji (reform) era in Japan

1864–1871 German unification

1825–1855 Repression in Russia

1870–1910 Expansion of commercial export economy in Latin America

1858 British Parliament assumes control over India

1846–1848 Mexican-American War

1870 Establishment of Japanese Ministry of Industry

1861 Emancipation of serfs in Russia; reform era begins

PART 5

Industrialization and Western Global Hegemony, 1750–1914

The period of world history that spans almost two centuries after 1750 was marked by unusually clear characteristics. These were the decades in which Western civilization (now embracing much of North America as well as western Europe) experienced the Industrial Revolution, which transformed the bases of production through new technology and new sources of power. Building on earlier Western developments, including the scientific revolution, industrialization brought massive changes to the West's economy and society.

Largely on the basis of industrialization the West attained a genuine, if fleeting, hegemony over most other civilizations in the world. In contrast to the early modern period, when Western power away from the seas was characteristically limited, particularly in and around most of Asia, no area could now escape the possibility of extensive European or United States penetration. Thus Africa, previously able to accommodate to Western power while strengthening internal political units, was now carved up into a patchwork of colonies. The West's new hegemony was also expressed through the rapid expansion of Western imperialism and the intensification of colonial controls even in many older holdings such as India. It was expressed through growing commercial penetration of areas such as much of China and the Ottoman Empire, not directly held as colonies. Western hegemony also continued to constrain Latin America, which ran against the tide in achieving independence from colonial

1884–1914 Russian industrialization

1898–1901 Boxer Rebellion in China

1871–1912 High point of European imperialism

1882 British takeover of Egypt

1890s Partition of East Africa

1911–1912 Revolution in China; abolition of empire

1903 Construction of Panama Canal begins

1890s European leases in China

1877–1878 Ottomans out of most of Balkans; Treaty of San Stefano

1898 Formation of Marxist Social Democratic Party in Russia

1908 Young Turk rising

1914 World War I

1879–1890s Partition of West Africa

1894–1895 Sino-Japanese War

1904–1905 Russo-Japanese War

1910 Japan annexes Korea

1886–1888 Slavery abolished in Cuba and Brazil

1905–1906 Revolution in Russia; limited reforms

1895 Cuban revolt against Spain

1901 Commonwealth of Australia

1885 Formation of National Congress Party in India

1898 Spanish-American War; U.S. acquires the Philippines, Puerto Rico, and Hawaii; U.S. intervenes in Cuba

1890 Japanese constitution

---

rule early in the 19th century. Finally, Western hegemony was expressed by the need of every civilization to come to terms with Western institutions and values, by figuring out what to try to imitate and how.

In a sense, the dominant themes of the imperialist era amplified tendencies already discernible in the early modern centuries. International commercial contacts increased, largely through Western merchant activity and shipping, enhanced now by major technological innovations in the transportation field—notably the steamship, railroad, and telegraph. Cultural contacts reflected Western power as well. Just as Christianity and commercial penetration had gone hand in hand in Latin America during the early modern period, by the end of the 19th century substantial

Industrial Development in Key Regional Centers, about 1900

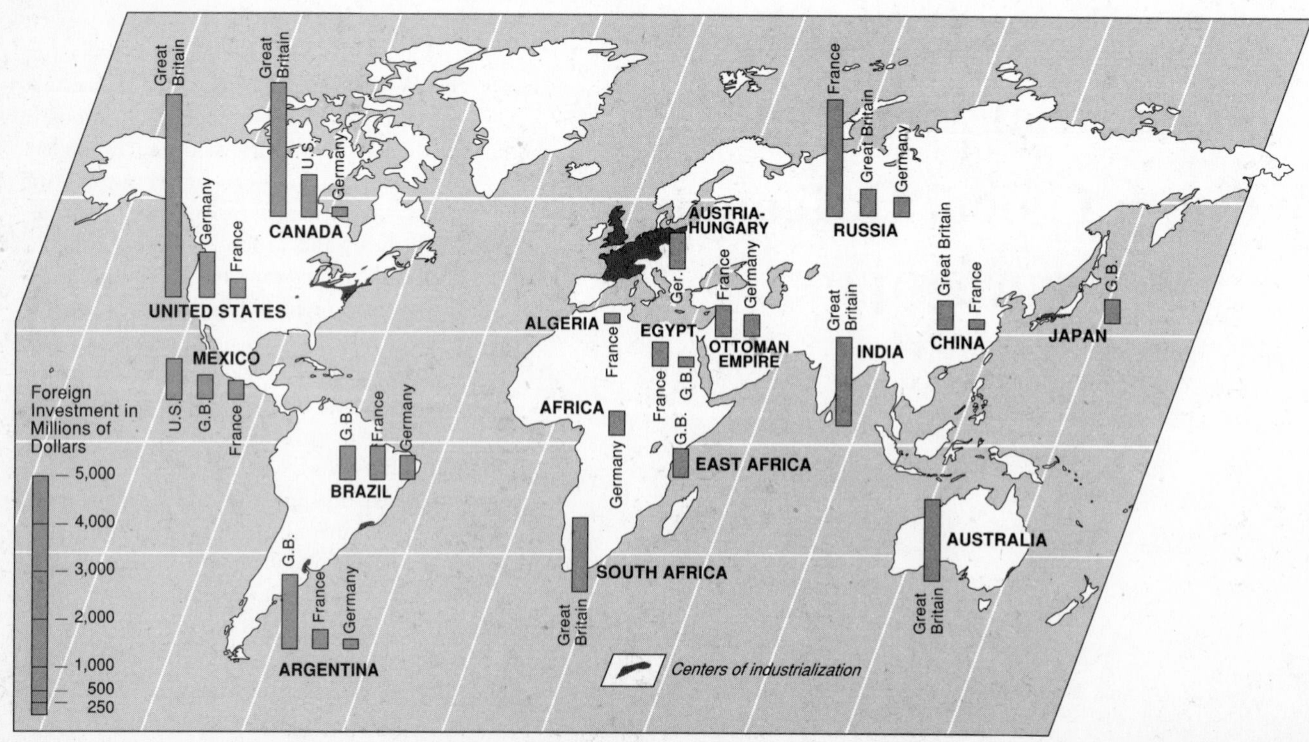

religious conversion began to accompany Western political and economic entry into Africa's heartlands.

Geographical rebalancing, in terms of the most obvious border shifts, also maintained the Western preeminence theme. Along with new levels of international exchange, boundary changes constitute one of the key criteria for defining a major period in world history, and during the 19th century they reflected the rise of Western power above all.

The decades of imperialism were not, however, simply a continuation of early modern trends in colonialism and the world economy. The dramatic new ingredient was the West's Industrial Revolution, which set the key themes of 19th-century world history by massively increasing the imperialist power of the West and by intensifying world economic contacts under the West's commercial sponsorship. By the 1850s the leading issues in all civilizations began to revolve around what to do about the West's new power—how and whether to resist, and what could or should be imitated. Western commercial interests generated the most obvious enhancement of international contacts, but missionary and other cultural conversion efforts played a role. These patterns, plus some common efforts at response, produced new parallels among major societies—as in growing interest in establishing new kinds of schools and, in a number of cases, even parliaments and constitutions. New geography, new contacts, and new parallels constitute the common stuff of world history periods, and in the 19th century they all took shape under Western influence.

CHRONOLOGY: FROM INDUSTRIAL REVOLUTION TO THE BEGINNINGS OF A WESTERN BREAKDOWN

The beginning point of this new period, 1750, focuses on no particular event, though it is true that the war that opened in that decade, pitting France against Britain as colonial powers and producing battles in Europe, North America, and India as well as on the seas, has some claim to being history's first global conflict. More important is the fact that it was during the 1750s that the forces that directly produced Europe's Industrial Revolution began to take shape: rapid population growth, expansion of manufacturing, a surge of new inventions. A real Industrial Revolution is properly dated a few decades later, but the second half of the 18th century captures its formative stages.

With Western industrialization under way, signs of its impact on the wider world followed relatively quickly. In 1798 a modest French expeditionary force seized Egypt from its Muslim rulers—a clear sign of a new power bal-

Main Colonial Holdings, about 1914

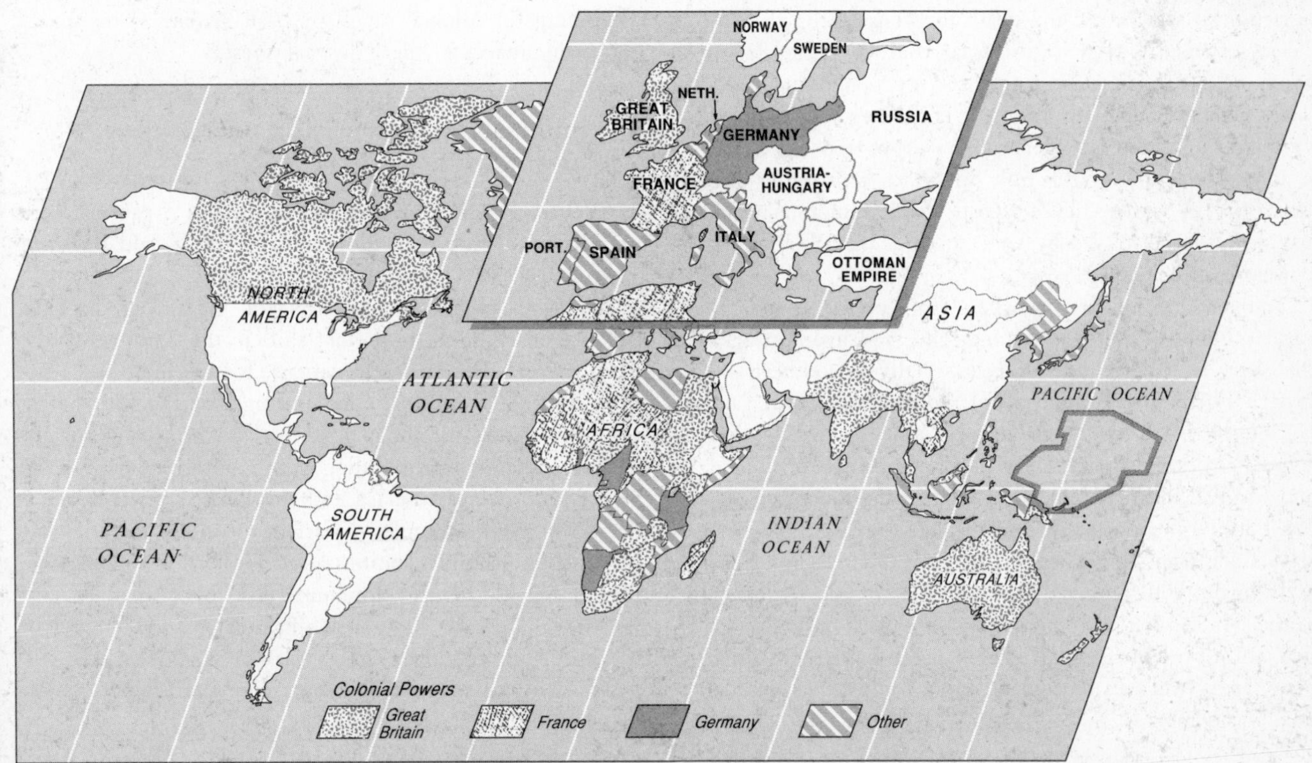

ance in the eastern Mediterranean and a warning, as a few Muslim leaders recognized even in the retreating Ottoman Empire, of a need to innovate in response. In the 1820s Britain's hold over India began to intensify. In the 1830s the West forced open China's markets, using the insistence on the right to sell opium in China as the unsavory entering wedge. In the 1850s Britain and France defeated Russia in a war in its own Crimean backyard, while the United States and Britain pried open Japanese markets under threat of naval bombardment. The American Civil War (1861–1865) saw the industrial north prevail over the slaveholding south. Also in the 1860s, the scramble for new African colonies effectively began. In the 1870s a new level of commercial penetration started to transform the Latin American economy and social relationships. Between the 1850s and 1900, the islands of Polynesia were brought under Western control as colonies; the Maoris of New Zealand were subjected to a government of European settlers.

Western industrialization and imperialism, supplemented by major policy changes in the Western states, led to huge shifts in the population structures of various parts of the world. In the West, including the United States, the birthrate began to decline to historically low levels, beginning in some cases before 1800 and accelerating after 1870. This "demographic transition" to low birthrates reflected the fact that child labor was being displaced by machines; children were far less useful than they had been in agricultural societies. Child death rates also declined in the West, especially after 1880, as a result of better living conditions—which caused a further reduction in birthrates. The changes in the definitions of children's purposes and emphasis on their lovableness also supported the demographic transition. With high birthrates continuing elsewhere in the world, the West's percentage of total world population began to slip by 1900, even as the West's world power reached its brief peak.

Industrialization drew workers from populous agricultural regions to the new factory centers. European areas that were slow to industrialize, especially in southern and eastern Europe, sent hundreds of thousands of immigrants to centers in Germany and France, and especially to the United States, Australia, and Canada. Italians, Portuguese, and Spanish immigrants also flooded to the more prosperous Latin American nations in the late 19th century. The slave trade from Africa was ended under British leadership early in the 19th century; only a trickle continued, mainly to the Middle East. Humanitarian considerations, plus the new abilities demonstrated by industrial factories to organize "free" workers more effectively for production, fed this development.

Various immigration patterns arose to replace the slave trade. European immigrants, as well as Asian immigrants, were recruited. New Asian minorities became important factors in various parts of the world, beginning a pattern that would continue in the 20th century. Though not slaves, most immigrants were poorly paid and often restricted by harsh contracts and employer controls that might include obligatory company-owned stores, where workers were required to shop at often inflated prices. Despite poor conditions, many eastern and southern Asian immigrants were able to rise as shopkeepers and other commercial agents in their new societies, another development that heightened the importance of the great population movements of the 19th century.

Demographic and immigration patterns reflected the strength of the basic causation that determined the leading developments in world history from 1750 to 1914. Western power allowed recruitment of labor from other societies without the crudeness of slavery. Western industrialization, causing major demographic redefinitions in the West itself, began to attract workers from other, poorer societies still locked in agricultural economies.

The industrial-imperialist period drew to a close with the outbreak of World War I in 1914 quite simply because, in the wake of this massive conflict, the West's world hold began to recede, and a new, if gradual and complex, pattern of global relationships began to take shape. Revolutions in Russia, Japanese expansion, and the beginnings of colonial revolt signaled the end of the undisputed dominance of the industrial West.

DIVERSITIES IN THE AGE OF WESTERN DOMINANCE

Western industrialization and imperialist expansion were not the only major developments in the world between 1750 and 1914. A major surge of popular conversion to Islam began in sub-Saharan Africa at the end of the 18th century, marking an important shift in the continent's religious map. Latin American nations, for the most part winning freedom from Spain and Portugal by the 1820s after a series of wars for independence, launched an important process of new-nation building that requires emphasis in its own right. Latin America and the United States formed the world's first examples of societies working to forge stable institutions and identities after Western colonial dominance. Significant developments elsewhere echoed more traditional themes. Thus in China, major social unrest in the mid-19th century recalled earlier periods of dynastic decline, in which rural elements rose against population pressure and unchecked landlord control.

The 19th century must not be simplified into the results of Western imperialist pressure alone. Nevertheless, the period's central themes are inescapable. The West's industrially fueled expansion did not command every trend, but it affected most of them.

The principal complexity in dealing with the period from 1750 to 1914 lies not in identifying the common international forces centered around the West's new expansion, but in detailing the diversities of reactions to the dominant trends. Amid growing Western influence and powerful pressures or inducements to imitate, the world remained diverse, and civilization boundaries continued to define distinctive experiences.

One reaction was incorporation into an expanded Western civilization. The West expanded during the 19th century through the emergence of strong immigrant societies in the United States, Canada, Australia, and New Zealand, each with its own important modifications of basic Western patterns.

Elsewhere, several other responses to the rise of the West predominated, and they revealed unexpected similarities among otherwise diverse societies. Two societies, Russia and Japan, undertook a substantial internal transformation amid great stress, which permitted them to imitate key Western gains without becoming Western outright. Another set of civilizations grappled more tentatively with reform, producing less definitive results amid growing weakness. A third set of societies were colonies outright and faced the twin issues of change and domination.

China and the Ottoman Empire both lost territories to Western imperialism, but preserved a degree of independence amid growing weakness, outside interference, and agonizing indecision about the most effective way to counter the challenge from the West. Latin American nations that were newly independent also grappled with reform currents but amid particularly intense economic constraints.

Most of the rest of the world, including North Africa, was either colonized outright or, as with Latin America, reduced to economic dependence on Western trade. Colonial rule was not a constant, having somewhat different effects in India, for example, than in Africa, where imperialism was a later arrival and where in some cases a harsher racism affected Western policy.

The different kinds of reactions to the industrial, imperialist West constituted an additional source of geographical change in the 19th century, helping to define the period particularly in its later phases. Areas that had previously cohered, at least loosely, as a single civilization zone now split apart.

Diverse responses to the West's fierce surge reflected prior civilization traditions. Some societies found it easier than others to imitate or to concentrate on technological change on the basis of preexisting cultural values or political forms. Diversity followed from different power bases in terms of political institutions and the extent and rapidity of Western economic penetration.

Finally, different patterns of response resulted also from changes in the West itself, in a chaotic if exhilarating period of Western history. What was the West: Was it Christianity or one of the newer political faiths such as nationalism or socialism? Was the Western political message liberal, or did it consist of tighter bureaucratic organization and more effective military force—both definite aspects of the West's 19th-century experience? Different Western faces would obviously appeal to different prior experiences, depending on the civilization involved and the manner in which the West was now encountered.

The analytical challenge of world history in the age of industrialization and Western global hegemony from 1750 to 1914 consists less in tracing the main themes, than in tracing, explaining, and assessing the significance of diverse responses to these themes. Only through this analysis can the dynamic of the 19th century history be grasped, as it ranged from eager embrace of what the West seemed to represent to horrified rejection. And only through this comparative analysis can the next stage of world history be properly anticipated; for in the 20th century world-historical trends became once again more complex with the decline of formal Western power amid the potent lingering effects of the West's economic and cultural examples and amid the worldwide impact of the industrial economy.

Chapters covering the industrial-imperialist age begin with the huge transformation of the West, where political upheavals associated with an age of democratic revolution joined the fundamental impact of the world's first industrial revolutions. The effects of industrialization on imperialism are presented in Chapter 30, with the new colonial patterns in India and Southeast Asia and the rapid acquisition of new swaths of territory from the Pacific to North Africa. The special pattern of Latin America stands in complex contrast to the various colonial settings, as economic dependence coexisted with newly independent nations. The two old civilizations not colonized outright, but faced with agonizing adjustment problems, China and Islam, are juxtaposed next. Finally, the startling responses of Russia and Japan, where Western pressures were deeply felt but actively countered, are compared. This concludes the treatment of a short period of world history made unusually dramatic by the economic revolution whose impact, reverberating around the globe, created important new economic inequalities from one society to the next along with new and intense connections.

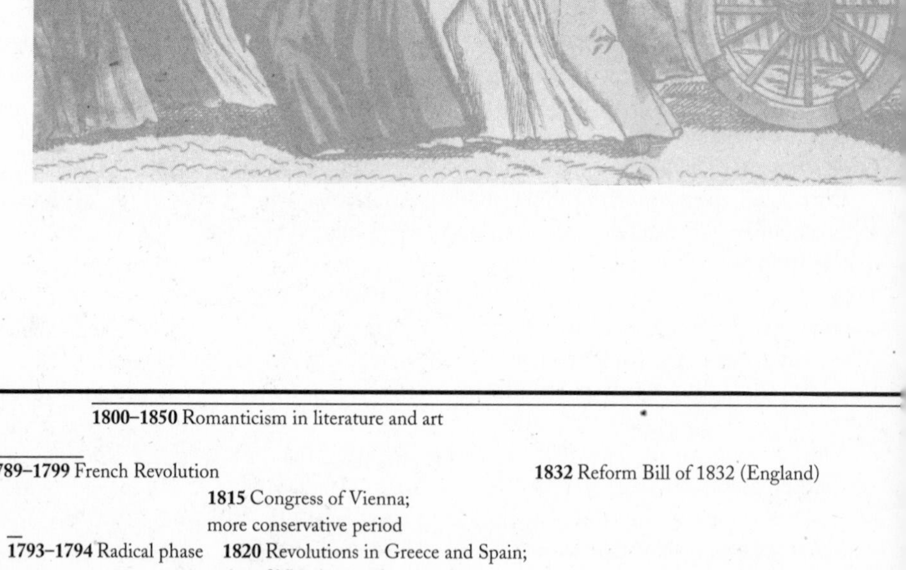

Western Europe

1730 ff. Massive population rise

c. 1770 James Watt's steam engine; beginning of Industrial Revolution

1789–1799 French Revolution

1793–1794 Radical phase

1799–1815 Reign of Napoleon

1800–1850 Romanticism in literature and art

1815 Congress of Vienna; more conservative period

1820 Revolutions in Greece and Spain; rise of liberalism and nationalism

1830, 1848 Revolutions in several European countries

1832 Reform Bill of 1832 (England)

Extensions of Western Civilization

1788 First convict settlement in Australia

1789 Washington, first president of the U.S.

1790 ff. Begin per capita birthrate decline

1793 First free European settlers in Australia

1803 The Louisiana Purchase (U.S.)

1810–1826 Rise of democratic suffrage in U.S.

1820s ff. Industrialization in U.S.

1823 First legislative council in Australia

1826–1837 Begin active European colonization in New Zealand

1829 Jackson, seventh president of the U.S.

29 The Industrialization of the West, 1760–1914

INTRODUCTION. In the century and a half after 1760, Western society went through a dizzying series of changes. A combustion of political and social revolutions reverberated throughout the society. The French Revolution of 1789 was in essence the first great modern revolution in world history, but it was paralleled by uprisings in North America and many other European states in a pattern that lasted through 1848. Dramatic new cultural styles developed, some challenging 18th-century Enlightenment thought, some building on it through scientific research or political theory. Changes in popular culture occurred as well, and ordinary Westerners thought and behaved quite differently in 1900 than in the mid-18th century. A host of diplomatic upheavals accompanied internal change. New Western states rose to power—the surge of Germany was particularly noteworthy—and at the end of the period a new alliance system brought the West to a catastrophic war.

The greatest change of all involved the West's industrialization. The Industrial Revolution featured the creation of radical new technological and economic structures, transforming agricultural society much as the Neolithic revolution had once transformed hunting-and-gathering cultures. The force of the industrial upheaval spilled over into all facets of Western life, changing intimate popular habits such as sexuality and family life and basic social processes such as the making of war.

1848 ff. Writings of Karl Marx; rise of socialism

1859–1870 Unification of Italy

1859 Darwin's *Origin of Species*

1864–1871 German unification

1870–1879 Institution of French Third Republic

1870s ff. Rapid birthrate decline

1870s ff. Spread of compulsory education laws

1871–1914 High point of European imperialism

1837 Rebellion in Canada

1837–1842 U.S.-Canada border clashes

1839 New British colonial policy

1840 Union act reorganizes Canada, provides elected legislature

1843–1848 First Maori War in New Zealand

1846–1848 Mexican-American War

1850 Australia's Colonies Government Act allows legislature and more autonomy

1852 New constitution in New Zealand; elected councils

1860–1870 Second Maori War

1861–1865 American Civil War

1863 Emancipation of slaves

1867 British North America Act, unites eastern and central Canada

This fundamental transformation of Western society, during what was by historical standards a surprisingly short span of time, had obvious significance for wider world history. The West was already established as one of the world's vigorous civilizations, so basic change had automatic importance simply as part of the ongoing human panorama. The West did not shake off all previous characteristics, but all traditions—for example, parliamentary political forms—had to be rethought and adapted.

More obviously still, the changes of the industrial period further enhanced Europe's power in the world. Important extensions of Western civilization arose not only in the young United States but also in Canada, Australia, and New Zealand. By the end of the 19th century, literally all areas were touched by Western economic and military strength, so that reactions to the West's transformation became a fundamental part of world history.

Finally, the changes the West experienced during these decades foreshadowed some of the issues and patterns that would affect other societies later on, even into our own day. The struggle to industrialize, to create appropriate new political forms, and to alter traditional family life would not take exactly the same shape everywhere, but some common themes were usually involved. In this sense, as in viewing the great French Revolution as the first of many modern revolutions around the world, change in the West can be used as an analogy, a base for comparison with other major civilizations from the late 19th century onward.

The Western pattern of change, partly because it had no full parallels in earlier human history—no society had ever industrialized before, no society had ever pulled the majority of its population into cities, no society had ever virtually eliminated death among young children—was inevitably complex. Not all changes easily related to each other. Political revolution, for example, began as a development separate from industrialization; in contrast the Industrial Revolution, taking shape first in Britain, occurred in a society that remained relatively stable (though not unchanging) in politics. Only gradually did the strands of political and industrial transformation merge.

The best way to untangle the complexity of the Western transformation is, not surprisingly, to proceed historically—that is, to identify key subperiods within the longer span. These subperiods involve a growing crisis, late in the 18th century, that helped create changes in a variety of areas from sex to machinery; then a phase of experimentation, roughly 1789 to 1850, in which political revolution vied for attention with the initial thrust of industrialization; and finally, from 1850 to 1914, a more mature stage in which the implications of industrial society were more fully worked out. This final subperiod seemed at the time tranquil after the alarms and excitements of the revolutionary decades, but it embodied subterranean tensions that would burst forth in the most dreadful war the world had ever known.

Through these three subperiods virtually every aspect of western Europe changed, with Britain, France, and Germany leading the way. Science gained ground, art was revolutionized by new styles, and religion on the whole declined further. Women's conditions were redefined, as was basic social structure. Recreation shifted from reliance on popular festivals, to a period of repression in the name of more diligent work habits, to an explosion of commer-

1879–1907 Alliance system: Germany-Austria (1879); Germany-Austria-Russia (1881); Germany-Italy-Austria (1882); France-Russia (1891); Britain-France (1904); Britain-Russia (1907)

1880s ff. High point of impressionism in art

1881–1889 German social insurance laws enacted

1912–1913 Balkan Wars

1914 Beginning of World War I

1881–1914 Build Canadian Pacific Railway

1882 U.S. excludes Chinese immigrants

1891–1898 Australia and New Zealand restrict Asian immigration

1893 U.S. annexes Hawaii

1893 Women's suffrage in New Zealand

1898 Spanish-American War; U.S. acquires Puerto Rico, Guam, Philippines

1899 U.S. acquires part of Samoa

1901 Commonwealth of Australia, creates national federation

1907 New Zealand dominion status in British Empire

1917 U.S. enters World War I

cialized mass leisure outlets at the end of the 19th century. Amid all these developments, two strands of change stand out, adding to the forces—such as the scientific revolution—that had already been reshaping the West. First, dramatic new technologies, the heart of the Industrial Revolution, transformed production and with it many other aspects of life. Second, new political forces brought a basic redefinition of the state and of peoples' relationships to the state.

THE CRISIS OF THE LATE 18TH CENTURY AND THE FRENCH REVOLUTION

The industrial transformation of Western society raises an obvious conundrum: Did it flow naturally from the previous shifts in this civilization, or was it a brutal jolt? The answer is "both." Western society had been changing rapidly since the 15th century through commercialization, the growth of the nation-state, and cultural redefinition. This is why the West was able to industrialize first, with no prior models to follow. At the same time, industrialization did involve important new directions that caused great strain, some of which continue to cause strain even in the late 20th century. This is why it is vital to see how a period of upheaval emerged, partly as a result of previous shifts and partly as a result of new factors that forced further, and sometimes agonizing, innovation.

FORCES OF CHANGE

The explosion of political revolution in France and the Industrial Revolution in Britain at the end of the 18th century seemed to some Western observers particularly startling in that so much of the previous century had been placid, at least on the surface. Western nations had quarreled over colonies, but most of the 18th-century wars had been fairly sedate, and the ascending position of the West in the wider world was unchallenged. Few major popular rebellions challenged the absolute monarchs of the continent, though it was true that the French monarchy, unable to reform a tax structure marked by exemptions for nobles and the Church, showed signs of stress. Parliamentary politics in Britain drew wide consensus, save for some agitation for wider voting rights in the 1760s.

Intellectual ferment, however, ran high. Enlightenment thinkers challenged regimes that did not grant full religious freedom, or that insisted on aristocratic privilege, and a few called for widespread popular voice in government. A gap had opened between leading intellectuals and established institutions, and this would play a role in the revolutions that lay ahead (as would a similar gap in revolutions elsewhere in the world after 1900).

Enlightenment thinkers agreed that traditional inequalities in law, which gave certain groups rights by birth, were wrong. They wanted governments to serve the general good and to protect various freedoms. Some also wanted governments to be open to participation by the people at large, through some kind of democratic vote. These ideas, a fundamental challenge to Europe's absolute monarchies, established churches, and privileged upper classes, lay behind much of the political agitation that drew the 18th century to a close.

A second source of disruption was occurring more quietly, at all social levels. Western Europe experienced a huge population jump after about 1730. Within half a century the population of France rose by 50 percent, that of Britain and Prussia rose a full 100 percent. This population revolution was itself caused by relatively stable conditions, including better border policing by the efficient nation-state governments that reduced the movement of disease-bearing animals. More important still was improved nutrition resulting from the growing use of the potato and other crops of American origin. Westerners had long resisted these new crops, but now shifted to them in order to allow more secure subsistence, often on smaller plots of land. The potato was particularly important because of the calories it yielded on limited acreage. These various factors reduced the death rate, particularly for children; instead of over 40 percent of all children dying by age two, the figure by the 1780s was nearer 33 percent. More children surviving also meant more people living to have children of their own, so the birthrate increased as well.

Population pressure at this level always has dramatic impact. In China recurrent population pressure had historically produced growing popular unrest, often leading to the collapse of a dynasty. In medieval Europe population growth had ultimately outstripped available resources, leading to subsequent decline. The 18th-century population surge, however, produced more innovative responses, though it certainly heightened popular grievances as well. Upper-class families, faced with more surviving children, tried to tighten their grip on existing offices. It became harder, in the later 18th century, for a nonaristocrat to gain a high post in the Church or state. This reaction helped feed demands for change by other groups. Business families faced with more children often decided to expand their operations, sometimes adopting new equipment in order to spur business success. Here was a source of a new willingness to take risks. For some ordinary peasants, population pressure caused a new interest in expanding market agriculture, as some peasants began to acquire more land and employ wage labor in order to take advantage of new opportunities. Above all, population pressure drove many people into the working-class proletariat, as they lost any real chance of inheriting property. These people were eager to take advantage of new labor opportunities simply to survive. They thus formed the nucleus of a new working class in agriculture and, above all, in manufacturing.

The population growth of the 18th century prompted a rapid expansion of domestic manufacturing throughout western Europe and also, by 1800, in the United States. Hundreds of thousands of people became full- or part-time producers of textile and metal products, working at home but in a capitalist system in which materials, work orders, and ultimate sales depended on urban merchants. This development has been called a process of *protoindustrialization* because of the importance of new market relationships and sheer manufacturing volume in advance of the technological revolution associated with industrialization. Some societies in the 20th century, still predominantly rural, may be in a somewhat analogous protoindustrial phase, so the concept may have wider applicability.

Population upheaval and the spread of a propertyless class working, where possible, for money wages certainly had a sweeping impact on a variety of behaviors in Western society, including North America. Many villagers began to modify their dress in favor of more urban styles—suggesting an early form of new consumer interest. Among groups with little or no property, the authority of parents began to decline because the traditional threat of denying inheritance now had no meaning. Youthful independence became more marked, and while this showed particularly in economic behavior as many young people now looked for jobs on their own, the new defiance of authority might have had political implications as well.

Sexual behavior changed as the West began, around 1780, to experience something of a sexual revolution particularly among the lower classes in cities and countryside. More young people began to have sex before marriage—resulting, among other things, in a rapid increase in the percentage of illegitimate births, which rose to as much as 10 percent of all births. There were more general signs that sexual expression was becoming more important, at least to young men, who now sought sexual pleasures to compensate for some of the uncertainties of life in other respects. Some women, saddled with unwanted children, may have suffered from this sexual revolution in which they often participated in hope of marriage, but others may have seen sex as a new badge of individual pleasure seeking. Certainly, traditional rules seemed to be changing.

The upheavals triggered by population growth plus the continuing spread of Enlightenment ideas had two more sweeping consequences, both of which became visible during the 1780s. First, the surge of revolutionary protest developed essentially because new grievances and changing beliefs butted against institutions that were incapable of major change, such as France's lackluster absolute monarchy, and against the inflexibility of many existing leaders who focused on closing off opportunities for people in other social layers. Second, the economic changes involved in protoindustrialization turned to outright economic revolution with a spate of fundamental new inventions developed primarily in Britain.

 DECADES OF FERMENT: THE TIDE OF REVOLUTION, 1789–1830

The placid politics of the 18th century was shattered by a series of revolutions that took shape in the 1770s and 1780s. The wave of revolutions reflected the disparity between social and ideological change on the one hand, and business-as-usual politics on the other. It also caught up a large number of social groups with very diverse motives, some eager to use revolution to promote further change, some hoping that the same revolution would allow them to turn back the clock and recover older values.

THE AMERICAN REVOLUTION

The first concrete development occurred when Britain's Atlantic colonies rebelled in 1775 in what was primarily a war for independence rather than a full-fledged revolution. A significant minority of American colonists resisted Britain's attempt to impose new taxes and trade controls on the colonies after 1763. Many settlers also resented restrictions on free movement into the frontier areas. Britain's moves also triggered objections in principle, as colonists invoked British political theory to argue that they should not be taxed without representation. Resentment against British rule and advocacy of national independence and self-government, were supplemented by internal grievances. Crowding along the eastern seaboard led some younger men to seek new opportunities, including political office, that turned them against the older colonial leadership. Growing commerce and money-making antagonized some farmers and artisans, who sought ways to defend older values of greater social equality and community spirit.

Colonial rebels set up a new government that issued the Declaration of Independence in 1776 and also authorized a formal army to pursue its war. The persistence of the revolutionaries (who introduced some tactics such as informal guerrilla-type raids on the more structured British army—tactics that would be developed more fully in 20th-century independence wars) combined with British strategic mistakes and significant aid from the French government designed to embarrass its key enemy. After several years of fighting the United States won its freedom, and in 1787 set up a new constitutional structure based on Enlightenment principles, with checks and balances between the legislature and the executive and formal guarantees of individual liberties. Voting rights, though limited, were widespread, and the new regime was for a time the most radical in the world. Socially, the revolution accomplished less; slavery was untouched in its strongholds. And new American leaders, bent on solidifying their nation, deliberately shunned elaborate contacts with the Old World of Europe. Nevertheless, American success did spur many Europeans to a sense that political upheaval could pay off.

1789

The next step in the revolutionary spiral focused on France. It was the French Revolution that most clearly set in motion the political restructuring of western Europe. Several factors conjoined in the 1780s in what became something of a classic pattern of revolutionary causation. Ideological insistence on change won increasing attention from the mid-18th century onward. Enlightenment thinkers urged the need to limit the powers of the Catholic church, to weaken the hold of the aristocracy—including their tax privileges—and possibly to give new political voice to the common man. They attacked the inefficiency and arbitrary behavior of the monarchy. Social changes reinforced the ideological challenge. Some middle-class people, proud of their business or professional success, wanted a greater political role. Many peasants, pressed by population growth, wanted fuller freedom from landlord exactions, while resenting the large estates directly controlled by aristocrats and the Church. These grievances added up to a social attack on remnants of manorialism and the privileged position of the Church.

At the same time growing commercial activity produced its own discontent. Many peasants were upset by the expansion of a minority of villagers, bent on buying land and dividing village common holdings in the name of market exploitation. Many craftworkers resisted the commercial motives of some artisans, who tried to speed their labor in order to take advantage of sales opportunities. The revolution, in other words, would combine protest by people rising in the market economy, who sought commensurate political voice, with protest by people who were suffering and who sought a return to older values—a "moral economy" in which commercial profit seeking and individualism would be set aside.

Amid the ferment, the government and upper classes proved incapable of reform. Aristocrats indeed tightened their grip in response to their own population pressure, while the government proved increasingly ineffective—a key ingredient in any successful revolution. Finally, a sharp economic slump in 1787 and 1788, triggered by bad harvests, set the seal on revolution.

The French king, Louis XVI, called a meeting of the traditional parliament in order to consider tax reform for his financially pinched regime. But middle-class representatives, inspired by Enlightenment ideals, insisted on turning this assembly (which had not met for 1½ centuries) into a modern parliament, with voting by head rather than by estate and within majority representation for nonnoble property owners. The fearful king caved in after some street riots in Paris in the summer of 1789, and the revolution was underway.

Events in the summer were crucial. The new assembly, with its middle-class majority, quickly turned to devising a new political regime. A stirring Declaration of Rights of Man and the Citizen proclaimed freedom of thought. A popular riot stormed a political prison, the Bastille, on July 14, in what became the Revolution's symbol—though ironically, almost no prisoners were in fact to be found. Soon after this, peasants, stirred by rumors of brigandage, but also correctly afraid that Paris would ignore their needs, seized manorial records and many landed estates. This triggered a general proclamation abolishing manorialism, giving peasants clear title to much land and also establishing equality under the law. While aristocrats survived for some time, the principles of aristocratic rule were undercut.

Amid all this excitement, the French uprising, like most revolutions, went through an initial moderate phase, and in this case (unlike 20th-century revolts where this first phase was typically short-lived) many lasting gains were pushed through. Peasants did not get all the land, but they were free from all traces of serfdom. Not only was aristocratic privilege abolished, but the privileges of the Church were also attacked, and Church property was seized. A new constitution proclaimed individual rights, including freedom of religion, press, and property. A strong parliament was set up to limit the king, with about one-half the adult male population—those with property—eligible to vote.

Here, then, was a sketch of a new political system, with an elected legislature in charge of policy and a constitution limiting arbitrary state action. At the same time, traditional local barriers to government authority—such as aristocratic courts—were torn down, so government officials won greater contact with ordinary citizens.

THE FRENCH REVOLUTION: RADICAL CHORDS AND AUTHORITARIAN CONSOLIDATION

By 1792 the liberal regime began to turn more radical. Initial reforms provoked massive opposition in the name of church and aristocracy, and civil war broke out in several parts of France. Monarchs in Britain, Prussia, and Austria trumpeted their opposition to this revolutionary nightmare, and France soon faced European war as well. The revolutionary leadership was also beleaguered by economic chaos at home, which caused further popular rioting. All these pressures led to a takeover by radical leaders, who wanted to press the Revolution further and to set up firmer authority in the Revolution's defense. The monarchy was abolished and the king was decapitated on the guillotine—a new device introduced, Enlightenment-fashion, to provide more humane executions but instead became a symbol of revolutionary bloodthirst. The radical leadership also attacked enemies at home and abroad. Several thousand people were executed in what was named the Reign of Terror—even though by later standards it was relatively mild.

Besides stiffening the Revolution and becoming a symbol of revolutionary excess, this radical phase introduced a new rhetoric. Its new constitution, never fully put into practice, proclaimed universal adult male suffrage. It discussed mass education and social reform, though it never envisaged an attack on private property. More concretely, the radicals introduced a metric system of weights and measures, the product of the rationalizing genius of the Enlightenment. They also proclaimed universal military conscription, on grounds that now that all citizens were free, they owed loyalty and service to the government that assured their freedom. And revolutionary armies, swelled by new numbers and also new officers who had not been able to rise in the aristocrat-dominated forces of the old regime, began to win major success. Not only were France's enemies driven out, but the revolution began to win new territory in the Low Countries, Italy, and Germany—spreading revolutionary gains still farther in western Europe.

A new spirit of popular nationalism surfaced during the Revolution's radical phase. Many French people felt an active loyalty to the new regime, to a state they believed they

Napoleon's Empire in 1812

helped create. Nationalism could replace older loyalties to church or locality.

Radical leadership was itself toppled in 1795, and after four years of more moderate government the final phase of the Revolution was ushered in with the victory of Napoleon Bonaparte, a leading general who soon converted the revolutionary republic to an authoritarian empire. Under Napoleon parliament was reduced to a rubber stamp, while a powerful police system limited freedom of expression. However, Napoleon confirmed other liberal gains, including religious freedom, while enacting substantial equality—though for men, not women—in a series of new law codes. To train bureaucrats, a centralized system of secondary schools and universities developed.

Goaded by insatiable ambition, Napoleon devoted most of his attention not to consolidation of the Revolution at home, though this was one of his key achievements, but to expansion abroad. A series of wars brought France against all of Europe's major powers, including Russia. At its height around 1812, the French empire directly held or controlled as satellite kingdoms most of western Europe, and its success spurred some reform measures even in Prussia and Russia. The French Empire crumbled after this point. An attempt to invade Russia in 1812 failed miserably, as French armies perished in the cold Russian winter even as they pushed deep into the empire. An alliance system organized by Britain crushed the emperor definitively in 1814 and 1815. Yet Napoleon's campaigns had done more than dominate European diplomacy for 1½ decades. They had also spread key revolutionary legislation—the idea of equality under the law, the attack on privileged institutions such as aristocracy, church, or craft guilds—throughout much of western Europe.

The Revolution and Napoleon encouraged popular nationalism outside of France as well as within. French military success continued to draw great excitement at home. Elsewhere, French armies tore down local governments, as in Italy and Germany, which whetted appetites for national unity. And the sheer fact of French invasion made many people more conscious of loyalty to their own nation; popular resistance to Napoleon, in parts of Spain and Germany, played a role in the final French defeat.

A CONSERVATIVE SETTLEMENT AND THE REVOLUTIONARY LEGACY

The allies who had brought the proud emperor down met at Vienna in 1815 to reach a peace settlement that would make further revolution impossible. They did not try to punish France too sternly, on grounds that the European balance of power should be restored. This act of generosity helped promote peace in Europe for many decades. Still, a series of stronger powers were established around France, which meant gains for Prussia within Germany and for the hitherto obscure nation of Piedmont in northern Italy. Italian and German nationalists were disappointed, but the old map was not restored and the realignments did ultimately facilitate unifications. Britain gained new colonial territories, confirming its lead in the scramble for empire in the wider world. Russia, newly important in European affairs as its own expansionist momentum resumed, confirmed its hold over most of Poland.

These territorial adjustments kept Europe fairly stable for almost half a century, a major achievement given the crisscrossed rivalries that long characterized Western society. But the Vienna negotiators were much less successful in promoting internal peace. The idea was to restore monarchy in France and to link conservative powers in a new war on revolutionary radicalism. A more formal conservative sentiment grew up in reaction to the quarter century of upheaval, urging the importance of king and church and arguing that change should come slowly and gradually, not through protest or rationalistic constitution-making.

The revolutionary era had stirred forces that could not be contained by the Vienna settlement or the conservative alliance formed by Napoleon's opponents. New political movements arose to challenge conservatism. All the forces promoted by the French Revolution, many of them following from Enlightenment political ideas, grew into more formal political movements during the 1820s and 1830s throughout the Western world.

Liberals focused primarily on issues of political structure, as they sought ways to limit state interference in individual life and also representation of propertied people in government. Liberals urged the importance of constitutional rule and protection for freedoms of religion, press, and assembly. They wanted parliaments to represent middle-class voters and check the power of kings. Many liberals also sought economic reforms, including better education that would promote industrial growth.

Radicals accepted the importance of most liberal demands, but they also wanted wider voting rights. Some advocated outright democracy. They also urged some social reforms in the interest of the lower classes. A smaller current of socialism urged an attack on private property in the name of equality and an end to capitalist exploitation of the working man.

Nationalists, finally, though often allied with one of the other "isms" urged the importance of national unity and glory. Nationalists spoke of their nation's liberty, and easily joined the wider liberal current, but they valued a collective identity that could conflict with liberal individualism.

Each of the new political movements gained ground in pressing Europe's established order; each would have a long life in Western political history. The key Western political issues shifted from the development of absolute monarchy to constitutional structure and political participation. While most articulate political agitators were drawn from the middle class and related student groups who sought a new voice for themselves as opposed to continued aristocratic dominance, popular protesters picked up new political demands as well. Many urban artisans in particular, worried about the continued inroads of commercialism on their older values of cooperation and skill and conscious of a growing threat from industrial machines that might unseat the artisans altogether, provided a recurrent force in the streets, matching the ideological leadership offered by the middle class. Artisans had a solid tradition of organization, and they could draw demands from the sense of traditional justice they now saw under attack; they were an ideal revolutionary force.

Revolutions broke out in several places in 1820 and again in 1830. The 1820 revolts involved a nationalist uprising in Greece against Ottoman rule—a key step in gradually dismantling the Ottoman Empire in the Balkans—and a rebellion in Spain. Revolutions in 1830 struck closer to the heart of Western society. The French rebelled again, installing a different king and a somewhat more liberal monarchy, though not producing a final balance among the conflicting ingredients of French politics. Risings also occurred in key states in Italy and Germany, though without durable result; a revolution in Belgium produced a liberal regime and a newly independent nation.

The Belgian Revolution of 1830 was a classic example of how new political forces could combine. Belgium had been placed under Dutch rule at the Congress of Vienna. Belgian nationalists, building on religious and language differences, found national independence an obvious target. Liberals chafed under Dutch restrictions on freedom of the press and teaching. Urban artisans, worried about rapid commercial change as Belgium began to develop factory production, sought new political rights.

Britain and the United States also participated in the process of political change, though without revolution. Key states in the United States granted universal adult male suffrage and other political changes in the 1820s, leading to the election of a popular president, Andrew Jackson, in 1828. In Britain the Reform Bill of 1832, prodded by considerable popular agitation, gave the parliamentary vote to most members of the middle class. This change ushered in a period in which urban governments gained new powers as they came under control of business leaders, while the aristocrats who still controlled the national ministries began to adopt measures that increasingly favored commercial development.

Through the 1830s the tides of revolution and the larger impact of new political movements had produced important changes in Western society. Regimes in France, Britain, Belgium, the United States, and several other countries now had solid parliaments (Congress in the United States), at least some guarantees for individual rights against arbitrary state action, considerable religious freedom not only for various Christian sects but also for Jews, and a voting system ranging from democratic (for men) to upper middle-class. Even more widely, movements representing liberal and other political views had spread throughout Western society, operating as political parties in the liberalized states, as agitators in central Europe. The revolutionary sequence had not ended—a major outburst was still to come in 1848—but it had already begun to interact with the other great Western transformation, the rise of industrialization.

THE INDUSTRIAL REVOLUTION

The essence of the Industrial Revolution was technological change, particularly the application of coal-powered engines (or, later, engines powered by other fossil fuels) to the production process. The new engines replaced people and animals as the key sources of energy in many branches of production. They were joined by new production equipment that could apply power to manufacturing through more automatic processes. Thus spindles were invented that wrapped fiber automatically into thread, and looms mixed thread automatically without direct human intervention. Hammering and rolling devices allowed application of power machinery to metals. And while in early industrialization textile and metallurgical production received primary attention, engines were also used in sugar refining, printing, and other processes.

The British Industrial Revolution resulted from a host of factors, including favorable natural resources and strong capital reserves won from previous trade. Industrialization was fed, also, by the late 18th-century crisis. Population pressure forced innovations at all social levels. Enlightenment beliefs encouraged faith in progress and in human ability to dominate nature. They also sanctioned a devotion to improving material life. Here were motivations for inventing new processes and applying them widely.

At the same time, the Industrial Revolution built on previous trends in Western society, including the large manufacturing sector and the huge advantages in world trade. Earlier commercialization played a role; British aristocrats were unusually tolerant of commerce, which helped center initial changes in the British Isles. Prior development of science set a basis for artisans to widen their efforts at technical innovation. Governments, already committed to policies of economic growth, also supported industrialization by instituting laws encouraging new inventions and new trading and banking systems.

ORIGINS OF INDUSTRIALIZATION, 1770–1840

The key inventions of early industrialization developed in Britain during the 18th century. Automatic machinery in textiles was initially intended for manual use in the domestic system. Then in the 1770s the Scottish artisan James Watt devised a steam engine that could be used for production, and the Industrial Revolution was off and running. Within a decade in Britain, the domestic production of key materials, such as cotton thread, was converted to factory-housed machines, at the expense of thousands of home workers, mostly women. Changes of this sort spurred the creation of new industries, to build machines, and also the rapid expansion of coal mining to fuel the new productive fires.

Additional inventions followed on the heels of the original set, for a key feature of the Industrial Revolution was recurrent technological change. Early machine spindles were expanded, so that a given worker could supervise even vaster output. American inventors devised a production system of interchangeable parts, initially for rifles, that helped standardize and so mechanize the production of machinery itself. Metallurgy advanced by use of coal and coke, instead of charcoal, for smelting and refining, allowing the creation of larger furnaces and greater output.

Technological change was quickly applied to transportation and communication, essential areas now that there were more goods to be moved and more distant markets to contact. The development of the telegraph, steam shipping, and the railway, all early in the 19th century, provided new speed in the movement of information and goods. These inventions were vital in facilitating a new stage in Western penetration of world affairs; they also kept the Industrial Revolution going in the West, by promoting mass-marketing techniques and providing direct orders for rails and other industrial goods.

While technological change lay at the heart of industrialization, several basic economic changes were inherent in the process as well. The Industrial Revolution depended on improvements in agriculture. Industrialization concentrated increasing amounts of manufacturing in cities, where power sources could be brought together with labor. City growth was dizzying during the first decades of industrialization, with sleepy villages—such as Manchester, England—growing to cities of several hundred thousand people. This kind of growth depended on better agricultural production, accomplished through improved equipment and seeds, plus growing use of fertilizers. Better agriculture freed up a growing percentage of the labor force for nonagricultural pursuits, and fairly soon in vigorous industrializers, such as Britain, manufacturing output surpassed that of farming in importance.

Industrialization also meant a factory system. Steam engines had to be concentrated, for their power could not be widely diffused until the later application of electricity. Factory labor separated work from the home—one of the basic human changes inherent in the Industrial Revolution. It also allowed manufacturers to introduce greater specialization of labor and more explicit rules and discipline, which along with the noisy machines permanently changed the nature of human labor.

Industrialization required new amounts of capital, which meant steady improvements in banking, and it required new marketing systems to handle rapidly growing output. Prices of manufactured goods fell because of new technologies that encouraged mass sales. The bigger industrial concerns began to set up nationwide, even with international sales organizations. Shops spread to villages where only occasional peddlers had previously brought in goods—as peasants began to produce more for urban markets, they tended to specialize and, thus, to buy clothing and equipment they once had made themselves. The first department stores opened in Paris in the mid-1830s, another response to the need for sophisticated marketing.

Overall, industrialization also promoted the development of increasingly large firms, though small operations might also benefit for a time from the Industrial Revolution's energy. Through the 19th century, large firms tended to promote more efficient use of engines and equipment, while also amassing needed stores of capital and developing efficient marketing and purchasing arrangements. Industrialization gradually promoted an economic organization that featured concentration, bureaucratic management, and a certain impersonality in directing the labor force.

Once Britain launched industrialization, other Western nations quickly saw the need to imitate. Britain's industrial power helped the nation hold out against Napoleon and led to huge profits for successful businessmen by the early 19th century. Hence both governments and individual entrepreneurs, in places such as Belgium, Germany, or New England, soon rushed to copy. Since most of the general factors that permitted industrialization were present in these areas as well, including population pressure and an ideology of material progress, industrialization proceeded relatively swiftly throughout much of the Western world.

On the European continent, French revolutionary laws helped unleash industrialization by destroying local restrictions on trade, protecting private property, and abolishing artisan guilds that had often tried to defend older production techniques. With guilds and manors destroyed, propertyless workers were commodities, to be used and paid as the market required.

Belgium and France began to industrialize in the 1820s, the United States and Germany followed soon thereafter. Industrialization did not immediately sweep all before it, even in Britain; artisan production actually expanded for a time as cities grew, and rural labor remained vital. But the forms of the Industrial Revolution gained ground steadily once implanted in the West, and factory workers and their managers became evermore important minorities in the general labor force.

Population growth, factory-promoted unemployment, and the growing potency of industrially produced alcoholic drinks helped create a slum life in English cities in the 18th and early 19th centuries.

THE DISRUPTIONS OF INDUSTRIAL LIFE

The causes of Western industrialization should not mislead us. Even though the phenomenon can be explained through earlier shifts in Western business, outlook, government policy, and labor supply—shifts that also explain why the Industrial Revolution occurred first in the West and often proved difficult to reproduce in other civilizations—the changes involved were massive, and they did not come easily.

The Industrial Revolution involved huge movements of people from countryside to city. Families were disrupted in this process, as young adults proved to be the prime migrants. Cities themselves, poorly equipped to begin with and now crowded beyond all precedent, became hellholes for many new residents. Health conditions worsened in poor districts because of packed housing and inadequate sanitation. Crime increased for a time. New social divisions opened up, as middle-class families sought to move away from the center-city poor, beginning a pattern of suburbanization that continued into the later 20th century.

Work became more unpleasant for many people. Not only was it largely separated from family, the new machines and factory rules compelled a rapid pace and coordination that pulverized traditional values of leisurely, quality production. First in Britain, then elsewhere, groups of workers responded to the new machines by outright attack; for example, Luddite protests, named after a mythical British machine-breaker called Ned Ludd, failed to stop industrialization, but they showed the stress involved. Many business and farm families were also appalled by the noise, dirt, and sheer novelty involved in the Industrial Revolution.

The early Industrial Revolution also forced new constraints on traditions of popular leisure. Factory owners, bent on getting as much work as possible from their labor force to help pay for expensive machines, deliberately reduced recreational aspects of work: They tried to ban singing, napping, drinking, and other customary frivolities on the job. Off the job, new business-led city governments, backed by expanding police forces, attacked popular festivals, animal contests, and gambling in the name of proper discipline and good order. Attempts were made to reduce social drinking as well, but they largely failed in light of workers' insistence on some recreational outlets. Nevertheless, the Industrial Revolution considerably reduced key leisure traditions and community ties, which made the early phases of the experience still more disorienting and grim for many people involved.

Family life changed, and in changing revealed some of the wider stresses of the industrialization process. Middle-class people quickly moved to enhance the redefinition of the family already begun in the early modern centuries: The family for them served as an image of affection and purity. Children and women were to be sheltered from the storms of the new work world. Women, traditionally active partners to merchants, now withdrew from formal jobs. They gained new roles in caring for children and the home, and their moral stature in many ways improved, but their sphere was more radically separate from that of men than had been true before. Children, too, were redefined. The middle class led in seeing education, not work and apprenticeship, as the logical role for children to prepare them for a complex future and, it was hoped, to maintain their innocence until they were prepared to cope with business or professional life.

The working-class family changed as well, though it could not afford all these indulgences. Young children, increasingly unnecessary on the job, were often sent to school. Women worked from adolescence until marriage, when they were often pulled away because of the demands of shopping, home care, and motherhood. Even when on the job, working-class women were more likely to be sent into domestic service in middle-class households than to factories, though there was an important minority of female factory hands. The working class, in sum, developed its own version of separate spheres, in part simply to compensate for the new distinction between jobs and home. Family life became more important than ever before, to provide homemaking services but also to offer some hope of emotional satisfaction in a confusing world. Marriages encountered new stresses, but the marriage rate went up fairly steadily.

The changes in family roles and values show how deeply the Industrial Revolution could reach into personal life, particularly for factory workers but also for other groups. The changes were not all bad, and many people found ways to use family satisfactions or community institutions such as neighborhood taverns to help compensate for a loss of power at work. Yet considerable confusion and anxiety remained; even businessmen, actively building the new industrial world, might be fearful of the effects of change. As a leading French industrialist noted, "Progress is not necessarily progressive. If it were not inevitable, it might be better to stop it."

DOCUMENT
WOMEN IN THE INDUSTRIAL REVOLUTION

The West's Industrial Revolution changed the situation of women in many ways. Some of the changes have occurred more recently in other civilizations, others were particularly characteristic of the 19th-century West. Industrialization cut into women's traditional work and protest roles (for example, in spearheading bread riots as attention shifted to work-based strikes), but it tended to expand educational opportunities. Some new work roles and protest outlets, including feminism, developed by 1914. Important changes occurred in the home as well. New ideas and standards at once elevated women's position and set up more demanding tasks. Relations among women were also affected by the growing use of domestic servants (the most common urban job for working-class women) and new attitudes by middle- and lower-class women alike. The first document that follows sketches the idealization of middle-class women; it comes from an American moral tract of 1837, anonymously authored, probably by a man. The second document, written by a woman in an English woman's magazine, shows new household standards of another sort, with a critical tone also common in middle-class literature. Finally, a British housewife discusses her servant problems, reflecting yet another facet of women's lives. How could women decide what their domestic roles were and whether they brought satisfaction or not?

WOMEN AS CIVILIZERS (1837)

As a sister, she soothes the troubled heart, chastens and tempers the wild daring of the hurt mind restless with disappointed pride or fired with ambition. As a mistress, she inspires the nobler sentiment of purer love, and the sober purpose of conquering himself for virtue's sake. As a wife, she consoles him in grief, animates him with hope in despair, restrains him in prosperity, cheers him in poverty and trouble, swells the pulsations of his throbbing breast that beats for honorable distinction, and rewards his toils with the undivided homage of a grateful heart. In the important and endearing character of mother, she watches and directs the various impulses of unfledged genius, instills into the tender and susceptible mind the quickening seeds of virtue, fits us to brave dangers in time of peril, and consecrates to truth and virtue the best affections of our nature.

MOTHERHOOD AS POWER AND BURDEN (1877)

Every woman who has charge of a household should have a practical knowledge of nursing, simple doctoring and physicianing. The professional doctor must be called in for real illness. But the Home

Doctor may do so much to render professional visits very few and far between. And her knowledge will be of infinite value when it is necessary to carry out the doctor's orders. . . .

THE MOTHER BUILDER

It is a curious fact that architects who design and builders who carry out their plans must have a training for this work. But the Mother Builder is supposed to have to know by instinct how to put in each tiny brick which builds up the "human." The result of leaving it to "instinct" is that the child starts out with bad foundations and a jerry-built constitution. . . .

When one considers that one child in every three born dies before the age of five years, it is evident how wide-spread must be the ignorance as to the feeding and care of these little ones. It is a matter of surprise to those who understand the constitution and needs of infants that, considering the conditions under which the large number of them are reared, the mortality is not greater. . . .

THE RISKS BABIES RUN

To begin with, the popular superstition that a young baby must be "hungry" because it lives on milk, and is on this plea the recipient of scraps and bits of vegetables, potato and gravy, crusts, and other heterogeneous articles of diet, has much to answer for. Then, the artistic sense of the mother which leads her to display mottled necks, dimpled arms, and chubby legs, instead of warmly covering these charming portions of baby's anatomy, goes hugely to swell the death-rate. Mistakes in feeding and covering have much to answer for in the high mortality of infants.

THE SERVANT "PROBLEM" (1860)

So we lost Mary, and Peggy reigned in her stead for some six weeks. . . .

But Peggy differed greatly from her predecessor, Mary. She was not clean in her person, and my mother declared that her presence was not desirable within a few feet. Moreover she had no notion of putting things in their places, but always left all her working materials in the apartment where they were last used. It was not therefore pleasant, when one wanted a sweeping brush, to have to sit down and think which room Peggy had swept the last, and so on with all the paraphernalia for dusting and scrubbing. But this was not the worst. My mother, accustomed to receive almost reverential respect from her old servants, could not endure poor Peggy's familiar ways. . . .

Now, though I am quite willing to acknowledge the mutual obligation which exists between the employer and employed, I do *not* agree with my charwoman that she is the only person who ought to be considered as conferring a favor. I desire to treat her with all kindness, showing every possible regard to her comfort, and I expect from her no more work than I would cheerfully and easily perform in the same time. But when I scrupulously perform my part of the bargain, both as regards food and wages, not to mention much thought and care in order to make things easy for her and which were not in the agreement at all, I think she ought not only to keep faith with me if possible, but to abstain from hinting at the obligation she confers in coming.

It is not pleasant, as my mother says, to beg and pray for the help for which we also pay liberally. But it is worse for my kitchen helper to be continually reminding me that she need not go out unless she likes, and that it was only to oblige me she ever came at all. I do not relish this utter ignoring of her wages, etc., or her being quite deaf because I choose to offer a suggestion as to the propriety of dusting out the corners, or when I mildly hint that I should prefer her doing something in my way. . . .

But if I were to detail all my experiences, I should never have done. I have had many good and willing workers; but few on whose punctuality and regularity I could rely.

Questions: In what ways did industrialization increase differences between women and men in the 19th century West? What were the main changes in women's roles and ideals? How did middle-class and working-class women differ?

INDUSTRIAL REVOLUTION AND POLITICAL REVOLUTION

The strands of political and industrial upheaval, initially somewhat separate, began to intertwine in the West by the 1830s. Both revolutions had of course responded to some of the same changes and crises in Western society. But their courses had not at first overlapped: Industry centered in Britain where politics was relatively stable, while political revolution elsewhere had actually detracted from economic development.

Yet there were important links. In the first place, political revolution helped clear the way for industrialization in places such as France. Revolutionaries did not deliberately plan industrial development, but many of them did hope for a more favorable business climate. By attacking the aristocracy, they increased the prestige of business life. By abolishing manorialism and guilds they created a labor force more open to market activities and freer to move to new work locations. Standardized law codes and more rational systems of measurement also promoted economic change. As in Russia early in the 20th century, the West's era of revolution resulted from the slowness of change at the top and created the conditions for more rapid innovation thereafter.

The early phases of industrialization, in turn, had strong political implications. Groups that benefited from industrial change usually sought a growing voice in government. This was a key pressure behind the British Reform Bill of 1832 that enfranchised the middle classes and gave them a means of representing their own interests in Parliament and in city administrations. A key result was a new tariff system in Britain that reduced protection for agriculture (and by facilitating food imports helped keep wages low). Other groups became more politically active as a slightly less obvious adjustment to industrialization. Lawyers, for example, and in many places also doctors, sought through political life a prestige and income that would help them compensate for the growing wealth and prestige of leading businessmen. Professional groups also pressed governments to provide better training and licensing facilities, in order to reduce competition from "unauthorized" practitioners.

Governments at various levels had to consider the process of industrialization in other respects. All major Western states shifted their economic policies to some extent during the first half of the 19th century. Some were not eager to embrace the Industrial Revolution outright, but all saw the need to sponsor certain activities that would help keep pace with Britain. All Western governments, for example, encouraged railway development; Prussia built many lines directly, while the United States government gave large land grants to promote a national rail system. All governments began to organize technical fairs and to promote engineering and science education. Most governments took an interest in education more generally, on grounds that a more literate work force would be more productive. Thus France, soon after the Revolution of 1830, began to encourage (though not yet require) primary schools throughout the nation, while state governments in the northern United States moved soon thereafter to make education compulsory. Another area that cried out for government attention involved urban conditions. Again by the 1830s, governments began to build new sewer systems, to promote some housing regulation and in general to launch the process of making the new cities minimally habitable. They also developed formal urban police forces, another vital extension of government power.

Important groups in the 19th century argued, in one version of the new liberal movement, that government activities should on balance decline. Many revolutionaries urged that governments should pull out of religious affairs, reduce economic regulation in the interest of promoting free competition, and even let the poor fend for themselves. In fact, only two Western governments actually scaled down their activities in the early 19th century: Britain and Norway. Other governments responded to political and industrial pressures by rebalancing their functions—with a net increase in the government role.

Political and industrial revolution intertwined in one final respect in the first half of the 19th century. Some lower-class groups, already mobilized through an interest in political rights, began to turn to the government as a means of compensating for industrial change and to revolt when the government seemed unresponsive. Artisans and workers in Britain generated a new movement to gain the vote in the 1830s and 1840s; this Chartist movement hoped that a democratic government would regulate new technologies and promote popular education. Artisans in France and Germany increased their revolutionary ardor because of their growing fears of displacement through industrialization. The political mood of the West became more fervent by the 1840s under the twin impact of unfulfilled popular revolutionary demands and the pressures and anxieties promoted by early industrialization.

THE 1848 REVOLUTIONS

The result was a final, extraordinary wave of revolutions in 1848 and 1849. Paris was again the center. In a popular uprising that began in February 1848, the French monarchy was once again expelled, this time for good, and a democratic republic was briefly established. Urban artisans pressed for serious social reform—perhaps some version of socialism and certainly government-supported jobs for the unemployed; groups of women schoolteachers, though fewer in number, agitated for the vote and other rights for women. This revolution, then, started on a more radical basis than had the great uprising of 1789, with a wider array of social demands and a democratic, rather than simply liberal, political platform.

Moreover, revolution quickly spread to other centers. Major revolts occurred in Germany, Austria, and Hungary. Revolutionaries in these areas sought liberal constitutions to modify conservative monarchies; artisans pressed for social reforms that would restrain industrialization; peasants sought a complete end to manorialism. Revolts in central Europe also pressed for nationalist demands, with German nationalists seeking the unity of their country, and various nationalities in Austria-Hungary, including Slavic groups, seeking greater autonomy. A similar liberal-nationalist revolt occurred in various parts of Italy. Significant agitation developed in other parts of western Europe.

The revolutionary fires burned only briefly. Nowhere did revolution win the kind of success the great French Revolution had achieved, partly because significant political changes had already been introduced. The social demands put forth by artisans and some factory workers, either for socialist gains or for a return to older guild structures, were quickly put down; not only conservatives but middle-class liberals opposed these efforts. Nationalist agitation also failed for the moment, as the armies of Austria-Hungary and Prussia restored the status quo to central Europe and Italy. Democracy persisted in France, but a nephew of the great Napoleon soon replaced the liberal republic with an authoritarian empire that lasted until 1870. Peasant demands were met, and serfdom was now fully abolished throughout western Europe. Many peasants, uninterested in other gains, now supported conservative forces.

The substantial failure of the revolutions of 1848 drew the revolutionary era in western Europe to a close. Failure taught many liberals and working-class leaders that revolution was too risky; more gradual methods should be used instead. Improved transportation reduced the chance of food crises, the traditional trigger for revolution in West-

In 1848 crowds, mainly urban artisans, stormed the military arsenal in Berlin during the last great revolution in the industrial West.

ern history. Bad harvests in 1846 and 1847 had driven up food prices and helped promote insurgency in the cities, but famines of this sort did not recur in the West. Many governments also installed better riot control police.

The ongoing social changes brought by industrialization also played a role in ending political revolution in the West. The artisan class, whose sense of organization and older values had been crucial to revolts, began to decline as factory industry continued to gain ground. Artisans did not disappear, but they lost some of their sense of mission. Many began to concentrate on personal advancement, or a solid but moderate craft trade unionism that sought improvements within the system rather than a different system. While many grievances continued on the part of new and old social groups, the belief that political upheaval could stem the tide of industrialization began to fade.

Finally, the experience of decades of recurrent revolution, plus industrialization itself, created new social divisions that made uprisings more difficult. The period of revolution had been predicated on old-style social divisions that pitted commoners against the privileges of the aristocracy, and on other institutions, such as unreconstructed monarchies or established churches that did not give ordinary people a voice. Divisions of interest obviously existed among commoners, depending on wealth or on urban as opposed to rural residence, but there could also be some shared interest in attacking the structures of the old regime. By 1850 an industrial class structure had come to predominate. Earlier revolutionary gains had reduced the legal privileges of the aristocracy, while the rise of business had eroded aristocrats' economic dominance. With industrialization social structure came to rest less on privilege and birth, and more on money. Key divisions by 1850 pitted middle-class property owners against workers of various sorts. The old alliances that had produced the revolutions were now dissolved. New social cleavages would produce important unrest, but not in the classic revolutionary mold. An era of transition had ended. Through intended and unanticipated results of earlier revolutions and the steady gains of an industrial economy, a new society had been created in the West—a society that, somewhat surprisingly, made revolution almost obsolete in the West from 1850 through the later 20th century.

THE CONSOLIDATION OF THE INDUSTRIAL ORDER, 1850–1914

In most respects, the 65 years after 1850 seemed calmer than the frenzied period of political upheaval and initial industrialization. Many people became accustomed to change. City growth continued in the West, and indeed several countries, starting with Britain, neared the 50 percent mark in urbanization, the first time in human history that more than a minority of a population had lived in cities. But the rate of city growth slowed. Furthermore, city government began to gain ground on the pressing problems growth had created. Sanitation improved, and death rates fell below birthrates for the first time in urban history. Parks, museums, effective regulation of food and housing facilities, more efficient police forces—all added to the safety and the physical and cultural amenities of urban life. Hosts of problems remained, but the horror stories of early industrialization did begin to abate. Revealingly, crime rates began to stabilize or even drop in several industrial areas, a sign of more effective social control but also a more disciplined population.

ADJUSTMENTS TO INDUSTRIAL LIFE

The theme of adjustment and stabilization applied to family life. Illegitimacy rates stopped rising—until 1960—which suggested that some earlier disruption in personal habits was easing. Within families, birthrates began to drop as Western society initiated a substantial *demographic transition* to a new system that promoted fairly stable population levels through a new combination of relatively low birthrates as well as low death rates. Led initially by the middle classes, the low birthrate involved a reassessment of the purposes of children. Children were now seen as a source of emotional satisfaction and considerable parental responsibility, not as contributors to a family economy. This meant that individual children would be highly valued, but the total number would be reduced. Other social groups soon bought into this reassessment, which reflected the progressive disappearance of child labor and promoted the economic well-being of all family members. Family life might still prove difficult, as expectations for improvements in standards of living or for emotional rewards might outpace reality. Merely effecting lower birthrates could be challenging, for while artificial birth control devices began to spread after 1850, they were still unfamiliar and not fully reliable, which meant that many families had to practice new levels of sexual restraint. Nevertheless, some of the starkest pressures did begin to yield in family life, as a result of significant adjustments to new realities.

Material conditions generally improved after 1850. There were important fluctuations; the industrial economy was unstable, and frequent depressions caused falling wages and unemployment. Huge income gaps also continued to divide various social groups. Nevertheless, the general trend was upward. By 1900 probably two-thirds of the

Western population enjoyed conditions above the subsistence level; people could afford a few amenities such as newspapers or family outings, and their diet and housing improved. Health got better. The decades from 1880 to 1920 saw a real revolution in children's health, thanks in part to better hygiene during childbirth and better parental care. Infancy and death separated for the first time in human history: Instead of one-third or more of all children dying by age 10, rates fell to under 10 percent and continued to plummet. Adult health also benefited from better nutrition and improved work safety. Discovery of germs by Louis Pasteur led by the 1880s to more conscientious sanitary regulations and procedures by doctors and other health care specialists; this reduced the deaths of women in childbirth. Women now began to outlive men by a noticeable margin, but men's health also improved.

While material life gained in several measurable respects, the workplace recurrently challenged established habits. Industrial jobs continued to involve a fast pace and severe limitations on worker autonomy. These characteristics worsened after 1850. New machines in textiles and metallurgy sped up work while reducing skill levels. The typical industrial worker was now semiskilled, trained in very limited areas that involved little sense of pride or creativity. New methods of supervision, often pioneered in the United States, involved detailed calculations by efficiency engineers designed to spur output and limit wasted motion. From this base, managers in industries such as automobile production introduced assembly-line procedures early in the 20th century, with workers deliberately reduced to machinelike repetitions.

Yet, as workers suffered under these new conditions—some to the point of severe depression—there were new ways to compensate. Important labor movements took shape among industrial workers by the 1890s, with massive strike movements by miners, metalworkers, and others from the United States to Germany. The new trade-union movement stressed the massed power of workers, and while often defeated by management-government coalitions, it did win some important gains and gave workers some sense of voice and dignity. Furthermore, both within the labor movement and as individuals, many workers learned to react to the new systems of work instrumentally. The instrumentalist reaction urged workers to regard their jobs not as ends in themselves, but as vehicles for other goals. Many workers, as instrumentalists, learned to bargain for better pay and shorter hours, so that less of their lives would be invested in the work process.

The theme of adjustment extended also to the countryside. Many European peasants gained new ability to use market conditions to their own benefit. Some, as in Holland and Denmark, developed cooperatives to market goods and purchase supplies efficiently; here was a sign of new rural organizing ability. Many peasants specialized in new cash crops such as dairy products. Still more widely, peasants began to send their children to school to pick up new knowledge that would facilitate farming operations. The traditional isolation of rural areas began to decline.

Rural conditions lagged behind those in the cities in many ways. European peasants also faced massive competition from the agricultural exports of the United States, Canada, Australia, and Argentina, which began to flood Western markets as ocean shipping improved and refrigeration was introduced in the 1870s. Here, as with urban labor, the theme of successful adjustment should not be exaggerated. Nevertheless, the raw confrontation with new pressures that had characterized important aspects of the transition decades before 1850 did yield to an extent. And in the countryside, as opposed to the cities, the amount of social protest declined as well, once manorialism was fully removed. Some important strikes by rural laborers occurred after 1890, and in the United States an important populist movement pitted many kinds of farmers against railroads and other manifestations of big business, but for the most part the rural world seemed fairly peaceful—and certainly more peaceful than rural populations in many other parts of the globe in the same decades.

The theme of consolidation is an obvious one, after the turmoil of the revolutionary decades. Vital changes continued—new technologies, the new work systems, new agricultural competition—but they were no longer startling to a population accustomed to the basic framework of industrial society. Adjustments by ordinary people, such as the radically new levels of birth control or the idea of instrumentalism, fed into consolidation as well: People were not being totally manipulated by forces beyond their control. Did adjustment mean that people were more contented than they had been when industrialization was new? Measuring contentment is always difficult, and certainly important expressions of grievance continued in Western society. The development of new expressions of social stress was a final feature of the decades after 1850 in the West.

POLITICAL TRENDS

The consolidation theme clearly applies to Western politics after the failures of the revolutions of 1848. Quite simply, issues that had dominated the Western political agenda for many decades were largely resolved within a generation. The great debates about fundamental constitutions and government structure, which had emerged first in the 17th century with the rise of absolutism and new political theory and then raged during the decades of revolution, at last grew quiet.

Many Western leaders worked to reduce the need for political revolution after 1850. Liberals decided that revolution was too risky and became more willing to compromise. Key conservatives strove to develop a new political consensus that would save elements of the old regime, including power for the landed aristocracy and the monarchy, but, through reform, would not engender resistance down the line. Conservatives realized that they could allow parliaments with limited powers, appeal to workers through limited social reforms, and even extend the vote without necessarily losing power. A British conservative leader, Benjamin Disraeli, thus in 1867 took the initiative of granting the vote to working-class males. Count Camillo di Cavour, in the Italian state of Piedmont, began even earlier to support industrial development and extend the powers of Parliament in order to please liberal forces. In Prussia a new prime minister, Otto von Bismarck, similarly began to work with a parliament and extend the vote to all adult males (though grouping them in wealth categories that protected the country from full democracy). These developments fell short of full liberal demands, in that parliaments did not have basic control over the appointment of ministries, but many groups gained some effective political voice. Other Prussian reforms granted freedom to Jews, extended (without guaranteeing) rights to the press, and promoted mass education. The gap between liberal and conservative regimes narrowed in the West, though it remained significant.

The new conservatives also began to use the force of nationalism to win support for the existing social order. Previously, nationalism had been a radical force, challenging established arrangements in the name of new loyalties. Many liberals continued to defend nationalist causes. Now, however, conservative politicians learned how to wrap themselves in the flag, often promoting an active foreign policy in the interests of promoting domestic calm. Thus British conservatives became champions of expanding the empire, while in the United States by the 1890s the Republican party became increasingly identified with imperialist causes.

The most important new uses of nationalism within the West occurred in Italy and Germany. Cavour, after wooing liberal support, formed an alliance with France that enabled him to attack Austrian control of northern Italian provinces in 1858. The war set in motion a nationalist rebellion in other parts of the peninsula that allowed Cavour to unite most of Italy under the Piedmontese king. This led to a reduction of the political power of the Catholic pope, already an opponent of liberal and nationalist ideas—an important part of the general reduction of Church power in Western politics.

Following Cavour's example, Bismarck in Prussia staged a series of wars in the 1860s that expanded Prussian power in Germany. A final war, against France, led to outright German unity in 1871. The new German Empire boasted a national parliament with a lower house based on uni-

The Unifications of Italy and Germany

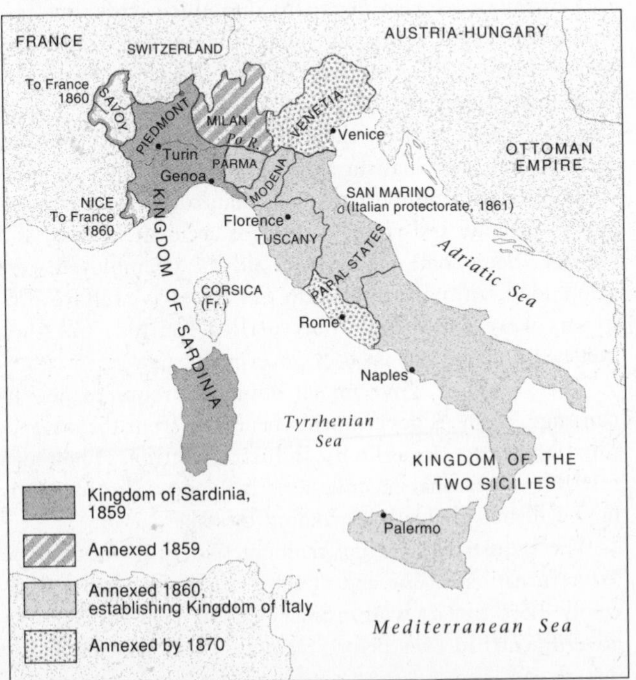

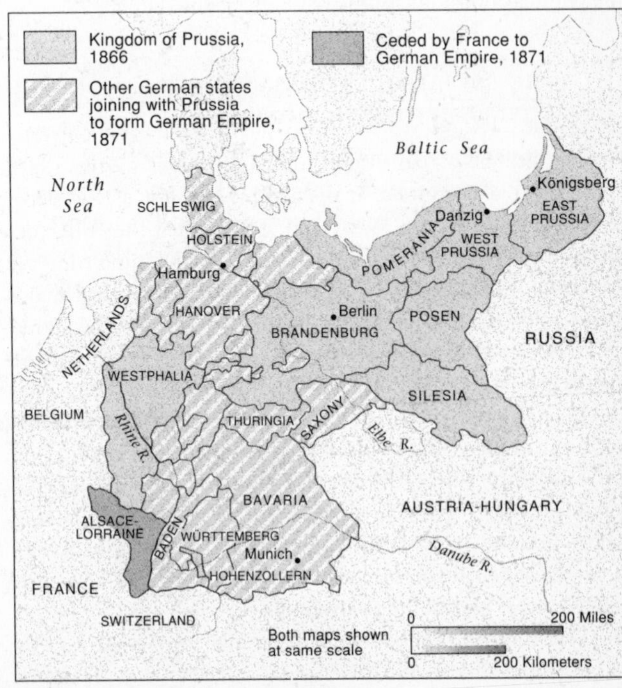

versal male suffrage and an upper house that favored conservative state governments. This kind of compromise, plus the dizzying joy of nationalist success, won support for the new regime from most liberals and many conservatives.

Other key political issues were resolved around the same time. The United States fought its bloody Civil War—the first war based extensively on industrial weaponry and transport systems, carefully watched by European military observers—between 1861 and 1865. The war resolved by force the simmering dispute over sectional rights between the North and South in the new nation, and also brought an end to slavery. France, after its defeat by Germany in 1870, overthrew its short-lived echo of the Napoleonic Empire and established a conservative republic—with votes for all adult men, a reduction of Church power, and expansion of education, but no major social reform or tampering with existing property relationships. Just as a conservative Bismarck could be selectively radical, so France proved that liberals could be very cautious.

With these changes, the war between conservatives and liberals yielded to petty skirmishes and sniper attacks. The big issues that divided the two groups were gone. Virtually the entire West now had a parliamentary system, usually a democracy of some sort, in which religious and other freedoms were widely protected. In this system, liberal and conservative ministries could alternate without major changes of internal policy. Indeed, Italy developed a process called *transformismo,* or transformism, in which parliamentary deputies, no matter what platforms they professed, were transformed once in Rome to a single-minded pursuit of political office and support of the status quo.

THE SOCIAL QUESTION AND NEW GOVERNMENT FUNCTIONS

The decline of basic constitutional disputes by the 1870s had two further results: It opened the way for a new set of political issues in the West, and it promoted the fuller development of an industrial-style state. At the same time the unifications of Italy and particularly of Germany had major impact on the diplomacy of western Europe. Germany, once unified, was immediately a dominant European power, with a rapidly expanding industrial base. Its ascendancy, plus the sheer addition of major diplomatic actors on the European stage, inevitably unsettled international relations among the Western states. Here, too, was an agenda item of growing importance after 1870, following many decades in which major diplomatic issues had been downplayed in favor of concentration on internal economic development and political challenge.

Government functions and personnel expanded rapidly throughout the Western world after 1870. All Western governments introduced civil service examinations to test applicants on the basis of talent, rather than on connections or birth alone—thus unwittingly imitating Chinese innovations over a thousand years before. With a growing bureaucracy and improved recruitment, governments began to extend their regulatory apparatus—inspecting factory safety, the health of prostitutes, hospital conditions, and even—through the introduction of passports and border controls—personal travel.

Schooling expanded, becoming generally compulsory up to age 12. Many American states by 1900 began also to require high school education, and most Western nations expanded their public secondary school systems. Here was a huge addition to the ways governments and individuals interacted. The new school systems promoted literacy, long gaining ground in the West and now becoming virtually universal; by 1900, 90 to 95 percent of all adults in western Europe and the United States could read. They promoted numerical skills and other job-related aptitudes. They also encouraged certain social agendas. Girls were carefully taught about the importance of home and women's moral mission; domestic science programs were designed to promote better nutrition and hygiene. Boys and girls alike were taught the advantages of medical science over other health measures, and in general, governments played a major role in promoting the use of doctors. Schools also carefully propounded nationalism, teaching the superiority of the nation's language and history as well as attacking minority or immigrant cultures.

Governments also began to introduce wider welfare measures, again replacing or supplementing traditional groups such as churches and families. Bismarck was a pioneer in this area too in the 1880s, as he sought to wean German workers from their attraction to socialism. His tactic failed, as socialism steadily advanced, but his measures had lasting importance. German social insurance began to provide assistance in cases of accident, illness, and old age. Soon some measures to aid the unemployed were also added, initially in Britain. These early welfare programs were small and their utility limited, but they sketched a major extension of government power.

The growth of government obviously required new financing. Western governments benefited from the advancing prosperity brought by industrialization. They also introduced personal income taxes by 1900, here too starting small but gradually expanding the take.

The industrial-style government widely introduced by Western nations at the end of the 19th century had considerably more contact with ordinary people than any Western government had ever before maintained. It also sought active loyalty, not mere calm. It began to take over many functions previously performed by families and communities, in part because these institutions had weakened or changed under the impact of industrialization.

Accompanying the quiet revolution in government functions was a realignment of the political spectrum in the Western world during the later 19th century that involved the replacement of constitutional issues by social issues—what people of the time called "the social question"—as the key criteria for political partisanship. Socialist and feminist movements surged to the political fore, placing liberals as well as conservatives in a new, though by no means unsuccessful, defensive posture.

The rise of socialism depended above all on the power of grievance of the working class, with allies from other groups. It also reflected a major redefinition of political theory accomplished, from 1848 through the 1860s, by one of the leading intellectuals of the century in the West, Karl Marx. Early socialist doctrine, from the Enlightenment through 1848, had focused on human perfectibility: Set up a few exemplary communities, where work and rewards would be shared, and the evils of capitalism would end as people exercised their rational judgment to choose the better way. Marx's socialism was tough-minded, and he blasted earlier theorists as giddy utopians. Marx saw socialism as the final phase of an inexorable march of history, which could be studied dispassionately and scientifically. History for Marx was shaped by the available means of production and who controlled those means—an obvious reflection of the looming role of technology in the industrial world forming at that time. Class struggle always pitted a group out of power with the group controlling the means of production; hence, in the era just passed, the middle class had battled the feudal aristocracy. Now the middle class had won; it dominated production and, through this, the state and culture as well. But it had created a new class enemy, the propertyless worker proletariat, that would grow until revolution became inevitable. Then, after a transitional period in which proletarian dictatorship would clean up the remnants of the bourgeois social order, full freedom would be achieved. People would benefit justly from their work, as essential equality would prevail, and the state would wither away; the historic class struggle would at last end because classes would be eliminated.

Marx's vision was a powerful one. It clearly identified capitalist evil. It told workers that their low wages were exploitative and unjust. It urged the need for violent action but also assured that revolution was part of the inexorable tides of history. Victory was assured, and the result would be heaven on earth—ultimately, an Enlightenment-like vision of progress.

Marx's message also came at a good time. Earlier socialist movements had withered in the collapse of the revolutions of 1848, partly because they seemed so impractical and partly because of government crackdowns on radical leaders. By the 1860s, when working-class activity began to revive, Marxist doctrine provided encouragement and structure. Marx himself continued to concentrate on ideological development and purity, but leaders in many countries translated his doctrine into practical political parties.

Germany led the way. As Bismarck extended the vote, socialist leaders in the 1860s and 1870s were the first to understand the implications of mass electioneering. Socialist movements were always strong in the provision of grassroots organization, available to constituents not only in election periods; they provided fiery speakers who courted popular support instead of appealing, as many liberals and conservatives did, on the basis of their elevated social station and the respect it deserved. By the 1880s socialists in Germany were cutting into liberal support, and by 1900 the party was the largest single political force in the nation. Socialist parties in Austria, France, and elsewhere followed a roughly similar course, everywhere emerging as a strong minority force. Only in Britain and particularly the United States did socialism lag somewhat, in part because workers already had the habit of looking to liberal movements as their political expression. In Britain, too, socialism became a significant third force by 1914.

The rise of socialism terrified many people in Western society, who took the revolutionary message literally. In combination with major industrial strikes and unionization, it was possible to see social issues portending outright social war. But socialism itself was not unchanging. As socialist parties gained strength, they often allied with other groups to achieve more moderate reforms, and in the main they became firm supporters of parliamentary democracy. A movement called *revisionism* arose, which argued that Marx's revolutionary vision was wrong—it needed revising—because industrial workers were not becoming a full majority and because success could be achieved by peaceful, gradual means. Revisionism was denounced by many socialist leaders, but in fact most behaved in revisionist fashion, putting their energies into building electoral victories rather than plotting violent revolution. Western socialism, in other words, while it reflected bitter grievances and class divisions as against a mood of consolidation and adjustment, worked to a great extent within the democratic political system.

Socialism was not the only challenge to the existing order. By 1900 powerful feminist movements arose, which sought various legal and economic gains for women, such

Agitating for the vote after 1900, militant "suffragettes" blocked public ways in England, provoking many confrontations with police.

as equal access to professions and higher education as well as the right to vote. Feminism won support particularly from middle-class women, who argued that the very moral superiority granted to women in the home should be translated into political voice. Many middle-class women also chafed against the confines of their domestic roles, particularly as family size declined. A small but important group of women entered the professions directly, challenging ideas of inherent male superiority; a still-larger number became teachers and nurses, increasingly dominating semiprofessions that gave women both a new work role, at least before marriage, and a new sense that their opportunities were unjustly limited. In several countries feminism combined with socialism, but in Britain, the United States, Australia, and Scandinavia a separate feminist current arose that petitioned widely and even conducted acts of violence in order to win the vote. Here, too, was a major threat to political adjustment, but here too was a threat that might be managed. Several American states and Scandinavian countries extended the vote to women by 1914, in a pattern that would spread to Britain, Germany, and the whole United States after 1918.

The politics of Western society remained lively, with new forces jostling older interests and assumptions. Outside of formal policy—for example, in some new cultural currents—tensions were even more pronounced, as against the mood of complacency—of confidence in industrial and political progress—that remained widespread around 1900.

POPULAR CULTURE AND HIGH CULTURE

Key developments in popular culture differentiated Western society after 1850 from the decades of initial industrialization. Better wages and the reduction of work hours gave ordinary people new flexibility to express themselves. Changes in social and economic structure also opened new doors. Alongside the working class grew a large white-collar labor force of secretaries, clerks, and salespeople, who serviced the growing bureaucracies of big business and the state. These people, some of them women workers, adopted many middle-class values, but they also insisted on interesting consumption and leisure opportunities. The middle class itself, freed from the work burdens of early industrialization, became more open, though with reservations, to the idea that pleasure could be legitimate.

Furthermore, the economy demanded change. Factories could now spew out goods in such quantity that popular consumption had to be encouraged simply to keep pace with production. Widespread advertising developed to promote a sense of need where none had before existed. Product crazes emerged. The bicycle fad of the 1880s, in which middle-class families flocked to purchase the new machine, was the first of many consumer fads in modern Western history. Bicycles were expensive; they altered previous social habits, as women needed less cumbersome garments and young couples could outpedal any potential chaperon during courtship; and people just had to have them. With consumerism spreading, becoming indeed a basic ingredient of the economy, older hesitations about pleasure seeking declined.

Mass leisure culture began to emerge. Popular newspapers, with bold headlines and compelling human-interest stories, won millions of subscribers in the industrial West. They featured shock and entertainment, more than appeals to reason or political principle. Crime, imperialist exploits, sports, and even comics became the items of the day. Popular theater soared. Comedy routines and musical reviews drew thousands of patrons to music halls; after 1900 some of these entertainment themes dominated the new medium of motion pictures. Vacation trips became increasingly common, and seaside resorts grew more and more to the level of big business.

Leisure outlets of these sorts were designed for fun. They appealed to impulse and escapism. Leisure was now a commodity to be enjoyed regularly, rather than through periodic festivals as in traditional society. With work increasingly disciplined, leisure was seen by many not as a chance for restraint and self-improvement, as the middle class still sometimes tried to insist, but as release.

The rise of team sports readily expressed the complexities of the late 19th century leisure revolution. Here was another Western-wide development, though one that soon had international impact. Soccer, football, and baseball all surged into new prominence, at both amateur and professional levels. These new sports reflected industrial life. Though based on traditional games, they were organized with rules and umpires. They taught the virtues of coordination and discipline, and could be viewed as useful preparation for work or military life. They were suitably commercial: Sports equipment, based on the ability to mass-produce rubber balls, and professional teams and stadia quickly became major businesses. But sports also expressed impulse and violence. They expressed irrational community loyalties and even, as Olympic Games were reintroduced in 1892, nationalist passions.

Overall, new leisure interests suggested a complex set of attitudes on the part of ordinary people in Western society. They demonstrated growing secularism. Religion still counted for something among some groups, but religious practice had declined markedly as people looked increasingly for worldly entertainments and gave allegiance to secular faiths such as nationalism or socialism or simply the growing prestige of science. Many people would have agreed that progress was possible on this earth, through rational planning and individual self-control. Yet mass leisure also suggested a more impulsive side to popular outlook, one bent on display of passion or at least, as spectators, vicarious participation in emotional release.

SCIENCE AND ART

A similar dualism, though a more formal one, developed in intellectual life in the West, with roots going back to the early 19th century. On the one hand, science continued to gain ground; on the other hand, a bewildering array of intellectual movements attempted to provide alternate views of reality and a less structured approach to human understanding. There were some common basic themes. The size of the intellectual and artistic community in the West expanded steadily, with rising prosperity and advancing educational levels. A growing audience existed for various intellectual and artistic products, making it more possible than ever before to hope to earn a living through painting or writing or scientific research. The bulk of the new activity was resolutely secular. Though new churches were built as cities grew, and missionary activity reached new heights outside the Western world, the churches no longer served as centers for the most creative intellectual life.

A major portion of Western cultural activity built on the traditions of rationalism that had been firmed up by the Enlightenment. Major political theories, such as liberalism,

Middle class and working class excursionists made trips to the seaside popular before costumes fully adjusted, as can be seen in this scene from Yarmouth, England.

assumed that people were basically rational and improvable, and that human society could be grasped through investigation of fundamental social laws. Thus liberals urged the importance of education and freedom of inquiry, while also urging that economic activity, for example, could be grasped through basic operations of supply and demand. Karl Marx, though arguing that large historical forces dominated individual action, also urged rational investigation, claiming that his revolutionary society would place rational human nature and benevolence in full command at last.

Continuing advances in science kept alive the rationalist tradition. Universities and other research establishments increasingly applied science to practical affairs, linking science and technology in the popular mind under a general aura of progress. Improvements in medical pathology and the germ theory linked science and medicine, though no breakthrough therapies as yet resulted. Science was applied to agriculture, with Germany and then the United States in the lead, through studies of seed yields and chemical fertilizers.

The great advance in theoretical science came in biology, with the evolutionary theory of Charles Darwin (whose major work was published in 1859). On the basis of careful observation, Darwin argued that all living species had evolved into their present form through the ability to adapt in a struggle for survival. Biological development could be scientifically understood as a process taking place over time, with some animal and plant species disappearing and others evolving from earlier forms. Darwin's ideas clashed with traditional beliefs that God had fashioned humankind as part of initial creation, and the resultant debate further weakened the intellectual hold of religion. Darwin's advance also created a more complex picture of nature than Newton's simple physical laws had suggested. Nature now worked through random struggle, and people were seen as animals with large brains, not as supremely rational. The theory of evolution confirmed the link between science and advancement of knowledge, and Darwin's theory was in fact compatible with a continued belief in progress.

Developments in physics continued as well, with work on electromagnetic behavior and then, around 1900, increasing knowledge of the behavior of the atom and its major components. New theories arose, based on complex mathematics, to explain the behavior of planetary motion and the movement of electrical particles, where Newtonian laws seemed too simple. After 1900 Albert Einstein's theory of relativity formalized this new work by adding time as a factor in physical measurement. Again, science seemed to be steadily advancing in its grasp of the physical universe, though it was also important to note that its complexity now surpassed the grasp even of educated laypeople.

The social sciences also continued to advance, on the basis of observation, experiment, and rationalist theorizing. Great efforts went into compilations of statistical data concerning populations, economic patterns, and health conditions. Sheer empirical knowledge about human affairs had never been more extensive. At the level of theory, leading economists tried to explain business cycles and the causes of poverty, while social psychologists studied the behavior of crowds. Toward the end of the 19th century the Viennese physician Sigmund Freud began to develop his theories of the workings of the human unconscious, arguing that much behavior is determined by impulses but that emotional problems can be relieved if they are brought into the light of rational discussion. Social scientists were thus complicating the traditional Enlightenment view of human nature by studying the animal impulses and unconscious strivings of human beings. Still, they continued to rely on standard scientific methods in their work, believing that human behavior can be described in rational categories; most social scientists asserted that ultimately human reason would pre-

Romantic painters delighted in evocative scenes and a mysterious Gothic presence, as depicted by Joseph Turner in "Tinturn Abbey."

vail. Social scientists claimed that personal and social problems alike could be reduced through knowledge and logical planning, and indeed the role of social science experts in advising governments and even individual families increased steadily.

Yet there was a second approach in the Western culture that developed in the 19th century. This approach emphasized artistic values and often glorified the irrational. To be sure, many novelists, such as Charles Dickens in England, bent their efforts toward realistic portrayals of human problems, believing that they could inform as well as improve the world around them. Many painters built on the discoveries of science, using knowledge of optics and color. Nevertheless, the central artistic vision, beginning with *romanticism* in the first half of the century, held that emotion and impression, not reason and generalization, were the keys to the mysteries of human experience and nature. Artists sought to portray intense passions, even madness, not calm reflection. Romantic novelists wanted to move readers to tears, not philosophical debate; painters sought empathy with the beauties of nature or the storm-tossed tragedy of shipwreck, not structured portrayal. Romantics and their successors after 1850 also deliberately endeavored to violate traditional Western artistic standards. Poetry did not have to rhyme; drama did not necessarily need plot; painting could be evocative, not literal (for literal portrayals, painters could now argue, use a camera). Each generation of artists proved more defiant than the last. By 1900 painters and sculptors were becoming increasingly abstract, while musical composers worked with atonal scales that defied long-established conventions. Some artists talked of an art for art's sake—arguing essentially that art had its own purposes, regardless of the larger society around it.

The development of modern artistic styles brought constant innovation into literature and art. This linked art to other facets of Western society where change and novelty were the name of the game, but it distressed many people who hoped art would confirm traditional values. After 1900 the new styles began to have an international influence, but they also pulled into the Western experience stylistic lessons from African and East Asian art, newly accessible as a result of growing cultural links.

Within the West itself, the split between rationalists and nonrationalists assured continued debate about the nature of truth. The debate had institutional implications: Most scientists and social scientists by 1900 worked in or around growing research universities, whereas artists often had no set institutional apparatus. Scientists were viewed as bastions of progress, as an essential part of industrial society, whereas artists might be seen as dangerous experimenters

Impressionists sought to escape literal representation, in favor of visual impressions of natural settings. This painting, *On the Seine at Bennecourt*, was completed by Claude Monet (1868) as the experimental style was getting underway.

or immoral vagabonds. Despite the imbalance, the modern art impulse continued to expand, which meant that many creative Westerners required a vision different from that of the established order and that elements of a wider public also wanted an outlet that would express some of the confusion of modern life and the human personality.

At neither the formal nor the popular levels, then, did Western culture produce a clear synthesis in the 19th century. New discipline and rationalism warred with impulse, even evocations of violence. The earlier certainties of Christianity or even the Enlightenment gave way to greater debate. The debate could be vigorous, and it seemed to reflect different facets of the industrial experience in the West; but some observers worried that it also expressed tensions that could become dangerous, between different kinds of observers or between different facets of the same modern mind. Perhaps the Western world was not put together quite so neatly as the adjustments and consolidations after 1850 might suggest.

ANALYSIS
THE UNITED STATES IN WORLD HISTORY

World history surveys often have some problems in integrating the United States, after some coverage of colonial origins as part of Western explorations and trade. World history already offers a full menu. American students always take some separate United States history courses. So why not simplify life and leave the United States out of world surveys?

This approach gains added support from the fact that until the late 19th century the United States, relatively isolated save for the arrival of immigrants, was not particularly important in the larger stream of world history. American preoccupation lay in internal development, including westward expansion. This brought clashes with Mexico, an important foretaste of the rebalancing in power between the United States and Latin America. Westward expansion also brought some posturing against European nations tempted to interfere in the Western hemisphere. The Monroe Doctrine (1820) warned against meddling in Latin America. In fact it was British policy and naval power that kept the hemisphere largely free from new colonialism.

The United States counted for little in world diplomacy. The nation's population, though growing, was small. Its economy, though developing, exported little until the great surge of agricultural exports followed by an industrial outflow in the 1870s and 1880s. The United States was a debtor nation, depending on loans from European banks for much of its development until 1914. The nation did play an important role in receiving European immigrants, just as it earlier had affected African history through its role in the slave trade. And the nation symbolized, especially to some Europeans, a land of freedom and prosperity; revolutionaries in 1848, for example, invoked American institutions, just as Latin American independence fighters had done around 1820. But while the United States depended on world currents of immigration, loans, and culture, it had yet to contribute much in detail.

By the end of the 19th century the tentativeness and isolation of the United States in world affairs, though they still affected American perceptions in promoting a belief that the nation could be shielded from international involvements, had really passed. American agriculture poured goods into the markets of Europe. American industry was rising, along with that of Germany, to the top of world output rankings. The United States had clearly become, along with western Europe, part of the dominant economic core in world trade. American naval power led to the acquisition of important colonies in Asia and the West Indies. As it gained in international impact, the United States, while retaining some of its earlier image as a revolutionary new nation, became increasingly similar to major west European powers in defending existing world power alignments.

Since the international importance of the United States did grow, leaving the nation out of world history until the late 19th century risks missing significant early patterns. But building United States history in, even after 1870, raises some conceptual as well as practical problems.

There is a legitimate historical question about whether to treat the United States as a separate civilization (along perhaps with Canada and other places that mixed dominant Western settlement with frontier conditions). Latin America, because of the peculiarities of its colonial experience, its ongoing position in the world economy, and above all its blending of European, Indian, and African influences, cannot be subsumed as part of an expanding Western civilization. Does the same hold true for the United States?

Because the United States is so often treated separately in history courses there is a ready assumption of American uniqueness. The United States had purer diplomatic motives than did western Europe—look at the idealism of Woodrow Wilson. It had its own cultural movements, such as the religious "great awakening" of the 18th century or transcendentalism in the 19th. The United States had the unique experience of wave after wave of immigrants reaching its shores, contributing great cultural diversity but also promoting considerable cultural and social integration under the banners of "Americanization." Many of these assumptions of uniqueness are mere reflexes, not supported by serious comparative study. There is, however, a more careful school of historians who argue for American *exceptionalism*—that is, the United States as its own civilization, not part of larger Western patterns. American exceptionalism need not contend that the United States was immune from contact with western Europe, which would be ridiculous, but it argues that this contact was incidental to the larger development of the United States on its own terms.

American exceptionalists can point to a number of factors that caused the development of a separate United States civilization. The Atlantic colonies gained political and cultural characteristics in relative isolation—they were, among other things, unusually democratic (among white males) compared to Europe at the time. Though colonial immigrants often intended to duplicate European styles of life, the vastness and wealth of the new land quickly forced changes. As a result American families gave greater voice to women and children, abundant land created a class of independent farmers rather than a traditionalist peasantry with its tight-knit villages. Even after the colonial era, distinctive institutions, created by the successful revolution and its federal Constitution, would continue to shape a political life different from that of western Europe. The frontier, which lasted until the 1890s and had cultural impact even beyond that date, would continue to make Americans unusually mobile and restless, while draining off some of the social grievances that arose in western Europe.

Distinctive causes, furthermore, produced distinctive results. There is no question that the United States, into the 20th century, had a different agricultural setup from that of western Europe. American politics—with the huge exception of the Civil War—emphasized relatively small disagreements between two major political parties, with third party movements typically pulled into the mainstream rather quickly. There was less political fragmentation and extremism than in western Europe, and more stability (some would add boredom). No strong socialist movement took shape. Religion was more important in American than in European life by the later 19th century. Religion served immigrants as a badge of identity and helped all Americans, building a new society, retain some sense of moorings. The absence of established churches in the United States kept religion out of politics, in contrast to Europe where churches got caught up in more general attacks on the political establishment.

The American exceptionalist argument often appeals particularly to things Americans like to believe about themselves—more religious, less socialistic, full of the competence that came from taming a frontier—but it must embrace some less savory distinctiveness as well. The existence of slavery, and then the racist attitudes and institutions that arose following its abolition, created ongoing issues in American life that had no direct counterpart in western Europe. Europe, correspondingly, had less direct contact with African culture; jazz was one of the key products of this aspect of American life.

The exceptionalist argument is powerful, particularly because Americans (and Europeans) are normally schooled to think of the United States history as a largely separate line of development. Yet from a world history standpoint, the United States must be seen also, and perhaps primarily, as an offshoot of Western civilization. The colonial experience showed the powerful impact of Western political ideas, culture, and even family styles. American history in the 19th century followed patterns common in western Europe. The development of parliamentary life and the spread of democracy, though unusually early in the United States, fits a larger Western trajectory. American industrialization was a direct offshoot of Europe and followed a basically common dynamic. American intellectuals kept in close contact with European developments, and there were few purely American styles. Conditions for women and wider patterns of family life, in areas such as birth control or disciplining children, were similar on both sides of the North Atlantic, which shows that the United States not only imitated western Europe but paralleled it.

In some important cases, because the United States was freer from peasant and aristocratic traditions, it pioneered developments that would soon surface in western Europe. This was true to an extent in politics; it was true in the development of mass consumer culture and mass media (for example, the popular press and popular films). In these areas the United States can be seen, not as distinctive to the point of forming a separate civilization, but as anticipating some developments that would become common in Western civilization in part because of American example.

American exceptions remain—the Civil War and racial issues, the absence of serious socialism (but not of trade unionism and bitter labor strife, quite similar to West European patterns), and the importance of religion. American distinctiveness remains in another respect: The United States was rising to world power just as key European nations, notably Britain, began to decline. The trajectory of American history is somewhat different from that of western Europe, and the 20th century revealed growing American ability to play power politics in western Europe itself. Just as American exceptionalists must admit special Western influences, so those who argue the United States as part of the West must work in special features and dynamics.

While the shared Western experience provides the most accurate framework, given not only mutual influence but so many common impulses, the main point is to analyze American history in careful comparative terms as part of removing the nation's history from the isolation in which it is so often taught and viewed.

There is, finally, one other vantage point, not definitive but suggestive, that uses the world history framework in the form of analogy. The United States here is Rome compared to West Europe's Greece. Like classical Greece, western Europe produced the basic cultural creativity of the civilization and its first expansion (the Atlantic of course replaced the Mediterranean). Like Greece, western Europe could never really unite, and its empires were fragile as a result. Like Rome, the United States went through a republican period in considerable isolation, full of stern virtue and the strengths of a solid farming community. It initially feared Western culture as corrupting. But as the United States gained power, like Rome, its initial political and social institutions gave way to a more powerful state, larger armies, and huge corporations (the equivalent of Rome's great estates). American power, like Roman, soon eclipsed the power of the civilization's source. Yet the United States never matched Europe's cultural creativity; its strength lay in highways, stadia, organizational ability, and brash self-confidence. Here, then, in analogy, is a restatement of American participation in Western history, but also of a distinctive American role. Is the analogy useful? Does it suggest the same last chapter: an American collapse that will affect the whole of Western civilization save perhaps for a "third Rome" somewhere else?

Questions: Which argument has the greater strength in describing 19th century history, the United States as a separate civilization, or the United States as part of the West? Have the United States and western Europe become more or less similar in the 20th century? Why?

THE EXPANSION OF THE WEST AND WESTERN DIPLOMACY

The Industrial Revolution, plus related improvements in bureaucratic organizing ability and science, prompted a major expansion of the West's power in the world. Western nations could pour out far more processed goods than before, which meant that they needed new markets. They also required new raw materials and agricultural products, which spurred the development of more commercial agriculture in places such as Africa and Latin America. The West's dominance in the world economy was greatly enhanced, and more areas of the world were brought into some kind of dependent relationship to it. The vast ships and communications networks created by industrial technology merely spurred the intensification of the Western-led world economy, while bringing additional profits back to Europe in the form of banking fees and merchant commissions.

Industrialization also extended the West's military advantage in the wider world. Steamships could navigate previously impassable river systems, bringing Western guns inland as never before. Invention of the repeating rifle and machine gun gave small bands of Western troops immense superiority over masses of local troops. These new means combined with new motives: European nations rivaled for new colonies as part of their nationalistic competition, businessmen sought new chances for profit, and missionaries sought opportunities for conversion. Haltingly before 1860, then rapidly, Europe's empires spread through Africa and Southeast Asia, plus parts of China and the Middle East.

Western dominance did not mean absolute sovereignty, and world history still had to be written in terms of the staying power of key civilizations even as they interacted with Western values. The working out of the West's imperialist century, then, must be treated not as part of Western history but as part of the civilizations affected.

NEW EUROPEAN SETTLEMENTS

In several areas, because of sparse previous settlement, Western expansion in the 19th century meant an extension of Western society itself, and not primarily a new cultural interchange. Already Britain's colonies on the Atlantic coast of North America had established an identifiable Western culture amid important new influences resulting from new interracial contacts and the frontier experience. During most of the 19th century the westward expansion of the new United States brought the American version of Western society across a whole continent. Early in the century Jefferson's purchase of Louisiana had opened a frontier across the Mississippi, and subsequent settlement plus war with Mexico had pushed the new nation to the Pacific coast.

At the same time, Canada, Australia, and New Zealand also filled with immigrants from Europe and established parliamentary legislatures and vigorous commercial economies that placed them in the general dynamic of Western civilization. Like the United States, these new nations looked primarily to Europe for cultural styles and intellec-

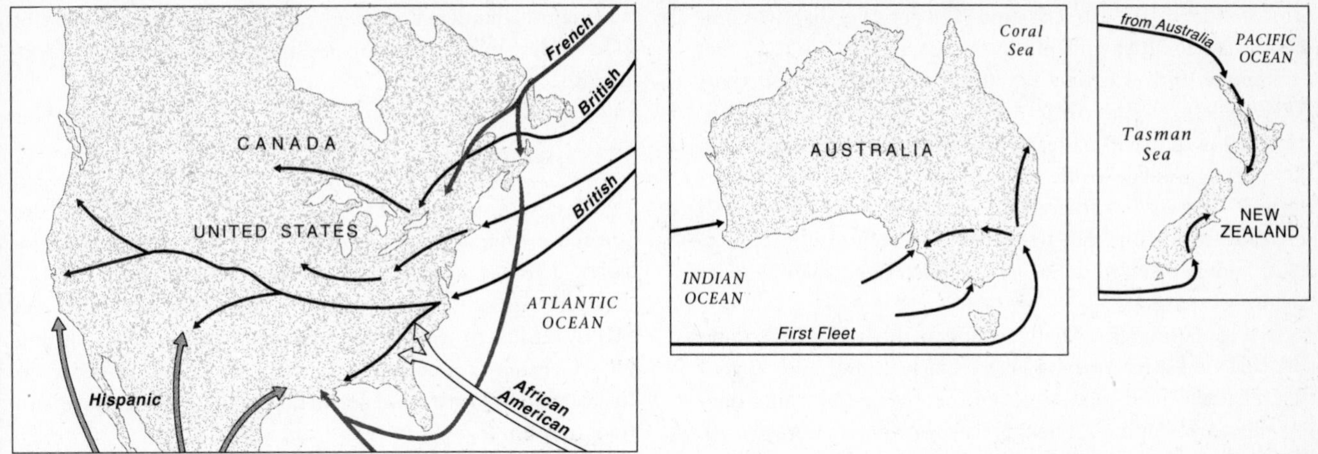

19th-Century Settlement and Consolidation in the United States, Canada, Australia, and New Zealand

tual leadership. They also followed common Western patterns in such areas as family life, the valuation of women, and the extension of mass education and culture. Unlike the United States, however, these nations remained part of the British Empire, though with growing autonomy.

Canada, won by Britain in wars with France in the 18th century, had been preserved from the contagion of the American Revolution. Religious differences between French Catholic settlers and British rulers and settlers troubled the area recurrently, and a number of uprisings occurred early in the 19th century. Determined not to lose this colony as it had lost the United States, the British began in 1839 to grant increasing self-rule. Canada set up its own Parliament and laws, while remaining attached to the larger empire. Initially this system applied primarily to the province of Ontario, but other provinces were included, creating a federal system that describes Canada to this day. French hostilities were eased somewhat by the creation of a separate province, Quebec, where the majority of French speakers were located. Massive railroad building, beginning in the 1850s, brought settlement to western territories and a great expansion of mining and commercial agriculture in the vast plains. As in the United States to the south, new immigrants from southern and particularly eastern Europe poured in during the last decades of the century, attracted by Canada's growing commercial development and spurring further gains.

Britain's Australian colonies originated in 1788 when a ship deposited convicts to establish a penal settlement at Sydney. Australia's only previous inhabitants had been a hunting-and-gathering people called the aborigines, and they were in no position to resist European settlement and exploration. By 1840 Australia had 140,000 European inhabitants, based mainly on a prosperous sheep-growing agriculture that provided needed wool for British industries. Exportation of convicts ceased in 1853, by which time most settlers were free immigrants. Discovery of gold in 1851 spurred further pioneering, leading to a population of over a million by 1861. As in Canada, major provinces were granted self-government with a multiparty parliamentary system. A unified federal nation was proclaimed on the first day of the 20th century. By this time considerable industrialization, a growing socialist party, and significant welfare legislation had occurred.

Finally, New Zealand, discovered by the Dutch in the 17th century and explored by the English in 1770, began to receive British attention after 1814. Here the Polynesian hunting-and-gathering people, the Maoris, were well organized politically. Missionary efforts converted many of them to Christianity between 1814 and the 1840s. The British government, fearful of French interest in the area, moved to take official control in 1840, and considerable European immigration followed. New Zealand settlers relied heavily on agriculture (including sheep growing), selling initially to Australia's booming gold-rush population and then to Britain. Wars with the Maoris plagued the 1860s, but after the Maori defeat, generally good relations were established, with Maoris winning some representation in Parliament. As in Canada and Australia, a parliamentary system was created that allowed the new nation to rule itself as a dominion of the British Empire, without interference from the mother country.

Like the United States, Canada, New Zealand, and Australia each had distinct national flavors and national issues. These new countries were far more dependent on the European, particularly the British, economy than was the

United States. Industrialization did not overshadow commercial agriculture and mining, even in Australia, so that exchanges with Europe remained unusually important. Nevertheless, despite their distinctive features, these countries followed basic patterns of Western civilization from this point onward, from political forms to key leisure activities. Currents of liberalism, socialism, modern art, and scientific education that described Western civilization to 1900 and beyond, thus largely characterized these important new extensions.

It was these areas, finally, along with the United States and part of Latin America, particularly Brazil and Argentina, that received new waves of European emigrants during the 19th century. Though Europe's population growth rate slowed after 1800, it still advanced rapidly on the basis of previous gains—that is, as more children reached adulthood and had children of their own. Europe's expansion was in fact greater than Asia's in percentage terms, with both continents relying heavily on the use of foodstuffs initially discovered in the New World, and Europe's export of people helped explain how Western societies could take shape in such distant areas.

The extension of Western society through most of North America as well as Australia and New Zealand depended on the fortuitous absence of large previous populations, compounded by the continued ravages of Western-imported diseases on the people who were present. Other parts of the world, more thickly inhabited, had quite different experiences under the impact of Western influence and some outright settlement. The spread of the West also reflected the new power of Western industrialization. Huge areas could now be settled quickly thanks to steamships and rails, while remaining in close contact with the Western home base in Europe. The expansion of the West revealed the power of Western values and institutions, as colonists deliberately introduced most of the patterns that had prevailed in Europe, from parliaments to Western-defined standards for women and children.

As a new century dawned in 1900, newspapers throughout the Western world—the new segments as well as the old—trumpeted the progress that had occurred during the past century and the bright prospects for the future. They noted the rise of mass education, improvements in material standards and health care, and the assurance of political freedoms and representation—the list seemed endless. Not all Westerners shared this rosy vision. Many workers as well as many women judged that progress had passed them by, though some expected to join the parade in the near future. Adjustments to industrial society had produced a noisy confidence on the part of many groups in the West. The same confidence showed in the facile implantation of essentially Western societies in other key parts of the world.

DIPLOMATIC TENSIONS

Western expansion had its limits, however, and these limits were beginning to tell on the Western heartland by 1900. The rise of new parts of the Western world, particularly the growing strength and assertiveness of the United States, added to the sense of national competition. Along with Germany's new-found muscle, American presence on the world diplomatic scene made rivalries for empire and trade more intense.

More important still at this point was the fact that by 1900 there were few parts of the world available for Western seizure. Latin America was independent but under extensive United States influence, so that a new intrusion of colonialism was impossible. Africa was almost entirely carved up. The few final colonies taken after 1900—Morocco by France and Tripoli (Libya) by Italy—caused great diplomatic furor on the part of other colonial powers worried about the balance of force on that continent. China and the Middle East were technically independent, but were in fact crisscrossed by rivalries among the Western powers and Russia (and in China's case, Japan). No agreement was possible on further takeovers.

Yet for several decades the growth of empire had served as a vital outlet for Western diplomatic and military energies. The tensions among the Western nation-states had escalated dangerously after the unifications of Italy and Germany. Bismarck, the architect of German unity, cleverly devised an alliance system during the 1870s and 1880s that neutralized France, a "natural enemy" that feared the growing power of the German neighbor and resented the loss of territories after the war in 1870–1871. Germany allied directly with Austria and Italy, and had had a separate understanding with Russia. This intricate alliance system was in fact preserved by the interest key nations took in overseas expansion. France worried less about the rivalry with Germany than about gaining new colonies in Africa and Indochina, while Germany itself entered the imperialist game by seizures in Africa and East Asia. Britain remained primarily preoccupied with colonial expansion.

Imperialist expansion, however, fed the sense of rivalry among key nation-states. Britain, in particular, grew worried about Germany's overseas drive, supplemented after 1890 by the construction of a large navy. Economic competition between a surging Germany and a lagging Britain added fuel to the fire. France, eager to escape the Bismarck-engineered isolation, was willing to play down traditional rivalries with Britain. The French also took the opportunity to ally with Russia, when after 1890 Germany dropped this particular alliance because of Russian-Austrian enmity.

By 1907 most major European nations were paired off in two alliance systems: Germany, Austria-Hungary, and Italy formed the Triple Alliance, while Britain, Russia, and France constituted the newer Triple Entente. Three against three seemed fair, but in fact Germany grew increasingly concerned about facing potential enemies both to the east (Russia) and west (France). All the powers steadily built up their military arsenals in what turned out to be the first of several arms races in the 20th century. All powers save Britain had instituted peacetime military conscription, to provide large armies and even larger trained reserves. Artillery levels and naval forces built steadily—the addition of a new kind of battleship, the Dreadnaught, to naval arsenals was a key escalation—while discussions about reducing armament levels got nowhere.

Each alliance system, furthermore, was dependent on an unstable partner. Russia suffered a revolution in 1905, and its allies worried that any further diplomatic setbacks might paralyze the eastern giant. Austria-Hungary was plagued by nationalities disputes, particularly by minority Slavic groups; German leaders fretted that a diplomatic setback might bring chaos. Both Austria and Russia were heavily involved, finally, in maneuverings in the Balkans—the final piece in what became a nightmare puzzle.

The arms race began around 1900. The massive "Dreadnought" battleship of 1911 was developed in Britain but provoked German buildup in response.

Small Balkan nations had won independence from the Ottoman Empire during the 19th century; as Turkish power declined, local nationalism rose, and Russian support for its Slavic neighbors paid off. But the nations were intensely hostile to each other. Furthermore, Balkan nationalism threatened Austria, which had a large southern Slav population. Russia and Austria nearly came to blows on several occasions over Balkan issues, for Austria felt that it must keep the Slavs in line while Russia looked to the Balkans as a place where it might pick up needed diplomatic prestige. Then in 1912 and 1913 the Balkan nations engaged in two internal wars, which led to territorial gains for several states but satisfied no one. Serbia, particularly, which bordered Austria to the south, had hoped for greater stakes. At the same time Austria grew nervous over the gains Serbia had achieved. In 1914 a Serbian nationalist assassinated an Austrian archduke on behalf of Serbian claims. Austria vowed to punish Serbia. Russia rushed to the defense of her little Slavic brother and mobilized its troops against Austria. Germany, worried about Austria and also eager to be able to strike against France before Russia's cumbersome mobilization was complete, called up her reserves, and then declared war on August 1. Britain hesitated briefly, then joined its allies. World War I had begun, and with it came a host of new problems for Western society.

CONCLUSION

DIPLOMACY AND SOCIETY

The tensions that spiraled into major war are not easy to explain. Diplomatic maneuverings can seem quite remote from the central concerns of most people, if only because key decisions—for example, with whom to ally—are made by a specialist elite. Even as the West became more democratic, few ordinary people placed foreign affairs high on their election agendas.

The West had long been characterized by political divisions and rivalries. This was, by comparison with some other civilizations, an endemic weakness of the Western political system. In a sense, what happened by the late 19th century was that the nation-state system got out of hand, encouraged by the absence of serious challenge from any other civilizations. The details of this development, involving the rise of Germany and the new tensions in the Balkans, are obviously important, but the link with a longer-term Western problem area should not be forgotten.

At the same time, the diplomatic escalation also had some links with the strains of Western society under the impact of industrialization. Obviously the fact that modern war proved so horrible, as had already been suggested in the American Civil War, stemmed directly from the destructive power of modern factory-produced weaponry, from massive new guns and ships to steady improvements in the explosive power of chemical combinations. The causes of war, also, related to industrial patterns.

Most obviously, established leadership in the West continued to worry about social protest and the growing visibility of the masses. Leaders tended as a result to seek diplomatic successes in order to distract. This procedure worked nicely for a few decades when imperialist gains came easily. But then it proved a straitjacket: German officials around 1914, fearful of the power of the socialists, wondered if war would not aid national unity, while British leaders, beset by feminist as well as labor unrest, failed to think through their own diplomatic options. Leaders also depended on military buildups for economic purposes. Modern industry, pressed to sell the soaring output of its factories, found naval purchases and army equipment a vital supplement.

The masses themselves had some role to play. Though some groups, particularly in the socialist camp, were hostile to the alliance system and to imperialism, many workers and clerks found the diplomatic successes of their nations exciting. In an increasingly disciplined and organized society, with work frequently routine if not downright boring, the idea of violence and energy, even of war, could find appeal. Mass newspapers that fanned nationalist pride with stories of conquest and tales of the evils of rival nations, helped shape this belligerent popular culture.

The consolidation of industrial society in the West, in other words, had continued to generate strain at various levels. Consolidation meant more powerful armies and governments, a more potent industrial machine. It also meant continued social frictions and an ongoing tug of war between rational restraint and a desire to break out, to dare something wild.

Thus it was that, just a few years after celebrating a century of material progress and relative peace, ordinary Europeans went to war almost gaily in 1914. Troops departed for the front convinced that war would be exciting with quick victories, their departure hailed by enthusiastic civilians who draped their trains with flowers. Four years later almost everyone would have agreed that war had been unmitigated hell. The complexities of industrial society were such, however, that war's advent seemed almost a welcome breath of the unexpected, a chance to get away from the disciplined stability of everyday life.

FURTHER READINGS

Two excellent studies survey Europe's industrial revolution: Sidney Pollard's *Peaceful Conquest: The Industrialization of Europe* (1981) and David Landes's *The Unbound Prometheus: Technological Change and Industrial Development in Western Europe from 1700 to the Present* (1969). See also Phyllis Dean's *The First Industrial Revolution* (1980), on Britain. On the demographic experience, see Thomas McKeown's *The Modern Rise of Population* (1977).

For the French Revolution and political upheaval, O. Connelly's *French Revolution—Napoleonic Era* (1979) is a useful introduction. Lynn Hunt's *Politics, Culture and Class in the French Revolution* (1984) is an important recent study. Other revolutionary currents are treated in George Rudé's *The Crowd in History: Popular Disturbances in France and England* (1981) and Peter Stearns's *1848: The Revolutionary Tide in Europe* (1974).

Major developments concerning women and the family are covered in Louise Tilly and Joan Scott's *Women, Work and Family* (1978) and Steven Mintz and Susan Kellogg's *Domestic Revolutions: A Social History of American Family Life* (1989). See also R. Evans's *The Feminists: Women's Emancipation in Europe, America and Australia* (1979). An important age group is treated in John Gillisk's *Youth and History* (1981).

For an overview on social change, see Peter Stearns and Herrick Chapman's *European Society in Upheaval* (1991). On labor history, see Michael Hanagan's *The Logic of Solidarity* (1981) and Albert Lindemann's *History of European Socialism* (1983). Eugen Weber's *Peasants into Frenchmen: The Modernization of Rural France* (1976) and Harvey Graff, ed., *Literacy and Social Development in the West* (1982) deal with important special topics.

On political and cultural history, see Gordon Wright's *France in Modern Times* (1981), Gordon Craig's *Germany, 1866–1945* (1978), and Louis Snyder's *Roots of German Nationalism* (1978). J. H. Randall's *The Making of the Modern Mind* (1976) is a useful survey; see also O. Chadwick's *The Secularization of the European Mind in the Nineteenth Century* (1976). On major diplomatic developments, see D. K. Fieldhouse's *Economics and Empire, 1830–1914* (1970) and David Kaiser's *Politics and War: European Conflict from Philip II to Hitler* (1990).

1619 Dutch establish trading post at Batavia in Java

1620s Sultan of Mataram's attacks on Batavia fail

1652 First Dutch settlement in South Africa at Cape Town

1661 British port-trading center founded at Bombay

1690 Calcutta established at center of British activities in Bengal

1707 Death of Mughal emperor, Aurangzeb; beginning of imperial breakdown

1739 Nadir Shah's invasion of India from Persia

1740–1748 War of Austrian Succession; global British-French struggle for colonial dominance

1750s Civil war and division of Mataram; Dutch become the paramount power on Java

1756–1763 Seven Years' War, British-French global warfare

1757 Battle of Plassey; British dominant power in Bengal

1769–1770 Great Famine in Benga

1775–1782 War for independence by American colonists; another British-French struggle for global preeminence

1786–1790 Cornwallis's political reforms in India

30 Industrialization and Imperialism: The Making of the European Global Order

INTRODUCTION. The process of industrialization that began to transform western European societies in the last half of the 18th century fundamentally altered the nature and impact of European overseas expansion. In the centuries of expansion before the industrial era, the Europeans went overseas because they sought material things they could not produce themselves and because they were threatened by powerful external enemies. They initially sought precious metals for which they traded in Africa and waged wars of conquest to control in the Americas. In the Americas they also seized land on which they could grow high-priced commercial crops such as sugar and coffee. In Asia, European traders and adventurers sought either manufactured goods, such as cotton and silk textiles (produced mainly in India, China, and the Middle East), or luxury items, such as spices, that would improve the living standards of the aristocracy and rising middle classes.

In the Americas, Africa, and Asia missionaries from Roman Catholic areas, such as Spain and Portugal, sought to convert what were regarded as "heathen" peoples to Christianity. Both the wealth gained from products brought home from overseas and the souls won for Christ were viewed as ways of strengthening Christian Europe in its long struggle with Muslim empires that threatened Europe from the south and east. Only on the eve of Columbus's voyage in 1492 were the Muslims driven from Spain into North Africa; and the Ottoman Empire remained a formidable foe of the European powers throughout the first two centuries of overseas expansion.

1790–1815 Wars of the Revolution and Napoleonic era

1798 Napoleon's invasion of Egypt

1815 British annex Cape Town and surrounding area

1830 Start of the Boers' Great Trek in South Africa

1835 Decision to give state support for English education in India; English adopted as the language of Indian law courts

1850s Boer republics established in the Orange Free State and Transvaal

1853 First railway line constructed in India

1857 Calcutta, Madras, and Bombay universities founded

1857–58 "Mutiny" or Great Rebellion in north India

1858 British Parliament assumes control over India from the East India Company

1867 Diamonds discovered in the Orange Free State

1869 Opening of the Suez Canal

c. 1879–1890s Partition of West Africa

1879 Zulu victory over British at Isandhlwana; defeat at Rourke's Drift

1882 British invasion of Egypt

1885 Indian National Congress Party founded in India; gold discovered in the Transvaal

1890s Partition of East Africa

1898 British-French crisis over Fashoda in the Sudan

1899–1902 Anglo-Boer War in South Africa

1914 Outbreak of World War I

In the industrial era, from roughly 1800 onward, the things that Europeans sought in the outside world as well as the source of the insecurities that drove them there changed dramatically. Raw materials—metals, vegetable oils, dyes, cotton, and hemp—needed to feed the machines of Europe, not spices or manufactured goods, were the main products the Europeans sought overseas. Industrialization made Europe for the first time the manufacturing center of the world, and overseas markets for machine-made European products became a key concern of those who pushed for colonial expansion. Christian missionaries, by then as likely to be Protestant as Roman Catholic, still sought to win converts overseas. But unlike the rulers of Portugal and Spain in the early centuries of expansion, European leaders in the industrial age rarely took initiatives overseas to promote Christian proselytization. In part this reflected the fact that western Europe itself was no longer seriously threatened by the Muslims or any other non-European people. The fears that fueled European imperialist expansion in the industrial age arose from internal rivalries between the European powers. Overseas peoples might resist the European advance, but the Europeans feared each other far more than even the largest non-European empires.

The contrast between European expansion in the preindustrial era and in the age of industrialization was also reflected in the extent to which the Europeans were able to sail to overseas areas, go ashore, and move inland. In the early centuries of overseas expansion, European conquests were concentrated in the Americas, whose long isolation left their peoples particularly vulnerable to the technology and diseases of the expansive Europeans (see Chapter 25). In much of the rest of the world (see Chapters 23, 26, and 28), European traders and conquistadores were confined largely to the sea-lanes, islands, and coastal enclaves. Now, industrial technology and techniques of organization and discipline associated with the increasing mechanization of the West gave the Europeans the capacity to reach and infiltrate any foreign land. From the populous, highly centralized, and technologically sophisticated Chinese Empire to small bands of hunters and gatherers struggling to survive in the harsh environment of Tierra del Fuego on the southern coast of South America, few peoples were remote enough to be out of reach of the steamships and railways that carried the Europeans to and across all continents of the globe. No culture was strong enough to remain untouched by the European drive for global dominance in this era, and none could long resist the profound changes unleashed by European conquest and colonization.

The shift from the preindustrial to the industrial phase of European overseas expansion was gradual and cumulative, extending roughly from 1750 to 1850. By the middle decades of the 19th century, few who were attuned to international events could doubt that a watershed had been crossed. The first section of this chapter will explore the initial stages of this momentous transformation. It will trace the advance of the Dutch inland on Java and the rise in India of what can be seen as the first empire of the industrial era. The middle sections of this chapter will be devoted to the forces in Europe and the outside world that led to the great burst of imperialist expansion, which was a dominant feature of global history in the last decades of the 19th century. The final sections will explore the patterns of European conquest and rule that persisted from earlier colonization efforts as well as the innovations that were dictated by the ambitions and aspirations of the European and American champions of the "new" imperialism. Special attention will be given to some of the key consequences of European domination for the societies and cultures of the colonized peoples of Africa and Asia.

THE SHIFT TO LAND EMPIRES IN ASIA

Though we usually use the term "partition" to refer to the European division of Africa at the end of the 19th century, the Western powers had actually been carving up the globe into colonial enclaves for centuries. In the early going, this process was haphazard and often quite contrary to the interests and designs of those in charge of European enterprises overseas. The "Directors," for example, who ran the Dutch and English East India Companies (which were granted monopolies of the trade between their respective countries and "the East" in the 17th and 18th centuries), had little interest in territorial acquisitions. In fact, they were actively opposed to involvement in the political rivalries of the Asian princes. Wars were expensive, and direct administration of African or Asian possessions was even more so. Both cut deeply into the profits gained through participation in the Asian trading system, and profits not empires were the chief concern of the Dutch or English Directors.

Whatever policies company Directors may have instructed their agents in Africa and Asia to follow, these men-on-the-spot were inevitably drawn into local power struggles. They had, after all, to defend their forts, warehouses, and occasionally their ships from the attacks of local lords who resented their competition or laid claim to the land that the Europeans occupied. Though the company Directors had to learn to write off these political entanglements as part of the overhead of their trading empires, they continued to resist initiatives by their overseas agents that would involve them in governing large numbers of Asians or Africans. But before the Industrial Revolution produced the telegraph and other methods of rapid com-

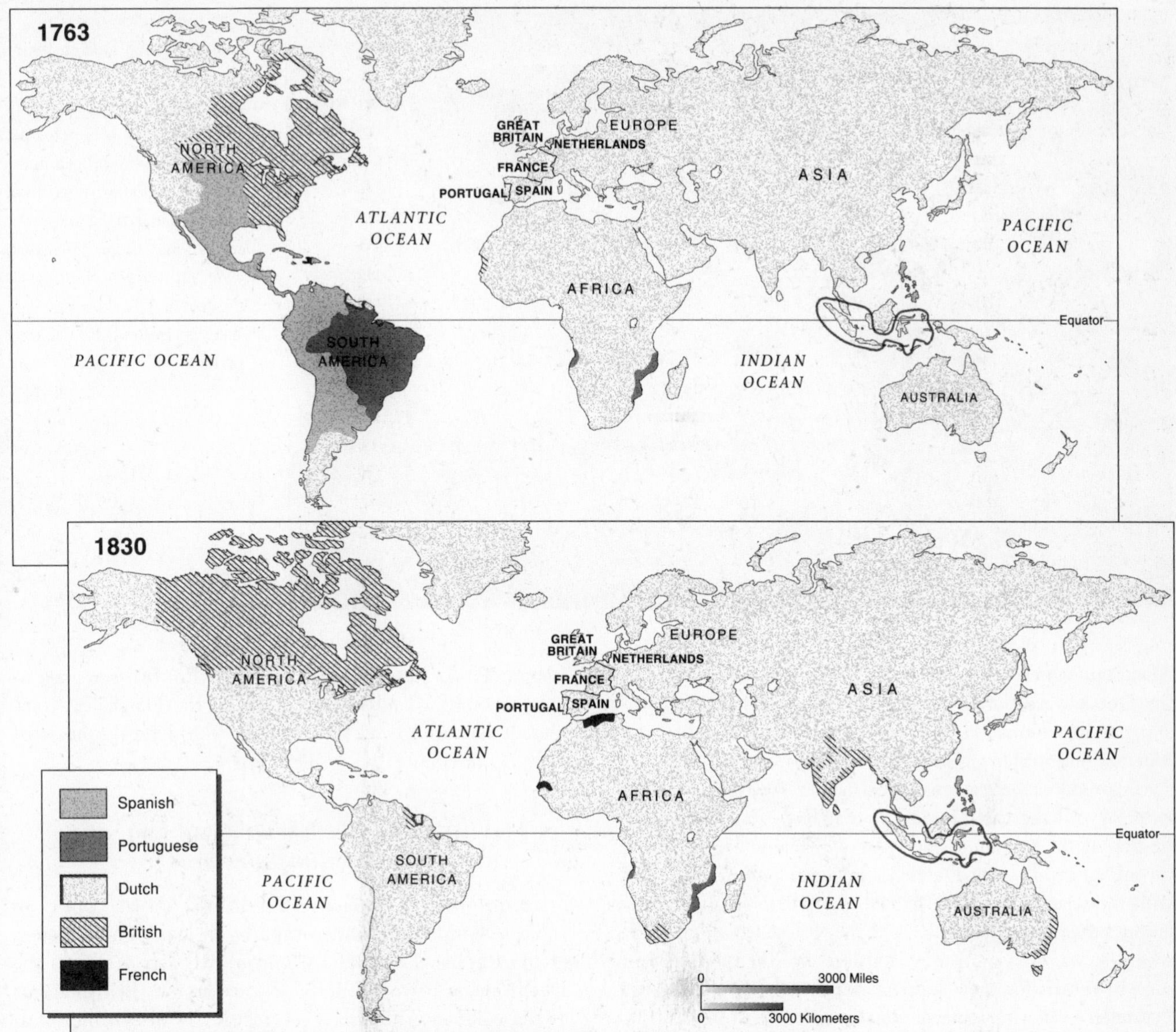

European Colonial Territories, before and after 1800

munication, company Directors or prime ministers in Europe had very little control over those who actually ran their trading empires. In the 18th century a letter took months to reach Calcutta from London; the reply took many more months. Thus, commanders in the field had a great deal of leeway. They could and did conquer whole provinces or kingdoms before home officials even learned that their armies were on the move. Thus, the land empires the European powers began to build were very much the product of initiatives by men-on-the-spot, often acting against the wishes and belated orders of their superiors in Europe.

PROTOTYPE: THE DUTCH ADVANCE ON JAVA

One of the earliest empires to be built in this fashion was that pieced together in the late 17th and 18th centuries by the Dutch in Java, the most populous of the chain of hundreds of islands that today makes up the country of Indonesia. In the early years after the Dutch established their Asian headquarters at Batavia on the northwest coast of the island in 1619, it was a struggle just to survive. After beating back major attacks against Batavia launched in the late 1620s by Sultan Agung—the ruler of the kingdom of

The great pride that 17th-century Dutch took in their overseas commerce and trading empire is evident in this portrait of a Dutch East India Company official and his wife—accompanied by a Western attired Javanese servant and large, Javenese-style umbrella—pointing to the fort and harbor of Batavia (present-day Jakarta) in Java.

Mataram, which controlled most of the Javanese interior—the Dutch were content to become the vassals of Mataram and pay an annual tribute. In the following decades, the Dutch concentrated on gaining monopoly control over the spices produced on the smaller islands of the Indonesian archipelago to the east. In the 1670s, however, an attempt by one of the vassals of the ruler of Mataram to seize the throne embroiled the Dutch in Javanese politics. Content with the security they had gained as a tributary of the Mataram sultans, the Dutch backed the threatened sultan and, when he was driven from his palace and died, his young son. In return for their support, the Dutch were ceded the Preanger territories south of Batavia in 1677.

This episode was the first of a long series of Dutch interventions in the wars of succession between the princes of Mataram. Dutch armies mainly comprised troops recruited from the island peoples of the eastern archipelago, who were led by Dutch commanders. Their superior organization and discipline, even more than their firearms, made the Dutch a potent ally of whichever prince was able to win them to his side. But the price the Javanese rulers paid was very high. Each succession dispute and Dutch intervention led to more and more land being ceded to the increasingly land-hungry Europeans. By the mid-18th century, the sultans of Mataram controlled only the south central portions of Java. A failed attempt by Sultan Mangkubumi to restore Mataram's control over the Dutch in the 1750s ended with a Dutch-dictated division of the kingdom that signified Dutch paramountcy over the entire island. Thus, just about the time the British were beginning to build a land empire in India, the Dutch had completed the capture of Java, which would be the heart of their Asian empire for the next 200 years.

PIVOT OF WORLD EMPIRE: THE RISE OF THE BRITISH RAJ IN INDIA

In many ways, the rise of the British as a land power in India resembled the Dutch capture of Java. The directors of the English East India Company were as hostile as the Dutch financiers to territorial expansion. But British agents of the company in India were repeatedly drawn into local wars, and all the more so as the great Mughal Empire disintegrated from the middle decades of the 18th century. In their wars of conquest, the British, adopting a practice pioneered by the French, relied heavily on Indian troops, called *sepoys,* recruited from peoples throughout the subcontinent. As had been the case in Java, Indian princes long regarded the British as allies that they could use *and* control to crush Indian rivals or put down usurpers who sought to seize their thrones. As had happened in Java, the European pawns gradually emerged as first a serious rival to the established Indian rulers and eventually the paramount power in the continent.

Partly because the struggle for India came later in time, there were also important differences between the patterns of colonial conquest in India and Java as well as the global repercussions of each. In contrast to the Dutch march in-

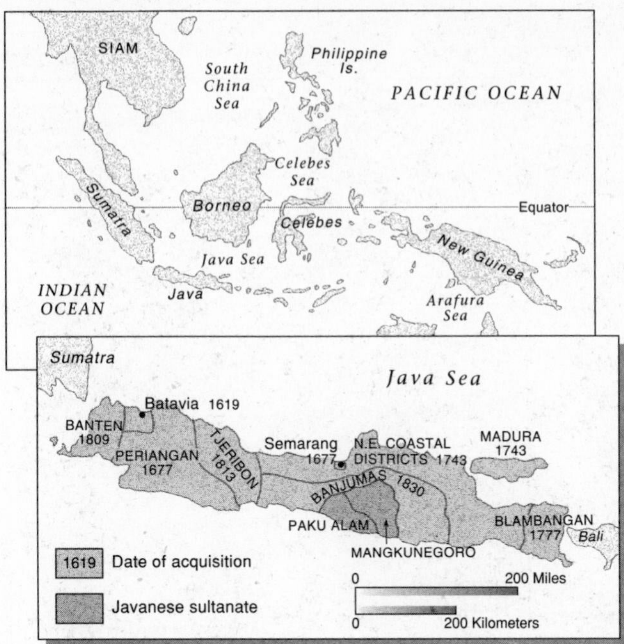

The Stages of Dutch Expansion in Java

land, which resulted largely from responses to local threats and opportunities, the rise of the British Raj in India owed much to the fierce global rivalry between the British and the French. In the 18th century the British and French found themselves on opposite sides in five major wars. These struggles were global in a very real sense. On land and sea, the two old adversaries not only fought in Europe, but they also squared off in the Caribbean where each had valuable plantation colonies, in North America, and on the coasts and bays of the Indian Ocean. With the exception of the American War of Independence (1775–1782), these struggles ended in British victories. The British loss of the American colonies in that ill-fated effort was more than offset by earlier victories in the Caribbean and especially in India, which gradually gave the British control of the entire South Asian subcontinent.

Though the first victories of the British over the French and the Indian princes came in the south in the late 1740s, their rise as a major land power in Asia hinged on victories won in Bengal to the northeast. The key battle at Plassey in 1757, in which fewer than 3000 British troops and Indian sepoys defeated an Indian army of nearly 50,000, is traditionally pictured as a heroic triumph of a handful of brave and disciplined Europeans over a horde of ill-trained and poorly led Asians. The battle pitted the *Nawab* Sirāj-ud-daula, who was then the ruler of Bengal, against Robert Clive, the architect of the British victory in the south. The prize was control of the fertile and populous kingdom of Bengal. The real reasons for Clive's famed victory, however, tell us a good deal more about the process of empire building in Asia and Africa than this white-hero-in-the-tropics cliché.

The numbers on each side and maneuvers on the field tell us little about a battle that was in a sense over before it had begun. Clive's well-paid Indian spies had given him detailed accounts of the divisions in Sirāj-ud-daula's ranks in the months before the battle. With money provided by Hindu bankers who were anxious to get back at the Muslim prince for unpaid debts and for confiscating their treasure on a number of occasions, Clive proceeded to buy off the Nawab's chief general and several of his key allies. Even the Nawab's leading spy was on Clive's payroll, which somewhat offset the fact that the main British spy had been bribed by Sirāj-ud-daula. The backing Clive received from the Indian bankers also meant that his troops were well paid, while those of the Nawab were not. Thus, when the understandably uneasy ruler of Bengal rode into battle on June 23, 1757, his fate had already been sealed. Though the troops under the French and one Indian commander fought well, the Nawab's major Indian allies defected to the British or remained stationary on his flanks when the two sides were locked in combat. These defections more or less wiped out the Nawab's numerical advantage, and Clive's skillful leadership and the superiority of his artillery did the rest. The British victors had once again foiled their French rivals, and they soon took over

Indian soldiers, or *sepoys*, made up a large portion of the rank-and-file troops in the armies of British India. Commanded by European officers, and armed, uniformed, and drilled according to European standards, troops like those pictured here were recruited from the colonized peoples and became one of the mainstays of all European colonial regimes.

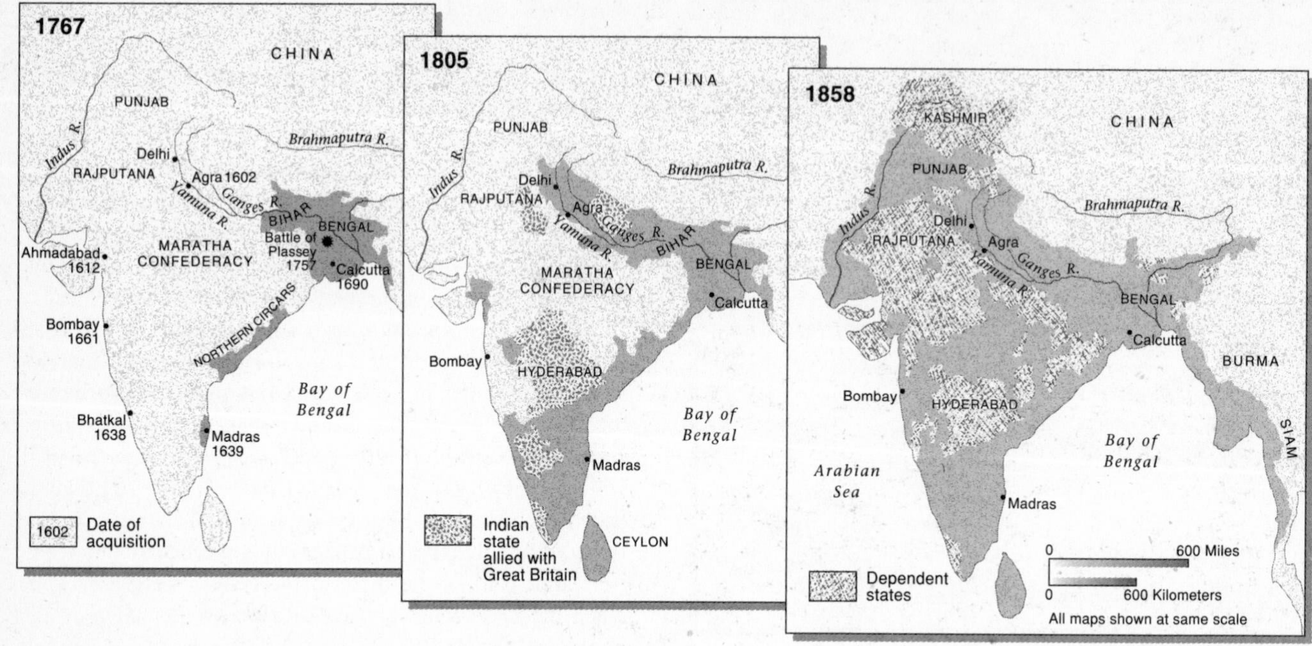

The Growth of the British Empire in India, from the 1750s to 1858

the direct administration of the sizeable Bengal-Bihar region. The foundations of Britain's Indian and global empire had been laid.

THE CONSOLIDATION OF BRITISH RULE

In the decades after Plassey, the British officials of the East India Company repeatedly went to war with Indian princes whose kingdoms bordered on the company's growing possessions, or, like the Dutch on Java, they became involved in succession disputes and ended up controlling the kingdoms being contested. All of these pulls grew stronger and stronger as the Mughal Empire broke down in the last decades of the century. In its ruins, regional Indian princes fought incessantly to defend or expand their territories at the expense of their neighbors. Involvement in these conflicts or assaults on war-weakened Indian kingdoms allowed the British to advance steadily inland from their three trading towns on the Indian coast—Madras, Bombay, and Calcutta. These cities became the administrative centers of the three Presidencies that eventually made up the bulk of the territory they ruled directly in India. In many areas, the British were content to leave defeated or allied Indian princes on their thrones and to control their kingdoms through agents stationed at the rulers' courts. By the time the British government took over direct control of India from the expiring East India Company in 1858, these "Princely States" made up over one-third of the British Indian Empire.

The British conquest of the Indian subcontinent was not completed until the 1850s. Thus, in the early industrial era the British took a century to colonize an area that was considerably smaller than the continent of Africa—an area that the more fully industrialized European powers would carve up in a matter of decades in the late 19th century. It is fashionable to downplay the role of industrialization in Britain's conquest of India. But there is little question that British armies, both those made up of soldiers recruited in Europe and those consisting of Indian sepoys, gained great advantage from modes of organization and bodily discipline promoted by industrialization. By the early 19th century, their more reliable field guns and the uniformity of their hand weapons also reflected advances in European metallurgy and machine tooling that their Indian adversaries were unable to match.

In attempting to prevent the conquest of their kingdoms by these forces, the princes of India, like those before them in Java, were handicapped in a number of critical ways. Because there was no India or sense of Indian national identity, it was impossible to appeal to the defense of the homeland or the need for unity to drive out the foreigners. Indian princes continued to fear and fight with each other despite the ever growing power of the British Raj. Old grudges and hatreds ran deeper than the new threat of the British, and there was a sense that the British would someday just go away. Many ordinary Indians were eager to serve in the British regiments, which had better weapons, brighter uniforms, and higher and more regular pay than all but a handful of the armies of the Indian rulers. The British were equally eager to recruit these volunteers, especially those drawn from Indian peoples whom the British deemed especially warlike, such as the Gurkhas of Nepal and the Sikhs of the Punjab. By the mid-19th century, Indian soldiers in the pay of the British outnumbered British officers and enlisted men in India by almost five to one.

From the first decades of the 19th century, India was clearly the pivot of the great empire being built by Britain on a global scale. Older colonies with large numbers of white settlers, such as Canada and Australia, contributed more space to the total square miles of empire the British were so fond of calculating, but India had by far the largest share of colonized peoples. Britain's largest and most powerful land forces were the armies recruited from the Indian peoples, and these were rapidly becoming the policemen of the entire British Indian Empire. In the middle of the 19th century, Indian soldiers were sent to punish the Chinese and Afghans, conquer Burma and Malaya, and begin the conquest of South and East Africa.

Indian ports were essential to British sea power east of the Cape of Good Hope, and the famous gunboats, which were a key instrument of British diplomacy in the 19th century, were more likely to sail from Bombay and Calcutta than from the British Isles. As the century progressed, India became the major outlet for British overseas investments and manufactured goods as well as a major source of key raw materials. India was the envy of the French and the Germans, and the acknowledged symbol of Britain's global empire, the largest that any people had ever built.

EARLY COLONIAL SOCIETY IN INDIA AND JAVA

Though they slowly emerged as the political masters of Java and India, the Dutch and British were at first content to leave the social systems of the peoples they now ruled pretty much as they had found them. The small numbers of European traders and company officials who actually lived in the colonies for any length of time simply formed a new class atop the social hierarchies that already existed in Java and different parts of India. Beneath them the aristocratic classes and often the old ruling families were preserved and left in charge of the day-to-day administration at all but the top levels. In most cases, European backing actually strengthened the control of the Javanese and Indian lords and middlemen over the peasantry, which continued to make up nearly 90 percent of the population in each area. Though Dutch monopolies and attacks by the sultans of Mataram on the northern coastal towns had decimated the Javanese trading classes, Chinese and Chinese-Javanese mestizo (mixed race) merchants soon emerged to take their place and increasingly allied themselves with the Dutch overlords. As we have seen, in India the links between East India Company officials and traders and Indian merchants and bankers were even more highly developed. Indian merchants and middlemen also recruited and controlled the handicraft laborers who produced the cotton textiles that remained the Company's chief export from India.

In order to survive in the hot tropical environments of South and Southeast Asia, the Dutch and English were forced to accommodate themselves to the ancient and sophisticated host cultures of their Asian colonies. After establishing themselves at Batavia, for example, the Dutch initially sought to create a little Holland in Java. They built high, close-packed houses overlooking canals, just like those they had left behind in Amsterdam and Rotterdam. But they soon discovered that the canals were splendid breeding grounds for insects and microbes that (though the Europeans did not make the connection until somewhat later) carried debilitating or lethal diseases like dysentery, malaria, and typhoid. By the late 17th century, the prosperous merchants and officials of Batavia had begun to move away from the unhealthy center of the city to villas in the suburbs, which were set in gardens and separated by rice paddies and palm groves. The tall houses of the inner city gave way to low, sprawling dwellings with many open spaces to catch the tropical breezes as well as long porches with overhanging roofs to block the heat and glare of the sun. Similar dwellings, from which we get our term *bungalow,* came into fashion in India in the 18th century.

Europeans living in the tropical colonies also adopted, to varying degrees, the dress, eating and work habits, and even the political symbols and styles of the Asian peoples they ruled. Though some Englishmen refused to give up their tight-fitting, woolen clothing—at least in public—many (one suspects most of those who survived) took to wearing looser fitting, cotton clothing. Dutch gentlemen even donned the long skirt-like *sarongs* of the Javanese aristocrats. British and Dutch officials learned to appreciate the splendid cuisines of India and Java, a taste that the Dutch would never lose and the British would revive at home in the postindependence era. Englishmen smoked Indian *hookahs,* or water pipes, and delighted in performances of Indian dancing girls. Adjusting to the heat of the colonies, both the Dutch and English worked hard in the relative cool of the morning, took a long lunch break (often with a siesta), and then returned to the office for the late afternoon and early evening. Impressive retinues followed Dutch colonial officials as they paraded about under umbrellas, which like those of the Javanese elite were colored and decorated in accordance with their rank. British governors rode about on lavishly attired elephants and received visitors in settings that would have done justice to the throne rooms of the more ostentatious Asian princes.

Though the Europeans usually lived in separate quarters within the factory towns or in villas in the countryside, they mingled quite freely with the indigenous peoples. They were waited on by large numbers of Asian servants, from cooks and coachmen to wet nurses and nannies who tended to their children. Dutch and British officials also struck up friendships with their peers among the subject populations. British officers and Indian princes played polo and enjoyed such "exotic" Indian pastimes as tiger and elephant fights.

Because the Europeans who went to Asia until the mid-19th century were overwhelmingly male, Dutch and British traders and soldiers commonly had liaisons with Asian women. In some cases these involved little more than visits to the local brothel, but very often European men lived with Asian women, and sometimes they married them. The mixed-blood Eurasian children who resulted from these liaisons were often abandoned by their fathers and ended up in orphanages when their destitute mothers proved unable to support them. Before the end of the 18th century, however, mixed marriages on the part of prominent traders or officers were widely accepted, particularly in Java. Some Eurasian children remained with their parents and found a place in the European sectors of the colonial world. Though examples of racial discrimination against the subject peoples on the basis of their physical appearance can certainly be found during the early decades of European overseas empire, the frequency of liaisons that cut across racial boundaries suggests a social fluidity and a degree of interracial interaction that would be unthinkable by the last half of the 19th century.

The close alliances that the European colonizers often struck with the "native" princes of conquered areas are graphically illustrated by this photo of the Susuhunan of Surakarta, a kingdom in central Java, standing arm-in-arm with a high Dutch official.

EDUCATION AND REFORM

Until the early 19th century neither the Dutch nor the British had much desire to push for changes in the social or cultural life of their Asian subjects. The British sanctioned and enforced the rigid divisions of the Hindu caste system, and both the British and Dutch made it clear that they had little interest in spreading Christianity among the Indians or Javanese. In fact, for fear of offending Hindu or Muslim religious sentiments, the British refused to allow Christian missionaries to preach in their territories until the second decade of the 19th century.

Beginning in the 1770s, however, rampant corruption on the part of company officials forced the British Parliament to enact significant reforms in the administration of the East India Company and its colonies. By that time most of those who served in India viewed their brief tenure as a chance to strike it rich quickly. They made great fortunes by cheating the company and exploiting the Indian peasants and artisans. The bad manners and conspicuous consumption of these upstarts, whom contemporaries scornfully dubbed *nabobs,* were satirized by novelists of the age, such as William Thackeray.

When the venality and misgovernment of the nabobs resulted in the catastrophic Bengal famine of 1770, when as much as one-third of the population of that once-prosperous province died, their abuses could no longer be ignored. Parliament passed a number of acts that restructured the company hierarchy and made it much more accountable to the British government. A succession of political reforms culminated in sweeping measures taken in the 1790s by the same Lord Cornwallis whose surrender at Yorktown had sealed Britain's loss of the American colonies. By cleaning up the courts and reducing the power of local British administrators, Cornwallis did much to check the widespread corruption that had hitherto made a sham of any pretence to good government on the part of the British. Unfortunately, because of his mistrust of Indians, his measures also severely constricted their participation in governing the empire.

In this same period forces were building, both in India and England, that caused a major shift in British policy regarding social reform among the subject peoples. The Evangelical religious revival, which had seen the spread of Methodism among the English working classes, soon spilled over into Britain's colonial domains. Evangelicals were in the vanguard of the struggle to put an end to the slave trade, and by the early years of the 19th century, they added the eradication of Indian social abuses to their campaigns for human improvement. Their calls for reforms were warmly supported by utilitarian philosophers such as Jeremy Bentham and James Mill, who believed that there were common principles by which human societies ought to be run if decent living conditions were to be attained by people at all class levels. Mill and other utilitarians were convinced that, though flawed, British society was far more advanced than Indian society. Thus, they pushed for the introduction of British institutions and ways of thinking in India as well as the eradication of what they considered Indian superstitions and social abuses.

Though the utilitarians had little use for the spread of Christianity that the Evangelicals saw as the ultimate solution to India's ills, both agreed that Western education was the key to revitalizing an ancient but decadent Indian civilization. Both factions had little use for Indian learning—the influential British historian, Thomas Babington Macaulay, put it the most bluntly when he declared in the 1830s that one shelf of an English gentleman's library was worth all the writings of Asia. Consequently the Evangelicals and utilitarians pushed for the introduction of English language education for the children of the Indian elite. In one sense, their advocacy of English was very self-serving. The British were in great need of Indians who were fluent in English to serve as clerks in their counting houses and as lower-level bureaucrats. But both Evangelicals and utilitarians also had more elevated motives. They firmly believed that English education would expose the Indian elite to Western learning in critical areas such as ethics, the sciences, and the creative arts. They envisioned this new class of English-educated Indians enlightening and reforming those beneath them in Indian society and thus playing critical roles in bringing India into the "modern" era.

The utilitarian and Evangelical determination to change Indian society went far beyond the introduction of Western learning. Officials of this persuasion pushed for major reforms in Indian society and advocated a large-scale infusion of Western technology. The period of their greatest influence was in the 1830s when they pushed through a number of reforms to correct major abuses that did in fact exist in Indian society. Ritual banditry, whose practitioners were known as thugs, was repressed, and human sacrifice among some of the hill peoples and certain Hindu sects was ended. A major effort was launched to end female infanticide, which was practiced by some high-caste groups who were fearful of financial ruin as the result of the huge expense of their daughters' marriage dowries.

The set piece of the reformers' campaign was the effort to put an end to sati, which, as we have seen, was the ritual immolation of Hindu widows on the funeral pyres of their deceased husbands. This practice, which was clearly a corruption of Hindu religious beliefs, had spread fairly widely among upper-caste Hindu groups by the era of the Muslim invasions in the 11th and 12th centuries A.D. In fact, the wives of proud warrior peoples, such as the Rajputs, had been encouraged to commit mass suicide rather than risk dishonoring their husbands by being captured and molested by Muslim invaders. By the early 19th century, some Brahmin castes and even lower-caste groups in limited areas had adopted the practice of sati.

In the 1830s, bolstered by the strong support and active cooperation of Western-educated Indian leaders such as Ram Mohun Roy, the British outlawed sati. A confrontation between the British and those affected by their efforts to prevent widow burnings provides a wonderful illustration of the confidence of the reformers in the righteousness of their cause and the sense of moral and social superiority over the Indians that the British in general felt in this era. A group of Brahmins complained to a British official,

Charles Napier, that his refusal to allow them to burn the widow of a prominent leader of their community was a violation of their social customs. Napier replied:

> The burning of widows is your custom. Prepare the funeral pyre. But my nation also has a custom. When men burn women alive, we hang them and confiscate all their property. My carpenters shall therefore erect gibbets on which to hang all concerned when the widow is consumed. Let us all act according to our national customs.

The range and magnitude of the reforms the British enacted in India in the first decades of the 19th century marked a watershed in global history. In these years the alien British, who had become the rulers of one of humankind's oldest centers of civilization, consciously began to transmit the ideas and inventions, modes of organization, and technology associated with western Europe's scientific and industrial revolutions to the peoples of the non-Western world. English education, social reforms, and railways and telegraph lines were only part of a larger project by which the British sought to remake Indian society along Western lines. India's croplands were measured and registered; its forests were set aside for "scientific" management; and its people were drawn more and more into the European-dominated global market economy. British officials promoted policies they believed would teach the Indian peasantry the merits of thrift and hard work. British educators lectured the children of India's rising middle classes on the importance of emulating their European masters in matters as diverse as being punctual, exercising their bodies, and mastering the literature and scientific learning of the West. Here was a far more sweeping, but also less spontaneous, Westernization process than Russia had attempted in the 19th century. The scientific and technological breakthroughs that had radically transformed western European civilization had begun to profoundly affect the lives of all the peoples of the globe.

ANALYSIS
WESTERN EDUCATION AND THE RISE OF AN AFRICAN AND ASIAN MIDDLE CLASS

To varying degrees and for many of the same reasons as the British in India, all European colonizers sought to educate the children of African and Asian elite groups in Western-language schools. The early 19th-century debate over education in India was paralleled, for example, by an equally hard-fought controversy among French officials and missionaries regarding the proper schooling for the peoples of Senegal in West Africa. The Dutch did not develop European language schools for the sons of the Javanese elite until the middle of the 19th century, and many young Javanese males continued to be educated in the homes of the Dutch residing in the colonies until the end of the century. Like the British, the French and Dutch needed administrative assistants and postal clerks, and they could neither recruit enough Europeans to fill these posts nor afford the wages European employees would have demanded.

One of the chief advantages of having Western-educated African and Asian subordinates—for they were always below European officials or managers in the office or on the parade ground—was that their salaries were considerably lower than what Europeans would have been paid for doing the same work. The Europeans had no trouble rationalizing this inequity. Africans and Asians served in their own lands and were thus accustomed to life in the hot, humid, insect- and disease-ridden tropics. For the Europeans who worked in the colonies, life in these environments was deemed difficult, even dangerous. Higher pay was thought to compensate them for the "sacrifices" involved in colonial service. The Europeans also had a higher standard of living than Africans or Asians, and colonial officials assumed that European employees would be more hardworking and efficient.

Beyond the need for government functionaries and business assistants, each European colonizer stressed different objectives in designing Western-language schools for the children of upper-class families. As we have seen, the transmission of Western scientific learning and production techniques was a high priority for the British in India. Educational policymakers, such as Macaulay, also sought to teach the Indians Western literature and manners and to instill in them a Western sense of morality. As Macaulay put it, they hoped that English-language schools would turn out brown English gentlemen, who would in turn teach their countrymen the ways of the West.

The French, at least until the end of the 19th century, went even further. They stressed the importance of Africans and other colonial students mastering the French language and the subtleties of French culture. When the lessons had been fully absorbed and the students fully assimilated to French culture, they could become full citizens of France, no matter what their family origins or the color of their skin. Though only a tiny minority of the population of any French colony had the opportunity for the sort of schooling that would qualify them for French citizenship, there were thousands of Senegalese and hundreds of

Vietnamese or Tunisians who could carry French passports, vote in French elections, and even run for seats in the French Parliament. Other European colonial powers adopted either the British or the French approach to education and its aims. The Dutch and Germans, for example, followed the British pattern, while the Portuguese pushed assimilation for even smaller numbers of the elite classes among the peoples they colonized.

Western education in the colonies succeeded in producing both clerks and railway conductors, and brown Indian gentlemen and black French citizens. It also had effects that those who shaped colonial educational policy did not intend, effects that would within a generation or two produce major challenges to the continuation of European colonial dominance. The population of most colonized areas was divided into many different ethnic, religious, and language groups with separate histories and identities. Western language schools gave the sons (and in limited instances, the daughters) of the leading families a common language in which to communicate. The schools also inculcated common attitudes and ideas and imparted to the members of diverse groups a common body of knowledge. In all European colonial societies, Western education led to similar occupational opportunities—in government service, with Western business firms, or as professionals (lawyers, doctors, journalists, etc.). Thus, within a generation after their introduction, Western-language schools had in effect created a new middle class in the colonies that had no counterpart in precolonial African or Asian societies.

Occupying social strata and economic niches in the middle range between the European colonizers and the old aristocracy on the one hand, and the peasantry and urban laborers on the other, Western-educated Africans and Asians within each colony became increasingly aware of the interests and grievances they had in common. They often found themselves at odds with the traditional rulers or the landed gentry, who ironically were often their fathers or grandfathers. Members of the new middle class also felt alienated from the peasantry, whose beliefs and way of life were so different from those they had learned in Western-language schools. For over a generation they clung to their European tutors and employers. Eventually, however, they grew increasingly resentful of their lower salaries, of European competition for scarce jobs, and of their social segregation from the Europeans, who often made little effort to disguise their contempt for even the most accomplished of the African or Asian students of Western ways. Thus, members of the new middle class in the colonies were caught between two worlds: the traditional ways and teachings of their fathers and the "modern" world of their European masters. Finding that they would be fully admitted to neither world, they rejected the first and set about supplanting the Europeans and building their own modern world.

Questions: Why did the Europeans continue to provide Western-language education for Africans and Asians once it was clear they were creating a class that might challenge their position of dominance? Why were challenges from this new class much more effective than resistance on the part of the peasantry or movements led by the traditional religious and political elites? Do you think the European colonial order would have lasted longer if Western-language education had been denied to colonized peoples?

INDUSTRIAL RIVALRIES AND THE PARTITION OF THE WORLD, C. 1870–1914

The spread of the Industrial Revolution from the British Isles to Continental Europe and North America greatly increased the already considerable advantages the Western powers possessed in manufacturing capacity and the ability to wage war relative to all other peoples and civilizations. These advantages resulted in ever higher levels of European—and American—involvement in the outside world and culminated in the virtually unchallenged domination of the globe by the Western powers by the last decades of the 19th century. Beginning in the 1870s, the Europeans indulged in an orgy of overseas conquests that reduced most of Africa, Asia, and the Pacific Ocean region to colonial possessions by the time of the outbreak of the First World War in 1914. During each year of that time period, an area larger than France was added to the empires of the different Western powers. By 1914 Europe and its colonial possessions occupied over 80 percent of the inhabitable lands of the earth. Areas not annexed directly, such as China and Persia, were forcibly "opened" to European trade and investment, and divided into informal "spheres of influence" of the various Western nations. The remaking of the world economic order to industrial Europe's specifications was completed. According to the new global division of labor, Europe and increasingly North America provided finance and machine capital, entrepreneurial and managerial talent, and manufactured goods. The rest of the world provided raw materials for Europe's factories, cheap labor, and abundant, if not always fertile, land. Thus, it was not without reason that the Europeans ultimately came to regard themselves as the "lords of humankind."

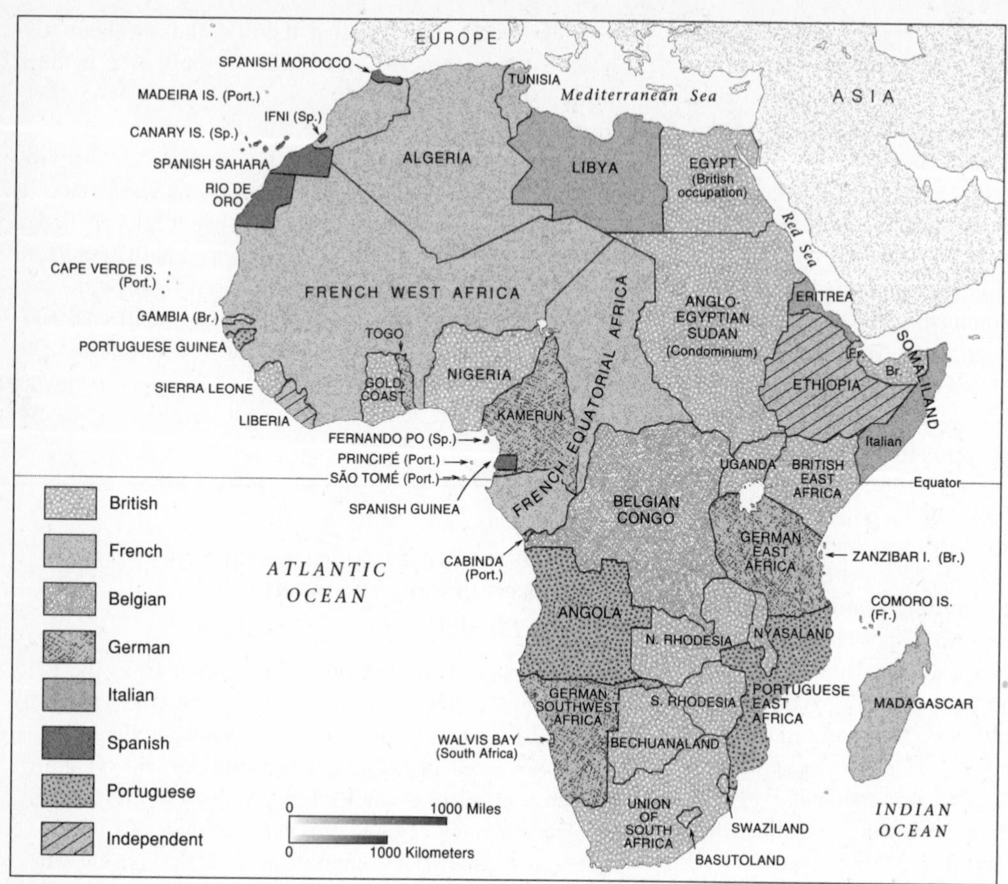

The Partition of Africa to

Though science and industry gave the Europeans the capacity to run roughshod over the rest of the world, they also heightened economic competition and political rivalries between the European powers. In the first half of the 19th century industrial Britain, with its seemingly insurmountable naval superiority, was left alone to dominate overseas trade and empire building. By the last decades of the century, Belgium, France, and especially Germany and the United States were challenging Britain's industrial supremacy and actively building (or in the case of France, adding to) colonial empires of their own. Many of the political leaders of these expansive nations viewed the possession of colonies as an essential attribute of states that aspired to great-power status. Colonies were also seen as insurance against raw material shortages and the loss of overseas market outlets to European or North American rivals.

Quarrels over the division of the colonial spoils were cited by those who sought to justify the arms buildup and general militarism of the age. Colonial rivalries greatly intensified the growing tension and paranoia that dominated great power interaction in the decades before World War I. As Europe divided into armed camps, successive crises over control of the Sudan, Morocco, and the Balkans (which the great powers treated very much like colonies) had much to do with the alliances that formed and the crisis mentality that contributed so much to the outbreak of the conflict in August, 1914.

MOTIVES BEHIND THE GLOBAL SCRAMBLE FOR COLONIES

Through much of the 20th century, historians have argued about the reasons for the unprecedented drive for colonial expansion that seized Europe and, to a lesser extent, the United States in the last decades of the 19th century. The majority of those engaged in this often heated debate have tended to join one of two camps: those who favor a political explanation for the outburst of territorial aggrandizement, and those who argue that it was fundamentally economic in origin. The truth may well be found by combining the two views—by recognizing that political leaders, not just businessmen, had to take into account economic concerns when deciding to intervene in disputes or to annex territories in Africa, Asia, or the South Pacific.

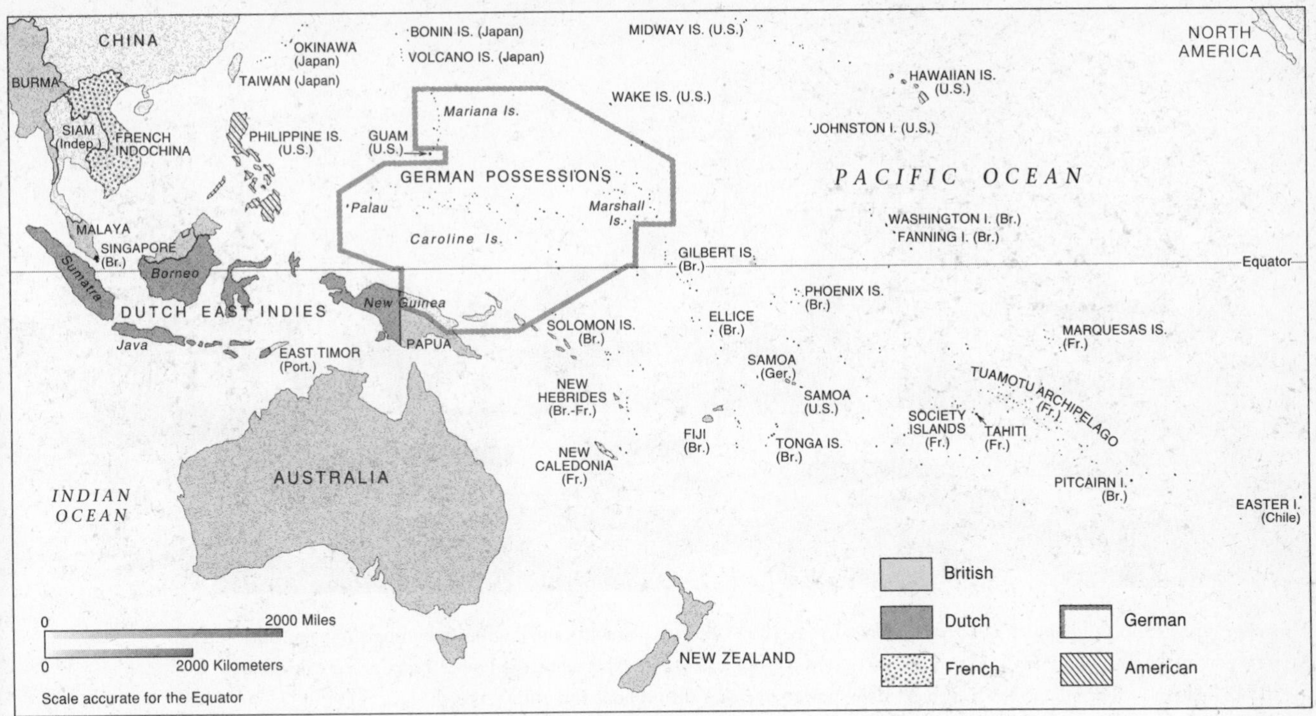

The Partition of Southeast Asia and the Pacific Islands to 1914

The British obsession with protecting strategic overseas naval stations, such as those in Malaya and in South Africa, for example, was linked to an underlying perception of growing threats to their Indian Empire. That empire was in turn more than just their "garrison in the east" and largest colonial possession. It was a major source of raw materials for British industries and a key outlet for both British manufactured goods and British overseas investment. Thus, political and economic motives were often impossible to separate; doing so unnecessarily oversimplifies and distorts our understanding of the forces behind the scramble for empire in the late 19th century.

It would also be a mistake to see a complete break between the pattern of European colonial expansion before and after 1870. Though a good deal more territory was annexed per year after that date, there were numerous colonial wars and additions to both the British and French empires all through the middle decades of the 19th century. One of the key differences between the two periods was that before 1870, Britain had only a weak France with which to compete in the outside world. This meant that the British were less likely than at the end of the century to be pushed into full-scale invasions and annexations because they feared that another European power was about to seize potentially valuable colonies. It also allowed the British to rely heavily on threats and gunboat raids rather than outright conquest to bring African kings or Asian emperors into line. With its "white" settler colonies (Canada, Australia, and New Zealand) and India, plus enclaves in Africa and Southeast Asia, the British already had all the empire they could handle. Most British politicians were cautious about or firmly opposed to adding more colonies. The British were wary of French advances in various parts of the globe, which were usually made to restore France's great-power standing following setbacks in Europe. But the French were far too weak economically and too politically divided to contest Britain's naval mastery or its standing as the greatest colonial power.

Once Germany was united in 1871, and the German Empire and the United States began to pass Britain as industrial powers, the situation was significantly altered. India and the rest of the empire were now seen as essential to Britain's maintenance of its great-power standing. British politicians worried that if Britain stood still while the rest of the powers built up overseas empires, it would soon be supplanted as the number one naval and colonial power. The concern here was economic as well as strategic. The last decades of the 19th century were a period of recurring economic depressions in Europe and the United States. The leaders of the newly industrialized nations had little

This engraving from the popular *Illustrated London News* shows British warships and gunboats bombarding the East African port of Mombasa in 1874. As in the early centuries of European expansion, sea power remained a critical way for the British and other colonizers to project their power overseas throughout the 19th century.

experience in handling the overproduction and unemployment that came with each of these economic crises. They were understandably deeply concerned about the social unrest and in some cases what appeared to them to be stirrings of revolution, that each phase of depression engendered. Some political theorists argued that as destinations to which unemployed workers might migrate and as potential markets for surplus goods, colonial possessions could serve as safety values to release the pressure built up in times of industrial slumps.

Thus, although a colony seemed to be of little economic value when it was annexed, it could prove a valuable asset later on. Industrial Europe's growing need for raw materials gave added credence to this line of reasoning. Each power felt compelled to conquer and annex vast territories—which often consisted of scantily populated, arid lands—because it feared that otherwise a rival would take them. In letting a competitor grab what might prove to be a mineral-rich colony, Britain or Germany might be foreclosing on its future chances to remain a global power.

Competition among the great powers had much to do with another major cause of the late 19th-century scramble for colonial possessions. Britain's successful application of gunboat diplomacy and indirect control over African and Asian kingdoms in the early 19th century depended heavily on the existence of reasonably strong African and Asian leaders who could enforce the demands made by the Europeans. With the intensification of European rivalries in the late 19th century, these leaders attempted to play the powers off each other. This reduced the value of their cooperation and often prompted one of the powers to invade their lands, remove them from power, and find less troublesome collaborators. In addition, in many areas, but particularly in Africa, decades and even centuries of European economic penetration and political interference resulted in the disintegration of indigenous governments and societies as a whole. Lack of a local center of power through which to exert their control as well as threats by growing social dislocations in areas where one or more of the powers had a strong strategic or economic stake caused European policymakers to conclude that military intervention and formal annexation were their only option.

As these motives suggest, in the era of the scramble for colonial possessions, political leaders in Europe played a much more prominent role in decisions to annex overseas territories than they had earlier, even in the first half of the 19th century. In part, this was due to improved communications. Telegraphs and railways not only made it possible to transmit orders from the capitals of Europe to men-on-the-spot in the tropics much more rapidly, they allowed ministers in Europe to play a much more active role in the ongoing governance of the colonies. More than politicians were involved in late 19th-century decisions to add to the colonial empires. The jingoistic "penny" press and the extension of the vote to the lower middle and working classes through much of industrial Europe and in the

United States made public opinion a major factor in foreign policy. Though stalwart explorers might on their own initiative make treaties with local African or Asian potentates who assigned their lands to France or Germany, these annexations had to be ratified by the home government. In most cases, ratification meant fierce parliamentary debates that often spilled over into press wars and popular demonstrations. Empires were no longer the personal projects of private trading concerns and ambitious individuals; they were the property and pride of the nations of Europe and North America.

UNEQUAL COMBAT: COLONIAL WARS AND THE APEX OF IMPERIALISM

Industrial change not only justified the Europeans' grab for colonial possessions, it made them much easier to acquire. By the last decades of the 19th century, scientific discoveries and technological innovations had catapulted the Europeans far ahead of all other peoples in the capacity to wage war. The Europeans could tap mineral resources that most peoples did not even know existed, and European chemists mixed ever more deadly explosives. Advances in metallurgy made possible the mass production of light and mobile artillery pieces that rendered suicidal the massed cavalry or infantry charges that were the mainstay of Asian and African armies. Advances in artillery were matched by great improvements in hand arms. Much more accurate and faster firing, breech-loading rifles replaced the clumsy muzzle-loading muskets of the first phase of empire building. By the 1880s, after decades of experimentation, the machine gun had become an effective battlefield weapon. Railroads gave the Europeans the mobility of the swiftest African or Asian horsemen as well as the ability to supply large armies in the field for extended periods of time. On the sea, Europe's already formidable advantages were awesomely increased by industrial transformations. After the opening of the Suez canal in 1869, steam power supplanted the sail, iron hulls replaced wood, and massive guns, capable of hitting enemy vessels miles away, were introduced into the fleets of the great powers.

The dazzling array of new weaponry with which the Europeans set out on their expeditions to the Indian frontiers or the African "bush" made the wars of colonial conquest very lopsided affairs. This was particularly true when the Europeans encountered resistance from peoples, such as those in the interior of Africa or the Pacific islands, who had been cut off from most preindustrial advances in technology and thus fought the European machine guns with spears, arrows, and leather shields. One African leader, whose people struggled with little hope to halt the German advance into East Africa, resorted to natural imagery to account for the power of the invaders' weapons:

> On Monday we heard a shuddering like Leviathan, the voice of many cannon; we heard the roar like waves of the rocks and rumble like thunder in the rains. We heard a crashing like elephants or monsters and our hearts melted at the number of shells. We knew that we were hearing the battle of Pangani; the guns were like a hurricane in our ears.

Not even peoples with advanced preindustrial technology and sophisticated military organization, such as the Chinese and Vietnamese, could stand against, or really comprehend, the fearful killing devices of the Europeans. In advising the Vietnamese emperor to give in to European demands, one of his officials, who had led the fight against the French invaders, warned:

> Nobody can resist them. They go where they choose. . . . Under heaven, everything is feasible to them, save only the matter of life and death.

Despite the odds against them, African and Asian peoples often fiercely resisted the imposition of colonial rule. West African leaders, such as Samory and Ahmadou Sekou, held back the European advance for decades, and when rulers, such as the Vietnamese emperors, refused to fight, local officials organized guerrilla resistance in defense of the traditional regime. Martial peoples, such as the Zulus in South Africa, had the courage and discipline to face and defeat sizeable British forces in set piece (or conventional and critical) battles, such as that at Isandhlwana in 1879. But conventional resistance eventually ended in defeat: The guerrilla bands in Vietnam were eventually run to the ground; even at Isandhlwana, 3000 Zulus lost their lives in the massacre of 800 British and 500 African troops. In addition, within days of the Zulu victory, a tiny force of 120 British troops held off an army of three or four thousand Zulus. Given the European advantages in conventional battles, guerrilla resistance, sabotage, and, in some cases, banditry proved the most effective means of fighting the Europeans' attempts to assert political control. Religious leaders were often in the forefront of these struggles. The magic potions and divine assistance they offered for the protection of their followers seemed to be the only way to offset the demoralizing killing power of the Europeans' weapons.

However admirable the courage of those who resisted the European advance and despite temporary setbacks, by the eve of World War I in 1914 there was very little of

This rather romantic depiction of the 1879 battle of Isandhlwana in the Natal province of South Africa shows that, despite their superior firepower, the Europeans could be defeated, if only temporarily, by well-organized and determined African or Asian resistance forces.

the earth left for the Europeans to conquer. Excepting Ethiopia, all of Africa had been divided between the European powers. Maps of the continent became a patchwork of colors—red for Great Britain, green for France, blue for Germany, and so on. In Southeast Asia, only Siam remained independent, in part because Britain and France could not decide which of them should have it. The Americans had replaced the Spanish as the colonial overlords of the Philippines, and the Dutch were completing the conquest of the "outer islands" of the Indonesian archipelago. Even the island clusters of the Pacific had been divided among the hungry industrial powers. China, Persia, and the Middle East had not yet been occupied, but many believed that the "informal" political and economic influences the European powers exerted in these areas were the prelude to formal annexation.

What was perhaps most striking was how easy this division of the world had been. There had been prolonged resistance in desolate places, such as the Sudan and the rain forests of Vietnam, but overall the Europeans had conquered most of the earth in a matter of decades with a remarkably low level of expense and loss of European lives. They had divided the world with little thought for the reactions of the peoples who came under their rule. European leaders quarreled and bargained at green, felt-topped tables in Paris or Berlin over lands they scarcely knew anything about. It was like a colossal game of *Diplomacy* or *Risk,* with armies and fleets moved, and colonies won, lost, and traded at the gaming tables of the European diplomats. To expand on an image offered by the arch-imperialist King Leopold of the Belgians, industrial technology had turned the world into a giant *gateau,* or cake, to be sliced up and divided between the European powers.

PATTERNS OF DOMINANCE: CONTINUITY AND CHANGE

By the end of the 19th century, the European colonial order was made up of two, quite different, kinds of colonies. The greater portion of the European empires consisted of "true" colonies in Africa, Asia, and the South Pacific in which small numbers of Europeans ruled large numbers of non-Western peoples. The true colonies represented a vast extension of the pattern of dominance the British, Dutch, and French had worked out earlier in India, Java, and African enclaves such as Senegal. Most of these had been brought, often quite suddenly, under European rule in the last decades of the 19th century and the first years of the 20th century. The following sections devoted to this form of colonization focus on the new forms of colonial rule and changing patterns of social interaction between colonizer and colonized that emerged in the decades of imperialist expansion before World War I.

Settlement colonies made up the second major type of European overseas possession, but within this type there were two different patterns of European settlement and indigenous response. The first pattern was exhibited by colonies such as Canada and Australia, which the British labeled the "White Dominions." The White Dominions accounted for a good portion of the land area but only a tiny minority of the population of Britain's global empire. The descendants of European settlers made up the overwhelming majority of the population in these colonies, in which small numbers of native inhabitants had been decimated by diseases and wars of conquest. These patterns of substantial European settlement and the precipitous decline of the indigenous population were also found in those portions of

North America that came to form the United States. Though Canada and Australia remained within the British Empire, each moved steadily toward self-government and parliamentary rule in the late 19th century.

In some areas where large numbers of Europeans had migrated, a second major variation on the settlement type of colony developed. Both in regions that had been colonized as early as North America, such as South Africa, and in those the Europeans and Americans had begun to occupy only in the mid- or late 19th century, such as Algeria, Kenya, New Zealand, and Hawaii, the key demographic characteristics of both the settler and the "true" colonies were combined. Temperate climates and relatively mild disease environments in these areas made it possible for tens or hundreds of thousands of Europeans to settle on a permanent basis. Despite the Europeans' arrival, large indigenous populations survived and then began to increase rapidly. As a result, in these areas for which the label *contested settler colonies* seems most apt, Europeans and indigenous peoples increasingly clashed over land rights, resource control, social status, and cultural differences. From the 19th century onward, the history of contested settler societies has been dominated by the interaction between European settlers and indigenous peoples. The last sections of this chapter are devoted to case studies of three of the most important and representative examples of the contested settler variation on the settlement colony pattern: South Africa, New Zealand, and Hawaii. Because the pattern of colonization involved in the White Dominions has been considered in some depth in Chapter 23, developments in Canada and Australia are covered largely through comparisons to patterns in South Africa and other contested settlement areas.

COLONIAL REGIMES AND AFRICAN AND ASIAN PEOPLES

As the Europeans imposed their rule over tens of millions of additional Africans and Asians in the late 19th century, they drew heavily on precedents set in older colonies, particularly India, in establishing administrative, legal, and educational systems. As in India (or in Java and Senegal), the Europeans exploited long-standing ethnic and cultural divisions between the peoples of their new African or Asian colonies to put down resistance and maintain control. In West and East Africa in particular, they used the peoples who followed animistic religions (those that focused on the propitiation of nature or ancestral spirits) or those who had converted to Christianity against the Muslim communities that existed in most colonies. In official reports and censuses, colonial administrators rigidified and enhanced existing ethnic differences by dividing the peoples in each colony into "tribes." The label itself, with its connotations of primitiveness and backwardness, says a great deal about general European attitudes toward the peoples of sub-Saharan Africa. In Southeast Asia, the colonizers sought to use hill dwelling "tribal" minorities against the majority populations that lived in the lowlands. In each colonial area, favored minorities, often Christians, were recruited into the civil service and police. Their collaboration not only resulted in a sense of loyalty to the colonizers, it antagonized less-favored ethnic and religious groups, thus bolstering the divide and rule strategy of the Europeans.

As had been the case in India, Java, and Senegal small numbers of Europeans, who lived mainly in the capital city and major provincial towns, oversaw the administration of the African and Asian colonies, which was actually carried out at the local level mainly by hundreds or thousands of African and Asian subordinates. Some of these—normally those in positions of the greatest authority—were Western educated, but the majority were recruited from indigenous elite groups, including village headmen, local notables, and regional lords. In Burma, Malaya, and East Africa, numerous Indian administrators and soldiers assisted the British in ruling new additions to their empire. The Europeans also recruited promising male youths in the newly colonized areas for Western schooling that would make them fit for jobs as government clerks or railway mechanics.

In contrast to Java and India, where schools were heavily state-supported, Western-language education in Africa was left largely to Protestant and Catholic missionaries. As a result of deep-seated racial prejudices held by virtually all the colonizers, higher education was not promoted in Africa, and in Africa college graduates were rare compared to India, the Dutch East Indies, or even smaller Asian colonies such as Burma and Vietnam. Of course, this policy stunted the growth of a middle class in black Africa, a consequence that European colonial officials increasingly intended. As nationalist agitation spread among the Western-educated classes in India and other Asian colonies, colonial policymakers warned against the dangers posed by college graduates. Those with advanced educations among the colonized, according to this argument, aspired to jobs that were beyond their capacity and were understandably disgruntled when they could not find employment.

CHANGING SOCIAL RELATIONS BETWEEN COLONIZER AND COLONIZED

In both long-held and newly acquired colonies, the growing tensions between the colonizers and the rising African and Asian middle classes reflected a larger shift in

This pointedly dramatized engraving of the submission in 1896 of King Prempeh of the powerful Asante kingdom in present-day Ghana underscores the importance European colonizers placed on alliances with or the forced submission of indigenous African rulers and local leaders.

European social interaction with the colonized peoples. This shift had actually begun long before the scramble for colonies in the late 19th century. Its causes are complex, but the growing size and changing makeup of European communities in the colonies were critical factors. As more and more Europeans went to the colonies, they tended to keep to themselves on social occasions rather than mixing with the "natives." New medicines and increasingly segregated living quarters made it possible to bring to the colonies the wives and families of government officials and European military officers (but not of the rank-and-file until well into the 20th century). Wives and families further closed the social circle of the colonized, and European women looked disapprovingly on liaisons between European men and Asian or African women. Brothels were put off-limits for upper-class officials and officers, and mixed marriages or living arrangements met with more and more vocal disapproval both within the constricted world of the colonial communities and back home in Europe. The growing numbers of missionaries and pastors for European congregations in the colonies obviously served to strengthen these taboos.

European women were once held to be the chief culprits in the growing social gap between colonizer and colonized, but male officials may well have been mainly responsible. They established laws restricting or prohibiting miscegenation and other sorts of interracial liaisons, and they pushed for housing arrangements and police practices designed specifically to keep social contacts between European women and the colonized at a minimum. These measures locked European women in the colonies into an almost exclusively European world. They still had lots of "native" servants and "native" nannies for their children, but they rarely came into contact with men or women of their own social standing from the colonized peoples. Occasions when they did were highly public and strictly formal.

The trend toward social exclusivism on the part of Europeans in the colonies and their open disdain for the culture of colonized peoples were reinforced by notions of white racial supremacy, which peaked in acceptance in the decades before the First World War. It was widely believed that the mental and moral superiority of whites over the rest of humankind, which was usually divided into racial types according to the crude criterion of skin color, had been demonstrated by scientific experiments. Because the inferior intelligence and weak sense of morality of non-Europeans were believed to be inherent and permanent, there seemed little motivation for Europeans to socialize with the colonized and lots of good reasons for fighting the earlier tendency to adopt elements of the culture and lifestyle of subject peoples. As photos from the late 19th century reveal, stiff collars and ties for men, and corsets and long skirts for women became obligatory for the respectable colonial functionaries and their wives. The colonizers' houses were filled with the overstuffed furniture and bric-a-brac that the late Victorians loved so dearly. European social life in the colonies revolved around the infamous clubs, where the only "natives" allowed were the servants. In the heat of the summer months, most of the administrators and virtually all of the colonizers' families retreated to the hill stations, where the cool air and the quaint architecture made it seem almost as if they were home again—or at least in a Swiss mountain resort.

SHIFTS IN METHODS OF ECONOMIC EXTRACTION

The relationship between the colonizers and the mass of the colonized remained much as it had been before. District officers, with the help of many "native" subordinates, continued to do their paternal duty to settle disputes between peasant villagers, punish criminals, and collect taxes. European planters and merchants still relied on African or Asian overseers and brokers to manage laborers and purchase crops and handicraft manufactures. But late 19th century colonial bureaucrats and managers sought to instruct African and Asian peasants in "scientific" farming techniques and to compel the colonized peoples more generally to work harder and more efficiently. Here was an important extension of dependent status in the Western-dominated world economy, as pressure for new work habits supported the drive for cheap raw materials (exports) and drew in a growing segment of the colonial labor force.

A wide range of incentives was devised in response to the expansion of production for export and also the abolition of prior forms of slavery. Some of these incentives benefited the colonized peoples, such as the cheap consumer goods that could be purchased with cash earned producing marketable crops or laboring on European plantations. In many instances, however, colonized peoples were simply forced to produce crops or raw materials that the Europeans desired for little or no remuneration. Head and hut taxes were imposed that could only be paid in ivory, palm nuts, or wages earned working on European estates. Villagers were forced to grow market produce on lands they normally devoted to food crops. Under the worst of these forced-labor schemes, such as those inflicted on the peoples of the Belgian Congo in the final decades of the 19th century, villagers were flogged and killed if they failed to meet production quotas, and women and children were held hostage to ensure that their menfolk would deliver the products demanded on time. Whether out of self-interest or fear, the colonial overlords were determined to draw their subjects into fuller participation in the European-dominated global market economy.

As increasing numbers of the colonized peoples were drawn into the production of crops or minerals intended for export to Europe, colonized areas in Africa, India, and Southeast Asia were reduced to dependence on the industrializing European economies. Roads and railways were built primarily to facilitate the movement of farm produce and raw materials from the interior of colonized areas to port areas where they could be shipped to Europe. Benefiting from Europe's technological advances, mining sectors grew dramatically in most of the colonies. Vast areas that were previously uncultivated or (more commonly) had been planted in food crops were converted to the production of commodities—such as cocoa, palm oil, rubber, and hemp—in great demand in the markets of Europe and, increasingly, the United States.

The profits from the precious metals and minerals extracted from Africa's mines or the rubber grown in Malaya went mainly to European merchants and industrialists. The raw materials themselves were shipped to Europe to be processed and sold or used in the manufacture of industrial products. The finished products were intended mainly for European consumers, whether these be members of middle and working class families or government contractors. The African and Asian laborers who produced these products were generally poorly paid—if indeed they were paid at all. The laborers and colonial economies as a whole were steadily reduced to dependence on the European-dominated global market. Thus, economic dependence complemented the political subjugation and social subordination of colonized African and Asian peoples in a world order loaded in favor of the expansionist nations of western Europe.

DOCUMENT
CONTRARY IMAGES: THE COLONIZER VS. THE COLONIZED ON THE "CIVILIZING MISSION"

Each of the following passages from novels written in the colonial era expresses a different view of the reasons behind and the consequences of European colonization in Africa and Asia. The first is taken from an adventure story written by John Buchan entitled *Prestor John,* a favorite in the pre-World War I decades among English schoolboys—many of whom would go out as young men to administer in the colonies. Davie, the protagonist in the story, is a "tall, square-set lad . . . renown [for his] prowess at Rugby football." He summarizes key elements of the "civilizing mission" credo by which so many European thinkers and political leaders attempted to justify their colonization of most of the rest of the world.

> I knew then [after Davie's struggle to thwart a "native" rising in South Africa] the meaning of the white man's duty. He has to take all the risks, reck[on]ing nothing of his life or his fortunes and well content to find his reward in the fulfillment of his task. That is the difference between white and black, the gift of responsibility, the power of being in a little way a king; and so long as we know this and practise it, we will rule not in Africa alone but wherever there are dark men who live only for the day and their own bellies. Moreover the work made me pitiful and kindly. I learned much of the untold grievances of the natives and saw something of their strange, twisted reasoning.

The second passage is taken from René Maran's *Batouala,* which was first published in 1921 just after the First World War. Though a French colonial official in West Africa, Maran was an African-American, born in Martinique, who was highly sensitive to the plight of the colonized in Africa. Here his protagonist, a local African leader named Batouala, complains of the burdens rather than the benefits of colonial rule, and mocks the self-important European agents of the vaunted civilizing mission.

> But what good does it do to talk about it? It's nothing new to us that men of white skin are more delicate than men of black skin.
>
> One example of a thousand possible. Everyone knows that the whites, saying that they are "collecting taxes," force all blacks of a marriageable age to carry voluminous packages from when the sun rises to when it sets.
>
> These trips last two, three, five days. Little matter to them the weight of these packages which are called "sandoukous." They don't sink under the burden. Rain, sun, cold? They don't suffer. So they pay no attention. And long live the worst weather, provided the whites are sheltered.
>
> Whites fret about mosquito bites. . . . They fear mason bees. They are also afraid of the "prakongo," the scorpion who lives, black and venomous, among decaying roofs, under rubble, or in the midst of debris.
>
> In a word, everything worries them. As if a man worthy of the name would worry about everything which lives, crawls, or moves around him.
>
> The whites, aha! The whites . . . didn't everyone know that their feet were just a stinking mass? And what a ridiculous idea to encase feet in black, white, or banana-colored skins! And if it were only their feet which stank! *Lalala*—their whole body smelled like a corpse.

Questions: What sorts of roles does Davie assume that the Europeans must play in the colonies? What benefits accrue to colonized peoples from their rule? What impression does he convey of the thinking and behavior of the colonized peoples? In what ways do Batouala's views of the Europeans conflict with Davie's assumptions about himself and other colonizers? Does Batouala agree with Davie's conviction that colonial rule is beneficial for the Africans? What sorts of burdens does Batouala believe it imposes? According to Batouala what advantages do Africans have over Europeans?

SETTLER COLONIES AND WHITE DOMINIONS: SOUTH AFRICA

The contested settler colonies that developed in Africa and the Pacific in the 19th century were in important ways similar to the White Dominions. In fact, the early history of South Africa, one of the largest of the contested settler colonies, exhibited interesting comparisons and contrasts with that of Canada and Australia, the largest of the White Dominions. European settlers began to move into the southwest corner of South Africa and eastern Canada in the middle decades of the 17th century, long before the settlement of Australia got under way in the 1840s. The initial Dutch colony at Cape Town was established to provide a way station where Dutch merchant ships could take on water and fresh foods in the middle of their long journey from Europe to the East Indies. In contrast to Canada, where French fur trappers and missionaries quickly moved into the interior, the small community of Dutch settlers stayed near the coast for decades after their arrival. But like the settlers in Australia, the Boers (or farmers), as the Dutch in South Africa came to be called, eventually began to move into the vast interior regions of the continent. Though the settlers in each of the three areas were confronted by wild, uncharted, and in some ways inhospitable frontier regions, they also found a temperate climate in which they could grow the crops and raise the livestock they were accustomed to in Europe. Equally important, they encountered a disease environment they could withstand.

The Boers and Australians found the areas into which they moved sparsely populated. In this respec t their experience was somewhat different from that of the settlers in Canada, where the Amerindian population, though far from dense, was organized into powerful tribal confederations. The Boers and Australians faced much less resistance as they took possession of the lands once occupied by hunting-and-gathering peoples. The Boer farmers and cattle ranchers enslaved these peoples, the Khoikhoi, while at the same time integrating them into their large frontier homesteads. Extensive miscegenation between the Boers and Khoikhoi in these early centuries of European colonization produced the sizeable "colored" population that exists in South Africa today, which is regarded as quite distinct from the black or African majority. The Australian and Canadian settlers drove the "aborigines" they encountered into the interior, eventually leaving those who survived their invasions the uneasy occupants of remote tracts of waste, which were not worth settling. In both cases, but particularly in Canada, the indigenous population was also decimated by many of the same diseases that had turned contacts with the Europeans into a demographic disaster for the rest of the Americas in the early centuries of expansion.

Thus, until the first decades of the 19th century, the process of colonization in South Africa paralleled that in Canada and Australia quite closely. Small numbers of Europeans had migrated into lands that they considered "empty" or undeveloped. After driving away or subjugating the indigenous peoples, the Europeans farmed, mined, and grazed their herds on these lands, which they claimed as their own. But while the settler societies in Canada and Australia went on to develop, rather peacefully, into loyal and largely self-governing dominions of the British empire, the arrival of the same British overlords in South Africa in the early 19th century sent the Boers reeling onto a very different historical course. The British captured Cape Town during the wars precipitated by the French Revolution in the 1790s when Holland was overrun by France, thus making its colonies subject to British attack. The British held the colony during the Napoleonic conflicts that followed and annexed it permanently in 1815 as a vital link on the route to India.

Made up mainly of people of Dutch and French Protestant descent, the Boer community differed from the British newcomers in almost every way possible. The Boers spoke a different language, and they lived mostly in isolated rural homesteads that had missed the scientific, industrial, and urban revolutions that had transformed British society and attitudes. Most critically, the Evangelical missionaries who entered South Africa under the protection of the new British overlords were deeply committed to eradicating slavery. They made no exception for the domestic pattern of enslavement that had developed in Boer homesteads and communities. By the 1830s missionary pressure and increasing British interference in their lives drove a handful of Boers to open, but futile, rebellion, and drove many of the remaining Boers to flee the Cape Colony.

In the decades of the Great Trek that followed, tens of thousands of Boer farmers migrated in covered wagons pulled by oxen, first east across the Great Fish River and then over the mountains into the *veld*, or rolling, grassy plains that make up much of the South African interior. In these areas, the Boers collided head-on with populous, militarily powerful, and well-organized African states built by Bantu peoples such as the Zulus and the Xhosa. Throughout the middle decades of the 19th century, the migrating Boers clashed again and again with the Bantu peoples, who were determined to resist the seizure of the lands where they pastured their great herds of cattle and grew subsistence foods. The British in effect followed the Boer pio-

This 1864 engraving shows well-to-do Afrikaner homes near Cape Town in South Africa. The abundance of mulatto servants, shown in the foreground, was typical of Boer homesteads, where color lines were quite permeable and miscegenation was not uncommon until well into the 19th century.

neers along the southern and eastern coast, eventually establishing a second major outpost at Durban in Natal. Tensions between Boers and Britain remained high, but the British were often drawn into the frontier wars against the Bantu peoples, even though they were not always formally allied to the Boers.

In the early 1850s the hard-liners among the Boers established two republics, the Orange Free State and the Transvaal, in the interior, which they sought to keep free of British influence. For over a decade they managed to keep the British out of their affairs. But when diamonds were discovered in the Orange Free State in 1867, British entrepreneurs, such as Cecil Rhodes, and prospectors began to move in, and tensions between Boers and British began to build anew. In 1880 and 1881, these tensions led to a brief war in which the Boers were victorious. The tide of British immigration into the republics, however, rose even higher after gold was discovered in the Transvaal in 1885.

Though the British had pretty much left the Boers to deal with the African peoples who lived in the republics as they pleased, British migrants and financiers grew more and more resentful of Boer efforts to limit their numbers and curb their civil rights. British efforts to protect the settlers and bring the feisty and independent Boers into line led to the republics' declaration of war against the British in late 1899, and Boer attacks on British bases in Natal, the Cape Colony, and elsewhere. The Boer War that resulted raged until 1902 and began the process of decolonization for the European settlers of South Africa, while at the same time it opened the way for their dominance over the African majority.

PACIFIC TRAGEDIES

The territories the Europeans, Americans, and Japanese claimed throughout the South Pacific in the 19th century were in some cases outposts of true empire, in others contested settler colonies. In both situations, however, the coming of colonial rule resulted in demographic disasters and social disruptions of a magnitude that had not been seen since the first century of European expansion into the Americas. Like the Amerindian peoples of the New World, the peoples of the South Pacific had long lived in isolation. This meant that like the Amerindians they had no immunities to many of the diseases European explorers and later merchants, missionaries, and settlers carried to their island homes from the 1760s onward. In addition, their cultures were extremely vulnerable to the corrosive effects of outside influences, such as new religions, different sexual mores, more lethal weapons, and sudden influxes of cheap consumer goods. Thus, whatever the intentions of the incoming Europeans and Americans—and they were by no means always benevolent—their contacts with the peoples of the Pacific islands almost invariably ushered in periods of social disintegration and widespread human suffering.

Of the many cases of contact between the expansive peoples of the West and the long isolated island cultures of the South Pacific, the confrontations in New Zealand and Hawaii are among the most informative. As we saw in Chapters 10 and 21, quite sophisticated cultures and fairly complex societies had developed in each of these areas. In addition, the two island groups contained, at the time of the European explorers' arrivals, some of the largest concentrations of population in the whole Pacific region. Both areas were subjected to European influences carried by a variety of agents from whalers and merchants to missionaries and colonial administrators. After the first decades of contact, the peoples of both New Zealand and Hawaii experienced a period of crisis so severe that their continued survival was in doubt. In both cases, however, the threatened peoples and cultures rebounded and found enduring solutions to the challenges from overseas that combined accommodation to outside influences and revivals of traditional beliefs and practices.

NEW ZEALAND. The Maoris of New Zealand actually went through two periods of profound disruption and danger. The first began in the 1790s when timber merchants and whalers established small settlements on the New Zealand coast. Maoris living near these settlements were afflicted with alcoholism and the spread of prostitution. In addition, they traded wood and food for European firearms that soon revolutionized Maori warfare—in part by rendering it much more deadly—and upset the existing balance among different tribal groups. Even more devastating was the impact of diseases, such as smallpox, tuberculosis, and even the common cold, that ravaged Maori communities throughout the north island. By the 1840s only eighty to ninety thousand Maoris remained of a population that had been as high as 130,000 less than a century earlier. But the Maoris survived these calamities and began to adjust to the imports of the foreigners. They took up farming with European implements, and grazed cattle purchased from European traders. They cut timber, built windmills, and traded extensively with the merchants who frequented their shores. Many even converted to Christianity, which the missionaries began to proselytize after their first station was established in 1814, though observers noted the Maoris' continuing adherence to their old beliefs and rituals.

The arrival of British farmers and herders in search of land in the early 1850s and the British decision to claim the islands as part of their global empire, again plunged the Maoris into misery and despair. Backed by the military clout of the colonial government, the settlers occupied some of the most fertile areas of the north island. The warlike Maori fought back, sometimes with temporary successes, but they were steadily driven back into the interior of the island. In desperation in the 1860s and 1870s, they flocked to religious prophets who promised them magical charms and supernatural assistance in their efforts to drive out the invaders. When the prophets also failed them, the Maoris seemed for a time to face extinction. In fact, some British writers, heavily influenced by the work of "social Darwinists," such as Herbert Spencer, predicted that within generations the Maoris, like the Arawaks and Tasmanians before them, would die out.

The Maoris displayed surprising resilience. As they built up immunities to new diseases, they also learned to use European laws and political institutions to defend themselves and preserve what was left of their ancestral lands. Because the British had in effect turned the internal administration of the islands over to the settlers' representatives, the Maoris' main struggle was with the invaders who had come to stay. Western schooling and a growing ability to win British colonial officials over to their point of view eventually enabled the Maoris to hold their own in their ongoing legal contests and daily exchanges with the settlers. A multiracial society has now evolved in which there is a reasonable level of European and Maori accommodation and interaction, and which has allowed the Maori to preserve much of value in their traditional culture.

HAWAII. The conversion of Hawaii to settler colony status followed familiar basic imperialist patterns, but with a number of specific twists. Hawaii did not become a colony until the United States proclaimed annexation in 1898, though an overzealous British official had briefly declared the islands for his nation in 1843. Hawaii came under increasing Western influence, however, from the late 18th century onward—politically at the hands of the British, culturally and economically from the United States whose westward surge quickly spilled into the Pacific Ocean.

While very occasional contact with Spanish ships during the 16th and 17th centuries is probable, Hawaii was effectively opened to the West through the voyages of Captain James Cook from 1777 to 1779. Cook was first welcomed as a god, partly because he had the good luck to land during a sacred period when war was forbidden. A later and less well-timed visit brought Cook's death, as Hawaiian warriors sought to take over his ship with its metal nails, much prized by a people whose elaborate culture rested on a Neolithic technology. Cook and later British expeditions convinced a young Hawaiian prince, Kamehameha, that some imitation of Western ways could produce a unified kingdom under his leadership, replacing the small and warring regional units that had previously prevailed. A series of vigorous wars, backed by British weapons and advisors, won Kamehameha his kingdom between 1794 and 1810. The new king and his successors promoted economic change, encouraging Western merchants to establish export trade in Hawaiian goods in return for increasing revenues to the royal treasury.

Hawaiian royalty began to imitate Western habits, in some cases traveling to Britain and often building Western-style palaces. Two powerful queens advanced the process of change by insisting that traditional taboos subordinating women be abandoned. In this context vigorous missionary efforts from Protestant New England, beginning in 1819, brought extensive conversions to Christianity. As with other conversion processes, religious change had wide implications. Missionaries railed against traditional Hawaiian costumes, insisting that women cover their breasts, and a new garment, the muumuu, was fashioned from homespun American nightgowns with the sleeves cut off. Backed by the Hawaiian monarchy, missionaries also quickly established an extensive school system, by 1831 serving 50,000 students from a culture that had not previously developed writing.

The combination of Hawaiian interest and Western intrusion produced creative political and cultural changes, though inevitably at the expense of previous values. Demographic and economic trends had more insidious effects. Western-imported disease, particularly venereal disease and tuberculosis, had the usual tragic consequences for a previously isolated people: By 1850 only about 80,000 Hawaiians remained of a prior population of about half a million. Westerners more consciously exploited the Hawaiian economy. Whalers helped create raucous seaport towns. Western settlers from various countries (called *haoles* by the Hawaiians) experimented with potential commercial crops, soon concentrating particularly on sugar. Many missionary families turned to leasing land or buying it outright, impatient with the subsistence habits of Hawaiian commoners. They did not entirely forget their religious motives—among other things, many American missionaries had a strong antislavery background and shunned the most intense forms of exploitation; but it remained true that many families who came to Hawaii to do good ended by doing well.

Western businesses were mainly encouraged by the Hawaiian monarchy, eager for revenues and impressed by the West's military power. In 1848 an edict called the Great Mahele imposed Western concepts of property on Hawaiian land that had previously been shared by commoners and aristocrats. Most of the newly defined private property went to the king and the nobles, who gradually sold most of it to investors from the West. As sugar estates spread, increasing numbers of Americans moved in to take up other commercial and professional positions—hence an increasingly "settler" pattern even in a technically independent state. Given Hawaiian population decline, it was also necessary to import Asian workers to staff the estates. The first Chinese contract workers were actually brought in before 1800, and after 1868 a larger current of Japanese swelled the immigrant throng.

Literal imperialism came as an anticlimax. The abilities of Hawaiian kings declined after 1872, in one case because of problems of disease and alcoholism. Under a weakened state, powerful planter interests pressed for special treaties with the United States that would promote their sugar exports, and the American government claimed naval rights at the Pearl Harbor base by 1887. As the last Hawaiian monarchs turned increasingly to the promotion of culture, writing a number of lasting Hawaiian songs but also spending considerable money on luxurious appointments, American planters concluded that their economic interests required outright United States control. An "annexation committee" persuaded American naval officers to "protect American lives and property" by posting troops around Honolulu in 1893, and the monarchy was disbanded. An imperial-minded United States Congress obligingly took over the islands in 1898.

As in New Zealand, Western control combined with considerable respect for Polynesian culture. Americans in Hawaii did not apply the same degree of racism that had described earlier relations with North American Indians or with African slaves. Hawaii's status as a settler colony was further complicated by the arrival of so many Asian immigrants. Nevertheless, Western cultural and particularly economic influence extended steadily, and the ultimate political seizure merely ratified the colonization of the islands.

CONCLUSION

THE PATTERN OF THE AGE OF IMPERIALISM

Though the basic patterns of domination in European colonial empires remained similar to those worked out in Java and India in the early industrial period, the style of colonial rule and patterns of social interaction between colonizer and colonized changed considerably in the late 19th century. Racism and social snobbery became pervasive in contacts between the colonizers and their African and Asian subordinates. The Europeans consciously renounced the ways of dressing, eating habits, and pastimes that had earlier been borrowed from or shared with the peoples of the colonies. The colonizers no longer saw themselves simply as the most successful competitors in a many-sided struggle for political power. They were convinced that they were inherently superior beings, citizens of the most powerful, civilized, and advanced societies on earth. Colonial officials in the age of "high imperialism" were much more concerned than earlier administrators to pull the peasants, who made up the overwhelming majority of the population of all colonized societies, into the market economy and teach them the value of hard work and discipline. Colonial educators were determined to impress upon the children of the colonized elite classes the superiority of Western learning and of everything from political organization to fashions in clothing.

In striving for these objectives, the European colonizers started with the assumption that it was their duty to impose their own views and ways of doing things, rather than learn from others—to remake the world, insofar as the abilities of the "natives" would allow, in the image of industrial Europe. But in pushing for change within colonized societies that had ancient, deeply rooted cultures and patterns of civilized life, the Europeans frequently aroused resistance to specific policies and to colonial rule more generally. Though the colonizers were able to put down protest movements led by displaced princes and religious prophets, much more enduring and successful challenges to their rule came, ironically, from the leaders their social reforms and Western-language schools had done much to nurture. These nationalists reworked European ideas and resurrected those of their own cultures, borrowed European organizational techniques, and made use of the communications systems and common language the Europeans had introduced into the colonies to contest European dominance. The overwhelming dependence of the Europeans on the collaboration of colonized peoples to govern and police their empires rendered the Europeans particularly vulnerable to these challenges from within.

FURTHER READINGS

There is vast literature on various aspects of European imperialism. Useful general histories on the different empires include Bernard Porter's *The Lion's Share: A Short History of British Imperialism 1850–1970* (1975), Raymond Betts's *Tricouleur* (1978), James J. Cooke's *The New French Imperialism, 1880–1910* (1973), and Woodruff D. Smith's *The German Colonial Empire* (1978). There is no really satisfactory general history of the growth of Dutch power on Java or the British Empire in India, but Edward Thompson and G. T. Garratt provide a reasonably lively chronology in the *Rise and Fulfillment of British Rule in India* (1962), which can be supplemented by the essays in R. C. Majumdar, ed., *British Paramountcy and Indian Renaissance* part I, (1963). More recent accounts of specific aspects of the rise of British power in India are available in C. A. Bayley's *Indian society and the making of the British Empire* (1988) and P. J. Marshall's *Bengal: The British Beachhead, 1740–1828* (1987), both part of *The New Cambridge History of India.*

Of the many contributions to the debate over late 19th century imperialism, some of the most essential are those by D. C. M. Platt, Hans-Ulrich Wehler, William Appleman Williams, Jean Stengers, D. K. Fieldhouse, and Henri Brunschwig, plus the earlier works by Lenin and J. A. Hobson. Winfried Baumgart's *Imperialism* (1982) provides a good overview of the literature and conflicting arguments. Very different perspectives on the partition of Africa can be found in Jean Suret-Canale's *French Colonialism in Tropical Africa, 1900–1945* (1971) and Ronald Robinson and John Gallagher's *Africa and the Victorians* (1961).

Most of the better studies on the impact of imperialism and social life in the colonies are specialized monographs, but Percival Spear's *The Nabobs* (1963) is a superb place to start on the latter from the European viewpoint, while the works of Frantz Fanon, Albert Memmi, and O. Mannoni provide much information on the plight of the colonized. The impact of industrialization and other changes in Europe on European attitudes toward the colonized are treated in a number of works, including Philip Curtin's *The Image of Africa* (1964), William B. Cohen's *The French Encounter with Africans* (1980), and Michael Adas's *Machines as the Measure of Men* (1989). Ester Boserup's *Women's Role in Economic Development* (1970) provides a good overview of the impact of colonization on African and Asian women and families, but it should be supplemented by more recent monographs on the position of women in colonial settings. One of the best of these is Jean Taylor's *The Social World of Batavia* (1983).

FROM COLONIES TO NATIONS

NEW NATIONS CONFRONT OLD AND NEW PROBLEMS

LATIN-AMERICAN ECONOMIES AND WORLD MARKETS, 1820–1870

DOCUMENT: Confronting the Hispanic Heritage: From Independence to Consolidation

SOCIETIES IN SEARCH OF THEMSELVES

ANALYSIS: Explaining Underdevelopment

THE GREAT BOOM, 1880–1920

CONCLUSION: New Nations, Old Problems

FURTHER READINGS

1792 Slave rebellion in St. Domingue (Haiti)

1804 Haiti declares independence

1808 Portuguese court flees Napoleon, arrives in Brazil; French armies invade Spain

1808–1825 Spanish-American wars of independence

1810 In Mexico, Father Hidalgo initiates rebellion against Spain

1821 Mexico declares independence; empire under Iturbide lasts to 1823

1822 Brazil declares independence; empire established under Dom Pedro I

1823 Monroe Doctrine indicates U.S. opposition to European ambitions in the Americas

1829–1852 Juan Manuel de Rosas rules Rio de la Plata

1830 Bolívar dies; Gran Colombia dissolves into separate countries of Venezuela, Colombia, and Equador

1846–1848 Mexican-American War

1847–1855 Caste War in Yucatan

1850s Beginnings of railroad construction in Cuba, Chile, and Brazil

1854 Benito Juárez leads reform in Mexico

31 The Consolidation of Latin America, 1830–1920

INTRODUCTION. The spread of Western imperialism, along with its consolidation in prior holdings such as Indonesia, had carved up much of the world during the 19th century. Africa, both north and south of the Sahara, was almost entirely swallowed up, in contrast to the much more limited colonial patterns established before 1800. Australia, New Zealand, and all the clusters of smaller Pacific islands, including Polynesia, were seized. Southeast Asia was taken, and in combination with earlier acquisitions this meant a solid colonial swatch from India in the west to the Philippines in the east.

Four major parts of the world, however, were not caught up in the full imperialist scramble, even though they were not "Western." Russia, most of the Middle East, and much of East Asia were exempt, though imperialist rivalries cut into the latter two civilizations to some extent. Vestiges of inherited political strength and/or new initiatives prevented Western control. The fourth exception, Latin America, was the most surprising of all, for in a century of imperialism this society cast off previous colonial controls. The force of the industrial West was deeply felt—like other non-Western and noncolonial areas, Latin America was substantially reshaped by the dominant international forces of the day. New and independent political and cultural initiatives also formed a major part of this civilization's 19th-century experience.

It was early in the 19th century that most of the nations of Latin America gained their political independence. These former American colonies of Spain and Portugal were swept by the same winds of change that brought about the transformation of Europe's society and economy and led to the separation of England's North American colonies. Although at present Latin America is sometimes

1862–1867 French intervention in Mexico

1865–1870 War of the Triple Alliance (Argentina, Brazil, and Uruguay against Paraguay)

1868–1878 Ten year war against Spain in Cuba

1869 First school for girls in Mexico

1876–1911 Porfirio Díaz rules Mexico

1886–1888 Cuba and Brazil finally abolish slavery

1889 Fall of Brazilian Empire; republic established

1895–1898 Cuban Spanish-American War; U.S. acquires Puerto Rico and Philippines

1903 Panamanian independence; beginning of Panama Canal (opens in 1914)

considered part of the "Third World" along with many Asian and African nations, in reality its political culture was formed in the 18th century by the ideas of the Western Enlightenment and the crisis of the traditional monarchy and social structure. Thus Latin-American leaders in the 19th century, despite their many differences, often shared with Western political figures a firm belief in the virtues of "progress," reform, representational and constitutional government, and the "sacred" rights of private property. At the same time Latin-American leaders were often faced with insurmountable problems different from those of Europe and the United States. The colonial heritage had left little tradition of participatory government among the majority of the Latin-American population. A highly centralized colonial state had intervened in many aspects of life and had created not only a dependence on central authority but a resentment of it as well. Class and regional interests deeply divided the new nations, and wealth was very unequally distributed. Finally, the rise of European industrial capitalism created an economic situation that often placed the new nations in a weak or dependent position. These problems and tensions will serve as the focus for our examination of Latin America in the 19th century.

FROM COLONIES TO NATIONS

By the late 18th century, the Creole elites expressed a growing self-consciousness as they began to question the policies of Spain and Portugal and the very necessity of remaining in a colonial relationship. At the same time, these elites were joined by the majority of the population in resentment of the increasingly heavy hand of government as expressed in the new taxes and administrative reforms of the 18th century. But the shared resentment was not enough to overcome class conflicts and divisions. Early movements for independence usually failed because of the reluctance of the colonial upper classes to enlist the support of the Indian, mestizo, and mulatto masses who might later prove too difficult to control. The actual movements were only set in motion when events in Europe precipitated actions in America.

CAUSES OF POLITICAL CHANGE

Latin-American political independence was achieved as part of the general Atlantic revolution of the late 18th and early 19th centuries, and Latin-American leaders were moved by the same ideas and influenced by the same trends as those seeking political change elsewhere in the Atlantic world. Four external events had a particularly strong impact on political thought in Latin America. The American Revolution from 1776 to 1783 provided a model of how colonies could break with the mother country. George Washington and Thomas Jefferson seemed to be examples of "Creole" leaders, and the revolutionary ideas of Jefferson, Thomas Paine, and the Declaration of Independence were eventually smuggled into Latin America. The French Revolution of 1789 provoked great interest in Latin America, and its slogans of "liberty, equality, and fraternity" appealed to some sectors of the population. As that revolution became increasingly radical, it was rejected by the Creole elites who could not support regicide, rejection of the Church's authority, and the social leveling implied by the Declaration of the Rights of Man.

The third external event was really an extension of the French Revolution. Torn by internal political conflict during the turmoil in France, the whites and free people of color in St. Domingue—France's great island sugar colony in the Caribbean—became divided. The slaves seized the moment in 1791 to stage a great general rebellion. Under able leadership provided by Toussaint L'Overture and other blacks, various attempts to subdue the island were defeated and in 1804 the independent republic of Haiti was proclaimed. For Latin-American elites, Haiti was an example to be avoided. The spectre of general social upheaval and of slaves becoming their own masters so frightened them that they became even more unwilling to risk political change. It was not accidental that neighboring Cuba and Puerto Rico, with plantations and slaves and acutely aware of events in Haiti, were among the last of Spain's colonies to eventually gain independence. For slaves and free people of color throughout the Americas, however, Haiti became a symbol of freedom and hope.

What eventually precipitated the movements for independence in Latin America was the confused Iberian political situation caused by the French Revolution and its aftermath. Portugal was invaded by the French in 1807, and in 1808 Napoleon placed the king of Spain and his son Ferdinand VII under arrest and forced them to abdicate in favor of his brother Joseph Bonaparte who then sought to rule Spain backed by French bayonets. A general insurrection erupted in 1808 and was followed by a long guerrilla war. During the fighting a central committee, or *junta central*, ruled in Ferdinand's absence, in opposition to Napoleon's brother who also claimed to be king.

Who was the legitimate ruler? By 1810 the confusion in Spain had provoked a crisis in the colonies. In a number of places such as Caracas, Bogotá, and Mexico, Creoles pretending to be loyal to captive Ferdinand set up juntas to rule in his name, but they effectively ruled on their own behalf. "The mask of Ferdinand" fooled few people and soon the more conservative elements of the population, those still loyal to Spain and royal officials, opposed the movements for autonomy and independence. A crisis of legitimacy reverberated throughout the American colonies.

SPANISH-AMERICAN INDEPENDENCE STRUGGLES

The independence movements divided into three major theaters of operation. In Mexico, a conspiracy among leading Creoles moved one of the plotters, the priest Father Miguel de Hidalgo, to call for help from the Indians and mestizos of his region in 1810. He won a number of early victories, but eventually lost the support of the Creoles who feared social rebellion more than they desired independence. Hidalgo was captured and executed, but the insurgency smoldered in various parts of the country. Eventually, after 1820 when events in Spain weakened the king and the central government, conservative Creoles in Mexico were willing to move toward independence by uniting with the remnants of the insurgent forces. Augustín de Iturbide, a Creole officer at the head of an army that had been sent to eliminate the insurgents, drew up an agreement with them instead, and the combined forces of independence occupied Mexico City in September, 1821. Soon thereafter, with the support of the army, Iturbide was proclaimed emperor of Mexico.

This was a conservative solution. The new nation of Mexico was born as a monarchy, and little recognition was given to the social aspirations and programs of Hidalgo and his movement. Central America was briefly attached to the Mexican Empire, which collapsed in 1824. Mexico became a republic, and the Central American states, after attempting union until 1838, split apart into independent nations.

In South America and the Caribbean the chronology of independence was a mirror image of the conquest of the 16th century. Formerly secondary areas like Argentina and Venezuela, slowest to be settled in the 16th century, were among the first to opt for independence and the best able to achieve it, while the old colonial center in Peru was among the last to break with Spain. The Caribbean islands of Cuba and Puerto Rico—among the first of Spain's American possessions—fearful of slave rebellion and occupied by large Spanish garrisons, remained loyal until the end of the 19th century.

In northern South America, a movement for independence centered in Caracas had begun in 1810. After early reverses, Simón Bolívar, a wealthy Creole officer, emerged as the leader of the revolt against Spain. With considerable military skill and a passion for independence, he eventually mobilized support, and between 1817 and 1822 he won a series of victories in Venezuela, Colombia, and Ecuador. Until 1830 these countries were united into a new nation called Gran Colombia. Political differences and regional interests led to the breakup of Gran Colombia. Bolívar became disillusioned and fearful of anarchy. "America is ungovernable," he said, and "those who have served the revolution have plowed the sea." To his credit, however, Bolívar rejected all attempts to crown him as king and remained until his death in 1830 firmly committed to the cause of independence and republican government.

Meanwhile in southern South America another movement had coalesced under José de San Martín in the Rio de La Plata. Buenos Aires had become a booming commer-

Simón Bolívar led the struggle for political independence in northern South America. Son of a wealthy Creole family, he became an ardent proponent of independence and a firm believer in the republican form of government.

cial center in the late 18th century and its residents, called *porteños,* particularly resented Spanish trade restrictions. Pushing for freedom of trade, they opted for autonomy in 1810 but tried to keep the outlying areas, such as Paraguay, under their control. The myth of autonomy rather than independence was preserved for a while. By 1816, however, the independence of the United Provinces of the Rio de la Plata had been proclaimed, although the provinces were far from united. Upper Peru (Bolivia) remained under Spanish control, Paraguay declared independence in 1813, and the Banda Oriental (Uruguay) resisted the central authority of Buenos Aires.

In Buenos Aires, José de San Martín had emerged as a military commander willing to speak and act for independence. From Argentina his armies crossed the Andes to Chile to help the patriot forces in that colony. With victories there, the patriot forces looked northward. Peru, the seat of the old viceroyalty and the scene of the Indian rebellion of Tupac Amaru in the 1780s, remained under Spanish rule. Its upper class was deeply conservative and little attracted to the movements for independence. San Martín's forces entered Peru and Creole adherence was slowly won. With victories like the battle of Ayacucho in 1824, royalist forces were defeated. By 1825 all of Spanish South America had gained its political independence. Despite various plans and programs to create some form of monarchy in many of the new states, all of them emerged as independent republics with representative governments. The nations of Spanish America were born of the Enlightenment and the ideas of 19th century liberalism.

BRAZILIAN INDEPENDENCE

Although the movement for independence in Brazil was roughly contemporaneous to those in Spanish America and many of the causes were similar, independence was achieved by quite a different process. By the end of the 18th century, Brazil had grown in population and economic importance and had clearly become the dominant part of the Portuguese colonial system. The expansion of European demand for colonial products, such as sugar, cotton, and cacao, contributed to that growth and also to the intensification of slave imports to the colony. While Brazilian planters, merchants, and miners sometimes longed for more open trade and fewer taxes, they feared that any upsetting of the political system might lead to a social revolution or, even worse, a Haitian-style general slave uprising. Thus incipient movements for independence in Minas Gerais in 1788 and Bahia in 1798 were unsuccessful. As one official said, "Men established in goods and property were unwilling to risk political change."

The Napoleonic invasions provoked a different outcome in Portugal than in Spain. When in 1807 French troops invaded Portugal, the whole Portuguese royal family and court were able to flee the country and, under the protection of British ships, sailed to Brazil. A new court was established at Rio de Janeiro, which then became the effective capital of the Portuguese Empire. Brazil was raised to equal status with Portugal, and all the functions of royal government were set up in the colony. As a partial concession to England and to colonial interests, the ports of Brazil were opened to world commerce, thus satisfying one of the main desires of the Brazilian elites. Unlike Spanish America, where the Napoleonic invasions provoked a crisis of authority and led Spanish Americans to consider ruling in their own name, in Brazil the transfer of the court brought royal government closer and tended to reinforce the colonial relationship.

From 1808 to 1820 the Portuguese king, Dom João VI, resided in Brazil and ruled his empire from there. Rio de Janeiro was transformed into a capital city with a public library, botanical gardens, and other improvements. Printing presses began to operate in the colony for the first time, schools were created, and commerce, especially with England, boomed in the newly opened ports. The Brazilian elite were given noble titles and offices in order to win their loyalty to the government, but the arrival of many Portuguese bureaucrats and nobles with the court also created jealousy and resentment. Still, during this period Brazil was transformed into the seat of empire, a fact not lost on its most prominent citizens.

Matters changed drastically in 1820 when, after the defeat of Napoleon in Europe and a liberal revolution in Portugal, the king was recalled and a parliament convoked. João VI, who loved Brazil, was reluctant to leave, but realizing that his return was inevitable, he left his young son Pedro as regent, warning him that if independence had to come, he should lead the movement and not some "adventurer." Although Brazilians were allowed representation at the Portuguese Parliament, it became clear that Brazil's new status was doomed and that it would be "recolonized." After demands that the prince regent also return to Europe, Pedro refused, and in September 1822 declared Brazilian independence. He became Dom Pedro I, constitutional emperor of Brazil. Fighting against Portuguese troops lasted a year, but Brazil avoided the long wars of Spanish America. Brazil's independence did not upset the existing social organization based on slavery nor did it radically change the political structure. With the brief exception of Mexico, all of the former Spanish-American colonies became republics, but Brazil became a monarchy under a member of the Portuguese ruling house.

NEW NATIONS CONFRONT OLD AND NEW PROBLEMS

By 1830 the former Spanish and Portuguese colonies had become independent nations. The roughly 20 million inhabitants of these nations looked hopefully to the future. Born in the crisis of the old regime and Iberian colonialism, many of the leaders of independence shared the ideals of representative government, careers open to talent, freedom of commerce and trade, the right to private property, and a belief in the individual as the basis of society. Generally there was a belief that the new nations should be sovereign and independent states, large enough to be economically viable and integrated by a common set of laws.

On the issue of freedom of religion and the position of the Church, however, there was less agreement among the leadership. Roman Catholicism had been the state religion and the only one allowed by the Spanish crown. While most leaders sought to maintain Catholicism as the official religion of the new states, some sought to end the exclusion of other faiths. The defense of the Church became a rallying cry for the conservative forces.

The ideals of the early leaders of independence were often egalitarian. Bolívar had received aid from Haiti and had promised in return to abolish slavery in the areas he liberated. By 1854 slavery had been abolished everywhere except Spain's remaining colonies of Cuba and Puerto Rico as well as in Brazil (all places where the economy was profoundly based on it). Early promises to end Indian tribute and taxes on people of mixed origin came much slower because the new nations still needed the revenue such policies produced. Egalitarian sentiments were often tempered by fears that the mass of the population was unprepared for self-rule and democracy. Early constitutions sought to balance order and popular representation by imposing property or literacy restrictions. Invariably, voting rights were reserved for males. Women were still disenfranchised and usually unable to hold public office. The Creole elite's lack of trust was based on the fact that in many places the masses had not demonstrated a clear preference for the new regimes and had sometimes fought in royalist armies mobilized by traditional loyalties and regional interests. While some mestizos had risen to leadership roles in the wars of independence, the old casta, or color distinctions, did not disappear easily. In Mexico, Guatemala, and the Andean nations, the large Indian population remained mostly outside of national political life. The mass of the Latin-American population—Indians and people of mixed origins—waited to see what was to come, and they were suspicious of the new political elite who were often drawn from the old colonial aristocracy but were now also joined by a new commercial and urban bourgeoisie.

POLITICAL FRAGMENTATION

The new nations can be grouped into a number of regional blocks. Some of the early leaders for independence had dreamed of creating a unified nation in some form, but regional rivalries, economic competition, and political divisions soon made that hope, and even more modest versions of it, impossible. Mexico emerged as a short-lived monarchy until a republic was proclaimed in 1823, but its government remained unstable until the 1860s because of military coups, financial failures, foreign intervention, and political turmoil. Central America broke away from the Mexican monarchy and did form a union, but regional antagonisms and resentment of Guatemala, the largest nation in the region, eventually led to dissolution of the union in 1838. Spain's Caribbean colonies, Cuba and Puerto Rico, suppressed early movements for independence and remained outwardly loyal. The Dominican Republic was occupied by its neighbor Haiti, and after resisting its neighbor as well as France and Spain, it finally gained independence in 1844. The Dominican example and the fear of a Haitian-style slave revolt tended to keep the Creole leaders of Cuba and Puerto Rico quiet.

In South America, as mentioned previously, the old colonial viceroyalty of New Granada became the basis for Gran Colombia—the large new state created by Bolívar that included modern Ecuador, Colombia, Panama, and Venezuela. The union, made possible to some extent by Bolívar's personal reputation and leadership, disintegrated as his own standing declined, and it ended in 1830, the year of his death. In the south, the viceroyalty of the Rio de la Plata served as the basis for a desired state that the peoples of Argentina hoped to lead. Other parts of the region resisted these hopes. Paraguay declared and maintained its autonomy under Dr. José Rodríguez de Francia, who ruled his isolated and landlocked country as a dictator until 1840. Modern Uruguay was formed by a revolution for independence against the dominant power of its large neighbors Argentina and Brazil. It became an independent buffer between those two nations in 1828. The Andean nations of Peru and Bolivia, with their large Indian populations and conservative colonial aristocracies, flirted with union from 1829 to 1839 under the mestizo general Andrés Santa Cruz, but once again regional rivalries and the fears of their neighbors undermined the effort. Finally, Chile, somewhat isolated and blessed by the opening of trade in the Pacific, followed its own political course in a relatively stable fashion.

Most attempts at consolidation and union failed. Enormous geographical barriers and great distances separated nations and even regions within nations. Roads were poor and transportation rudimentary. To move goods 200 miles from Guayaquil on the coast to Quito in the Andes was an enormous task, and to send a message from Mexico City to Monterrey, California, took weeks. Geography, regional interests, and political divisions were too strong to overcome. Then too, the colonial heritage, in which the Spanish crown had protected some interests and regions at the expense of others and had left the mass of the population outside the political process, carried over into the new regimes. The problems of national integration were daunting. What is striking is not that Spanish America became 18 separate nations, but that it did not separate into even more.

"CAUDILLOS," POLITICS, AND THE CHURCH

The problems confronting the new nations were many. Over a decade of warfare in places, such as Venezuela, Colombia, and Mexico, had disrupted the economies and devastated wide areas. The mobilization of large armies whose loyalty to regional commanders was often based on their personal qualities, rather than their rank or politics, led to the rise of *caudillos,* independent leaders who dominated local areas by force in defiance of national policies and who sometimes seized the national government itself to impose their concept of rule. In situations of intense division among civilian politicians, a powerful regional commander of the army became the arbiter of power, leading sometimes to a situation of "praetorian politics" in which the army made and unmade governments. Keeping the army in the barracks became a preoccupation of governments, and the amount of money spent on the military in national budgets far exceeded needs.

Military commanders and regional or national caudillos were usually interested in power for their own sake, but they could represent or mobilize different groups in society. Many often defended the interests of regional elites, usually landowners, but others were populists who mobilized and claimed to speak for Indians, peasants, and the poor and sometimes received their unquestioning support. A few, such as the conservative Rafael Carrera, who ruled Guatemala from 1839 to 1865, sincerely took the interest of the Indian majority to heart, but in other matters there was a disregard for the normal workings of an open political system and the rule of law among these personalist leaders.

Other common issues confronted many of the new nations. With the exception of Brazil and briefly Mexico, the political leaders were agreed on the republic as the basic form of government, but what kind of republic? A struggle often developed between centralists—who wished to create strong, centralized national governments with broad powers—and federalists—who wanted policies, especially fiscal and commercial ones, to be set by regional governments. Other tensions developed between liberals and conservatives. Liberals stressed the rights of the individual and attacked the corporate (membership in a group or organization) structure of colonial society. They dreamed of a secular society and looked to the models of the United States or France. Often they wanted a decentralized or federalist form of government. Conservatives usually believed in a strong centralized state, and they often wished to maintain aspects of colonial society. They believed that a structure in which corporate groups (such as the Indians), artisan guilds, or institutions (such as the Church) provided the most equitable basis of social action should be recognized in law. Rather than a society based on open competition and individualism, society for the conservatives was organic—each group was linked to the other like parts of a body whose health depended on the proper functioning of each part. Not all conservatives resisted change, and some—such as the Mexican intellectual and politician, Lucas Alamán—were among the most "enlightened" leaders in terms of economic and commercial reforms, but as a group the conservatives were skeptical of secularism and individualism and strove to keep the Catholic Iberian heritage alive.

The role of the Church became a crucial issue in politics. The secularization of society and the role of the Church was a key matter that divided pro-clerical conservatives from the more secular liberals. In Mexico, for example, the Church had played a major role in education, the economy, and politics. Few questioned its dogma, but liberals sought to limit its role in civil life. The Church fought back with the aid of its pro-clerical supporters and with the power of the Papacy, which until the 1840s refused to fill vacant positions in the hierarchy or to cooperate with the new governments.

Political parties, often calling themselves Liberal or Conservative, sprang up throughout Latin America. They struggled for power and sought to impose their vision of the future on society. Their leadership, however, was usually drawn from the same social class of landowners and urban bourgeoisie with little to differentiate them except their position in the Church or on the question of federalism vs. centralization. The general population might be mobilized by the force and personality of a particular leader such as Juan Manuel de Rosas in Argentina or Antonio López de Santa Anna in Mexico, but political ideology was rarely an issue for most of the population.

The result was political turmoil and insecurity in much of Latin America in the first 50 years following independence. Presidents came and went with sad rapidity. Written constitutions, which both Liberals and Conservatives thought were a positive thing, were often short-lived and overturned with a change in government because the margin for interpretation of the constitution was slight. To some extent this was due to the Roman legal heritage that pervaded Hispanic law and emphasized written laws rather than the more interpretative common-law tradition. Great efforts were made to make constitutions precise, specific, and definitive, but this resulted in an attempt to change or at least modify the constitution each time there was a change in government. Some nations avoided the worst aspects of instability. Chile, after enacting a constitution in 1833 that gave the president broad powers, established a functioning political system that allowed for compromise. Brazil with its monarchical rule, despite a period of turmoil from 1832 to 1850, was able to maintain a political system of compromise, although it was dominated by the Conservatives who were favored by the emperor. Its 1824 constitution remained in force until 1889.

It is fair to say that in much of Latin America the basic questions of government and society remained unresolved after independence. Some observers attributed these problems to personalism, a lack of civic responsibility, and other defects in the "Latin" character. Nevertheless, the parallel experience of later emerging nations in the 20th century suggests that these problems were typical of former colonial dependencies searching for order and economic security in a world in which their options were constrained by their own potential and by external conditions.

LATIN-AMERICAN ECONOMIES AND WORLD MARKETS, 1820–1870

The former colonies of Spain and Portugal now entered the world of diplomatic relations and international commerce. The new nations sought diplomatic recognition and security. In the 1820s, while Europe was undergoing the post-Napoleonic conservative reaction and monarchies were being restored, various plans to help Spain recolonize Latin America were put forward. Great Britain, however, generally opposed these ideas, and since Great Britain was the dominant power at sea, its recognition of Latin-American sovereignty was crucial. Moreover, the newly independent United States also felt an affinity and sympathy for the new nations to the south. The Monroe Doctrine of 1823 stated clearly that any attempt of a European power to colonize in the Americas would be considered an unfriendly act by the United States. The United States at the time probably could have done little to prevent such actions, but Britain could, and its support of Latin-American independence provided needed protection.

There was a price for this support. During the turmoil of the 1820s, British foreign minister Lord Canning had once said, "Spanish America is free and if we do not mismanage our affairs sadly, she is English." He was referring to the broad economic and commercial advantages that the new nations offered. British commerce had penetrated the area in the 18th century when various concessions for trade had been won from the Spanish government, and Britain had profited from illegal trade as well. Now it could afford to offer its diplomatic recognition in exchange for the freedom to trade with the new nations. While little capital was directly invested in Latin America prior to 1850, Latin-American governments turned to foreign governments and banks for loans. Meanwhile, Britain became a major consumer of Latin-American products. In return Britain sold about £5 million of manufactured goods to the new nations each year, about half of which went to Brazil where British merchants were especially strong. While some historians argue that this was a rather small portion of Britain's overseas trade, it was crucial for Latin America. In some ways Britain replaced Spain as a dominant economic force over the area in a sort of neocolonial commercial system. Although other nations, notably France and the United States, also traded with Latin America, prior to 1860 Britain remained predominant.

Open ports and the influx of foreign goods, often of better quality and cheaper than local products, benefited the port cities that controlled customhouses and the large landowners whose hides, sugar, and other products were exported. But these policies tended to damage local industries or regions that had specialized in producing for internal markets. Little capital was available for investment in local industries, and often the governments controlled by liberal free traders or conservative landowners refused or were unable to impose tariffs on imports needed to protect or stimulate local industry. Latin America became increasingly dependent on foreign markets and foreign imports, and as it did, it reinforced the old colonial economic heritage in which land was the basis of wealth and prestige.

MID-CENTURY STAGNATION

From about 1820 to 1850 the economy of Latin America was stagnant. Its mining sector was slow to recover after the wars of independence, its transportation network and port facilities were still underdeveloped, and it lacked capital for investment or found that so much capital was tied up in land that it was unavailable for investment in industry. Only Cuba with its booming sugar economy experienced expansion, but Cuba was still a colony of Spain. After 1850, however, this situation began to change as the expansion of the European economy created new demands for Latin-American products. Coffee cultivation in Brazil, hides and beef in Argentina, and minerals and grains in Chile provided the basis of growth and allowed some Latin-American governments to address social issues. Peru, for example, exploited enormous guano (bird droppings) deposits on islands off its coast. Between 1850 and 1880, exports of this fertilizer earned Peru over £10 million, and this income allowed the government to end Indian tribute and to abolish slavery by compensating the owners. Latin-American cities began to grow and provide good internal markets, and the introduction of steamships and railroads began to overcome the old problems of transportation. By the 1840s steamship lines improved communications within countries and opened up new possibilities for international commerce, and by the 1860s railroads were being constructed, usually to link export-producing regions to the ports. Landed wealth and exports continued to characterize the economies of the region as they had in the colonial era, and as the levels of exports and the governments' dependence on them increased, the vulnerability of Latin America to the vagaries of the world economy increased as well.

Without detailing all the complex changes within the Latin-American nations during the 19th century, a few general patterns can be discerned. After the turmoil of independence, a number of Liberal reformers attempted to institute a series of programs in the 1820s and 1830s intended to break the patterns of the colonial heritage and to follow the main social and economic trends of western Europe. These ideas were often imposed on societies and economies unprepared for drastic change, especially since the strength of opposing institutions, such as the Church and the army, remained intact. By the 1840s Conservatives had returned to power in many places to slow or stop the reform measures. Some of them attempted to speak for the lower classes or Indians, who wished to see the paternal aspects of the old colonial state reimposed to protect them from the reforms of the liberals. In some ways, an alliance

The drive for progress made Latin-American nations anxious to accept foreign investment. Railroads were important for economic growth in that they often linked key exports to the ports and were designed principally to serve the needs of foreign capital.

between the landowners and the peasantry emerged in opposition to the changes suggested by the middle class and urban "modernizers."

ECONOMIC RESURGENCE AND LIBERAL POLITICS

By the last quarter of the century, as the world economy entered into a phase of rapid expansion, there was a shift in attitude and possibilities in Latin America. Liberals returned to power in many places in Latin America and initiated a series of changes that began to transform their nations. The ideological basis of the new liberal surge was also changing. Based on the ideas of *positivism* of the French philosopher Auguste Comte, who stressed observation and a scientific approach to the problems of society, Latin-American politicians and intellectuals found a guiding set of principles and a justification of their quest for political stability and economic growth.

This shift was due in large part to the general economic expansion of the "second" Industrial Revolution and the age of imperialism. The application of science to industry created new demands for Latin-American products, such as copper and rubber, to accompany the increasing demand for its consumer products such as wheat, sugar, and coffee. The population of Latin America doubled to over 43 million inhabitants in the 60 years between 1820 and 1880. After 1850 economies grew rapidly. Timing, of course, varied greatly but the expansion of exports in places, such as Colombia, Argentina, and Brazil, stimulated prosperity for some and a general belief in the advantages of the Liberal programs. The desire to participate in the capitalist expansion of the Western economy dominated the thinking of Latin-American leaders. Foreign entrepreneurs and bankers joined hands with philosophical liberals, landowners, and urban merchants in Latin America to back the Liberal programs, which now became possible because of the increased revenues generated by exports.

The leaders of the post-1860 governments were a new generation of politicians who had matured, not in the age of independence, but during the chaotic years of postindependence politics. Their inspiration came from England, France, and the United States. They were firm believers in progress, education, and free competition within a secular society, but they were sometimes distrustful of the mass of their own people, who seemed to represent an ancient "barbarism" in contrast to the "civilization" of progress. That distrust and their sometimes insensitive application of foreign models to a very different reality in their own countries—what one Brazilian author has called "ideas out of place"—prevented many from achieving the progress they so ardently desired.

Economic growth and "progress" were costly. Responding to international demand, landowners increased their holdings, often aided by the governments they controlled or influenced. Peasant lands were expropriated in Chile, Peru, and Bolivia; small farmers were displaced in Brazil and Costa Rica; and Church lands were seized in Mexico. Labor was needed. Immigrants from Europe flooded into Argentina and Brazil, while in other countries new forms of tenancy, peonage, and disguised servitude developed.

DOCUMENT

CONFRONTING THE HISPANIC HERITAGE: FROM INDEPENDENCE TO CONSOLIDATION

Simón Bolívar (1783–1830) "The Liberator" was a man of determination and perception. His campaigns for independence were defeated on a number of occasions, yet he did not despair. In 1815 while in exile on the island of Jamaica, he penned a letter to a newspaper that gave his evaluation of Latin America's situation and his vision for the future for its various parts. He advocated a republican form of government and rejected monarchy, but he warned against federalism and against popular democracies that might lead to dictatorships. "As long as our countrymen do not acquire the abilities and political virtues that distinguish our brothers to the north, wholly popular systems, far from working to our advantage, will, I greatly fear, bring about our downfall." Spain had left America unprepared, and in this letter Bolívar summarized many of the complaints of Latin Americans against Spanish rule and underlined the difficulty of the tasks of liberation—political, social, and economic. The famous "Letter of Jamaica" is one of the most candid writings by a leader of Latin-American independence. The following excerpts suggest its tone and content.

"BOLÍVAR'S JAMAICA LETTER" (1815)

We are a young people. We inhabit a world apart, separated by broad seas. We are young in the ways of almost all the arts and sciences, although, in a certain manner, we are old in the ways of civilized society. I look upon the present state of America as similar to that of Rome after its fall. Each part of Rome adopted a political system conforming to its interest and situation or was led by the individual ambitions of certain chiefs, dynasties, or associations. But this important difference exists: those dispersed parts later reestablished their ancient nations, subject to the changes imposed by circumstances or events. But we scarcely retain a vestige of what once was; we are, moreover, neither Indian nor European, but a species midway between the legitimate proprietors of this country and the Spanish usurpers. In short, although Americans by birth we derive our rights from Europe, and we have to assert these rights against the rights of the natives, and at the same time we must defend ourselves against the invaders. This places us in a most extraordinary and involved situation. . . .

The role of the inhabitants of the American hemisphere has for centuries been purely passive. Politically they were nonexistent. We are still in a position lower than slavery, and therefore it is more difficult for us to rise to the enjoyment of freedom. . . . States are slaves because of either the nature or the misuse of their constitutions; a people is therefore enslaved when the government, by its nature or its vices infringes on and usurps the rights of the citizen or subject. Applying these principles, we find that America was denied not only its freedom but even an active and effective tyranny. . . .

We have been harassed by a conduct which has not only deprived us of our rights but has kept us in a sort of permanent infancy with regard to public affairs. If we could have at least managed our domestic affairs and our internal administration, we could have acquainted ourselves with the processes and mechanics of public affairs. We should also have enjoyed a personal consideration, thereby commanding a certain unconscious respect from the people, which is so necessary to preserve amidst revolutions. That is why I say we have even been deprived of an active tyranny, since we have not been permitted to exercise its functions.

Americans today, and perhaps to a greater extent than ever before, who live within the Spanish system occupy a position in society no better than that of serfs destined to labor, or at best they have no more status than that of mere consumers. Yet even this status is surrounded with galling restrictions, such as being forbidden to grow European crops, or to store products which are royal monopolies, or to establish factories of a type the Peninsula (Spain) itself does not possess. To this add the exclusive trading privileges, even in articles of prime necessity, and the barriers between the American provinces, designed to prevent all exchange of trade, traffic, and understanding. In short, do you wish to know what our future held?—simply the cultivation of the fields of indigo, grain, coffee, sugar cane, cacao, and cotton; cattle raising on the broad plains, hunting wild game in the jungles; digging in the earth to mine its gold—but even these limitations could never satisfy the greed of Spain. So negative was our existence that I can find nothing comparable in any other civilized society. . . .

By mid-century Latin American political leaders were advocating "progress" and seeking to bring Latin America closer to the norms of life set by Europe. For liberals like the Argentine soldier, statesman, and author Domingo F. Sarmiento (1811–1888) his nation's task was to overcome the "barbarism" of rural life and implant the "civilization" of the Europeanized cities. Sarmiento saw in the bands of mounted rural workers, or *gauchos*, and their caudillo leaders an anachronistic way of life that held the nation back. His comparison of the gauchos, to the Berbers of North Africa demonstrates the ancient hostility of "civilized" urban-dwellers to the nomadic way of life. In a way, Sarmiento saw the dictatorship of Juan Manuel de Rosas as a result of the persistence of the gauchos and the manipulation of the lower classes, a sort of living example of what Bolívar had warned against. The following excerpt from Sarmiento's classic *Life in the Argentine Republic in the Days of the Tyrants or Civilization and Barbarism* (1868) demonstrates his admiration for European culture including that of Spain, and his desire it model his nation on it. That such a program might involve economic and cultural dependency did not concern Sarmiento and others like him.

THE SEARCH FOR PROGRESS

Before 1810 two distinct, rival, and incompatible forms of society, two differing kinds of civilization existed in the Argentine Republic: one being Spanish, European, and cultivated, the other barbarous,

American, and almost wholly of native growth. The revolution which occurred in the cities acted only as the cause, the impulse, which set these two distinct forms of national existence face to face, and gave occasion for a contest between them, to be ended, after lasting many years, by the absorption of one into the other.

I have pointed out the normal form of association, or want of association, of the country people, a form worse a thousand times, than that of a nomad tribe. I have described the artificial associations formed in idleness, and the sources of fame among the gauchos—bravery, daring, violence and opposition to regular law, to the civil law, that is, of the city. These phenomena of social organization existed in 1810, and still exist, modified in many points, slowly changing in others, and yet untouched in several more. These foci about which were gathered the brave, ignorant, free, and unemployed peasantry, were found by thousands through the country. The revolution of 1810 carried everywhere commotion and the sound of arms. Public life, previously wanting in this Arabo-Roman society, made its appearance in all the taverns, and the revolutionary movement finally brought about provincial, warlike associations, called *montoneras* [mounted gaucho guerrilla bands] legitimate offspring of the tavern and the field, hostile to the city and to the army of revolutionary patriots. As events succeed each other, we shall see the provincial montoneras headed by their chiefs; the final triumph, in Facundo Quiroga [a caudillo leader], of the country over the cities throughout the land; and by their subjugation in spirit, government, and civilization, the final formation of the central consolidated despotic government of the landed proprietor, Don Juan Manuel de Rosas, who applied the knife of the gaucho to the culture of Buenos Aires, and destroyed the work of centuries—of civilization, law, and liberty. . . .

They [revolutions for independence] were the same throughout America, and sprang from the same source, namely, the progress of European ideas. South America pursued that course because all other nations were pursuing it. Books, events, and the impulses given by these, induced South America to take part in the movement imparted to France by North American demands for liberty, and to Spain by her own and French writers. But what my object requires me to notice, is, that the revolution—except in its external symbolic independence of the king—was interesting and intelligible only to the Argentine cities, but foreign and unmeaning to the rural districts. Books, ideas, municipal spirit, courts, laws, statutes, education, all points of contact and union existing between us and the people of Europe, were to be found in the cities, where there was a basis of organization, incomplete and comparatively evil, perhaps, for the very reason it was incomplete, and had not attained the elevation which it felt itself capable of reaching, but it entered into the revolution with enthusiasm. Outside the cities, the revolution was a problematical affair, and [in] so far [as] shaking off the king's authority was shaking off judicial authority, it was acceptable. The pastoral districts could only regard the question from this point of view. Liberty, responsibility of power, and all the questions which the revolution was to solve, were foreign to their mode of life and to their needs. But they derived this advantage from the revolution, that it tended to confer an object and an occupation upon the excess of vital force, the presence of which among them has been pointed out, and was to add a broader base of union than that to which throughout the country districts the men daily resorted. These Spartan constitutions, that warlike nature hitherto ill-satisfied by the free use of the dagger, that Roman-like idleness which could only be exchanged for the activity of the battle-field, that utter impatience of judicial control, were all to have at last a fit sphere of action in the world. . . .

Its [the caudillo band's] essence was individual action; its exclusive weapon, the horse; its stage, the vast pampas. The Bedouin hordes which in our day disturb the Algerian frontier by their war-cries and depredations, give us an exact idea of the Argentine montonera, which has been made use of by men of sagacity, as well as by noted desperadoes. In Africa, at the present day, there exists the same struggle between civilization and barbarism: the Bedouin band and the montonera are distinguished by the same characters, the same spirit, the same undisciplined strategy. . . .

The only explanation of the montonera is to be discovered in the examination of the society from which it proceeded. Artigas [caudillo leader of the Uruguayan rebels] the scout and outlaw, at war with the authorities of the city, but bought over as provincial commandant and chief of equestrian bands, presents a type reproduced with little change in each provincial commandant who came to be like a partisan leader. Like all civil wars in which deep differences in education, belief, and motives divide the parties engaged in them, the internal warfare of the Argentine Republic was long and obstinate, until one of the elements of the strife was victorious. The Argentine Revolutionary War was twofold: first, a civilized warfare of the cities against Spain; second, a war against the cities on the part of the country chieftains with the view of shaking off all political subjugation and satisfying their hatred of civilization. The cities overcame the Spaniards, and were in their turn overcome by the country districts. This is the explanation of the Argentine Revolution, the first shot of which was fired in 1810, and the last is still to be heard.

Questions: To what extent did the leaders of independence see their problems as a result of their Hispanic heritage? What would have been the reaction of the mass of the population to Sarmiento's idea of progress? Were the leaders naive about Latin America's possibilities for political democracy?

MEXICO: INSTABILITY AND FOREIGN INTERVENTION

After the short monarchical experiment, a Mexican republic was established. Its constitution of 1824, based on the examples of France, the United States, and Spain was a federalist document that guaranteed basic civil rights. Nevertheless, this constitution did not address the nation's continuing social problems and needs: the maldistribution of land, the status of the Indians, the problems of education, and the situation of vast numbers of indigent poor among the approximately seven million people in Mexico, the most populous of the new nations. Politics soon became a complicated struggle between the Conservative centralists and the Liberal federalists and was made even more complicated by the rival jockeying for advantage by commercial agents of Great Britain and the United States. Control by the Conservatives led to some financial and economic improvements under the intelligent and innovative Lucas Alamán, but General Antonio López de Santa Ana staged a coup and then, after being elected president, turned the government over to the Liberals. For a short period from 1832 to 1835, the Liberals, led by Valentin Gómez Farias, were in control and tried to institute a series of sweeping social and economic reforms, but their attack on the Church led to violent reaction and the return of Santa Ana—this time as a defender of the Church.

The mercurial Santa Ana remained until his death the maker of Mexican politics. He was an archetype of the caudillo; the personalist, autocratic leader. But Mexico's instability was not only due to his personality. Santa Ana was merely the symptom of deeper problems.

These in fact were many. Mexico's instability and financial difficulties made it a target for foreign intervention. A Spanish invasion was repulsed in 1829, and a French expedition landed to collect unpaid debts in 1838. More serious, Texas, the vast area of Mexico's northern frontier was increasingly occupied by Anglo-American settlers who brought their language, customs, and religion despite restrictions on the latter. Although the Texans at first sought more autonomy as federalists within the Mexican nation, as had been done in Yucatán and other Mexican provinces, ethnic and religious differences as well as Santa Ana's attempts to suppress the Texans in 1836 led to widespread fighting and the declaration of Texan independence. Santa Ana, captured for a while by the Texans, returned to dominate Mexican politics, but the question of Texas festered and became acute when in 1845 the United States, with its eye on California and moved by "manifest destiny"—a belief that it was destined to rule the continent from coast to coast—voted to annex Texas.

The result was war. A border dispute and the breakdown of negotiations over California led to hostilities in 1846. Santa Ana, who had been in exile, returned to lead the Mexican forces, but United States armies seized California, penetrated northern Mexico, and eventually occupied the Mexican capital. Mexico was forced to sign the disadvantageous Treaty of Guadalupe-Hidalgo (1848) in which the United States acquired about one-half of Mexico's national territory—but less than five percent of its population. The Mexican-American War and the treaty left a bitter legacy of distrust of the northern neighbor, not only in Mexico but throughout the region. For Mexico there was also a serious loss of economic potential, but the heroic battle against the better-equipped Americans produced a sense of nationalism and a desire to confront the nation's serious internal problems, which also bore some responsibility for the war and the defeat.

Politics could not return to the situation before the war. Santa Ana did return to office for a while, more mercurial and despotic than ever, but now he was opposed by a new generation of Liberals: intellectuals, lawyers, and some rural leaders, many of them from middle class backgrounds, some of them mestizos and even a few Indians. Perhaps the most prominent of them was Benito Juárez (1806–1872), a humble Indian who had received a legal education and who had eventually become the governor of his state. He shared the Liberal vision of a secular society based on the rule of law in which the old privileges of the Church and the army would be eliminated as a way of promoting economic change and growth. The Liberal revolt, called *La Reforma*, began in 1854, and within a year the Liberals had taken Mexico City. In a series of laws integrated into a new constitution in 1857, the Liberals set the basis for their vision of society. Military and clerical privileges were curtailed and Church property was placed on sale. Indian communal lands were also restricted, and the government forced the sale of these lands to individuals—it was hoped to Indians. The goal of these programs was to create a nation of small independent farmers. The lands, however, were often bought up by speculators or already wealthy hacendados, and the result, in fact, was that the peasants and Indians lost what land they had. By 1910 about half of Mexico's rural population was landless. Good intentions had brought disastrous results.

The Liberal program produced the expected Conservative reaction. The Church threatened to excommunicate those who upheld the new constitution. Civil war erupted, and in reaction, Juárez, now president, pushed forward even more radical measures, including confiscation of Church properties and the secularization of marriage and burial. Losing ground in the war, the Conservatives turned to Europe and convinced Napoleon III of France to intervene. Attracted by possible economic advantage, dreams of empire, and a desire to please Catholic opinion in France, Napoleon III justified French intervention by claims of a shared "Latin" culture (this was the origin of the term "Latin America"). Under cover of a joint expedition, French forces landed in 1862 and soon took the capital. At French urging Maximilian von Habsburg, an Austrian archduke, was convinced to take the throne of Mexico. Well-intentioned but ineffective, Emperor Maximilian tried to get the support of Juárez and the Liberals and even kept many of the laws of the *Reforma* in place, to the dismay of his Conservative supporters. But Juárez absolutely rejected the idea of a foreign prince ruling Mexico. French bayonets and the United States' preoccupation with its own Civil War allowed Maximilian and his Empress Carlota to rule until 1867. When French troops were withdrawn, however, the regime crumbled. Maximilian and his loyal generals were captured and executed in 1867.

Juárez returned to office, but his administration was increasingly autocratic—a reality that he felt was unavoidable after so long a period of instability. By his death in 1872,

Benito Juárez, an Indian from southern Mexico, rose to the presidency and began a series of sweeping reforms designed to break the old colonial structures. His uncompromising resistance to foreign intervention and monarchy has made him a symbol of Mexican sovereignty and independence. Here he is portrayed in a mural by Diego Rivera.

the force of his personality, his concern for the poor, and his nationalist position against foreign intervention had identified Liberalism with nationalism in Mexico and made Juárez a symbol of the nation. By 1880 Mexico was poised on the edge of a period of strong central government and relative political stability, which under the virtual dictator Porfirio Díaz led to rapid economic growth, penetration of the economy by foreign capital, the expansion of the large landed estates, political repression, and a revolution.

ARGENTINA: THE PORT AND THE NATION

Whereas Mexico and its silver had been the core of Spain's empire in America, the rolling plains, or pampas, of the Rio de la Plata in southern South America had been a colonial backwater until the 18th century when direct trade had begun to stimulate its economy. The Rio de la Plata was dominated by the port of Buenos Aires and its merchants, but the other areas of the region had their own interests and resented the power and growth of the port city and its surrounding countryside. The United Provinces of the Rio de la Plata, which declared their independence in 1816, soon split apart, and local caudillos, able to call on the support of gauchos, dominated each region. In Buenos Aires, the Liberals gained control in the 1820s and under Bernardino Rivadavia (1780–1857), a Europeanized lawyer, instituted a series of broad reforms in education, finance, agriculture, and immigration. These included a program of public land sales that stimulated the growth of cattle ranches and the power of the rancher class.

In many ways the secular and progressive program of Rivadavia in Argentina paralleled the program of Gómez Farias in Mexico and produced a similar negative reaction from Conservatives and the Church, especially when Church lands were confiscated and freedom of religion was legislated. But Rivadavia's main sin was centralism, a desire to create a strong national government. Centralists (called Unitarians in the Argentine context) provoked the reaction of the federalists, who by 1831 had taken power under Juan Manuel de Rosas, who commanded the loyalty of the gaucho employees of the stockmen.

Under Rosas the federalist program of a weak central

Emperor Maximilian was finally captured after his attempt with French help to reestablish a monarchy in Mexico. Well-meaning, he eventually lost the support of the conservatives, and Juárez refused to spare his life, as a warning to other ambitious nations that Mexico would remain independent.

government and local autonomy was instituted, but Rosas's federalism favored the ranchers of the Buenos Aires province and the merchants of the great port. He campaigned against the Indians to the south in order to open new lands to the cattle ranchers. Exports of hides and salted meat increased, but the revenues collected at the port were not shared with the other provinces. Although popular with the gauchos and the urban poor and remembered today as a nationalist who resisted British and French economic pressure, Rosas proved to be a despotic leader, crushing his opponents and forcing people to display his slogan, "Death to the savage, filthy Unitarians." His brand of populist, authoritarian, personalist politics drove Liberal opponents into exile where they plotted his overthrow. Meanwhile his policies continued to favor the ranching and meat exporting interests of Buenos Aires. Eventually, the Liberal exiles joined forces with the caudillos who, while federalists, resented Rosas's brand of federalism that had so favored the Buenos Aires province. In 1852 this coalition defeated Rosas and drove him from power.

There followed a confused decade of rival governments, because the questions of federalism and the role of Buenos Aires within the nation remained unresolved. A new constitution was issued in 1853 under the influence of Juan Bautista Alberdi, an able and progressive journalist who was also a strong believer in the need to encourage immigration. This constitution incorporated the programs of the federalists but guaranteed national unity through the power of the presidency over the provincial governors. By 1862 after considerable fighting, a compromise was worked out and the new, unified nation, now called the Argentine Republic, entered into a period of prosperity and growth under a series of Liberal presidents whose programs paralleled the *Reforma* in Mexico. The age of the Liberals was now in full swing.

Between 1862 and 1890, able and intelligent presidents, such as Bartolomé Mitre (1821–1876) and Domingo F. Sarmiento (1811–1888), initiated a wide series of political reforms and economic measures designed to bring "progress" to Argentina. Sarmiento was an archetype of the liberal reformers of the mid-century. A great admirer of England and the United States, a firm believer in the value of education, and an ardent supporter of "progress," Sarmiento had been a constant opponent of Rosas and had been driven into exile. During that time, he had written *Facundo,* a critique of the caudillo politics of the region, in which the "barbarism" of the gauchos and their leaders was contrasted to the "civilization" of the liberal reformers. (See the document in this chapter.)

Now in power, Sarmiento and the other liberal leaders were able to put their programs into practice. They were aided by a number of factors. Political stability made investment more attractive to foreign banks and merchants. The expansion of the Argentine economy, especially exports of beef, hides, and wool, created the basis for prosperity. Foreign trade in 1890 was five times as great as it had been in 1860. The population tripled to over three million as the agricultural expansion, high wages, and opportunities for mobility attracted large numbers of European immigrants. With increased revenues the government could initiate reforms in education, transportation, and other areas, often turning to foreign models and foreign investors. Then too there was an increased feeling of national unity. A long and bloody war waged by Argentina, Brazil, and Uruguay against their neighbor Paraguay from 1865 to 1870 created a sense of unity and national pride that was previously absent.

That sense was also heightened by the final defeat of the Indians south of Buenos Aires by 1880 as more land was opened to ranching and agriculture. At about the same time as in the United States, the railroad, the telegraph, and the repeating rifle brought an end to Indian resistence and opened their lands to settlement. The Indians, who were pushed far to the south, and the gauchos, whose way of life was displaced by the tide of immigrants, received little sympathy from the Liberal government. By 1890 Argentina seemed to represent the achievement of a Liberal program for Latin America.

THE BRAZILIAN EMPIRE

It was sometimes said that, despite its monarchical form, Brazil was the only functioning republic in South America in the 19th century. At first glance it seemed that Brazil did avoid much of the political instability and turmoil found elsewhere in the continent, and that through the mediation of the emperor a political compromise was worked out. Beneath that facade, however, problems and patterns similar to those in Spanish America were apparent. The transition to nationhood was relatively smooth, and thus the basic foundations of Brazilian society—slavery, large landholdings, and an export economy—remained securely in place, reinforced by a new Brazilian nobility created for the new empire.

Brazilian independence had been declared in 1822, and by 1824 a relatively liberal constitution had been issued by Dom Pedro I, the young Brazilian monarch, although not without resistance from those who wanted a republic or at least a very weak constitutional monarch. But Dom Pedro I was an autocrat, still surrounded by Portuguese courtiers, and when his expansionist policies in the Rio de la Plata and his scandalous personal life began to wear away his

The tremendous boom in the Argentine economy was reflected in the growth of Buenos Aires, the so-called "Paris of the Americas," as a cosmopolitan urban center.

popularity, pressures built up against him. In 1831 he was forced to abdicate in favor of his young son, Pedro (later to become Dom Pedro II), but the boy was too young to rule and a series of regents directed the country in his name. What followed was an experiment in republican government, although the facade of monarchy was maintained.

The next decade was as tumultuous as any in Spanish America. The issues of liberalism vs. conservatism were complicated by the existence of monarchist and antimonarchist factions in Brazil. The centralism of the government in Rio de Janeiro was opposed by the provinces, and a series of regional revolts erupted, some of which took on aspects of social wars as slaves, peasants, and free people of color were mobilized in the fighting. The southernmost province of Brazil, Rio Grande do Sul, attempted to break away and declare its independence over federalist issues. In northeastern Brazil, a strong republican tradition had led to rebellions in 1817 and 1824, and now the region generated a series of revolts against the central government. All of these were suppressed by the imperial government, and the territorial unity of Brazil remained intact. By 1840, however, the politicians were willing to see the young Dom Pedro II begin to rule in his own name.

Meanwhile, Brazil had been undergoing an economic transformation brought about by a new export crop, coffee. Brazil had long been an exporter of minerals and agricultural products, a position reinforced by the trade agreements made with Great Britain in the 19th century. Coffee provided a new basis for agricultural expansion in southern Brazil. In the provinces of Rio de Janeiro and then São Paulo, coffee estates, or *fazendas,* began to spread toward the interior as new lands were opened. By 1840 coffee made up over 40 percent of Brazil's exports, and by 1880 that figure reached 60 percent.

Along with the expansion of coffee growing came an intensification of slavery, Brazil's primary form of labor. For a variety of humanitarian and economic reasons Great Britain pressured Brazil to end the slave trade from Africa during the 19th century, but the slave trade continued on an enormous scale up to 1850. Over 1.4 million Africans were imported in the last 50 years of the trade, and even after the trans-Atlantic slave trade ended, slavery continued. At mid-century about one-fourth of Brazil's population were still enslaved. While some reformers were in favor of ending slavery, a real abolitionist movement did not develop in Brazil until after 1870. Brazil did not finally abolish slavery until 1888.

As in the rest of Latin America, the years after 1850 witnessed considerable growth and prosperity in Brazil. Dom Pedro II proved to be an enlightened man of rather bourgeois middle-class habits who was anxious to reign over a tranquil and progressive nation, even if that tranquility was based on slave labor. Dom Pedro II favored the Conservatives in his appointment of ministers, but Liberals were given enough access to government to avoid direct confrontations. The trappings of a monarchy, a court, and noble titles kept the elite attached to the regime. Meanwhile railroads, steamships, and the telegraph began to change the nature of communication and transportation. Foreign companies invested in these projects as well as in banking and other activities. In growing cities like Rio de Janeiro and São Paulo merchants, lawyers, and a middle and urban working class began to exert pressure on the government. Less wedded to landholding and to slavery, these new groups were a catalyst for change, even though the right to vote was still very limited. Moreover, the nature of the labor force was changing.

After 1850 a tide of immigrants, mostly from Italy and Portugal, began to reach Brazil's shores, increasingly attracted by government immigration schemes. Between 1850 and 1875 over 300,000 immigrants arrived in Brazil and over two-thirds of them went to work in the coffee trees of southern Brazil. Their presence lessened the dependence on slavery, and by 1870 the abolitionist movement was gaining strength. A series of laws freeing children and the aged, the sympathy of Dom Pedro II himself, the agitation by abolitionists (both black and white), and the efforts of the slaves (who began to overtly resist and run away in large numbers) brought in 1888 an end to slavery in Brazil, the last nation in the Western Hemisphere to abolish it.

The Brazilian monarchy rested on the support of the planter aristocracy, but after 1870 their commitment and that of other groups began to wither. The long war of the Triple Alliance against Paraguay (1865–1870) had become unpopular, and the military began to take an active role in politics. Squabbles with the Church undercut support from the clergy. The planters now turned increasingly to immigrants for their laborers, and some began to modernize their operations. The ideas of positivism, a modernizing philosophy that sought to bring about material progress through the application of scientific principles to government and society, attracted many intellectuals and key members of the army. Politically, a Republican party, formed in 1871, began to gather support in urban areas from a wide spectrum of the population. The Brazilian monarchy could not survive the abolition of slavery. In 1889 a virtually bloodless military coup deposed the emperor and established a republic under military men strongly influenced by positivist intellectuals and Republican politicians.

SOCIETIES IN SEARCH OF THEMSELVES

As colonial subjects of Spain and Portugal, the elites of Latin America had shared the culture and values of Europe. Recognition of that shared experience continued among the upper classes who still looked to Europe for their inspiration, but political independence also provoked feelings of Americanism and at least a partial separation from, and rejection of, the old forms. Many times, however, this was simply a denial of the Hispanic traditions associated with the old colonial status and an acceptance of English and French models that seemed to represent the new age.

CULTURAL LIFE AND POLITICS

In Latin America, there was little separation between intellectual life and politics. The *pensador,* or thinker, who might write poetry, history, essays, and novels and combine that activity with political action, public office, and military command, was a common and highly respected figure.

The end of colonial rule opened up Latin America to direct influences from the rest of Europe. Scientific observers, travelers, and the just plain curious often accompanied by artists came to see and record, and while doing so introduced new ideas and fashions. Artistic and cultural missions were sometimes brought directly from Europe by Latin-American governments.

The tastes and fashions of Europe were adopted by the elite in the new nations. The battles and triumphs of independence were celebrated in paintings, hymns, odes, and theatrical pieces in the neoclassical style in an attempt to use Greece and Rome as a model for the present. In this Latin Americans followed the lead of Europe, especially France. The same neoclassical tradition was also apparent in the architecture of the early 19th century.

In the 1830s the generation that came of age after independence turned to romanticism and found the basis of a new nationality in historical images, the Indian, and local customs. This generation often had a romantic view of "liberty." They emphasized the exotic as well as the distinctive aspects of American society. In Brazil, for example, the poet Antônio Gonçalves Dias (1823–1864) used the Indian as a symbol of Brazil and America. In Cuba, novels sympathetic to slaves began to appear by mid-century. In Argentina, writers celebrated the pampas and its lonely open spaces. Sarmiento's critical account of the caudillos in *Facundo* described in depth the life of the gauchos, but it was José Hernández who wrote *Martin Fierro* in 1872, a romantic epic poem about the end of the way of the gaucho. Historical themes and the writing of history itself became a political act, because the analysis of the past became a way of setting out a proper program for the present. Many of Latin America's leading politicians were also excellent historians—Mitre in Argentina, Alamán in

Mexico, and a remarkable group of liberal Chilean historians deeply influenced by positivism.

By the 1870s a new realism emerged in the arts and literature more in line with the scientific approach of positivism and the modernization of the new nations. As the economies of Latin America surged forward, novelists appeared who were unafraid to deal with human frailties such as corruption, prejudice, and greed. The Chilean Alberto Blest Gana and the Brazilian mulatto J. Machado de Assis (1839–1908) wrote critically about the social mores of their countries during this era.

Throughout the century, the culture of the mass of the population had been little affected by the trends and taste of the elite. Popular arts, folk music, and dance flourished in traditional settings, demonstrating a vitality and adaptability to new situations that was often lacking in the more imitative fine arts. Sometimes authors in the romantic tradition or poets like Hernández turned to themes for their subject and inspiration, and in that way increasingly brought these traditions to the attention of their class and of the world. For the most part, however, popular artistic expressions were not appreciated or valued by the traditional elites, by the modernizing urban bourgeoisie, or by the newly arrived immigrants.

Machado de Assiz (1839–1908) was a gifted African-Brazilian author of humble origins whose psychological short stories and novels won him acclaim as Brazil's greatest novelist of the 19th century.

GENDER, CLASS, AND RACE

While significant political changes make it appealing to deal with the 19th century as an era of great change and transformation in Latin America, it is necessary to recognize the persistence of old patterns and sometimes their reinforcement. Changes took place to be sure, but their effects were not felt equally by all classes or groups in society, nor were all groups attracted by the promises of the new political regimes and their views of progress.

Women, for example, gained little ground during most of the century. They had participated actively in the independence movements. Some had taken up arms or aided the insurgent forces, and some—such as the Colombian Policarpa (La Pola) Salvatierra, whose final words were "Do not forget my example"—had paid for their activities on the gallows. Following independence, there was virtually no change in the predominant attitudes toward women's proper role. Expected to be wives and mothers, women could not vote, hold public office, become lawyers, or, in some places, testify in a court of law. While there were a few exceptions, unmarried women less than 25 years of age remained under the power and authority of their fathers. Once married they could not work, enter into contracts, or control their own estates without permission of their husbands. As in the colonial era, marriage, politics, and the creation of kinship links were essential elements in elite control of land and political power, and thus women remained a crucial resource in family strategies.

Lower-class women had more economic freedom—often controlling local marketing—and also more personal freedom than elite women under the constraints of powerful families. In legal terms, however, their situation was no better—and in material terms, much worse—than their elite sisters. Still, women were by the 1870s an important part of the work force.

The one area in which the situation of women began to change significantly was in public education. There had already been a movement in this direction in the colonial era; at first the idea behind it was that since women were responsible for the education of their children, they should be educated so that the proper values could be passed to the next generation. By 1842 Mexico City required girls and boys of age 7 to 15 to attend school, and in 1869 the first girls' school was created in Mexico. Liberals in Mexico wanted secular public education to prepare women for an enlightened role within the home, and similar sentiments were expressed by liberal regimes elsewhere. Public schools appeared throughout Latin America, although their impact was limited. Brazil, for example, had a population of 10 million in 1873 but only about one million men and half that number of women were literate.

The rise of secular public education created new opportunities for women. The demand for teachers at the primary level created the need for schools in which to train teachers. Since most teachers were women, these teacher training schools provided women access to advanced education; and while the curriculum often emphasized traditional female roles, an increasing number of educated women began to emerge who were dissatisfied with the legal and social constraints on their lives. By the end of the 19th century these women were becoming increasingly active in advocating womens' rights and other political issues.

The new nations, in most cases, legally ended the old "society of castes" in which legal status and definition depended on color and ethnicity, but in reality much of that system continued. The stigma of skin color and former slave status created barriers to advancement. Indians in Mexico, Bolivia, and Peru often continued to labor under poor conditions and to suffer the effects of government failures. There was conflict. In Yucatán, a great rebellion broke out, pitting the Maya against the central government and the whites, in 1839 and then again in 1847. It smoldered for ten years. Despite the intentions of governments, Indians proved resistant to changes imposed from outside their communities and willing to defend their traditional ways. The word "Indian" was still an insult in most places in Latin America. For some mestizos and others of mixed origin, the century presented opportunities for advancement in the army, professions, and commerce, but these cases were exceptions.

In many places expansion of the export economy resulted in a continuation and intensification of old patterns. Liberalism itself changed during the century, and once its program of secularization, rationalism, and rights of property were implanted as law, it displayed a more restrictive nature. Positivists of the end of the century still hoped for economic growth, but some were willing to gain it at the expense of individual freedoms. The motto, "Order and Progress," chosen for the flag of the Brazilian republic reflected that willingness. The positivists were generally convinced of the benefits of international trade for Latin America, and large landholdings increased in many areas at the expense of small farms or Indian communal lands as a result. A small, white Creole, landed upper class controlled the economies and politics in most places and they were sometimes joined in the political and economic functions by a strata of urban middle class merchants, bureaucrats, and other bourgeois types. The landed and mercantile elite tended to merge over time to create one group that, in most places, controlled the government. Meanwhile, there were new social forces at work. The flood of immigration, beginning in earnest in the 1870s, to Argentina, Brazil, and a few other nations began to alter the social composition of those places. Increasingly, rapid urbanization also changed the nature of these societies. Still, Latin America, though politically independent, began the 1880s as a group of predominantly agrarian nations with rigid social structures and a continuing dependency on the world market.

ANALYSIS
EXPLAINING UNDERDEVELOPMENT

Whether we use the word *underdeveloped*, the more benign *developing*, or the old-fashioned *backward*, it is usually clear that the term describes a large number of nations in the world that seem to be beset by a series of economic and social problems. Because Latin America was the first part of what we now call the Third World to establish its independence and begin to compete within the world economy, it had to confront the reasons for its relative position and problems quite early and without many alternative models to follow. The documents included in this chapter offer two visions of Latin America's early problems that are similar because both emphasize the Hispanic cultural heritage, as well as its supposed deficiencies or strengths, as a key explanation for the region's history. Such cultural explanations were popular among 19th-century intellectuals and political leaders, and they continue today, though other general theories based on economics and politics have become more popular.

At the time of Latin-American independence the adoption of European models of economy, government, and law seemed to offer great hope. But as "progress," republican forms of government, free trade, and liberalism failed to bring about general prosperity and social harmony, Latin Americans and others began to search for alternative explanations of their continuing problems as a first step in resolving them. Some critics condemned the Hispanic cultural legacy; others saw the materialism of the modern world as the major problem and called for a return to religion and idealism. By the 20th century, Marxism provided a powerful analysis of Latin America's history and present reality—though Marxists themselves could not decide if Latin-American societies were essentially feudal and needed first to become capitalist, or if they were already capitalist and ready for socialist revolution.

Throughout these discussions and debates Latin Americans often implicitly compared their situation to that of the United States and tried to explain the different economic positions of the two regions. At the beginning of the 19th century both regions were still primarily agricultural, and while a few places in North America were starting small industries, the mining sector in Latin America was far stronger than that of its northern neighbor. In 1850 Latin America had a population of 33 million in comparison to 23 million in the United States, and the per capita income in both regions was roughly equal; by 1940, however, Latin America's population was much larger, and its economic situation far worse than in the United States. Why and how this disparity arose preoccupied observers. Was there some flaw in the Latin-American character, or were the explanations to be found in the economic and political differences of the two areas and how could these differences be explained? The answers to these questions were not easy to obtain, but increasingly they were sought not in the history of individual countries but in analyses of a world economic and political system.

While there had long been a Marxist critique of colonialism and imperialism, the modern Latin-American analysis of underdevelopment grew from different origins. During the 1950s, a number of European and North American scholars developed the concept of "modernization," or "Westernization." Basing their ideas on the historical experience of Western Europe, they believed that development was a matter of increasing per capita production in any society, and that as development took place various kinds of social changes would follow. The more industrialized, urban, and modern a society became, the more social change and improvement were possible as traditional patterns and attitudes were abandoned or transformed. Technology, communications, and the diffusion of material goods were the means by which the transformation would take place. Some scholars also believed that as this process occurred, there would be a natural movement toward more democratic forms of government and popular participation.

Modernization theory held out the promise that any society could move toward a brighter future by essentially following the path taken earlier by Western Europe. Its message was one of improvement through gradual rather than radical or revolutionary change, and thus it tended to be politically conservative. It also tended to disregard cultural differences, internal class conflicts, and struggles for power within nations. Moreover, it was sometimes adopted by military regimes that believed, that by imposing order, they could best promote the economic changes necessary for modernization.

The proponents of modernization theory had a difficult time convincing many people in the "underdeveloped" world, where the historical experience had been considerably different from that of western Europe. In 19th century Latin America, for example, early attempts to develop industry had been faced with competition from the cheaper and better products of already industrialized nations such as England and France, and so a similar path to development was impossible. Critics argued that each nation did not operate individually, but was part of a world system that operated to keep some areas "developed" at the expense of others.

These ideas were first and most cogently expressed in Latin America. After World War II, the United Nations established an Economic Commission for Latin America (ECLA). Under the leadership of the Argentine economist Raul Prebisch, the ECLA began to analyze the Latin-American economies. Prebisch argued that "unequal exchange" between the developed nations at the center of the world economy and those like Latin America created structural blocks to economic growth. The ECLA suggested various policies to overcome the problems, especially the development of industries that would overcome the region's dependence on foreign imports.

From the structural analysis of the ECLA and from more traditional Marxist critiques, a new kind of explanation, usually called *dependency theory*, began to emerge in the 1960s. Rather than seeing underdevelopment or the lack of economic growth as the result of failed modernization, some scholars in Latin America began to argue that development and underdevelopment were not stages but part of the same process. They believed that the development and growth of some areas, such as Western Europe and the United States, were achieved at the expense of, or because of, the underdevelopment of dependent regions such as Latin America. Agricultural economies at the periphery of the world economic system were always at a disadvantage in dealing with the industrial nations of the center, and would thus become relatively poorer as the industrial nations got richer. The industrial nations would continually draw products, profits, and cheap labor from the periphery. This basic economic relationship of dependency meant that production, capital accumulation, and class relations in a dependent country were all essentially determined by external forces. Some theorists went even further and argued that Latin America and other nations of the Third World were also culturally dependent in their consumption of ideas and concepts. Both modernization theory and Mickey Mouse were seen as the agents of a cultural domination that was simply an extension of economic reality. These theorists usually argued that socialism was the only hope to break out of the dependency relationship.

These ideas, which dominated Latin-American intellectual life, were broadly appealing to other areas of Asia and Africa that had recently emerged from colonial control. Forms of dependency analysis became popular in many areas of the world in the 1960s and 1970s. By the 1980s, however, dependency theory was loosing its appeal. As an explanation of what had happened historically in Latin America, it was useful; but as a theory that could predict what might happen elsewhere and what to do, it provided little help. Marxists argued that it overemphasized the circulation of goods (trade) rather than how things were produced and that it ignored the class conflicts they felt were the motor force of history. Moreover, with the rise of multinational corporations the nature of capitalism itself was changing, and thus an analysis based on trade relationships between countries became somewhat outdated.

Whether development can be widely diffused as modernization theory argued or whether the underdevelopment of some countries is inherent in the nature of the capitalist world economy as the dependency theorists believe, is still a matter of dispute, but recent events in Eastern Europe have thrown the socialist alternative into question as well. A search for new explanations and new solutions to the problems of development will characterize the decade of the 1990s as peoples throughout the world seek to improve their lives.

Questions: In what sense was 19th-century Latin America a dependent economy? Which explanation or prediction about dependency best fits world economic trends today?

THE GREAT BOOM, 1880–1920

Between 1880 and 1920 Latin America, like certain areas of Asia and Africa, experienced a tremendous spurt of economic growth, stimulated by the increasing demand in industrializing Europe and the United States for raw materials, foodstuffs, and specialized tropical crops. Latin America was well prepared for this export-led economic expansion. The Liberal ideology of individual freedoms, an open market, and limited government intervention in the operation of the economy had triumphed in many places. Whereas this ideology had been the expression of the middle class in Europe, in Latin America it was adopted not only by the small urban middle sectors of lawyers, retailers, bureaucrats, and professionals, but also by the large landowners, miners, and export merchants linked to the rural economy and the traditional patterns of wealth and landowning. In a number of countries a political alliance was forged between the traditional aristocracy of wealth and the new urban elements. Together they controlled the presidential offices and the congresses and imposed a business-as-usual approach to government at the expense of peasants and a newly emerging working class.

The expansion of Latin American economies was led by exports. Each nation had a specialty: bananas and coffee from Central America; tobacco and sugar from Cuba; rubber and coffee from Brazil; henequen (a fiber for making rope), copper, and silver from Mexico; wool, wheat, and beef from Argentina; and copper from Chile. In this era of strong demand and good prices these nations experienced high profits. This allowed for the import of large quantities of foreign manufactures, and it provided funds for the beautification of cities and other government projects. But export-led expansion was always risky because the world-market prices of Latin-American commodities were ultimately determined by conditions outside the region. In that sense, these economies were particularly vulnerable and in some ways dependent.

The expansion of Latin-American trade was remarkable. It increased by about 50 percent between 1870 and 1890. Argentina's trade was increasing at about 5 percent a year in this period, one of the highest rates of growth ever recorded for a national economy. "As wealthy as an Argentine," became an expression in Paris, reflecting the fortunes that wool, beef, and grain were earning for some in Argentina. In Mexico an "oligarchic dictatorship," which maintained all the outward attributes of democracy but imposed "law and order" under the dictator Porfirio Díaz, created the conditions for unrestrained profits. Mexican exports doubled between 1877 and 1900. Similar figures could be cited for Chile, Costa Rica, and Bolivia.

This rapidly expanding commerce attracted the interest of foreign investors anxious for high returns on their capital. British, French, German, and North American businessmen and entrepreneurs invested in mining, railroads, public utilities, and banking. Over half the foreign investments in Latin America were British, which alone increased to over £750 million by 1913, or to ten times as much as had been invested in 1870. But British leadership was no longer uncontested; Germany and increasingly the United States provided competition. The United States was particularly active in the Caribbean region and Mexico, but not until after World War I would United States capital predominate in the region.

Foreign investments provided Latin America with needed capital and services, but tended to place key industries, transportation facilities, and services in foreign hands. These were thus vulnerable to external influences and decisions. Foreign investments also constrained Latin-American governments in the social, commercial, and diplomatic policies which they could follow.

MEXICO AND ARGENTINA

We can use these two large Latin-American nations as examples of different responses within the same general pattern. In Mexico the Liberal triumph of Juárez had set the stage for economic growth and constitutional government. In 1876 Porfirio Díaz, one of Juárez's generals, was elected president and for the next 35 years he dominated politics either as president or as the power behind the scenes. Díaz suppressed regional rebellions and imposed a strong centralized government. Using foreign capital, the railroad system grew rapidly, providing a new way of integrating Mexican regional economies, moving goods to the ports for export, and allowing the movement of government troops to keep order. Industrialization began to take place. Foreign investment was encouraged in mining, transportation, and other sectors of the economy, and financial policies were changed to promote investments. United States investments, for example, expanded from about 30 million pesos in 1883 to over 1 billion by 1911.

The forms of Liberal democracy were maintained but were subverted in order to keep Díaz in power and to give his development plans an open track. Behind these policies were a number of Díaz's advisors, who were strongly influenced by positivist ideas and who wished to impose a scientific approach on the national economy. These *cientificos* set the tone for Mexico while the government suppressed any political opposition to these policies. Diaz's Mexico projected an image of modernization led by a Europeanized elite who greatly profited from the economic growth and the imposition of order under Don Porfirio.

Growth was often bought at the expense of Mexico's large rural peasantry and its growing urban and working classes. This population was essentially native, since unlike in Argentina and Brazil few immigrants came to Mexico. They participated very little in the prosperity of export-led growth. The expansion of henequen production in Yucatán displaced peasants, and their attempts at resistence led to arrests and deportation as convict laborers to Cuba. Indian rebellions in the north were similarly crushed. In Morelos in central Mexico, modernization of sugar production with the use of steam-powered mills increased the capacity of the haciendas. Their expansion at the expense of peasants and Indian communal lands created a volatile situation.

Strikes and labor unrest increased, particularly among railroad workers, miners, and textile workers. An especially violent strike took place at the American-owned Cananea Copper mines from 1906 to 1908. In the countryside a national police force, the *Rurales*, maintained order and the army was mobilized when needed. At the regional level political bosses linked to the Díaz regime in Mexico City delivered the votes in rigged elections.

For 35 years Díaz reigned supreme and oversaw the transformation of the Mexican economy. His opponents were arrested or driven into exile while the small middle class, the landowners, miners, and foreign investors celebrated the progress of Mexico. In 1910, however, a middle-class movement with limited political goals seeking electoral reform began to mushroom into a more general uprising in which the frustrations of the poor, the workers, the peasants, and nationalist intellectuals of various political persuasions erupted in a bloody ten-year civil war, the Mexican Revolution.

At the other end of the hemisphere Argentina followed an alternate path of economic expansion. By 1880 the Indians on the southern pampa had finally been conquered and vast new tracts of land opened to ranching. The strange relationship between Buenos Aires and the rest of the nation had finally been resolved when Buenos Aires had been made a federal district. With a rapidly expanding economy it became "the Paris of South America," an expression that reflected the drive by wealthy Argentines to establish their credentials as a modern nation. By 1914 Buenos Aires had over two million inhabitants, or about one-fourth of the national population. Its political leaders, the "Generation of 1880," were the inheritors of the Liberal program of Sarmiento and Mitre, and they were able to enact their programs because of the high levels of income generated by the expanding economy.

Technological changes contributed to Argentine prosperity. Refrigerated ships allowed fresh beef to be sent directly to Europe, and this along with wool and wheat provided the basis of expansion. Labor was provided by a flood of immigrants. Some were *golondrinas,* which literally means swallows, who were able to work one harvest in Italy and then a second in Argentina because of the differences in seasons in the two hemispheres, but many immigrants elected to stay. Almost 3.5 million immigrants stayed in Argentina between 1857 and 1930, and unlike in Mexico, by 1914 about one-third of the Argentine population was foreign-born. Italians, Germans, Russians, and

Jews came to "hacer America"—that is, "to make America"—and remained. In a way, quite unlike Mexico they really did Europeanize Argentina, introducing the folkways and ideologies of the European rural and working classes. The result was a fusion of cultures that produced not only a radical workers' movement, but also the distinctive music of the "tango" which combined Spanish, African, and other musical elements in the cafés and red-light districts of Buenos Aires. The tango became the music of the Argentine urban working class.

As the immigrant flood increased, workers began to seek political expression. A Socialist party was formed in the 1890s, seeking to elect representatives to office. Anarchists hoped to smash the political system and called for strikes and walkouts. Moved to some extent by European ideological battles, the struggle spilled into the streets. Violent strikes and government repression characterized the decade after 1910, culminating in a series of strikes in 1918 that led to extreme repression. Development had its social costs.

The Argentine oligarchy was capable of some internal reform, however. Critics of corruption emerged within the political system, and a new party representing the emerging middle class began to organize. It was aided by an electoral law in 1912 that called for secret ballots, universal male suffrage, and compulsory voting. With this change the Radical party, promising political reform and more liberal policies for workers, came to power in 1916, but faced with labor unrest it acted as repressively as its predecessors. The oligarchy made room for middle-class politicians and interests, but the problems of Argentina's expanding labor force remained unresolved, and Argentina's economy remained closely tied to the international market for its exports.

With considerable variations, similar patterns of economic growth, political domination by oligarchies formed by traditional aristocracies and "progressive" middle classes, and a rising tide of labor unrest or rural rebellion can be noted elsewhere in Latin America. Modernization and "progress" were not welcomed by all sectors of society. Messianic religious movements in Brazil, Indian resistance to the loss of lands in Colombia, and banditry in Mexico were all to some extent reactions to the changes being forced on the societies by national governments tied to the ideology of progress and often insensitive to its effects.

UNCLE SAM GOES SOUTH

After its Civil War, the United States began to take a more direct and active interest in the politics and economic situation of Latin America. Commerce and investments began to expand rapidly in this period, especially in Mexico and Central America. American industry was seeking new markets and raw materials, while the growing population of the United States created a demand for Latin-American products. Attempts were made to create inter-American cooperation, but a major turning point came in 1898 with the outbreak of war between Spain and the United States, which now began to join the nations of western Europe in the age of imperialism.

The war centered on Cuba and Puerto Rico, Spain's last colonies in the Americas. The Cuban economy had boomed in the 19th century based on its exports of sugar and tobacco grown with slave labor. A ten-year civil war for independence beginning in 1868 had failed in its main objective but had won the island some autonomy. A number of ardent Cuban nationalists, such as the journalist and poet José Marti, had gone into exile to continue the struggle. Fighting erupted again in 1895 and the United States joined in 1898, declaring war on Spain and occupying Cuba, Puerto Rico, and the Philippines.

In fact, United States investments in Cuba had been rapidly increasing prior to the war, and the United States had become a major market for Cuban sugar. The Cuban Spanish-American War now opened the door to direct United States involvement in the Caribbean. The Cuban army was treated poorly by its American allies, and a United States government of occupation was imposed on Cuba and Puerto Rico. When the occupation ended in 1902, a series of onerous conditions were imposed on independent Cuba that made it a virtual American dependency, a status that was, in fact, legally imposed in Puerto Rico.

For strategic, commercial, and economic reasons Latin America, particularly the Caribbean and Mexico, began to attract American interest at the turn of the century. These considerations lay behind the drive to construct a canal across Central America that would shorten the route between the Atlantic and Pacific. When Colombia proved reluctant to meet American proposals, the United States backed a Panamanian movement for independence and then signed a treaty with its representative that granted the United States extensive rights over a trans-isthmus canal. President Theodore Roosevelt was a major force behind the canal, which opened to traffic in 1908.

The Panama Canal was a remarkable engineering feat and a fitting symbol of the technological and industrial strength of the United States. North Americans were proud of these achievements and hoped to demonstrate the superiority of the "American way," a feeling fed to some extent by racist ideas and a sense of cultural superiority. Latin Americans were now wary of American power and intentions in the area. A number of intellectuals cautioned against the expansionist designs of the United States and

José Martí (1853–1895), an ardent Cuban patriot, used his talents as a poet, journalist, and lawyer for the cause of Cuban independence. While living a long exile in the United States, he became critical of U.S. ambitions in the Caribbean. He died in the early stages of the Spanish-American War.

against what they viewed as the materialism of American culture. The Uruguayan José Enrique Rodó, in his essay *Ariel* (1900), compared the spirituality of Hispanic culture to the materialism of the United States. Others, elsewhere in Latin America, offered similar critiques.

Latin-American criticism had a variety of origins: nationalism, a Catholic defense of traditional values, and also some socialist attacks on expansive capitalism. In a way, Latin America, which had achieved its political independence in the 19th century and had been part of European developments, was able to articulate clearly the fears and the reactions of the areas that had become the colonies and semicolonies of western Europe and the United States in the age of empire.

CONCLUSION

NEW NATIONS, OLD PROBLEMS

During the 19th century the nations of Latin America moved from the status of colonies to that of independent nation-states. The process was sometimes exhilarating and often painful, but during the course of the century, these nations were able to construct governments and begin to address many social and economic problems. These problems were inherited from the colonial era and intensified by internal political and ideological conflicts and by foreign intervention. Moreover, the Latin-American nations also had to resuscitate their economies after the struggles for independence and to confront their position within the world economic system as suppliers of agricultural products and consumers of manufactured goods.

The heritage of the past weighed heavily in Latin America. Political and social changes were many, and pressures for these changes came from a variety of sources such as progressive politicians, modernizing military men, a growing urban population, dissatisfied workers, and disadvantaged peasants. Still, in many ways Latin America remained remarkably unchanged. Revolts were frequent but revolutions that altered the structure of society or the distribution of land or wealth were few, and the reforms intended to do this were usually unsuccessful. The elite controlled most of the economic resources, a growing but still small urban sector had emerged politically but either remained weak or had to accommodate the elite, and the vast majority of the population continued to labor on the land with little hope of improvement. Latin America was a distinctive civilization—culturally and politically sharing much of the Western tradition, yet economically functioning more like areas of Asia and Africa. Latin America was the first non-Western area to face the problems of decolonization, and many aspects of its history that seemed so distinctive in the 19th century proved to be previews of what would follow—decolonization and nation-building elsewhere in the world in the 20th century.

FURTHER READINGS

Stanley J. and Barbara Stein's *The Colonial Heritage of Latin America* (1970) is a hard-hitting interpretation of colonial and 19th-century Latin America that emphasizes its continued dependency and its neocolonial status after independence. David Bushnell and Neil Macauley's *The Emergence of Latin America in the Nineteenth Century* (1988) provides an excellent overview that is critical of the dependency thesis. The classic study from the dependency perspective is Fernando Henrique Cardoso and Enzo Faletto's *Dependency and Development in Latin America* (1979). Roberto Cortés Conde's *The First Stages of Modernization in Spanish America* (1974) provides a good economic analysis. The movements for independence are described in John Lynch's *The Spanish American Revolutions* (1973). Tulio Halperin Donghi's *The Aftermath of Revolution in Latin America* (1973) analyzes the first half of the 19th century. Claudio Veliz's *The Centralist Tradition in Latin America* (1980) tries to explain the divergent development of Latin America and western Europe, while E. Bradford Burns's *Poverty or Progress. Latin America in the Nineteenth Century* (1973) provides a challenging attack on the liberal programs and a defense of a "folk" political tradition. Jean Franco's *The Modern Culture of Latin America. Society and the Artist* (1967) is a lively discussion of literature and the arts. Volumes 3 to 5 of the *Cambridge History of Latin America* (1985–1986) contain up-to-date essays on major themes and individual countries. A good essay from the collection is Robert Freeman Smith's "Latin America, the United States, and the European Powers, 1830–1930," vol. IV, 83–120.

There are an enormous number of single-volume country histories as well as monographs on particular topics. David Rock's *Argentina* (1985), E. B. Burns' *A History of Brazil* (1980), Michael Meyer and William Sherman's *The Course of Mexican History* (1979), and Herbert Klein's *Bolivia* (1982) are good examples of national histories. There are excellent rural histories, such as Stanley Stein's *Vassouras. A Brazilian Coffee County*, (2d ed., 1989), Charles Berquist's *Coffee and Conflict in Colombia, 1886–1910* (1978), and Arnold Bauer's *Chilean Rural Society* (1975). Silvia Arrom's *The Women of Mexico City* (1985) is a fine example of the growing literature in women's history, some of which is also seen in June Nash and Helen Safa, eds., *Sex and Class in Latin America* (1980). Hobart Spalding, Jr.'s *Organized Labor in Latin America* (1977) surveys urban labor, while Charles Berquist's *Labor in Latin America* (1986) is a comparative interpretative essay.

1644 Manchu nomads conquer China; Qing dynasty rules

1664–1722 Reign of the Kangxi emperor in China

1727 First printing press set up in the Ottoman Empire

1736–1799 Reign of the Qianlong emperor in China

1768–1774 Disastrous Ottoman war with Russia

1772 Safavid dynasty falls in Persia

1780s Early efforts at reform in the Ottoman Empire

1789–1807 Reign of Ottoman Sultan Selim III

1798 British embassy to Qianlong emperor in China; French invasion of Egypt; Napoleon defeats Egypt's Mameluk rulers

1805–1849 Reign of Muhammad Ali in Egypt

1807–1839 Reign of Ottoman Sultan Mahmud II

1826 Ottoman Janissary corps destroyed

1834 Postal system established in Ottoman Empire

1838 Ottoman treaty with British removing trade restrictions in the empire

1839–1841 Opium War in China

1839–1876 *Tanzimat* reforms in the Ottoman Empire

1839–1897 Life of Islamic thinker Al-Afghani

32 Civilizations in Crisis: The Ottoman Empire, the Islamic Heartlands, and Qing China

INTRODUCTION. Conditions in those parts of Asia that were not outright European colonies differed in many ways from those in Latin America during the century and a half after 1750. Problems of political decline and reactions of highly successful traditional cultures to new challenges predominated, particularly in the great empires of China and the Middle East. The threat of Western imperialism was more menacing, though larger problems of dealing with the West's industrial lead and the intensified world economy overlapped with issues in Latin America.

By the early decades of the 18th century, it appeared that two of the civilizations—Middle Eastern Islamic and Chinese—still capable of contesting the European drive for global dominance were headed in very different directions. Under the Manchu rulers, whose seizure of the Chinese throne in the mid-17th century was noted in Chapter 28, China was enjoying yet another early dynastic period of growth and general prosperity. The territory controlled by the Manchus was greater than that claimed by any Chinese dynasty since the Tang in the 7th century. China's population was growing steadily, and its trade and agricultural production were keeping pace. China's border defenses were strong; its huge armies, led by the elite "banner" units made up of ethnic Manchu soldiers, appeared capable of defending the empire against any outside threat. Like other "barbarian" peoples, the Europeans were closely controlled by the functionaries of the ruling Qing dynasty. European traders were confined to the ports of Macao and Canton on China's south coast. In the early 18th century, the Qing emperor had severely curtailed

1849–1905 Life of Muhammad Abduh

1870 Ottoman legal code reformed

1908 Young Turks seize power in Istanbul

1898–1901 Boxer Rebellion in China; 100 Days of Reform in China

1883 Mahdist victory over British-led Egyptian expeditionary force at Shakyan

1882 British invasion and occupation of Egypt; failed revolt led Orabi in Egypt

1850–1864 Taiping rebellion in China

1876 Constitution promulgated for Ottoman Empire

1869 Opening of the Suez Canal

1877 Treaty of San Stefano; Ottomans driven from most of the Balkans

1905 Fatherland Party established in Egypt

1856–1860 Anglo-French war against China

1866 First railway begun in Ottoman Empire

1889 Young Turks established in Paris

1898 British-Egyptian army defeats the Mahdist army at Omdurman

1854–1856 Crimean War

1876–1908 Reign of Ottoman Sultan Abdul Hamid

missionary activities in China without fear of foreign reprisals. Thus, despite signs of growing poverty and social unrest in some districts, the Manchus appeared not only to have restored good government and the well-being of the general populace but to have carried China to a new level of political and cultural dominance in East Asia.

At the other end of Asia, the fate of the Ottomans appeared to be exactly the reverse. After centuries of able rule and expansion at the expense of their Christian and Muslim neighbors (see Chapter 26), the Ottomans were in full retreat by the first decades of the 18th century. From the west the Austrian Habsburgs chipped away at the Ottomans' European possessions, while a revived Russia closed in from the north. Muslim kingdoms in North Africa broke away from the empire, and imperial governors and local notables throughout the Arab portions of the Middle East grew more and more independent of the ruling Sultan in Istanbul. Political decline was accompanied by rising economic and social disruption. Inflation was rampant throughout much of the empire, and European imports were rapidly destroying what was left of the already battered Ottoman handicraft industries. The empire was racked by social tensions, crime, and rebellion in some areas. The divided Ottoman elite could not agree on a strategy to reinvigorate state and society or to drive back the Christian infidels whose advance was undoing centuries of hard-won conquests. With its Ottoman defenders reduced, the very heartlands of the Islamic world were increasingly at risk.

In a little over a century, the very different paths these two civilizations appeared to be following suddenly converged, and then the Ottomans gained strength as China fell apart. A combination of internal weaknesses and growing pressure from the industrializing European powers threw China into a period of prolonged crisis in the early 19th century. If anything, Chinese civilization was revealed as even more exposed and vulnerable than the Islamic world the Ottomans sought to defend in the face of internal decay and European inroads. While the Ottomans began to find new sources of leadership and to introduce reforms on the basis of Western precedents, the Manchus were paralyzed by the shock of devastating defeats at the hands of the European "barbarians." Overpopulation, drug addiction—particularly that which afflicted members of the scholar-gentry elite—and massive rebellions sapped China's strength from within, while European gunboats and armies broke down its outer defenses. By the end of the 19th century, internal disruptions and external pressures had literally demolished the foundations of Chinese civilization, a civilization whose development we have traced over nearly four millennia.

As old China died, its leaders struggled to find a new and viable system to put in its place. That struggle would be carried on throughout a half century (roughly from 1898 to 1949) of foreign invasion, revolution, and social and economic breakdown that produced suffering on a scale unmatched in all human history. In sharp contrast, by the end of the 19th century new leaders had emerged in the Ottoman Empire who were able to overthrow the sultanate with a minimum of bloodshed and to begin the process of nation making in the Turkish portions of the empire (largely the present-day nation of Turkey). Unfortunately, Ottoman weaknesses in earlier decades left the rest of the Middle East exposed to European inroads, and a larger Islamic crisis proved impervious to Turkish solutions.

The early sections of this chapter will focus on attempts to revive the declining Ottoman Empire and the emergence of groups within the Ottoman elite dedicated to the overthrow of the sultanate and the establishment of a new state on the basis of Turkish nationalism. In dealing with these patterns we will also look at developments in the central Islamic lands, from the great changes set in motion by Napoleon's invasion of Egypt in 1798, to the differing responses of Islamic thinkers and political leaders, to the growing threat of industrial Europe. The second half of the chapter will concentrate on the forces that led to the collapse of Chinese civilization in the last half of the 19th century. We will also look at some of the early Chinese responses to the profound crisis engendered by this collapse and examine the legacy of the fall of the Qing, China's last imperial dynasty, in the first years of the 20th century.

ANALYSIS
WESTERN DOMINANCE AND THE DECLINE OF CIVILIZATIONS

With Europe's emergence as the dominant global power from the 18th century onward, the patterns of the rise and fall of civilizations established in the classical age were fundamentally altered. As we have seen in our examination of the forces that have led to the breakup of the great civilizations in human history, each civilization has a unique history, but a number of general patterns, such as those set out in Chapter 11, have been associated with the decline of civilizations. Both internal weaknesses and external pressures have acted over a period of time to erode the institutions and break down the defenses of even the largest and most sophisticated civilizations that humans have created. In the preindustrial era, slow and vulnerable communications systems were a major barrier to the long-term cohesion of the political systems that held civilizations together. Ethnic, religious, and regional differences, which were overridden by the confidence and energy of the founders of civilizations, reemerged as self-serving corruption and the pursuit of pleasure gradually eroded the sense of purpose of the elite groups that played a pivotal role in civilized development. The deterioration in governance and military strength that followed both exacerbated social tensions and undermined rather fragile preindustrial economies.

Growing social unrest from within was paralleled by increasing threats from without. A major factor in the fall of virtually every great civilization, from those of the Indus valley and Mesopotamia to Rome and the civilizations of Mesoamerica, was an influx of nomadic peoples, whom the civilized peoples invariably regarded as barbarians. Nomadic assaults not only revealed the ineptness of the ruling elites and destroyed their military base, but barbarian raids disrupted the agricultural routines and smashed the public works on which all civilizations rested. Normally, the nomadic invaders stayed on as the rulers of the sedentary peoples they had conquered, as happened repeatedly in China, Mesoamerica, and the Islamic world. Elsewhere, as after the destruction of the Indus valley civilization in India and the fall of Rome, the vanquished civilization was largely forgotten or lay dormant for centuries. But over time the invading peoples living in its ruins managed to restore patterns of civilized life that were quite different from, though sometimes influenced by, the civilization their incursions had helped to destroy centuries earlier.

Neighboring civilizations sometimes clashed in wars on their frontiers, but it was rare for one civilization to play a major part in the demise of another. In areas like Mesopotamia, where civilizations were crowded together in space and time in the last millennia B.C. (see Chapter 2), older, long dominant civilizations had been overthrown and absorbed by upstart rivals. In most cases, however, and often in Mesopotamia, external threats to civilizations came from nomadic peoples. This was true even of Islamic civilization, which proved the most expansive before the emergence of Europe and whose rise and spread brought about the collapse of a number of long-established civilized centers. The initial Arab explosion from Arabia that felled Sassanid Persia and captured Egypt was very much a nomadic enterprise. But the incursions of the Arab bedouins differed from earlier and later nomadic assaults on neighboring civilizations because the new religion that they carried with them from Arabia provided the basis for a new civilization which incorporated the older ones they conquered. Thus, like other nomadic conquerors, they borrowed heavily from the civilizations they overran.

The emergence of western Europe as an expansive global force radically altered the patterns of interaction between civilizations as well as between civilizations and nomadic peoples. From the first years of overseas exploration, the aggressive Europeans proved a threat to other civilizations. Within decades of Columbus's arrival in 1492, European military assaults had destroyed two of the great centers of high civilization in the Americas—the Aztec and Inca empires. The previous isolation of the Amerindian societies and their consequent susceptibility to European diseases and weapons made them more vulnerable than most of the peoples the Europeans encountered overseas. Thus, in the first centuries of expansion, most of the existing civilizations in Africa and Asia proved quite capable of standing up to the Europeans—except on the sea. With the scientific discoveries and especially the technological innovations that transformed Europe in the 17th and 18th centuries, all of this gradually changed. The unparalleled extent of the western Europeans' mastery of the natural world gave them new sources of power for resource extraction, manufacture, and war. By the end of the 18th century, this power was being translated into the economic, military, and increasingly the political domination of other civilizations.

A century later, the Europeans had either conquered most of these civilizations outright or reduced them to spheres they controlled indirectly and threatened to annex. The adverse effects of economic influences emanating from the West and Western political domination proved highly corrosive to the very fabric of civilizations as diverse as those of West Africa, the Islamic heartlands, and China. For a span of several decades before the First World War, it appeared that the materially advanced and expansive West would level all other civilized centers. In that era, most leading European, and some African and Asian, thinkers and political leaders believed that the rest of humankind had no alternative (except perhaps a reversion to savagery or barbarism) but to follow the path of development pioneered by the West.

As we shall see in this chapter and the ones that follow, the many challenges European global domination posed for other civilizations provoked a wide variety of responses. These ranged from those that stressed a retreat into an idealized past free of European influences to responses that presumed the need for the extensive transformation of non-Western societies along European lines. The leaders and thinkers of all non-Western peoples debated how extensively their societies must adopt Western ways to survive the onslaught of the European imperialist powers and whether it would be possible to confine Western influences to certain spheres. They also struggled to come up with ways of mobilizing popular support for movements aimed at resisting the advance of the European powers and driving them from areas in Africa and Asia where they were already in control. As we shall see in the examples drawn from the Middle East and China in the sections that follow, some of these modes of resistance were more successful than others—some civilizations managed to adapt and survive, while others collapsed entirely. But all non-Western peoples became preoccupied with coping with the powerful challenges the industrial West posed for the survival of their civilized past and the course of their future development.

Questions: Can you think of instances where one preindustrial civilization was a major factor in the collapse of another? Why do you think such an occurrence was so rare? Discuss the advantages that the Amerindians' isolation from civilizations in Europe, Africa, and Asia gave the European intruders in the 16th century. What kinds of advantages did the scientific and industrial revolutions give the Europeans over all other civilized peoples from the 18th century onward? Is the West losing these advantages today, and, if so, what do you think the consequences will be?

BETWEEN THE WESTERN POWERS: THE STRUGGLE OF THE OTTOMAN EMPIRE FOR SURVIVAL

By the early 18th century, the days of the Ottoman Empire appeared numbered. In part the crisis was brought on by a succession of weak rulers within a political and social order that was centered on the sultan at the top. Inactive or inept sultans opened the way for seemingly endless power struggles between rival ministers, religious experts, and the commanders of the Janissary corps. Competition between factions of the elite further eroded effective leadership within the empire, exposing it to external assaults by its European enemies and weakening its control over the population and resources it claimed to rule. Provincial officials colluded with the local landowning classes, the ayan, to cheat the sultan of a good portion of the taxes due him, and they skimmed all the revenue they could from the already impoverished peasantry in the countryside. As in other preindustrial civilizations, the peasants responded to these threats to their livelihood with flight (if open lands or less exacting landlords were within reach), banditry, and outright rebellions in various parts of the empire.

At the same time, the position of the artisan workers in the towns deteriorated due to competition from imported manufactures from Europe. This led, particularly in the 18th and early 19th centuries, to urban riots in which members of artisan guilds or young mens' associations often took a leading role. Merchants within the empire, especially those who belonged to minority religious communities, such as the Jews and Christians, grew more and more dependent on commercial dealings with their European counterparts. This pattern accelerated the influx of Western manufactured goods that was steadily undermining handicraft industries within the empire, thereby increasing Ottoman economic dependence on some of its most threatening European political rivals.

With the Ottoman leaders embroiled in internal squabbles and their armies deprived of the resources needed to match the great advances in weaponry and training made by European rivals, the far-flung Ottoman possessions proved an irresistible temptation for their neighbors. In the early decades of the 18th century, the Austrian Habsburg dynasty was the main beneficiary of Ottoman decadence. The long-standing threat to Vienna was forever vanquished, and the Ottomans were pushed out of Hungary and the northern Balkans.

In the later 1700s, the Russian Empire, strengthened by Peter the Great's forced Westernization (see Chapter 24), became the main threat to the Ottomans' survival. As military setbacks mounted and the Russians advanced across the steppes toward warm water ports in the Black Sea, the Ottomans' weakness was underscored by their attempts to forge alliances with other Christian powers. As the Russians gobbled up poorly defended Ottoman lands in the

The Ottoman Empire in the Late 18th Century

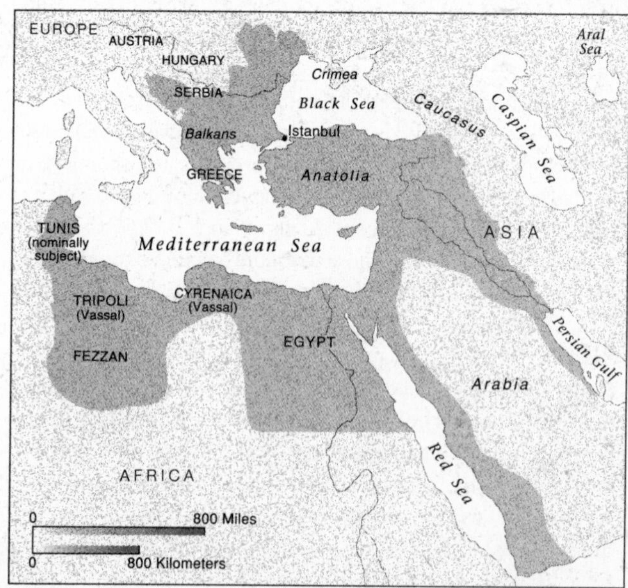

Caucasus and Crimea, the subject Christian peoples of the Balkans grew more and more restive under Ottoman rule. In 1804 a major uprising broke out in Serbia that was repressed after years of difficult and costly military campaigns. Military force could not quell the Greek revolt that broke out in the early 1820s, and by 1830 the Greeks had regained their independence after centuries of Ottoman rule. By 1867 Serbia was also free, and by the late 1870s the Ottomans had been driven from virtually the whole of the Balkans and thus most of the European provinces of their empire. In the following decades Istanbul itself was repeatedly threatened by Russian armies or those of the smaller Balkan States.

REFORM AND SURVIVAL

Despite almost two centuries of unrelieved defeats on the battlefield and steady losses of territory, the Ottoman Empire somehow managed to survive into the 20th century. In part this was due to divisions between the European powers, each of which feared that the others would gain more from the total dismemberment of the empire. In fact the British concern to prevent the Russians from controlling Istanbul—thus gaining direct access to and threatening British naval dominance in the Mediterranean—led them to prop up the tottering Ottoman regime repeatedly in the last half of the 19th century. Ultimately, the Ottomans' survival depended on reforms from within—reforms initiated by the sultans and their advisors at the top of the imperial system and carried out in stages over most of the 19th century. At each stage, reform initiatives intensified tensions within the ruling elite: Some advocated far-reaching change along European lines; others argued for reforms based on precedents from the early Ottoman period; and still others had a vested interest in blocking change of any sort.

These deep divisions within the Ottoman elite rendered reform a dangerous enterprise. Though modest innovations, including the introduction of the first printing press in 1727, had been enacted in the 18th century, Sultan Selim III (1789–1807) believed that bolder initiatives were required if the dynasty and empire were to survive. But his reform efforts, which were aimed at improving administrative efficiency and building a new army and navy capable of reversing a century of defeats at the hands of the European powers, angered powerful factions within the bureaucracy. They were also viewed by the Janissary corps, which had long been the dominant force within the Ottoman military (see Chapter 26), as a direct and vital threat. Selim's modest initiatives cost him his throne—he was toppled by a Janissary revolt in 1807—and his life.

The European view of the Ottoman Empire as an exotic and bizarrely antique land is captured in this late 18th-century engraving of the Ottoman sultan entertaining the French ambassador and his entourage.

Two decades later, a more skillful sultan, Mahmud II, succeeded where Selim III had failed. After secretly building a small professional army with the help of European advisors, in 1826 Mahmud II ordered his agents to incite a mutiny of the Janissaries. This began when the angry Janissaries overturned the huge soup kettles in their mess area. With little thought of preparation, the Janissaries poured into the streets of Istanbul, more a mob than a military force, where they were shocked to be confronted by the sultan's well-trained new army. The confrontation ended in the slaughter of the Janissaries, their families, and the Janissaries' religious allies.

After cowing the ayan or provincial notables into at least formal submission to the throne, Mahmud II launched a program of much more far-reaching reforms than Selim III had attempted. Though the ulama, or religious experts, and some of Mahmud's advisors argued for self-strengthening through a return to the Ottoman and Islamic past, Mahmud II patterned his reform program on Western precedents. After all, the Western powers had made a shambles of his empire. He established a diplomatic corps on Western lines and exchanged ambassadors with the European powers. The Westernization of the army was expanded from Mahmud's secret force to the whole military establishment. European military advisors, both army and navy, were imported to supervise the overhaul of Ottoman training, armament, and officers' education.

In the following decades, Western influences were pervasive at the upper levels of Ottoman society, particularly during the period of the Tanzimat reforms between 1839 and 1876. University education was reorganized on Western lines, including the introduction of training in the European sciences and mathematics. State-run postal and telegraph systems were introduced in the 1830s and railways were begun in the 1860s. Newspapers were established in the major towns of the empire, extensive legal reforms were enacted, and in 1876 a constitution, based heavily on European prototypes, was promulgated. These legal reforms greatly improved the position of minority religious groups, whose role in the Ottoman economy increased steadily.

Some groups were adversely affected by these changes that opened the empire more and more to Western influences. This was especially true of the artisans, whose position was gravely weakened by an 1838 treaty with the British that removed import taxes and other barriers to foreign trade that had protected indigenous producers from competition from the West. Other social groups gained little from the Tanzimat reforms. This was particularly true of women. Though proposals for women's education and the end to seclusion, polygamy, and veiling were debated in Ottoman intellectual circles from the 1860s onward, few improvements in the position of women—even among the elite classes—were won until after the fall of the dynasty in 1908.

REPRESSION AND REVOLT

Though the reforms initiated by the sultans and their advisors did improve somewhat the Ottomans' ability to fend off, or at least deflect, the assaults of foreign aggressors, they increasingly threatened the dynasty responsible for them. Western-educated bureaucrats, military officers, and professionals came increasingly to view the sultanate as a major barrier to even more radical reforms—some of which involved proposals for constitutional checks on the rulers' authority—and the full transformation of society. The new elites also clashed with conservative but powerful groups, such as the ulama and ayan, who had a vested interest in preserving as much as possible of the old order. There were also divisions within the new elite between those who had derived great benefit from the early reforms and were wary of further changes, and those who saw the reforms already enacted as the entering wedge for a much more radical restructuring of Ottoman institutions and society.

The Ottoman Sultan Abdul Hamid responded to the growing threat from Westernized officers and civilians by attempting to return to despotic absolutism during his long reign from 1878 to 1908. He nullified the constitution, restricted civil liberties, particularly the freedom of the press, and deprived Westernized elite groups of the considerable initiative they had gained in the formulation of imperial policies. Legal safeguards were flaunted as dissidents or even suspected troublemakers were summarily imprisoned, and sometimes tortured and killed. But the deep impact that decades of reform had made upon the empire was demonstrated by the fact that even Abdul Hamid continued to push for Westernization in certain areas. The military continued to adopt European arms and techniques, increasingly under the instruction of German advisors. In addition, railways, including the famed line that linked Berlin to Baghdad, and telegraph lines were constructed between the main population centers, more often than not under the aegis of German investors and supervisors. Western-style educational institutions continued to grow, and judicial reforms continued. Under Abdul Hamid the old bureaucratic apparatus remained largely in place and social reforms were minimal, but the military and communications infrastructure for a modern state was established.

The despotism of Abdul Hamid came to an abrupt end in the nearly bloodless coup of 1908. Resistance to his authoritarian rule had led exiled Turkish intellectuals and political agitators to found an organization, the Ottoman Society for Union and Progress, in Paris in 1889. Though professing their loyalty to the Ottoman regime, the Young Turks, as members of the society came to be known, were determined to restore the 1876 constitution and resume far-reaching reforms within the empire. Clandestine printing presses operated by the Young Turks turned out tracts denouncing the regime and outlining the further steps to be taken to modernize and thus save the empire. Assassinations were attempted and coups plotted, but until 1908 all were undone by a combination of divisions within the ranks of the Westernized dissidents and police countermeasures.

The fascination that the Young Turks and what appeared to be their revolutionary movement held for European intellectuals is reflected in the cover drawing and story of a 1909 edition of the popular French periodical *Le Petit Parisien*. It is also suggested by the radical or avant-garde connotations that the label "Young Turk" has had from the early 20th century to the present day.

Sympathy within the military for the 1908 coup had much to do with its success, as did the fact that only a handful of the sultan's supporters were willing to die defending the regime. Though a group of officers came to power, they restored the constitution and press freedoms and promised reforms in education, administration, and even the status of women. The sultan was retained as a political figurehead and the highest religious authority in Islam.

Unfortunately, the officers soon became embroiled in factional fights that took up much of the limited time remaining before the outbreak of World War I. In addition, their hold on power was shaken as they lost a new round of wars in the Balkans and against Italy over the Ottomans' last remaining possession in North Africa, Libya. Just as the sultans had before them, however, the Young Turk officers managed to stave off the collapse of the empire with last-gasp military victories and by playing the hostile European powers against each other.

Though it is difficult to know how the Young Turks would have fared if it had not been for the outbreak of the First World War, their failure to resolve a number of critical issues did not bode well for the future. They had overthrown the sultan, but they could not bring themselves to give up the empire ruled by Turks for over 600 years. The peoples most affected by their decision to salvage what was left of the empire were the Arabs of the Fertile Crescent and coastal Arabia who still remained under Ottoman control. Arab leaders in Beirut and Damascus had initially favored the 1908 coup because they believed it would bring about the end of their long domination by the Turks. To their dismay, the Arabs discovered that the Young Turks not only meant to continue their subjugation, but that they were determined to enforce state control to a degree unthinkable to the later Ottoman sultans. The quarrels between the leaders of the Young Turk coalition and the growing resistance in the Arab portions of what was left of the Ottoman Empire were quite suddenly cut short by a much larger global crisis brought on by the outbreak of general war in Europe in August 1914. Turkish entry into and defeat in the First World War brought about the dissolution of the Ottoman Empire. This also gave rise to the leader, Mustafa Kemal or Ataturk, and some of the forces that proved critical in the emergence of the modern nation of Turkey from the ruins of the empire. However able a military commander he might have been, Ataturk's successes would not have been possible without the struggles and reforms of the last century and a half of the Ottoman Empire.

WESTERN INTRUSIONS AND THE CRISIS IN THE ARAB ISLAMIC HEARTLANDS

By the early 1800s, the Arab peoples of the Fertile Crescent, Egypt, coastal Arabia and North Africa had lived for centuries under Ottoman-Turkish rule. Though most Arabs resented Turkish domination, they could identify with the Ottomans as fellow Muslims, who were both ardent defenders of the faith and patrons of Islamic culture. Still, the steadily diminishing capacity of the Ottomans to defend the Arab Islamic heartlands left them exposed to the danger of conquest by the aggressive European powers. The European capture of outlying, but highly developed, Islamic states from those in the Indonesian archipelago and India to Algeria in North Africa engendered a sense of crisis among the Islamic faithful in the Middle Eastern heartlands. From the terror of Christendom and the encirclers of its European bastion, the Muslims had become the besieged. Islam had been displaced by

Europe as the leading civilization in a wide range of endeavors from scientific inquiry to monumental architecture. Much of the Muslim community was forced to live under infidel European overlords; what remained was threatened by European conquest.

The profound crisis of Islamic confidence brought on by successive reverses and the ever-increasing strength of their old European rivals gave rise to a wide variety of responses in the Islamic world. Islamic thinkers debated the best way of reversing the decline and driving back the Europeans. Some argued for a return to the Islamic past; others favored a large-scale adoption of Western ways; while still others sought to find ways to combine the two approaches. Reformist leaders, such as those in 19th-century Turkey, tried to graft on elements of Western culture while preserving the old state and society pretty much intact. Religious leaders, sometimes proclaiming themselves divinely appointed prophets, rose up to lead their followers in jihads, or holy wars, against the advancing Europeans. Though it is not possible to examine all of these responses in each of the Islamic lands, the following sections focus on key responses on the part of Arab peoples in Egypt and the Sudan in the 19th century. In these areas, European involvement was intense and the growing challenges posed by the West generated important attempts to find ways of reversing the decline of Islamic civilization and restoring it to its former glory.

FRENCH INVASION AND MAMLUK DEFEAT

Though it did not establish a permanent European presence in the Islamic heartlands, Napoleon's invasion of Egypt in 1798 sent shock waves across what remained of the Muslim world. Significantly, Napoleon's motives for launching the expedition had little to do with designs for empire in the Middle East itself. Rather he saw the Egyptian campaign as the prelude to the destruction of British power in India, where, as we have seen, the French had come out on the short end of earlier wars for empire. Whatever his calculations, Napoleon managed to slip his fleet past the British blockade in the Mediterranean and put ashore his armies in July 1798. There followed one of the most lopsided military clashes in modern history. As they advanced inland, Napoleon's forces were met by tens of thousands of cavalrymen bent on defending the Mamluk regime that then ruled Egypt as a vassal of the Ottoman sultans. The term Mamluk literally meant slave, and it suggested the Turkic origins of the regime in Egypt. Beginning as slaves who served Muslim overlords, the Mamluks had centuries earlier risen in the ranks as military commanders to the point where they were able to seize power in their own name. Murad, the head of the coalition of Mamluk households that shared power in Egypt at the time of Napoleon's arrival, dismissed the invader as a donkey boy whom he would soon drive from his lands.

Though courageous and determined to drive back the French invaders at the Battle of the Pyramids, the undisciplined Mamluk cavalrymen proved no match for the drilled marksmen and massed artillery of Napoleon's armies.

Murad's contempt for the talented young French commander was symptomatic of the profound ignorance of events in Europe that was characteristic of many leaders of the Islamic world at that time. Murad's ignorance led to a series of crushing defeats, the most famous of which came in a battle fought beneath the pyramids of the ancient Egyptian pharaohs. In the brief but bloody battle, the disciplined firepower of the French legions devastated the ranks of Mamluk horsemen clad in medieval armor, wielding spears against the artillery Napoleon used with such devastating effect.

Because the Mamluks had long been regarded as fighters of great prowess in the Islamic world, their rout was literally traumatic. It brutally revealed just how vulnerable even the Muslim core areas were to European aggression and how far the Muslims had fallen behind the Europeans in the capacity to wage war. Ironically, the successful invasion of Egypt brought little advantage to Napoleon or the French. The British caught up with the French fleet and sunk most of it at the Battle of Aboukir in August of 1798. With his supply line cut off, Napoleon was forced to abandon his army and sneak back to Paris, where his enemies were attempting to use his reverses in Egypt to put an end to his rise to power. Thus, Egypt was spared European conquest—for a time. The reprieve brought little consolation, since the British, not Egypt's Muslim defenders, had been responsible for the French retreat.

THE RISE OF MUHAMMAD ALI

In the chaos that followed the French invasion and eventual withdrawal in 1801, the Mamluk survivors fought with local notables for political control. The unexpected winner of these struggles was a young officer of Albanian origins named Muhammad Ali. He was a member of the Ottoman expeditionary force that had been sent to drive the French from Egypt. Having consolidated his base in the Cairo area by 1805, Muhammad Ali was master of Egypt after his soldiers slaughtered 300 Mamluk chieftains in 1811. Deeply impressed by the weapons and discipline of the French armies, the Albanian upstart devoted his energies and the resources of the land that he had brought under his rule to building an up-to-date European-style military force. He introduced Western-style conscription among the Egyptian peasantry, hired French officers to train his troops, imported Western arms, and adopted Western tactics and modes of organization and supply. Within years he had put together the most effective fighting force in the Middle East. With it, he flaunted the authority of his nominal overlord, the Ottoman sultan, by successfully invading Syria and building a modern war fleet that threatened Istanbul on a number of occasions.

By the 1830s Muhammad Ali's armies had been so successful that they were threatening the Ottoman regime itself. Twice, intervention by European powers was necessary to rescue the regime at Istanbul and foil Muhammad Ali's dreams of becoming the paramount lord of the Arab Muslim heartlands. Once again, the Europeans, not Muslim leaders, emerged as the arbiters of the destiny of the Arab world.

Though Muhammad Ali's efforts to introduce reforms patterned after Western precedents were not confined to the military, they fell far short of a fundamental transformation of Egyptian society. To shore up his economic base, he ordered the Egyptian peasantry to expand their production of cotton, hemp, indigo, and other crops that were in growing demand in industrial Europe. Efforts to improve Egyptian harbors and extend irrigation works met with some success and led to modest increases in the revenues that could be devoted to the continuing modernization of the military. Attempts to reform education were ambitious but limited in what was actually achieved. Many of the most significant innovations in schooling were linked to Muhammad Ali's military projects. His frequent schemes to build up an Egyptian industrial sector were eventually frustrated by the opposition of the European powers and by the intense competition from imported, Western-manufactured goods.

To secure his home base, Muhammad Ali also found that he had little choice but to ally with the powerful rural landlords, the ayan, to control the peasantry. He eliminated the tax farmers and claimed all land as state property, but despite these measures within decades a hereditary landlord class was firmly entrenched in the rural areas. His forcible confiscations of the peasants' produce to pay for the rising costs of the military establishment and for his foreign entanglements further impoverished an already hard-pressed rural population.

The limited scope of Muhammad Ali's reforms ultimately checked his plans for territorial expansion and left Egypt open to inroads by the European powers. He died in 1848, embittered by the European opposition that had prevented him from mastering the Ottoman sultans and well aware that his empire beyond Egypt was crumbling. Lacking his ambition and ability, his successors were content to confine their claims to Egypt and the Sudanic lands that stretched away from the banks of the Upper Nile to the south. Intermarrying with Turkish families that had originally come to Egypt to govern in the name of the Ottoman sultans, Muhammad Ali's descendants provided a succession of rulers, known as khedives after 1867, who were the formal rulers of Egypt until they were overthrown by the military coup that brought Nasser to power in 1952.

BANKRUPTCY, EUROPEAN INTERVENTION, AND STRATEGIES OF RESISTANCE

Muhammad Ali's successors made a muddle of his efforts to reform and revitalize Egyptian society. While cotton production increased and the landlord class grew fat, the great majority of the peasants went hungry or starved. The long-term consequences of these developments were equally troubling. The great expansion of cotton production at the expense of food grains and alternative market crops rendered Egypt dependent on a single export and vulnerable to fluctuations in demand on the European markets to which most of it was exported. Some further educational advances were made, mainly at elite schools where French was the language of instruction. But the advances were too limited to benefit the populace by making government more efficient or stimulating public works projects and improved health care.

Much of the revenue the khedives managed to collect, despite the resistance of the ayan, was wasted on extravagant pastimes and fruitless military campaigns to assert Egyptian authority over the Sudanic peoples along the Upper Nile. The increasing inability of the khedives to balance their books led in the middle decades of the 19th century to their growing indebtedness to European financiers. The latter lent money to the profligate khedives and members of the Turkish elite because the financiers desired both continued access to Egypt's cheap cotton and, by the 1850s, a share in the potentially lucrative schemes to build a canal across the Isthmus of Suez that would connect the Mediterranean and Red seas. The completion of the Suez Canal in 1869 shortened the distance by sea between Europe and Asia and allowed steamboats to replace sailing vessels, which had earlier proven better able to weather the rough passage around Africa.

The ineptitude of the khedival regime and the Ottoman sultans, who were their nominal overlords, prompted a good deal of discussion among Muslim intellectuals and political activists as to how they might find the leadership and means to ward off the growing European menace. Egypt, and particularly Cairo's ancient Muslim University of al-Azhar, became in the middle decades of the 19th cen-

The construction of a canal over the desert wastes of the Isthmus of Suez was a remarkable engineering feat. As this contemporary photo illustrates, a massive investment in up-to-date technology was essential to the success of the venture.

tury one of the key meeting places of these thinkers from throughout the Islamic world. Some prominent Islamic scholars called for a jihad to drive the infidels from Muslim lands. They also argued that the Muslim world could be saved only by a return to the patterns of religious observance and social interaction that they believed had existed in the "golden age" of the Prophet.

Other thinkers, such as al-Afghani (1839–1897) and his disciple Muhammad Abduh (1849–1905), stressed the need for Muslims to borrow scientific learning and technology from the West and to revive their earlier capacity to innovate. They argued that Islamic civilization had once taught the Europeans much in the sciences and mathematics, including such critical concepts as the Indian numerals. Thus, it was fitting that Muslims learn from the advances the Europeans had made with the help of Islamic borrowings. Those who advocated this approach also stressed the importance of the tradition of rational inquiry in Islamic history. They strongly disputed the views of fundamentalist theorists who contended that the Quran was the source of all truth and should be interpreted literally.

One of the oldest universities in the world, al-Azhar in Cairo has been one of the main centers of Muslim intellectual ferment in the modern era.

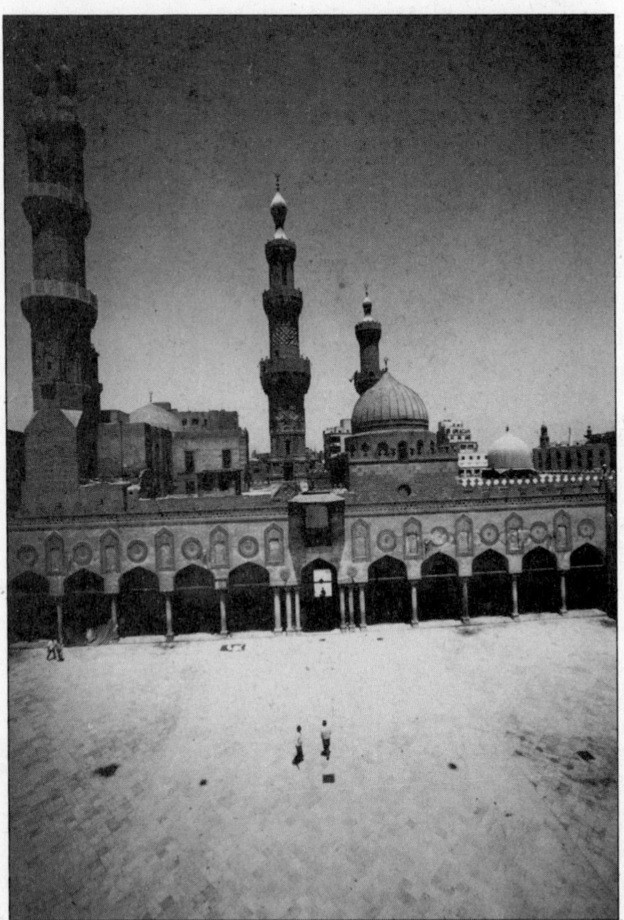

Though both fundamentalists and those who stressed the need for imports from the West agreed on the need for Muslim unity in the face of the growing European threat, they could not reconcile their very different approaches to Islamic revival. Their differences and the uncertainties they have injected into Islamic efforts to cope with the challenges of the West remain central problems in the Muslim world today.

The mounting debts of the khedival regime and the strategic importance of the canal gave the European powers, particularly Britain and France, a growing stake in the stability and accessibility of Egypt. French and British bankers, who had bought up a good portion of the khedive's shares in the canal, urged their governments to intervene militarily when the khedives proved unable to meet their loan payments. At the same time, French and British diplomats quarreled over how much influence their nations should exercise within Egypt. In the early 1880s a genuinely nationalist challenge to both the puppet khedival regime and the European powers prompted the British to intervene militarily to the chagrin of the French, who at that point were in no position to do likewise.

The challenge was mounted by the supporters of a charismatic young Egyptian officer named Achmad Orabi. The son of a small farmer in lower Egypt, Orabi had attended Quranic school and studied under the reform-minded Muhammad Abduh at al-Azhar. Though a native Egyptian, Orabi had risen in the ranks of the khedival army and had become increasingly critical of the fact that the officer corps was dominated by Turks with strong ties to the khedival regime. An attempt by the khedive to save money by disbanding Egyptian regiments and dismissing Egyptian officers sparked a revolt led by Orabi in the summer of 1882. Riots in the city of Alexandria, associated with mutinies in the Egyptian armies, drove the frightened khedive to seek British assistance. After bombarding coastal batteries set up by Orabi's troops, the British sent ashore an expeditionary force that crushed Orabi's rebellion and secured the position of the khedive. Though Egypt was not formally colonized, the British intervention began decades of dominance by both British consuls, who ruled through the puppet khedives, and British advisors to all high-ranking Egyptian administrators. British officials controlled Egypt's finances and foreign affairs, and British troops ensured that their directives were heeded by Egyptian administrators. Direct European control over the Islamic heartlands had begun.

JIHAD: THE MAHDIST REVOLT IN THE SUDAN

As Egypt fell under British control, the invaders were inevitably drawn into the turmoil and conflict that gripped the Sudanic region to the south in the last decades of the 19th century. Egyptian efforts to conquer and rule the Sudan, beginning in the 1820s, were fiercely resisted, particularly by the camel and cattle herding nomads who occupied the vast, arid plains that stretched west and east from the Upper Nile. The sedentary peoples who worked the narrow strip of fertile land along the river were more easily dominated. Thus, Egyptian authority, insofar as it existed at all, was concentrated in these areas and in river towns such as Khartoum, which was the center of Egyptian administration.

Even in the riverine areas Egyptian overlordship was greatly resented. The Egyptian regime was notoriously corrupt and its taxes placed a heavy burden on the peasants compelled to pay them. The Egyptians were clearly carpetbagging outsiders, and the favoritism they showed some of the Sudanic tribes was guaranteed to alienate the others. In addition, virtually all groups in the Muslim areas in the north Sudan were angered by Egyptian attempts in the 1870s to eradicate the slave trade. The trade had long been a great source of profit for both the merchants of the Nile towns and the nomads, who attacked non-Muslim peoples, such as the Dinka in the south, in order to capture slaves. British advisors at the khedive's court had strongly pushed for the antislavery effort, and an English commander, George Gordon, had taken charge of the campaign and on occasion employed very heavy-handed methods to suppress the trade.

By the late 1870s Egyptian oppression and British intervention had aroused deep resentment and hostility, particularly among the Muslim peoples of the northern Sudan. But a leader was needed to unite the diverse and often divided peoples of the region and to provide an ideology that would give focus and meaning to rebellion. The son of a boat builder named Muhammad Achmad, who had been educated by the holy man head of a local Sufi brotherhood, proved to be that leader. The fact that his family claimed descent from the Prophet and that he had the physical signs—a cleft in his teeth and a mole on his right cheek—that the local people associated with the promised deliverer did much to advance his reputation. The visions he began to experience, after he had broken with his Sufi master and established his own sectarian following, also suggested that a remarkable future was in store. What was seen to be a miraculous escape from a bungled Egyptian effort to capture and imprison Muhammad Achmad soon led to his widespread acceptance as a divinely appointed leader of revolt against the foreign intruders.

The jihad that Muhammad Achmad, who was known to his followers as the Mahdi (the promised deliverer), proclaimed against both the Egyptian heretics and British infidels was one of a number of such movements that had swept sub-Saharan Africa since the 18th century. It represented the most extreme and violent Islamic response to what was perceived as the dilution of Islam in the African environment and the growing threat of Europe. Muhammad Achmad promised to purge Islam of what he viewed as superstitious beliefs and degrading practices that had built up over the centuries and to return Islam to what he claimed was its original purity. He led his followers in a violent assault on the Egyptians, whom he believed professed this corrupt version of the faith, and the European infidels. At one point, his successors dreamed of toppling the Ottoman sultans and invading Europe itself.

The Mahdi's skillful use of guerrilla tactics and the confidence his followers placed in his blessings and magical charms earned his forces a number of stunning victories over the Egyptians. In 1883 the Mahdi's commanders drew a force of 8000 Egyptians, led by British officers, deep into the desert wilderness and ambushed and destroyed it in a desolate valley called Shaykan. By the end of 1883 the Mahdi's forces controlled most of the northern Sudan and were besieging the Egyptians' last major stronghold at Khartoum. In both ignorance and arrogance, the British sent a single officer, General Gordon, who had earlier overseen the suppression of the slave trade, up the Nile to Khartoum to command the Egyptian garrison and put down the Mahdist rebellion. Just under a year after Gordon's arrival, the city was taken and he was killed by the Mahdi's followers. The Mahdists had driven off the Egyptians, slaughtered their British commanders, and were now the masters of the Sudan.

At the peak of his power, the Mahdi fell ill from typhus and died just months after the capture of Khartoum. In contrast to many movements of this type, which have collapsed rapidly after the death of their prophetic leaders, the Mahdists found a capable successor to Muhammad Achmad in the Khalifa Abdallahi, one of his most skillful military commanders. Under Abdallahi, the Mahdists built a strong, expansive state and a closely controlled society, where smoking, dancing, and alcoholic drink were forbidden and theft, prostitution, and adultery were severely punished. For nearly a decade, Mahdist armies attacked or threatened neighboring states on all sides, including the Egyptians to the north, whose territories the Mahdists planned to invade. But in the fall of 1896, famed British General Kitchener was sent with an expeditionary force to put an end to what was one of the most serious threats to European domination in Africa. The spears and magical garments of the Mahdist forces proved no match for the machine guns and artillery of Kitchener's columns, and at the battle of Omdurman in 1898 the bulk of the Mahdist cavalry and Abdallahi himself were slaughtered. The Mahdist state collapsed and British power advanced still farther into the interior of Africa.

RETREAT AND ANXIETY: ISLAM IMPERILED

The 19th century was a time of severe reverses for the peoples of the Islamic world. Outflanked and outfought by their old European rivals, Islamic leaders either became puppets of European overlords or their lands passed under the rule of infidel colonial rulers. Diverse forms of resistance, from the reformist path taken by the Ottoman sultans to the prophetic rebellions of leaders such as Muhammad Achmad, slowed but could not halt the European advance. European products and demands steadily eroded the economic fabric and heightened social tensions in Islamic lands. The stunning military and economic successes of the Christian Europeans cast doubts on Muslim claims to possession of the one true faith. By the century's end it was clear that neither the fundamentalists, who called for a return to a purified Islam free of Western influences, nor the reformers, who argued that some borrowing from the West was essential for survival, had come up with a successful formula for dealing with the powerful challenges posed by the industrial West. Failing to find adequate responses and deeply divided within, the Islamic community grew increasingly anxious over the dangers that lay ahead. Islamic civilization was by no means defeated, but its continued viability was clearly threatened by the powerful neighbor that had become master of the world.

THE LAST DYNASTY: THE RISE AND FALL OF THE QING EMPIRE IN CHINA

By the early decades of the 19th century a major collision between the aggressive and ever-expanding European industrial powers and the largest and most enduring of preindustrial civilizations, China, was unavoidable. For centuries the rulers of China had superciliously resisted European attempts to "open up" their rich lands and vast population to Christian missionary campaigns or the market economy the Europeans had extended over much of the globe. European traders were confined to two ports, Macao, which had been established by the Portuguese in the 16th century, and Canton, where their activities were strictly supervised by Chinese officials. The Chinese refused to accept European ambassadors or even to recognize nations, such as Britain and France, as their equals. Chinese officials treated European merchants and emissaries with the contempt that they felt the "southern (because they came by sea from the south) barbarians" deserved. Because they believed the Europeans had little to offer in the way of civilized attainments, the rulers of China made little ef-

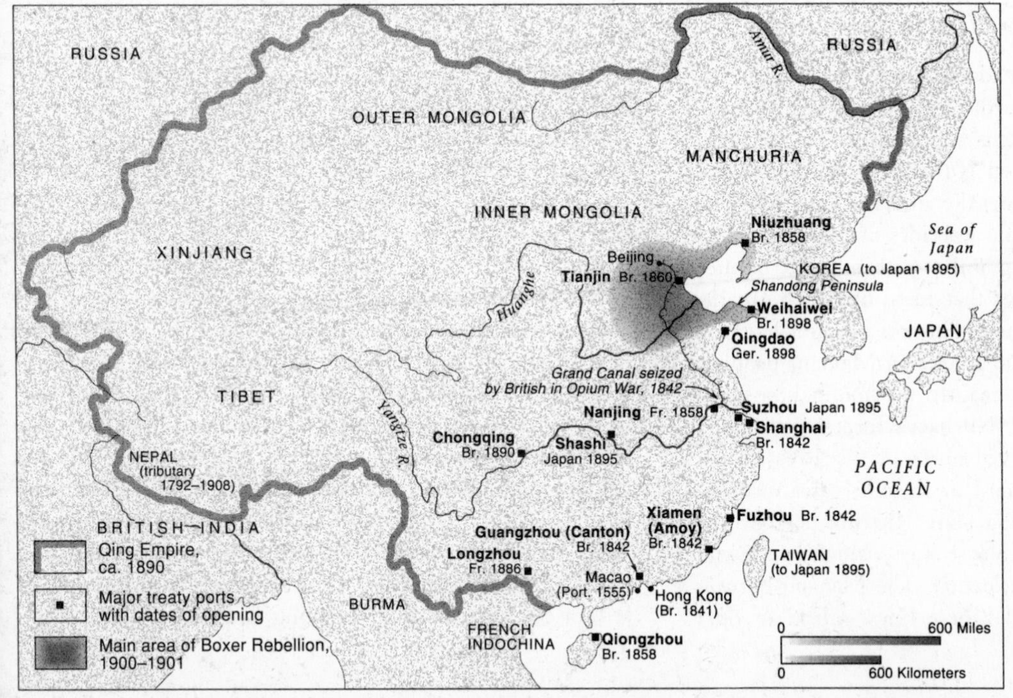

China during the Qing Era

fort to learn about the nation-states they represented. They knew next to nothing about the Renaissance and Reformation, and not much more about the scientific and industrial revolutions. As a result, when the Chinese were confronted by armed intervention of the European powers in the first decades of the 19th century, they struck out in blindness against adversaries whose motives they could not understand and whose power they were not at all prepared to reckon with.

Though China had been strong enough to get away with its policies of isolation and attitudes of disdain in the early centuries of expansion, by the late 18th century these were outmoded and dangerous. Not only had the Europeans grown incomparably stronger than they had been in the early centuries of expansion, but Chinese society was crumbling from within. Over a century of strong rule by the Manchus and a high degree of social stability, if not prosperity, for the Chinese people gave way to rampant official corruption, severe economic dislocations, and social unrest by the last decades of the 18th century. Each of these phases will be considered in the first sections of the following discussion of Chinese history in the Qing era. The next sections will be devoted to the growing tensions between the Chinese and the Europeans, particularly the British, and the series of 19th-century wars that resulted. The remaining portions of this chapter on the crises of Europe's two greatest rival civilizations, Islam and China, will explore the consequences of Europe's forcible entry into China and the slow demise of the last Chinese dynasty.

THE MAKING OF THE MANCHU IMPERIUM

Though the Manchu nomads had been building an expansive state of their own north of the Great Wall for decades, their conquest of China was both unexpected and sudden. A local leader named Nurhaci (1559–1626) was the architect of unity among the quarrelsome Manchu tribes. He combined the male warriors of each tribe into extremely cohesive fighting units within eight banner armies, named after the flags that identified each. In the first decades of the 17th century, Nurhaci brought much of Manchuria, including a number of non-Manchu peoples, under his rule. Though he remained the nominal vassal of the Chinese Ming emperor, Nurhaci's forces continually harassed the Chinese who lived north of the Great Wall, steadily driving them southward or in some cases incorporating them into his growing state. In this period, the Manchu elite's adoption of Chinese ways, which had begun much earlier, was greatly accelerated. The Manchu bureaucracy was organized along Chinese lines, Chinese court ceremonies were adopted, and numerous Chinese scholar-officials found lucrative employment in the growing barbarian state north of the Great Wall. Though less affected by Chinese influences, Manchu commoners had some exposure to Chinese ways, and though most remained nomadic herders, a fair percentage had become sedentary farmers by the time of the conquest of China proper.

The weakness of the declining Ming regime, rather than the Manchus' own strength, provided the opportunity to seize control in China. The Manchu entry into China resulted from a bit of luck. In 1644 an official of the Ming government in charge of the northern defenses called in the Manchus to help him put down a widespread rebellion in the region near the Great Wall. Having allowed the Manchus to pass through the wall, the official found that they were even a greater threat than the rebels. Exploiting the political divisions and social unrest that were in the process of destroying what was left of Ming authority, the Manchus boldly advanced on the Ming capital at Beijing, which they captured within the year. Though it took nearly two decades before centers of Ming and rebel resistance in the south and west were destroyed by the banner armies, the Manchus soon found themselves the masters of China.

They quickly proved that they were up to the challenge of ruling the largest empire in the world. Their armies forced submission by nomadic peoples far to the west and compelled tribute from kingdoms such as Vietnam and Burma to the south. Within decades, the Manchu regime, which had taken the dynastic name *Qing* before their conquest of China, ruled an area larger than any previous Chinese dynasty with the exception of the Tang.

To reconcile the ethnic Chinese who made up the vast majority of their subjects, the Manchu rulers shrewdly retained much of the political system of their Ming predecessors. They added to the court calendar whatever Confucian rituals they did not already observe. They made it clear that they wished the scholar-officials who had served the Ming to continue in office, and the Manchus even pardoned many who had been instrumental in prolonging resistance to their conquest. At the same time, however, the new rulers assumed a much more direct role in the appointment of local officials than had the Ming, and somewhat reduced the tax exemptions and privileges of these functionaries. For much of the first century of the dynasty, Chinese and Manchu officials were paired in appointments to most of the highest posts of the imperial bureaucracy, and Chinese officials predominated at the regional and local levels. Though Manchus, who made up less than two percent of the population of the Qing Empire, occupied a dis-

This Western engraving after a Chinese drawing portrays the first Manchu emperor, Kangxi, whose long reign between 1654 and 1722 brought such power and prosperity to China that European writers like Voltaire compared him to the philosopher-king who was the ideal of Plato.

proportionate number of the highest political positions, there were few limits as to how high talented ethnic Chinese could rise in the imperial bureaucracy.

Unlike the Mongol conquerors who abolished it, the Manchus retained the examination system and had their own sons educated in the Chinese classics. The Manchu emperors styled themselves the Sons of Heaven and rooted their claims to be the legitimate rulers of China in their practice of the traditional Confucian virtues. The early Manchu rulers were generous patrons of the Chinese arts and at least one, Kangxi (1661–1722), was a significant Confucian scholar in his own right. Kangxi and other Manchu rulers employed thousands of scholars to compile great encyclopedias of Chinese learning.

Despite the Manchus' high degree of Sinification and efforts to conciliate the Chinese scholar-gentry elite, resentment of them persisted. The burden of maintaining garrisons of their troops in the major cities of the empire was a very real one, and many ethnic Chinese never forgave the Manchus the humiliation of an edict that forced all Chinese males to shave their foreheads and wear their hair braided in the back. When the empire was strong and prosperous, most of the Manchus' subjects were willing to put up with these burdens. But when the Qing dynasty went into decline in the late 18th century, its foreign origins became a rallying point for risings from below.

ECONOMY AND SOCIETY IN THE EARLY CENTURIES OF QING RULE

The Manchu determination to preserve much of the Chinese political system was paralleled by an equally conservative approach to Chinese society as a whole. In the early centuries of their reign the writings of Zhu Xi, which had been so influential in the preceding dynastic eras, continued to dominate official thinking. Thus, long-nurtured values such as respect for rank and acceptance of hierarchy—that is, old over young, male over female, scholar-bureaucrat over commoner—were emphasized in education and imperial edicts. Among the elite classes, the extended family remained the core unit of the social order, and the state grew increasingly suspicious of any forms of social organization, such as guilds and especially secret societies, that rivaled it.

The lives of women at all social levels remained centered or wholly confined to the household, where the dominance of elder males was upheld by familial pressures and the state. Male control was enhanced by the practice of choosing brides from families slightly lower in social status than those of the grooms. Because they were a loss to their parents' household at marriage and usually required a sizeable dowry, daughters continued to be much less desirable than sons. Despite the poor quality of the statistics relating to the practice, there are indications that the incidence of female infanticide rose in this period. In the population as a whole males considerably outnumbered females—the reverse of the balance between the two in contemporary industrial societies.

Beyond the family compound the world pretty much belonged to men, though women from lower-class families continued to labor in the fields and sell produce in the local markets. The best a married woman could hope for was strong backing from her father and brother after she had gone to her husband's home, as well as the good luck in the first place to be chosen as the wife rather than as a second or third partner in the form of a concubine. If they bore sons and lived long enough, wives took charge of running the household, and in elite families they exercised considerable control over other females and even younger males. In contrast to India where widow remarriage was all but prohibited, especially among the higher castes, in China it was permitted since widows were seen as a burden on family resources.

Some of the strongest measures the Manchus took after conquering China were aimed at alleviating the rural distress and unrest that had become so pronounced in the last years of Ming rule. Taxes and state labor demands were lowered, and incentives, such as tax-free tenure, were offered to those willing to resettle lands that had been abandoned in the turmoil of the preceding decades. A sizeable chunk of the imperial budget (up to ten percent in the early years of the dynasty) was devoted to the repair of existing dikes, canals, and roadways and the extension of irrigation works. Peasants were encouraged to plant new crops, including those for which there was a considerable market demand, and to grow two or even three crops per year on their holdings. Like a number of the earlier dynasties, the Qing sought to check the accumulation of great estates by rural landlords or, failing that, to at least strengthen the position of the tenant classes.

Given the growing pressure of population on the available cultivable acreage and the virtual disappearance in most areas of open lands that could be settled, the regime had very little success in these laudable endeavors. After several decades of holding steady, the landed classes found that they could add to their estates with impunity by calling in loans to peasants or simply buying them out. With a surplus of laborers desirous of their positions, tenants had less and less bargaining power in their dealings with landlords. If they objected to the share of the crop the landlords offered, they were turned off the land and replaced by those willing to accept even less. As a result of these patterns, the gap between the rural gentry and ordinary peasants, not to mention the impoverished laborers, increased noticeably. One could not miss the old and new rich in the rural areas, as they rode, decked out in silks and furs, to make social calls on their peers. To further impress their superior social standing upon those whom they encountered, many males of the gentry class let their nails grow long to demonstrate that they never engaged in physical labor.

The sector of Chinese society over which the Qing were able to exercise the least control was also the most dynamic. The commercial and urban expansion that had begun in the Song era gained new strength in the long peace China enjoyed during the first century and a half of Manchu rule. Regional diversification in crops such as tea was matched by the development of new ways of financing agricultural and artisan production. Until the end of the 18th century, both the state and the mercantile classes profited enormously from the great influx of silver that poured into China in payment for its exports of tea, porcelain, and silk textiles. European and other foreign traders flocked to Canton, and Chinese merchants, freed from the restrictions against overseas travel of the late Ming, found lucrative market outlets in the Philippines, Siam, and elsewhere in Southeast Asia. The influx of silver meant some inflation, but until the latter half of the 18th century the much more market-oriented and sophisticated Chinese economy was better able to handle rising prices than its Islamic counterparts were. Overseas trading links gave rise to a wealthy new group of merchants, the *compradors,* who specialized in the import-export trade on China's south coast. In the 19th century, these merchants proved to be one of the major links between China and the outside world. The inability of the Qing regime to control this growing commercial class effectively both undermined the regime's attempts to prohibit the import of harmful substances, such as opium, and deprived the regime of substantial tax revenues.

ROT FROM WITHIN: BUREAUCRATIC BREAKDOWN AND SOCIAL DISINTEGRATION

By the late 18th century, it was clear that, like so many Chinese dynasties of the past, the Qing was in decline. The signs of decline were pervasive and familiar. The bureaucratic foundations of the Chinese Empire were rotting from within. The exam system, which had done well in selecting able and honest bureaucrats in the early decades of the dynasty, had become riddled with cheating and favoritism. Despite formal restrictions, sons of high officials were often ensured a place in the ever-growing bureaucracy. Even more disturbing was the fact that virtually anyone with enough money could buy a post for sons or brothers.

Impoverished scholars could be paid to take the exams for poorly educated or not so bright relatives, and examiners could be bribed to approve their credentials or look the other way when candidates consulted cheat sheets while taking their exams. In one of the most notorious cases of cheating, a merchant's son won high honors, despite the fact that he had spent the days of testing in a brothel hundreds of miles from the examination.

Cheating had become so blatant as early as the first decades of the 18th century that in 1711 students who had failed the exams at Yangzhou held a public demonstration to protest bribes given to the exam officials by wealthy salt merchants. The growing influx of merchant and poorly educated landlords' sons into the bureaucracy was particularly troubling because few of these had received the classical Confucian education that stressed the responsibilities of the educated ruling classes and their obligation to serve the people. Increasingly, positions in the bureaucracy were regarded by the wealthy as a means of exerting influence over local officials and judges as well as a way of enhancing family fortunes without regard for the effects of bureaucratic decisions on the peasantry and urban laborers.

Over a period of decades, the diversion of revenue from state projects to the enrichment of individual families had a devastating impact on Chinese society. For example, funds needed to maintain the armies and fleets that defended the huge empire fell off sharply, resulting in a noticeable drop in the training and armament of the military. Even more critical for the mass of the people were reductions in spending on public works projects. Of these, the most vital were the great dikes that confined the Yellow River in northern China. Over the millennia, the silting of the river bottom and the constant repair of and additions to the dikes created a situation where river and dikes were raised high above the densely populated farmlands through which they passed. Thus, when neglected for lack of funds and proper official supervision of repairs, leaking dikes and rampaging waters of the great river meant catastrophe for much of northeastern China.

Nowhere was this disaster more apparent than in the region of the Shandong peninsula. Before the mid-19th century, the Yellow River emptied into the sea south of the peninsula. By the 1850s, however, the neglected dikes had broken down over much of the area and the river had flooded hundreds of square miles of heavily cultivated farmland. By the 1860s the main channel of the river flowed north of the peninsula. The lands in between had been flooded and the farms wiped out. Peasants in the millions were left without livestock or land to cultivate; tens, perhaps hundreds, of thousands of peasants died of famine and disease.

As the condition of the peasantry deteriorated in many parts of the empire, further signs of dynastic decline appeared. Food shortages and landlord exactions prompted mass migrations; vagabond bands clogged the roads and beggars crowded the city streets. Banditry, long seen by the Chinese as one of the surest gauges of the extent of dynastic decline, became a major problem in many districts. As the following verse from a popular ditty of the 1860s illustrates, the government's inability to deal with the bandits was seen as a further sign of Qing weakness:

> *When the bandits arrive, where are the troops?*
> *When the troops come, the bandits have vanished.*
> *Alas, when will the bandits and troops meet?*

The assumption then widely held by Chinese thinkers—that the dynastic cycle would again run its course with the Manchus being replaced by a new and vigorous dynasty—was belied by the magnitude of the problems confronting the leaders of China. The belief that China's future could be predicted by the patterns of its past history ignored the fact that, in a number of ways, there were no precedents for the critical changes that had occurred in China under Manchu rule. Some of these changes had their roots in the preceding Ming era (see Chapter 28) in which, for example, food crops from the New World had set in motion a population explosion. An already large population had nearly doubled to reach a total of over 200 million in the first century (c. 1650–1750) of Manchu rule; in the following century it doubled again to reach 410 to 415 million. However successful they had been in the past, Chinese social and economic systems were simply not capable of carrying a population of this magnitude. China desperately needed innovations, breakthroughs in technology and organization that would increase its productivity to the point where its exploding population could be supported at a reasonable level. The corrupt and highly conservative late-Manchu regime was increasingly an obstacle to, rather than a source of, these desperately needed changes.

BARBARIANS AT THE SOUTHERN GATES

A second major difference between the forces sapping the strength of the Manchus and those that had brought down earlier dynasties was the nature of the so-called barbarians who threatened the empire from outside. As we have seen, nomadic incursions had traditionally played a large role in the dynastic cycle. Their bolder and more frequent incursions into the agrarian regions protected by the Great Wall was one of the surest signs of the impending end of a dynasty. But in the past the nomads, even when—like the Manchus—they had established themselves as the new rulers of China, had soon been assimilated to China's more sophisticated culture and society and absorbed into the much larger Chinese population.

Though the Chinese, out of ignorance, treated the Europeans much like the nomads and other peoples whom they regarded as barbarians, the Europeans presented a very different sort of challenge. They came from a civilization that was China's equal in sophistication and complexity. In fact, though European nation-states like Great Britain were much smaller in population (in the early 19th century England had seven million people to China's 400 million), they could, thanks to the scientific and industrial revolutions, compensate for their smaller numbers with better organization and superior technology. As tensions built up between the Europeans—who demanded that restrictions on their trading and religious proselytization in China be removed—and the Chinese—who were determined to limit foreigners' activities within the empire—the Europeans' advantages in technology and knowledge of the wider world became increasingly decisive. When violent clashes between the two led to wars between 1839 and 1842 as well as 1856 and 1860, the underlying vulnerabilities of Chinese civilization were brutally exposed.

DOCUMENT
THE LETTER OF THE QIANLONG EMPEROR TO KING GEORGE III

One of the most fascinating and important documents from the early decades of European imperialist involvement in China was the letter sent in 1793 from the emperor of China to King George III of England. Excerpts of the letter follow:

> We have perused the text of your state message and the wording expresses your earnestness. From it your sincere humility and obedience can clearly be seen. . . . As to what you have requested in your message, O King, namely to be allowed to send one of your subjects to reside in the Celestial Empire to look after your country's trade, this does not conform to the Celestial Empire's ceremonial system, and definitely cannot be done. . . . If it is said that your object, O King, is to take care of trade, men from your country have been trading at Macao for some time and have always been treated favorably. For instance, in the past Portugal and Italy and other countries have several times sent envoys to the Celestial Empire with requests to look after their trade, and the Celestial Empire, bearing in mind their loyalty, treated them with great kindness. Whenever any matter concerning trade has arisen which affected those countries it has always been fully taken care of.
>
> The Celestial Empire, ruling all within the four seas [the world], simply concentrates on carrying out the affairs of the Government properly, and does not value rare and precious things. Now you, O King, have presented various objects to the throne, and mindful of your loyalty in presenting offerings from afar, we have specially ordered the Department of Foreign tribute to receive them. In fact, the virtue and power of the Celestial Dynasty has penetrated afar to the myriad kingdoms, which have come to render homage, and so all kinds of precious things from "over mountain and sea" have been collected here, things which your chief envoy and others have seen for themselves. Nevertheless, we have never valued ingenious articles, nor do we have the slightest need of your country's manufactures. Therefore, O King, as regards your request to send someone to remain at the capital, while it is not in harmony with the regulations of the Celestial Empire we also feel very much that it is of no advantage to your country. Hence we have issued these detailed instructions and have commanded your tribute envoys to return safely home. You, O King, should simply act in conformity with our wishes by strengthening your loyalty and swearing perpetual obedience so as to ensure that your country may share the blessings of peace.

Questions: What do these excerpts tell you about the Chinese view of themselves, the English, and the wider world at the time? How well do these attitudes correspond to the actual situation? Why were they likely to cause serious problems for the Chinese?

THE ORIGINS OF THE OPIUM WAR

The issue that was responsible for the initial warfare between China and the British did little credit to the latter. For centuries British merchants had eagerly exported silks, fine porcelains, tea, and other products from the Chinese Empire. Finding that they had little in the way of manufactured goods or raw materials that the Chinese were willing to take in exchange for these products, the British were forced to surrender growing amounts of silver bullion to obtain the products they wanted. Unhappy about the unfavorable terms of trade in China, British merchants hit on a possible solution in the form of opium that was grown in the hills of eastern India. Though opium was also cultivated in China, the Indian variety was far more potent and soon in great demand in the Middle Kingdom. By the first decades of the 19th century an average of 4500 chests of opium, each weighing 133 pounds, were sold, either legally or illicitly, to merchants on the south China coast. By 1839, on the eve of the Opium War, nearly 40,000 chests were imported by the Chinese.

Though the British had found a way to reverse the trade balance in their favor, the Chinese soon realized that the opium traffic was a major threat to their economy and social order. Within years China's favorable trade balance with the outside world was reversed and silver began to flow in large quantities out of the country. As sources of capital for public works and trade expansion decreased, agricultural productivity stagnated or declined and unemployment spread, especially in the hinterlands of the coastal trading areas. Wealthy Chinese, who could best afford it, squandered increasing amounts of China's wealth to support their opium habits, and opium dens spread in the towns and villages of the empire at an alarming rate. By 1838, it has been estimated, one percent of China's better than 400 million people were addicted to the drug. Strung out officials neglected their administrative responsibilities, the sons of prominent scholar-gentry families lost their ambition, and even laborers and peasants abandoned their work for the debilitating pleasures of the squalid opium dens.

From early in the 18th century, Qing emperors had issued edicts forbidding the traffic, but little had been done to enforce them. By the first years of the 19th century, it was clear to the court and high officials that the opium trade must be stopped. When serious efforts were finally undertaken in the early 1820s, they only served to drive the opium dealers from Canton to nearby islands and other clandestine locations on the coast. Finally, in the late 1830s the emperor sent one of the most distinguished officials in the empire, Lin Zexu, with orders to use every means available to stamp out the trade. Lin, who was famed for his incorruptibility, took his charge quite seriously. After being rebuffed in his attempts to win the cooperation of European merchants and naval officers in putting an end to the trade, Lin ordered the European trading areas in Canton blockaded, their warehouses searched, and all the opium that was confiscated destroyed.

Not surprisingly, these actions enraged the European merchants, and they demanded military action to avenge their losses. Arguing that Lin's measures violated both the property rights of the merchants and principles of free

This mid-19th-century European engraving depicts the criminal atmosphere and dissolution associated with Chinese opium dens. Victorian sensibilities made it difficult for contemporary artists to capture fully the depths of despair and degradation that addicts reached in these centers of unchecked vice.

trade, the British ordered the Chinese to put an end to their antiopium campaign or risk military intervention. When Lin persisted, war broke out in late 1839. In the conflict that followed the Chinese were first routed on the sea, where their now-antiquated war junks were no match for British gunboats; then they were soundly defeated in their attempts to repel an expeditionary force the British sent ashore. With British warships and armies threatening the cities of the Yangze River region, the Qing emperor was forced to sue for peace and send Lin into exile in a remote province of the empire.

Their victories in the Opium War and a second conflict, which erupted in the late 1850s, allowed the European powers to force China to open trade and diplomatic exchanges. After the first war, Hong Kong was established as an additional center of British commerce, and European trade was permitted at five other ports, where the Europeans were given land to build more warehouses and living quarters. By the 1890s, 90 ports of call were available to over 300,000 European and American traders, missionaries, and diplomats. Britain, France, Germany, and Russia had won long-term leases over several ports and surrounding territory, as imperialist expansion pressed China directly.

Though the treaty of 1842 made no reference to the opium trade, following China's defeat the drug poured unchecked into China. By the middle of the century, China's foreign trade and customs were overseen by British officials. They were careful to ensure that European nationals had favored access to China's markets and that no protective tariffs, such as those the Americans were using at the time to protect their young industries, were established by the Chinese. Most humiliating of all for the Chinese was the fact that they were forced to accept European ambassadors at the Qing court. Not only were ambassadors traditionally (and usually quite rightly) regarded as spies, but the exchange of diplomatic missions was a concession that European nations were equal in stature to China. Given the deeply entrenched Chinese conviction that their Middle Kingdom was the civilized center of the earth and that all other peoples were barbarians, this was indeed a very difficult concession to make. European battleships and firepower gave them little choice.

A CIVILIZATION AT RISK: REBELLION, FAILED REFORMS, AND THE FALL OF THE QING

Though it was not immediately apparent, China's defeat in the Opium War greatly contributed to a building crisis that threatened not just the Qing dynasty but Chinese civilization as a whole. Defeat and the dislocations in south China brought on by the growing commercial encroachments of the West spawned a massive rebellion that convulsed much of south China in the 1850s and early 1860s, and at one point threatened to overthrow the Qing dynasty. Led by a mentally unstable, semi-Christianized prophet named Hong Xiuquan, the Taiping rebellion exacerbated the already considerable stresses within Chinese society and further drained the diminishing resources of the ruling dynasty. Though widespread peasant risings, incited by the members of secret societies like the White Lotus, had erupted as early as the 1770s, the Taiping movement was the first to pose a serious alternative not only to the Qing dynasty but to Confucian civilization as a whole. In contrast to a number of contemporary rebellions to the west of China, the Taipings offered sweeping programs for social reform, land redistribution, and the liberation of women. They also attacked the traditional Confucian elite and the learning on which its claims to authority rested. Taiping rebels smashed ancestral tablets and shrines, and proposed a simplified script and mass literacy that would have undermined one of the scholar-gentry's chief sources of power.

Their attack on the scholar-gentry, in fact, was one of the main causes of the Taipings' ultimate defeat. Left no option but to rally to the Manchu regime, the provincial gentry became the focus of resistance to the Taipings. Honest and able Qing officials, such as Zeng Guofan, raised more effective, provincially based military forces just in time to beat off the Taiping assault on northern China. Zeng and his allies in the government also sought to carry out much-needed reforms to root out corruption in the bureaucracy and revive the stagnating Chinese economy.

In the last decades of the 19th century, these dynamic provincial leaders were the most responsible for China's self-strengthening movement, which was aimed at countering the challenge from the West. They encouraged Western investment in railways and even factories in the areas they governed, and sought to modernize their armies. Combined with the breakdown of Taiping leadership and the declining appeal of a movement that could not deliver on the promises it made to its followers, the efforts of the gentry brought about the eventual but very bloody suppression of the Taiping rebellion. Other movements were also crushed and banditry was brought under control for a time. But like the Ottoman sultans and their advisors, the Chinese gentry introduced changes that they viewed as limited, aimed at preserving the existing order, not fundamentally transforming it. They continued to profess loyalty to the gravely weakened Manchu regime because they saw it as a defender of the traditional order. At the same time, their own power grew to the point that the Manchus could control them only with great difficulty. Resources were increasingly drained from the court center to the provincial governors, whose growing military and political power posed a potential threat to the Qing court. The basis of China's political fragmentation was building behind the crumbling facade of Manchu rule.

Despite their clearly desperate situation by the last decades of the 19th century, including a shocking loss in a war with Japan in 1894 and 1895, the Manchu rulers stubbornly resisted the far-reaching reforms that were the only hope of saving the regime, and, as it turned out, Chinese civilization. Manchu rulers on occasion moved to back those officials who pushed for extensive political and social reforms, some of which were inspired by the example of the West. But their efforts were repeatedly frustrated by the backlash of members of the imperial household who allied themselves to the great majority of the scholar-gentry, who were determined to preserve the old order with only minor changes and to make no concessions to the West.

The last decades of the dynasty were dominated by the ultra-conservative dowager empress Cixi, who became the power behind the throne. In 1898 she and her faction crushed the most serious move toward reform from the top. Her nephew, the emperor, was imprisoned in the Forbidden City, and leading advocates for reform were executed or driven from China. On one occasion, Cixi flaunted the Westernizers by rechanneling funds that had been raised to build modern warships to defend China into the building of a huge marble boat in one of the lakes in the imperial gardens. With genuine reform blocked by Cixi and her faction, the Manchus relied on divisions between the provincial officials as well as between the European powers to maintain their position. The involvement of members of the Qing household in popular outbursts aimed at forcibly expelling the foreigners from China—such as the Boxer Rebellion that broke out in 1898 and was only put down through the intervention of the imperialist powers in 1901—resulted in further military setbacks and enhanced the control of the Europeans and the power of the provincial officials.

By the first years of the 20th century, the days of the Manchus were clearly numbered. With the defeat of the Taipings, resistance to the Qing came to be centered in rival secret society organizations such as the Triads and the Society of Elders and Brothers. These underground organizations inspired numerous local risings against the dynasty in the last decades of the 19th century, which failed for lack of coordination and sufficient resources. But some of the secret society cells became a valuable training ground that prepared the way for a new sort of resistance to the Manchus. By the end of the 19th century, the sons of some of the scholar-gentry and especially of the comprador merchants in the port cities were becoming more and more involved in secret society operations and other activities aimed at the overthrow of the regime. Because many of these young men had received European-style educations, their resistance was aimed at more than just getting rid of the Manchus. They envisioned power passing to Western-educated, reformist leaders who would build a new and strong nation-state in China patterned after those of the West, rather than simply establishing yet another imperial dynasty. For aspiring revolutionaries such as Sun Yat-sen, who emerged as one of their most articulate spokesmen, their seizure of power was also seen as a way of enacting desperately needed social programs to relieve the misery of the peasantry and urban workers.

Though they drew heavily on the West for ideas and organizational models, the revolutionaries from the rising middle classes were deeply hostile to the involvement of the imperialist powers in Chinese affairs and condemned the Manchus for their failure to control the foreigners. The young rebels cut off their queues in defiance of Manchu order that all ethnic Chinese wear their hair in this fashion, and joined in uprisings fomented by the secret societies or plotted assassinations and acts of sabotage on their own. Attempts to coordinate an all-China rising floundered on a number of occasions due to personal animosities or amateurish incompetence. But in late 1911, opposition to the government's reliance on the Western powers for railway loans led to secret society uprisings, student demonstrations, and mutinies on the part of imperial troops. When a number of key provincial officials refused to put down the spreading rebellion, the Manchus had no choice but to abdicate. In February of 1912 the last emperor of China, a small boy named Puyi, was deposed, and one of the more powerful of the provincial lords was asked to establish a republican government in China.

THE END OF A CIVILIZATION?

The revolution of 1911 toppled the Qing dynasty, but in many ways a more important watershed for Chinese civilization was crossed in 1905. In that year the civil service exams were given for the last time. Reluctantly, even the ultraconservative advisors of the empress Cixi had concluded that solutions to China's predicament could no longer be found in the Confucian learning the exams tested. The abandonment of the exams in effect signaled the end of a pattern of civilized life the Chinese had nurtured, improved, and held to for nearly 2500 years. The mix of philosophies and values that had come to be known as the Confucian system, the massive civil bureaucracy, rule by an educated and cultivated scholar-gentry elite, and even the artistic accomplishments of the old order were to come under increasing criticism in the early years of the 20th century. Many of these hallmarks of the most enduring civilization that had ever existed would be vehemently discarded, violently destroyed. As we shall see in Chapter 41, however, even though Confucian civilization like so many before it passed into history, many of its ideas, attitudes, and ways of approaching the world survived. Some of these played critical roles in the violent and painful struggle of the Chinese people to build a new civilization to replace the one that had failed them. The challenge of blending and balancing the two remains to the present day.

CONCLUSION

ISLAMIC AND CHINESE RESPONSES TO THE CHALLENGE OF THE WEST COMPARED

Though both Chinese and Islamic civilizations were severely weakened by internal disruptions in the 18th and 19th centuries, each was thrown into prolonged crisis by the growing challenges posed by the West. A number of key differences in the interaction between each civilization and the West do much to explain why Islam, though badly shaken, survived, while Chinese civilization collapsed under the burden of domestic upheavals and foreign aggression. For the Muslims, who had been warring and trading with Christian Europe since the Middle Ages, the Western threat had long existed. What was new was the much greater strength of the Europeans in the ongoing contest, which resulted from their global expansion and their scientific and industrial revolutions. For China, the challenges from the West came suddenly and brutally. Within decades, the Chinese had to revise their estimate of their empire as the center of the world and the source of civilization itself to take into account severe defeats at the hands of peoples they once dismissed as barbarians.

The Muslims could also take comfort from the fact that in the Judeo-Christian and Greek traditions they shared much with the ascendant Europeans, and that elements of their own civilization had played critical roles in the rise of the West. This made it easier to justify Muslim borrowing from the West, which in any case could be set in a long tradition of exchanges with other civilizations. Though some Chinese technology had passed to the West, Chinese and Western leaders were largely unaware of early exchanges but deeply impressed by the profound differences between their societies. For the Chinese, borrowing from the barbarians required a painful reassessment of their place in the world—a reassessment many were unwilling to make.

In countering the thrusts from the West, the Muslims gained from the fact that they had many centers to defend—the fall of a single dynasty or regime did not mean the end of Islamic independence. The Muslims also gained from the more gradual nature of the Western advance. They had time to learn from earlier mistakes and try out different responses to the Western challenges. For the Chinese, the defense of their civilization came to be equated with the survival of the Qing dynasty—a line of thinking that the Manchus did all they could to promote. When the dynasty collapsed in the early 20th century, the Chinese lost faith in the formula for civilization they had successfully followed for over two millennia. Again timing was critical. The crisis in China seemed to come without warning. Within decades, the Qing went from the arrogant controller of the barbarians to a defeated and humbled pawn of the European powers.

When the dynasty failed and it became increasingly clear that the barbarians had outdone the Chinese in so many fields of civilized endeavor, the Chinese had little to fall back on. Like the Europeans, they had excelled in social and political organization and mastery of the material world. Unlike the Hindus or the Muslims, they had no great religious tradition with which to counter the European conceit that worldly dominance could be equated with inherent superiority. In the depths of their crisis, Muslim peoples clung to the conviction that they possessed the true faith, the last and fullest of God's revelations to humankind. That faith became the basis of their resistance and of their strategies for renewal, the key to the survival of Islamic civilization and its continuing efforts to meet the challenges of the West in the 20th century.

FURTHER READINGS

The best general introductions to the Ottoman decline and the origins of the nation of Turkey remain Bernard Lewis's *The Emergence of Modern Turkey* (1961) and the chapter on "The Later Ottoman Empire" by Halil Inalcik in the *Cambridge History of Islam,* vol. 1 (1973). Other recent studies of importance on specific aspects of this process include C. V. Findley's studies of Ottoman bureaucratic reform and the development of a modern civil service in what is today Turkey, Ernest Ramsaur's *The Young Turks* (1957), Stanford Shaw's *Between Old and New* (1971), and David Kusher's essay on *The Rise of Turkish Nationalism* (1977). On Egypt and the Islamic heartlands in this period, see P. M. Holt's *Egypt and the Fertile Crescent, 1516–1922* (1965) or P. J. Vatikiotis's *The History of Egypt* (1985). On the Mahdist movement in the Sudan see P. M. Holt's *The Mahdist State in the Sudan* (1958) or the fine summary by L. Carl Brown in Robert Rotberg and Ali Mazrui, eds., *Protest and Power in Black Africa* (1970). The latter also includes many informative articles on African resistance to European conquest and rule. On women and changes in the family in the Ottoman realm, see Nermin Abadan-Unat's *Women in Turkish Society* (1981), and in the Arab world, see Nawal el Saadawi's *The Hidden Face of Eve* (1980).

On the Manchu takeover in China, see Frederic Wakeman, Jr.'s *The Great Enterprise* (1985) and Jonathan Spence and John E. Willis, eds., *Ming to Ch'ing* (1979). On Qing rule, among the most readable and useful works are Spence's *Emperor of China: Portrait of K'ang-hsi* (1974) and the relevant sections in his recent study on *The Search for Modern China* (1990); Susan Naquin and Evelyn Rawski's *Chinese Society in the 18th Century* (1987); and the essays in John Fairbank, ed., *Cambridge History of China: Late Ch'ing 1800–1911* (1978). A good survey of the causes and course of the Opium War is provided by Chang Hsin-pao's *Commissioner Lin and the Opium War* (1964). The Taiping rebellion is covered in Jen Yu-wen's *The Taiping Revolutionary Movement* (1973), and the first stages of the Chinese nationalist movement are examined in the essays in Mary Wright, ed., *China in Revolution: The First Phase* (1968). The early sections of Elisabeth Croll's *Feminism and Socialism in China* (1980) provide an excellent overview of the status and condition of women in the Qing era.

RUSSIA'S REFORMS AND INDUSTRIAL ADVANCE

DOCUMENT: Russian Conservatism and the West

PROTEST AND REVOLUTION

JAPAN

ANALYSIS: The Separate Paths of Japan and China

CONCLUSION: Japan, Russia, and World War I

FURTHER READINGS

Russia

1812 Failure of Napoleon's invasion

1815 Russia reacquires Poland through the Treaty of Vienna; Alexander I and the Holy Alliance

1825 Decembrist Revolt

1825–1855 Heightening of repression by Tsar Nicholas I

1829–1878 Serbia gains increasing autonomy in Ottoman Empire, then independence

1830–1831 Polish nationalist revolt repressed

1831 Greece wins independence after revolt against Ottomans

1833, 1853 Russian-Ottoman wars

Japan

1720 End ban on Western books

1800–1850 Growth of "Dutch school"

1841–1843 Brief shogun reform effort

33 Russia and Japan: Industrialization Outside the West

INTRODUCTION. Two important nations defied the common pattern of growing Western domination during the 19th century: Russia and Japan. Both did so only after a heightened threat of Western interference, and both had to accept Western advisors and other intrusions. Russia and Japan did, however, manage to launch significant industrialization by 1914, along with other changes designed to strengthen their political and social systems and preserve national independence. Neither Russia nor Japan rivaled the industrial might of the West at this point; both were trying to catch up after a late start. Their achievement was economic autonomy—not yet a share in the West's core position—which enabled both nations to gain sufficient power to wield important political and military influence, participating in the imperialist scramble of the late 19th century.

Most of the non-Western world, as we have seen, was described largely in terms of growing vulnerability in the face of Western advance during the 19th century. A host of territories were either newly seized colonies or existing colonies controlled with new rigor. Latin America, a special case, won independence and admittedly enjoyed some growing economic success by the later 19th century, but amid firm commercial and diplomatic constraints from western Europe and the United States. China and the Islamic Middle East, technically independent amid important territorial loss, hesitated in their response to new

1854–1856 Crimean War
1856 Romania gains virtual independence
1860s–1870s Alexander II reforms
1861 Russian emancipation of serfs
1865–1876 Russian conquests in central Asia
1867 Russia sells Alaska to U.S.
1875–1877 Russian-Ottoman war, Russia wins new territory
1878 Bulgaria gains independence
1881–1905 Growing repression, attacks on minorities
1881 Anarchist assassination of Alexander II
1884–1887 New gains in central Asia
1884–1914 Beginnings of Russian industrialization; near-completion of trans-Siberian railway (full linkage 1916)
1892–1903 Sergey Witte, minister of finance
1898 Formation of Marxist Social Democratic Party
1904–1905 Loss in Russo-Japanese War
1905–1906 Revolution results in peasant reforms and duma
1914 World War I
1917 Revolution and Bolshevik victory

1853 Perry expedition to Edo Bay
1854 Follow-up American and British fleet visits
1860–1868 Civil strife
1867 Mutsuhito, emperor of Japan
1868–1912 Meiji period
1870–1940 Population growth
1870 Ministry of Industry established
1872 Universal military service established
1877 Final samurai rising
1890 New constitution and legal code
1894–1895 Sino-Japanese war
1902 Loose alliance with Britain
1904–1905 Russo-Japanese War
1910 Annexation of Korea
1912 Growing party strife in Parliament
1914 Entry to World War I
1916–1918 Seizure of former German holdings in Pacific and China

Western power, though Turkish reformers and Arab nationalists sketched some promising alternatives by 1900. Russia and Japan were different, though they too experienced new Western threats.

The early industrial revolutions of Japan and Russia as well as the forces that prompted them constitute important phenomena in that here were major cases of change in significant societies. These changes are also interesting in showing what societies could do, and had to do, in order to launch the kind of transformation the West had pioneered—without becoming fully Western.

Yet the distinctiveness of the Russian and Japanese patterns must also be recognized. These were the only societies outside the West to begin a wholesale process of industrialization before the 1960s. Other societies changed in many ways, but for various reasons, including Western interference, their transformations did not include this economic centerpiece. This means, in turn, that some special factors must be grasped in Japan and Russia, involving not just their industrialization but also their earlier history and their evolution during the early 19th century, in order to explain their unusual reactions to the West's industrial example.

The pairing of Russia and Japan was in many ways unexpected. The two societies had little to do with each other in the past, and they had scant contact even as they began to industrialize. Furthermore, their processes of change were quite different, based on different institutional structures and cultures. Japan displayed much more political flexibility than Russia did, and, once committed to reforms, Japan undertook a more sweeping transformation. Change in Russia more obviously heightened social strains, leading to a significant revolution in 1905 and a major upheaval in 1917. Japan had no outright revolution, which in a way made its ability to change all the more remarkable.

Japan must also be compared to other East Asian societies, particularly China, with which it shared many characteristics—the fruit of earlier imitation—but from which it began to diverge. Simply put, Japanese industrialization and related reforms seemed less expected in light of previous patterns than did Russia's, where an awareness of Western models and an interest in selective borrowing had developed by 1700. Japan pulled away from its larger civilization area at least for a time, whereas Russia continued a pattern of expanding influence in eastern Europe and central Asia.

Nevertheless, while Russia and Japan cannot be dealt with in a single sketch, their pairing is not random. Industrialization involved some common processes, and as late industrializers—chasing a considerable Western lead—Japan and Russia displayed still more similarities. Further, while Japan avoided revolution it did not escape serious strain; its differentiation from Russia should be not exaggerated on this score. Reactions to the West's Industrial Revolution obviously could shake up earlier civilizational alignments—such as in pulling Japan farther away from Chinese patterns.

Finally, in general but important ways Russia and Japan did have some common characteristics, which help explain why both could maintain economic and political independence during the West's century of power. They both had prior experience of imitation, Japan from China, Russia from Byzantium and then the West. They knew that learning from outsiders could be profitable and need not necessarily destroy their native cultures. They both had improved their political effectiveness during the 17th and 18th centuries, through the Tokugawa shogunate and tsarist empire. This would aid both in dealing with change from the basis of some political strength, though it did not deflect a need for further political reform, and it would allow both nations to use the state to sponsor changes that in the West had rested in part with private groups such as businessmen.

Ironically, soon after the reform period began in both countries, Russia and Japan met in new ways, as expansionist interests brought a clash over influence in Korea. The resultant Russo-Japanese War symbolized the growing importance of both societies in world affairs and their common involvement in unsettling change, though it also showed Japan's greater success in military modernization. The war promoted further change, convincing Japanese leaders that they were on the right course, while weakening a beleaguered Russian establishment.

RUSSIA'S REFORMS AND INDUSTRIAL ADVANCE

Neither Russia nor Japan generated significant changes during the first half of the 19th century. Both countries were bent on maintaining the status quo, though in Russia's case this involved pulling apart from Western patterns more fully than had been necessary in the previous century. Yet the early 19th century in both countries must be briefly probed in order to explain the ability and willingness to react decisively to a new Western challenge after 1850.

RUSSIA BEFORE REFORM

Russia's new fearfulness about Western patterns started in the governing elite and it was rooted in the shock generated by the French Revolution. Russian rulers, beginning with Catherine the Great in her later years, sought means to protect the country from Western revolutionary contagion, and in the process the sense that Western policies might serve as models for Russia faded dramatically. Napolean's 1812 invasion of Russia also produced new concern with defense. This turn toward renewed isolation was supported by conservative intellectuals who seized the opportunity to vaunt Russian values over those of the chaotic West. In the eyes of these aristocratic writers, Russia knew the true meaning of community and stability. The system of serfdom provided ignorant peasants with the guidance and protection of paternalistic masters—an inaccurate social analysis, but a comforting one. To combat Napoleon's pressure early in the 19th century some improvements in bureaucratic training were introduced, and city administrations were granted somewhat greater authority. A new tsar, Alexander I, flirted with liberal rhetoric, but he also sponsored the Holy Alliance idea at the Congress of Vienna that grouped the conservative monarchies of Russia, Prussia, and Austria in defense of religion and the established order. The idea of Russia as a bastion of sanity in a Europe gone mad was an appealing one.

The defense of the status quo produced some important new tensions, however. A number of intellectuals remained fascinated with Western progress, though they typically criticized certain aspects of it. Some praised political freedom and educational and scientific advance, while deploring the West's neglect of social issues amid the squalor of early industrialization. Others focused more purely on Western cultural styles. Early in the 19th century, Russia began to contribute creatively to European cultural output. The poet Pushkin, for example, descended from an African slave, used romantic styles to celebrate the beauties of the Russian soul and the tragic dignity of the common people. Because of its compatibility with the use of folklore and a sense of nationalism, the romantic style took deep root in eastern Europe. Russian musical composers would soon begin their contributions, again using folk themes and sonorous sentimentality within an essentially Western stylistic context.

While Russia's ruling elite continued to welcome Western artistic styles and took great pride in Russia's growing cultural respectability, they increasingly censored intellectuals who tried to incorporate liberal or radical political values. Many intellectuals were jailed or exiled to the West, in a pattern that to some extent has continued until very recently.

Western values also inspired a minor but disturbing political revolt, the Decembrist uprising in 1825. A group of middle-level army officers, many of whom had served in western Europe during the Napoleonic wars and who deplored Russia's backwardness compared to Western bureaucratic efficiency and political liberalism, rose up in the name of change. The officers were not well organized, and they were divided between a majority who wanted political improvements and nothing more and a minority who talked vaguely of more sweeping social change including peasant reforms. The revolt was easily put down, but it inspired the new tsar, Nicholas I, to still more adamant conservatism. Repression of political opponents stiffened, and the secret police expanded. Newspapers and schools, already confined to a small minority, were tightly supervised. What political criticism there was flourished mainly in exile in places such as Paris or London, and had little impact on Russia.

Partly because of political repression, Russia was spared the wave of revolutions that spread through Europe in 1830 and 1848. There was no substantial middle class to spearhead liberal protest, and police activity prevented the kind of ideological buildup that preceded revolution in the West. The artisan class was small and lacked strong organizational traditions. The huge peasant majority had grievances aplenty, and it continued to break out in periodic regional revolts against landlord exactions, but these revolts were not substantial enough to trigger a larger uprising. Russia seemed to be operating in a different political orbit from that of the West, to the great delight of most Russian officials. In its role as Europe's conservative anchor, Russia even intervened in 1849 to help Austria put down the nationalist revolution in Hungary—a blow in favor of monarchy but also a reminder of Russia's eagerness to flex its muscles in wider European affairs.

In the military Decembrist revolt in St. Petersburg, Loyalist troops ultimately put down the revolting regiments in 1825.

Russian Expansion, 1815–1914

While turning more fiercely conservative than it had been in the 18th century, Russia maintained its tradition of territorial expansion. Russia had confirmed its hold over most of Poland at the Congress of Vienna in 1815 after Napoleon had briefly sponsored a separate Polish duchy. While technically a separate entity under the tsar, the Polish territory was ruled with a heavy hand. Nationalist sentiment, inspired by the growth of romantic nationalism in Poland and backed by many Polish landowners with ties to the West, roused recurrent Polish opposition to Russian rule. An uprising occurred in 1830 and 1831, triggered by news of the revolutions in the West and led by liberal aristocrats and loyal Catholics who chafed under the rule of an Orthodox power. Tsar Nicholas I put down this revolt with great brutality, driving many leaders into exile.

Russia was clearly bent on maintaining full authority over its new European holdings. At the same time the Russians continued pressure on the Ottoman Empire, whose weakness attracted eager attention. A war in the 1830s led to some territorial gains, though Western powers, fearful of a Russian advance on Constantinople that would provide easy access to the Mediterranean, forced some limitations. France and Britain recurrently tried to prop up Ottoman authority in the interest of countering Russian aggression. Russia also supported many nationalist movements in the Balkans, including the Greek independence war in the 1820s—a desire to cut back the Turks here outweighed Russia's commitment to conservatism. Overall, while no massive acquisitions marked the early 19th century, Russia continued to be a dynamic diplomatic and military force.

ECONOMIC AND SOCIAL PROBLEMS: THE PEASANT QUESTION

Russia's economic position, however, did not keep pace with its diplomatic aspirations. As the West industrialized and central European powers, such as Prussia and Austria, introduced at least the beginnings of industrialization, including some rail lines, Russia largely stood pat—this meant that it began to fall increasingly behind the West in technology and trade. The patterns of the 18th century, which had suggested growing Russian economic dependence on the West, resumed with a vengeance. Russian landlords eagerly took advantage of Western markets for grain, but they increased their exports not by improving their techniques but by tightening the labor obligations on their serfs. This was a common pattern in much of eastern Europe in the early 19th century, as Polish and Hungarian nobles also increased labor service in order to gain ground in the export market. In return for low-cost grain exports, Russia and other East European areas imported some

Western machinery and other costly equipment, as well as luxury goods for the great aristocrats to display as badges of cultured respectability. A few isolated factories were opened up using Western equipment, but there was no significant change in overall manufacturing or transportation mechanisms. Russia remained a profoundly agricultural society based on essentially unfree labor, but it was now a visibly stagnant society as well. Many Russian leaders were aware of the West's great economic innovation and dynamism, but they papered over the differences by their enthusiastic embrace of European cultural styles, keeping up to date on the latest in costume, dance, or painting, while in some cases offering criticisms of the social injustice of industrialization.

The widening gap between Russia and the West was dramatically driven home by a fairly minor war in the Crimea between 1854 and 1856. Nicholas I had provoked conflict with the Ottoman Empire in 1853, arguing among other things that Russia had the responsibility for protecting Christian interests in the Holy Land and that the Ottomans were not assuring the rights of churches and monasteries there. Essentially this attack resumed the long-standing Russian attempt to gain ground in the area. This time, however, France and Britain were not content with diplomatic maneuverings to limit Russian gains, but came directly to the sultan's aid. Britain was increasingly worried about any great power advance in the region that might threaten its hold on India, while France sought diplomatic glory and also represented itself as the Western champion of Christian rights. The resultant Crimean War was fought directly in Russia's backyard on the Black Sea, yet the Western forces won, driving the Russian armies from their entrenched positions. The loss was shocking and profoundly disturbing to Russian leadership, for the West won this little war not because of great tactics or inspired principles, but essentially because of their industrial advantage. They had the ships to send masses of military supplies long distances, and their artillery and other weapons were vastly superior to Russia's home-produced models. Here was a severe blow to a regime that prided itself on military vigor, and a frightening portent for the future.

The Crimean War helped convince Russian leaders, including the new tsar, Alexander II, that it was time for a change. Reform was essential not to copy the West, but to allow sufficient economic adjustments for Russia to keep pace in the military arena. And reform meant, first and foremost, some resolution of Russia's leading social issue, the issue that most distinguished Russian society from that of the West: serfdom. Only if the status of serfs changed could Russia develop a more vigorous and mobile labor force and so be able to contemplate some version of industrialization. Russian concern paralleled attacks on slavery in the Americas in the same period, reflecting a desire to meet Western humanitarian standards and a need for cheap, flexible labor.

Other factors argued for reform of the serfs as well. Some aristocrats were convinced that a freer labor system would motivate serfs to work hard and thus produce higher agricultural profits. Several leaders were also stung by repeated Western-inspired criticisms of the injustice of Russian society, which focused on the harsh conditions of servile labor. Even more aristocrats were concerned by the periodic peasant uprisings that focused on lack of freedom, undue obligations, and lack of land. Stability required some dramatic new moves that would protect the essentials of the social order while contenting the peasantry to a greater degree. Peasant uprisings increased in the 1850s, triggered in part by some bad harvests—unlike the West at this point, Russia was still vulnerable to famine when crops failed—and in part by the discontents of returning peasant veterans from the Crimea.

So Russia returned, for two decades, to a policy of reform, based in part on Western standards and examples—manorialism had been fully abolished in western Europe after 1789 and in east-central regions such as Prussia and Hungary, in the aftermath of the revolutions of 1848. As before, however, the intention was not to duplicate Western measures down the line, but to protect distinctive Russian institutions including the landed aristocracy and tightly knit peasant communities. The result was an important series of changes that, with tragic irony, created more grievances than they resolved while opening the way to further economic change.

THE REFORM ERA AND EARLY INDUSTRIALIZATION

The final decision to emancipate the serfs in 1861 came at roughly the same time that the United States and, soon, Brazil decided to free slaves. Neither slavery nor rigorous serfdom suited the economic needs of a society seeking an independent position in Western-dominated world trade.

In some ways the emancipation of the serfs was more generous than the liberation of slaves in the Americas. While aristocrats retained part of the land, including the most fertile holdings, the serfs got most of it—in contrast to slaves who received their freedom but nothing else. Russian emancipation, however, was careful to preserve essential aristocratic power; the tsar was not interested in destroying the nobility, who remained his most reliable political ally and the source of most bureaucrats. Even more, emancipation was designed to retain the tight grip of the tsarist state. The serfs obtained no new political rights at a national level. They were still tied to their villages until they could pay for the land they were given—the redemption money going to the aristocrats to help preserve this class. Redemption payments added greatly to peasants' material hardship, and they were infuriating, for peasants thought the land belonged to them with no need to pay for its return. Enforcement of redemption obligations meant many peasants could still not move freely or even sell their land, though some became more mobile. High redemption payments, in addition to state taxes that increased as Russia sought funds to build railroads and factories, kept most Russian peasants miserably poor.

Emancipation did bring change; it helped create a larger urban labor force. But it did not spur a revolution in agricultural productivity, as most peasants continued to use traditional methods on their small plots. And it did not bring contentment: Indeed, peasant uprisings became more common as hopes for a brighter future now seemed dashed by the limits of change. Rural unrest in Russia was furthered also by substantial population growth, as some of the factors that had earlier swelled the West's population now spread to Russia, including growing use of the potato. Peasant crowding would by itself have created hardship, while also providing new migrants in search of other work; in combination with grievances about emancipation, it was a truly explosive force.

This roadside scene in the late 19th century depicts the poverty of a Russian peasant village.

Russia, in sum, provided after 1861 a classic case of a society in the midst of rapid change where reform did not go far enough—perhaps, given traditions and established interests, it could not go far enough—to satisfy key protest groups. Peasants used their village structures so often praised by Russian conservatives to provide organization and goals for recurrent attacks on landlords and state tax officials, while usually still professing loyalty to the tsar.

To be sure, the reform movement did not end with emancipation. Alexander II introduced a host of further measures in the 1860s and early 1870s. New law codes cut back traditional punishments now that serfs were legally free in the eyes of the law (though subject to important transitional restrictions). The tsar created local political councils, the *zemstvoes,* that had a voice in regulating roads, schools, and other regional policies. Some form of local government was essential now that the nobles no longer directly ruled the peasantry. The zemstvoes gave some Russians, particularly middle-class people such as doctors and lawyers, new political experience, and they undertook important inquiries into local problems. The councils, however, had no influence on national policy, where the tsar resolutely maintained his own authority and that of his extensive bureaucracy. Another important area of change was the army, where the Crimean War had shown the need for reform. The officer corps were improved through promotion by merit and a new organization of essential services. Recruitment was extended, and many peasants learned new skills, including literacy, through their military service. Some strides were made also in providing state-sponsored basic education, though schools spread unevenly.

These adjustments, like emancipation itself, were important. They imitated some Western principles; the new law codes, for example, included a more humanitarian approach to punishment for crime as well as technical equality before the law. The reforms were sufficient to spur the beginnings of Russian industrialization. They were not sufficient to provide a stable social base for this inherently traumatic economic upheaval.

From the reform era onward, literacy spread rapidly in Russian society. A new market developed for popular reading matter that had some similarities to the mass reading culture developing in the West. Interestingly, Russian potboiler novels, while displaying a pronounced taste for excitement and exotic adventure, also attested to distinctive values; Russian "bad guys" for example were never glorified in the end, but always were either returned to social loyalty or condemned for their obduracy, a clear sign of the limits to individualism. Women gained new positions in the climate of change. Some won access to higher education, and, as in the West, a minority of women mainly from the upper classes began to penetrate professions such as medicine.

As these examples suggest, Russia had been launched on a process of considerable transformation, going well beyond the official political reforms. Even sexual habits began to change, as had occurred in the West a century before. Fathers' control over their children's behavior loosened a bit, particularly where non-agricultural jobs were available, and sexual activity before marriage increased.

The move toward industrialization was part of the wider process of change. The tsar's government was not always in agreement over industrialization goals, with some conservatives rightly fearing the impact of economic change on the existing social and political structure. On the whole, however, state support for industrialization continued even after the reform era ended in the late 1870s. And state support was vital for this shift toward industrialization, for Russia lacked a preexisting middle class and substantial capital; state enterprises had to make up part of the gap, in the tradition of economic activity that went back to Peter the Great.

The first step toward industrialization came with railroads, a clear necessity for military and political coordination as well as economic development in the vast land. Russia began to create an extensive railroad network in the 1870s. The establishment of the trans-Siberian railroad, which connected European Russia with the Pacific, was the crowning achievement of this drive when it was substantially completed by the end of the 1880s. The railroad boom directly stimulated expansion of Russia's iron and coal sectors. Rails also allowed fuller utilization of Russia's rich holdings in both minerals, for in contrast to England and Germany (and to an extent the United States) Russia lacked waterways that could do the job, as the north-south flow of rivers did not link up coal and iron deposits. Railroad development also stimulated the export of grain to the West, which now became essential to earn foreign currency needed in payment for advanced Western machinery. The railroads also opened Siberia up to new development, which in turn brought Russia into a more active and contested Asian role.

By the 1880s, when Russia's railroad network had almost quintupled compared to 1860, modern factories were beginning to spring up in Moscow, St. Petersburg, and several Polish cities, and an urban working class was growing apace. Printing factories and metalworking shops expanded the skilled artisanry in the cities, while new works in metallurgy and textiles created a still-newer, semiskilled industrial labor force from the troubled countryside.

Under Count Witte, minister of finance from 1892 to 1903 and an ardent economic modernizer, the government enacted high tariffs to protect new Russian industry, improved its banking system, and encouraged Western investors to build great factories with advanced technology. As Witte put it, "The inflow of foreign capital is . . . the only way by which our industry will be able to supply our country quickly with abundant and cheap products." By 1900 approximately half of Russian industry was foreign-owned and much of it was foreign-operated, with British, German, and French industrialists taking the lead. Russia became a debtor nation as huge industrial development loans piled up. And while an important class of Russian industrialists emerged, the early phases of Russian industrialization did not clearly improve Russia's autonomy in the world economy. Witte and others were confident that strong government controls could keep the foreigners in line rather than converting Russia into a new imperialist playground, and certainly foreign influence over basic government policy was not extensive. While the foreign presence and foreign profit-taking created resentments from workers and conservatives alike, there was some clear payoff: By 1900 Russia had surged to fourth rank in the world in steel production, and was second to the United States in the newer area of petroleum production and refining. Russian textile output was also impressive. Longstanding Russian economic lags were beginning to yield.

This was still an industrial revolution in its early stages. Russia's world rank was a function more of its great size and population, along with its very rich natural resources, than of really thorough mechanization. Many Russian factories were vast—on average, the largest in the world—but they were not usually up to Western technical standards, nor was the labor force highly trained. Many workers continued to go back and forth from factory to countryside, which helped ease the adjustment to often appalling urban and factory conditions but did not encourage full conversion to new work regimes. Agriculture also remained backward, as peasants, often illiterate, had neither capital nor motives to change their ways. Poor agriculture limited the growth of cities—which did surge forward impressively nevertheless—and made famine a recurrent threat.

Other reforms also produced ambiguous results. Russia remained a traditional peasant society in many ways. Beneath official military reorganization, many peasant-soldiers continued to regard their officers as landlord-patrons. Discipline and military efficiency were lax. It was not clear that the Russian masses had experienced the kinds of attitudinal changes that had occurred in the West around the time of initial industrialization or even before. Even more obvious was the absence of a large, self-confident middle class of the sort that had arisen earlier in the West. Businessmen and professional people grew in numbers, but they were often dependent on state initiatives—through zemstvo employment for doctors, or economic guidance for businessmen—and simply lacked the class size and tradition to become as assertive as their Western counterparts had been, for example, in challenging aristocratic power and values. The limitations of change in Russia reflected the recency of the process; by 1914 Russia was really only

Early Russian industrialization is depicted in this 1888 photo of the commercial department of the Abrikosova and Son factory.

DOCUMENT

RUSSIAN CONSERVATISM AND THE WEST

Russian conservatives continued to define a special Russian tradition in contrast to Westernizing initiatives up to the 1917 revolution. Their arguments help explain why Russia avoided basic political change; their assumptions about popular support seem somewhat fanciful in light of ultimate revolution. Yet the attempt to argue for an alternative to Western forms was important, not only in explaining Russian policies for several decades, but in suggesting reasons that people in various societies—including Russia itself even after 1917—might seek to avoid a strict Western model. The statement that follows, written in the shock of Alexander II's assassination in 1881, comes from a speech by a leading Slavophile, Ivan Aksakov.

The Emperor is murdered; the same Emperor who was the greatest benefactor to his country, who emancipated, bestowing upon them human and civil rights, tens of millions of Russian peasants. He is murdered; not from personal vengeance, not for booty, but precisely because he is the Emperor, the crowned head, the representative, the first man of his country, that vital, single man, who personified the very essence, the whole image, the whole strength and power, of Russia. From time immemorial that power constituted the strength of the country. The attempt directed against the person of the Tsar is always directed against the whole people; but in this case the whole historical principle of the national life has been attacked, the autocratic power bestowed upon the Emperor by the country itself. Who are those who dared to bring that awful shame upon the people, and, as if by mockery, in the name of the people? . . .

Can it be anything else but the logical, extreme expression of that Westernism which, since the time of Peter the Great, demoralized both our government and our society, and has already marred all the spiritual manifestations of our national life? Not content to profit by all the riches of European thought and knowledge, we borrowed her spirit, developed by a foreign history and foreign religion. We began idolizing Europe, worshiping her gods and her idols! Who is to be blamed? Some forty years ago has not Khomiakov warned us, threatening us with Divine punishment for 'deserting all that is sacred to our hearts'? But really, what are these 'Anarchists,' 'Social Democrats,' and Revolutionists, as they call themselves? Have they the smallest particle of Russian spirit in all their aspirations and aims? Is there the slightest shade in their teachings of a protest against the real shortcomings of which Russia is suffering? Just the opposite; what they despise most is precisely the Russian people. . . .

Our peasantry, forming almost eighty per cent of the whole realm, now possess land, organization, and the most complete self-government. To this very day, that fourth class is the keeper of our historical instinct, of our religion, and of the whole element of our political organism. They, and not the so-called 'Intelligentsia,' are the real supporters of our country. . . . Who accepts the causes has also to accept their logical consequences. Who accepts the Western Constitution has also to bear the last expression of Western political life, viz., social revolution with all its manifestations.

Worse than all the external calamities was the moral treason of its leading class, powerful through knowledge and development. The reforms of Peter the Great weakened our memory and disabled us from understanding our own history—so very different from that of the West. Conquest is not at the bottom of our historical life, as is the case in all the Western countries. Our history begins with quite a voluntary and rational appeal to power. The same appeal was repeated much later, in 1612, and gave the foundation to the present reigning dynasty, empowered with autocracy, and nothing and nobody could induce the country to alter that shape of government. Such was the will, such was the inspiration of the national spirit.

Our history does not possess, therefore, that fundamental fact, which characterizes the political life of the Western powers of Europe, the antagonism between the people and a power imposed by conquest. That antagonism, however, is the very foundation of Western constitutionalism. It is a mere agreement; a compromise between two camps hostile to each other, mistrusting each other; a kind of treaty, surrounded with all sorts of conditions. To evade those conditions *without contradicting the letter of the agreement*, constitutes the great talent of the rulers as well as of those who are ruled. Struggle for power—that is the real sense of the political life of European countries. The foundation of their administration is a kind of mechanical apparatus; the center of power and mind, or an *unlimited power*, belongs to the majority of voices based upon the numbers of the representatives. Thus some ten voices—often bribed and bought—automatically decide the destinies of the people, forming the actual majority, in comparison of which the parliamentary majority is a few grains of sand compared to the sandy wilderness of Sahara. But that autocrat, composed of several numerical units, bears no moral responsibility before its conscience and the country, responsibility which falls heavily on the one personal representative of the supreme power.

During the First Republic the French Representative Assembly declared—quite legally as far as the form was concerned, and in the name of the people—that worship addressed to God was null, and replaced by adoration of the 'Goddess of Reason'; and all that in the face of tens of millions of true believers, but of men deprived of any legal voice, and thus unable to protest at all. The same thing happened in France the other day. It is ordered now to put in all the primary schools, instead of the word God, the word *Nature*. Is this not a study illustrative of popular Western representation? What is the use of political rights which allow, in the name of liberty and law, such a revolting infraction of freedom and truth?

Such are the kinds of freedom promised to Russia by worshipers of European liberal institutions. But the instincts and the notions of freedom in the Russian people are higher and broader than in any part of the world, because they are free from the conventional and formal element, and are based on *moral truth*. They are easily traced in our self-government, the broadest of Europe, and in the largest application of the *elective element*. . . .

The Russian people has not entrusted full power to a heartless, soulless, mechanical apparatus, but to the 'holiest of beings'—to a man with a human soul, with a Russian heart, and a Christian conscience. The people know, and know well, the drawbacks of every human institution, but feel at the same time the power to overcome and improve them. And our former Tsars have not deceived their hopes and confidence; they held majestically and rigorously their imperial tide. . . . There was no mentioning any political rights, or supporting any kind of political doctrine. It was the regular, the natural manifestation of national life itself. Neither the people nor the autocratic Tsar ever thought themselves otherwise than in a constant moral and intellectual alliance of unity.

Questions: In what ways does Aksakov define the special Russian spirit? Why, in this judgment, are Western values inferior to Russian traditions? What kind of political system, according to this view, works best in Russia?

in its third decade of outright industrial revolution. It also reflected distinctive features of the process itself, and of earlier Russian tradition.

 PROTEST AND REVOLUTION

A rising tide of unrest accompanied Russia's period of transformation. Alexander II's reforms, plus economic change with the greater population mobility it involved, helped encourage demands by minority nationalities in the great empire. Intellectuals explored the cultural traditions of Ukrainians and other groups. This cultural nationalism could lead to political demands, particularly at a point when state power, through military recruitment and school expansion, was beginning to increase. Nationalist beliefs were initially imported from western Europe, but here, and elsewhere in eastern Europe, they encouraged divisive minority agitation that multinational states, such as Russia or Austria-Hungary, found very hard to handle. Nationalist pressures were not the main problem in Russia, but in combination with other kinds of protest and given Russia's mainstream nationalist insistence on the distinctive superiorities of a Russian tradition, they did cause problems.

A RANGE OF DISCONTENT

Social protest was more vigorous still, and it was heightened not only by the limitations of reform but by industrialization itself. Peasant discontent was not a constant force, but it continued to burst forth. Recurrent famines regularly provoked uprising. Peasants deeply resented redemption payments and taxes and frequently attacked and burned the records that indicated what they "owed." Peasants' sense of natural justice, heightened by population pressure, also turned them against aristocratic estates.

Many educated Russians, including some aristocrats, also clamored for revolutionary change. Two strands developed. Many business and professional people, while not extremely aggressive, began to seek a fuller political voice and new rights such as greater freedom in the schools and press; they thus argued for liberal reforms. At the same time a group of radical *intelligentsia*—a Russian term denoting articulate intellectuals as a class—building on earlier intellectual discontent, became increasingly active. The intelligentsia formed a self-conscious group bent on radical change; the group was more distinct than in the West if only because the middle-class reform tradition, to which intellectuals might attach their efforts, was so limited. As Russian universities expanded, student groups grew as well, and many were extremely impatient with Russia's slow development and with the visible restrictions on political activity.

Some intellectuals later toned down their goals as they entered the bureaucracy or business life. But many remained inspired by radical doctrines, and more than a few devoted their lives to a revolutionary cause. This kind of intellectual alienation, while it utilized some of the principles that had earlier disturbed intellectuals in the West, went deeper in the Russian case. It was the first example of a kind of intellectual radicalism, capable of motivating outright terrorism, that would characterize other societies caught in uncompleted change during the 20th century. The goals and motives of the Russian intelligentsia varied, but in general they wanted political freedom and deep social reform while maintaining a Russian culture different from that of the West, which they saw as hopelessly plutocratic and materialistic. Their radicalism may have stemmed from the demanding task they set themselves: simultaneously to attack key Russian institutions while building a new society that would not reproduce the injustices and crippling limitations of the Western world.

The radical intelligentsia claimed that a spirit of community lay deep in the Russian soul, and this could serve both as the basis for social justice in Russia and as the foundation for an egalitarian society free from the exploitation and competitive individualism of the capitalist West. Many Russian radicals were anarchists, who sought the abolition of all formal government. While anarchism was not unknown in the West, it took on particular force in Russia in opposition to unyielding tsarist autocracy. Many early anarchists in the 1860s hoped that they could triumph by winning peasant support, and a host of upper-class radicals fanned out to teach the peasantry the beauties of political activism. They found however that peasants were largely uninterested in political change and not at all eager to take lessons from upper-class leaders, revolutionary or not. This failure led many anarchists to violent methods, forming the first large terrorist movement in the modern world. Given the lack of popular support and of other political outlets, assassinations and bombings seemed the only way to attack the existing order. Anarchist tactics indeed often focused more on destruction than on coherent political goals for the future; terrorism could become an end in itself. As the anarchist leader Bakunin put it:

> We have only one plan—general destruction. We want a national revolution of the peasants. We refuse to take any part in the working out of schemes to better the conditions of life; we regard as fruitless solely theoretical work. We consider destruction to be such an enormous and difficult task that we must devote all our powers to it, and we do not wish to deceive ourselves with the dream that we will have enough strength and knowledge for creation.

Not surprisingly, the recurrent waves of terrorism merely confirmed the tsarist regime in its resolve to avoid further political change, in what became a vicious circle in 19th-century Russian politics.

By the late 1870s Alexander II was pulling back from his reform interest, fearing that change was getting out of hand. Censorship of newspapers and political meetings tightened; many dissidents were arrested and sent to Siberia. Alexander II was assassinated by a terrorist bomb in 1881, after a series of botched attempts. His successors, while escalating the effort to industrialize, continued to oppose further political reform. New measures of repression were also directed against minority nationalities, partly to dampen their unrest but partly to gain the support of upper-class conservatives who were wary of the industrialization process and could be contented only by vigorous backing for Russian dominance in language and culture. The Poles and other groups were carefully supervised. Russian language instruction was forced on people such as the Ukrainians. Persecution of the large Jewish minority was stepped up, resulting in many executions—called *pogroms*—and seizures of property; as a consequence, many Russian Jews emigrated. The regime also tried to Christianize many Jewish children by force. All of this, of course, spurred additional, underground protest among various nationalities.

By the 1890s the protest currents were complicated by two other ultimately related developments. In the first place, Marxist doctrines spread from the Western socialist movement to a segment of the Russian intelligentsia. There was no unity here, and anarchists and other peasant-oriented revolutionaries bitterly disputed Marxist insistence on careful revolutionary organization and a focus on the working class. Nevertheless small Marxist groups formed, some in exile, committed to a tightly organized proletarian revolution. One of the most active Marxist leaders was Vladimir Ilyich Ulyanov, known as Lenin. Lenin, from a bureaucratic family whose brother had been killed by the political police, introduced important innovations in Marxist theory to make it more appropriate for the Russian scene. He argued that, because of the spread of international capitalism, a proletariat was developing worldwide in advance of industrialization. Russia, then, could have a proletarian revolution without going through a distinct middle-class phase. Lenin also insisted on the importance of disciplined revolutionary cells that could maintain doctrinal purity and effective action even amid severe police repression. Small but dedicated revolutionary cadres, not the mass electioneering of the Western socialist parties whose revisionism Lenin detested, would be the path to the future. Lenin's approach animated the group of Russian Marxists known as *Bolsheviks,* or majority party (though ironically they were actually a minority in the Russian Marxist movement as a whole, much of which remained more wedded to the idea of an initial middle-class revolution). The approach proved ideal for Russian conditions.

Working-class unrest in the cities developed apace with the new currents among the intelligentsia. Russian workers became far more radical than their Western counterparts. They formed unions and conducted strikes—all illegal—but many of them also had firm political goals in mind. Their radicalism stemmed partly from the absence of legal political outlets. They stemmed partly from rural unrest, for these new workers pulled in peasant grievances against the existing order. They stemmed partly from the severe conditions of early industrialization, exacerbated by large factories and frequent foreign ownership. While many workers were not linked to any particular doctrine, some became interested in one of the revolutionary agendas—including Bolshevism—and they were urged on by passionate organizers.

By 1900 the contradictory currents in Russian society may have made revolution inevitable. The forces demanding change were not united, but the importance of mass protest both in countryside and city, plus the radical intelligentsia, made it difficult to find a compromise position that might content some while isolating others. Furthermore, the regime remained resolutely uninterested in compromise. Vigorous conservative ministers urged a policy of resistance and repression; this kept most uprisings in hand, but it fed further pressure from below.

THE REVOLUTION OF 1905

Military defeat in 1904 and 1905 finally lit this tinderbox. Russia had maintained its expansionist foreign policy through the later 19th century, in part because of tradition and in part because diplomatic success might draw the venom from some internal unrest. It also wanted to match the imperialist strides of the Western great powers. A war with the Ottoman Empire in the 1870s brought substantial gains, which were then pushed back at the insistence of France and Britain. Russia also successfully aided the creation of new Slavic nations in the Balkans, such as Serbia and Bulgaria, the "little Slavic brothers" that filled nationalist hearts with pride. Some conservative writers even talked in terms of a Pan-Slavic movement that would unite the Slavic people, under Russian leadership of course. Russia participated vigorously in other Middle Eastern and central Asia areas. Russia and Britain both increased their influence in Persia and Afghanistan, reaching some uneasy truces that divided spheres of activity early in the 20th century. Russia was also active in China. The development of the trans-Siberian railroad encouraged Russia to incorporate some northern portions of Manchuria, violating the 18th century Amur River agreement. Russia also joined Western powers in obtaining long-term leases to Chinese territory during the 1890s.

These were important gains, but they did not satisfy growing Russian ambitions, and they also brought trouble. Russia risked now an overextension, as its diplomatic aspirations were not backed by real increases in military power. The problem first came to a head in 1904. Japan, increasingly powerful in its own right, became worried about further Russian expansion in northern China and efforts to extend influence into Korea. War broke out in 1904. Against all expectation, save Japan's, the Japanese won. Russia could not move her fleet quickly to the Pacific, and her military organization in general proved too cumbersome to oppose more effective Japanese maneuvers. Japan gained the opportunity to move into Korea, as the balance of power in the Far East began to shift.

Unexpected defeat in war unleashed massive protests on the home front in the Revolution of 1905. Urban workers mounted well-organized general strikes designed above all for political gains. Peasants produced a tumultuous series of insurrections, while liberal groups also agitated. After first trying brutal police repression—which only infuriated the urban crowds—and worried about the reliability of the peasant-based army, the tsarist regime had to change course. It granted little to the workers, for new rights for unions and Marxist political parties were almost immediately stripped away—though not before worker organizations gained further ground. But liberals were wooed through the creation of a national parliament, the *duma*. And the minister Stolypin introduced an important series of reforms for the peasantry. The emancipation system was greatly loosened. Peasants gained greater freedom from redemption payments and village controls. They could buy and sell land quite liberally. The goal here was to create a stratified, market-oriented peasantry in which successful farmers would move away from the peasant masses, becoming rural capitalists. Indeed, peasant unrest did die down, and a minority of aggressive entrepreneurs, called *kulaks*, began to increase agricultural production and buy additional land. Yet the reform package overall quickly came unglued. Not only were workers' rights withdrawn, triggering a new series of strikes and underground activities, but the duma was progressively stripped of power. Nicholas II, a weak man who was badly advised, simply could not surrender the tradition of autocratic rule, and the duma became a hollow institution, representing and satisfying no one. Police repression also resumed, creating new opponents to the regime.

Pressed in the diplomatic arena by the closing of the Far Eastern theater through Japanese advance, yet eager to counter paralyzing internal pressures by some foreign policy success, the Russian government turned once again to the Ottoman Empire and the Balkans. Various stratagems to acquire new rights of access to the Mediterranean and to back Slavic allies in the Balkans yielded no concrete results, but they did stir the pot in this vulnerable area and helped lead to World War I. And this war, in which Russia participated in order to maintain her diplomatic standing and live up to the billing of Slavic protector while hoping for new territorial gains, led to one of the great revolutions of modern times.

RUSSIA AND EASTERN EUROPE

Russia was not the whole of eastern Europe, of course, but in many respects Russian patterns were paralleled in smaller states such as Hungary (joined to Austria but autonomous after 1866), Romania, Serbia, Bulgaria, and Greece. These were new nations—unlike Russia—and emerging after long Ottoman dominance, they had no access to the diplomatic influence of their giant neighbor. Most of the new nations established parliaments, in imitation of Western forms, but carefully restricted voting rights and parliamentary powers. Kings—some of them new, as the Balkan nations had set up monarchies after gaining independence from the Ottoman Empire—ruled without much check. Most East European nations followed Russia's lead in emancipating serfs, but landlord power remained more extensive than in Russia, and the usual result of recurrent peasant unrest followed. Most of the smaller East European nations industrialized much less extensively than Russia, and so they remained, as agricultural exporters, far more dependent on Western markets.

Yet amid all the problems, eastern Europe enjoyed a period of glittering cultural productivity in the late 19th century, with Russia in the lead. Utilization of the romantic tradition and other Western styles continued. National dictionaries and histories helped the smaller Slavic nations gain a sense of their heritage, along with the collection of folk tales and music. The Russian novel enjoyed a period of unprecedented brilliance. Westernizers such as Turgenev wrote realistic novels that vaunted what they saw as modern values, while writers such as Tolstoy and Dostoevsky displayed more ambiguity about Western values and tried to portray a special Russian spirit. Russian music moved from the romanticism of Tchaikovsky to more innovative, atonal styles early in the 20th century. Polish composers such as Chopin and Liszt also made an important mark. Russian painters began participating in modern art currents, producing important abstract work. Finally, scientific work advanced at levels of fundamental importance. A Czech scientist, Gregor Mendel, advanced the understanding of genetics, while a Russian physiologist, Ivan Pavlov, experimenting on conditioned reflexes, explained unconscious responses in human beings.

Eastern Europe thus participated more fully than ever before in a cultural world shared with the West, though with some distinctive emphases. This fruitful juncture was not matched by comparable developments in the political and social spheres, however, and it was complicated by attempts to define a special Russian or Slavic essence.

Furthermore, the masses in eastern Europe, mainly peasant, remained firmly attached to a largely separate popular culture, including the Orthodox religion, that was different from the traditions of the West and from those of the partially Westernized upper classes. Peasant culture was not unchanging, as the openness to some new radical loyalties demonstrated, but it was not easily manipulable. And popular resentment against growing Western cultural as well as economic influence contributed to the revolutionary tides during and after World War I.

By 1900, then, Russia and much of the rest of eastern Europe represented a distinctive amalgam of tradition and change. Principles of authoritarian rule remained virtually unaltered, but they were now joined with diverse political opposition bent in the main on sweeping revolution rather than on purely liberal reforms. The tradition of territorial expansionism, though checked by resistance from the West and Japan, still ran strong. Pan-Slavic sentiments indeed encouraged new Russian influence in southeastern Europe. Massive social change had resulted from emancipation and industrialization, but East European society continued to be more agricultural and in many ways more traditionalist than its Western counterpart. Finally, a larger ambivalence toward Western values persisted. East European intellectuals contributed creatively to general European artistic and scientific work, but a desire to define distinctive features and to resist full Westernization remained lively in many quarters, both elite and popular. Eastern Europe was, in sum, developing its own pattern of change as it entered the industrial age. This pattern would soon embrace a distinctive kind of revolution as well.

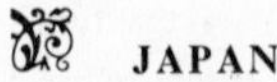

JAPAN

Like Russia, Japan faced new pressure from the West during the 1850s, though it took the form of a demand for more open trade rather than outright military conflict. Japan's response was more direct than Russia's and, on the whole, more immediately successful. Despite its long history of isolation, Japanese society was better adapted than Russia's to the challenge of industrial change. Market forms were more extensive, reaching into peasant agriculture; levels of literacy were higher. Nevertheless, Japan had to rework many of its institutions during the final decades of the 19th century, and the process produced significant strain. The result, by 1900, was different both from purely Western patterns and from the more obvious tensions of Russian society.

THE FINAL DECADES OF THE SHOGUNATE

On the surface, Japan experienced little change during the first half of the 19th century, and certainly this was a quiet time, compared to the earlier establishment of the Tokugawa shogunate or the transformation introduced after the 1850s. Some scholars have argued that the shogunate was becoming less effective, and there were some signs of deterioration. It is also important to note ongoing currents of change that continued from the 17th and early 18th centuries. These developments help explain why Japan was able to adjust so quickly when a new challenge, requiring major adjustments, became apparent.

During the first half of the 19th century, the shogunate continued to combine a central bureaucracy with semifeudal alliances between the regional daimyos and the samurai. The government recurrently ran into financial problems. Its taxes were based on agriculture, despite the growing commercialization of the Japanese economy; this was a severe constraint. At the same time, maintaining the feudal shell was costly. The samurai were paid government stipends in return for their loyalty. Loans from merchants frequently bridged the gap between expenditure and income, but this system also required periodic reform movements that would limit the budget and introduce greater stringency. These reform periods would then yield to a more openhanded mood. A long reform spurt late in the 18th century built a successful momentum for a time, but a shorter effort between 1841 and 1843 was notably unsuccessful. This weakened the shogunate into the 1850s and hampered its response to the crisis induced by Western pressure. Until that point, however, the balance between central bureaucrats and regional lords had lasted surprisingly well, with neither group trying to undercut the authority of the other. It was true that bureaucratization advanced in some spheres, as in the collection of taxes from the samurai domains (on the basis of which the government paid the samurai) and in a proliferation of administrative codes and attendant hierarchies of offices and paperwork. But the bureaucracy itself was reserved for the samurai, which eased the tension between the principles of centralization and ongoing feudal privilege.

Japanese intellectual life and culture also continued to develop under the Tokugawa regime, though the major literary figures of earlier centuries were not equaled. Confucianism continued to gain, among the ruling elite, at the expense of Buddhist fervor. Japan became more secular, though gradually and particularly among the upper classes: This was an important precondition for the nation's response to the Western challenge in that it precluded a strong religious-based resistance to change. Various Confucian schools actively debated into the mid-19th century, which kept Japanese intellectual life relatively creative—in contrast to the increasing sterility, including rote, examination-based memorization, characteristic of China in the same decades. Schools and academies expanded, reaching well below the upper class through commoner schools, or *terakoya,* that taught reading, writing, and the rudiments of Confucianism to ordinary people. By 1859 over 40 percent of all adult men and over 15 percent of all women were literate—a far higher percentage than anywhere else in the world outside the West, including Russia, and on a par with some of the fringe areas of the West (including the American South). Here was a fruitful basis for the development of new attitudes that could shape labor activities as well as official policies when the Western challenge arrived.

While Confucianism remained the dominant intellectual strand, there were important rivals. Tensions between traditionalists and reformist intellectuals were emerging, as in Russia in the same decades. A national studies group praised Japanese traditions, including the office of emperor, over the fascination with Chinese values and the institutions of the shogunate. Here was a seedbed for a special nationalist feeling, including praise for the Shinto tradition—Japan's indigenous animist, ceremonial religion—and scorn for Chinese narrowness and artificiality. One national studies writer expressed a typical sentiment late in the 18th century: "The 'special dispensation of our Imperial Land' means that ours is the native land of the Heaven-Shining Goddess who casts her light over all countries in the four seas. Thus our country is the source and fountainhead of all other countries, and in all matters it excels all the others." The influence of the national studies school grew somewhat in the early 19th century and played some role in promoting the office of emperor during the subsequent Meiji restoration; more important, it helped inspire ultranationalist sentiment at the end of the century and beyond.

A second minority group consisted of what the Japanese called Dutch Studies. While major Western works had been banned when the policy of isolation was adopted, a group of Japanese translators kept alive knowledge of Dutch in order to deal with the traders at Nagasaki. The ban on Western books was ended in 1720, and thereafter a group of Japanese scholars interested in "Dutch medicine" created a new interest in Western scientific advance—based on the realization that Western anatomy texts were superior to the Chinese. In 1850 there were schools of Dutch studies in all major cities, and their students urged freer exchange with the West and an attack on Chinese medicine and culture. "Our general opinion was that we should rid our country of the influences of the Chinese altogether. Whenever we met a young student of Chinese literature, we simply felt sorry for him." Here, obviously, was the basis for a much fuller interest in the West, including Western science, in later decades, for already a knowledge of Western physics, geography, and chemistry were entering Japan along with the knowledge of medicine. Not surprisingly, the Dutch schools expanded rapidly in reaction to the concern aroused by the visit of Western fleets after 1853.

Just as Japanese culture showed an important capacity for lively debate and fruitful internal tension, so the Japanese economy continued to develop into the 19th century. Commerce continued to expand, as big merchant companies established monopoly privileges in many centers. Manufacturing gained ground in the countryside, in such consumer-goods industries as soy sauce and silks, and much of this was organized by city merchants. Some of these developments were comparable to slightly earlier changes in the West and have given rise to arguments that, economically, Japan had a running start on industrialization once the Western challenge showed the necessity of further economic change. Obviously also, the Japanese economy was significantly more commercial than that of Russia, and not at all touched before the 1850s by any dependency on cheap exports; here too was an advantage in coping with subsequent change that helps explain the absence of severe revolutionary pressures.

The Japanese economy was not growing rapidly by the 1850s, however; its earlier surge had trailed off somewhat. Some scholars have, as a result, stressed Japan's backwardness compared to the West. The population was stagnant because of constraints on agricultural expansion given available technology. Frequent infanticide plus abortion and birth control achieved this result, which limited the strain on resources but also provided little motive for rapid growth. Poor families, especially, were careful to restrict their effective birthrate. At the same time rural riots increased in many regions, from the late 18th century onward. They were not overtly political, but rather directed against wealthy peasants, merchants, and landlord controls; they included resentment against commercial practices. Increasingly violent protests, which extended into the 1860s, weakened the Tokugawa shogunate and helped explain its demise. While authorities put down unrest with little difficulty, the protests contributed to a willingness to consider change when they were joined by challenge from the outside.

THE CHALLENGE

Some Japanese had become increasingly worried about potential outside threats. In 1791 a book was issued advocating a strong navy. Fears about the West's growing power and particularly Russia's Asian expansion fed these concerns in subsequent decades.

Fear became reality in 1853, when the American commodore Matthew Perry arrived with a fleet in Edo Bay near Tokyo and insisted by threats of bombardment that Americans be allowed to trade. The United States, increasingly an active part of the West's core economy, thus launched for Japan the same kind of pressure the Opium War had created for China—due to the heightened military superiority of the West and its insistence on opening markets for its burgeoning economy. In 1854 Perry returned and won the right to station an American consul in Japan; through a formal treaty, two ports were opened to commerce. Britain, Russia, and Holland quickly won similar rights. As in China this meant that Westerners living in Japan would be governed by their own representatives, not by Japanese law. Other privileges soon followed. Leading Western nations simply insisted on their need and right to trade as part of the expanding world economy, while also seeking fishing rights in Japanese waters. Russian pressure was a problem as well, as the nation's eastward expansion had already produced a few small clashes over control of islands in the north Pacific.

The bureaucrats of the shogunate had seen no alternative but to open up Japan, given the superiority of Western navies now including steamships. And there were of course Japanese who had grown impatient with strict isolation, whose numbers swelled as Dutch schools began to expand. On the other hand the daimyos, intensely conservative, were opposed to the new concessions, which forced the shogun to appeal to the emperor for support. Soon, samurai opponents of the bureaucracy were also appealing to the emperor, who began to emerge from his centuries-long confinement as a largely religious and ceremonial figure. While most daimyos defended the status quo, samurai were

This Japanese cartoon portrays American Admiral Perry as a greedy warlord.

more divided, some seeing opportunity in change including unseating the shogunate. The fact was that the complex shogunate system had depended on the isolation policy: It could not survive the stresses of foreign influence and internal reactions. The result was not immediate collapse; indeed into the late 1850s Japanese life seemed to go on much as before.

In the 1860s a political crisis came into the open, involving a clash between the feudal lords and the shogunate exacerbated by disagreements over the appointment of a new shogun. The crisis was spiced by samurai attacks on foreigners, including one murder of a British official, matched by Western naval bombardments of feudal forts. Virtual civil war broke out in 1866 as the samurai eagerly armed themselves with American Civil War surplus weapons, causing Japan's aristocracy to come to terms with the superiority of Western armaments. When the samurai defeated a shogunate force, a number of Japanese finally were shocked out of their traditional reliance on their own superiority, with one author arguing that the nation was, compared to the West with its technology, science, and humane laws, only half-civilized.

This multifaceted crisis came to an end in 1868, with the proclamation of rule by a new emperor named Mutsuhito but commonly called Meiji, or Enlightened One. Backed by some samurai leaders, the new emperor managed to put down the troops of the shogunate and gradually built up support. The crisis period had been shocking enough to allow further changes in Japan's basic political structure—changes that went much deeper at the political level than those introduced by Russia from 1861 onward. One reason Japan avoided political revolution as part of its transformation process involved this early crisis and its sweeping results. Unlike Russia, Japan joined restructuring of the central state and the upper class to its other reforms.

ANALYSIS
THE SEPARATE PATHS OF JAPAN AND CHINA

Japan's ability to change in response to new Western pressure contrasted strikingly with the sluggishness of Chinese reactions into the 20th century. The contrast draws particular attention because China and Japan had been part of the same civilization orbit for so long, which means that some of the assets Japan possessed in dealing with change were present in China as well. Indeed Japan turned out to benefit, by the mid-19th century, from having become more like China in key respects during the Tokugawa period. The link between Chinese and Japanese traditions should not be overdrawn, of course, and earlier differences help explain the divergence that opened so clearly in the later 19th century. A problem of interpretation remains, however, as the East Asian world now split apart, with Japan seizing eagerly on Chinese weakness to target a series of attacks from the 1890s to 1945—which of course merely made China's troubles worse.

Japan and China had both chosen isolation from larger world currents from about 1600 until the West forced new openings between 1830 and 1860. Japan's isolation was the more complete. Both countries lagged behind the West because of their self-containment, which was why Western industrialization caught them unprepared. China's power and wealth roused Western greed and interference first, which gave Japan some relative leeway.

China, however, surpassed Japan in some areas that should have aided it in reacting to the Western challenge. Its leadership, devoted to Confucianism, was more thoroughly secular and bureaucratic in outlook. There was no need to brush aside otherworldly commitments or feudal distractions in order to deal with the West's material and organizational power. Government centralization, still an issue in Japan, had a hoary history in China. With a rich tradition of technological innovation and scientific discovery in its past as well, China might appear to be a natural to lead the Asian world in responding to the West.

That role, however, fell to Japan. Several aspects of Japanese tradition turned out to give it a flexibility that China lacked. It already knew the benefits of imitation, which China, save for its period of attraction to Buddhism, had never acknowledged. Japan's slower government growth had allowed a stronger, more autonomous merchant tradition, even as both societies became more commercial in the 17th and early 18th centuries. Feudal traditions, though declining under the Tokugawa shogunate, also limited the heavy hand of government controls while stimulating some sense of competitiveness—as in the West. China's government, in contrast, probably tried to control too much by the 18th century and squashed initiative in the process.

China was also oppressed by massive population growth from the 17th century onward. This population pressure consumed great energy, leaving scant capital for more fundamental economic initiatives. Japan's population stability into the 19th century, though a sign of economic sluggishness, was more manageable and pressed resources less severely. Japan's island status made the nation more sensitive to Western naval pressures.

Finally, China and Japan were enmeshed in somewhat different trajectories when the Western challenge intruded in the mid-19th century. China was suffering one of its recurrent dynastic declines. Government became less efficient, intellectual life stagnated, and popular unrest surged. Quite possibly a cycle of renewal would have followed, with a new dynasty seizing more vigorous reins. But Western interference distorted this process, complicating reform and creating various new discontents that ultimately overturned the imperial office. China's sluggish leadership, convinced of the nation's superiority, finally provoked reformers to radical action as they saw their country torn apart by foreign imperialists.

Japan, in contrast, maintained considerable political and economic vigor into the 19th century. There were some new political challenges and an increase of peasant revolt. Whereas by the late 19th century China ironically needed Western guidance simply to handle such bureaucratic affairs as tariff collection or repression of peasant rebellion, Japan suffered no such breakdown of authority, using foreign advisors far more selectively.

Once a different pattern of response was established, every decade increased the gap. Western exploitation of Chinese assets as well as dilution of government power made conditions more chaotic, while Japanese strength steadily grew after a very brief period of uncertainty. By the 20th century the two nations were not only enemies—with Japan, for the first time, the stronger—but seemed to be in different orbits. Japan was an increasing industrial success, with a conservative state that would yield after World War II to a more fully parliamentary form. China, after decades of revolution, finally won its 20th century political solution, in communism.

Yet today, near the arrival of the 21st century, it becomes possible to wonder if East Asia was split as permanently as 19th and early 20th century developments had suggested. Japan's industrial lead remains, but China's economy begins perhaps to stir, along with other innovations along Asia's Pacific coast. Common cultural habits of group cooperation and decision making remind us that beneath different political systems, a fruitful shared heritage continues to operate—a heritage quite different from that of the West, but seemingly fully adaptable to the demands of economic change. And so Westerners begin to wonder if a Pacific century is about to dawn.

Questions: What civilization features had Japan and China shared before the 19th century? In what ways were Japanese political institutions more adaptable than Chinese institutions? Why was Russia able to change earlier and more fundamentally than 19th-century China?

THE MEIJI STATE AND INDUSTRIAL DEVELOPMENT

The new Meiji government promptly set about abolishing feudalism, replacing the domains of the daimyos in 1871 with a system of nationally appointed prefects (carefully chosen from different regions). Political power was effectively centralized, and from this base in turn the Meiji rulers—the emperor and his close advisors drawn from loyal segments of the aristocracy—began to expand the power of the state to effect economic and social change.

Quickly, the Japanese government sent samurai officials abroad, to western Europe and the United States, to study economic and political institutions and technology. These samurai, deeply impressed by what they saw, pulled back from the earlier antiforeign mood and gained increasing voice over other officials in the government. Their basic goal was Japan's domestic development, accompanied by a careful diplomatic policy that would avoid antagonizing the West.

POLITICAL CHANGE

The restructuring of the state and its new policy commitments were accompanied by a fundamental improvement in government finance. Between 1873 and 1876 the Meiji ministers introduced a real social revolution. They abolished the samurai class and the stipends this group had received. The tax on agriculture was converted to a wider tax, payable in money. The samurai were conciliated by government-backed bonds, but these decreased in value and most samurai became impoverished. This development sparked renewed conflict, with a final samurai uprising in 1877. However, the government had by this point introduced an army based on national conscription, and by 1878 the nation was militarily secure. Individual samurai found new opportunities in political and business areas, as they amplified their reaction to change. The continued existence of the samurai—reflecting Japan's lack of outright revolution—would leave diverse results in subsequent Japanese history.

The final capping of the process of political reconstruction came in 1889. Many former samurai had organized political parties, which had room to operate in district assemblies established in 1878. At the same time, Meiji leaders traveled abroad to gain suggestions about appropriate modern political forms. In 1884 they created a new conservative nobility, stocked by former nobles and Meiji leaders, that would operate a British-style House of Peers. Next the bureaucracy was reorganized, insulated from political pressures, and opened to talent on the basis of civil service examinations. The bureaucracy simultaneously began rapidly to expand; it would grow from 29,000 officials in 1890 to 72,000 in 1908. Finally, the constitution, issued in 1889, assured major prerogatives for the emperor along with limited powers for the lower house of the Diet (as the new Parliament was called). Here Germany provided the model, for the emperor commanded the military directly (served by a German-style general staff) and also directly named his ministers. The Diet could pass laws (upon agreement of both houses) and could approve budgets, but failure to pass a budget would simply reinstate the budget of the previous year. Parliament could thus advise government, but it could not control it. Finally, the conservative tone of this parliamentary experiment was confirmed by high property qualifications set for voting rights.

Only about five percent of the adult male population had enough wealth to be allowed to vote for representatives to the lower house.

Japan's political structure thus came to involve centralized imperial rule, wielded by a handful of Meiji advisors, combined with limited representative institutions copied from the West. This combination gave great power to an oligarchy of wealthy businessmen and former nobles, who influenced the emperor and also pulled strings within Parliament. The structure was radically new, and it greatly strengthened government authority while opening opportunities to new people. But it also retained a traditional flavor by relying on cooperation at the top rather than persistent political competition, and by building in a great deal of deference to the authority of the upper classes. Political parties arose, but a coherent oligarchy overrode their divisions into the 20th century. Japan thus followed its new policy of imitating the West, but it retained its own identity. It also devised a structure that appeased many former samurai, by giving them a voice in Parliament, while creating the effective central government necessary to reorganize military and economic affairs. Finally, the Japanese political solution compared interestingly to Russian institutions after Alexander II's reforms: Both states were centralized and authoritarian, but Japan's institution had incorporated business leaders into its governing structure while Russia defended a more traditional social elite.

JAPAN'S INDUSTRIAL REVOLUTION

Political decisions were essential following the crisis of the 1860s, but they were soon matched by other initiatives. The new army, based on the universal conscription of young men, was further improved by formal officer training—as older feudal fighting traditions were put aside—and by upgrading armaments according to Western standards. With the aid of Western advisors, a modern navy was established.

Attention also focused on creating the conditions necessary for industrialization. New banks were created by the government to fund growing trade and to provide capital for industry. State-built railroads spread across the country, and the islands were connected by rapid steamers. The market emphasis in agriculture increased, as new methods were introduced to raise output to feed the people of the growing cities.

The new economic structure depended on destruction of many older restrictions. Guilds and internal road tariffs were abolished to create a national market. Land reform created clear individual ownership for many farmers, which helped motivate expansion of production and the introduction of new fertilizers and equipment. Rice production grew rapidly. Rural Japan included progressive landlords, enterprising peasants, and a growing group of tenants—a class stratification not totally unlike that of the West, though based on different crops and more labor-intensive methods.

Government initiative dominated manufacturing, not only in the creation of transportation networks but also in state operation of mines, shipyards, and metallurgical plants. Scarce capital and the unfamiliarity of new technology seemed to compel state direction—as occurred in Russia at the same time. Government control also helped check the many foreign advisors early Japanese industry required, and here Japan maintained closer supervision than its Russian neighbor. Japan established the Ministry of Industry in 1870, and it quickly became one of the key government agencies, setting overall economic policy as well as operating specific sectors. By the 1880s model shipyards, arsenals, and factories, though not yet capable of substantial output, provided experience in new technology and disciplined work systems for many Japanese. Finally, by expanding technical training and education, setting up banks and post offices, and also by regularizing commercial laws the government provided a structure within which Japan could develop on many fronts. Measures in this area largely copied established practices in the West, but with adaptation suitable for Japanese conditions; thus, well before any European university, Tokyo Imperial University had a faculty of agriculture.

Private enterprise quickly played a role in Japan's growing economy, particularly in the vital textiles sector. Some businessmen came from older merchant families, though some of the great houses had been ruined along with the financial destruction of the samurai class. There were also newcomers, some rising from peasant ranks. Shuibuzawa Eiichi, for example, born a peasant, became a merchant and then an official of the Finance Ministry. He turned to banking in 1873, using other people's money to set up cotton-spinning mills and other textile operations. Chemicals, construction material, and food products (including beer) were other areas dominated by private entrepreneurs, many of whom however had government experience. By the 1890s huge new industrial combines, later known as *zaibatsu*, were being formed as the result of accumulations of capital and far-flung merchant and industrial operations.

By 1900 the Japanese economy was fully launched in an industrial revolution. It rested on a political and social structure different from that of Russia, and one that had in most respects changed more substantially. Japan's success in

This silk factory, based on imported technology and designed mainly for the burgeoning export trade to the West, is representative of early Japanese industrialization.

organizing industrialization, including its careful management of foreign advice and models, proved to be one of the great developments of later 19th-century history. Toward the end of the 20th century many Americans, pressed by Japanese competition, would fondly imagine that Japan's economic success was due to American guidance and generosity after 1945. The fact was that industrialization came about through largely Japanese efforts, as indeed must be the case given the fundamental transformation involved.

It is important to keep these early phases of Japanese industrialization in perspective. Pre–World War I Japan was far from the West's equal. It depended on substantial imports of Western equipment, and also of raw materials such as coal—for Japan was, for industrial purposes, a resource-poor nation. While economic growth and careful government policy allowed Japan to avoid Western domination, Japan was newly dependent on world economic conditions and often at a disadvantage in the process. Exports were vital to pay for machine and resource imports, and these in turn required hordes of inexpensive labor. Silk production grew rapidly, the bulk of it destined for Western markets. Much of this production was based on poorly paid workers laboring at home or in sweatshops, not in mechanized factories. Correspondingly the Japanese economy, in this fragile transition period, had little leeway for expansive social measures. A few big companies provided social organizations and other benefits for their employees, which helped maintain low-wage policies but also translated group loyalty traditions from the feudal past. Most workers, however, were given a poor salary and nothing more. Efforts at labor organization or other means of protest were greeted by vigorous repression. This exploitative mood was not a permanent feature of Japanese industrialization, but it was widely characteristic of this first period, which meant that the social impact of Japan's industrial revolution had much in common with its earlier counterpart in the West or in contemporary Russia.

In some respects, Japan's early industrialization was distinctive, compared either to the West or to Russia. The need to rely on low-paid labor to produce manufacturing exports had some similarity to Western practice during the 18th century, but the fact that Japan had no prior capital built up from earlier foreign trade sharpened this characteristic. The export momentum also differed from the Russian case, for Russia's industrialization could utilize earnings from grain exports; Russia's industry was not geared in this direction. The Russian focus rested on heavy industry and production for domestic use, including government purchases for rails and military expansion. Japan produced ships and heavy industrial goods and built up its military forces; but it was inevitably more involved, because of its lack of domestic energy sources, in a vigorous drive to sell manufactured goods abroad, even though this was a very new enterprise for the Japanese. These differences between Japanese and Russian industrial patterns would have ongoing implications in the 20th century, affecting relationships with the wider world as well.

SOCIAL AND ECONOMIC EFFECTS OF INDUSTRIALIZATION

The industrial revolution and the wider extensions of manufacturing and commercial agriculture, along with political change, had significant ramifications within Japanese culture and society. The Japanese government introduced a universal education system, providing primary schools for all. This education stressed the discipline of science and the importance of technical subjects along with political loyalty to the nation and emperor. Elite students at the university level also took courses that emphasized science, and many of the Japanese students went abroad to study technical subjects in other countries. The rapid assimilation of a scientific outlook built on and enhanced the earlier secularization of Japanese elite culture, but it was a major new ingredient.

In the Meiji era in the late 19th century, Japanese women learned Western musical forms and how to play Western instruments. Note the Western impact on Japanese fashions.

As in the West earlier, industrialization altered social structure. While an important group of aristocrats and people from the samurai warrior class entered the ranks of successful businessmen and officials, a new elite was formed that embraced leading entrepreneurs for the first time. Among the masses, the rise of a huge, propertyless class of urban workers was a new development. Both peasants and workers endured low wages and high taxes, as Japanese leaders required profits and tax revenue to amass the capital needed for further investment. Japan's industrial success did not come easily as far as the lower classes were concerned. And while the new elite did not cultivate the luxurious life-style of Western business magnates, being content with lower profit rates, it did insist on retaining power. Unions and lower-class political parties began to emerge by 1900 but made only slow headway, and a militant socialist movement was outlawed. Periodic strike movements were brutally repressed, though a legacy of serious class bitterness remained.

Japanese society was also disrupted by massive population growth. Better nutrition and new medical provisions reduced death rates, while the upheaval of the rural masses cut into traditional restraints on births. The result was a steady population surge that strained Japanese resources and stability, though it also assured an ongoing supply of low-cost labor.

Many Japanese copied Western fashions as part of the effort to become modern. Western-style haircuts replaced the samurai shaved head with a top knot—another example of the fascinating pattern of the Westernization of hair in world history. Western standards of hygiene spread, and the Japanese became enthusiastic toothbrushers and consumers of patent medicines. Japan also adopted the Western calendar and the metric system. Few Japanese converted to Christianity, however, and despite fads for Western popular culture, the Japanese managed to preserve an emphasis on their own values. What the Japanese wanted and got from the West involved practical techniques; they planned to infuse these with a distinctively Japanese spirit. As an early Japanese visitor to the American White House wrote in a self-satisfied poem that caught part of the national mood:

> *We suffered the barbarians to look upon*
> *The glory of our Eastern Empire of Japan.*

Western-oriented enthusiasms, in other words, were not meant to destroy a distinctive Japanese spirit.

Japanese family life retained many traditional emphases. The birthrate dropped as rapid population growth forced increasing numbers of people off the land. Meanwhile the rise of factory industry, separating work from home, made the labor of children less useful. Here was a trend, developed earlier in the West, that seems inseparable from successful industrialization. There were new signs of family instability as well. Many men moved to cities, leaving wives behind in rural manufacturing: The result in 1900, until legal changes made procedures more difficult, was the highest divorce rate in the world. On the more traditional side, however, the Japanese were eager to maintain the inferiority of women in the home. The position of Western women repelled them. Japanese government visitors to the United States were appalled by what they saw as the bossy ways of women: "The way women are treated here is like the way parents are respected in our country." Standards of Japanese courtesy also contrasted with the more open and boisterous behavior of Westerners—particularly Americans. "Obscenity is inherent in the customs of this country," noted another samurai visitor to the United States. Other basic features of Japanese life, including diet, were maintained in the face of Western influence. Certain Japanese religious values were also preserved. Buddhism lost some ground, though it remained important, but Shintoism, which appealed to the new nationalist concern with Japan's distinctive mission and the religious functions of the emperor, won new interest.

Japan's transformation had not brought the country to Western levels, and the Japanese remained intensely fearful for their independence. Economic change and the tensions, as well as the power it generated, did, however, produce a shift in Japanese foreign policy. With only one previous exception, the Japanese had never before been interested in territorial expansion, but by the 1890s they joined the ranks of imperialist powers. Partly this shift was an imitation of Western models, and at the same time an effort to prevent Western encroachment. Imperialism also relieved some strains within Japanese society, giving displaced samurai a chance to exercise their military talents elsewhere and providing symbols of nationalist achievement for the populace as a whole. The Japanese economy also required access to markets and raw materials. Because Japan was poor in many basic materials, including coal and oil for energy, the pressure for expansion was particularly great.

Japan's quick victory over China, in the quarrel for influence over Korea in 1894 and 1895, was a first step toward expansion. Japan convincingly demonstrated its new superiority over all other purely Asian powers. Humiliated

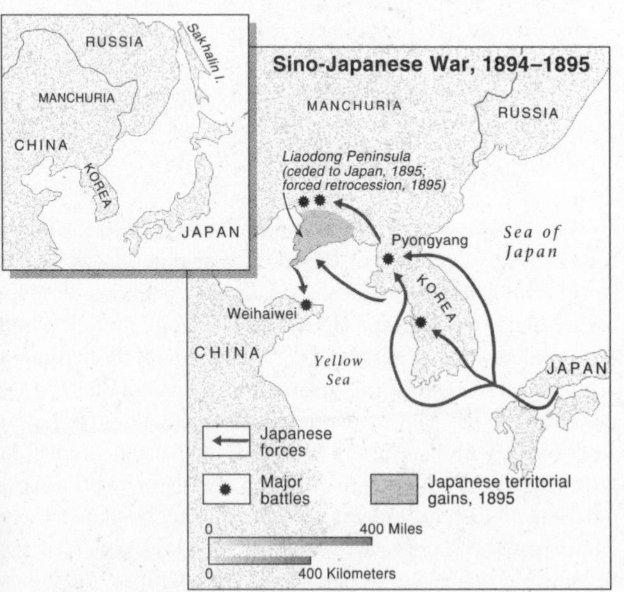

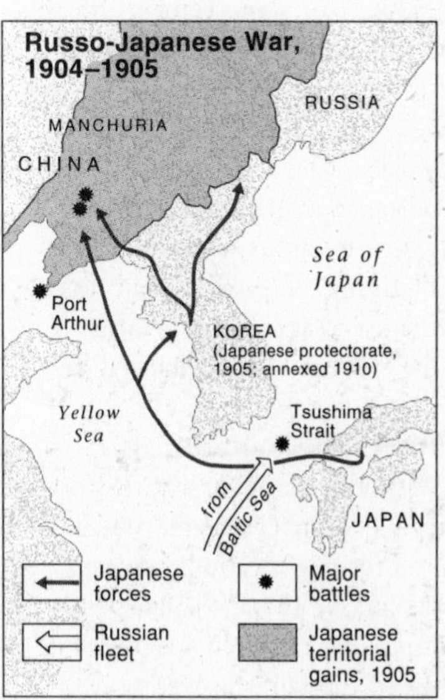

Japanese Colonial Expansion to 1914

by Western insistence that it abandon the Liaotung peninsula it had just won, the Japanese planned a war with Russia as a means of striking out against the nearest European power. A 1902 alliance with Britain was an important sign of Japan's arrival as an equal nation in the Western-dominated world diplomatic system. The Japanese were also eager to dent Russia's growing strength in East Asia, after the development of the trans-Siberian railroad. Disputes over Russian influence in Manchuria and Japanese influence in Korea led to the Russo-Japanese War in 1904, which Japan won handily on the basis of its superior navy. Japan annexed Korea in 1910; with this annexation, Japan was now not only a modern industrial power, but a new imperialist power as well.

THE STRAIN OF MODERNIZATION

Japan's success in a scant three decades was amazing. Its victories over China and then Russia surprised virtually every outside observer. There is no question that Japan's rapid transformation, like its more recent success in becoming one of the most advanced industrial societies in the world, constitutes a unique achievement. Furthermore, the Japanese—unlike Russia or major parts of the West—prepared the groundwork for industrialization without serious threat of revolution.

Yet this achievement, even blended as it was with substantial continuities from earlier Japanese culture and political styles, had its costs. Many Japanese conservatives resented the passion some of their countrymen displayed for Western fashions. Their concern helped assure that Japanese women, initially the subject of some reform interest, would be mainly confined to family roles. Nevertheless, disputes between generations, with the old clinging to traditional standards and the young more interested in Western styles, were commonplace, and very troubling in a society that stressed the importance of parental authority. Social tensions added to the strain, as expectations rose more rapidly than standards of living. Crowded conditions in the growing cities produced misery at least as great as in earlier Western slums. The high divorce rates showed another kind of strain.

Some tension entered political life. Political parties in Japan's Parliament clashed with the emperor's ministers over rights to determine policy. The government frequently had to dissolve the Diet and call for new elections, seeking a more workable parliamentary majority. Political assassinations and attempted assassinations reflected grievances, including direct action impulses in the samurai tradition.

Another kind of friction emerged in intellectual life. Many Japanese scholars copied Western philosophies and literary styles, and there was enough adaptation to prevent the emergence of a full, Russian-style intelligentsia. In addition to their interest in more traditional forms, other intellectuals expressed a deep pessimism about the loss of identity in a changing world. Some wanted the government to become more fully Western; many were concerned about jobs, as universities tended to turn out more graduates than the economy could handle. The underlying theme was confusion about a Japan that was no longer traditional, but not Western either. What was it? Thus some writers spoke of Japan heading for a "nervous collapse from which we will not be able to recover." Others dealt with more personal conflicts like those in the following poem:

> *Do not be loved by others; do not accept their charity, do not promise anything. . . . Always wear a mask. Always be ready for a fight—be able to hit the next man on the head at any time. Don't forget that when you make friends with someone you are sooner or later certain to break with him.*

As an antidote to social and cultural insecurity, Japanese leaders urged national loyalty and devotion to the emperor, and with considerable success. The official message promoted Japanese virtues of obedience and harmony that the West lacked. School texts thus stressed:

> Our country takes as its base the family system: the nation is but a single family, the imperial family is our main house. We the people worship the unbroken imperial line with the same feeling of respect and love that a child feels toward his parents. . . . The union of loyalty and filial piety is truly the special character of our national polity.

Nationalism was a partially new force in Japan, and of course it was common in the West and other parts of the world. But Japanese nationalism built on traditions of superiority and cohesion, and deference to rulers, as well as on the new tensions generated by rapid change. It became a deep force, probably in Japan more than elsewhere, that played a unique role in justifying sacrifice and struggle in a national mission to preserve independence and dignity in a hostile world. Nationalism, along with firm police repression of dissent and the sweeping changes of the early Meiji years, certainly helps explain why Japan avoided the revolutionary pressure that hit Russia, China, and other countries after 1900, and also avoided the kind of unrest that had characterized early Western industrialization around 1848.

Japan's traditions thus enabled it to foster rapid change through initiatives by the state and the elite, without the need for revolution. The result by 1900 was a dynamic country newly powerful on the world scene, shaping a distinctive kind of industrial society.

Yet Japan's very success reminds us of how unusual it was. No other society outside the Western world was yet able to match its achievements. Russia, responding to Western example in its own way, continued its growth as a world power, but amid such social disarray that further upheaval was inevitable. Most of the rest of the world, including independent Latin America, was not yet in a position to ask the Japanese question—how to industrialize without losing essential values—as it faced the more immediate concern of adjusting to or combating Western dominance. Even today, when classic Western imperialism has become largely a thing of the past and many societies are striving toward greater industrialization, the ability to emulate the Japanese pattern of rapid change seems very limited—concentrated, interestingly enough, in other small East Asian and Southeast Asian nations.

CONCLUSION

JAPAN, RUSSIA, AND WORLD WAR I

The beginnings of serious industrialization in Russia and Japan, and the unprecedented entry of Japan into world affairs, contributed important new ingredients to the world diplomatic picture by the early 20th century. Developments in both countries, along with the rise of the United States, added to the growing sense of rivalry among the established Western powers. Japan's surge, and particularly its surprising military victories, promoted a fear in the West of a new "yellow peril" that should be opposed through greater imperialist efforts. Outright colonial acquisitions by the new powers added directly to the competitive atmosphere, particularly in the Far East. Japan, to be sure, was not yet a major world player, but it was beginning to make its muscle felt.

Furthermore, the strains of early industrialization, including the need to appease embittered conservative aristocrats as well as aggrieved masses, made both Russia and Japan increasingly dependent on diplomatic success. After 1912, for example, Japan faced growing political party competition in Parliament, with frequent if futile parliamentary defiance of the emperor's ministers. Massive popular protest added fuel to the fire as Japanese workers and peasants developed new political expectations and allegiances. It was in this setting that Japan joined the Allied side in World War I, hoping not for a significant military role but for the chance to seize German colonies in the Pacific—which it quickly gobbled up. Russia, of course, launched into the war from the outset, as a central actor, as its narrowing diplomatic options combined with internal pressures to preclude any alternative. Japan and Russia were not unique in finding diplomacy affected by new domestic rifts—the Western industrial leaders faced some similar tensions—but they were unquestionably caught up in a new spiral.

THE STRAINS OF WAR

The war itself, finally, exacerbated problems in both countries. Japan's participation as an ally to Britain and France encouraged new liberal and democratic sentiments along with an increased pro-Western sentiment. This alarmed conservatives, who were also disappointed that Japan did not win full great-power status from the war. Here were seeds of new political tensions in Japan.

Involvement in World War I was no mere prelude in Russia: Building on the existing tensions in Russian society, it brought major revolution. Russia fared badly in the war, losing important territory to Germany. Furthermore, the Russian economy, after an initial year of solid performance, simply could not sustain the effort of a modern total war. Hunger became widespread and, along with military setbacks and the incompetence of the tsar and his advisors, this produced by 1916 a growing wave of strikes and discontent. Yet in 1916 the tsar adjourned the duma and proceeded to rule alone, making even moderate political groups discontent. Then in March 1917 strikes broke out in the major cities, backed by growing unrest in the peasant countryside. The duma had to be recalled and soon took over the government, while Marxists and other radical leaders improved their organization among the urban workers. The Russian Revolution was under way.

Russia and soon Japan were thus embroiled in new adventures in the wake of World War I. Their new directions reflected the stresses of rapid change in the context of a complicated world diplomatic and economic system. Given the importance of the nations and their newfound industrial power, changes both in Russia and in Japan would have major repercussions in the world.

THE WORLD IN 1914

As World War I broke out, despite the industrial stirrings of the latecomers, the world was still largely under the Western thumb. Japan and Russia had figured out their own special relationship to the West's industrially driven surge, which gave them unusual freedom of action. Their increasing industrialization would progressively challenge unadulterated Western domination, and it constituted an important qualification to Western triumphs even in 1914. It remained true that the world's most important quarrels in 1914 were among Western powers, not between the West and other societies—simply because of Western economic, political, and military power.

Western imperialism and economic outreach had operated as the major forces in world history for a full century by 1914, substantially altering world patterns and the dynamic of individual societies. Significant divisions opened between societies directly under imperialist control and those, such as China and the Ottoman Empire, touched by imperialism but technically independent. New distinctions arose in East Asia, between China's sluggish response to the new world environment and Japan's modernization surge. Russia continued its own rise to greater power, now grafting early industrialization onto this process. Latin America was another scene of important change, as political independence and cultural identity were combined with the growing commercialization of a dependent economy. As a result of imperialism plus reactions to Western example, some common changes were beginning to take shape around the world. Educational systems spread in most societies. Traditional forms of unfree labor, including rigorous serfdom and slavery, largely disappeared, though low-paying wage labor on estates and in factories provided new thralls for many workers. A new element of nationalism surfaced almost everywhere.

Yet in 1900, the world's diversity remained striking, as it blended long-standing differences in cultural and political traditions with the variety of responses to Western imperialism and industrial example. Some of the divisions taking shape between industrializers, including "early latecomers" such as Japan, and more dependent economies would have continuing influence in world history. Other divisions between an India open to forced Western influence and a more traditionalist China would be complicated or superseded by later developments. What was becoming clear was the new set of divisions among civilizations, based no longer on evolving tradition alone, but also on response to change and challenge. What would become clear when war broke out in 1914 was that rivalries within the West, tragically played out on battlefields in Europe, would combine with new reactions elsewhere to close the era of Western supremacy. The new chapter that then opened in world history would give fuller rein to changes and diversities in other societies, including the new power bases being prepared in Russia and Japan.

FURTHER READINGS

Several studies deal with Russian industrialization. W. Blackwell's *The Industrialization of Russia* (1982) provides useful overview. An older collection deals with Russian change in terms of modernization theory: C. Black, ed., *The Transformation of Russian Society* (1960). Economic backwardness and latecomer reactions are taken up in A. Gerschenkron's *Economic Backwardness in Historical Perspective* (1962).

A number of historians have advanced understanding of Russia's workers: See R. Zelnik's *Labor and Society in Tsarist Russia, 1855–1870* (1971) and Victoria Bonnell, ed., *The Russian Worker: Life and Labor under the Tsarist Regime* (1983). On rural conditions, see T. Emmons's *The Russian Landed Gentry and the Peasant Emancipation of 1861* (1968). Political agitation is discussed in A. B. Ulam's *Russia's Failed Revolutionaries* (1981). Army service and protest form the subject of John Bushnell's *Mutiny and Repression: Russian Soldiers in the Revolution of 1905–1906* (1983). Barbara Engel's *Mothers and Daughters: Women of the Intelligentsia in Nineteenth Century Russia* (1983) takes up another vital topic. Finally, on popular culture, see Jeffrey Brooks's *When Russia Learned to Read: Literacy and Popular Culture* (1987) and Ben Eklof's *Russian Peasant Schools: Officialdom, Village Culture, and Popular Pedagogy, 1864–1914* (1986).

For general coverage of Japan in the period, consult G. Akita's *Foundations of Constitutional Government in Modern Japan, 1868–1900* (1967) and W. G. Beasley's *The Meiji Restoration* (1973). Several books cover economic trends: G. C. Allen's *A Short Economic History of Modern Japan* (1958), W. W. Lockwood's *The Economic Development of Japan* (1954), and R. Dore, ed., *Aspects of Social Change in Modern Japan* (1967).

Japanese industrial structure has received much recent attention from worried Americans: See J. C. Abegglen's *The Japanese Factory: Aspects of Its Social Organization* (1985), Hugh Patrick, ed., *Japanese Industrialization and*

Its Social Consequences (1973), and the careful study by Andrew Gordon, *The Evolution of Labor Relations in Japan* (1985). On culture, E. O. Reischauer's *Japan, the Story of a Nation* (1981) is unusually readable, and M. Miyoshi's *Accomplices of Silence: The Modern Japanese Novel* (1974) is good. See also R. H. Myers and M. R. Beattie, eds., *The Japanese Colonial Empire 1895–1945* (1984).

1910–1920 Mexican Revolution

1914–1918 World War I

1917 Russian Revolution

1919 Versailles peace settlement; League of Nations

1921 Foundation of Chinese Communist party

1912 African National Congress party formed in South Africa

1920 Treaty of Sèvres reorganizes Middle East

1917 United States' entry to World War I

1919 Revolt in Egypt; first Pan-African Nationalist Congress

1912 Fall of Qing dynasty in China; beginning of Chinese revolution

1917 Balfour Declaration promises Jews a homeland in Palestine

1916 Arab revolts against Ottomans

1930–1945 Vargas regime in Brazil

1933–1939 New Deal in United States

1933 Nazis rise to power in Germany

1931–1947 Gandhi-led resistance in India

1934–1940 Cárdenas reform period in Mexico

1937 Army officers in power in Japan; invasion of China

1929–1933 Height of Great Depression

1931 Japan invades Manchuria

1927–1928 Stalin heads Soviet Union; five-year plans and collectivization

1935 German rearmament; Italy conquers Ethiopia

On July 26 and 27, 1941 the night skies over the Kremlin were illuminated during German raids.

1939–1945 World War II

1946–1974 Decolonization in Asia, Africa, and Oceania

1948 Division of Korea

1945 Formation of United Nations

1949 Formation of NATO

1948 Israel-Palestine partition; first Arab-Israeli war

1960s Civil rights movement in U.S.; revival of feminism

1959 Cuban Revolution

1968–1973 Student protests in West

1942–1945 Holocaust

1950–1953 Korean War

1951 End U.S. occupation of Japan

1957 Ghana becomes first independent African nation

1965–1968 Cultural revolution in China

1945–1948 Soviet takeover of Eastern Europe

1939 Nazi-Soviet pact

1955 Bandung conference; nonaligned movement

1947 India and Pakistan gain independence

1956 Partial end of Stalinism

1945 Atomic bomb

1949 Communist victory in China

1941 United States enters war

1947–1975 Cold war; Marshall Plan

1946 Philippines proclaim independence

1945 Communists proclaim Vietnam independence

1947 Peronism in Argentina

1955 Warsaw Pact

1957 European Economic Community (Common Market)

1965–1973 U.S. military intervention in Vietnam

1962 Algeria declares independence

PART 6

The 20th Century in World History

Pinpointing the 20th century as a time period is one of the most challenging tasks facing a historian, particularly a world historian. We are so close to the patterns involved that reasoned judgment is difficult. Previous periods, though they generate continued debate, at least constitute stories whose endings are known. We can easily see, for example, that the Industrial Revolution ushered in profound changes for the West and some other parts of the world by 1900. We can even more easily see that during the 19th century Western nations gained unprecedented power in the world at large, building on earlier colonialism but also measurably surpassing it. It is not difficult, in other words, to define the 19th century in terms of its contrasts with the early modern period, to see what its new ingredients were and how many of them turned out.

We ourselves are engaged in the 20th century, which makes judgment far more tentative. In the 19th century, for example, many people were not explicitly aware of the Industrial Revolution, even when they were involved in it. They would be much more likely to point to some recent political event or cultural current in defining their era. Most historians, however, now take a different view, and argue that what people thought was significant may have been somewhat less vital than the underlying processes of which contemporaries were only dimly aware. Knowing this, we must admit uncertainty in trying to pinpoint our own age. How significant in world history, for example, was the surge of Nazism of the 1930s? Here was a fearsome new political movement that at the time seemed to

1975–1989 Democratic regimes spread in Latin America

1989 Reform movement in South Africa

1980–1988 Iran-Iraq War

1990 Reunification of Germany

1973, 1979 Oil crises; height of OPEC power

1985 ff. Gorbachev heads Soviet Union; reforms and unrest through Eastern Europe

1976 Death of Mao; new reform pattern in China

1992 Full economic integration of Common Market

1979 Iranian Revolution; spread of Islamic fundamentalism

1990–1991 Iraq invades Kuwait; Persian Gulf crisis; U.S.-Allied defeat of Iraq

1975 Communist victory in Vietnam

1989 New regimes throughout Eastern Europe

threaten some permanent changes in political trends and that disrupted two decades and, through World War II, contributed to undeniably important shifts in many parts of the world. Almost any historian, at least in the Western world, writing in the 1950s would have seen the rise of Nazism as a major turning point. Yet from the vantage point of the 1990s Nazism seems one of a number of developments that mark a key subperiod, rather than a fundamental feature of the whole century, though some similar racist movements still survive. Many Americans in the 1990s would rate the rise of Japan to the status of industrial superpower far more important in creating a novel international context for our century than Nazism was. Nazism's decisive focus has diluted with the passage of time—which is another way of reminding us that our judgment of the 20th century in terms of world history periodization is highly conditioned by how we feel about world conditions now.

Given the problems of perspective, two contradictory impulses can affect historians' efforts to place their century as part of a larger scheme of periodization. One impulse is to emphasize the continuities, lest we be misled into exaggerating the novelty of our time and perhaps forget the importance of the past. At the end of the 1980s, amid a host of changes in Russia and Eastern Europe, nationalist sentiment revived in the Balkans and a number of other ethnic regions. Bulgaria tried to eliminate a Turkish minority (by expelling them or making them adopt Bulgarian names); Romanians clashed with Hungarians. Despite more than 50 years of war, revolution, and massive attendant political change in this region, passions dating from at least the 19th century remained lively. Which is more important: all the new developments or the fact that, in the minds of many, basic loyalties had changed so little?

At the other extreme, some historians and many other observers caught in a modern culture that emphasizes rapid and fundamental change as a condition of contemporary life are prone to see the 20th century as a decisive new stage in human history. They write of the 20th century as a "third revolution," comparable only to the Neolithic and Industrial Revolutions of the past in setting up basic new conditions for human existence. Or they see the 20th century defined by the final exhaustion of human frontiers (at least on this planet), as a result of massive population growth and new technologies. As the remaining tropical forests are being chopped down at a fearsome rate, and as human crowding reaches proportions never before imagined, these historians stress the extent to which the 20th century has altered the human condition in ways that have no clear precedent at all. We are moving into uncharted waters. It is certainly useful to discuss whether 20th-century developments can be compared to a few key changes in the past (like the previous transformations of economic modes) or whether they are moving toward unprecedented novelty. We will discuss some of these extremely important and complex contemporary issues in the final chapter of this final unit of the text.

For the moment, however, it seems safest to avoid the most extreme predictions, most of which pick up on fairly recent developments (for example, advent of computers in the postindustrial revolution model) or on catastrophes that have not yet definitively occurred, and recognize that at most points in world history a balance of continuity and change must be embraced to capture reality. This has been the case heretofore—even during the throes of the Industrial Revolution—and may prove to characterize the 20th century as well, regardless of all the real and apparent innovations.

The key question, to make the change and continuity formula more precise, is whether the 20th century opened up a new basic period in world history, or whether it added lots of modifications to the fundamental patterns of the 19th century without, however, altering the basic framework. Here, despite all the appropriate caveats about not exaggerating change, the answer seems clear: The 20th century has provided one of those relatively rare breaks in world history, comparable in scope to the 15th century or to the 5th century. The contemporary period in world history is just taking shape even in the 1990s, and so it is harder to define than earlier watersheds; we cannot be sure of some ultimate directions. It may prove distinctive also in that some unprecedented force—a sweeping new technology or environmental degradation—will pull the 20th century away from prior historical patterns. It is, however, assessable as a period in world history, and this can prepare a more extended inquiry.

Previous periods in world history, at least since the great classical age, have met three criteria: They have involved basic geographic rebalancing among major civilization areas; they have measurably increased the intensity and extent of contact among civilizations; and they have, partly as a result of new contacts, demonstrated some new and roughly parallel patterns among many if not all of these major civilizations. The 20th century fits this definition, as a result of developments that can be traced to the events involved in World War I and its aftermath; this is why its position as the launching pad for a new periodization schema seems secure.

THE REPOSITIONING OF THE WEST

The 20th-century shift in balance among civilizations has featured the relative decline of the West. This resulted in part from the two intensely destructive internal wars fought in the West between 1914 and 1945, which in each case expanded into global conflict. The West's relative decline also reflected the patterns of change and development in a number of other societies (including of course the two—Russia and Japan—that had begun an industrial revolution even before 1900). The rise of the United States to new international importance maintained Western influence to some extent, but this merely enhanced Western Europe's relative decline and did not prevent the relative slippage of the West as a whole. Despite great Western strength, including European revival after 1945 and again in the 1990s, the pattern of the 19th century prevailed no more. The rise of the West to steadily more powerful international positions—militarily, commercially, and politically—stopped and then reversed during the 20th century, even with the United States added to the West's leadership ranks.

The West's relative decline showed in several areas. Western population (including that of the United States), began to fall back rapidly as a percentage of world totals, reversing a pattern that had begun to develop in the 12th century. Western birth control (matched to be sure in a few other areas, such as the Soviet Union and Japan) combined with rapid population growth rates elsewhere to produce this result. What the long-term outcome of the West's population slide will be remains unclear; many analysts argue that since the Industrial Revolution, rapid population growth is a source of weakness, not a strength. At the very least, the West's population stagnation opened Europe and the United States to rapid immigration from other societies. Here was a new pattern that might either add to Western dynamism or lead to crippling new tensions.

More specific than population rebalancing was the decline and then virtual end of the great Western empires, a process clearly under way by the 1920s and then culminating after 1945. The West, which dominated most of the world directly or indirectly by 1920, ruled little beyond its own borders by 1980. Its influence remained very great—change in this area was complex; but literal political control unquestionably receded, again reversing a centuries-long trend. Monopoly over the most advanced weapons systems, a key Western advantage since the 16th century, also ended, though key Western nations—led after 1945 by the United States—retained a major share in leadership. Japan and then the Soviet Union joined the West as world military giants, while other societies though not quite as advanced, gained ground. Further, alternate forms of warfare—particularly guerrilla tactics used in colonial struggles, but to some extent terrorism as well—allowed certain technologically inferior regions to counter Western military supremacy. In terms of warfare, the world (from a Western standpoint) became more complicated, after centuries of a steadily advancing edge in raw power.

In 1991 the United States and various allies decisively defeated the nation of Iraq in the Persian Gulf War, using a variety of high-technology weaponry. Clearly, Western-dominated military advances were again demonstrated, as only a few hundred allied soldiers died in combat compared to possibly 100,000 Iraqis. But even this war showed how the 20th century had become more complex than the easy days of Western imperialism. It took months of military buildup, a force of over half a million men and women, plus expenditures of over $50 billion to defeat (overwhelmingly, to be sure) a medium-sized Arab state.

The West also lost its unchallenged preeminence as world trader and manufacturer. Of course, much of the world economic system established in the 16th century persisted. Important regions still sent cheap raw materials—based on low-paid labor—into international trade, which constrained not only their economic levels but also their political independence. Nations with heavy international debts thus faced substantial outside intervention in a 20th-century version of international inequality. Only a few societies won the bulk of the profits from international trade because they ran the shipping and banking facilities and produced the most expensive processed products. In this basic sense, there was substantial continuity from earlier periods in world history. But the actors changed, which is where the West's relative decline showed up. While the West continued to be among the dominant economic agents, it was joined, by the 1960s, by Japan and an increasing number of other East Asian centers.

Clearly, on a number of fronts the rise of the West, one of the leading processes in world history since the 15th century, leveled off, with the 1920s and 1930s forming a key turning point. The results of this change were diffuse. No single civilization emerged by the 1990s to claim the kind of growing world leadership the West had long produced. In part this was because the West itself still remained quite strong with its influence pervasive on many international fronts. Parts of East Asia now matched the West economically, but other areas generated new international influence in military or cultural sectors. As with the decline of Arab civilization earlier in world history, a number of new centers of power emerged. Perhaps one center will ultimately take primary leadership as the West had ultimately done after Arab recession, but this is not inevitable and is not likely to be speedy.

More obvious was the increased autonomy the West's relative decline made possible for a number of regional centers. This allowed places such as Brazil, India, and the Middle East to develop new combinations of tradition and change that had some relationship to Western models but were not dictated by them. The proliferation of new nations around the world in the decades after 1945 was a revealing index of opportunities for political innovation; a host of states had to establish political legitimacy and decide on appropriate state structures. Even in the economic area, where Western and Japanese prominence remained extremely influential, a number of world regions managed to generate substantial internal economic growth and win a place as exporters of manufactured goods. Brazil, for example, became the world's fourth largest computer exporter by the 1990s, behind only the high-tech leaders: Japan, the United States, and Western Europe. These patterns will be explored in the chapters that follow.

World Distribution of Manufacturing, 1930

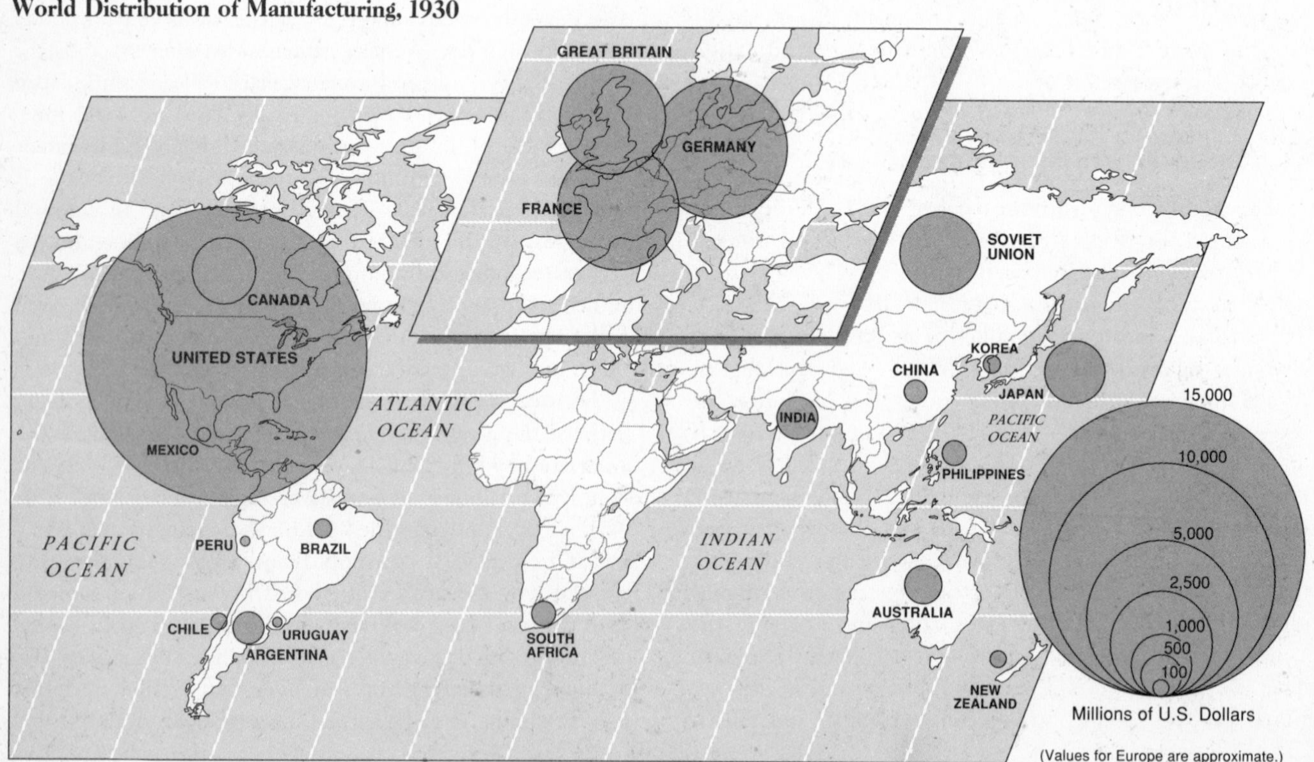

INTERNATIONAL CONTACTS

Along with rebalancing among civilizations, with a vigorous West now challenged by great vitality in other regions, came intensifying international contacts. A few areas pulled back into relative isolation: This was true of the Soviet Union from the late 1920s through the 1970s when a largely independent national economy was forged with little involvement in wider world trade; it also characterized China, especially in the decades after 1956. Nevertheless, even relative isolation was difficult, for the dominant trends urged increasing interaction. Technology was critical: Innovations included faster communication via wireless radio and, later, satellite and computer; faster transport, using the airplane; and larger capacity for both communication and movement of goods. World-trade levels steadily increased, and more and more corporations (particularly from the West and Japan) operated on an international basis.

World wars and peacetime alliances demonstrated the new levels of international contact on other fronts. Great diversity of interests remained, but diplomatic contacts were internationalized as never before; thus the intensity and importance of United States-Chinese diplomacy, to choose one example, rivaled the relationships between Britain and Germany a century before. International cultural influences also increased in tandem with improved communications and the efforts of multinational corporations. Films, scientific research, and artistic styles all spread widely at both popular and elite levels. The result was not a single world culture, for extent of penetration and regional reactions varied widely. But most cultures had to come to some terms with the impact of Hollywood movies, Parisian art, or British-American popular music. International sports interest constituted another unprecedented development across civilization lines: soccer football won mass enthusiasm virtually everywhere; the Olympic Games, which were reestablished in the 1890s and gradually shifted from an initial Western dominance to global participation, both symbolized and promoted this facet of new cultural contacts.

INTERNATIONAL CHALLENGES IN POLITICS AND CULTURE

Parallelisms in patterns of change resulted partly from outright imitation, particularly of Western models, but also from regional efforts to push back Western dominance. One result was a sweeping pattern of political change. Almost no society aside from some of the more stable Western nations (United States, Britain, and Scandinavia) had the same form of government by 1990 that it had maintained in 1900. Monarchies crumbled, replaced by democracies, totalitarian governments, or authoritarian regimes. The results were varied, but the fact of innovation was virtually universal, as major civilizations tried to come to terms with Western example while also developing governments vigorous enough to gain or maintain independence. More concretely, revolutions and decolonization compelled political experiments almost everywhere outside the West as well as in key areas within Western society. Moreover, along with new political forms came new functions. Governments generally took on new roles in trying to further economic growth. They also accepted new and unprecedented responsibilities in areas such as education and health care, and their contact with masses of citizens increased greatly as a result. Regardless of prior political traditions and ongoing diversity, the governments of the 20th century world innovated in several common directions.

Changes or modifications in previous belief systems formed another current that swept over many national and civilizational boundaries. Most of the world's people in 1850 adhered to one of the great religions or philosophical systems created during the classical or postclassical eras: Confucianism, Christianity, Islam, and the like. These systems were still lively in 1950 and some were even winning new converts. In most parts of the world, however, they had been modified or challenged by new systems of beliefs that were more strictly secular in orientation, such as liberalism, nationalism, or communism. Quite widely, they were also challenged by growing interest in science, a staple of the burgeoning mass education systems. As with politics, belief changes took no single direction, but the encounter with fundamentally novel ideas was a genuinely international experience—and one of the key developments of 20th-century world history.

Changes in ideas and politics related to a third general international current: the displacement of long-standing beliefs in rigid social inequalities. All the great agricultural civilizations had developed highly structured systems of inequality, though some of the civilizations complicated these systems through religious beliefs in the spiritual equality of all souls. Western ideas, expressed in great movements such as the French Revolution of 1789, had attacked assumptions of structured inequality and legal privilege. Also, the abolition of slavery through most of the world in the 19th century signaled the end of another traditional institution of inequality. The further spread of Western ideas plus new movements such as Russian and Chinese communism and the nationalisms of Asia and Africa brought a more widespread attack on rigid inequalities in the 20th century. Caste systems and aristocracies "officially" crumbled, with only rare exceptions. Societies turned to new efforts at equality or at least equality of opportunity, including widespread voting rights, though countercurrents such as racist beliefs or gender inequalities complicated the picture. Inequality did not end, but older ideas that had sanctified it did yield to new beliefs.

Patterns of economic change were more diverse: Despite a general interest in improving production levels, some societies remained largely agricultural, while others began to move into industrial ranks. Nevertheless, efforts at change as well as the influence of international corporations and trade prompted some widespread social effects. Most societies witnessed new levels of social mobility, as earlier caste or class lines loosened. The social status of women was almost everywhere reconsidered, as a result of new levels of education and new involvement in work outside the home, though again specific results varied.

No single world society existed, even in embryo, by the 1990s. Differences among civilizations remained great: Some of them reached deep into earlier traditions, while others reflected diverse experiences in the 20th century itself. India and China differed, thus, because of patterns inherited from the classical and postclassical eras and because one society underwent revolution while the other experienced a somewhat less traumatic decolonization in the middle decades of the 20th century. The developments highlighted in this unit on the contemporary era must be evaluated both in terms of the distinctive features of major civilizations, old features as well as new ones, and in terms of their common participation in international phenomena such as political change or gender redefinition.

USING THE 20TH CENTURY AS A NEW PERIOD IN WORLD HISTORY

Understanding the 20th century as the starting point of a new period in world history, comparable to a few key transition periods in the past, helps explain why the last eight decades have been so very dramatic, not simply in one or two particularly dynamic or troubled areas, but almost across the board. Other shaping factors add ingredients to the sense of overall global change: the impact of massive, though somewhat uneven, population growth; environmental change in an unprecedentedly populous, mechanized, urbanized, and interconnected human community; new and potentially devastating forms of warfare, involving nuclear weapons and rocketry; and what may turn out to be a radically novel technological framework as postindustrial systems replace the steam-driven machinery of an industrial age. Any one of these ingredients, and particu-

The World in 1991

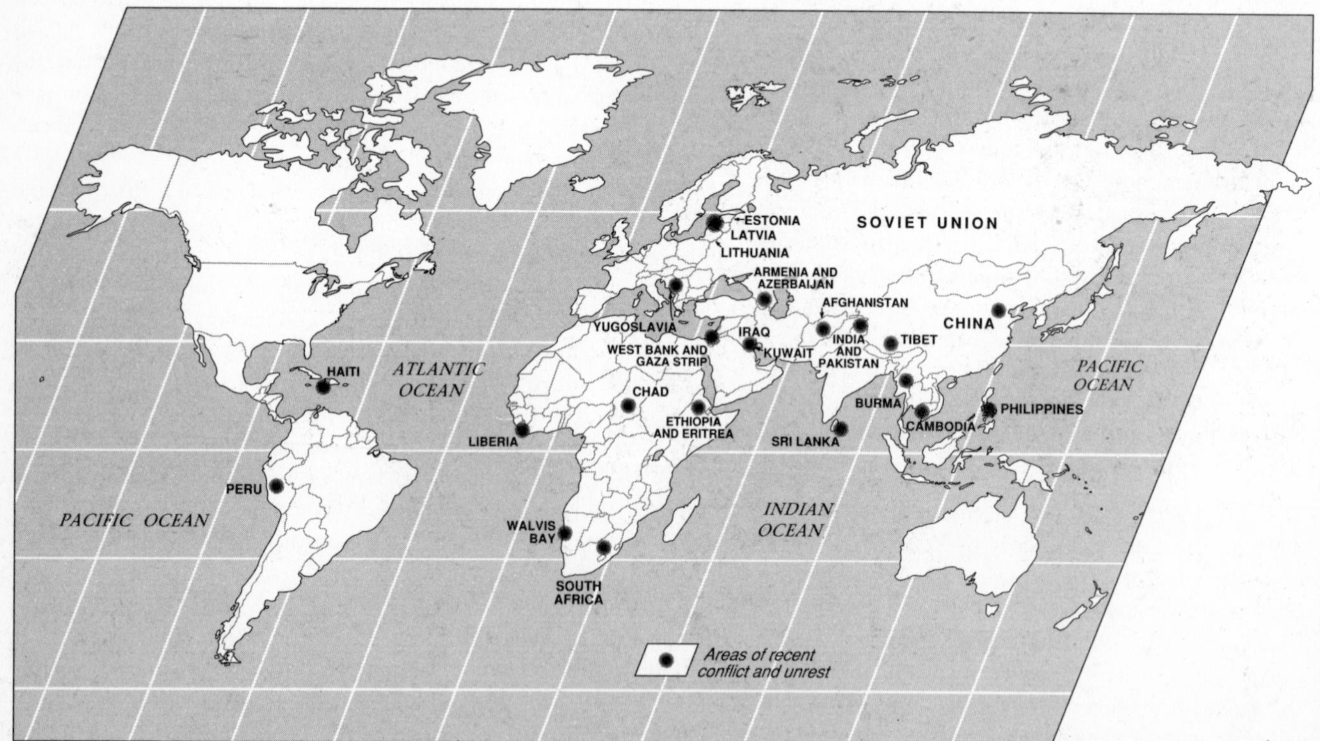

larly their combination, may turn out to dwarf the civilizational rebalancings and parallelisms discussed here. Or, more probably, these processes can be seen in conjunction with the new world history framework, enhancing international contacts and creating additional impulses toward change.

The 20th century as a new period in world history unfolded in at least two phases. Between 1914 and 1945 the world was shaken by a series of catastrophic events—two world wars and an international depression—that can be seen as the birth pains of the new international order, causing and reflecting the West's relative decline and facilitating the emergence of new centers of activity. Several political revolutions accompanied the West's crises, ushering in new regimes in Russia, Mexico, China, and (if a top-down revolution may be included) Turkey. After 1945 the West began to adjust to a new world order in which decolonization created a host of novel governments. These were the decades in which new social mobility, changes in gender relations, and redefinitions of government functions moved to center stage, although some had been suggested during the crisis period as well.

The following chapters deal first with the crisis era, in terms of basic international events and processes of the decades of war and depression. Then individual civilizations are treated: first the West and its most obvious rivals for power—the Soviet Union and Eastern Europe as well as the Pacific Rim states dominated by Japan. Latin America is something of a special case in that decolonization had already occurred, but industrialization remained elusive; nevertheless, the 20th century was a period of fundamental change in this region, including a number of key revolutions in Mexico, Cuba, and several Andes nations. Areas dominated by decolonization and the formation of new nations include much of southern Asia, the Middle East, and Africa, where the hold of distinctive traditions reflected continued diversity in combination with some common problems and opportunities. China and its neighbors require separate treatment because of the special importance of complex revolutionary processes. Finally, some trends and prospects for the later 20th century and beyond return to the more general dynamic of world history in its emerging new period.

One basic corollary of 20th-century periodization must be kept in mind. Many people in the world today argue that change has accelerated, and this may be true; nevertheless, most new periods in world history have taken at least two centuries or more to clarify. The history of the 20th century allows us to see the forces overturning the old framework; it permits only glimpses of what the new one will be. We know that the new period will not be Western-dominated to the extent the previous one turned out to be, but we cannot be sure whether a successor will emerge, or what the successor will be. Precisely because of the uncertainties of transition, many pundits offer beguiling simplicities: Will the next West be East Asia or, perhaps, Brazil? Then again everyone will be computer-linked anyway so separate traditions won't matter much. The chapters in this unit flesh out a periodization scheme for the 20th century, describing frameworks applicable to many different areas. These frameworks, however, also demonstrate that the century has been exceedingly complex thus far, its implications diverse. Grasping what has happened already in the most recent period of world history is the best basis for discussing what may yet come.

1914–1918 World War I

1919–1939 Period of United States isolation

1917 British Balfour Declaration promises Jews a homeland in Palestine

1923 Treaty of Lausanne recognizes independence of Turkey

1918 German emperor abdicates

1916 Beginning of Arab revolt against Ottoman Empire

1920 Treaty of Sèvres dissolves Ottoman Empire; French and British mandates set up in Middle East

1917 Russian Revolution

1918 Treaty of Brest-Litovsk; Russia withdraws from war

1919 Versailles conference and treaty; League of Nations established

1915 Italy enters war

1919 Treaty of St. Germain recognizes Czechoslovakia, Yugoslavia, Poland, and Hungary

1917 United States enters war

One-half Century of Crisis, 1914–1945

INTRODUCTION. This chapter focuses on key developments in international military, diplomatic, and economic spheres in the crucial time period framed by the two world wars and filled by an agonizing global economic depression.

These developments illustrate the extent to which the world network had intensified. There had been previous wars with international ramifications—European conflict in the Seven Years' War spilled over to struggles in the colonies in North America and India, as well as on the seas; the same held true for the battles against Napoleon early in the 19th century. The two world wars, however, were more genuine international conflicts in that they directly covered a larger portion of the globe and, though heavily centered on struggles within Europe, involved nations from several different civilizations as major combatants as well as victims. The explosion of the international economy was perhaps less novel since many regions of the world already had been tied to each other economically, but the sudden embroilment of so many different economies in the Great Depression had qualities of its own.

This chapter, in other words, covers key disruptions in the international framework, at a point in which the importance of this framework requires assessment before turning to developments in individual civilizations. International crises lay behind new directions in the world economy and massive political change, marking the 20th century as a crucial break in global periodization.

The international framework was still skewed by the fact that some civilizations were economically and militarily more powerful than others. World War I was mainly a

---

- **1929–1939** Great Depression
- **1931** Japan invades Manchuria
- **1933** Nazis to power in Germany
- **1935** Germany rearms; Italy invades Ethiopia
- **1936–1939** Spanish Civil War
- **1937** New Japanese attack on China; beginning of war in Asia
- **1938** Germany's union (Anschluss) with Austria; Germany invades Czechoslovakia; Munich conference
- **1939** Nazi-Soviet Pact
- **1939** World War II begins; Germany and Soviet Union invade Poland
- **1940** Axis agreement (Germany, Italy, Japan)
- **1940** Fall of France
- **1941** German invasion of Soviet Union
- **1941** Japanese attack Pearl Harbor; United States enters war
- **1942–1945** Allied conferences in Teheran, Yalta, Potsdam
- **1942** Tide begins to turn in both war theaters; Soviet Union repulses attack on Stalingrad; Allies invade North Africa
- **1944** Invasion of France by Allies
- **1945** End of World War II
- **1945** Atomic bomb dropped on Japan
- **1945** United Nations established
- **1946** United States grants Philippines independence
- **1947** Cold war begins between United States and Soviet Union
- **1947** Wider decolonization begins with independence of India and Pakistan

European conflict, though it involved participants from the colonies and had independent areas of operations in the Pacific region and the Middle East. The Great Depression was more generally international, as it stemmed from economic problems in various parts of the world; here again, however, the focus of the collapse was on western Europe and the United States. World War II, finally, saw decisive activity in Asia and Europe as well as on the high seas. International events, in other words, drew in a growing number of active participants, most notably Japan and the United States (along with Europe including Russia), but also other parts of Asia and portions of Africa. The impact of international events was wider yet, even when, as in both depression and war, some areas were primarily victims of other areas' disasters rather than being directly responsible.

The chapter does not attempt to cover all major aspects of world historical development between 1914 and 1945; subsequent chapters will turn to the major individual civilizations. Each society was marked, however, by the great international events that are the focus of this chapter. Grasping these events is vital to tracing their more particular impacts that would last well beyond 1945.

THE RISE OF THE UNITED STATES

The growing international role of the United States was a crucial ingredient of the new century. American power had been building since the 1870s. By then, the nation's sectional conflict had ended and overland expansion to the West was nearing completion. Fueled by new immigration, population levels soared. Most important, the United States became a major player in the international economy, sending both farm and factory exports abroad. From 1890 until after 1960, exports consistently exceeded imports. Though still a debtor nation until World War I, the United States expanded its investments abroad, more than quadrupling the level between 1897 and 1914. Finally, national confidence soared. American missionaries worked in Africa and Asia; the number in China alone rose from 436 in 1874 to 5462 in 1914. American nationalist pride easily kept pace with the nation's religious sense.

These developments propelled the United States into the imperialist scramble by the 1890s. Following involvement by merchants and missionaries, Hawaii and some other Pacific islands were seized. The Spanish-American War brought the Philippines plus vital territory in the Caribbean under the United States' protection. The United States' intervention in Central America became commonplace, leading among other things to construction and control of the Panama Canal. American muscle began to affect great power diplomacy. Theodore Roosevelt sponsored the conference that ended the Russo-Japanese War, winning the Nobel Peace Prize for his efforts and also signaling American concern about Japanese expansion.

Full American entry into world affairs awaited World War I. Even then, many Americans remained unsure of their international role, eager to continue to benefit from world trade but inclined to return to diplomatic isolation at crucial junctures. The first half of the 20th century was an experimental period for the United States internationally. Even apart from debates over involvement, Americans also oscillated between conventional great-power maneuvers and some desire to bring a special idealism to the diplomatic process. It was not always easy for other parts of the world to adjust to the American style; here too, the period from 1900 to 1950 required experimentation.

DECADES OF DISASTER

Despite innovative developments, such as the new United States' role in the world, the overriding tone of the period from 1900 to 1950 must be gloomy. Wars became bloodier and more international in scope. The 20th century showed that man's ability to kill man, woman, and child had reached new levels of gruesome sophistication. The depression devastated not only whole economies, but countless personal lives. This was a time of troubles in world history.

This chapter will reflect and explain how so many disasters occurred. Here, however, oversimplification is dangerous. As in earlier periods of world history, international trends were not uniform and certainly could vary in their impact. This half-century was a period of exciting—if sometimes chaotic and bloody—revolution in a number of countries. Societies in revolution, particularly Soviet Russia, were assuredly affected by the larger international trends but in distinctive ways. Even where the theme of hardship more fully predominated, clouds could have silver linings. Latin America, for example, profoundly hurt by worldwide depression (though not by the international wars), was able to respond to the disaster by new and constructive forms of government policy, opening a new chapter in the civilization's political history and at least a modification of its long-standing inferiority in international trade.

The disasters of the age particularly affected the West's power position in the world, and this meant opportunities for many dependent or colonial societies to strike out in new ways. Nationalism in India and the Middle East became more confident and effective. Here too, the international framework—though undeniably difficult—offered novel hopes, not crushing despair. Correspondingly the most agonized reactions to the half-century of crisis were voiced in the West, by people who suffered directly and who forecast further decline in their civilization.

Yet even in the West, the crisis half-century was not the final historical word. The results did diminish the West's role in the world, opening a complex rebalancing among civilizations after 1945. Nevertheless, Western society rebounded, creating a political and economic vitality that contrasted markedly with the agonies of the previous 40 years. Thus, while some people (particularly in the West) who lived through the decades of crisis thought that civilization was coming to an end, and while crises did reflect and cause huge changes in the international framework, they did not dictate the tone for world history after 1945. This tone will be discussed in Chapter 42.

For now, the key point to note is the complexity of the results of worldwide crises. These events created a new set of problems but also important new opportunities. The ensuing agenda can be summed up after dealing with the crises themselves, starting with World War I.

THE FIRST WORLD WAR

To many Western observers shortly before 1914, the main trends in world history seemed both clear and benign. During the previous century or more, Western society had become unquestionably richer and by many measurements more open and just. Mass education had become a fact of life. Health had improved, and the death of infants, long a constant in human history, was becoming increasingly rare. New political rights gave most adult men a direct voice in government, while protecting freedoms of religion and press. Knowledge advanced steadily, with increasing understanding of the physical universe. Dark corners of the universe existed still, but it was reasonable to assume that scientific planning, leavened by humanitarian concern, could reduce them steadily. Certainly, in this vision, catastrophic war had no place—people and governments should be too enlightened to allow more than minor discord.

CONFIDENCE AND INTERNATIONALISM ON THE WAR'S EVE

The optimism of many Westerners focused mainly on what they saw as progress in their own civilization, but there was also an international dimension to their belief in progress. Imperialists believed that Western leadership was bringing new enlightenment to the inferior peoples of the rest of the world, though they did not nake it clear whether these peoples might someday learn enough to take care of themselves according to Western standards. Beyond outright imperialism, there had been during the later 19th century some interesting first steps at international organization, which might foreshadow a more smoothly and peacefully functioning world.

In 1851, for example, an International Statistical Congress began meeting to standardize the practices of statistical services of the European governments. A more informal committee met in 1863 to prepare policies on the rights of neutral parties to aid the wounded during wars, and an official diplomatic conference redrafted these policies in 1864 at the Geneva Convention, establishing the Red Cross, an international agency for humanitarian service in wartime. The Telegraphic Union of 1865 blazed a new trail, followed ten years later by the Postal Union—both unions set agreed-upon international procedures for regular exchanges of letters and messages. Some of these steps constituted serious modifications of the idea that an individual national government could do as it pleased, and the practical agreements certainly facilitated the further development of international business arrangements. The habit of thinking internationally seemed to spread increasingly. Scientists met often in international conferences; industrialists showed their wares at international fairs and exhibitions, starting with London's great Crystal Palace display in 1851 and extending through regular world's fairs in various parts of Europe and the United States. Western socialists formed an international movement, based on the idea that working peoples should unite across national boundaries. Athletes gained a new forum for international competition with the establishment of the modern Olympic Games in 1890.

These various moves toward internationalization constituted an important development in world history, both recognizing and furthering the intensification of the world network. Many of the international systems and habits established from the later 19th century still facilitate world exchanges today—some, like easy international mailing, are so routine that they barely merit thought.

Despite genuine significance, however, the international movement had two related weaknesses. First, it was heavily based on Western dominance and control of empires. A few other governments fit in—from North America, Latin America, and Asia—but most of the initial arrangements were primarily set by Europeans and for Europeans. The process of weaning internationalism from Western control would be a long and painful one, focused particularly on the decades after 1945. Internationalization, furthermore, gained ground at the same time that European nationalism was at a height, as well as at a time when the idea of national independence and pride was spreading to new areas such as India. Here was another limit on internationalist thinking, quickly visible in areas such as the Olympic Games, which turned into an international forum for fierce athletic competition among rival nations.

The limits on internationalism showed clearly when the movement turned away from economic and goodwill areas to more directly political matters. In 1898 the Russian tsar urged the calling of a peace conference, designed to seek agreement on reducing armaments levels among the world's great powers. The move was prompted in part by Russia's economic problems, as a nation just beginning to industrialize, and its difficulty in keeping up with the arms costs escalating among the Western nations. Nevertheless, the discussions, held in The Hague in 1899, amplified international agreements on the treatment of war prisoners, temporarily prohibited weapons thrown from balloons, and banned gas warfare and some other new technologies (these latter measures were ignored in the great world war that broke out 15 years later). Disarmament and the idea of a compulsory arbitration of international disputes were shunted aside. But a permanent court of arbitration was established that nations could use to settle disputes. This court, now called the World Court, still sits in The Hague and has ruled on conflicts in such areas as economic rights or minor boundary questions. Obviously, however, the promising move toward more genuine international discussion of the issues that might cause war was not possible, given intense national rivalries at the time and since.

It remains true that an optimistic observer before 1914 could legitimately believe that a more rational approach toward international problems was in the works. The strides that had occurred in setting up international mechanisms were limited but not entirely illusory. Interestingly, though the international movement did not prevent massive 20th-century war, it also did not die—it was reinvoked, indeed, as part of the effort to settle World War I.

Still, the main point is the gap between confident assumptions in the West, about internal and international progress alike, and the disaster that beckoned in 1914. How did the West collapse into near-total war, dragging much of the world along with it? The advent of an unprecedented kind of war seemed to make a mockery of widely held optimism, causing all the more havoc because so many people had fervently believed that such man-made catastrophes were impossible.

THE ONSET OF WORLD WAR I

Diplomatic tensions had escalated fairly steadily among the major European powers—Britain, France, Russia, Germany, and Austria-Hungary—since the 1890s (see Chapter 29). Two rival alliances had formed, theoretically pitting the first three nations against the last two plus Italy. Rapid imperialist gains in Africa and Asia had accustomed all the European nations to territorial expansion and easy diplomatic prestige, yet by 1900 most of the world's available territory had already been carved up. Inevitably, tensions within Europe became prominent once again. Many nations tended to use military growth—such as the big battleship-building rivalry that seized Britain and Germany—and diplomatic victories as a means of distracting people from difficult social tensions at home. This was particularly tempting in central and eastern Europe. Austria-Hungary was beset by bitter national struggles among a number of Slavic groups against the control of German and Hungarian leadership. Russia faced a revolutionary mood among workers and peasants—revolution had burst out directly in 1905—producing a belief that diplomatic success was essential. More stable nations, such as France, were so burdened by fears of rivals, such as Germany, that they refused to pull back from their less stable allies. The two alliance systems focused increasingly on the leading European trouble spot, the Balkans in the southeast, where a number of bitterly competitive small nations fought two wars in 1912 and 1913. Russia was directly interested in these struggles because of her vaunted kinship with other Slavic peoples; Austria-Hungary was interested because it feared the same south-Slavic nationalism.

The stage for war, in other words, was set by a combination of explicitly diplomatic rivalries and an unusually inflexible, though theoretically defensive, alliance system. It was also fed by the social tensions of industrial Europe among Western powers, who had become accustomed to big armaments expenses as one means of supporting heavy industry, and among several East European nations caught in the stresses of an earlier phase of industrialization. It was fed finally by ethnic tensions in eastern Europe, where a variety of Slavic groups and small nations, such as in the Balkans, competed for influence and tried to undermine multinational empires like Austria-Hungary.

The spark for war occurred, not surprisingly, in the troubled Balkans. In July 1914 a Serbian nationalist shot the Austrian archduke Ferdinand, the emperor's nephew, hoping to strike a blow for Serbian acquisition of Slavic territories controlled by Austria. After years of tension, this was the last straw for Austria-Hungary: Serbia had to be attacked. Germany supported Austria, partly out of loyalty to a weak ally and partly because some leaders believed that world war was inevitable and sooner was better than later, because both France and Russia were in early stages of military reforms that would strengthen them in the long run. Russia refused to let Austria bully Serbia, lest it lose all Balkan influence, and France vowed to support Russia come what might. When Austria declared war on Serbia on July 28, Russia declared a general mobilization—Russia believed it had to prepare because its procedures were slow. Mobilization frightened Germany, whose strategy called for a quick defeat of France before turning to Russia, so Germany declared war on both allies on August 1. Britain hesitated, hoping for peace, but in fact the nation was heavily committed to France and then was frightened and offended by Germany's invasion of Belgium, which was part of Germany's plan to knock France out quickly by attacking from the north as well as the east. Britain entered the fray on August 4. After a century of considerable peace in Europe, the nation-states had once again launched a general war. But this one, fed by the new powers of the state, by new nationalist passions, and by the devastating armaments produced by industrialization, would have far more awesome consequences than any previous struggle.

PATTERNS OF WAR IN EUROPE

Quickly, two major fronts were established as hostilities opened. One, mainly in France, pitted attacking German troops against French and British defenders. The second developed in eastern Europe, particularly in Russian Poland, where German armies battled Russian forces while trying also to support the weaker Austrian-Hungarian army to the south. After 1915 when Italy entered the war on the side of France and Britain, wooed by promises of territory to be seized from Austria and in the Middle East, a third front developed between Italians and Austrians. There was also an important contest for the seas. The large German surface fleet was bottled up by the British for most of the war, but German submarines played havoc with Atlantic sea-lanes, particularly through 1916. German attacks on United States ships bringing people and supplies to Britain were the most important single cause of American entry into the war in 1917.

FIELDS OF BATTLE

France thrust briefly into Germany in the late summer of 1914, but on the western front, the German conquest of Belgium and advance through northern France were the big news. For a brief moment, as French forces pulled back in panic from their own offensive, it looked as though German hopes for a quick Western settlement might be met. But France rallied, aided by British reinforcements and by heroic civilian support, including a famous troop convoy organized by Parisian cabdrivers. Soon northern France was pockmarked with trenches, from which little advance was possible. The awesome technology of modern war was revealed in all its power, as devastating artillery, the withering fire of machine guns, barbed-wire fences, and the use of poison gas defined the deadening stalemate. By 1916 stagnation on the western front had

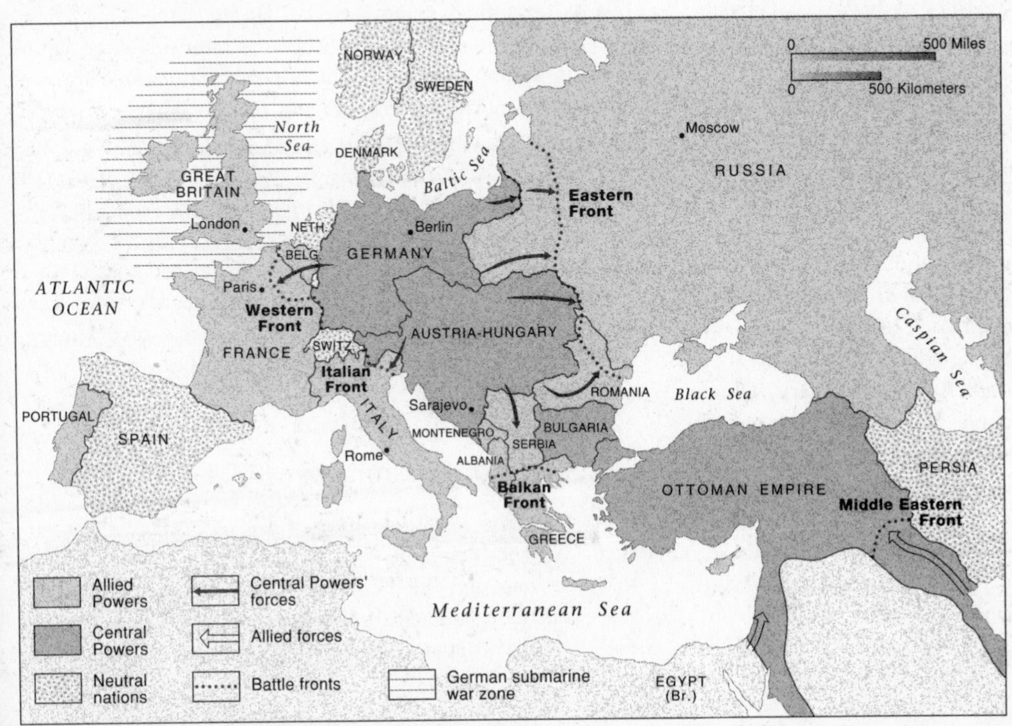

World War I Fronts in Europe and the Middle East

The horrors of trench warfare are clearly visible in this photo from World War I.

turned into a nightmare as the Germans lost 850,000 men, the French 700,000, and the British 410,000—without any appreciable change in the lines of battle. A German novelist later described life in the rat-infested trenches:

> The front is a cage in which we must await fearfully whatever may happen. We lie under the network of arching shells and live in a suspense of uncertainty. Over us Chance hovers.

Other fronts were slightly more mobile, although they too took huge tolls in lives. The Italian front also produced trench warfare, though it moved back and forth in northeastern Italy. In eastern Europe, Germany fought off a Russian offensive but had to aid Austria-Hungary, which was outclassed by Russian troops. Most of the fighting on the eastern front took place in the western portions of Russia, with some momentous battles. Fighting also spread to the Balkans, where Austria crushed Serbia and the other small states aligned variously in hopes of local advantage.

Along both the western and eastern fronts, the intensity of involvement among the combatants ran high. The conscripted and professional soldiers of the mass armies were most heavily engaged, of course, and even those who survived would long be marked by physical and psychological scars, often including a resentment against civilian authorities, politicians above all, who could not have known what the horror of war was. Yet civilian commitment was considerable, as each nation-state showed its power of mobilization to the fullest. Governments increasingly organized the major sectors of the economy to ration resources and production and to prevent crippling labor disputes. Whole industrial sectors, such as railroads in the United States, were administered outright by the state. Within government, the executive branch increasingly took over from parliament—particularly in Germany, where by 1917 a top general virtually ran the country. Governments also leaned heavily on public opinion. Dissent was censored, and dissenters were arrested. Newspapers and other media were manipulated to create the most favorable public opinion possible. Thus the British (and through them, the Americans) were regaled with exaggerated stories of German violence, while Germans were so carefully shielded from military setbacks after 1917 that many did not know they were losing until the end actually came. The power of governments to command resources and also beliefs and passions made this truly the first total war.

The war in essence sped up many developments already visible in industrial society. The power of organization increased, particularly through the new interventions of governments. To keep the social peace, socialists and trade unions were given new recognition, serving on governing boards for industry and the like. By the same token, however, many labor leaders also became more involved in the existing system, which heightened revolutionary discontent among a minority of workers and others. Women's participation in the labor force increased greatly, although this proved to be a fragile trend as men recaptured many jobs at the war's end. At the same time, the war brought material shortages, even famine, to many people in the belligerent nations, while imposing great tensions on soldiers and civilians alike. These hardships, plus feverish hopes for a better world after war had ended, brought a revolutionary or near-revolutionary mood to many European nations after four years of struggle.

THE WAR OUTSIDE EUROPE

World War I was essentially a European conflict, a particularly cruel result of the political divisions and rivalries that had long marked the Western experience and had been exacerbated by nationalism and other new forces during the 19th century. Nevertheless, given the West's world dominance, it was inevitable that the war spilled over into other areas, or that it had some of its most important effects outside Europe proper.

British dominions, notably Canada, Australia, and New Zealand, were drawn into the war effort early on as loyal members of the British Empire. Forces from these countries fought bravely on several fronts and in the process brought their new nations into greater world involvements.

World War I also brought the United States into world power politics as a major player, culminating a development that had been brewing for some time. By 1914 the United States was turning decisively away from a largely regional diplomatic role, with its Asian empire, centering on Hawaii and the Philippines, complementing its forceful activities in Central America and the West Indies. The advent of world war, however, caught the United States in a mood of considerable ambivalence. Distant from these battlefields, Americans also disagreed over which side, if either, was in the right. American businessmen, in the meantime, profited greatly from the war by selling goods to the various combatants and taking advantage of European distraction to gain new ground in other world markets. Rapidly rising exports, combined with loans to European governments that needed credit in order to buy war materials and food, converted the United States from an international debtor to a creditor nation essentially for the first time in the nation's history. Despite all the gains resulting from noninvolvement, American leadership was on balance decidedly pro-British. Clumsy German attempts to influence American opinion as well as the submarine warfare that affected American ships, including passenger vessels, moved the country toward a more interventionist mood. In 1917 the United States entered the war, soon sending fresh troops as well as needed supplies to the western front, and unquestionably helping to turn the tide against the Germans. The United States also brought into the war a new current of idealism, choosing to see their unaccustomed role as a battle for international justice and democracy; this input, too, would play an important role in the war's results.

AFRICA AND ASIA

The involvement of the United States and the British Commonwealth was only part of the war's international story. Minor skirmishes in the war were fought around the German colonies in Africa, but the major African involvement came in the use by Britain and France of many African troops in their armies on the European front. Britain also used important contingents from India. Experience in fighting in a European war could be an important one for the Africans and Asians involved, by increasing awareness of European standards and the contradiction between fierce nationalist pride in Europe and the subjection of their own peoples. It was no accident that the first Pan-African Nationalist Congress occurred in 1919, as emerging African leaders pursued nationalist goals similar to those they had seen in Europe, though without the internal divisiveness.

The war also spread to East Asia, where it fit into a new pattern of conflict. Japan entered the war on the side of Britain and France, honoring its previous alliance with Britain. The main Japanese purpose was to seize Germany's Far Eastern colonies—Pacific islands and holdings in China—to advance its imperialist role and strengthen itself in relation to China. Australia and New Zealand seized German Samoa to forestall Japanese advance to the south. China declared war on Germany in 1917, hoping not to be ignored by the European powers. But Japan was the big gainer in the region, moving into German holdings in China's Shantung province and presenting additional demands for Chinese concessions. World War I in the Far East, then, advanced already aggressive Japanese policy, setting the stage for further conflict.

Large numbers of troops from India fought for the British in Europe. Indian nationalists backed the war effort, hoping that a British victory would promote India's freedom. Allied wartime declarations about national liberation inspired hope in India as in Africa and elsewhere, again promoting new issues for the future.

World War I had wider ramifications still in the Middle East. The Ottoman Empire, long attached to German military advisors, joined Germany in the war effort. The Germans even hoped that the Turks could sponsor a Muslim uprising against British and French holdings in North Africa, though this did not materialize. Rather, the war weakened the already feeble Ottoman state. Britain sponsored an attack on the Dardanelles, near Constantinople, hoping to open an additional front to rescue the smaller Balkan states. The campaign was a failure, yet it cost 150,000 British and colonial troops. Nevertheless, the British did sponsor Arab nationalists against their Ottoman overlords, winning important allies along the eastern Mediterranean. They also promised support to Jewish settlers in Israel, in the Balfour Declaration of 1917. Allied actions set in motion various forces hostile to Ottoman rule and eager for some kind of independence, though they also encouraged contradictory goals in the Middle East itself.

Overall, the war's international ramifications constituted a substantial diminution of Europe's world power. Two new players, the United States and Japan, gained ground, winning new prestige or new territory. Europe's need for colonial support and its devotion to belligerent nationalism encouraged many other people in India, Africa, and the Middle East to a higher level of awareness of their own national rights and merits.

THE WAR'S END

The international context, save for the United States' entry, did not play a massive role in the central theaters of war, where attention riveted once more on the two major fronts by 1917. In March 1917, the pressures of war, added to the earlier massive strains in Russian society, caused a major revolution that toppled the tsarist government (see Chapter 36). The new government, strongly committed to Western-style liberalism, vowed to live up to Russian obligations under the alliance, but in fact the Russian war effort began to falter even further. Moreover, popular hostility to the impositions of war helped produce more radical agitation, aided by the activities of communist leaders such as Lenin who had been transported to Russia from a Swiss exile by the German government precisely in hopes of fomenting trouble. The result was a new revolt, in October 1917, that brought Lenin and the communists to power. This leadership, bent on restructuring Russian society, wanted to escape the pressures of war. In March 1918 it signed the Brest-Litovsk treaty with the Germans, giving the Germans substantial territories in western Russia in return for peace.

This proved to be the peak of German success, however, and indeed the treaty was a partial mistake. The Germans had to commit more troops to occupying its new territory than was sensible, reducing the abilities of a thoroughly war-torn nation to push new energy into the crucial western front. Heavy fighting there during 1917 caused massive losses on both sides, prior to the arrival of fresh American troops. A last-ditch German offensive in 1918 failed, leaving the nation with no reserves. Then a French-British-American counteroffensive pressed forward, aided by the collapse of Austrian forces in Italy and the Balkans. The German military generals, by now effectively running the country, installed a new civilian government so that blame for defeat would not fall directly on their forces. This government, led ultimately by socialists when the German emperor abdicated, had no choice but to sue for peace in November 1918.

THE PEACE AND THE AFTERMATH

Settlement of the war was difficult, even with the military apparatus of Germany temporarily dismantled or underground. Diplomats of the victorious nations convened at Versailles, near Paris, where they debated the fate of much of the world, with Russia, Germany, and indeed most of the world unrepresented. France was bent on revenge against Germany and assurance that Germany would be so weakened that it could not attack a third time. It got back the provinces surrendered after its 1871 war loss, but not the security it yearned for. Italy wanted new territory in abundance; it received some, but not enough and emerged unsatisfied as well. Japan hoped for a great power role but was largely ignored, which heightened Japanese discontent despite concrete war gains. The United States, led by President Woodrow Wilson, espoused great ideals, hoping for just settlement of all nationalist issues—particularly in eastern Europe where many nationalities struggled for recognition—and a new League of Nations to deal with future disputes and to make war unnecessary. But ideals were hard to put into practice amid the welter of conflicting interests, and opinion back home prevented the United States from taking a consistently active role. The nation did not even join the League of Nations its representatives had devised. American isolationism contributed to French and British fears for the future, in a peacetime that was badly born.

The big losers at Versailles were of course Germany and Austria-Hungary in Europe. In Asia China suffered particularly because of its losses to a surging Japan and internal unrest that followed the war, as China refused to sign away the Shantung province to Japan but was powerless to resist. The Austro-Hungarian Empire collapsed entirely, as nationalist groups carved out the new nations of Czechoslovakia and Hungary, plus Yugoslavia as an enlarged south Slavic state—leaving a somewhat fragile Germanic Austria, cut off from its traditional markets, as one of many small countries in a weakened region of Europe. Germany lost Alsace-Lorraine to France, as well as territory to a revived Polish state in the east. It was also blamed for causing the war and faced huge reparation payments to the Allies, particularly France and Belgium. The level of military forces was limited, and the region west of the Rhine was supposed to remain demilitarized entirely. These various impositions created huge discontent in Germany, with many leaders vowing revenge on France as the leader of the punitive peacemakers. Russia, ignored as a communist pariah after its revolution in 1917, was also cut back through the creation of additional small states in eastern Europe at its expense—Poland and several Baltic republics. Here too was potential for future trouble. The Versailles peace settlement thus set up important preconditions for future diplomatic strife in Europe by creating new categories of discontented great powers, insecure or disappointed victors, and a new series of small states in parts of eastern Europe that might tempt future expansionists.

LARGER DISLOCATIONS

The legacy of World War I involved more, however, than a difficult diplomatic heritage. The war had devastated Europe's economy and society. More than ten million people had died, meaning that almost every European family had a death to mourn. Never before had a war approached this level of devastation. Countries such as France and Serbia, particularly hard hit, lost over one-tenth of their total populations. Truly, this war was "the blood red dawn of the 20th century." The loss of young men was an economic as well as a psychological blow, for these men were the potential cream of the upcoming labor force and leadership groups. Loss of men also hampered the European birthrate, for families that might have formed now could not start. Massive destruction of industrial property and agricultural land temporarily dislocated many economies, leading to a period of postwar instability that ended only in 1923. More serious than these largely repairable setbacks was an imbalance produced by the methods of financing the war. Most combatant regimes had borrowed heavily, unwilling to raise taxes too much lest civilian morale be destroyed. Even during the last years of war, despite government restrictions, prices began to rise because of the inflationary impact of increased government spending and money supply. And after the war, in many countries inflation soared. Although some groups could profit from rapidly rising prices, many people with fixed savings were nearly wiped out, while others, such as many farmers, were encouraged to borrow unwisely, which would later leave them strapped for funds and wondering how to solve their economic problems. In various ways, then, the war introduced basic dislocations that promised, and later produced, further trouble.

The peace settlement also set in motion the forces that would launch western Europe's decline in the wider world. To be sure, there was little outright loss of colonies, and indeed the 1920s constituted (on paper) the apogee of Western imperialism. Germany's African colonies were taken over and much of the Middle East was divided between France and Britain, but the new "colonies" were held as mandates of the League of Nations, not outright possessions. The implication was that, although colonial administrations might in fact be established, they were only temporarily responsible, with an obligation under international scrutiny to prepare for independence. In the Middle East and elsewhere, nationalist leaders seized on Wilsonian principles of self-determination, asking why they were applied only within Europe and not to the wider world. Here was a vital pressure for heightened agitation against imperialist rule.

The Postwar World in 1920

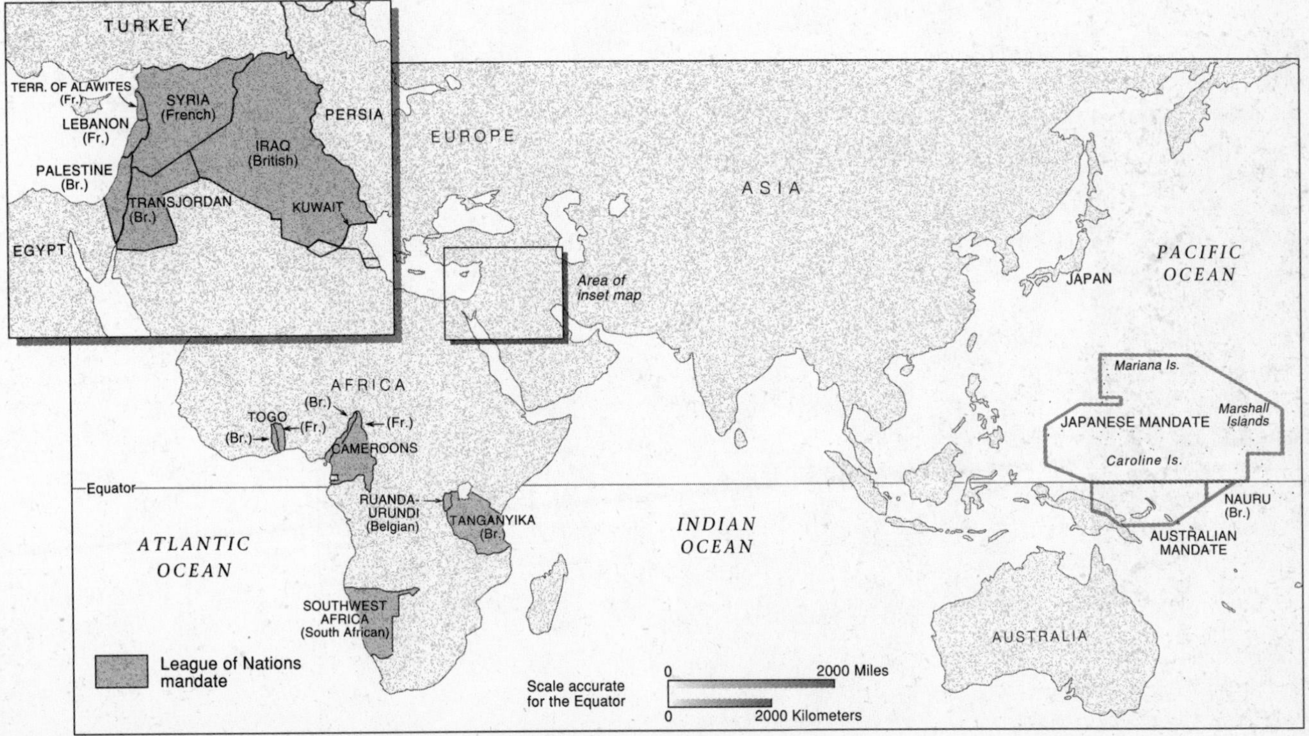

Leadership in the peace settlements also passed from strictly European hands. The United States role, though ultimately confused by isolationism, was vital. Japan gained international status as a wartime ally of Britain and France, though Japanese leaders emerged (like almost everyone else) dissatisfied with their rewards and infuriated at exclusion from the European-United States great power conclaves, eager to resume a quest for expansion.

A crucial area of change involved the Middle East. The Ottoman Empire effectively collapsed. Italy and Greece led an initial effort to carve up even those areas around Constantinople where Turks were in the majority, but a vigorous new Turkish republic by 1923 repulsed these efforts through war and negotiation. The rest of the Ottoman holdings, however, were divided up as mandates of the League of Nations, with Britain taking Palestine and Iraq, and France gaining Syria and Lebanon. A few new monarchies, notably the kingdom of Saudi Arabia, sprang up outside the old Ottoman domains. The Middle East was recreated as a series of separate fragments—a legacy that would burn through world affairs later in the 20th century. Here, as in central Europe, the settlement simply asked for further trouble.

Beyond the peace settlement itself, the international economic results of the war continued to reverberate. American and Japanese businessmen had captured many European export markets, which complicated Europe's immediate postwar recovery and, even when the continent had regained greater health, forced an unprecedented amount of international competition. Britain, particularly, never recovered the export position on which its eminence had so long depended. Debts to impatient United States creditors further complicated the international economic mix.

Overall, the results of the war and its settlement, in addition to provoking a host of new tensions within Europe, set the stage for further change in the larger world balance. The European nations remained major actors, their role exaggerated by Russian preoccupation with its internal revolution and the United States' refusal to attend consistently to international affairs. Nationalist agitation in the colonies, new economic imbalances, and the heightened power of Japan and the United States all portended a new world structure that was not, however, clearly defined.

The war also sketched a new international organization. The League of Nations established a number of subsidiary groups, dealing with issues such as protecting minimum

At the Paris Peace Conference of 1919, the Arabs sought a new voice. The Arab representations included Prince Feisel of Jordan and an Iraqi general. The Arabs did not win full application of the principles of national self-determination to their homelands.

working conditions, that effectively gathered information and focused international social concerns. The league itself, however, proved to be little more than a discussion group, as real diplomacy continued on a nation-to-nation basis. Several disarmament conferences held in the 1920s, designed particularly to reduce naval competition, were ultimately ineffective as well. The international idea advanced, in sum, but it lacked muscle.

The peace settlement after World War I is routinely and correctly criticized for its failure to handle European tensions well. Too many small countries were created near dissatisfied great powers, notably the Soviet Union and Germany. Further conflict was inevitable. The peace settlement took insufficient account of Europe's reduced position in the world, blithely assuming in fact that imperialism was at most slightly modified. In fact, the war had roused nationalist ambitions virtually worldwide, and this was perhaps its most lasting legacy. The war taught Africans, Arabs, Jews, and a host of different Asians that nationalism was legitimate; by creating new European weakness it also held out the hope that non-European nationalisms might also be feasible.

THE GREAT DEPRESSION

The next step in a mounting spiral of international crisis came with the onset of a global economic depression, which hit the headlines with the crash of key Western banks in 1929 but which in fact had begun, sullenly, in many parts of the world economy even earlier.

The depression resulted from new problems in the industrial economy of Europe and the United States, combined with the long-term weakness in economies, like those of Latin America, that depended on sales of cheap exports in the international market. The result was a worldwide collapse that spared only a few economies and brought political and economic pressures on virtually every society.

CAUSATION

The impact of the First World War on the European economy had led to several rocky years into the early 1920s. War-induced inflation was a particular problem in Germany, as prices soared daily and ordinary purchases required huge quantities of currency. Forceful government action finally resolved this crisis in 1923, but only by a massive devaluation of the mark, which did nothing to restore lost savings. More generally, a sharp, brief recession in 1920 and 1921 had reflected other postwar dislocations, though by 1923 production levels had regained or surpassed prewar levels. Great Britain, an industrial pioneer that was already victim of a loss of dynamism before the war, recovered more slowly, in part because of its unusually great dependence on an export market now open to wider competition.

Structural problems affected other areas of Europe besides Britain and lasted well beyond the predictable readjustments to peacetime. Farmers throughout much of the Western world including the United States faced almost chronic overproduction of food and resulting low prices. Food production had soared in response to wartime needs, and then during postwar inflation many farmers, both in western Europe and in North America, borrowed heavily to buy new equipment, overconfident that their good markets would be sustained. But rising European production combined with large imports from the Americas sent prices down, which made debts harder to repay. One response was continued flight from the countryside, as urbanization continued. Remaining farmers were hard-pressed and unable to sustain high demand for manufactured goods.

Thus, although economies in nations such as France and Germany seemed to have recovered by 1925, there were continued problems: the fears inflation had generated, which in turn limited the capacity of governments to respond to other problems, plus the weaknesses in the buying power of key groups. In this situation, part of the mid-decade prosperity rested on exceedingly fragile grounds. Loans from United States banks to various European enterprises helped sustain demand for goods, but on condition that additional loans pour in to help pay off the resultant debts.

Furthermore, most of the dependent areas in the world economy, colonies and noncolonies alike, were suffering badly. Pronounced tendencies toward overproduction developed in the smaller nations of eastern Europe, which sent agricultural goods to western Europe, as well as among tropical producers in Africa and Latin America. Here, continued efforts to win export revenue drove local estate owners to drive up output in such goods as coffee, sugar, and rubber. As European governments and businessmen organized their African colonies for more profitable exploitation, they set up large estates devoted to goods of this type. Again, production frequently exceeded demand, which drove prices and earnings down not only in Africa but also in Latin America. This meant in turn that many colonies and dependent economies were unable to buy many industrial exports, which weakened demand for Western products precisely when output tended to rise amid growing United States and Japanese competition.

Governments of the leading industrial nations provided scant leadership during the emerging crisis of the 1920s. Knowledge of economics was often feeble amid a Western leadership group not noteworthy for its quality even in more conventional areas. Nationalistic selfishness predominated. Western nations were more concerned about insisting on repayment of any debts owed to them or about constructing tariff barriers to protect their own industries than in facilitating balanced world economic growth. Protectionism, in particular, as practiced even by traditionally free-trade Great Britain and by the many new nations in eastern Europe, simply reduced market opportunities and made a bad situation worse. By the later 1920s employment in key export industrial sectors in the West—coal (also beset by new competition from imported oil), iron, and textiles—began to decline, the foretaste of more general collapse.

THE DEBACLE

The formal advent of depression occurred in October 1929, when the New York stock market crashed. Stock values tumbled, as investors quickly lost confidence in issues that had been pushed ridiculously high. United States banks, which had depended heavily on their stock investments, rapidly echoed the financial crisis, and many institutions failed, dragging their depositors along with them. Even before this collapse, Americans had begun to call back earlier loans to Europe. Yet the European credit structure depended extensively on American loans, which had fueled some industrial expansion but also less productive investments such as German reparation payments and the construction of fancy town halls and other amenities. In Europe, as in the United States, many commercial enterprises existed on the basis not of real production power but of continued speculation. When one piece of the speculative spiral was withdrawn, the whole edifice quickly collapsed. Key bank failures in Austria and Germany followed the American crisis. Throughout most of the industrial West, investment funds dried up as creditors went bankrupt or tried to pull in their horns.

With investment receding, industrial production quickly began to fall, beginning in the industries that produced capital goods and extending quickly to consumer products fields. Falling production—levels dropped by as much as one-third by 1932—meant falling employment and lower wages, which in turn withdrew still more demand from the economy and led to further hardship. The existing weakness of some markets, such as the farm sector or the non-industrial world, was exacerbated as demand for foods and minerals plummeted. New and appalling problems developed among workers—now out of jobs or suffering from reduced hours and reduced pay—as well as the middle classes. The depression, in sum, fed on itself, growing steadily worse from 1929 to 1933. Even countries initially less hard hit, such as France and Italy, saw themselves drawn into the vortex by 1931.

In itself, the Great Depression was not entirely unprecedented. Previous periods had seen slumps triggered by bank failures and overspeculation, yielding several years of falling production, unemployment, and real hardship. But the intensity of the Great Depression had no precedent in the brief history of industrial societies. Its duration was also unprecedented; in many countries full recovery came only after a decade, and only with the forced production schedules provoked by World War II. The depression was also more marked than its antecedents because it came on the heels of so much other distress—the economic hardships of war, for example, and the catastrophic inflation of the 1920s—and because it caught most governments utterly unprepared to cope.

The depression was more, of course, than an economic event. It reached into countless lives, creating hardship and tension that would be recalled even as the crisis itself eased. Loss of earnings, loss of work, or simply fears that loss would come could devastate people at all social levels. The suicides of ruined investors in New York were paralleled by the vagrants' camps and begging that spread among displaced workers. The statistics were grim: up to one-third of all blue-collar workers in the West lost their jobs for prolonged periods. White-collar unemployment, though not quite as severe, was also unparalleled. In Germany 600,000 of four million white-collar workers had lost their jobs by 1931. Graduating students could not find work or had to resort to jobs they regarded as insecure or demeaning. Figures of six million overall unemployed in Germany and 22 percent of the labor force unemployed in Britain were statistics of stark misery and despair. Families were disrupted, as men felt emasculated at their inability to provide and women and children were disgusted at authority figures whose authority was now hollow. In some cases wives and mothers found it easier to gain jobs in a low-wage economy than their husbands did, and although this development had some promise in terms of new opportunities for women, it could also be confusing for standard family roles. Again, the agony and personal disruption of the depression constituted no short shock. For many it was desperately prolonged, with renewed recession around 1937 and with unemployment still averaging ten percent or more in many countries by 1939.

Just as World War I had been, the depression was an event that blatantly contradicted the optimistic assumptions of the later 19th century. To many, it showed the fragility of any idea of progress, any belief that Western civilization was becoming more humane. To still more it challenged the notion that standard Western governments—the parliamentary democracies—were able to control their own destinies. And because it was a second catastrophic event within a generation, the depression led to even more ex-

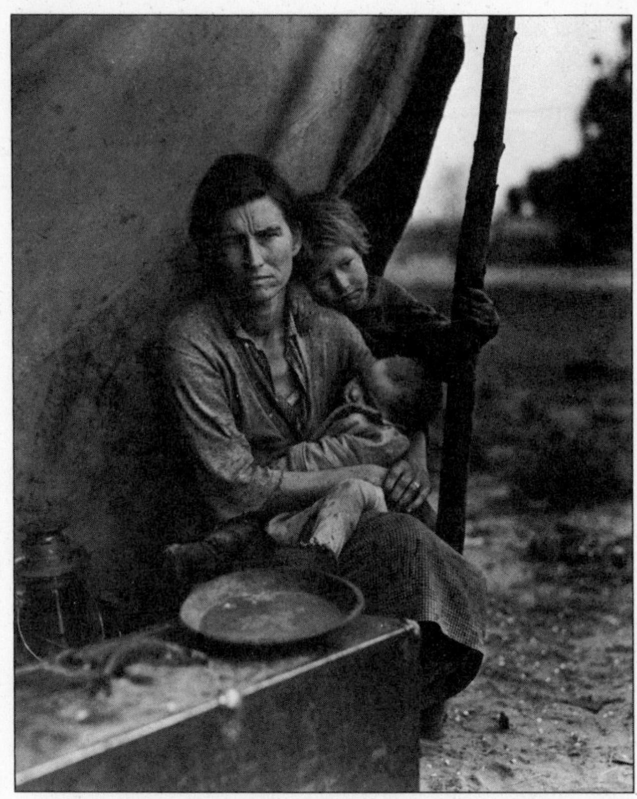

A United States woman reflects unemployment and poverty during the Great Depression.

treme results than the war itself had done—more bizarre experiments, more paralysis in the face of deepening despair.

WORLDWIDE IMPACT

Just as the depression had been caused by a combination of specifically Western problems and wider weaknesses in the world economy, so its effects had both Western twists and international repercussions.

A few economies were buffered from the depression. The Soviet Union, busy building an industrial society under communist control, had cut off all but the most insignificant economic ties with other nations under the heading "socialism in one country." The result placed great hardships on many Russian people, called to sustain rapid industrial development without outside capital, but it did prevent anything like a depression during the 1930s. Soviet leaders pointed with pride to the lack of serious unemployment and steadily rising production rates, in a telling contrast with the miseries of Western capitalism at the time.

For most of the rest of the world, however, the depression worsened an already bleak economic picture. Western markets could absorb fewer commodity imports as production fell and incomes dwindled. Hence the nations that produced foods and raw materials saw prices and earnings drop even more than before. Unemployment rose rapidly in the export sectors of the Latin American economy, creating a major political challenge not unlike that faced by the Western leaders.

Japan, as a new industrial country still heavily dependent on export earnings for financing its imports of essential fuel and raw materials, was hit hard too. The Japanese silk industry, an export staple, was already suffering from the advent of artificial silk-like fibers produced by Western chemical giants. Now luxury purchases collapsed, leading to severe unemployment and, again, a crucial political crisis.

Between 1929 and 1931, the value of Japanese exports plummeted by 50 percent. Workers' real income dropped by almost one-third, and there were over three million unemployed. Depression was compounded by bad harvests in several regions, leading to rural begging and near-starvation.

The Great Depression, though most familiar in its Western dimensions, was a truly international collapse, a sign of the tight bonds and serious imbalances that had developed in world trading patterns. The results of the collapse, and particularly the varied responses to it, are best traced in individual cases. For Latin America, the depression marked a pronounced stimulus to new kinds of effective political action, and particularly greater state involvement in planning and direction. New government vigor did not cure the economic effects of the depression, which escaped the control of most individual states, but it did set an important new phase in the civilization's political evolution. For Japan, the depression increased suspicions of the West and helped promote new expansionism designed among other things to win more assured markets in Asia. In the West the depression led to new welfare programs that stimulated demand and helped restore confidence, but it also led to radical social and political experiments such as German Nazism. What was common in this welter of reactions was the intractable global quality of the depression itself, which made it impossible for any purely national policy to restore full prosperity. Even Nazi Germany, which boasted of regaining full employment, continued to suffer from low wages and other dislocations aside from its obvious and growing dependence on military production.

The reactions to the depression, including a sense of weakness and confusion in many quarters inside and outside policy circles, finally helped to bring the final great crisis of the first half of the 20th century: a second, and more fully international, world war.

DOCUMENT
THE LEADER OF THE SOVIET UNION EVALUATES THE DEPRESSION

In March 1939 Joseph Stalin, uncontested leader of the Soviet state, spoke to the 18th Communist Party Congress on the state of the world and the implications for the Soviet Union. His evaluation of the nature of the depression and its implications were central to his overall policy statement.

NEW ECONOMIC CRISIS IN THE CAPITALIST COUNTRIES. INTENSIFICATION OF THE STRUGGLE FOR MARKETS AND SOURCES OF RAW MATERIAL, AND FOR A NEW REDIVISION OF THE WORLD

The economic crisis which broke out in the capitalist countries in the latter half of 1929 lasted until the end of 1933. After that the crisis passed into a depression, and was then followed by a certain revival, a certain upward trend of industry. But this upward trend of industry did not develop into a boom, as is usually the case in a period of revival. On the contrary, in the latter half of 1937 a new economic crisis began which seized the United States first of all and then England, France and a number of other countries.

The capitalist countries thus found themselves faced with a new economic crisis before they had even recovered from the ravages of the recent one.

This circumstance naturally led to an increase of unemployment. The number of unemployment in capitalist countries, which had fallen from 30,000,000 in 1933 to 14,000,000 in 1937, has now again risen to 18,000,000 as a result of the new crisis.

A distinguishing feature of the new crisis is that it differs in many respects from the preceding one, and, moreover, differs for the worse and not for the better.

Firstly, the new crisis did not begin after an industrial boom, as was the case in 1929, but after a depression and a certain revival, which, however, did not develop into a boom. This means that the present crisis will be more severe and more difficult to cope with than the previous crisis.

Further, the present crisis has broken out not in time of peace, but at a time when a second imperialist war has already begun; when Japan, already in the second year of her war with China, is disorganizing the immense Chinese market and rendering it almost inaccessible to the goods of other countries; when Italy and Germany have already placed their national economies on a war footing, squandering their reserves of raw material and foreign currency for this purpose; and when all the other big capitalist powers are beginning to reorganize themselves on a war footing. This means that capitalism will have far less resources at its disposal for a normal way out of the present crisis than during the preceding crisis.

Lastly, as distinct from the preceding crisis, the present crisis is not universal, but as yet involves chiefly the economically powerful countries which have not yet placed themselves on a war economy basis. As regards the aggressive countries, such as Japan, Germany and Italy, who have already reorganized their economies on a war footing, they, because of the intense development of their war industry, are not yet experiencing a crisis of overproduction, although they are approaching it. This means that by the time the economically powerful, nonaggressive countries begin to emerge from the phase of crisis the aggressive countries, having exhausted their reserves of gold and raw material in the course of the war fever, are bound to enter a phase of very severe crisis. . . .

The Soviet Union is the only country in the world where crises are unknown and where industry is continuously on the upgrade. Naturally, such an unfavorable turn of economic affairs could not but aggravate relations among the powers. The preceding crisis had already mixed the cards and sharpened the struggle for markets and sources of raw materials. The seizure of Manchuria and North China by Japan, the seizure of Abyssinia by Italy—all this reflected the acuteness of the struggle among the powers. The new economic crisis was bound to lead, and is actually leading, to a further sharpening of the imperialist struggle. It is no longer a question of competition in the markets, of a commercial war, of dumping. These methods of struggle have long been recognized as inadequate. It is now a question of a new redivision of the world, of spheres of influence and colonies, by military action. It is a distinguishing feature of the new imperialist war that it has not yet become universal, a world war. The war is being waged by aggressor states, who in every way infringe upon the interests of the nonaggressive states, primarily Britain, France and the U.S.A., while the latter draw back and retreat, making concession after concession to the aggressors.

Thus we are witnessing an open redivision of the world and spheres of influence at the expense of the nonaggressive states, without the least attempt at resistance, and even with a certain connivance, on their part.

Incredible, but true.

To what are we to attribute this one-sided and strange character of the new imperialist war?

How is it that the nonaggressive countries, which possess such vast opportunities, have so easily and without resistance abandoned their positions and their obligations to please the aggressors?

Is it to be attributed to the weakness of the nonaggressive states? Of course not! Combined, the nonaggressive, democratic states are unquestionably stronger than the fascist states, both economically and militarily.

To what then are we to attribute the systematic concessions made by these states to the aggressors?

It might be attributed, for example, to the fear that a revolution might break out if the nonaggressive states were to go to war and the war were to assume world-wide proportions. The bourgeois politicians know, of course, that the first imperialist world war led to the victory of the revolution in one of the largest countries. They are afraid that the second imperialist world war may also lead to the victory of the revolution in one or several countries.

Questions: How did Stalin compare his nation's economy to that of the capitalist leaders? How did he relate the depression to the diplomatic crisis? Was his judgment accurate, or was it unduly biased by communist theory? What would be the implications of this kind of analysis for Soviet foreign policy by 1939?

WORLD WAR II

World War II, which broke out formally in 1939 but was actually prepared by a series of wars and clashes through the 1930s, was fed by two active agents and an excessively passive one. Deliberate strides toward military expansion on the part of new regimes in Japan and Germany formed the active causes, bringing the clouds of war to Asia and the Pacific as well as to Europe and the Mediterranean quite directly. The passivity centered on the most logical opponents to the new aggressors—the other powerful states in Europe and North America. Here, nationalistic and ideological divisions, including widespread Western suspicion of the communist regime in the Soviet Union, limited an ability to act. So did weak leadership and paralyzing internal political disputes, which made positive response difficult until a late hour. Amid ineffective responses, the inability of the League of Nations to take more than rhetorical action was a foregone conclusion, and the league progressively withered as a policy instrument during the prewar decade.

Underlying all the factors contributing to war was the prior experience of war and economic depression. The aggressive regimes resulted from the tensions in Germany and Japan caused by economic collapse, supplemented in Germany's case by the wounds of prior defeat and a harsh peace. Western passivity followed also from the confusions engendered by prior crises. World history, or at least those facets dominated by the great powers, seemed locked in a spiral of growing tragedy.

THE NEW REGIMES

The first scenes of this new tragedy involved the advent of new, militaristic governments as key national actors plus an important supporting player. The early phases of the depression had triggered growing political fragmentation in Japan, particularly through the rise of various ultranationalist groups. Some opposed Western values in the name of Shintoism and Confucianism, while others urged a Nazi-style authoritarian government free from parliamentary restraint and undue tradition. A military group, backed by many younger officers, urged a "defense state" under their control. It was this group in 1932 that attacked key government and business offices and killed the prime minister. The result, satisfactory to no major group, was four years of moderate military rule under an older admiral, followed in 1936 and 1937 by a tougher military regime after another officer rebellion had failed. Japanese voters continued to prefer more moderate parties, but effective leadership fell increasingly into militaristic hands.

The advent of military rule developed in a context of regional diplomatic crisis. During the later 1920s, Chinese nationalist forces seemed to be gaining ground in their effort to unify their chaotic nation after the 1911 revolution. Their success worried Japan's army leaders, who wanted to be able to influence the Manchurian province of China as a buffer between their colony of Korea and the Soviet Union. Japan had, in fact, dominated the Manchurian warlord since its victory over Russia in 1905. Fearful of losing ground, and unimpeded by the weak civilian government in Tokyo, the Japanese army marched into Manchuria in 1931, proclaiming it an independent state. Japan's action was condemned by the League of Nations—which, however, was unable to take effective action—and in consequence Japan simply withdrew from the league. The resulting atmosphere of crisis aided the military's advance in domestic politics, for other leaders were reluctant to damage national military strength, and this advance in turn set the scene for the next round of crisis—effectively, the outbreak of World War II in the Far East—in 1937.

In the meantime, however, a more decisive change of regime had occurred in Germany. Here too, a trend toward growing conservatism and suspicion of parliamentary government had developed by the late 1920s, and then the advent of full depression triggered near-chaos politically. The National Socialist (Nazi) party, led by Adolf Hitler, began to pick up strength after nearly fading from existence during the mid-1920s. Nazis advocated many things, but among their leading goals were an authoritarian state under a single leader as well as an aggressive foreign policy that would reverse the humiliation of the Versailles treaty and gain Germany military glory and new territory for expansion. As German parliamentary leaders bickered among themselves and failed to provide decisive policies to address the depression, and as communist strength grew on the left, Nazis were able to win a growing minority of votes in general elections, while also disrupting normal political meetings and winning quiet support from many business and military leaders. Sponsored by conservatives who erroneously thought they could control him, Hitler was able to take power legally in 1933, and soon abolished the parliamentary regime and constructed a totalitarian state with himself at the helm.

The Nazi state was a radically new kind of regime. Hitler attacked competing sources of power within Germany, abolishing free trade unions as well as opposition political parties. Many political opponents were placed in concentration camps, and new political police added to the terror. Attacks on Jews, the so-called enemies of true Germans, mounted steadily, as part of Hitler's racist ideology. During World War II these attacks escalated into what Hitler called his "final solution," as millions of Jews were forced into concentration camps and then murdered in gas chambers. Nazism also meant construction of a war machine. Hitler expanded armaments production, creating new jobs in the process, and also built up the army and separate Nazi military forces. In Hitler's view, the essence of the state was authority, and the function of the state was war.

Hitler's advent galvanized the authoritarian regime of a near-great power, Italy. Here, a fascist state had been formed in the 1920s, led by Benito Mussolini. Mussolini had, like Hitler, promised an aggressive foreign policy and new nationalist glories, but in fact his first decade had been rather moderate diplomatically. With Hitler in power, however, Mussolini began to experiment more boldly, if only to avoid being overshadowed completely. Here, then, was another destabilizing element in world politics.

THE STEPS TOWARD WAR

Hitler moved first. He suspended German reparation payments, thus renouncing this part of the Versailles settlement; he walked out of a disarmament conference and withdrew from the League of Nations. In 1935 he announced German rearmament and in 1936 brought military forces into the Rhineland—both moves in further violation of Versailles. When these challenges were greeted by loud verbal protests from France and Britain, but nothing more serious, Hitler was poised for the further buildup of German strength and further diplomatic adventures that would ultimately lead to World War II.

In 1935 Mussolini attacked Ethiopia, planning to avenge Italy's failure to conquer this ancient land during the imperialist surge of the 1890s. Again the League of Nations condemned the action, but again neither it nor the democratic powers in Europe and North America took action. Consequently, after some hard fighting, the Italians won their new colony.

In 1936 a civil war engulfed Spain, pitting authoritarian and military leaders against republicans and leftists. Germany and Italy quickly moved to support the Spanish right, sending in supplies and troops, gaining not only new glory but also precious military training in such specialties as bombing civilian targets. France, Britain, and the United States, in contrast, though vaguely supporting the Spanish republic, could agree on no concrete action. Only the Soviet Union sent effective government support, and by 1939 the republican forces had been defeated.

In 1938 Hitler proclaimed a long-sought union, or *Anschluss*, with Austria as a fellow German nation. Western powers complained and denounced but did nothing. In the same year Hitler marched into a German-speaking part of Czechoslovakia. War threatened, but a conference at Munich convinced French and British leaders that Hitler might be satisfied with acquiescence. Czechoslovakia was dismembered and the western (Sudeten) region was turned over to Germany, as the British prime minister, Neville Chamberlain, duped by Hitler's apparent eagerness to compromise, proclaimed that his appeasement had won "peace in our time." ("Our time" turned out to be slightly over a year.) Emboldened by Western weakness, in March 1939 Hitler took over all of Czechoslovakia and began to press Poland for territorial concessions. He also concluded an agreement with the Soviet Union, which was not ready for war with Germany and had despaired of Western resolve. The Soviets also coveted parts of Poland, the Baltic states, and Finland for their own, and when Hitler invaded Poland, Russia launched its own war to undo the Versailles settlement. Hitler attacked Poland on September 1, 1939, not necessarily expecting general war but clearly prepared to risk it; Britain and France, now convinced that nothing short of war would stop the Nazis, made their own declaration in response.

War had already broken out in China. Japan, continuing to press the ruling Chinese government lest it gain sufficient strength to threaten Japanese gains, became involved in a skirmish with Chinese forces in the Beijing area in 1937. Fighting spread, initially quite unplanned. Most Japanese military leaders opposed more general war, arguing that the nation's only interest was to defend Manchuria and Korea. However, influential figures on the General Staff held that China's armies should be decisively defeated to prevent trouble in the future. This view prevailed, and Japanese forces quickly occupied the cities and railroads of eastern China. The Chinese army refused to give in, and a stalemate resulted that lasted in effect until 1945, with neither side capable of major new advance.

In 1940 the two main areas of conflict, Europe and the Pacific, drew together, when Germany and Italy (already uneasy allies) signed an agreement with Japan. Japanese leaders had long admired Germany and welcomed Hitler's basic hostility to the Soviet Union and communism. Full alliance was prevented by the Nazi-Soviet agreement, which briefly drove Japan to try to resolve disputes with the United States. But the United States insisted that the Japanese evacuate China, so full reconciliation was impossible. Meanwhile, early German successes in the European war and Japanese realization that expansion in the Pacific would pit them against the United States combined to argue for a more formal alliance. A Tripartite Pact was signed by Germany, Japan, and Italy in September 1940. In fact, Japan and Germany never collaborated closely. Notably, Japan refused to participate in Germany's ultimate war with the Soviet Union, despite long-standing opposition to Russian strength. Nevertheless, the union of the aggressor states, however hollow in practice, seemed to align the powers of the world between those on the attack and those legitimately on the defense—a symbolism particularly influential for the United States.

As war broke out from 1937 to 1939, the powers most interested in preserving the status quo remained unprepared, hopeful that war could be deflected by talk and concessions. France and Britain continued to feel the debilitating effects of World War I and were not eager for another conflict. Depression-induced tensions made it difficult to agree on any active policy, and political leftists and conservatives even disagreed over which was the greater enemy, Germany or the Soviet Union. The United States was less polarized, but eager to maintain its policy of isolationism in order not to complicate the delicate process of constructing a new set of government programs to fight the depression. Only by late 1938 did Western leaders begin to admit that war was likely, launching some measures of military preparedness including army expansion and aircraft production. Britain took the lead here, and its efforts proved vital in allowing successful defense of the nation in the first stages of the war with Germany, but the Western effort was too little and too late to stop war itself.

THE COURSE OF THE WAR: JAPAN'S ADVANCE AND RETREAT

The background to World War II made it obvious that war would be fought in two major centers—the Pacific and the European regions, the latter spilling over into North Africa and the Middle East. The background also made it inevitable that the first years of the war would feature almost unremitting German and Japanese success against ill-prepared opponents. Only in 1942 and 1943 did the tide begin to change, based on the fact that the powers that had been drawn into war were essentially more powerful, economically and in population size, than their ambitious taunters.

The bitter war in Asia, pitting Japan against the United States with Britain in an important supporting role, followed a fairly simple course of thrust and counterthrust. Stalemated in China, Japan used the outbreak of war in Europe as an occasion to turn its attention to other parts of Asia. It seized Indochina from France's troops. The alliance with Germany and Italy, along with continued expansion in Southeast Asia as the Japanese attacked Malaya and Burma, put the Japanese on a collision course with the United States, which as a Pacific power was unwilling to

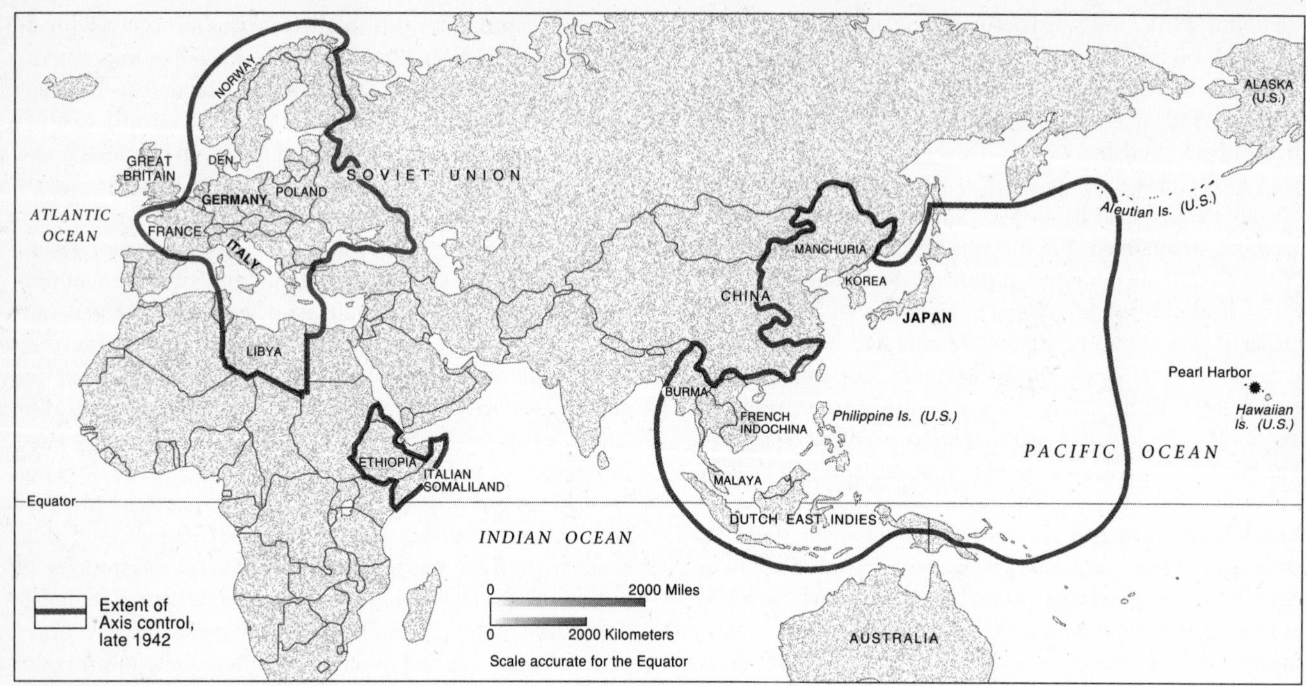

The Main Theaters of World War II

allow Japan to become a predominant force in the Far East. United States' holdings in Hawaii and the Philippines, plus American attempts to withhold materials necessary to Japan's war economy, convinced Japanese leaders that a clash was inevitable. Negotiations with the United States broke down with American insistence that Japan renounce all gains acquired since 1931. It was in this setting that the Japanese attacked Pearl Harbor on December 7, 1941, and then in the following months seized American possessions in the eastern Pacific, including the Philippine Islands. Only toward the end of 1942 did the United States begin to gain the initiative, using its greater numbers and superior level of industrialization. Scattered islands were reconquered in 1943, and the Philippines were regained in 1944, while massive air raids began an onslaught on Japan itself. Meanwhile American, British, and Chinese forces continued to tie down a considerable Japanese army on the Asian mainland.

Japan's military buildup included marine machine-gun squads such as this one in occupied Shanghai, China.

GERMANY OVERREACHES

In Europe the early years of World War II carried key trends of the 1930s toward even deeper tragedy. Germany seemed unstoppable and the Western democracies suffered accordingly. German strategy focused on the *blitzkrieg*, or "lightning war," involving rapid movement of troops, tanks, and mechanized carriers. With this the Germans crushed Poland and, after a brief lull, pushed early in 1940 into Denmark and Norway. The next targets were Holland, Belgium, and France, with invasion prepared by massive bombardments of civilian targets. Rotterdam, for example, was flattened at the cost of 40,000 lives.

German dynamism was matched, again as in the 1930s, by Allied weakness. France fell surprisingly quickly, partly because the French were unprepared for war and reliant on

These Japanese soldiers were captured by Chinese forces in the interior of China after a bitter battle in 1942.

an outdated defensive strategy, and partly because French troops were quickly demoralized due to the deep tensions within their own society. By the summer of 1940 most of France lay in German hands, while a semifascist collaborative regime, based in the city of Vichy, ruled the remainder. Only Britain stood apart, able to withstand Hitler's air offensive and win the contest for its skies known as the Battle of Britain. Imaginative air force tactics combined with solid new leadership, under a coalition government headed by Winston Churchill, as well as the iron resolve on the part of British citizens to resist the devastating air raids. Hitler's hopes for a British collapse were dashed.

In 1940 Germany controlled the bulk of the European continent. It aided its ally, Italy, in a conquest of Yugoslavia and Greece. It moved into North Africa to press British and French holdings. Conquered territories were forced to supply materials, troops, and compulsory slave labor to the German war machine. Hitler also stepped up his campaign against the Jews, aiming at a "final solution" that meant mass slaughter in Germany as well as its tribute territories. Even as Germany ground out its war effort, it forced six million Jews from all parts of Europe into concentration camps and gas chambers. This holocaust was the most shocking aspect of the war, an attempt at genocide on an unprecedented scale.

The balance in the war began to shift slightly in 1941. Blocked from invasion of Britain, Hitler turned toward the tempting target of Russia, viewed as an inferior Slavic state in Nazi racial ideology. Germany's attack began in June, all pretense of alliance abandoned, and the Germans easily penetrated into central Russia. Yet the Soviet forces, while giving ground amid massive loss of life, did not collapse. They moved back, relocating Soviet industry eastward. As with Napoleon's invasion attempt over a century before, weather also came to the Russians' aid, as a harsh winter caught the Germans off guard, counting on another quick victory. As in Britain, civilian morale in Russia greatly aided the war effort, and although German forces continued to advance through 1942, the knockout blow eluded them. The invasion attempt also stretched German resources very thin, revealing how ill-prepared Hitler's economy was for a long-haul effort and how inefficient the economy was in many aspects of war production.

Late 1941 also brought the United States' entry into the war, spurred initially by the Japanese attack on Pearl Harbor, which in fact took place against German wishes. The United States' leadership had already supported Britain with loans and supplies, and they now eagerly used the bombing of Pearl Harbor to enter the war in Europe and Asia against what seemed a clear threat to Western democracy, perhaps to Western civilization itself. American involvement, delayed because of lack of full prior preparation, began to make itself felt in 1942 when American and British forces challenged the Germans in North Africa. The Soviet Union, in the same year, pushed back an intensive German siege of the city of Stalingrad, which if successful might have opened the way to the Ural Mountains and Russia's new industrial heartland. Over one-third of the German force surrendered, and the Red armies began a gradual push westward that would take them past their own borders, through eastern Europe, and by 1945 deep into Germany itself.

In the meantime, British and American forces moved into the Italian peninsula from North Africa, ousting Mussolini, while also bombing German industrial and civilian targets. Then in 1944 the Allies invaded France, again pushing the Germans back with the aid of French forces hostile to fascism. Amid bitter fighting—Hitler decided to resist as fiercely as possible, goaded in part by Allied insistence that Germany surrender without conditions—the Anglo-American forces gradually surged into western Germany. In late April 1945, Russian and American troops met on the Elbe River. On April 30 Hitler committed suicide in his Berlin bunker, and in the following month German military commanders surrendered their country to the victorious invaders.

Within months after this the war in the Pacific also ended. This conflict had become primarily a duel between Japan and the United States, but British and Chinese forces were also engaged and, after the European theater of operations closed, the Soviet Union turned its attention eastward as well. Japan's surrender was precipitated by

American use of atomic bombs on two cities, Hiroshima and Nagasaki, which forced a full Japanese surrender and a period of American occupation.

HUMAN COSTS

World War II had been a huge killer, with wanton cruelty adding to the effect of unprecedented weapons. Japanese troops in China had killed hosts of civilians, often after torturing them, when they captured cities that had tried to hold out; in Nanking, for example, as many as 300,000 were killed after the city had fallen. Hitler's decision to eliminate Jews throughout Europe led to six million dead in the gas chambers of the Holocaust. Hitler's forces also deliberately attacked civilian centers through bombing raids, in the usually mistaken belief that such destruction would destroy morale. Allied forces, as they became more powerful, paid back in kind. The British air force firebombed the German city of Dresden in retaliation for earlier German raids. Firebombing of Japanese cities led to as many as 80,000 dead in a single raid. The American decision to drop its newly developed atomic bomb on Japan was taken in this atmosphere. American officials wanted to force Japan to surrender without needlessly costly invasion, and they also hurried to prevent Soviet advance in Asia. Bombing of Hiroshima killed over 78,000 civilians, and the raid on Nagasaki two days later also killed tens of thousands. Radiation fallout ultimately killed thousands more, as the new American President, Harry Truman, termed the bombing "the greatest thing in history." Overall, at least 35 million people were killed in the war—20 million in the Soviet Union alone.

ANALYSIS
TOTAL WAR

In the earlier history of civilization—quite clearly by the classical period—the nature of war changed, losing its ritual characteristics and becoming more commonly an all-out battle in which any tactics and weapons that would aid in victory were now countenanced. War, in other words, became less restrained than it had been among more "primitive" peoples who often enjoyed bluff and scare more than all-out violence. All sorts of wars were fought between the classical era and the 20th century, as weapons and military organization changed and varied. Particularly bloody episodes often involved peoples from different cultures, including Westerners battling what they conveniently regarded as "savages." Sometimes, at the other extreme, a ritual element might return, as in the carefully uniformed parades of troops who fought Europe's battles in the 18th century, recognizing the importance of stylized maneuvers over random bloodshed.

It was the 20th century, however, that most clearly saw the introduction of a fundamentally new kind of war—total war, in which vast resources and emotional commitments of the belligerent nations were marshaled to support military effort. The two world wars were thus novel not only in their geographical sweep, but in their mobilization of the major combatants. The features of total war also fed some regional conflicts later in the 20th century, such as the long Iran-Iraq War in the Middle East in the 1980s. They also colored other forms of struggle, helping to explain brutal guerrilla and terrorist acts among groups not powerful enough to mount total wars but nonetheless affected by their methods and passions.

Total war can be seen as resulting from the impact of industrialization on military effort, reflecting both the technological innovation and the organizational capacity that accompanied the industrial economy from its early stages. Key steps in the development of total war thus emerged in the West from the end of the 18th century onward. The French Revolution, building new power for the state in contact with ordinary citizens, introduced mass conscription of men, forming larger armies than had ever before been possible. New citizen involvement was reflected in incitements to nationalism and stirring military songs including—a new idea itself—aggressive national anthems. Industrial technology was first applied to war on a large scale in the American Civil War. Railroads allowed wider movement of mass armies, while mass-produced guns and artillery made a mockery of earlier cavalry charges and might redefine the kind of personal bravery needed to fight in war.

It was World War I, however, that fully revealed the nature of total war. Steadily more destructive technology included battleships, submarines, tanks, airplanes, poison gas (this theoretically banned by international agreement prior to the war), machine guns, and long-range artillery. Organization for war included not only massive, compulsory recruitment—the draft—but also government control of economic activity, via obligatory planning and rationing, that altered management policy, labor relations, and personal consumption options. It included unprecedented control of media, not only through effective censorship and the jailing of dissidents but through powerful propaganda designed to incite passionate, all-out commitment to the national cause and deep, unreasoned hatred of the enemy. Vivid posters, flaming speeches and outright falsehood combined in the emotional mobilization effort. All of these features returned with a vengeance, of course, in World War II, from the new technology of bombing, rocketry, and ultimately the atomic bomb to the enhanced economic mobilization effort organized by government planners.

The people most affected by the character of total war were the troops themselves, who directly endured—bled from and died from—the new technology. But one measure of total war was a blurring of the distinction between military and civilians, a distinction that had often restrained war's impact earlier in world history. Whole civilian populations, and not just those unfortunate enough to be near front lines, were now forced into certain types of work, urged to certain types of beliefs. The bombing raids, including the German rockets directed against British cities late in World War II, subjected civilians to some of the most lethal weapons available, as many belligerents deliberately focused attacks on densely populated cities. Correspondingly psychological suffering, though less common among civilians than among frontline soldiers, could arise quite widely in the populations involved in war.

Total war, like any major historical development, had mixed results. Greater government economic direction often included new measures to protect workers and give them a voice on management boards. Labor force mobilization often produced at least temporary breakthroughs for women. And intense efforts to organize technological research often produced side results of more general economic benefit, as in the invention of new materials such as synthetic rubber.

Still, total war was notable especially for its devastation. The idea of throwing all possible resources into a military effort and having the organizational ability and transporta-

This British government cartoon appealed for loans from the public. It shows a simple, almost sportive and jocular war, with a British Tommy confronting a ridiculous German emperor.

tion capacity to do so made war typically more economically disruptive than had been the case before, at least in terms of short-term impact. The possibilities unleashed in total war produced embittered veterans who might vent their anger by attacking established political values. It certainly made postwar diplomacy more difficult. One result of total war was a tendency to be inflexible in negotiations at war's end: People who fought so hard found it difficult to treat enemies generously, and the results of a quest for vengeance often produced new tensions that led directly, and quickly, to further conflict. War-induced passions and disruptions could also spark new violence at home, as crime rates often soared not only right after the war ended (a traditional result), but more durably. Trying to determine how much the passions sparked by total war altered basic processes, such as diplomacy, crime, or even family life, yields a set of key questions about wider aspects of 20th-century history. How much of the nature of life has been determined by the consequences of total war?

Questions: How did being a soldier in a total war differ from being a soldier in a more traditional war? How did the experience of total war affect social and political patterns after the war's end? Why do many historians believe that total war made rational peacetime settlements more difficult than earlier in history?

THE SETTLEMENT OF WORLD WAR II

World War II did not produce the sweeping peace settlement, untidy as it was, that had officially ended World War I. The major Allies opposed to Germany and Japan did meet on several occasions, earnestly trying to construct a peace that would avoid the mistakes of Versailles. There was agreement that a new international organization, the United Nations, should be set up, with better representation than had characterized the League of Nations. The United States pledged to join, and indeed ultimately it housed the United Nations headquarters in New York. The Soviet Union was included, and China (represented by the Nationalist government) attained great power status for the first time in modern history. Britain and France rounded out the key group of great powers that would have a permanent seat on the Security Council—the steering committee for the new organization. Internationalism now moved beyond the conventional Western orbit, though the Western leaders sought to retain dominance. Like the league, the United Nations had as its primary mission provision of a forum for negotiating disputes, but it also took over the apparatus of more specialized international agencies that addressed world problems in agriculture, labor, and the like.

Beyond agreeing on a new, if ultimately fairly modest, international apparatus, the wartime Allies found it increasingly difficult to reach accord on the shape of the postwar world. Some leaders wanted virtually to destroy Germany's industrial structure, to prevent any recurrence of threat from this quarter, but others held out for milder measures—though all agreed that Hitler's regime must go and that Germany must surrender unconditionally, a stance that may have discouraged some peace movements within the German military. The key problem that emerged involved growing tension between the Soviet Union and the United States along with British representatives who feared Soviet ambitions.

Initial discussions among United States, British, and Soviet governments began in 1942, focusing at first on purely military issues. Heads of the three states met in 1943, in Teheran, Iran, where the Soviet government pressed the Western powers to open a new front in France, which was of course done with the invasion of Normandy in 1944. The decision to focus on France rather than moving up from the Mediterranean in effect gave the Soviet forces a free hand to move through the smaller nations of eastern Europe as they pushed the Nazi armies back. Britain negotiated separately with the Soviets to assure Western preponderance in postwar Greece as well as equality in Hungary and Yugoslavia, with Soviet control of Romania and Bulgaria—but the United States resisted this kind of un-Wilsonian scorn for the rights of small nations.

With the war nearly over, the next settlement meeting took place in Yalta in the Soviet Crimea early in 1945. Franklin Roosevelt of the United States was eager to press the Soviet Union for assistance against Japan, and to this end the Soviets were promised important territorial gains in Manchuria and the northern Japanese islands. The organization of the United Nations was confirmed. As to Europe, however, agreement was more difficult. The three powers easily arranged to divide Germany into four occupation zones (liberated France getting a chunk), which would be disarmed and purged of Nazi influence. Britain, however, resisted Soviet zeal to eliminate German industrial power, seeing a viable Germany as a potential ally in a subsequent Western-Soviet contest. Bitter disagreement also raged over the smaller nations of Eastern Europe. That they should be friendly to their Soviet neighbor was uncontested, but the Western leaders also wanted them to be free and democratic. Stalin, the Soviet leader, had to make some concessions by including noncommunist leaders in what was already a Soviet-controlled government in liberated Poland—concessions that he soon violated.

The final postwar conference occurred in Potsdam, a Berlin suburb, in July 1945. Russian forces now occupied not only most of Eastern Europe but eastern Germany as well. This de facto situation prompted agreement that the Soviet Union could take over much of what had been eastern Poland, with the Poles gaining part of eastern Germany in compensation. Germany was divided pending a final peace treaty (which was not to come for over 40 years). Austria was also divided and occupied, gaining unity and independence only in 1956 on condition of neutrality between the United States and the Soviet Union. Amid great difficulty, treaties were worked out for Germany's other allies, including Italy, but the United States and, later, the Soviet Union signed separate treaties with Japan.

All these maneuvers had several results. Japan was occupied by the United States. Its wartime gains were stripped away, and even Korea, taken earlier, was freed—but divided between United States and Soviet zones of occupation (the basis for the North-South Korea division still in effect today). Former Asian colonies were returned to their old "masters," though often quite briefly as new independence movements quickly challenged the control of the weakened imperialist powers. China regained most of its former territory, though here too stability was quickly challenged by renewed fighting between communist and Nationalist forces within the nation, aided by the Soviet Union and the United States, respectively.

The effort to confirm old colonial regimes applied also to the Middle East, India, and Africa. Indian and African troops had fought for Britain during the war, though Britain imprisoned key nationalist leaders and put independence plans on hold. African leaders had participated constructively in the French resistance to its authoritarian wartime government. The Middle East and North Africa had been shaken by German invasions and Allied counterattacks. Irritability increased, and so did expectations for change. With Europe's imperial powers further weakened by their war effort, adjustments seemed inevitable, as in those parts of Asia invaded by the Japanese.

In Europe the boundaries of the Soviet Union pushed westward, with virtually all the losses after World War I erased. Independent nations created in 1918 were for the most part restored (though the former Baltic states of Latvia, Lithuania, and Estonia became Soviet provinces because they had been Russian provinces before World War I). Except for Greece and Yugoslavia, the new nations

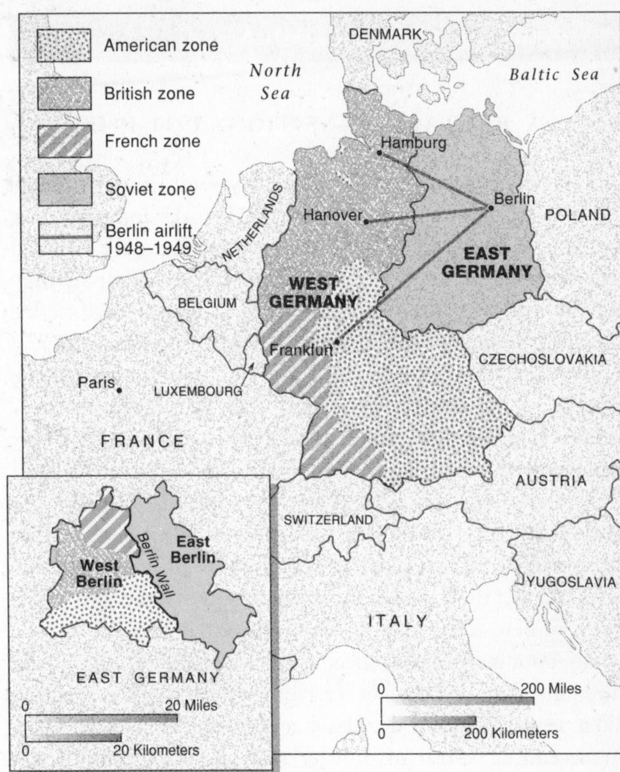

The World after World War II

quickly fell under Soviet domination, with communist governments forced upon them and Soviet troops in occupation. The nations of Western Europe were free to set up or confirm democratic regimes, but most of them lived under the shadow of growing United States influence, manifested in continued occupation by American troops, substantial economic aid and coordination, and no small amount of outright policy manipulation.

The stage was set, in other words, for two of the great movements that would shape the ensuing decades in world history: the challenges by subject peoples to the tired vestiges of control by the great European empires—the movement known as decolonization that in a few decades would create scores of new nations in Asia, Africa, and the West Indies; and the confrontation between the two great powers that emerged from the war, the United States and the Soviet Union, each with new international influence and new military might. This confrontation was dubbed the "cold war," and many believed it would soon become a war in a more literal and devastating sense. That these trends constituted a peace settlement was hard to imagine in 1945 or 1947, yet they seemed the best that could be done.

CONCLUSION

A BRUTAL TRANSITION, 1914–1945

The framework for world history established through the two world wars and the Great Depression was only that—a framework. It must be explored by more detailed consideration of developments in key individual areas during the first half of the 20th century. Understanding of the framework itself requires more detailed probing. War and depression, for example, did not inevitably produce the horrors of Nazism in Germany; other factors must be explored even in the connections between war, depression, and renewed war.

The consequences of the war-torn international framework must also be explored by probing the major trends of the century's second half, which were by no means all anticipated by the tense war settlement that emerged after 1945. Then, after examining individual regions of the world both before and after 1945, we can return to the question of the kind of overarching global context that has taken shape in recent decades—a context that is freer from the ascending spiral of disaster that seemed to engulf the world between 1914 and 1945.

The best way to capture the essential results of the many events that marked the first half of the 20th century is to view them as part of an exceedingly painful transition from Western world dominance to a different kind of world order. Whether this transition would have occurred had the major powers of Europe not tried twice to destroy each other, oblivious to the impact on their wider world role, cannot be determined. Certainly the transition would not have occurred so quickly.

The world wars weakened and distracted the nations that had long formed the core of Western civilization. They allowed new powers—the United States and the Soviet Union, as well as Japan despite the crushing defeat in 1945—to gain new roles. They allowed new independence movements and revolutionary uprisings. The Japanese forces that invaded Vietnam, the Philippines, and Indonesia during the early 1940s were often cordially detested by their new subjects, but they did teach that the Western overlords could be defeated and that a nonwhite people could put the West on the run. The lessons were important in supporting nationalist demands that had already stirred. World wars and depression broke the political framework western Europe had established during the preceding century, without at all restoring what had been before; and they dented, though less simply and decisively, the older Western-dominated world economic framework as well. The major events of the decades after 1914 constituted the death throes of one world order and the bloody birth pains of a new one.

This is why, for each of the individual societies still operating during the 20th century, a set of common questions can be asked. How did world wars and resultant international rebalancing affect the society? What was the impact of depression in shaping new political and social responses?

Yet the world wars, particularly, had one further long-range result beyond stirring new expectations and resentments and reducing Europe's world role. They also raised the specter of war itself to a new level.

Two world wars in a single generation had to haunt the world's people in 1945, particularly those in Europe, China, Japan, the Soviet Union, and even the United States (spared direct combat on its own soil) who had lived through one or both wars so directly. The lack of complete settlement after World War II was profoundly troubling as well, because it resulted from the almost immediate crescendo of a new conflict between the United States and the Soviets. Finally, war had become increasingly terrible, its destructive power mounting with every passing year. Again, the end of World War II, with the inauguration of the two atomic bombs dropped on Japan, could only stir a feeling of dread. Even optimistic Americans went through at least six years of pressing anxiety, as they tried to come to terms with the nuclear monster they had created.

Yet the end of World War II brought new leadership to almost every part of the globe as a result of new elections, toppling of colonial regimes, the discrediting of defeated governments, and a new revolutionary surge in China. Many new leaders vowed to undo some of the mistakes of the past, though they disagreed profoundly over what the mistakes had been and how they should be remedied. How new leadership confronted the issues that had brought depression and war to world dominance during the first half of the 20th century raises another set of questions that must be addressed to almost every major society in exploring its most recent history.

FURTHER READINGS

A number of important books have dealt with the origins of World War I. L. Lafore's *The Long Fuse* (1965) is a very readable introduction; see also James Joll's *Origins of World War I* (1984), which is slightly more up to date. A controversial interpretation is F. Fischer's *Germany's Aims in the First World War* (1967); see also P. Kennedy's *The Rise of the Anglo-German Antagonism 1860–1914* (1980). I. Geiss's *July 1914* (1967) is a collection of documents on the subject.

For a wider perspective, G. Barraclough's *An Introduction to Contemporary History* (1968) is extremely interesting. On the war's cultural impact, P. Fussell's *The Great War and Modern Memory* (1975) is a brilliant treatment. See also R. J. Sontag's *A Broken World, 1919–1939* (1971) for a survey of the period, mainly dealing with Europe. On the war itself see K. Robbins's *The First World War* (1984); see also J. Williams's *The Other Battleground: The Home Fronts, Britain, France, and Germany, 1911–1918* (1972) and R. Wohl's *The Generation of 1914* (1979). On the peace settlement, see A. J. Mayer's *The Politics and Diplomacy of Peacemaking* (1968).

On the depression, C. Kindleberger's *The World in Depression, 1929–1939* (1973), is a solid introduction. See also J. Galbraith's *The Great Crash of 1929* (1980) and, for a useful collection of articles, W. Laqueur and G. L. Mosse, eds., *The Great Depression* (1970). Japan's experience is covered in I. Morris, ed., *Japan, 1931–1945: Militarism, Fascism, Japanism?* (1963).

A good introduction to World War II is Gordon Wright's *The Ordeal of Total War, 1939–1945* (1968); see also W. Murray's *The Change in the European Balance of Power* (1984). On the war itself, see B. H. Liddell Hart's *History of the Second World War*, vol. 2 (1971). The United States' role is the subject of R. A. Divine's *The Reluctant Belligerent: American Entry into World War II* (1979). On the Asian front, see J. H. Boyle's *China and Japan at War, 1937–1945* (1972) and R. Butow's *Japan's Decision to Surrender* (1954). See also S. Ienaga's *The Pacific War* (1978) and Chi Hsi-sheng's *Nationalist China at War* (1982).

On the war's immediate aftermath, see H. Feis's *From Trust to Terror: The Onset of the Cold War, 1945–1950* (1970) and Martin Sherwin's *A World Destroyed: The Atomic Bomb and the Grand Alliance* (1975). For a more general assessment of war's role in the 20th century, see Raymond Aron's *Century of Total War* (1985).

1918–1923 Postwar adjustments; new republic in Germany; economic recession and recovery; emergence of communist movement

1922 Mussolini takes power in Italy

1925 Locarno agreements regularize Germany's diplomatic relations

1928 Kellogg-Briand Pact

1930 Rapid rise of Nazi party

1933–1957 New Deal in United States

1933 Hitler becomes chancellor of Germany

1935 Nuremberg laws deprive German Jews of citizenship

1936 Popular Front government in France

1938 Attacks on German Jews increase

1942 Hitler decides on extermination of European Jews

1945 End of World War II

1945–1948 New constitutions in Italy, Germany, and France; Labour party victory in Britain; basic measures of welfare states

1947–1974 Decolonization

1947–1960s Emergence and most intense phase of cold war

1947 Marshall Plan

1948 Publication of *The Second Sex*

1948 East and West German regimes established

1949 North Atlantic Treaty Organization established

A.D. 1915 A.D. 1935

35 The West in the 20th Century

INTRODUCTION. The theme of Western history during the last part of the 19th century was a new consolidation of political and social forms as the industrialization process matured. Tensions among social classes worked in part within the existing system, while the state took on new functions that met some pressing needs and also allowed new kinds of discipline through schools and military recruitment.

With the shock of World War I and its unsettling results, the consolidation focus was replaced by new confusions, bordering on the chaotic. The three decades after 1914 are among the most troubled in Western history. Political forms that had seemed so successful, revolving around some kind of representative institutions, were cast aside in favor of new radical regimes, or simply stopped functioning with any efficacy. Cultural emphases dating from the Enlightenment and building on beliefs in human rationality were challenged by new movements that deliberately appealed to the vicious and impulsive traits in human nature.

During the decades between the world wars, conflicts and paralysis within western Europe encouraged the development of new challenges to the West's world supremacy. European power within Western civilization also declined, in favor of the surging United States—which, however, was not ready to take a leadership role directly. These rebalancing effects within the West, and for the West in the world, proved durable and were only enhanced by the results of renewed struggle during World War II.

1957 Establishment of European Economic Community (Common Market)

1958 De Gaulle's Fifth Republic in France

1960s Civil rights movement in U.S.

1960s Emergence of new feminist movement

1968–1973 Massive student protests

1970s Democratic regimes in Spain, Portugal, and Greece

1973, 1979 Oil crises

1979 Thatcher and new conservatism in Britain

1979 Significant recession

1981 Reagan president in U.S.

1992 End of economic restrictions within Common Market

Other elements of the West's interwar experience, however, proved less persistent. The dominant events of world history between 1914 and 1945 did not set a rigid framework for the internal development of the West thereafter. Western society, both in Europe and the United States, found new sources of dynamism after 1945 as older themes combined with new departures in politics, while a new economic and social structure was gradually developed. The West was hardly problem-free in the decades after World War II, among other things because adjustments to its new world position raised uncertainties and concrete issues. But the level of conflict and confusion was far less great, with a newly constructive spirit dominating the 1950s and 1960s, and people responding positively in the workplace to this constructive strain.

Western history in the 20th century thus divides into two periods in which marked deterioration contrasts with considerable resurgence. Western history was dominated, between 1914 and 1945, by the impact or imminence of wars and depression, but somewhat surprisingly it shook off much of this context after 1945. Despite the West's decline in the world at large—a decline partially balanced by the emergence of the United States as a world power—Western patterns continued to play a disproportionate role in world affairs. The West's problems during the 1920s and 1930s gave other regions an opportunity to assert new independence. Western revival after 1945, while it did not stem the loss of colonies, maintained the West as a pacesetter in culture, technology, and to a degree in political style. Thus, even in a period of world history when the West lost its 19th-century preeminence, it is logical to begin the examination of recent world patterns by examining the recent, and oddly complex, evolution of this civilization.

Western development, particularly since the late 1940s, reminds us that the West's position in the world has slipped only relatively during the 20th century, given new economic competition from the Pacific Rim states and the independence and regional political strength of many former colonies. Important adjustments occurred in diplomatic and political forms that, despite many new problems, greatly heightened the West's internal strengths. Both the United States (plus Canada, Australia, and New Zealand) and the leading nations of Western Europe displayed considerable flexibility in dealing with major political and economic issues. The West also continued to provide leadership in scientific research and in the elaboration of popular consumer culture. In these various areas Western patterns continued to have influence well beyond the borders of the civilization itself.

 THE WEST'S DISARRAY, 1914–1945

World War I quickly shattered the confidence many Europeans had maintained around the turn of the century. It also brought serious structural damage to the European economy, diplomatic relations among Western states, and political systems in many individual countries.

While the ultimate effects of World War I involved Europe's world position, it also brought tremendous dislocation within Europe, and though some of the damage was quickly repaired, much persisted for the subsequent two decades. The key battlegrounds for four bloody years had been in Europe. The sheer rate of death and maiming, as well as the frustration of nearly four years of virtual stalemate, had a devastating material and psychological impact on the European combatants. More than ten million Europeans had died. In key countries, such as Britain, France, and Germany, the percentage killed had a serious demographic impact, reducing the number of young men available. Vast amounts of property had been destroyed. Most governments had failed to tax their populations enough to pay for the war effort—lest they weaken domestic support—so huge debts accumulated, leading to inflationary pressure even before the war was over. Key prewar regimes were toppled when the German emperor abdicated and the Habsburg Empire collapsed.

THE ROARING '20s

Despite all the disruptions, a brief period of stability, even optimism emerged in the mid-1920s. Diplomatic tensions eased somewhat within Europe, as Germany made some moves to accommodate its reduced position in return for partial relief from the reparations payments. While Germany refused definitively to accept its new eastern boundaries, it did promise friendship all around. Hopes that the Versailles settlement could be permanent ran so high that an American and a French leader coauthored a treaty outlawing war forever (the Kellogg-Briand Pact of 1928, which a number of nations dutifully ratified)—a sign of the shallow hopes of the decade.

Internal politics also seemed to calm. The war's end and immediate economic dislocations, plus the impact of the Russian Revolution, had inspired a new political polarization in many countries. Many veterans joined groups on the far right that wanted an authoritarian government and recovery of national honor; the labor movement on the left split, with a minority wing becoming communist, taking cues from the revolutionary regime in the Soviet Union. Both radical factions scared each other, further complicating parliamentary life. Germany produced an admirable constitution for its new democratic republic, but many groups did not accept it and there were understandable fears for its life. Even Britain, long known for its political stability, saw a major shift as the Labour party replaced the Liberals as the second major political force. Generally, the liberal middle sector of European politics was weakened. Nevertheless, the middle years of the 1920s brought a brief respite, as the extremist groups declined in force. Few leaders of great stature emerged, as even in the United States a series of colorless presidents captured the political timidity of the decade.

Economic prosperity buoyed hopes in the middle of the decade. The worst inflationary pressures were resolved at the cost of wiping out the value of savings for many propertied groups. Industrial production boomed, though more markedly in the United States than in western Europe. Mass consumption standards rose for several years. New products such as rayon, an artificial fiber, and radios spread widely. Particularly in the United States, the automobile became a mass consumption item, with effects ranging from reducing rural isolation to changing teenage dating habits. Household appliances proliferated, as technology's impact on daily life reached a new level.

This magazine cover by John Held, Jr., depicts the coed of 1926 as a combination of sweetness and sophistication.

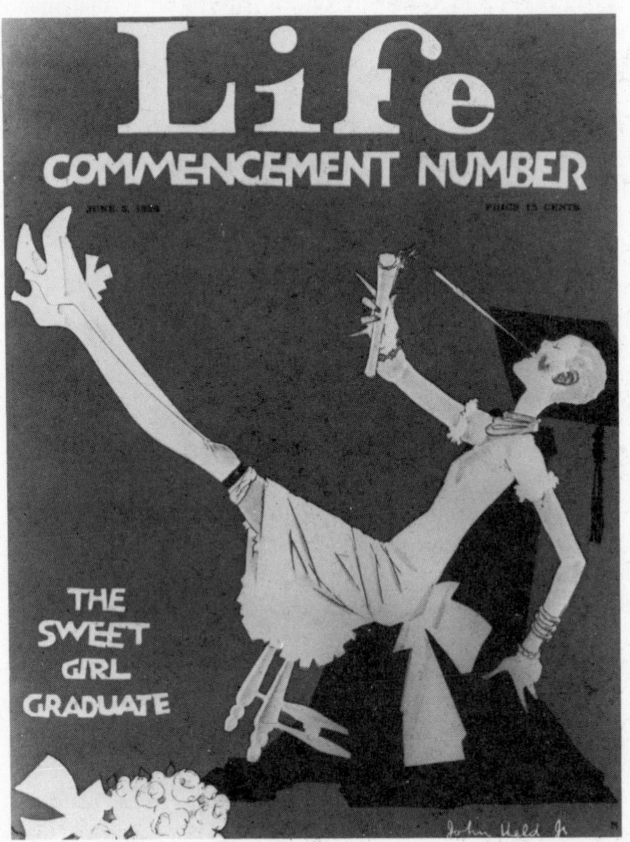

Finally, the 1920s saw a burst of cultural creativity in many parts of the West. Filmmakers experimented with this genre for artistic expression as well as mass entertainment. Modern artists developed geometrical cubist styles and other innovations. Writers and playwrights pioneered new forms, reducing plot lines and, in the case of drama, often seeking audience involvement. In retrospect the mood of the 1920s, in terms of high culture and popular culture alike, seemed somewhat frenzied, as if people sought escape from the tragic destiny that awaited. There was, however, no denying major new strides in art and science, as well as a significant development of mass consumer habits.

Women, particularly in the middle class, registered important change. Women's involvement in the labor force during the war was short-lived as men pushed them out at war's end. However, postwar legislation granted suffrage in Britain, Germany, and the United States. Further, prosperity and the still falling birthrate gave many women the chance to develop new leisure habits and less restrictive fashions. Young women in the United States began to date more freely, as a preliminary to courtship. Wives in Britain wrote of new interests in sexual pleasure, while maintaining commitment to marriage. Here were developments, like the more general rise of consumerism, that would gain momentum later on.

THE DEPRESSION'S IMPACT

All the hopeful signs seemed to vanish with the onset of depression in 1929—and the Great Depression revealed that neither the economic nor the political achievements of the mid-20s had been as solidly based as had been hoped. Political consequences were inevitable, with so many people out of work or threatened. The relatively weak Western governments responded to the onset of the catastrophe counterproductively. National tariffs were raised to keep out the goods of other countries, but this merely worsened the international economy and weakened sales for everyone. Most governments tried to cut spending, because with falling production their own revenues went down. They were concerned about avoiding renewed inflation, but in fact their measures further reduced economic stimulus and pushed additional workers—government employees—out of jobs. Confidence in the normal political process deteriorated. And the depression in many countries heightened political polarization. People sought solutions from radical parties or movements, both on the left and the right. Support for communist parties went up in many countries, and in important cases an authoritarian movement on the radical right gained increased attention. Even in relatively stable countries, such as Britain, battles between conservative and labor movements made decisive policy difficult.

There were a few cases of constructive political response. Scandinavian states, directed by moderate socialist movements, increased government spending, providing new levels of social insurance against illness and unemployment and foreshadowing the modern welfare state. In the United States, Franklin Roosevelt's New Deal, from 1933 onward, enacted a number of social insurance measures and used government spending to stimulate the economy. The New Deal did not cure the American depression, but it alleviated the worst effects and provided new hope that forestalled persistent political pressure against the established order. The New Deal also brought the United States more in line with the government traditions of other Western nations by increasing the power of the state in what had been, by European standards, a rather loosely governed society. Under Roosevelt the government became much more active, regulating banks and other economic activities and sponsoring huge public works. A new social security system provided some assistance to the unemployed and retirees; older people began, correspondingly, to expect less economic support from their families, and more from the state.

In key cases, however, the Great Depression led to one of two effects: a parliamentary system that became increasingly incapacitated, unable to come to grips with the new economic dilemma and too divided to take vigorous action even in more familiar areas such as foreign policy; or the outright overturning of the parliamentary system itself.

France was a prime example of the first pattern. The French government responded sluggishly to the depression. Voters responded to the depression by moving toward political extremes. Socialist and then Communist parties expanded. Rightist movements calling for a strong leader and fervent nationalism grew, often disrupting political meetings in order to discredit the parliamentary system. In response, Liberal, Socialist, and Communist parties allied in a Popular Front in 1936, winning the election. The Popular Front government, however, was unable to take strong measures of social reform because of the ongoing strength of conservative republicans and the authoritarian right. The same paralysis crept into foreign policy, as Popular Front leaders, initially eager to support the new liberal regime in Spain that was attacked by conservative army leaders in the Spanish Civil War, found themselves forced to pull back. The Popular Front fell in 1938, but even before this France was close to a standstill.

FASCISM

In Germany, the impact of the depression led directly to the new fascist regime. Germany had suffered the shock of loss in World War I, enhanced by treaty arrangements that cast blame for the war on the German nation. This was a country in which modern parliamentary traditions were recent and shaky. A number of factors combined to make Germany a breeding ground for fascism, though it took the depression to bring this current to the fore.

Fascism was a product of the war. The movement's advocates, many of them former veterans, attacked the weakness of parliamentary democracy and the corruption and class conflict of Western capitalism. They proposed a strong state ruled by a powerful leader, who would revive the nation's forces through vigorous foreign and military policy. Fascists vaguely promised social reforms to alleviate class antagonisms, and their attacks on trade unions as well as Socialist and Communist parties pleased landlords and business groups. A first fascist regime took power in Italy in 1923, and Fascist parties complicated the political process in a number of other nations during the 1920s and beyond. It was the advent of the National Socialist, or Nazi, regime in Germany under Adolf Hitler that made this new political movement a major force in world history. Here, a modern Western commitment to liberal, democratic political forms was challenged and reversed.

In his vote-gathering campaigns, Hitler repeated standard fascist arguments about the need for unity and the hopeless weakness of parliamentary politics. The state should provide guidance, for it was greater than the sum of individual interests, and the leader should guide the state. Hitler promised many groups a return to more traditional ways; thus many artisans voted for him in the belief that preindustrial economic institutions, such as the guilds, would be revived. Middle-class elements, including big business leaders, were attracted to Hitler's commitment to a firm stance against socialism and communism. Hitler also focused grievances against various currents in modern life, from big department stores to feminism, by attacking Jewish influences in Germany. And he promised a glorious foreign policy to undo the wrongs of the Versailles treaty. Finally, Hitler represented a hope for effective action against the depression. While the Nazis never won a majority vote in a free election, his party did win the largest single slice in 1932, and this enabled Hitler to make arrangements with other political leaders for his rise to power legally in 1933.

Once in power, Hitler quickly set about constructing a *totalitarian* state—that is, a new kind of government that would exercise massive, direct control over virtually all the activities of its subjects. Hitler eliminated all opposition

German Nazis moved the orchestrated mass rally to a high art form, profoundly influencing those who participated as well as those who could feel its power and solidarity through the radio or the movie screen.

parties; he purged the bureaucracy and military, installing loyal Nazis in many posts. His secret police, the *Gestapo*, arrested hundreds of thousands of political opponents. Trade unions were replaced by government-sponsored bodies that tried to appease low-paid workers by offering full employment and various welfare benefits. Government economic planning helped restore production levels, with particular emphasis on armaments construction. Hitler cemented his regime by constant, well-staged propaganda bombardments, strident nationalism, and an incessant attack on Germany's large Jewish minority.

Hitler's hatred of Jews ran deep; he blamed them for various personal misfortunes and also for movements such as socialism and excessive capitalism that in his view had weakened the German spirit. Obviously, anti-Semitism served as a catchall for a host of diverse dissatisfactions, and as such it appealed to many Germans. Anti-Semitism also played into Hitler's hands by providing a scapegoat that could rouse national passions and distract the population from other problems. Measures against Jews became more and more severe, as they were forced to wear special emblems, their property was attacked and seized, and increasing numbers were sent to concentration camps. After 1940 Hitler's policy insanely turned to the literal elimination of European Jewry, as the Holocaust raged in the concentration camps of Germany and conquered territories.

Hitler's foreign and military policies were based on preparation for war. He wanted not only to recoup Germany's World War I losses but to create a land empire that would extend across much of Europe, particularly toward the east against what he saw as the inferior Slavic peoples. Progressively Hitler violated the limits on German armaments and annexed neighboring territories, provoking only weak response from the Western democracies. When war finally resulted in 1939, Hitler's forces pressed forward for three years before his opponents were able to regroup. By late 1942 Soviet armies had recovered from German invasion, with some assistance in the form of armaments from the United States, and pressed inexorably toward Germany's eastern borders. American and British forces, aided by resistance movements against Nazi occupation, drove Germany first from North Africa, then gradually from Italy. In 1944 a massive invasion moved across the English Channel into France, and within a year the Allies entered Germany from the west, finally meeting Soviet forces along the Elbe River—Germany's new divide. Hitler committed suicide, and the war in Europe drew to a close.

The years from one world war through the next read like a tragic drama in Western history. One dire event led almost inexorably to the next, with none of the major participants able to tamper with fate.

PATTERNS IN WESTERN HISTORY, 1914–1945

Amid this sequence of events it is important to discern some key patterns. In the first place, the relentless unfolding of the Western tragedy had three key sources. The escalation of national conflicts, visible already in the later 19th century, was one such source. World War I, creating new grievances and imbalances, simply enhanced this nationalist tension within Western civilization. Secondly, the nature of war now changed, with the advent of total war, and had more sweeping effects on societies involved in combat than earlier wars had done. Propaganda bombarded civilians, often raising false hopes and encouraging new hatreds of foreign enemies as well as internal suspects such as leftists or capitalist profiteers. The economy was massively enmeshed in the war effort, making subsequent recovery difficult. Also, the weaponry of war involved unprecedented capacity to kill and damage. Finally, weaknesses in Western democracy and industrialization, exacerbated by war, came home to roost. From an economic standpoint the Western economies tolerated too much poverty, in addition to depending on exports to poor countries, to be entirely secure: Sales could easily plummet. From a social standpoint a number of groups continued to be suspicious of industrial conditions, eager in a crisis either to attack capitalism in the name of socialism or to urge a return to older values and authority.

Conditions of women, for example, continued to provoke fundamental disagreements from both genders. Some women were delighted with new consumer and life-style opportunities that opened up during the 1920s (along, in many countries, with the right to vote). Women began to smoke and drink in public and to enjoy new dance crazes and other leisure options. Yet other women continued to protest the limitations on women's roles, and particularly their inequality in work opportunities, as a brief wartime surge of female employment was pushed back during the 1920s. These feminist grievances, though less pronounced than before World War I, could feed leftist sentiment. Still other Westerners were aghast at the changes that had arrived, urging that women return to more purely domestic roles and traditional, modest costumes and habits. This sentiment provided some support for fascist movements. The West, in sum, remained deeply affected by the innovations brought by industrialization, and the resultant divisions helped sharpen political dispute.

Industrialization, however, continued to advance. The interwar decades saw continued gains for assembly-line production and big business forms. Huge combines developed in key industries, both in Europe and the United States, while managers learned new ways to coordinate and discipline masses of workers in factories, offices, and sales outlets. Major new product lines developed with artificial fibers and other consumer goods, including British-pioneered television production in the 1930s. In terms of industrial development and big business, Nazi Germany, despite anticapitalist rhetoric, promoted change as well, somewhat ironically weakening many of the more conservative sectors of German society. Capitalist control of industry and marketing advanced under Hitler, further reducing the role of small shops and artisans, while peasant agriculture was squeezed by support for large estates. The Nazi regime did dispute dominant Western cultural trends. It attacked modern art, urging more realistic, heroic styles often in the classical mode, and even challenged scientific education with praise for sports and physical training over intellectual life.

In the main, however, Western culture continued to develop along earlier lines. Fundamental discoveries in physics confirmed the earlier work of Einstein and led to additional work on atomic structure—which Nazi Germany supported because of its relevance to military power—while new discoveries in medicine advanced understanding of tissues and glands. The link between science and progress was confirmed as medicine introduced new inoculations for childhood diseases and new therapies, based at first on sulfa drugs, that greatly reduced the death rates from respiratory disease. The interwar period, in sum, did not see a total reversal of technical and intellectual development, even as dire events accumulated and a special mood of despair gripped Westerners—particularly in Europe—at many social levels.

DOCUMENT
THE RESISTANCE SPIRIT

In most countries occupied by Nazi Germany, resistance movements sprang up during the war to contest the short-lived empire. Resistance fighters in Holland, France, and elsewhere also formulated plans for a new Europe after the war that would redress the social and diplomatic tensions that had bedeviled the West for decades. This resistance spirit was far from fully realized as Europe rebuilt after 1945, but it helps explain some of the West's new directions and unexpected comeback. The first of the following selections comes from a document adopted by the French National Resistance Council in 1944, representing various movements. The second selection contains excerpts from underground newspapers in the previous year.

THE RESISTANCE COUNCIL PLEDGED TO REMAIN UNITED AFTER THE WAR

In order to assure: the establishment of the broadest possible democracy by allowing the people to voice their desires through the reestablishment of universal suffrage; full liberty of thought, conscience and expression; freedom of the press—an honest press, independent of the State, powerful economic interests and foreign influences; freedom of association, freedom to meet and demonstrate; the inviolability of the home and of private correspondence; respect for the individual; absolute equality of all citizens before the law.

In order to effect the necessary reforms:

a. Economic: the establishment of a true economic and social democracy, with the requisite eviction of the great economic and financial feudatories from the direction of the economy; rational organization of the economy, assuring the subordination of special interests to the general interest, and freed from the professional dictatorship installed in the image of the fascist states; the development of national production following a state plan, established after consultation with the representatives of all interested groups; the return to the nation of the great monopolies, fruits of the labor of all, of energy resources, of the underground riches of the country, of the insurance companies and the major banks; the development and support of producers', buyers', and sellers' cooperatives in both agriculture and manufacturing; the right of qualified workers to rise to administrative and management positions in businesses, and workers' participation in the running of the economy.
b. Social: the right to work and the right to leisure, in particular by the reestablishment and the improvement of labor contracts; a major readjustment of wages and the guarantee of a level of wages and working conditions which will assure every worker and his family security, dignity, and the chance of a decent life; a complete social security system, providing all citizens with the means of existence when they are unable to secure it themselves—a system whose management is shared by those concerned and by the State; a meaningful opportunity for all French children to have the benefits of education and access to the best of French culture, whatever their family's financial status, so that the highest positions in society are truly open to all those with the capacity to fill them, thus bringing into being a real elite, of merit rather than of birth, constantly renewed from the people.

FROM LA REVUE LIBRE AND L'ECOLE D'URIAGE, 1943

The visible causes of the war are not the main causes: racist imperialism, megalomania of the totalitarian leaders, etc. All these factors stem from an essential main cause, to wit the need for people to adapt their social and economic organization to the progress of science and technology. . . .

Like it or not, this war is revolutionary, in several senses.

First, it destroys the last vestiges of the decaying capitalist order. . . . Under the Nazi oppression the masses in Europe, long so apathetic, are gradually regaining the taste for liberty. To use their energies we must give this war a goal, which can rouse their enthusiasm, to win their agreement to the construction of a world where they are no longer pariahs, but with the completion of democracy, truly sovereign. . . .

As to France, we think that some kind of Western grouping effected with us, mainly on an economic basis and as extensive as possible, can offer great advantages. Such a grouping, extended in Africa, in close relations with the Orient and notably the Arab states which legitimately seek to unite their interests, and for which the English Channel, the Rhine, the Mediterranean will be like arteries, can constitute a chief center in the worldwide organization of production, exchange and security.

Questions: What did resistance leaders identify as Europe's big problems? How might resistance thinking help explain European recovery after 1945?

AFTER WORLD WAR II: INTERNATIONAL SETTING FOR THE WEST

World War II was fully as total a war as its predecessor, and it left Western Europe in shambles. The sheer physical destruction, caused particularly by bombing raids, disrupted housing and transportation. Downed bridges and rail lines complicated food shipments, leaving many people in places such as France and Germany ill-fed and unable to work at full efficiency. German use of forced foreign labor plus the many boundary changes generated hundreds of thousands of refugees trying to return home or find a new home. For at least two years after 1945, it was unclear that recovery would be possible, as sheer survival proved difficult enough. In the long run, Europe's postwar weakness, after three decades of strife, helped trigger a crescendo of nationalist sentiment directed against the West, plus the fuller emergence of the United States and the Soviet Union, whose size and building industrial strength finally overshadowed Europe's proud nation-states.

EUROPE AND ITS COLONIES

Two larger changes provoked by the war quickly intruded on the West: decolonization and the cold war. Colonies outside Europe, roused by the war, proved increasingly restive. Colonial powers returned where they had been dislodged—such as the British to Malaya and the Dutch to Indonesia—but they found a more hostile climate, with well-organized nationalist resistance. It was soon clear that many colonies could be maintained only at great cost, and in the main the European nations decided that the game was not worth the candle. A few cases proved messy. France tried to defend its holdings in Vietnam against communist guerrillas, yielding only in 1954 after some major defeats. The French clung even more fiercely to Algeria, its oldest African colony, and one with a large European minority. The French military joined Algerian settlers in insisting on a war to the death against nationalist forces, and bitter fighting went on for years. Tension even threatened civil war in France, until a new president, Charles de Gaulle, realized the hopelessness of the struggle and negotiated Algeria's independence in 1962.

Overall, decolonization proceeded more smoothly than in Algeria between the late 1940s and the mid-1970s, without prolonged fighting that might drain the Western nations themselves. Western governments typically retained important cultural relations with their former colonies and sometimes provided administrative and military help as well. Both France and Belgium, for example, frequently intervened in Africa after decolonization was officially complete. Finally, Western economic interests remained strong in most former colonies—particularly in Africa, which exploited mineral and agricultural resources in a pattern of trade not radically different from colonial days.

The impact of decolonization on the West should not, however, be minimized. Important minorities of former settlers and officials came home embittered, though except briefly in France they were not a significant political force. Europe's overt power in the world was dramatically reduced. Efforts by Britain and France to attack independent Egypt in 1956, to protest Egypt's nationalization of the Suez Canal, symbolized the new state of affairs. The United States and the Soviet Union forced a quick end to hostilities, and what was once a colonial lifeline came under non-Western hands. Yet, while decolonization was a powerful change in world affairs, it did not, at least in the short run, overwhelm the West, as neither economic growth nor internal political stability suffered greatly.

THE COLD WAR

The final new ingredient of Europe's diplomatic framework, the cold war between the United States and the Soviet Union, had a more durable ongoing influence on politics and society within the West. The conflict shaped up between 1945 and 1947. The last wartime meetings among the leaders of Britain, the United States, and the Soviet Union had rather vaguely staked out the dimensions of postwar Europe, which were certainly open to varied interpretations. By the war's end Russian troops firmly occupied most Eastern European countries, and within three years the Russians had installed communist regimes to their liking, while excluding opposition political movements. Thus an *eastern bloc* shaped up that included Poland, Czechoslovakia, Bulgaria, Romania, and Hungary. And Soviet boundaries themselves had pushed west, reversing the decisions of the post-World War I Versailles conference. The Baltic states disappeared, and Poland lost territory to Russia, gaining some former German lands as compensation. Finally, Soviet occupation of the eastern zone of Germany gave Russia a base farther toward the heart of Europe than the tsars had ever dreamed possible.

Offended by Russia's heavy-handed manipulation of Eastern Europe, United States and British policymakers tried to counter. The new American president, Harry Truman, was less eager for smooth relations with the Soviets than Franklin Roosevelt had been; he was emboldened by the United States' development in 1945 of the atomic bomb. Britain's wartime leader, Winston Churchill, had long feared communist aggression; it was he in 1946 who coined the phrase *iron curtain* to describe the division between free and repressed societies that he saw taking shape in Europe. But Britain frankly lacked the power to resist Soviet pressure, and under the Labour government it explicitly left the initiative to the United States.

The United States responded to Russia's power plays with vigor. It criticized Russian policies and denied Russian applications for reconstruction loans. It bolstered regimes in Iran, Turkey, and Greece that were under Soviet pressure. In Greece, particularly, Americans took over British resistance to a powerful communist guerrilla campaign. Then in 1947 the United States proclaimed its Marshall Plan, a program of substantial loans that was designed to aid Western nations in rebuilding from the war's devastation. In Soviet eyes, the Marshall Plan was a vehicle for American economic dominance, and indeed there is little question that in addition to humanitarian motives the United States intended to beat back domestic communist movements in countries such as France and Italy by promoting economic growth.

The focal point of the cold war in these early years was in Germany. Soviet policy in Germany initially concentrated on seizing goods and factories as reparation. The Western Allies soon prevented Russian intervention in their own zones and turned to some rebuilding efforts in the interests of playing a modest "German card" against growing Soviet strength in the east. That is, although the West, led by the United States, did not intend to resurrect a powerful Germany, it soon began to think in terms of constructing a viable political and economic entity. Allied collaboration started building a unified West Germany in 1946, and local followed by more national political structures were established through elections. When in 1947 the West moved to promote German economic recovery by creating a stable currency, the Soviet Union responded by blockading the city of Berlin, the divided former capital that sat in the midst of the Russian zone. The United States responded with a massive airlift to keep the city supplied, and the crisis finally ended in 1948, with two separate Germanies—East and West—beginning to take clear shape along a tense, heavily fortified frontier.

Cold war divisions spread from Germany to Europe more generally with the formation of two rival military alliances. The North Atlantic Treaty Organization (NATO) was formed in 1949, under United States' leadership, to group most of the Western European powers plus Canada in a defensive alliance against possible Soviet aggression. The NATO pact soon legitimated some rearmament of West Germany in the context of resistance to communism. It also legitimated the continued maintenance of a substantial United States military presence in Germany and in other member nations. In response, the Soviet Union organized the Warsaw Pact among its Eastern European satellites, and when in 1949 the Soviets developed their own nuclear capability, the world—particularly, the European world—seemed indeed divided between two rival camps, each in turn dominated by its own superpower. Numerous American and Soviet military units were permanently stationed in Europe on either side of the cold war divide.

The cold war had a number of implications for Western Europe. It brought new pressures from the United States on internal as well as foreign policy. Americans pressed, through the 1950s and beyond, for acceptance of German rearmament (though under some agreed-upon limits); it lobbied for higher military expenditures in its old allies France and Britain; and it pressed for acceptance of American forces and weapons systems. The United States' wishes were not always met, but the Americans had vital negotiating leverage in the economic aid they offered (and might withdraw), in the troops they stationed in Europe, and in the nuclear "umbrella" they developed (and might, in theory, also withdraw). The nuclear weapons seemed to offer the only realistic protection should the Soviet Union venture direct attack. The Soviets, for their part, influenced Western Europe not only through perceived aggressive intent, but also by funding and supporting substantial communist movements in France and Italy, which in turn affected but did not overwhelm the political process.

The cold war did not maintain the intensity it reached in its early years. Centers of conflict shifted in part outside Europe as Korea, then Vietnam, and recurrently the Middle East became flashpoints. A few European states, in special circumstances, managed to stay out of strict cold war alignment. Sweden and Switzerland maintained traditions of neutrality; Finland, a capitalist democracy on Soviet borders, was neutral perforce. Austria regained independence in 1956—in a period of lessening cold war dispute—on condition of neutrality; and Yugoslavia, though communist, pulled away increasingly from the Soviet camp. Finally, the main Western powers themselves, once launched on recovery, found increasing room to maneuver. After 1958, France became more and more restive under what it viewed as Anglo-American dominance of NATO, and it finally withdrew its forces from the joint NATO command, requiring also that American troops leave French soil. In the 1970s Germany opened new negotiations with the Soviet Union and eastern bloc countries, toward increasing export opportunities and reducing diplomatic tension.

The fact was that the cold war and the resultant alliance system continued to describe much of the framework of East-West relations in Europe from the end of World War II into the 1990s. France might have gained partial independence from NATO, but it did not withdraw entirely. Although tensions often receded after the high point of the late 1940s, fear of possible Soviet aggression remained; for this reason the United States' military presence was deemed essential by leading policymakers, if not the entire European public. Western Europe could no longer plan on defending itself against a major outside enemy. Although Great Britain and, after 1958, France developed small nuclear capabilities, they simply could not afford the massive stockpiles and rockets of the two superpowers. To some extent, indeed, Western Europeans ultimately grew rather comfortable in their reliance on United States' protection. Not only during the lean postwar recovery years, but even after prosperity returned, European nations kept military budgets relatively modest, compared to United States or Soviet spending, which meant a degree of vulnerability to outside military and diplomatic pressures that had no precedent in modern European history.

A vital feature of this diplomatic realignment obviously involved the rise of the United States to preeminence within the West. This was a development long in the making. America's industrial surge had already brought it new influence by the late 19th century, as key United States firms—Singer sewing machines, for example—quickly established a worldwide base with branches heavily influencing the economies of several European nations. Economic power was enhanced by agricultural exports and, after World War I, the power of American banking and credit. Following World War II, when the dollar became standard international currency, the economic supremacy of the United States among the Western nations seemed assured, and for a time many experts worried that Europe would never regain economic autonomy, doomed always to poor relative status vis-à-vis the giant American cousin. This situation proved temporary, as we will see, but even in the 1980s the economic power of the United States continued to surpass that of Western Europe.

The diplomatic and military ascendancy of the United States showed more checkered progress. The nation flexed its muscles during the First World War but then pulled back; only after 1941 did its full international potential stand revealed. The leadership role played by the United States in the postwar Western alliance—while it produced grievances and protests within Europe from various groups, both conservative nationalists and leftist supporters of nuclear disarmament—was never seriously challenged. The rise of the United States qualified the general pattern of declining world power for the West, though there were those by the late 1980s who argued that this nation, too, had become overcommitted and was destined to pull back. This same rise signaled the reduced status of what had been the Western heartland in Europe and raised questions about whether the West would remain coherent, not just diplomatically but also culturally, under unfamiliar American leadership.

The shifting balance between America and Europe produced a crisscrossing of military relationships, whatever the larger implications of the shift. As Western Europe abandoned military preeminence, the United States, never before a major peacetime military power, devoted growing resources to its military capacity and gave a growing voice to its military leaders. Regardless of the political party in power, the percentage of the United States government budget going to the military remained stable from the 1950s to the 1980s—when it went up. In contrast, some European leaders boasted that their societies had made a transition toward preeminence of civilian values and goals. Although American and European values and institutions became more similar in key respects after World War II, the difference in military roles signaled ongoing distinctions within Western society.

AFTER WORLD WAR II: NEW DIRECTIONS IN THE WEST

While the shifts in the West's external environment triggered by World War II were not catastrophic, they constituted major readjustments. Ironically, Western Europe's domestic development in this same period was considerably more positive, a strong contrast not only to the reduction in world status but also to the massive troubles that had followed World War I. Immediately after the war, Western Europe suffered tremendous dislocation, amid grinding poverty and painful rebuilding, made worse by the new cold war division of the European map and strong fears of a new superpower clash.

Though postwar problems left their mark, Western Europe demonstrated surprising resiliency. A new set of leaders emerged in many countries, some from wartime resistance movements eager to avoid the mistakes that had led to depression and war. While their vision was not always realized, from 1945 onward Western Europe did move forward on three important fronts: the extension of democratic political systems; a modification of nation-state rivalries within Europe; and a commitment to rapid economic growth that reduced previous social and gender tensions.

THE SPREAD OF LIBERAL DEMOCRACY

In politics, defeat in war greatly discredited fascism and other rightist movements that had opposed parliamentary democracy. Vestiges of these movements continued, periodically surfacing in countries such as France and Italy, but rarely with much muscle. At the same time, key leftist groups, including the strong communist movements that emerged from the war in France and Italy, were committed to democratic politics. While social protest continued, outright revolutionary sentiment declined. Finally, several new political movements surfaced, notably an important Christian Democratic current, which was wedded to democratic institutions and moderate social reform. While great national variations existed, in general Western Europe experienced a shift in the political spectrum toward fuller support for democratic constitutions and greater agreement on the need for government planning and welfare activities.

New regimes had to be constructed in Germany and Italy after the defeat of fascist and Nazi leadership, while France established a new republic once occupation ended. In Germany, political reconstruction was delayed by the division of the nation by the victorious Allies. As the cold war took shape, however, France, Britain, and the United States progressively merged their zones into what became the Federal Republic of Germany (West Germany), encouraging a new constitution that would avoid the mistakes of Germany's earlier Weimar Republic by outlawing extremist political movements. The new constitutions set up after 1945 in many European countries, while varied in particulars, uniformly established effective parliaments with universal (now always including female) suffrage. And the regimes endured. Only France, pressed by the Algerian War, changed its constitution in 1958, forming a Fifth Republic, still democratic but with stronger presidential authority.

Western Europe's movement toward more consistent democracy was extended in the 1970s when Spain and Portugal shifted from their authoritarian, semifascist constitutions, following the deaths of longtime strongmen to democratic, parliamentary systems. Greece, increasingly linked to the West, followed the same pattern. By the 1980s Western Europe had become more politically uniform than ever before in history. Party dominance shifted, with conservatives including Christian Democrats alternating with Socialist coalitions, but all major actors agreed on the constitutional system itself.

THE WELFARE STATE

The consolidation of democracy also entailed a general movement toward a welfare state. Resistance ideas and the shift leftward of the political spectrum helped explain the new activism of the state in economic policy and welfare issues. Wartime planning in the British government had pointed to the need for new programs to reduce the impact of economic inequality and to reward the lower classes for their loyalty. Not surprisingly, the governments that emerged at the war's end—Britain's Labour party and communist-socialist-Christian Democrat coalitions in France and Italy—quickly moved to set up a new government apparatus that would play a vigorous role in economic planning and develop new social activities as well. By 1948 the basic nature of the modern welfare state had been established throughout Western Europe, as not only the new regimes but also established reformists (as in Scandinavia) extended a variety of government programs. The United States, though somewhat more tentative in welfare measures, added to its New Deal legislation in the 1960s, under President Lyndon Johnson's *Great Society* programs, creating medical assistance packages for the poor and the elderly. Canada enacted a still more comprehensive medical insurance plan.

The welfare state elaborated a host of social insurance measures. Unemployment insurance was improved. Medical care was supported by state-funded insurance or, as in Britain where it became a centerpiece to the new Labour program, the basic health-care system was nationalized. State-run medical facilities provided free care to the bulk of the British population from 1947 onward, although some small fees were later introduced. Family assistance was another category, not entirely new, that was now greatly expanded. All Western European governments provided payments to families with several children, the amount increasing with family size. Because the poor now tended to have the largest families, family-aid programs both encouraged population growth—of particular concern to countries such as France—and helped redistribute some of the general tax revenues toward the neediest groups. In the 1950s a French worker's family with low earnings and five children (admittedly an unusual brood by this point) could improve its income by as much as 40 percent through family aid. Governments also became more active in the housing field—a virtual necessity given wartime destruction and postwar population growth. Britain embarked on an ambitious program of *council housing*, providing many single-family units that deliberately mixed working-class and middle-class families in new neighborhoods. By the 1950s over one-fourth of the British population was housed in structures built and run by the government.

The welfare state that emerged in the postwar years was a compromise product. It recognized a substantial private sector and tried to limit and cushion individual initiative rather than replace it with state action alone as in the communist system. It provided aid for citizens at many income levels. Middle-class people might benefit from family assistance, and they certainly used state medical insurance. They also disproportionately benefited from the expanded educational systems and university scholarships that developed along with the welfare state. In other words, although the welfare state focused particularly on problems of workers and the poor, it won support from other groups by dealing with some of their special needs as well.

Relatedly, although some aspects of the welfare state redistributed income, the welfare state did not generally make a huge dent on Western Europe's unequal class system. Though taxes rose, they were not always steeply graduated. Furthermore, starting with France, a supplementary tax system was installed, beginning in the late 1950s, that was not graduated at all. This "value-added" tax system, which quickly spread through Europe, levied taxes on each stage of the production process, operating essentially as a super-sales tax ultimately paid by consumers.

The welfare state was, in sum, an important new definition of government functions, but hardly a device for social revolution. It cushioned citizens against big expenses and unusual hardships, rather than rearranging overall social structure. It protected the purchasing power of the very poor against catastrophe, and it contributed to improved health conditions generally. It also, of course, increased contacts between government and citizen, and it produced a host of new regulations that framed European life.

Despite many criticisms from both the left and the right, the welfare state initially seemed to win wide acceptance. The British, for example, became quickly attached to their new health system, making major revision impossible. For the most part political debate centered on tinkering with the welfare state, not revolutionizing it in any particular direction. Socialist parties, when in power, extended welfare measures by improving their coverage and benefits. Conservative parties, for their part, often cut back a bit and promised more efficient administration. Into the 1970s, no major political movement attacked the new state root and branch.

The welfare state was undeniably expensive. It greatly expanded government bureaucracies, in addition to channeling tax monies to new purposes. By the 1950s, up to 25 percent of the gross national product of countries such as France or Holland was going to welfare purposes, and the figure tended to rise with time. As military expenses began to stabilize, welfare commitments became far and away the largest component of Western government budgets outside the United States. Here was a clear indication of the extent to which the Western European state had altered its relationship to the wider society.

An increased governmental role in economic policy paralleled the welfare state. Most postwar governments nationalized some sectors of industry outright. Most European countries also set up new planning offices, responsible for developing multiyear economic projections and for setting goals and the means to meet them. By coordinating tax concessions and directing the flow of capital from state banks, government planners had genuine power to shape, although not directly to run, economic activity. Planning extended to agriculture as well as industry. Planning offices regulated crop sizes and encouraged consolidation of land for greater efficiency, and they could require farmers to participate in cooperatives that would improve marketing and purchasing procedures.

Planning involved European governments more directly than ever before in commitments to economic growth, full employment, and avoidance of damaging recessions. It was also aimed at improving the economic development of laggard regions. Italy thus tried to direct increasing industrialization toward the south while France industrialized toward the west, in both cases with partial success.

Of the Western nations, only the United States shunned an economic planning office, though it maintained government regulation of the financial system. American government growth consisted more of expanding military activities and piecemeal welfare measures, though American elections, like European, usually hinged on the electorate's judgment of how well the nation was doing economically.

Despite important variations, the role of the state loomed unprecedentedly large throughout the West from the 1940s onward. A new breed of bureaucrat, often called a *technocrat* because of intense training in engineering or economics and because of a devotion to the power of national planning, came to the fore in the offices of the government. Some state initiatives undoubtedly reflected the potential overzealousness of the new breed. Housing authorities forced workers out of old but comfortable slums into anonymous high-rise structures that, however elegant on paper, never felt right to residents. Peasants, no friend of distant central governments even before, often lamented heavy-handed requirements. Yet here too, as with the welfare state, no particularly coherent political disputes took shape, at least until the 1960s. The new state seemed to work well enough that it was difficult to attack categorically.

POLITICAL STABILITY AND THE QUESTION MARKS

The fact was that big, contentious political issues were notable for their absence through most of Europe during the 1950s and 1960s, except for the polarizing experience of the Algerian War in France. Reformist governments of the immediate postwar years tended to give way to more conservative regimes during the 1950s. Labour, for example, lost the 1951 election in Britain and, even earlier, communists had been forced out of coalitions in France and Italy. But the conservative regimes were generally content to support the existing definition of state functions. Also, when socialist or labor governments gained renewed access to power, as in Britain in the 1960s, they too, typically, had no dramatic new programs to offer. For better or worse, Europeans seemed to accept the state's new social and economic role as well as its constitutional structure. Political debates were often fierce, and partisan loyalties intense, but few sweeping issues were raised.

The Western pattern of political compromise around the mechanisms of parliamentary democracy and the welfare state were, however, severely jolted by a series of student protests that developed in the late 1960s. Even before this, in the United States a vigorous civil rights movement had developed to protest unequal treatment of African Americans. Massive demonstrations, particularly in southern cities, attacked segregation and limitations on African-American voting rights.

Campus unrest was a Western-wide phenomenon in the 1960s. At major American universities, campus unrest focused on the nation's involvement in the war in Vietnam. Young people in Europe and the United States also targeted the materialism of their societies, including the stodginess of the welfare state, seeking more idealistic goals and greater justice. Student uprisings in France in 1968 created a near revolution. By the early 1970s, new rights for students as well as other reforms, combined with police repression, ended the most intense student protests, while passage of civil rights legislation in the United States ultimately reduced urban rioting and demonstrations. The flexibility of postwar Western democracy seemed triumphant. Some additional political concerns, including a new

During the civil rights movement in the United States, African-American leaders pressed for voting rights and other movements toward legal and educational equality through vivid demonstrations. Here, a voter registration drive in 1965 features a march from Selma to Montgomery, Alabama.

wave of feminism focusing on economic rights and dignity for women and environmentalist movements, entered the arena during the 1970s, partly as an aftermath of the student explosion. The rise of the Green movement in several countries in the 1970s signaled a new political tone, hostile to uncontrolled economic growth; Green parliamentary deputies in Germany refused even to wear coats and ties in their efforts to defy established political habits.

Observers in many countries speculated that a shift in basic political alignments might be in the making if old parties failed to deal adequately with the new issues. In some West European countries, also, a terrorist movement, targeting political and business leaders, caused recurrent anxiety. As economic growth slowed in the 1970s, and the Western world faced its greatest economic recession since the immediate postwar years, other signs of political change emerged. New leadership sprang up within the British Conservative party and the United States Republican party. In 1979 British Conservative leader Margaret Thatcher began the longest-running prime-ministership in history, working to cut welfare and housing expenses and to promote free enterprise. Neither she nor her American counterpart, Ronald Reagan, fully dismantled the welfare state, but they did reduce its impact.

Despite all the portents of change, however, the main lines of postwar government persisted into the 1990s. Democratic institutions often failed to command great excitement, as voting levels went down throughout the West (particularly in the United States), but they roused no widespread, coherent resistance either. New political movements, while interesting, had yet to dislodge mainstream Conservative and Socialist (or, in the United States, liberal) parties. The Western world has unquestionably remained freer from major political upheavals than have most other civilizations in the postwar decades, and freer than Western society itself had been during the 1920s and 1930s. Has Western society achieved a durable new harmony, or were the postwar decades a period of deceiving tranquility before some yet-to-be-defined storm?

THE DIPLOMATIC CONTEXT

Along with the extension of democracy and the development of the welfare state, the West showed postwar vigor in addressing some traditional diplomatic problems, notably the recurrent bugbear of nationalistic rivalry plus specific manifestations such as French-German enmity. United States guidance combined with innovative thinking in the new European governments.

Many resistance leaders had, during the war, tempered their hatred of Nazism with a plea for a reconstruction of the European spirit. The Christian Democratic movement, particularly, produced important new advocates of harmony among European nations. Early postwar reforms, however, concentrated primarily on internal changes. While cold war rivalries prevented a formal European peace settlement, initial impulses on the part of the victorious Allies suggested a harsh treatment of Germany, possibly a permanent dismemberment, as the means of avoiding a repetition of the two previous world wars—not a more fundamental rethinking of Western conventions.

Yet the demands of the cold war and pressure from the United States forced second thoughts, which ultimately revived elements of resistance idealism. By 1947, as American leaders grew eager to spur Western Europe's economic recovery, they judged that coordination across national boundaries was an essential precondition. Thus the American Marshall Plan required discussion of tariffs and other development issues among recipient nations. With simultaneous American insistence on the partial rearmament of Germany and German participation in NATO, the framework for diplomatic reform was complete.

Faced with these pressures and aware of the failure of nationalistic policies between the wars, several French statesmen took a lead in proposing coordination between France and Germany as a means of setting up a new Europe. The nations of the Low Countries and Italy were soon linked in these activities. The idea was to tie German economic activity to an international framework so that the nation's growing strength would not again threaten European peace. Institutions were established to link policies in heavy industry and later to develop atomic power. A measure to establish a united European military force proved too ambitious and collapsed under nationalist objections. But in 1958 the six West European nations (West Germany, France, Italy, Belgium, Luxembourg, and the Netherlands) set up the European Economic Community, or Common Market, to begin to create a single economic entity across national political boundaries. Tariffs were progressively reduced among the member nations, while a common tariff policy was set for the outside world. Free movement of labor and investment was encouraged. A Common Market bureaucracy was established, ultimately in Brussels, to oversee these operations. The Common Market set up a court system to adjudicate disputes and prevent violations of coordination rules; it also administered a development fund to spur economic growth in laggard regions such as southern Italy or western France.

The Common Market did not move quickly toward a single government. Important national disputes limited the organization's further growth. France and Germany, for example, routinely quarreled over agricultural policy, with France seeking more payments to farmers as a matter of obvious self-interest. The establishment of the Fifth Re-

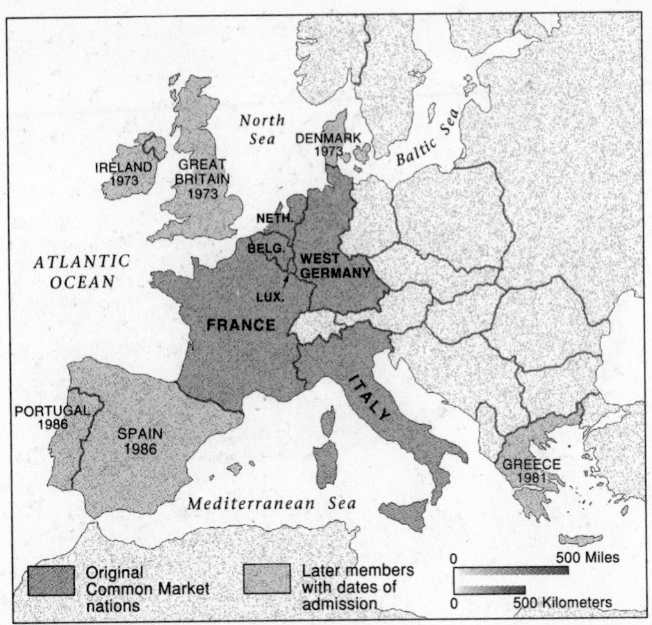

The Common Market and Its Growth; NATO Boundaries and Neutral Nations

public in France, under Charles de Gaulle, indeed signaled an increase of French nationalism. But while the Common Market did not turn into full unity, it did survive and, on the whole, prosper. It even established an advisory international Parliament, ultimately elected by direct vote. Further, in the 1980s, firm arrangements were made to dismantle all trade and currency exchange barriers among member states in 1992, creating essentially complete economic unity. And the Common Market's success expanded its hold within Western Europe. After long hesitations, Britain, despite its tradition of proud island independence, decided to join, as did Ireland, Denmark, and later Greece, Spain, and Portugal. Nationalist tensions within Europe receded to a lower point than ever before in modern European history. After the worst scares of the cold war, focused mainly on the division between the communist East and the semicapitalist West, Europe became a diplomatically placid continent, enjoying one of the longest periods of complete internal peace in its history.

ECONOMIC EXPANSION

Accompanying political and diplomatic change was striking economic growth, after a short, if agonizing, postwar rebuilding. The welfare state and Common Market may have encouraged this growth by improving purchasing power for the masses and facilitating market expansion across national boundaries; economic growth encouraged the success of new political and diplomatic systems.

There was no question that, by the mid-1950s, Western Europe had entered a new economic phase. Agricultural production and productivity increased rapidly as peasant farmers, backed by the technocrats, adopted new equipment and seeds. European agriculture was still less efficient than that of North America, which necessitated some hotly debated tariff barriers by the Common Market. But food production easily met European needs, often with some to spare for export. Retooled industries poured out textiles and metallurgical products. Expensive consumer products such as automobiles and appliances supported rapidly growing factories. Western Europe also remained a leading center of weapons production, trailing only the United States and the Soviet Union in exports.

Overall growth in gross national product surpassed the rates of any extended period since the Industrial Revolution began; it also surpassed the growth rates of the United States economy during the 1950s and 1960s. The German economy, once some basic reconstruction and currency stabilization had occurred by 1948, took off at a six percent annual expansion during the 1950s; with few modest setbacks this pace continued into the early 1970s. France attained an eight percent growth rate by the late 1950s, maintained almost this level during the 1960s, and returned to rates of over seven percent annually by the early 1970s. By 1959 the Italian economy, a newcomer to the industrial big leagues, was expanding at an 11 percent annual rate. These were, admittedly, the clearest success stories. Scandinavian growth was substantial but more modest, and Britain, also expanding but falling rapidly in rank among the European national economies, managed at best a four percent increase annually. Even this, however, contrasted markedly with the stagnation of the 1920s and early 1930s.

Growth rates of the sort common in Western Europe, their impact heightened by the absence of major depressions, depended on rapid technological change. Europe's rising food production was achieved with a steadily shrinking agricultural labor force. France's peasant population—16 percent of the labor force in the early 1950s—fell to 10 percent two decades later, but overall output was much higher than before. During the 1950s the industrial work force grew as part of factory expansion, but by the 1960s, despite rising production, the relative proportion of factory workers also began to drop. Workers in the service sector, filling functions as teachers, clerks, medical personnel, insurance and bank workers, and performers and other "leisure industry" personnel, rose rapidly in contrast. Europe, like the United States, began to convert technological advance into the provision of larger bureaucracies and service operations without jeopardizing the expanding output of goods. In France, by 1968 half of all paid workers were in the service sector, and the proportion rose steadily thereafter.

The high rates of economic growth also assured relatively low unemployment after the immediate postwar dislocations passed. Even Britain, with lagging development, averaged no more than four percent unemployment per year during the 1950s and 1960s, while countries such as France and Germany featured rates of two percent to three percent a year. Indeed, many parts of the continent were labor-short and had to seek hundreds of thousands of workers from other areas—first from southern Europe, then, as this region industrialized, from Africa, the Middle East, and parts of Asia. The rise of immigrant minorities was a vital development in Western Europe and also the United States, where the influx of Asian and Latin-American immigrants stepped up markedly.

Unprecedented economic growth plus low unemployment meant unprecedented improvements in incomes, even with the taxation necessary to sustain welfare programs. Per-capita disposable income rose 117 percent in the United States between 1960 and 1973, while soaring 258 percent in France, 312 percent in Germany, and 323 percent in Denmark. Scandinavia, Switzerland, and the Federal Republic of Germany indeed surpassed the United States in standards of living by the 1980s, while France, long an apparent laggard in modern economic development, pulled even. New spending money rapidly translated

In the United States, as well as in Japan and Western Europe, advertisements increasingly evoked a good life to be fulfilled through buying the right goods. The newest car was associated with a prosperous home, a loving family, and even happy pets.

into huge increases in the purchase of durable consumer goods, as virtually the whole of Western civilization became an "affluent society." By 1969 two of every ten people in Britain, Sweden, West Germany, and France owned an automobile. Ownership of television sets became virtually universal. France and other countries indulged in a mania for household appliances. Shopping malls and supermarkets, the agents of affluence and extensive but efficient shopping that had first developed in the United States, spread widely, at the expense of more traditional, specialist small shops. A West German company, in fact, took over a key American grocery chain in the late 1970s, on grounds that Europeans now knew mass marketing as well as or better than the American consumer pioneers.

Europe had unquestionably developed a framework of affluent consumerism as fully as had the United States, with at least as much impact on basic social patterns and

TABLE 35.1

Two Measures of Rising Consumer Prosperity in Europe, 1957 and 1965

Automobiles	1957	1965
France	3,476,000	7,842,000
Germany (Federal Republic)	2,456,288	8,103,600
Italy	1,051,004 (1956)	5,469,981
The Netherlands	375,676	1,272,890
Sweden	796,000	1,793,000
Televisions	**1957**	**1965**
France	683,000	6,489,000
Germany	789,586	11,379,000
Italy	367,000	6,044,542
The Netherlands	239,000	2,113,000
Sweden	75,817	2,110,584

Sources: Adapted from *The Europa Year Book 1959* (London: Europa Publications, 1959) and *The Europa Year Book 1967*, vol. 1 (London: Europa Publications, 1967).

habits of thought. Advertising was not quite as ubiquitous in Europe as across the Atlantic, particularly because most television channels were state-run and noncommercial. But promptings to buy, to smell good, to look right, to express one's personality in the latest car style, began quickly to describe European life. The frenzy to find good vacation spots was certainly intense. Literally millions of Germans poured annually into Italy and Spain, seeking the sun. Britons thronged to Spanish beaches. Europeans were bent on combining efficient work with indulgent leisure.

The West's economic advance was not without some dark spots. Inflation was a recurrent headache, when demand outstripped production. And inflation in the 1970s, affecting even the cautious Germans who were eager to avoid this specter from the past, caused serious dislocation. Pockets of unemployment were troubling. Many immigrant workers from Turkey, North Africa, Pakistan, and the West Indies suffered very low wages and unstable employment. These immigrants, euphemistically labeled "guest workers," were often residentially segregated and victims of discrimination by employers and police, as racism continued to be an important factor in Western society.

More troubling still was the slowing of economic growth in the 1970s. In 1973 the oil-producing states of the Middle East cut their production and raised prices, initially in response to a Middle Eastern war with Israel. Many nations were hit hard by higher energy prices, but Western Europe, heavily dependent on imports, was particularly pressed. A second orchestrated oil crisis in 1979 led to a severe recession throughout Western society, with unusually high rates of unemployment. Growing competition from East Asia and other areas cut into traditional staples such as steel and automobile production, making it difficult to recover the dynamism of the two postwar decades.

Western leaders were able to respond to new crises with some success. Conservation measures reduced dependence on imported oil, and by the 1980s energy prices fell back. Several European nations embarked on rapid development of nuclear energy production. European productivity rates continued to improve, with nations such as France introducing the use of robots on assembly lines at a particularly rapid pace. The economic climate had become tighter, however. This spurred some renewed labor agitation, directed, for example, at governments that closed inefficient factories. Yet even by 1990, the ongoing impact of dramatic economic growth lingered, giving Western Europe as well as the United States a source of new satisfactions and interests, as well as a vigorous presence in the world power structure even as colonies disappeared and sheer military dominance receded.

THE SOURCES OF WESTERN VITALITY

No single factor explained the post-1945 vigor of Western society in political, diplomatic, and economic structure. The West, including the United States, continued to benefit from technological leadership in the world economy even as it faced new competition from Japan. It built on its existing industrial base, in contrast to most other societies still trying to industrialize for the first time. It also spread and adapted democratic and parliamentary traditions, another heritage from the 19th century and before. Emphasis on scientific training, particularly strong in Europe, followed from prior intellectual change; it made Westerners open to new ideas and techniques.

The West was not involved in revolutionary adaptation, even as it pulled out of the doldrums of the decades from 1914 to 1945. Yet there were major changes resulting from innovative leadership—the fruit of new groups ascending to power after World War II plus the role of the United States in influencing key adjustments. The reduction of nationalism in favor of regional cooperation was a basic step. So was the more active posture of the state in promoting and guiding change. Even as Western politics became less contentious, political leadership became more central in shaping the patterns of Western society.

CULTURE AND SOCIETY IN THE WEST

Political and economic changes in Western society progressively altered the contours of earlier industrial development. They also smoothed out a number of earlier differences within Western society, particularly between the United States and Western Europe, as the two key Western spaces converged in many respects. The West became the first example of an advanced industrial society, especially from the 1950s onward, and both the United States and Western Europe shared in leading facets of change.

SOCIAL STRUCTURE

Economic growth, bringing increasing prosperity to most groups, eased some earlier social conflicts throughout the West. Workers were still propertyless, but they had substantial holdings as consumers. Social lines were also blurred by rapid social mobility, as educational opportunities opened further and the size of the white-collar sector expanded. Much unskilled labor was left to immigrants. Economic and political change also altered conditions for West Europe's peasantry. Peasants became commercial, eager for improvements in standards of living, and, through car trips and television, participants in urban culture. They also became more attuned to bureaucracies, as state regulations pushed them into cooperative organizations.

Social distinctions remained, to be sure. Middle-class people had more abundant leisure opportunities and a more optimistic outlook than did most workers. Signs of tension continued. Crime rates went up throughout Western society after the 1920s, though the levels were particularly high in the United States. Race riots punctuated American life in the 1950s and 1960s and exploded in immigrant sections of British cities in the 1980s.

There were strong signs that what was happening in Western society, at least by the 1960s, was not so much a resolution of older issues—how to fit peasants into modern society or what to do about worker grievances—as the establishment of a new social system, a second version of industrial society or, as some held, a postindustrial society. The majority of the labor force in the West was now engaged in services and management hierarchies, not working as producers in either farm or factory. It was drawn less to the older ethic of hard work than to new ideas of high consumption and expressive leisure. The West, in sum, continued to change, whether for good or ill.

THE WOMEN'S REVOLUTION

A key facet of postwar change involved women and the family, and again both Western Europe and the United States participated fully in this upheaval. While family ideals persisted in many ways—with workers, for example, urging that "a loving family is the finest thing, something to work for, to look to and to look after"—the realities of family life changed in many ways. Family leisure activities expanded. Extended family contacts were facilitated by telephones and automobiles. More years of schooling increased the importance of peer groups for children, and the authority of parents undoubtedly declined.

The clearest innovation in family life came through the new working patterns of women. World War II brought increased factory and clerical jobs for women, as the earlier world war had done. After a few years of downward adjustment, the trends continued. From the early 1950s onward, the number of working women, particularly married women, rose steadily both in Western Europe and in the United States and Canada. Women's earlier educational gains had improved their work qualifications; the growing number of service jobs created a need for additional workers—and women, long associated with clerical jobs and paid less than men, were ideal candidates. Many women also sought entry into the labor force as a means of adding to personal or family income, to afford some of the consumer items now becoming feasible but not yet easy to buy, or as a means of personal fulfillment in a society that associated worth with work and earnings.

The growing employment of women, which by the 1970s brought the female segment of the labor force up to 44 percent of the total in most Western countries, represented particularly the employment of adult women, most of them married and many with children. Teenage employment dropped as more girls stayed in school, but long-term work commitments rose steadily. This was not, to be sure, a full stride to job equality. Women's pay lagged behind men's pay. Most women were concentrated in clerical jobs rather than spread through the occupational spectrum, despite a growing minority of middle-class women who were entering professional and management ranks. Clearly, however, the trends of the 19th-century Industrial Revolution, to keep women and family separate from work outside the home, had yielded to a dramatic new pattern.

Other new rights for women accompanied this shift. Where women had lacked the vote before, as in France, they now got it; only Switzerland, of the West European nations, doggedly refused this concession at the national level until 1971. Gains in higher education were considerable, though again full equality remained elusive. Women constituted 23 percent of German university students in 1963, and under socialist governments in the 1970s the figure rose. Preferred subjects, however, remained different from those of men, as most women stayed out of engineering, science (except medicine), and management. Family rights improved, at least in the judgment of most

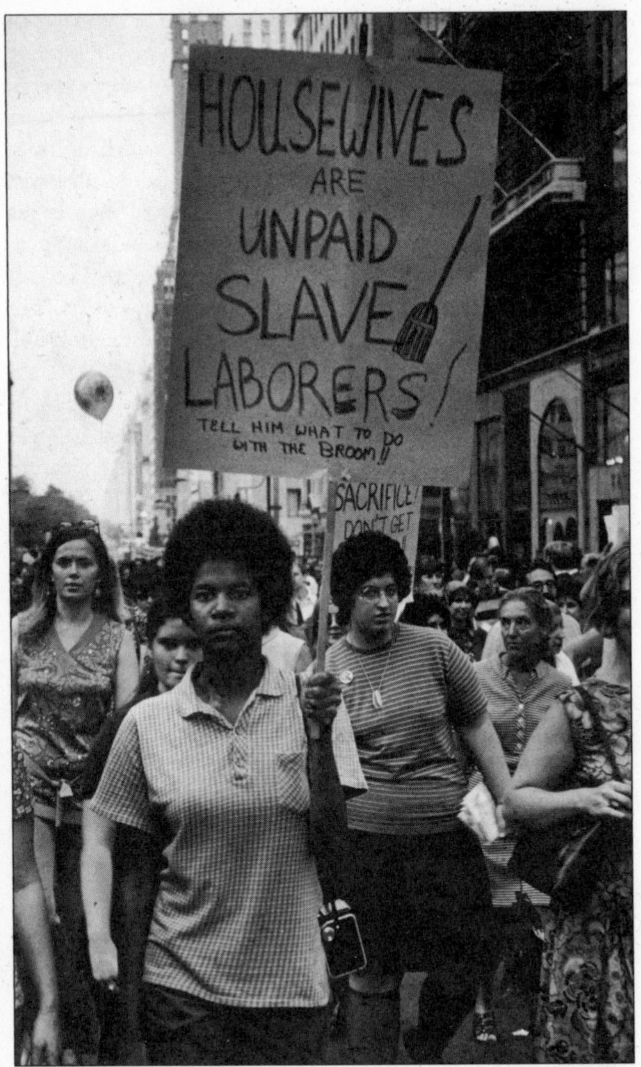

The feminist movement focused particularly on economic gains for women and a rejection of purely domestic roles. The movement first gained momentum in the United States in the late 1960s, in the wake of civil rights agitation, but soon spread to Western Europe.

women's advocates. Access to divorce increased, which many observers viewed as particularly important to women. Abortion law eased, though more slowly in countries of Catholic background than in Britain or Scandinavia; it became increasingly easy for women to regulate their birthrate. Development of new birth-control methods, such as the contraceptive pill introduced in 1960, plus growing knowledge and acceptability of birth control, decreased unwanted pregnancies. Sex and procreation became increasingly separate considerations. Although women continued to differ from men in sexual outlook and behavior—over twice as many French women as men, for example, hoped to link sex, marriage, and romantic love, according to 1960s polls—more women than before tended to define sex in terms of pleasure.

Predictably, of course, changes in the family, including the roles of women, brought new issues as well as redefined ideals of companionship. The first issue involved children. A brief increase in the Western birthrate ended in the early 1960s, and a rapid decline ensued. Women working and the desire to use income for high consumer standards mitigated against children, or very many children, particularly in the middle class, where birthrates were lowest. Those children born were increasingly sent, often at an early age, to day-care centers, one of the amenities provided by the European welfare state and particularly essential where new fears about population growth began to surface. European families had few hesitations about replacing maternal care with collective care, and parents often claimed that the result was preferable for children. At the same time, however, some observers worried that Western society, and the Western family, were becoming indifferent to children in an eagerness for adult work and consumer achievements. American adults, for example, between the 1950s and 1980s, shifted their assessment of family satisfaction away from parenthood by concentrating on shared enjoyments between husbands and wives.

Family stability also opened new cracks. Pressures to readjust family roles, women working outside the family context, and growing legal freedoms for women, caused men and women alike to turn more readily to divorce. In 1961 nine percent of all British marriages ended in divorce; by 1965 the figure was 16 percent and rising. By the late 1970s one-third of all British marriages ended in divorce, and the United States' rate was higher still.

Finally, even aside from divorce, the changing roles of women raised questions about family values. Expectations lagged behind reality. Polls taken of German women in the 1960s indicated that a solid majority believed mothers with children under 12 should stay home; yet in fact a solid majority of such mothers were working. Gaps of this sort, between ideals and practice, suggested that, like Western society generally, the family was in a new transition, its end state far from clear.

The development of a new surge of feminist protest, although it reflected far wider concerns than family life alone, showed the strains caused by women's new activities and continued limitations. Growing divorce produced many cases of impoverished women combining work and child care. New work roles revealed the persistent earnings gap between men and women. More generally, many women sought supporting values and organizations as they tried to define new identities less tied to the domestic roles and images of previous decades.

A new feminism began to take shape with the publication in 1949 of *The Second Sex* by the French intellectual Simone de Beauvoir. Echoed in the 1950s and 1960s by other works, such as American Betty Friedan's *The Feminine Mystique,* a new wave of women's rights agitation arose after three decades of relative calm. The new feminism tended to emphasize a more literal equality that would play down special domestic roles and qualities; therefore, it promoted not only specific reforms but more basic redefinitions of what it meant to be male or female.

The new feminism did not win all women, even in the middle class, which was feminism's most avid audience. It also did not cause some of the most sweeping practical changes that were taking place, as in the new work roles. But it did support the revolution in roles. From the late 1960s onward it pressed Western governments for further change, raising issues that were hard to fit into established political contexts. The movement both articulated and promoted the gap between new expectations and ongoing inequalities in gender. And the new feminism expressed and promoted some unanswered questions about family functions. In a real sense, later 20th-century feminism seemed to respond to the same desire for individuality and work identity in women that had earlier been urged on men as part of the new mentality suitable for a commercialized economy. Family remained important in the evolving outlook of women, although some feminist leaders attacked the institution outright as hopelessly repressive. Even for many less ideological women, however, family goals were less important than they had been before.

Thus, even as social class tensions declined in the West, compared to the century of industrialization, new divisions surged forward. Gender conflict was an obvious new issue, but so was the gap between racial minorities, new or old, and established white populations.

ANALYSIS
THE DECLINE OF THE WEST?

At various points in the 20th century, various kinds of Westerners have worried about the decline of Western society. Sometimes their concern focuses on the undeniable relative decline of the West in the world, which sets the 20th century off from the periods in world history between 1450 and 1920. In the 1980s, for example, various United States news magazines began to trumpet the idea of an emerging "Pacific century," dominated by East Asian powers, that would replace the period of Western (and recently, American) preponderance.

The idea of absolute decline has had its proponents as well. The West's relative loss of power over the past 60 years, with decolonization and the rise of Japanese exports, may produce absolute decline compared to earlier Western leadership. Some societies—such as the Roman Empire or the Ottoman Empire—depended on continued expansion to provide labor or booty for the upper class and then began to lose their vitality when further growth became impossible. The West no longer requires colonies to provide slaves, but it might have become so dependent on its ability to dominate other economies that relative decline will spell the beginning of a new period of internal woes.

Furthermore, there have been numerous periods in which developments within the West provoked gloom. Early in the 20th century, pondering the growing pleasure seeking of Western culture and its internal divisions, a German philosopher named Oswald Spengler wrote a book called the *Decline of the West* in which he predicted that Western civilization was going the way of Rome, doomed to fall before the onslaught of such vigorous but less civilized peoples as the Russians or the Americans. His book was hugely popular after World War I, when it looked as if Western nations had indeed inflicted grievous injury on their own society. Other historians, though somewhat less cosmically pessimistic than Spengler, have picked up the theme of what they see as an inevitable decline of societies following periods of vigor. The theme seemed to fit Western Europe again immediately after World War II, when both victors and vanquished were suffering through the immense problems of reconstruction. It was revived again in the late 1980s, when the world dominance of the United States seemed in retreat.

Other observers, though less systematic, discerned internal decay. Some focused on cultural trends, bemoaning the lack of standards in art—the tendency to play with novel styles, however frivolous, simply to win attention. Or they might bemoan popular culture for what they claimed was a shallow materialism and vulgar sexuality; some critics saw analogies between Western commercialism and the Roman "bread and circuses" approach to the urban masses that, they argued, had weakened the empire's moral fiber and reduced its capacity for work and military valor.

Analogies, however, are inexact, and the role of moral decline in causing Rome's downfall is debatable in any event. One of the problems in comparing current Western trends to past cases of decline—even subtler cases, such as the gradual reduction of Arab vitality in the later postclassical era—is that modern conditions as shaped by industrialization may weaken the applicability of past standards.

Western demography is a case in point. There is no question that the demographic vitality of the West weakened in the late 19th and 20th centuries, with the baby boom era, from 1943 to 1963, a brief if interesting exception. Birthrates have gone down fairly steadily, in the 1930s and again by the 1980s reaching a point close to bare reproduction. Indeed some Western nations, such as Germany, were by the 1980s coming close to falling beneath reproduction levels, with birthrates so low that population decline would soon set in unless compensated by further immigration. Moreover, slow or zero population growth was accompanied by increased aging, the result of advancing life expectancy combined with the relatively small number of children being born. In most historic situations, slowing population growth has signaled a general decrease in vitality, causing further decline as competition and the opportunity provided by population increase waned. Unquestionably, the West's demographic trends reduced its percentage of world population, which might relate to its relative decline and certainly opened it to new immigration from various parts of the world. But the total package was hard to measure, for in the context of an industrial society, which provided a variety of technical aids to human labor and was a heavy consumer of resources, stable populations might prove a source of strength, not weakness, while rapid population increase might be a fateful burden that limited effective development.

Judgments about decline, finally, are complicated by the cycles of Western history during the 20th century and the nature of modern Western expectations. Periods of great disarray, like the 1930s, have not thus far led to long-term chaos, as Western nations have seemed able to bounce back. Other decades roused anxieties mainly because of the heavy Western commitment to steady progress. Thus during the 1970s, when economic growth slowed, many polls showed that Americans had stopped believing that their society would advance in the future (though interestingly they still believed that their own lives would get better). Yet the 1970s brought no huge crisis, simply a slowing in the pace of improvement. The Western habit of expecting steady economic advance could easily lead to temporary exaggerations of what 1970s Americans called "malaise."

Clearly, to paraphrase Mark Twain, reports of the death of the West seemed premature. Yet past examples from world history suggest one other caution: Social decline, if it does set in, typically takes a long time to work through. Rome declined for three centuries before it "fell"; the Ottoman Empire began to turn downward two centuries before it became known as "sick." The first century of decline may be hard to perceive, yet particularly important to monitor in case restorative measures are necessary.

Question: Has the West shown signs of cultural decline in the 20th century? What is the best case for arguing that 20th-century Western history does <u>not</u> suggest cultural decline? If the West is in decline by the late 20th century, what might be done about it? Does world history suggest that decline is reversible?

WESTERN CULTURE

As with leading social trends, Western culture in the 20th century displayed important creativity and change, but also signs of tension. Artists and composers stressed stylistic innovation, as against older traditions and even the efforts of the previous generation. Scientific work flourished, as the West remained the center of most fundamental inquiry in the theoretical sciences. But complex discoveries, such as the principle of relativity in physics, qualified older ideas that nature can be captured in a few sweeping scientific laws. And the sheer specialization of scientific research removed much of it from ready public understanding. Because no clear unifying assumptions captured the essence of formal intellectual activity in the contemporary West, neutral terms such as *modern* or *postmodern* were used even in the artistic field. Disciplines that once provided an intellectual overview, such as philosophy, declined in the 20th century or were transformed into specialized research fields; many philosophers, for example, turned to the scientific study of language, while sweeping political theory virtually disappeared. And while work in theology continued among both Catholic and Protestant thinkers, it no longer commanded center stage in intellectual life. No emphasis was placed on an integrated approach, as Western intellectual life developed with specialized branches, and no agreement was reached on what constitutes an essential understanding of human endeavor.

The dynamism of scientific research continued to form the clearest central thread in Western culture after 1920. Growing science faculties commanded greatest prestige in the expanding universities. Individual scientists made striking discoveries, while a veritable army of researchers cranked out more specific findings than scientists had ever before produced. In addition, the wider public continued to maintain a faith that science held the keys to understanding nature and society and to improving technology and human life. Finally, while scientific findings varied widely, a belief in a central scientific method persisted: Form a rational hypothesis, test that hypothesis through experiment or observation, and emerge with a generalization that will show regularities in physical behaviors and thus provide human reason with a means of systematizing and even predicting such behaviors. No other approach to understanding in Western culture has had such power or widespread adherence.

By the 1930s, physicists began to experiment with bombarding basic matter with *neutrons,* or particles that carry no electric charge; this work was to culminate during World War II in the development of the atomic bomb. Research in physics continued after World War II with a combination of increasingly sophisticated means of observation, made possible by improved telescopes, atom smashers, and then lasers and space satellites, and the complex mathematical theories facilitated by the theory of relativity. Astronomers made substantial progress in identifying additional galaxies and other phenomena in space; the debate also continued about the nature of matter.

Breakthroughs in biology primarily involved genetics. The identification in the 1860s of principles of inheritance received wide attention only after 1900. By the 1920s, researchers who used the increasingly familiar fruit fly had exact rules for genetic transmission. Discovery in the 1950s by British and American scientists of the structure of the basic genetic unit, the famous "double helix" pattern of deoxyribonucleic acid (DNA), advanced the understanding of how genetic information is transmitted and how it can be altered.

Fundamental discoveries in physics and biology, though hard to grasp even by the educated public, promoted the idea of science as penetrating the mysteries of the universe. They also furthered the relationship between science and technology. Physicists spearheaded research into atomic weaponry and atomic power. During and after World War II, they helped develop missiles and other spacecraft. Biologists produced major improvements in health care. New drugs, beginning with penicillin in 1928, revolutionized the treatment of common diseases, while immunization virtually eliminated scourges such as diphtheria. Genetics itself, by the 1970s, gave rise to a host of industries that utilized scientific principles to produce new medicines, seeds, and pesticides.

The new science displayed some troubling features, even apart from its use in the weapons of destruction or its sheer complexity. The physical world was no longer considered to be neatly regulated as it had been by Newtonian physics. Many other phenomena came to be perceived as relative and unpredictable. Genetics made it clear that evolution proceeded by a series of random accidents, not through any consistent pattern. Use of the rational, scientific method thus has not produced the kind of tidy world view that was prevalent a century or so ago, and the resultant uncertainties have influenced some artists in their attempts to convey an irrational, relativist universe. Yet in the public mind, partly because the new science is so hard to understand, the belief in progress, defined both as better technology and as rational penetration of nature, largely persisted.

The rational method, broadly conceived, also advanced in the social sciences from 1920 onward. In economics, while sweeping theories were downplayed, quantitative models of economic cycles or business behavior increasingly gained ground. Work by the British economist John Keynes, stressing the importance of government spending to compensate for loss of purchasing power during a depression, played a great role in the policies of the American New Deal and efforts by European planners to control the economic cycles after World War II. In psychology, the work by Sigmund Freud on the human unconscious and its role in mental disturbance gained increasing attention; while no single psychological theory predominated, the idea of using research to probe both conscious thought and irrational impulse won growing acceptance.

Like the sciences, the social sciences became increasingly diverse and specialized. Like the sciences also, many social scientists sought practical applications for their work. Psychologists became involved, for example, not only in dealing with mental illness but in trying to promote greater work efficiency. Governments called on economists for their advice, particularly after World War II when their forecasting attempts formed the basis of economic planning. Great diversity existed within the social sciences, and many individual researchers, like their scientific counterparts, worked on small problems of data gathering and manipulation. The rise of anthropology in the 1920s, and the development of social history as a branch of inquiry into human behavior, swam against the social scientific current by pointing to the importance of diversity and chronology in understanding human life. Most leading social scientists, however, continued to emphasize the quest for consistency in human and social behavior. After World War II the increasing use of mathematical models and laboratory experiments in the social sciences enhanced this emphasis.

Most 20th-century artists, concerned with capturing the world through impressions, worked against the grain of science and social science. Painting became increasingly nonrepresentational. The cubist movement, headed by Pablo Picasso, rendered familiar objects as geometrical shapes; after cubism, modern art moved even further from normal perception, stressing purely geometrical design or wild swirls of color. The focus was on mood, the individual reaction of viewers to the individual reality of the artist. Musical composition involved the use of dissonance and experimentation with new scales; after World War II, a growing interest in electronic instrumentation added to this diversity. In poetry the use of unfamiliar forms, ungrammatical constructions, and sweeping imagery continued the movement of the later 19th century. In literature the novel remained dominant, but it turned toward the exploration of moods and personalities.

Marcel Duchamp, using a modified cubist style, sought dramatic visual effect in an approach characteristic of Western art from the 1920s onward.

The arts in the 20th-century West were thus characterized by unprecedented diversity, by a conscious effort to seek new forms, and by a focus on the individual and mood, rather than on some agreed-upon objective reality. These emphases, as noted earlier, joined with science in certain ways: They provided the artistic equivalent of relativity, and they certainly stressed the importance of the unconscious. But a vast gulf grew between the scientific approach and the artistic framework as to how reality can be captured and, to an extent, what constitutes reality.

Many people ignored the leading modern artists and writers in favor of more commercial artistic productions and popular stories. The gap that had opened earlier between avant-garde art and public taste generally continued. Some politicians, including Adolf Hitler, campaigned against what they saw as the decadence and immorality of modern art, urging a return to more traditional styles. And certainly art did not hold its own against the growing prestige of science.

Yet the artistic vision was not simply a preoccupation of artists. Designs and sculptures based on abstract art began to grace public places from the 1920s onward; furnishings and films also reflected the modernist themes. Most revealing of a blend between art, modern technology, and public taste was the development of a characteristic 20th-century architectural style, the "modern" or "international" style. Use of new materials, such as reinforced concrete and massive sheets of glass, allowed the abandonment of much that was traditional in architecture. Need for new kinds of buildings, particularly for office use, and the growing cost of urban space also encouraged the introduction of new forms such as the skyscraper, pioneered in the United States. In general, the modern style of architecture sought to develop individually distinct buildings—sharing the goal of modern art to defy conventional taste and cultivate the unique—while conveying a sense of space and freedom from natural constraints. Soaring structures, free-floating columns, and new combinations of angles and curves were features that described leading Western buildings in the 20th century. Following World War II, when reconstruction in Europe and the expansion of new centers in the West and Southwest of the United States provided massive opportunities for building, the face of urban space in Western society was greatly transformed.

Artistic innovation thus played an important role in Western society in the 20th century. Inherently controversial, it seemed to provide an alternative to the regularized world of mechanized industry and rationalistic science. The result has been no unified culture, but a set of tensions and options that can be creative for society as a whole, as well as meaningful to many individuals.

There have been a few unifying themes between the artistic and the scientific approaches, as both explored elements of the human unconscious or reflected a growing uncertainty about the benevolence and clear rationality of nature and human nature. A constant quest for the new has been another feature, as artists sought new styles and scientists sought new discoveries. Furthermore, Western culture in the 20th century, both in art and in science, has become largely secular. Individual artists, writers, and scientists may proclaim religious faith, but the churches have long since lost control over basic style or content. In Western Europe, despite an important reform movement within the Catholic church that cut down traditional ceremonies in favor of more direct contact between priests and worshipers,

The skyscraper, launched first in the United States, became a major expression of artistic innovation and dramatic new structural materials, including novel uses of glass. This Chicago tower was designed by the European master, Ludwig Mies van der Rohe.

religion played a minor role in both formal and popular culture. Regular church attendance fell, attracting only five percent of the British population, for example, by the 1970s. Increasing use of cremation, rather than burial, showed radical change in traditional Christian approaches to death. In the United States, religion maintained a greater hold, and both church attendance and popular belief remained at higher levels than elsewhere in Western society. The United States also saw, both in the 1920s and again after World War II, a greater variety of popular revival movements and attempts to use religion to maintain or restore traditional values.

On the whole, however, Western people participated in ongoing change in beliefs in the 20th century, with the secular focus predominating. Here was one area where the West actively participated in and helped to shape larger world trends. Before 1950 new beliefs often came in the form of political ideologies, with passionate commitments to fascist nationalism or to communism. More pervasive was the growing attachment to consumer goods and to a scientific outlook. Feminism, for example, strived for the same kind of material rewards and opportunities for individual expansion for women as for men. Growing use of doctors and hospitals showed a desire to place illness and death in a scientific framework, as Western nations began, after 1945, to pay up to 15 percent of their total incomes into efforts to stave off disease. While sweeping ideologies declined in the West, the commitment to a secular value system advanced steadily.

Western culture was not a monopoly of European civilization in the 20th century. Western art forms, particularly in architecture, spread widely, because of their practicality and their currency in what remained a highly influential society. The achievements of Western science, at least those related to technology and medicine, often had to be taken into account by societies seeking their own industrial development. Western art and science were, by the same token, greatly enriched by many practitioners from other cultures—by Japanese artists, for example, or Indian medical researchers and computer scientists. Elements of Western culture thus have now become international, and we will have to trace their interweaving into a number of other civilizations. Yet no other culture, not even the Japanese, created quite the same balance between an overwhelming interest in science and a frenzied concern for stylistic innovation and individual expression in the arts.

CONCLUSION

WILL THE REAL WEST PLEASE STAND UP?

To some observers the West in the 20th century was dominated by the futilities and barbarianisms of the interwar years: No superficial recovery could undo these wounds or make good these failures. This despairing judgment might be compounded by the renewed uncertainties of Western life in the 1970s and 1980s and the growing impact of the decline in world dominance that the interwar years had launched.

Other observers saw Western trends in terms of some ongoing dilemmas raised by industrialization. They noted the dualism present in formal culture and popular outlook since the 19th century. Western intellectuals thus insisted on the primacy of rational inquiry, while relying on artistic forms that seemed bent on portraying a world gone mad. Ordinary Europeans and Americans accepted a disciplined work environment that stressed control over emotion while reveling in scenes of violence and sexual ecstasy in their leisure hours, sometimes embellished as well by the use of drugs.

ADJUSTING TO INDUSTRIAL SOCIETY

Contemporary Western society reflected tensions between industrial values and Western traditions that were exacerbated in the 20th century. On the one hand, the society encouraged children to think of themselves as individuals, to rise above their parents' achievements if possible, to adjust to new work opportunities. Leisure interests appealed to individual pleasure seeking. But individualism was severely curtailed by the growing bureaucratization of society. Most jobs involved routine activities, controlled by an elaborate supervisory apparatus; individual initiative counted for little in factories as well as in the offices of giant corporations. Leisure, appealing to individual self-expression in one sense, generally meant mass, commercially manipulated outlets for all but a handful of venturesome souls. By the 1950s television watching had become far and away the leading recreational interest of Western peoples, and most television fare was deliberately standardized. Ironically, individualism and its outlets in consumer behavior often made collective protest against bureaucratization and routine extremely difficult. One of the reasons for the decline of organized labor throughout the West was workers' growing need to spend time earning money for a new car or using the new car they had.

To critics within Western society and without, Western society at times seemed badly confused. Poverty and job boredom coexisted with affluence and continued appeals to the essential value of work. Youth protest—including defiant costumes and pulsating rock music—family instability, and growing crime might be signs of a fatally flawed society. Rising rates of suicide and increasing incidence of mental illness were other troubling symptoms. At the least, Western society continued to display the strains of change.

Western civilization, in sum, continued to be distinctive for a mixture of old and new reasons. Headed by the United States, it led the world, by the 1960s, in the use of mind-altering drugs. The burgeoning leisure culture involved many Westerners with an interest in sexuality and sexual symbolism profoundly shocking to people from many other societies. The West also maintained a distinctive commitment to liberal democracy, and when Latin America and then Eastern Europe looked to political change in the 1970s and 1980s, they turned largely to Western models. Germany reunited in 1990, for example, as East Germans sought both the affluence and the political freedom they saw among their western cousins.

The West also remained closely tied to larger world currents. It continued to organize much world trade, as its economy fairly steadily expanded. Western developments in technology, science, and popular culture continued to have international impact. Western feminism, a newer force, helped inspire feminist interests in other societies, such as Japan. At the same time, growing rates of immigration to the West and the increasing impact of economic competition from industry in other societies made it clear that the West's links to the rest of the world were not entirely determined by the West itself.

A POSTINDUSTRIAL AGE?

Many people in Western society, indeed, believe they are facing greater changes than ever before, whether for better or for worse. By the late 1960s a new concept of a postindustrial society took shape both in Western Europe and in North America. The idea was that Western society was leading in a transformation as fundamental as the Industrial Revolution had been. The rise of a service economy, according to this argument propounded by people in different strata of the country, promised as many shifts as the rise of an industrial economy had done. Control of knowledge, rather than control of goods, would be the key to the postindustrial social structure. Technology would allow expansion of factory production with a shrinking labor force, and attention would shift to the generation and control of information. The advent of new technology, particularly the computer, supported the postindustrial concept by applying to knowledge transmission the same potential technological revolution the steam engine had brought to manufacturing.

Changes in the role of women paralleled the postindustrial concept, and some observers began to talk of a postindustrial family in which two equal spouses would pool their earnings in a high-consumption life-style. Postindustrial cities would increasingly become entertainment centers, as most work could now be decentralized in suburbs, linked by the omnipresent computer. Postindustrial politics were less clearly defined, though some commentators noted that the old party structure might loosen as new, service-sector voters sought issues more appropriate to their interests. The rise of environmental and feminist concerns, which cut across older political alignments, thus might prove an opening wedge to an unpredictable future for the West.

The postindustrial society is not established fact, of course. Important continuities with earlier social forms, including political values and cultural directions, suggest that new technologies might modify rather than revolutionize Western industrial society. It is clear, however, that Western society has taken on important new characteristics, ranging from age brackets to occupational structure, that differentiate it from the initial industrial patterns generated in the 19th century. And this fact, even if more modest than the visions of some postindustrial forecasters, raises a vital question for the West and the world: How would a rapidly changing, advanced industrial society fit in a world that has yet fully to industrialize? How could the concerns of an affluent, urban, fad-conscious Westerner coexist with the values of the world's peasant majority?

FURTHER READINGS

For an excellent general survey see Robert Paxton's *Europe in the 20th Century* (1985). See also Morris Janowitz's *The Last Half Century: Social Change and Politics in America* (1978). A good factual compendium is Tony Howarth's *Twentieth-Century History: The World Since 1900* (1979).

Some excellent national interpretations enhance coverage. See A. F. Havighurst's *Twentieth-Century Britain* (1982) and John Ardagh's highly readable *The New French Revolution: A Social and Economic Survey of France* (1968) plus *France in the 1980's* (1982). Volker Berghahn's *Modern Germany: Society, Economy and Politics in the 20th Century* (1983) is also useful.

On Europe between the wars, Charles Maier's *Recasting Bourgeois Europe* (1975) is a penetrating comparative approach. On fascism and Nazism, see F. Carsten's *The Rise of Fascism* (1980) and S. Payne's *Fascism: Comparison and Definition* (1984). David Schoenbaum's *Hitler's Social Revolution* (1980) is an excellent study of how Nazism worked in practice. See also Gerald Fleming's *Hitler and the Final Solution* (1984), on the holocaust. R. Stromberg's *Intellectual History of Modern Europe* (1966) and K. D. Bracher's *Age of Ideologies: A History of Political Thought in the Twentieth Century* (1989) provide a factual framework in a complex area. See also H. S. Hughes's *Consciousness and Society* (1976).

On post–World War II social and economic trends see C. Kindleberger's *Europe's Postwar Growth* (1967); V. Bogdanor and R. Skidelsky, eds., *The Age of Affluence* (1970); and R. Dahrendorf, ed., *Europe's Economy in Crisis* (1982). On the welfare state, see Stephen Cohen's *Modern Capitalist Planning: The French Model* (1977) and E. S. Einhorn and J. Logue's *Welfare States in Hard Times* (1982).

Important overviews of recent European history are Walter Laqueur's *Europe Since Hitler* (1982), R. von Albertini's *Decolonization* (1982), Helen Wallace and others' *Policy-Making in the European Community* (1983), and Alfred Grosser's *The Western Alliance* (1982).

THEMES IN EASTERN EUROPE

EASTERN EUROPE AND THE WORLD

THE RUSSIAN REVOLUTION

- **ANALYSIS:** 20th-Century Revolutions

BUILDING SOVIET SOCIETY

- **DOCUMENT:** Socialist Realism

THE SOVIET UNION AS A SUPERPOWER

THE EXPLOSION OF THE 1980S AND 1990S

- **CONCLUSION:** What Next?
- **FURTHER READINGS**

1917 Russian Revolution; Bolshevik takeover (October)

1918–1919 Independent smaller nations in eastern Europe

1921 Lenin's New Economic Policy

1923 New constitution in Russia

1927 Stalin in full power

1928 Beginning of collectivization of agriculture and five-year plans

1936–1938 Stalin's great purges

1939 Signing of Russo-German pact; Soviet invasion of eastern Poland and Finland

1941 German invasion of Soviet Union

1943 Soviet army pushes west

1945–1948 Soviet takeover of Eastern Europe

1949 Soviet Union develops atomic bomb

1953 Stalin's death

1955 Formation of Warsaw Pact

1956 Stalinism attacked by Khrushchev

1956 Hungarian revolt and its suppression

36

The Soviet Union and Eastern Europe

INTRODUCTION. East European history in the 20th century has been dominated by the glare of Russia's 1917 revolution, one of the great upheavals of modern times. The varied discontents that had swelled during the later 19th century, heightened by the stresses of early industrialization, partial reform, and an inept tsarist administration, came together in a rush in 1917, under the further pressure of world war. Much of Russian history thereafter, particularly during the 1920s and 1930s but to some extent into the 1990s, derived from the revolution's impact and the attempt to build a society on new, communist principles.

Russia's history merged unprecedentedly with that of the rest of Eastern Europe after 1945, as Soviet-dominated regimes were installed in most of the smaller countries after a confused interwar period. Soviet control was not complete, and important discontents boiled to the surface particularly after 1985, but there were more common directions in East European institutions than ever before in the region's history.

There are two reasons why Soviet history also had an unprecedented importance in wider world history during the 20th century. The Russian Revolution seemed to many people, in many parts of the world, a vital beacon; the example of the revolution, as well as the rise of communist movements to some extent patterned after and guided by Russian leadership, played a vital role in the history of most societies after 1917. China and Cuba used Russian models though adding their own twists; revolutionaries elsewhere in Latin America and Asia, and also in Africa and the West, drew inspiration from the Soviet system.

Spurred by the revolution and ongoing industrialization, the new Soviet Union also emerged after 1945 as one of the two great world powers. Soviet economic and military

1961 Berlin Wall erected

1962 Cuban missile crisis

1968 Revolt in Czechoslovakia and its repression; Soviet policy (Brezhnev doctrine) proclaims right to intervene in any Socialist country

1979 Uprisings in Poland and their suppression

1979 Soviet invasion of Afghanistan

1985 Gorbachev to power

1988 New Soviet constitution; establishment of the Congress of People's Deputies

1988–1989 Liberalization movements throughout Eastern Europe; new constitutions, economic reforms; nationalities agitation in Soviet Union

1990 Gorbachev selected as President; new elections throughout much of Eastern Europe; economic unification in Germany

A.D. 1960 A.D. 1980

influence burst beyond Europe and Asia to have direct effects literally around the globe, as a Soviet-United States rivalry set a basic framework for world diplomacy in the post-World War II decades. The Soviet role must thus be added to the factors considered in the intensifying world exchange of the 20th century. For several decades after 1945, as Western colonial controls receded, Soviet ideological influence seemed to rival the West's cultural outreach in the world at large.

Soviet history during the century involves several major themes. Russia, already an important civilization, should be examined in relationship to its own past. The revolution commands analysis in its own right as one of the great phenomena in contemporary history. The Soviet role as world power must be assessed, but so should its failure to match Western economic dynamism after the 1950s, as Eastern Europe, though industrialized, settled into growing stagnation. Finally, an explosion of new uncertainties, opening up after 1985, raises vital questions not only about the Soviet Union, but about the cold war, Eastern Europe, and the future of revolution.

One means of sorting out the complex history of the Soviet Union and its 20th-century role involves division into four subperiods. The years from 1917 to 1928 were dominated by the revolution and its initial installation. Then, from 1928 to 1945, the dictatorship of Joseph Stalin commandeered the revolutionary process. During the first part of this period, the Soviet Union attempted considerable isolation from wider world contacts, and the aftermath of this isolation affected later Soviet history. The years from 1945 to 1985, as Stalinism was modified, saw the emergence of the Soviet Union as a world superpower and the incorporation of Eastern Europe into the Soviet empire. Finally, since 1985 a host of innovations and uncertainties have shaken the Soviet system, dissolved its empire, and raised questions about survival of the Soviet state itself.

THEMES IN EASTERN EUROPE

The Russian Revolution of 1917 and the spread of communism throughout most of Eastern Europe after World War II embraced several subsidiary themes. The revolution redefined Russia's relationship with Western civilization, but it did not end the ambivalent attraction-rejection reactions that had surfaced earlier. The theme of Russian expansion resumed in the postrevolutionary decades, after a retreat during an initial consolidation period. To Western eyes Russian expansion seemed an obvious resumption of older tsarist goals, though to Soviet leaders themselves a different set of criteria, including the importance of spreading revolutionary truth and the need to prevent a recurrence of German attack, seemed more salient.

Revolutionary Russia also resumed and quickened the process of industrialization, at the same time temporarily removing Russia from the intricate involvements with the world economy that had been taking shape during the 19th century. Russian industrialization after 1917 resembled industrializations elsewhere in many ways, with some common social results including the rapid growth of cities and changes in family styles. It was also a unique product, however, concentrating unusually on heavy industry and designed to protect Russia's independence from the world economy and Western modes of exchange, rather than to gain new power within the world commercial network. As the Soviets built their society and completed the basic industrialization framework, they greatly enhanced their strength in world affairs, but on somewhat distinctive foundations.

The theme of change dominates East European history during the 20th century, because of the great revolution that opened the contemporary era in this region and then the extension of Russian influence to virtually the entire civilization. Yet even great changes must be balanced against continuities from the past. Earlier political and foreign policy traditions intertwined with the effects of revolution within the Soviet Union. Communist rule and industrialization greatly altered the lives of Russian peasants, but a peasant problem remained, in an interesting if muted echo from tsarist days. Aspects of Western culture were embraced more eagerly than before, particularly in scientific areas, but new ambiguities surfaced in relation to Western art and popular culture—again a redefinition of an older theme. The smaller East European nations also recalled their past in different kinds of relationships with Soviet military dominance and political guidance. Seldom had conditions of life changed as rapidly in Eastern Europe as they did in the decades after 1917, yet earlier values persisted as well, including intense ethnic identities. The ferment after 1985 showed how many traditional impulses had survived, even as another new era dawned.

EASTERN EUROPE AND THE WORLD

The Russian Revolution and the later extension of Soviet control over Eastern Europe isolated this region in world affairs to some extent. Russian revolutionaries, initially hopeful of sparking risings elsewhere, pulled back by the later 1920s, arguing that they could build an industrial, socialist society by themselves. Russia's post–World War II empire in Eastern Europe, correspondingly, was closed off by walls and fences.

Yet developments in Eastern Europe had considerable impact on the 20th-century world. The example of the Russian Revolution inspired many radicals in Asia, Africa, and Latin America—as well as in the West—as a sign that a society could throw off a Western aura and carve out its own path to independence and justice. The Soviet Union's superpower status after World War II brought it into new economic, cultural, and diplomatic contact with various regions of the world. Smaller East European nations participated in this outreach as well. Russian influence on China, Vietnam, Cuba, and other regions was considerable and constituted a new force in contemporary world history.

By the same token Russian isolation could not ultimately be preserved. It contradicted the Soviet Union's far-flung activities as a superpower. The growing strength of international economic and cultural contacts attracted many Russians—leaders and ordinary people alike—who gained some sense of the wider world around them. When the Soviet empire exploded in the 1980s, its collapse resulted in part from expectations fed by international contacts, and it opened the whole region to unprecedented new international influences.

East European history in the 20th century has an undeniable flavor of its own, combining earlier traditions and distinctive events in the region. At the same time, East European developments helped shape the new world framework and was shaped by it in turn.

THE RUSSIAN REVOLUTION

In March 1917, strikes and food riots broke out in Russia's capital, St. Petersburg (later renamed Leningrad, briefly known as Petrograd in an effort to Russianize and secularize its original name, and renamed St. Petersburg in 1991). The outbursts, spurred by wartime misery but more basically protesting the conditions of early industrialization set against incomplete rural reform and an unresponsive political system, quickly assumed revolutionary proportions. The rioters called not just for more food and work but for a new political regime. A council of workers, called a *soviet,* took over the city government and arrested the tsar's ministers, after some brutal attempts at military repression. Unable to rely on his own soldiers the tsar abdicated, thus ending the long period of imperial rule.

LIBERALISM TO COMMUNISM

For eight months a liberal provisional government struggled to rule the country. Russia seemed thus to launch its revolution on a basis similar to France in 1789, where a liberal period set change in motion. Like Western liberals, revolutionary leaders such as Alexander Kerensky were eager to see genuine parliamentary rule, religious and other freedoms, and a host of political and legal changes. But liberalism was not deeply rooted in Russia, if only because of the small middle class, so the analogies with the first phase of the French Revolution cannot be pressed too far. Furthermore, Russia's revolution took place in far more adverse circumstances, given the pressures of participation in the world war. The initial liberal leaders were eager to maintain their war effort, which associated their link with democratic France and Britain. Yet the nation was desperately war weary, and prolongation drastically worsened economic conditions while public morale plummeted. Liberal

Moscow workers guard the Bolshevik headquarters during the Russian Revolution of 1917.

leaders also held back from the massive land reforms expected by the peasantry, for in good middle-class fashion they respected existing property arrangements and did not wish to rush into social change before a legitimate new political structure could be established. Hence serious popular unrest continued, and in November (October, by the Russian calendar) a second revolution took place that expelled liberal leadership and soon brought to power the radical, Bolshevik wing of the Social Democratic party (soon renamed the Communist party) and Lenin, its dynamic chief.

The revolution was a godsend to Lenin, though he had long been writing of Russia's readiness for a communist revolt because of the power of international capitalism and its creation—even in a society that had not directly passed through middle-class rule—of a massive proletariat. Lenin quickly gained a strong position among the urban workers' councils in the major cities. This corresponded to his rooted belief that revolution should come not from literal mass action, but from tightly organized cells whose leaders boasted a coherent plan of action.

Once the liberals were toppled, Lenin and the Bolsheviks faced several immediate problems. One problem, the war, they handled by signing a humiliating peace treaty with Germany that gave up huge sections of western Russia in return for an end of hostilities. This treaty was soon nullified by Germany's defeat at the hands of the Western allies, but Russia was ignored at the Versailles peace conference—treated as a pariah by the fearful Western powers—and found considerable territory converted into nation-states. A revived Poland built heavily on land Russia had controlled for over a century, and new, small Baltic states cut into even earlier acquisitions. Still, while Russia harbored deep grievances against the Versailles treaty, which would later help motivate renewed expansionism, the early end to the war was vital to Lenin's consolidation of power.

The second problem faced at the end of 1917 was that Lenin and the Bolsheviks, though they had gained a majority role in the leading urban soviets, were not the most popular revolutionary party. The November seizure of power had created the Council of People's Commissars, headed by Lenin and drawn from soviets across the nation, to govern the state. But a parliamentary election had already been called, and this produced a clear majority for the Social Revolutionary party, which emphasized peasant support and rural reform. Lenin, however, shut down the Parliament, replacing it with a Bolshevik-dominated Congress of Soviets. He pressed the Social Revolutionaries to disband, arguing that "the people voted for a party which

Other voices of revolution were heard at a 1917 women's demonstration. Well into the 1920s, revolutionary committees debated major reforms in the lives of women, and a variety of women's groups added strong voices to the ferment of change.

Eastern Europe and the Soviet Union, 1919–1939

no longer existed." Russia was thus to have no Western-style, multiparty system but rather a Bolshevik monopoly in the name of the true people's will. Indeed, Communist control of the government apparatus persisted from this point to 1989, a record for continuity far different from the fate of revolutionary groups earlier in the Western past.

Russia's revolution did, however, produce a familiar backlash that revolutionaries in other eras would have recognized quite easily: foreign hostility and, even more important, domestic resistance. The world's leading nations were appalled at the Communist success, which threatened principles of property and freedom they cherished deeply. They also, as settled regimes, disliked the unexpected, and some were directly injured by Russia's renunciation of its heavy foreign debts. So there was an attempt at intervention, recalling the attacks on France in 1792. Britain, France, the United States, and Japan all sent troops, but this intervention, while it heightened Russian suspicion of outsiders, did relatively little damage. The Western powers, exhausted by World War I, pulled out quickly, and even Japan, though interested in lingering in Asiatic Russia, stepped back fairly soon.

The internal civil war, which foreign troops slightly abetted, was a more serious matter, as it raged from 1918 to 1921. Tsarist generals, religiously faithful peasants, and many minority nationalities made common cause against the communist regime. Their efforts were aided by continuing economic distress, the normal result of revolutionary disar-

Civil war and peasant resistance to collectivization measures dramatically reduced food supplies, ultimately forcing a temporary change in government policy. Children were the victims of the famine of 1922.

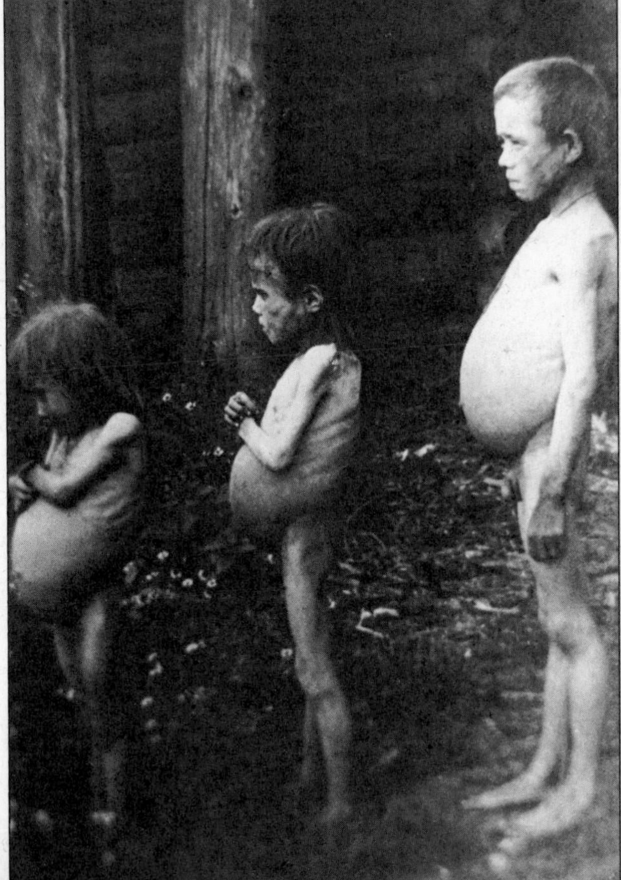

ray but heightened by earlier communist measures. Lenin had quickly decreed a redistribution of land to the peasantry and also launched a *nationalization*, or state takeover, of basic industry. Many already landed peasants resented the loss of property and incentive, and in reaction lowered food production and the goods sent to markets. Industrial nationalization somewhat similarly disrupted manufacturing. Famine and unemployment created more economic hardship than the war had generated, which added fuel to the civil war fires. Even workers revolted in several cities, threatening the new regime's most obvious social base as well as its ideological mainstay.

STABILIZATION OF THE NEW REGIME

Order was restored, however, on several key foundations. First, a powerful new army was constructed under the leadership of Leon Trotsky, which recruited able generals and masses of loyal conscripts. This Red Army was an early beneficiary of two ongoing sources of strength for Communist Russia: a willingness to use people of humble background but great ability, who could rise to great heights under the new order but who had been doomed to immobility under the old system; and a capacity to inspire mass loyalty in the name of an end to previous injustice and a promise of a brighter future. Next, economic disarray was reduced in 1921 when Lenin issued his New Economic Policy (NEP). Intended as a stopgap measure in recognition of the real-life barriers to immediate construction of communism, the NEP promised considerable freedom of action for small businessmen and peasant landowners. The state continued to set basic economic policies, but its efforts were now combined with individual initiative. Under this temporary policy, food production began to recover and the regime gained time to prepare the more durable structures of the Communist system.

By 1923 the Bolshevik Revolution was an accomplished fact. A new constitution set up a federal system of socialist republics. This system recognized the multinational character of the nation, known now not as Russia but the Union of Soviet Socialist Republics. The dominance of ethnic Russians was preserved in the central state apparatus, however, and certain groups, notably Jews, were given no distinct representation. Since the separate republics were firmly controlled by the national Communist party, and since basic decisions were as firmly centralized, the impact of the new nationalities policy was somewhat mixed. It was also true, however, that direct nationalities protest declined notably from the 1920s until the late 1980s.

The apparatus of the central state was another mixture of appearance and reality. A Supreme Soviet had many of the trappings of a parliament and was elected by universal suffrage. But competition in elections was normally prohibited, which meant that the Communist party easily controlled this body that, in any event, served mainly to ratify decisions made by the party's central executive. Parallel systems of central bureaucracy and party bureaucracy further confirmed the Communist monopoly on power and the ability to control major decisions from the center. The Soviet political system was elaborated over time. A new constitution in the 1930s spoke glowingly of human rights. In fact, the Communists had quickly reestablished an authoritarian system, making it more efficient than its tsarist predecessor had been, complete with updated versions of political police to assure loyalty.

Along with its political and constitutional construction, the Soviet regime grappled with other key definitional issues early in the 1920s. Rivalries among leaders at the top had to be sorted out. Lenin sickened and then died in 1924, creating an unexpected leadership gap. A number of key lieutenants jostled for power, including the Red Army's flamboyant Trotsky and a Communist party stalwart of worker origins who had taken the name Stalin, meaning steel. After a few years of jockeying, Stalin emerged as undisputed leader of the Soviet state, his victory a triumph also for party control over other branches of government. Stalin's accession was more than a personal bureaucratic issue, however, for Stalin represented a strongly nationalist version of communism, in contrast to the more ideological and international visions of many rivals. At the revolution's outset Lenin had believed that the Russian rising would be merely a prelude to a sweeping Communist upheaval throughout the Western, industrial world. Many revolutionary leaders actively encouraged Communist parties in the West and set up a *Comintern*, or Communist International office, to guide this process. But revolution did not spill over, despite a few brief risings in places such as Hungary and Germany right after World War I. Under Stalin, the revolutionary leadership, while still committed in theory to an international movement, pulled back to concentrate on Russian developments pure and simple—building "socialism in one country," as Stalin put it. Stalin in many ways represented the anti-Western strain in Russian tradition, though in new guise. Rival leaders were killed or expelled, and rival visions of the revolution were downplayed.

The Russian Revolution was one of the most successful uprisings in human history. Building on widespread if diverse popular discontent and a firm belief in centralized leadership, the Bolsheviks beat back powerful odds to create a new, though not totally unprecedented, political regime. They used features of the tsarist system, but they managed to propel a wholly new leadership group to power not only at the top, but at all levels of the bureaucracy and army. The tsar and his hated ministers were gone, mostly executed, but so was the overweening aristocratic class that had loomed so large in Russian history for centuries. And after the first years the revolutionaries never had to look backward; they avoided even a partial restoration of the "old regime" as had occurred in England after its 17th-century Civil War as well as in France after Napoleon's defeat. The Bolsheviks, in contrast, managed to create a new political, economic, and cultural structure without serious internal challenge between the initial, chaotic years and the late 1980s.

Serious revolutions, however, do not end quickly. While the formal revolutionary period consumed but a few vivid years, the actual force of the revolution continued easily until the mid-1930s—that is, through a period of fascinating experimentation during the 1920s and into the establishment of a full Stalinist regime from 1928 onward.

ANALYSIS
20TH-CENTURY REVOLUTIONS

Never in world history have there been as many revolutions, in not one but a host of different civilizations, as in the 20th century. The roster includes a minor and a major revolution in Russia; one or perhaps two major revolutions in China (the question concerns whether to view the whole span from 1911 to 1947 as a single revolutionary process or a sequence of two outbreaks); a major upheaval in Mexico; then, much later, significant revolutions in Cuba, Bolivia, and Nicaragua; and quite recently a revolution in Iran. In addition to these major cases, other possible candidates include the Philippines, where the replacement of strongman rule in 1986 had revolutionary overtones but where it remains too soon to judge whether significant changes in social arrangements are involved. These revolutions do not count the important shifts to and from authoritarian and democratic regimes in other Latin-American countries, as well as in Africa and the Middle East, where the heavy popular involvement characteristic of a revolution as opposed to a coup d'etat was not fully present. Also omitted are the recent, largely nonviolent transformations in Eastern Europe.

The abundance of 20th-century revolutions raises vital questions about possible patterns and common causation, which are easier, however, to evoke than to answer. Contemporary revolutions occur in societies where significant changes are under way—such as the earliest phases of industrialization in Russia, the economic development undertaken by the prerevolutionary regime in Iran, or the initial political and educational changes in China—but where these changes have not yet had a chance to coalesce. The revolutionary moment, in other words, sees some groups antagonized by the shifts that have occurred and other groups eager for still more rapid change. Relatedly, 20th-century revolutions, like earlier revolts, always involve a number of different groups with diverse demands and revolutionary attributes, some capable of assuming political controls, others willing to participate in street violence or rural uprisings. Most of the 20th-century revolutions have a strong peasant component and take place where landlord controls had helped spur rural grievances (in contrast to poor regions where peasant ownership predominated).

The wave of 20th-century revolutions has always involved a prior intellectual buildup. Doctrines of democracy and liberalism, nationalism, or some form of socialism (most often Marxism) have provided the most common ideological spurs, but the Iranian revolution—one of the most distinctive in the group—was dominated by Islamic fundamentalism. Revolutions also, though this is an obvious point, require an absence of effective political outlets for key groups plus a weakening of the established state; strong governments can repress discontent, though it is always possible that too many years of repression will raise new doubts and uncertainties and so lead to a softening of the established order. Most revolutionary cases involve a government structure strong in principle but recently deteriorated due to weak new leaders (the tsarist case, for example) or the aging of an authoritarian figure (as in Mexico, Cuba, and Iran).

Some historians have sought to develop a standard revolutionary dynamic, based, however, on earlier Western models more than 20th-century cases. In this model, revolutions begin with initially liberal impulses, seeking greater freedom and control from below. Then as economic problems continue, and often civil strife and even foreign intervention, the liberal phase gives way to greater authority, even outright dictatorship. Elements of this pattern are visible in several 20th-century cases (such as China, Russia to an extent, Mexico, and Iran briefly) but the authoritarian strand in most instances emerges very quickly. This in turn often reflects an absence of a significant basis for liberalism in the host society, the decline of liberalism as a revolutionary doctrine, and the presence of more experienced revolutionary leaders who know that they must seize the state and use its power if the revolution is to have a chance.

An important common ingredient of 20th-century revolutions is the need to come to terms with Western influence and often to reassert greater national autonomy. Mexico, Russia, and China all grappled with growing Western economic control and cultural influence in the early 20th century, and all tried to come up with alternative development models. Though an array of internal issues is involved in each revolution, the problem of reacting to the West, as well as the objections to the responses developed by the existing regime (often friendlier to Western involvement or at least weaker in its face than the revolutionaries desire), serves as a common bond. Many revolutions thus heighten anti-Western sentiment, at least for a time, and all try to reduce the Western power to interfere with internal affairs. Thus the Russian Revolution reduced foreign business involvement, while Stalinism went on the attack against "decadent" Western cultural influence.

This revolutionary feature helps explain why 20th-century revolutions have generally occurred in societies that had not been Western colonies, at least in their recent past, for in such colonies national independence movements could serve some of the purposes revolutions served elsewhere. Colonial administration often brought some of the changes revolutionaries sought elsewhere, in unseating old-fashioned monarchies for example; independence movements brought new leaders to power and gave larger groups a sense of national pride that made revolution for a time less salient. This may explain why India and most of Africa have avoided revolution to date in the 20th century (just as Latin America did during its first century of independence after 1820).

No sense of a schema for 20th-century revolutions should, however, ignore two basic points. First, each revolution, including of course the Russian, had its own flavor—its own specific causes, its own outcomes. Individual flavor came from distinctive cultural traditions, social balances, and individual leadership. Not every revolution, for example, had a Lenin who could unify and galvanize the whole experience. Second, while 20th-century revolutions share some common ingredients, including previous government heavy-handedness, ideological buildup, peasant or other mass discontent, and anti-Western reactions, it remains impossible to predict where revolution will strike next. Understanding what revolutions are like once they occur, as well as grasping certain common features such as a period of radical isolation and truculence with foreign intervention, is possible on the basis of a sketch of the common revolutionary dynamic. And it is possible to suggest that certain societies are unlikely to face revolution because of the strength of government, social balance, or recency of major change. But revolutions involve enough accident, a sufficiently unusual blend of factors, that precise forecasting defies expertise—whether the expertise comes from the historian or the intelligence community employed by one of the established powers fearful of revolutionary explosion. Right before World War I, an Austrian banker urged investment in the Russian Empire because it had endured so well compared to the harassed regimes of Western Europe; right before the Iranian Revolution, the American Central Intelligence Agency sent back rosy reports of the government's solidity. Revolutions do have patterns, and these patterns suggest a great deal about the dynamic of 20th-century world history in which the phenomenon of revolution has loomed so large. Revolutions must also be evaluated through their spontaneous qualities, their capacity to make predictions look ridiculous.

Questions: How do 20th-century revolutions compare with "liberal" Western revolutions from 1789 to 1848? Will revolutions affect other societies in the 21st century, or has the revolutionary movement exhausted itself?

BUILDING SOVIET SOCIETY

The mid-1920s constituted a lively, experimental period in Soviet history, partly because of jockeying for power at the top of the power pyramid. Despite the absence of Western-style political competition, a host of new groups found a voice. The Communist party, though not eager to recruit too many members lest it lose its tight organization and elite status, encouraged all sorts of subsidiary organizations. Youth movements, women's groups, and particularly organizations of workers all actively debated problems in their social environment and what directions future planning should take. Workers were able to influence management practices, while women's leaders helped carve legal equality and new educational and work opportunities for their constituents.

The atmosphere of excited debate spilled over into such areas as family policy. At various points Soviet policy seemed to downplay the importance of family in favor of individual rights, thus making it easy to obtain divorces or abortions. Ultimately, by the 1930s the pendulum swung back toward greater conservatism, featuring protection of the family unit and an effort to encourage the birthrate, but only after some fascinating fluctuations and experimentalism. One key to the creative mood of these years was the rapid spread of education promoted by the government, plus educational and propaganda activities sponsored by various adult groups. Literacy gained ground quickly. The new educational system was also bent on reshaping popular culture away from older peasant traditions and, above all, religion, and toward beliefs in Communist political analysis and in science. Access to new information, new modes of inquiry, and new values encouraged controversy.

STALINISM

The experimental mood began to fade after 1927, when Joseph Stalin acquired full power over potential rivals. Stalin, eager for authoritarian control, was also anxious to renew the momentum toward socialism that had been deflected by the New Economic Policy and the surge of discussion among many mass organizations. By this point the bulk of the land lay in the hands of a minority of wealthy, commercially oriented peasants, the *kulaks*, who were particularly attuned to a profit-based market agriculture. Rural Russia seemed inclined to parallel earlier Western experience, in dividing the peasantry among relatively innovative owners and a mass of laborers—and this was not socialism. Even in industry, state-run enterprises and planning had only limited effect, as opposed to small private businesses. Stalin devoted himself to a double task: to make the Soviet Union a fully industrial society, and to do so under full control of the state, rather than through private initiative and individual ownership of producing property. In essence, Stalin wanted modernization, but with a revolutionary, noncapitalist twist. And while he was willing to borrow Western techniques and advice, importing a small number of foreign engineers for example, he insisted on Russian control and largely Russian endeavor.

ECONOMIC POLICIES

A massive program to collectivize agriculture began in 1928. *Collectivization* meant the creation of large, state-run farms rather than individual holdings as in the West. Communist party agitators pressed peasants to join in collectives. The collective movement was not only distinctively socialistic; it further offered, at least in theory, the chance to mechanize agriculture most effectively, as collective farms could group scarce equipment such as tractors and harvesters. Collectivization also allowed more efficient control over peasants themselves, as the Soviet state continued (in radical new form) a Russian reluctance to leave peasants to their own devices. Government and party control was desirable not only for political reasons, but also because Stalin's hopes for a speedup of industrialization required that resources be taken from peasants, through taxation, in order to provide capital for industry.

The Russian peasantry responded to collectivization with a decidedly mixed voice. Many laborers, resentful of kulak wealth, initially welcomed the opportunity to have more direct access to land. But most kulaks refused to cooperate voluntarily, often destroying livestock and other property rather than submit to collectivization. Devastating famine resulted from Stalin's insistence on pressing forward. In addition, millions of kulaks were killed or deported to Siberia during the early 1930s, in one of the most brutal oppressions of what turned out to be a brutal century in world history. Gradually, rural resistance collapsed and production began to increase once again; the decimation of the kulaks may indeed have weakened opportunities to oppose Stalin's increasingly authoritarian hold for a generation or more. But collectivization, though increasingly thorough, was not a smash success, for even those peasants who participated often seemed relatively unmotivated. While the collective farms allowed peasants small plots of their own, plus job security and considerable propagandizing by the omnipresent party members, they created an atmosphere of factory-like discipline and rigid planning from above that antagonized many. The centralized planning process allowed few incentives for special efforts and often complicated a smooth flow of supplies and equipment, a problem also exacerbated by the Stalinist regime's priority concentration on the industrial sector. Agricultural production remained a major weakness in the Soviet economy, demanding a higher percentage of the labor force than was common under industrialization.

The collective farms did, however, allow normally adequate if minimal food supplies once the messy transition period had ended, and they did free excess workers to be channeled into the ranks of urban labor. The late 1920s and early 1930s saw a massive flow of unskilled workers into the cities, as Russia's industrialization shifted into high gear.

If Stalin's approach to agriculture had serious flaws, his handling of industry was in most ways a smashing success. A system of five-year plans under the state planning commission began to set clear priorities for industrial development, including expected output levels and new facilities. The government constructed massive factories in metallurgy, mining, and electric power to make Russia an industrial country independent of Western-dominated world banking and trading patterns, with the productive infrastructure also suitable for modern war. There was more than a hint of Peter the Great's policies here, in updating the economy without really Westernizing it, save that industrialization constituted a more massive departure than anything Peter had contemplated. The focus, as earlier, was on heavy industry, which built on Russia's great natural resources and also served to prepare for possible war with Hitler's anti-Communist Germany. This distinctive industrialization, which slighted consumer goods production, was to remain characteristic of the Soviet version of industrial society. Further, Stalin sought to create an alternative not simply to private business ownership but to the profit-oriented market mechanisms of the West. Thus he relied not on price competition but on formal, centralized resource allocation to distribute equipment and supplies. This led to many bottlenecks and considerable waste, as quotas for individual factories were set in Moscow, but there was no question that rapid industrial growth occurred. During the first two five-year plans, to 1937—that is, during the same period the West was mired in the depression—Russia's output of machinery and metal products grew fourteenfold. Russia had become the world's third industrial power, behind Germany and the United States. A long history of backwardness seemed to have ended.

TOWARD AN INDUSTRIAL SOCIETY

The Russian industrialization process, for all its distinctive features, produced many results similar to those in the West. Increasing numbers of Russians were crowded into cities, often cramped in inadequate housing stock—for Russian planners, like earlier Western capitalists, were reluctant to put too many resources into mass housing. Factory discipline was strict as Communist managers sought to instill new habits in a peasant-derived work force. Incentive procedures were introduced to motivate higher production. Particularly capable workers received bonuses and also elaborate public awards for their service to society. At the same time, Communist policy quickly built up a network of welfare services, surpassing the West in this area as well as reversing decades of tsarist neglect. Workers had meeting houses and recreational programs, plus protection in cases of illness and old age. Soviet industrial society provided only modest standards of living at this point, but a host of collective activities compensated to some degree. Finally, while Soviet industry was directed from the top, with no legal outlet for worker grievances—strikes were outlawed, and the only trade union movement was controlled by the party—worker concerns were studied, and identified problems were addressed. Stalinist Russia used force and authority, but it also recognized the importance of maintaining worker support—so, informally, it consulted as well.

TOTALITARIAN RULE

Stalin combined his industrialization program with a new intensification of government police procedures, as he used the party and state apparatus to monopolize power, even more thoroughly than Hitler's totalitarian state attempted. Opponents and imagined opponents of his version of communism were executed. During the great purge of party leaders that culminated in 1937 and 1938, hundreds of people were intimidated into confessing imaginary crimes against the state, and most of them were put to death. Many thousands more were sent to Siberian labor camps. Any possibility of vigorous internal initiative was crushed, as both the state and the Communist party were bent under Stalin's suspicious will. News outlets were monopolized by the state and the party, and informal meetings also risked a visit from the ubiquitous secret police, renamed the MVD (Ministry of Internal Affairs) in 1934. Party congresses and meetings of the executive committee, or *Politburo,* became mere rubber stamps. An atmosphere of terror spread in Russian society.

Stalin's purges, which included top army officials, ironically weakened the nation's ability to respond to growing foreign policy problems, notably the rising threat of Hitler. Soviet diplomatic initiatives after the revolution had been unwontedly modest, given the nation's traditions, largely because of the intense concentration on internal development. Diplomatic relations with major nations were gradually reestablished, as the fact of Communist leadership was accepted, and the Soviet Union was allowed into the League of Nations. A few secret military negotiations, as with Turkey in the early 1920s, showed a flicker of interest in more active diplomacy, and of course the nation continued to encourage and often guide internal Communist party activities in many other countries.

Hitler's rise was a clear signal that more active concern was necessary. A strong Germany was inevitably a threat to Russia from the west, and Hitler was vocal about his scorn for Slavic peoples and communism, about his desire to create a "living room" for Germany to the east. Stalin initially hoped that he could cooperate with the Western democracies in blocking the German threat. The Soviet Union thus tried to participate in a common response to German and Italian intervention during the Spanish civil war in 1936 and 1937. But France and Britain were incapable of forceful action and were in any event almost as suspicious of the Soviets as of the Nazis. So the Soviet Union, unready for war and greatly disappointed in the West, signed the historic agreement with Hitler in 1939. This pact bought some time for greater war preparation, and also enabled Russian troops to attack eastern Poland and Finland in an effort to regain territories lost in World War I. Here was the first sign of a revival of Russia's long interest in conquest, which would be intensified by the experience of World War II.

The awkward honeymoon with Hitler did not last. The Nazis, having completed their sweep of France but blocked from invading Britain, quickly regained their eastern appetites, sharpened by concern about the Soviet Union's territorial gains. The invasion of the Soviet Union was launched in 1941 and soon brought a new Soviet alliance with the Western powers including, by the end of the year, the United States.

The war itself was devastating but also exhilarating for the Soviet Union. Russia's new industrial base, hastily relocated in the Ural Mountains and beyond, proved vital in providing the material needed for war, but the effort was extremely costly. Great cities such as Leningrad and Stalingrad were besieged by the Germans for months, with huge loss of life. The war heightened Russia's age-old fear of invasion and foreign interference, already enhanced by World War I and Western intervention during the revolution. But as the Red Army pressed westward after 1943, finally penetrating to the Elbe River in Germany, there was new opportunity for aggrandizement. Russia was able to regain its former western boundaries at the expense of nations such as Poland; some small states set up by the Treaty of Versailles were swallowed entirely. Larger eastern European states were allowed to remain intact, but their regimes were quickly brought under the control of Communist parties backed by the Soviet occupation forces.

DOCUMENT

SOCIALIST REALISM

One of the most fascinating features of the Soviet system was the attempt to create a distinctive art, different from Western culture now regarded as decadent, and appropriate to the Communist mission. This effort involved a great deal of censorship and forced orthodoxy, but it constituted also an attempt to resolve earlier Russian problems of relating formal culture to the masses and of trying to preserve distinctiveness amid the seductions of Western influence. The following effort to define Soviet artistic policy was written by Andrey Zhdanov in 1934, the year Stalin made him the party's spokesman at the Congress of Soviet Writers.

. . . There is not and never has been a literature making its basic subject-matter the life of the working class and the peasantry and their struggle for socialism. There does not exist in any country in the world a literature to defend and protect the equality of rights of the working people of all nations and the equality of rights of women. There is not, nor can there be in any bourgeois country, a literature to wage consistent war on all obscurantism, mysticism, hierarchic religious attitudes and threats of hell-fire, as our literature does.

Only Soviet literature could become and has in fact become such an advanced, thought-imbued literature. It is one flesh and blood with our socialist construction. . . .

What can the bourgeois writer write or think of, where can he find passion, if the worker in the capitalist countries is not sure of his tomorrow, does not know whether he will have work, if the peasant does not know whether he will be working on his bit of land or thrown on the scrap heap by a capitalist crisis, if the working intellectual is out of work today and does not know whether he will have work tomorrow?

What can the bourgeois author write about, what source of inspiration can there be for him, when the world, from one day to the next, may be plunged once more into the abyss of a new imperialist war?

The present position of bourgeois literature is such that it is already incapable of producing great works. *The decline and decay of bourgeois literature derive from the decline and decay of the capitalist system and are a feature and aspect characteristic of the present condition of bourgeois culture and literature*. The days when bourgeois literature, reflecting the victories of the bourgeois system over feudalism, was in the heyday of capitalism capable of creating great works, have gone, never to return. Today a degeneration in subject matter, in talents, in authors and in heroes, is in progress. . . .

A riot of mysticism, religious mania and pornography is characteristic of the decline and decay of bourgeois culture. The "celebrities" of that bourgeois literature which has sold its pen to capital are today thieves, detectives, prostitutes, pimps and gangsters. . . .

The proletariat of the capitalist countries is already forging its army of writers and artists—revolutionary writers, the representatives of whom we are glad to be able to welcome here today at the first Soviet Writers' Congress. The number of revolutionary writers in the capitalist countries is still small but it is growing and will grow with every day's sharpening of the class struggle, with the growing strength of the world proletarian revolution.

We are firmly convinced that the few dozen foreign comrades we have welcomed here constitute the kernel, the embryo, of a mighty army of proletarian writers to be created by the world proletarian revolution in foreign countries. . . .

Comrade Stalin has called our writers "engineers of the human soul." What does this mean? What obligations does such an appellation put upon you?

It means, in the first place, that you must know life to be able to depict it truthfully in artistic creations, to depict it neither "scholastically" nor lifelessly, nor simply as "objective reality," but rather as reality in its revolutionary development. The truthfulness and historical exactitude of the artistic image must be linked with the task of ideological transformation, of the education of the working people in the spirit of socialism. This method in fiction and literary criticism is what we call the method of socialist realism.

Our Soviet literature is not afraid of being called tendentious, for in the epoch of class struggle there is not and cannot be "apolitical" literature.

And it seems to me that any and every Soviet writer may say to any dull-witted bourgeois, to any philistine or to any bourgeois writers who speak of the tendentiousness of our literature: "Yes, our Soviet literature is tendentious and we are proud of it, for our tendentiousness is to free the working people—and the whole of mankind—from the yoke of capitalist slavery."

To be an engineer of the human soul is to stand four-square on real life. And this in turn means a break with oldstyle romanticism, with the romanticism which depicted a non-existent life and non-existent heroes, drawing the reader away from the contradictions and shackles of life into an unrealizable and utopian world. Romanticism is not alien to our literature, a literature standing firmly on a materialistic basis, but ours is a romanticism of a new type, revolutionary romanticism.

We say that socialist realism is the fundamental method of Soviet fiction and literary criticism, and this implies that revolutionary romanticism will appear as an integral part of any literary creation, since the whole life of our Party, of the working class and its struggle, is a fusion of the hardest, most matter-of-fact practical work, with the greatest heroism and the vastest perspectives. The strength of our Party has always lain in the fact that it has united and unites efficiency and practicality with broad vision, with an incessant forward striving and the struggle to build a communist society.

Soviet literature must be able to portray our heroes and to see our tomorrow. This will not be utopian since our tomorrow is being prepared by planned and conscious work today. . . .

Questions: What were the reasons for culture according to Stalinist intellectuals? How did Soviet cultural leaders analyze Western intellectual life?

THE SOVIET UNION AS A SUPERPOWER

By 1945 Soviet foreign policy had several ingredients. Desire to regain tsarist boundaries (though not carried through regarding Finland) joined with traditional interest in expansion and in playing an active role in European diplomacy. Genuine revulsion at Germany's two invasions prompted a feverish desire to set up buffer zones under Soviet control. As a result of Soviet industrialization and its World War II push westward, the nation also emerged as a world power, like the newcomer United States. Continued concentration on heavy industry and weapons development, plus strategic alliances and links to Communist movements in various parts of the world, helped maintain this status.

Russian participation in the late phases of the war against Japan brought an opportunity to seize some islands in the northern Pacific. Russia established a protectorate over the Communist regime of North Korea to match the American protectorate in South Korea. Russian aid to the victorious Communist party in China brought new influence in that country for a time, and in the 1970s Russia was to gain a new ally in Communist Vietnam, which among other things provided naval bases for the Russian fleet. Russia's growing military and economic strength gave the postwar Soviet Union new leverage in the Middle East, Africa, and even parts of Latin America; alliance with newly Communist Cuba was a key step here during

Soviet and East European Boundaries by 1948

the 1960s. The Soviet Union's superpower status was confirmed by its development of the atomic and then hydrogen bombs from 1949 onward and by its deployment of missiles and naval forces to match the rapid expansion of United States arsenals. Russia had become a world power.

THE NEW SOVIET EMPIRE IN EASTERN EUROPE

While the Soviet Union, as a superpower, developed increasing worldwide influence, with trade and cultural missions on all inhabited continents and military alliances with several Asian, African, and Latin-American nations, the clearest extension of the Soviet sphere developed right after World War II in Eastern Europe, and here the Soviets made it clear that they intended to stay, pushing Russia's effective sphere of influence farther to the west than ever before in history. Soviet insistence on this empire helped launch the cold war, as the Soviet Union demonstrated its willingness to confront the West rather than relax its grip.

The small nations of eastern Europe, mostly new or revived after World War I, had gone through a troubled period between the world wars, and this helped make them vulnerable to Nazi and then Soviet advances. Most were consumed by nationalist excitement at independence by 1918, as well as by intense grievances about territories not acquired. Hence there were bitter rivalries among the East European states, which weakened them diplomatically and economically. Most of the new nations began the interwar period with some form of parliamentary democracy in imitation of the West but soon converted to authoritarian rule, either through a dictator (as was the pattern in Poland) or by a monarch's seizure of new power (as in Yugoslavia, the new nation expanded from Serbia). This political pattern resulted from more underlying social tensions. Most East European countries remained primarily agricultural and heavily dependent on sales to western Europe. They were hard hit by the collapse of agricultural prices in the 1920s, and then they were further damaged by the depression. Furthermore, most countries also refused to undertake serious land reform, despite widely professed intentions. Aristocratic estate owners thus sought desperately to repress peasant movements, which brought them to the support of authoritarian regimes complete, often, with vaguely fascist trappings. Peasant hunger to own land and continued problems of poverty and illiteracy were simply not addressed in most cases.

Only Czechoslovakia stood as an exception, where an unusually advanced industrialization process and extensive urban culture, combined with substantial land reform, produced the basis for an effective parliamentary-democratic regime. Only Czechoslovakia, relatedly, clearly maintained the East European borderland impulse to look primarily to the West for models and interaction. Most of the rest of eastern Europe remained caught between Western patterns that seemed impossible or irrelevant and a revolutionary Soviet Union now feared for its communism as well as its Russian strength. The situation was predictably impossible. While the interwar experience served to enhance nationalist loyalties, it did not create a viable economic or diplomatic system for the region.

Then came the Nazi attack and ineffective Western response. Czechoslovakia, Poland, and Yugoslavia were seized by German or Italian forces. Several other East European authoritarians allied directly with Hitler, because of shared ideological leanings and a fear of the Soviet Union plus Germany's great economic voice as primary importer and exporter. Eastern Europe fell under Nazi control for four years, compelled to provide troops and labor and brought under Hitler's holocaust attack on the Jews.

The Red Armies came next, directly liberating all of eastern Europe plus the eastern part of Germany to the Elbe River, except for Greece and Yugoslavia, remaking the East European map. Through the combination of Soviet military might and collaboration with local Communist movements in the nations that remained technically independent, opposition parties were crushed and non-Communist regimes were forced out by 1948. Only three East European nations stood out from the common pattern: Greece, which moved toward the Western camp in diplomatic alignment and political and social systems; Albania, which formed a rigid Stalinist regime that ironically brought it into disagreement with Russia's post-Stalinist leaders; and Yugoslavia, where a Communist regime formed under the resistance leader Tito quickly proclaimed its neutrality in the cold war, defying Soviet direction and trying to form a more open-ended, responsive version of the Communist economic and social system.

Through most of Eastern Europe, after the essential Soviet takeover, a standard development dynamic emerged by the early 1950s. The new Soviet-sponsored regimes attacked possible rivals for power, including where relevant the Roman Catholic church. Mass education and propaganda outlets were quickly spread. Collectivization of agriculture ended the large estate system without creating a property-owning peasantry. Industrialization was pushed through successive five-year plans, though with some limitations due to Soviet insistence on access to key natural resources (such as Romanian oil) on favorable terms. After the formation of NATO in Western Europe, the relevant East European nations were also enfolded in a common defense alliance, the Warsaw Pact, and a common economic planning organization. Soviet troops continued to be stationed in most East European states both to confront the Western alliance and to monitor the new regimes and their loyalty to the common cause.

The imposition of the Soviet system, while it responded to many social problems in the smaller nations of Eastern Europe as well as to the desire of the Soviet Union to expand its influence and guard against German or more general Western attack, created obvious tensions. Dissatisfaction with particularly tight controls in East Germany brought a workers' uprising in 1953, vigorously repressed by Soviet troops, and widespread exodus to West Germany until a Berlin wall was built in 1961 to contain the flow. All along the new borders of Eastern Europe barbed wire fences and armed patrols served to keep the people in. Relaxation of Stalinism within the Soviet Union in 1956 created new hopes that controls might be loosened. More liberal Communist leaders arose in Hungary and Poland, with massive popular backing, seeking to create states that, while Communist, would permit greater diversity and certainly more freedom from Soviet domination. In Poland, the Russians accepted a new leader more popular with the Polish people; among other results, Poland was allowed to halt agricultural collectivization, establishing widespread peasant ownership in its place, while the Catholic church, now the symbol of Polish independence, gained greater tolerance. A new regime in Hungary, however, was cruelly crushed by the Russian army and replaced by hard-line Stalinist leadership.

Yet Soviet control over Eastern Europe did loosen slightly overall, for the heavy-handed repression cost considerable prestige. East European governments were given a freer hand in economic policy and were allowed limited room to experiment with greater cultural freedom. Several countries thus began to outstrip the Soviet Union in industrialization levels and consumer prosperity. Contacts with the West expanded in several cases, with greater trade and tourism. Eastern Europe remained, with the Soviet Union, a somewhat separate economic bloc in world trade, but there was room for limited diversity. Individual nations such as Hungary developed new intellectual vigor, while experimenting with slightly less centralized economic planning. The Communist political system remained in full force, however, with its single-party dominance and strong police controls, and diplomatic and military alignment with the Soviet Union remained essential.

The limits of experimentation in Eastern Europe were brought home again in 1968, when a more liberal regime came to power in Czechoslovakia. Again the Russian army responded, expelling the reformers and setting up a particularly rigid leader in their stead. A challenge came again from Poland in the late 1970s in the form of widespread Catholic unrest plus an independent labor movement called Solidarity, all against the backdrop of a stagnant economy and low morale. Here response was slightly more muted, though key agitators were arrested; the Polish army took over the state, under careful Soviet supervision.

Eastern Europe had, by the 1980s, been vastly transformed by several decades of Communist rule. Important national diversity remained, visible both in industrial levels and in political styles. Important discontents remained as well. Yet a Communist-imposed social revolution had brought considerable economic change and real social upheaval, through the abolition of the once-dominant aristocracy and the remaking of the peasant masses through collectivization and industrial, urban growth. Earlier cultural ties with the West, though still greater than in the Soviet Union itself, had been lessened; Russian, not French or English, was the first foreign language learned.

The expansion of Soviet influence answered important foreign policy goals, both traditional and new. The Soviets retained military presence deep in Europe, which among

As Soviet troops moved into Hungary to crush the revolt of 1956, freedom fighters in Budapest headed for the front with whatever weapons they could find.

other things reduced very real anxiety about yet another German threat. East European allies aided Soviet ventures in other parts of the world, providing supplies and advisors for activities in Africa, Latin America, and elsewhere. The recurrent unrest in Eastern Europe served as something of a check on Soviet policy as well; the need for continued military presence may have diverted Soviet leaders from emphasizing expansionist ambitions in other directions, particularly where direct commitment of troops might be involved.

EVOLUTION OF DOMESTIC POLICIES

Within the Soviet Union, the Stalinist system remained intact during the initial postwar years. The war encouraged growing use of nationalism as well as appeals for Communist loyalty, as millions of Russians responded heroically to the new foreign threat. Elements of this mood were sustained as the cold war with the United States took shape after 1947, with news media blasting America as an evil power and a distorted society. Many Russians, fearful of a new war that American aggressiveness seemed to threaten, agreed that strong government authority remained necessary. This attitude helped sustain the difficult rebuilding efforts after the war, which proceeded rapidly enough for the Soviet Union to regain its prewar industrial capacity and then proceed, during the 1950s, to impressive annual growth rates. The attitude also helped support Stalin's rigorous efforts to shield the Soviet population from extensive contact with foreigners or foreign ideas. Strict limits on travel, outside media, or any uncensored glimpse of the outside world kept the Soviet Union unusually isolated in the mid-20th century world; its culture, like its economy, was largely removed from world currents.

Stalin's political structure continued to emphasize central controls and the ever-present party bureaucracy, leavened by the adulation accorded to Stalin himself and the aging leader's endemic suspiciousness. Moscow-based direction of the national economy, along with the steady extension of education, welfare, and police operations, expanded the bureaucracy both of the government and of the parallel Communist party. Recruitment from the ranks of peasant and worker families continued into the 1940s, as educational opportunities, including growing secondary school and university facilities, allowed talented young people to rise from below. Party membership was the ticket to bureaucratic promotion, and the party deliberately kept its membership low, at about six percent of the population, to assure selection of the most dedicated elements. New candidates for the party, drawn mostly from the more broadly based Communist youth organizations, had to be nominated by at least three party members. They vowed unswerving loyalty and group consciousness. A 1939 party charter stated the essential qualities:

> The Party is a united militant organization bound together by a conscious discipline which is equally binding on all its members. The Party is strong because of its solidarity, unity of will and unity of action, which are incompatible with any deviation from its program and rules, with any violation of Party discipline, with fractional groupings, or with double-dealing. The Party purges its ranks of persons who violate its program, rules or discipline.

Through the party apparatus, the Soviet system became characterized by careful hierarchy and elaborate bureaucracy. The party was run by the Politburo, consisting of 20 people who were the real power brokers in the nation—operating, of course, under Stalin's watchful eye. Most Politburo members also held key ministries or top positions in the secret police or army. The Politburo apparatus helped coordinate these various branches and balance their interests and ambitions. Both party and state, as overlapping governing bodies, spread gradations of authority from the top committees through the regional governments to local industries, cities, and collective farms. Decisions were made at the top, often in secret, and then transmitted to lower levels for execution; little reverse initiative, with proposals coming from lower bureaucratic agencies, was encouraged.

The Stalinist version of this system, indeed, engendered particular bureaucratic caution. Innovative proposals, much less criticisms, were risky. Top officials who kept their posts tended to be colorless figures, competent but above all extremely loyal both to official ideology and to Stalin as leader. One durable foreign minister, Molotov, for example, was described by Stalin as having a "mind like a file clerk."

The Communist government built on the precedent of tsarist authoritarianism. As with the tsars, political contests and open-ended agencies such as multiparty parliaments were shunned. Carefully worded constitutions gave Russians the vote and required participation in elections, but mainly to rubber-stamp official candidates and policies. The Supreme Soviet, like the earlier duma, had no power to initiate legislation or block official decisions; it served to ratify and praise.

SOVIET CULTURE: PROMOTING NEW BELIEFS

The Soviet government was also a new product, and an impressive one. It carried on a much wider array of functions than the tsars had ventured, not only in fostering industrialization but also in reaching out for the direct loyalties of individual citizens. The direction of agriculture was itself a new initiative that the tsars had never attempted. The government and party also maintained an active cultural agenda. While this had been foreshadowed by the church-state links of tsarist days, it had no full precedent. The regime quickly declared war on the Orthodox church and other religions, seeking to shape a secular population that would maintain a Marxist, scientific orthodoxy; vestigial church activities remained but under tight government regulation. Artistic and literary styles, as well as purely political writings, were carefully monitored to assure the party line. The educational system was used to train and recruit technicians and bureaucrats, as well as to create a loyal, right-thinking citizenry. New mass ceremonies, such as May Day parades, stimulated devotion to Russia and communism.

While the new regime did not attempt to abolish the Orthodox church outright, it greatly limited the church's outreach. Thus the church was barred from giving religious instruction to anyone under the age of 18, while state schools vigorously preached that religion is mere superstition. While loyalties to the church persisted, they now seemed concentrated in a largely elderly minority. The Soviet regime also limited freedom of religion for the Jewish minority, often holding Jews up as enemies of the state in what was, in fact, a manipulation of traditional Russian anti-Semitism. The larger Muslim minority was given greater latitude, on condition of careful loyalty to the regime. On the whole, the traditional religious orientation of Russian society was severely tested in favor of a scientific outlook and Marxist explanations of history in terms of class conflict.

The Soviet state also opposed the strong Western cultural orientation of the 19th-century tsarist elite, which had never widely touched the masses in any event. Modern Western styles of art and literature were attacked as decadent. Earlier styles, appropriated as Russian, were maintained. Thus Russian orchestras performed a wide variety of classical music, and the Russian ballet, though rigid and conservative by 20th-century Western norms, commanded wide attention and enforced rigorous standards of excellence. Soviet culture emphasized a new style of "Socialist realism" in the arts, bent on glorifying heroic workers, soldiers, and peasants. A vigorous strand of modern art in prerevolutionary and 1920s Russia was repulsed under Stalin in favor of grandiose, neoclassical paintings and sculpture. Russian architecture, though careful to preserve older buildings, emphasized functional, classical lines, with a pronounced taste for the monumental. Socialist realist principles spread to Eastern Europe after World War II, particularly in public displays and monuments. With some political loosening and cold war thaw after 1950, however, Soviet and East European artists began to interact somewhat more with Western styles. At the popular level, jazz and rock music bands began to emerge by the 1980s, though official suspicion persisted.

Russian literature remained diverse and creative, despite official controls sponsored by the Communist-dominated Writers' Union. Leading Russian authors wrote movingly of the travails of the civil war and World War II, maintaining the earlier tradition of sympathy with the Russian people, great patriotism, and a concern for the Russian soul.

In his 1949 painting, *Creative Fellowship*, Shcherbakov shows the cooperation of scientists and workers in an idealized factory setting.

The most creative Soviet artists, and particularly the writers, often skirted a fine line between conveying some of the sufferings of the Russian people in the 20th century and courting official disapproval. Their freedom also varied, depending on leadership mood; thus censorship eased after Stalin, and then tightened somewhat though not to previous levels. Yet even authors critical of aspects of the Soviet regime maintained distinctive Russian values. Aleksandr Solzhenitsyn, for example, who was exiled to the West because of publication of his trilogy on Siberian prison camps, *Gulag Archipelago,* found the West too materialistic and individualistic for his taste. Though barred from his homeland, he continued to seek some alternative both to Communist policy and to Westernization, with more than a hint of a continuing belief in the durable solidarity and faith of the Russian common people and the national soul.

Along with interest in the arts and a genuine diversity of expression despite official party lines, Soviet culture placed strong emphasis on science and social science. Scientists enjoyed great prestige and wielded considerable power. Social scientific work, heavily colored by Marxist theory, nonetheless produced important analyses of current trends and history. Scientific research was even more heavily funded, and Soviet scientists generated a number of fundamental discoveries in physics, chemistry, and mathematics. At times scientists felt the heavy hand of official disapproval. Biologists and psychiatrists, particularly, were urged to reject Western theories that called human rationality and social progress into question. Thus Freudianism was banned, and under Stalin biologists who overemphasized the uncontrollability of genetic evolution were jailed. But Russian scientists overall enjoyed considerable latitude as well as real prestige. As in the West, their work was often linked with advances in technology and weaponry. After the heyday of Stalinism, scientists gained greater freedom from ideological dictates, and exchanges with Western researchers became more common in what was, at base, a common scientific culture.

Shaped by substantial state control, 20th-century Soviet culture overall proved neither traditional nor Western. Considerable ambivalence about the West remained, as Russians continued to utilize many art forms they developed in common with the West, such as the ballet, while instilling a comparable faith in science. Fear of cultural pollution, particularly of course through non-Marxist political tracts but also through modern art forms, remained lively, as Soviet leaders sought a culture that would enhance their goals of building a socialist society separate from the capitalist West.

In this example of Socialist realism, heroic women workers labor at a bustling, productive factory. Their stalwart energy was an inspiration to the Soviet people.

ECONOMY AND SOCIETY

The Soviet Union became a fully industrial society between the 1920s and 1950s. Rapid growth of manufacturing and the rise of city populations to over 50 percent of the total were measures of this development. Most of the rest of Eastern Europe was also fully industrialized by the 1950s. East European modernization, however, had a number of distinctive features. State control of virtually all economic sectors was one key element. No other industrialized society gave so little leeway to private initiative. The unusual imbalance between heavy industrial goods and consumer items was another distinctive aspect. The Soviet Union lagged in the priorities it placed on consumer goods—not only Western staples such as automobiles, but also housing construction and simple items such as bathtub plugs. Consumer-goods industries were poorly funded and did not achieve the advanced technological level that characterized the heavy manufacturing sector. The Soviet need to amass capital for development, in a traditionally poor society, helped explain the inattention to consumer goods; so did the need to create a massive armaments industry to rival that of the United States, in a society that remained poorer overall. Thus, despite an occasional desire to beat the West at its own affluent-society game, Eastern Europe did not develop the kind of consumer society that came to characterize the West. Living standards improved greatly, and extensive welfare services provided security for some groups that was lacking in the West, but complaints about poor consumer products and long lines to obtain desired goods remained a feature of Soviet life.

The Communist system throughout Eastern Europe also failed to resolve problems with agriculture. Capital that might have gone into farming equipment was often diverted to armaments and heavy industry. The arduous climate of northern Europe and Asia was a factor as well, dooming a number of attempts to spread grain production to Siberia, for example. It also seemed clear that the East European peasantry continued to find the constraints and lack of individual incentive in collectivized agriculture a deterrent to maximum effort. Thus, Eastern Europe had to retain a larger percentage of its labor force in agriculture than was true of the industrial West and still encountered problems with food supply and quality.

Despite the importance of distinctive political and economic characteristics, Eastern European society echoed a number of the themes of contemporary Western social history—simply because of the shared fact of industrial life. Work rhythms, for example, became roughly similar. Industrialization in Russia brought massive efforts to speed the pace of work and introduce regularized supervision. The incentive systems designed to encourage able workers resembled those used in Western factories. Along with similar work habits came similar leisure activities. Sports provided excitement for the peoples of Eastern Europe, as did mass media such as films and television. Family vacations to the beaches of the Black Sea became cherished respites. Here too there were some distinctive twists, as the Communist states boosted sports efforts as part of their political program (in contrast to the Western view of sports as a combination of leisure and commercialism).

East European social structure also grew closer to that of the West, despite the continued importance of the rural population and despite the impact of Marxist theory. Particularly interesting was a tendency to divide urban society along class lines, between workers and a better-educated, managerial middle class. Wealth divisions remained much less great than in the West, to be sure, but the perquisites of managers and professional people—particularly if they were Communist party members—set them off from the standard of living of the masses.

Finally, the Soviet family reacted to some of the same pressures of industrialization the Western family experienced. Massive movement to the cities and crowded housing focused the nuclear family unit, as ties to a wider network of relatives loosened. The birthrate dropped. Official Soviet policy on birthrates varied for a time, but the basic pressures became similar to those in the West. Declining infant death rates due to improved diets and medical care, plus growing periods of schooling and some increase in consumer expectations, made large families less desirable than before. Wartime dislocations contributed to birthrate decline as well. By the 1970s the Russian growth rate was about the same as that of the West. As in the West, also, some minority groups, particularly Muslims in southern Russia, maintained higher birthrates than the majority ethnic group—in this case, ethnic Russians—a differential that caused some concern about maintaining Russian cultural dominance in the future.

Patterns of child rearing showed some similarities to those in the West, as parents, especially in the managerial middle class, devoted great attention to promoting their children's education and assuring good jobs for the future. At the same time children were more strictly disciplined than in the West, both at home and in school, with an emphasis on authority that had political implications. Russian families never afforded the domestic idealization of women that had prevailed in the West during industrialization. Most married women worked, an essential feature of an economy struggling to industrialize and offering relatively low wages to individual workers. As in the peasant past, women performed many heavy physical tasks. They also dominated some professions, such as medicine, though these were far lower in status than their male-dominated counterparts in the West. Russian propagandists took pride in the constructive role of women and their official equality, but there were signs that many women suffered burdens from demanding jobs with little help from their husbands at home.

The features Russian society shared with the West, because of common urban and industrial experience, showed in aspects of popular culture. Concerns about acquisition, romance, and school success could have a very Western, or more properly modern-industrial, ring. Thus 1970s graffiti on a church wall in Leningrad—a traditional site of wish lists since the last tsarist days—displayed familiar personal aspirations:

> "Lord, grant me luck, and help me to be accepted into the Art Academy in four years."—"Happiness and health to me and Volodya."—"Lord strangle Tarisyn."—"Lord, help me get rid of Valery."—"Lord, help me in love."—"Lord make Charlotte fall in love with me."—"Lord, I'm hungry."—"Lord, help me pass the exam in political economics."—"Lord, help me pass the exam in: (1) electrical technology; (2) electrical vacuum instruments; (3) Marxism-Leninism."—"Help me pass my driver's license test, Lord."—"Lord, take the arrogance out of my wife."—"Lord, help me win a transistor radio, model AP-2-14, in the lottery." (Added on by another person:) "All we have is P-20-1. Archangel Gabriel."

Overall, Soviet society and culture displayed a distinctive blend of basic features. Several key traditions persisted, like beliefs in a Russian soul. Revolutionary emphases produced unique artistic forms (though later imitated in other Communist societies) and the large bureaucratic class. Industrialization generated many familiar forms of urban life, even in such intimate areas as family behavior and personal aspirations.

DE-STALINIZATION

The rigid government apparatus, created by Stalin and sustained after World War II by frequent arrests and exiles to forced labor camps, was put to a major test after Stalin's death in 1953. The results gradually loosened, without totally reversing, Stalinist cultural isolation.

Focus on one-man rule might have created immense succession problems, and indeed frequent jockeying for power did develop among aspiring candidates. Yet the system held together. Years of bureaucratic experience gave most Soviet leaders a taste for coordination and compromise, along with a reluctance to strike out in radical new directions that might cause controversy or arouse resistance from one of the key power blocs within the state. Stalin's death was answered by a ruling committee that balanced interest groups, notably the army, the police, and the party apparatus. This mechanism encouraged conservatism, as each bureaucratic sector defended its existing prerogatives, but it also assured fundamental stability.

In 1956, however, a new Soviet leader, Nikita Khrushchev, emerged from the committee pack to gain primary power, though without seeking to match Stalin's eminence. Khrushchev indeed attacked Stalinism for its concentration of power and arbitrary dictatorship, in a stirring speech delivered to the party congress. Khrushchev condemned Stalin for his treatment of political opponents, for his narrow interpretations of Marxist doctrine, even for his failure adequately to prepare for World War II. The implications of this startling blast modified the Soviet political climate and led to some decentralization of decision making. Little concrete institutional reform occurred, however. Political trials became less common, and the most overt police repression eased. A few intellectuals were allowed to raise new issues, dealing for example with the purges and other Stalinist excesses. Outright critics of the regime were less likely to be executed and more likely to be sent to psychiatric institutions or, in the case of internationally visible figures such as a handful of novelists, exiled to the West or confined to house arrest. Party control and centralized economic planning remained intact. Khrushchev indeed planned a major extension of state-directed initiative by opening new Siberian land to cultivation; his failure in this costly effort, plus his antagonization of many Stalinist loyalists, led to his quiet downfall.

After the de-Stalinization furor and Khrushchev's fall from power, patterns in the Soviet Union remained stable into the 1980s, verging at times on stagnant. Economic growth continued, but with no dramatic breakthroughs and with recurrent worries over sluggish productivity and especially over periodically inadequate harvests, which compelled expensive grain deals with Western nations including the United States. A number of subsequent leadership changes occurred, as party chieftains aged and died, but the transitions were handled smoothly.

Cold war policies eased somewhat upon Stalin's death. Khrushchev vaunted Soviet ability to outdo the West at its own industrial game, bragging on a visit to the United States that "we will bury you." The Khrushchev regime did produce one of the most intense moments of the cold war with the United States, as it probed for vulnerabilities. Exploiting the new alliance with Cuba the Soviets installed missiles there, yielding only to firm American response in 1962. Khrushchev had no desire for war, and both before and after the Cuban missile crisis he promoted a new policy of peaceful coexistence. He hoped to beat the West economically and actively expanded the Soviet space program: Sputnik, the first manned spacecraft, was sent into space in 1957, well in advance of the United States' equivalent. Khrushchev maintained a competitive tone, but he shifted away from the exclusive military emphasis. Lowered cold war tensions with the West permitted a small influx of Western tourists by the 1960s, plus greater access to the Western media and a variety of cultural exchanges that gave some Russians a renewed sense of contact with a wider world and restored some of the earlier ambiguities about Russia's relationship to Western standards.

At the same time the Soviet leadership continued a steady military buildup, adding increasingly sophisticated rocketry and bolstered by its unusually successful space program. The Soviets maintained a lead in manned space flights into the late 1980s. Both in space and in the arms race the Soviet Union demonstrated great technical ability combined with a willingness to settle for somewhat simpler systems than those the United States attempted, which helped explain how it could maintain superpower parity even with a less prosperous overall economy. An active sports program, resulting in a growing array of victories in Olympic Games competition, also showed the Soviet Union's new ability to compete on an international scale and its growing pride in international achievements.

The nation faced a number of new foreign policy problems, while maintaining superpower status. A growing rift with China, from the mid-1950s onward, pitted against each other two great Communist nations who also shared a massive border. Successful courtship of many other nations—such as Egypt, a close diplomatic friend during the 1960s—often turned sour, though these developments sometimes were balanced by new alignments elsewhere. The rise of Muslim awareness in the 1970s was deeply troubling to the Soviet Union, with its own large Muslim minority; this prompted an invasion of Afghanistan, to promote a friendly puppet regime, which bogged down amid guerrilla warfare into the late 1980s. On balance, the Soviet Union played a normally cautious diplomatic game, almost never engaging directly in warfare but maintaining a high level of preparedness.

Problems of work motivation and discipline loomed larger in Russia than in the West by the 1980s, after the heroic period of building an industrial society under Stanlinist exhortation and threat. With highly bureaucratized and centralized work plans, plus an absence of abundant consumer goods, many workers found little reason for great diligence. High rates of alcoholism, so severe as to cause an increase in death rates particularly among adult males, also burdened work performance and caused great concern to Soviet leaders. More familiar were problems of youth agitation. While Russian statistics tended to conceal crime problems, it was clear that many Russian youths became impatient with the disciplined life and were eager to have greater access to Western culture, including rock music and blue jeans.

Russian output continued to grow, though the Russian economy by 1980 was lagging behind the West and Japan in adopting new technologies such as computers (aside from military application). Military and space technology still kept pace with Western levels, as both sides fed the arms race. A higher percentage of Russian output had to go to military use than in the West because of the continued differential in per capita wealth, but until the 1980s most Russians seemed to accept that the higher percentage was necessary, given what they were told about the West's aggressive intentions and their own memory of invasion in World War II.

Some skepticism about the existing system showed in the minority of beleaguered intellectuals who occasionally ventured criticisms of domestic and foreign policies, including armaments policies. Cynicism cropped up also in humor magazines and popular jokes, which poked fun at the luxurious living of Communist officials and the inefficiencies of the bureaucracy. Humor may at the same time have provided some outlet for grievances that might otherwise have festered.

THE EXPLOSION OF THE 1980S AND 1990S

From 1985 onward, the Soviet Union entered a period of intensive reform. This was soon matched by a host of new political movements in Eastern Europe that effectively dismantled the Soviet Empire. The initial cause of this extraordinary and unanticipated upheaval lay in the deteriorating Soviet economic performance, intensified by the costs of military rivalry with the United States.

THE ECONOMIC SETTING

There were reasons for pride in the Soviet system, and many observers believed that public attitudes by the 1980s were shaped much less by terror than by satisfaction with the Soviet Union's world prestige and the improvements the Communist regime had fostered in education and welfare. But to a degree unperceived outside the Soviet Union the economy was grinding to a standstill. Forced industrialization had produced extensive environmental deterioration throughout Eastern Europe. According to Soviet estimates, half of all rivers were severely polluted, and over 40 percent of all agricultural land was endangered by the late 1980s; over 20 percent of Soviet citizens lived in regions of "ecological disaster." Rates and severity of respiratory and other diseases rose, impairing both morale and economic performance. Infant mortality rates also rose in several regions, sometimes matching the highest levels anywhere in the world.

More directly still, industrial production began to stagnate and even drop as a result of rigid central planning, health problems, and poor worker morale. Growing inadequacy of housing and common goods resulted, yet further worsened motivation. As economic growth stopped, the percentage of resources allocated to military production escalated toward one-third of all national income. This reduced funds available for other investments or for consumer needs. Younger leaders began to recognize, at first privately, that the system was near collapse.

THE AGE OF REFORM

The Soviet system was not changeless, despite its heavy bureaucratization. Problems and dissatisfactions, though controlled, could provoke response beyond renewed repression. In 1985, after a succession of leaders whose age or health precluded major initiatives, the Soviet Union brought a new, younger official to the fore. Mikhail Gorbachev quickly renewed some of the earlier attacks on Stalinist rigidity and replaced some of the old-line party bureaucrats. He conveyed a new and more Western style, dressing in fashionable clothes (and accompanied by his wife who did the same), holding relatively open press conferences, and even allowing Soviet media to engage in active debate and report on problems affecting the country as well as successes.

Gorbachev also further altered the Soviet Union's modified cold war stance. He urged a reduction in nuclear armament, and in 1987 negotiated a new agreement with the United States that limited medium-range missiles in Europe. He ended the war in Afghanistan, bringing Soviet troops home. Internally, Gorbachev proclaimed a policy of *glasnost,* or openness, which implied new freedom to comment and criticize. He pressed particularly for a reduction in bureaucratic decision making and the use of some market incentives to stimulate greater output. The sweep of Gorbachev's reforms, as opposed to an undeniable new tone in Soviet public relations, remained difficult to assess. Strong limits on political freedom persisted, and it was unclear whether Gorbachev could cut through the centralized planning apparatus that controlled the main lines of the Soviet economy. There was also uncertainty about how well the new leader could balance reform and stability.

Questions about Gorbachev's prospects, indeed, recalled many basic issues in Russian as well as Soviet history. In many ways Gorbachev's policies constituted a return to a characteristic ambivalence about the West as he reduced Soviet isolation while continuing to criticize aspects of Western political and social structure. Gorbachev clearly hoped to use some Western management techniques and was open to certain Western cultural styles, without intending to abandon basic controls of the Communist state. Western analysts wondered if the Soviet economy could improve worker motivations without embracing a Western-style consumerism, or whether computers could be more widely introduced without admitting wider freedom to information exchange.

Gorbachev also sought to open the Soviet Union to fuller participation in the world economy, recognizing that isolation in a separate empire had restricted access to new technology and limited motivation to change. While the new leadership did not rush to make foreign trade or investment too easy—considerable suspicion persisted—the economic initiatives brought symbolic changes, such as the opening of a McDonald's restaurant in Moscow, and a whole array of new contacts with foreigners for various Soviet citizens.

Gorbachev's initial policies, while not successful in quickly stirring the Soviet economy, had immediate political impacts—some of which the reform leader had almost certainly not anticipated. The keynote of the reform program was *perestroika*, or economic restructuring, which Gorbachev translated into more leeway for private ownership and decentralized control in industry and agriculture. Farmers, for example, won the chance to lease land for 50 years with rights of inheritance, while industrial concerns were authorized to buy from either private or state operations. Foreign investment was newly encouraged. Gorbachev pressed for reductions in Soviet military commitments, particularly through agreements with the United States on troop reductions as well as limitations on nuclear weaponry, in order to free resources for consumer goods industries. He urged more self-help among the Russians, including a reduction in drinking, arguing that he wanted to "rid public opinion of . . . faith in a 'good Tsar,' the all powerful center, the notion that someone can bring about order and organize perestroika from on high." Politically, he encouraged a new constitution in 1988, giving considerable power to a new Parliament, the Congress of People's Deputies, and abolishing the Communist monopoly on elections. Important opposition groups developed both inside and outside the party, pressing Gorbachev between radicals wanting faster reforms and conservative hard-liners. Gorbachev was elected to a new, powerful Presidency of the Soviet Union in 1990.

Reform, amid continued economic stagnation, provoked agitation among minority nationalities in the Soviet Union from 1988 onward. Muslims and Armenian Christians rioted in the south, both against each other and against the central state. Baltic nationalists and other European minorities also stirred, some insisting on independence (notably in Lithuania), some pressing for greater autonomy. In early 1991 a number of regions, including Lithuania as well as Georgia in the south, voted for independence, though their efforts were at least temporarily thwarted by the central state. Again, results of this diverse unrest were hard to forecast, but some observers predicted the end to Russian control of central Asia and the European borderlands.

Even social issues were given uncertain new twists. Gorbachev noted that Soviet efforts to establish equality between the sexes had burdened women with a combination of work and household duties. His solution—to allow women to "return to their purely womanly missions" of housework, child rearing, and "the creation of a good family atmosphere"—had a somewhat old-fashioned ring to it.

DISMANTLING THE SOVIET EMPIRE

Gorbachev's new approach, including his desire for better relations with Western powers, prompted more definitive results outside the Soviet Union than within, as the smaller states of Eastern Europe uniformly moved for greater independence and internal reforms. Bulgaria opted for economic liberalization in 1987 but was held back by the Soviets; pressure resumed in 1989 as the Bulgarian party leader was ousted and free elections were arranged. Hungary changed leadership in 1988 and installed a non-Communist president. A new constitution and free elections were planned in Hungary as the Communist party renamed itself Socialist. Hungary also reviewed its great 1956 uprising, formally declaring it "a popular uprising . . . against an oligarchic system . . . which had humiliated the nation." Hungary moved rapidly toward a free-market economy.

Poland installed a non-Communist government in 1988 and again worked quickly to dismantle the state-run economy; prices rose rapidly as government subsidies were withdrawn. The Solidarity movement, born a decade before through a merger of non-Communist labor leaders and Catholic intellectuals, became the dominant political force. East Germany displaced its Communist government in 1989, expelling key leaders and moving rapidly toward

During the revolts of the late 1980s, Lithuanians demonstrated for national independence from the Soviet Union, in the capital city of Vilnius.

unification with West Germany. The Berlin wall was dismantled, and in 1990 non-Communists won a free election. Full German unification occurred toward the end of 1990. Czechoslovakia installed a new government in 1989, headed by a playwright, and again sought to introduce free elections and a more market-driven economy.

While mass demonstrations played a key role in several of these political upheavals, only in Romania was there outright violence, as an exceptionally authoritarian Communist leader was swept out by force. As in Bulgaria, the Communist party retained considerable power, though under new leadership, and reforms moved less rapidly than in places such as Hungary and Czechoslovakia.

New divergences in the nature and extent of reform in Eastern Europe were exacerbated by clashes among nationalities—as in the Soviet Union itself. Change and uncertainty brought older attachments to the fore. Romanians and ethnic Hungarians clashed, while Bulgarians attacked a Turkish minority left over from the Ottoman period. Yugoslavia witnessed bitter clashes among rival Slavic groups.

Amid this rapid and unexpected change, prospects for the future were in many ways very unpredictable. Few of the new governments fully defined their constitutional structures, while amid innovation the range of new political parties almost compelled later consolidations. Like the Soviet Union itself, all the East European states suffered from sluggish production, and economic problems might well lead to new political discontents. Environmental issues were also massive. Diplomatic linkages among small states—a critical problem area between the two world wars—also had yet to be resolved. What was clear was the massive change in Soviet policy. Gorbachev reversed postwar imperialism completely, stating that "any nation has the right to decide its fate by itself." In several cases, notably Hungary, Soviet troops were rapidly withdrawn, and generally it seemed unlikely that a change of heart, toward a repressive attempt to reestablish empire, would be possible.

SHOCKS IN 1991

The uncertainties of the situation within the Soviet Union were confirmed in the summer of 1991, when an attempted coup was mounted by military and police elements. Gorbachev's presidency and democratic decentralization were both threatened. Massive popular demonstrations, however, asserted the strong democratic current that had developed in the Soviet Union since 1986. The contrast with earlier Soviet history and with the suppression of democracy in China two years before was striking.

The failed coup led to new attacks on the Communist party and to new independence movements by minority nationalities. The Baltic republics declared independence again, this time with wide international recognition. How many other regions might split away, even from a loose union, and what political forces might replace the Communist party in organizing the political process within the huge Russian republic moved to the top of the agenda in an ongoing process of change and redefinition.

CONCLUSION

WHAT NEXT?

Inevitably, Soviet and East European history in the 1990s is dominated by the surprising events of the most recent periods, and by huge uncertainties about their consequences. Recent events made clear that much less had changed in this region during the 20th century than had been recognized—even by Soviet citizens themselves. Soviet law had long trumpeted women's equality, and indeed Soviet women played vital roles in the labor force, but inequality in household chores continued while unavailability of reliable birth-control devices—a result of shoddy consumer goods production—forced a high rate of abortions. Soviet constitutions had featured a system of federated republics, but in fact central government control and Russian ethnic dominance spurred minority nationalism, and nationalist hostilities burned brightly. Nationalism in the Soviet Union and among newly independent East European nations threatened to divide the region profoundly.

Religion also remained a vital force, despite decades of secularization. Catholicism in the smaller nations and in the Western republics of the Soviet Union plus Islam in central Asia provided important loyalties.

Revolution and a totalitarian state had gained limited impact, despite theories of absolute control and undeniable police terror in key periods. The same system had made less of a dent in traditional attraction to Western values and standards than might have been imagined. Several East European states indeed rushed to proclaim a Western-style devotion to individual liberty as well as a market economy. Though nationalist loyalties and economic lags might well limit openness to Westernization in the long run, it seemed unlikely that isolation could be resumed—a sign both of older East European interests in the West and the new intensity of international contacts.

The excitement of recent change, however, and the huge uncertainties of Eastern Europe's future are not the whole story of the 20th century. The Soviet Union had been an expansionist state, building on an older Russian tradition of expansionism. It had been a cautious superpower in most respects, avoiding outright war after 1945, save in Afghanistan—more careful in this respect than the United States. Economic problems prompted a pullback under Gorbachev, but questions remained about the permanence of this reorientation. Concern about outside threats, plus the temptation to use military means to defend a beleaguered empire, might change Soviet moderation in the future, and undue rigidity by the United States might have the same effect. Alternatively, some observers worried that the Soviet Union might split into hostile republics, several with sophisticated atomic weaponry; this would be novel, but at least as threatening as former cold war maneuvering.

Communist domestic policies might also survive the turmoil of transition. The conservative Soviet bureaucracy remains suspicious of loss of control. Gorbachev tried to construct a powerful presidency, legally protected from public "insult," to balance greater political freedom, thus displaying strong attachment to authoritarian structure, as have new leaders in Bulgaria and Romania. Use of the Soviet army to put down dissident nationalities within the Soviet Union in 1991—particularly in Lithuania and Georgia— increased the conservative strain in the new Soviet regime. Even other areas, such as Poland, might return to authoritarianism, as they had before World War II, if economic pressures should persist, for liberal experience is limited. Change in several areas brought new opportunities for ruthless ambition, and the prospects for democratic leadership were by no means secure.

Continuities or potential continuities are not confined to leadership ranks. East Europeans and Soviet citizens value the welfare protections of Communist society and the limitations on social inequality. Many hope to combine elements of collective protection with a larger dollop of capitalism. Many continue to attack aspects of Western individualism that seem unattractive—such as high crime rates and youth unrest—even as these very trends gain ground in East European society. And many citizens appreciate the earlier achievements of the Soviet system, in destroying the landlord class, for example, and in revolutionizing educational access. Soviet people also display antagonism to blatant individual profiteering, maintaining earlier communal traditions that predated communism; for some, equality in poverty seems preferable to individual self-seeking.

Prospects in Eastern Europe remain unclear not only because of the shock of recent changes and the magnitude of economic and environmental issues, but also because of holdovers from earlier revolutionary institutions and the expectations they had fostered. The restructuring born in the fires of earlier revolution is open to drastic change, but it is unlikely to be obliterated. Tensions in relationships with Western values, an old theme redefined under communism, may persist as well.

Eastern Europe had been a dynamic factor in world history for centuries, which means that the questions about its future, unanswerable in the early 1990s, affect far more than the region itself. Throughout the turmoil of 20th-century war and revolution, the Soviet Union retained a pivotal position in European and Asian power balances, and ultimately in world affairs more widely. Is this role to be redefined, or will it gradually recede—and with what consequences?

FURTHER READINGS

On the Russian Revolution, Sheila Fitzpatrick's *The Russian Revolution, 1917–1932* (1982) is a recent overview with a rich bibliography. See also A. Rabinowitch's *The Bolsheviks Come to Power* (1976), Robert Tucker's *Stalin as Revolutionary* (1972), and R. Conquest's *The Great Terror* (1968). Edmund Wilson's *To the Finland Station* (1972) offers a dramatic account of the revolution's early phase. On nationalities issues see R. Pipes's *The Formation of the Soviet Union* (1964).

More recent Soviet history is treated in Richard Barnet's *The Giants: Russia and America* (1977); A. Rubinstein's *Soviet Foreign Policy Since World War II* (1981); Alec Nove's *The Soviet Economic System* (1980); Stephen Cohen and others, eds., *The Soviet Union Since Stalin;* and Ben Eklof's *Gorbachev and the Reform Period* (1988).

Other parts of Eastern Europe are treated in H. Setson Watson's *Eastern Europe between the Wars* (1962), F. Fetjo's *History of the People's Democracies: Eastern Europe Since Stalin* (1971), J. Tampke's *The People's Republics of Eastern Europe* (1983), Timothy Ash's *The Polish Revolution: Solidarity* (1984), H. G. Skilling's *Czechoslovakia: Interrupted Revolution* (1976) (on the 1968 uprising), and B. Kovrig's *Communism in Hungary from Kun to Kadar* (1979).

A major interpretation of the Communist experience is T. Skocpol's *States and Social Revolutions* (1979). On the early signs of explosion in Eastern Europe, see K. Dawisha's *Eastern Europe, Gorbachev and Reform: The Great Challenge* (1988). Bohdan Nahaylo and Victor Swoboda's *Soviet Disunion: A History of the Nationalities Problem in the USSR* (1990) provides important background. On women's experiences, see Barbara Engel and Christine Worobec, eds., *Russia's Women: Accommodation, Resistance, Transformation* (1990).

1923 Tokyo earthquake

1923 Defeat of Japanese bill for universal suffrage

1931 Rebellion in Korea; Japanese repression

1931 Rise of nationalism, new hostility to West

1931 Height of depression, impact on Japan; bad harvests

1936 Assassination of several Japanese political leaders; young army officer rebellion

1938 Japan's war budget; state control of economic life

1937 Increasingly open rule by military officers; arrest of opposition politicians

37 Japan and the Pacific Rim

INTRODUCTION. The rise of coastal areas in eastern Asia to world importance forms one of the major facets of the rebalancing of major societies in the 20th century. Unmarked by formal revolution—in contrast to Russia—the Pacific Rim gained momentum as an economic rather than a military superpower, particularly following the upheaval of World War II. The dynamism of Asia's Pacific Coast centered in several societies long in China's shadow as East Asian civilization was redivided and redefined, and the same societies began to influence international patterns in unprecedented ways. Societies that had been shaped by Confucian influence began to take very different paths.

This chapter covers several political units in eastern Asia—Japan, Korea, Taiwan, and the city-states of Singapore and Hong Kong—that are joined by their common ability to generate unusual economic growth during the second half of the 20th century. The Pacific Rim states also reflect some common heritage that had included considerable Chinese influence. The Pacific Rim category was still tentative by the 1990s, for it was not clear how much these different nations would prove to have in common, or how permanent their splitting away from other East Asian societies would be, notably China and Vietnam (see Chapter 41). Yet the Pacific Rim states were undeniably important in their own right, becoming along with the West the center of the world's greatest economic strength, and challenging the West through new competition. The Pacific Rim states also shared a fascinating effort to blend successful industrial forms with a distinctive cultural and political tradition—providing the clearest alternative to the West of what a vigorous modern society might look like.

The key actor was Japan, which had diverged from Chinese patters in the previous period. Japan's rise to new eminence had been launched in the 19th century with the

1945 Japan defeated; American occupation

1946–1948 Kuomintang (Nationalist) regime consolidates in Taiwan

1948 Korea divided

1950–1953 Korean War after invasion of North Korea

1951 American occupation ends in Japan

1954 U.S.-Taiwan defense treaty

1955 Japanese production reaches prewar levels

1955 Merger forms Liberal Democratic party in Japan

1959 Singapore declares independence

1961 Military regime in South Korea

1965 Growing Hong Kong autonomy

1980 End U.S.-Taiwan treaty alliance

1984 British-Chinese agreement to return Hong Kong to China in 1999

1988–1989 Growing student agitation for liberal political reform in South Korea; elected civilian government installed reforms of the Meiji era, the beginnings of industrialization, and then the military push that brought Japanese victories over China and Russia and profitable participation on the Allied side in World War I. During the 1930s the Japanese military surge continued with attacks on China and big stretches of southeast Asia and the Pacific. After defeat in World War II and a new series of internal reforms, Japanese influence returned, this time in the guise of dynamic economic growth that by the 1960s made Japan a major world competitor—the first Asian nation to reach this position since the onset of the Industrial Revolution. Japan became a leading factor in international markets of all sorts—in banking, in foreign investment both in raw materials areas and in the United States, and in foreign economic aid—as the relatively small, resource-poor island nation reached toward control of almost one-fifth of total world trade. Japanese competition challenged the United States and Western Europe, while its demand for raw materials figured prominently in Canada, Latin America, and the Middle East as well as Asia.

After World War II, Japan's success was mirrored by the rapid rise of other centers in eastern Asia, some of which became the first successful entrants to the ranks of industrial economies for virtually a century—since Japan and Russia had begun their surge. South Korea, Taiwan, and the city-states of Hong Kong and Singapore, though not yet attaining Japanese levels of prosperity and influence, gained ground rapidly, challenging the Japanese lead in certain export sectors and making a profound impact on international markets.

The rise of the Pacific Rim nations commands attention in 20th-century history because of their success in breaking the previous Western monopoly on industrial leadership—not only in sheer volume of production and export trade, but in technological innovation as well. Many observers predicted that coastal East Asia, perhaps joined by parts of China and other areas, would replace the West in world leadership. This has not yet occurred by the early 1990s, though the Pacific Rim unquestionably generates significant new competition. It was revealing, nevertheless, that many Western businesses and political leaders advocated imitation of certain Japanese methods of organization and personality style, on grounds that the Japanese had leapfrogged over the West in the habits essential to successful modern life. "Japanization" has not become a word, and Japan's ability to provoke imitation has not yet reached Westernization levels in the world at large; Japan, indeed, continues its earlier interest in selective adoption of Western attributes even as it serves as a model in other respects. Nevertheless, the Pacific Rim's presence seems to increase with every passing year during the final quarter of the 20th century. Japan has begun to earn the combination of envy and resentment the West itself had produced during its period of growing influence.

The emergence of a Pacific Rim also commands interest because it has formed such a challenging exception to the general difficulty faced by 20th-century societies that were still to enter into a genuine industrial revolution. And it commands interest because successful industrialization has not led to full Westernization. In political styles and a host of personal values, the Pacific Rim states, headed by Japan, have provided a laboratory for testing what social features were inherent in industrial advance, and what features could diverge from Western patterns on the basis of distinctive traditions and ongoing experience. Japan and increasingly other nations such as South Korea were at once highly industrial, setting new standards for the most advanced versions of industrial society, and highly Asian, adapting a host of regional traditions quite different from contemporary Western patterns.

Overall, the Pacific Rim has formed a distinctive grouping of societies amid the larger patterns of the 20th-century world, particularly after the upheavals of World War II and its immediate aftermath. Pacific Rim societies differ from the West, from Eastern Europe, and from most of the rest of Asia.

DECADES OF TURMOIL: THE WORLD WARS AND THEIR CONSEQUENCES

During the initial decades of the 20th century, Japan concentrated heavily on diplomatic and military gains plus the difficult process of adjusting to the parliamentary, constitutional government established during the Meiji period. During the 1890s the various branches of the central government had faced serious problems of cooperation, while opposition parties in the Parliament tried to gain ground at the expense of the executive ministries. In 1900 the government leaders formed their own political party, winning a majority in the lower house of Parliament. Over the next 22 years the leadership party struggled to maintain a working majority against various opposition factions. Japan was by this point an expansionist power; it formally annexed Korea in 1910. Japan ruled its new Asian colonies firmly, exacting considerable taxes and raw materials while securing markets for its growing industrial output. In no sense did the new Japanese empire lead directly to a united or vigorous Pacific Rim, though the disruption of established dependence on China did add an important new ingredient to Korean development.

JAPAN'S ONGOING DEVELOPMENT

Along with international gains came continued industrial advance. Japanese industry continued to lag behind Western levels, relying heavily on low-wage labor and the export of a relatively small number of items such as silk cloth; silk production, at 16 million pounds in 1900, soared to 93 million pounds in 1929. Agricultural productivity improved steadily, led by progressive landlords who introduced fertilizers and new equipment. Rice production more than doubled between the 1880s and the 1930s. Modern industry advanced more slowly, though it passed well beyond the pilot phase of the late 19th century. Great industrial combines—the *zaibatsu*—sponsored rapid expansion in fields such as shipbuilding, usually relying heavily on tight links with the government bureaucracy, but there were daring individual entrepreneurs as well. Between 1905 and 1918, Japan enjoyed a considerable industrial boom, with rapid advances not only in light industries such as silk, but also in electrical power, iron, and coal. Japanese life expectancy began to improve, fueled by a higher standard of living. A popular consumer culture was sketched, at least in the cities, as workers began to attend movies and read newspapers. Education advanced rapidly, with primary-school attendance universal in the relevant age groups by 1925. Enrollments in secondary schools and technical colleges swelled, improving the capacity to assimilate the newer Western technologies.

Limits on Japanese economic advance included vulnerability to economic conditions abroad. Because Japan exported relatively few items to the West, but continued to require considerable imports of raw materials, including fuels, as well as sophisticated equipment, a slump in demand for a product such as silk cloth could be disastrous. In this sense, Japan bore some resemblance to dependent economies in the world, despite industrial progress. Population growth was another burden, or at least a mixed blessing. Japan's population soared from 30 million in 1868, to 45 million in 1900, and then to 73 million by 1940. This was a tribute to agricultural advance, as the size of the farm population remained constant, and it facilitated a low-wage industrial economy. It also restricted further improvements in standard of living and created social dislocation in the crowded, migrant-filled cities. Periodic protests through strikes, demonstrations, and some socialist agitation were met with vigorous police response. Conditions worsened (see Chapter 34) in the first phase of the Great Depression of the 1930s. The economy recovered quickly, however, under the twin stimuli of a new export boom and government-organized military procurement as Japan began to beef up its war machine.

By 1937 Japan boasted the third largest and the newest merchant marine in the world. The nation became self-sufficient in machine tools and scientific equipment, the fruit of the growth in technical training. The quality of Japanese industrial goods rose, producing the first Western outcry against Japanese exports—even though in 1936, the Japanese controlled only 3.6 percent of world trade. The basis had been set for the more significant economic surge of the later 20th century, delayed by Japan's dash into World War II.

POLITICAL CRISIS

While the economy gained, however, political crisis seized center stage, leading in turn to a new and risky round of military and diplomatic experiments that culminated in World War II. Social tensions played a role in this transition, as Japan moved further from its basic tradition of noninvolvement in elaborate foreign ventures. Tokyo was virtually destroyed by an earthquake in 1923, and 100,000 people died. Six years later, the initial impact of the depression caused great misery, as exports fell by two-thirds. Half of all factories were idled by 1931. Widespread poverty and fears of social unrest helped produce an atmosphere in which new measures, including military aggression, seemed essential. In some areas in 1931, children were reduced to begging for food from passing trains, while farmers were forced to eat the inner bark of pine trees. Despite these dire conditions, social protest did not surge to dangerous proportions and the depression was soon successfully countered by an active government policy; Japan suffered far less, as a result, than many Western nations did during the depression decade as a whole. Under the 1930s minister of finance, Korekiyo Takahashi, the government increased its spending to provide jobs, which in turn generated new demands for food and manufactured items, yielding not only the export boom but also the virtual elimination of unemployment by 1936. The same policy helped support government military purchasing, but it is not clear that this constituted an essential response.

The key to Japan's new initiatives rested rather with ongoing difficulties in assimilating a generally accepted political structure—difficulties that had not been resolved during the first decades of the 20th century. Military leaders began to take a growing role in setting general diplomatic policy from the mid-1920s onward, at the expense of the civilian parties and politicians. Japan's oligarchic political structure, in which elite groups negotiated with each other for appropriate policy rather than fully yielding to any single agency, such as Parliament, permitted this kind of realignment. From the Meiji period onward, military leaders, though weaned fully from the samurai tradition, had remained separate from the civilian bureaucracy. They were trained in separate schools and regarded themselves as true guardians of the modern Japanese state as well as older traditions. They reported not to civilian authority, but directly to the emperor. Like military leaders in the West during the 1920s, but with greater vigor, they resented what they regarded as the selfishness and accommodation to special interests of the political parties, as the latter increasingly converted to mass political campaigns and vote-getting strategies. Reduction of military budgets during the 1920s hit military leaders hard, and army prestige declined to the point that officers wore civilian clothing when off base. Naval officers, at the same time, were appalled at decisions accepted from a great power Naval Conference in 1930 that limited fleet levels. In essence, Japan experimented during the 1920s with a liberal political pattern, which seemed to give primacy to party maneuverings and electoral appeals, but which also antagonized the military (and other conservative elite groups) while failing to subject them to new controls. This was the context in which military officials began to make separate decisions about Manchuria, leading to the 1931 seizure of this key Chinese region, while the civilian government tried to equivocate.

Then, as political divisions increased in response to the initial impact of the depression, a variety of nationalist groups emerged, some advocating a return to Shintoist or Confucian principles against the more Western values of urban Japan. This was more than a political response to the depression. As in Germany, a variety of groups used the occasion for a more sweeping protest against parliamentary forms; nationalism here seemed a counterpoise to alien Western values. Older military officers joined some bu-

During the early stages of World War II in Asia, Shanghai, China, was bombed by the Japanese in 1937.

reaucrats in urging a more authoritarian state that could ignore party politics; some wanted further military expansion to protect Japan from the uncertainties of the world economy by providing secure markets.

In May 1932, a group of younger army officers attacked key government and banking officers and murdered the prime minister. They did not take over the state directly, but for the next four years moderate military leaders headed the executive branch, frustrating both the military firebrands and the political parties. Another attempted military coup in 1936 was put down by forces controlled by the established admirals and generals, but this group, including the vigorous General Tojo Hideki, increasingly interfered with civilian cabinets, blocking the appointment of most liberal bureaucrats. The result, after 1936, was a series of increasingly militaristic prime ministers.

Japan gained a great deal of novel political experience during the 1920s and 1930s, and moderate political parties won widespread support. The Japanese electorate, though strongly nationalistic and loyal to the emperor, were not enthusiastic expansionists. These ingredients would reemerge in Japanese politics after World War II. For the moment, however, the military superseded civilian politics, particularly when renewed wars broke out between Japan and China in 1937. By the end of 1938, Japan controlled a substantial regional empire including Manchuria, Korea, and Taiwan, within which the nation sold half its exports and from which it bought over 40 percent of all imports, particularly food and raw materials. Both the military leadership, eager to justify further modernization of Japan's weaponry and to consolidate political control, and economic leaders, interested in rich resources of other parts of Asia—such as the rubber of British Malaya or the oil of the Dutch East Indies—soon pressed for wider conquests as Japan surged into World War II.

OTHER AREAS IN THE PACIFIC RIM

During the interwar decades, the experiences of other parts of eastern Asia were diverse. Japan's firm control over Korea created important resentments, and Japanese economic policies did little to stimulate major new developments in the Korean economy. The period of Japanese rule did have important results in disrupting Korean traditions, including the tendency to look toward Chinese superiority and the fact of monarchy itself. The Korean king, prior to full Japanese annexation in 1910, had attempted to protest growing interference, but Western powers had ignored his appeals. The Japanese had replaced the monarch with his feebleminded son in 1908, and then, when a Korean patriot assassinated the resident general in 1909, they abolished the monarchy altogether. Korea's elaborate court aristocracy was undermined in this process. Colonial status, which lasted until Japan's World War II defeat in 1945, prevented the generation of new, alternative institutions, but there was new potential for innovation after the long centuries of Yi dynasty rule.

Economically and culturally, the Japanese annexation of Korea ushered in an era of virtually unchecked exploitation of its land and people. For most of the 3½ decades the Japanese ruled the peninsula, it was governed by military leaders who put down all resistance quite brutally. Almost from the outset, the Japanese launched a concerted effort to suppress Korean culture and promote adoption of Japanese ways. Korean language newspapers were banned, Korean teachers were required to wear Japanese uniforms and carry swords, and Japanese money, weights and measures, and language instruction were introduced throughout the country. Korean resources were put at the disposal of Japanese industrialists, many of whom invested in factories in the new colony. The Korean peasantry was compelled to concentrate on rice production for export to Japan and other foreign markets. With much of their labor devoted to producing rice for others to eat, the impoverished Koreans increasingly found that they could only afford millet (a grain they had traditionally considered quite inferior to rice) for their own consumption. In the Great Depression when the world market for rice contracted rapidly and the price plunged as a consequence, the concentration on rice production proved disastrous. The long-suffering Korean peasant bore the brunt of the misery caused by Japanese miscalculations.

Peasants also bore the brunt of the Japanese effort to speed up exploitation of Korea's resources and labor as the Japanese advanced into China in the late 1930s and the Pacific war with America approached. Korea became the strategic pivot of Japanese empire building in East Asia, a vast warehouse devoted to supplying Japanese military forces. Army officers instructed the dreaded Japanese military police to forcibly conscript increasing numbers of Korean youths for labor gangs and troops to support their expanding war effort. The population was exhorted to join the Japanese people in "training to endure hardship." Japanese military rituals were given great prominence and the cult of the Japanese god-emperor was celebrated in schools and community centers across the colony. Throughout the 1930s and early 1940s, the Korean people were forced to endure hardships and the loss of tens of thousands of youth for an emperor who had usurped the powers of their own and a cause that had nothing to do with them. The state in which the long Japanese occupation left the country only prolonged the suffering and multiplied the casualties.

In March 1919 the Korean people declared their independence and rose in revolt against Japanese imperialism. Many Koreans were executed by Japanese police during the movement.

Singapore, a city with a largely Chinese population held as part of Britain's colony of Malaya, underwent important development during the late 1930s as the British tried to build it into an "invulnerable" naval base. Singapore served as a growing international seaport linked by road and rail to the rubber- and tin-producing areas of Malaya, though its people remained separate in identity and loyalty from the Muslim Malays themselves. It suffered greatly during the Japanese World War II occupation, emerging with massive unemployment and poverty.

Overall, the first decades of the 20th century brought important changes to various parts of East Asia, largely though not exclusively as the result of new Japanese initiatives. China, long the dominant East Asian force, was consumed by its complex process of internal revolution and was of course itself beset by the Japanese; it lost much of its traditional regional hold in the process. Japan led the way in economic development, despite difficulties and setbacks, gaining new international as well as regional importance—witness its unusual ability to bounce back from the depression as most Western nations foundered. World War II obviously increased pressures for change in the region, as the Japanese temporarily dislodged Western colonial rule in places such as Malaya. Japan's defeat, and the hostility it had generated in its colonies along with admiration for its ability to defy the West, challenged the patterns that had developed by 1945, while assuring the need for further change.

DOCUMENT

JAPAN AND THE LOSS IN WORLD WAR II

Japan's defeat obviously brought a great deal of moral as well as material confusion. The government was so uncertain of the intentions of the victorious Americans that it evacuated its female employees to the countryside. The following document, from the 1945 diary of Miss Yoshizawa Hisako (who became a writer on home economics), indicates something of more popular attitudes and the mixed ingredients that composed them. The passage also suggests how the American occupation force tried to present itself and the reception it received.

August 15. As I listened to the Emperor's voice announcing the surrender, every word acquired a special meaning and His Majesty's voice penetrated my mind. Tears streamed down my cheeks. I kept on telling myself that we must not fight ourselves and work hard for our common good. Yes, I pledged myself, I must work [for Japan's recovery].

The city was quiet.

I could not detect any special expression in people's faces. Were they too tired? However, somehow they seemed brighter, and I could catch an expression showing a sign of relief. It could have been a reflection of my own feelings. But I knew I could trust what I saw. . . .

The voluntary fighting unit was disbanded, and I was no longer a member of that unit. Each of us burned the insignia and other identifications.

I cannot foresee what kind of difficulty will befall me, but all I know is that I must learn to survive relying on my health and my will to live.

August 16. People do not wear expressions any different from other days. However, in place of a "good morning" or "good afternoon," people are now greeting each other with the phrase "What will become of us?"

During the morning, the city was still placed under air-raid alert.

My company announced that until everything becomes clearer, no female employees were to come to work, and urged all of us to go to the countryside, adding that we should leave forwarding addresses. This measure was taken to conform to the step already taken by governmental bureaus. Are they thinking that the occupation army will do something to us girls? There are so many important questions we have to cope with, I cannot understand why governmental officials are so worried about these matters.

We did not have enough power and lost the war.

The Army continued to appeal to the people to resist the enemy to the end. This poses a lot of problems. People can show their true colors better when they are defeated than when they win. I just hope we, as a nation, can show our better side now.

Just because we have been defeated, I do not wish to see us destroying our national characteristics when we are dealing with foreign countries.

August 17. It was rumored that a number of lower echelon military officers were unhappy with the peace, and were making some secret moves. There were other rumors, and with the quiet evacuation of women and children from the cities, our fear seemed to have intensified. After all we have never experienced a defeat before. Our fear may simply be the manifestation of fear of the unknown.

Our airplanes dropped propaganda leaflets.

One of the leaflets was posted at the Kanda Station which said: "Both the Army and Navy are alive and well. We expect the nation to follow our lead." The leaflet was signed. I could understand how those military men felt. However, we already have the imperial rescript to surrender. If we are going to rebuild, we must open a new path. It is much easier to die than to live. In the long history of our nation, this defeat may become one of those insignificant happenings. However, the rebuilding after the defeat is likely to be treated as a far more important chapter in our history.

We did our best and lost, so there is nothing we have to say in our own defense. Only those people who did not do their best may now be feeling guilty, though.

Mr. C. said that everything he saw in the city was so repugnant that he wanted to retreat to the countryside. I was amazed by the narrowness of his thought process. I could say that he had a pure sense of devotion to the country, but that was only his own way of thinking. Beautiful perhaps, but it lacked firm foundation. I wish men like him would learn to broaden their perspectives.

August 18. Rationed bread distribution in the morning. I went to the distribution center with Mrs. A.

August 21. We heard that the allied advance units will be airlifted and arrive in Japan on the 26th. And the following day, their fleet will also anchor in our harbors. The American Army will be airlifted and land in Atsugi airport.

According to someone who accompanied the Japanese delegation which went to accept surrender conditions, Americans behaved like gentlemen. They explained to the Americans that certain conditions were unworkable in light of the present situation in Japan. The Americans immediately agreed to alter those conditions. They listened very carefully to what the Japanese delegation had to say.

An American paper, according to someone, reported that meeting as follows: "We cooked thick beefsteak expecting seven or eight Japanese would appear. But seventeen of them came, so we had to kill a turkey to prepare for them. We treated them well before they returned. . . ." When I hear things like this, I immediately feel how exaggerated and inefficient our ways of doing things are. They say that Americans will tackle one item after another at a conference table, and do not waste even 30 seconds. . . .

In contrast, Japanese administration is conducted by many chairs and seals. For example when an auxiliary unit is asked to undertake a task for a governmental bureau, before anything can be done, twenty or thirty seals of approval must be secured. So there is no concept of not wasting time. Even in war, they are too accustomed to doing things the way they have been doing, and their many seals and chairs are nothing but a manifestation of their refusal to take individual responsibilities.

The fact of a defeat is a very serious matter and it is not easy to accept. However, it can bring some positive effects, if it can inculcate in our minds all the shortcomings we have had. I hope this will come true some day, and toward that end we must all endeavor. Even if we have to suffer hunger and other tribulations we must strive toward a positive goal.

Questions: How did Japanese attitudes in defeat help prepare Japan for postwar redevelopment? What other kinds of reactions might have been expected? How would you explain the rather calm and constructive outlook the passage suggests? Would American reactions to a Japanese victory have been similar?

EAST ASIA IN THE POSTWAR SETTLEMENTS

The victors in World War II had some reasonably clear ideas about how East Asia was to be restructured. Korea, was divided between a Russian zone of occupation in the north and an American zone in the south. Taiwan was restored to China, which was in principle ruled by a Kuomintang government headed by Chiang Kai-shek. The United States regained the Philippines, with a pledge to grant independence quickly—retaining some key military bases. European powers restored controls over their holdings in Vietnam, Malaya, and Indonesia. Japan was occupied by American forces bent on introducing major changes that would prevent a recurrence of military aggression.

NEW DIVISIONS AND THE END OF EMPIRES

Not surprisingly, given the complex impact of the war plus the complication of the new cold war struggle between the United States and the Soviet Union, the Pacific regions of Asia did not quickly settle into agreed-upon patterns. A decade after the war's end, not only the Philippines but also Indonesia and Malaya were independent—part of the postwar tide of decolonization. Taiwan was still ruled by Chiang Kai-shek, but the Chinese mainland was in the hands of a new and powerful Communist regime. Chiang's Nationalist regime claimed a mission to recover China, but in fact Taiwan was now a separate republic. Korea remained divided, but had undergone a brutal north-south conflict in which only United States intervention preserved South Korea's independence. Japan, rather ironically, was one of the few Pacific regions where matters had proceeded somewhat according to plan, as the nation began to recover while also adjusting to a considerably altered political structure.

East Asia's postwar turmoil forms a complex story, only part of which is directly relevant to the emergence of the Pacific Rim economy. The Communist phase of China's revolution maintained a separation between China and the parts of its traditional regional hinterland that showed little interest in communism; Vietnam's decolonization struggles also demand special attention. The Pacific Rim turned out

The United States advanced on Japan with the invasion and capture of Okinawa in March, 1945.

to be composed of areas traditionally influenced to some degree by Chinese culture but not brought under Communist control. This somewhat complex definition was forged in part by the actual experience of key Pacific regions during the period of postwar confusion.

JAPANESE RECOVERY

Japan in 1945 was in shambles. Its cities were burned, its factories destroyed or idle, its people impoverished and also shocked by the fact of surrender and by the trauma of bombing, including the atomic devastation of Hiroshima and Nagasaki. However, like the industrial nations of the West, Japan was capable of reestablishing a vigorous economy with surprising speed. And its occupation by United States forces, eager to reform Japan but also eager to avoid punitive measures, provided an opportunity for a new period of selective Westernization.

The American occupation government, headed by General Douglas MacArthur, worked quickly to tear down Japan's wartime political structure. The military forces were disbanded, the police decentralized, a number of officials removed, and political prisoners released. For the long run, American authorities pressed for a democratization of Japanese society by giving women the vote, encouraging labor unions, and abolishing Shintoism as a state religion. Several economic reforms were also introduced, breaking up landed estates for the benefit of small farmers, who quickly became politically conservative, and dissolving the holdings of the zaibatsu combines, a measure that had little lasting effect as Japanese big business quickly regrouped.

A new constitution tried to cut through older limitations by making Parliament the supreme government body, from which the cabinet was appointed; a variety of civil liberties were guaranteed, along with gender equality in marriage and collective bargaining rights; military forces with "war potential" were abolished forever, making Japan a unique major nation in its limited military strength; and the emperor was made merely a symbolic figurehead, without political power and with no claims to Shinto divinity. Even as Japan accepted many political and legal concepts, it inserted its own values into the new constitution. Thus a 1963 law inscribed special social obligations to the elderly, in obvious contrast to Western approaches to this subject, at the statutory level: "The elders shall be loved and respected as those who have for many years contributed toward the development of society, and a wholesome and peaceful life shall be guaranteed to them. . . ."

These new constitutional measures were in the main embraced by the Japanese people, many of whom became avid opponents of any hint of military revival. Japan did ultimately create a self-defense force and military capacity qui-

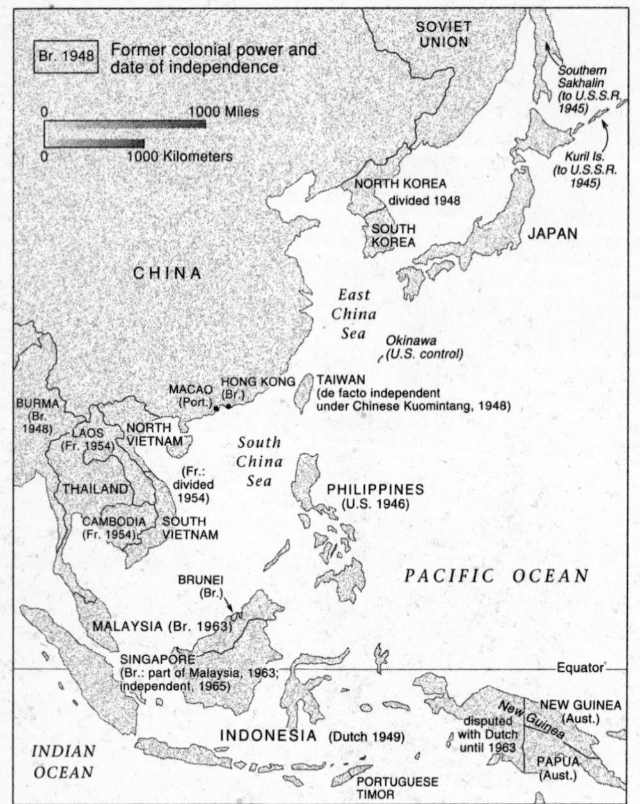

The Pacific Rim Areas by 1960

etly grew well beyond what the constitution intended, but military expenditures remained a minuscule part of the overall budget. Military power and responsibility in the region were retained by the United States, which long after the occupation period kept important bases in Japan. Many of the political features of the new constitution worked smoothly, in large part, of course, because the Japanese had experienced parliamentary and political party activity for extended periods in previous decades. Two moderate parties, both with substantial prewar traditions, vied for power during the late 1940s, with the Liberal party holding sway; in 1947 a minority Socialist party gained ground by winning 26 percent of the vote in the first postwar elections. The Socialist threat indeed spurred a 1955 merger of the moderate parties into the new Liberal Democratic party that would monopolize Japan's government into the 1990s.

Amid political reconstruction, Japan's economy gradually recovered. By 1955 production in the major industrial branches regained prewar levels. At that point many experts anticipated a moderation of growth, but in fact a huge surge ensued that propelled Japan into the first rank of world industrial powers. By this point, of course, the postwar adjustment period was clearly past, a fact expressed by the signing in 1951 of a peace treaty between Japan and 48 of its former wartime opponents; American occupation ended in the following year, with an agreement on postwar bases. The Soviet Union, now locked in the cold war (which in fact had spurred the United States to convert Japan from defeated enemy to dependent ally) did not officially make peace, and its continued occupation of former Japanese islands was a source of serious friction. Nevertheless the Soviets acquiesced in the new arrangements de facto, leaving Japan free from major diplomatic distractions.

KOREA: INTERVENTION AND WAR

Korea's postwar adjustment period was far more troubled than Japan's. Leaders of the great Allied powers during World War II had agreed in principle that Korea should be restored as an independent state. But United States' eagerness to obtain Soviet help against Japan, plus long-standing Russian interest in the area, determined that the northern part of the peninsula was occupied by the Soviet Union after the war. As the cold war intensified, American and Soviet authorities could not agree on unification of the zones, and in 1948 the United States sponsored a Republic of Korea in the south, matched by a Soviet-dominated People's Democratic Republic of Korea in the north. North Korea's regime drew on an earlier Korean Communist party founded in exile in the 1920s. North Korea quickly became a Communist state with Stalinist-type emphasis on the power of the leader, Kim Il-Sung. The South Korean regime, bolstered by ongoing American military presence, was headed by the nationalist Syngman Rhee, another politician who had earlier worked in exile against Japanese occupation. Rhee's South Korea developed parliamentary institutions in form, but maintained a strongly authoritarian tone.

In June 1950, North Korean forces attacked the south, hoping to impose unification on Communist terms. The United States, eager to maintain South Korea as protection for its deeper interests in Japan, reacted quickly (after some confusing signals about whether or not South Korea was inside the United States' "defense perimeter"). President Truman insisted on drawing another line against Communist aggression, and orchestrated United Nations sponsorship of a largely American "police action" in support of South Korean troops. Under General MacArthur's leadership, Allied forces pushed North Korea back, driving on toward the Chinese border; this in turn roused concern on the part of China's Communist regime, which sent "volunteers" that drove American troops back toward the south. The front stabilized in 1952 near the original north-south border. The stalemate dragged on until 1953, when a new American administration was able to agree to an armistice.

Korea then continued its dual pattern of development. North Korea produced an unusually isolated version of one-man rule, as Kim concentrated powers over the only legal political party, the military, and the government. Even Soviet liberalization in the late 1980s brought little change. South Korea and the United States concluded a mutual defense treaty in 1954; American troops levels were reduced, but the South Korean army gained more sophisticated military equipment and the United States poured considerable economic aid into the country, initially to prevent starvation in a war-ravaged land. The political tenor of South Korea continued to be authoritarian, but with sporadic protests in behalf of a more genuine democracy. In 1961 army officers took over effective rule of the country, though sometimes a civilian government served as a facade. Economic change, however, began to gain ground in the south, ushering in a new phase of activity and international impact. Tensions between the two Koreas continued to run high, with many border clashes and sabotage, but outright warfare was avoided.

TAIWAN, HONG KONG, AND SINGAPORE

Postwar adjustments in Taiwan involved yet another set of issues. As the Communist revolutionary armies gained the upper hand in mainland China, between 1946 and 1948 the Kuomintang (Nationalist) regime prepared to fall back on its newly reacquired island, which the Communists could not threaten because they had no navy. The result was imposition over the Taiwanese majority of a new leadership, bureaucracy, and massive military force drawn from the mainland and, particularly in its early years but in principle for several decades, devoted to the task of regaining mainland authority from the Communists.

The authoritarian political patterns the Nationalists had developed in China, centered on Chiang Kai-shek's personal control of the government, were amplified by the

This tank unit of the North Korean Peoples Army assembled in September 1950.

need to keep disaffected Taiwanese in check. Tensions with the Communist regime across the Taiwan Strait ran high. In 1950 the United States sent its Seventh Fleet to protect the island, and in 1954 a mutual defense treaty was signed (ended only in 1980, in the aftermath of United States diplomatic recognition of the Communist regime). In 1955 and 1958 the Communists bombarded two small islands controlled by the Nationalists, Quemoy and Matsu, and wider conflict threatened as the United States backed up its ally. Tensions were defused when China agreed to fire on the islands only on alternate days, while United States ships supplied them on the off-days, thus salvaging national honor. Finally, the United States induced Chiang to renounce any intentions of attacking the mainland, and conflict eased into mutual bombardments of propaganda leaflets. During this period, as in South Korea, the United States devoted considerable economic aid to its Taiwanese ally, ending assistance only in the 1960s when growing prosperity (and increasing competition with United States firms in the manufacture of inexpensive consumer items) seemed assured.

Two other ultimate participants in Pacific Rim economic advance were distinguished by special ties to Britain. Hong Kong remained a British colony after World War II; only in the 1980s was an agreement reached between Britain and China for its 1997 return to the Chinese fold. Hong Kong gained increasing autonomy from direct British rule. Its Chinese population, already considerable, swelled at various points after 1946 as a result of flights from Communist rule. Singapore retained a large British naval base until 1971, when Britain abandoned all pretense of significant power in East Asia. Even before this a merger with independent Malaya (granted self-government in 1957) collapsed on racial grounds. Because Singapore's presence made the Chinese in the whole of Malaysia a plurality (44 percent to the Malay 41 percent), Malay nationalists rejected the association with Singapore, which gained independence as a vigorous free port in 1959.

Overall, by the end of the 1950s a certain stability had emerged in the political situation of the smaller East Asian nations with the vital exception of Vietnam and its neighbors in Indochina. Despite unresolved problems, such as Korean unity or Taiwanese-Chinese relations, a number of nations had acquired de facto independence or, like Japan, had accepted important alterations in previous political and military structures. Several of these nations in turn had received special Western attention and economic support during this same adjustment period. It was from the 1960s onward that some of these same areas, combining Western contacts with important earlier traditions of group activity and vigorous group loyalty, moved from impressive economic recovery to new international influence on the basis of manufacturing and trade.

 JAPAN, INCORPORATED

As Japanese politics developed under its postwar constitution, its chief emphasis lay in a rather conservative stability. The Liberal Democratic party, formed by the merger of two conservative units in response to Socialist challenge, held the reins of government from 1955 onward. This meant that Japan, uniquely among the democratic nations of the postwar world, had no experience with shifts in party administration. Changes in leadership, which at times were frequent, were handled through negotiations among the Liberal Democratic elite, not directly as a result of shifts in voter preference.

THE DISTINCTIVE POLITICAL STYLE

Clearly, this system revived many of the oligarchic features of Meiji Japan and the Japan of the 1920s, in which parliamentary rule was mediated through the close ties among the members of the elite. The system also encouraged cooperation between government bureaucracy and big business combines, based on shared participation in the leadership group. The Liberal Democrats also revived some other features of Japan's previous political tradition. In the late 1950s, for example, it recentralized the police force. Socialist opponents of these programs reacted bitterly, protesting what they termed a revival of authoritarianism; Japan's political atmosphere for a time turned venomous, and there were many strikes and street demonstrations to protest government policies. During the 1960s, however, the Liberal Democrats shifted to avoid needless confrontations, and they strongly emphasized policies of economic development. During the prosperous 1970s and 1980s, economic progress plus the Liberal Democrats' willingness to consult opposition leaders about major legislation reinforced Japan's effective political unity. Only at the end of the 1980s, when a number of Liberal Democratic leaders were branded by corruption of various sorts and Socialist strength revived somewhat, were new political questions raised.

Japan's distinctive political atmosphere, even under a Western-influenced constitution, showed clearly in the array of functions the government undertook in cooperation with business leaders. Economic planning was extensive, and the state set production and investment goals while actively lending public resources to encourage investment and limit imports. There was scant sense of division between public and private spheres, another reminder of older Japanese traditions in this case encouraged by Confucian principles. The government-business coordination to promote economic growth and export expansion prompted the half-admiring, half-derisory Western label of "Japan, Incorporated."

Close business and political interaction resulted in part from the needs of postwar reconstruction and from Japan's precarious resource position, as the nation needed to import petroleum and most other vital raw materials and so depended on success in the export sector to an unusual degree. Government initiative extended also to the demographic sphere, as postwar leaders realized that, with Japanese imperial expansion ended, it was vital to control population size. The government actively campaigned to promote birth control and abortion, and demographic growth, though still somewhat higher than Western levels, slowed notably. Here again was a product of the strong national tradition of group cohesion: While it did not prevent strong political party differences, this tradition united many Japanese in a sense of common purpose with the government. Later, however, Japan's aging population prompted the government to try to limit birth control by making a number of common methods illegal; here Japan's people proved more recalcitrant, as high costs of living kept families small.

Expansion of the educational system was another practical contact between state and citizens. The extensive school system developed from the Meiji era was further expanded, giving many more Japanese an opportunity to attend secondary schools and universities, which in turn were strongly oriented toward technical subjects. Japanese children were encouraged to achieve academic success, with demanding examinations for entry into universities defining much of the youth of ambitious men and women. The scientific and technical focus encouraged further secularization in Japanese culture, with strong emphasis on rational inquiry and practical knowledge. Not only growing creativity in science and technology, as Japan began to generate innovative discoveries instead of specializing in clever imitation of ideas developed elsewhere, but the unusually high I.Q. scores of Japanese children, showed the deep impact of this cultural focus. Again, traditional elements entered the picture, as education stressed somewhat mechanical group learning, based on disciplined memorization, over more eccentric individual achievements.

Japanese culture more generally preserved other important traditional elements that provided aesthetic and spiritual satisfactions amid rapid economic change and an ongoing interest in Western forms. Customary styles in poetry, painting, tea ceremonies, and flower arrangements continued; each New Year's Day, for example, the emperor presided at a poetry contest, and masters of traditional arts were honored by being designated as "Living National Treasures." Kabuki and No theater also flourished. Japanese films and novels often recalled earlier history, including the age of the samurai warriors; they also stressed group loyalties, as opposed to individuality or strong assertions of will. Japanese painters and architects participated actively in the "international style" pioneered in the West, but they often infused it with earlier Japanese motifs such as stylized nature painting. City orchestras played the works of Western composers, both classical and contemporary, and also native compositions with passages played on the Japanese flute and zither. Both Buddhism and Shinto-

The hot sand baths at Kyushu exemplify traditional practices of health and relaxation in Japan.

Traditional settings are found in modern Japan. The yomei-mon gateway, at the mausoleum of Ieyasu in Nikko, is a traditional place for contemplation.

ism remained significant forces in Japanese life as well, despite the strong secular emphasis. Overall, Japan in the later 20th century blended new cultural interests, which allowed the Japanese to incorporate many Western forms, with distinctive recollections of strictly national ways. At the same time, aside from interior decoration and film, Japanese contributions to world culture were negligible; this was not where national creativity showed an international face.

THE ECONOMIC SURGE

Particularly after the mid-1950s, it was rapid economic growth that produced Japan's clearest mark internationally and commanded the most intense energies at home. By 1983 the total national product was equal to the combined totals of China, both Koreas, Taiwan, India, Pakistan, Australia, and Brazil. Per capita income, though still slightly behind the leading Western nations such as West Germany, had passed that of many centers, including Britain. Annual economic growth reached at least 10 percent regularly from the mid-1950s onward, surpassing the regular levels of every other nation during the 1960s and 1970s, as Japan became one of the top two or three economic powers in the world. Leading Japanese corporations, such as the great automobile manufacturers and electronic equipment producers, became known not simply for their volume of international exports but for the high quality of their goods.

A host of factors fed this astounding economic performance. Active government encouragement was a vital ingredient, as the government made economic growth its top priority. Cheap loans for technological innovations and direct technical research in government laboratories, as well as carefully favorable international trade policies, translated this priority directly. Educational expansion played a vital role, as Japan began to turn out far more engineers than did more populous competitors such as the United States. Foreign policy also played a role. Japan was able to devote virtually its whole capital to investment in productive technology, for its military expenses were negligible given reliance on United States' protection. Labor was a central feature. Japan had a growing available labor force based on continued if slower population growth and a rapid reduction of the agricultural population (from 47 percent in 1945 to the standard advanced-industrial rate of about 10 percent by the mid-1980s).

Workers were not only abundant but highly organized mainly, however, in company unions that engaged in important social activities and some serious bargaining for improved benefits but remained careful not to impair their companies' productivity. Leading corporations solidified this cooperation, which spurred zealous work from most employees. Few days were lost to strikes because of paternalistic policies that provided important benefits to workers despite wages that remained slightly low by Western standards. Social activities promoted and expressed group loyalty (including group exercise sessions before the start of the working day), and managers displayed active interest in suggestions by employees. The Japanese system also assured lifetime employment to an important part of the labor force, a policy aided by economic growth, low average unemployment rates, and a relatively early retirement age. This network of policies and attitudes made Japanese labor seem both less class-conscious and less individualistic than labor forces in the advanced industrial nations of the West; it reflected older traditions of group solidarity in Japan, going back to feudal patterns. Other popular habits encouraged economic growth, including a high (20 percent) savings rate born of a cautious attitude toward materialist acquisitiveness and the need to set aside money for old age. The result was considerable capital for investment in further innovation.

Japanese management displayed a distinctive spirit, again the result of adapting older traditions of leadership. There was more group consciousness, including a willingness to abide by collective decisions once made, and less concern for quick personal profits than was characteristic of the West and particularly the United States. Few corporate bureaucrats changed firms, which meant that their own efforts concentrated on their company's success.

Japan, in other words, produced a distinctive economic culture that was clearly compatible with impressive results, that responded to particular Japanese needs and traditions, and that differed in important ways from Western norms. It had costs: Workers faced intense pressure to produce and were deprived of much protest outlet. Personal consumer standards did not rise as rapidly as national output did, because of the concentration on savings and group benefits and the government-sponsored push to promote exports rather than drain output toward internal use. Leisure life remained meager by Western standards, and many Japanese even proved reluctant to take regular vacations.

Not surprisingly, the society that developed under the rapid industrial spurt showed features similar to the West's slightly earlier experience. Japanese women, though increasingly well educated and experiencing an important decline in birthrates, did not follow Western patterns precisely. A feminist movement was confined to a small number of intellectuals. Women's work outside the home was slightly less common and considerably more segregated than in the postwar West. Within the family, women shared fewer leisure activities with their husbands, concentrating more heavily on domestic duties and intensive child rearing than was true in the West by the 1970s. Divorce rates were lower (merely one-third of United States levels), a sign of Japanese family stability after the disruptions of earlier stages of modernization, but this stability was predicated on the acceptance of considerable differences in gender roles and power.

Japanese methods of child rearing reflected distinctive family values. Conformity to group standards was emphasized far more than in the West or in Communist China. A comparative study of nursery schools thus showed Japanese teachers bent on effacing their own authority in the interests of developing strong bonds among the children themselves. Shame was directed toward nonconformist behaviors—a disciplinary approach the West had largely abandoned in the early 19th century. Japanese television game shows, superficially copied from the West, accordingly imposed elaborate, dishonoring punishment on losing contestants.

The same group-oriented culture shone through in diverse facets of Japanese life. The nation had few lawyers, for it was assumed that people could make and abide by firm arrangements through mutual agreement. In the psychological area, psychiatrists reported far fewer problems of loneliness and individual alienation than in the West, as the Japanese remained devoted to group activities. Conversely, situations that promoted competition among individuals, such as the university entrance tests, produced far higher stress levels than did analogous Western experiences. The Japanese had particular ways to relieve tension, as well. Bouts of heavy drinking were more readily tolerated than in the West, as a time when normal codes of conduct could be suspended under the helpful eyes of friends. Businessmen and some politicians had recourse to traditional geisha houses for female-supplied cosseting, as a normal and publicly accepted activity. Japanese teenagers participated in higher rates of sexual activity than was common in the West, another sign perhaps of a distinctive Japanese combination of hard work with recreational release.

Japanese popular culture was not static, both because of ongoing attraction to Western standards and because of rapid urbanization and economic growth. The United States' presence after World War II brought a growing fascination with baseball, and a number of professional teams were set up. Individual Japanese athletes began also to excel in such sports as tennis and golf. In popular as well as more formal culture, change and Westernization continued to cause concern among conservatives who worried that vital traditions might be lost for good. In the mid-1980s the government, appalled to discover that a majority of Japanese children did not use chopsticks to eat (preferring knives and forks in order to eat more rapidly), invested considerable money to promote chopstick training in the schools—a minor development, but indicative of the ongoing tension between change, with its Western connotations, and a commitment to Japanese identity. At the end of the 1980s a new assertion of women's political power against some Japanese politicians who kept mistresses suggested the possibility that a more Western-style feminist consciousness might gain ground as part of Japan's ongoing evolution and its growing awareness, through cultural imports and also growing tourism abroad, of the standards of other societies. Veneration of old age was challenged by some youthful assertiveness and also by the sheer cost of the rapidly growing percentage of older people—for Japan relied heavily on family support for elders. Questions abounded about how Japan would combine distinctiveness with its industrial achievement in the future, but to Western eyes the Japanese ability to adapt traditions to change and imitation remained the most striking characteristic of the nation as the end of the 20th century neared.

Japan's continued success in international competition remained the dominant theme. Many nations both in the West and Asia resented Japanese competition and the Japanese reluctance to open their own markets to outside goods. Calls for retaliation by erecting tariff barriers against Japan were a recurrent threat, and the Japanese tried to respond—for example by increasing their economic aid to developing nations and by investing directly in the United States and Europe—without changing their policies entirely. By the 1960s, pollution became a serious problem as cities and industry expanded rapidly; traffic police, for example, sometimes wore protective masks to protect their lungs, though the government (eager to preempt a potential opposition issue) paid increasing attention to environmental issues after 1970. Some Japanese experts, worried that the nation's economic vigor would prove fragile amid such problems as growing fuel costs, foreign hostility, and internal problems, wrote articles with such titles as "The Short, Happy Life of Japan as a Superpower." Western observers continued at times to expect that Japan would soon become like the West, that is, would experience the same level of crime, strikes, individualism, family instability, youth unrest, and feminist assertiveness as the West had come to know. This expectation combined a certain amount of wishful thinking—that a wider array of problems would slow Japan up—with an implicit belief that industrialization must in the long run produce the same kinds of society regardless of the starting point.

Crowding and commerce in contemporary Japan are depicted in this photo of the lively Shinjuku district of Tokyo at night.

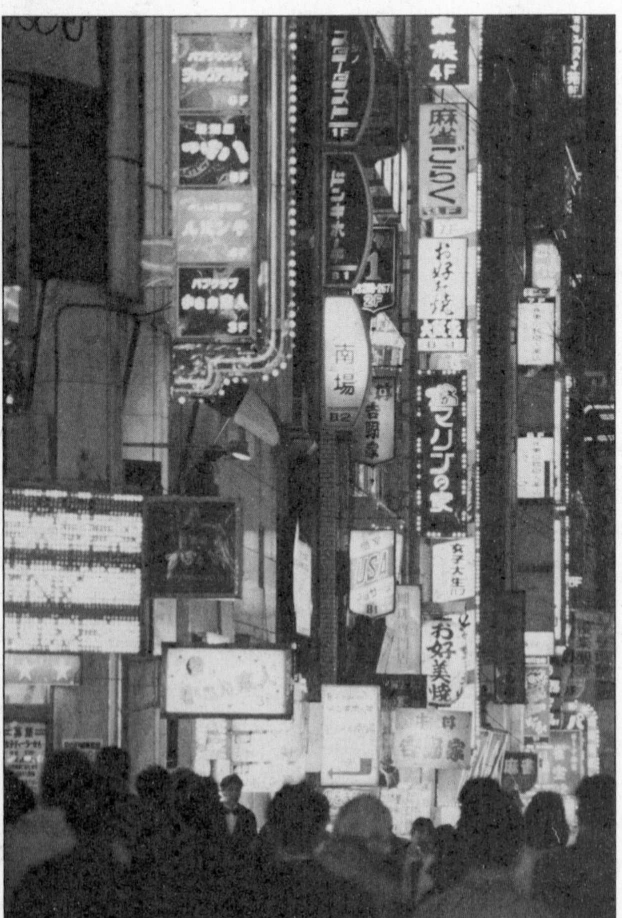

Increasing recognition developed, however, that Japan must be understood in its combination of change with distinctiveness. Some observers even advocated that the West copy key Japanese values, particularly in the areas of diligence and group loyalty. Quite possibly, now that advanced industrialization had ceased being a Western monopoly, Japanese models would gain an increasing audience, though how much the West could or would imitate remained unclear. What was obvious, though confusing to many in the West, was Japan's achievement in reaching full economic equality—in becoming a genuine economic superpower—without adopting all Western forms of politics, family life, or personal values.

THE PACIFIC RIM: NEW JAPANS?

Economic and to some extent political developments in several other middle-sized nations and city-states on Asia's Pacific coast mirrored important elements of Japan's 20th-century history, though at a slightly later date. Political authoritarianism was characteristic, though usually with periodic bows to parliamentary forms and with recurrent protest from dissident elements who wanted greater freedom. Government functions extended to careful economic planning and promotion and to rapid expansions of the educational system, with the emphasis on technical training. Group loyalties promoted diligent labor and a willingness to work hard for relatively low wages. Economic growth burgeoned.

THE KOREAN MIRACLE

South Korea was the most obvious exemplar of the spread of new economic dynamism to other parts of the Pacific Rim. The Korean government rested normally in the hands of a political strongman, usually from army ranks. Syngman Rhee was forced out of office by massive student demonstrations in 1960, but a year later a military general, Chung-hee, seized power. He retained his authority until his assassination in 1979 by his director of intelligence. Then another general seized power. Intense student protest, backed by wider popular support, pressed the military from power at the end of the 1980s, but a conservative politician won the ensuing general election and it was not clear how much the political situation had changed. Opposition activity was possible in South Korea, though usually heavily circumscribed with many leaders jailed. There was some freedom of the press except for publications from Communist countries.

As in postwar Japan, the South Korean government from the mid-1950s onward placed its primary emphasis on economic growth, which in this case started from a much lower base after the Korean War and previous Japanese exploitation. Huge industrial firms were created by a combination of government aid and active entrepreneurship. Exports were actively encouraged and by the 1970s, when Korean growth rates began to match those of Japan, Korea was competing successfully, in the area of cheap consumer goods as well as in steel and automobiles, in a variety of international markets. In steel, Korea's surge—based on the most up-to-date technology, a skilled engineering sector, and low wages—indeed pushed past Japan. The same held true in textiles, where Korean growth (along with that of Taiwan) erased almost one-third of the jobs held in the industry in Japan.

Huge industrial groups like Daewoo and Hyundai resembled the great Japanese holding companies before and after World War II and wielded great political influence. Hyundai, for example, is the creation of the entrepreneur Chung Ju Yung, a modern folk hero who walked 150 miles to Seoul, South Korea's capital, from his native village to take his first job as a day laborer at the age of 16. By the 1980s, when Chung was in his sixties, his firm had 135,000 employees and embraced 42 overseas offices throughout the world. Hyundai virtually governed Korea's southeastern coast. It built ships, including petroleum supertankers; it constructed thousands of housing units given to relatively low-paid workers at below-market rates; it built schools, a technical college, and an arena for the practice of the traditional Korean martial art, Tae Kwon Do. With their lives carefully provided for, Hyundai workers responded in kind, putting in six-day weeks with three vacation days per year and participating in almost-worshipful ceremonies when a fleet of cars was shipped abroad or a new tanker launched.

South Korea's rapid entry into the ranks of newly industrialized countries produced a host of more general changes. Population growth soared, as by the 1980s over 40 million people lived in a nation about the size of the state of Indiana, producing the highest population density on earth, about 1000 people per square mile. Here was one reason that, even amid growing prosperity, many Koreans emigrated, while the government gradually began to encourage couples to limit their birthrates. Seoul expanded to embrace nine million people, with intense air pollution and a hothouse atmosphere of deals and business maneuvers. Per capita income advanced despite demography, rising almost ten times from the early 1950s to the early 1980s—but to a level still only one-ninth of that of Japan. Huge fortunes coexisted with massive poverty in this setting, though the poverty itself had risen well above levels characteristic of less-developed nations.

ADVANCES IN TAIWAN AND THE CITY-STATES

The Republic of China, as the government on Taiwan came to call itself, experienced a rate of economic development similar to that in Korea, though slightly less impressive in terms of outright industrialization. Productivity in both agriculture and industry increased rapidly, the former spurred by substantial land reform that benefited small commercial farmers. The government concentrated increasingly on economic gains, as its involvement in plans for military action against the mainland Communist regime declined. As in Japan and Korea, formal economic planning reached high levels, though not at the expense of considerable latitude for private business. Massive investments were also poured into education, with basic literacy rates and levels of technical training rising rapidly. The result was important cultural and economic change for the Taiwanese people. Traditional medical practices and ritualistic popular religion remained lively, but expanded to allow simultaneous use of modern, Western-derived medicine and some of the urban entertainment forms popular elsewhere.

The assimilation of rapid change gave the Taiwanese government considerable stability despite a host of new concerns. United States recognition of the People's Republic of China brought with it a steadily decreasing official commitment to Taiwan. In 1978 the United States severed diplomatic ties with the Taiwanese regime, though unofficial contacts—through the American Institute in Taiwan and the Coordination Council for North American Affairs established by the republic in Washington—remained strong. The Taiwanese also built important regional contacts with other governments in eastern and southeastern Asia that facilitated trade; Japan, for example, served as the nation's most important single trading partner, purchasing foodstuffs, manufactured textiles, chemicals and other industrial goods.

Taiwan also developed some informal links with the Communist regime in Beijing, though the latter continued to claim the island as part of its territory. The republic survived the death of Chiang Kai-shek and the accession of his son, Chiang Ching-kuo, to power in 1978. The young Chiang emphasized personal authority less than his father had, and reduced somewhat the gap between mainland-born military personnel and native Taiwanese in government ranks. A strong authoritarian strain, however, continued, and political diversity was not encouraged.

Conditions in the city-state of Singapore, though less enveloped in echoes of great-power politics, resembled those in Taiwan in many ways. The prime minister, Lee Kuan Yew, took office in 1959, when the area first gained independence, and held power for the next three decades. The government established tight controls over its citizens—here going beyond anything attempted elsewhere in the Pacific Rim. Sexual behavior and potential economic corruption, as well as more standard aspects of municipal regulation and economic planning, were carefully scrutinized, as the government proclaimed the necessity of unusual discipline and restraint given a large population crowded into limited space. One result was unusually low reported crime rates; another was a limitation on tensions between the Chinese majority and other ethnic groups; and still another was the virtual impossibility of serious political protest. The authoritarian strain in politics developed increasingly, after an initially democratic constitution; the dominant People's Action party suppressed opposition movements, though there was some easing in the late 1980s. Authoritarian politics were rendered somewhat more palatable by extraordinarily successful economic development, based on a combination of government controls and initiatives and free enterprise. Already the world's fourth largest port, Singapore saw manufacturing and banking surpass shipping as sources of revenue. Electronics, textiles, and oil refining joined shipbuilding as major sectors. By the 1980s Singapore's population enjoyed the second highest per capita income in Asia. Educational levels and health conditions improved commensurately. Government regulation and propaganda combined to reduce population growth, which leveled off notably.

Finally, Hong Kong retained its status as a major world port and branched out increasingly as a center of international banking, serving as a bridge between the Communist regime in China and the wider world. Export production combined high-speed technology with low wages and long hours for the labor force, yielding highly competitive results. While textiles and clothing formed 39 percent of total exports by the 1980s, other sectors, including heavy industry, had developed impressively as well. As in other Pacific Rim nations, a large and prosperous middle class had developed, with cosmopolitan links to many other parts of the world, Western and Asian alike.

COMMON THEMES IN THE PACIFIC RIM

Overall, the Pacific Rim states, including Japan as a special case of advanced industrial success, had more in common than their rapid growth rates and expanding exports. They all stressed group loyalties against excessive individualism and in support of hard work and somewhat limited consumer demands. Confucian morality was often utilized, implicitly or explicitly, as part of this effort, for all the Pacific Rim states were either Chinese or had been strongly influenced by Chinese values. Pacific Rim areas thus sought to merge rapid change and considerable imitation of Western ways with preservation of core standards that were distinctly East Asian. Pacific Rim states also shared, despite diverse specific political systems, considerable reliance on government planning and direction, amid limitations on dissent and instability.

ANALYSIS
THE PACIFIC RIM AS A UNITED STATES POLICY ISSUE

Whenever power balances change among nations or larger civilizations, a host of policy issues arise for all parties involved. The rise of the Pacific Rim economies posed some important dilemmas for the West, and particularly, because of its military role in the Pacific as well as its world economic role, for the United States. The United States had actively promoted economic growth in Japan, Korea, and Taiwan as part of its desire to sponsor solid regional development that would discourage the spread of communism. While American aid was not alone responsible for Pacific Rim advance, and while it tapered off by the 1960s, the United States took some satisfaction in the fruits of its efforts and in the demonstration of the vitality of non-Communist economies. The United States was also not eager to relinquish its military superiority in the region, which gave it a stake in continued conciliation of Asian opinion; it did not want to see tensions translated into outright hostility that might threaten American bases (as in South Korea) or lead to independent military efforts (a potential in the case of Japan).

Yet the threats posed by growing Pacific Rim economic competition, if more subtle than the military challenges more characteristic of changing power balances, were real and growing. Japan seemed to wield a permanent balance of payments superiority; exports to the United States regularly exceeded imports by the 1970s and 1980s, which contributed greatly to the United States' unfavorable overall trade balance. Japanese investment in American companies and real estate, while helping to bridge the international payments deficit by bringing yen for dollars, increased the United States' growing indebtedness to foreign nations. Symbolic problems were real as well. Japanese observers pointed out with some justice that Americans seemed more worried about Japanese investments than about larger British holdings in the United States—an imbalance that smacked of racism. Certainly Americans found it harder to accept Asian competition than they did European, if only because it was less familiar. Thus a Korean advertisement for a major firm, placed in a 1984 copy of Fortune magazine, featured tales of technological prowess and also pictures of three leading executives wearing the sweatshirts of their American university alma maters (MIT, Wisconsin, and Cal Tech)—a combination that rankled many Americans both because of the boasts and because of the partially justified sense that the United States' know-how was being used against it. More concretely, Japanese ability to gain near-monopolies in key industries such as electronic recording systems—in some of which initial inventions still came from the United States, but their successful implementation shifted to Asia—and the growing Korean challenge in steel and automobiles meant or seemed to mean loss of jobs and perhaps a threat of more fundamental economic decline in years to come.

Several general lines of response were suggested to deal with the new competitive balance between the United States and the Pacific Rim. Some observers downplayed any sense of crisis. They argued that some readjustment was acceptable—the United States did not have to maintain its brief economic superiority worldwide and could not indeed do so. They urged that acceptance of Japanese economic vigor in tandem with American military strength in East Asia was a viable combination—each society specialized in areas it had talent for, to the benefit of both.

Other observers, far more concerned about a worsening economic imbalance, urged American imitation of the bases of Pacific Rim success: The United States should open more partnerships between government and private industry and do more economic planning; it should teach managers to commit themselves to group harmony rather than individual profit seeking; and it should build a new concord between management and labor based on mutual respect, greater job security and cooperative social programs. Some United States' firms did introduce certain Japanese management methods, including more consultation with workers, with some success.

A final set of observers, also concerned about long-term erosion of American power on the Pacific Rim, urged a more antagonistic stance. A few wanted the United States to pull out of costly Japanese and Korean bases, so that the Pacific Rim would be forced to shoulder more of its own defense costs. Others wanted to mount tariffs against Asian goods, at least until Pacific Rim nations made it easier for American firms to compete in Asian markets. Some limits on Asian competition were introduced by law during the 1980s, and Japan occasionally agreed to stabilize exports lest more hostile restrictions ensue. Aggrieved American workers sometimes smashed imported cars and threatened Asian immigrants, though many Americans, as consumers, continued to prefer Pacific Rim products and many American firms set up production in Japan or Korea—with an eye toward export back to the home market—in order to maintain profits while using superior Pacific Rim technology and advantageous labor costs. The options were complex, and American policy continued to veer among them.

Pacific Rim nations also faced choices about orientation toward the West, and here too particularly the United States'. Questions that had arisen earlier about what Western patterns to copy and what to avoid continued to be important—as the Japanese concern about forks and chopsticks suggests. Added now were issues about how to express pride and confidence in modern achievements against what was seen as Western tendencies to belittle and patronize. In 1988 the summer Olympic Games were held in South Korea, a sign of Korea's international advance and a source of great national satisfaction. During the games, a great deal of Korean nationalism flared against United States' athletes and television commentators, based on real or imagined tendencies to seek out faults in Korean society. South Korea, like Japan, continued to look heavily toward Western markets and United States military assistance, but there was clearly a desire to put the relationship on a more fully equal footing. This desire reflected widespread public opinion, and it could have policy implications.

Questions: How great were the challenges posed by the Pacific Rim to the United States' world position and well-being? What are the most likely changes in American-Pacific Rim relations over the next two decades?

CONCLUSION

PACIFIC RIM AS EXCEPTION OR AS MODEL

The rise of the Pacific Rim nations was based on a combination of several factors. First, the nations shared in aspects of the Chinese cultural and political heritage, mediated, as in Japan, by many prior adaptations and additions. A roughly common culture helped account for similar tendencies to emphasize cooperation, to build tight links between state and society, and to seek to maintain distinctive identity even amid change and imitation of aspects of Western technical and social forms. Second, the Pacific Rim nations shared some special contacts with the West through unusually intense interaction with the British or through postwar dealings with the United States. These contacts provided a certain amount of economic and/or military support at key junctures, and also some unusual opportunities to grasp aspects of the West's technology, politics, and even popular culture. Finally, the principal Pacific Rim centers, including Japan, had been rocked by 20th-century events, which virtually forced considerable rethinking and innovation.

The shared features of the Pacific Rim were very general. The region was not unified geographically or in any other way, though growing mutual trade provided an important bond in some instances. Japan was far more advanced industrially than the rest of the Pacific Rim. Political structures and diplomatic and military contexts varied considerably. The apparent similarities of Pacific Rim nations might therefore prove temporary. Certainly, even in the short run, there was mutual rivalry, most obviously in the economic competition between Japan and Korea exacerbated by mutual memories of Japanese occupation.

At least for an important moment in the later 20th century, however, the emergence of the Pacific Rim nations involved important innovations both in the cultural and political map of East Asia, newly divided between Communist and other, and in the economic map of the world as a whole. The Pacific Rim, headed by Japan but joined by the self-sustaining industrializations achieved elsewhere, provided the clearest challenge to the West's long international economic leadership. Though not wedded to commensurate military prowess, the Pacific Rim's economic surge might foreshadow wider international influence later on, as cultural forms and values, for example, begin spreading both ways instead of primarily mainly west to east. And what of China, and possibly Vietnam, where different issues dominated much of the 20th century but where many features were shared or could be resurrected that would mesh with the factors responsible for Pacific Rim dynamism? As China experimented with new economic forms in the late 1970s and early 1980s, many observers wondered if this Asian giant, or at least its coastal cities, would soon join in the Pacific Rim ascendancy. What would happen, for example, when Hong Kong was rejoined to China in 1997, assuming the Communist regime kept its pledge to give the city-state considerable latitude? Would this encourage more general Chinese adaptation to a more mixed economic structure that in turn could propel more rapid economic growth?

Certainly the success of the Pacific Rim states after World War II raised substantial questions about the contrast to China, questions that linked history to present patterns. Confucian traditions were clearly not only compatible with rapid industrial advance but could actually contribute to it. Chinese zest for commerce showed directly in Hong Kong, Taiwan, and Singapore. Huge population pressure and a long period of foreign exploitation did not hold South Korea back. Was East Asia durably divided between industrial states and societies that, while changing, remained largely agricultural, or between non-Communist and Communist? Here is a key question for Hong Kong as it prepares to accept Chinese rule in 1997. And here is a larger question for the future, where recent experience and long-term tradition suggest different answers.

The possibility also exists that economic dynamism similar to that of the Pacific Rim states may take hold in other small, non-Communist societies in southeast Asia, even though religious traditions and ethnic makeup differ from the Pacific Rim proper. By the 1980s economic growth rates in Malaysia and Thailand spurted forward, suggesting the possibility of an industrialization process beyond more piecemeal technological change.

Ongoing evolution within the Pacific Rim states raises a final set of questions. Both Japan and South Korea continue to express tension between change and considerable imitation of Western forms, on the one hand, and periodic traditionalist-nationalist reactions. Usually, to be sure, a compromise has prevailed that maintains distinctive social forms without preventing rapid change. Japan's interwar experience, and some of the political frustrations visible in South Korea late in the 1980s, remind us that adaptive compromise might not always be successful.

Even without these speculations for the future, the entry of the Pacific Rim into the mainstream of international trade represented a vital new development both for the region itself and for the world economy. Unsupported by military might after World War II and not joined as yet by any missionary culture of the sort that helped propel the

Arabs or West Europeans in the past, the rise of the Pacific Rim was an unusual development in world history, quite apart from its contrast with the region's substantial isolation in earlier eras. It is not surprising that it provokes questions about a wider ultimate international role. If a choice has to be made for the next internationally dominant region—and it is not clear that it is sensible to project a choice in the early 1990s—East Asia seems the most obvious single candidate.

FURTHER READINGS

The best account of contemporary Japanese society and politics is E. O. Reischauer's *The Japanese* (1988). For a recent history, see M. Howe's *Modern Japan: A Historical Survey* (1986). On the economy, consult H. Patrick and H. Rosovsky's *Asia's New Giant: How the Japanese Economy Works* (1976); E. F. Vogel's *Japan as Number One: Lessons for America* (1979); and K. Ohkawa and H. Rosovsky's *Japanese Economic Growth: Trend Acceleration in the Twentieth Century* (1973).

Several novels and literary collections are accessible and useful. J. Tanizaki's *The Makioka Sisters* (1957) deals with a merchant family in the 1930s; see also H. Hibbett, ed., *Contemporary Japanese Literature: An Anthology of Fiction, Film and Other Writing Since 1945* (1977). An important study of change, focusing on postwar rural society, is G. Bernstein's *Haruko's World: A Japanese Farm Woman and Her Community* (1983). Another complex 20th-century topic is assessed in R. Storry's *The Double Patriots: A Story of Japanese Nationalism* (1973).

On the Pacific Rim concept and its implications in terms of the world economy, see David Aikman's *Pacific Rim: Area of Change, Area of Opportunity* (1986); Philip West and others, eds., *Pacific Rim and the Western World: Strategic, Economic and Cultural Perspectives* (1987); Stephen Haggard and Chung-in Moon's *Pacific Dynamics: The International Politics of Industrial Change* (1988); Ronald A. Morse and others' *Pacific Basin: Concept and Challenge* (1986); and Staffan B. Linder's *Pacific Century: Economic and Political Consequences of Asian-Pacific Dynamism* (1986).

Excellent introductions to recent Korean history are Bruce Cumings's *The Two Koreas* (1984) and David Rees's *A Short History of Modern Korea* (1988). A variety of special topics are addressed in Marshall R. Pihl, ed., *Listening to Korea* (1973). See also David Steinberg's *The Republic of Korea: Economic Transformation and Social Change* (1989), Paul Kuznets's *Economic Growth and Structure in the Republic of Korea* (1977), and Dennis McNamara's *The Colonial Origins of Korean Enterprise 1910–1945* (1990).

For a fascinating exploration of cultural change and continuity in Taiwan around issues in health and medicine, see Arthur Kleinman's *Patients and Healers in the Context of Culture* (1979). On Singapore, Janet W. Salaff's *State and Family in Singapore* (1988) is an excellent study; see also R. N. Kearney, ed., *Politics and Modernization in South and Southeast Asia* (1975).

1920–1940 Mexican muralist movement active

1910–1920 Mexican Revolution

1934–1940 President Cárdenas enacts many of the reforms promised by the Mexican Revolution

1917 Mexican Constitution includes revolutionary changes

1932 Women win voting rights in Cuba and Brazil

1929 Women get the right to vote in Ecuador

1910 Madero's revolt

1933 Death of Augusto César Sandino, leader of Nicaraguan resistance to U.S. occupation

1911 Zapata promises land reform

1930 Revolution in Brazil brings Getúlio Vargas to power

1914 Panama Canal opens

1930 Military takes control of the Argentine government

38

Latin America: Revolution and Reaction in the 20th Century

INTRODUCTION. The focus of the previous three chapters—the West, Eastern Europe, and the Pacific Rim—involved societies with very different 20th-century institutions and experiences, but with one common bond: the experience of industrialization or its elaboration. The following chapters deal with societies grouped in what is sometimes termed the Third World in contrast to the capitalist industrial nations of the First World and the Communist industrial nations of the Second World. Third World societies displayed great diversity, depending on political tradition—the presence or absence of revolutionary experience, for example—and on cultural emphasis. They all, however, faced issues of economic development and inequality—of relating to economically more powerful societies—as part of their 20th-century history.

Latin America fit the Third World definition closely, despite great regional variety, but it also demonstrated how very loose this definition was. During the 20th century, Latin America continued to demonstrate its intermediate position between the nations of the North Atlantic and the developing countries of Asia and Africa. While Latin America shared many problems with these other areas of the Third World, its earlier political independence and its often more Western social and political structures placed it in a distinct category. During the course of the century, the Latin-American elites led their nations into closer ties with the growing international capitalist economy, although admittedly over increasing objections from critics within their nations. Investments and initiative often came from Europe and the United States, and Latin-American economies continued their concentration on exports. As a result, Latin America became increasingly vulnerable to changes in the world financial system.

1938 Mexico nationalizes its petroleum resources

1942 Brazil joins the Allies; sends troops to Europe

1944–1954 Arevalo and Arbenz reforms in Guatemala

1947 Juan Peron elected president of Argentina

1952–1964 Bolivian Revolution

1954 Arbenz overthrown with help from U.S.

1959 Castro leads revolution in Cuba

1961 U.S.-backed invasion of Cuba is defeated

1964 Military coup topples Brazilian government

1970–1973 Salvador Allende, Socialist government in Chile; overthrown and assassinated by the military in 1973

1979 Sandinista Revolution takes control in Nicaragua

1982 Argentina and Great Britain clash over the Falkland Islands (Malvinas Islas)

1983 U.S. invades Grenada

1989 Sandinistas lose election in Nicaragua

1989 U.S. invades Panama, deposes General Noriega

For many Latin Americans, this "dependency" on the markets, the financial situation, and economic decisions made outside the region was also reflected in a political and even cultural dependency in which foreign influence and foreign models shaped all aspects of national life.

Throughout the century, Latin Americans grappled with the problem of finding a basis for social justice, cultural autonomy, and economic security either by adopting ideologies from abroad or by developing a specifically Latin-American approach to the problem. Thus, in Latin America the struggle for decolonization has been primarily one of economic disengagement and a search for political and cultural forms appropriate to Latin-American realities, rather than being a process of political separation and independence as in Asia and Africa.

New groups began to appear on the political stage. While Latin America continued its 19th-century emphasis on agrarian and mineral production, there was also a growth of an industrial sector in some places, and as this movement gathered strength, worker organizations began to emerge as a political force. Industrialization was accompanied by continued immigration to some countries and urban growth in many places. A growing urban middle class linked to commerce, industry, and the expanding state bureaucracies also began to play a role in the political process.

With considerable variation from country to country, overall the economy and the political process were subject to a series of broad shifts. There was a pattern to these shifts, with economic expansion (accompanied by relatively conservative regimes that, although sometimes willing to make gradual reforms, hoped to maintain a political status quo) alternating with periods of economic crisis during which various attempts were made to provide social justice or to break with old social and political patterns. Thus the political pendulum swung broadly across the region and often affected a number of countries at roughly the same time, indicating the relationship between international trends and the internal events in these nations.

Latin Americans have long debated the nature of their societies and the need for change. While much of the rhetoric of Latin America has stressed radical reform and revolutionary change in the 20th century, the fact is that the region has remained remarkably unchanged as the old institutions and patterns of politics and economy have adapted to new situations and provided a sometimes disheartening continuity. Revolutionaries have not been lacking, but the task of defeating the existing political and social order and creating a new one upon which the majority of the population will agree is a difficult one, especially when this must be done within an international as well as a national context. Thus the few revolutionary political changes that have had long-term effects stand in marked contrast to the general trends of the region's political history. At the same time, however, there have been significant changes in education, social services, the position of women, and the role of industry that have taken place over the course of the century and have gradually begun to transform many areas of Latin-American life.

THE MEXICAN REVOLUTION AND THE GREAT WAR

Two cataclysmic events launched Latin America into the 20th century and set in motion trends that would determine much of the region's subsequent history. The first of these events was the ten-year civil war and political upheaval of the Mexican Revolution, which erupted because of the internal situation in that country. Eventually, however, the Mexican Revolution was also influenced by the other major event, the outbreak of World War I. While most Latin-American nations avoided direct participation in the Great War, as World War I was called at the time, the disruption of traditional markets for Latin-American exports and the elimination of European sources of manufactures caused a realignment of the economies of a number of nations in the region. Forced to rely on themselves, a spurt of manufacturing continued the process begun after 1870, and some small steps were taken to overcome the traditional dependence on outside supply. Finally, at the end of World War I, the United States emerged as the dominant foreign power in the region replacing Great Britain in both economic and political terms. That position created a reality that Latin Americans could not ignore and that greatly influenced economic and political options in the region.

MEXICO'S UPHEAVAL

The event that announced a new age in Latin America and launched it into the 20th century was the Mexican Revolution of 1910. The regime of Porfirio Díaz had been in power since 1876 and seemed unshakable. During the Díaz dictatorship, tremendous economic changes had been made, and foreign concessions in mining, railroads, and other sectors of the economy had created a sense of prosperity among the Mexican elite. This progress, however, had been bought at considerable expense. Foreigners controlled large sectors of the economy. The hacienda system of extensive landholdings dominated certain regions of the country. The political system was wholly corrupt and any complaint was stifled. The government took repressive measures against workers, peasants, and Indians who opposed the alienation of their lands or the unbearable working conditions. Political opponents were often imprisoned or forced into exile. In short, Díaz ruled with an iron fist through an effective political machine.

By 1910, however, Díaz was 80 years old and seemed willing to allow some political opposition. Francisco Madero, a wealthy son of an elite family, proposed to run against Díaz. Madero was no radical, but he believed that some moderate democratic political reforms would relieve social tensions and allow the government to continue its "progressive" economic developments with a minimum of popular unrest. Madero's moderate challenge was not much, but it was more than Díaz could stand. Madero was arrested, a rigged election put Díaz back in power; and things returned to normal. When Madero was released from prison, he called for a revolt.

A general rebellion developed. In the north, small farmers, railroaders, and cowboys coalesced under the colorful former bandit and able commander, Pancho Villa. In Morelos, an area of old conflicts between Indian communities and large sugar estates, a peasant-based guerrilla movement began under Emiliano Zapata whose goal of land reform was expressed in his motto "Tierra y Libertad" (Land and Liberty). Díaz was driven from power by this coalition of forces, but it soon became apparent that Madero's moderate programs would not resolve Mexico's continuing social problems. Zapata rose in revolt demanding a sweeping land reform and Madero steadily lost control of his subordinates. In 1913, with at least tacit agreement of the American ambassador in Mexico, a military coup removed Madero from government and he was then assassinated.

General Victoriano Huerta sought to reimpose a Díaz-type dictatorship supported by the large landowners, the army, and the foreign companies, but the tide of revolution could not be stopped so easily. Villa and Zapata rose again against the government and were joined by other middle-class political opponents of Huerta's illegal rule. By 1914 Huerta was forced from power, but the victorious leaders now began to fight over the nature of the new regime and the mantle of leadership. An extended period of warfare followed as the tides of battle continually shifted. The railroad lines built under Díaz now moved large numbers of troops and their accompanying women *soldaderas* who sometimes shouldered arms. Matters were also complicated by United States intervention and by diplomatic maneuverings after the outbreak of World War I in Europe. Villa and Zapata remained in control in their home territories, but they could not wrest the government from control of the more moderate political leaders in Mexico City. Alvaro Obregón, an able general who had learned the new tactics of machine guns and trenches from the war raging in Europe and had beaten Villa's cavalry in a series of bloody battles in 1915, emerged as leader of the government.

As much as the Mexican Revolution had its own internal dynamic, it is interesting to note that it was roughly contemporaneous with revolutions in other agrarian societies which had also just undergone a period of rapid and disruptive modernization. The Boxer Rebellion in China (1899–1901) and the toppling of the emperor in 1911, the 1905 revolution in Russia and a revolution in Iran in the same year underlined the rapid changes in these societies, all of which had received large foreign investments from either the United States or western Europe. In each of these countries governments had tried to establish strong

The Mexican Revolution mobilized large segments of the population, both men and women. The Villista forces shown here included soldaderas among the railroad workers, peasants, cowboys, and townsfolk who took up arms in northern Mexico.

centralized control and had sought rapid modernization, but in doing so had made their nations increasingly dependent on foreign investments and consequently on world financial markets. Thus a world banking crisis like that of 1907 and 1908 cut Mexico and these other countries off from their needed sources of capital and created severe strains on their governments. This kind of dependency, and the fact that in Mexico over 20 percent of the nation's territory was owned directly by United States' citizens or companies, fed a growing nationalism that spread through many sectors of society. That nationalist sentiment played a role in each of these revolutions.

By 1920 the period of civil war was ended and Mexico began to consolidate the changes that had taken place in the previous confused and bloody decade. Obregón was elected president in that year, and he was then followed by a series of presidents from the new "revolutionary elite" who sought to consolidate the new regime. There was much to be done. The revolution had devastated the country: one-half million people had died, major industries were destroyed, ranching and farming were disrupted. But there was great hope because the revolution also promised (although it did not always deliver) real changes.

What were some of these changes? A new constitution of 1917 promised land reform, limited the foreign ownership of key resources, guaranteed the rights of workers, placed restrictions on clerical education and Church ownership of property, and promised educational reforms. The workers who had been mobilized were organized in a national confederation and were given representation in the government. The promised land reforms were slow in coming, but under President Lázaro Cárdenas (1934-1940) over 40 million acres were distributed, most of it in the form of *ejidos*, or communal holdings. The government launched an extensive program of primary and especially rural education.

CULTURE AND POLITICS IN POSTREVOLUTIONARY MEXICO

Nationalism and *indigenism*, or the concern for the Indians and their contribution to Mexican culture, lay beneath many reforms. Having failed to integrate the Indians into national life for a century, Mexico now sought to "Indianize" the nation through secular schools that emphasized nationalism and a vision of the Mexican past that glorified its Indian heritage and denounced Western capitalism. Artists such as Diego Rivera and José Clemente Orozco recaptured that past and outlined a social program for the future in stunning murals on public buildings designed to inform, convince, and entertain at the same time. The Mexican muralist movement had a wide impact on artists throughout Latin America even though, as Orozco himself stated, it sometimes created simple solutions and strange utopias by mixing a romantic image of the Indian past with Christian symbols and Communist ideology. Novelists

During and after the Mexican Revolution, artists like David Alfaro Siqueiros called for murals in public places, worker neighborhoods, and sport stadiums, as well as on large buildings to record the history of Mexico and to emphasize the actions of the people. Siqueiros's *Struggle for the Banner* (1957) portrays workers and peasants seizing the national flag from the hands of oppressors.

such as Mariano Azuela found in the revolution itself a focus for the examination of Mexican reality. Popular culture celebrated the heroes and events of the revolution in scores of ballads that were sung to celebrate and inform. In literature, music, and the arts, the revolution as well as its themes provided a stimulus to a tremendous burst of creativity.

The gains of the revolution were not made without considerable opposition. While it had preceded the Russian Revolution of 1917 and had no single ideological model, many of the ideas of Marxian socialism were held by leading Mexican intellectuals and a few politicians. The secularization of society and especially education met strong opposition from the Church and the clergy, especially when in some states Socialist rhetoric and anticlericalism was extreme. In the 1920s a conservative peasant movement backed by the Church erupted in central Mexico. These "Cristeros," backed also by conservative politicians, fought to stop the slide toward secularization. Fighting lasted for years until a compromise was reached.

The United States had intervened diplomatically and militarily during the revolution. An incident provoked a short-lived United States seizure of Veracruz in 1914, and when Pancho Villa's forces had raided across the border, the United States sent an expeditionary force into Mexico to catch him. The mission failed. For the most part, however, the war in Europe had distracted American foreign policy until 1918. The United States was suspicious of the new government and a serious conflict arose when American-owned oil companies ran into problems with workers. The companies called for United States intervention or pressure when President Cárdenas expropriated the companies in 1934. An agreement was worked out, however, and Mexico nationalized its petroleum industry in a state-run monopoly. This nationalization of natural resources was considered a declaration of economic independence. It symbolized the nationalistic basis of many of the revolution's goals.

As in any revolution, the question of continuity arose when the fighting ended. The revolutionary leadership hoped to institutionalize the new regime by creating a one-party system. This organization, presently called the Party of the Institutionalized Revolution (PRI), developed slowly during the 1920s and 1930s into a dominant force in Mexican politics. It incorporated labor, peasant, military, and middle class sectors and proved flexible enough to incorporate new interest groups as they developed. While Mexico became in theory a multiparty democracy, in real-

These graphs reflect party membership by sectors. Note that the population shifted away from rural areas and that labor remained fairly steady.

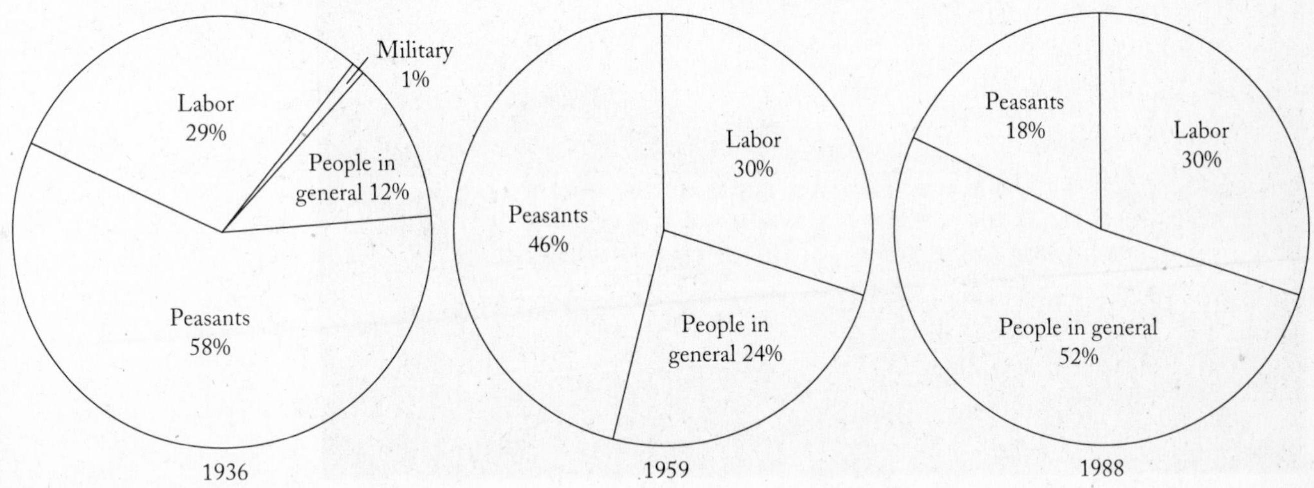

ity the PRI controlled politics and, by accomodation and sometimes repression, maintained its hold on national political life. Some presidents governed much like the strong men in the 19th century had done, but the party structure and the need to incorporate various interests within the government coalition limited the worst aspects of caudillo, or personalist, rule. Presidents were strong, but the policy of limiting the presidency to one six-year term ensured some change in leadership. The question of whether a revolution could be institutionalized remained in debate. By the last decades of the century, many Mexicans believed that little remained of the principles and programs of the revolutionaries of 1910.

LATIN-AMERICAN ECONOMIES AND WORLD WAR I

The Mexican Revolution had a limited immediate impact beyond the borders of Mexico, but the outbreak of World War I affected most of the region directly. Throughout much of Latin America, the effects of the economic boom of the late 19th century had continued into the first decades of the 20th century. Each nation had its specialized crop or set of exports—coffee for Colombia, Brazil, and Costa Rica; minerals from Bolivia, Chile, and Peru; bananas from Ecuador and Central America; and sugar from Cuba. As long as European demand remained high, groups in control of these exports greatly profited.

For a while, World War I produced some immediate effects on the Latin-American economies. Cut off from supplies of traditional imports, a spurt of industrial growth took place in what economists call "import substitution industrialization." Latin Americans had to produce for themselves some of what they had formerly imported. Most of this involved "light" industry such as textiles. Latin America continued to suffer from a lack of capital, limited markets (because so many people had so little to spend), and low technological levels. Still, changes had taken place. Moreover, during the war there was also increased European demand for some products. World War I had provided a stimulus to the economy but it was a false start. After the war a general inflationary trend meant that the real wages of the working classes declined and their worsening condition contributed to increasing political unrest.

That unrest also resulted from population growth, which was rapid in some countries. Immigrants continued to pour into Argentina, Brazil, and some of the other temperate countries, swelling the ranks of the rural and urban

Latin America experienced industrial growth with light industries such as textiles. This painting of a Mexican factory is from the mid-19th century.

working classes. Cities grew in size and importance. Often the old pattern of a capital city and its port dominating the rest of the country became reinforced during this period. This has been a continuing problem in Latin America, where cities such as Lima, Montevideo, Quito, and Mexico City have so dominated the economic and political resources of their countries that growth outside the capital has been difficult. By 1920, for example, 20 percent of Argentina's total population lived in Buenos Aires; 14 percent of the population of Chile and Cuba lived in their capitals of Santiago and Havana. Latin America had a strong urban tradition since colonial times, but in the 20th century rapid urban growth created a series of social problems that reflected the transformation of Latin America from basically agrarian to industrializing societies.

NEW POLITICAL ACTORS: LABOR AND THE MIDDLE CLASS

The rising importance of an urban labor force and the growth of an urban middle class led to changes in the political structure of some Latin-American nations. The traditional landowning oligarchy in countries such as Argentina, Chile, and Brazil began to open up the political system in order to meet the desire of the growing middle class to share political power. In Argentina, for example, a new electoral law in 1912 resulted in the 1916 triumph of the middle-class-based Radical party. After some preliminary attempts to forge an alliance with workers, however, that strategy was abandoned in favor of closer ties with the traditional elites. In Brazil, after the establishment of a republic in 1889, a series of conservative presidents from the Republican party in the wealthiest and most powerful states held control of the government. This alliance of traditional landed interests and urban middle classes maintained political stability and a business-as-usual approach to government, but it began to encounter a series of opponents during the 1920s. Reformist military officers, disaffected state politicians, social bandits, and millenarian peasant movements seeking a return to a golden age, all acted in different ways against the political system and the system of export-import capitalism that seemed to produce increasing inequality while it produced great wealth. Similar criticisms were voiced elsewhere throughout Latin America.

As in western Europe, in Latin America the growing industrial and urban labor forces began to exert some influence on politics in the first decades of the century. Not surprisingly, many of these workers were engaged in the production of exports or in related transportation activities. Immigrants from Spain, Italy, and elsewhere in Europe sometimes came with well-developed political goals and ideologies from anarchism, which wished to smash the state entirely by using the weapon of the general strike to gain power, to syndicalism, which hoped to use the organization of labor to achieve that goal. Railroad, dock, and mining workers were often among the most radical and the first to organize and were usually met with force. Hundreds of miners in Iquique, Chile, striking against awful conditions in 1907, were shot down by government forces. Between 1914 and 1930 a series of general strikes and labor unrest swept through much of Latin America. Sometimes, as in Argentina in 1919 during the "Tragic Week" government reaction to "revolutionary workers," many of whom were foreign-born, led to brutal repression under the guise of nationalism.

A growing sense of class conflict developed in Latin America as it had in western Europe in this period. Some gains were made, however, as it became increasingly clear that governments now had to consider organized labor as a force that had to be confronted or incorporated. It should be emphasized that, unlike in western Europe, the vast majority of workers in Latin America were still agrarian and for the most part were not organized. Thus, the history of the labor movement tells only a small part of the story.

IDEOLOGY AND SOCIAL REFORM

In the 1920s and 1930s the failures of liberalism were becoming increasingly apparent. A middle class had emerged and had begun to enter politics, but unlike its western European counterpart, it gained power only in conjunction with the traditional oligarchy and/or the military. In Latin America the ideology of liberalism we discussed in Chapter 31 was not an expression of the strength of this class, but rather a series of ideas, "out of place," not particularly suited to the realities of Latin America where large segments of the population were landless, uneducated, and destitute. Increasing industrialization did not dissolve the old class boundaries, nor did public education and other classic liberal programs produce as much social mobility as had been expected.

Disillusioned by liberalism and by the destruction of Europe in the Great War, artists and intellectuals who had looked to Europe for inspiration turned to Latin America's own populations and history for values and solutions to Latin-American problems. Increasingly, during the 1920s intellectuals complained that Latin America was embarked on a race to nowhere. Books such as Paulo Prado's *Portrait of Brazil* (1928) or the Argentine Eziquiel Martínez's

X-Ray of the Pampa (1933) examined the pseudo-European regimes, the corruption, and the seeming failure of these "co-optive democracies" that provided the forms of democratic government but little of the substance to the vast majority of the population. In literature and the arts the ideas of rationality, progress, and order associated with liberalism were under attack.

Ideas of reform and social change were in the air. University students in Cordoba, Argentina, began a reform of their university system that gave the university more autonomy and students more power within it. This movement soon spread to other countries. Movements for social reform gathered strength in Brazil, Chile, and Uruguay. Many of those who criticized the failure of the Liberal regimes claimed that Latin America should seek its own solutions and paths rather than import ideas and models from Europe. There were other responses as well. Socialist and Communist parties were formed or grew in strength in a number of Latin American nations in this period, especially after the Russian Revolution of 1917. The strength of these parties of the left originated in local conditions, but was sometimes aided by the international Communist movement. While criticism of existing governments and of liberalism as a political and economic philosophy came from these left-leaning parties, it also came from traditional elements in society such as the Roman Catholic church, which disliked the secularization a capitalist society represented.

POPULIST POLITICS: THE CASE OF PERU

We can use Peru as an example of this ferment. That Andean nation, with its predominantly Indian population, had followed the general trend of export-oriented development based on nitrates and a few agricultural products. The foreign capital that was invested controlled many crucial transportation facilities and vital industries. The elites profited from economic expansion, but a war with Chile (the War of the Pacific, 1879–1883) led to the loss of territory and nitrate resources. Many peasants were landless and government graft and corruption were rampant. By the 1920s critics had emerged. José Carlos Mariateguí (1895–1930), a young essayist, wrote nationalistic analyses of Peru's ills from a Socialist perspective that glorified the Indian past and denounced political and economic conditions in Peru. His *Seven Essays of Peruvian Reality* (1928) became a classic of social criticism.

Another young Peruvian, Victor Raul Haya de la Torre (1895–1979) created a new party called American Popular Revolutionary Alliance (APRA) in 1924. This party, drawing on the models of the Mexican Revolution, socialism, and nationalism, as well as some aspects of Mussolini's fascism, aimed at being an international party throughout the hemisphere. Its greatest success, however, was in Peru itself where by the 1930s its members had made an impact on politics. Anti-imperialist, nationalistic, and in favor of nationalizing lands and basic industries, APRA's program won wide support. Haya de la Torre depended on his own personal charisma and on middle-class and proletarian support for the success of APRA. This was a mix of personal qualities and programs that could be seen in a number of Latin-American regimes in the period. Electoral battles and a virtual political war between right and left in the 1930s kept APRA from power. Although opposed by the military and other sectors of society, *Apristas* remained a force in Peruvian politics and finally gained the presidency in 1985 with the victory of Alan García, but the origins of the movement were tied to the political disillusionment of the period between the wars.

APRA represented the new populist political parties in Latin America that began to mobilize mass support among workers, small farmers, and urban sectors under the direction of personalist leaders. Populism was usually nationalist and seemingly antiestablishment. It gained broad support from urban masses and rural peasants, but it was often led by politicians from the military or the elites who channeled this support into policies that did not challenge the structure of government. With an emphasis on personal charisma, direct appeals to the masses, and the political mobilization of people previously excluded from politics, Populist leaders, such as Juan Perón in Argentina, became powerful forces in the region.

THE GREAT CRASH AND LATIN-AMERICAN RESPONSES

The economic dependency of Latin America and the internal weaknesses of the Liberal regimes were made abundantly clear by the great world financial crisis of 1929. After the crash, the foreign investments so essential to the continued growth of the Latin-American economies ceased, and purchases of the region's products declined. Unemployment and economic dislocation were general. The Liberal political and economic programs that had brought the changes of the late 19th and early 20th centuries were now literally bankrupt. Within three years, there were violent military coups in 12 countries as new alternatives were sought to the deepening crisis of the area. Among these alternatives were various adaptations of socialism or *corporatism*, a political ideology that emphasized the organic nature of society and made the state a mediator, adjusting the interests of different social groups. This philosophy often appealed to conservative groups in society and to the military because it stressed cooperation and the avoidance of class conflict and because it placed the state at the center of power. Moreover, the fact that corporatism was adopted by Catholic European regimes, such as Italy, Spain, and Portugal, contributed to its popularity in Latin America. Aspects of Italian and later German fascism also appealed to conservatives in Latin America. During the 1930s Fascist groups formed, complete with their own militant rhetoric and uniforms, and sometimes gained considerable political power in Brazil, Mexico, and Chile.

Unrestrained capitalism had created deep social divisions. By the 1930s many Western societies, including Latin America, began to moderate the principles and policies of unbridled laissez-faire capitalism by attempting to provide some kind of social reform in order to provide a broader basis for governments. The New Deal in the United States and the corporatist governments of Italy and Spain were responses to the failures and problems of capitalism. Latin America also participated in this trend.

PROMISES OF SOCIAL REFORM

New regimes or a new concern with social problems characterized much of Latin America in the 1930s. We have already mentioned the reforming administration of President Cárdenas (1934–1940) in Mexico, when land reform and many of the social aspects of the revolution were finally initiated on a large scale. Cárdenas distributed over 40 million acres of land and created communal farms and a credit system to support them. He expropriated foreign oil companies that refused to obey Mexican law and created a state oil monopoly. He expanded rural education programs. These measures made him broadly popular in Mexico and seemed to give the promise of the revolution substance.

Cárdenas was perhaps the most successful example of the new political tide in Latin America. In Cuba, for example, a Nationalist revolution in 1933 aimed at social reform and breaking the tutelage of the United States took power, and although it soon was taken over by moderate elements, important changes and reforms did take place. To some extent such new departures underlined both the growing force of nationalism and the desire to integrate new forces into the political process. Nowhere was this more apparent than in the populist regimes of Brazil and Argentina.

THE VARGAS REGIME IN BRAZIL

In Brazil, a contested political election in 1929 in which the state elites could not agree on the next president, resulted in a short civil war and the emergence of Getúlio Vargas (1872–1954) as the new president. The Brazilian economy, based on coffee exports, was a shambles due to the impact of the 1929 crash on coffee exports. Vargas had promised liberal reforms and elimination of the worst abuses of the old system. Once in power, he launched a new kind of centralized political program, imposing federal administrators over the state governments. He held off attempted coups by the Communists in 1935 and by the green-shirted Fascist "Integralists" in 1937. With the support of the military, Vargas then imposed a new constitution in 1937 that established the *Estado Novo* (New State), based on ideas from Mussolini's Italy. It imposed an authoritarian regime within the context of nationalism and economic reforms, limiting immigration and eliminating parties and groups that resisted national integration or that opposed the government.

For a while Vargas played off Germany and the Western powers in hopes of securing armaments and favorable trade arrangements. Despite Vargas's authoritarian sympathies, he eventually joined the Allies, supplied bases to the United States, and even sent troops to fight against the Axis powers in Italy. In return, Brazil obtained arms, financial support for industrial development, and trade advantages. Meanwhile, Vargas ran a corporatist government allowing some room for labor negotiations, but under strict government supervision. Little open opposition to the government was allowed. The state, moreover, organized many other aspects of the economy. Opposition to Vargas and his repressive policies was building in Brazil by 1945, but by then he was turning increasingly to the left, seeking support from organized labor and coming to terms with the Communist party leaders whom he had imprisoned.

In 1945 Vargas was deposed by a military coup, but he did not disappear from Brazilian political life. After an interim of five years, Vargas returned to the presidency, this time on a program of nationalism and with support from the left and from a new Workers' party (PTB). Under his supporter, João Goulart, the party mobilized the urban labor force. Limitations were put on foreign profit-making in Brazil. As in Mexico and Argentina, a state monopoly of petroleum was established. Vargas's Nationalist and Populist stance had a broad appeal, but his policies were often more conservative than his statements. Under attack and criticism from both the political right and left, Vargas committed suicide in 1954. His suicide note emphasized his Populist ties and blamed his death on Brazil's enemies:

> Once more the forces and interests which work against the people have organized themselves again and emerge against me. . . . I was a slave to the people, and today I am freeing myself for eternal life. But this people whose slave I was will no longer be slave to anyone. My sacrifice will remain forever in their souls and my blood will be the price of their ransom. . . .

Much of Brazilian history since Vargas has been a struggle over his mantle of leadership. In death, Vargas became a martyr and a Nationalist hero even to those groups that he had repressed and imprisoned in the 1930s.

ARGENTINA: POPULISM, PERÓN, AND THE MILITARY

Argentina was somewhat of an anomaly. In Argentina, the middle-class Radical party that had held power during the 1920s fell when the economy collapsed in 1929. A military coup backed by a strange coalition of Nationalists, Fascists, and Socialists seized power, hoping to return Argentina to the golden days of the great export boom of the 1890s. The coup failed. Argentina became more dependent, as foreign investments increased and markets for Argentine products declined. Industry, however, was growing, and with it grew the numbers and strength of industrial workers, many of whom had migrated from the countryside. By the 1940s the workers were organized in two major labor federations. Conservative governments backed by the traditional military held power through the 1930s, but in 1943 a military group once again took control of government.

The new military rulers were Nationalists who wished to industrialize and modernize Argentina and make it the dominant power of South America. Some were admirers of the Fascist powers and their programs. While many of them were distrustful of the workers, the man who became the dominant political force in Argentina recognized the need to create a broader basis of support for the government. Colonel Juan D. Perón (1895–1974) emerged as a power in the government. Using his position in the Ministry of Labor, he appealed to workers, raising their salaries, improving their benefits, and generally supporting their demands. Attempts to displace him failed, and he increasingly gained popular support, aided by his wife Eva Duarte, known as Evita. She became a public spokesperson for Perón among the lower classes. During World War II Peron's admiration for the Axis powers was well known. In 1946 Perón successfully manipulated an attempt by the United States to discredit him because of his pro-Fascist sympathies into Nationalist support for his presidential campaign.

Perón forged an alliance of interest among the workers, the industrialists, and the military. Like Vargas, he learned the effectiveness of the radio, the press, and public speeches in mobilizing public support. He depended on his personal charisma and on repression of opponents to maintain his rule. The Peronist program was couched in nationalistic terms. The government nationalized the foreign-owned railroads and telephone companies as well as petroleum resources. The foreign debt was paid off and for a while the Argentine economy boomed in the immediate postwar years. But by 1949, there were economic problems again. Meanwhile Perón ruled by a combination of inducements and repression while his wife Evita became a symbol

The populist politics of Juan Perón and his wife Evita brought new forces, especially urban workers, into Argentine politics. Their personal charisma attracted great support among groups formerly excluded from politics but eventually led to opposition from the Argentine military and Perón's overthrow in 1955.

to the *descamisados*, or the poor and downtrodden who saw in Peronism a glimmer of hope. Her death in 1952 at age 33 was the cause for national mourning.

Perón's regime was a populist government with a broader base than had ever been attempted before in Argentina. Nevertheless, holding the interests of the various components of the coalition together became increasingly difficult as the economy worsened. A democratic opposition developed and complained of Perón's control of the press and his violation of civil liberties. Industrialists disliked the strength of labor organizations. The military worried that Perón would arm the workers, and so they feared Perón would begin to cut back on the military's gains. The Peronist party became more radical and began a campaign against the Catholic church. In 1955 anti-Perón military officers drove him into exile.

Argentina then lived the next 20 years in the shadow of Perón. The Peronist party was banned, and a succession of military-supported civilian governments tried to resolve the nation's economic problems and continuing political instability. But Peronism could survive even without Perón, and the mass of urban workers and the strongly Peronist unions continued to agitate for his programs, especially as austerity measures began to affect living conditions of the working class. Perón and his new wife Isabel returned to Argentina in 1973, and they won the presidential election in that year (she as vice president). When he died the following year, however, it was clear that Argentina's problems could not be solved by the old formulas. Argentina slid once more into military dictatorship.

RADICAL OPTIONS IN THE 1950S

The Argentine and Brazilian cases begun by Vargas and Perón were symptomatic of the continuing problems of Latin America, but their personalistic authoritarian solutions were only one possible response. By the 1940s frustration had built up considerable pressure for change throughout much of Latin America. Across the political spectrum there was a desire to improve the social and economic conditions throughout the region and a general agreement that "development" and economic strength were the keys to a better future. How to achieve those goals, however, remained in question. In Mexico, one-party rule continued, and the "Revolution" became increasingly conservative and interested in economic growth rather than social justice. In a few countries, such as Venezuela and Costa Rica, reform-minded democratic parties were able to win elections in an open political system. In other places such a solution was less likely or less attractive to those who wished to bring about reform. Unlike the Mexican revolutionaries of 1910 through 1920, those seeking change in the post-World War II period could turn to the well-developed political philosophy of Marxian socialism as a guide. Such models, however, were fraught with dangers because of the context of the cold war and the ideological struggle between Western Europe and the Soviet bloc.

Throughout Latin America, the failures of political democratization, economic development, and social reforms led to the consideration of radical and revolutionary solutions to national problems. During the 1950s, three major attempts at radical change were made in Latin America with very different results.

GUATEMALA: REFORM AND UNITED STATES INTERVENTION

The first place where more radical solutions were tried was Guatemala. This predominantly Indian nation suffered from some of the worst features of the region's problems. Its population was mostly illiterate and suffered poor health conditions and high rates of mortality. Land and wealth were very unequally distributed, and the whole economy depended on the highly volatile prices for its main exports of coffee and bananas. In 1944 a coalition of middle class and labor elected a reformer, Juan José Arevalo as president. With a new constitution he began a series of programs within the context of "spiritual socialism" that included land reform and an improvement in the rights and conditions of rural and industrial workers. An income tax, the first in the nation's history, was projected and educational reforms were planned. These programs and his sponsorship of an intense nationalism brought the Arevalo government into direct conflict with foreign interests operating in Guatemala, especially the United Fruit Company, the largest and most important foreign concern there. That company had operated in Guatemala from the turn of the century and had acquired extensive properties. It also controlled transportation and shipping facilities. Its workers were often better paid than the average, and their health and other benefits were more extensive, but because it was a foreign company with such a powerful role in Guatemala, United Fruit was the target of nationalistic anger.

In 1951, after a free election, the presidency passed to Colonel Jacobo Arbenz, whose Nationalist program was more radical and whose public statements against foreign economic interests and the landholding oligarchy were more extreme than under Arevalo. Arbenz announced a number of programs to improve or to nationalize the transportation network, the hydroelectric system, and other areas of the economy. A move to expropriate unused lands on large estates in 1953 provoked opposition from the landed oligarchy and from United Fruit, which was eventually threatened with the loss of almost half a million acres of "reserve" land. The United States government, fearing "Communist" penetration of the Arbenz government and under considerable pressure from United Fruit Company, denounced the changes and began to impose economic and diplomatic restrictions on Guatemala. At the same time, the level of Nationalist rhetoric intensified and the government increasingly received the support of the political left in Latin America and in the Socialist bloc.

In 1954, with the help of the Central Intelligence Agency, a dissident military force was organized and invaded Guatemala. The Arbenz government fell, and the pro-American regime that replaced it then turned back the land reform and negotiated a settlement favorable for United Fruit. The reform experiment was thus brought to a halt. In retrospect, by the standards of the 1960s, the programs of Arevalo and Arbenz seemed rather mild, although undoubtedly Arbenz's statements and his acceptance of arms from eastern Europe had contributed to the United States' intervention. The reforms promised by the United States-supported governments were minimal. Guatemala continued to be characterized by a low standard of living, especially for its Indian population. The series of military governments following the coup failed to address the nation's social and economic problems. That failure led to continual violence and political instability. A coalition of coffee planters, foreign companies, and the military controlled political life. A guerrilla movement grew and provoked brutal military repression, which once again fell particularly hard on the rural Indian population. Guate-

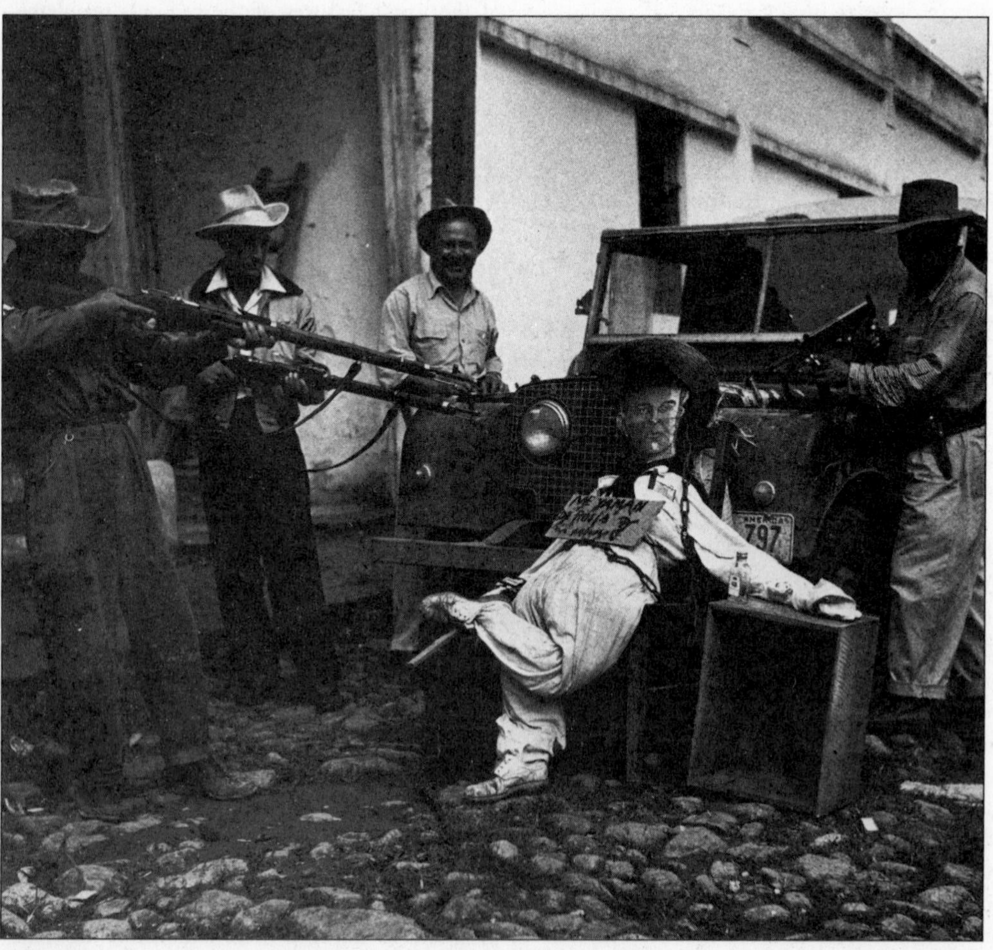

U.S. fears of Soviet influence in Guatemala and sweeping land reforms that threatened U.S. interests led to the coup of 1954. Members of the U.S.-supported "Liberation Army" train their guns on an effigy of the overthrown leftist president, Arbenz. The sign on the effigy reads, "I am going back to Russia with Arevalo."

mala's attempt at radical change, an attempt that began with an eye toward improving the conditions of the people, failed because of external intervention.

THE BOLIVIAN REVOLUTION: A LOSS OF DIRECTION

Another predominantly Indian nation, Bolivia, was the scene of a similar movement for revolutionary change, but its outcome differed. Long characterized by political instability, and with an economy considerably weakened after the loss of territory and access to the sea in the War of the Pacific against neighboring Chile (1879–1883), Bolivia experienced a period of expansion in the 1920s as demands for its major products, silver and tin, increased. Foreign companies, such as Standard Oil of New Jersey, secured concessions to exploit its major resources, and the government took large loans from United States banks to finance various projects. With the world financial crisis of 1929 and a drop in the price of tin, the Bolivian economy was thrown into crisis. To make matters worse, a war broke out with neighboring Paraguay over the disputed region of the Chaco, which blocked Bolivia's access to the rivers leading to the Atlantic and which was thought to contain rich petroleum deposits. The Chaco War (1932–1935) led to high casualties on both sides and more political instability in Bolivia, as defeat by Paraguay led to disillusionment.

Through the 1920s and 1930s, despite rhetoric to the contrary, little was done to lessen the great social gap between the mass of the Indian population and the urban elites or to improve the conditions of the miners, the backbone of the nation's work force. As late as 1950 over 90 percent of the land was owned by six percent of the population, and Indians were often treated like serfs. Conditions in the mines were abysmal, and to a large extent three foreign-owned or controlled mining companies regulated that sector of the economy. Little could be done to change this situation. Because of literacy requirements and gender exclusion for voting, less than seven percent of the population was entitled to cast a ballot.

After an army coup to forestall the electoral victory of a Reformist and Nationalist political coalition called the National Revolutionary Movement (MNR), a revolt erupted in 1952. Although initially an urban political movement, it soon became a real revolution as Indian peasants and mining workers joined in, taking up arms and seizing lands and mines. This was a violent social movement in which armed workers and peasants joined with students and radical middle class interests against the army, the mine owners, and the landed elite. Winning the government, the MNR initiated a series of reforms including universal suffrage, nationalization of the mines, land expropriation and redistribution, and the movement of population from the Andes to unused lands in the nation's eastern lowlands. The mines, long-controlled by three great companies, were nationalized, and the government raised wages and benefits. Land redistribution was extensive. With militant and armed worker and peasant organizations, the government cut back on support for the military, whose power was greatly reduced for a while. The United States, faced with these revolutionary changes, acted cautiously, but since the level of Socialist rhetoric was relatively muted and there seemed to be no direct "external" involvement, the United States recognized the revolutionary government and offered financial assistance, sometimes in large amounts.

The momentum of revolutionary change could not be maintained, however. The mining and agricultural sectors were disrupted by the changes and by poor world prices in the 1960s for tin and other Bolivian minerals. Fearing the radical unions, the government allowed the military to regain some of its power, and then the MNR began to maneuver to ensure its continuance in power. By 1964 the military stepped in again. Since then a series of military governments has ruled for most of the time. While a few of the governments have promised reforms and continuation of the principles of the 1952 revolution, most have been more interested in the maintenance of order. By the 1980s little was left of the revolutionary program, and, more sinisterly, new cartels of cocaine producers linked to the government and the military emerged. The Bolivian Revolution did not fail because of outside intervention as much as it did from the mistakes of its leadership, the weight of the nation's past, and its problems that continued to the present day.

THE CUBAN REVOLUTION: SOCIALISM IN THE CARIBBEAN

The differences between Cuba and Bolivia or Guatemala underline the diversity of Latin America. The island nation had a population of about six million, most of whom were the descendants of Spaniards and the African slaves who had been imported to produce the sugar, tobacco, and hides that were the colony's mainstays. Cuba had a relatively large middle class, and levels of literacy and health care were better than in most of the rest of the region. Rural areas lagged behind in these matters, however, and there the working and living conditions were poor, especially for the workers on the large sugar estates. Always in the shadow of the United States, Cuban politics and economy were rarely free of American interests. By the 1950s about three-fourths of what Cuba imported came from the United States; American investments in the island were heavy during the 1940s and 1950s. While the island experienced periods of prosperity, fluctuations in the world market for Cuba's main product, sugar, revealed the tenuous basis of the economy. Moreover, the disparity between the countryside and the growing middle class in Havana underlined the nation's continuing problems.

From 1934 to 1944 Cuba had been ruled by Fulgencio Batista, a strong-willed, authoritarian reformer who had risen from the lower ranks of the army. Among his reforms were a democratic constitution of 1940 that promised major changes, nationalization of natural resources, full employment, and land reform. Batista's programs of reform, however, began to founder on the shoals of graft and corruption, and when in 1952 he returned to the presidency, there was little left of the reformer but a great deal of the dictator. Opposition developed in various sectors of society. Among the regime's opponents was Fidel Castro, a young lawyer, experienced in leftist university politics and an ardent critic of the Batista government and the ills of Cuban society. On July 26, 1953, Castro and a few followers launched an unsuccessful attack on some military barracks. Captured, Castro faced a trial, an occasion he used to expound his revolutionary ideals, which were mostly aimed at a return to democracy, social justice, and the establishment of a less-dependent economy.

Released from prison, Castro fled to exile in Mexico where, with the aid of Ernesto "Che" Guevara, a militant Argentine revolutionary, a small military force was gathered. They landed in Cuba in 1956 and slowly began to gather strength in the mountains. By 1958 the "26th of July Movement" had found support from students, some labor organizations, and rural workers and was able to conduct operations against Batista's army. The bearded rebels, or *barbudos*, won a series of victories. The dictator, under siege and isolated by the United States (which refused to support him any longer), was driven from power, and the rebels took Havana amid wild scenes of genuine joy and relief.

What happened next is highly debatable, and Castro himself has offered alternate interpretations at different times. Whether Castro was already a Marxist-Leninist and had always intended to introduce a Socialist regime (as he now claims), or whether the development of this program was the result of a series of pragmatic decisions is in question. Rather than simply returning to the Constitution of 1940 and enacting moderate reforms, Castro launched a program of sweeping change that altered the nature of Cuba. Foreign properties were expropriated, farms were

Fidel Castro and his guerrilla army finally brought the downfall of the Batista government in January 1959, to the wild acclaim of many Cubans. Castro began to initiate sweeping reforms in Cuba that eventually led to the creation of a socialist regime and the hostility of the U.S.

collectivized, and a centralized Socialist economy was put in place. Most of these changes were accompanied by a Nationalist and anti-imperialist foreign policy. Relations with the United States were broken off in 1961, and Cuba increasingly depended on the financial support and arms of the Soviet Union to maintain its revolution. With that support in place, Castro was able to survive the increasingly hostile reaction of the United States. That reaction included a disastrous United States sponsored invasion by Cuban exiles in 1961 and an embargo on trade with Cuba. Dependence on the Soviet Union led to a crisis in 1962, when Soviet nuclear missiles were discovered in Cuba and a confrontation between the superpowers ensued. Despite these problems, to a large extent the Cuban Revolution survived because the politics of the cold war provided Cuba with a protector and a benefactor.

The results of the revolution have been mixed. The social programs were extensive. Education, health, and housing have greatly improved and rank Cuba among the world's leaders—quite unlike most other nations of the region. This is especially true in the long-neglected rural areas. A wide variety of social and educational programs has mobilized all sectors of the population. To some extent the achievements have been accompanied by severe restrictions of basic freedoms.

Attempts to diversify and strengthen the economy have been less successful. An effort to industrialize in the 1960s failed, and Cuba turned again to its ability to produce sugar. The world's falling sugar and rising petroleum prices led to a disastrous situation. Only a subsidy for Cuban sugar and the supply of petroleum below the world price has enabled the Soviet Union to maintain the Cuban economy, which has become increasingly dependent on the Soviet Union and the nations of Eastern Europe. Despite these problems, the Cuban Revolution has offered an example that has proven attractive to those seeking the transformation of Latin-American societies. Early direct attempts to spread the model of the Cuban Revolution, such as Che Guevara's guerrilla operation in Bolivia where he lost his life in 1967, were failures, but the Cuban model and the island's ability to resist the pressure of a hostile United States has proven attractive to other nations in the Caribbean and Central America, such as Grenada and Nicaragua that have also sought the revolutionary option.

DOCUMENT
THE PEOPLE SPEAK

Scholarly analysis of general trends often cannot convey the way in which historical events and patterns affect the lives of people, or the fact that history is made up of the collective experience of individuals. It is often very difficult to know about the lives of common people in the past or to learn about their perceptions of their lives. In recent years in Latin America, however, a growing literature of autobiographies, interpreted autobiographies (when another writer puts the story down and edits it), and collections of interviews have provided a vision of the lives of common people. These statements, like any historical document must always be used carefully because their authors or editors sometimes have political purposes, because they reflect individual opinions, or because the events they report may be atypical. Nevertheless, these personal statements do put flesh and blood on the bones of history and provide an important perspective from those whose voice in history is often lost.

A BOLIVIAN WOMAN DESCRIBES HER LIFE

Domitilia Barrios de Chungara was a miner's wife who became politically active in the mine workers' political movement. Her presence at the United Nations-sponsored International Woman's Year Tribunal in 1975 moved a Brazilian journalist to organize her statements into a book about her life. This excerpt provides a picture of the everyday struggle for life.

My day begins at four in the morning, especially when my compañero is on the first shift. I prepare his breakfast. Then I have to prepare *salteñas* [small meat pastries] because I make about one hundred *salteñas* every day and I sell them on the street. I do this in order to make up for what my husband's wage doesn't cover in terms of our necessities. The night before, we prepare the dough and at four in the morning I make the *salteñas* while I feed the kids. The kids help me.

Then the ones that go to school in the morning have to get ready, while I wash the clothes left soaking over night.

At eight I go out to sell. The kids that go to school in the afternoon help me. We have to go to the company store and bring home the staples. And in the store there are immensely long lines and you have to wait there until eleven in order to stock up. You have to line up for meat, for vegetables, for oil. So it's just one line after another. Since everything is in a different place, that's how it has to be.

From what we earn between my husband and me, we can eat and dress. Food is very expensive: 28 pesos for a kilo of meat, 4 pesos for carrots, 6 pesos for onions. . . . Considering that my compañero earns 28 pesos a day, that's hardly enough is it?

We don't ever buy ready made clothes. We buy wool and knit. At the beginning of each year, I also spend about 2,000 pesos on cloth and a pair of shoes for each of us. And the company discounts some of that each month from my husband's wage. On the pay slips that's referred to as the "bundle." And what happens is that before we finish paying the "bundle" our shoes are worn out. That's how it is.

Well, from eight to eleven in the morning I sell

salteñas. I do the shopping in the grocery store, and I also work at the Housewives Committee, talking with the sisters who go there for advice.

At noon, lunch has to be ready because the rest of the kids have to go to school.

In the afternoon I have to wash clothes. There are no laundries. We use troughs and have to get the water from a pump.

I've got to correct the kids' homework and prepare everything I'll need to make the next day's *salteñas*.

FROM PEASANT TO REVOLUTIONARY

Rigoberta Menchú, a Quiché Indian from the Guatemalan highlands, came from a peasant family that had been drawn into politics during the repression of Indian communities and human rights in the 1970s. In these excerpts she reveals her disillusionment with the government and her realization of the ethnic division between Indians and *ladinos*, or mestizos, that complicates political action in Guatemala.

The CUC [Peasant Union] started growing; it spread like wildfire among the peasants in Guatemala. We began to understand that the root of all our problems was exploitation. That there were rich and poor and that the rich exploited the poor—our sweat, our labor. That's how the rich got richer and richer. The fact that we were always waiting in offices, always bowing to the authorities was part of the discrimination that we Indians suffered.

The situation got worse when the murderous generals came to power although I did not actually know who was the president at the time. I began to know them from 1974 when General Kjell Langerud came to power. He came to our region and said: "We're going to solve the land problem. The land belongs to you. You cultivate the land and I will share it out among you." We trusted him. I was at the meeting when [he] spoke. And what did he give us? My father tortured and imprisoned.

Later I had the opportunity of meeting other Indians. Achi Indians, the group that lives closest to us. And I got to know some Mam Indians too. They all told me: "The rich are bad. But not all *ladinos* are bad." And I started wondering: "Could it be that not all *ladinos* are bad? . . ." There were poor *ladinos* as well as rich *ladinos*, and they were exploited as well. That's when I began recognizing exploitation. I kept on going to the *finca* [large farm] but now I really wanted to find out, to prove if that was true and learn the details. There were poor *ladinos* on the *finca*. They worked the same, and their children's bellies were swollen like my little brother's. . . . I was just beginning to speak a little Spanish in those days and I began to talk to them. I said to one poor *ladino:* "You are a poor *ladino*, aren't you?" And he nearly hit me. He said: "What do you know about it, Indian?" I wondered: "Why is that when I say poor *ladinos* are like us, I'm spurned?" I didn't know then that the same system which tries to isolate us Indians also puts barriers between Indians and *ladinos*. . . . Soon afterwards, I was with the nuns and we went to a village in Uspantán where mostly *ladinos* live. The nun asked a little boy if they were poor and he said: "Yes, we're poor but we're not Indians." That stayed with me. The nun didn't notice, she went on talking. She was foreign, she wasn't Guatemalan. She asked someone else the same question and he said: "Yes, we're poor but we're not Indians." It was very painful for me to accept that an Indian was inferior to a *ladino*. I kept on worrying about it. It's a big barrier they've sown between us, between Indian and *ladino*. I didn't understand it.

Questions: What was distinctive about lower-class life and outlook in late 20th-century Latin America? How had life of the lower class changed from the 19th century?

THE SEARCH FOR REFORM AND THE MILITARY OPTION

The revolutionary attempts of the 1950s, the durability of the Cuban Revolution, and the general appeal of Marxist doctrines in the Third World underlined Latin America's proclivity for revolutionary change, so long as real reforms in its economic and social structures remained unchanged. How could the traditional patterns of inequality and international dependency be overcome? What was the best path to the future?

For some, the answer was political stability, imposed if necessary, in order to assure conditions for capitalist economic growth. The one-party system of Mexico demonstrated its capacity for repression when student dissidents were brutally killed during disturbances in 1968. Mexico enjoyed some prosperity from its petroleum resources in the 1970s, but poor financial planning, corruption, and foreign debt had again caused problems by the 1980s, and the PRI seemed to be loosing its ability to maintain control of Mexican politics.

For others the Church, long a power in Latin America, provided a guide. Christian Democratic parties formed in Chile and Venezuela in the 1950s, hoping to bring reforms through popularly based mass parties that would preempt the radical left. The Church, in fact, was often divided politically, but the clergy took an increasingly "engaged" position, arguing for social justice and human rights, often in support of government opponents. A few, such as Father Camilo Torres in Colombia, actually joined armed revolutionary groups in the 1960s.

More common was the emergence within the Church hierarchy of an increased concern for social justice. By the 1970s a "Liberation theology" combined Catholic theology and Socialist principles in an effort to bring about improved conditions for the poor. When criticized for promoting communism in his native Brazil, Dom Helder da Camara, archbishop of Pernambuco, remarked: "The trouble with Brazil is not an excess of Communist doctrine, but a lack of Christian justice." The position of the Church in Latin-American societies was changing, but there was no single program for this new stance nor even agreement among the clergy about its validity. Still, this activist position provoked attacks against clergymen such as the courageous Archbishop Oscar Romero of El Salvador who was assassinated in 1980. The Church also played an important role in the fall of the Paraguayan dictatorship in 1988.

OUT OF THE BARRACKS: SOLDIERS TAKE POWER

The success of the Cuban Revolution also impressed and worried those who feared revolutionary change within a Communist political system. The military forces in Latin America had been involved in politics since the days of the caudillos in the 19th century, and in a number of nations military interventions had been relatively common. As the Latin-American military became more professionalized, however, a new philosophy underlay the military's involvement in politics. The soldiers began to see themselves as above the selfish interests of political parties and as the "true" representatives of the nation. With considerable technical training and organizational skills, military officers by the 1920s and 1930s believed that they were best equipped to solve their nations' problems, even if that meant sacrificing the democratic processes and imposing martial law.

In the 1960s the Latin-American military establishments, made nervous by the Cuban success and the swing to leftist or Populist regimes, began to intervene directly in the political process, not simply to clean out a disliked president or party, as they had done in the past, but to take over government itself. In 1964 the Brazilian military (with the compliance of the United States and supported by the middle class) overthrew the elected president after he threatened a number of sweeping social reforms. In Argentina, growing polarization between the Peronists and the middle class led to a military intervention in 1966. In Chile, the Socialist government of President Salvador Allende was overthrown in 1973 by the Chilean military, which until then had remained for the most part out of politics. Allende had nationalized industries and banks and had sponsored peasant and worker expropriations of lands and factories. His government was caught in an increasing polarization between groups trying to halt these changes and those pushing for faster and more radical reforms. By 1973 the economy was in serious difficulty, undermined by resistence in Chile and by United States policies designed to isolate the country. Allende was killed during the military coup against him, and throughout Latin America there were demonstrations against the military and United States involvement. But Chile was not alone. Similar coups took place in Uruguay in 1973 and in Peru in 1968.

The soldiers in power imposed a new type of "bureaucratic authoritarian regime." Their governments were supposed to stand above competing demands of various sectors and establish economic stability. Now, as arbiters of politics, the soldiers would place the national interest above "selfish interests" by imposing dictatorships. Government was essentially a presidency controlled by the military in which policies were formulated and applied by a bureaucracy organized like a military chain of command. Political repression and torture were used to silence critics, and stringent measures were imposed in order to control inflation and strengthen the economies. While laws limited political freedoms, repression often was brutal and illegal. In Argentina, violent opposition to military rule led to a counteroffensive and a "dirty war" in which thousands of people were "disappeared" [kidnapped] and brutally tortured or killed by government security forces.

Government economic policies fell heaviest on labor and the working class. The goal of the military in Brazil and Argentina was "development" and to some extent, in Brazil at least, considerable economic improvements took place, although income distribution became even more unequal than it had been. Inflation was reduced, industrialization increased, and gains were made in literacy and health, but basic structural problems such as landownership and social conditions for the poorest members of society remained unchanged.

There were variations within these military regimes. All were nationalistic. The Peruvian military tried to create a mass base for its programs and sought to mobilize popular support among the peasantry. It had a real social program, including extensive land reform, and was not simply a surrogate for the conservatives in Peruvian society. In Chile and Uruguay, the military was fiercely anti-Communist. In Argentina, nationalism and a desire to gain popular support in the face of a worsening economy led to a confrontation with Great Britain over the Falkland Islands (Islas Malvinas), which both nations claimed. A short war in 1982 resulted in an Argentine defeat and a loss in the military's credibility that contributed to its loss of authority.

THE NEW DEMOCRATIC TREND

In Argentina and elsewhere in South America, by the mid-1980s, the military had begun to return government to civilian politicians. Continuing economic problems and the pressures of containing opponents wore heavily on the military leaders, who began to realize that their solutions were no more destined to success than those of civilian governments. Moreover, the Populist parties, such as the Peronists and Apristas, seemed less of a threat, and the fear of Cuban-style communism had diminished. In Argentina, elections were held in 1983. Brazil began a process to restore democratic government after 1985 and in 1989 chose its first popularly elected president since the military takeover. The South American military bureaucrats and modernizers were returning to their barracks.

The process of redemocratization was not easy, nor was it universal. In Peru, "Sendero Luminoso (Shining Path)," a long-sustained leftist guerrilla movement controlled areas of the countryside and tried to disrupt national elections in 1990. In Central America, the military cast a long shadow over the government in El Salvador. After the elections of 1990, which removed the Sandinistas from control in Nicaragua, an uneasy truce continued between them and the centralist government of Violeta Chamorro, the newly elected president. The United States demonstrated its continuing power in the region in its invasion of Panama and the arrest of its strongman leader Manuel Noriega.

Latin-American governments in the 1980s faced tremendous problems. Large foreign loans taken in the 1970s for the purposes of development, sometimes for unnecessary projects, had created a tremendous level of debt that threatened the economic stability of countries such as Brazil, Peru, and Mexico. High rates of inflation provoked social instability as real wages fell. Pressure from the international banking community to curb inflation by cutting government spending and reducing wages often ignored the social and political consequences of such actions. Programs to control inflation, such as that introduced by Brazilian president Fernando Collor de Mello, were shock treatments that often disrupted the economy as a whole.

By the late 1980s an international commerce in drugs, which produced tremendous profits, stimulated criminal activity and created powerful international cartels that could even threaten national sovereignty as they did in Colombia. In countries as diverse as Cuba, Panama, and Bolivia the narcotics trade penetrated the highest government circles.

THE UNITED STATES AND LATIN AMERICA

As a backdrop to the political and economic story we have traced thus far stands the continuing presence of the United States. After World War I, the United States had emerged as the predominant power in the hemisphere, a position it had already begun to assume at the close of the 19th century with the Cuban-Spanish-American War and the building of the Panama Canal. European nations were displaced as the leading investors in Latin America by the United States. In South America, private investments by American companies and entrepreneurs, as well as loans from the American government, were the chief means of United States influence. United States investments rose to over five billion dollars by 1929, or over one-third of all United States investments abroad.

In Cuba and Puerto Rico, of course, there was direct United States involvement and almost a protectorate status. But in the Caribbean and Central America, the face of United States power, economic interest, and disregard for the sovereignty of weaker neighbors was most apparent. Military interventions to protect United States-owned properties and investments became common. There were over 30 prior to 1933. Haiti, Nicaragua, the Dominican Republic, Mexico, and Cuba all witnessed one or more direct interventions by United States troops. Central America was a peculiar case because the level of United States private investments of companies such as United Fruit was very high and the economies of these countries were so closely tied to the United States. Those who resisted the United States' presence were treated as "bandits" by expeditionary forces. In Nicaragua Augusto Sandino led a resistance movement against occupying troops until his assassination by the United States-trained Nicaraguan National Guard in 1934. His struggle against American intervention made him a hero and the figurehead of the Sandinista party, which carried out a Socialist revolution in Nicaragua in the 1980s.

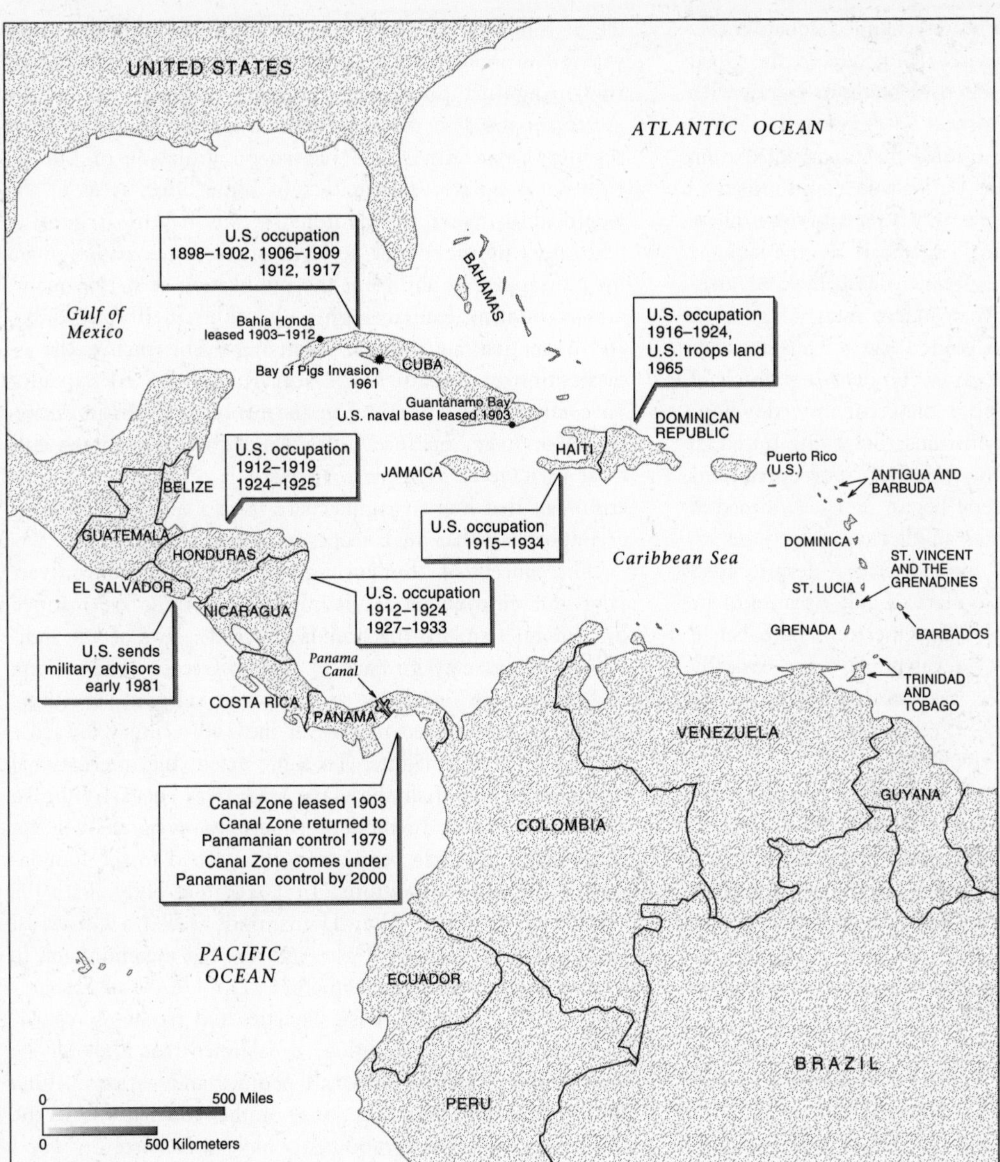

Intervention in Central America and the Caribbean, 1898–1981

The grounds for these interventions were economic, political, strategic, and ideological. The direct interventions were usually followed by the creation or support of conservative governments, often dictatorships that would be "friendly" to the United States. These became "Banana Republics," a reference not only to their dependence on the export of tropical products, but also to their often subservient and corrupt governments.

Foreign interventions contributed to a growing Nationalist reaction. Central America with its continuing political problems became a symbol of Latin America's weakness in the face of foreign, especially United States, influence and interference. The Nobel Prize-winning Chilean Communist poet Pablo Neruda, in his poem "The United Fruit Co." (1950), spoke of the dictators of Central America as "circus flies, wise flies, learned in tyranny" who buzzed over the graves of the people. He wrote the following eight lines with passion:

> When the trumpet sounded, all was prepared in the land,
> and Jehovah divided the world between Coca Cola Inc.,
> Anaconda, Ford Motors, and other companies:
> United Fruit Co. reserved for itself the juiciest part,
> the central coast of my land,
> the sweet waist of America
> and baptized again its lands
> as Banana Republics. . . .

The actions of the United States changed considerably after 1933, when President Roosevelt introduced the Good Neighbor Policy that promised to deal more fairly with Latin America and to stop direct interventions. After World War II, however, the United States' preoccupation with containment of the Soviet Union and communism as an ideology led to new strategies in Latin America. These included participation in regional organizations, the support of governments that at least expressed democratic or anti-Communist principles, the covert undermining of governments considered unfriendly to United States interests, and, when necessary, direct intervention. Underlying much of this policy was also a firm belief that economic development would eliminate the conditions that contributed to radical political solutions. Thus, United States programs such as the Alliance for Progress, begun in 1961, aimed at the development of the region as an alternative to those solutions. The alliance had only limited success despite good intentions and over ten billion dollars of aid. Because of its record, Latin Americans and North Americans both began to question the assumption that "development" was basically a problem of capital and resources, and that appropriate strategies would lead to social and economic improvement, which in turn would forestall revolution.

During the 1970s and 1980s, United States policy was often "pragmatic," accepting Latin America "as it was," which meant dealing on friendly terms with the military dictatorships. President Jimmy Carter (1976-1980) made a new initiative to deal with Latin America and to influence governments there to observe civil liberties. Most significantly, a treaty was signed with Panama ceding to that nation eventual control of the Panama Canal.

Increasing violence in Central America in the 1980s and the more conservative presidencies of Ronald Reagan and George Bush have led the United States back to policies based on strategic, economic, and defense considerations in which direct intervention or support of counterrevolutionary forces have played a part. Thus in 1989 and 1990 the United States toppled a government in Panama—authoritarian but defiant of United States policies, including control of drug smuggling—replacing it with a cooperative regime backed by American troops.

ANALYSIS
HUMAN RIGHTS IN THE 20TH CENTURY

In Latin America the question of "human rights" became a burning issue in the decade of the 1960s and continued thereafter. The use of torture by repressive governments, the mobilization of death squads and other vigilante groups with government acquiescence, and the employment of terrorism against political opponents by the state and by groups opposed to the state became all too common in the region. Latin America's record on violation of human rights was no worse than that of some other areas of the world. However, the demonstrations by the Argentine "Mothers of the Plaza del Mayo" to focus attention on their disappeared children; the publication of prison memoirs recounting human rights violations in Brazil, Cuba, and Argentina; and films dramatizing events such as the assassination of Archbishop Oscar Romero in El Salvador have all focused attention on the problem in Latin America. Moreover, because Latin America shares in the cultural heritage of Western societies it is difficult to make an argument that human rights there have a different meaning or importance than in Europe or North America.

The concept of "human rights," that is, certain universal rights enjoyed by all people because these are justified by a moral standard that stands above the laws of any individual nation, may go back to ancient Greece. The concept of "natural law" and the protection of religious or ethnic minorities also moved nations in the 19th century toward a defense of human rights. To some extent the international movement to abolish the slave trade was an early human rights movement. In modern times, however, the concept of human rights has been strongly attached to the foundation of the United Nations. In 1948, that body, with the experience of World War II in mind, issued a Universal Declaration of Human Rights and created a commission to oversee the human rights situation. The Universal Declaration, which guaranteed basic liberties and freedoms regardless of color, sex, or religion, proclaimed that it should be the "common standard for all peoples and nations." One critic has stated, however, that of the 160 nations in the United Nations, only about 30 have a consistently good record on the matter of human rights.

A major problem for the international community has been enforcement. The United Nations commission did not have any specific powers of enforcement, and much debate subsequently has taken place on the power of the United Nations to intervene in the internal affairs of any nation. More recently, various regional organizations have tried to establish the norms that should govern human rights and to create institutions to enforce these norms. The European community established a body to deal with human rights in the 1950s. Since 1969, under the auspices of the Organization of American States, the American Convention on Human Rights has been active in the Americas. More recently, in the 1980s, the Organization of African Unity has created a similar body. In addition there are private groups such as Amnesty International, which seeks to investigate and reveal abuses. Throughout much of the world there is a growing feeling that the issue of human rights transcends national boundaries.

One specialist has claimed that "human rights is the world's first universal ideology." The defense of human rights would seem to be a cause that most people and governments would be able to accept without hesitation, but the question is, in fact, a complex one. While the rights to life, liberty, security, and to be free from torture or degrading punishment are generally accepted in principle by all nations, other "rights" remain open to question. What is a "right," and to what extent are definitions of "rights" determined by culture?

The question of universality versus relativism quickly emerged in the debate over human rights. What seemed to be obvious human rights in Western societies were less obvious in other parts of the world where other priorities were held. Laws prohibiting child labor, for example, were enforced by most Western societies, but throughout the world perhaps 150 million children worked, often in unhealthy and exploitative conditions. They worked often because of economic necessity but in some societies they also worked because such labor was considered moral and proper. Such cultural differences have led to a position of relativism, which recognizes that there are profound cultural variations in what is considered moral and just. Critics of the original Universal Declaration, for example, have contended that its advocacy of the right to own property and the right to vote imposed Western political and economic values as universals, which in fact they were not. Cultural relativism had the advantage of recognizing the variety of cultures and standards in the world, but it has at times also been used as a shield to deflect criticism and to continue to violate human rights.

The definition of human rights is also political. The West has placed considerable emphasis on civil and political rights of the individual. The Socialist nations have placed social and economic justice above individual rights, although by the 1990s movements in Eastern Europe and China indicated that there was considerable pressure to modify this approach. In the Third World an argument for "peoples' rights" has emerged in which the "right to development," which calls for a major structural redistribution of the world's resources and economic opportunities, is a central concept. As Leopold Senghor of Senegal put it: "Human rights begin with breakfast"; or as a report on Ghana stated: "'One man, one vote,' is meaningless unless accompanied by the principle of 'one man, one bread.'" Needless to say, while the "right to development" is seen as a human right in the Third World, it is viewed instead as a political and economic demand in wealthier nations of the West.

Another dimension of human rights is the extent to which it influences national foreign policies. Governments may make statements pledging respect for human rights in their foreign policy, but often considerations of national defense, sovereignty, or goals, such as the maintenance of peace, may move human rights concerns into a secondary position. Sometimes disputes over the role of human rights in foreign policy have been posed as a conflict between "moralistic utopians" who see the world as it should be and "pragmatists" who see the world as it is. Neither approach necessarily denies the importance of human rights, but there are differences in priority and strategy. Pragmatists might argue that it is better to maintain relations with a nation violating human rights in order to be able to exercise some influence over it in the future, or that other policy considerations must be weighed along with those of human rights in establishing foreign policy. Moralists would hope to bring pressure by isolating and condemning a nation that violates international standards.

These different approaches have been reflected in United States policy shifts toward Latin America. In the 1950s human rights considerations were secondary to opposing the spread of communism in the hemisphere, and the United States was willing to support governments that violated human rights so long as they were staunch anti-Communist allies. During the 1960s this policy continued, but increasing and systematic abuses by military regimes in Brazil, Uruguay, Chile, Nicaragua, and elsewhere in Latin America began to elicit some changes. In 1977 President Carter initiated a new policy in which human rights considerations would be given high priority in United States foreign policy. The United States' refusal to support or aid governments that violated human rights contributed to the weakening of some regimes and stimulated resistance to human rights violations in Latin America, but by the 1980s a more pragmatic approach had returned to United States policy. Criticism of human rights violations was sometimes made selectively, dismissing abuses in "friendly" governments. The extent to which human rights concerns must be balanced against issues such as security, the maintenance of peace, and nonintervention continues to preoccupy policymakers.

During the 1990s attention to human rights will play an increasingly important role in international affairs. Problems of definition still remain and there is no universal agreement on the exact nature of human rights. Controversy on the relative weight of political and civil rights and social, cultural, and economic ones continues to divide richer and poorer nations. Still, the United Nations Declaration of Human Rights, to which 160 nations are signatories, provides a basic guideline and an outline for the future.

Questions: Why might various regimes oppose human rights, and on what basis? Is the human rights movement a Western replacement for imperialism as a means of international political influence? Have international human rights movements produced political change?

SOCIETIES IN SEARCH OF CHANGE

Despite the structural, political, and international conditions that have frustrated Latin-American attempts at profound reform there have been considerable changes during the 20th century. Problems of ethnicity, gender, and class continue to influence many of these societies. The movement of populations and their settlement has also been a major feature of the century. These two aspects of social life represent just two of the continuing historical processes of Latin America.

Social and gender relations have changed during the century. We have already seen how countries such as Mexico, Peru, and Bolivia sought to enfranchise their Indian populations during this century in different ways and with differing degrees of success. National ideologies and actual practice are often not the same, and discrimination on the basis of ethnicity continues in many places. To be called "Indian" is still an insult in many places in Latin America. While ethnic and cultural mixture characterizes many Latin-American populations and makes Indian and African elements important features of national identity, relations with Indian populations often continue to be marked by exploitation and discrimination in nations as diverse as Brazil, Nicaragua, and Guatemala.

WOMEN'S ROLES

The role of women has changed considerably but relatively slowly. In the years following World War I, women in Latin America continued to live under disabilities in the work place and in politics. Women were denied the right to vote anywhere in Latin America until Ecuador enfranchised women in 1929 and Brazil and Cuba did the same in 1932, but throughout most of the region those examples were not followed until the decades of the 1940s and 1950s. In some nations, the traditional associations of women with religion and the Catholic church in Hispanic life made reformers and revolutionaries fear that women would become a conservative force in national politics. This attitude, combined with traditional male attitudes that women should be concerned only with home and family, led to a continued exclusion of women from political life. In response, women formed various associations and clubs and began to push for the vote and other issues of particular interest to them.

Feminist organizations, suffrage movements, and international pressures eventually combined to bring about change. In Argentina 15 bills for female suffrage were introduced into the senate before the vote was won in 1945. Sometimes the victory was a matter of political expediency for those in power. In a number of places such as the Dominican Republic, enfranchisement of women was a strategy used by conservative groups to add more conservative voters to the electorate in an effort to hold off political change. In Argentina recently enfranchised women became a major pillar of the Peronist regime, although that regime was not averse to suppressing female political opponents such as Victoria Ocampo, editor of the important literary magazine, *Sur*.

Women eventually discovered that the ability to vote did not by itself guarantee political rights or the ability to have their specific issues heard. After achieving the vote, women tended to join the national political parties, where traditional prejudices against women in public life limited their ability to influence political programs. In Argentina, Brazil, Colombia, and Chile, for example, the integration of women into national political programs has been slow, and women have not participated in proportion to their numbers. In a few cases, however, such as in the election of Perón in Argentina in 1946 and Eduardo Frei in Chile in 1964, or in the popular opposition to Salvador Allende in 1973, women played a crucial role.

Some of the earliest examples of mobilization of women and their integration into the national labor force of various Latin-American nations came in the period just before the First World War and continued thereafter. The classic roles of women as homemakers, mothers, and part of the agricultural work force were increasingly expanded as women entered the industrial labor force in growing numbers. By 1911 in Argentina, for example, women made up almost 80 percent of the textile and clothing industry's workers. But women found that their salaries were often below those of comparable male workers and that their jobs, no matter the skill levels demanded, were considered "unskilled" and thus less well paid. Under these conditions women, like other workers, joined the Anarchist, Socialist, and other labor unions and organizations.

Labor organizations are only a small part of the story of women in the labor force. In countries such as Peru, Bolivia, and Ecuador, market women control much small-scale commerce and have become increasingly active politically. In the growing service sectors women have also become an important part of the labor force. Shifts in attitudes about women's roles have come more slowly than political and economic changes. Even in revolutionary Cuba, where a Law of the Family guaranteed equal rights and responsibilities within the home, enforcement has been difficult.

By the mid-1980s, the position of women in Latin America stood closer to the status of women in Western Europe and North America than it did to the other areas of the world. Women made up nine percent of the legislators in Latin America, a percentage higher than in any other region of the world. They also held nine percent of the cabinet posts, a figure only behind North America (12 percent). In terms of demographic patterns, health, education, and place in the work force, the comparative position of women reinforced Latin America's intermediate position between the "developed nations" and the Third World.

THE MOVEMENT OF PEOPLE

In 1950 the populations of North America (United States and Canada) and Latin America were both about 165 million, but by 1985 Latin America's population had grown to over 400 million compared to 165 million for North America. Declining mortality and continuing high fertility were responsible for this situation.

While at the beginning of the 20th century the major trend of population movement was immigration to Latin America, the region has long experienced internal migration and the movement of people within the hemisphere. By the 1980s this movement had reached significant levels, fed by the flow of workers seeking jobs, the demands of capital for cheap labor, and the flight of political refugees seeking basic freedoms. Large numbers of West Indians from Jamaica, Barbados, and other islands have migrated to Great Britain or the United States. In the 1920s Mexican workers crossed the border to the United States in large numbers at the same time that Guatemalans crossed the border to Mexico to work on coffee estates. During World War II government programs to supply laborers were set up between the United States and Mexico, but these were always accompanied by a considerable amount of extralegal migration, which fluctuated with the economy. Conditions for migrant laborers were often deplorable, although the extension of social welfare to them in the 1960s began to address some of the problems. By the 1970s over 750,000 illegal Mexican migrants a year were crossing the border—some more than once—as the United States continued to attract migrants.

This internationalization of the labor market was comparable in many ways to the movement of workers from poorer countries such as Turkey, Morocco, Portugal, and Spain to the stronger economies of West Germany and France. In Latin America it also reflected the fact that industrialization in the 20th century depended on highly mechanized industry that did not create enough new jobs to meet the needs of the growing population. Much of the migration has been to the United States, but there has also been considerable movement across Latin-American frontiers, as Haitians migrate to work in the Dominican Republic or Colombians illegally migrate to Venezuela. By the 1970s about five million people per year were migrating in Latin America and the Caribbean.

Politics has also been a major impulse for migration. Haitians fleeing political repression and abysmal conditions have risked great dangers in small open boats to reach the United States. One of the great political migrations of the century has been caused by the Cuban Revolution. Beginning in 1959 with the middle class fleeing socialism, but continuing into the 1980s with the flight of Cuban workers, close to one million Cubans have left the island. The revolutionary upheaval in Nicaragua and political violence in Central America have contributed to the flight of refugees. Often, it is difficult to separate political and economic factors in the movement of people from their homelands.

International migration is only part of the story. During the century there has been a marked movement in Latin America from rural to urban areas. While in the 19th century Latin America had been an agrarian region, by the 1980s about one-half of the population lived in cities of over 20,000, and over 25 of these cities had populations of over one million. Some of these cities had reached enormous size. In 1988 Mexico City had over 16 million inhabitants, São Paulo had 10 million, and Buenos Aires had 8 million. Latin America was by far the most urbanized area of the developing world and only slightly less urbanized than Western Europe.

The problem is not one simply of size but of the rate of growth. The urban populations have grown at a rate about three times that of the population as a whole, which itself was growing rapidly. Urban economies have not been able to create enough jobs for the rapidly increasing population. Often recent migrants lived in marginal neighborhoods or in shantytowns, which have become characteristic of the rapid urban growth of Latin America. These *favelas,* to give the Brazilian term for them, have created awful living conditions, but over time some have become poorer neighborhoods within the cities in which community cooperation and action have taken place to secure basic urban services.

In Socialist Cuba, a concerted effort to de-emphasize Havana and other large cities and reverse the rural-urban migration pattern was made, but in most of the region, urbanization has continued as growing populations seek better opportunities. In part, this movement is explained by a general population growth rate of over 2.5 percent per year since the 1960s.

TABLE 38-1

Population of Capital Cities as a Percentage of Total Population in Ten Latin-American Nations

Nation	Capital	1880	1905	1930	1960	1983
1. Brazil	Rio	3	4	4	7	(4)
2. Mexico	Mexico City	3	3	5	15	20
3. Argentina	Buenos Aires	12	20	20	32	34
4. Colombia	Bogotá	1	2	2	8	11
5. Peru	Lima	3	3	5	19	27
6. Chile	Santiago	6	10	13	22	37
7. Uruguay	Montevideo	12	30	28	31	40
8. Venezuela	Caracas	3	4	7	20	18
9. Cuba	Havana	13	15	15	18	20
10. Panama	Panama City	7	14	16	25	20

( ) = no longer capital city

Source: From J. P. Cole, *Latin America: An Economic and Social Geography* (1965), 417.

While Latin-American urbanization has increased rapidly since 1940, the percentage of its people living in cities is still less than in Western Europe but more than in Asia and Africa. Unlike the 19th-century European experience, the lack of employment in Latin-American cities has kept rural migrants from becoming part of a laboring class with a strong identification with fellow workers. Those who do succeed in securing industrial jobs often join paternalistic labor organizations that are linked to the government. Thus there is a separation between the chronically underemployed urban lower class and the industrial labor force. Whereas industrialization and urbanization promoted a strong class solidarity in 19th-century Europe that led to the gains of organized labor, in contemporary Latin America Nationalist and Populist politics have weakened the ability of the working class to operate effectively in politics.

CULTURAL REFLECTIONS OF DESPAIR AND HOPE

Latin America remains an amalgamation of cultures and peoples seeking to adjust to changing world realities. Protestant denominations have made some inroads, but the vast majority of Latin Americans are still nominally Roman Catholics. Hispanic traditions of family, gender relations, business, and social interaction influence everyday life and help to determine responses to the modern world.

Latin-American popular culture remains vibrant. It draws on African and Indian traditional crafts, images, and techniques but arranges them in new ways. Also part of popular culture are various forms of Latin-American music. The Argentine tango of the turn of the century developed from the music halls of lower-class working districts of Buenos Aires into an international craze. The African-influenced Brazilian *samba* and the Caribbean *salsa* have been widely diffused, a Latin-American contribution to world civilization.

The struggle for social justice, economic security, and political formulas in keeping with the cultural and social realities of their nations has provided a dynamic tension that has produced tremendous artistic achievements. Latin-American poets and novelists have gained worldwide recognition. We have already noted the artistic accomplishments of the Mexican Revolution. In 1922 Brazilian artists, composers, and authors staged a Modern Art Week in São Paulo, which emphasized a search for a national artistic expression that reflected Brazilian realities.

That theme also preoccupied authors elsewhere in Latin America. The social criticism of the 1930s produced powerful realist novels that revealed the exploitation of the poor, the peasantry, and the Indians. Whether in the heights of the Andes or in the dark streets of the growing urban slums, the plight of the common folk provided a generation of authors with themes worthy of their effort. Social and political criticism has remained a central feature

Latin-American artists such as Colombian Fernando Botero (b. 1932) used surrealism and irony to depict Latin-American realities. The dominance of military regimes in the 1970s called forth the imaginative parody of the soldiers reflected in this painting.

of Latin-American literature and art and has played an important role in the development of newer art forms such as filmmaking.

The inability to bring about social justice or to influence politics has also sometimes led Latin-American artists and intellectuals to follow other paths. In the 1960s a "boom" of literature took place in which novels that mixed the political, the historical, the erotic, and the fantastic were produced by a generation of authors who found the reality of Latin America too absurd to be described by the traditional forms or logic. Writers such as the Argentine Jorge Luis Borges (b. 1899) and the Colombian Gabriel García Marquez (b. 1928) won acclaim throughout the world for their literary ability. García Marquez's *One Hundred Years of Solitude* (1967) used the history of a family in a mythical town called Macondo as an allegory of Latin America and traced the evils that befell the family and the community as they moved from naive isolation to a maturity that included oppression, exploitation, war, revolution, and natural disaster, but which never subdued the spirit of its people. In that way, his book outlined the trajectory of Latin America in the 20th century.

CONCLUSION

STRUGGLING TOWARD THE FUTURE

By the last decade of the 20th century Latin America continued to search for economic growth, social justice, and political stability. No easy solutions were available. In many ways, Latin-American societies remained "unrevolutionary," unable to bring about needed changes because of deeply entrenched class interests, international conditions, or power politics. The struggle for change had, however, produced some important results. The Mexican and Cuban revolutions brought profound changes in those countries and had a broad impact over the rest of the hemisphere, either as models to copy or dangers to be avoided. Other nations, such as Bolivia, Peru, and Nicaragua, attempted their own versions of radical change with greater or lesser success. New forms of politics, sometimes Populist and sometimes militarist, were tried and new political and social ideas like those of "Liberation Theology" grew out of the struggle to find a just and effective formula for change. Latin-American authors and artists served as a conscience for their societies and received worldwide recognition for their depiction of the sometimes surreal reality they observed. While tremendous problems continued to face the region, Latin America remained the most advanced part of the developing world.

FURTHER READINGS

There is a considerable literature in many disciplines that deals with Latin America as a whole, as well as many country-specific studies. Two good introductory texts, both of which present variations of the "dependency" interpretation, are E. Bradford Burns's *Latin America: A Concise Interpretative History* (4th ed., 1986) and Thomas E. Skidmore and Peter H. Smith's *Modern Latin America* (1989). An excellent overview of Latin-American literature and art is provided by Jean Franco's *The Modern Culture of Latin America* (2d ed., 1970). Aspects of population history are discussed in Nicholas Sánchez-Albornoz's *The Population of Latin America* (1970) and Magnus Morner's *Adventurers and Proletarians: The Story of Migrants in Latin America* (1985). The role of women is presented briefly in June Hahner's *Women in Latin American History* (1976).

The economic history of Latin America is summarized in the classic by Brazilian economist Celso Furtado, *Economic Development of Latin America* (2d ed., 1976) and in John Sheahan's *Patterns of Development in Latin America* (1987). Two excellent studies of labor that have essentially different emphases are Hobart Spalding, Jr.'s *Organized Labor in Latin America* (1977) and Charles Berquist's *Labor in Latin America* (1986).

There are many good studies of Latin American politics, but Guillermo O'Donnell's *Modernization and Bureaucratic Authoritarianism* (1973) has influenced much recent scholarship. The role of the United States is discussed in Abraham Lowenthal's *Partners in Conflict: The United States and Latin America* (1987). Lester D. Langley's *The United States and the Caribbean in the Twentieth Century* (4th ed., 1989) gives a clear account of the recent history in that region, while Walter La Feber's *Inevitable Revolutions* (1984) is a critical assessment of United States policy in Central America. Lars Schoultz's *Human Rights and United States Policy toward Latin America* (1981), details how human rights have influenced foreign policy.

A few good monographs on important topics can serve to indicate the high level of scholarship on Latin America. Alan Knight's *The Mexican Revolution*, 2 vols. (1986) and John M. Hart's *Revolutionary Mexico* (1987) provide excellent analyses of that event. Florencia Mallon's *The Defense of Community in Peru's Central Highlands* (1983) looks at national change from a community perspective. Robert Potash's *The Army and Politics in Argentina 1945–1962* (1980) is one of the best in-depth studies of a Latin-American military establishment, while Richard Gott's *Guerilla Movements in Latin America* (1972) presents analysis and documents on the movements seeking revolutionary change.

THE INDIAN PROTOTYPE: THE MAKINGS OF THE NATIONALIST CHALLENGE TO THE BRITISH RAJ

EGYPT AND THE RISE OF NATIONALISM IN THE MIDDLE EAST

- **DOCUMENT:** Lessons for the Colonized from the Slaughter in the Trenches

WORLD WAR I AND THE POSTWAR CRISIS OF THE EUROPEAN EMPIRES

- **ANALYSIS:** Women in Asian and African Nationalist Movements

ANOTHER GLOBAL WAR AND THE COLLAPSE OF THE EUROPEAN WORLD ORDER

- **CONCLUSION:** The Limits of Decolonization
- **FURTHER READINGS**

1876 Madras famine in India

1882 Orabi revolt in Egypt; British occupation of Egypt

1885 Founding of the Indian Congress party

1890s First Egyptian political parties formed

1897 World Zionist Organization founded; West African Aborigines Rights Protection Society founded

1904–1905 Japanese victory over Russia; British partition of the province of Bengal in India

1906 Dinshawai incident in Egypt; Muslim League founded in India

A.D. 1880 | A.D. 1890 | A.D. 1900

39 Decolonization and the Decline of the European World Order

INTRODUCTION. All of the great civilizations of Asia and Africa had been shaken to their foundations by Europe's rise to global hegemony in the 18th and 19th centuries. European political, economic, and later cultural dominance forced the thinkers and leaders of ancient centers of civilized development—from China and the Islamic heartlands to South Asia and Sudanic Africa (see Chapters 29, 30 and 32)—to reappraise their own beliefs, institutions, and traditions. However reluctantly, many of these thinkers and politicians came to the realization that if their civilizations were to be revitalized and freed from European domination, hard decisions had to be made as to what could be preserved of their own cultures and what could be rejected, what needed to be borrowed from the Europeans and what could be refused.

Most accounts of African and Asian solutions to these dilemmas stress ideas such as nationalism and modes of political organization that the colonized peoples borrowed from the Europeans. But African and Asian responses, which eventually forced the Europeans to relinquish their colonial empires, were also deeply rooted in their own religions, long-standing patterns of political mobilization, and other facets of their traditions of civilization. Reinvigorating and reformulating these distinctive civilized traditions has proven one of the central challenges for 20th-century African and Asian leaders, both in the era of decolonization and the postcolonial period that followed.

In the decades at the end of the 19th century when Europe's global domination peaked, forces were beginning to build that would eventually lead to the loss of its colonial empires and bring its world domination to an end. Some

1909 Morley-Minto political reforms in India

1913 Rabindranath Tagore wins the Nobel Prize for literature

1914–1918 World War I; main theaters of war in European colonies: Mesopotamia, Arabia and Palestine, and Africa

1915–1916 McMahon-Hussein correspondence

1917 Balfour Declaration

1919 Revolt in Egypt, women a major force in demonstrations; Montagu-Chelmsford reforms in India; Rowlatt Act in India; first all-India civil disobedience movement

1920s Pan-African Congresses in Paris; beginnings of the négritude movement

1921 René Maran wins the French Prix Goncourt for *Batouala*

1922 British granted the League of Nations mandate for Palestine; first stage in Egyptian independence

1927 Simon Commission in India

1930s Great Depression

1931 Gandhi-led Salt March revives Indian Nationalist movement; strikes and rebellion in Sierra Leone

1935 Government of India Act

1936–1939 Arab risings in Palestine

A.D. 1910 | A.D. 1920 | A.D. 1930 | CONTINUED

of these forces came from within the colonies as a sense of community and common cause began to build among the Western-educated, middle-class groups that emerged in colonized Asia and Africa (see Chapter 30). The political organizations established by these groups and their efforts to arouse mass nationalist sentiments increasingly challenged the right of the Europeans to subjugate African and Asian lands and peoples.

Though violence was sometimes employed, particularly in colonial societies with settler populations, African and Asian nationalists relied mainly on peaceful mass demonstrations, economic boycotts, and constitutional maneuvers in their struggles for independence. In these struggles, leaders such as Mohandas Gandhi and Kwame Nkrumah deftly turned the Europeans' own principles and values, such as those stressing human dignity and civil rights, against the colonial overlords. At the same time they employed indigenous religious beliefs and traditional symbols of legitimacy to rally mass support to their cause. The fact that European colonial regimes had been built in collaboration with indigenous elite groups—including princes, landlords, and the new middle classes—and depended for their survival on these groups, as well as on soldiers and policemen recruited from the colonized peoples, rendered them particularly vulnerable to growing challenges from within.

In addition to internal forces that eroded the European colonial order, growing conflicts between the Western powers dealt heavy blows to the imperial edifice. The rivalries between the great powers that helped cause the late 19th-century scramble for colonies also contributed to the outbreak of the series of global conflicts that set the framework for 20th-century global history. Thus, World War I cast doubt on the Europeans' claims that they were the fittest of all peoples to rule. It also strengthened the arguments of nationalist leaders who sought to disprove prevailing myths of European invincibility and superiority. Even before 1914 those myths had been badly damaged by the rise of Japan as an industrialized, global power. Japan's decisive victory over the Russians in the Russo-Japanese War of 1904 and 1905 thrilled nationalists from Vietnam to Egypt and gave them confidence that the European colonizers could be overcome.

The social and economic disruptions caused by the war in key colonies, such as Egypt, India, and the Ivory Coast, made it possible for nationalist agitators to build a mass base for their anticolonial movements. The Great Depression of the 1930s, which hit most of the colonies very hard, gave further strength to the nationalist cause. It also brought on harsh repression in many colonies on the part of European administrators, who became deeply worried about their capacity to preserve European dominance in Africa and Asia. Despite the ultimate victory of the old colonial powers over Nazi Germany and Japan, World War II dealt a series of crushing blows to the European colonial order. Within decades of the end of that conflict, most of Africa and Asia had been liberated from European rule.

This chapter will explore each of these phases of the decolonization process, beginning with the first stirrings of nationalism in India and Egypt in the late 19th century. The sections that follow will examine the interplay between international events, such as those associated with the two world wars and the Great Depression, and conditions and movements in the colonies. Since it is impossible to relate the history of the independence struggles in each of the colonies, key movements, such as those in India, Egypt, and British and French West Africa, will be considered in some depth. These specific movements will then be related to broader patterns in African and Asian decolonization or, in the case of South Africa, the winning of independence for a small minority of the colonial population. The case of Vietnam, which makes an interesting comparison with its equally revolutionary neighbor, China, will be considered in Chapter 41.

1941–1945 World War II; main theaters of war in European colonies: North Africa, Southeast Asia, and Pacific Islands

1941 Fall of Singapore to the Japanese

1942 Cripps Mission to India; Quit India movement

1947 India and Pakistan gain independence

1948 Israel-Palestine partition, first Arab-Israeli war; beginning of apartheid legislation in South Africa

1957 Ghana established as first independent African nation

1958 Afrikaner Nationalist party declares independence of South Africa

1960 Congo granted independence from Belgian rule

1962 Algeria wins independence

A.D. 1940 A.D. 1950 A.D. 1960

THE INDIAN PROTOTYPE: THE MAKINGS OF THE NATIONALIST CHALLENGE TO THE BRITISH RAJ

Because India and much of Southeast Asia had been colonized long before Africa, movements for independence arose in Asian colonies somewhat earlier than in their African counterparts. By the last years of the 19th century, the Western-educated minority of the colonized had been organized politically in India and the Philippines for decades and were beginning to form associations to give voice to their political concerns in Burma and the Netherlands Indies. Because of India's size, the pivotal role it played in the British Empire (by far the largest of the European imperialist empires) as a whole, and the large numbers and sophistication of India's Western-educated elite, the Indian nationalist movement pioneered patterns of nationalist challenge and European retreat that were later followed in many other colonies. Local conditions elsewhere in Asia and in Africa made for important variations on the sequence of decolonization worked out in India. But key themes, such as the lead taken by Western-educated elites, the importance of charismatic leaders in the spread of the anticolonial struggle to the peasant and urban masses, and a reliance on nonviolent forms of protest, were repeated again and again in other colonial settings, often in conscious emulation of strategies that had achieved great success in India.

The Indian Congress party, which led the Indians to independence and has governed through most of the postcolonial era, grew out of regional associations of Western-educated Indians that were more like study clubs than political organizations in any meaningful sense of the term. These associations were centered in the cities of Bombay, Poona, Calcutta, and Madras. The Congress party that Indian leaders formed in 1885 had the blessing of a number of high-ranking British officials. These officials viewed it as a forum through which the opinions of educated Indians could be made known to the government, thereby heading off potential discontent and political protest.

For most of its first decades, the Congress party served these purposes quite well. The organization had no mass base and very few ongoing staff members or full-time politicians who could sustain lobbying efforts on issues raised at its annual meetings. Some members of the Congress party voiced concern for the growing poverty of the Indian masses and the drain of wealth from the subcontinent to Great Britain. But the Congress party's debates and petitions to the government were dominated by elite-centric issues such as the removal of barriers to Indian employment in the colonial bureaucracy and increased Indian representation in all-Indian and local legislative bodies. Most of the members of the early Congress party were firmly loyal to the British rulers and confident that once their grievances were made known to the government, they would be remedied.

British India in the Nationalist Era

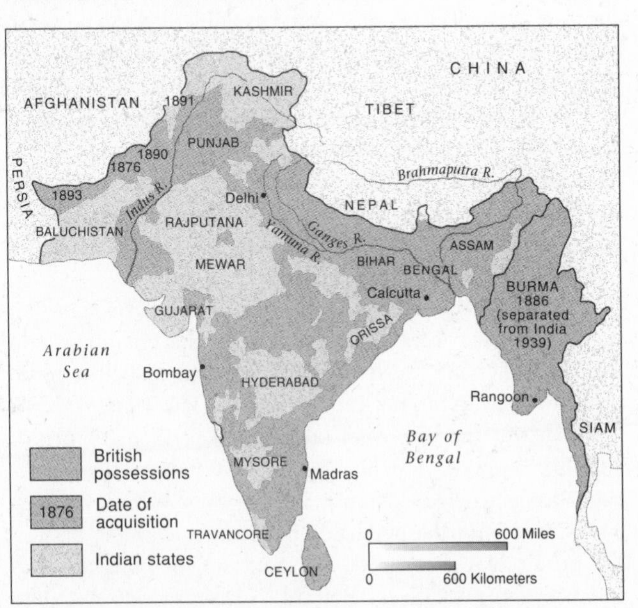

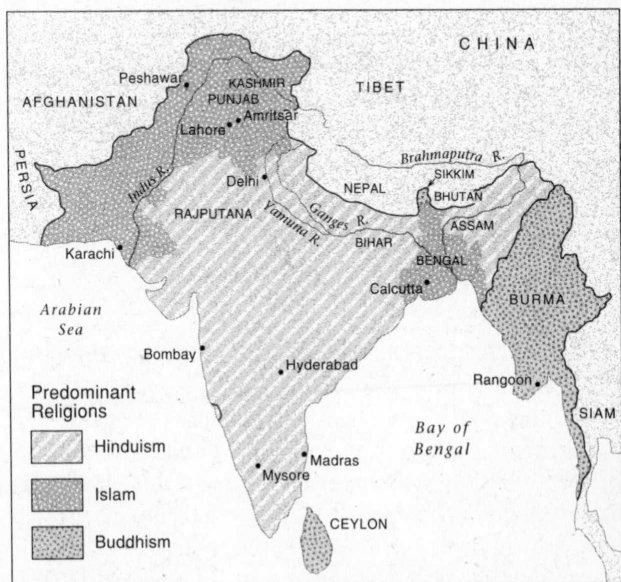

As this photograph of some of the leaders of the "Non-Cooperative" Congress party illustrates, by the early 1920s even moderate Indian nationalist leaders were moving away from loyalty to the British and extensive Anglicization. In the next decades the mix of Western coats and ties and Indian headgear and dhotis increasingly gave way to apparel that was entirely Indian, even among highly Anglicized nationalist families like the Nehrus.

Many Western-educated Indians were increasingly troubled, however, by the growing virulence of British racism, which they were convinced had much to do with their poor salaries and limited opportunities for advancement in the colonial administration. In their annual meetings, members of the Congress party, who were now able to converse and write in a common English language, discovered that from wherever they came in India, they were treated in a similar fashion. The Indians' common grievances, their similar educational and class backgrounds, and their growing contacts through the Congress party gave rise to a sense of common Indian identity that had never existed before among the diverse linguistic and religious groups in the Indian subcontinent.

SOCIAL FOUNDATIONS OF A MASS MOVEMENT

By the last years of the 19th century, the Western-educated elites had also begun to grope for causes that would draw a larger segment of the Indian population into their growing nationalist community. Over a century of British rule had generated in many areas of India the social and economic disruptions and the sort of discontent that produced substantial numbers of recruits for the nationalist campaigns. Indian businessmen, many of whom would become major financial backers of the Congress party, were angered by the favoritism the British rulers showed to British investors in establishing trade policies in India. Tariffs or taxes on British imports into India were set low, which kept the price of British goods down and made it difficult for Indian producers of such competing products as cotton textiles to shift to modern industrial techniques. Indian investors were also incensed by advantages, in the form of tax incentives and contracts, given to their British rivals. In their ever sharper attacks on British policies, Indian political leaders increasingly stressed these inequities and the more general loss to the Indian people resulting from what they termed the "drain" of Indian resources under colonial rule. Though the British rebutted that a price had to be paid for the peace and good government that had come with colonial rule, nationalist thinkers pointed out that the cost was very high indeed.

A large portion of the government of India budget went to cover the expenses of the huge army that mainly fought wars elsewhere in the British Empire that had little to do with the welfare of the Indian people. The Indian people also paid for the very high salaries and pensions of British administrators, who manned posts that Indians themselves could have managed at much lower wages. Whenever possible, such as in the purchase of railway equipment or steel for public works projects, the government bought goods manufactured in Great Britain. This practice not only served to buttress a British economy that was fast losing ground to the United States and Germany; it ensured that the classic colonial relationship between a manufacturing European colonizer and its raw-material-producing overseas dependencies was maintained.

In the villages of India, the shortcomings of British rule were equally apparent by the last decades of the 19th century. The needs of the British home economy had often dictated policies that pushed the Indian peasantry toward the production of cash crops such as cotton, jute, and indigo. The decline in food production that invariably resulted played a major role in the regional famines that struck repeatedly in the pre-World War I period. Radical Indian nationalists frequently charged that the British were callously indifferent to the suffering caused by food shortages or outbreaks of epidemic disease, and that they did far too little to alleviate the suffering that resulted. In many areas landlessness and chronic poverty, already a problem before the establishment of British rule, increased markedly. In most places, British measures to control indebtedness and protect small landholders and tenants were too little and came too late.

One clear symptom of the worsening condition of the agrarian classes was the rash of localized riots and rebellions against moneylenders and landlords that shook the imperial peace in the late 19th century. Ironically, discontent among agrarian groups was most pronounced among the more prosperous smallholders and tenants, whose hard work and shrewdness had made them major beneficiaries of great increases in market production in the last half of the 19th century. When the global demand for many kinds of Indian agricultural produce fell at the end of the century, these groups began to rethink their loyalty to the British overlords and respond to the organizational appeals of the Indian nationalists. In many parts of India, these market producers were to provide the key organizers and the ongoing core of the popular support aroused by Gandhi and other nationalist leaders in the war years and decades thereafter.

THE RISE OF MILITANT NATIONALISM

While the issues, such as cow protection, that nationalist leaders selected in their campaigns to build a mass base had great appeal to devout Hindus, they often strongly alienated other religious groups, especially the Muslims, who made up nearly one-fourth of the population of the Indian Empire. Some leaders, such as B. G. Tilak, were little concerned by this split. They believed that since Hindus made up the overwhelming majority of the Indian population, nationalism should be built on appeals to Hindu religiosity. Tilak worked to promote the restoration and revival of what he believed to be the ancient traditions of Hinduism. On this basis, he opposed women's education and the raising of the (very low) marriage age for women.

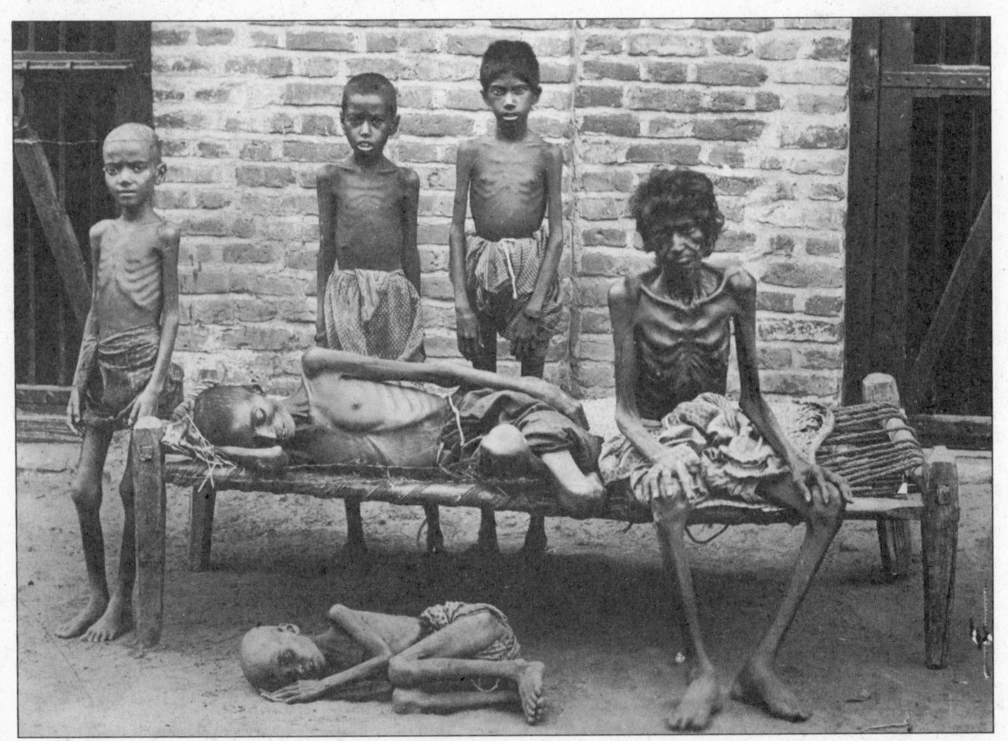

Despite widespread railway construction, government relief measures often proved too little and too late to avert horrific famines in the Indian countryside in the late 19th century. As in Ireland in the same period, British ineptitude in providing famine relief provided Indian nationalist leaders with compelling arguments for the struggle to end alien colonial rule.

Tilak also turned festivals for Hindu gods into occasions for mass political demonstrations. He broke with more moderate leaders of the Congress party by demanding (long before Gandhi) the boycott of British-manufactured goods and insisting that Indians refuse to serve in the colonial administration and military. He demanded full independence, with no deals or delays, and threatened violent rebellion if the British failed to comply.

Tilak's oratorical skills and religious appeals made him the first Indian nationalist leader with a genuine mass following, though that was confined mainly to his home base in Bombay and surrounding areas in western India. At the same time, his strong views alienated most of the moderates, and his promotion of a very reactionary sort of Hinduism offended and frightened Muslims, progressive Hindus, and the followers of other religions such as Sikhism. When evidence was found connecting Tilak's writings to underground organizations that advocated violent revolt, the British, who had grown increasingly uneasy about his radical demands and mass appeal, arrested and imprisoned him. Though mass protests against Tilak's conviction and six-year jail term erupted in western India, they were quickly suppressed. Six years in a prison in Burma, during which Tilak's wife died, took much of the fire out of India's first populist leader.

The other major threat to the British in India before World War I also came from Hindu communalists who advocated the violent overthrow of the colonial regime. But unlike Tilak and his followers, those who joined the terrorist movement favored clandestine operations over mass demonstrations. Though terrorists were active in several parts of India by the last decade of the 19th century, those in Bengal built perhaps the most extensive underground network. Considerable numbers of young Bengalis, impatient with the gradualist approach advocated by moderates in the Congress party, were attracted to secret societies led by quasi-religious, guru-style leaders who exhorted them to build up their physiques with Western-style calisthenics and learn how to use firearms and make bombs. British officials and government buildings were the major targets of terrorist assassination plots and sabotage, though on occasion the young revolutionaries also struck at European civilians and collaborators among the Indian population. But the terrorists' small numbers and limited support among the colonized populace as a whole rendered them highly vulnerable to British repressive measures. The very considerable resources the British devoted to crushing these violent threats to their rule had broken or greatly weakened the secret organizations by the outbreak of the First World War.

The alternative approaches to protest, which Gandhi developed first in South Africa in the early 1900s and then in India in the years after the war, further sapped the strength of violent populists, such as Tilak, as well as the communalist terrorists. Tilak's removal and the repression campaigns against the terrorists strengthened the hand of the more moderate politicians of the Congress party in the years before the war. Western-educated Indian lawyers came to be the dominant force in nationalist politics, and—as the careers of Gandhi, Jinnah, and Nehru demonstrated—they would provide many of the movement's key leaders throughout the struggle for independence.

The approach of those who advocated a peaceful, constitutionalist route to decolonization was given added appeal by timely political concessions on the part of the British. The Morley-Minto reforms of 1909 provided educated Indians with considerably expanded opportunities to elect and to serve on local and all-India legislative councils. The moderates also sought ways to expand their political base by both backing local protest movements and increasing their criticisms of the economic and social policies of the British colonizers. In addition, they dropped their loyalist attachment to the colonial overlords. By 1914, prominent moderate politicians were actually demanding Home Rule for India—but Home Rule within the larger British Empire. Though mass agitation that was genuinely nationalist rather than communalist only emerged with the rise of Gandhi after World War I, much of the organizational basis for Gandhi's early campaigns had been laid in the prewar decades.

EGYPT AND THE RISE OF NATIONALISM IN THE MIDDLE EAST

Egypt is the one country in the Afro-Asian world in which the emergence of nationalism *preceded* European conquest and domination. The risings touched off by the mutiny of Ahmad Orabi and other Egyptian officers (see Chapter 32), which led to the British occupation in 1882, were aimed at the liberation of the Egyptian people from their alien Turkish overlords as well as the meddling Europeans. In contrast to the other peoples who shared an Arab and Islamic cultural tradition, the Egyptians long had a strong sense of separate identity that was anchored in their view of themselves as the descendants of the builders of the great ancient Egyptian civilizations. The concentration of the Egyptians along the Nile River and their geographical separation from other Islamic centers enhanced this sense of a distinctive identity. After the British occupa-

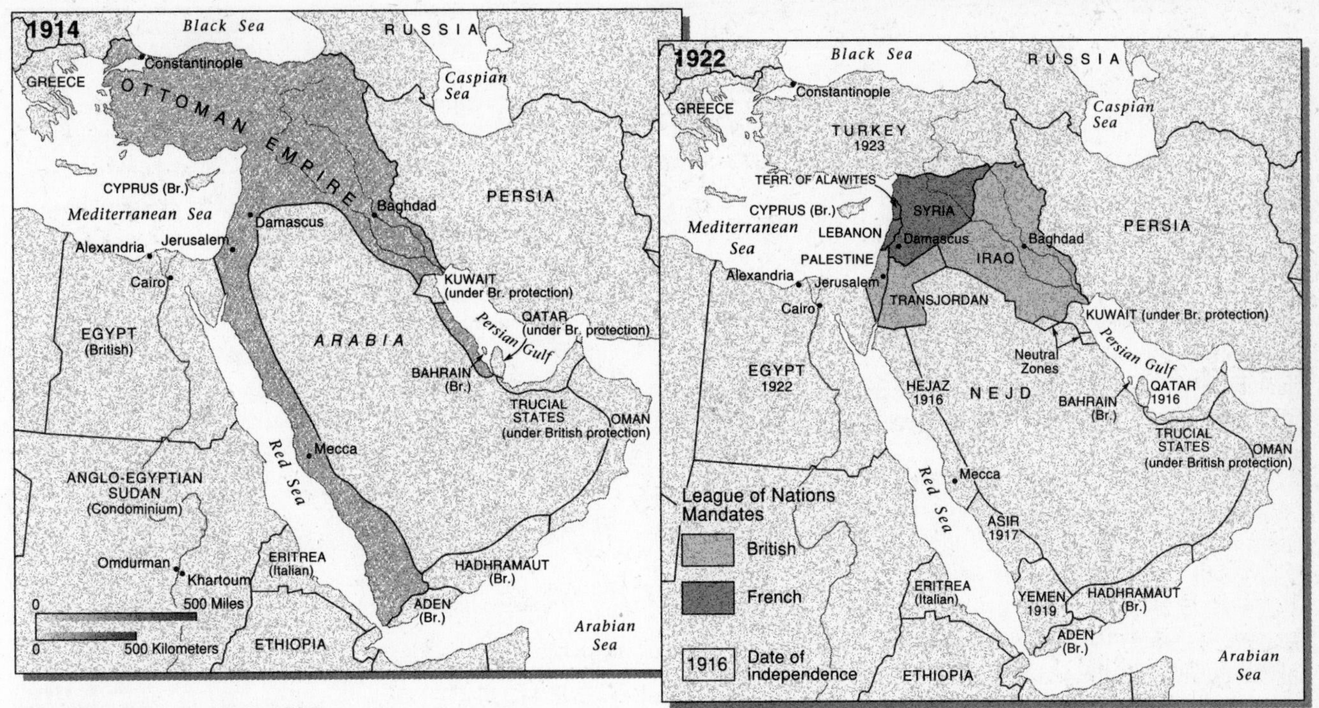

The Middle East, 1914–1922

tion in 1882, this identity was further reinforced by railway and telegraph systems that were aimed at establishing communication links within the Nile valley rather than with other Islamic centers such as those in Syria-Lebanon and the Fertile Crescent. Egyptian distinctiveness was also strengthened by the growing struggle against the British occupation, which other Arabs had not experienced, and the preoccupation of Arab leaders in Syria-Lebanon and the Fertile Crescent with opposition to Ottoman rule.

SOURCES OF EGYPTIAN NATIONALISM

British occupation meant, in effect, double colonization for the Egyptian people by the Turkish khedives (who were left in power) and their British advisors. In the decades following the British conquest, government policy was dominated by the strong-willed and imperious Lord Cromer, who pushed for much-needed economic reforms that reduced but could not eliminate the debts of the khedival regime, for sweeping reforms in the khedival bureaucracy, and for the construction of irrigation systems and other public works projects. But the prosperity the British congratulated themselves for having brought to Egypt by the first decade of the 20th century favored the tiny middle and elite classes, often at the expense of the mass of the population. The leading beneficiaries included foreign merchants, the Turco-Egyptian political elite, a small Egyptian bourgeoisie in Cairo and other towns in the Nile delta, and the ayan, the great landlords in the rural areas.

The latter were clearly one of the biggest gainers. The British had been forced to rely heavily on established local, estate-owning notables in extending their control into the rural areas. As a result, the ayan, not the impoverished mass of rural cultivators and laborers, received most of the benefits of the new irrigation works, the spread of the railway, and the increasing orientation of Egyptian agriculture to the production of raw cotton for the export market. Unfettered by legal restrictions for decades, the ayan had greedily amassed ever larger estates by turning smallholder owners into landless tenants and laborers. As their wealth grew, the contrast between the landlords' estate houses and the thatch and mud-walled villages of the great mass of the peasantry became more and more pronounced. Bored by life in the provinces, the well-heeled landed classes spent most of their time in the fashionable districts of Cairo or in resort towns such as Alexandria. Their estates were run by hired managers who, as far as the peasants were concerned, were little more than rent collectors.

DOCUMENT

LESSONS FOR THE COLONIZED FROM THE SLAUGHTER IN THE TRENCHES

The prolonged and horrific slaughter of the youth of Europe in the trench stalemate on the western front did much to erode the image of Europeans as superior, rational, and more civilized beings that they had worked hard to propagate among the colonized peoples in the decades before the Great War. The futility of the seemingly endless slaughter cast doubts on the Europeans' rationality and fitness to rule themselves, much less the rest of the world. The destructive uses to which their science and technology were put brought into question the Europeans' long-standing claims that these material advancements tangibly demonstrated their intellectual and organizational superiority over all other peoples. The following quotations, taken from the writings of some of the leading thinkers and political leaders of the colonized peoples of Africa and Asia, reflect their disillusionment with the West as a result of the war and the continuing turmoil in Europe in the postwar era.

1. Rabindranath Tagore, Bengali poet, playwright, and novelist, who was one of the earliest non-European recipients of the Nobel Prize for literature:

> Has not this truth already come home to you now when this cruel war has driven its claws into the vitals of Europe? When her hoard of wealth is bursting into smoke and her humanity is shattered on her battlefields? You ask in amazement what she has done to deserve this? The answer is, that the West has been systematically petrifying her moral nature in order to lay a solid foundation for her gigantic abstractions of efficiency. She has been all along starving the life of the personal man into that of the professional.

2. Mohandas Gandhi, who emerged in the years after the war as India's leading nationalist figure:

> India's destiny lies not along the bloody way of the West, but along the bloodless way of peace that comes from a simple and godly life. India is in danger of losing her soul. . . . She must not, therefore, lazily and helplessly say, "I cannot escape the onrush from the West." She must be strong enough to resist it for her own sake and that of the world. I make bold to say that the Europeans themselves will have to remodel their outlooks if they are not to perish under the weight of the comforts to which they are becoming slaves.

3. Léopold Sédar Senghor, Senegalese poet and political leader, who is widely regarded as one of the finest writers in the *French* language of the 20th century:

> *Lord, the snow of your Peace is your proposal to a divided world to a divided Europe*
> *To Spain torn apart. . . .*
> *And I forget*
> *White hands that fired the shots which brought the empires crumbling*
> *Hands that flogged the slaves, that flogged You [Jesus Christ]*
> *Chalk-white hands that buffeted You, powdered painted hands that buffeted me*
> *Confident hands that delivered me to solitude to hatred*
> *White hands that felled the forest of palm trees once commanding Africa, in the heart of Africa. . . .*
>
> (From *Snow Upon Paris*)

4. Aimé Cesaire, West-Indian poet and founder of the *négritude*, or the assertion of black culture, movement in the late 1920s:

> *Heia [Praise] for those who have never invented anything*
> *those who never explored anything*
> *those who never tamed anything*
>
> *those who give themselves, up to the essence of all things*
> *ignorant of surfaces but struck by the movement of all things*
>
> (From *Return to My Native Land*)

Questions: On the basis of this sample, what aspects of the West's claims to superiority would you say were called into question by the suicidal conflict of the leading powers within European civilization? What aspects of their own civilizations do these writers, both implicitly and explicitly, champion as alternatives to the ways of the West? Are these writers in danger of stereotyping both the West and their own civilizations?

With the khedival regime and the great landlords closely allied to the British overlords, resistance to the occupation was left mainly to the middle class that had been growing in the towns since the middle of the 19th century. With the memory of Orabi's revolt in 1882 still fresh, the cause of Egyptian independence was taken up mainly by the sons of the *effendi*, the prosperous business and professional urban families. Even nationalist leaders who came from rural ayan families built up their following from among the urban middle classes. In contrast to India where lawyers predominated in the nationalist leadership, in Egypt, journalists (a number of them educated in France) led the way. In the 1890s and early 1900s numerous newspapers in Arabic (and to a lesser extent French and English) vied to expose the mistakes of the British and the corruption of the khedival regime. Egyptian writers also attacked the British for their racist arrogance and their monopolization of well-paying positions in the Egyptian bureaucracy, which could just as well have gone to university-educated Egyptians. In the 1890s the first nationalist party was formed, but, again in contrast to India where the Congress party dominated the nationalist movement from the outset, a variety of rival parties proliferated in Egypt. There were three main alternatives by 1907, and none could be said to speak for the great majority of the Egyptians, who were illiterate, poorly paid, and largely ignored urban laborers and rural cultivators.

NATIONALIST AGITATION BEFORE WORLD WAR I

Despite the failure of the nationalist parties to unite or build a mass base in the decades before the First World War, the extent of the hostility felt by the Egyptian masses was demonstrated by the Dinshawai incident that occurred in 1906. Most Egyptian villages raised large numbers of pigeons, which served as an important supplement to the meager peasant diet. Over the years, some of the British had turned the hunting of the pigeons of selected villages into a holiday pastime. A party of British officers on leave were hunting the pigeons of the village of Dinshawai in the Nile delta when they accidentally hit the wife of the prayer leader of the local mosque. The angry villagers mobbed the greatly outnumbered shooting party, which in panic fired on the villagers. In the scuffle both the villagers and the British soldiers suffered casualties. In reprisal for the death of one of the officers, the British summarily hung four of the villagers and publicly flogged or punished with hard labor numerous others.

The harsh British reprisals in turn aroused a storm of

By the early 1920s, Mohandas Gandhi had become a pivotal figure in Indian politics. The Mahatma attracted crowds whenever he appeared in public, and this mass appeal gave him unprecedented leverage in dealing with the British as well as other nationalist politicians.

protest in the Egyptian press and among the nationalist parties. Some Egyptian leaders later recounted how the incident convinced them that cooperation with the British was totally unacceptable and fixed their resolve to agitate for an end to Egypt's occupation. Popular protests in a number of areas and the emergence of ayan support for the nationalist cause also suggested the possibility of building a mass base for anti-British agitation. In the years before the outbreak of World War I in 1914, heavy-handed British repression was necessary on several occasions to put down student riots or in reprisal for assassination attempts on high British and Turco-Egyptian officials. By 1913, the British had been sufficiently intimidated by the rising tide of Egyptian nationalism to grant a constitution and representation in a parliament elected indirectly by the men of wealth and influence. World War I and the British declaration of martial law put a temporary end to nationalist agitation. But, as in India, the war unleashed forces in Egypt that could not be stopped and that would soon lead to the revival of the drive for independence with even greater strength than before.

WORLD WAR I AND THE POSTWAR CRISIS OF THE EUROPEAN EMPIRES

The nationalist struggle against European colonial domination was given a great boost by the long and devastating war between the great powers of Europe that broke out in 1914. Though the European powers had frequently quarreled over colonial possessions in the late 19th century, during the war they actually fought each other in the colonies for the first time. Major theaters of conflict developed during the war in West and East Africa and especially in the Middle East. British naval supremacy denied the Germans access to their colonies in Africa and the Pacific. With the blockade on their side, the British, French, and Belgians were able to draw heavily on their colonies for soldiers, laborers, and raw materials.

African and Asian soldiers in the hundreds of thousands served both on the western front and in the far-flung theaters of war from Egypt, Palestine, and Mesopotamia to East Africa. The French recruited tens of thousands of African and Asian laborers to replace workers in French industrial centers who had been conscripted into the armies fighting on the western front. The colonies also supplied food for the home populations of the Entente powers and vital raw materials such as oil, jute, and cotton. Contrary to long-standing colonial policy, the hard-pressed British even encouraged a considerable expansion of industrial production in India to supplement the output of their overextended home factories. Thus, the war years contributed to the development in India of the largest industrial sector in the colonized world.

World War I presented the subjugated peoples of Africa and Asia with the spectacle of the self-styled civilizers of humankind sending their young men by the millions to be slaughtered in the horrific and barbaric trench stalemate on the western front. For the first time, African and Asian soldiers were ordered by their European officers to kill other Europeans. In the process, the deep divisions between and the vulnerability of the seemingly invincible Europeans were starkly revealed. During the war years, European troops in the colonies were withdrawn to meet the need for manpower on the many war fronts. The garrisons that remained were dangerously understaffed. The need to recall administrative personnel from both British and French colonies meant that colonial officials were compelled to fill their vacated posts with African and Asian administrators, many of whom enjoyed real responsibility for the first time.

To maintain the loyalty of their traditional allies among the colonized and to win the support of the Western-educated elites or new allies such as the Arabs, the British and French made many promises regarding the postwar settlement. Because these concessions often seriously compromised their prewar dominance or plans for further colonial expansion, the leaders of victorious allies repeatedly reneged on them in the years after the war. The betrayal of these pledges understandably contributed a great deal to postwar agitation against the continuance and spread of European colonial domination.

INDIA: GANDHI AND THE NATIONALIST STRUGGLE

In the months after the outbreak of the war, the British could take great comfort from the way in which the peoples of the empire rallied to their defense. Though already well on the way to independence, their subjects in the White Dominions—Canada, Australia, and New Zealand—lost no time in declaring war on the Central Powers and raising armies. Dominion troops served with distinction in both the Middle Eastern and European theaters of war, though botched campaigns like those at Gallipoli and the costly offensives on the Somme severely strained relations between the British high command and the colonials. Of the many colonies in the "true" empire, none played as critical a role in the British war effort as India. The Indian princes offered substantial war loans; Indian soldiers bore the brunt of the war effort in East Af-

This contemporary photograph shows the hangings that were carried out in reprisal for the attacks on British soldiers at the village of Dinshawai. The conical tower in the distance behind the scaffold was the roost for the pigeons that were the original and intended targets of the ill-fated hunting party.

rica and the Middle East; and nationalist leaders, including Gandhi and Tilak, toured India selling British war bonds. But as the war dragged on and Indians died on the battlefield or went hungry at home to sustain a conflict that had little to do with them, signs of unrest spread throughout the subcontinent.

Wartime inflation had adversely affected virtually all segments of the Indian population. Indian peasants were angered at the ceilings set on the price of their market produce, despite rising costs, and often their inability to sell it due to shipping shortages linked to the war. Indian laborers saw their already meager wages drop steadily in the face of rising prices. At the same time, their bosses grew rich from profits earned in war production. Many localities suffered from famines that were exacerbated by wartime transport shortages that impeded relief efforts.

Moderate Indian politicians were frustrated by the British refusal to honor promises that if they continued to support the war effort, India would move steadily after the war to self-government *within the empire*, just as Canada had one-half century earlier. Indian hopes for the fulfillment of these promises were raised by the Montagu-Chelmsford reforms of 1919, which increased the powers of Indian legislators at the all-India level and placed much of the provincial administration of India under local ministries controlled by legislative bodies with substantial numbers of elected Indians. But the concessions granted in the reforms were offset by the passage later in the year of the Rowlatt Act, which placed severe restrictions on key Indian civil rights such as freedom of the press. These conditions fueled localized protest during and immediately after the war; Gandhi soon built the protest into an all-India campaign directed against the policies of the colonial overlords.

Gandhi's remarkable appeal to the masses and the Western-educated nationalist politicians was due to a number of personal traits as well as to the strategy for protest that had been worked out a decade earlier in opposing restrictive laws imposed on the Indian migrant community in South Africa. Gandhi combined the experience of a Western-educated lawyer, having considerable world exposure and a rather astute understanding of the British colonizers, with the attributes of a traditional Hindu holy man, which served as a reminder of the glories of India's past civilizations. The former made it possible for him to build up a strong following among middle-class, Western-educated Indians who, as we have seen, had long been the dominant force behind nationalist campaigns. Gandhi's stress on nonviolent, but quite aggressive, protest tactics endeared him both to the moderates and more radical elements within the nationalist movement. His advocacy of peaceful boycotts, strikes, noncooperation, and mass demonstrations—which he labeled collectively *satyagraha*, or truth force—proved a viable way of weakening British control while limiting opportunities for violent reprisals that would allow the British to make full use of their superior military strength.

These tactics also required the involvement of ever-increasing numbers of the Indian people in the nationalist cause. The holy man image Gandhi projected was critical in arousing this mass support from peasants and laborers alike, many of whom walked for miles when Gandhi was on tour to do honor to a saint rather than listen to a political speech. Gandhi's widespread popular appeal in turn gave him even greater influence among nationalist politicians, who were very much aware of the leverage this mass base gave to them in their negotiations with British officials.

THE RISE OF COMMUNALISM AND THE BEGINNINGS OF POLITICAL FRAGMENTATION

Gandhi's holy man side did, however, hamper his efforts to reach out to all Indians. Despite his constant stress on religious tolerance and communal harmony, many Muslims mistrusted this Hindu *guru* and the Congress party politicians who organized his civil disobedience campaigns. The less well-educated Muslim minority had been suspicious of the Hindu-dominated Congress party from the outset, even though a number of Muslims had been and continued to be prominent leaders in the organization. To better support their demands for separate electorates and legislative seats, a number of mostly well-educated and well-to-do Muslims founded a separate party, the Muslim League, in 1906. Though the League represented only a small percentage of even the Muslim minority until the 1940s, its presence signified a dangerous potential division within the Indian national movement. Its intransigence was matched on the Hindu side by a number of extremist, communalist parties that were equally mistrustful of united action and vehemently opposed to Gandhi's call for tolerance and Hindu power sharing with minority religious groups. All the charisma and wisdom Gandhi could muster was not sufficient to bring these fringe groups into the Congress party's mainstream. The Muslims would destroy his vision of a united India; a Hindu extremist would eventually take his life.

The success of Gandhian satyagraha tactics in a number of local protest movements paved the way for his sudden emergence as the central figure in the all-Indian nationalist struggle. The India-wide campaign to repeal the Rowlatt Act demonstrated both the strengths and weaknesses of the Gandhian approach. Congress party organizers rallied mass support for boycotts, noncooperation, and civil disobedience throughout the subcontinent that stunned the British and put them on the defensive. But a lack of time and sufficient numbers of trained followers to instruct protesters in the discipline of passive resistance led inevitably to violent reprisals for police repression. Convinced that satyagraha could not be truly carried out under these conditions, Gandhi delighted the British and angered other nationalist politicians, such as Nehru, by calling off the anti-Rowlatt campaign. His withdrawal allowed the British to round up and imprison Gandhi and other nationalists whom they had identified as the ring leaders of the movement.

Although it would be nearly a decade before Gandhi and the Congress party would be able to launch a campaign on a scale comparable to the postwar satyagraha, British relief at the successful repression of dissent was short-lived. Throughout the 1920s, urban lawyers and peasant associations made use of Gandhian tactics to protest colonial policies and local abuses by both British and Indian officials. By the early 1930s, British insensitivity and the mounting effects of the global Great Depression paved the way for a revival of the civil disobedience campaign on an all-India basis. The establishment in 1927 of the all-white Simon Commission to consider future government responses to nationalist demands angered and unified, for a brief period, nationalist politicians on both the left and the right and those representing both Hindus and Muslims. The depression left openings for the revival of the mass struggle for decolonization. The sharp fall in the early 1930s in the price of agricultural products hit virtually all segments of the rural population, which made up well over 80 percent of the total Indian population.

Astutely gauging the mood of the Indian masses, Gandhi launched another round of all-India civil disobedience campaigns with the dramatic Salt March and satyagraha in early 1931. The British alternated between mass jailings and forcible repression and roundtable negotiations in the next half decade, but ended by making major concessions to nationalist demands. These were embodied in the Government of India Act of 1935. Though retaining control of the central administration, the British agreed to turn the provincial governments over to Indian leaders who would be chosen by a greatly expanded electorate. Their assumption of office by 1937 brought an end to the already much diminished civil disobedience agitation and a British-nationalist accommodation that lasted until another global war shook the foundations of the European colonial order.

THE MIDDLE EAST: BETRAYAL AND THE GROWTH OF ARAB NATIONALISM

In the years after World War I, resistance to European colonial domination that had been confined largely to Egypt in the prewar years spread to much of the Middle East. With Turkish rule in the area ended by their defeat in the war, Arab nationalists in Beirut, Damascus, and Baghdad turned to face the new threat presented by the victorious Entente powers, France and Britain. Betraying promises to preserve Arab independence that Henry McMahon, the British High Commissioner in Egypt, had made in 1915 and early 1916 to Hussein, the *sherif* of Mecca, French and British forces occupied much of the Middle East in the years after the war. Because Hussein had used these promises to convince Arabs to rise in support of Britain's war against the Turks, who were fellow Muslims, their violation by the Allies humiliated and deeply angered Arabs throughout the Middle East. The occupying European powers faced stiff resistance from the Arabs in each of the mandates they carved out in Syria, Iraq, and Lebanon under the auspices of the League of Nations. The Arabs' sense of humiliation and anger was greatly intensified by the disposition of Palestine, where the British occupation was coupled with promises of a Jewish homeland.

The fact that the British had appeared to promise Palestine, for which they received a League of Nations mandate in 1922, to both the Jewish Zionists and the Arabs during the war greatly complicated an already confused situation. British promises to the Arabs have already been discussed, but some background is necessary to understand their pledge to the Zionists and determination to occupy the area themselves. Zionist aspirations to return to their ancient Middle Eastern homeland had been nurtured by the Jews of the diaspora for millennia. But political organizations, created to restore the Jewish home in Palestine, were largely a product of the persecution of the Jews of eastern Europe in the last decades of the 19th century. Particularly vicious pogroms, or violent assaults on the Jewish communities of Russia and Romania in the 1860s and 1870s, convinced Jewish intellectuals such as Leon Pinsker that assimilation into or even acceptance by Christian European nations was impossible. Pinsker and other thinkers called for a return to the Holy Land. Like-minded individuals founded Zionist organizations, such as the Society for the Colonization of Israel, to promote Jewish migration to Palestine in the last decades of the 19th century. Until World War I, the numbers of Jews returning were small—in the tens of thousands—though Zionist communities were established on lands purchased in Palestine.

Until the late 1890s, the Zionist effort was generally opposed by Jews in Germany, France, and other parts of western Europe, who enjoyed citizenship and extensive civil rights, and many of whom had grown prosperous and powerful in their adopted lands. A major defection to the Zionists occurred in 1894 after Theodor Herzl, an established Austrian journalist, witnessed angry mobs shouting "Death to the Jews" as they taunted the hapless French army officer Alfred Dreyfus, a Jew who had been falsely accused of passing military secrets to the Germans. Soon after this incident, Herzl and a number of other western European Jews joined with prominent eastern Jews in forming the World Zionist Organization in 1897. As Herzl made clear in his writings, the central aim of his increasingly well funded organization was to promote Jewish migration to and settlement in Palestine until the point was reached when a Zionist state could be established in the area. Herzl's nationalist ambitions, as well as his indifference to the Arabs already living in the area, were captured in his often quoted view that Palestine was "a land without people for a people [the Jews] without a land."

British motivations for claiming Palestine in the postwar settlement arose from the dangers posed by Turkish offensives during the war against Britain's crucial lifeline at Suez. These offensives convinced the British of the need to occupy Palestine as an additional buffer zone. The situation was further complicated in 1917 when Lord Balfour, the British foreign secretary, assured prominent Zionist leaders that the British would promote the establishment of a Jewish homeland in the region after the war. Lord Balfour's promises to the Zionists and the British takeover of Palestine struck the Arabs as a double betrayal of McMahon's assurances that Arab support for the Entente powers against the Turks would guarantee them independence after the war. This sense of betrayal was a critical source of the growing hostility the Arabs felt toward Jewish emigration to Palestine and their purchase of land in the area.

Rising Arab opposition convinced many British officials, especially those who actually administered Palestine, to constrict severely the rather open-ended pledges that had been made to the Zionists during the war. This shift only led to Zionist mistrust of and open resistance to British policies, as well as a determination to build up their own defenses against the increasingly violent Arab resistance to the Zionist presence in Palestine. But British attempts to limit Jewish emigration and settlement were not matched by efforts to encourage, through education and consultation, the emergence of strong leadership within the Arab population of Palestine. Consequently, in the critical struggles and diplomatic maneuvers of the 1930s and 1940s, the Arabs of Palestine rarely spoke for themselves. They were represented by Arab leaders from neighboring lands, who did not always understand their needs and desires, and who often acted more in the interest of Syrian or Lebanese Arabs than that of the Arabs of Palestine.

REVOLT IN EGYPT

Because Egypt was already occupied by the British when the war broke out and had been formally declared a protectorate in 1914, it was not included in the promises made by McMahon to the sherif Hussein. As a result, the anticolonial struggle in Egypt was rooted in earlier agitation and the heavy toll the war had taken on the Egyptian people, particularly the peasantry. During the war, the defense of the Suez Canal was one of the top priorities for the British. To guard against possible Muslim uprisings in response to Turkish calls for a holy war, martial law was declared soon after hostilities began, and throughout the war large contingents of Entente and empire forces were garrisoned in Egypt. These proved a heavy drain on the increasingly scarce food supplies of the area. Forced labor and confiscations by the military of the precious draft animals of the peasantry also led to widespread discontent. As the war dragged on, this dissidence was further inflamed by spiraling inflation and by food shortages and even starvation in some areas. The wartime cotton boom enriched a tiny mercantile elite, which included many Europeans and Egyptian Christians, and further alienated the mass of peasants and workers from the British and their loyal khedival allies.

By the end of the war, Egypt was ripe for revolt. Mass discontent strengthened the resolve of the educated nationalist elite to receive a hearing at Versailles, where the victorious Allies were struggling to reach a postwar settlement. Like many of the leaders of the colonial world, the Egyptians were also inspired by Woodrow Wilson's principle of self-determination. What they failed to understand was that Wilson's belief that subjugated ethnic groups should have the right to freely elect their own leaders and form their own nations was intended only for Poles and Czechs, not Arabs, Indians, or Africans. When a delegation, or *Wafd* in Arabic, of Egyptian leaders was denied permission to travel to France to put the case for Egyptian self-determination to the peacemakers at Versailles, most Egyptians resigned from the government and called for mass demonstrations. What followed shocked even the most nervous British officials. Student-led riots touched off outright insurrection over much of Egypt. At one point Cairo was cut off from the outside world, and much of the countryside was hostile territory for the occupying power. Though the British army was able, at the cost of scores of deaths, to restore control, it was clear that some hearing had to be given to Egyptian demands. The emergence of the newly formed Wafd party under its hard-driving leader Sa'd Zaghlūl provided the nationalists with both unity and a mass base that far excelled any they had attracted in the prewar decades.

When a special British commission, sent to inquire into the causes of the upheaval in Egypt, met with widespread civil disobedience and continuing violent opposition, it recommended that the British begin negotiations for an eventual withdrawal from Egypt. Years of bargaining followed, which led to a highly qualified independence for the Egyptians that came in stages beginning in 1922 and culminating in the British withdrawal to the Suez Canal zone in 1936. The British pulled out of Egypt proper, but the khedival regime was preserved and the British reserved the right to reoccupy should Egypt be threatened by a foreign aggressor.

Though they had won a significant degree of political independence, the Egyptian leaders of the Wafd party, as well as its rivals in the Liberal Constitutionalist and Union parties that were formed in the 1920s, did little to relieve the increasing misery of the great majority of the Egyptian people. Most Egyptian politicians regarded the winning of office as an opportunity to increase their own and their families' fortunes. Many politicians, both those from ayan households and those from the professional and merchant classes, used their influence and growing wealth to amass huge estates, which were worked by landless tenants and laborers. Locked in personal and interparty quarrels, as well as the ongoing contest with the khedival regime for control of the government, few political leaders had the time or inclination to push for the land reforms and public works projects that the peasantry so desperately needed. Though entrepreneurs and landlords were adversely affected by the slump in the cotton market that hit Egypt during the Great Depression, most were able to pass along their losses to laborers and tenants, who had no choice but to accept lower wages or pay higher rents.

The utter social bankruptcy of the 40 years of nationalist political dominance that preceded Nasser's revolution in 1952 is suggested by some revealing statistics compiled by the United Nations in the early 1950s. By that time, nearly 70 percent of Egypt's cultivable land was owned by six percent of the population. Some 12,000 families alone controlled 37 percent of the farmland. As for the mass of the people, 98 percent of the peasants were illiterate; malnutrition was chronic among both the urban and rural population; and an estimated 95 percent of rural Egyptians suffered from eye diseases. Such was the legacy of the very unrevolutionary process of decolonization in Egypt.

THE BEGINNINGS OF THE LIBERATION STRUGGLE IN AFRICA

Although most of Africa had only come under European colonial rule in the decades just before the outbreak of World War I, precolonial missionary efforts had produced small groups of Western-educated Africans in parts of

West and south-central Africa by the end of the 19th century. Like their counterparts in India, most western-educated Africans were staunchly loyal to their British and French overlords during the First World War. With the backing of both Western-educated Africans and the traditional rulers, many of whom found that their powers actually increased under colonial rule, the British and especially the French were able to draw on their African possessions for manpower and raw materials throughout the war. But this reliance took its toll on their colonial domination in the long run. In addition to local rebellions in response to the forcible recruitment of African soldiers and laborers, the war effort seriously disrupted newly colonized African societies. African merchants and farmers suffered from shipping shortages and the sudden decline in demand for crops, such as cocoa, some of which had been heavily dependent on German markets before the war. African villagers were not happy to go hungry so that their crops could feed the armies of the Allies. The sudden removal of European administrators and policemen from the colonies led to widespread and dangerous rumors that the Europeans were withdrawing for good or that they had run out of manpower in Europe itself. As Lord Lugard pointed out, the desperate plight of the British and French also forced them to teach tens of thousands of Africans:

> . . . how to kill white men, around whom [they had] been taught to weave a web of sanctity of life. [They] also know how to handle bombs and Lewis guns and Maxims—and [they have] seen the white men budge when [they have] stood fast. Altogether [they have] acquired much knowledge that might be put to uncomfortable use someday.

The fact that the Europeans kept few of the promises of better jobs and public honors after the war, which they had made to induce young Africans to enlist in the armed forces or serve in the colonial administration, contributed a good deal to the unrest of the postwar years. In the French colonies—where opportunities for political organization, much less protest, were severely constricted—there were major strikes and a number of riots in the interwar period. In the British colonies, where there was considerably more tolerance for political organization, there were also strikes and a major uprising in Sierra Leone in 1931, protesting colonial taxes and the hardships caused by the sharp fall in prices paid for cash crops due to the Great Depression. The economic slump brought on by the depression also contributed to the refusal of cocoa producers in the Gold Coast colony (later called Ghana) to market their crops for the much-reduced prices offered by the merchants in the port towns. The growing political involvement of the cocoa farmers and other cash-crop producers was to prove a major factor in the nationalists' ability to build a popular base for anticolonialism in the post–World War II era.

Though Western-educated politicians did not link up with urban workers or peasants in most African colonies until the 1940s, disenchanted members of the emerging African elite began to organize in the 1920s and 1930s. In the early stages of this process, charismatic black American political figures, such as Marcus Garvey and W. E. B. Du Bois, had a major impact on emerging African nationalist leaders, including those who were delegates to international conferences in Paris and other Western capitals. Unlike Indian or Egyptian nationalist leaders, African nationalists had to struggle with the question of the level at which their political energies ought to be focused. In the 1920s much effort was placed into attempts to arouse all-Africa loyalties and build Pan-African organizations. The fact that the leadership of these organizations was more American and West Indian than African, and that African delegates faced very different challenges in different colonies, rendered Pan-Africanism unworkable. But its well-attended conferences did much to arouse anticolonial sentiments among Western-educated Africans.

By the mid-1920s, nationalists from French and British colonies were pretty much going separate ways. Due to restrictions in the colonies and the fact that small, but well-educated, groups of Africans were represented in the French Parliament, French-speaking West Africans concentrated their organizational and ideological efforts in Paris in this period. The négritude literary movement nurtured by these exiles did much to combat the racial stereotyping that had so long held the Africans in psychological bondage to the Europeans. Writers such as L. S. Senghor, Léon Damas, and the West Indian Aimé Cesaire celebrated the beauty of black skin and the African physique. They argued that in the precolonial era African peoples had built societies where women were freer, old people were better cared for, and attitudes towards sex were far healthier than they had ever been in the so-called civilized West. Though there was no literary movement comparable to négritude in the British colonies, authors such as Edward Blyden and J. E. Casely Hayford stressed Africa's contributions to the civilized development of all humankind in their books and essays. These and other writers made good use of the press, which was a good deal freer in the British colonies.

Western-educated Africans in British colonies were also given greater opportunities to organize political associations within Africa itself. Early organizations that linked the

In the post–World War I era, African and African-American intellectuals like Léopold Sédar Senghor (pictured here), W.E.B. Du Bois, and Aimé Césaire explored in their writings the ravages wrought by centuries of suffering inflicted on the people of Africa by the slave trade and the forced diaspora that resulted. These intellectuals sought to affirm the genius of African culture and patterns of social interaction.

emerging nationalists of different British colonies, such as the National Congress of British West Africa, gave way in the late 1920s to political groupings concerned primarily with issues confined to single colonies such as Sierra Leone, the Gold Coast, or Nigeria. After the British granted some representation in colonial advisory councils to Western-educated Africans in this period, these types of political groupings became even more pronounced. Though most of these early political organizations were too loosely structured to be considered true political parties and their members spent most of their energies getting elected to the colonial legislative councils, there was a growing recognition on the part of some leaders of the need to build a mass base. In the 1930s a new generation of leaders not only made much more vigorous attacks on the policies of the British, but through their newspapers and political associations they sought to reach out to the ordinary African villagers and the young, who had hitherto played little role in nationalist agitation. The disruptions of yet another world war and the emergence of a new generation of much more radical nationalist leaders would turn these early efforts at outreach to the masses into the more broadly supported movements that won independence in both British and French Africa in the 1950s and 1960s.

ANALYSIS
WOMEN IN ASIAN AND AFRICAN NATIONALIST MOVEMENTS

One important, but often neglected, dimension of the liberation struggles that Asian and African peoples waged against their colonial overlords was the emergence of a stratum of educated, articulate, and politically active women in most colonial societies. In this process, the educational opportunities provided by the European colonizers often played as vital a role as they had in the formation of male leadership in nationalist movements. Though confined in the early stages of European involvement in Africa and Asia to the daughters of low-class or marginal social groups, missionary girls' schools had by the end of the 19th century become quite respectable for women from the growing Westernized business and professional classes. In fact, in many cases, some degree of Western education was essential if Westernized males were to find wives with whom they could share their career concerns and intellectual pursuits.

The seemingly insurmountable barriers that separated Westernized Asian and African males from their traditional—and thus usually without formal education—wives became a stock theme in the novels and short stories of the early nationalist era, a theme perhaps best exemplified by the works of Rabindranath Tagore. The problem was felt so acutely by the first generation of Indian nationalist leaders that many took up the task of teaching their wives English and Western philosophy and literature at home. Thus, for many upper-class Asian and African women colonization proved a liberating force. This trend was often offset by the male-centric nature of colonial education and the "domestic" focus of much of the curriculum in women's schools.

Although women played little role in the early, elitist stages of Asian and African nationalist movements, they frequently became more and more prominent as the early study clubs and political associations reached out to build a mass base. In India, women who had been exposed to Western education and European ways, such as Tagore's famous heroine in the novel *The Home and the World,* came out of seclusion and took up supporting roles, though still usually behind the scenes. Gandhi's campaign to supplant imported, machine-made British cloth with homespun Indian cloth, for example, owed much of whatever success it had to female spinners and weavers. As nationalist leaders moved their anticolonial campaigns into the streets, women became involved in mass demonstrations. Throughout the 1920s and 1930s, Indian women braved the *lathi,* or billy club, assaults of the Indian police, suffered the indignities of imprisonment, and launched their own newspapers and lecture campaigns to mobilize female support for the nationalist struggle.

In Egypt, the British made special note of the powerful effect that the participation of both traditional veiled women and more Westernized upper-class women had on mass demonstrations in 1919 and the early 1920s. These outpourings of popular support did much to give credibility to the Wafd's demands for British withdrawal. In both India and Egypt, female nationalists addressed special appeals to British and American suffragettes to support their peoples' struggles for political and social liberation. In India in particular, their causes were advanced by feminists such as the English champion of Hinduism, Annie Besant, who became a major figure in the nationalist movement both before and after the First World War.

When African nationalism became a popularly supported movement in the post-World War II period, women, particularly the outspoken and fearless market women in West Africa, emerged as a major political force. In settler colonies such as Algeria and Kenya, where violent revolt proved necessary to bring down deeply entrenched colonial regimes, women took on the dangerous tasks of messengers, bomb carriers, and guerrilla fighters. As Frantz Fanon argued decades ago, and as it was later beautifully dramatized in the film "The Battle of Algiers," for women who had been in seclusion right up until the time of the revolutionary upsurge this transformation was particularly painful. The cutting of their hair, as well as the wearing of lipstick and Western clothes, often alienated them from their own fathers and brothers, who equated such practices with prostitution.

In many cases, women's participation in struggles for the political liberation of their people was paralleled by campaigns for female rights in societies that, as we have seen, were dominated by males. Upper-class Egyptian women founded newspapers and educational associations that pushed for raising the age of marriage, educational opportunities for women, and an end to seclusion and veiling. Indian women took up many of these causes and also sought to develop programs to improve hygiene and employment opportunities for lower-caste women. These early efforts, as well as the prominent place of women in nationalist struggles, had much to do with the granting of rights to women, including suffrage and legal equality that were key features of the constitutions of many newly independent Asian and African nations. Though the great majority of women in the new states of Africa and Asia have yet to enjoy most of these rights, their recognition in constitutions and laws provides crucial backing for the struggle for women's liberation in much of the present-day Third World.

Questions: Why might missionary education for women in the colonies have stressed domestic skills? In what ways do you think measures to "modernize" colonial societies might have been oriented to males? Can you think of women who have been or are major political figures in the contemporary Third World? Why have there not been more? What sorts of traditional constraints hamper the efforts of women to achieve economic and social equality and major political roles in the Third World today?

ANOTHER GLOBAL WAR AND THE COLLAPSE OF THE EUROPEAN WORLD ORDER

The effects of a second global conflict, brought on by the expansionist ambitions of Hitler's Germany and imperial Japan, proved fatal to the already badly battered European colonial empires. The Nazi rout of the French and the stunningly rapid Japanese capture of the French, Dutch, British, and American colonies in Southeast Asia put an end to whatever illusions the colonized peoples of Africa and Asia had left about the strength and innate superiority of the colonial overlords. Because the Japanese were non-Europeans, their early victories over the Europeans and Americans played a particularly critical role in destroying the myth of the white man's invincibility. The fall of the "impregnable" fortress at Singapore on the southern tip of Malaya and the Americans' reverses at Pearl Harbor and in the Philippines proved to be blows from which the colonizers never quite recovered, even though they went on to eventually defeat the Japanese. The sight of tens of thousands of British, Dutch, or American troops, struggling under the supervision of the victorious Japanese to survive the "death marches" to prison camps in their former colonies, left an indelible impression on the Asian villagers who saw them pass by. The colonized peoples were also disenchanted by the feeble defense against the Japanese invaders put up by their former masters. The harsh regimes and heavy demands the Japanese conquerors imposed on the peoples of Southeast Asia during the war further strengthened their determination to fight for self-rule and look to their own defenses after the conflict was over.

The devastation of World War II—a total war fought in the cities and countryside over much of Europe—drained the resources of the European powers and sapped their citizens' will to hold increasingly resistant African and Asian peoples in bondage. The war also greatly enhanced the power and influence of the two giants on the European periphery, the United States and the Soviet Union. In Africa and the Middle East, as well as in the Pacific, the United States approached the war as a campaign of liberation. American propagandists made no secret of Franklin Roosevelt's hostility to colonialism in their efforts to win Asian and African support for the Allied war effort. In the Atlantic Charter of 1941, which sealed an alliance between the United States and Great Britain that the latter desperately needed to survive, Roosevelt persuaded a reluctant Churchill to include a clause that recognized the "right of all people to choose the form of government under which they live." The Soviets were equally vocal in their condemnation of colonialism, and even more forthcoming with material support for nationalist campaigns after the war. In the cold war world of the superpowers that emerged after 1945, there was little room for the domination the much-reduced powers of Western Europe had once exercised over much of the globe.

THE WINNING OF INDEPENDENCE IN SOUTH AND SOUTHEAST ASIA

The outbreak of the Second World War soon put an end to the accommodation between the Indian Congress party and the British in the late 1930s. Congress party leaders offered to support the British war effort, if the British would give them a significant share of power at the all-India level and commit themselves to Indian independence once the conflict was over. These conditions were staunchly rejected both by the viceroy in India and at home by Winston Churchill, who headed the coalition government that led Britain through the war. Labour members of the coalition government, however, indicated that they were quite willing to negotiate India's eventual independence. As tensions built between the nationalist leaders and the British rulers, hard-pressed in the early 1940s by their defeats both in Southeast Asia and the Mediterranean, Sir Stafford Cripps was sent to India in early 1942 to see if a deal could be struck to bring the Indians fully behind the British in the war effort. Indian divisions and British intransigence led to the collapse of Cripps's initiative and the renewal of mass civil disobedience campaigns under the guise of the Quit India movement, which began in the summer of 1942.

The British responded with repression and mass arrests, and for much of the remainder of the war Gandhi, Nehru, and other major Congress party politicians were imprisoned. Of the Indian nationalist parties, only the Communists—who were committed to the anti-Fascist alliance and, more ominously, the Muslim League—rallied to the British cause. The League, now led by a former Congress party politician, the dour and uncompromising Muhammad Ali Jinnah, won much favor from the British for its wartime support. As their demands for a separate Muslim state in the subcontinent hardened, the links between the British, Jinnah, and other League leaders became a key factor in the struggle for decolonization in South Asia.

The Second World War brought disruptions to India similar to those caused by the 1914 to 1918 conflict. Inflation stirred up urban unrest, while a widespread famine in 1943 and 1944, brought on in part by wartime transport shortages, engendered much bitterness in rural India. Though successful, the repression of the nationalists during the war convinced many British politicians and even the viceroy of India in the mid-1940s that they had neither the resources nor the will to hold India by force. Churchill's defeat in the 1945 elections, in large part because of his determination to resist India's move toward independence, brought to power a Labour government ready to deal with the nationalist leaders. With independence in effect conceded in the near future, the process of decolonization between 1945 and 1947 focused on what sort of state or states would be carved out of the subcontinent after the British withdrawal. Jinnah and the Muslim League had begun to build a mass following among the Muslims on the basis of their claims that a single Indian nation would be dominated by the Hindu majority, with the Muslims an oppressed minority. It was therefore essential, they insisted, that a separate Muslim state called Pakistan be created from those areas in northwest and east India where Muslims were in the majority.

As communal rioting, which only the physical presence of Gandhi was capable of checking, spread throughout India, the British and key Congress party politicians reluctantly concluded that only partition—the creation of two nations in the subcontinent, one secular, one Muslim—

could avert a bloodbath. Thus, in the summer of 1947 the British handed power over to the leaders of the majority Congress party, who headed the new nation of India, and to Jinnah, who became the first president of Pakistan. In part because of the haste with which the British withdrew their forces from the deeply divided subcontinent, a bloodbath occurred anyway. Vicious Hindu-Muslim and Muslim-Sikh communal rioting, in which neither women nor children were spared, took the lives of hundreds of thousands in the searing summer heat of the plains of northwest India. Whole villages were destroyed; trains pulled into railway stations that were packed with corpses hacked to death by armed bands of rival religious adherents. These atrocities fed a massive exchange of refugee populations between Hindu-Sikh and Muslim areas that may have totaled ten million people. Those who fled were so terrified that they were willing to give up their land, their villages, and most of their worldly possessions.

Partition was compounded by the fact that there was soon no longer a Gandhi to preach tolerance and communal coexistence. On January 30, 1948, Mohandas Gandhi was shot by a Hindu fanatic while on his way to one of his regular prayer meetings. Ironically, Gandhi's prayer sessions had always begun with prayers from each of the many faiths observed by the peoples of the Indian subcontinent.

In granting independence to India, the British in effect removed the keystone from the arch of an empire that spanned three continents. Burma (known today as Myanmar) and Ceylon (now named Sri Lanka) won their independence peacefully in the following years. India's independence and Gandhi's civil disobedience campaigns, which had done so much to win a mass following for the nationalist cause, also inspired African leaders such as Nkrumah, Kenyatta, and Nyerere in the 1950s and 1960s.

The retreat of the greatest of the imperial powers could not help but contribute to the weakening of lesser empires such as those of the Dutch, French, and Americans. In fact, the process of the transfer of power from United States officials to moderate, middle-class Filipino politicians was well under way before the Second World War broke out. The loyalty to the Americans most Filipinos displayed during the war, as well as the stubborn guerrilla resistance they put up against the Japanese occupation, did much to bring about the rapid granting of independence to the Philippines once the war was ended. The Dutch and French were less willing to follow the British example and relinquish their colonial possessions in the postwar era. From 1945 to 1949, the Dutch fought a losing war to destroy the nation of Indonesia, which nationalists in the Netherlands Indies had claimed when the Japanese hold over the islands broke down in mid-1945. The French struggle to retain Indochina will be discussed in Chapter 41, which focuses on the Communist revolutions in East Asia that also emerged victorious in the postwar period. No sooner had the European colonizers suffered those losses than they were forced to deal with new threats to the last bastions of the imperial order in Africa.

THE LIBERATION OF NONSETTLER AFRICA

The Second World War proved even more disruptive to the colonial order imposed on Africa than the first global conflict of the European powers. Forced labor and confiscations of crops and minerals returned, and inflation and controlled markets again cut down on African earnings. African recruits in the hundreds of thousands were drawn once more into the conflict and had even greater opportunities to use the latest European weapons to destroy Europeans. African servicemen, who had witnessed British and French defeats in the Middle East and Southeast Asia and fought bravely only to experience again racial discrimination once they returned home, became in some colonies the staunchest supporters of postwar nationalist campaigns. The swift and humiliating rout of the French and Belgians by Nazi armies in the spring of 1940 shattered whatever was left of the colonizers' reputation for military prowess. It also led to a bitter and, in the circumstances, embarrassing struggle between the forces of the puppet Vichy regime and those of de Gaulle's *Free French*, or those who continued fighting the Nazis, which was fought out mainly in France's North and West African colonies.

The wartime needs of both the British and the Free French led to major departures from long-standing colonial policies that had restricted industrial development throughout Africa. Factories to process urgently needed vegetable oils, foods, and minerals were established in West and south-central Africa. These in turn contributed to a growing migration on the part of African peasants to the towns and a sharp spurt in African urban growth. The inability of many of those who moved to the towns to find employment made for a reservoir of disgruntled, idle workers that would be skillfully tapped by nationalist politicians in the postwar decades.

There were essentially two main paths to decolonization in nonsettler Africa in the postwar era. The first was pioneered by Kwame Nkrumah and his followers in the British Gold Coast colony, which, as the nation of Ghana, became the first independent black African state in 1957. Nkrumah epitomized the more radical sort of African leader that emerged throughout Africa after the war. Edu-

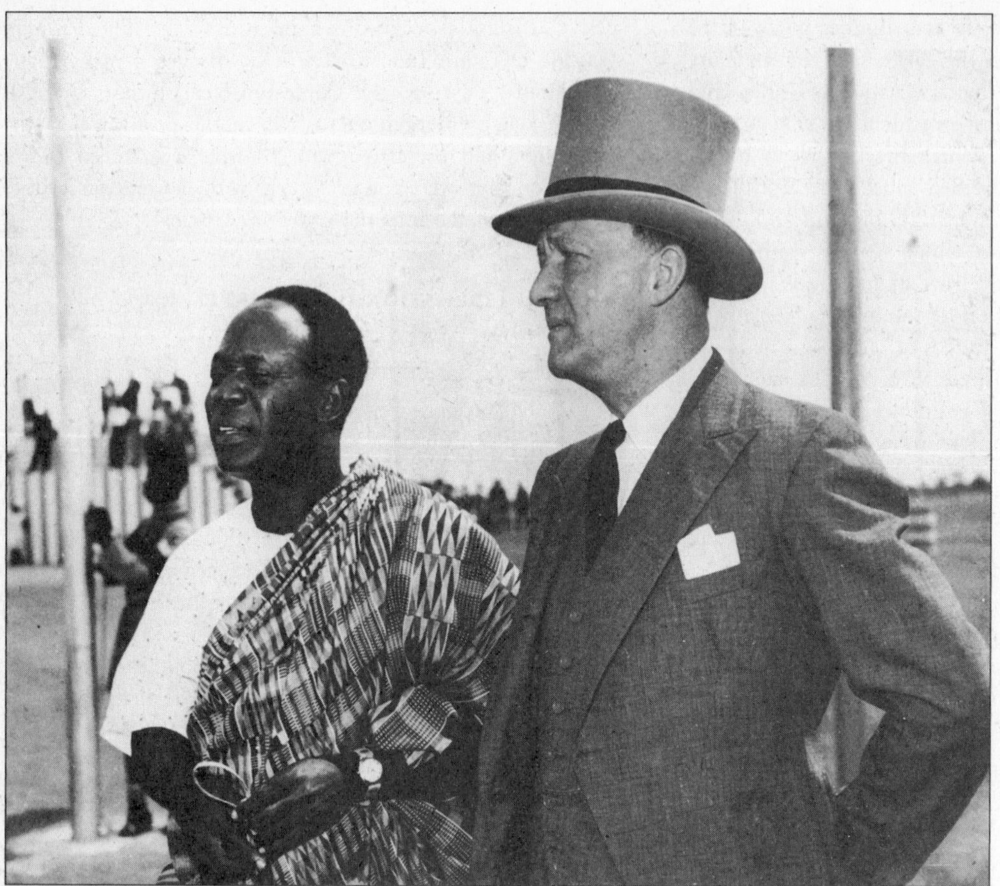

The scene depicted in this photo was played out tens of times in the decades after World War II. British Home Secretary R. A. Butler is greeted by Kwame Nkrumah, whom Butler soon installs as the leader of the first independent nation, Ghana, to be carved out of Britain's African colonies.

cated in African missionary schools and the United States, he had established wide contacts with nationalist leaders in both British and French West Africa and civil rights leaders in America prior to his return to the Gold Coast in the late 1940s. He returned to a land in ferment. The restrictions of government-controlled marketing boards and their favoritism for British merchants had led to protests and then, after the police fired on a peaceful demonstration of ex-servicemen, to widespread rioting in 1948. Though both urban workers and cash crop farmers had supported the unrest, Western-educated African leaders were slow to organize their dissidents into a sustained mass movement. Their reluctance arose in part from their fear of losing major political concessions, such as seats on colonial legislative councils, that the British had just made. Sweeping aside the fears of more established political leaders regarding the radical nature of the popular protest, Nkrumah resigned his position as chairman of the dominant political party in the Gold Coast and established his own Convention Peoples party (CPP). Even before the formal break, Nkrumah had signaled the arrival of a new style of politics by organizing mass rallies, boycotts, and strikes—inspired, as he readily admitted, by the tactics of Gandhi and the Indian nationalists. In the mid-1950s, Nkrumah's growing stature as a leader who would not be deterred by imprisonment or British threats and his mass following won repeated concessions from the British. Educated Africans were given more and more representation in legislative bodies, and gradually they took over administration of the colony. The British acknowledgement of Nkrumah as the prime minister of an independent Ghana in 1957 simply concluded a transfer of power from the European colonizers to the Western-educated African elite that had been under way for nearly a decade.

The peaceful devolution of power to African nationalists—often led by charismatic figures, such as Nkrumah, who were capable of mobilizing mass protest when the British stalled—led to the independence of the British nonsettler colonies in black Africa by the mid-1960s. Independence in the comparable areas of the French and Belgian empires in Africa came in a somewhat different way. Pressed by costly military struggles to hold on to their colonies in Indochina and Algeria, the French took a much more conciliatory line in dealing with the many peoples they ruled in West Africa. Ongoing negotiations with leaders, such as Senegal's Senghor and the Ivory Coast's Felix Houphouët-Boigny, led to reforms and political concessions that ensured that moderate African leaders, who were eager to retain French economic and cultural ties, dominated the nationalist movement in French West Africa. Between 1956 and 1960, the French colonies moved by stages toward nationhood, a process that sped up after de Gaulle's return to power in 1958. By 1960, all of France's African colonies, with the exception of Algeria, where there was a European settler community nearly one million strong, had been granted their independence.

In the same year, the Belgians completed an even hastier retreat from their huge colonial possession in the Congo (now called Zaire). Their rapid retreat is evidenced by the fact that there was little in the way of an organized nationalist movement to pressure them into concessions of any kind. In fact, by design there were scarcely any well-educated Congolese to lead resistance to Belgian rule. At independence in 1960, there were only 16 African college graduates in a Congolese population that exceeded 13 million. Though the Portuguese still clung to their impoverished and scattered colonial territories, by the mid-1960s the European colonial era had come to an end.

REPRESSION AND GUERRILLA WAR: THE STRUGGLE FOR THE SETTLER COLONIES

The pattern of relatively peaceful withdrawal by stages that characterized the process of decolonization in most of Asia and Africa proved unworkable in areas such as Algeria, Kenya, and Southern Rhodesia, where substantial numbers of Europeans had gone to settle permanently in the 19th and early 20th centuries, and in South Africa, which had begun to be settled by Europeans centuries earlier. In each case, the presence of European settler communities, varying in size from millions of whites in South Africa and Algeria to tens of thousands in Kenya and Southern Rhodesia, blocked both the rise of indigenous nationalist movements and concessions on the part of the colonial overlords. Because the settlers regarded the colonies to which they had emigrated as their permanent homes, they fought all attempts to turn political control over to the African majority or even to grant them civil rights. They also doggedly refused all reforms by colonial administrators that required them to give up any of the lands they had occupied, often dispossessing the indigenous Africans in the process. Unable to make headway through nonviolent protest tactics, which were forbidden, or negotiations with British or French officials, who were fearful of angering the highly vocal settler minority, many African leaders turned to violent, revolutionary struggles to win their peoples' independence.

The first of these erupted in Kenya in the early 1950s. Impatient with the failure of the nonviolent approach adopted by Jomo Kenyatta and the leading nationalist party, the Kenya African Union (KAU), an underground organization, coalesced around a number of more radical leaders to win meaningful concessions from the settler-dominated regime. Some of these leaders had fought with the British in Burma and were disgusted by the British failure to reward their services with a fair hearing on such key issues as land confiscations by the settlers. After forming the Land Freedom Army, they mounted, beginning in 1952, a campaign of terror and guerrilla warfare against the British, the settlers, and Africans who were considered collaborators. At the height of the struggle in 1954, some 200,000 rebels were in action in the capital at Nairobi and in the forest reserves of the central Kenyan highlands. The British responded with an all-out effort to crush the guerrilla movement—which was dismissed as an explosion of African savagery and labeled, menacingly, the Mau Mau. In the process they imprisoned Kenyatta and his KAU organizers, thus eliminating the nonviolent alternative to the guerrillas.

Though the rebel movement had been militarily defeated by 1956 at the cost of thousands of lives, the British were now in a mood to negotiate with the nationalists, despite strong objections from the European settlers. Kenyatta was released from prison, and he emerged as the spokesman for the Africans of Kenya. By 1963 a multiracial Kenya had won its independence, and under virtually one-party rule it remained until the mid-1980s one of the most stable and more prosperous of the new African states.

The struggle of the Arab and Berber peoples of Algeria for independence was longer and even more vicious than that in Kenya. Algeria had for decades been regarded by the French as in integral part of France, a department just like Provence or Brittany. The presence of more than one million European settlers in the colony only served to bolster the resolve of French politicians to retain it at all costs. When sporadic rioting in the years after the war turned to sustained guerrilla resistance, led by the National Liberation Front (FLN) in the mid-1950s, the French army saw the defeat of the movement as a way to restore a reputation that had been badly tarnished by recent defeats in Vietnam. As in Kenya, the rebels were defeated in the field, but they gradually negotiated the independence of Algeria after de Gaulle came to power in 1958. The French people soon wearied of the seemingly endless war, and de Gaulle became convinced that he could not restore France to great power status as long as its resources were drained by the Algerian conflict.

In contrast to Kenya, the Algerian struggle was prolonged and brutalized by a violent settler backlash, led after 1960 by the Secret Army Organization (OAS), directed against the Arabs and Berbers as well as Frenchmen who favored independence for the colony. With strong support from elements in the French military, earlier settler resistance had managed to topple the government in Paris in 1958, thereby putting an end to the Fourth Republic. In the early 1960s, the OAS came close to assassinating de Gaulle and overthrowing the Fifth Republic, which his accession to power brought into existence. In the end Algeria was granted its independence in 1962. After the bitter civil war, the multiracial accommodation worked out in Kenya appeared out of the question for the settlers. Over 900,000 left the new nation within months after its birth.

In southern Africa, violent revolutions had also put an end to white settler dominance in the Portuguese colonies of Angola and Mozambique in 1975 and in Southern Rhodesia (now Zimbabwe) by 1980. Only in South Africa has the white minority managed to maintain its position of supremacy. Its ability to do so rests on a number of factors that distinguish it from other settler societies. To begin with, the white population of South Africa, roughly equally divided between the Dutch-descended Afrikaners and the more recently arrived English speakers, was a good deal larger than that of any of the other settler societies. Though only a small minority in a country of 23 million black Africans and 3½ million East Indians and coloreds (mulattos in American parlance), by the mid-1980s South Africa's settler-descended population had reached 4½ million. Unlike the settlers in Kenya and Algeria, who had the option of retreating to Europe as full citizens of France or Great Britain, the Afrikaners in particular have no European homeland to fall back upon. They have lived in South Africa as long as Europeans have lived in North America and consider themselves quite distinct from the Dutch. Over the centuries, the Afrikaners had also built up what was for them a persuasive ideology of white racist supremacy, which, though crude by European or American standards, is far more explicit and elaborate than that developed by the settlers in any other colony. The Afrikaner ideology is grounded in selected biblical

Algerians celebrate in Oran as French barricades, designed to confine the Arab-Berber population to non-European quarters of the city, are torn down by the local militia and civilians just after independence is announced in July 1962.

quotations and the celebration of their historic struggle to "tame a beautiful but hard land" in the face of opposition from both the African "savages" and the British "imperialists."

Ironically, their defeat by the British in the Boer War from 1899 to 1902 (see Chapter 30), also contributed much to the capacity of the white settler minority to maintain its place of dominance in South Africa. A sense of guilt, arising especially from their treatment of Boer women and children during the war—tens of thousands of whom died of disease in what the British called "concentration camps"—led the British to make major concessions to the Afrikaners in the postwar decades. The most important of these was internal political control, which included turning over the fate of the black African majority to the openly racist supremist Afrikaners. Not surprisingly, the continued subjugation of the black Africans became a central aim of the Afrikaner political organizations that emerged in the 1930s and 1940s, culminating in the Afrikaner National party. From 1948, when it emerged as the majority party in the all-white South African legislature, the National party devoted itself to winning complete independence from Britain (which came without violence in 1961) and to establishing lasting white domination over the political, social, and economic life of the new nation.

A rigid system of racial segregation (which will be discussed more fully in the following chapter), called *apartheid* by the Afrikaners, was established after 1948 through the passage of thousands of laws. Among other things, this legislation reserved the best jobs for whites and carefully defined the sorts of contacts permissible between different racial groups. Not only was the vote and political representation denied to the black Africans and ultimately to the coloreds and Indians, it was illegal for them to hold mass meetings or to organize political parties or labor unions. These restrictions, combined with very limited opportunities for higher education for black Africans, obviously hampered the growth of black African political parties and mass mobilization for decolonization efforts. The Afrikaners' establishment of a vigilant and brutal police state to uphold apartheid and their opportunistic cultivation of divisions between the diverse peoples in the black African population also contributed to their ability to preserve a bastion of white supremacy in a liberated continent. Thus far, despite the opening of political dialogue under the current de Klerk regime, decolonization in South Africa has been meaningful only for the privileged white majority. Black, colored, and Indian South Africans struggle to the present day to win their freedom from bondage under a regime that is as exploitative and oppressive as any that existed in the era of European colonial dominance.

CONFLICTING NATIONALISMS: ARABS, ISRAELIS, AND THE PALESTINIAN QUESTION

Though virtually all Arab peoples who were not yet free by the end of the Second World War were liberated by the early 1960s, the fate of Palestine continued to present special problems. Hitler's campaign of genocide against the European Jews had provided powerful support for the Zionists' insistence that the Jews must have their own homeland, which was increasingly conceived in terms of a modern, national state. The brutal persecution of the Jews also won international sympathy for the Zionist cause—in part because the leaders of many nations were reluctant to admit Jews fleeing the Nazi terror into their own countries. As Hitler's henchmen stepped up their race war against the Jews, the tide of Jewish immigration to Palestine rose sharply. But growing Arab resistance to Jewish settlement and land purchases in Palestine, which was often expressed in communal rioting and violent assaults on Zionist communities, led to increasing British restrictions on Jewish entry into the colony. A major Muslim revolt between 1936 and 1939, which the British only managed to put down with great difficulty, both decimated the leadership of the Palestinian Arab community and further strengthened the British resolve to stem the flow of Jewish immigrants to Palestine. Government measures to keep out Jewish refugees from the Holocaust led in turn to violent Zionist resistance to the British presence in Palestine. The Zionist assault was spearheaded by several underground terrorist organizations, including the Stern Gang and the Haganah.

By the end of World War II, the major parties claiming Palestine were locked into a deadly stalemate. The Zionists were determined to carve out a Jewish state in the region. The Palestinian Arabs and their allies in neighboring Arab lands were equally determined to transform Palestine into a multireligious nation, in which the position of the Arab majority would be ensured. Having badly bungled their mandatory responsibilities and under attack from both sides, the British wanted more than anything else to scuttle and run. The 1937 report of a British commission of inquiry supplied a possible solution—partition; the newly created United Nations provided an international body that could give a semblance of legality to the proceedings. In 1948, with sympathy for the Jews running high due to postwar revelations of the horrors of Hitler's Final Solution, the member nations of the United Nations, with the United States and the Soviet Union in rare agreement, approved the partition of Palestine into Arab and Jewish states.

The Arab states that bordered on the newly created nation of Israel had vehemently opposed the United Nation's action and attacked from all sides. Though heavily outnumbered, the Zionists proved to be better armed and much better prepared to defend themselves than almost anyone could have expected. They not only held on to the tiny, patchwork state they had been given by the United Nations, they expanded it at the Arabs' expense. The brief but bloody war that ensued created hundreds of thousands of Arab refugees from Palestine and engendered the abiding hostility between Arabs and Israelis that has been the all-consuming issue in the region and a major international problem throughout the postwar era. In Palestine, conflicting strains of nationalism had collided, and the legacy of colonialism proved even more of a liability to social and economic development than in the rest of the newly independent Third World.

CONCLUSION

THE LIMITS OF DECOLONIZATION

Given the rather fragile foundations on which it rested, the rather rapid demise of the European colonial order is not really surprising. The winning of political freedom in Asia and Africa also represented less of a break with the colonial past than the appearance of many new nations on the map of the world might lead one to assume. The decidedly nonrevolutionary, elite-to-elite transfer of power that was central to the decolonization process in most colonies, even those where there were violent guerrilla movements, limited the amount of change that accompanied the decolonization process. The Western-educated African and Asian classes moved into the offices and jobs, and often the former homes, of the European colonizers. But social gains for the rest of the population in most new nations were minimal or nonexistent. In Kenya, Algeria, and Zimbabwe (formerly Southern Rhodesia), abandoned European lands were distributed to Arab and African peasants and laborers, but in most ex-colonies, especially in Asia, the big landholders were indigenous, and they have held on tenaciously to their holdings. Though educational reforms were carried out to include more sciences in school curricula and the history of Asia or Africa rather than Europe, Western cultural influences have remained strong in almost all of the former colonies. Indians with a higher education continue to communicate in English; some of the most prominent of the leaders of West African states continue to pride themselves on their impeccable French, decorate their presidential palaces with French antiques, and keep closely in touch with trends in French intellectual circles.

The liberation of the colonies also did little to disrupt Western dominance of the terms of international trade or the global economic order more generally. In fact, in the negotiations that led to decolonization Asian and African leaders often explicitly promised to protect the interests of Western merchants and businessmen in the postindependence era. As we shall see in the next chapter, these and other limits that sustained Western influence and often dominance, even after freedom was won, greatly reduced the options open to nationalist leaders struggling to build viable and prosperous nations. Though new forces have also played important roles, the postindependence history of the Third World cannot be understood without taking into account the lingering effects of the colonial interlude.

FURTHER READINGS

The best introduction to the massive literature that has developed on the Indian nationalist movement, as well as a good general historical chronology of the struggle for independence, can be found in Sumit Sarkar's *Modern India 1885–1947* (1983). Louis Fischer's biography of *Gandhi* (1950) still yields valuable insights into the personality of one of the great nationalist leaders and the workings of nationalist politics; Judith Brown's studies of Gandhi's political career, including *Gandhi's Rise to Power* (1972), provide an approach more in tune with current research. The poems and novels of Tagore yield wonderful insights into the social and cultural life of India through much of this era.

P. J. Vatikiotis's *The History of Egypt* (especially the 1985 edition) has excellent sections on the nationalist era in that country. Interesting, but less reliable, is Jacque Berque's *Colonialism and Nationalism in Egypt* (1972). George Antonius's *The Arab Awakening* (1946) is essential reading on the Palestine question. It can be balanced by Aaron Cohen's *The Arabs and Israel* (1970) and Fred Khouri's survey of the roots of *The Arab-Israeli Dilemma* (1968). The early stages of the nationalist struggle in West Africa are covered by Michael Crowder's *West Africa under Colonial Rule* (1982), while the final drives for decolonization are surveyed by Ali A. Mazrui and Michael Tidy in *Nationalism and New States in Africa* (1984), J. D. Hargreaves's *Decolonization in Africa* (1988), and W. R. Louis and P. Gifford, eds., *Decolonization in Africa* (1984). On specific movements, see Alstair Horne's *A Savage War of Peace* (1977) on Algeria, C. Rosberg and J. Nottingham's *The Myth of 'Mau Mau'* (1966) on Kenya, and the writings of Terrence Ranger on Rhodesia. Of the many works on South Africa, the general histories of S. Throup, B. Bunting, T. D. Moodie, and L. Thompson provide a good introduction to the rise of Afrikaner power.

THE CHALLENGES OF INDEPENDENCE

- **ANALYSIS:** Women and the Struggle to Build New Societies in the Third World

PATHS TO DEVELOPMENT

- **DOCUMENT:** Cultural Creativity in the Third World: Some Literary Samples
- **CONCLUSION:** The Third World Experience in Historical Perspective
- **FURTHER READINGS**

1912 African National Congress party formed

1928 Founding of the Muslim Brotherhood in Egypt

1930s Free Officers movement develops in Egypt

1947 India and Pakistan achieve independence

1948 First Arab-Israeli War; Afrikaner Nationalist party to power in South Africa; beginnings of apartheid legislation

1949 Hassan al-Banna assassinated in Egypt

1951 India's first Five-Year Plan for economic development launched

1952 Farouk and khedival regime overthrown in Egypt; Nasser and Free Officers to power

1955 Bandung Conference; beginning of Non-Aligned movement

1956 Abortive British-French intervention in Suez

A.D. 1920 | A.D. 1940 | A.D. 1950

40

Africa and Asia in the Era of Independence

INTRODUCTION. In Gillo Pontecorvo's moving film on the struggle for independence in Algeria, "The Battle of Algiers," one member of the high command of the National Liberation Front (FLN) reflects on the nature of the revolutionary struggle in a conversation with a young guerrilla fighter, the protagonist of the film. When the young man expresses his anxieties about the outcome of the general strike then taking place in the city of Algiers, the thoughtful leader of the FLN seeks to put the immediate crisis in a larger perspective. Revolutions, he muses, are difficult to get going and even harder to sustain. But the real tests, he concludes, will come when the revolutionary struggle has been successfully concluded, when the makers of the movement must assume power and face the greatest challenges of all—those involved in building viable nations and prosperous societies for peoples disoriented and deprived by decades or in many cases centuries of colonial rule.

These reflections on the process of decolonization anticipated the actual experience of the peoples in the new nations carved out of the ruins of the European colonial empires. Once the European colonizers had withdrawn and the initial euphoria of freedom had begun to wear off, Western-educated nationalist leaders were forced to confront the sobering realities of the fragile state structures and underdeveloped economies they had inherited. With the common European enemy gone, the deep divisions between the different ethnic and religious groups that had been thrown uneasily together in the postcolonial states became more and more apparent and disruptive. The Western-educated leaders soon realized how small a proportion of the population had gen-

1958 South Africa completely independent of Great Britain

1960 Sharpeville shootings in South Africa

1966 Nkrumah overthrown by a military coup in Ghana

1966–1970 Biafran secessionist war in Nigeria

1967 Six-Day War between Israel and the Arabs

1970s Peak period for the OPEC cartel

1971 Bangladesh revolt against West Pakistan; Indo-Pakistani War

1972 Bangladesh becomes an independent nation

1973 Third Arab-Israeli War

1979 Shah of Iran overthrown; Khomaini-led Islamic republic declared

1980–1988 Iran-Iraq War

1989 De Klerk charts a path of peaceful reform in South Africa

1990 Nelson Mandela released from prison; Iraqi invasion of Kuwait

1991 First Gulf War

uinely committed themselves to the nationalist identity and goals that had formed the backbone of the drive for independence. They were often startled by how shallow loyalty to a common nation was, even among the Westernized elite classes that had led the decolonization struggle.

The leaders of the new nations found their efforts to spur economic growth constricted by concessions made to the departing colonizers and the very nature of the international economy, in which the terms of investment and trade heavily favored the industrialized nations. They saw their ambitious schemes to improve living standards among formerly colonized peoples frustrated by a shortage of expertise and resources and by population growth rates that quickly ate up whatever modest advances could be made. Many of the nationalist leaders despaired as hungry peasants flocked to the rapidly growing cities where there was little employment to be had, and bad weather and market reverses resulted in famines and mounting debts that left their nations even more at the mercy of the industrialized world. The leaders of the new nations lamented the continuing intellectual and cultural dependence of their societies on the United States and Western Europe. This dependence was reflected in all manner of things from the architecture of African and Asian cities and the literary output of their novelists, playwrights, and movie directors to university curricula and the pop music and blue jeans the children of the elite classes consumed as avidly as their counterparts in the West.

Increasing poverty, official corruption, and a growing concern for the breakdown of traditional culture and social values produced widespread social unrest and often violence between different religious and ethnic groups. Dissent and civil disturbances called into question the leadership abilities of nationalist politicians who had won independence but floundered as heads of new nations. Challenges to the existing order came both from Communist parties on the left and religious revivalist movements on the right. In order to remain in power and to ensure that they would be able to realize their visions of economic and social development in the postcolonial era, Western-educated nationalist leaders adopted various strategies to beat back these threats. These strategies ranged from attempts by leaders such as Sukarno of Indonesia and Nkrumah of Ghana to establish themselves as charismatic strongmen at the head of unopposed populist movements to the state-directed reform and development programs nurtured by Nehru in India, where civil rights and democracy were preserved. As we shall see, these strategies met with widely varying degrees of success. The price for failure was often a fall from power and at times the execution of former nationalist heroes. In many instances, their places were taken by military commanders who assumed dictatorial powers, forcibly silenced dissent, and suppressed interethnic and religious rivalries. In a limited number of cases, the champions of religious revival and resistance to Western influences, most notably those in Iran, swept moderate reformers and dictators from power.

The many nations carved out of the colonial empires were invariably lumped together as members of the Third World. This grouping of what were very diverse societies and political systems reflected the common dilemmas these nations had to face. They became contested ground between the wealthy First World of the West and Japan and the militant and aspiring states of the Second World, the Communist bloc, which was united in the years right after the war behind the Soviet Union and the Peoples Republic of China. The newly independent states of Africa and Asia also shared a common experience of colonization and the struggle for freedom, and they came to independence with underdeveloped economies and consequently high levels of poverty, illiteracy, and population growth.

Though most of the Latin-American countries have often been included in the Third World category, they had actually won their political independence much earlier. Because the Latin-American struggles for development and social justice have been discussed in some depth in Chapter 38, this chapter focuses on responses to these challenges in the newly independent states of Asia and Africa. In some cases similar social and economic problems have produced comparable responses, but it is vital to keep in mind the great diversity of Third World societies—a diversity grounded in the very different precolonial histories and colonial experiences of various African and Asian peoples. For that reason, after the common challenges that faced Third World societies in the early independence era are surveyed in the opening sections of this chapter, the remaining sections will be devoted to the varying solutions different leaders of African and Asian nations devised to deal with the urgent and complex problems they faced.

THE CHALLENGES OF INDEPENDENCE

The nationalist movements that won independence for most of the peoples of Africa and Asia usually involved some degree of mass mobilization. Peasants and working-class townspeople, who hitherto had little voice in politics beyond their village boundaries or local labor associations, were drawn into political contests that toppled empires and established new nations. To win the support of these groups, nationalist leaders promised them jobs, civil rights, and equality once independence was won. The leaders of many nationalist movements nurtured visions of postindependence utopias in the minds of their followers. They were told that once the Europeans, who monopolized the best jobs, were driven away and their exploitative hold on the economies of colonized peoples was brought to an end, there would be enough to give everyone a good life.

Unfortunately, the realities of the postindependence situation in virtually all new African and Asian nations made it impossible for nationalist leaders to fulfill the expectations they had aroused among their followers and in varying degrees the colonized populace at large. Even with the Europeans gone and terms of economic exchange with more developed countries somewhat improved, there was simply not enough to go around. Thus, the socialist-inspired ideologies that had often been embraced by nationalist leaders and propagated to their followers proved misleading. The problem was not just that goods and services were unequally distributed, leaving some people rich and the majority poor. The problem was that there were not sufficient resources to take care of everybody, even if it had been possible to distribute them equitably.

When utopia failed to materialize, personal rivalries and long-standing divisions between different classes and ethnic groups, which had been more or less successfully muted by the common struggle against the alien colonizers, resurfaced or intensified. In almost all of the new states, these rivalries and differences became dominant features of political life. They produced political instability and often threatened the viability of the nations themselves. They also consumed resources that might have been devoted to economic development and blocked—in the name of the defense of subnational interests—measures designed to build more viable and prosperous states. Absorbed by the task of just holding their new nations together, African and Asian politicians neglected problems—such as soaring population increases, uncontrolled urban growth, rural landlessness, and ecological deterioration—that soon loomed as just as great a threat as political instability to their young nations.

BUILDING NATIONS AND NATIONAL IDENTITIES

A pernicious precedent was set at the very beginning of the decolonization process. Neither Gandhi, nor the British, nor the compromises offered by Congress party politicians could break Jinnah's resolve, and in 1947 India

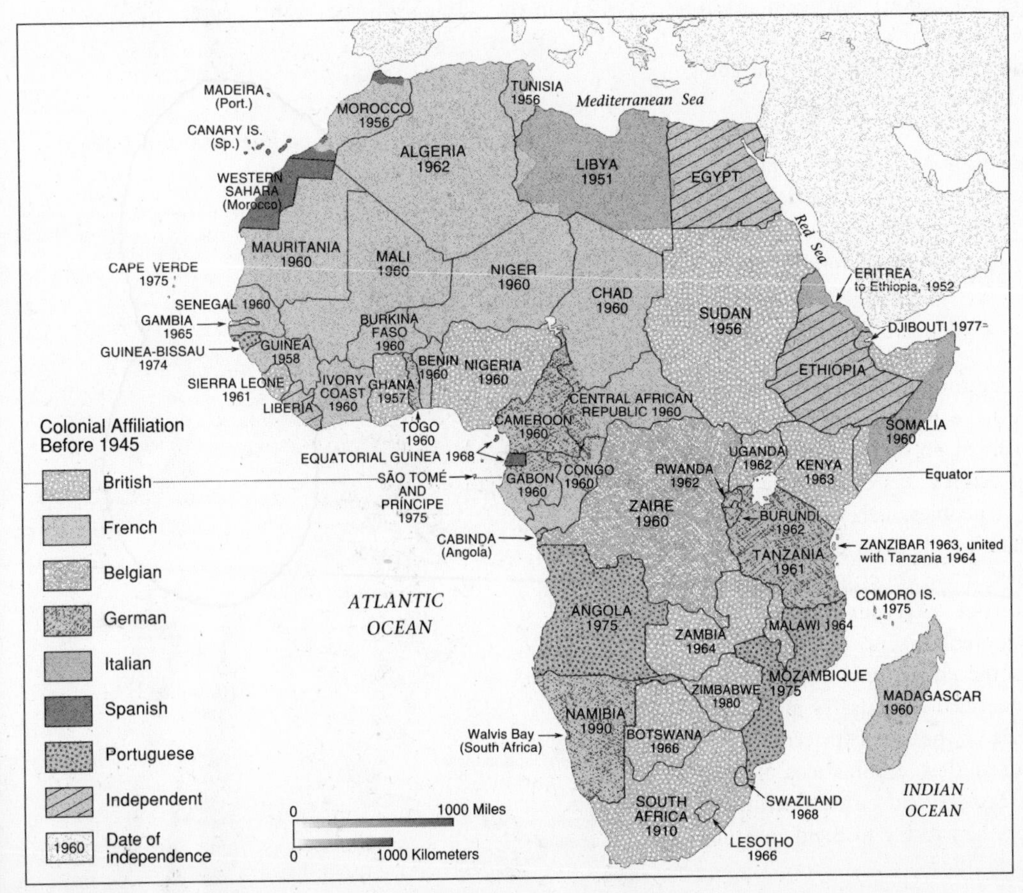

Colonial Division of Africa and the Emergence of New Nations

became two hostile nations rather than a unified state in which Hindus, Muslims, Sikhs and other religious groups strove to live together in peace. The communal rivalries and centuries-old hatred and mistrust that surfaced in the era of decolonization in India could be found in equal or even greater measure in virtually all of the colonies that made up the European overseas empires. The way the empires had been built and their boundaries demarcated ensured that this would be the case. European generals conquered and European explorers staked out claims to territories in ways that rarely, if ever, took into account the interests or history of the peoples who occupied these lands. In most colonies, the pattern that had been set in India prevailed. Peoples who had traditionally lived in separate states and developed very different cultures were thrown together under the same colonial regime. India at least was bound by common institutions, such as the caste system, and Hindus and Muslims had lived together there for centuries before the coming of the British.

In Africa, which was grabbed by the rival European powers in much greater haste, peoples who had little in common except wars over slaves and territory found themselves thrown together as subjects of alien colonizers. As Lord Salisbury, one of the most prominent late 19th century champions of imperialist expansion, confessed in the 1890s, the conquerors knew next to nothing about the lands they divided up around the green-felt tables at conferences in Berlin, Paris, and other European capitals:

> We have been engaged in drawing lines upon maps where no white man's foot ever trod; we have been giving away mountains and rivers and lakes to each other [Europeans] only hindered by the small impediment that we never knew exactly where the mountains and rivers and lakes were. . . .

If they could not locate the mountains and rivers, European diplomats could hardly have been expected to know much about the peoples who lived on or along them. As a consequence, the division of Africa was completely arbitrary. Colonial boundaries cut peoples such as the Yoruba of West Africa and the Somalis of the horn of East Africa apart, and they tossed together tens, sometimes hundreds, of very different—often hostile—African peoples. The roads and railways built by the colonizers, the marketing systems they established, and the educational policies they pursued all hardened the unnatural boundaries and divisions established in the decades of the late 19th century. It was these artificial units, these motley combinations of peoples that defied the logic of history and cultural affinity, that African nationalist leaders had to try to meld into nations in the decades after World War II.

In virtually all of the new states that have emerged from the European colonial empires, ethnic rivalries and communal violence have been endemic. In some cases, the unnatural creations of the colonizers did not long survive the transfer of power to indigenous leaders. The most spectacular collapse of a new state came in Pakistan, the unwieldy patchwork of a nation the British had thrown together at the last minute in 1947 to satisfy Jinnah's demands for majority rule in Muslim areas of the Indian subcontinent. A glance at the map revealed the vulnerability of Pakistan, split into two parts, West and East Pakistan that were separated by over 1000 miles of hostile Indian territory. Some attention to the history of the two halves that made up Pakistan would have made clear the problems in store.

Bengal in the east was a region shaped by the tropical monsoons. Its language was akin to Hindi, one of the official languages of India; it was written in a script derived from ancient Sanskrit, the sacred language of the Hindus. The Muslim Bengalis in East Pakistan followed a less fundamentalist, much more Hindu-influenced variant of the Islamic faith than the Muslim peoples of the other half of Pakistan far to the west. The Bengalis were physically closer to the peoples of south India and parts of Southeast Asia than the lighter-skinned, taller peoples of West Paki-

The Partition of South Asia: The Formation of India, Pakistan, Bangladesh, and Sri Lanka

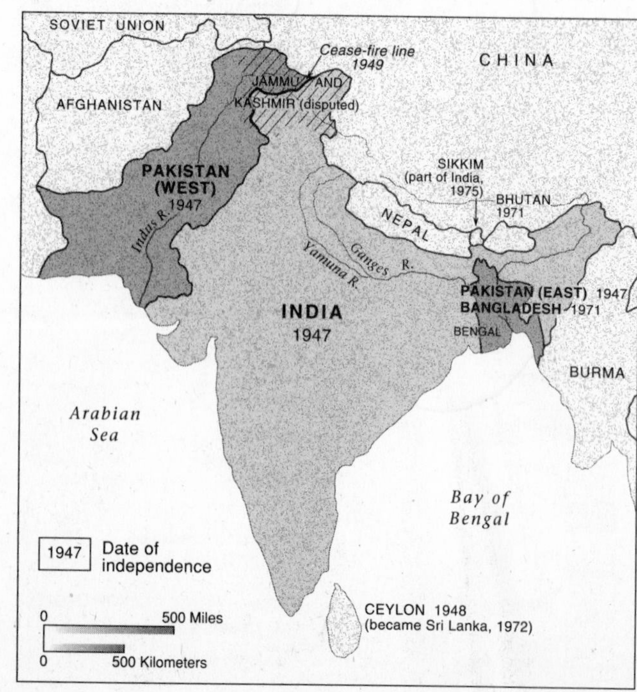

stan. The latter, molded by the hard, dry climate of the regions they inhabited, were a very different sort of people than the Bengalis. Their main language was Urdu, written in a script derived from Persian; they were more prone to embrace Islamic fundamentalism, more resistant to Hindu influences. Many traced their descent from the Muslim peoples who invaded the Indian subcontinent a millennium earlier. This heritage contrasted sharply with that of the Bengalis, most of whom descended from Hindu and Buddhist peoples who had converted to Islam during the early centuries after the Muslims' arrival. Thus, even the Islamic religion that the people of the two halves of Pakistan shared and that had been responsible for them being combined in the same country in the first place differed significantly from west to east.

Though efforts had been made to bridge differences between the two Pakistans and especially to ensure that political power was shared equally between the two regions, the politicians and military leaders of the West soon gained the upper hand. Though the export of jute and other crops from the East brought in most of the foreign currency earned by Pakistan, the West absorbed a lion's share of state revenues, especially those spent on economic development schemes. West Pakistanis held a far greater portion of positions at the upper levels of the national bureaucracy and in the military forces than they warranted in view of the larger population in East Pakistan. In the 1960s, under a succession of military leaders, West Pakistanis sought to limit civil liberties in and further curtail the political influence of East Pakistanis. By the 1970s, the heavy handed, often outright arrogant policy of the West Pakistanis had generated resistance movements in East Pakistan. A brutal attempt in 1971 by the military strongman Yahya Khan to crush this resistance triggered an all-out revolt in East Pakistan against West Pakistani dominance. Backed by the Indians, always eager to weaken their Pakistani rivals, the East Pakistanis won a war of secession that led to the establishment of the independent nation of Bangladesh in 1972.

The contrasting lush tropical and arid semidesert environments of East and West Pakistan underscore the great differences between the two areas—differences that eventually led to the violent breakaway of East Pakistan and the creation of the nation of Bangladesh.

At various points in their history, most of the new nations of Africa and Southeast Asia have been threatened by similar secessionist movements. In fact, India, which relished the chance to contribute to the breakup of Pakistan, has itself been repeatedly threatened by civil strife between different linguistic, religious, and ethnic groups. At the present time, Sikh guerrillas carry on a violent campaign for separation in the north, and the Indian government has been forced to intervene militarily in the violent struggle between different ethnic and religious groups in Sri Lanka (Ceylon), its neighbor to the south.

In Africa, where there was often even less of a common historical and cultural basis on which to build nationalism than in South or Southeast Asia, separatist movements have been a prominent feature of the political life of new states. Secessionist movements currently rage from Morocco in the northwest to Ethiopia in the east and Angola in the south. Civil wars, such as the current struggle of the non-Muslim peoples of the southern Sudan against the Muslim rulers from the northern parts of that country, have also abounded. Thus far, none of the secessionist movements have succeeded, though that of the Ibo peoples of eastern Nigeria, who proclaimed an independent state of Biafra in 1967, led to three years of bloody warfare in Africa's most populous nation.

Though African leaders have been acutely aware of the injustices and persecutions of minority groups that have often precipitated these conflicts, none has seriously suggested altering the unnatural boundaries established in the colonial era. The reverse, in fact, is the case. These divisions have become sacrosanct, because each African leader fears that a successful secession movement in another country or a redrawing of boundaries elsewhere could provide precedents for dissident minorities in their own country or for neighboring leaders to claim boundary adjustments that would work to their disadvantage.

In all cases, the artificial nature of the new nations of the Third World has proved costly. In addition to internal divisions, boundary disputes between newly independent nations have often led to border clashes and on a number of occasions to open warfare. India and Pakistan have fought three such wars since 1947. Iraq's Saddam Hussein justified his 1990 annexation of Kuwait with the argument that the tiny, but oil-rich, Arab "sheikhdom" was an artificial creation of the British colonizers, who had carved out land that had historically been part of Iraq. These disputes have done much to confirm the West's view of the Third World as a region of unrest and instability. But it is important to remember that "developed" countries, such as the United States, took decades and numerous boundary disputes (with, for example, the British over Canada) and outright wars, such as that with Mexico, to reach their current size and contours.

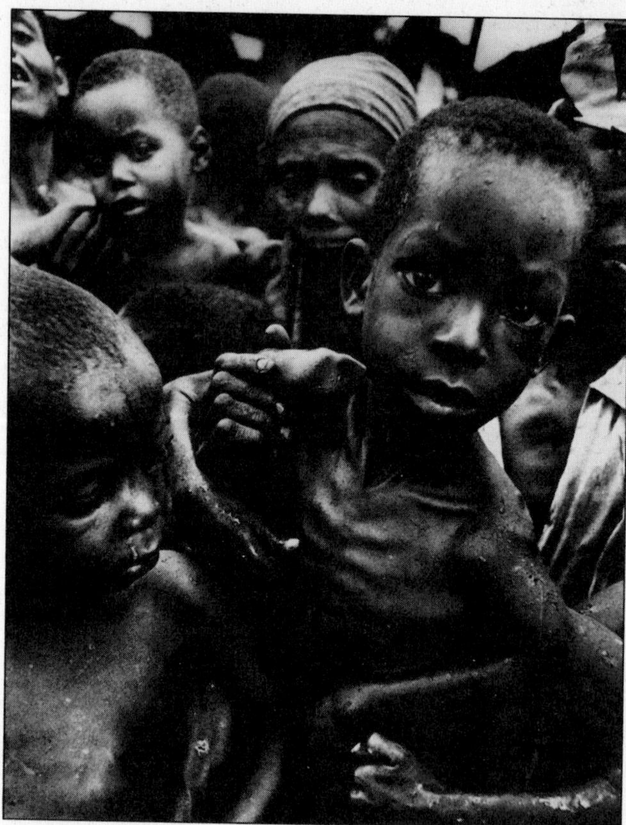

In the late 1960s, posters and photos such as this, which graphically depicted the ravages of the Nigerian civil war, served as reminders of the artificiality and instability of the new states that had been hastily carved out of the European colonial empires.

Democracy has often been one of the main victims of the tensions between rival ethnic groups within Africa and Asian nations and threats from neighbors without. Politicians in virtually all of the new states have been quick to play upon ethnic and religious loyalties as well as fears to win votes. The result has been that freely elected legislatures have often been dominated by parties representing these special interests. Suspicions that those in power were favoring their own or allied groups led to endless bickering and stalemated national legislatures, which became tempting targets for the coup attempts of military strongmen. One of the more persuasive reasons these usurpers have given for dictatorial rule was the need to contain communal conflict, which had only been whipped up by democratic election campaigns. Ironically, this was one of the key rationales given by the European colonizers to justify the continuation of colonial rule. The threats from rival ethnic and religious groups felt by those in power have also contributed to exorbitant military spending by Asian and African leaders—spending that their impoverished societies can rarely afford. In countries where civil wars have actually occurred, such as Ethiopia, Mozambique, and Angola, economic development has ground to a virtual standstill, while disease and famine have reduced their peoples to levels of misery and despair that even the most well-funded of international agencies often can do little to alleviate.

THE POPULATION BOMB

The nationalist leaders who led the Third World peoples to independence had firmly committed themselves to promoting rapid economic development once colonial restraints were removed. In keeping with their Western-educated backgrounds, most of these leaders envisioned their nations following the path of industrialization that had brought national prosperity and international power to much of Western Europe and the United States. This course of development was also fostered by representatives of the Soviet bloc, who had emphasized heavy industry in their state-directed drives to "modernize" their backward economies and societies. Of the many barriers to the rapid economic breakthroughs Third World leaders hoped for, the most formidable and persistent were the spiraling increases of population that often overwhelmed whatever economic advances the peoples of the new nations managed to make.

Factors making for sustained population increases in already quite densely populated areas of Asia and Africa had begun to take effect even before the era of high colonialism. Food crops, mostly from the New World, had contributed to dramatic population growth in China and India as early as the 17th century. They also helped sustain high levels of population in areas such as the Niger delta in West Africa, despite heavy losses of both males and females as a result of the slave trade. The coming of colonial rule reinforced these upward trends in a number of ways. It ended local warfare that had caused population losses and, perhaps more significantly, had indirectly promoted the spread of epidemic diseases and famine. The new railroad and steamship links established by the colonizers in order to foster the spread of the market economy also cut down on regional famines that had been a major check against sustained population increase since ancient times. Large amounts of food could now be shipped from areas where harvests were good to those where drought or floods threatened the local inhabitants with starvation.

With war and famine—two of the main checks that Malthus and others had identified as major barriers to population increase—much reduced, growth began to speed up, particularly in areas such as India and Java that had been under European control for decades. The death rate declined, but the birthrate remained much the same, leaving more and more sizeable net increases. Improved hygiene and medical treatment played little part in this rise until the first decades of the 20th century. From that time, efforts to eradicate tropical diseases, as well as global scourges such as smallpox, and to improve sewage systems and purify drinking water have given further impetus to sharp upswings in population, particularly in sub-Saharan Africa.

Virtually all the leaders of the emerging Third World nations headed states in which the population was increasing at unprecedented levels. This increase continued in the early years of independence. In much of Asia, it has begun to level off in recent decades. But in most of Africa population growth continues at very high rates. In some cases, most notably South Asia, rather moderate growth rates have produced prodigious total populations because they were adding to an already large base. As a result, in the 1970s population experts predicted that at the then-current rates, South Asia's population of over 600 million would more than double by the year 2000. With over one billion people by the late 1980s, the prophecy appears well on the way to fulfillment.

In Africa, by contrast, which began with relatively low population levels, given its large land area, very high birthrates and diminished mortality rates have resulted in population increases of alarming proportions in recent decades. The magnitude of this increase can be envisioned if one considers the predictions of some population experts that, if present growth rates continue, by the middle of the next century Nigeria will have a population equal to that of present-day China and Kenya will have a population double that of the United States in the mid-1980s. Some indication of the size of the human calamities that are likely to result is suggested by the fact that the 400 million peoples of Africa are currently supported by a continental economy with a productive capacity equal to just six percent of the present United States' economy, or roughly equal to that of the state of Illinois.

On the face of it the conquest of the Malthusian checks to sustained population growth throughout much of human history—war, disease, and famine—was one of the great

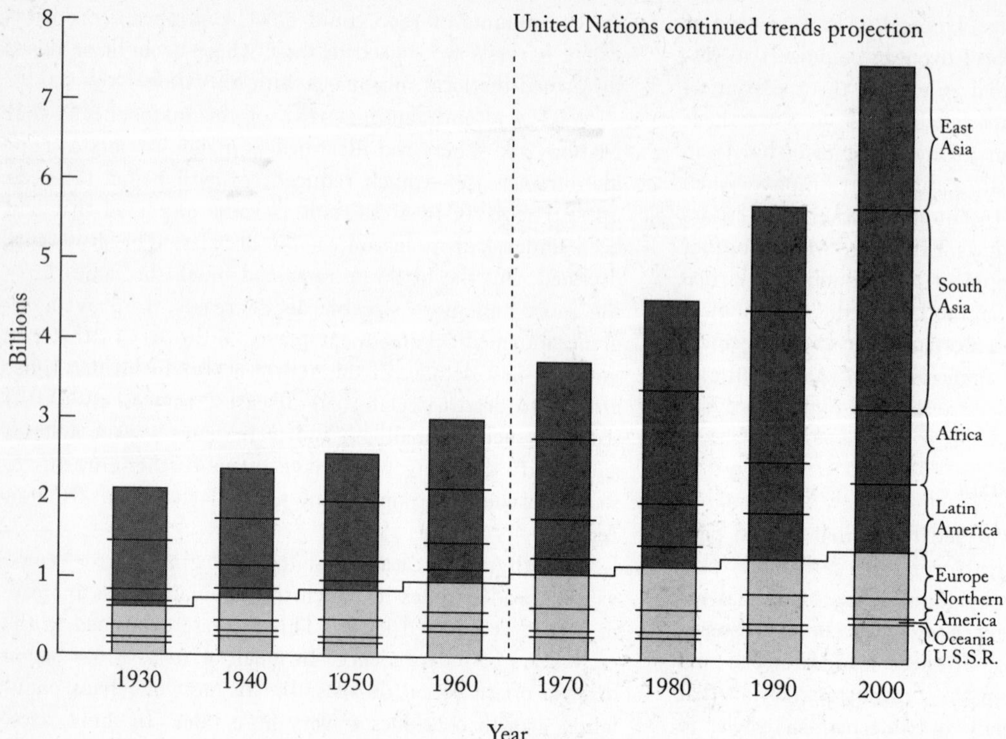

Numerical growth of world population, 1930-2000.

achievements of European colonial regimes. It was certainly an accomplishment that colonial officials never tired of citing in defense of the perpetuation of European dominance. But another side of the colonial legacy rendered this increase a trap in which most of the Third World nations were soon to find themselves caught. The European policy of limiting industrialization in their colonial dependencies meant that one of the key ways by which Europe had met its own population boom in the 19th and early 20th centuries was not available to the new nations of the Third World. They lacked the factories to employ the exploding population that moved to the cities from the rural areas, as well as the technology to produce the necessities of life for more and more people. Unlike the Europeans and the Americans, the Third World nations found it difficult to draw food and mineral resources from the rest of the world to feed this ever-proliferating population. In fact, these were the very things the colonized peoples had been set up to sell to the industrialized countries. Even in countries such as India, where impressive advances in industrialization were made in the postcolonial era, gains in productivity were rapidly swallowed up by the population explosion.

In most Third World countries there has been considerable resistance to birth control efforts aimed at bringing runaway population growth in check. Some of this resistance is linked to deeply entrenched social patterns and religious beliefs. In many Third World societies, procreation is seen as a key marker of male virility, and the capacity to bear children, preferably male children, continues to be critical to the social standing of adult women. In some cases, resistance to birth control is linked to specific cultural norms. Hindus, for example, believe that a deceased man's soul cannot begin the cycle of rebirth until his eldest son has performed special ceremonies over his funeral pyre. This belief both increases the already considerable pressure on Indian women to have children, and it encourages families to have several sons in order to ensure that at least one survives the father.

In Africa children are seen as indispensable additions to the lineage—the extended network of relatives (and deceased ancestors) that, much more than the nuclear family, makes up the core social group over much of the subcontinent. As in India, sons are essential for, among other things, the continuation of the patrilineal family line and the performance of burial and ancestral rites. Their key roles in agricultural production and marketing make female offspring more highly valued in Africa than in many Asian societies, where high dowries and occupational restrictions limit their contribution to family welfare.

Before the 20th century, the high incidence of stillbirths and high rates of infant mortality more generally meant that mothers could expect to lose many of the children to whom they gave birth—ten or 12 deaths of 15 or 16 children conceived was not unheard of. Beyond the obvious psychological scars left by these high death rates, they also fostered the conviction that it was necessary to have many children to ensure that some would outlive the parents. In societies where welfare systems and old-age pensions were meager or unknown, surviving children took on special urgency because they were the only ones who would care for their parents once they could no longer work for themselves. The persistence of these attitudes in recent decades, when medical advances have greatly reduced infant mortality, has been a major factor contributing to soaring population growth.

In the early decades after independence, many Third World leaders were deeply opposed to state measures to promote family planning and birth control. Some saw these as Western attempts to meddle in their internal affairs; others proudly declared that the socialist societies they were building would be able to take care of the additional population. As it has become increasingly clear that excessive population increase renders significant economic advances impossible, many Third World leaders have begun to reassess their earlier attitudes toward birth control. A particular cause for alarm is the fact that in many Third World countries a high percentage of the population is under the age of 15 (as high as 40 percent in some countries) and thus dependent on others for support. But even for those who now wish to actively promote family planning, the obstacles are staggering. In addition to the cultural and social factors making for resistance discussed above, Third World leaders often find they lack sufficient resources and the educated personnel required to make these programs effective. High rates of illiteracy, particularly among women, need to be overcome, but education is expensive. Perhaps no form of financial and technical assistance from the industrialized to the developing world will be as critical in the coming decades as that devoted to family planning to defuse the global population bomb.

PARASITIC CITIES AND ENDANGERED ECOSYSTEMS

As population increase in the rural areas of Third World countries outstripped the land and employment opportunities available to the peasantry, mass migrations to urban areas ensued. The massive movement of population from overcrowded villages to the cities was one of the most dramatic developments in the postcolonial history of most Third World nations. Ambitious youths and the rural poor crowded into port centers and capital cities in search of jobs and a chance to win the "good life" that the big hotels and restaurants and the neon lights of the city center appeared to offer to all comers. But because Third World cities lacked the rapidly expanding industrial sectors that had made possible the absorption (with considerable difficulty) of a similar migrant influx earlier in the West, they were often dead ends for migrants from the rural areas. There were few jobs, and heavy competition for these ensured that wages would remain low for most workers. The growing numbers of underemployed or unemployed turned to street vending, scavenging, huckstering, begging, or petty crime to survive. The idleness and despair of the urban underclass has been a prominent theme in the novels and plays of Third World writers such as Mochtar Lubis of Indonesia, Cyprian Ekwensi of Nigeria, and V. S. Naipaul, who was born of Indian parents in the Caribbean and has written about many Third World countries.

In the independence era, the urban poor has become a volatile factor in the political struggles of the elite, willing for a price to cheer on one contender or jeer down another, ready to riot and loot in times of government crisis. In deeply divided societies, the poor, working-class, or idle youths of the urban areas have often formed the shock troops in communal clashes between rival ethnic and religious groups. Fear of outbursts by urban "mobs" has also forced Third World regimes to expend considerable portions of their scarce resources to subsidize and thus keep low the price of staple foods, such as bread, and other necessities.

The great and sudden influx of population from the rural areas to cities without the jobs or infrastructure to support them has greatly skewed urban growth in the Third World. Within decades, Asian cities have become some of the largest in the world, while African urban areas have sprawled far beyond their modest limits of colonial times. The wealth of the glitzy hotel and high-rise dominated enclaves of the upper- and middle-class minorities in Third World societies contrasts disturbingly with the poverty of the vast slums that stretch in all directions from the city centers. Little or no planning was possible for the slum quarters that expanded as squatters erected makeshift shelters wherever open land or derelict buildings could be found. Originally, most of the slum areas lacked electricity, running water, or even the most elementary sewage facilities. As shanties were gradually converted into ramshackle dwellings, many Third World governments scrapped plans to level slum settlements and sought instead to provide them with some semblance of electrical and sanitary systems. As an increasing number of development specialists have reluctantly concluded, slums often provide the only housing urban dwellers are likely to find for some time to come. Only substantially higher levels of economic growth will give most Third World nations the resources to replace them with planned housing at some future date.

In the urbanized areas of the Third World, the contrast between the wealth of the few and the poverty of the majority is starkly revealed by the juxtaposition of the high-rise apartments of the affluent middle classes and the ramshackle shantytowns of the urban poor.

These conditions have burdened most Third World societies with parasitic rather than productive cities, which are heavily dependent for survival on food and resources drawn from their own countryside or from abroad. In contrast to the cities of Western Europe and North America—even during the decades of rapid urban expansion in the 19th century—few Third World cities have had the manufacturing base required to generate growth in their surrounding regions or the nation as a whole. They take from the already impoverished countryside, but they are able to give little in return, though in the more industrialized societies of the Third World, such as India, cement and steel for dam and road construction and farm implements have made some contribution to rural development. Urban dependence on the countryside further stretches the already overextended resources of the rural areas.

Rural overpopulation in the decades after independence has led to the depletion of soils in many areas that have been worked for centuries or millennia. It has also resulted in an alarming rate of deforestation throughout the Third World, as peasant villagers cut trees for fuel or to clear land for farming and their flocks. Deforestation and overgrazing not only pose major threats to the wild animal life, ranging from tigers to elephants, they also upset the balance in fragile tropical ecosystems, producing further soil depletion and erosion and encouraging desertification. This environmental degradation is intensified by industrial pollution, both from developed countries and Third World nations themselves. Though the industrial sectors in the latter are generally small, pollution tends to be proportionally greater than in the developed world because Third World nations rarely have the means to afford the anti-pollution technology introduced in Western Europe, Japan, and North America.

ANALYSIS

WOMEN AND THE STRUGGLE TO BUILD NEW SOCIETIES IN THE THIRD WORLD

The example of both the Western democracies and the Communist republics of Eastern Europe, where women had won the right to vote in the middle decades of the 20th century, encouraged the founders of the nations of the Third World to write female suffrage into their constitutions. The very active part women played in many nationalist struggles was perhaps even more critical to their earning the right to vote and run for political office. Female activism also produced some semblance of equality in terms of legal rights, education, and occupational opportunities under the laws of many new nations.

The equality that was proclaimed on paper, however, often bore little resemblance to the actual rights that the great majority of African and Asian women could exercise or had little bearing on the conditions under which they lived their daily lives. Despite the media attention given to Third World women such as Indira Gandhi, Corazon Aquino, and Benazir Bhutto who have emerged as national leaders, political life in most African and Asian countries continues to be dominated by males. The overwhelming majority of elected officials and government administrators, particularly at the upper levels of state bureaucracies, are males. Because they are usually less well educated than their husbands, women in societies where genuine elections are held often do not exercise their right to vote, or they simply vote for the party and candidates favored by their spouses. In many Third World societies in which coups or one-party dominance have put an end to democratic politics, female suffrage is meaningless.

Even the rise to power of individual women like Indira Gandhi, who proved to be one of the most resolute and powerful of all Third World leaders, is deceptive. In every case, female heads of state in the Third World entered politics and initially won political support because they were connected to powerful males. Indira Gandhi was the daughter of Jawaharlal Nehru, India's first prime minister; Corazon Aquino's husband was the martyred leader of the Filipino opposition to Ferdinand Marcos; and Benazir Bhutto's father was a domineering Pakistani prime minister who had been toppled by a military coup and was executed in the late 1970s. Lacking these sorts of connections, the vast majority of Third World women have been at best relegated to peripheral political positions, and at worst, they are allowed no participation in the political process whatsoever.

The limited real gains made by Third World women in the political sphere are paralleled by the second-class position to which most are consigned in many societies. In some respects their handicaps are comparable to those that constrict women in the industrialized democracies and communist nations. But the obstacles to female self-fulfillment, and in many cases just survival, in Third World societies are usually much more blatant and fundamental than the child-rearing patterns, educational and job discrimination, and other sexist restrictions women have to contend with in developed societies. To begin with, the fact that early marriage ages for women and large families are still the norm in most Third World societies means that women spend their youthful and middle-age years having children. There is little time to think of higher education or a career.

In many Third World societies, large numbers of women are still confined to the home, a trend that has been reinforced by the spread of religious fundamentalism in recent decades. Even in India, which is officially a secular state, it was estimated that decades after independence in 1947, as high as 20 percent of all women were still in *purdah*, or domestic seclusion. In Islamic lands, the proportion of women confined to the home is often a good deal higher. This trend has not been followed in most of sub-Saharan Africa, where women were traditionally more independent and free to follow occupations outside the home. It has also been resisted by women of the middle and elite classes in many Third World countries, who have had the resources to pursue higher education and professional careers. As the experience of the Iranian revolution suggests, "liberated" women from these classes are likely to lose these outlets in areas where religious fundamentalism takes hold.

Because of the low level of sanitation in many Third World communities and food scarcity, all but upper-class women experience endemic anxiety regarding such basic issues as sufficient and nutritional meals for their hungry children and their susceptibility to disease. The persistence of male-centric customs directly affects the health and life expectancy of women themselves. The Indian tradition, for example, which dictates that women first serve their husbands' and sons' meals and then eat what is left, has obvious disadvantages. The quantity and nutritional content of the leftovers is likely to be lower than of the original meals, and in tropical environments flies and other disease-bearing insects are more likely to have fouled the food.

The consequences of these social patterns can be quite injurious for women. In the 1970s, for example, it was estimated that as high as 20 percent of the female population of India was malnourished and that as much as another 30 percent had a diet that was well below acceptable United Nations levels. In sharp contrast to the industrial societies of Japan, North America, and Europe, where women outnumber (because on the average they outlive) men, in India there are only 930 females for every 1000 males.

In most Third World societies, the disadvantages women traditionally faced within the household and in terms of career opportunities were compounded by the prejudices and policies of colonial officials. Whatever education, particularly higher and technical education, that was provided was geared to males. Colonial development schemes and links to the global markets also favored males. Thus, in societies like those of West Africa and Southeast Asia, where women had traditionally played significant roles in farming and marketing, their position actually declined in the colonial era.

Traditional religious restrictions on women often remained after independence, and they lagged far behind men in the degree to which they were able to take advantage of what might have been countervailing educational and occupational opportunities. As late as 1975, for example, there were only 300,000 women in India with bachelors degrees in a total population of some 600 million.

Though the highly secular property and divorce laws many new states promulgated after independence gave women much greater rights, many of these have been ignored in practice, and very often Third World women have neither the education nor the resources to exercise their legal rights. The spread of religious fundamentalism has in many cases further eroded these rights, most notably in Islamic areas, though advocates of a return to tradition often argue that practices such as veiling and stoning for women (but not men) caught in adultery actually enhance the dignity and status of women. Wherever one comes down in these disputes, there is little doubt that most Third World women continue to be dominated by male family members, are much more constricted than males in terms of career opportunities, and are likely to be less well-fed, educated, and healthy than males at a comparable social level.

Questions: In what ways would the persistence of some of the traditional religious beliefs of African and Asian societies, which we have discussed in earlier chapters, contribute to the limitation of women's rights and career opportunities in the Third World? Are there comparable obstacles in the religious and secular belief systems of the West? What sorts of programs and measures could be undertaken by international agencies, such as the United Nations, and Third World governments to speed the liberation of African and Asian women?

"NEOCOLONIALISM," COLD WAR RIVALRIES, AND UNDERDEVELOPMENT

The schemes of nationalist leaders aimed at building an industrial base that would provide adequate support for the rapidly increasing populations of their new nations soon floundered amid the economic realities of the postcolonial world. Not only did most of the nations that emerged from colonialism have little in the way of an industrial base, their means of obtaining one were depressingly meager. In order to buy the machines and hire or train the technical experts they needed to get industrialization going, Third World countries needed to earn capital they could invest for these ends. Some funds could be accumulated by saving a portion of the state revenues collected from the peasantry. In most cases, however, there was precious little left once bureaucrats had been given their salaries, essential public works and the extension of education had been funded, and other state expenses had been met. Thus, most Third World countries have relied on the sale of cash crops and minerals to earn the foreign exchange they need to finance industrialization. As their leaders soon discovered, the structure of the world market was heavily loaded against them.

The pattern of exchange promoted in the colonial era left most Third World countries dependent on the export production of two or three food or industrial crops—such as cocoa, palm oil, coffee, or jute and hemp—or minerals—such as copper, bauxite, and oil—for which there was a high demand in the industrialized economies of Europe, North America, and increasingly Japan. Since the Second World War, the prices of this sort of export—which economists call primary products—have not only fluctuated widely, they have steadily declined when compared to the prices of most of the manufactured goods Third World countries usually buy from the industrialized nations. Price fluctuations have created nightmares for planners in the Third World. Revenue estimates from the sale of coffee or copper in years when the price is high are used to plan government projects for the construction of roads, factories, and dams. Market slumps can wipe out these critical funds—thereby retarding economic growth—and throw Third World countries deeply into debt. These setbacks are doubly frustrating because in order to get industrialization going, Third World countries are often forced to export precious and finite mineral resources that they themselves will require if they succeed in industrializing.

Except with oil, the leaders and planners of Third World countries have had little success in improving the terms under which they participate in the global market economy. Even the gains made by the oil cartel have tended to be confined to a select few Third World nations and to be temporary. They were also soon rolled back to a large degree by divisions between the oil-producing states. These differences, including those partly responsible for Iraq's invasion of Kuwait in 1990, have made it difficult to maintain the production quotas that were essential to the great rise in the price of oil in the mid-1970s. Third World leaders have been quite ready to blame the legacy of colonialism and what they have termed the "neocolonial" structure of the global economy for the limited returns yielded thus far by their development schemes. Though there is much truth to these accusations, they do not tell the whole story. Third World leaders and elites must also share the responsibility for the slow pace of economic development in much of the Third World. To begin with, few leaders of the new nations had the technical or scientific training to tackle the mundane but complex tasks involved in development. To some extent their deficiencies can be blamed on the low level of technical education available in most colonies. But even in areas like India where it was available, the rising Western-educated classes rarely pursued it, preferring instead the training in Western languages and the humanities that opened to them well-paying careers in government, law, and business.

In addition, members of the educated classes that came to dominate the political and business life of newly independent nations often used their positions to enrich themselves and their relatives at the expense of their societies as a whole. Corruption has been notoriously widespread in most of the new nations. Government controls on the import of goods, such as automobiles, television sets, and stereos, which are luxury items for most of the people, have often been lax. As a result, tax revenues and export earnings that could have fueled development have often gone to provide "the good life" for small minorities within Third World societies. The inability or refusal of many Third World regimes to carry out key social reforms such as land redistribution, which would spread the limited resources available more equitably over the population, has contributed vitally to the persistence of these patterns. Leaders who have defied the interests of the elite classes from which they came and pushed for sweeping reforms have often fallen victim to coups and even assassination plots.

Badly strapped for investment funds and essential technology, Third World nations have often turned to international organizations, such as the World Bank and the International Monetary Fund, and the rival great powers for assistance. Though considerable resources for development have been generated in this way, the price for international assistance has often been high. Both the United States and the Soviet Union, as well as their allies, have normally extracted major concessions in return for their aid. These have ranged from commitments to buy the products of and favor investors from the lending countries to entering into alliances and permitting military bases on the territory of the client state. Loans from international lending agencies have almost invariably been granted only after the needy nation agreed to what are called "conditionalities." These are regulations that determine how the money is to be invested and repaid, and they usually involve promises to undertake major "reforms" in the economy of the borrowing nation.

In recent years, these promises have often included a commitment to remove or reduce state subsidies on food and other essential consumer items. State subsidies were designed to keep prices for staple goods at a level that the urban and rural poor—the great majority of the people in virtually all Third World countries—could afford. When carried through, subsidy reductions have frequently led to widespread social unrest, violent riots, and the collapse or near collapse of Third World regimes. These violent outbursts have served as dramatic reminders both of just how precarious social stability is in much of the Third World, and of how limited and perilous solutions to the problems facing the new states spawned by decolonization have proved.

PATHS TO DEVELOPMENT

However much the leaders of the new Third World countries might have blamed their nations' woes on the recently departed colonizers, they soon felt the need to deliver on the promises of social reform and economic well-being that had done so much to rally support to the nationalist cause. Different leaders adopted different approaches, and some tried one strategy after another. Depending on their own skills, the talents of their advisors and lieutenants, and the resources at their disposal, Third World leaders tackled the awesome task of development with varying degrees of success. Though it is obviously impossible to deal with all of these efforts at nation-building and economic development in depth, the basic elements of several distinctive strategies will be considered in sections that make up the second half of this chapter. Discussion of each strategy will focus on a single, prominent case example, and some attempt will be made to assess the merits and drawbacks of each approach. As this overview clearly reveals, though some countries have done a good deal better than others, successful overall strategies to deal with the challenges facing the nations of the Third World have yet to be devised.

Solutions to specific problems, such as the Green Revolution in agriculture that many development experts credit with averting global famine in the last two decades, have often given rise to new problems. Ways have been found to raise the living standards of some of the population of Third World nations, but these have rarely benefited the majority. Revolutionary movements aimed at genuine redistribution and the benefit of all have thus far floundered due to planning errors and insufficient resources. It may be too early to judge the outcomes of many development schemes, but thus far none has proven a path to the social justice and general economic development that nationalist leaders envisioned as the ultimate outcome of struggles for decolonization.

CHARISMATIC POPULISTS AND ONE-PARTY RULE

One of the least successful responses on the part of Third World leaders who found their dreams for national renewal frustrated was a retreat into authoritarian rule, which was disguised by calculated, charismatic appeals for support from the disenfranchised masses. Perhaps the career of Kwame Nkrumah, the leader of Ghana's independence movement, illustrates this pattern as well as that of any Third World politician. There can be little question that Nkrumah was genuinely committed to social reform and economic uplift for the Ghanaian people during the years of his rise to the position of the first prime minister of Ghana in 1957. After assuming power, he moved vigorously to initiate programs that would translate his high aspirations for his people into reality. But his ambitious schemes for everything from universal education to industrial development soon ran into trouble. Rival political parties, some of them representing regional interests and ethnic groups long hostile to Nkrumah, repeatedly challenged his initiatives and sought to block efforts to carry out his schemes. His leftist leanings won support from the Soviet bloc, but frightened away Western investors who had a good deal more capital to plow into his economy. They also led to growing hostility on the part of the United States, Great Britain, and other influential noncommunist countries. Most devastatingly, soon after independence the price of cocoa, by far Ghana's largest export crop, began to fall sharply. Tens of thousands of Ghanaian cocoa farmers were hard hit and the resources for Nkrumah's development schemes suddenly dried up.

Many monumental statues of Kwame Nkrumah like this one rose in the towns and villages of Ghana as he attempted to cover the failure of his socialist-inspired development programs with dictatorial rule and self-glorification.

Nkrumah's response to these growing problems was increasingly dictatorial. He refused to give up or cut back on his development plans. As a result, most failed miserably due to lack of key supplies and to official mismanagement. In the early 1960s he forcibly crushed all political opposition by banning rival parties and jailing other political leaders. He assumed dictatorial powers and ruled through functionaries in his own Convention Peoples party.

Nkrumah also sought to hold on to the loyalty of the masses and mobilize their energies by highly stage-managed "events" and the manipulation of largely invented symbols and traditions that were said to be derived from Ghana's past history. Thus, he sought to justify his policies and leadership style with references to a uniquely African brand of socialism and the need to revive African traditions and African civilization. Even before independence he had taken to wearing the traditional garb of the Ghanaian elite. The very name of Ghana, which Nkrumah himself had proposed for the new nation that emerged from the former Gold Coast colony, had been taken from an ancient African kingdom that had actually been centered much farther to the north and had little to do with the peoples of the Gold Coast.

Nkrumah went about the country giving fiery speeches, dedicating monuments to the "revolution," which often consisted of giant statues of himself, and taking a prominent role in the nonaligned movement that was then sweeping the Third World. As the French journalist Jean Lacouture reported in the mid-1960s, Nkrumah's posturing had become a substitute for his failed development schemes. His followers' adulation knew no bounds. Members of his captive Parliament compared him to Confucius, Muhammad, Shakespeare, and Napoleon and predicted that his birthplace would serve as a "Mecca" for all of Africa's statesmen. But his suppression of all opposition and his growing ties to the Communist party, coupled with the rapid deterioration of the Ghanaian economy, increased his enemies, who laid low and waited for a chance to strike. That chance came early in 1966 when Nkrumah went off on one of his many trips, this time a peace mission to Vietnam. In his absence, he was deposed by a military coup. Nkrumah died in exile in 1972, and Ghana moved in a very different direction under its new military rulers.

MILITARY RESPONSES: DICTATORSHIPS AND REVOLUTIONS

Nkrumah is just one of many civilian leaders in the Third World who have fallen victim to military coups. In fact, it is far more difficult to find African and Asian (or, as we have seen in Chapter 38, Latin-American) countries that have remained under civilian regimes since independence than those that have experienced military takeovers of varying durations. India, the Ivory Coast, Kenya, Zambia, and Zimbabwe are some of the more notable of the former; much of South and Southeast Asia and the rest of Africa have been or are now governed by military regimes. Given the difficulties confronted after independence by leaders such as Nkrumah and a number of advantages the military have in crisis situations, the proliferation of coups in the Third World is not all that surprising.

The armed forces in Third World countries have at times been divided by the religious and ethnic rivalries that have proved such a disruptive force in new nations. But the regimentation and emphasis on discipline and in-group solidarity in military training have often rendered soldiers more resistant to these forces than other social groups. In conditions of political breakdown and social conflict, the military possesses the monopoly—or near monopoly—of force that is often essential for restoring order. Their occupational conditioning not only makes soldiers more ready than civilian leaders to use the force at their disposal, but less concerned with its destructive consequences. Military personnel also tend to possess some degree of technical training, which as we have seen was usually lacking in the humanities-oriented education of civilian nationalist leaders. Because most military leaders have been staunchly anticommunist, they have often attracted covert technical and financial assistance from Western governments.

Once in control, military leaders have banned civilian political parties and imposed military regimes of varying degrees of repression and authoritarian control. Yet the ends to which these regimes have put their dictatorial powers have differed considerably. At their worst, military regimes—such as those in Uganda, Burma (now Myanmar), and Zaire—have quashed civil liberties, while making little attempt to reduce social inequities or improve living standards. These regimes have existed mainly to enrich the military strongmen, as well as their cronies and lackeys, who control them. Regimes of this sort have been notorious for official corruption and the imprisonment and brutal torture or outright elimination of political dissidents. Understandably uneasy about being overthrown, they have diverted a high proportion of their nations' meager resources that might have gone for economic development into expenditures on expensive military hardware, which the Western democracies and the countries of the Soviet bloc have been only too eager to sell to them. Military leaders of this type have also been ready to use quarrels and sometimes military conflicts with neighboring regimes to divert attention from the bankruptcy of their domestic policies.

In a few cases, military leaders have proven quite radical with regard to economic and social reform. Perhaps none was more so than Gamal Abdul Nasser, who took power in Egypt following a military coup in 1952. As we have seen, the Egyptians had won their independence, except for the lingering British presence in the Suez Canal zone in the mid-1930s. But self-centered civilian politicians and the corrupt khedival regime had done little to improve the standard of living of the mass of the Egyptian people. As conditions worsened and Egypt's governing parties did little but rake in wealth for their limited, largely elitist memberships, two revolutionary forces emerged in Egyptian society.

The first was the Muslim Brotherhood, a party founded by Hasan al-Banna in 1928. Though committed to a fundamentalist approach to Islam, al-Banna's organization was also devoted to social uplift and sweeping reform. The Muslim Brotherhood became involved in a wide range of activities, from promoting trade unions and building medical clinics to educating women and pushing for land reform. By the late 1930s, the Brotherhood's social service had become highly politicized. Al-Banna's followers fomented strikes and urban riots and set up militant youth organizations and paramilitary assassination squads. Though stunned by the murder of al-Banna by the khedive Farouk's hit men in 1949, the members of the Brotherhood continued to expand its influence among both middle-class youth and the impoverished masses into the early 1950s. Its ultimate goal of the seizure of power, however, was thwarted by the second revolutionary force that emerged in this period.

The Free Officers movement, which evolved from a secret organization established by officers in the Egyptian army in the 1930s, was for many decades loosely allied to the Muslim Brotherhood. Founded by idealistic young officers of Egyptian, rather than Turco-Egyptian, descent, the secret Revolutionary Command Council studied conditions in the country and prepared to seize power in the name of a genuine revolution. Following Egypt's humiliating defeats in the first Arab-Israeli War in 1948 and in a clash with the British over the latter's continuing occupation of the Suez Canal zone in 1952, mass anger with a discredited khedival and parliamentary regime gave the officers their chance. In July of 1952, an almost bloodless military coup toppled the corrupt and "well-padded" khedive Farouk from his jewel-encrusted throne.

The revolution had begun. The monarchy was ended, and the Egyptians ruled themselves for the first time since the 6th century B.C. By 1954, all political parties had been disbanded—including the Muslim Brotherhood, which had clashed with its former allies in the military—and had been suppressed after an attempt on the life of Nasser. Nasser was only one of several officers as the head of the Free Officers movement, and by no means was he initially the most charismatic. After months of internal power struggles in the officer corps, however, he emerged as the head of a military government that was deeply committed to revolution.

The growing Egyptian resistance to the continuing British occupation of the Suez Canal zone was dramatically expressed in this effigy of a British soldier that was strung up on a Cairo street corner in January 1952. Within months mass demonstrations and a military coup freed Egypt from the British occupation and the repressive khedival regime.

Nasser and his fellow officers used the dictatorial powers they had won in the coup in an attempt to uplift the long oppressed Egyptian masses. They believed that only the state possessed the power to carry out essential social and economic reforms, and thus they began to intervene in all aspects of Egyptian life. Land reform measures were enacted: limits were placed on how much land an individual could own, and excess lands were seized and redistributed to landless peasants. State-financed education was made available to Egyptians through the college level. The government became Egypt's main employer—by 1980 over 30 percent of Egypt's work force was on the state payroll. State subsidies were used to lower the price of basic food staples such as wheat and cooking oil. State-controlled development schemes were introduced that emphasized industrial growth, just like the Five-Year Plans of the Soviet Union. In order to establish Egypt's economic independence, stiff restrictions were placed on foreign investment, and in some cases foreign properties were seized and redistributed to Egyptian investors. Nasser also embarked on an interventionist foreign policy that stressed the struggle to destroy the newly established Israeli state, forge Arab unity, and foment socialist revolutions in neighboring lands. His greatest foreign policy coup came in 1956, when he rallied international opinion to oust finally the British (and their French allies) from the Suez Canal zone. Despite the setbacks suffered by Egyptian military forces, Nasser made good use of the rare combined backing of the United States and the Soviet Union to achieve his aims in the crisis.

However well-intentioned, many of Nasser's initiatives misfired. Land reform efforts were frustrated by bureaucratic corruption and the clever stratagems devised by the landlord class to hold on to their estates. State development schemes often lacked proper funding and failed due to mismanagement and miscalculations. Even the Aswân Dam project, which was the cornerstone of Nasser's development drive, was something of a fiasco. Egypt's continuing population boom quickly canceled out the additional cultivable lands the dam produced. The dam's interference with the flow of the Nile resulted in an increase in parasites that spread blindness, as well as in a decline in the fertility of farmlands in the Lower Nile delta that were deprived of the rich silt annually washed down by the river. Foreign investment funds from the West, which Egypt desperately needed, soon dried up. Aid from the much poorer Soviet bloc could not begin to match what was lost, and much of this assistance was military. In the absence of sufficient foreign investment and with Egypt's uncontrolled population rising at an alarming rate, the state simply could not afford all the ambitious schemes to which Nasser and the revolutionary officers had committed it. The gap between aspirations and means was increased in the later years of Nasser's reign (in the 1960s) by the heavy costs of his mostly failed foreign adventures, including the disastrous Six-Day War with Israel that Egypt was drawn into in 1967.

Though he had to move slowly at first, Nasser's successor, Anwar Sadat, had little choice but to dismantle the massive state apparatus that had been created. He favored private rather than state initiatives, and during his tenure in office the middle class, which had been greatly restricted by Nasser, emerged again as a powerful force. Sadat also moved, after fighting the Israelis to a stalemate in 1973, to end the costly confrontation with Israel and Egypt's support for revolutionary movements in the Arab world. Sadat expelled the Russians and opened Egypt to aid and investment from the United States and Western Europe.

Sadat's shift in direction has been continued by his successor and the present leader of Egypt, Hosni Mubarak. But neither the attempt at genuine revolution led by Nasser nor the retreat to capitalism and more pro-West positions under his successors has done much to check Egypt's alarming population increases and the corruption of its bloated bureaucracy. Neither path to development has had much effect on the glaring gap between the living conditions of Egypt's rich minority and its impoverished masses.

THE INDIAN ALTERNATIVE: DEVELOPMENT FOR SOME OF THE PEOPLE

Although the approach to nation building and economic development followed by the leaders of independent India has shared the Nasserite emphasis on socialism and state intervention, India's experience has diverged from Egypt's in a number of very significant respects. To begin with, the Indians have managed to preserve civilian rule throughout the four decades since they won their independence from Great Britain. In fact, in India the military has consistently defended secular democracy against religious extremism and other would-be authoritarian trends. In addition, though India, like Egypt, has been saddled with a crushing burden of overpopulation, it came to independence with a larger industrial and scientific sector, a better communications system and bureaucratic grid, and a larger and more skilled middle class in proportion to its total population than any other Third World country.

During the first decades of its freedom, India had the good fortune to be governed by leaders, such as Jawaharlal Nehru and his allies in the Congress party, who were deeply committed to social reform and economic development as well as the preservation of civil rights and democracy. India's success at the latter has been nothing short of remarkable. Despite continuous threats of secession by religious and linguistic minorities, as well as massive poverty, unemployment, and recurring natural disasters, India remains the world's largest functioning democracy. Except for brief periods of rule by coalitions of opposition parties, the Congress party has ruled at the center for most of the independence era. But opposition parties have controlled many state and local governments, and they remain vocal and active in the national Parliament. Civil liberties, exemplified by a very outspoken press and free elections, have been upheld to an extent that sets India off from much of the rest of the Third World. Their staying power was perhaps most emphatically demonstrated by the heavy political price that Nehru's daughter, Indira Gandhi, and more dictatorially-prone successor paid for attempting to curtail press and political freedoms in the mid-1970s, an attempt that led to the one of the rare election defeats the Congress party has suffered thus far.

Nehru's less dictatorial approach to government and development also differed from Nasser's in his more moderate mix of state and private initiatives. Nehru and his successors pushed state intervention in some sectors, but also encouraged foreign investment from countries in both of the rival blocs in the cold war. As a consequence, India has been able to build on its initial advantages in industrial infrastructure and its skilled managerial and labor endowment. Its significant capitalist sector has encouraged ambitious farmers like those in the Panjab in the northwest to invest heavily in the improved seed strains, fertilizers, and irrigation that are at the heart of the Green Revolution. The new techniques associated with the Green Revolution have produced much higher yields in key crops such as rice, wheat, and corn throughout much of the Third World in recent decades. Considerable industrial and agrarian growth have generated the revenue for the Indian government to promote literacy and village development schemes, as well as family planning, village electrification, and other improvement projects in recent decades.

Despite its very considerable successes, India has suffered from the same gap between needs and resources that all Third World nations have had to face. Whatever the government's intentions—and India has been hit by corruption and self-serving like most polities—there have simply not been the resources to raise the living standards of even a majority of its huge population. The middle class has grown, perhaps as rapidly as that of any Third World nation. Its presence is striking in the affluent neighborhoods of cities like Bombay and Delhi and proclaimed by the Indian film industry, the world's largest, in innumerable sitcoms and dramas about the woes in the lives of yuppies, Indian-style. But as high as 60 percent of India's people have gained little or nothing from the development schemes and economic growth that have occurred since independence.

In part, this has been because population growth has wiped out economic gains. But social reform has been slow in most areas, both rural and urban. Groups like the wealthy landlords, who supported the nationalist drive for independence, have continued to dominate the great mass of tenants and landless laborers, just as they did in the pre-colonial and colonial eras. Some development measures, most notably those associated with the Green Revolution, have greatly favored those cultivators with the resources to invest in new seeds and fertilizer. They have increased the gap between well-off and poor people over much of rural India. India's literacy rate remains well below that of China (the only rival with which it can be reasonably compared given the size of each and the magnitude of the problems they face), and a far larger proportion of India's population remains malnourished. Thus, the poor have paid and will continue to pay the price for Indian gradualism, and those favoring more revolutionary solutions to India's social inequities and mass poverty have plenty of ammunition with which to attack the ruling parties.

DOCUMENT
CULTURAL CREATIVITY IN THE THIRD WORLD: SOME LITERARY SAMPLES

Despite, or perhaps because of, political instability and chronic economic difficulties, Third World societies have generated a high level of artistic creativity over the past decades. Nowhere has this creativity been more prominent and brilliant than in literary productivity, for which Third World writers have earned Nobel Prizes and deservedly won a wide readership far beyond their own nations. The selections that follow provide only a small sample of the vast and varied talent Third World writers have displayed, from poetry and drama to novels and short stories.

Much of the literature of Third World writers focuses on the predicament of the Western-educated African and Asian elites who dominate the new nations that emerged from the European colonial empires. In the following stanza from the poem "I Run Around with Them," the Indonesian poet, Chairil Anwar, reflects on the lack of purpose and malaise he believed to be widespread among the children of these elite groups.

I run around with them, what else can I do, now—
Changing my face at the edge of the street, I use their eyes
And tag along to visit the fun house:
These are the facts as I know them
(A new American flic at the Capitol,
The new songs they dance to).
We go home: there's nothing doing
Though this kind of Death is our neighbor, our friend, now.
Hanging around at the corner, we wait for the city bus
That glows night to day like a gold tooth;
Lame, deformed, negative, we
Lean our bony asses against lamp poles
And jaw away the years.

In the next quotation from the novel *No Longer at Ease*, the widely read Nigerian author, Chinua Achebe, identifies another dilemma, the pull between Western culture and the ancient civilization of one's own land.

> Nothing gave him greater pleasure than to find another Ibo-speaking student in a London bus. But when he had to speak in English with a Nigerian student from another tribe he lowered his voice. It was humiliating to have to speak to one's countryman in a foreign language, especially in the presence of the proud owners of that language. They would naturally assume that one had no language of one's own. He wished they were here today to see. Let them come to Umuofia [the protagonist's home village] now and listen to the talk of men who made a great art of conversation. Let them come and see men and women and children who knew how to live, whose joy of life had not yet been killed by those who claimed to teach other nations how to live.

Like a number of the more famous Third World novelists, V. S. Naipaul is an expatriot who was born in the Caribbean and now lives in rural England. In his moving account of his return to his Indian ancestral home, entitled *An Area of Darkness*, Naipaul confronts the problem of massive poverty and the responses of foreigners and the Indian elite to it.

> . . . to see [India's] poverty is to make an observation of no value; a thousand newcomers to the country before you have seen and said as you. And not only newcomers. Our own sons and daughters, when they return from Europe and America, have spoken in your very words. Do not think that your anger

and contempt are marks of your sensitivity. You might have seen more: the smiles on the faces of the begging children, that domestic group among the pavement sleepers waking in the cool Bombay morning, father, mother and baby in a trinity of love, so self-contained that they are as private as if walls had separated them from you; it is your gaze that violates them, your sense of outrage that outrages them. . . . It is your surprise, your anger that denies [them] humanity.

Questions: Can you think of parallels in American history or contemporary society for the situations and responses conveyed in these passages from recent African and Asian writings? Do they suggest that it is possible to communicate even intimate feelings across cultures or do you find them alien, different?

IRAN: RELIGIOUS REVIVALISM AND THE REJECTION OF THE WEST

No path of development adopted by a Third World society has provided more fundamental challenges to the existing world order than revolutionary Iran under the direction of Ayatollah Khomaini. In many respects, the Khomaini revolution of 1979 represents a throwback to the religious fervor of such anticolonial resistance movements as that led by the Mahdi of the Sudan in the 1880s. The emphasis on religious purification and the rejoining of religion and politics that leaders such as the Mahdi and Khomaini have seen as central to the Islamic tradition provided the core motivations for the followers of both movements. The call for a return to the kind of society believed to have existed in the past "golden age" of the prophet Muhammad was central to the policies pursued by both the Mahdist and Iranian regimes once they had gained power. Both movements were aimed at Western-backed governments: the Mahdist at the Anglo-Egyptian presence in the Sudan, and Khomaini's against the autocratic Iranian shah and the Pahlavi dynasty, which were pictured as advocates of secularization and unchecked Westernization as well as puppets of America.

Though from the Sunni and Shi'ite religious traditions respectively, both the Mahdi and Khomaini claimed to be divinely inspired deliverers who would rescue the Islamic faithful from imperialist Westerners and corrupt and heretical leaders within the Muslim world. Both leaders promised their followers magical protection and instant paradise should they fall waging the holy war against the heretics and infidels. Each movement sought to build a lasting state and social order on the basis of what were believed to be Islamic precedents. Thus, each movement aimed at the defense and restoration of what its leaders believed to be the true beliefs, traditions, and institutions of Islamic civilization. The leaders of both movements sought to spread their revolutions to surrounding areas, both Muslim and infidel, and each believed he was setting in motion forces that would eventually sweep the entire globe.

Though proclaimed as an alternate path for development that can be followed by the rest of the Third World, Khomaini's revolution owed its initial success in seizing power to a number of circumstances that were more or less unique to Iran. Like China, Iran had not been formally colonized by the European powers, but rather reduced to a sphere of informal influence, divided between Great Britain and Russia. As a result, neither the bureaucratic nor the communications infrastructures that accompanied colonial takeovers were highly developed there. Nor did a substantial Western-educated middle class emerge. Thus, the impetus for "modernization" came suddenly and was imposed from above by the Pahlavi shahs. The initiatives taken by the second shah in particular, which were supported by Iran's considerable oil wealth, wrenched Iran out of the isolation and backwardness in which most of the nation lived until the mid-20th century. The shah sought to impose economic development and social change by government directives. Though advances occurred, the regime managed to alienate the great mass of the Iranian people in the process.

The shah's dictatorial and repressive regime deeply offended the emerging middle class, whom he considered his strongest potential supporters. His flaunting of Islamic conventions and neglect of Islamic worship and religious institutions enraged the ayatollahs, or religious experts, and mullahs, or local prayer leaders and mosque attendants, who guided the religious and personal lives of the great majority of the Iranian population. The favoritism he showed foreign investors and a handful of big Iranian entrepreneurs, who had personal connections to highly placed officials, angered the smaller bazaar merchants, who had long maintained close links with the mullahs and other religious leaders. The shah's halfhearted land reform schemes alienated the landowning classes without really doing much to improve the condition of the rural poor. Even the urban workers, who benefited most from the boom in construction and light industrialization the shah's development efforts had stimulated, were disaffected in the years before the 1979 revolution by a fall in oil prices that had led to an economic slump and widespread unemployment.

Though he had treated his officers well, the shah had badly neglected the military rank-and-file, especially in the army. So when the crisis came in 1978, the shah found that few of his countrymen were prepared to defend his regime. His armies refused to fire on the growing crowds that demonstrated for his removal and the return of Khomaini, then in exile in Paris. Dying of cancer and disheartened by what he viewed as betrayal by his people and allies such as the United States, the shah fled without much of a fight. Khomaini's revolution triumphed over a regime that looked powerful, but in fact proved to be exceptionally vulnerable.

After coming to power, Khomaini, defying the predictions of most Western "experts" on Iranian affairs, followed through on his promises of radical change. Constitutional and leftist parties allied to the revolutionary movement were brutally repressed. Moderate leaders were quickly replaced by radical religious figures, eager to obey Khomaini's every command. The "satanic" influences of the United States and Western Europe were purged; at the same time Iran also distanced itself from the atheistic communist world. Secular influences in law and government were supplanted by strict Islamic legal codes, which included such punishments as the amputation of limbs for theft and stoning for women caught in adultery, and rule by the mullahs and ayatollahs. Veiling became obligatory for all females, and the career prospects for women of the educated middle classes, who had been among the most favored by the shah's reforms, were suddenly greatly constricted.

Khomaini's planners also drew up grand schemes for land reform, religious education, and economic development that accorded with the dictates of Islam. Most of these measures came to little because soon after the revolution, Saddam Hussein, the military leader of neighboring Iraq, sought to take advantage of the turmoil in Iran by annexing its western, oil-rich provinces. The war that resulted has swallowed up Iranian energies and resources for virtually the entire decade since Khomaini came to power. Though clearly initially the fault of the invading Iraqis, the struggle became a highly personal vendetta for Khomaini, who was determined to destroy Hussein and punish the Iraqis. His refusal to negotiate peace caused heavy losses and untold suffering to the Iranian people. This suffering continued long after it was clear that the Iranians'

Women played a vital role in the mass demonstrations that toppled the shah and brought Ayatollah Khomaini to power. The fundamentalist version of Islam pursued by Khomaini and his allies, expressed, for example, by the return to veiling for women shown here, divided many of the highly Westernized women of the new Iranian middle classes from those of the urban working and merchant classes as well as the peasant class.

aging military equipment and handful of allies were no match for Hussein's more advanced military hardware and an Iraqi war machine bankrolled by its oil-rich Arab neighbors, who were fearful that Khomaini's revolution might spread to their own countries.

As the support of the Western powers, including the United States (despite protestations of neutrality), for the Iraqis increased, the position of the isolated Iranians became increasingly intolerable. Hundreds of thousands of poorly armed and half-trained Iranian conscripts, including tens of thousands of untrained and virtually weaponless boys, died before Khomaini finally agreed to a humiliating armistice in 1988. Peace found revolutionary Iran in shambles: Few of its development initiatives had been pursued, and shortages in food, fuel, and the other necessities of life were widespread.

Iran's decade-long absorption in the war makes it impossible to assess the potential of the religious revivalist, anti-Western option for Third World nations. What had seemed at first to be a viable path to genuinely independent development for African and Asian peoples has become mired in brutal internal repression and littered with the wreckage of a losing war.

SOUTH AFRICA: DEFENDING AND CHALLENGING THE GARRISON STATE

South Africa was by no means the only area still under some form of colonial dominance decades after India became the first of the former European colonies to gain its independence in 1947. Portugal, the oldest and long considered the weakest of the European colonizers, held onto Angola, Mozambique, and its other African possessions until the mid-1970s. Zimbabwe (formerly Southern Rhodesia) was run by white settlers, who had unilaterally declared their independence from Great Britain, until 1980. Southwest Africa only became fully free of South African control in 1989, and some of the smaller islands in the West Indies and the Pacific remain under European or American rule to the present day.

By the 1970s, however, South Africa was by far the largest, most populous, richest, and most strategic area where the great majority of the population had yet to be liberated from colonial domination. Since the 1940s, the white settlers, particularly the Dutch-descended Afrikaners, have solidified their internal control of the country under the leadership of the Nationalist party. In stages and through a series of elections in which the blacks, who made up the great majority of South Africans, were not allowed to vote, the Nationalists won complete independence from Great Britain in 1960. From 1948, when the Nationalist party first came to power, the Afrikaners moved to institutionalize white supremacy and white minority rule by the passage of thousands of laws that, taken together, made up the system of apartheid that dominates all aspects of South African life today.

The system of apartheid was designed not only to ensure a monopoly of political power and economic dominance for the white minority, both British and Dutch descended, but also to impose a system of extreme segregation on all races of South Africa, in all aspects of their lives. Separate and patently unequal facilities were established for different racial groups for recreation, education, housing, work, and medical care. Dating or sexual intercourse across racial lines was strictly prohibited; skilled and high-paying jobs were reserved for white workers; and nonwhites were required to carry passes that listed the parts of South Africa where they were allowed to work and reside. If caught by the police without their passes or in areas where they were not permitted to travel, nonwhite South Africans were routinely given stiff jail sentences.

Spacial separation was also organized on a grander scale by the creation of numerous homelands within South Africa, each designated for the main ethno-linguistic or "tribal" groups within the black African population. Though touted by the Afrikaners as the ultimate solution to the racial "problem," the homelands scheme would leave the black African majority with a small percent of some of the poorest land in South Africa. Because the homelands are overpopulated and poverty stricken, the white minority is guaranteed a ready supply of cheap black labor to work in their factories and mines and on their farms. Denied citizenship in South Africa proper, these laborers are

The blatant segregation of public facilities was a key feature of the apartheid regime in South Africa. The police stood ready to enforce the multitude of laws that confined the blacks to designated areas and a very limited range of low-paying occupational roles.

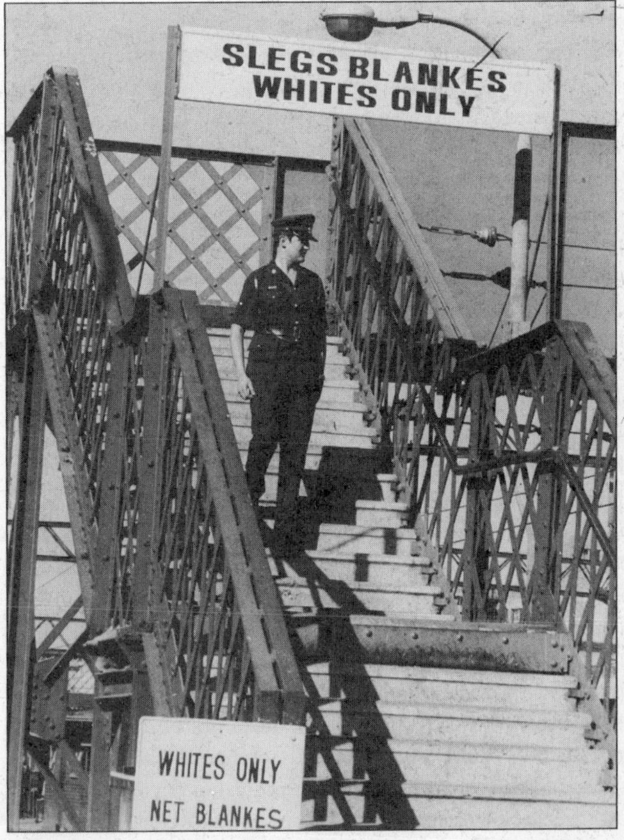

forced eventually to return to the homelands, because they have left their wives and children there while emigrating in search of work.

To maintain the blatantly racist and inequitable system of apartheid, the white minority has had to build a police state and expend a large portion of the federal budget on a sophisticated and well-trained military establishment. Because of the land's great mineral wealth, the Afrikaner nationalists have thus far been able to find the resources to fund their garrison state. Until the late 1980s, the government prohibited all forms of black protest and brutally repressed even nonviolent resistance. Black organizations, such as the African National Congress, were declared illegal, and African leaders, such as Walter Sisulu and Nelson Mandela, were shipped off to maximum-security prisons. Other leaders, such as Steve Biko, one of the young organizers of the Black Consciousness movement, died under very suspicious circumstances while in police custody.

Through spies and police informers, the regime sought to capitalize on personal and ethnic divisions within the black majority community. Favoritism was shown to some leaders and groups to keep them from uniting with others in all-out opposition to apartheid. With all avenues of constitutional negotiation and peaceful protest closed, many advocates of black majority rule in a multiracial society have turned to guerrilla resistance in recent decades. The South African government responded in the 1980s with a state of emergency, which simply intensified the restrictions already in place in the garrison state. The government has repeatedly justified its draconian repression by labeling virtually all black protest as communist inspired and playing on the racial fears of the white minority.

Through most of the 1970s and early 1980s, it appeared that the hardening hostility between the unyielding white minority and the frustrated black majority was building to a major and very violent upheaval. This may still prove the end result of apartheid and the Afrikaners' garrison state. In recent years, however, there have been signs that some Afrikaner leaders are beginning to realize that these solutions are dead ends. Reforms give some hope that apartheid can be dismantled. The release of key black political prisoners, such as the dramatic freeing of Nelson Mandela in 1990, and permission for peaceful mass demonstrations are signs that those in power, most notably the Afrikaner-descended president de Klerk, may finally be willing to listen to and negotiate a settlement with black leaders.

Black African leaders are understandably wary after so many years of oppression and repression, but so far most have been willing to wait and explore peaceful ways to put pressure on the regime. The differences between the two sides remain colossal, and more radical and violence-prone alternatives threaten both those in power and the more moderate leaders of the black majority. Bitter interethnic rivalries within the black majority community, which flared into bloody battles between Zulus and Xhosas in the summer of 1990, also threaten to be a major obstacle to a peaceful settlement. It is still possible for the stalemate to intensify and massive civil war to erupt. Yet for the first time since the white majority won their independence in the 1940s and 1950s, there are signs that the internal colonization that has continued for the great majority of the peoples of South Africa under apartheid may be breaking down. Its demise may well pave the way to the peaceful creation of a truly free, multiracial society in South Africa.

CONCLUSION

THE THIRD WORLD EXPERIENCE IN HISTORICAL PERSPECTIVE

Although the years of independence for the nations that have emerged from the colonial empires have been filled with political and economic crises and social turmoil, it is important to put recent Third World history in a larger perspective. Most of these new nations have been in existence only a few decades, and they came to independence with severe handicaps, many of which were a direct legacy of their colonial experiences. Some observers have been tempted to question whether Africans and Asians are able to govern themselves, given the widespread occurrence of communal violence, civil strife, and military takeovers in the new states. But if we consider that the far smaller, much better resource endowed, and relatively homogenous population that made up the young American republic in the late 18th century was so deeply divided for nearly 100 years that only a massive civil war could salvage the union in the 1860s, the political tensions in Third World nations do not seem so exceptional. If one takes into account the artificial nature of these states, most have held together rather well. This is especially striking if they are compared to European nations, such as Yugoslavia, still shaken periodically by regional and religious clashes, despite the fact that the peoples who make them up have a lot more in common historically and culturally than the populations of most Third World countries.

India's success is particularly striking here. In size—both population and ethnic—as well as in linguistic and religious diversity, India is a continent comparable to Western Europe. Yet, few see Europe's long centuries of national rivalries, quarrels, and wars as a sign that the Europeans are incapable of governing themselves. India's continuing unity contrasts sharply with Europe's disunity, but India's very considerable political achievements are passed over in favor of sensationalist accounts of religious and regional strife in the subcontinent.

What is true in politics is true of all other aspects of the Third World experience. With much lower populations and far fewer or no industrial competitors, as well as drawing on the resources of much of the rest of the world, European and North American nations had to struggle to industrialize and thereby achieve a reasonable standard of living for most of their people. Even with their advantages, the human cost in terms of horrific working conditions and urban squalor was enormous, and we are still paying the high ecological price. Third World countries (and, as you saw in Chapter 33, Japan) have had few or none of the West's advantages. They have begun the "great ascent" to development burdened by excessive and rapidly increasing populations that overwhelm their limited resources, which must be exported to earn the capital to buy food and machines. They struggle to establish a place in the world market system that is heavily loaded in favor of the established industrial powers in terms of pricing and investment. Their efforts to build modest industrial sectors are frustrated by competition from the many nations that have industrialized ahead of them.

Despite the cultural dominance of the West, which was one of the great legacies or burdens of the colonial era, Third World thinkers and artists have achieved a great deal. If much of this—such as African and Asian political organizations and economic planning—has been dependent on Western models, one should not be surprised given the educational backgrounds and personal experiences of the first generations of African and Asian leaders.

The challenge for the coming generations will be to find genuinely Third World solutions to the problems that have stunted political and economic development and to the dependence on the West that once had checked intellectual originality. If the promise Iran once seemed to offer in this respect has faded after a decade of brutal internal repression, economic retreat, and war, the conviction among Third World leaders and thinkers that other options must emerge is growing. The solutions reached are likely to vary a great deal, given the diversity of the nations and societies of the Third World. They are also more likely to be forged from a combination of Western and indigenous influences than from the Iranian Revolution, whose leaders have been so determined to ban and destroy all Western influences, even those that might be critical to building viable and prosperous nations. They are also likely to draw heavily on the ancient and distinguished traditions of civilized life that have been nurtured by African and Asian peoples for millennia.

FURTHER READINGS

Much of the very large literature on political and economic development in the Third World is focused on individual nations, and it is more helpful to know several cases in some depth rather than try to master them all. Robert Heilbroner's writings, starting with his *The Great Ascent* (1961), still provide the most sensible introduction to challenges to the new states in the early decades of independence. Peter Worsley's *The Third World* (1964) provides a provocative, if somewhat disjointed, supplement to Heilbroner's many works. Though focused mainly on South and Southeast Asia, Gunnar Myrdal's *Asian Drama*, 3 vols. (1968), is the best exploration in a single cultural area of the complexities of the challenges to development. A good overview of developments in India can be found in W. N. Brown's *The United States and India, Pakistan, and Bangladesh* (1984 ed.), despite its misleadingly Western-centric title. Michael Brecher's *Nehru: A Political Biography* (1969) is a very readable account of Indian history in the Nehru years after independence. Ali Mazrui and Michael Tidy's *Nationalism and New States in Africa* (1984) gives a good overview of developments throughout Africa. Also useful are S. A. Akintoye's *Emergent African States* (1976) and H. Bretton's *Power and Politics in Africa* (1973). For the Middle East, John Waterbury's *The Egypt of Nasser and Sadat* (1983) provides a detailed account of the politics of development, and Peter Mansfield's *The Arabs* (1978) supplies a decent (if now a bit dated) overview.

On military coups, see Ruth First's *The Barrel of a Gun* (1971) and S. Decalo's *Coups and Army Rule in Africa* (1976). Shaul Bakash's *The Reign of the Ayatollahs* (1984) is perhaps the most insightful of several books that have appeared on Iran since the revolution. Brian Bunting's *The Rise of the South African Reich* (1964) traces the rise of the apartheid regime in great (and polemical) detail, while Gail Gerhart's *Black Power in South Africa* (1978) is one of the better studies devoted to efforts to tear that system down. Among the many fine Third World authors whose works are available in English, some of the best include (for Africa) Chinua Achebe, Wole Soyinka, and Ousmane Sembene; (for India) A. K. Narayan and V. K. Naipaul; (for Egypt) Nawal el Saadawi and Neguib Mahfouz; and (for Indonesia) Mochtar Lubis and P. A. Toer. For white perspectives on the South African situation, the works of Nadine Gordimer and J. M. Coetzee are superb.

THE STRUGGLE FOR CHINA

MAO'S CHINA AND BEYOND

- **DOCUMENT:** Women in the Revolutionary Struggle

DECOLONIZATION AND REVOLUTION IN VIETNAM

- **ANALYSIS:** Decolonization with and without Social Revolution
- **CONCLUSION:** Revolutions and Civilization in China and Vietnam
- **FURTHER READINGS**

1770s Tayson rebellion in Vietnam

1802 Establishment of the Nguyen dynasty; Vietnam unified

1858–1862 Beginning of the French conquest of Vietnam

1883 French conquest of Vietnam is completed

1911 Revolution in China

1912 Fall of the Qing dynasty in China

1919 May Fourth Movement begins; founding of Guomindang or Nationalist party

1921 Communist party of China founded

1925 VNQDD founded in Vietnam; first Communist organization established in Vietnam

1927 Nationalists capture Shanghai; purge of Communists and workers

1929 Failed VNQDD-inspired uprising

1930 Failed Communist uprising in Vietnam

1931 Japanese invasion of Manchuria

1937 Japanese invasion of China proper

41 War and Revolution in China and Vietnam

INTRODUCTION. In many respects the recent histories of China and the peoples of Japan, Korea, and Vietnam whose cultures were so profoundly affected by Chinese civilization have been fundamentally different from that of much of the rest of the Third World. Particularly in the past century, the experience of the Japanese has diverged the most from those of other African and Asian peoples (see Chapters 33 and 37). The ethnically homogenous, politically unified, and militarily adept Japanese were not only able to beat off Western imperialist advances against their island home; they have been one of the few non-Western peoples to achieve a high level of industrialization. Within decades of the forced "opening" of Japan by the United States in the 1850s, Japan also became the only African or Asian nation to join the ranks of the great powers, and in imitation of Western rivals, it embarked on its own campaign of imperialist expansion overseas. Though Korea was colonized early in the 20th century by its powerful Japanese neighbor, in the decades since the Second World War it has emerged as one of the new industrial centers on the Pacific Rim (see Chapter 37).

In contrast to industrialized Japan and to Korea in the past two decades or so, with their relatively high standards of living and global economic power, the recent histories of China and Vietnam have had much in common with the rest of the Third World. Both China and Vietnam suffered heavily from the assaults and exploitative terms of exchange imposed by imperialist powers, both Western and Japanese. Each has had to contend with underdevelopment, overpopulation, poverty, and environmental degradation. Moreover, in contrast to most of the rest of the Third World,

1942 Japanese occupation of French Indochina

1945 Ho Chi Minh proclaims the Republic of Vietnam

1949 Victory of the Communists in China; People's Republic of China established

1950–1951 Purge of the landlord class in China

1950–1953 Korean War

1953 Beginning of China's first Five-Year Plan

1954 French defeated at Dien Bien Phu; Geneva accords, French withdrawal from Vietnam; beginning of the Sino-Soviet split

mid-1950s Build-up of U.S. advisors in South Vietnam

1957 "Let a Thousand Flowers Bloom" campaign in China

1958–1960 "Great Leap Forward" in China

1963 Beginning of state family planning in China

1965–1968 Era of the Cultural Revolution in China

1965–1973 Direct U.S. military intervention in Vietnam

1968 Tet offensive in Vietnam

1975 Communist victory in Vietnam; collapse of the Republic of South Vietnam

1976 Death of Zhou Enlai and Mao Zedong; purge of the Gang of Four

China and Vietnam have had to deal with these awesome challenges in the midst of the utter collapse of the patterns of civilized life each had followed for thousands of years.

However disruptive imperialist conquest and its effects proved in the rest of the African-Asian world, most colonized peoples managed to preserve much of their precolonial cultures and modes of social organization. The defense and revival of traditional customs, religious beliefs, and social arrangements played a key role in the struggle for decolonization. This was not the case in China and Vietnam, where a combination of external aggression and internal upheavals discredited and destroyed the Confucian system that had long been synonymous with the preservation of civilized life.

With their traditional order in shambles, the peoples of China and Vietnam had no choice but to embark on full-scale revolutions that would clear away the rubble of the failed Confucian system, remove the obstacles posed by imperialist dominance, and provide the means to build new and viable states and societies. In contrast to much of the rest of the colonized world, the countries of China and Vietnam derived few benefits from European domination, either informal or formal. Imperialist pressures eroded and smashed their political institutions, rather than building up a bureaucratic grid and imparting political ideologies that could form the basis for nation building.

For differing reasons, neither China nor Vietnam developed a large middle class, though each had wealthy commercial groups. In each society, the weakness of the bourgeoisie, coupled with the establishment of highly repressive regimes in the region in the late 19th and early 20th centuries, greatly constricted constitutionalist and nonviolent political options. The magnitude of the disruption and hardships the Chinese and Vietnamese peoples endured in this period also discredited gradualism and reformist democracy in the eyes of many emerging intellectuals and political leaders. Young students, such as Mao Zedong (Tsetung) and Nguyen Ai Quoc (alias Ho Chi Minh), became convinced that the salvation of their peoples and the restoration of civilized life in their lands could be won only through armed revolution and radical social transformations.

The distinctive forces that made for revolutionary upheavals in China and Vietnam will be examined in this chapter. Special attention will be given to why revolutionary rather than gradualist, reformist alternatives emerged victorious in each case. In the case of China, which has had a great impact on much of the Third World, we will also explore the history of the period after the revolutionaries took power. In considering these patterns, emphasis will be placed on key themes in the history of Chinese civilization and that of its Vietnamese neighbor over the past century, including the changing position of women; the impact of invasion, civil war, and natural calamities; and the struggle to develop new forms of intellectual and cultural expression. Perhaps more than any other part of the modern world, China and Vietnam provide us with the opportunity to study why civilizations break down and how new civilizations are fashioned from the ruins of the old. An awareness of their experience is crucial to an understanding of present changes and the future course of civilized development in the world as a whole.

THE STRUGGLE FOR CHINA

The abdication of Puyi, the Manchu boy-emperor in 1912, marked the end of a century-long losing struggle on the part of the Qing dynasty to protect Chinese civilization from foreign invaders and revolutionary threats from within like the massive Taiping movement (see Chapter 32). The fall of the Qing opened the way for an extended struggle over which a leader or movement would be able to capture the mandate to rule the ancient society that had for millennia ordered the lives of one-fourth of the population of humankind. The loose alliance of students, middle-class politicians, secret societies, and regional military commanders that overthrew the Manchus quickly splintered into a number of hostile contenders for the right to rule China.

The best positioned of the contenders for power were the military commanders, or warlords, who would play a leading role in Chinese politics for the next three decades. Many of the warlords combined in cliques or alliances, both to protect their own territories and to crush neighbors and annex their lands. The most powerful of these cliques was centered in north China, and headed by the unscrupulous Yuan Shikai, who hoped to seize the vacated Manchu throne and found a new dynasty. By virtue of their wealth, the merchants and bankers of coastal cities like Shanghai and Canton made up a second power center in post-Manchu China. As had been the case in the late-Confucian era, their involvement in politics resulted from their eagerness to bankroll both favored warlords and Western-educated, middle-class politicians like Sun Yat-sen.

Sometimes supportive of the urban civilian politicians, sometimes wary of them, university students and their teachers, as well as independent intellectuals, provided yet another factor in the complex political equation. Though the intellectuals and students played critical roles in shaping new ideologies to rebuild Chinese civilization, they were virtually defenseless in a situation in which force was essential to those who hoped to exert political influence. Deeply

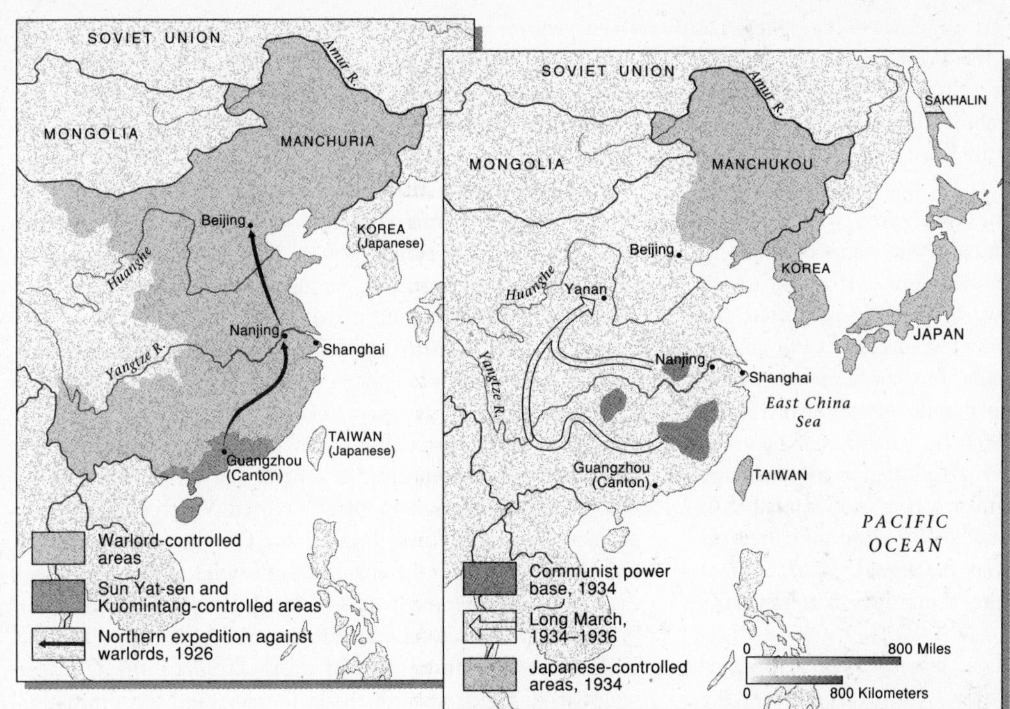

China in the Era of Revolution and Civil War

divided, but very strong in some regions, the secret societies represented another contender for power. Like the military, they envisioned the restoration of monarchical rule, but under a Chinese not a foreign dynasty like that of the Manchus. As if the situation were not already confused enough, it was further complicated by the continuing intervention of the Western powers anxious to profit from China's divisions and weakness. Their inroads, however, were increasingly overshadowed by entry into the contest for the control of China by the newest imperialist power, Japan. From the mid-1890s, when the Japanese had humiliated their much larger neighbor by easily defeating them in war, until 1945, when Japan's surrender ended World War II, the Japanese were a major factor in the long and bloody contest for mastery of China.

THE MAY FOURTH MOVEMENT AND THE FAILURE OF LIBERALISM

Sun Yat-sen, who headed the Revolutionary Alliance, a loose coalition of anti-Qing political groups that had spearheaded the 1911 revolt, claimed that he and the parties of the alliance were rightful successors to the fallen Manchus. But he could do little to assert civilian control in the face of warlord opposition. The Revolutionary Alliance had little power and virtually no popular support outside the urban trading centers of the coastal areas in central and south China. Even in these areas they were at the mercy of the local warlords. The alliance formally elected Sun president at the end of 1911, set up a parliament modeled after those in Europe, and chose cabinets with great fanfare, but their decisions had little effect on warlord-dominated China.

Sun Yat-sen conceded this reality when he resigned the acting presidency in favor of the northern warlord Yuan Shikai in 1912. As the most powerful of the northern clique of generals, Yuan appeared to have the best chance to unify China under a single government. He at first feigned sympathy for the democratic aims of the alliance leaders, but soon revealed his true intentions. He took foreign loans to build up his military forces and buy out most of the bureaucracy in the capital at Beijing. When Sun and other leaders of the Revolutionary Alliance called for a second revolution to oust Yuan in the years after 1912, he made full use of his military power and more underhanded methods, such as assassinations, to put down their opposition. By 1915, it appeared that Yuan was well on his way to realizing his ambition of becoming China's next emperor. His schemes were foiled, however, by the continuing rivalry of other warlords, republican nationalists like Sun, and the growing influence of Japan in China, which increased dramatically as a result of the First World War.

As England's ally according to terms of a 1902 treaty, Japan immediately entered the war on the side of the Entente powers. Moving much too quickly for the comfort of the British and the other Western powers, the Japanese seized German-held islands in the Pacific and occupied the Germans' concessionary areas in China. With all the great powers except the Americans embroiled in war, the Japanese seized the chance to establish a dominant hold over their giant neighbor. In early 1915 they presented Yuan's government with Twenty-One Demands, which, if accepted, would have reduced China to the status of a dependent protectorate. Though Sun and the Revolutionary Alliance lost much support by refusing to repudiate the Japanese demands, Yuan was no more decisive. He neither accepted nor rejected the demands, but concentrated his energies on an effort to trump up popular enthusiasm for his accession to the throne. Disgusted by Yuan's weakness and ambition, one of his warlord rivals plotted his overthrow. Hostility to the Japanese won Yuan's rival widespread support, and in 1916 Yuan was forced to retreat and then resign the presidency. His fall was the signal for a free-for-all power struggle between the remaining warlords for control of China.

As one of the victorious Allies, Japan managed to solidify its hold on northern China by winning control of the former German concessions in the Versailles Treaty of 1919, which ended the war. However, the Chinese had also allied themselves to the Entente powers during the war. Enraged by what they viewed as a betrayal by the Allied powers, students and nationalist politicians organized mass demonstrations in numerous Chinese cities on May 4, 1919. The demonstrations began a prolonged period of protest against Japanese inroads, which included strikes and mass boycotts of Japanese goods. May 4, the day when the resistance began, gave its name to a movement in which intellectuals and students played a leading role. Initially at least, the May Fourth movement was aimed at transforming China into a liberal democracy. Its program was enunciated in numerous speeches, pamphlets, novels, and newspaper articles. Confucianism was ridiculed and rejected in favor of a wholehearted acceptance of all that the Western democracies had to offer. Noted Western thinkers, such as Bertrand Russell and John Dewey, toured China, extolling the merits of science, industrial technology, and democratic government and basking in the cheers of their packed Chinese audiences. Chinese thinkers called for the liberation of women, the simplification of the Chinese script in order to promote mass literacy, and the promotion of Western-style individualism. Many of these themes are

Spearheaded by students and intellectuals in China's urban areas, the May Fourth demonstrations in 1919 proclaimed the end of nearly 2000 years of Confucian dominance in China and the opening of the country to ideologies from the West, both democratic and Marxist.

captured in the literature of the period. In the novel *Family* by Ba Jin, for example, a younger brother audaciously informs his elder sibling that he will not accept the marriage partner the family has arranged for him. He clearly sees his refusal as part of a more general revolt of the youth of China against the ancient Confucian social code.

> Big Brother, I'm doing what no one in our family has ever dared do before—I'm running out on an arranged marriage. No one cares about my fate, so I've decided to walk my own road alone. I'm determined to struggle against the old forces to the end. Unless you cancel the match, I'll never come back. I'll die first. . . .

However enthusiastically the program of the May Fourth movement was adopted by the urban youth of China, it was soon clear that mere emulation of the liberal democracies of the West could not provide effective solutions to China's prodigious problems. Civil liberties and democratic elections were meaningless in a China that was ruled by warlords; gradualist solutions were folly in a nation where the great mass of the peasantry was destitute, much of it malnourished or dying of starvation. Even if fair elections could be held and a Western-style parliament installed as China's effective rulers, China's crisis had become so severe that there was little time for legislators to squabble and debate. The ministers of an elected government with little military clout would hardly have been able to implement well-meaning programs for land redistribution and subsidies for the poor in the face of deeply entrenched regional opposition from the landlords and the military. It soon became clear to many Chinese intellectuals and students, as well as to some of the nationalist politicians, that more radical solutions were needed. In the 1920s this conviction gave rise to the Communist left within the Chinese nationalist movement.

THE RISE OF THE COMMUNIST ALTERNATIVE

The example of the Russian Revolution, not careful readings of the writings of Karl Marx and Fredrich Engels, made a number of Chinese thinkers aware of possible Marxist solutions to China's ills. In fact, before the Russian upheavals of 1917 and Lenin's launching of a state-directed drive for the social and economic transformation of backward Russia, the few Chinese who knew about Marx or even less radical socialist theorists felt they had little to offer impoverished, agrarian societies like China. Marx, after all, had foreseen socialist revolutions occurring in the more advanced industrial societies with well-developed working classes and a strong proletarian consciousness. He had thought that there would be little chance for revolution in Russia. In China, with its overwhelmingly rural, peasant population (and Marx viewed the peasantry as a reactionary or at best a conservative, petty bourgeois social element), the prospects for revolution looked even more dismal. But the October revolution in Russia that brought Lenin and the Bolsheviks to power changed all of this. For the first time, a Marxist regime governed, and it had come to power in backward, largely peasant Russia, not in western Europe or North America.

The Bolshevik victory and the programs launched to rebuild Russia prompted Chinese intellectuals, such as Li Dazhao, to give serious attention to the works of Marx, Engels, Trotsky, and Lenin and the potential they offered for the regeneration of China. A number of societies devoted to the study of Marxism developed just after the May Fourth movement around thinkers like Li, who headed the study circle at the University of Beijing. Li's borrowings from European communist thinkers placed heavy emphasis on Marxism's capacity for renewal and its ability to harness the energy and vitality of a nation's youth. In contrast to Lenin, Li saw the peasants rather than the urban workers as the vanguard of the revolution. He justified this shift from the orthodox Marxist emphasis on the working classes, which made up only a tiny fraction of China's population at the time, by characterizing Chinese society as a whole as proletarian. All of China, he argued, had been exploited by the bourgeois, industrialized West. Thus, the oppressed Chinese as a whole needed to unite and rise up against their exploiters.

Li's version of Marxism, with alterations or emphasis on elements that made it suitable for China, had great appeal for the students, including the young Mao Zedong, who joined his study circle. They too were angered by what they perceived as China's betrayal by the imperialist great powers. They shared Li's hostility (very much a throwback to the attitudes of the Confucian era) to merchants and commerce, which appeared to dominate the West. They too longed for a return to a political system, like the Confucian, where those who governed were deeply committed to social reform and social welfare, and an authoritarian state was expected to intervene in all aspects of the peoples' lives.

The societies that developed around Li Dazhao and other Marxist intellectuals soon spawned a number of more broadly based, politically activist organizations. The Marxists' capture of prominent periodicals, such as *New Youth* magazine, did much to spread the ideas of Marx and Lenin among the politically active youth of China's coastal cities. With support from Sun Yat-sen, Marxist intellectu-

Though he received no formal military training, Mao Zedong's adoption of a soldier's uniform reflected the importance of force in the highly militarized and deeply divided society that China had become by the early 20th century.

als established the Socialist Youth Corps in 1920, which was dedicated to recruiting the urban working classes. Students like Mao returned to their provincial bases to win supporters for the leftist cause and foment resistance to the oppressive rule of the local warlords.

In the summer of 1921, in an attempt to unify the growing Marxist wing of the nationalist struggle, a handful of leaders from different parts of China met in secret in the city of Shanghai. At this meeting, closely watched by the agents of the local warlord and rival political organizations, the Communist party of China was born. In Paris a year earlier, Zhou Enlai, who like Mao was later to become one of the main Communist leaders, and a number of other Chinese expatriot students had founded the Communist Youth Corps. In Paris and inside China itself, the development of Communist organizations was supported by both the advisors and funds of the Comintern, the international arm of the Bolshevik or Communist party of the Soviet Union. Though minuscule in terms of the numbers of their supporters, and at this time fixed on a revolutionary program fatally oriented to the working classes, the Communists at least offered a clear alternative to fill the ideological and institutional void left by the collapse of the Confucian order.

THE SEIZURE OF POWER BY THE GUOMINDANG, OR NATIONALIST PARTY

In the years when the Communist movement in China was being put together by urban students and intellectuals, the Guomindang, or Nationalist party, which was to prove the Communists' great rival for the mandate to rule in China, was struggling to survive in the deep south. Sun Yat-sen, who was the acknowledged head of the nationalist struggle from the 1911 revolution until the time of his death in early 1925, had gone into exile in Japan in 1914, while warlords, such as Yuan Shikai, consolidated their regional power bases. After returning to China, Sun and his followers sought in 1919 to join the diverse political organizations struggling for political influence in China by reorganizing the revolutionary movement and naming it the Nationalist Party of China (the Guomindang).

The Nationalists began the slow process of forging alliances with key social groups and building an army of their own, which they now viewed as the only way to rid China of the warlord menace. Sun strove to enunciate a nationalist ideology that gave something to everyone. It stressed the need to unify China under a strong central government, bring the imperialist intruders under control, and enact social reforms that would alleviate peasant poverty and the oppressive working conditions of laborers in China's cities. Unfortunately for the great majority of the Chinese people, for whom social reforms were the main concern, the Nationalist leaders concentrated on political and international issues and neglected internal reforms.

In this early stage, Sun and the Nationalists built their power primarily on the support provided by urban businessmen and merchants in coastal cities such as Canton. Though it received little publicity, the Nationalist party also drew support from local warlords and the criminal underworld, especially the notorious Green Gang headquartered in Shanghai. After much and very time-consuming factional infighting, Sun had more or less secured control over the party, if not the warlords in the neighborhood of Canton. He forged an alliance with the Communists that was officially proclaimed at the first Nationalist party conference in 1924. For the time being at least, the Nationalist leaders were content to let the Communists serve as their major link to the peasants and the urban workers.

Disappointed in their early hopes of assistance from the Europeans and the United States, Nationalist leaders turned to Soviet Russia. Lenin and the Bolsheviks were eager to support a revolutionary movement in neighboring China. They not only sent advisors and gave material assistance, they encouraged the fledgling Communist party to join with the larger and richer Nationalists in a common struggle to seize power.

From 1924, when the Whampoa Military Academy was founded with Soviet help and partially staffed by Russian instructors, the Nationalists added a critical military dimension to their political maneuvering. The first head of the academy was an ambitious young military officer named Chiang Kai-shek. The son of a poor salt merchant, Chiang had fought his way up in the world through the military and by virtue of connections with powerful figures in the Shanghai underworld. He had received some military training in Japan and managed by the early 1920s to work his way into Sun Yat-sen's inner circle of advisors. Chiang was not happy with the Communist alliance but was willing to bide his time until he had the military strength to deal with both the Communists and the warlords, who remained the major obstacles to the Nationalist seizure of power.

Absorbed by all these political machinations, Sun and other Nationalist leaders had little time left for serious attention to the now severe deterioration of the Chinese economy and the huge population whose sufferings mounted as a result. Though urban laborers worked for pitiful wages and lived in appalling conditions, the social condition of the peasantry, which made up nearly 90 percent of China's population, was perhaps the most pressing issue facing China's aspiring national leaders. Patterns of landowning varied considerably in different parts of China. Over a century of corruption and weak Manchu rule, however, and then the Manchu collapse in 1911 and the depredations of the warlords had left the peasantry in many regions of China in misery. Big landlords and rich peasants rapaciously amassed great landholdings, which they rented out at exorbitant rates that left the tenants who worked them little to feed and clothe their families. In times of flood and drought when the crops failed, tenants, landless laborers, and even small landowners simply could not make ends meet. Tenants and smallholders were turned off their lands, and landless laborers could not find crops to harvest. Famine and disease stalked China's heavily populated provinces, while its ancient irrigation systems fell into disrepair. Corrupt warlords and bureaucrats, including those allied to the Nationalist party, colluded with the landlords to extract the maximum taxes and labor services from the peasantry.

As they had for millennia, dispossessed peasants took to banditry or vagabondage to survive. Many joined the hordes of beggars and unemployed in the towns; many more perished—swept away by floods, famine, disease, or the local warlord's armies. Children were sold into slavery by their parents, so that both might have a chance to survive. A growing number of cases of cannibalism were reported, which occurred after the bark and leaves had been stripped off all the trees to make the scarcely digestible "stew" that the peasants ate to put something in their bellies. Many peasants were too poor to perform the most basic of social duties, such as burying their deceased parents, whose bodies were often left to be devoured by vultures and packs of wild dogs. Given the great reverence for family and parents that had been instilled by Confucian teachings for millennia, the psychological scars left by the nonperformance of such critical obligations must have been deep and lasting.

Though rural China cried out for strong leadership and far-reaching economic and social reform, China's leaders bickered and plotted, but did little. Sun gave lip service to the Nationalist party's need to deal with the peasant problem. But his abysmal ignorance of rural conditions was revealed by statements in which he denied that China had large landlords and his refusal to believe that there were "serious difficulties" between the great mass of the peasantry and the landowners. Communists such as Mao Zedong were an exception to the general Nationalist pattern of ignorance and neglect. But the numbers of peasants the Communists could assist were limited by the small size of the party at that time and the obstacles thrown up by the landlords and warlords. Nonetheless, Mao and his fellow Communists persisted in their work of rural reconstruction in areas such as Hunan in south-central China.

Though the son of a fairly prosperous peasant, Mao had rebelled early in his life against his father's exploitation of the tenants and laborers who worked the family fields. Receiving little assistance from his estranged father, Mao was forced to make his own way and educate himself in the history, philosophy, and economic theory that most other nationalist and revolutionary leaders mastered in private schools. Having made his way to Beijing in the post–May Fourth era, Mao came under the influence of thinkers such as Li Dazhao, who placed considerable emphasis on solutions to the peasant problem as one of the keys to China's survival. As the following passage from Mao's early writings reveals, almost from the outset he was committed to revolutionary solutions that depended on peasant support.

A revolution is an insurrection, an act of violence by which one class overthrows another. A rural revolution is a revolution by which the peasantry overthrows the power of the feudal landlord class. Without using the greatest force, the peasants cannot possibly overthrow the deep-rooted authority of the landlords which has lasted for thousands of years.

Throughout most of the 1920s, however, Mao's vision of a rural revolution remained a minority and much repudiated position even with the Communist party. Rivals such as Li Lisan, who favored a more orthodox strategy based on the urban working classes who had formed the core of support for the Bolshevik revolutionaries in Russia, dominated party policy-making. Ironically, the move by Chiang and the Nationalist leaders to destroy all of the Communists in the late-1920s would pave the way for Mao's rise to leadership in the party.

The Nationalists' successful drive for national power began only after Sun Yat-sen's death in 1925 opened the way for their counterparts among the warlords, Chiang Kai-shek and his cronies, to seize control of the party. After winning over or eliminating the military chiefs in the Canton area, Chiang marched north with his newly created armies in a campaign that culminated in the Nationalists' seizure of the Yangtze River valley and Shanghai in early 1927. Later his forces also captured the capital at Beijing and the rest of the Yellow River basin. The refusal of most of the warlords to end their long-standing feuding meant that Chiang could defeat them or buy them out, one by one. By the late 1920s, he was the master of China—in name and international standing, if not in actual fact. He was, in effect, the head of a warlord hierarchy, but most political leaders within China and in the outside world recognized him as the new president of China.

Since there were no elections, the people had no say in the matter. Nor had Chiang's political rivals, whom he ruthlessly purged even while he was still settling scores with the warlords. The most fateful of these purges came while Chiang's armies were occupying Shanghai in the spring of 1927. After clearing the Communists out of the

The Guomindang's brutal suppression of the workers' organizations in Shanghai in 1927 marked a watershed in the history of modern China. The Guomindang-Communist alliance was shattered, and Mao Zedong's call for a peasant-based revolution became imperative as the vulnerability of the small Chinese working class was exposed.

Nationalist Central Committee, where they had been represented since 1924, Chiang ordered his troops and gangster allies in Shanghai to round up the workers, despite the fact that their mass demonstrations had done so much to make possible the city's capture by the Nationalist armies. In some of the most brutal scenes of an era when violence and human suffering were almost commonplace, Chiang's soldiers and hired toughs machine-gunned and beheaded Communist supporters wherever they could be found throughout the city. Though the Communists' Soviet advisors continued to insist that they cooperate with the Nationalists, Chiang's extension of the bloody purge to other cities and into the countryside precipitated an open civil war between the two main branches of the nationalist movement that, despite temporary and halfhearted truces, ended only with the Communist victory in 1949.

REACTION VS. REVOLUTION: THE STRUGGLE FOR CHINA

At the outset, all signs appeared to favor the Nationalist party in its violent contest with the Communists for control of China. Despite the fact that Chiang did not fully control the more powerful regional warlords, as the heir of Sun Yat-sen and the architect of the victorious northern campaign he had the support of the richest and most powerful social groups in China. These included the urban businessmen and merchants, most of the intellectuals, and a large portion of the university students, the rural landlords, and the military. Chiang could also count on the services of the bureaucrats and police throughout China, and he launched a calculated public relations campaign to win sympathy in the United States and the other Western democracies. The urban workers, who preferred the Communists or other radical parties, had been beaten into submission. The peasants, who longed for stable government and state-sponsored relief, were willing, for the time being at least, to wait and see if the Nationalists would act to alleviate their distress.

Despite his ruthless betrayal of the Communists, Chiang continued to receive assistance from the Soviet Union, where Stalin had emerged as the unchallenged dictator of a totalitarian state. Possibly because he preferred a weak China under the Nationalist party to a revolutionary one under the Communists, Stalin gave little assistance to his alleged comrades and continued to push policies that left them at the mercy of Chiang and his henchmen. With what seemed to be insurmountable advantages, Chiang moved to eliminate what was left in the way of rivals for power, most especially the shattered remnants of the Communist party.

The smashing of the workers' movement in Shanghai and other urban centers greatly strengthened Mao's hand in his ongoing struggle with Li Lisan and other orthodox ideologues within the Communist party. Mao and much of what was left of the Communist leadership retreated into the countryside and set to work carrying out land reform and improving life in China's tens of thousands of impoverished villages.

In the late 1920s the center of Communist operations came to be the south-central province of Hunan, where the Communists established soviets (named after the revolutionary workers' and soldiers' organizations in Russia) and "liberated" zones. This area became the main target of a succession of military campaigns that Chiang launched against the Communists in the early 1930s. Though the Communists successfully resisted the early campaigns, Chiang's reliance on German military advisors and his command of the resources and manpower of the rest of China eventually wore the Communists down. By the autumn of 1934, it was clear that if the remaining Communists did not break out of the Nationalist encirclement and escape from Hunan, they would be eliminated. At the head of over 90,000 party stalwarts, Mao set off on the Long March across thousands of miles of the most difficult terrain in China to Shaanxi in northwestern China, where a smaller number of peasant soviets had been established. At the end of the following year, Mao and only about 20,000 followers fought their way into the rugged, sparsely populated terrain of Shaanxi, which was the center of the Communist movement in China until the mid-1940s.

By the end of the Long March, Mao was firmly established as the head of the Chinese Communist party. The heroic and successful struggle for survival in the Long March on the part of those who supported his peasant-based strategy of revolution greatly enhanced his stature and fired his followers with the conviction that whatever the odds, they could not be defeated. Chiang obviously did not agree. Soon after the Communists were established in Shaanxi, he launched a new series of extermination campaigns. Again, the peasant supporters of the Communists fought valiantly, but Chiang's armies were beginning to get the upper hand by early 1937.

Just as he was convinced that he was on the verge of total victory, Chiang's anti-Communist crusade was rudely interrupted by the all-out Japanese invasion of the Chinese mainland. Obsessed with the Communists, Chiang had done little to block the steady advance of Japanese forces in the early 1930s into Manchuria and the islands along China's coast. Even after the Japanese launched their massive assaults aimed at the conquest of all of China, Chiang wanted to continue the struggle against the Communists.

Forced by his military commanders to concentrate on the Japanese threat, Chiang grudgingly formed a military alliance with the Communists. Though he did all he could to undermine the alliance and continue the anti-Communist struggle by underhanded means, for the next seven years the war against Japan took priority over the civil war in the contest for control of China.

Though it brought yet further suffering to the Chinese people, the Japanese invasion proved enormously advantageous for the Communist party. This turned out to be so vital to the ultimate Communist victory that some writers have speculated Mao chose Shaanxi in the northwest partly out of the calculation that it would put his forces in the probable path of the anticipated Japanese advance. Whatever his thinking, the war against the Japanese greatly strengthened his cause, while weakening his Nationalist rivals. The Japanese invaders captured much of the Chinese coast, where the trading cities were the centers of the business and mercantile backers of the Nationalists. Chiang's conventional military forces were pummeled by the superior air, land, and sea forces of the Japanese. The Nationalists' attempts to meet the Japanese in conventional, set-piece battles led to disaster; their inability to defend the coastal provinces lowered their standing in the eyes of the Chinese people. Chiang's hasty and humiliating retreat to Chongqing in the interior of China further eroded his aura as the savior of the nation and rendered him more dependent than ever on his military allies and the rural landlords.

The guerrilla warfare the Communists waged against the Japanese armies proved far more effective than Chiang's conventional approach. With the Nationalist extermination campaigns suspended, the Communists used their anti-Japanese campaigns to extend their control over large areas of north China. By the end of World War II, the Nationalists controlled mainly the cities in the north—they had become (as Mao prescribed in his political writings) islands surrounded by a sea of revolutionary peasants. The Communists' successes and determination to fight the Japanese, while Chiang and his advisors vacillated, won them the support of most of China's intellectuals and many of the students who had earlier looked to the Nationalists for China's salvation. By 1945, the balance of power within China was clearly shifting in the Communists' favor. In the four-year civil war that followed, Communist soldiers, who were well treated and fought for a cause, consistently routed the much-abused soldiers of the Nationalists, who went over in droves to the Communist side. By 1949, it was over. Chiang and what was left of his armies fled to the island of Formosa (renamed Taiwan) off the China coast, and Mao proclaimed the establishment of the Peoples Republic of China in Beijing.

The Japanese invasion proved critical in the Communist drive to victory. But equally important were the Communists' social and economic reform programs that eventually won the great majority of the peasantry, the students and intellectuals, and even many of the bureaucrats to their side. While Chiang, whatever his intentions, was able to do little to improve the condition of the great mass of the people, Mao made the peasants' uplift the central element in his drive for power. Land reforms, access to education, and improved health care gave the peasantry a real stake in Mao's revolutionary movement and good reason to defend the soviets against both the Nationalists and the Japanese. In contrast to Chiang's armies, whose arrival meant theft, rape, and wanton murder to China's villagers, Mao's soldiers were indoctrinated with the need to protect the peasantry and win their support. Lest they forget, harsh penalties were levied, such as execution for so much as stealing an egg.

As guerrilla fighters, Mao's soldiers had a much better chance to survive and advance in the ranks than the forcibly conscripted, brutally treated rank-and-file of the Nationalists. Mao and the commanders around him, such as Lin Biao who had been trained at Chiang's Whampoa Academy in the 1920s, proved far more gifted—even in conventional warfare—than the often corrupt and inept Nationalist generals. Thus, though the importance of the Japanese invasion cannot be discounted, the Communists won the mandate to govern China because they offered solutions to China's fundamental social and economic problems, and they actually put their programs into action in the areas that came under their control. In a situation where revolutionary changes appeared to be essential, the Communists alone convinced the Chinese people that they had the leaders and program that could affect them.

MAO'S CHINA AND BEYOND

In assuming power in 1949, the Communists faced the formidable task of governing a vast nation in ruins. Over a century of foreign invasions, civil warfare, and natural calamities had ravaged China's cities and villages, destroyed much of its economic infrastructure, and left its population physically exhausted and deeply demoralized. The confidence of Mao and the Communist leaders that they could build a better future did much to lift spirits and rally popular support for the ambitious projects of the new regime.

The Communists could also draw on the enthusiastic support of those peasants, students, and soldiers who had already been liberated by the experience of living in Communist-controlled areas during the mid-1930s and the years of Japanese occupation. In these zones, land reforms had already been put into effect, mass literacy campaigns had been mounted, and young people, both male and female, had enjoyed opportunities to rise in the party ranks on the basis of hard work and personal talents. Thus, in contrast to the Bolsheviks, who seized power in 1917 in Russia quite easily but then had to face years of civil war and foreign aggression, the Communists in China claimed a unified nation from which foreign aggressors had been expelled. Unlike the Bolsheviks, the Communist leadership in China could move directly to the tasks of social reform and economic development that China so desperately needed, and they could build on the base they had established in the "liberated" zones during their long struggle for power.

POLITICS AND SOCIAL REVOLUTION

Although deep social divisions remained, the Chinese faced far less serious splits between different religious and ethnic groups than most other new nations of Africa and Asia. Millennia of common history and common cultural development had given the peoples of China a sense of identity and a tradition of political unity. The long struggle against foreign aggressors had strengthened these bonds and impressed upon the Chinese the importance of maintaining a united front against outsiders if they were to avoid future humiliations and exploitation. The Communists' "long march" to power had left the party with a strong political and military organization that was rooted in the party cadres and the Peoples Liberation Army. The continuing importance of the army was indicated by the fact that most of China was administered by military officials for five years after the Communists came to power. But the army remained clearly subordinate to the party, with cadre advisors attached to military contingents at all levels and the central committees of the party dominated by nonmilitary personnel.

With this strong political framework in place, the Communists moved quickly to both assert China's traditional preeminence in East and much of Southeast Asia. Potential secessionist movements were forcibly repressed in Inner Mongolia and Tibet, though resistance in the latter has erupted periodically and continues to the present day. In the early 1950s, the Chinese intervened militarily in the conflict between North and South Korea, an intervention that was critical in forcing the United States to settle for a stalemate and a lasting division of the peninsula. Refusing to accept a similar, but far more lopsided, two-nation outcome of the struggle in China itself, the Communist leadership has periodically threatened to invade the Nationalists' refuge on Taiwan, in a number of cases touching off international incidents in the process. China also played an increasingly important role in the liberation struggle of the Vietnamese to the south, though that would not peak until the height of American involvement in the conflict in the 1960s.

By the late 1950s, the close collaboration between the Soviet Union and China that marked the early years of Mao's rule had broken down. Border disputes, focusing on territories the Russians had seized during the period of Manchu decline, and the Chinese refusal to play second fiddle to Russia, especially after Stalin was succeeded by the less imposing Khrushchev, were key causes of the split. These causes of the breakdown in collaboration greatly exacerbated differences resulting from the disappointingly meager economic assistance provided by the Soviet "comrades" and Mao's sense that, with the passing of Stalin, he was the number-one theoretician and leader of the communist world. In the early 1960s, the Chinese flexed their very considerable military and technological muscle by thrashing India in a brief war that resulted from a border dispute and more startlingly by exploding the first nuclear device developed by a nonindustrial nation.

On the domestic front, the new leaders of China moved with equal vigor, though with a good deal less success. Their first priority was to complete the social revolution in the rural areas that had been, to some extent, carried through in Communist controlled areas during the wars against the Japanese and Guomindang. Between 1950 and 1952, the landlord class and the large landholders, most of whom had been spared in earlier stages of the revolution, were dispossessed and purged. Village tribunals, overseen by party cadre members, gave tenants and laborers a chance to get even for decades of oppression. Perhaps as many as three million people who were denounced as members of the exploitative landlord class were executed. At the same time, the land taken from the landowning classes was distributed to peasants who had none or little. For a brief time at least, one of the central pledges of the communist revolutionaries was fulfilled: China became a land of peasant smallholders.

Communist planners, however, saw rapid industrialization, not peasant farmers, as the key to successful development. With the introduction of the first Stalinist-style Five-Year Plan in 1953, the Communist leadership turned away from the peasantry, which had brought them to power, to the urban workers as the hope for a new China. With little foreign assistance from either the West or the Soviet bloc, the state resorted to stringent measures to draw resources from the countryside to finance industrial growth. Though some advances were made in industrialization, particularly in heavy industries such as steel, the shift in direction had consequences that were increasingly unacceptable to Mao and his more radical supporters in the party. State planning and centralization were stressed, party bureaucrats greatly increased their power and influence, and an urban-based privileged class of technocrats began to develop. These changes and the external threat to China posed by the American intervention in Korea and continuing United States-China friction led Mao and his followers to force a change of strategies in the mid-1950s.

Mao had long nurtured a deep hostility toward elitism, which he associated with the discredited Confucian system. He had little use for Lenin's vision of revolution from above, led by a disciplined cadre of professional political activists. He distrusted intellectuals, disliked specialization, and clung to his faith in the peasants rather than the workers as the repository of basic virtue and the driving force of the revolution. Acting to stem the trend toward an elitist, urban-industrial focus, Mao and his supporters introduced the Mass Line approach, beginning with the formation of agricultural cooperatives in 1955. In the following year, cooperatives became farming collectives that soon accounted for over 90 percent of China's peasant population. The peasants had enjoyed their own holdings for less than three years. As had occurred earlier in the Soviet Union, the leaders of the revolution that had originally won the land for the mass of the peasants, later took it away from them through collectivization.

In 1957 Mao struck at the intellectuals through what may have been a miscalculation or perhaps a clever ruse. Announcing that he wished to "let a thousand flowers bloom," Mao encouraged professors, artists, and other intellectuals to speak out on the course of development under Communist rule. His request stirred up a storm of angry protest and criticism of communist schemes. Having flushed the critics into the open, if the campaign was indeed a ruse, or having been shocked by the vehemence of the response, the party struck with demotions, prison sentences, and banishment to hard labor on the collectives. The flowers rapidly wilted in the face of this betrayal.

With political opposition within the party and army apparently in check (or in prison), Mao and his supporters launched the Great Leap Forward in 1958. The programs of the Great Leap represented a further effort to revitalize the flagging revolution by restoring its mass, rural base. Rather than huge plants located in the cities, industrialization would be pushed through small-scale projects integrated into the peasant communes. Instead of siphoning off the communes' surplus to build steel mills, industrial de-

The famous backyard steel furnaces became a central symbol of China's failed drive for self-sufficiency during the "Great Leap Forward" in the late 1950s.

velopment would be aimed at producing tractors, cement for irrigation projects, and other manufactures needed by the peasantry. Enormous publicity was given to efforts to produce steel in "backyard" furnaces, relying on labor— rather than machine-intensive techniques. Mao preached the benefits of backwardness and the joys of mass involvement, and looked forward to the withering away of the meddling bureaucracy. Emphasis was placed on self-reliance within the peasant communes, and all aspects of the lives of their members were regulated and regimented by the commune leaders and the heads of the local labor brigades.

Within months after it was launched, all indicators suggested that the Great Leap Forward and rapid collectivization were leading to economic disaster. Peasant resistance to collectivization, the abuses of commune leaders, and the dismal output of the backyard factories combined with the failure of the rains to turn the Great Leap into a giant step backward. The worst famine of the Communist era spread across China. For the first time since 1949 China had to import large amounts of grain to feed its people. And the numbers of Chinese to feed continued to grow at an alarming rate. Defiantly rejecting Western and United Nations proposals for family planning, Mao and like-thinking radicals charged that socialist China could care for its people, no matter how many they were. Birth control was viewed as a symptom of capitalist selfishness and inability to provide a decent living for all of the people.

Like those of India, China's birthrates were actually a good deal lower than many Third World nations. Also like India, however, the Chinese were adding people to a massive population base. At the time of the Communist rise to power, China had approximately 550 million people. By 1965, this had risen to approximately 750 million. If that rate of growth had continued, some experts predicted that China would have 1.8 billion people by the year 2000.

In the face of the environmental degradation and overcrowding that this leap in population inevitably produced, even the party ideologues came around to the view that something must be done to curb the birthrate. Beginning in the mid-1960s, the government launched a nationwide family planning campaign designed to limit urban couples to two children and those in rural areas to one. By the early 1970s, these targets had been scaled back to two children for either urban or rural couples. But by the 1980s, just one child per family was allowed. Though there is considerable evidence of official excesses—undue pressure for women to have abortions, for example—these programs have greatly reduced the birthrate and have begun to slow China's overall population increase. But again, the base to which new births are added is already so large that China's population will not stabilize until well into the next century when there will be far more people than even now to educate, feed, house, and provide with productive work.

Advances made in the first decade of the new regime were lost through amateurish blunders, excesses of overzealous cadre leaders, and students' meddling. China's national productivity fell by as much as 25 percent. Population increase soon overwhelmed the stagnating productivity of both the agricultural and industrial sectors. By 1960, it was clear that the Great Leap must be ended and a new course of development adopted. Mao lost his position as State Chairman (though he remained the head of the party's Central Committee). The "pragmatists," including Mao's old ally Zhou Enlai along with Liu Shaoqui and Deng Xiaoping, came to power determined to restore state direction and market incentives at the local level.

"WOMEN HOLD UP HALF OF THE HEAVENS"

In Mao's struggles to renew the revolutionary fervor of the Chinese people, his wife, Jiang Qing, played an increasingly prominent role. Mao's reliance on her, which had become dependence by the time of his death in 1976, was quite consistent with the commitment to the liberation of Chinese women he had acted upon throughout his political career. As a young man he had been deeply moved by a newspaper story about a young girl who had committed suicide rather than be forced by her family to submit to the marriage they had arranged for her with a rich but very elderly man. From that point onward, women's issues and the support of women for the Communist movement became important parts of Mao's revolutionary strategy. Here he was drawing on a well-established revolutionary tradition, for women had been very active in the Taiping Rebellion of the mid-19th century, as well as the Boxer revolt in 1900 and the 1911 revolution that had toppled the Manchu regime. One of the key causes taken up by the May Fourth intellectuals, who had a great impact on the youthful Mao Zedong, was women's rights. Their efforts put an end to foot-binding. They also did much to advance campaigns to end female seclusion, win legal rights for women, and open educational and career opportunities to them.

The attempts by the Nationalists in the late-1920s and 1930s to reverse many of the gains made by women in the early revolution brought many women into the Communist camp. Led by Chiang's wife, Madam Chiang Kai-shek, the Nationalist counteroffensive (like comparable movements in the Fascist countries of Europe at the time) sought to return Chinese women to the home and hearth. Madam Chiang proclaimed a special Good Mother's Day, and declared that "virtue was more important [for women] than learning." She taught that it was immoral for a wife to criticize her husband (an ethical precept she herself apparently ignored).

The Nationalist campaign to restore Chinese women to their traditional domestic roles and dependence on males contrasted sharply with the Communists' extensive employment of women to advance the revolutionary cause. Women served as teachers, nurses, spies, truck drivers, and laborers on projects ranging from growing food to building machine-gun bunkers. Though the party preferred to use them in these support roles, in moments of extreme crisis women became soldiers on the front lines, where many won distinction for their bravery under fire. Some rose to become cadre leaders, and many were prominent in the antilandlord campaigns and agrarian reform. Their contribution to the victory of the revolutionary cause truly bore out Mao's early dictum that the energies and talents of women had to be harnessed to the national cause because, after all, "women hold up half of the heavens."

As was the case in many other African and Asian countries, the victory of the revolution brought women legal equality with men—in itself a revolutionary development in a society like China. Women were expected to choose their marriage partners without familial interference. But arranged marriages persist today, especially in rural areas, and the need to have party approval for all marriages represents a new form of control beyond the choice of the couple involved.

Women were also expected to work outside the home. Their opportunities for education and professional careers have greatly improved. As in other Socialist states, however, openings for employment outside the home have proved something of a burden for Chinese women. Until the late 1970s, traditional attitudes toward child rearing and home care prevailed. As a result, women were required not only to hold down a regular job, but also to raise a family, cook meals, clean, and shop—and all without the benefit of the modern appliances available in Western societies. Though considerable numbers of women held cadre posts at the middle and lower levels of the party and bureaucracy, the upper echelons of both were overwhelmingly controlled by males.

As in other developing societies, the rather brief but very considerable power amassed by Mao's wife, Jiang Qing, in the early 1970s runs counter to the overall dominance of males in politics and the military. In any case, like her counterparts elsewhere, Jiang Qing got to the top because she was married to Mao. She exercised power mainly in his name and was toppled soon after his death when she tried to rule in her own right. Women have come far in China, but, as is the case in most other societies in both the "developed" and "developing" worlds, they have by no means attained full equality with males in career opportunities, social status, or political power.

DOCUMENT
WOMEN IN THE REVOLUTIONARY STRUGGLE

Even more than in the nationalist movements in colonized areas such as India and Egypt, women were drawn in large numbers into violent, revolutionary struggles in areas such as China and Vietnam. The breakdown of the political system and social order not only weakened the legal and family restrictions that had subordinated women and limited their career choices, but it ushered in decades of severe crisis and brutal conflict in which the very survival of women depended on them assuming radically new roles and actively involving themselves in revolutionary activities. The following quotations are taken from Vietnamese and Chinese revolutionary writings and interviews with women involved in the revolutionary movements in each country. They express the women's goals, their struggle to be taken seriously in the uncharacteristic political roles they had assumed, and some of the many ways women found self-respect and redress for their grievances as a result of the changes wrought by the spread of the new social order.

1. Women must first of all be masters of themselves. They must strive to become skilled workers . . . and, at the same time, they must strictly observe family planning. Another major question is the responsibility of husbands to help their wives look after children and other housework. . . .

2. We intellectuals had had little contact with the

peasants and when we first walked through the village in our Chinese gowns or skirts the people would just stare at us and talk behind our backs. When the village head beat gongs to call out the women to the meetings we were holding for them, only men and old women came, but no young ones. Later we found out that the landlords and rich peasants had spread slanders among the masses saying "They are a pack of wild women. Their words are not for young brides to hear."

3. . . . brave wives and daughters-in-law, untrammelled by the presence of their menfolk, could voice their own bitterness . . . encourage their poor sisters to do likewise, and thus eventually bring to the village-wide gatherings the strength of "half of China" as the more enlightened women, very much in earnest, like to call themselves. By "speaking pains to recall pains," the women found that they had as many if not more grievances than the men, and that given a chance to speak in public, they were as good at it as their fathers and husbands.

4. In Chingtsun the work team found a woman whose husband thought her ugly and wanted to divorce her. She was very depressed until she learned that under the Draft Law [of the Communist party] she could have her own share of land. Then she cheered up immediately. "If he divorces me, never mind," she said. "I'll get my share and the children will get theirs. We can live a good life without him."

Questions: On the basis of these quotations, what traditional roles and attitudes of women (explored in earlier chapters on China and Vietnam) did those who opposed revolutionary movements in China and Vietnam seek to defend? Which of these roles and attitudes do the revolutionaries reject? What do they believe is essential if women are to gain equality with men? How similar and different are the demands of the women supporting these revolutionary movements in Asia to those of women's rights advocates in the United States?

MAO'S LAST CAMPAIGN AND THE FALL OF THE "GANG OF FOUR"

Having lost his position as head of state but still powerful in the Communist party and by far the most charismatic and popular of the Communist leaders, Mao worked throughout the early 1960s to establish grass roots support for yet another renewal of the revolutionary struggle. He fiercely opposed the efforts of Deng Xiaoping and his pragmatist allies to scale back the communes, promote peasant production on what were in effect private plots, and push economic growth over political orthodoxy. By late 1965, Mao was convinced that his support among the students, peasants, and military was strong enough to launch what would turn out to be his last campaign, the Cultural Revolution. With mass student demonstrations paving the way, he launched an all-out assault on the "capitalist-roaders" in the party.

Waving "little red books" of Mao's pronouncements on all manner of issues, the infamous Red Guard student brigades publicly ridiculed and abused Mao's political rivals. Liu Shaoqui was killed, Deng Xiaoping was imprisoned, and Zhou Enlai was driven into seclusion. The aroused students and the rank and file of the Peoples Liberation Army were used to pull down the bureaucrats from their positions of power and privilege. College professors, plant managers, and the children of the bureaucratic elite were berated and forced to confess publicly their many crimes against "the people." Those who were not imprisoned or, more rarely, killed were forced to do manual labor on rural communes to enable them to understand the hardships endured by China's peasantry. In cities such as Shanghai, the workers seized control of the factories and local bureaucracy. As Mao had hoped, the centralized state and technocratic elites that had grown steadily since the first revolution won power in 1949 were being torn apart by the rage of the people.

However satisfying for an advocate of continuing revolution like Mao and supporters like his wife Jiang Qing, who saw her power grow by leaps and bounds as Mao's former compatriots were purged, it was soon clear that the Cultural Revolution threatened to return China to the chaos and vulnerability of the prerevolutionary era. The rank-and-file threat to the leaders of the Peoples Liberation Army proved in the end decisive in prompting countermeasures that forced Mao to call off the campaign by late 1968. The heads of the armed forces moved to bring the rank and file back into line; the student and worker move-

In launching the Cultural Revolution in the mid-1960s, Mao Zedong and his allies sought to restore the revolutionary fervor of the 1930s and 1940s that they felt had been eroded by the growing bureaucratization of China. In this photo a crowd of Mao's young supporters rally in Beijing.

ments were disbanded and in some cases forcibly repressed. By the early 1970s, Mao's old rivals had begun to surface again, and until the mid-1970s a hard-fought struggle was waged at the upper levels of the party and the army for control of the government. The reconciliation between China and the United States negotiated in the early 1970s suggested that, at least in foreign policy, the pragmatists were gaining the upper hand over the ideologues. Deng's growing role in policy formation from 1973 onward also represented a major setback for Jiang Qing and her three allies, who made up the notorious "Gang of Four" that increasingly contested power on behalf of the aging Mao.

The death in early 1976 of Zhou Enlai, who was second only to Mao in stature as a revolutionary hero and who had consistently backed the pragmatists, appeared to be a major blow to those whom the Gang of Four had marked out as "capitalist-roaders" and betrayers of the revolution. But Mao's death later in the same year cleared the way for an open clash between the rival factions. While the Gang of Four plotted to seize control of the government, the pragmatists acted in alliance with some of the more influential military leaders. The Gang of Four were arrested, and their supporters' attempts to foment popular insurrections were easily foiled. Later tried for their crimes against the people, Jiang Qing and the members of her clique were purged from the party and imprisoned for life, after having death sentences commuted.

In the past decade, the pragmatists have been ascendant, and leaders such as Deng Xiaoping have opened China to Western influences and considerable capitalist development, if not yet democratic reform. Under Deng and his allies the farming communes have been discontinued and private peasant production for the market encouraged. Private enterprise has also been encouraged in the industrial sector, and experiments have been made with such arch-capitalist institutions as a stock exchange and foreign hotel chains.

Though it has become fashionable to dismiss the development schemes of the Communist states as misguided failures, the achievements of the Communist regime in China over the past four decades have been considerable. Despite severe economic setbacks, political turmoil, and a low level of foreign assistance, the Communists have managed a truly revolutionary redistribution of the wealth of the country. China's very large population remains poor, but in education, health care, housing, working conditions, and the availability of food, most of it is far better off than it was in the prerevolutionary era. The Chinese have managed to provide a decent standard of living for a higher proportion of their people than perhaps any other large developing country. They have also achieved higher rates of industrial and agricultural growth than neighboring India, with its mixed state-capitalist economy and democratic polity. And the Chinese have done all of this without leaving up to half their people in misery, and with much less foreign assistance than most Third World nations. If the pragmatists remain in power and the champions of the market economy are right, China's growth in the coming decades should be even more impressive. But the central challenge for China's leaders will be how to nurture that growth as well as the improved living standards without a recurrence of the economic inequities and social injustice that made for the revolution in the first place.

DECOLONIZATION AND REVOLUTION IN VIETNAM

Like most of the peoples of the African and Asian world, the Vietnamese, as well as their neighbors in Laos and Cambodia, were brought under European colonial rule in the 19th century. But because the Vietnamese had long modeled their polity on the Confucian system of their giant neighbor to the north and borrowed heavily from China in the social and cultural spheres, their encounter with the expansive West had much in common with that of the Chinese. The Vietnamese were also shocked by the sudden and forcible intrusion into their formerly rather sheltered world by one of the European imperialist powers, in this instance France bent on restoring its world empire after defeats in Europe. As was the case in China, the failure of Vietnam's Confucian emperor and bureaucracy to successfully repel the foreign invaders discredited and eventually led to the complete collapse of the system around which the Vietnamese had organized civilized life for nearly two millennia.

As in China, the Vietnamese nationalists who emerged in the 1890s and early 1900s soon realized that their rejection of the traditional order meant radical solutions rather than gradualist, reformist measures would be required to liberate Vietnam and build a viable social order for its people. The French refusal to encourage the growth of moderate political parties and to tolerate constitutional or peaceful mass agitation also served to channel Vietnamese political energies into revolutionary channels. The highly exploitative nature of French rule in Vietnam, which was excessive even by colonial standards, also gave rise to economic distress and social dislocations that rendered the status quo unbearable for most of the Vietnamese and won widespread support for those who offered revolutionary alternatives. Therefore, in contrast to much of the rest of the colonized world, the Vietnamese drive to win independence and build a new nation was dominated by violent insurrections, long decades of guerrilla warfare, and far-reaching social and economic transformations.

As if the struggle against the French and reactionary elements in Vietnam itself were not enough, the Vietnamese also had to contend with the intervention of the American goliath in their affairs and nearly a decade of armed struggle against the world's leading military power. Though a tribute to their endurance and dedication, the ultimate victory of the Vietnamese in that struggle left the nation in shambles and isolated from much of the rest of the world.

THE NGUYEN DYNASTY AND THE RISE OF FRENCH COLONIAL DOMINANCE

French interest in Vietnam reached back as far as the 17th century. Driven from Japan by the founders of the Tokugawa Shogunate, French missionaries fell back on coastal Vietnam. Vietnam attracted them both because its Confucian elite seemed deceptively similar to that of the Japanese, and because the continuing wars between rival dynastic houses in the Red River valley and central Vietnam gave the missionaries ample openings for their conversion efforts. From this time onward, French rulers, who styled themselves the protectors of the Catholic missions overseas, took an interest in Vietnamese affairs. As the numbers of converts grew into the tens of thousands and French merchants began to trade at Vietnamese ports, the French stake in the region increased.

By the last decades of the 18th century, French involvement had become distinctly political as a result of the power struggles that convulsed the whole region. In the south, a genuine peasant rebellion, the Tayson, toppled the Nguyen dynasty in the late 1770s. In the following years, the northern rival of the Nguyen, the Trinh dynasty, was also dethroned. The Tayson controlled most of the country, eliminated the Trinh, and all but wiped out the Nguyen. Seeing a chance to win influence in the ruling house, the French head of the Vietnam mission, the Bishop of Adran, threw his support behind the one surviving prince of the southern house, Nguyen Anh.

Anh had fled into the Mekong wilderness with a handful of supporters, thus escaping death at the hands of the Tayson. With the arms and advice of the French, he rallied local support for the dynasty and soon fielded a sizeable army. After driving the Tayson from the south, Nguyen Anh launched an invasion of Tayson strongholds in the north. His task of conquest was made easier by bit-

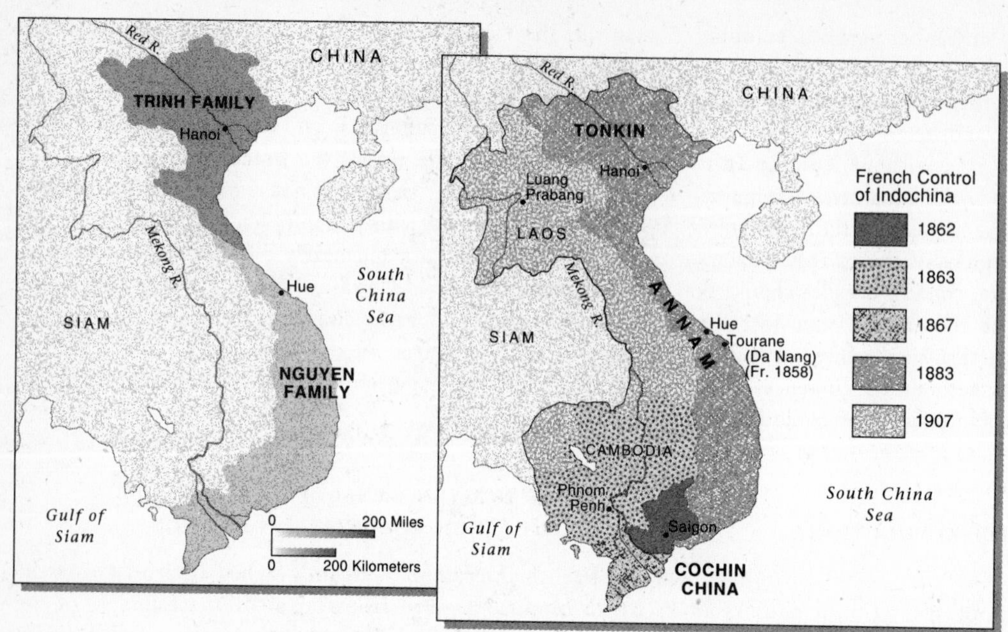

Vietnam: Divisions in the Nguyen and French Periods

ter quarrels among the Tayson leaders. By 1802 the Nguyen armies had prevailed, and Nguyen Anh proclaimed himself the Gia Long emperor of Vietnam.

Nguyen Anh made the old Nguyen capital at Hue in central Vietnam the imperial capital of a unified Vietnam. His French missionary allies were rewarded with a special place at court, and French traders were given greater access to the port of Saigon, which was rapidly emerging as the leading city of the Mekong River valley region in the south. The Nguyen dynasty was the first in centuries to rule all of Vietnam and the first to rule a Vietnamese kingdom that included both the Red River and Mekong deltas. In fact, the Mekong region had only begun to be settled extensively by Vietnamese in the century or so before Nguyen Anh rose to power.

Nguyen Anh and his successors proved to be arch-traditionalists deeply committed to strengthening Confucianism in Vietnam. Their capital at Hue was intended to be a perfect miniature of the imperial palace at Beijing. The dynasty patronized Confucian schools and built its administration around scholar-bureaucrats well-versed in Confucian learning. The second emperor Minh Mang (1820–1841) prided himself on his knowledge of the Confucian classics and his mastery of the Chinese script. He even had the audacity to criticize the brushwork of the reigning Chinese emperor, who after all was not any more Chinese than Minh Mang but descended from Manchu nomads. All of this proved deeply disappointing to the French missionaries, who had been counting on baptizing Nguyen Anh and then carrying out the sort of top-down conversion of the Vietnamese the Jesuits had hoped for ever since their arrival in Asia. Things actually got worse. Gia Long's ultra-Confucian successor Minh Mang came to view the Catholics as something of a fifth column, which he believed posed a substantial danger to the dynasty. His persecution of the Vietnamese Catholic community not only enraged the missionaries, but it contributed to the growing political and military intervention of the French government in the region.

Pushed both by political pressures at home and military defeats in Europe, French adventurers and soldiers exploited quarrels with the Nguyen rulers to justify the piecemeal conquest of Vietnam and neighboring Cambodia and Laos, beginning in the late 1840s. By the 1890s, the whole of the country was under French control and the Nguyen dynasty had been reduced to the status of puppet princes. In the following decades, the French concentrated on drawing revenue and resources from Vietnam, while providing very little in return.

The French determination to make Vietnam a colony that was profitable for the homeland exacerbated social and economic problems that were already bad under the Nguyen rulers. Most of the densely packed peasant population of the north lacked enough land to even eke out a subsistence livelihood. French taxes and the burden of obligatory purchases by each village of set amounts of government-sold opium and alcohol drove many peasants into labor in the mines. Even larger numbers left their ancestral villages and migrated to the Mekong region to work on the plantations established there by French and Chinese entrepreneurs, or to become tenants on the great estates that had been carved out of sparsely settled frontier regions by Vietnamese and Chinese landlords. Migration brought little relief. Plantation workers were paid little and treated much like slave laborers. The unchecked demands of the Mekong landlords left their tenants with scarcely enough of the crops they grew to feed, clothe, and house their families. The blatantly exploitative nature of French colonialism in Vietnam was graphically revealed by the statistics the French themselves collected. These showed a sharp drop in the food consumed by the peasantry in all parts of the colony between the early 1900s and the 1930s—a drop that occurred despite the fact that Vietnam became, in these years, one of the world's major rice-exporting areas.

VIETNAMESE NATIONALISM: BOURGEOIS DEAD ENDS AND COMMUNIST SURVIVAL

The failure of the Nguyen rulers after Minh Mang to rally the forces of resistance against the French did much to discredit the dynasty. But from the 1880s into the first decades of the 20th century, guerrilla warfare was waged in various parts of the country in support of the Save the King movement. Because this resistance was localized and small-scale, the French were able to crush it on a piecemeal basis. In any case, French control over the puppet emperors who remained on the throne at Hue left the rebels with little cause worth fighting for. The failure of the Nguyen and the Confucian bureaucratic classes to defend Vietnam against the French did much to discredit the old order in the eyes of the new generations that came of age in the early decades of French rule. Perhaps because it was imported rather than homegrown, the Vietnamese were quicker than the Chinese to reject Confucianism once its failings were clear, and they did it with a good deal less trauma. But its demise left an ideological and institutional vacuum that the Vietnamese, again like the Chinese, would struggle decades to fill.

In the first years of the 20th century, a new Western-educated middle class, similar to that found in other colonial settings (see Chapters 30 and 39) was formed by the children of the traditional Confucian elite and the emerging landlord class in the Mekong region. Some, taking advantage of their parents wealth, went to French schools and emerged speaking fluent French and with a taste for French fashions and frequent holiday jaunts to Paris and the French Riviera. Many of these went to work for the French as colonial administrators, bank managers, and even labor recruiters. Others pursued independent professional careers as lawyers, doctors, and journalists. Many who opted for French educations and French life-styles were soon drawn into nationalist organizations. Like their counterparts elsewhere in the colonies, the members of these organizations initially concentrated on protesting French racism and discrimination, improving their wages, and gaining access to positions in the colonial government held by Frenchmen.

As in other colonies, nationalist newspapers and magazines proliferated. These became the focal point of an extended debate regarding the approach that should be taken

Though violent Vietnamese resistance to French rule never really died out, as this cartoon illustrates, some Vietnamese—mostly from the landlord and commercial middle classes—were willing not only to collaborate with the colonizers but also to adopt their dress and social conventions.

toward winning freedom from French rule and, increasingly, what needed to be done to rebuild Vietnam as a whole. Because the French forcibly repressed all attempts to mount peaceful mass demonstrations or organize constitutional agitation, those who argued for violent resistance eventually gained the upper hand. In the early 1920s the nationalist struggle was centered in the clandestine Vietnamese Nationalist party (Vietnamese Quoc Dan Dong or VNQDD), which was committed to violent revolution against the French colonizers. Though the VNQDD made some attempt to organize urban laborers and peasant villagers, party members were drawn overwhelmingly from the children of the landlord elite and urban professional classes. Their secret codes and elaborate rituals proved little protection against the dreaded Sûreté or French Secret Police. A series of failed uprisings, culminating in a 1929 attempt to spark off a general revolution with the assassination of a much-hated French official in charge of labor recruitment, decimated the party. It was particularly hard-hit by the following all-out French campaign of repression, execution, and imprisonment. From that point onward, the bourgeois nationalists were never again the dominant force in the independence struggle.

The demise of the VNQDD left its major rival, the Communist party, as the main focus of nationalist resistance in Vietnam. As in China and Korea, the Communist wing of the nationalist movement had developed in Vietnam during the 1920s, often at the initiative of leaders in exile. By the late 1920s, the party was dominated by the charismatic, young Nguyen Ai Quoc, who would later be known as Ho Chi Minh. Ho had discovered Marxism while studying in France and Russia during and after World War I. Disillusioned by his failure to gain a hearing for his plea to the victorious Allies at the Versailles Peace Conference for the Vietnamese right to self-determination, Ho dedicated himself to a revolutionary struggle to drive the French from Indochina.

In the early 1930s the Communist party still held to the rigid, though unrealistic, orthodox vision of a revolution based on the urban working classes. Since the workers in Vietnam made up as small a percentage of the population as they had in China, the orthodox strategy made little headway. A sudden shift in the early 1930s to a peasant emphasis, in part to take advantage of widespread but non-Communist inspired peasant uprisings in central Vietnam, led to a disaster almost as great as that which had overtaken the VNQDD a year before. French repression smashed the Communist party hierarchy and drove most of the major Communist leaders into exile. But the superior underground organization of the Communists and the support they received from Comintern helped them survive a French onslaught. Slowly, during the late 1930s, the discredited Ho reestablished his place in the party, and the party won growing peasant support due to its programs for land reform, higher wages for laborers, mass education, and health care. When the French were weakened by the Japanese invasion of Indochina in 1941, the Communists were ready to use the colonizers' setbacks to advance the struggle for national liberation.

THE WAR OF LIBERATION AGAINST THE FRENCH

During World War II, operating out of bases in south China, the Communist-dominated nationalist movement, known as the Viet Minh, established liberated areas throughout the northern Red River delta. As in Korea, the abrupt end of Japanese rule left a vacuum in Vietnam, which only the Viet Minh was prepared to fill. Its programs for land reform and mass education had wide appeal among the hard-pressed peasants of the north, where they had been propagated during the 1930s and especially the war years. The fact that the Viet Minh actually put their reform and community building programs into effect in the areas they controlled won them very solid support among much of the rural population. The Viet Minh's efforts to provide assistance to the peasants during the terrible famine of 1944 and 1945 also convinced the much-abused Vietnamese people that here at last was a political organization that was genuinely committed to improving their lot.

Under the leadership of General Giap, the Viet Minh skillfully employed guerrilla tactics similar to those devised by Mao in China. These offset the advantages that first the French and then the Japanese enjoyed in conventional firepower. With a strong base of support in much of the rural north and the hill regions, where they had won the support of key non-Vietnamese "tribal" peoples, the Viet Minh forces advanced triumphantly into the Red River delta as the Japanese withdrew. By August, 1945, the Viet Minh were in control of Hanoi, where Ho Chi Minh proclaimed the establishment of the independent nation of Vietnam.

Though the Viet Minh had liberated much of the north, they had very little control in the south, where a variety of Communist and bourgeois nationalist parties jostled for power. The French, anxious to reclaim their colonial empire and put behind them their humiliations at the hands of the Nazis, were quick to exploit this turmoil. With British assistance, the French reoccupied Saigon and much of south and central Vietnam. In March 1946 they denounced the August declaration of Vietnamese independence and moved to reassert their colonial control over the whole of Vietnam and the rest of Indochina. An unsteady truce between the French and the Viet Minh quickly broke down, and Vietnam was soon consumed by a renewal of the Viet Minh's guerrilla war for liberation, as well as bloody infighting between the different factions of the Vietnamese. After nearly a decade of indecisive struggle, the Viet Minh had gained control of much of the Vietnamese countryside, while the French, with increasing American financial and military aid, clung to the fortified towns. In 1954 the Viet Minh decisively defeated the French at Dien Bien Phu in the mountain highlands near the Laotian border. The victory won the Viet Minh control of the northern portions of Vietnam as a result of an international conference at Geneva in the same year. At Geneva, elections throughout Vietnam were promised within two years to decide who should govern a reunited north and the still politically fragmented south.

ANALYSIS
DECOLONIZATION WITH AND WITHOUT SOCIAL REVOLUTION

As we have seen, independence was won in most of the nonsettler colonized world with a minimum of violence and only very limited changes in Africa and Asian economies and social hierarchies. Vietnam provides a sharp contrast to this dominant pattern, despite the fact that it had few French settlers and was colonized by the French in much the same way as the rest of Africa and Asia under European rule. The reasons for the divergent path to independence taken by the Vietnamese tell us much about the origins of revolutionary as opposed to gradualist, reformist political change. They are rooted in the differences between Vietnam, China and its other satellite civilizations in East Asia, and most of the rest of the Afro-Asian world. They are also tied to the extraordinarily exploitative and excessively repressive nature of colonial rule under the French in Vietnam as well as the consequences of the brief period of Japanese control in the area.

Like the other peoples of East Asia, the Vietnamese already had a unified state, a common written and spoken language, and a strong sense of common identity long before the expansive Europeans broke into their comparatively isolated world. There were sharp cultural and political divisions between the lowland-dwelling, wet-rice growing Vietnamese and the multitude of slash-and-burn cultivating peoples who lived in the hills. But the Vietnamese made up an overwhelming majority of the people who occupied the areas that would eventually comprise the nation of Vietnam. French rule promoted Vietnamese dominance over the hill peoples as well as over the lowland peoples of neighboring Laos and Cambodia. It also intensified the traditional Vietnamese sense of identity, both by providing a foreign target for them to resist and by enriching that sense of identity with the European concepts of the nation and patriotism. Like all peoples who had been deeply influenced by China's Confucian tradition, the Vietnamese found their political subjugation to the "barbarian" Europeans intensely galling. Their own long tradition of violent resistance to political foreign domination, whether by the Chinese, the Mongols, or the Manchus, also fed the Vietnamese determination to fight against the French conquest.

In contrast to colonial India, Africa, and most of the rest of Southeast Asia, from the outset Vietnamese cooperation with the French was branded by those who resisted French rule as a betrayal of the Vietnamese people and tradition. Also in contrast to other colonized areas, the Vietnamese continued to violently resist the imposition of French rule long after the initial wars of conquest and "pacification" had ended. There was to be no early colonial period of peace and submissiveness in Vietnam. From the outset, the Vietnamese fought the French encroachments into their country with fierce determination. This violent struggle continued through most of the period of French rule.

The crumbling of the Confucian order and the nature of French rule in Vietnam made it essential for those who sought to mobilize opposition to the French to promise far-reaching social and economic transformations. As in China and Korea, the failure of the Confucian elite in Vietnam to ward off the intrusions of the West led to the rejection of Confucian civilization as a whole. As a result and in contrast to the peoples of most of the rest of the Afro-Asian world, the Vietnamese were left without a "tradition" to defend and to revive as an alternative to European colonialism. Unlike Islam, Hinduism, and Buddhism elsewhere, the depoliticized, eclectic, and rather amorphous variant of Buddhism in Vietnam was simply not seen by the emerging nationalists of the country as a viable base on which to build a postcolonial order. The fact that the breakdown of the Confucian system was paralleled by the worsening condition of the peasantry resulting from French exploitative policies rendered mere political responses insufficient. The substitution of French-educated, middle class, Vietnamese politicians for French colonial officials would do little to alleviate the misery of the peasant farmers of the north or the plantation workers in the south.

In any case, the middle class could make little headway even in the political sphere against determined repression by the French. In contrast to the policies followed in most other nonsettler colonies, the French prohibited all but the most innocuous political organizations. The Vietnamese press was tightly controlled; even moderate political parties were smashed; and mass demonstrations of any kind were strictly prohibited. The French doggedly refused to negotiate seriously with, much less make any significant constitutional concessions to, the bourgeois nationalists, whose collaboration was a major prop of their continued domination in Indochina. Under these circumstances the gradual transfer of power from the colonizers to the nationalists, which had been a key factor in peaceful decolonization in other areas, was out of the question. As a consequence, underground terrorist and guerrilla organizations like the VNQDD and the Communist party dominated the struggle for independence by the 1920s.

Even the Japanese takeover in the 1940s, which proved so crucial to the strengthening of moderate, constitutional nationalist organizations in Burma, Indonesia, the Philippines and other areas they occupied, had the reverse effect in Indochina. For most of the period of occupation, the Japanese were content to let French collaborators, linked to the Nazi-puppet Vichy regime then in power in France (see Chapter 34), continue to run the colony under their supervision. As a result, the policy of repressing nationalist organizations continued. Thus, any hopes for building a nonviolent, moderate party that could rival the Communist-dominated Viet Minh were again crushed. The violent struggle against the Japanese, the French, and later the Americans only served to reinforce the revolutionary orientation of the Vietnamese Communist party.

Questions: Compare the precolonial sense of identity and political unity in Vietnam with the situation found in most of the rest of the colonized world. How have the differences between the two made for very different paths of political development in Vietnam, as opposed to patterns of colonial dominance and nation-building in much of the rest of the Third World? If the French had been more tolerant of moderate nationalist agitation, do you think that revolutionary parties like the Communists would have dominated the independence movement? Why or why not?

THE WAR OF LIBERATION AGAINST THE UNITED STATES

The promise at Geneva that free elections would be held to determine who should govern a united Vietnam was never kept. Like the rest of East Asia, Vietnam had become entangled in the cold war maneuvers of the United States and the Soviet Union. Despite very amicable cooperation between the Viet Minh and United States armed forces during the war against Japan, American support for the French in the First Indochina War and the growing fame of Ho Chi Minh as a Communist leader drove the two further and further into opposition. The anti-Communist hysteria in the United States in the early 1950s fed the perception of influential American leaders that, like South Korea, South Vietnam must be protected from Communist takeover.

The search for a leader to build a government in the south that the United States could prop up with economic and military assistance led to Ngo Dinh Diem. Diem appeared to have impeccable nationalist credentials. In fact, he had gone into exile rather than give up the struggle against the French. His sojourn in the United States in the 1940s and the fact that he was a Catholic also recommended him to American politicians and churchmen. Unfortunately, these same aspects would alienate him from the great majority of his countrymen.

With American backing, Diem was installed as the president of Vietnam, a status he tried to legitimatize in the late-1950s by holding rigged elections in the South, in which the Communists were not permitted to run. Diem also mounted a series of campaigns to eliminate by force all possible political rivals in the South. Because the Communists posed the biggest threat (and were of the greatest concern to Diem's American backers), the suppression campaign increasingly focused on the Communist cadres that remained in the South after Vietnam had been divided at Geneva. By the mid-1950s, the Viet Cong (as the Diem regime dubbed the Communist resistance) were threatened with extermination. In response to this threat, the Communist regime in the north began to pump weapons, advisors, and other resources into the southern cadres, which were reorganized as the National Liberation Front in 1958.

As guerrilla warfare spread and Diem's military responses expanded, both the United States and the North Vietnamese escalated their support for the warring parties. When Diem proved unable to stem the Communist tide in the countryside, the United States gave the go-ahead for the military to overthrow him and take direct charge of the war. When the Vietnamese military could make little headway, the United States stepped up its military intervention.

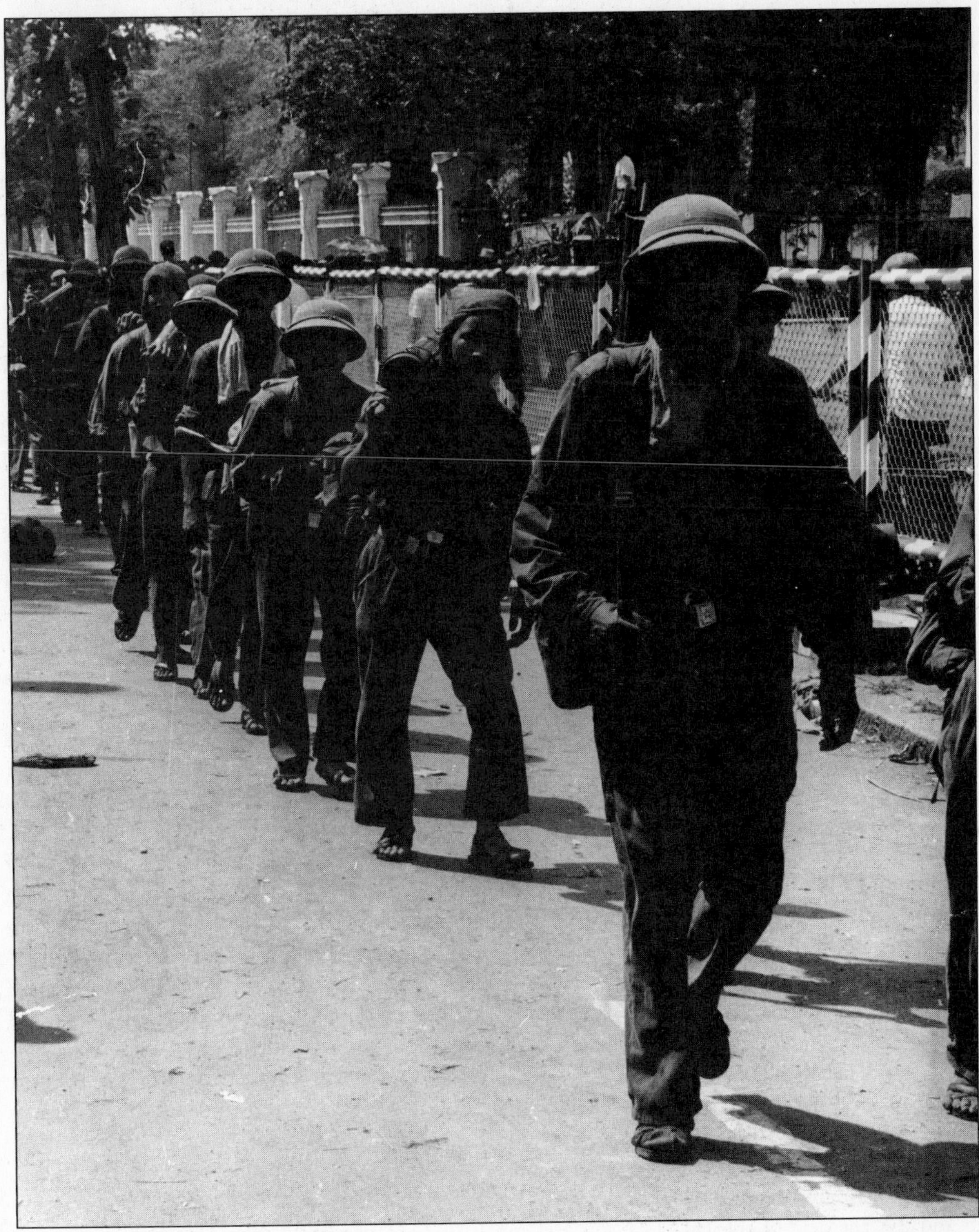

After decades of struggle against foreign invaders, Vietnamese guerrillas march with the regular forces of the North Vietnamese army into Saigon in May 1975. The capture of the city marked the end of the long wars to free a unified Vietnam.

From thousands of special advisors in the early 1950s, the American commitment rose to nearly 500,000 men and women, who made up a massive force of occupation by 1968. But despite the loss of nearly 60,000 American lives and hundreds of thousands of Vietnamese casualties, the Americans could not defeat the communist movement. In part, their failure resulted from their very presence, which made it possible for the Communists to convince the great majority of the Vietnamese people that they were fighting for their independence from yet another imperialist aggressor.

Though more explosives were dropped on tiny Vietnam, North and South, than in all of the theaters of the Second World War, and America resorted to chemical warfare against the very environment of the South Vietnamese they claimed to be trying to save, the Communists would not yield. The indomitable Vietnamese emerged as the victors of the Second Indochina War. In the early 1970s, American diplomats negotiated an end to direct American involvement in the conflict. Without that support, the unpopular military regime in the South fell apart by 1975.

The Communists united Vietnam under a single government for the first time since the late-1850s. But the nation they governed was shattered and impoverished by decades of civil war, revolution, and armed conflict with two major colonial powers and the most powerful nation of the second half of the 20th century.

CONCLUSION

REVOLUTIONS AND CIVILIZATION IN CHINA AND VIETNAM

There can be little doubt that the ancient civilizations of both China and Vietnam have undergone revolutionary transformations in the 20th century. Monarchies or autocratic colonial regimes have been replaced by Communist party cadres who seized power in the name of the peasants and workers. Whole social classes, such as the scholar-gentry and the large landlords, have been eliminated. Elite-centric education and writing systems have been replaced by mass-oriented schooling and simplified scripts designed to promote general literacy. Women have greatly improved their legal status and position within the family, and a wide range of career opportunities, most of which would have been unthinkable under the prerevolutionary Confucian order, have opened to them. Marxism-Leninism—blended in recent years with experiments in Western-style capitalism—has replaced Confucianism as the state ideology and provided the philosophical underpinnings for the new social order.

The breadth and profundity of these changes might lead one to conclude that the patterns of civilized life China and Vietnam nurtured for over two millennia disappeared as completely as Harappa vanished from the Indian landscape in the 2d millennium B.C. But upon closer examination, it becomes clear that much more has been preserved than these gauges of radical change and the rhetoric of the ruling parties of China and Vietnam might lead one to believe. Both societies, for example, have retained deeply ingrained suspicions of the commercial and entrepreneurial classes. Both continue to stress that those who wield political power are obligated to rule in ways that promote the welfare of the mass of the people. Both China and Vietnam still adhere to ideological systems that stress the secular, social harmony, and life in this world rather than religious concerns and life hereafter. In each case these continuities between the prerevolutionary patterns and those of the postrevolutionary era exemplify important affinities between Marxist-Leninist and Confucian thought. They explain why Marxism had such a strong appeal to Chinese and Vietnamese intellectuals and revolutionary leaders.

The persistence of the ancient civilized traditions of China and Vietnam extends far beyond areas of agreement between Marxism and Confucianism. At times it runs directly counter to Marxist-Leninist internationalism. The continuing Chinese sense of cultural superiority to even more powerful nations, such as the United States and Japan, and Mao's conviction that he, not Stalin or Trotsky, should be the leading authority on Marxian revolutionary thought are but two notable examples of this persistence. The repeated reassertion of elitist thinking and bureaucratic control over all aspects of social life, which Mao railed against in the last decades of his career, provides additional evidence of the strength of prerevolutionary patterns of civilization. Resistance in both China and Vietnam to the full liberation of women, to restrictions on the number of children each married couple is allowed to have, and to state attempts to break down extended family ties are important manifestations of the persistence of these patterns in society more generally.

These continuities caution us, as we have argued in the introduction to this section on the 20th century, against overstating the extent to which the history of the present century marks a decisive break with the past. Just as the Bolsheviks in Russia drew on the political traditions of the Tsarist era and nationalists in India and Africa invoked the ancient symbols and beliefs of their societies, Chinese and Vietnamese revolutionaries struggled to build "new" societies that owed much to their Confucian past. These continuities also remind us of the resilience of ideas and patterns of civilized life that have been nurtured over centuries and, in the cases of China and Vietnam, over millennia. Civilizations weave dense and complex webs of human interaction. These may be profoundly altered by the sort of revolutionary upheavals that have occurred in the 20th century. But more often than not the changes are less sweeping and much more is preserved than revolutionary leaders would like to admit.

FURTHER READINGS

Some of the best general studies on China in the 20th century include Lucian Bianco's *The Communist Revolution in China* (1967), C. P. Fitzgerald's *The Birth of Commu-*

nist China (1964), Wolfgang Franke's *A Century of Chinese Revolution* (1970), and Jonathan Spence's *The Search for Modern China* (1990). For firsthand accounts of conditions in the revolutionary era, see especially Graham Peck's *Two Kinds of Time* (1950), Edgar Snow's *Red Star Over China* (1938), and Theodore White and Analee Jacoby's *Thunder Out of China* (1946). Mark Selden's *The Yenan Way to Revolution in China* (1971) provides the fullest account of the development of the Communist movement after the Long March. Of the growing number of works on China after the Communists came to power, Maurice Meisner's *Mao's China* (1977) and Michael Gasster's *China's Struggle to Modernize* (1987 ed.) are the most useful. Rodney Macfarquhar's two-volume study of the *Origins of the Cultural Revolution* (1974, 1983) is essential for an understanding of the last years of Mao's rule. Elisabeth Croll's *Feminism and Socialism in China* (1978) is by far the best single work on the position of women in revolutionary China.

There is substantial literature on Vietnamese history during the Nguyen and French period, as well as, of course, a large number of works on Vietnam during the Second Indochina War. Alexander Woodside's *Vietnam and the China Model* (1971) remains the place to start on the pre-French period, and Buttinger's *Political History of Vietnam* (1968) also remains useful for general background. Woodside, Huynh Kim Khanh, David Marr, Milton Osborne, William Duiker, and Hue Tam Ho-Tai have all made important contributions to the rise of nationalism and communism in Vietnam. On U.S. intervention in the area, see the works by George Kahin and Lloyd Gardner. On the conduct of the war, Jeffrey Race and Malcolm Browne are among the most insightful of many accounts.

- **PERIODIZATION: NEW EVENTS AND UNCERTAINTY**
- **TRENDS IN WORLD SOCIETIES**
- **THE WORLD'S FUTURE AS PROMISE OR THREAT**
- **THE ZIPPY FORECAST**
- **REGIONS, CIVILIZATIONS, AND WORLD FORCES**
  - **CONCLUSION:** Asking Questions
  - **FURTHER READINGS**

42

Toward the Future: World History Yet to Come

INTRODUCTION Since the formation of civilizations, the history of the world has involved relatively rapid change—sometimes in directions already set, but sometimes in new trajectories. This pattern obviously continues as we near the 21st century. Indeed, some people would argue that the pace of change has sped up, as new discoveries and new technologies press against older ideas and habits. World history, in other words, offers no convenient stopping point at which one can lean back and say, This is what it all means. Contemporary world history provides no magic vantage point, either, on what is to come. The only thing we know for sure about the future is that we do not know what it will bring.

People in various civilizations have attempted to devise schemes to look beyond their present. From the time of the ancient river-valley civilizations to the 20th century, some people have used astrology or other divinations to predict the future. More systematically, some scholars have assumed that time moves in cycles, so that one could count on repetition of basic patterns. This was a common assumption in Chinese historical thought and also among Muslim historians in the postclassical period. Others, including Christian thinkers and advocates of more secular faiths such as Marxism, have looked toward some great change in the future: the Last Judgment, for example, or the classless society to which history is steadily working. The idea of some master plan guiding history, moving it in a steady direction and toward a purpose, runs deep in the thought of several cultures, including our own. Whatever the approach, the human impulse to know what we cannot definitely know seems inescapable.

Yet all the evidence suggests that our vision of the future remains cloudy at best. It has been calculated that well over 60 percent of all predictions or forecasts offered by serious social scientists in the United States since 1945—called upon to sketch future business cycles, family trends, or political currents, for instance—have been wrong. How many observers just 50 years ago could have predicted such basic recent transformations as decolonization; the rise of new kinds of authoritarianism; fundamental revolutions in China, Iran, and Cuba; the challenge to communist rule in the Soviet Union; the invention of computer and genetic engineering technologies; or the industrial breakthroughs of many Pacific coast regions of Asia? A few of these events could be discerned in advance, to be sure, but many were great surprises. And other developments that were confidently predicted have not come to pass: Americans are not normally riding about in helicopters rather than automobiles (an image of the 1940s), nor have families been replaced by promiscuous communes (a forecast of the 1960s).

Even though we cannot know the future, we can use history to develop a framework for evaluating it and partially anticipating it as it unfolds: We can know what factors to monitor. Recent patterns and their relationship to older themes in world history allow an orientation toward what is to come. This final chapter suggests several vantage points from which to relate past to present to future. We deal with issues of progress and deterioration, with the ongoing tensions between separate civilizations and forces that impact throughout the world, and with trends in the basic political, cultural, economic, and social functions of human society.

This chapter presents several methods of approaching the future, all of which require historical knowledge and analytical skills in assessment. No method offers certainty, which is why some historians refuse to deal with forecasting in any form, lest it corrupt their true craft. All the approaches, however, promote further thinking, not only about the future but about the various kinds of historical trends that are shaping it.

We begin first with the easiest relationship between recent past, present, and future: extrapolating from recent trends. We then turn to two more dramatic forms: the moral evaluation based on judgments of whether world society is getting better or worse and the dramatic forecast based on a revolutionary factor that will provoke a major disruption between future and past. Finally, we look at the future in terms of a set of issues fundamental to world history for many centuries, though taking new form in our own era.

PERIODIZATION: NEW EVENTS AND UNCERTAINTY

What we know about 20th-century history both helps and hinders use of the recent past to organize some sense of the future. It seems clear that in the 1920s and 1930s a new phase in world history began to take shape by the usual periodization criteria: parallel developments in major civilizations, reshuffling of geographical boundaries including changes in the roster of particularly influential civilizations, and intensification of international contacts. More extensive trade, unprecedented worldwide alliance systems, and the new variety of cultural exchanges readily illustrate the international intensification theme. Geographical changes include the loosening of Western domination through the decolonization movement and the new sources of industrial competition; they also include realignments in the societies of East and Southeast Asia and new configurations of the Middle East and the Indian subcontinent. Developments that cut across diverse societies include shared technologies (despite continuing gaps in overall technological levels), new political forms, and a tendency toward cultural secularization. The patterns add up, as we have seen, to a break in world history at least as great as the one that occurred in the 15th century, as Arab dominance yielded and new empires and trade patterns emerged.

The fact of a major break in world history, and of such recent vintage, means that many patterns familiar from the 19th century will almost surely continue to recede—we need not expect a revival of Western colonial dominance, for example. More positively, it is reasonable to expect continuing intensification of many world contacts: the necessary technology is increasingly available with international computer linkages and air-delivery systems, and the increase in contacts has formed a fairly steady trend in world history for at least 1000 years. Societies in the 20th century that have tried to isolate themselves from larger world currents—the Soviet Union in the 1930s to an extent as well as China under Mao, for example—have usually found it necessary to open somewhat more fully, lest they lose the technological and economic benefits of contact.

The fact that the 20th century launches a major new period, however, automatically limits more precise prediction. We may know that the West's relative dominance has declined, but we do not know whether it will continue to do so. Events in the early 1990s, including the reunification of Germany, hopes for firmer West European unity, and Westernized leadership for many of the newly independent East European nations, point to a European revival—not back to 19th-century imperialist levels, but well beyond what could have been foreseen just two decades ago. Analogies for a Western decline drawn from Roman or even Arab experience in the classical and postclassical periods may be totally misplaced. By the same token, there may be no single center of dominance—of the sort Arab and then Western civilization represented—in this emerging period in world history. The world of the future may continue the present pattern of several major centers of power and influence.

Other forecasts, based on recent trends, are also uncertain. The century has seen growing secularization of belief in otherwise varied societies. Trends are not uniform, given Muslim and Christian missionary activity in Africa as well as the Islamic resurgence elsewhere, but the general point—describing the spread of communism, consumer materialism, and nationalism—has been clear. Yet the idea of a world without dominant religions is so strange to some observers that they predict a major religious revival—perhaps under some new doctrine—for the coming century. Who is to say they are wrong? The point is that a new period in world history inevitably produces doubt about the directions of the future precisely because old patterns are shaken up and emerging trends are hard to gauge.

MAKING SENSE OF RECENT DEVELOPMENTS

Events themselves establish uncertain directions. The biggest political development of the late 1980s involved the explosions in the communist world. China experimented through the entire decade with a range of interactions with the capitalist world and with the introduction of more market devices into its own economy. Consumer interest grew in Chinese cities, while a number of peasant entrepreneurs amassed considerable earnings by catering to market demand in their agricultural production. Gorbachev's ascent to leadership in the Soviet Union in 1985 triggered sharper change (see Chapter 36). Reforms and protest vied within the Soviet Union, and the smaller East European states burst from Soviet Europe.

This was almost unprecedented ferment. Most observers, including seasoned intelligence experts, were astounded at the events throughout the communist system, precisely because they overturned settled assumptions about Soviet power and the hold of what had been effective police states. While it was essential to recast these assumptions, it was not clear how to predict subsequent patterns. Would Gorbachev succeed in reforming Soviet politics and coping with his country's admitted economic doldrums and massive environmental problems? His policies triggered important worker strikes for higher earnings and even more urgent nationalist protests from minority peoples long subject to Russian dominance. Here was a reminder of continuities of cultural identity and political interest, even amid apparent change. Indeed, the demands of regional nationalities in Eastern Europe by 1990 recalled tensions in the area before World War I; not only Soviet groups, but Bulgarians, Turks, Hungarians, Serbs, Croats, and Romanians began to raise intense and conflicting territorial demands. It was possible that the weakening of the Soviet empire would bring new diplomatic and even military turmoil to key parts of the world.

Within the Soviet Union, it was not clear that Gorbachev could survive the varied sources of discontent, and many predicted that a more authoritarian regime, bent on protecting the integrity of the Soviet empire, would replace him. If Gorbachev fell or changed his policies, what would happen to the new regimes in places such as Poland and Hungary? Further, could Soviet and East European economies break out of a limited industrial framework to the newer technologies and affluence of the advanced industrial societies of the West or of the Pacific Rim?

In China, meanwhile, a massive student demonstration in 1989 in favor of greater democracy was brutally repressed. Would China remain an exception to trends in European communism, or had a seed of liberalization been planted that must someday flower more fully?

Historical understanding aids in sorting out possibilities, but only to a point simply because the future does not cleanly reproduce the past and the past itself offers various models. Some experts emphasized Russia's long authoritarian tradition and the more specific antecedents of Stalinist communism: Gorbachev's reformism must fail, in this view, because it countered Russian officialdom's commitment to a strong state and a controlled social order. Others, however, argued that Gorbachev was reviving an important Russian tradition of looking to partial Western models and experimenting on this base, an impulse visible not only in pre-Soviet experience but during the 1920s. Here was a more optimistic rendering that could be supplemented by the possibility that new factors, including the nation's productivity problems, could wipe away some historical precedents. The failure of the 1991 coup, amid democratic resistance to revived authoritarianism, emphasized the extent of real change in Russian political culture. Prognostication about China was no easier. It was nice to believe that democratic agitation, once launched, could not be permanently repressed, particularly if China continued a policy of economic reforms and contacts with the wider world economy. On the other hand, China's traditions of control and the specific precedents of Maoism might support a long period of suppression. It was also worth noting that student protest movements in 1989 had not precisely called for Western-style politics anyway, for they were directed in part toward smoother and less corrupt bureaucratic procedures, evoking Confucianism as much as Western liberalism.

Upheavals in Eastern Europe and potentially in China raised questions about the future of communism and the world balance of power. The rise of the Soviet Union and the United States had followed on the decline of Western Europe by the late 1940s. However, by the 1990s the Soviet Union was in partial eclipse and the United States, burdened by heavy international debt, found its international activities somewhat constrained. With the cold war and its leading practitioners receding, what global pattern would follow? Analogy could be suggestive: Recall that the first initiative that briefly replaced Arab dominance in the 15th century—the Chinese surge in international trade—proved to be a false start. Perhaps the cold war, with the United States and Soviet international rivalry, would be a similar episode, revealing the decline of the older West European dominance but not providing more than a temporary alternative. This possibility does not, however, predict what patterns may prove more durable, nor does it forecast the extent of Soviet decline or American constraint.

THE TRIUMPH OF THE WEST?

A few popularizers, to be sure, tried to make sense of complex trends as the 20th century neared its close. One writer from the American State Department, briefly popular among official United States government circles, projected an "end to history." He argued that the cold war had ended with a Western victory; all parts of the world were bent on imitating Western institutions. With this development, history with its massive conflicts and ideological competitions had ended. Peace would prevail through a somewhat boring eternity, sparked mainly by marketplace competitions in a thoroughly capitalist world. Such a prospect might be comforting, particularly as it seemed to glorify Western values. Yet the attempt to judge the future on the basis of recent events, while simplifying those events in turn, might also be judged foolhardy. Various Western historians have periodically attempted to postulate an end to the normal ups and downs of history. Middle-class liberals—the British Whig school—argued over a century ago that bourgeois values of education, social mobility, and political rights would lead to such general justice or satisfaction that there would be no reason for further change: All of history had been pointing to this moment of supreme enlightenment. Marx, of course, anticipated an end to historical process through communism's victory, though he did not claim to be quite so clear about the details of the future order. Hopes for a simpler future based on real or imagined recent trends thus has a pedigree; whether it greatly aids understanding or intelligently uses what we know of the past to predict the future, is doubtful.

Indeed the decline of the cold war clearly encouraged realignments in troubled regions, now that superpower rivalry no longer served as constraint. German reunification in 1990, resulting from the expulsion of the Communist regime from East Germany and creating a powerful state in Europe's center, raised some questions about European tensions, though plans for full economic unity in the Common Market proceeded. Iraq's ambitious leader, Saddam Hussein, judged the moment opportune for a more daring realignment in the Middle East. He invaded the small, oil-rich nation of Kuwait and may have hoped to use invasion to spearhead Muslim unity in the whole region, in the tradition of earlier conquerors such as the caliphs or the Ottomans. A United States led coalition defeated Hussein, changing the balance of power in the area but again making future arrangements extremely unpredictable. The victorious American president called for a "new world order" of stability, but the prospects for regional disruptions in the Middle East and elsewhere may have become more likely rather than less, as various leaders probed the decline of superpower rivalry.

TRENDS IN WORLD SOCIETIES

Prediction based on dramatic recent events is both essential and frustrating; the complication of the larger issues of 20th-century periodization recur constantly. One forecasting mode, however, seeks to cut through some of the problems by focusing on processes rather than events and by identifying strong current trends in order to gain some sense of the future's shape or at least of the questions that might be sensibly asked about it.

Trend extrapolation can be quite precise. Within a particular society such as the West or Japan, for example, it is easy to predict an expansion of problems associated with retirement and old age costs in the near future, based on current patterns and the almost-certain further results of low birthrates and growing longevity. The problems are present already, and they will increase. Only unforeseen changes, such as a spurt in the birthrate or new policies that deny medical care for older adults and so reduce longevity gains, can throw such short-term projections off.

Extrapolating vaguer trends, as well as adding an international basis, is obviously riskier. Nevertheless, several common questions or issues had emerged in the later 20th century that provide a valid framework for anticipating ongoing opportunities or problems.

POLITICAL ISSUES

In the political sphere, the changing balance between democracy and other 20th-century government forms, notably communism and authoritarianism, provided the most obvious link between recent trends and future prospects.

Democratic parliamentarianism is now a well-established tradition in much of the West. Extremist movements still challenge it in some countries, and the fact that democratic trends were dislodged by Nazism in Germany scarcely one-half century ago reminds us not to be too complacent. Major economic setbacks might again call the regimes into doubt. But while there are many problems with Western politics, the regimes do seem firmly rooted. They have withstood massive shocks such as loss of colonies. Indian and Japanese democracies are more recent and possibly less rooted in prior political forms; Japanese democracy still combines somewhat uneasily with the tradition of upper-class dominance, while Indian democracy seeks to accommodate the old tendency toward regional fragmentation plus new class and religious tensions. Here too, however, comparative stability has by now described a span of several decades.

More generally, there is no question that a democratic impulse was spreading in the world by the late 1980s, as it had in the first flush of decolonization in the 1940s and 1950s. New currents in the communist world suggested a clear link between democracy and economic reform, which resulted in widespread popular aspiration toward a democratic system.

The authoritarian form of government also showed new weaknesses. Authoritarian forms in the 20th century had resulted from the tensions experienced by many new nations after the destruction of earlier political institutions and from sources of available leadership such as the military. Authoritarianism has a strong base in Latin-American tradition, where it goes back to the 19th century and where it has proved capable of both change and popularity. By the 1980s, however, democratic institutions had effaced authoritarianism in all but a few cases in Latin America. Again in the 1980s attacks on authoritarianism in the Philippines, Korea, and Pakistan raised new doubts about the system's future, though particularly in Korea authoritarian overtones remained even under an elected president. Early in the 1990s new democratic movements challenged authoritarianism in many African states.

Buoyed by the trends, some observers argued that a form of liberal democracy would prove to be the only viable political style for modern nations, because of the prestige it carried and because of the flexibility it allowed in responding to rapid social and economic change. Arguments of this sort were not new, but they gained increasing credibility with the overturning of authoritarian regimes in Latin America during the 1970s and then the upheaval of the communist world. Certainly a worldwide turn to democracy would have simplified political analysis, yet doubts about the forecast remained, because of the distinctiveness—both traditional and recent—of Chinese political systems, for example, or the stubborn persistence of authoritarian regimes in the Middle East.

CULTURAL ISSUES

The idea of a set of cultural issues affecting the world's future is hardly commonplace. We are instead accustomed to thinking about political and military scenarios or the tensions of economic development. Furthermore, many cultural patterns apply primarily to individual civilizations, which are defined more clearly by cultural styles than by any other characteristic.

A few cultural themes cut across civilizations, however, raising questions about what is to come. Many people have periodically wondered or worried about the results of pressures for homogeneity, as the trappings of consumer culture, the popularity of Western fads, and the impact of the leading international artistic and architectural styles continue to spread. It is possible to travel to most of the world's cities today and stay in hotels, eat in restaurants, and buy goods that would scarcely differentiate downtown Chicago from downtown Istanbul. The dissemination of English as a world-currency language for travel, business, and science adds to the impression of growing homogeneity. The popularity of Western-dominated cultural styles has raised issues for Japan, it has added to the confusions of growing up in modern African cities, and it has helped divide Islamic societies. So the issue of balancing international modes and distinctive traditions has wide applicability. To date, most civilizations have maintained their own tone, even as they selectively use international fads and products. But the further spread of global customs will probably intensify the friction between tradition and modernity, while possibly undermining diversity around the world. Further internationalization might also, at the same time, promote greater understanding; already, at their best, the modern Olympic Games, based on an internationalization of key sports, have bridged some gaps that political leaders cannot close.

A more subtle issue involves the role of expressions such as art or music in human life. Industrialization forces such concentration on economic and technical needs and involves such uprooting of established habits through emphasis on technical training that the arts may be pushed to the periphery. This concern, of course, is phrased in various ways, depending on the civilization. Westerners worry that a rich popular cultural tradition has been replaced by commercialized, shallow entertainments designed to sell goods. The most creative artists may have become unusually remote from public taste. Non-Western intellectuals worry that their cultural traditions are being displaced by urban squalor or Westernization, or that government controls bend culture to purposes of political obedience. Japanese intellectuals sometimes lament the materialism of their own

This photo of downtown Lagos, Nigeria, shows the Western influence on international urban architecture.

culture where traditional art survives but, again, may play a less central role than in the past. Some dissident Russian intellectuals have expressed the same concern about their industrial society, while Africans worry that traditional art degenerates into mass-produced trinkets for tourists.

The problem of integrating science with more traditional religious and artistic endeavors constitutes a related theme. Science has long been part of the intellectual arsenal of most civilizations, but it played a role subordinate to religious and esthetic interpretations of nature and human nature. Starting with the West, modern intellectual history has involved a steady upgrading of science, which became linked to the broader process of technical and industrial development. Yet even in the West, science has not satisfied all human needs, and at the same time it has not provided as encompassing a framework as traditional religion once did for relating separate portions of the human cultural experience. The result in the West, during the past two centuries, has been enduring tension, dividing science from the arts or humanistic disciplines. Several societies outside the West have lagged in developing scientific research to match better-established interests in arts, religion, and literature, or, as with Islamic fundamentalism, they have insisted on the primacy of a religious view. Tensions between science and nonscience may be healthy; they certainly seem inevitable; but in various ways in different major cultures, they raise important issues about the integration of intellectual outlook for the future.

World culture in the future must also deal with technological change. The omnipresence of the radio is already an accomplished fact; most villages, not to mention urban families, have their transistors. Television too is becoming a global medium, as over half the world's population has relatively ready access to a TV set. The potential spread of computer-based information systems raises an additional prospect for the future. Most people in the later 20th century are contending with standardized sources of information and with increased amounts of information. The question of the ongoing impact of new transmission technologies on popular culture as well as on creativity in the sciences and nonsciences alike, forms a final open-ended issue for the world's cultural evolution at the end of the 20th century and beyond.

ECONOMIC ISSUES

Economic problems and prospects form the most familiar framework for discussing the future. Will the agricultural civilizations, as in Africa or Latin America, manage to industrialize? Can the environment withstand mounting industrialization? How will the growing parity between the West and East Asia in industrial development work out—will the West decline, or can it live with a new balance? Has East European development, so vigorous earlier in the century, reached a plateau, and if so, what will the results be in terms of Russian politics and diplomacy?

The gap that opened between early industrializing societies—including those initial latecomers, Russia and Japan—and those that are still industrializing remains stubbornly wide. Several major civilizations besides the industrial pioneers—most notably India, China, and Southeast Asia—have been generating economic growth above population increase in recent decades. They have invested substantially in agriculture and in manufacturing. The industrial world continues to undergo change as well, as the advent of postindustrial technologies and labor-force structures attests.

The economic divisions of the contemporary world are more subtle than the convenient dichotomy between industrial and developing nations suggests. Gaps have opened among industrial nations, depending on use of the newest technology; thus Eastern Europe again lags, as in the 18th and 19th centuries, which is an important source of the recent turmoil. Important differences divide nations struggling for agricultural subsistence from those involved in rapid economic transformation. A few smaller nations, particularly on Asia's Pacific Rim, have joined the ranks of industrialized states, while other nations, such as Brazil, have developed strong industrial sectors amid many severe economic problems. Economic inequalities are complex, and they remain a concern. In a world increasingly interconnected, the political and military tensions resulting from economic differences can be acute. Unequal levels of wealth among major civilizations are no novelty in history, but disparities in levels of development in such a tightly linked global economy constitutes a novel combination. The stresses of playing catch-up in the economic development game and the resentments that can result on all sides—including those in wealthy nations seeking to preserve their lead—are an important if incalculable ingredient in the world's future.

Economic imbalances also helped explain other important developments in the later 20th century for which no clear end was in sight. The international drug trade picked up steam from the 1920s onward. Supplies came largely from countries with poor peasantries and desperate need for foreign exchange, plus in some cases weak governments. Between the world wars, countries such as Turkey and China served as key suppliers; after World War II, as these countries moved toward greater economic development, areas such as northwestern Latin America moved toward center stage. Demand for the drugs resulted from tensions in several industrial societies, as the burgeoning trade served as a perverse link among quite different kinds of economies in the interconnected world market.

The world's economic imbalances, plus different rates of population growth, also generated new pressures for immigration. Arabs and South Asians moved toward the oil-rich states of the Middle East. Growing minorities from Africa, Latin America, and Asia gravitated toward the United States and Western Europe. Japan, though leery of immigrants, admitted laborers and also prearranged brides from various Asian countries. The result of these movements has been a cross-civilization mixture of peoples unusual in world history and often associated with considerable tension and confusion. Continued relocation pressures form vital issues for many societies, including those that depend on sending excess labor elsewhere.

SOCIAL ISSUES

Diverse civilizations and unequal levels of industrial and urban development produce radically different social forms. Concern about family stability in the West and Africa contrasts with substantial family stability (and undue traditionalism?) in India and Latin America. Pressures of economic development have called some traditional social forms into question; most societies now attempt to encourage some social mobility as part of an effort to recruit talented leadership, spread education, and promote social justice. But specific social issues continue to vary greatly: India faces persistent, if now informal, gaps among castes, Communist societies uneasily accommodate a managerial or bureaucratic middle class, peasant unrest continues in parts of Latin America, and the West worries about racial tensions surrounding new or traditional minorities. Even relations among the generations vary, with most industrial societies gradually coming to terms with a growing old-age segment, and most agricultural civilizations still focusing on problems of nurturing and educating the young.

A few fundamental questions do apply to all societies. Industrialization has involved city growth, and urbanization now in many cases races ahead of other economic change. City life, in turn, poses some basic challenges, such as problems of dealing with crowding, problems of providing appropriate entertainment, and problems of dealing with psychological stress stemming from the excitement and tension of city life. At times, though not invariably, urbanization brings heightened crime. It certainly reduces traditional community control over behavior, so that other devices, including formal policing, must be extended. The impact of urbanization, both its promise and its difficulties, thus raises global questions for the present and future alike. Urbanization also creates new divisions between rural and urban people, a source of heightened misunderstanding, and, in many societies, a neglect of farming populations and even of agriculture.

Economic change and the spread of mass education also affect the family, including conditions for women and the position of other groups. Young people are subjected to examples other than those of their immediate relatives. Children who are better educated than their parents or who work outside the home often develop a taste for independence—a theme that, in the contemporary world, runs from Hong Kong to Nairobi to St. Louis. While the West, as the first industrializer, faced the changing role of children somewhat earlier than other societies, it has hardly resolved the resulting issues, and some common concerns about youth unrest and family solidarity have cut across a number of cultures, including that of the Soviet Union in recent decades.

Another trend to monitor involves social structure. Control of the land becomes steadily less important as the basis for social position. Aristocracies and landlord classes loom less large in late 20th-century world history than at any time since the dawn of civilization. Urbanized societies tend to place emphasis on wealth, knowledge, and managerial control as the basis of social prestige. This has been the clear pattern in the West and in Communist Eastern Europe; the pattern seems to be emerging in Africa and Asia as well. Division between wealthy managerial classes and laboring groups with little or no property and inferior education forms a set of tensions that cuts across several different civilizations. Educational access and attainment, for example, become everywhere more important as a basis for upward mobility, though this is a less novel phenomenon in Chinese tradition than, say, in Latin American tradition.

In sum: What we know about industrialization patterns and the impact of efforts to industrialize in various parts of the world suggests some ongoing questions about social and family structure that apply to a number of societies despite vastly different specific patterns. The social structures of the world range from remnants of India's caste system to the managerial bureaucracies of China and the Soviet Union, and from highly urbanized Japan to societies where urban elites struggle to control rural majorities. Quite generally, however, tension between expectations of opportunity and ongoing social hierarchies raises another set of leading questions for the future.

THE WORLD'S FUTURE AS PROMISE OR THREAT

Talking about future issues on the basis of recent trends provides a vital connection between what we know about the later 20th century and the issues we can anticipate in the 21st century. The strategy can be applied to a vast range of specific issues and specific societies, beyond the general points raised in the previous section. The approach lacks flair, however, and many observers prefer a different and more dramatic means of linking society past and society to come.

One mode, and a tempting way to end a world history text, is to offer glowing words of hope about the achievements and bright prospects of humankind. Moral judgments here substitute for precise forecasts. Contemporary Western culture continues to value optimism and to believe that students, especially, should be inspired to think well of the society around them, hopeful as they face their own future. Yet the message of history, including contemporary history, is decidedly ambiguous on the question of hopefulness.

THE BRIGHT SIDE

World history is without question a record of impressive, even inspiring, human achievement. Through art, music, and literature, people have created moments of great beauty. Through religion and science, people have gained new understanding of the world they live in; the daily environment is surely a less fearful and more intelligible habitat for us than it was for our hunting-and-gathering ancestors. Political institutions have been generated that at certain times at least brought impressive stability and mechanisms of justice to many people. Technological mastery of nature has increased fairly steadily in human history. Certainly our species has learned how to support ever greater numbers of people, as agricultural techniques and then industrialization provided more reliable means of subsistence. Humankind, at first a rather frail competitor for survival, now easily outnumbers any of the other complex mammalian species, and thus has, to date, handily passed this basic biological test of success.

The 20th century has contributed at least its share to the record of progress. Advances in industry and agriculture have permitted the birth and survival of more people in our century than in all previous centuries combined. Life expectancy has risen notably in all societies, not just those with a sophisticated industrial apparatus. New seeds and fertilizers in the agricultural "green revolution" have greatly improved food supplies in otherwise "poor" societies such as India. Scientific discoveries add greatly to our knowledge as well as to our technology, though some civilizations continue to value nonscientific ways of viewing the world. Experts in virtually every nation know more about the functioning of the human body, about weather and climate patterns, about astronomy, and indeed about human history than any society has ever known before. The capacity to organize large groups of people has also improved, at least in certain respects. Most societies today can operate larger businesses or school systems or census-taking operations than ever before. Along with this bureaucratic achievement come some probable improvements in certain aspects of social relationships. Slavery has been almost fully eradicated. Although great variety persists, women have been granted new opportunities in many parts of the world in terms of political rights and less complete confinement to domestic functions. No one would argue that injustice has been eliminated, but there may be some measurable gains. The spread of education, another general development in the 20th century, also provides a basis for claiming a genuine increase in human knowledge, not just at the level of advanced research but also among peasants and workers.

Many of these developments provide additional hope for the future. Better medical care and nutrition may broaden the human potential. Mass schooling, still a relative novelty in many societies, may join with electronic technologies, such as radio and television, to bring formal education even to remote regions that remain largely agricultural. Additional research gains seem virtually assured, as physicists, for example, make almost daily discoveries about the nature of the universe. Unquestionably, the human potential remains vast. It seems likely, though not certain, that women in most societies will continue to gain new rights and functions, based on worldwide trends of rising educational levels, falling birthrates and greater legal and suffrage equality. Women's conditions may vary considerably according to the particular standards of each civilization, but there are some general trends away from traditional patriarchy—in Africa, China, and parts of the Middle East as well as in industrial societies.

THE OTHER SIDE

Yet history is also, unquestionably, the record of humankind's inhumanity to its own members. The historical record is peppered with acts of massive cruelty and bitter hatreds that have divided nations and races. While certain civilizations may claim to have tamed some destructive impulses, and while certain cruelties like deliberate human sacrifice have ended, it is hard to argue that the overall record of world history reveals measurable improvements in human relationships.

The 20th century has generated particularly troubling questions about human impulses wedded to awesome technologies and wider contacts among peoples. The century has produced the bloodiest wars on record; 60 million people were killed in World War II alone. Even small wars produced great carnage, such as the 100,000 Iraqis killed by Western bombing in 1991's Persian Gulf conflict. The introduction of sophisticated weaponry, combined with ongoing political tensions, has resulted in massive slaughter even aside from formal wars: the deaths of hundreds of thousands as part of revolution in Russia and China; Hitler's insane efforts to exterminate the Jews; and the execution of additional hundreds of thousands stemming from racial or religious conflict in Uganda, Cambodia, and on the Indian subcontinent, for example. Less massive but surely menacing has been the rise of new kinds of terrorism in the West, the Middle East, and parts of Asia, as political fanatics attack civilian populations to dramatize their desire for social revolution or redress of nationalist grievances. The 20th century has been a violent period, surpassing even the most ravaged periods of the past in the sheer volume of slaughter if only because of the availability of technologies for mass killing. A number of societies, as a result of revolutionary or other tensions, developed new nonchalance about killing during key periods of tension. Even India, long a tolerant civilization and known in the 20th century for emphasis on nonviolence, exhibited unusual levels of internal religious warfare, intolerant hatreds, and attendant killing.

Our violent century has also generated a nuclear capability that makes the prospect of future war a new shadow on world history. Humankind may now have the weaponry necessary to destroy itself as a species and to destroy its habitat, planet Earth, as well. The atomic bomb has been used only once, by the United States, and it is possible to hope that the fearsomeness of the nuclear arsenal will teach world leaders to avoid all-out war in the future. But the peace many regions of the world have enjoyed since 1945 rests on a balance of terror more than on demonstrable enlightenment, and most efforts to negotiate serious nuclear disarmament have at best slowed rates of arsenal expansion, not reversed the trend of growing weapons sophistication.

We can hope that further escalation of human violence will not occur. Amid the new economic problems in the Soviet Union and budget pressures in the United States, greater willingness to reduce some weapons stocks emerged at the end of the 1980s, though both superpowers continued research into lasers and space shields. While almost one-half century without direct major-power warfare was encouraging, it hardly offered guarantees for the future. Further, spreading nuclear and chemical warfare capacity in other nations such as Iran, Iraq, and South Africa heightened anxieties about escalating tensions in some future regional conflict. Dependence of nations such as the United States and France on export sales of advanced weaponry added to a host of area arms races. Although most people have learned to carry on their lives without anxieties about nuclear disaster, no one can believe the world is secure.

The first true thermonuclear explosion in 1945 introduced the nuclear age.

The pattern of 20th-century war, terror, and weaponry forms the clearest blot on any idea of overall progress, but there are other nightmares. In the first place, the technologies that allow more people to survive in our world have also generated frightening levels of pollution and created potential imbalances in the natural environment. The daily elimination of acres of natural vegetation in expanding societies, such as those of Latin America and Africa, hinders the natural production of oxygen through photosynthesis, while in other regions industrial plants lower air and water quality and the increased output of human wastes produces still other environmental problems. Our ability to sustain growing populations, though unquestionable in recent history despite warfare, may be jeopardized in the future, or at least the amenities to which many people have become accustomed may be reduced.

Major environmental accidents during the 1980s pointed up the severity of the problems. Many different societies were involved in the generation of these accidents. A Russian nuclear reactor at Chernobyl in the Ukraine experienced partial meltdown, devastating the immediate regions with radiation and increasing radioactive levels in a wide area of Europe. An American chemical plant in Bhopal, India, suffered a huge explosion, killing hundreds of

The rain forest is threatened by each new road through the Amazon. Economic development vs. world ecological balance is a major problem of the region.

people and maiming even more. In 1989 a series of oceanic oil spills around the United States, including a particularly extensive accident in Alaska, severely damaged shorelines and marine life. The 1991 Persian Gulf War resulted in massive oil spills and oil fires. More general findings, about penetration of the ozone layer because of chemical pollution and about widely anticipated global warming because of the growing use of hydrocarbons, demonstrated the international scope of environmental issues and the lag between policy controls and the acceleration of problems.

Other areas of concern more directly involve human relations. Improvements in bureaucratic capacity have brought new means of police control over many people around the world, most obviously in some authoritarian and Communist nations but also in places such as the United States that maintain unusually large prison populations. Human freedom is hard to measure over time, but it would certainly be difficult to assert that it has steadily increased in recent decades. The 20th century also stands open to some attack for its relative neglect of spiritual and esthetic expressions, though here, of course, evaluation is particularly subjective. Crowding, war, and the sheer concentration on economic development may have tended to shunt artistic and religious creativity to the side, reducing the beauty available in many human lives. Critics who worry about the undermining of African cultural traditions and those who bemoan the mindless mass entertainments of the contemporary West may be identifying an important common problem in our own time and in our future.

New formulations of social and economic inequalities also support a pessimistic rendition of recent history. Slavery and caste systems were officially gone, to be sure. But the deteriorating position of unskilled wage labor, including much immigrant labor, within individual nations such as the United States, and the growing worldwide gaps between labor standards of the industrial and the less developed nations posed troubling new trends. Freedom from want was not uniformly increasing.

A review of both optimistic and pessimistic cases provides useful ways of summing up historical patterns and deciding what one's own standards of evaluation are. But it seems fatuous to pretend that either an optimistic or a pessimistic approach is so clear-cut as to define the meaning of recent world history or the world's probable future. Some of humankind's most hopeful recent endeavors have not worked out particularly well: the United Nations organization, for example, has not produced serious mechanisms for conflict resolution, though it has usefully facilitated discussion. On the other hand, some of humankind's direst recent fears have not come to pass either: world population has not yet overwhelmed the available food supply, the United States and the Soviet Union have not as yet yielded to some inevitable cataclysm, and Nazi-style racism and

The greatest nuclear disaster to date occurred at Chernobyl, Soviet Union, in 1986. The nuclear plant was in ruins after the reactor's explosion.

brutality have not gained ground in the world's repertoire of political movements.

THE ZIPPY FORECAST

Another common approach to the future, sometimes related to optimism or pessimism, involves identification of an overwhelming causal factor that will fundamentally alter the framework in which the societies of the world operate. Just as some historians have long sought a basic factor to explain historical change—through technology, trade levels, or cultural values—so the most dramatic breed of forecasters points to the single emerging revolutionary factor that will make almost everything different. The resultant dramatic forecast differs from general extrapolation from trends by seizing on one decisive ingredient and by anticipating massive contrasts between future and present.

THE OVERCROWDING SCENARIO

In the 1960s and early 1970s, gloomy "population bomb" predictions received a considerable audience. Experts correctly noted the unprecedented size and growth rates of world population, and argued that, unchecked, the sheer number of people would outstrip available resources, produce unmanageable environmental degradation, and create rivalries for space that could usher in a series of bitter wars. Concern about world population trends, though still lively, had lessened by 1990, in part because growth rates had slowed. Some experts claimed that resources could expand with population growth, and noted that historically population expansion had often been a major source of innovation and creativity. Some also claimed a racist element in population bomb forecasts, insofar as these involved Western pundits urging people of color to have fewer babies. Population bomb forecasts had not been discounted entirely, and environmentalists picked up some of their concerns. As a tool for gauging the future, however, the "bomb" approach was yesterday's fad, though it remained true in 1990 that world population continued to grow at a rate of 250,000 new people per day.

A variant on the population bomb approach, though less widely publicized, played up the exhaustion of frontiers. Only by the later 20th century, some world historians argued, had human societies fully run out of room to expand—pending as yet unrealized space travel. Each previous period of world history had featured expansions into relatively empty spaces; thus the postclassical period saw movements into eastern Europe and western China plus Bantu migrations southward in Africa, while the 19th century had climaxed the history of human frontiers with the fuller peopling of the Americas and Australia and Rus-

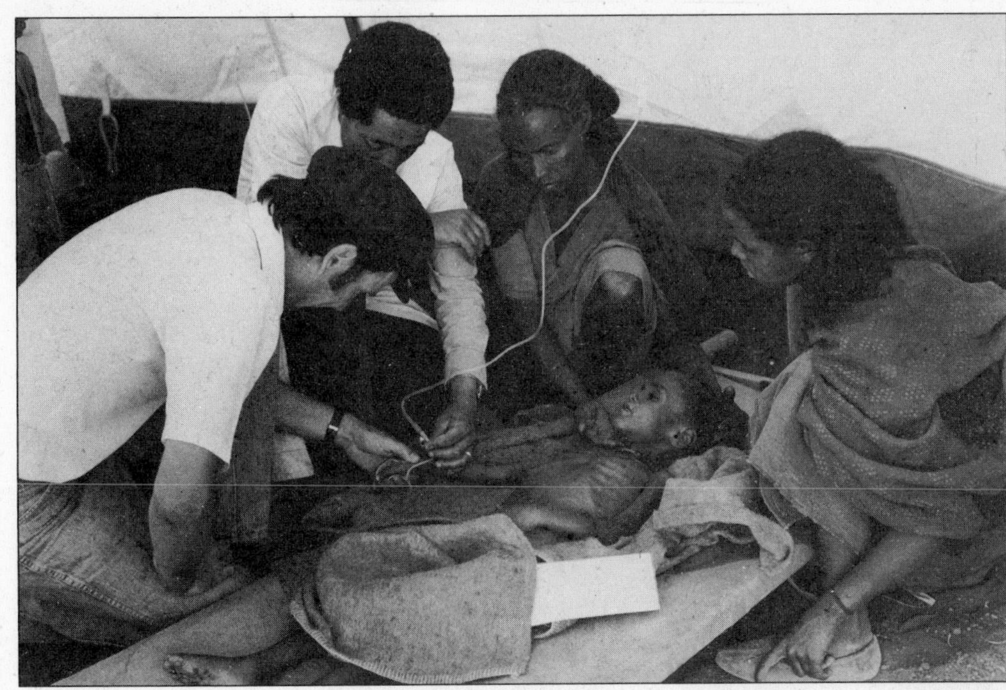

World hunger and international aid. Ethiopian famine victims receive aid at a Red Cross center in 1984.

sian settlement in Siberia. With frontiers gone by the late 20th century, organized societies bumped against each other far more than ever before, while immigration inevitably meant movement not into relatively unsettled terrain, but into highly populous, often suspicious host societies. The implications for potential conflict, environmental exhaustion, and efforts to impede human movement were considerable, if this major factor is viewed as a basic distinction between society future and society past.

A POSTINDUSTRIAL WORLD

Another effort to identify deterministic causation highlights a revolutionary wave of technological change associated with computers, genetic engineering, robotics, and new devices for transmitting energy. According to some popular forecasters, late 20th-century society entered a postindustrial revolution fully as dramatic as the Industrial Revolution two centuries ago or the Neolithic revolution 10,000 years ago—with exactly the same potential for altering the whole framework of human existence. As technology continues to take over production, postindustrial society will feature service occupations dealing with people and information exchange, as not only agriculture but also industrial production is handled largely by machines. Social status will depend on technical knowledge, not money or landed property. Cities will change, becoming centers for meetings and recreation, not basic points of exchange and production. This picture is dramatic, and some observers have claimed to find ample evidence of its accuracy in existing trends. The postindustrial vision is also usually optimistic in assuming that key industrial problems will be resolved in the new order. Routine, repetitive work, for example, will be eliminated by automation, and computers will allow labor to become more varied and individualized.

Critics of the postindustrial vision raise several objections. They are not sure that the transformation discernible in the United States or Western Europe, for example, is as fundamental as the analogies to the Industrial Revolution suggest. Change is occurring, to be sure, but it preserves management and labor structures similar to the patterns of industrial society. There is no relocation of people as massive as industrial-based urbanization had involved and no need for such fundamental shifts in habits of thought. Computers can make work more routine, not less, as rigorous supervision becomes automated. Corporate and government bureaucracies continue to expand. New technology, in other words, does not necessarily change most basic trends, and technological determinism should not be pressed too far. Further, if distinctive postindustrial societies are developing, they concentrate in very few parts of the world—the West and Japan; postindustrialization mainly exacerbates the economic inequalities among major areas that had already arisen as part of the world economy. How useful, then, is the concept for forecasting overall world history?

The computer age comes to life at an office of the International Business Machines corporation.

Dramatic forecasting of this sort—whether imbued with postindustrial optimism or population-bomb gloom, relies heavily on a single basic casual factor—technology or population determines all, and everything falls into place once this factor is established. Yet most historians reject this kind of determinism. The analysis of the past shows the power of considerable continuity, rather than some single-minded transformation. Major changes do occur, but they result from the confluence of several factors, not a single cause. Though some cataclysm is always possible, most historians assume that complexity will continue. Eye-catching forecasts can help organize thinking about what makes history tick and how present relates to past, but there are other orientations toward the future as well.

REGIONS, CIVILIZATIONS, AND WORLD FORCES

A final set of issues for the future returns us to more complex prospects, different from the stark drama of all-or-nothing forecasts and their reliance on one primary source of causation. These final issues really involve another assessment based on current trends but of a special sort that reaches not only into developments of the late 20th century but well back into world history and its fundamental dynamics.

Since the classical period, world history has involved a tension between the operations of individual civilizations and wider international forces that shape the way people think and behave across civilizational boundaries and sometimes almost through the entire world. As a new period in world history, the 20th century raises important new questions about this tension. As usual when large but inherently uncertain interpretive problems are at stake, some polar positions are available. It is possible to predict a new splintering among civilizations, even a new selfish regionalism, with each area emphasizing its own flavor now that the hothouse period of Western dominance is cooling down. There are also new centripetal forces, however, that may reduce the scope for individual cultures in favor of more literally international trends.

THE QUEST FOR SEPARATE IDENTITIES

Because the history of civilization began against a backdrop of widely separated communities, whether agricultural villages or hunting-and-gathering bands, patterns of aggregation and of building larger units form an underlying theme in the larger world-historical process. Yet aggregation into regions or whole civilizations has never been a constant. Empires and even cultural units fragment. The great multinational empires of the early modern period—

the Mughal, Ottoman, and now Russian, for example—all split apart. Events in the 1980s raised the prospect of new fragmentations to a surprising level: Peoples in relatively small regions showed that old loyalties persisted fiercely. Thus Slavic groups in Eastern Europe, even in a single small nation such as Yugoslavia, turned on each other with demands for separation or at least autonomy. French descendants in Quebec, seeking greater independence, encountered hostility from their English-descended neighbors elsewhere in Canada. A host of established units, including of course the Soviet Union, were newly vulnerable to regional ethnic, linguistic, and religious loyalties.

Amid the welter of new or newly recognized issues in the 20th century, it was easy to forget the persistence of many separate traditions. Various societies were grouped under common headings—such as *nonindustrial*, *overpopulated*, and *authoritarian*—and these labels had real meaning.

Nevertheless, regional patterns still counted, and in some cases they were supplemented by distinctive recent experiences—such as India's interaction with Britain in the 19th and early 20th centuries, compared to China's more complex contacts with the West. Areas where traditional religion remained intense, as in the Middle East and India, might share some results in the relatively low status of women, but they also divided depending on what the religion was. Islam's role in the Middle East thus helped differentiate this region from Hindu-majority India. Artistic styles picked up other long-standing distinctions, as did commitment to political centralization versus emphasis on greater regional autonomy. Even revolutionary China showed the hand of its particular past, despite great changes, in the continued emphasis on an embracing central state and the extensive reliance—interrupted only during Mao's cultural revolution—on elders in political leadership.

Developments after 1950 continued to reflect civilization boundaries. Thus both China and India newly struggled against high birthrates. The Indian government, however, proved relatively ineffective, given traditional resistance to state involvement, whereas Chinese efforts, though far from completely successful against older family habits, could build on earlier patterns of state intervention. Japan's avoidance of lawyers, in favor of reliance on honor and group loyalty, reflected inherited values different from those of the more contract-minded West.

Regions and civilizations have not remained changeless, but they combine distinctive traditions, distinctive recent experiences, and a distinctive filter by which even common experiences are modified. This pattern survives in the later 20th century. Thus the Indian interpretation of the problem of economic development differs from that of the Chinese, while the Chinese interpretation of what a Communist society involves turns out to differ from that of Soviet Russia. Moreover, despite important common themes, including nationalism, mass education, and attempts to improve agricultural and industrial technology, no overriding pattern of modernization has yet obliterated key boundaries among the major civilizations.

A basic theme of 20th-century history, almost certain to extend into the 21st century, thus involves an understanding of how each major civilization will interpret the forces of modern politics and industrialization to create its own amalgam. We can begin to see that this process may well resemble the earlier interplay between the spread of agriculture and local cultures, when a similar force of economic change—in this case, from hunting and gathering to farming—generated a variety of political, religious, and family institutions, all of which differed from the hunting past. Correspondingly, any common international process—for example, the forces that work toward modification of a patriarchal structure for women—must be evaluated specifically for each civilization. Generalization about the whole world could easily misfire in light of separate traditions (such as the specific forms of patriarchy) and distinctive recent experience.

A key result of decolonization and the growing challenge to Western dominance was, in fact, a reassertion of the cultural independence of several civilizations. The end of the cold war enhanced the prospects for new regional separations. This was a strong ingredient both of the Iranian revolution, bent on guiding a reinvigoration of Islam more generally, and of Chinese Communist reactions to the protest currents at the end of the 1980s, where renewed claims to China's separate and superior path surfaced quickly.

The quest for cultural autonomy in several major societies is particularly marked in contrast to the homogenizing impulses of modern mass culture. Indian films reproduce the themes and spirit of the great Hindu sagas in the world's largest movie industry. Islamic societies, quite like other Third World areas in many respects, maintain particularly vigorous religious strains, expressed also in distinctive birthrates and family patterns. Latin-American intellectuals deal with problems of identity and loneliness that derive from this civilization's particular past. Japan uses habits of group loyalty to generate modes of industrial governance different from those of the West, within an equally successful economic framework.

One key theme for the future, then, involves identifying separate paths for major civilizations and regions, including new ingredients and new vitalities as well as outright continuities from the past—as has long been the pattern in world history. It is certainly not possible to predict an international spread of a Western-type women's rights movement, though it is valid to note that conditions for women are changing everywhere. Formal feminism may depend heavily on prior political and cultural traditions, and though Western feminism has had some international echoes, it may not emerge as a strong popular force in Japan or Egypt. Again, each specific civilizational context balances larger world trends.

Yet the emphasis on distinctive civilizations, increasingly conscious of their unique qualities, is not the only focus of world history as we approach the future. In the first place, there is little assurance that the civilization areas identifiable in the late 20th century will remain constant. Societies do collapse and merge, and they may split apart. The differences between China and Japan in recent centuries prevent ongoing reference to a single East Asian pattern, and the emergence of a Pacific Rim adds further complexities. In another case, Turkey at the end of the 1980s applied for admission to the European Common Market. Without renouncing Islam, but building on the special relationship Turks have long maintained with the West, Turkey asked essentially to become part of the West. The application roused great anxieties in Western Europe,

The surge of feminism led to this women's rights rally in the United States in the 1970s.

concerned not only about Turkey's backwardness despite considerable recent industrial advance, but also about its strangeness. Possibly, however, the map of the Middle East was about to be redrawn once again, in terms of a division among separate identities.

The most important question for the future, however, involves the civilizational framework itself, as it has been elaborated over a 5000-year span, and whether it will persist. Civilizations, long functioning as forms that integrated more disparate and smaller regions to some degree, now may see a similar process pulling them into closer synchronism on a global basis.

THE FORCES OF INTERNATIONAL INTEGRATION

Previous crosscutting forces in world history, from agricultural technologies to the great world religions to new foodstuffs or inventions, such as the printing press, all promoted transformation *within* the separate civilizations. Even the rise of Western-dominated world trade did not fuse the civilizations into a single basic pattern. Arab or Western dominance reduced the autonomy of most civilizations only modestly, save in special cases such as Latin America where a prior civilization was substantially destroyed. Even in Latin America international contact brought massive change, but not full merger into Western cultural, political, or economic forms.

This balance, between separate regional and civilizational identities and international pressure, may now be changing decisively. The crosscutting forces of the past century or so have unquestionably stepped up the impact of international forces. One sign of this is the difficulty major societies have in trying to isolate themselves for whatever ideological reason. While the distinct features of individual civilizations can readily be discerned even in the way apparently common ideas, such as feminism, are handled, this may not always be the case. International movements of women, computer hackers, or soccer fans clearly override civilization boundaries, and they may gradually make those boundaries less distinct.

The internationalization of the world embraces a number of familiar ingredients. The speed of modern transportation and communication brings societies closer together, as does the rising volume of world trade. International artistic styles, particularly in urban architecture, have more vitality than ever before. The popularity of Western fads and fashions, from clothes to television to sports, leads to cultural contact among ordinary people in daily activities. In this sense the rise of the West continues to reverberate even as its relative dominance recedes. The diplomatic framework created for the world by the cold-war rivalry between the United States and Russia touches virtually every regional conflict in ways that no single international pattern ever did before. At the elite level, if not at the level of mass culture, the spread of scientific training cuts across cultural boundaries as no world religion ever did.

The fact of growing world contacts and a spreading array of global forces produced the understandable, but erroneous, attempt a generation ago to simplify recent world history into a study of how rapidly each society yielded to the inevitable impulse to become essentially Western. Thus serious scholars assumed that the Western version of modernization, including industrialization, mass education, democratic parliamentary politics, low birthrate, a consumer society, and greater equality for women, would take hold around the world. Each civilization could thus be measured by the speed at which it generated the standard modern (meaning Western) features. This analytical approach confused some undeniably common impulses, including the desire to alter traditional patterns in the name of nationalism and economic development, with homogeneity. And it did not, moreover, allow for the revived force of traditional values in societies such as Islam.

Still, if the simplest modernization model has proved clearly inaccurate, as the world's civilizations continue to handle certain common impulses distinctively, the sense that a new simplifying framework may be right around the corner persists. Will one of the new technologies taking hold, for example, do the trick? This is a crucial aspect of any postindustrial argument applied at a world level. The spread of computer networks is sometimes held to foreshadow new, common patterns of organization, research, and thinking, bringing far greater similarities to the societies involved than the rhythms of the factory or the farm ever did. Some advocates even believe that agricultural societies can shift to a computer system for production and communication without going through a classic industrial phase. The idea of a computer-generated system of organization providing new common ground among civilizations applies most readily to the West and Japan, where structural changes have already brought similarity without obliterating vital diversities. But technologies have cut across cultural divides before, and possibly the power and speed of the computer revolution will have even more sweeping impacts.

Common cultures generate other forces through which specific international communities are obliterating civilizational distinctions. Scientists and social scientists from almost every society can now meet and discuss common methods and common basic assumptions. Political or other divisions may complicate this harmony, but a fundamental international community exists with a shared frame of reference. At another level, soccer football and a few other sports elicit very similar enthusiasms around much of the world, even though they also express competition among the societies fielding the teams.

International business constitutes another integrating force. As Japanese and Korean firms join Americans and Europeans in setting up branches of production in almost every regional market, and as business leaders strive to imitate each other's organizational forms and labor policies, civilizational boundaries retreat considerably.

On several different fronts, then, the intensification of international networks, itself part of a long and varied process in world history, has proceeded to the point that various scholars could seriously see in the late 20th century the beginning of the end for the civilizational form. World diversities and inequalities will obviously persist amid new international communities, but coherent regional civilizations may gradually pull apart at the seams.

For the moment, separate civilizations are still very much alive. An equilibrium between distinct civilizations and unifying developments provides the most obvious interpretive basis for asking questions about the future. Increasingly rapid and intense contacts around the world have not created a single framework for world history. The pull of regional as well as civilizational loyalties remains strong. The revival of divisive allegiances in many parts of the world in the early 1990s surely reflects a human need to find a way to counterbalance the large, impersonal forces stemming from international developments. The world, in some ways growing smaller, is becoming no less complex. Distinctive traditions continue to modify, sometimes to reverse, seemingly powerful unifying forces, though these forces persist as well.

CONCLUSION

ASKING QUESTIONS

Whatever the vantage point, questions easily outweigh answers in contemplating the future. The power of particular models—such as Western democracy or mass culture—and the international power of industrial business and technology pose new challenges to particular civilizations. This is not a mere replay of earlier tensions between world currents and separate civilizational traditions. Yet continuities from the past—the surge of religious sentiment in Eastern Europe, for example—and possibly new needs for smaller-scale identities make predictions of an imminent triumph of a single world framework sheer folly. We know that tensions between international forces and needs, as well as the distinct reactions of individual societies, will shape the future, and that the tensions have some different ingredients in this newest period of world history from earlier periods. We know that the resultant interplay will be an important part of the future, along with new technologies and crucial environmental issues—for such interplay between contacts and divisiveness has shaped world history for many centuries. We do not know, however, what the precise results will be.

History contributes more than an understanding of the traditions and patterns that will continue to play some role in the future. Through analogies to past situations—such as earlier interactions between individual societies and a world economy—and through an understanding of changing trends, history improves our ability to ask good questions about the future and to evaluate the major types of forecasting available. We can count on the emerging world future to challenge our understanding, but we can also learn to use a grasp of the world past as a partial guide.

FURTHER READINGS

Several serious books (as well as many more simplistic popularized efforts) attempt to sketch the world's or the West's future. On the postindustrial society concept, see Daniel Bell's *The Coming of Post-Industrial Society* (1974). For other projections, consult R. L. Heilbroner's *An Inquiry into the Human Prospect* (1974) and L. Stavrianos's *The Promise of the Coming Dark Age* (1976).

On environment and resource issues, D. H. Meadows and D. L. Meadows's *The Limits of Growth* (1974) and L. Herbert's *Our Synthetic Environment* (1962) are worthwhile. M. ul Haq's *The Poverty Curtain: Choices for the Third World* (1976) and L. Solomon's *Multinational Corporations and the Emerging World Order* (1978) cover economic issues, in part from a non-Western perspective.

On military and diplomatic issues, A. Sakharov's *Progress Coexistence and Intellectual Freedom*, rev. ed. (1970), is an important statement by a Russian dissident; other useful texts include S. Hoffman's *Primacy or World Order. American Foreign Policy Since the Cold War* (1978),

S. Melman's *The Peace Race* (1961), and W. Epstein's *The Last Chance. Nuclear Proliferation and Arms Control* (1976).

On a leading social issue, see P. Hudson's *Third World Women Speak Out* (1979). A major interpretation of the 20th century world is Theodore von Laue's *The World Revolution of Westernization* (1989).

Glossary

Abbas the Great: Safavid ruler from 1587 to 1629; extended Safavid domain to greatest extent; created slave regiments based on captured Russians who monopolized firearms within Safavid armies; incorporated Western military technology. (26)

Abdallahi, Khalifa: Successor of Muhammad Achmad as leader of Mahdists in Sudan; established state in Sudan; defeated by British General Kitchener in 1898. (32)

Abduh, Muhammad: Disciple of al-Afghani; Muslim thinker at end of the 19th century; stressed need for adoption of Western scientific learning and technology, importance of tradition of rational inquiry. (32)

Abdul Hamid: Ottoman sultan who attempted to return to despotic absolutism during reign from 1878 to 1908; nullified constitution and restricted civil liberties; deposed in coup in 1908. (32)

absolute monarchy: Concept of government developed during rise of nation-states in western Europe during the 17th century; featured monarchs who passed laws without parliaments, appointed professionalized armies and bureaucracies, established state churches, imposed state economic policies. (22)

African National Congress: Black political organization within South Africa; pressed for end to policies of apartheid; sought open democracy leading to black majority rule; until the 1990s declared illegal in South Africa. (40)

Afrikaner National party: Emerged as the majority party in the all-white South African legislature after 1948; advocated complete independence from Britain; favored a rigid system of racial segregation called apartheid. (39)

Akbar: Son and successor of Humayan; oversaw building of military and administrative systems that became typical of Mughal rule in India; pursued policy of cooperation with Hindu princes; attempted to create new religion to bind Muslim and Hindu populations of India. (26)

al-Afghani: Muslim thinker at the end of the 19th century; stressed need for adoption of Western scientific learning and technology, importance of tradition of rational inquiry. (32)

Ali, Muhammad: Won power struggle in Egypt following fall of Mamluks; established mastery of all of Egypt by 1811; introduced effective army based on Western tactics and supply; by 1830s able to challenge Ottoman government in Constantinople; died in 1848. (32)

Allende, Salvador: President of Chile; nationalized industries and banks; sponsored peasant and worker expropriations of lands and foreign-owned factories; overthrown in 1973 by revolt of Chilean military with the support of the United States. (38)

Alliance for Progress: Begun in 1961 by the United States to develop Latin America as an alternative to radical political solutions; enjoyed only limited success; failure of development programs led to renewal of direct intervention. (38)

Álvares Cabral, Pedro: Portuguese leader of an expedition to India; blown off course in 1500 and landed in Brazil. (25)

Amaru, Tupac: Mestizo leader of Indian revolt in Peru; supported by many among lower social classes; revolt eventually failed because of Creole fears of real social revolution. (25)

American Civil War: Fought from 1861 to 1865; first application of Industrial Revolution to warfare; resulted in abolition of slavery in the United States and reunification of North and South. (29)

American exceptionalism: Historical argument that the development of the United States was largely individualistic; contact with western Europe was incidental to the larger development of the United States on its own terms. (29)

American Revolution: Rebellion of English American colonies along Atlantic seaboard between 1775 and 1783; resulted in independence for former British colonies, eventual formation of United States of America. (29)

amigos del país: Clubs and associations dedicated to improvements and reform in Spanish colonies; flourished during the 18th century; called for material improvements rather than political reform. (25)

anarchists: Political groups that sought the abolition of all formal government; particularly prevalent in Russia; opposed tsarist autocracy; eventually became a terrorist movement responsible for assassination of Alexander II in 1881. (33)

Anglican church: Form of Protestantism set up in England after 1534; established by Henry VIII with himself as head at least in part to obtain a divorce from his first wife; became increasingly Protestant following Henry's death. (22)

Anschluss: Hitler's union of Germany with the German-speaking population of Austria; actually took place in 1938, despite complaint of other European nations. (34)

apartheid: Policy of strict racial segregation imposed in South Africa to permit the continued dominance of whites politically and economically. (40)

appeasement: Policy of Neville Chamberlain, British prime minister; particularly applied to Munich Conference agreements; hoped to preserve peace in the face of German aggression; failed when Hitler invaded Poland in 1939. (34)

Arevalo, Juan José: Elected president of Guatemala in 1944; began series of Socialist reforms including land reform; Nationalist program directed against foreign-owned companies such as United Fruit Company. (38)

Argentine Republic: Replaced state of Buenos Aires in 1862; result of compromise between centralists and federalists. (31)

Asante Empire: Established in Gold Coast among Akan people settled around Kumasi; dominated by Oyoko clan; many clans linked under Osei Tutu after 1650. (27)

asantehene: Title taken by ruler of Asante Empire; supreme civil and religious leader; authority symbolized by golden stool. (27)

Asian sea trading network: Prior to intervention of Europeans consisted of three zones: Arab zone based on glass, carpets, and tapestries; India with cotton textiles; and China with paper, porcelain, and silks. (28)

Atlantic Charter of 1941: Treaty between the United States and Britain creating an alliance; included a clause that recognized the right of all people to choose the form of government under which they live; indicated sympathy for decolonization. (39)

Atlantic colonies: British colonies in North America; originally restricted to coastline of Atlantic Ocean from New England to Georgia. (23)

audiencia: Royal court of appeals established in Spanish colonies of New World; there were ten in each viceroyalty; part of colonial administrative system; staffed by professional magistrates. (25)

Aurangzeb: Son and successor of Shah Jahan in Mughal India; determined to extend Mughal control over whole of subcontinent; wished to purify Islam of Hindu influences; incessant warfare exhausted empire despite military successes; died in 1707. (26)

Babur: Founder of Mughal dynasty in India; descended from Turkic warriors; first led invasion of India in 1526; died in 1530. (26)

Balboa: First Spanish captain to begin settlement on the mainland of Mesoamerica in 1509; initial settlement eventually led to conquest of Aztec and Inca empires by other captains. (23)

Balfour Declaration: British minister's promise of support for the establishment of Jewish settlement in Palestine during the First World War; issued in 1917. (34)

Balkan nationalism: Movements to create independent nations within the Balkan possessions of the Ottoman Empire; provoked a series of crises between the European alliance system; eventually led to the First World War. (29)

Banana Republics: Term given to conservative governments supported or created by the United States in Latin America; believed to be either corrupt or subservient to U.S. interests. (38)

Bangladesh: Founded as an independent nation in 1972; formerly East Pakistan. (40)

banner armies: Eight armies of the Manchu tribes identified by separate flags; created by Nurhaci in early 17th century; utilized to defeat Ming emperor and establish Qing dynasty. (32)

Batavia: Dutch fortress located after 1620 on the island of Java. (28)

Batista, Fulgencio: Dictator of Cuba from 1934 to 1944; returned to presidency in 1952; ousted from government by revolution led by Fidel Castro. (38)

Belgian Revolution of 1830: Produced Belgian independence from the Dutch; established a liberal constitutional monarchy. (29)

Berlin Wall: Built in 1961 to halt the flow of immigration from East Berlin to West Berlin; immigration in response to lack of consumer goods, close Soviet control of economy, failed workers' uprising in 1953. (36)

Biafra: Founded as an independent nation in eastern Nigeria where the Ibo people were most numerous; suppressed as an independent state and reincorporated into Nigeria in 1970. (40)

Bismarck, Otto von: Conservative prime minister of Prussia; architect of German unification under Prussian king in 1870; utilized liberal reforms to attract support for conservative causes. (29)

blitzkrieg: German term for lightning warfare; involved rapid movement of troops, tanks, and mechanized carriers; resulted in early German victories over Belgium, Holland, and France. (34)

Boer republics: Transvaal and Orange Free State; established to assert independence of Boers from British colonial government in Cape Colony in 1850s; discovery of diamonds and precious metals caused British migration into the Boer areas in 1860s. (30)

Boer War: Fought between 1899 and 1902 over the continued independence of Boer republics; resulted in British victory, but began the process of decolonization in South Africa. (30)

Boers: Dutch settlers in Cape Colony. (23)

Bolívar, Simon: Creole military officer in northern South America; won series of victories in Venezuela, Colombia, and Ecuador between 1817 and 1822; military success led to creation of independent state of Gran Colombia. (31)

Bolsheviks: Literally the majority party; the most radical branch of the Russian Marxist movement; led by V. I. Lenin and dedicated to his concept of social revolution; actually a minority in the Russian Marxist political scheme. (33)

Bonaparte, Joseph: Brother of Napoleon; placed on Spanish throne during Napoleonic Wars; disruption of Spanish monarchy contributed to Latin-American movements for liberation. (31)

Bonaparte, Napoleon: Rose within the French army during the wars of the French Revolution; eventually became general; led a coup that ended the French Revolution and established the French Empire under his rule; defeated and deposed in 1815. (29)

Boxer Rebellion: Popular outburst aimed at expelling foreigners from China; failed due to intervention of armies of Western powers in China; defeat enhanced control of Europeans and the power of provincial officials. (32)

Brest-Litovsk: Treaty signed between the revolutionary government of Russia and Germany in March 1918; Russia withdrew from the First World War and granted substantial territories to Germany in return for peace. (34)

British East India Company: Joint stock company that obtained government monopoly over trade in India; acted as virtually independent government in regions it claimed. (23)

British Raj: Government of the British East India Company; developed as a result of the rivalry between France and Britain in India. (30)

Calcutta: Headquarters of British East

India Company in Bengal in Indian subcontinent; located on Ganges; captured in 1756 during early part of Seven Years' War; later became administrative center for all of Bengal. (23)

Calvin, Jean: French Protestant who stressed doctrine of predestination; established center of his group at Swiss canton of Geneva; encouraged ideas of wider access to government, wider public education; spread from Switzerland to northern Europe and North America. (22)

candomble: African religious ideas and practices in Brazil, particularly among the Yoruba people. (27)

Canton: One of two ports in which Europeans were permitted to trade in China during the Ming dynasty. (28)

Cape Colony: Dutch colony established at Cape of Good Hope in 1652 initially to provide a coastal station for the Dutch seaborne empire; by 1770 settlements had expanded sufficiently to come into conflict with Bantus. (23)

Cape of Good Hope: Southern tip of Africa; first circumnavigated in 1488 by Portuguese in search of direct route to India. (23)

captaincies: Strips of land along Brazilian coast granted to minor Portuguese nobles for development; enjoyed limited success in developing the colony. (25)

caravels: Slender, long-hulled vessels utilized by Portuguese; highly maneuverable and able to sail against the wind; key to development of Portuguese trade empire in Asia. (28)

Cárdenas, Lázaro: President of Mexico from 1934 to 1940; responsible for redistribution of land, primarily to create ejidos or communal farms; also began program of primary and rural education. (38)

Caribbean: First area of Spanish exploration and settlement; served as experimental region for nature of Spanish colonial experience; encomienda, system of colonial government initiated here. (25)

Casa de Contratación: Spanish Board of Trade operated out of Seville; regularized commerce with New World, supplied colonial provisions. (25)

castas: People of mixed origin in Spanish colonial society; relegated to secondary status in social system; constituted potentially revolutionary group. (25)

Castro, Fidel: Cuban revolutionary; overthrew dictator Fulgencio Batista in 1958; initiated series of reforms to establish Socialist reforms; came to depend almost exclusively on USSR. (38)

Catherine the Great: German-born Russian tsarina; ruled after assassination of her husband; gave appearance of Enlightened rule; accepted Western cultural influence; converted nobility to service aristocracy by granting them new power over peasantry. (24)

Catholic Reformation: Restatement of Orthodox Catholic beliefs in response to Protestant Reformation; established councils that revived Catholic doctrine and refuted Protestant beliefs. (22)

caudillos: Independent leaders who dominated local areas by force in defiance of national policies; sometimes seized the national governments to impose their concept of rule; typical throughout newly independent countries of Latin America. (31)

Cavour, Count Camillo di: Architect of Italian unification in 1858; formed an alliance with France to attack Austrian control of northern Italy; resulted in creation of constitutional monarchy under Piedmontese king. (29)

centralists: Those Latin-American politicians who wished to create strong, centralized national governments with broad powers; often supported by those politicians who described themselves as conservatives. (31)

Chaldiran: Site of battle between Safavids and Ottomans in 1514; Safavids severely defeated by Ottomans; checked western advance of Safavid Empire. (26)

Charles III: Spanish enlightened monarch; ruled from 1759 to 1788; instituted fiscal, administrative, and military reforms in Spain and its empire. (25)

Chartist movement: Attempt on the part of artisans and workers in Britain to gain the vote during the 1840s; demands for reform beyond the Reform Act of 1832 were incorporated into a series of petitions; the movement failed. (29)

Chiang Ching-kuo: Son and successor of Chiang Kai-shek as ruler of Taiwanese government in 1978; continued authoritarian government; attempted to lessen gap between followers of his father and indigenous islanders. (37)

Chongzhen: Last of the Ming emperors; committed suicide in 1644 in the face of a Jurchen invasion of the Forbidden City at Beijing. (28)

Christian Democratic movement: Political movement common to many Western European nations after World War II; wedded to democratic institutions and moderate social reform. (35)

Churchill, Winston: British prime minister during World War II; responsible for British resistance to German air assaults. (34)

cientificos: Advisors of government of Porfirio Díaz who were strongly influenced by positivist ideas; permitted government to project image of modernization. (31)

Cixi: Ultraconservative dowager empress who dominated the last decades of the Qing dynasty; supported Boxer Rebellion in 1898 as a means of driving out Westerners. (32)

Clive, Robert: Architect of British victory at Plassey; established foundations of British Raj in northern India. (30)

co-optive democracies: Governments that offered forms of democratic government but little of the substance of democracy to the majority of the population; typical in Latin America in the 20th century. (38)

cold war: The state of relations between the United States and its allies and the Soviet Union and its allies between the end of World War II to 1990; based on creation of political spheres of influence and a nuclear arms race rather than actual warfare. (35)

collectivization: Creation of large, state-run farms rather than individual holdings; allowed more efficient control over peasants; part of Stalin's economic and political planning; occasionally adopted in other Communist regimes. (36)

Colombian exchange: Biological and ecological exchange that took place following Spanish establishment of colonies in New World; peoples of Europe and Africa came to New World; animals, plants, and diseases of two hemispheres transferred. (25)

Columbus, Christopher: Genoese captain in service of king and queen of Castile and Aragon; successfully sailed to New World and returned in 1492; initiated European discoveries in Americas. (23)

Comintern: International office of communism under USSR dominance established to encourage the formation of Communist parties in Western Europe. (36)

commercio libre: Policy established during reign of Charles III; opened trade in ports of Spain and Indies to all Spanish merchants; undercut monopoly of consulados. (25)

Communist party of Vietnam: Originally a wing of the nationalist movement; became primary nationalist party after decline of VNQDD in 1929; led in late 1920s by Nguyen Ai Quoc, alias Ho Chi Minh. (41)

compradors: Wealthy new group of Chinese merchants under the Qing dynasty; specialized in the import-export trade on China's south coast; one of the major links between China and the outside world. (32)

Comte, Auguste: French philosopher; founder of positivism, a philosophy that stressed observation and scientific approaches to the problems of society. (31)

Comunero Revolt: One of popular revolts against Spanish colonial rule in New Granada (Colombia) in 1781; suppressed due to divisions among rebels. (25)

Congress of Soviets: Lenin's parliamentary institution based on the soviets and Bolshevik domination; replaced the initial parliament dominated by the Social Revolutionary party. (36)

Congress of Vienna: Meeting in the aftermath of the Napoleonic Wars to restore political stability in Europe; at first attempted to restore status quo. (33)

consulado: Merchant guild of Seville; enjoyed virtual monopoly rights over goods shipped to America and handled much of the silver received in return. (25)

contested settler colonies: Featured large-scale European settlement despite the existence of large, indigenous populations; generally resulted in clashes over land rights, resource control, social status, and differences in culture; typical of South Africa, New Zealand, Kenya, Algeria, and Hawaii. (30)

Cook, Captain James: Made voyages to Hawaii from 1777 to 1779 resulting in opening of islands to the West; convinced Kamehameha to establish unified kingdom in the islands. (30)

Copernicus: Polish monk and astronomer; disproved Hellenistic belief that the earth was at the center of the universe. (22)

core nations: Nations, usually European, that enjoyed profit from world economy; controlled international banking and commercial services such as shipping; exported manufactured goods for raw materials. (23)

Cornwallis, Lord Charles: Reformer of the East India Company administration of India in 1790s; reduced power of local British administrators, checked widespread corruption. (30)

Coronado, Francisco Vázquez de: Leader of Spanish expedition into northern frontier region of New Spain; entered what is now United States in search of mythical cities of gold. (25)

corporatism: Political ideology that emphasized the organic nature of society and made the state a mediator, adjusting the interests of different social groups; appealed to conservative groups in Latin-American societies and to the military. (38)

Cortés, Hernán: Led expedition of 600 to coast of Mexico in 1519; conquistador responsible for defeat of Aztec Empire; captured Tenochtitlan. (25)

cossacks: Peasants recruited to migrate to newly seized lands in Russia, particularly in south; combined agriculture with military conquests; spurred additional frontier conquests and settlements. (24)

Council of People's Commissars: Government council composed of representatives from soviets across Russia and headed by Lenin; form of government initially established after November 1917. (36)

Council of the Indies: Body within the Castilian government that issued all laws and advised king on all matters dealing with the Spanish colonies of the New World. (25)

Creole slaves: American-born descendants of "salt water" slaves; result of sexual exploitation of slave women or process of miscegenation. (27)

Creoles: Whites born in the New World; dominated local economies; ranked just beneath peninsulares. (25)

Crimean War: Fought between 1854 and 1856; began as Russian attempt to attack Ottoman Empire; opposed by France and Britain as well; resulted in Russian defeat in the face of Western industrial technology; led to Russian reforms under Tsar Alexander II. (33)

Cristeros: Conservative peasant movement in Mexico during the 1920s; most active in central Mexico; attempted to halt slide toward secularism; movement resulted in armed violence. (38)

Cromer, Lord: British adviser in khedival Egypt; pushed for economic reforms that reduced but failed to eliminate the debts of the khedival regime. (39)

cubist movement: 20th-century art style; best represented by Spanish artist Pablo Picasso; rendered familiar objects as geometrical shapes. (35)

Cultural Revolution: Movement initiated in 1965 by Mao Zedong to restore his dominance over pragmatists; used mobs to ridicule Mao's political rivals; campaign was called off in 1968. (41)

da Gama, Vasco: Portuguese captain who first reached India in 1497; established early Portuguese dominance in Indian Ocean. (23)

Dahomey: Kingdom developed among Fon or Aja peoples in 17th century; center at Abomey 70 miles from coast; under King Agaja expanded to control coastline and port of Whydah by 1727; accepted Western firearms and goods in return for African slaves. (27)

Darwin, Charles: Biologist who developed theory of evolution of species; argued that all living species evolved into their present form through the ability to adapt in a struggle for survival. (29)

De la Cruz, Sor Juana Inés: Author, poet, and musician of New Spain; eventually gave up secular concerns to concentrate on spiritual matters. (25)

Decembrist uprising: Political revolt in Russia in 1825; led by middle-level army officers who advocated reforms; put down by Tsar Nicholas I. (33)

Declaration of the Rights of Man and the Citizen: Adopted during the liberal phase of the French Revolution; stated the fundamental equality of all French citizens; later became a political source for other liberal movements. (29)

Deism: Concept of God current during the scientific revolution; role of divinity was to set natural laws in motion, not to regulate once process was begun. (22)

dependency theory: Belief that development and underdevelopment were not stages but part of the same process; that development and growth of some areas such as western Europe were achieved at the expense of underdevelopment of dependent regions such as Latin America. (31)

dependent economic zones: Those regions within the world economy that produced raw materials; dependent on European markets and shipping; tendency to build system of forced, inexpensive labor. (23)

Descartes, Rene: Established importance of skeptical review of all received wisdom; argued that human reason could then develop laws that would explain the fundamental workings of nature. (22)

Deshima: Island port in Nagasaki Bay; only port open to non-Japanese after closure of the islands in the 1640s; only Chinese and Dutch ships were permitted to enter. (28)

Díaz, Porfirio: One of Juárez's generals; elected president of Mexico in 1876; dominated Mexican politics for 35 years; imposed strong central government. (31)

Diem, Ngo Dinh: Political leader of southern Vietnam established as president with the support of the United States in the 1950s; opposed Communist government of northern Vietnam; overthrown by military coup supported by the United States. (41)

Dien Bien Phu: Most significant victory of the Viet Minh over French colonial forces in 1954; gave the Viet Minh control of northern portions of Vietnam. (41)

Diet: Japanese parliament established as part of the new constitution of 1889; part of Meiji reforms; could pass laws and approve budgets; able to advise government, but not to control it. (33)

Din-i-Ilahi: Religion initiated by Akbar in Mughal India; blended elements of the many faiths of the subcontinent; key to efforts to reconcile Hindus and Muslims in India; failed to accomplish reconciliation of religions. (26)

Dinshawai incident: Clash between British soldiers and Egyptian villagers in 1906; arose over hunting accident along Nile River where wife of prayer leader of mosque was accidentally shot by army officers hunting pigeons; led to Egyptian protest movement. (39)

Disraeli, Benjamin: Leading conservative political figure in Britain in the second half of the 19th century; took initiative of granting vote to working-class males in 1867; typical of conservative politician making use of popular politics. (29)

Duarte, Eva: Also known as Evita Perón; first wife of Juan Perón; became public spokesperson for Perón among the poor until her death in 1952. (38)

duma: A national parliament created in Russia in the aftermath of the Revolution of 1905; progressively stripped of power during the reign of Tsar Nicholas II; failed to forestall further revolution. (33)

Dutch East India Company: Joint stock company that obtained government monopoly over trade in Asia; acted as virtually independent government in regions it claimed. (23)

Dutch Studies: Group of Japanese scholars interested in implications of Western science and technology beginning in the 18th century; urged freer exchange with West; based studies on few Dutch texts available in Japan. (33)

Dutch trading empire: Based on control of fortified towns and factories, warships on patrol, and monopoly control of limited number of products—particularly spices. (28)

eastern bloc: Nations that remained favorable to the Soviet Union in Eastern Europe—particularly Poland, Czechoslovakia, Bulgaria, Rumania, and Hungary. (35)

eastern front: Most mobile of the fronts established during the First World War; lacked trench warfare because of length of front extending from Baltic to southern Russia; after early successes, military defeats led to downfall of the tsarist government in Russia. (34)

edict of Nantes: Grant of tolerance to Protestants in France in 1598; granted only after lengthy civil war between Catholic and Protestant factions. (22)

Edo: Tokugawa capital city; modern-day Tokyo; center of the Tokugawa shogunate. (28)

effendi: Class of prosperous business and professional urban families in khedival Egypt; as a class generally favored Egyptian independence. (39)

Einstein, Albert: Developed mathematical theories to explain the behavior of planetary motion and the movement of electrical particles; after 1900 issued theory of relativity. (29)

El Mina: Most important of early Portuguese trading factories in forest zone of Africa. (27)

emancipation of the serfs: Tsar Alexander II ended rigorous serfdom in Russia in 1861; serfs obtained no political rights; required to stay in villages until they could repay aristocracy for land. (33)

encomendero: Holder of an encomienda; able to use Indians as workers or to tax them. (25)

encomienda: Grants of Indian laborers made to Spanish conquerors and settlers in Mesoamerica and South America; basis for earliest forms of coerced labor in Spanish colonies. (25)

English Civil War: Conflict from 1640 to 1660; featured religious disputes mixed with constitutional issues concerning the powers of the monarchy; ended with restoration of the monarchy in 1660 following execution of previous king. (22)

Enlightenment: Intellectual movement centered in France during the 18th century; featured scientific advance, application of scientific methods to study of human society; belief that rational laws could describe social behavior. (22)

European Economic Community: The Common Market; an alliance of six European nations (Germany, France, Italy, Belgium, Luxembourg, and the Netherlands) set up to begin creation of a single economic entity across national boundaries in 1958; later joined by Britain, Ireland, Denmark, Greece, Spain, and Portugal. (35)

factories: Portuguese trading fortresses and compounds with resident merchants; utilized throughout Portuguese trading empire to assure secure landing places and commerce. (27)

factory system: Not to be confused with the fortified ports of the commercial revolution; intensification of all processes of production at a single site during the Industrial Revolution; involved greater organization of labor and firmer discipline. (29)

fascism: Political philosophy that became predominant in Italy and then Germany during the 1920s and 1930s; attacked weakness of democracy, corruption of capitalism; promised vigorous foreign and military programs; undertook state control of economy to reduce social friction. (35)

fazendas: Coffee estates that spread within interior of Brazil between 1840 and 1860; created major export commodity for Brazilian trade; led to intensification of slavery in Brazil. (31)

Federal Republic of Germany: What became the nation of West Germany; created by the merging of the zones of occupation held by France, Britain, and the United States. (35)

federalists: Those Latin-American politicians who wanted policies, especially fiscal and commercial regulations, to be set by regional governments rather than centralized national administrations; often supported by those politicians who described themselves as liberals. (31)

feminist movements: Sought various legal and economic gains for women, including equal access to professions and higher education; came to concentrate on right to vote; won support particularly from middle-class women; more active in western Europe at the end of the 19th century. (29)

Ferdinand of Aragon: Along with Isabella of Castile, monarch of largest Christian kingdoms in Iberia; marriage to Isabella created united Spain; responsible for reconquest of Granada, initiation of exploration of New World. (25)

final solution: Hitler's term for the genocide of European Jews; led to incarceration of millions of Jews in concentration camps and their eventual slaughter in gas chambers devised for mass executions. (34)

five-year plans: Stalin's plans to hasten industrialization of USSR; constructed massive factories in metallurgy, mining, and electric power; led to massive state-planned industrialization at cost of availability of consumer products. (36)

Francia, Dr. José Rodríguez de: Ruler of independent Paraguay; ruled country as dictator until 1840. (31)

Francis I: King of France; regarded as Renaissance monarch; patron of arts, imposed new controls on Catholic church; ally of Ottoman sultan against holy Roman emperor. (22)

Frederick the Great: Prussian king; attempted to introduce Enlightenment reforms into Germany; built on military and bureaucratic foundations of his predecessors; introduced freedom of religion; increased state control of economy. (22)

Free Officers movement: Military nationalist movement in Egypt founded in the 1930s; often allied with the Muslim Brotherhood; led coup to seize Egyptian government from khedive in July 1952. (40)

French Revolution: Revolution in France between 1789 and 1800; resulted in temporary overthrow of Bourbon monarchy; ended with establishment of French Empire under Napoleon Bonaparte; source of many liberal movements and constitutions in Europe. (29)

French Revolution of 1830: Second rebellion against Bourbon monarchy; essentially a liberal movement resulting in the creation of a bourgeois government under a moderate monarchy. (29)

French Revolution of 1848: Overthrew the monarchy established in 1830; briefly established a democratic republic; failure of the republic led to the reestablishment of the French Empire under Napoleon III in 1850. (29)

Freud, Sigmund: Viennese physician; developed theories of the workings of the human unconscious; argued that behavior is determined by impulses. (29)

Fulani: Pastoral people of western Sudan; adopted purifying Sufi variant of Islam; under Usuman Dan Fodio in 1804, launched revolt against Hausa kingdoms; established state centered on Sokoto. (27)

Galileo: Published Copernicus's findings; added own discoveries concerning laws of gravity and planetary motion; condemned by the Catholic church for his work. (22)

galleons: Large, heavily armed ships used to carry silver from New World colonies to Spain; basis for convoy system utilized by Spain for transportation of bullion. (25)

Gálvez, José de: Spanish Minister of the Indies and chief architect of colonial reform; moved to eliminate Creoles from upper bureaucracy of the colonies; created intendants for local government. (25)

Gandhi, Mohandas K.: Western-educated Indian lawyer and nationalist politician; took on attributes of traditional Indian holy man; stressed nonviolent tactics such as boycotts, strikes, and noncooperation; tactics eventually led to Indian independence; assassinated by Hindu fanatic shortly after Indian independence was achieved. (39)

Gang of Four: Jiang Qing and four political allies who attempted to seize control of Communist government in China from the pragmatists; arrested and sentenced to life imprisonment in 1976 following Mao Zedong's death. (41)

gauchos: Bands of mounted rural workers in the region of the Rio de la Plata; aided local caudillos in splitting apart the United Provinces of the Rio de la Plata after 1816. (31)

Giap, General Vo Nguyen: Chief military commander of the Viet Minh; architect of the Vietnamese victory over the French at Dien Bien Phu in 1954. (41)

Glorious Revolution: English overthrow of James II in 1688; resulted in affirmation of parliament as having basic sovereignty over the king. (22)

Goa: Portuguese factory or fortified trade town located on western India coast; sites for forcible entry into Asian sea trade network. (28)

Good Neighbor Policy: Established by Franklin D. Roosevelt for dealing with Latin America in 1933; intended to halt direct intervention in Latin-American politics. (38)

Gorbachev, Mikhail: USSR ruler after 1985; renewed attacks on Stalinism; urged reduction in nuclear armament; proclaimed policies of glasnost and perestroika. (36)

Gordon, General George: English commander in Sudan and leader of antislavery effort at khedival court of Egypt; killed at Khartoum by forces of Mahdi. (32)

Government of India Act of 1935: British agreed to retain control of the central administration in return for turning over the provincial governments to Indian leaders chosen by expanded electorate. (39)

Gran Colombia: Independent state created in South America as result of military successes of Simon Bolívar; existed only until 1830 at which time Colombia, Venezuela, and Ecuador became separate nations. (31)

Great Depression: International economic crisis following the First World War; said to have begun with collapse of American stock market in 1929; actual causes began with collapse of agricultural prices in 1920s; included collapse of banking houses in the United States and western Europe, massive unemployment; contradicted optimistic assumptions of 19th century. (34)

Great Leap Forward: Economic policy of Mao Zedong introduced in 1958; proposed industrialization of small-scale projects integrated into peasant communes; led to economic disaster; ended in 1960. (41)

Great Mahele: Hawaiian edict issued in 1848; imposed Western concept of property on Hawaiian land previously shared among Hawaiians; much of private property sold off to Western commercial interests by Hawaiian monarchy. (30)

great trek: Movement of Boer settlers in Cape Colony of southern Africa to escape influence of British colonial government in 1834; led to settlement of regions north of Orange River and Natal. (27)

Greek Revolution: Rebellion in Greece against the Ottoman Empire in 1820; key step in gradually dismantling the Ottoman Empire in the Balkans. (29)

Green Revolution: Attempt to introduce improved seed strains, fertilizers, and irrigation as a means of producing higher yields in crops such as rice, wheat, and corn; particularly important in the densely populated countries of Asia. (40)

guano: Bird droppings utilized as fertilizer; exported from Peru as a major item of trade between 1850 and 1880; income from trade permitted end to Indian tribute and abolition of slavery. (31)

Guevara, Ernesto "Che": Argentine revolutionary; aided Fidel Castro in overthrow of Fulgencio Batista; died while directing guerrilla movement in Bolivia in 1967. (38)

guillotine: Introduced as a method of humane execution; utilized to execute thousands during the most radical phase of the French Revolution known as the Reign of Terror. (29)

Guomindang: Chinese Nationalist party founded by Sun Yat-sen in 1919; drew support from local warlords and Chinese criminal underworld; initially forged alliance with Communists in 1924; dominated by Chiang Kai-shek after 1925. (41)

Gutenberg, Johannes: Introduced movable type to western Europe in 15th century; credited with greatly expanded availability of printed books and pamphlets. (22)

Habsburg, Archduke Maximilian von: Proclaimed emperor of Mexico following intervention of France in 1862; ruled until overthrow and execution by liberal revolutionaries under Benito Juárez in 1867. (31)

haciendas: Rural estates in Spanish colonies in New World; produced agricultural products for consumers in America; basis of wealth and power for local aristocracy. (25)

Harvey, John: English physician who demonstrated the circular movement of blood in animals, function of heart as pump. (22)

Haya de la Torre, Victor Raul: Peruvian politician; founder of APRA (American Popular Revolutionary Alliance) in 1924; aimed at establishing an international party throughout Western Hemisphere. (38)

Henry the Navigator: Portuguese prince responsible for direction of series of expeditions along the African coast in the 15th century; marked beginning of western European expansion. (23, 27)

Herzl, Theodor: Austrian journalist and Zionist; formed World Zionist Organization in 1897; promoted Jewish migration to Palestine and the formation of a Jewish state. (39)

Hidalgo, Father Miguel de: Mexican priest who established independence movement among Indians and mestizos in 1810; despite early victories, was captured and executed. (31)

Hideyoshi, Toyotomi: General under Nobunaga; succeeded as leading military power in central Japan; continued efforts to break power of daimyos; constructed series of alliances that made him military master of Japan in 1590; died in 1598. (28)

Hiroshima: One of two Japanese cities on which the United States dropped atomic bombs in 1945; devastation of these cities caused Japanese surrender without invasion of home islands. (34)

Hispaniola: First island in Caribbean settled by Spaniards; settlement founded by Columbus on second voyage to New World; Spanish base of operations for further discoveries in New World. (25)

Hitler, Adolf: Nazi leader of fascist Germany from 1933 to his suicide in 1945; created a strongly centralized state in Germany; eliminated all rivals; launched Germany on aggressive foreign policy leading to World War II; responsible for attempted genocide of European Jews. (34)

Ho Chi Minh: Communist nationalist leader of Vietnam; Western-educated; devoted to violent revolution against French colonialism; shifted to Maoist strategy of basing revolution on peasantry during 1930s; defeated France by 1954; led war to reunite Vietnam against United States. (41)

Holocaust: Term for Hitler's attempted genocide of European Jews during World War II; resulted in deaths of six million Jews. (34)

Holy Alliance: Alliance between Russia, Prussia, and Austria in defense of religion and the established order; formed at Congress of Vienna by most conservative monarchies of Europe. (33)

homelands: Areas in South Africa designated for ethno-linguistic groups within the black African population; such areas tend to be overpopulated and poverty stricken. (40)

Hong Kong: British colony on Chinese mainland; major commercial center; agreement reached between Britain and People's Republic of China will return colony to China in 1999. (37)

Hong Xiuquan: Leader of the Taiping rebellion; converted to specifically Chinese form of Christianity; attacked traditional Confucian teachings of Chinese elite. (32)

Hongwu: First Ming emperor in 1368; originally of peasant lineage; original name Zhu Yuanzhang; drove out Mongol influence; restored position of scholar-gentry. (28)

Huancavelica: Location of greatest deposit of mercury in South America; aided in American silver production; linked with Potosí. (25)

Huerta, Victoriano: Sought to reestablish centralized dictatorship in Mexico following the removal of Madero in 1913; forced from power in 1914 by Villa and Zapata. (38)

human rights: Certain universal rights enjoyed by all people because these are justified by a moral standard that stands above the laws of any individual nation. (38)

humanism: Focus on humankind as center of intellectual and artistic endeavor; method of study that emphasized the superiority of classical forms over medieval styles, in particular the study of ancient languages. (22)

Humayan: Son and successor of Babur; expelled from India in 1540, but restored Mughal rule by 1556; died shortly thereafter. (26)

Hussein, Saddam: Military ruler of Iraq; led Iraq in ten-year war with Iran; attempted to annex Kuwait into Iraq in 1990; defeated by coalition of American, European, and Arabic forces in 1991 in Persian Gulf War. (40)

Hyundai: Example of huge industrial groups that wield great power in modern Korea; virtually governed Korea's southeastern coast; vertical economic organization with ships, supertankers, factories, schools, and housing units. (37)

Ieyasu, Tokugawa: Vassal of Toyotomi Hideyoshi; succeeded him as most powerful military figure in Japan; granted title of shogun in 1603 and established Tokugawa shogunate; established political unity in Japan. (28)

imams: According to Shi'ism, rulers who could trace descent from Ali. (26)

import substitution industrialization: Typical of Latin-American economies; production of products during the 20th century that had previously been imported; led to light industrialization. (38)

Indian Congress party: Grew out of regional associations of Western-educated Indians; originally centered in cities of Bombay, Poona, Calcutta, and Madras; became political party in 1885; focus of nationalist movement in India; governed through most of postcolonial period. (39)

Indies piece: Term utilized within the complex exchange system established by the Spanish for African trade; referred to the value of an adult male slave. (27)

Industrial Revolution: Series of changes in economy of western Europe between 1740 and 20th century; stimulated by rapid population growth, increase in agricultural productivity, commercial revolution of 17th century, and development of new means of transportation; in essence involved technological change and the application of machines to the process of production. (29)

instrumentalist reaction: Workers began during the Industrial Revolution to regard their jobs not as ends, but as vehicles for other goals; workers learned to bargain for better pay and shorter hours. (29)

intelligentsia: Russian term denoting articulate intellectuals as a class; group bent on radical change in Russian political and social system; wished to maintain a Russian culture distinct from the West. (33)

internationalization: Idea that peoples should unite across national boundaries; gained popularity during the mid-19th century; led to establishment of international Red Cross, Telegraphic Union, Postal Union, series of international fairs. (34)

iron curtain: Phrase coined by Winston Churchill to describe the division between free and repressed societies taking shape in Europe after 1946. (35)

Isabella of Castile: Along with Ferdinand of Aragon, monarch of largest Christian kingdoms in Iberia; marriage to Ferdinand created united Spain; responsible for reconquest of Granada, initiation of exploration of New World. (25)

Isandhlwana: Location of battle fought in 1879 between the British and Zulu armies in South Africa; resulted in defeat of British; one of few victories of African forces over western Europeans. (30)

Isfahan: Safavid capital under Abbas the Great; planned city laid out according to shah's plan; example of Safavid architecture. (26)

Ismail: Sufi commander who conquered city of Tabriz in 1501; first Safavid to be proclaimed shah or emperor. (26)

Italian front: Front established in World War I; generally along Italian border with Austria-Hungary; also produced trench warfare; somewhat greater mobility than on western front. (34)

Iturbide, Augustín de: Conservative Creole officer in Mexican army who signed agreement with insurgent forces of independence; combined forces entered Mexico City in 1821; later proclaimed emperor of Mexico until its collapse in 1824. (31)

Ivan III: Also known as Ivan the Great; prince of Duchy of Moscow; claimed descent from Rurik; responsible for freeing Russia from Mongols after 1462; took title of tsar or Caesar—equivalent of emperor. (24)

Ivan IV: Also known as Ivan the Terrible; confirmed power of tsarist autocracy by attacking authority of boyars; continued policy of Russian expansion; established contacts with western European commerce and culture. (24)

Janissaries: Ottoman infantry divisions that dominated Ottoman armies; forcibly conscripted as boys in conquered areas of Balkans; legally slaves; translated military service into political influence, particularly after 15th century. (26)

Jesuits: A new religious order founded during the Catholic Reformation; active in politics, education, and missionary work; sponsored missions to North America and Asia. (22)

Jiang Qing: Wife of Mao Zedong; one of Gang of Four; opposed pragmatists and supported Cultural Revolution of 1965; arrested and imprisoned for life in 1976. (41)

Jinnah, Muhammad Ali: Muslim nationalist in India; originally a member of the National Congress party; became leader of Muslim League; traded Muslim support for British during World War II for promises of a separate Muslim state after the war; first president of Pakistan. (39)

João VI, Dom: Portuguese monarch who established seat of government in Brazil from 1808 to 1820 as a result of Napoleonic invasion of Iberian peninsula; made Brazil seat of empire with capital at Rio de Janeiro. (31)

Joseph II: Enlightened monarch of Austria; attempted to introduce reforms into Austria such as limitation of powers of Catholic church, restructuring of peasantry. (22)

Juárez, Benito: Indian governor of state of Oaxaca in Mexico; leader of liberal rebellion against Santa Ana; liberal government defeated by French intervention under Emperor Napoleon III of France and establishment of Mexican Empire under Maximilian; restored to power in 1867 until his death in 1872. (31)

Kamehameha I: Fought series of wars backed by British weapons and advisors resulting in unified Hawaiian kingdom by 1810; as king he promoted economic change encouraging Western merchants to establish export trade in Hawaiian goods. (30)

Kangxi: Confucian scholar and Manchu emperor of Qing dynasty from 1661 to 1722; established high degree of Sinification among the Manchus. (32)

Kellogg-Briand Pact: A treaty coauthored by American and French leaders in 1928; outlawed war forever; ratified subsequently by other nations. (35)

Kenyatta, Jomo: Leader of the nonviolent nationalist party in Kenya; organized the Kenya African Union (KAU); failed to win concessions because of resistance of white settlers; came to power only after suppression of the Land Freedom Army or Mau Mau. (39)

Kerensky, Alexander: Liberal revolutionary leader during the early stages of the Russian Revolution of 1917; sought development of parliamentary rule, religious freedom. (36)

Keynes, John: British economist who stressed importance of government spending to compensate for loss of purchasing power during a depression; played role in the policies of the American New Deal and European economic planning after World War II. (35)

Khartoum: River town that was administrative center of Egyptian authority in Sudan. (32)

khedives: Descendants of Muhammad Ali in Egypt after 1867; formal rulers of Egypt despite French and English intervention until overthrown by military coup in 1952. (32)

Khomaini, Ayatollah: Religious ruler of Iran following revolution of 1979 to expel the Pahlavi shah of Iran; emphasized religious purification; sought to eliminate Western influences and establish purely Islamic government. (40)

Khrushchev, Nikita: Stalin's successor as head of the USSR; attacked Stalinism for concentration of power and arbitrary dictatorship; failure of Siberian development program and antagonism of Stalinists led to downfall. (36)

Korean War: Fought from 1950 to 1953; North supported by USSR and later People's Republic of China; South supported by United States and small international United Nations force; ended in stalemate and continued division of Korea. (37)

Korekiyo Takahashi: Minister of finance in Japan during the 1930s; increased government spending to provide jobs; created export boom and elimination of unemployment by 1936; helped support military purchasing. (37)

kulaks: Agricultural entrepreneurs who utilized the Stolypin reforms to increase agricultural production and buy additional land. (33)

L'Overture, Toussaint: Leader of slave rebellion on the French sugar island of St. Domingue in 1791; led to creation of independent republic of Haiti in 1804. (31)

La Reforma: The name given to the liberal rebellion of Benito Juárez against the forces of Santa Ana. (31)

lançados: Collection points for Portuguese trade in the interior of Africa; provided essential links between economies of African interior and factories on the coast. (27)

Land Freedom Army: Radical organization for independence in Kenya; frustrated by failure of nonviolent means, initiated campaign of terror in 1952; referred to by British as the Mau Mau. (39)

Las Casas, Bartolomé de: Dominican friar who supported peaceful conversion of the Native American population of the Spanish colonies; opposed forced labor and advocated Indian rights. (25)

League of Nations: International diplomatic and peace organization created in the Treaty of Versailles that ended the First World War; one of the chief goals of President Woodrow Wilson of the United States in the peace negotiations; the United States was never a member. (34)

Lee Kuan Yew: Ruler of Singapore from independence in 1959 to present; established tightly controlled authoritarian government; ruled through People's Action party to suppress political diversity. (37)

Lepanto: Naval battle between the Spanish and the Ottoman Empire resulting in a Spanish victory in 1571; demonstrated European naval superiority over Muslims. (23)

Lesotho: Southern African state that survived mfecane; not based on Zulu model; less emphasis on military organization, less authoritarian government. (27)

letrados: University-trained lawyers from Spain in the New World; juridical core of Spanish colonial bureaucracy; exercised both legislative and administrative functions. (25)

Li Dazhao: Chinese intellectual who gave serious attention to Marxist philosophy; headed study circle at the University of Beijing; saw peasants as vanguard of revolutionary communism in China. (41)

liberal: Political viewpoint with origins in western Europe during the 19th century; stressed limited state interference in individual life, representation of propertied people in government; urged importance of constitutional rule and parliaments. (29)

Liberal Democratic party: Monopolized Japanese government from its formation in 1955 into the 1990s; largely responsible for economic reconstruction of Japan. (37)

Liberation theology: Combined Catholic theology and Socialist principles in effort to bring about improved conditions for the poor in Latin America. (38)

Lin Zexu: Distinguished Chinese official during the early 19th century; charged with stamping out the opium trade in southern China; ordered European trading areas in Canton blockaded and confiscation of opium; sent into exile following Opium War. (32)

Locke, John: English philosopher during 17th century; argued that people could learn everything through senses; argued that power of government came from the people, not divine right of kings; offered possibility of revolution to overthrow tyrants. (22)

Long March: Communist escape from Hunan province during civil war with Guomindang in 1934; center of Communist power removed to Shaanxi province; firmly established Mao Zedong as head of the Communist party in China. (41)

Louis XIV: French monarch who personified absolute monarchy. (22)

Louis XVI: Bourbon monarch of France who was executed during the radical phase of the French Revolution. (29)

Luanda: Portuguese factory established in 1520s south of Kongo; became basis for Portuguese colony of Angola. (27)

Luddites: Workers in Britain who responded to replacement of human labor by machines during the Industrial Revolution by attempting to destroy the machines; named after a fictional British worker named Ned Ludd. (29)

Luo: Nilotic people who migrated from Upper Nile valley; established dynasty among existing Bantu population in lake region of central eastern Africa; center at Bunyoro. (27)

Luther, Martin: German monk; initiated Protestant Reformation by nailing 95 theses to door of Wittenberg church; emphasized primacy of faith over works stressed in Catholic church; urged state control of Church. (22)

Luzon: Northern island of Philippines; conquered by Spain during the 1560s; site of major Catholic missionary effort. (28)

Macao: One of two ports in which Europeans were permitted to trade in China during the Ming dynasty. (28)

MacArthur, General Douglas: American commander in Pacific campaign of World War II; headed American occupation government of Japan after the war; later commanded international forces during Korean War. (37)

Machiavelli, Niccolo: Author of *The Prince;* emphasized realistic discussions of how to seize and maintain power; one of most influential authors of Italian Renaissance. (22)

Madero, Francisco: Moderate democratic reformer in Mexico; proposed moderate reforms in 1910; arrested by Porfirio Díaz; initiated revolution against Díaz when released from prison; temporarily gained power, but removed and assassinated in 1913. (38)

Magellan, Ferdinand: Spanish captain who in 1519 initiated first circumnavigation of the globe; died during the voyage; allowed Spain to claim Philippines. (23)

Mahdi: Muhammad Achmad, head of a Sudanic Sufi brotherhood; claimed descent from Prophet; proclaimed both Egyptians and British as infidels; launched revolt to purge Islam of impurities; took Khartoum in 1883. (32)

Mahmud II: Ottoman sultan; built a private, professional army; fomented revolution of Janissaries and crushed them with private army; destroyed power of Janissaries and their religious allies; initiated reform of Ottoman Empire on Western precedents. (32)

Malacca: Portuguese factory or fortified trade town located on the tip of the Malayan peninsula; traditionally a center for trade among the southeastern Asian islands. (28)

Manchus: Jurchen people from region to the northeast of the Chinese empire; seized power following collapse of Ming dynasty; established Qing dynasty, last of imperial houses. (28)

mandates: Governments entrusted to European nations in the Middle East in the aftermath of World War I; Britain occupied mandates in Syria, Iraq, Lebanon, and Palestine after 1922. (39)

manifest destiny: Belief of the government of the United States that it was destined to rule the continent from coast to coast; led to annexation of Texas and Mexican-American War. (31)

Mao Zedong: Communist leader in revolutionary China; advocated rural reform and role of peasantry in Nationalist revolution; influenced by Li Dazhao; led Communist reaction against Guomindang purges in 1920s culminating in Long March of 1934; seized control of all of mainland China by 1949; initiated Great Leap Forward in 1958. (41)

Marquis of Pombal: Prime minister of Portugal from 1755 to 1776; acted to strengthen royal authority in Brazil; expelled Jesuits; enacted fiscal reforms and established monopoly companies to stimulate the colonial economy. (25)

Marshall Plan: Program of substantial loans initiated by the United States in 1947; designed to aid Western nations in rebuilding from the war's devastation; vehicle for American economic dominance. (35)

Marx, Karl: German socialist; blasted earlier socialist movements as utopian; saw history as defined by class struggle between groups out of power and those controlling the means of production; preached necessity of social revolution to create proletarian dictatorship. (29)

mask of Ferdinand: Term given to movements in Latin America allegedly loyal to the displaced Bourbon king of Spain, Ferdinand VII; actually Creole movements for independence. (31)

mass leisure culture: An aspect of the later Industrial Revolution; based on newspapers, music halls, popular theater, vacation trips, and team sports. (29)

Mass Line: Economic policy of Mao Zedong; led to formation of agricultural cooperatives in 1955; cooperatives became farming collectives in 1956. (41)

Mataram: Kingdom that controlled interior regions of Java in 17th century; Dutch East India Company paid tribute to the kingdom for rights of trade at Batavia; weakness of kingdom after 1670s allowed Dutch to exert control over all of Java. (30)

May Fourth movement: Resistance to Japanese encroachments in China began on this date in 1919; spawned movement of intellectuals aimed at transforming China into a liberal democracy; rejected Confucianism. (41)

Mehmed II: Ottoman sultan called the "Conqueror"; responsible for conquest of Constantinople in 1453; destroyed what remained of Byzantine Empire. (26)

Meiji restoration: Restoration of the power of the emperor in Japan in 1868; new emperor named Mutsuhito, but called Meiji or Enlightened One; put down troops of shogunate; marked beginning of creation of centralized Japanese government. (33)

mercantilism: Economic theory that stressed governments' promotion of limitation of imports from other nations and internal economies in order to improve tax revenues; popular during 17th and 18th centuries. (22)

mestizos: People of mixed European and Indian ancestry in Mesoamerica and South America; particularly prevalent in areas colonized by Spain; often part of forced labor system. (23)

Mexican Constitution of 1917: Promised land reform, limited foreign ownership of key resources, guaranteed the rights of workers, and placed restrictions on clerical education; marked end of Mexican Revolution. (38)

Mexican Revolution: Fought over a period of ten years from 1910; resulted in ouster of Porfirio Díaz from power; opposition forces led by Pancho Villa and Emiliano Zapata. (38)

Mexican-American War: Fought between Mexico and the United States from 1846 to 1848; led to devastating defeat of Mexican forces; loss of about one-half of Mexico's national territory to the United States. (31)

Mexico City: Capital of New Spain; built on ruins of Aztec capital of Tenochtitlan. (25)

mfecane: Wars of crushing and wandering in southern Africa; created by Zulu expansion under Shaka; revolutionized political organization of southern Africa. (27)

Middle Passage: Slave voyage from Africa to the Americas; generally a traumatic experience for black slaves, although it failed to strip Africans of their culture. (27)

Minas Gerais: Region of Brazil located in mountainous interior where gold strikes were discovered in 1695; became location for gold rush. (25)

Mindanao: Southern island of Philippines; a Muslim kingdom that was able to successfully resist Spanish conquest. (28)

Minh Mang: Second emperor of a united Vietnam, successor of Nguyen Anh; ruled from 1820 to 1841; sponsored emphasis of Confucianism; persecuted Catholics. (41)

miscegenation: Practice of interracial marriage; found in virtually all colonial ventures. (30)

mita: System of labor drafts that replaced encomienda system in Spanish colonies during the 16th century; particularly important in providing labor for mines. (25)

MNR: The National Revolutionary Movement; Reformist and Nationalist political coalition in Bolivia; seized power as a result of a revolution in 1952; initiated series of reforms including universal suffrage, nationalization of mines, land redistribution; cut back power of military; replaced by military government in 1964. (38)

Moctezuma II: Last independent Aztec emperor; killed during Hernán Cortés's conquest of Tenochtitlan. (25)

modernization theory: The belief that the more industrialized, urban, and modern a society became, the more social change and improvement were possible as traditional patterns and attitudes were abandoned or transformed; used as a blueprint for development in Latin America. (31)

Monroe Doctrine: American declaration stated in 1823; established that any attempt of a European country to colonize in the Americas would be considered an unfriendly act by the United States; supported by Great Britain as a means of opening Latin-American trade. (31)

Montagu-Chelmsford reforms: Increased the powers of Indian legislators at the all-India level and placed much of the provincial administration of India under local ministries controlled by legislative bodies with substantial numbers of elected Indians; passed in 1919. (39)

Morley-Minto reforms of 1909: Provided educated Indians with considerably expanded opportunities to elect and to serve on local and all-Indian legislative councils. (39)

Mughal dynasty: Established by Babur in India in 1526; the name is taken from the supposed Mongol descent of Babur, but there is little indication of any Mongol influence in the dynasty; became weak after rule of Aurangzeb in first decades of 18th century. (26)

mullahs: Local mosque officials and prayer leaders within the Safavid Empire; agents of Safavid religious campaign to convert all of population to Shi'ism. (26)

Munich Conference: Meeting concerning Germany's occupation of portions of Czechoslovakia in 1938; after receiving Hitler's assurances that he would take no more land, Western leaders agreed to the division of Czechoslovakia. (34)

Murad: Head of the coalition of Mamluk households in Egypt; opposed Napoleonic invasion of Egypt and suffered devastating defeat; failure destroyed Mamluk government in Egypt and revealed vulnerability of Muslim core. (32)

Muslim Brotherhood: Egyptian nationalist movement founded by Hasan al-Banna in 1928; committed to fundamentalist movement in Islam; fostered strikes and urban riots against the khedival government. (40)

Muslim League: Founded in 1906 to better support demands of Muslims for separate electorates and legislative seats in Hindu-dominated India; represented division within Indian nationalist movement. (39)

Mussolini, Benito: Italian fascist leader; actually created first fascist government based on aggressive foreign policy and new nationalist glories. (34)

Mvemba, Nzinga: King of Kongo south of Zaire River from 1507 to 1543; converted to Christianity and took title of Alfonso I; under Portuguese influence attempted to Christianize all of kingdom. (27)

nabobs: Name given to British representatives of the East India Company who went briefly to India to make fortunes through graft and exploitation. (30)

Nadir Khan Afshar: Soldier-adventurer following fall of Safavid dynasty in 1722; proclaimed himself shah in 1736; established short-lived dynasty in reduced kingdom. (26)

Nagasaki: One of two Japanese cities on which the United States dropped atomic bombs in 1945; devastation of these cities caused Japanese surrender without invasion of home islands. (34)

Nasser, Gamal Abdul: Took power in Egypt following a military coup in 1952; enacted land reforms and used state resources to reduce unemployment; ousted Britain from the Suez Canal zone in 1956. (40)

Natal: British colony in South Africa; developed after Boer trek north from Cape Colony; major commercial outpost at Durban. (30)

National Liberation Front (FLN): Radical nationalist movement in Algeria; launched sustained guerrilla war against France in the 1950s; success of attacks led to independence of Algeria in 1958. (39)

National Socialist party: Also known as the Nazi Party; led by Adolf Hitler in Germany; picked up political support during the economic chaos of the Great Depression; advocated authoritarian state under a single leader, aggressive foreign policy to reverse humiliation of the Treaty of Versailles; took power in Germany in 1933. (34)

nationalism: Political viewpoint with origins in western Europe in the 19th century; often allies with one of other "isms"; urged importance of national unity; valued a collective identity based on race or ethnic origin. (29)

négritude: Literary movement in Africa; sought to combat racial stereotypes of African culture; celebrated the beauty of black skin and African physique; associated with origins of African nationalist movements. (39)

Nehru, Jawaharlal: One of Gandhi's disciples; governed India after independence; committed to program of social reform and economic development; preserved civil rights and democracy. (40)

neocolonial economy: Economy that results from continued dominance of the First and Second World nations of the world's economy; ability of the First and Second World nations to maintain economic colonialism without political colonialism. (40)

New Deal: President Franklin Roosevelt's precursor of the modern welfare state; program to combat economic depression enacted a number of social insurance measures and used government spending to stimulate the economy; increased power of the state and the state's intervention in social and economic life. (35)

New Economic Policy: Initiated by Lenin in 1921; state continued to set basic economic policies, but efforts now combined with individual initiative; policy allowed food production to recover. (36)

new feminism: New wave of women's rights agitations dating from 1949; emphasized more literal equality that would play down domestic roles and qualities for women; promoted specific reforms and redefinition of what it meant to be female. (35)

New France: French colonies in North America; extended from St. Lawrence along Great Lakes and down Mississippi River valley system. (23)

New Spain: Spanish colonial possessions in Mesoamerica; included most of central Mexico; based on imperial system of Aztecs. (25)

New Youth: Marxist periodical in China; did much to spread the ideas of Marx and Lenin among the politically active youth of China's coastal cities. (41)

Newton, Isaac: English scientist during the 17th century; author of *Principia;* drew the various astronomical and physical observations and wider theories together in a neat framework of natural laws; established principles of motion; defined forces of gravity. (22)

Nguyen Anh: Last surviving member of Nguyen dynasty following Tayson Rebellion in Vietnam; with French support retook southern Vietnam; drove Tayson from northern Vietnam by 1802; proclaimed himself emperor with capital at Hue. (41)

Nkrumah, Kwame: African nationalist during period of decolonization; responsible for creation of first independent, black African state of Ghana in 1957; established power through his own party—Convention Peoples party (CPP). (39)

Nobili, Robert di: Italian Jesuit missionary; worked in India during the early 1600s; introduced strategy to convert elites first; strategy later widely adopted by Jesuits in various parts of Asia; mission eventually failed. (28)

Nobunaga: Japanese daimyo; first to make extensive use of firearms; in 1573 deposed last of Ashikaga shoguns; unified much of central Honshu under his command; killed in 1582. (28)

North Atlantic Treaty Organization (NATO): Created in 1949 under United States leadership to group most of the Western European powers plus Canada in a defensive alliance against possible Soviet aggression. (35)

Northern Renaissance: Cultural and intellectual movement of northern Europe; began later than Italian Renaissance c. 1450; centered in France, Low Countries, England, and Germany; featured greater emphasis on religion than Italian Renaissance. (22)

Nur Jahan: Wife of Jahangir; amassed power in court and created faction of male relatives who dominated empire during later years of Jahangir's reign. (26)

Nurhaci: Architect of Manchu unity; created distinctive Manchu banner armies; controlled most of Manchuria; adopted Chinese bureaucracy and court ceremonies in Manchuria; entered China and successfully captured Ming capital at Beijing. (32)

obeah: African religious ideas and practices in the English islands. (27)

obrajes: Small textile workshops established in Spanish colonies in New World; produced common cloth usually with Indian women's labor; supplied American demand. (25)

Obregón, Alvaro: Emerged as leader of the Mexican government in 1915; elected president in 1920. (38)

obruk: Labor obligations of Russian peasants to either their aristocratic landlords or to the state; typical of increased labor burdens placed on Russian peasantry during the 18th century. (24)

old believers: Russians who refused to accept the ecclesiastical reforms of Alexis Romanov; many exiled to Siberia or southern Russia where they became part of Russian colonization. (24)

Opium War: Fought between the British and Qing China beginning in 1839; fought to protect British trade in opium; resulted in resounding British victory, opening of Hong Kong as British port of trade. (32)

Orabi, Achmad: Student of Muhammad Abduh; led revolt in 1882 against Turkish influence in Egyptian army; forced khedive to call on British army for support. (32)

Ormuz: Portuguese factory or fortified trade town located at southern end of Persian Gulf; site for forcible entry into Asian sea trade network. (28)

Orozco, José Clemente: Mexican muralist of the period after the Mexican Revolution; like Rivera, his work featured romantic images of the Indian past with Christian symbols and Communist ideology. (38)

Ottoman Society for Union and Progress: Organization of political agitators in opposition to rule of Abdul Hamid; also called "Young Turks"; desired to restore 1876 constitution. (32)

Ottomans: Turkic people who advanced from strongholds in Asia Minor during 1350s; conquered large part of Balkans; unified under Mehmed I; captured Constantinople in 1453; established empire from Balkans that included most of Arab world. (26)

Pacific Rim states: Japan, Korea, Singapore, Hong Kong, Taiwan; typified by rapid growth rates, expanding exports, and industrialization; either Chinese or strongly influenced by Chinese values; considerable reliance on government planning and direction, limitations on dissent and instability. (37)

Palmares: Kingdom of runaway slaves with a population of 8,000 to 10,000 people; located in Brazil during the 17th century; leadership was Angolan. (27)

Panama Canal: An aspect of American intervention in Latin America; resulted from United States support for a Panamanian independence movement in return for a grant to exclusive rights to a canal across the Panama isthmus; provided short route from Atlantic to Pacific Ocean. (31)

Partition of Poland: Three separate divisions of Polish territory between Russia, Prussia, and Austria in 1772, 1793, and 1795; eliminated Poland as an independent state; part of expansion of Russian influence in eastern Europe. (24)

Pasteur, Louis: Discoverer of germs; led to more conscientious sanitary regulation by the 1880s. (29)

Paulistas: Backwoodsmen from São Paulo in Brazil; penetrated Brazilian interior in search of precious metals during 17th century. (25)

Pearl Harbor: American naval base in Hawaii; attack by Japanese on this facility in December 1941 crippled American fleet in the Pacific; caused entry of United States into World War II. (34)

Pedro I, Dom: Son and successor of Don João VI in Brazil; aided in the declaration of Brazilian independence from Portugal in 1822; became constitutional emperor of Brazil. (31)

peninsulares: People living in the New World Spanish colonies but born in Spain. (25)

People's Democratic Republic of Korea: Northern half of Korea dominated by USSR; headed by Kim Il-Sung; attacked south in 1950 and initiated Korean War; retained independence as a Communist state after the war. (37)

Peoples Liberation Army: Chinese Communist army; administered much of country under Peoples Republic of China. (41)

Peoples Republic of China: Communist government of mainland China; proclaimed in 1949 following military success of Mao Zedong over forces of Chiang Kai-shek and the Guomindang. (41)

perestroika: Policy of Mikhail Gorbachev calling for economic restructuring in the USSR; more leeway for private ownership and decentralized control in industry and agriculture. (36)

Perón, Evita: Also known as Eva Duarte; first wife of Juan Perón; became public spokesperson for Perón among the poor until her death in 1952. (38)

Perón, Juan D.: Military leader in Argentina who became dominant political figure after military coup in 1943; used position as Minister of Labor to appeal to working groups and the poor; became president in 1946; forced into exile in 1955; returned and won presidency in 1973. (38)

Perry, Matthew: American commodore who visited Edo Bay with American fleet in 1853; insisted on opening ports to American trade on threat of naval bombardment; won rights for American trade with Japan in 1854. (33)

Peter I: Also known as Peter the Great; son of Alexis Romanov; ruled from 1689 to 1725; continued growth of absolutism and conquest; included more definite interest in changing selected aspects of economy and culture through imitation of western European models. (24)

Pinsker, Leon: European Zionist who believed that Jewish assimilation into Christian European nations was impossible; argued for return to Middle Eastern Holy Land. (39)

Pizarro, Francisco: Led conquest of Inca Empire of Peru beginning in 1535; by 1540 most of Inca possessions fell to Spanish. (25)

Plassey: Battle in 1757 between troops of the British East India Company and an Indian army under Sirāj-ud-daula, ruler of Bengal; British victory resulted in control of northern India. (30)

Politburo: Executive committee of the Communist party; 20 members. (36)

Popular Front: Combination of Socialist and Communist political parties in France; won election in 1936; unable to take strong measures of social reform because of continuing strength of conservatives; fell from power in 1938. (35)

population revolution: Huge growth in population in western Europe beginning about 1730; prelude to Industrial Revolution; population of France increased

50 percent, England and Prussia 100 percent. (29)

positivism: French philosophy based on observation and scientific approach to problems of society; adopted by many Latin-American liberals in the aftermath of independence. (31)

Potosí: Mine located in upper Peru (modern Bolivia); largest of New World silver mines; produced 80 percent of all Peruvian silver. (25)

Potsdam Conference: Meeting between leaders of the United States, Britain, and the Soviet Union just before the end of the war in 1945; Allies agreed upon Soviet domination in eastern Europe; Germany and Austria to be divided among victorious Allies. (34)

pragmatists: Chinese Communist politicians such as Zhou Enlai, Deng Xiaoping, and Liu Shaoqui; determined to restore state direction and market incentives at the local level; opposed Great Leap Forward. (41)

Presidencies: Three districts that made up the bulk of the directly ruled British territories in India; capitals at Madras, Calcutta, and Bombay. (30)

PRI: Party of the Institutionalized Revolution; dominant political party in Mexico; developed during the 1920s and 1930s; incorporated labor, peasant, military, and middle-class sectors; controlled other political organizations in Mexico. (38)

primary products: Food or industrial crops for which there is a high demand in industrialized economies; prices of such products tend to fluctuate widely; typically the primary exports of Third World economies. (40)

Princely States: Indian princes allied with the British Raj; agents of the East India Company were stationed at the rulers' courts to ensure compliance; made up over one-third of the British Indian Empire. (30)

proletariat: Class of people without access to producing property; typically manufacturing workers, paid laborers in agricultural economy, or urban poor; product of economic changes of 16th and 17th centuries. (22)

Protestantism: General wave of religious dissent against Catholic church; generally held to have begun with Martin Luther's attack on Catholic beliefs in 1517; included many varieties of religious belief. (22)

protoindustrialization: Preliminary shift away from agricultural economy; workers become full- or part-time producers of textile and metal products, working at home but in a capitalist system in which materials, work orders, and ultimate sales depended on urban merchants; prelude to Industrial Revolution. (29)

Pugachev rebellion: During 1770s in reign of Catherine the Great; led by cossack Emelyan Pugachev who claimed to be legitimate tsar; eventually crushed; typical of peasant unrest during the 18th century and thereafter. (24)

Puyi: Last emperor of China; deposed as emperor while still a small boy in 1912. (32)

radical: Political viewpoint with origins in western Europe during the 19th century; advocated broader voting rights than liberals; in some cases advocated outright democracy; urged reforms in favor of the lower classes. (29)

Recopilación: Body of laws collected in 1681 for Spanish possessions in New World; basis of law in the Indies. (25)

Red Army: Military organization constructed under leadership of Leon Trotsky, Bolshevik follower of Lenin; made use of people of humble background. (36)

Red Guard: Student brigades utilized by Mao Zedong and his political allies during the Cultural Revolution to discredit Mao's political enemies. (41)

Red Heads: Name given to Safavid followers for distinctive red headgear. (26)

Reform Bill of 1832: Legislation passed in Great Britain that extended the vote to most members of the middle class; failed to produce democracy in Britain. (29)

Republic of Korea: Southern half of Korea sponsored by United States following World War II; headed by nationalist Syngman Rhee; developed parliamentary institutions, but maintained authoritarian government; defended by UN forces during Korean War; underwent industrialization and economic emergence after 1950s. (37)

revisionism: Socialist movement that disavowed Marxist revolutionary doctrine; believed social success could be achieved gradually through political institutions. (29)

Revolutions of 1848: Generally refers to those nationalist and liberal movements within the Habsburg Empire—specifically in Italy, Germany, Austria, and Hungary; after temporary success, the revolutions failed. (29)

Rhodes, Cecil: British entrepreneur in South Africa; manipulated political situation in South Africa to gain entry to resources of Boer republics; initiated Boer War as means of destroying Boer independence. (30)

Ricci, Matteo: Along with Adam Schall, Jesuit scholar in court of Ming emperors; skilled scientist; corrected calendars, forged cannons, fixed clocks; won few converts to Christianity. (28)

Rio de Janeiro: Brazilian port; closed to mines of Minas Gerais; importance grew with gold strikes; became colonial capital in 1763. (25)

Rivadavia, Bernardino: Liberal leader in Buenos Aires in 1820s; instituted series of reforms in education, finance, agriculture, and immigration; attempted to create a strong central government. (31)

Rivera, Diego: Mexican artist of the period after the Mexican Revolution; famous for murals painted on walls of public buildings; mixed romantic images of the Indian past with Christian symbols and Communist ideology. (38)

Romanov, Alexis: Second Romanov tsar; abolished assemblies of nobles; gained new powers over Russian Orthodox church. (24)

Romanov dynasty: Dynasty elected in 1613 at end of Time of Troubles; ruled Russia until 1917. (24)

romanticism: Artistic and literary movement of the 19th century in western Europe; held that emotion and impression, not reason, were the keys to the mysteries of human experience and nature; sought to portray passions, not calm reflection. (29)

Roosevelt, Theodore: American president; sponsored the conference that ended the Russo-Japanese War; winner of the Nobel Peace Prize; efforts indicated first American concern with Japanese expansion in Pacific. (34)

Rosas, Juan Manuel de: Federalist leader in Buenos Aires; took power in 1831; commanded loyalty of gauchos; restored local autonomy. (31)

Rowlatt Act: Placed severe restrictions on key Indian civil rights such as freedom of the press; acted to offset the concessions granted under Montagu-Chelmsford reforms of 1919. (39)

Royal African Company: Chartered in 1660s to establish a monopoly over the slave trade among British merchants; supplied African slaves to colonies in Barbados, Jamaica, and Virginia. (27)

Russian Communist party: The Bolshevik wing of the Social Democratic party in Russia in 1917; came to power under Lenin after the November expulsion of Kerensky's liberal government. (36)

Russian Revolution of 1905: Consisted of strikes by urban workers and widespread insurrections among the peasantry; resulted in some temporary reforms such as the creation of the duma. (33)

Russo-Japanese War: War between Japan and Russia over territory in Manchuria beginning in 1905; Japan defeated the Russians, largely due to superior naval power; Japan annexed Korea in 1910 as a result of military dominance. (33)

Sadat, Anwar: Successor of Gamal Abdul Nasser as ruler of Egypt; acted to dismantle costly state programs; accepted peace treaty with Israel in 1973; opened Egypt to investment by Western European nations. (40)

Safavid dynasty: Originally a Turkic nomadic group; family originated in Sufi mystic group; espoused Shi'ism; conquered territory and established kingdom in region equivalent to modern Iran; lasted until 1722. (26)

Safi al-Din: Early 14th century Sufi mystic; began campaign to purify Islam; first member of Safavid dynasty. (26)

"salt water" slaves: Slaves transported from Africa; almost invariably black. (27)

San Martín, José de: Leader of independence movement in Rio de la Plata; led to independence of the United Provinces of the Rio de la Plata by 1816; later led independence movement in Chile and Peru as well. (31)

Sandinista party: Nicaraguan Socialist movement named after Augusto Sandino; successfully carried out a Socialist revolution in Nicaragua during the 1980s. (38)

Sandino, Augusto: Led a guerrilla resistance movement against U.S. occupation forces in Nicaragua; assassinated by Nicaraguan National Guard in 1934; became national hero and symbol of resistance to U.S. influence in Central America. (38)

Santa Ana, General Antonio López de: Seized power in Mexico after collapse of empire of Mexico in 1824; after brief reign of liberals, seized power in 1835 as caudillo; defeated by Texans in war for independence in 1836; defeated by United States in Mexican-American War in 1848; unseated by liberal rebellion in 1854. (31)

Santa Cruz, Andrés: Mestizo general who established union of independent Peru and Bolivia between 1829 and 1839. (31)

Sarmiento, Domingo F.: Liberal politician and president of Argentine Republic; author of *Facundo*, a critique of caudillo politics; increased international trade, launched internal reforms in education and transportation. (31)

satyagraha: Literally "truth-force"; Gandhi's policy of nonviolent opposition to British colonialism. (39)

Schall, Adam: Along with Matteo Ricci, Jesuit scholar in court of Ming emperors; skilled scientist; corrected calendars, forged cannons, fixed clocks; won few converts to Christianity. (28)

school of National Learning: New ideology that laid emphasis on Japan's unique historical experience and the revival of indigenous culture at the expense of Chinese imports such as Confucianism; typical of Japan in 18th century. (28)

scientific revolution: Culminated in 17th century; period of empirical advances associated with the development of wider theoretical generalizations; resulted in change in traditional beliefs of Middle Ages. (22)

Secret Army Organization: Organization of French settlers in Algeria; led guerrilla war following independence during the 1960s; assaults directed against Arabs, Berbers, and French who advocated independence. (39)

Selim III: Sultan who ruled Ottoman Empire from 1789 to 1807; aimed at improving administrative efficiency and building a new army and navy; toppled by Janissaries in 1807. (32)

sepoys: Troops that served the British East India Company; recruited from various warlike peoples of India. (30)

Seven Years' War: Fought both in continental Europe and also in overseas colonies between 1756 and 1763; resulted in Prussian seizures of land from Austria, English seizures of colonies in India and North America. (22)

Shaka: Ruler and reformer of Nguni peoples after 1818; reformed loose forces into regiments organized by lineage and age; created Zulu chiefdom that began to absorb or destroy its neighbors in southern Africa. (27)

siege of Stalingrad: Turning point in Germany's assault on Soviet Union in 1942; despite massive losses, Russians successfully defended the city; over one-third of German army surrendered. (34)

Simon Commission: In 1927 considered future Indian colonial government responses to nationalist demands; served to unify nationalist politicians on both right and left of independence movement as well as healed rift between Muslims and Hindus. (39)

Singapore: Originally held by British as part of colony of Malaya; largely Chinese population; British attempted to create invulnerable naval base; captured by Japanese during World War II; emerged after war as independent port. (37)

Sino-Japanese War: War fought between Japan and Qing China between 1894 and 1895; resulted in Japanese victory; frustrated Japanese imperial aims due to Western insistence that Japan withdraw from Liaotung peninsula. (33)

Smith, Adam: Established new school of economy; argued that government should avoid regulation of economy in favor of the operation of the laws of market forces. (22)

social question: Issues relating to repressed classes in western Europe during the Industrial Revolution, particularly workers and women; became more critical than constitutional issues after 1870. (29)

Social Revolutionary party: Winners of the parliamentary majority of the first election held following the November 1917 Bolshevik seizure of power; emphasized peasant support and rural reform; expelled in favor of Bolsheviks. (36)

socialism: Political viewpoint with origins in western Europe during the 19th century; urged an attack on private property in the name of equality; wanted state control of means of production, end to capitalist exploitation of the working man. (29)

socialism in one country: Joseph Stalin's concept of Russian communism based solely on the Soviet Union rather than the Leninist concept of international revolution; by cutting off the Soviet Union from other economies, the USSR avoided worst consequences of the Great Depression. (34)

Socialist realism: Attempt within the USSR to relate formal culture to the masses in order to avoid the adoption of Western European cultural forms; begun under Joseph Stalin; fundamental method of Soviet fiction and literary criticism. (36)

Socialist Youth Corps: Formed in 1920 in China; dedicated to recruiting urban working classes to the nationalist revolution in China. (41)

sociedad de castas: American social system based on racial origins; Europeans or whites at top, black slaves or Indians at bottom, mixed races in middle. (25)

Solidarity: Polish labor movement formed in 1970s under Lech Walesa; challenged USSR-dominated government of Poland. (36)

Solzhenitsyn, Aleksandr: Russian author critical of the Soviet regime; published trilogy on the Siberian prison camps—*Gulag Archipelago.* (36)

soviet: Council of workers formed to seize city government in Petrograd in 1917; basis for early political organization of Russian Revolution. (36)

Spanish Civil War: War between authoritarian and military leaders in Spain against republicans and leftists between 1936 and 1939; Germany and Italy supported the royalists; the Soviet Union supported the republicans; led to victory of the royalist forces. (34)

Spanish-American War: War fought between Spain and the United States beginning in 1898; centered on Cuba and Puerto Rico; permitted American intervention in Caribbean, annexation of Puerto Rico and the Philippines. (31)

Sputnik: First manned spacecraft in 1957; sent up during Khrushchev government; initiated space race with the United States. (36)

St. Petersburg: New capital of Russia established during the reign of Peter the Great. (24)

Stalin, Joseph: Successor to Lenin as head of the USSR; strongly nationalist view of communism; represented anti-Western strain of Russian tradition; crushed opposition to his rule; established series of five-year plans to replace New Economic Policy; fostered agricultural collectivization; led USSR through World War II; initiated cold war with Western Europe and the United States; died in 1953. (36)

Stolypin reforms: Reforms introduced by the Russian minister for which they are named; basically reforms intended to placate the peasantry in the aftermath of the Revolution of 1905; included reduction in redemption payments, attempt to create market-oriented peasantry. (33)

submarine warfare: Use of the relatively new sea weapon was a major aspect of the German naval effort against the western allies in the First World War; unrestricted submarine warfare was major factor in bringing the United States into active participation. (34)

Suez Canal: Built across Isthmus of Suez connecting Mediterranean with the Red Sea in 1869; financed by European investors; with increasing indebtedness of khedives, permitted intervention of British into Egyptian politics to protect their investment. (32)

Sun Yat-sen: Head of Revolutionary Alliance, organization that led 1911 revolt against Qing dynasty in China; briefly elected president in 1911, but yielded in favor of Yuan Shikai in 1912; created Nationalist party of China (Guomindang) in 1919; died in 1925. (41)

Supreme Soviet: Parliament of Union of Soviet Socialist Republics; elected by universal suffrage; actually controlled by Communist party; served to ratify party decisions. (36)

Suriname: Formerly a Dutch plantation colony on the coast of South America; location of runaway slave kingdom in 18th century; able to retain independence despite attempts to crush guerrilla resistance. (27)

Swazi: New African state formed on model of Zulu chiefdom; survived mfecane. (27)

syndicalism: Government based on the organization of labor; imported in Latin America from European political movements; militant force in Latin-American politics. (38)

Taiping rebellion: Broke out in south China in the 1850s and early 1860s; led by Hong Xiuquan, a semi-Christianized prophet; sought to overthrow Qing dynasty and Confucian basis of scholar-gentry. (32)

Taiwan: Island off Chinese mainland; became refuge for Nationalist Chinese regime under Chiang Kai-shek as Republic of China in 1948; successfully retained independence with aid of United States; rapidly industrialized after 1950s. (37)

Taj Mahal: Most famous architectural achievement of Mughal India; originally built as a mausoleum for the wife of Shah Jahan, Mumtaz Mahal. (26)

Tanzimat reforms: Series of reforms in Ottoman Empire between 1839 and 1876; established Western-style university, state postal system, railways, extensive legal reforms; resulted in creation of new constitution in 1876. (32)

Tayson Rebellion: Peasant revolution in southern Vietnam during the late 1770s; succeeded in toppling the Nguyen dynasty; subsequently unseated the Trinh dynasty of northern Vietnam. (41)

technocrat: New type of bureaucrat; intensely trained in engineering or economics and devoted to the power of national planning; came to fore in offices of governments following World War II. (35)

Teheran Conference: Meeting between leaders of the United States, Britain, and the Soviet Union in 1943; agreed to the opening of a new front in France. (34)

terakoya: Commoner schools founded during the Tokugawa shogunate in Japan to teach reading, writing, and the rudiments of Confucianism; resulted in high literacy rate approaching 40 percent of Japanese males. (33)

Thatcher, Margaret: Conservative British prime minister from 1979 to 1991; held office longer than any other person; worked to cut welfare and housing expenses, promote free enterprise. (35)

third Rome: Russian claim to be successor state to Roman and Byzantine empires; based in part on continuity of Orthodox church in Russia following fall of Constantinople in 1453. (24)

Third World: Those nations outside the capitalist industrial nations of the First World and the industrialized Communist nations of the Second World; generally less economically powerful, but with varied economies. (38)

Thirty Years' War: War within the Holy Roman Empire between German Protestants and their allies (Sweden, Denmark, France) and the emperor and his ally, Spain; ended in 1648 after great destruction with Treaty of Westphalia. (22)

Tilak, B. G.: Believed that nationalism in India should be based on appeals to Hindu religiosity; worked to promote the restoration and revival of ancient Hindu traditions; offended Muslims and other religious groups; first Populist leader in India. (39)

Time of Troubles: Followed death of Ivan IV without heir early in 17th century; boyars attempted to use vacuum of power to reestablish their authority; ended with selection of Michael Romanov as tsar in 1613. (24)

Tojo Hideki: Japanese general; put down attempted military coup in 1936; increasingly interfered with civilian cabinets to block appointment of liberal bureaucrats; helped create increasingly militaristic series of prime ministers after 1936. (37)

total war: Warfare of the 20th century; vast resources and emotional commitments of the belligerent nations were marshaled to support military effort; resulted from impact of industrialization on the military effort reflecting technological innovation and organizational capacity. (34)

totalitarian state: A new kind of government in the 20th century that exercised massive, direct control over virtually all the activities of its subjects; existed in Germany, Italy, and the Soviet Union. (35)

Tragic Week: Occurred in Argentina in 1919; government response to general strike of labor forces led to brutal repression under guise of nationalism. (38)

trans-Siberian railroad: Constructed in 1870s to connect European Russia with the Pacific; completed by the end of the 1880s; brought Russia into a more active Asian role. (33)

transformismo: Political system in Italy that promoted alliance of conservatives and liberals; parliamentary deputies of all parties supported the status quo. (29)

Treaty of Gijanti: Signed in 1757; reduced remaining Javanese princes to vassals of Dutch East India Company; allowed Dutch to monopolize production of coffee on Java. (28)

Treaty of Guadalupe-Hidalgo: Agreement that ended the Mexican-American War; provided for loss of Texas and California to the United States; left legacy of distrust of the United States in Latin America. (31)

Treaty of Paris: Arranged in 1763 following Seven Years' War; granted New France to England in exchange for return of French sugar islands in Caribbean. (23)

Treaty of Tordesillas: Signed in 1494 between Castile and Portugal; clarified spheres of influence and rights of possession in New World; reserved Brazil and all newly discovered lands east of Brazil to Portugal; granted all lands west of Brazil to Spain. (25)

Treaty of Versailles: Ended the First World War; provided for the League of Nations; also punished Germany with loss of territories and the payment of reparations as a result of their "war guilt"; Russia also lost territories with the reestablishment of eastern European nations such as Poland. (34)

Treaty of Westphalia: Ended Thirty Years' War in 1648; granted right to individual rulers within the Holy Roman Empire to choose their own religion —either Protestant or Catholic. (22)

triangular trade: Commerce linking Africa, the New World colonies, and Europe; slaves carried to America for sugar and tobacco transported to Europe. (27)

Tripartite Pact: Alliance of Japan, Germany, and Italy signed in September 1940; created alliance system for World War II. (34)

Triple Alliance: Alliance between Germany, Austria-Hungary, and Italy at the end of the 19th century; part of European alliance system and balance of power prior to the First World War. (29)

Triple Entente: Alliance between Britain, Russia, and France at the outset of the 20th century; part of European alliance system and balance of power prior to the First World War. (29)

true colonies: Western European possessions in Africa, Asia, and the South Pacific in which small numbers of Europeans ruled large numbers of non-Western peoples; mostly brought under European control during the last decades of the 19th century and the first years of the 20th century. (30)

Truman, Harry: American president from 1945 to 1952; less eager for smooth relations with the Soviet Union than Franklin Roosevelt; authorized use of atomic bomb during World War II; architect of American diplomacy that initiated the cold war. (35)

Tutu, Osei: Member of Oyoko clan of Akan peoples in Gold Coast region of Africa; responsible for creating unified Asante Empire; utilized Western firearms. (27)

Ulyanov, Vladimir Ilyich: Better known as Lenin; most active Russian Marxist leader; insisted on importance of disciplined revolutionary cells; leader of Bolsheviks. (33)

Union of Soviet Socialist Republics: Federal system of socialist republics established in 1923 in various ethnic regions of Russia; firmly controlled by Communist party; diminished nationalities protest under Bolsheviks. (36)

United Fruit Company: Most important foreign economic concern in Guatemala during the 20th century; attempted land reform aimed at United Fruit caused U.S. intervention in Guatemalan politics leading to ouster of reform government in 1954. (38)

United Nations: International organization formed in the aftermath of World War II; included all of the victorious Allies; its primary mission was to provide a forum for negotiating disputes. (34)

Valdivia, Pedro de: Spanish conquistador; conquered Araucanian Indians of Chile and established city of Santiago in 1541. (25)

Vargas, Getúlio: Elected president of Brazil in 1929; launched centralized political program by imposing federal administrators over state governments; held off coups by Communists in 1935 and Fascists in 1937; imposed a new constitution based on Mussolini's Italy; leaned to Communists after 1949; committed suicide in 1954. (38)

viceroyalties: Two major divisions of Spanish colonies in New World; one based in Lima, the other in Mexico City; direct representatives of the king. (25)

Vichy: French collaborationist government established in 1940 in southern France following defeat of French armies by the Germans. (34)

Viet Cong: Name given by Diem regime to Communist guerrilla movement in southern Vietnam; reorganized with northern Vietnamese assistance as the National Liberation Front in 1958. (41)

Viet Minh: Communist-dominated Vietnamese nationalist movement; operated out of base in southern China during World War II; employed guerrilla tactics similar to the Maoists in China. (41)

Vietnamese Nationalist party: Also known as the Vietnamese Quoc Dan Dong or VNQDD; active in 1920s as revolutionary force committed to violent overthrow of French colonialism. (41)

Villa, Pancho: Mexican revolutionary and military commander in northern Mexico during the Mexican Revolution; succeeded along with Emiliano Zapata in removing Díaz from power; also participated in campaigns that removed Madero and Huerta. (38)

vizier: Ottoman equivalent of the Abbasid wazir; head of the Ottoman bureaucracy; after 15th century often more powerful than sultan. (26)

Vodun: African religious ideas and practices among descendants of African slaves in Haiti. (27)

Wafd party: Egyptian nationalist party that emerged after an Egyptian delegation was refused a hearing at the Versailles Treaty negotiations following World War I; led by Sa'd Zaghlūl; negotiations eventually led to limited Egyptian independence beginning in 1922. (39)

War of the Spanish Succession: Resulted

from Bourbon family's succession to Spanish throne in 1701; ended by Treaty of Utrecht in 1713; resulted in recognition of Bourbons, loss of some lands, grants of commercial rights to English and French. (25)

Water Margin, The; Monkey;* and *The Golden Lotus: Novels written during the Ming period in China; recognized as classics in their own time; established standards for Chinese prose literature. (28)

Watt, James: Devised a steam engine in 1770s during the Industrial Revolution that could be used for production; utilized in textile industries, mining, and railroads. (29)

welfare state: New activism of the state in economic policy and welfare issues after World War II; introduced programs to reduce the impact of economic inequality; typically included medical and civil rights programs. (35)

western front: Front established in World War I; generally along line from Belgium to Switzerland; featured trench warfare and horrendous casualties for all sides in the conflict. (34)

Whampoa Military Academy: Founded in 1924; military wing of the Guomindang; first head of the academy was Chiang Kai-shek. (41)

White Dominions: Colonies in which European settlers made up the overwhelming majority of the population; small numbers of native inhabitants typically reduced by disease and wars of conquest; typical of British colonies in North America and Australia. (30)

white racial supremacy: Belief in the inherent mental, moral, and cultural superiority of whites; peaked in acceptance in decades before First World War; supported by social science doctrines of social Darwinists such as Herbert Spencer. (30)

Wilberforce, William: British statesman and reformer; leader of abolitionist movement in English parliament; led abolition of English slave trade in 1807. (27)

witchcraft hysteria: Reflected resentment against the poor, uncertainties about religious truth; resulted in death of over 100,000 people between 1590 and 1650; particularly common in Protestant areas. (22)

Witte, Count: Russian minister of finance from 1892 to 1903; economic modernizer responsible for high tariffs, improved banking system; encouraged Western investors to build factories in Russia. (33)

Wollstonecraft, Mary: Enlightenment feminist thinker in England; argued that new political rights should extend to women. (22)

World Court: Developed during period of internationalization; permanent court of arbitration established at the Hague in 1899; intended to remove causes of war; failed to resolve problems of international conflict in 20th century. (34)

world economy: Established by Europeans by the late 16th century; based on control of seas including the Atlantic and Pacific; created an international exchange of foods, diseases, and manufactured products. (23)

World War I: Fought from 1914 and 1919; involved almost all European nations and their respective colonies; arose over conflict in the Balkans; resulted in victory of allied countries of Britain, France, Italy, and the United States; ended with Treaty of Versailles. (34)

World War II: Fought from 1939 to 1945 on fronts including western Europe, northern Africa, the Middle East, Eurasia, southwestern Asia, China, and the Pacific; ended with defeat of Germany and Japan in 1945. (34)

Xavier, Francis: Spanish Franciscan missionary; worked in India in 1540s among the outcaste and lower caste groups; made little headway among elites. (28)

Yalta Conference: Meeting between leaders of the United States, Britain, and the Soviet Union in 1945; agreed to Soviet entry into the Pacific war in return for possessions in Manchuria, organization of the United Nations; disputed the division of political organization among the eastern European states to be reestablished after the war. (34)

yellow peril: Western term for perceived threat of Japanese imperialism; met by increased Western imperialism in region. (33)

Yuan Shikai: Warlord in northern China after fall of Qing dynasty; hoped to seize imperial throne; president of China after 1912; resigned in face of Japanese invasion in 1916. (41)

zaibatsu: Huge industrial combines created in Japan in the 1890s as part of the process of industrialization. (33)

Zapata, Emiliano: Mexican revolutionary and military commander of peasant guerrilla movement centered in Morelos; succeeded along with Pancho Villa in removing Díaz from power; also participated in campaigns that removed Madero and Huerta; demanded sweeping land reform. (38)

zemstvoes: Local political councils created as part of reforms of Tsar Alexander II; gave some Russians, particularly middle-class professionals, some experience in government; councils had no impact on national policy. (33)

Zhenghe expeditions: Series of seven overseas trade expeditions under third Ming emperor, Yunglo; led by court eunuch Zhenghe between 1405 and 1423; last Chinese attempt to create worldwide trade empire. (28)

Zionism: Movement originating in eastern Europe during the 1860s and 1870s that argued that the Jews must return to a Middle Eastern Holy Land; eventually identified with the settlement of Palestine. (39)

Credits

LITERARY CREDITS

CHAPTER 24

From *Documents of Catherine the Great* edited by W. F. Reddaway, pp. 216, 258 & 293. Copyright © 1931 by Cambridge University Press. Reprinted by permission.

Cited in *Imperial Russia: A Source Book, 1700–1917* edited by Basil Dymtryshyn. Copyright © 1967 by Harcourt, Brace, Jovanovich.

CHAPTER 25

From *Florentine Codex*, Book VI. Reprinted by permission of The University of Utah Press.

CHAPTER 27

From *Africa Remembered* by Philip D. Curtin, pp. 92–94. Copyright © 1967 by the Regents of The University of Wisconsin. Reprinted by permission.

Table from *Transformations in Slavery* by Paul E. Lovejoy, pp. 45 & 47. Copyright © 1983 Cambridge University Press. Reprinted by permission.

CHAPTER 28

From *Cultural Atlas of Japan* by Martin Collcutt, et al., 1988. Copyright © 1988. Reprinted by permission of Andromeda Oxford Ltd., Abington, UK.

PART 5

Adaptation of map "The Development of the World Economy" cited in *The Times Atlas of World History* edited by G. Barraclough. Copyright © 1985 by Times Books Ltd.

CHAPTER 30

From *Britain and Germany in Africa* edited by P. Gifford et al, p. 670. Copyright © 1967 Yale University Press. Reprinted by permission.

Cited in *Patterns of Vietnamese Response to Foreign Intervention: 1858–1900* by Truong Buu Lam. Copyright © 1967 by Yale Southeast Asia Studies.

Map "Dutch Penetration in Java, 1619–1830" cited in *A Short History of Indonesia* by Ailsa Zainu'ddin. Copyright © 1968 by Greenwood Publishing.

CHAPTER 33

From *Cultural Atlas of Japan* by Martin Collcutt, et al., 1988. Copyright © 1988. Reprinted by permission of Andromeda Oxford Ltd., Abington, UK.

PART 6

Adaptation of map "Industrialization Outside Europe and North America" cited in *The Times Atlas of World History* edited by G. Barraclough. Copyright © 1985 by Times Books Ltd.

CHAPTER 36

From *Readings in Russian Civilization,* V.III edited by Thomas Riha. Copyright © 1969 The University of Chicago Press. Reprinted by permission.

Adaptation of Map "The Civil War" from *The World Atlas of Revolutions* by Andrew Wheatcroft. Text copyright © 1983 by Andrew Wheatcroft, Cartography © 1983 by Hamish Hamilton Ltd. Reprinted by permission of Simon & Schuster.

CHAPTER 39

From Poem "Snow Upon Paris" from *Selected Poems* by Léopold Sédar Senghor, Translated and Introduced by John Reed and Clive Wake. Copyright © 1974 Oxford University Press. Reprinted by permission of Oxford University Press.

Excerpt of poem cited in *Return to My Native Land* by Aime Cesaire. Copyright © 1956 by Penguin Books Ltd.

CHAPTER 40

Abridgement of "I Run Around With Them" cited in *The Complete Poetry and Prose of Chairil Anwar* edited & translated by Burton Raffel. Copyright © 1970 by State University of New York Press.

CHAPTER 41

Letter "Big Brother" from *Family* by Pa Chin, Copyright © 1972 by Doubleday.

Adaptation of map "The Northern Expedition 1926–27" cited in *The Times Atlas of World History,* revised edition edited by G. Barraclough. Copyright © 1985 by Times Books Ltd.

Adaptation of Map from *Histoire du Vietnam* par André Masson, p. 86. Copyright © 1949 Presses Universitaires de France. Reprinted by permission.

PHOTO CREDITS

Unless otherwise acknowledged, all photographs are the property of ScottForesman. Page abbreviations are as follows: (T)top, (C)center, (B)bottom, (L)left, (R)right.

PART 4

488 The Metropolitan Museum of Art; **496** Historical Pictures Service, Chicago

CHAPTER 22

499 The Granger Collection, New York; **505** The Granger Collection, New York; **508** The Granger Collection, New York; **512** The Granger Collection, New York; **515** The Granger Collection, New York

CHAPTER 23

518 Bibliothèque Nationale; **521** North Wind Picture Archives; **522** North Wind Picture Archives; **532** The Granger Collection, New York; **533** Asian Art Museum of San Francisco; **535** Courtesy of The Newberry Library, Chicago; **537** By courtesy of the Victoria & Albert Museum; **540** Mansell Collection

CHAPTER 24

544 SOVFOTO; **548R** Novosti/SOVFOTO; **548L** Novosti/SOVFOTO; **548L** SOVFOTO; **550** Courtesy of the Trustees of the British Museum; **551** The Bettmann Archive; **553** Novosti/SOVFOTO; **557** SOVFOTO; **558** Novosti/SOVFOTO

CHAPTER 25

564 Pierpont Morgan Library; **567** Library of Congress; **576** Laurie Platt Winfrey/Carousel, Inc., NY; **578** Det Kongelige Bibliotek Kobenhavn; **580** The Granger Collection, New York; **584** Castillo de Chapultepec Mexico City/ Museo Nacional de Historia, Mexico City; **587** Historical Pictures Service, Chicago

CHAPTER 26

592 Robert Frerck/Odyssey Productions, Chicago; **595** Bibliothèque Nationale; **600** National Maritime Museum, Greenwich, England; **603** Courtesy of the Trustees of the British Museum; **605** Dr. Laurence Lockhart/Cambridge, England; **609** New York Public Library, Astor, Lenox and Tilden Foundations; **611L** Museum of Fine Arts, Boston/Francis Bartlett Donation of 1912 and Picture Fund

CHAPTER 27

616 Library of Congress; **619** Courtesy of the Trustees of the British Museum; **624** Courtesy of the Newberry Library, Chicago; **629** Local History Museum/ Durban South Africa; **634** Courtesy of the Newberry Library, Chicago; **635** UPI/Bettmann; **636** Fowler Museum of Cultural History/University of California at Los Angeles

CHAPTER 28

638 Rene Burri/Magnum Photos; **643** Giraudon/Art Resource, NY; **645** Culver Pictures; **649** THE MIDDLE KINGDOM Vol 1, S. Wells William LL.D, Carles Scribner's Sons. 1883; **652** Courtesy of the Trustees of the British Museum; **653** The Art Institute of Chicago. All Rights Reserved./Gift of Guy Mitchell; **659** The Granger Collection, New York; **660** The Granger Collection, New York

PART 5

664 The Art Institute of Chicago. All Rights Reserved.

CHAPTER 29

670 Bulloz; **680** The Metropolitan Museum of Art, Harris Brisbane Dick Fund, 1932; **684** The Granger Collection, New York; **690** The Hulton-Deutsch Collection/The Hulton Picture Company; **691** By courtesy of the Victoria & Albert Museum; **692** Courtesy of the Trustees of the British Museum; **693** The Art Institute of Chicago. All Rights Reserved. The Potter Palmer Collection; **699** The Hulton-Deutsch Collection/The Hulton Picture Company

CHAPTER 30

702 APA Photo Agency; **706** The Granger Collection, New York; **707** The Hulton-Deutsch Collection/The Hulton Picture Company; **710** Royal Tropical Institute/APA Photo Agency; **716** Mary Evans Picture Library; **718** National Army Museum, London; **720** The Hulton-Deutsch Collection/The Hulton Picture Company

CHAPTER 31

728 Culver Pictures; **741** Robert Frerck/Odyssey Productions, Chicago; **742** Mannheim Municipal Art Museum; **744** Historical Pictures Service, Chicago; **746** The Granger Collection, New York; **752** The Granger Collection, New York

CHAPTER 32

754 The Hulton-Deutsch Collection/The Hulton Picture Company; **759** Mary Evans Picture Library; **761** Mary Evans Picture Library; **762** Réunion des Musées Nationaux; **764** Mary Evans Picture Library; **765** Woodfin Camp & Associates; **769** Historical Pictures Service, Chicago; **773** Historical Pictures Service, Chicago

CHAPTER 33

778 Novosti Press Agency; **781** Novosti Press Agency; **784** Keystone Mast Collection/California Museum of Photography of California, Riverside/University of California; **786** Novosti Press Agency; **797** The Metropolitan Museum of Art, Gift of Lincoln Kirstein, 1989; **798** The Granger Collection, New York

PART 6

804 Life Magazine Time Warner Inc.

CHAPTER 34

812 AP/Wide World; **818** Trustees of The Imperial War Museum, London; **822** The Bettmann Archive; **825** Dorothea Lange Collection/Library of Congress; **830** AP/Wide World; **833** Trustees of the Imperial War Museum, London

CHAPTER 35

838 Fenno Jacobs/Black Star; **841** John Held, Jr./Life Magazine Time Warner Inc.; **843** Pix Publishing; **851** James H. Karales (c)1965 LOOK/Library of Congress; **854** The Granger Collection, New York; **857** Burt Glinn/Magnum Photos; **861** Philadelphia Museum of Art Collection/Louise and Walter Arensberg Collection; **862** Hedrich-Blessing

CHAPTER 36

866 SOVFOTO; **869** Bildarchiv Preussischer Kulturbesitz; **870** SOVFOTO; **871** Tass from SOVFOTO; **881** United Press Photo; **883** SOVFOTO; **884** SOVFOTO; **889** Leh/Saukkomaa/Woodfin Camp & Associates

CHAPTER 37

892 Nathan Benn/Woodfin Camp & Associates; **896** Hulton/UPI/Bettmann; **898** UPI/Bettman; **901** Camera Press/Globe Photos, Inc.; **903** The Bettmann Archive; **905** Mike Yamashita/Woodfin Camp & Associates; **906** Palmer Pictures; **908** AP/Wide World

CHAPTER 38

914 Almasy; **917** FPG; **920** Laurie Platt Winfrey/Carousel, Inc., NY; **924** UPI/Bettmann; **926** UPI/Bettmann; **928** UPI/Bettmann; **938** Marlborough Gallery/Private Collection

CHAPTER 39

940 Margaret Bourke-White/Life Magazine Time Warner Inc.; **944** The Bettmann Archive; **945** The Bettmann Archive; **949**

ACME/UPI/Bettmann; **951** The Granger Collection, New York; **956** Camera Press/Globe Photos, Inc.; **960** UPI/Bettmann; **962** AP/Wide World

CHAPTER 40

966 Shandiz/Sygma; **972** UPI/Bettmann; **976** Sygma; **980** UPI/Bettmann; **982** UPI/Bettmann; **986** AP/Wide World; **987** William Campbell/Sygma

CHAPTER 41

990 Culver Pictures; **994** Eastfoto/SOVFOTO; **996** AP/Wide World; **998** Hoover Institution Archives/Jay Calvin Huston Collection; **1002** Eastfoto/SOVFOTO; **1006** AP/Wide World; **1009** Yale University Library/Maurice Durand Collection of Vietnamese Art; **1013** Sygma

CHAPTER 42

1016 Jaques Pavlovsky/Sygma; **1022** AP/Wide World; **1026** Los Alamos National Laboratory; **1027** Loren McIntyre; **1028** Sygma; **1029** WIlliam Campbell/Sygma; **1030** Courtesy of IBM; **1032** Los Angeles Times Photo

Index